Related Books of Interest

WebSphere Engineering

A Practical Guide for WebSphere Support Managers and Senior Consultants

by Ying Ding

ISBN-13: 978-0-13-714225-5

The Practical, End-to-End Guide to WebSphere® Infrastructure Engineering and Technical Management. Drawing on his tremendous real-world expertise, Ying Ding shows how to maximize the WebSphere platform's reliability, stability, scalability, and performance for large enterprise systems. You'll find insightful discussions of each option and strategy for managing WebSphere, including practical guidance on making the right tradeoffs for your environment.

Whether you're a WebSphere administrator, developer, consultant, support manager, engineer, or architect, this book brings together the information you need to run your WebSphere infrastructure with maximum effectiveness and efficiency.

WebSphere Business Integration Primer

Process Server, BPEL, SCA, and SOA

by Ashok Iyengar, Vinod Jessani, and Michele Chilanti

ISBN-13: 978-0-13-224831-0

Using WebSphere® Business Integration (WBI) technology, you can build an enterprise-wide Business Integration (BI) infrastructure that makes it easier to connect any business resources and functions, so you can adapt more quickly to the demands of customers and partners. Now there's an introductory guide to creating standards-based process and data integration solutions with WBI.

WebSphere Business Integration Primer thoroughly explains Service Component Architecture (SCA), basic business processes, and complex long-running business flows, and guides you to choose the right process integration architecture for your requirements. Next, it introduces the key components of a WBI solution and shows how to make them work together rapidly and efficiently. This book will help developers, technical professionals, or managers understand today's key BI issues and technologies, and streamline business processes by combining BI with Service Oriented Architecture (SOA).

Related Books of Interest

The New Language of Business

SOA & Web 2.0

By Sandy Carter

ISBN-13: 978-0-13-195654-4

In *The New Language of Business*, senior IBM executive Sandy Carter demonstrates how to leverage SOA, Web 2.0, and related technologies to drive new levels of operational excellence and business innovation.

Writing for executives and business leaders inside and outside IT, Carter explains why flexibility and responsiveness are now even more crucial to success — and why services-based strategies offer the greatest promise for achieving them.

You'll learn how to organize your business into reusable process components — and support them with cost-effective IT services that adapt quickly and easily to change. Then, using extensive examples — including a detailed case study describing IBM's own experience — Carter identifies best practices, pitfalls, and practical starting points for success.

Listen to the author's podcast at:
ibmpressbooks.com/podcasts

Executing SOA

A Practical Guide for the Service-Oriented Architect

by Norbert Bieberstein, Robert G. Laird, Dr. Keith Jones, and Tilak Mitra

ISBN-13: 978-0-13-235374-8

In Executing SOA, four experienced SOA implementers share realistic, proven, "from-the-trenches" guidance for successfully delivering the largest and most complex SOA initiative. This book follows up where the authors' best-selling *Service-Oriented Architecture Compass* left off, showing how to overcome key obstacles to successful SOA implementation and identifying best practices for all facets of execution—technical, organizational, and human. Among the issues it addresses include introducing a services discipline that supports collaboration and information process sharing; integrating services with preexisting technology assets and strategies; choosing the right roles for new tools; shifting culture, governance, and architecture; and bringing greater agility to the entire organizational lifecycle, not just isolated projects.

Listen to the author's podcast at:
ibmpressbooks.com/podcasts

IBM Press™

Visit ibmpressbooks.com for all product information

Related Books of Interest

Rapid Portlet Development with WebSphere Portlet Factory

Step-by-Step Guide for Building Your Own Portlets

by David Bowley

ISBN-13: 978-0-13-713446-5

Portlet development traditionally has been difficult and time-consuming, requiring costly resources and specialized expertise in multiple technologies. IBM® WebSphere® Portlet Factory simplifies and accelerates portlet development, enabling developers to build world-class portlet solutions without in-depth knowledge of portal technology.

Expert developer David Bowley walks you through several of today's most common portlet development scenarios, demonstrating how to create powerful, robust portlets quickly and cost-effectively. Each walkthrough contains all the step-by-step instructions, detailed guidance, fast answers, and working sample code you need to get tangible results immediately.

Enterprise Messaging Using JMS and IBM WebSphere

Yusuf

ISBN-13: 978-0-13-146863-4

IBM WebSphere System Administration

Williamson, Chan, Cundiff, Lauzon, Mitchell

ISBN-13: 978-0-13-144604-5

Outside-in Software Development

Kessler, Sweitzer

ISBN-13: 978-0-13-157551-6

Enterprise Master Data Management

Dreibelbis, Hechler, Milman, Oberhofer, van Run, Wolfson

ISBN-13: 978-0-13-236625-0

Enterprise Java Programming with IBM WebSphere, Second Edition

Brown, Craig, Hester, Pitt, Stinehour, Weitzel, Amsden, Jakab, Berg

ISBN-13: 978-0-321-18579-2

Service-Oriented Architecture (SOA) Compass

Bieberstein, Bose, Fiammante, Jones, Shah

ISBN-13: 978-0-13-187002-4

IBM WebSphere

Barcia, Hines, Alcott, Botzum

ISBN-13: 978-0-13-146862-7

IBM® WebSphere® DataPower® SOA Appliance Handbook

IBM® WebSphere® DataPower® SOA Appliance Handbook

Bill Hines
John Rasmussen
Jaime Ryan
Simon Kapadia
Jim Brennan

IBM Press
Pearson plc
Upper Saddle River, NJ • Boston• Indianapolis • San Francisco
New York • Toronto • Montreal • London • Munich • Paris • Madrid
Cape Town • Sydney • Tokyo • Singapore • Mexico City

ibmpressbooks.com

IBM Press Program Managers: Steven M. Stansel, Ellice Uffer

Cover design: IBM Corporation

Associate Publisher: Greg Wiegand

Marketing Manager: Kourtnaye Sturgeon

Publicist: Heather Fox

Acquisitions Editor: Katherine Bull

Development Editor: Ginny Bess Munroe

Managing Editor: Kristy Hart

Designer: Alan Clements

Senior Project Editor: Lori Lyons

Copy Editor: Editorial Advantage

Indexer: WordWise Publishing Services LLC

Compositor: TnT Design

Proofreader: San Dee Phillips

Manufacturing Buyer: Dan Uhrig

Published by Pearson plc

Publishing as IBM Press

IBM Press offers excellent discounts on this book when ordered in quantity for bulk purchases or special sales, which may include electronic versions and/or custom covers and content particular to your business, training goals, marketing focus, and branding interests. For more information, please contact:

U. S. Corporate and Government Sales

1-800-382-3419

corpsales@pearsontechgroup.com.

For sales outside the U. S., please contact:

International Sales
international@pearsoned.com.

Library of Congress Cataloging-in-Publication Data

IBM websphere datapower SOA appliance handbook / Bill Hines ... [et al.].
p. cm.
ISBN 978-0-13-714819-6
1. WebSphere. 2. Web site development. I. Hines, Bill.
TK5105.8885.W43I265 2008
004.6—dc22

2008042957

Pearson Education, Inc
Rights and Contracts Department
501 Boylston Street, Suite 900
Boston, MA 02116
Fax (617) 671 3447

ISBN-13: 978-0-13-714819-6

ISBN-10: 0-13-714819-4

Text printed in the United States on recycled paper at R.R. Donnelley in Crawfordsville, Indiana.
First printing December 2008

To my mother Carol, who inspired me to learn and read, encouraged me to write, and who put up with me all of those years; and to my wonderful wife Patty who puts up with me now; and my children Jennifer, Brittany, and Derek, of whom I am so proud. Lastly, to my sisters Donna and Patty, and my brother-in-law Marty, who are always there for our fun weekends after a long week at work.

—Bill Hines

To my mother Marilyn, who has shown me the strength and joy of family and the skills of perseverance; and in memory of my father James, an Officer and a Gentleman, "born on the crest of a wave and rocked in the cradle of the deep," who taught me to fish, and so much more; and most of all, to my sons Alex and Nick, who provide me with continuous pride and joy.

—John Rasmussen

To my wife Danielle, who dealt with all the late nights and busy weekends; to my parents, who instilled a hunger for knowledge in general and books specifically; and to my extended family and friends, who supported me through good times and bad. Last, but not least, to Andrew.

—Jaime Ryan

To my darling wife Wioletta, for putting up with the long nights and grumpy mornings; and to my three glorious children, Andrew, Victoria, and Christopher, that they may find their path in life as rewarding as I have found mine, and that they may be inspired in whichever field they choose to work. Finally, to my parents.

—Simon Kapadia

To my beautiful wife Jennifer and wonderful children Emily and Patrick, who have all been very patient and supportive of my goals and aspirations even when it meant weekends and late nights away from them. Also to my parents, who always encouraged me to learn and persevere.

—Jim Brennan

Contents at a Glance

Contents

Foreword by Eugene Kuznetsov

> "The proper planning of any job is the first requirement. With limited knowledge of a trade, the job of planning is doubly hard, but there are certain steps that any person can take towards proper planning if he only will."
> —Robert Oakes Jordan, *Masonry*

I founded a company called DataPower® in the spring of 1999 to build products based on several distinct ideas. The first idea involved applying reconfigurable computing and dynamic code generation to the problem of integrating disparate applications. The second idea centered on the concept of data-oriented programming (DOP) as the means to achieve direct and robust data interchange. The third idea involved delivering middleware as a network function, enabled by the DOP technology and inspired by the successful models of ubiquitous connectivity. The product's journey since has been remarkable, and this great book is another milestone for the entire team behind DataPower. Before more discussion of the book itself, a few words on these three ideas.

Rapidly adapting to change is key for everything and everyone in today's world, and IBM SOA appliances are no exception. Whether it's a policy, a transformation map, a schema, or a security rule, DataPower will try to put it into effect with as little delay and interruption as possible. Popular methods for maintaining this kind of flexibility come with a large performance penalty. However, by dynamically generating code and reconfiguring hardware based on the current message flow, it became possible to achieve both flexibility and near-optimal performance. At any given point, the device operates as a custom engine for a particular task, but when the task changes, it can rapidly become a different custom engine underneath the covers.

This dynamic adaptability is especially useful when combined with DOP. Stated briefly, DOP emphasizes formally documenting data formats and using them directly, instead of encapsulation or abstraction, to integrate or secure different modules or systems. Today, XML is probably one of the most successful and readily recognized examples of DOP, but the principles are more universal than any particular technology. Another example of DOP is the way DataPower XI50 processes binary data, by using high-level format descriptors instead of adaptors.

These, in turn, enable the creation of network hardware (also known as appliance) products that operate on whole application messages (rather than network packets) to integrate, secure, or control applications. Greater simplicity, performance, security, and cost-effectiveness were envisioned—and are now proven—with the appliance approach. Beyond the appliance design discipline, the success of IP & Ethernet networking in achieving universal connectivity has much to teach about the best way to achieve radically simplified and near-universal application integration.

Reading this book will enable you to benefit from the previous three ideas in their concrete form: the award-winning IBM products they became. From basic setup to the most powerful advanced features, it covers DataPower appliances in a readable tone with a solid balance of theory and examples. For example, Chapter 6 does a great job in explaining the big-picture view of device operation, and Chapter 22 gives a detailed how-to on extending its capabilities. With some of the most experienced hands-on DataPower practitioners among its authors, it provides the kind of real-world advice that is essential to learning any craft.

When learning IBM DataPower, there is one thing that may be more helpful and rewarding than remembering every particular detail, and that is developing an internal "mental model" of how the devices are meant to operate and fit into the environment. Especially when troubleshooting or learning new features, this "mental model" can make device behavior intuitive. Reading the following pages with an eye toward not just the details but also this mental model will speed both productivity and enjoyment.

In conclusion, I would like to use this occasion to thank the entire team, past and present, who made and continues to make DataPower possible. Their work and the passion of DataPower users is an inspiring example of how great people and a powerful idea can change the world for the better.

—**Eugene Kuznetsov**, Cambridge, MA Founder of DataPower Technology, Inc. served as President, Chairman, and CTO at various points in the company's history, and then served as director of Product Management and Marketing, SOA Appliances at IBM Corporation.

Figure 1 DataPower's first office is on the right. (*Photo courtesy of Merryman Design.*)

Foreword by Jerry Cuomo

It all started when I was asked to co-host an IBM Academy Conference on "Accelerators and Off-Loading" in 2004. I was feeling a little out of my element, so I decided to take some of the focus off me and put it on others. I had been reading about some of the new XML-centered hardware devices and was intrigued. I have always been interested in system performance. With XML dominating our emerging workloads (e.g., Service Oriented Architecture), the impact of XML performance on system performance was becoming increasingly important. Hence, I thought it would be a good idea to invite a handful of these XML vendors to our conference.

At the conference, the DataPower presentation was quite different from the others. It wasn't about ASICs or transistors; it was about improving time to value and total cost of operation. The DataPower presentation focused on topics that were also near and dear to me, such as systems integration, configuration over programming, and the merits of built-for-purpose systems. In essence, Eugene Kuznetsov, the DataPower founder and presenter, was talking about the value of *appliances*. While very intriguing, I couldn't help but feel curious about whether the claims were accurate. So, after the conference I invited Eugene to come to our lab in Research Triangle Park in North Carolina to run some tests.

I have to admit now that in the back of my mind, I operated on the principle of "keeping your friends close and your enemies closer." Behind my intrigue was a feeling of wanting to understand their capabilities so that we could outperform vendors with WebSphere® Application Server. The tests went well; however, the DataPower team was somewhat reluctant to dwell on the raw XML performance capabilities of their appliance. Feeling a little suspicious, I had my team run some raw performance experiments. The results were off the charts. Why wasn't the DataPower team flaunting this capability? This is when I had my "ah-ha" moment. While performance measured in transactions per second is important and part of the value equation, the overall performance metrics found while assessing time to value and overall cost of operation and ownership are the most critical performance metrics to a business. This is where the DataPower appliances outperform. I read a paper, written by Jim Barton, CTO and co-founder of Tivo, called "Tivo-lution." The paper was inspiring as it confirmed the motivations and aspirations that I've had ever since I led IBM's acquisition of DataPower in 2005. In the paper, Barton describes the challenges of making complex systems usable and how "purpose-built" computer systems are one answer to the challenge:

> "One of the greatest challenges of designing a computer system is in making sure the system itself is 'invisible' to the user. The system should simply be a conduit to the desired result. There are many examples of such purpose-built systems, ranging from modern automobiles to mobile phones."

The concept of purpose-built systems is deeply engrained in our DNA at IBM. The name of our company implies this concept: International *Business Machines*.

IBM has a long history of building purposed machines, such as the 1933 Type 285, an electric bookkeeping and accounting machine. I can imagine this machine being delivered to an accountant, plugging it in, immediately followed by number crunching. The accountant didn't have to worry about hard drive capacity, operating system levels, compatibility between middleware vendors, or application functionality. It just did the job. I can also imagine it followed the 80/20 rule. It probably didn't do 100% of what all accountants needed. But it probably did 80% of what all accountants needed very well. Users just dealt with the remaining 20%, or learned to live without it.

"Business Machines, Again" is my inspiration. Our customers respond positively to the re-emergence of this approach to engineering products. It's all about time-to-value and total cost of operation and ownership. Appliances such as our WebSphere DataPower XI50 are leading the way in delivering on these attributes.

At the extreme, purpose-built systems, such as a Tivo DVR and a XI50, are built from the ground up for their purposes. While they might use off-the-shelf parts, such as an embedded Linux® OS, it is important that all parts are "right sized" for the job. Right-sizing source code in a hardware appliance is more like firmware (with strong affinity to the underlying hardware) than it is software. As such, the Tivo-lution paper describes the need to own every line of source code to ensure the highest level of integration and quality:

> "...by having control of each and every line of source code...
>
> Tivo would have full control of product quality and development schedules. When the big bug hunt occurred, as it always does, we needed the ability to follow every lead, understand every path, and track every problem down to its source."

The Tivo team even modified the GNU C++ compiler to eliminate the use of exceptions (which generate a lot of code that is seldom used) in favor of rigid checking of return code usage in the firmware. DataPower similarly contains a custom XML compiler that generates standard executable code for its general-purpose CPUs, as well as custom code for the (XG4) XML coprocessor card.

A physical appliance has the unparalleled benefit of being hardened for security. Jim talks about this in his Tivo paper:

> "Security must be fundamental to the design...We wanted to make it as difficult as possible, within the economics of the DVR platform, to corrupt the security of any particular DVR."

The DataPower team has taught me the meaning of "tamper-proof" appliances, or more precisely "tamper-evident." Like the 1982 Tylenol scare, we can't stop you from opening the box, but we can protect you, if someone does open it. In fact, the physical security characteristics of the DataPower XS40 make it one of the only technologies some of our most stringent customers will put on their network Demilitarized Zone (DMZ). If a DataPower box is compromised and opened, it basically stops working. An encrypted flash drive makes any configuration data, including security keys, difficult to exploit. "DP is like the roach motel; private keys go in, but never come out" is the way we sometimes describe the tamper-proof qualities of the XS40.

But the truth is, DataPower is not a DVR. DataPower is a middleware appliance. Middleware is a tricky thing to make an appliance out of. Middleware is enabling technology and by its nature is not specific to any application or vendor. The Tivo appliance is a specific application (TV and guide) that makes it somewhat easier to constrain:

> "Remember, it's television. Everybody knows how television works."
>
> "Television never stops, even when you turn off the TV set. Televisions never crash."

Hence, the challenge (and the art) in building a middleware appliance involves providing the right amount of constraint, without rendering the appliance useless. For example, DataPower does not run Java™ code (which is the primary means of customizing much of the WebSphere portfolio); instead, it uses XML as the primary mode of behavior customization. So, at some level, DP is not programmed, but instead it is configured. Now, for those who have used XML (and its cousin XSLT), you know that it's more than configuration; however, it is a constraint over Java programming, which has unbounded levels of customizability. The new combined team of IBM and DataPower have been bridging this gap (of special to general purpose) effectively. We have recently added features to DP to allow it to seamlessly connect to IBM mainframe software (IMS™ and DB2®) as well as capabilities to manage a collection of appliances as if they were one.

IBM has a healthy general-purpose software business. Our WebSphere, Java-based middleware is the poster child for general-purpose middleware (write once, run almost everywhere). However, there is a place for business machines that are purposed built and focus on providing the 80 part of the 80/20 rule. We are heading down this path in a Big Blue way.

This book represents an important milestone in the adoption of DataPower into the IBM family. The authors of this book represent some of IBM's most skilled practitioners of Service Oriented Architecture (SOA). This team is a customer facing team and has a great deal of experience in helping our customers quickly realize value from our products. They have also been among the most passionate within IBM of adopting the appliance approach to rapidly illustrating the value of SOA to our customers. The authors have unparalleled experience in using DataPower to solve some of our customers' most stringent systems integration problems. This book captures their experiences and best practices and is a valuable tool for deriving the most out of your WebSphere DataPower appliance.

—**Jerry Cuomo**, IBM Fellow, WebSphere CTO

Foreword by Kyle Brown

I can still remember the day in late 2005 when Jerry Cuomo first called me into his office to tell me about an acquisition (then pending) of a small Massachusetts company that manufactured hardware devices.

"Wait a minute. *Hardware??!?"*

That's the first incredulous thought that went through my mind. Jerry was the CTO of the WebSphere brand in IBM, which had become the industry-leading brand of middleware based on Java. Why were we looking at a company that made hardware? Echoing the immortal words of Dr. "Bones" McCoy from the classic Star Trek series, I then thought,

"I'm a software engineer, not a hardware engineer, dang it!"

But as I sat in his office, Jerry wove me a story (as he had for our executives) that soon had me convinced that this acquisition did, in fact, make sense for WebSphere as a brand and for IBM as a whole. Jerry had the vision of a whole new way of looking at SOA middleware—a vision that encompassed efficient, special-purpose appliances that could be used to build many of the parts of an SOA. Key to this vision was the acquisition of DataPower, which gave us not only a wealth of smart people with deep experience in Networking, XML, and SOA, but an entry into this field with the DataPower family of appliances—notably the XI50 Integration appliance.

Since that day, I've never regretted our decision to branch out the WebSphere brand well beyond its Java roots. The market response to the introduction of the DataPower appliances to the brand has been nothing short of phenomenal. Far from distracting us, the ability to provide our customers with an easy-to-use, easy-to-install, and remarkably efficient hardware-based option for their ESB and security needs has turned out to be an asset that created synergy with our other product lines and made the brand stronger as a whole. It's been an incredible journey, and as we begin to bring out new appliances in the DataPower line, we're only now beginning to see the fundamental shift in thinking that appliance-based approaches can give us.

On this journey, I've been accompanied by a fantastic group of people—some who came to us through the DataPower acquisition and some who were already part of the WebSphere family—who have helped our customers make use of these new technologies. Bill, John, and the rest of the author team are the true experts in this technology, and their expertise and experience show in this book.

This book provides a wealth of practical information for people who are either novices with the DataPower appliances, or who want to learn how to get the most from their appliances. It provides comprehensive coverage of all the topics that are necessary to master the DataPower appliance, from basic networking and security concepts, through advanced configuration of the Appliance's features. It provides copious, detailed examples of how the features of the appliances work, and provides debugging help and tips for helping you determine how to make those examples (and your own projects) work. But what's most helpful about this book is the way in which the team has given you not just an explanation of *how* you would use each feature, but also *why* the features are built the way they are. Understanding the thinking behind the approaches taken is an enormous help in fully mastering these appliances. The team provides that, and provides you with a wealth of hints, tips, and time-saving advice not just for using and configuring devices, but also for how to structure your work with the devices.

This book is something the DataPower community has needed for a long time, and I'm glad that the authors have now provided it to the community. So sit back, crack open the book, open up the admin console (unless you have yet to take the appliance out of the box—the book will help you there, too!) and begin. Your work with the appliances is about to get a whole lot easier, more comprehensible, and enjoyable as well.

—**Kyle Brown**, Distinguished Engineer, IBM Software Services and Support

Acknowledgments

The Author Team:
We thank the IBM management team for allowing us to access the resources necessary to write the book.

We thank the people at IBM Press and Pearson Education, the publishers and staff who have helped market and complete the production work that goes into publishing a book like this. At IBM Press, we thank Tara Woodman and her team. At Pearson Education, we'd like to thank Katherine Bull, who acted in the role of senior editor to get our work in line and meet the standards. We thank development editor Ginny Bess Munroe for her eye on comprehensiveness and for helping us express ourselves better, and we thank Arif Siddiqui, Ken Hygh, David Shute, Trey Williamson, Ozair Sheikh, and Rich Groot for their technical reviews. We also thank the production and marketing teams at Pearson who helped make the book come alive.

The author team would like to thank the following people for technical contributions, clarifications, and suggestions for this book: Shiu-Fun Poon, Russell Butek, Trey Williamson, Arif Siddiqui, Colt Gustafson, David Maze, David Shute, Eugene Kuznetsov, Gari Singh, Greg Truty, Henry Chung, Joel Smith, John de Frie tas, Corey Scobie, John Graham, Julie Salamone, Ozair Sheikh, Ken Hygh, Keys Botzum, Rich Groot, Marcel Kinard, Rich Salz, Steve Hanson, Tom Alcott, Naipaul Ojar, Davin Holmes, and Jon Harry.

Bill Hines:
I'd like to thank my manager Al Scardino for being supportive during this process, and putting up with my sleep-deprived ill temper and rants—and also his manager, my second line, Bruce Eppinger for hiring me into the best job in the best company in the world (and giving me the opportunity to see that world). Thanks to Keys Botzum for being my role model for work ethic and integrity, and being my mentor throughout my IBM career. I'd like to thank my immediate and extended family for being supportive and understanding during the tough times. Last, I'd like to thank my author team for sticking with this project during the many months, nights, and weekends of heated debates and stress. You were all picked for a reason, and I think the fact that you have all put up with me, and we have been through what we have and emerged still good friends with tremendous respect for each other, attests to those decisions being good ones. I'm extremely proud of the job you've done.

John Rasmussen:
I'd like to thank my manager Ken McCauley for his support and encouragement during the writing of this book. I would like to thank Eugene Kuznetsov for making this all possible and for providing me with the opportunity to participate. To Rich Salz for his generosity of time and knowledge and the many contributions he has made to DataPower. To the many individuals whom I've come to respect and to rely on in tough times such as; Jan-Christian Nelson, Gari Singh, David Maze, John de Freitas, Holger Reinhardt, John Shriver, James Ricotta, and many others within the DataPower family. To my fellow authors who have truly gone above and beyond. And a special word of appreciation to Bill Hines. There is no doubt that without Bill's tremendous effort and continuous dedication this book would not have happened. Finally, I'd like to say a special thanks to Renè, and my friends and family who have supported me and who have put up with and without me during this endeavor.

Jaime Ryan:
I'd like to thank my colleagues in Sales and my former colleagues in Services for proving that a team is always more capable than any individual—I've learned an incredible amount from all of you. Thanks to Ken Hygh for introducing me to IBM in all the right ways, and Corey Scobie and Amir Assar for a painless and exciting transition to the world of Sales. When I was going through a rough patch, I was supported by my current manager Steve Loscialpo, Brian Bell, and Philippe Riche, all of whom I consider my friends. Gari, John, Rich, Arif, Diego, and Dave—you guys are always there for me. I'd like to thank my co-authors, for putting heart and soul into this project, and especially Bill Hines, without whom none of this would have been possible. I'm proud of the entire DataPower extended family, and I look forward to the future!

Simon Kapadia:

I'd like to thank my co-authors above all else, for being patient and understanding, for encouraging and pushing and driving. Especially thanks to Bill Hines, without whom this book would not have happened. Thank you to my friends in IBM, especially Dave Artus, Tom Alcott, Keys Botzum, Martin Lansche, Paul Ilechko, Richard Groot, and Ken Hygh, all of whom contributed to this book even if they didn't realize it, by exploring ideas with me and discussing technical details. Thank you to my family and friends for ignoring me sleeping in the corner, and especially to Wiola for explaining why. Thank you to my children, Andy, Vicky, and Chris, for providing inspiration. And finally, thank you to all the musicians deceased and living whose recorded music kept me going through the long nights and gray mornings.

Jim Brennan:

I'd like to thank my manager Shiretta Shaw for being supportive and understanding during this endeavor. I would like to thank all of my co-authors for including me in the writing of this book and making it the best that it could be. I would especially like to thank Bill Hines for leading this effort and cracking the whip when it needed to be cracked. I would like to thank my family and friends for being understanding and supportive when the stress seemed to be getting the best of me.

About the Authors

Bill Hines is a Consulting I/T Specialist with IBM's Software Services for WebSphere organization in the Software Division, working as a mobile consultant out of Hershey, PA (Chocolatetown, USA). He has several years of DataPower experience in both customer engagements and developing and delivering internal DataPower training to the IBM consulting, engineering, support, QA, and technical sales teams. He also has WebSphere Application Server experience dating back to 1998 and across all versions from 2.x to 6.x in areas of specialty including installation, configuration, tuning, dynacache, security, troubleshooting, and design/architecture of enterprise J2EE applications using WebSphere family development tools. He is a co-author of the highly acclaimed IBM Press book *IBM WebSphere: Deployment and Advanced Configuration* as well as several articles published in *WebSphere Technical Journal* and developerWorks®, and his background includes more than twenty years of information technology experience in many platforms and languages, as well as degrees from New York Institute of Technology and Tulsa Jr. College.

John Rasmussen is a Senior I/T Specialist with IBM Software Services for WebSphere organization, Software Division in Cambridge, MA. John was first introduced to DataPower devices in 2001 while working as an engineer with Fidelity Investments developing XML/XSLT/JAXP applications for Internet-enabled mobile devices. John has been with IBM/DataPower since that time, and has worked as a product development engineer (where he created and developed the original WebGUI Drag and Drop Policy Editor) and as a product specialist assisting many clients in the implementation of DataPower devices. John has an extensive career in software development, including work with McCormack & Dodge/D&B Software and as an independent consultant and independent developer of application software and security systems. John has a degree from the University of Massachusetts at Amherst, and lives in Gloucester, Massachusetts, with his sons Alex and Nick.

Jaime Ryan is a DataPower Specialist for the IBM WebSphere Software Group, currently in Technical Sales for the Western United States. He has worked with all aspects of customer-oriented Services, Sales, and Education for DataPower SOA Appliances at some of IBM's largest and most strategic accounts. He has more than eight years of experience in the creation of high performance Web Services registry, routing, acceleration, BPM, and EAI products. Jaime's background includes a strong focus on Service Oriented Architectures from multiple perspectives: software development, independent consulting, and technical documentation. He received Computer Science and Cognitive Science degrees from the University of California, San Diego, where he met his lovely wife, Danielle.

Simon Kapadia is the Security Lead for IBM Software Services for WebSphere (ISSW) in Europe. He works on designing and implementing large distributed computer systems for IBM customers. Simon holds a Bachelor's degree in English and Drama and a Master's in Computing Science. He has owned a computer since six years of age and has turned a lifelong hobby into a career. Prior to joining IBM, Simon developed software for digital exchanges at Bell Laboratories, managed networks and Web applications at an ISP, and supported and consulted on DCE, DFS™, and Encina® for Transarc Corporation. You can reach Simon at simon.kapadia@uk.ibm.com or via his public Web site at http://www.kapadia.pl.

Jim Brennan is an IBM I/T Specialist with IBM Software Services for WebSphere. He is a mobile consultant out of Hackettstown, NJ specializing in DataPower administration and configuration. Jim has assisted in developing and delivering internal DataPower education material to IBM consultants and engineers. Jim has also been an application developer working with several different programming languages and platforms ranging from COBOL to Java. Jim has been a J2EE developer for several years specializing in J2EE development for WebSphere Application Server. He also has several years of experience with WebSphere Application Server installation, configuration, troubleshooting, and administration. Jim has more than ten years of I/T experience with a certificate from the Chubb Institute of Technology and also attended Felician College in Lodi, NJ.

PART I

DataPower Introduction

CHAPTER 1

An Introduction to DataPower SOA Appliances

Let's get one thing straight right from the top—these are not your mother's appliances!

Let's use that opening statement as a springboard for our discussion on exactly what SOA appliances are, how they are used, and how they are similar and dissimilar to traditional household appliances. The use of the term *appliance* to describe this new class of IT products is no accident. It is meant to convey certain parallels to the term that is familiar to us. Think about it—what are the characteristics of your typical household appliances? Visualize the appliances of yesteryear rather than the more complex ones we see on the market today. Certain attributes should come to mind:

- **Purpose-built**—Appliances at home are typically for specialized uses—one for washing clothes, one for keeping food cold, and so on.
- **Simple**—Most appliances have few knobs and controls. They have simple designs due to the dedicated purpose for which they are designed. They are also reliable, so they don't need to be serviced or replaced often.

Get the picture? Now let's move the discussion to a realm where we as IT professionals are more comfortable—for many, that is *not* the realm of domestic chores!

There is a current trend in IT shops to use specialized appliances wherever possible. This is due to several factors, the primary ones being total cost of ownership (TCO), return on investment (ROI), performance, integration, ease of use, and security. To get started, we introduce you to IBM's WebSphere DataPower SOA appliances, and then talk about how appliances can help in each of these areas. Of course, we go into much greater detail throughout this book.

Meet the Family!

The primary[1] three products in the DataPower family are the DataPower XA35, XS40, and XI50, as shown in Figure 1-1. As you can see, the products are outwardly similar in appearance. Each is a hardened 1U rack-mount device in a tamper-proof case with four RJ-45 Ethernet ports, a DB-9 serial port, and a power switch. We are speaking about the base configuration—there are options available, such as adding a Hardware Security Module, which could alter the outward physical profile. There are also replaceable fan trays, batteries, power supplies, and compact flash cards or hard drives.

Figure 1-1 The DataPower product family.

In the following sections, we discuss the feature set for each model and then move on to scenarios in which appliances can be of great value before taking a closer look at what's under the covers.

DataPower XA35

The DataPower XA35 (on the bottom in Figure 1-1) is the entry level product in the line and most representative of the beginnings of the product and DataPower company. The appliance is green, which represents its primary function: to make XML "go faster." This is also the impetus behind the designation of the "A" in XA; it stands for acceleration. The XA35 is at its core a highly efficient XML processing engine. It makes use of DataPower's purpose-built features, such as optimized caches and dedicated SSL hardware to process XML at near wire-speed.

[1] There are also specialized, derivative appliances, such as the XB60 Business-to-Business and XM70 Low Latency Messaging devices, which are discussed in Appendix C, "DataPower Evolution."

The XA35 is a hardened appliance, but it has limited security processing functionality; for example, it does not have the full XML threat protection or encryption/digital signature capabilities as the other models that we discuss. For these reasons, it generally sits behind the DMZ,[2] in the trusted zone to augment the processing of XML files. For example, it may be configured to do validation and transformation of XML before it reaches (or for traffic flowing between) the backend servers. It should be used in-line in the network topology, not as a co-processor hanging off a particular server (although this latter usage is how the appliances were first designed). A popular usage is to receive XML responses from backend servers and transform those into HTML before continuing the response to the client. It has full SSL and SNMP capabilities to fit into the network infrastructure.

DataPower XS40

The DataPower XS40 (in the middle in Figure 1-1) is called the security appliance, and justifiably it is yellow, which represents caution or yield. The "S" in XS stands for security. This model is often found in the DMZ, as its security capabilities are extensive.

The XS40 has all the capabilities of the XA35, plus the following:

- Encryption/decryption utilizing purpose-built hardware for RSA operations
- Digital signature creation/verification
- Fine grained Authentication, Authorization, and Auditing (AAA)
- Full XML threat protection
- Tivoli® Access Manager (TAM) integration option
- Hardware Storage Module (HSM) option
- Dynamic routing
- Message filtering
- Fetching content from remote servers
- MIME, DIME, and Message Transmission Optimization Mechanism (MTOM) attachment processing
- XML Generation 4 (XG4) accelerator module option
- Web services management
- Service level monitoring

DataPower XI50

The DataPower XI50 (at the top in Figure 1-1) is truly the star of the show. It is the integration appliance, as represented by the "I" in XI, and it is IBM blue (what else!) in color. Due to its integration capabilities, it is often found in the backend private network, functioning in an ESB

[2] A DMZ is generally the front-facing "perimeter" of a network, where client traffic enters. Because it's the first point of entry into your network, and hackers have access, it must be hardened.

capacity but is just as suitable for the DMZ. The majority of this book focuses on the XI50, as it is a superset of the other two models.

The XI50 has all the features of the XS40 (and hence the XA35) plus the following:

- WebSphere MQ client option
- WebSphere Java Message Service (JMS) Jetstream protocol connectivity
- TIBCO Enterprise Message Service (EMS) connectivity
- IBM IMS Connect client
- Database option (DB2, Sybase, Oracle, SQL Server)
- Optimized run-time engine for non-XML transformations

This might seem like a short list compared to all the capabilities that the XS40 heaps on what the XA35 had, but these are some big-ticket items! Throughout this book, you will see just how important these features are and how to leverage them.

Now that we've had our brief introduction, let's talk about where appliances are being used in corporate information technology shops, and what kinds of problems they can help solve.

Typical Usages of Appliances

While the appliances are quite versatile and can thus be used to solve many different types of problems (and implementers have been quite creative in this regard), we find there are a few common use cases that are typical. These generally focus around security, performance, cost savings, and integration. In the following sections, we discuss each of these in more detail.

Solving Security Problems

Let's think about what it would take to deploy a software-based proxy product in the DMZ. Each of the layers of the 'typical server' shown in Figure 1-2 requires specialized skills to install and maintain. Particularly for DMZ deployments, the server hardware itself must be hardened. In highly secure environments, this can involve removing any components that might allow information to be taken from the server, such as USB ports and writeable CD/DVD drives. The operating system must also be hardened, removing components such as telnet and sendmail.[3] Often, this results in other layers of the software stack not installing or operating properly! If you are successful in installing the application software stack, it must be hardened as well. These are common requirements for high security environments such as financial companies, intelligence services, and military applications.

[3] The Center for Internet Security (http://cisecurity.org/) has papers showing how to harden various platforms, as well as scoring tools to see how well your platform is hardened.

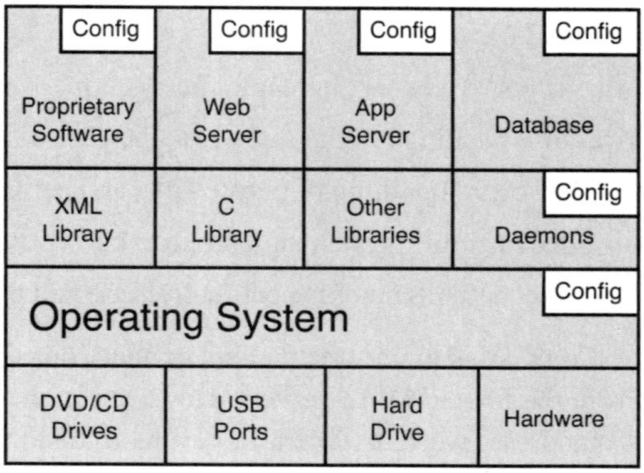

Figure 1-2 Typical server components.

Although software-based DMZ components can be hardened successfully, it is a lot of work. Compare this with the simplicity of installing a dedicated, highly secure hardware appliance, purpose built to do a few things well with fairly simple administrative interfaces, as shown in Figure 1-3.

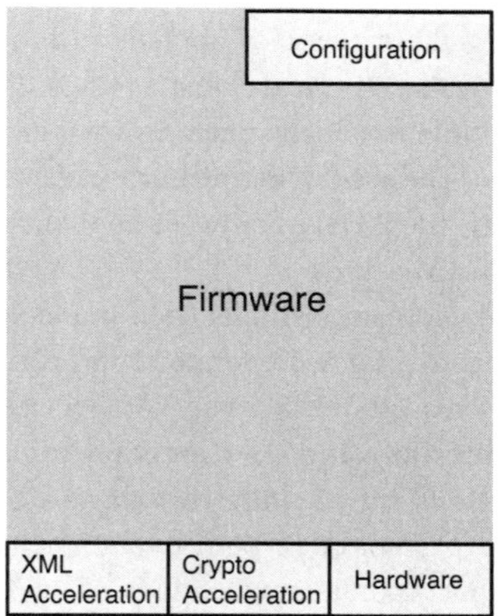

Figure 1-3 High-level SOA appliance components.

The appliances are hardened out of the box. For example:

- They are designed with security in mind from the ground up, before anything else.
- They are shipped secure by default; virtually every feature is disabled, including the network adapters and administrative interfaces (except for the serial port used to do initial bootstrap). If you want something, *you* must turn it on!

- They have an encrypted file system.
- They have no Java, print services, or shareable file system.
- They are tamper-proof—backing out the screws on the case disables the appliance.
- They have specialized secure handling of crypto keys and certificates.
- They have an embedded operating system, not prone to known exposures of common OSs.
- They reject messages by default, unless specifically accepted by configured policies.

The age-old rule for the DMZ is to terminate client connections there and then proxy connections to the backend from the trusted DMZ servers. However, in the field we find even more stringent security policies that do not warrant *any* traffic (even proxied through these secure intermediaries) to the backend until the client is authenticated and authorized. This is referred to as *perimeter security* and is an increasingly common requirement, driving sales of DMZ security products such as TAM. Later, we show how DataPower appliances can also solve this problem.

Another requirement for DMZ components is to virtualize or hide the implementation details of backend servers and applications. Typical DMZ products interact only with the protocol layer of the network stack, so they can hide things like hostname/IP, ports, and URIs, whereas XML-centric application proxies such as DataPower appliances can virtualize on a much more intelligent basis and can analyze the entire message stream.

A strong reason for using these types of appliances is the burgeoning risk of systems becoming compromised by XML-based threats. Just as once upon a time we felt HTTP to be innocuous, today we are susceptible to underestimating what can be done by virtue of XML. In Chapter 20 "XML Threats," we show how entire infrastructures can be brought down using small, simple, well-formed XML files. Only hardware appliances have the processing power to check for the many variations of XML threats.

Another common security problem is a mismatch in the specification levels or credential formats of various technologies across large corporate IT infrastructures. For example, consider a marketing IT silo running on Microsoft®.NET using WS-Security 1.0 and SPNEGO credentials for identity and a manufacturing silo using IBM WebSphere Application Server (WAS), WS-Security 1.1, and LTPA credentials for identity. In today's ESB-driven SOA architectures, a single transaction may have to pass through both environments, so this presents challenges. Because DataPower appliances incorporate a wide range of the latest specification implementations and credential formats, they can be used to transform messages and credentials to fit the target each step of the way. Notice that this can be used to achieve cross-platform single-signon (SSO), although that also depends on other factors such as having a common registry.

To Lower Total Cost of Ownership (TCO)

Refer back to the scenario in Figure 1-2, where there are numerous skills required to install and maintain a typical server and software stack. Now think of this in terms of the staff required and cost to the organization. With self-contained appliances where the operating system and file system characteristics are irrelevant from an administrative perspective, this becomes much less work. The function of the appliances is dedicated and streamlined, hence the administrative tasks and interfaces tend to be as well. For example, in the scenario in Figure 1-2, you have to continually install fixes and updates at every layer of the stack. However, for appliances, you typically do this by uploading a small firmware update and rebooting, which takes only minutes. In the server scenario, you have multiple different administrative consoles to manage the layers of the stack; with the appliances, you have only one console.

The TCO return does not solely manifest itself in the setup and administration of the platform. Consider the silo example in the prior section—where various areas of a corporate IT infrastructure are running Web services across different platforms, such as those from IBM, Microsoft, and BEA. If the corporation has one set of policies for security and SLM that need to be implemented across all these platforms, then it must be done multiple times, by multiple people, with skills on each platform. Not only is the configuration redundant and therefore expensive, but this problem is repeated each time it needs to change, and there is always the risk that the policy will not be implemented exactly the same on each platform, which can lead to security holes or application failures. This is depicted in Figure 1-4.

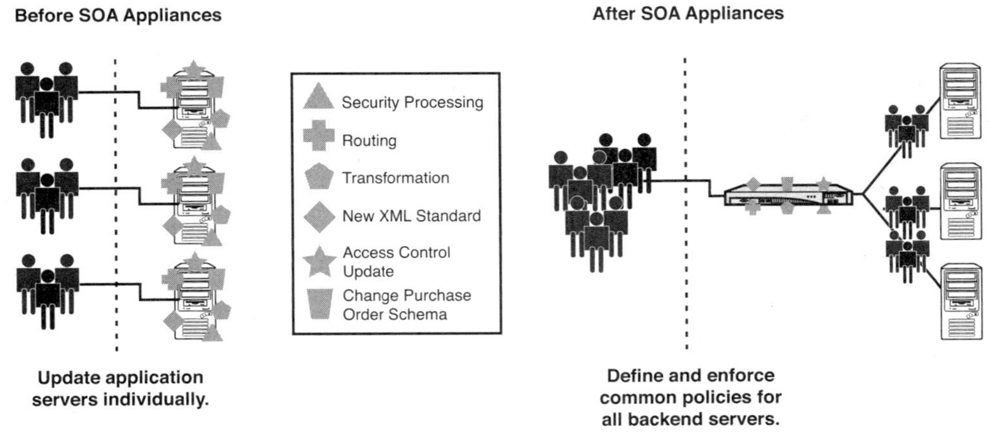

Figure 1-4 Redundant administration versus simplified appliance model.

A more concrete example can be implemented by creating a single service that acts as a Web service proxy on the DataPower appliance, importing the WSDL files for the Web services providers on each of those backend platforms, and then applying the security and SLM policies on the proxy, thereby gaining policy definition and enforcement one time for all platforms. All this is based on standards that we discuss later, not only Web services itself, but also the accompanying standards such as WS-Security for security, WS-Policy for policy definition, WS-Addressing for endpoint resolution, and WS-Management and WSDM[4] for management.

[4] WSDM (Web Services Distributed Management) is a Web service standard for managing and monitoring the status of Web services.

Enhancing Performance

XML is the foundation on which many modern architectures are built—it has evolved into SOAP for Web services and is found across the breadth and depth of the SOA stack and related specifications. Over time, it has evolved from a simple markup language to something quite complex and sophisticated. Of course, the problem as far as performance is concerned is that XML is fairly easy for humans to read, but not for computers. It is a verbose representation of data and typically requires significant resources in terms of CPU power and memory to process. This overhead is typically found in parsing the XML document into an in-memory representation and in validating the XML against its schema file.[5]

Consider the impact of parsing and validating the storm of XML/SOAP documents that hit your systems during peak production levels. Now consider the overhead of security that may be embedded in those messages—validating client identities against LDAP servers, verifying digital signatures, and decrypting encrypted data. This requires a tremendous amount of processing power and time and robs precious cycles away from what your backend systems should really be doing—focusing on transactional business logic! Also consider the absolute waste of expending these cycles for messages that come in badly formed, with schema violations or illegitimate security issues. The cycles expended on processing them and handling the errors are wasted. Figure 1-5 shows a graph demonstrating the CPU overhead of various common tasks. (Notice the parsing level is low here—the main hit when parsing is memory utilization.) Notice the impact of security operations. This can be helped somewhat with hardware-assisted acceleration, but the cost-benefit of hardware acceleration boards is often debated. Also note that abusing these security features to consume CPU resources is one way of mounting attacks.

A grand solution for this, of course, is to use appliances to do all that heavy lifting at near wire speed. As you will see when we discuss the appliance characteristics, they are amazingly fast and can handle these tasks at orders of magnitude faster than software-based solutions running on standard servers. Now focus on another scenario—one where the appliance makes sure that only clean traffic gets to the backend systems. Imagine the huge differential in available processing power on the backend if the validation and security tasks are done by the time the traffic gets there. The appliances can validate schemas, verify signatures, decrypt the data, and more. This can often result in huge performance returns, depending on considerations such as message sizes, cipher strengths, network latency, and so forth.

Speaking of message sizes, this is often another major stumbling block for Java-based software systems processing XML. In modern day real-world systems, we are now seeing huge SOAP messages on the order of hundreds of megabytes or even gigabytes in size. The conundrum is how to process these, given constraints on maximum JVM heap sizes in many platforms. Due to aggressive built-in streaming and compression, appliances can handle messages larger than their actual memory space.

[5] An XML schema definition file (XSD) is a set of rules for how the file should look and what it should contain, including optional and required elements.

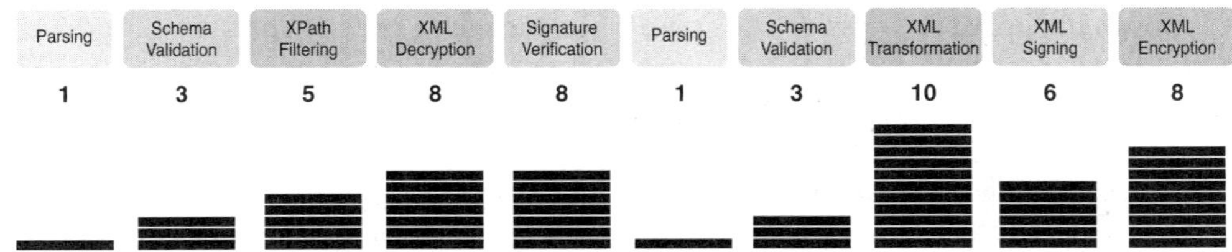

Figure 1-5 Security impact of common tasks.

On another message-related topic, consider applications that do XML transformation between differing schemas; for example, an application that consumes XML purchase orders and must understand a variety of incoming purchase order formats from business partners, and then transforms each into the one "golden" purchase order schema that this company uses. These transformations can be quite expensive to process (see Figure 1-5) and result in bloated application code. We all know that line-for-line, application code is expensive in terms of programmer time, testing, and debugging. Now consider the effect on the application if the transformations were moved out to the appliance on the frontend so that the backend application now gets only the one "golden" schema format. Yes, our application has gone on quite a diet, is less expensive to maintain, and is much faster. One field scenario consisted of a frontend cluster of Java EE applications to do such transformations to keep the cluster of business logic applications behind it lightweight. However, since this was running on a platform that charged for CPU time, and given the overhead of XML transformations shown in Figure 1-5, it was expensive. The solution was to move the transformation layer out to DataPower appliances. The result was a huge cost savings and orders of magnitude faster processing.

Integrating Platforms

In the previous section, we discussed a scenario in which the appliance could be used to bridge differences in standards specifications (WS-Security v1.0 versus. v1.1) and identity credentials (SPNEGO versus LTPA) across systems. This is one good example of easily integrating disparate platforms, particularly when the standards and specifications are in flux. It is difficult for software-based solutions running on standard servers and products to keep up with this. On the appliance, you load a firmware update to get the latest and greatest.

> **NOTE—FIRMWARE VERSIONS USED FOR THIS BOOK**
>
> The recommendations, advice, and practices shown in this book are generally applicable to firmware versions 3.6.0 through 3.7.2 (and likely future releases) and based on the DataPower XI50. However, much of the information in this book is "timeless" in that it represents information that is generally accepted as "best practices" in our experience for most situations, and unrelated to specific firmware versions.

However, there are other issues that arise when integrating different platforms. Consider a scenario in which a medium-sized business XYZ Corp has its infrastructure running on legacy platforms and technologies, perhaps mainframe-based EDI. The business partners that they depend on have long since moved their platforms to Web services and are telling poor XYZ Corp that they can no longer afford to support XYZ's legacy interface to that system, and they must provide a modern SOA or Web services interface or lose the business. This puts XYZ in a bad position; what will it cost to retrain its programmers, rewrite its COBOL applications, and revamp the backends to its Java EE platforms? Likely, it would be a staggering amount! A common solution to this problem is to place appliances at the front of the network as proxies, cook up a WSDL file to describe some Web services, begin receiving the ASCII SOAP messages from the now-happy business partners, and convert them on-the-fly to EBCDIC EDI or COBOL Copybook messages and send them over MQ or IMS Connect to the legacy backend. The backend does not have to change, and no programs have to be rewritten—a win-win!

Due to the variety of protocols (HTTP(S), FTP, MQ, JMS/JFAP, IMS, NFS, TIBCO, MQ, ODBC, SNMP, and so on) supported by the DataPower appliances, there is a wealth of opportunity for protocol bridging, content enrichment, and integration between platforms. Notice that the previous scenario involved message transformation. The XI50 DataPower appliance can handle either XML-to-XML or non-XML transformation scenarios, meaning that messages can be transformed to the appropriate format for any intended backend.

Another common and age-old scenario related to integrating platforms is dynamic routing. Because it is often a requirement to make dynamic routing decisions "on the edge of the network," we have DMZ Web servers, proxies, and load balancers handle this. The problem is that they can understand only the protocol and not the payload of the message. To accomplish the goal, applications place some value in the protocol header to facilitate the content-based routing. As an example, if we want any purchase orders over one million dollars to be routed to high-priority servers, the sending application would place a cookie or attribute in an HTTP header or URL parameter. The Web server, proxy. or load balancer in the DMZ would be configured to check for this and then route the traffic accordingly. The problem with this scenario is that you have to put this hack in the applications and the HTTP payload, potentially disclose message data to attackers, and involve the sender/client. This solution doesn't scale because if you continually do this, the HTTP header and application code bloat.

Because SOA appliances are XML-savvy and can use technologies such as XPath, they can check *inside* the message payload to look for the actual <po_value> element rather than alter the application and HTTP header. If the message is encrypted, you don't need to expose this by externalizing the data; you can just decrypt the message and check the value, and then route accordingly. The client in this case does not have to be complicit—the routing is truly dynamic and transparent. The XML Aware Network layer is shown in Figure 1-6.

One last important feature in regard to the integration story is the use of appliances as ESBs. The appliances fulfill the model of an ESB by virtue of their strong routing, transformation, mediation, and protocol-switching capabilities. IBM has other ESB products capable of implementing the ESB pattern—WebSphere Message Broker (WMB) and WebSphere Enterprise Service Bus (WESB). Each of these have unique capabilities that may suit them for particular usages. Although DataPower may be thought of as a highly secure and performant ESB, the others have features that DataPower does not have in the arenas of transactionality, persistent message handling, and the capability to work in other programming languages. We discuss ESBs in Chapter 5, "Common DataPower Deployment Patterns," and Chapter 9, "Multi-Protocol Gateway."

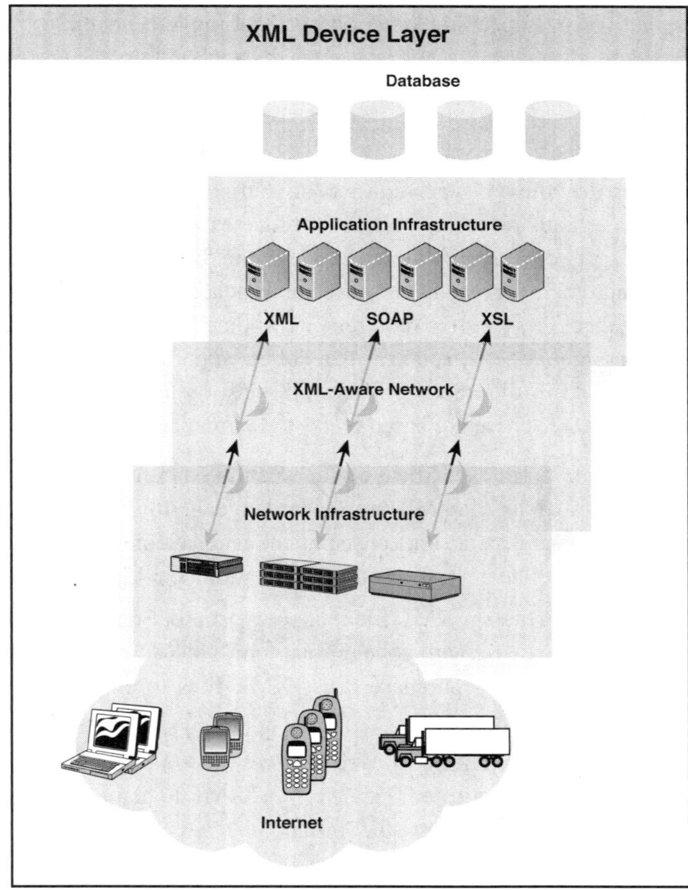

Figure 1-6 XML Aware Network layer.

A Closer Look at the DataPower Products

Now that you have a general idea what "SOA Appliances" are, and have some familiarity with the IBM offerings in this space and what they are used for, we will describe them in more detail.

Physical Characteristics of Appliances

As stated earlier, and demonstrated in Figure 1-1 appliances are "pizza-box," rack-mountable 1U (1.75-inch thick) hardware devices. The only external interfaces are a power switch, 9-pin serial port, and four RJ-45 Ethernet ports. (Appliances with HSM will have a Pin Entry Device [PED] connector.)

Software Architecture of Appliances

As Figure 1-3 illustrates, the software architecture is simple from the user perspective. There is a customized, hardened, native-code operating system kernel that implements the appliance's core functionality. The OS resides in firmware that can be updated by applying small firmware update files.

On top of this is a layer of functionality that is implemented in XSLT stylesheets, which are read-only and used by the system to implement certain functionality. We get into more detail in Chapter 2, "DataPower Quick Tour and Setup."

The next layer up the software stack consists of configurations developed by the user; these are the application proxies and processing policies to process message traffic for your applications. Configuration files and application artifacts can reside in the directory structure on the file system or they can be hosted on remote servers and retrieved and cached at start-up time so that they do not ever reside on the appliance file system (a requirement in some highly secure environments).

Although the operating system itself and many of the appliances' implementation details are custom and proprietary, outwardly, the appliances are built on a standards-based model. A few important ones are listed here. These are based on a single foundation, XML.

- **XML**—A general purpose specification for creating other markup languages—and many are built upon it, such as MathML (a markup language to describe mathematics). It is a combination of data and metadata, consisting of tagged elements to not only show the data but to describe and delineate it; for example, <po_number>12345</po_number>.
- **XSD**—A set of rules that an XML file must conform to. So if you want to define a purchase order XML file to use with your applications, you can create an XSD file to be used to validate those incoming purchase order XML files to ensure they have the proper structures.
- **SOAP**—A message format used by Web services for sending and receiving XML-based messages. It is more sophisticated than "normal" XML in that its construct provides for a message header and body, among other things.
- **WSDL**—A language for describing Web services. It defines the services, ports, bindings, and operations that constitute the Web service, along with the endpoint information (hosts, ports, URIs) and perhaps other metadata such as policy information.
- **XPath**—XPath for XML is somewhat analogous to SQL for databases.[6] XPath allows for searching and retrieving information (nodesets) from XML documents based on some criteria.

[6] A newer and related XML specification named XQuery is much closer to true SQL capability.

- **XSLT**—An XML language for transforming XML documents from one format to another. If you want to transform a vendor's XML purchase order format to your own company's XML format, you can write a set of instructions in XSLT to do so.
- **EXSLT**—A community extension to XSLT to provide a library for things like string manipulation, date/time functions, and other miscellaneous library functions.

Administrative Model

As part of the "secure by default" DataPower mantra, all remote administrative interfaces are shut down by default. The only way to enable them is by bootstrapping the appliance via the serial port. We show how to do this in Chapter 2. After you do this, you have several options for administrative interfaces. These are described in detail in Chapter 12 "Device Administration" and Chapter 13 "Alternate Management Interfaces," but we give a brief overview in the following list:

- **Command-shell Admin**—This can be accessed using telnet, secure-shell (SSH), or the serial port. The Command Line Interface (CLI) is an IOS-like interface, which will be familiar to many network administrators. In the most ultra-secure environments, all remote administrative interfaces are disabled, forcing all administration to be done only by those with physical access to the appliances in the datacenter. For security purposes, telnet normally remains disabled.
- **XML Management Interface**—The XML Management interface provides a way to administer the appliance and obtain status information via XML-based SOAP requests. There are several different specifications that can be used, including DataPower's own SOAP Configuration Management,[7] WS-Management, and WSDM. This interface is commonly used for automated, programmatic, or custom approaches to administration.
- **WebGUI Admin Console**—This is a standard browser-based administrative interface. It is the most commonly used way to administer the appliances. However, in some high security or production environments, browser-based administration is not permitted and is allowed only in development environments as a convenience for developers. You can see in Figure 1-7 that the WebGUI is well laid out, attractive, and intuitive.[8]

The administrative WebGUI is not only used for administering the appliance, it is also used to create the application proxies that are the raison d'être (justification for existence) for the product. You can use the drag-and-drop capabilities of the Processing Policy editor to create work-flow type rules for requests and responses, to carry out various actions as traffic flows through the device. Figure 1-8 shows the simplicity of dragging an Encrypt Action from the upper palette row of actions to the processing rule to encrypt a message as it passes through to its destination. From here, only the certificate to be used for the encryption needs to be identified, although there are

[7] This has in the past been referred to as SOMA, which is shorthand for SOap MAnagement.

[8] This is the admin interface for an XI50; the other models will have fewer features.

many other advanced options that can be chosen, such as the encryption algorithm to use. Compare the ease of this to creating policies to encrypt a message on other platforms (and then factor in the performance difference). Notice in this figure that the other types of actions can be just as easily applied for tasks such as message filtering, creating or validation digital signatures, transforming messages, dynamic routing, and AAA. The Advanced Action contains a great deal more.

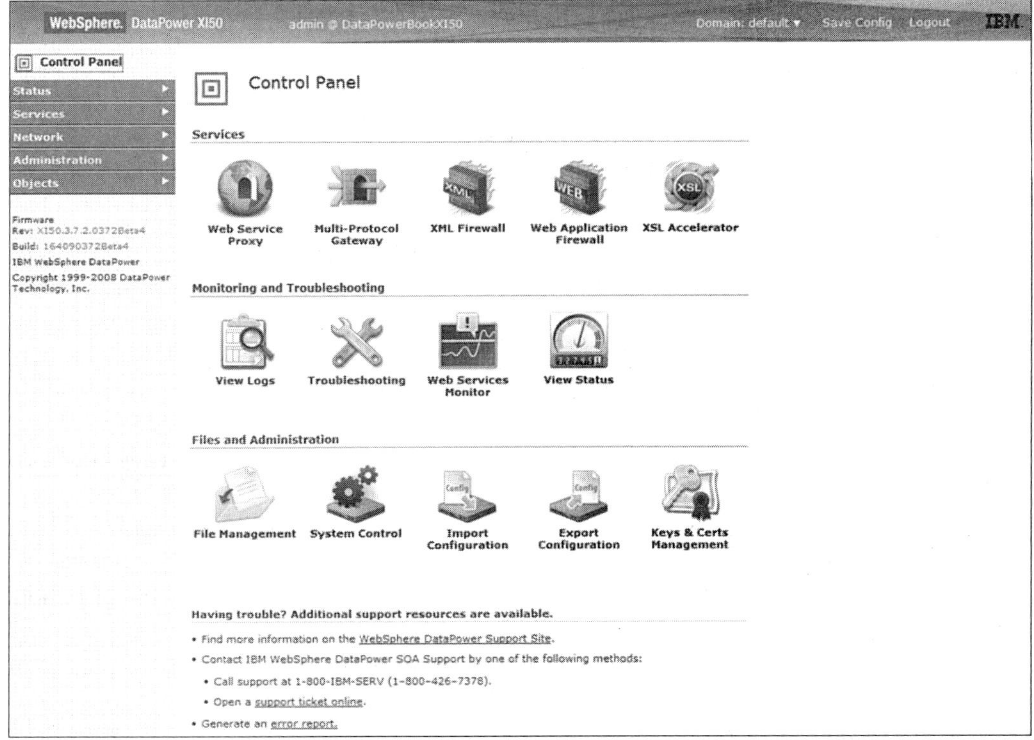

Figure 1-7 DataPower Web Admin console.

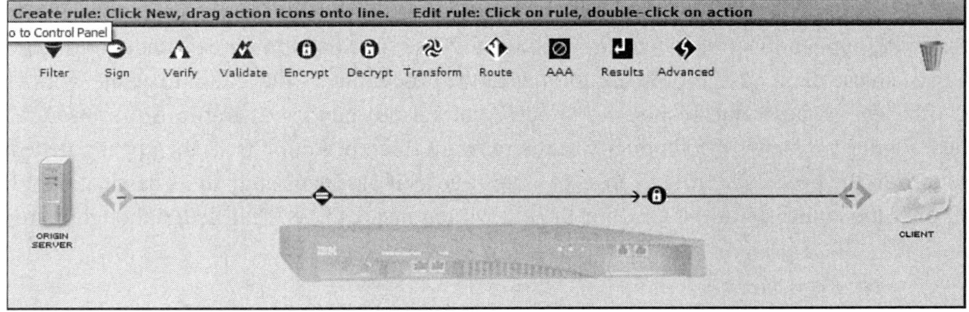

Figure 1-8 Drag-and-drop policy editor.

Often, the browser-based console is used only in development environments for easily building proxies, and from there, automated, scripted processes are used to deploy these configurations to test, QA and production environments, leveraging either the command-line, or SOAP-based administrative interfaces. These techniques are described in Chapter 15, "Build and Deploy Techniques."

Programming Model

As shown in the previous section, most of the work in configuring the appliances is done using the friendly drag-and-drop paradigm of the Processing Policy editor. For any customized scenarios not covered by the GUI, the devices can be programmed.

As the appliance is XML-centric, the custom programming model for DataPower is XSLT, which is a full Turing-complete programming language. Any custom programming is done in this language.

XPath is an important technology for these XML-centric products. Aside from custom programming done in XSLT, XPath expressions are used frequently in building configurations using the WebGUI. For example, if you are building a policy to sign and/or encrypt selected nodesets in an XML or SOAP document, you simply provide DataPower an XPath expression so that it can locate those nodesets. For nonprogrammer types, the DataPower WebGUI provides an easy-to-use XPath tool that enables you to load a sample document and click on the element or nodeset, and the XPath statement is generated for you.

The DataPower appliances offer much more than what standard XSLT and EXSLT have in their libraries. The appliances support crypto operations and many different protocols that are outside the domain of XSLT and EXSLT. To provide for custom programming that leverages the full scope of functionality on the appliances, they include a complete library of extension functions and elements that can be used for XSLT custom programming. These are covered in the chapters in Part VI, "DataPower Development."

Of course, all the power of XML, SOAP, and many of the WS-* specifications/standards are available on the appliance. Some of the key WS- specifications are

- **WS-Security**—A specification to enable message integrity, message privacy, and non-repudiation,[9] typically using digital signatures and encryption.
- **WS-Addressing**—A specification to enable Web services to communicate endpoint and addressing information between themselves.
- **WS-Policy**—A specification that allows Web services to advertise and enforce policies for things like security and quality of service.
- **WS-ReliableMessaging**—A specification that enables Web services to reliably transmit SOAP messages, even when there are problems in the infrastructure that would otherwise lead to failure.

[9] Many security experts find non-repudiation to be a weak concept.

DataPower as a Member of the Network Infrastructure

At their physical core, the DataPower appliances are network devices. Certainly, by looking at them, this would be one's presumption. In Figure 1.1, the most apparent feature is the set of four network interface jacks on the front of the appliance. On the appliance, these are labeled MGMT, ETH0, ETH1, and ETH2. They can be split up any way you choose; for example, it is common to dedicate the Management port to the administrative subnet. From there, the remaining three can be split up so that two receive client traffic and the third connects to the backend private network, thereby segregating the network data for network security.

There are also a number of network protocols supported on the appliance. These include HTTP, HTTPS, FTP, FTPS, SFTP, NFS, MQ, MQ/SSL, JMS, and Tibco EMS for application traffic, and SNMP, SMTP, sFTP, and others for administrative usage.

We've mentioned SNMP a few times, which is ubiquitous and useful for infrastructure monitoring. The appliance comes with SNMP MIB files that can be imported into your monitoring tools to set up monitoring policies, and the appliances can send out SNMP traps when critical events occur. Monitoring can also be achieved by using SOAP, as is the case with the integration with Tivoli ITCAM for SOA (see Figure 1-9). There are also objects built in that are useful for monitoring and auditing, such as message count and duration monitors and sophisticated service-level management tools. Most logging is done off-device, utilizing protocols such as syslog and

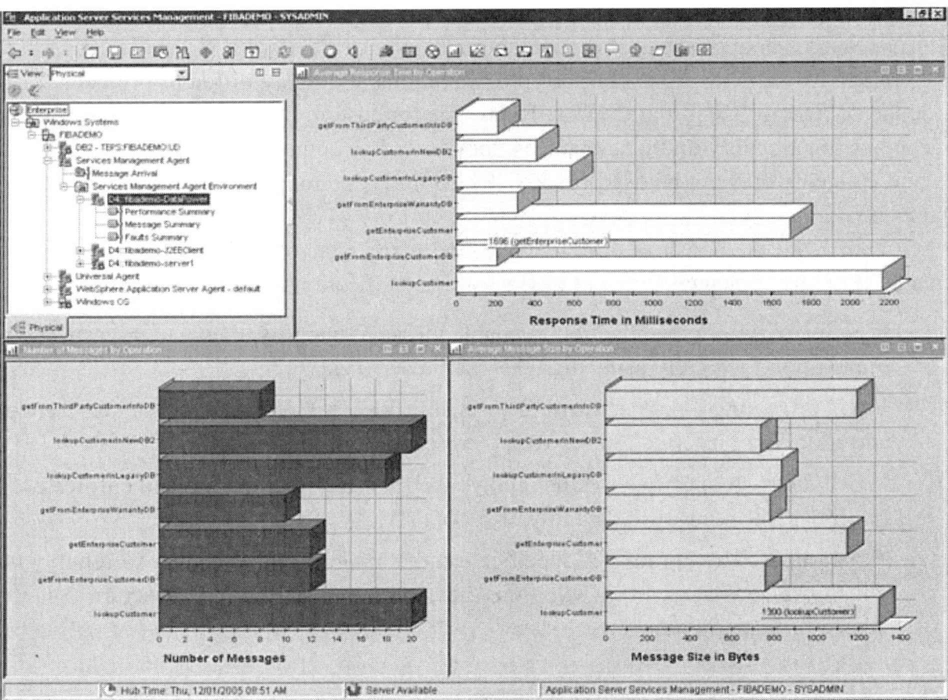

Figure 1-9 Monitoring DataPower appliances with Tivoli ITCAM for SOA.

syslog-NG, or by writing logs to a remote NFS mount. (DataPower never shares its own file system, but can connect to shared file systems on other servers.) There is a full suite of logging formats and protocols for your use, as well as a model for specifying event notifications on various levels of granularity.

Included with the appliances is a utility for managing multiple devices, ITCAM SE for DataPower, which is based on a cut-down version of the Tivoli ITCAM product built on the Tivoli Enterprise™ Monitoring Server (TEMS). This fat-client utility is installed on a server or workstation and enables appliances to be grouped into managed sets in order to keep their firmware levels and configurations in sync. This can be used to cluster application proxies for high availability and better levels of service. It also backs up the configurations when it detects changes.

Similar management features are also included in the WAS 7.0 administrative console. Both utilities are covered in Chapter 29, "Multiple Device Management Tools."

Summary

This chapter served as an introduction and overview of the IBM WebSphere DataPower SOA appliances. We introduced you to the product family and ran through some use cases where the strengths of this platform are emphasized, and then took a closer look and discussed at a glance how the appliances fit in with the rest of the network infrastructure. We expand on all these principles in the following chapters. Although we cannot cover every aspect of these unique devices, we hope to describe those most-often used in your enterprise deployments.

CHAPTER 2

DataPower Quick Tour and Setup

In Chapter 1, "An Introduction to DataPower SOA Appliances," we outlined what an SOA Appliance (specifically, a DataPower SOA appliance) is and what it is used for (or should be!). We focused that discussion primarily at the conceptual, more abstract level. Let's dive in and get our hands dirty. In this chapter, we take a closer look at the devices, and then show you what you should do to get up and running.

Getting Started with Your New Appliance

It is not unlike many technical practitioners to be in a hurry to rip open and install new products as they arrive from the shipping dock. Certainly, lengthy corporate procurement processes can help to build the anticipation! And as we know, many in the technical space prescribe to the mantra "Documentation be damned!"

However, despite their reputation for simplicity, appliances like any other product should be carefully planned for and implemented to prevent later rework and reconfiguration. Let's take a walk through the process.

Hey Bert, Got a Package for You...

For those of us who get excited about technology, it's a great moment when the device finally arrives in its well-padded shipping container. The contents yield the following:

- DataPower appliance
- Rack-mount kit
- Power cords
- Reference Kit and Documentation CD-ROMs

- 6' null-modem female-female serial cable
- Printed installation manual

The installation manual has the usual dire electrical warnings and other good advice such as not to use the appliance for a "shelf or workspace." (So you'll have to find another place for those pictures of the kids.)

> **TIP—READ THE MANUAL!**
>
> Although experience shows that folks too often don't, it's a good idea to temper your excitement for a few moments and read through the short install manual, even though we guide you through the process in this chapter.

The Resource CD has a great deal of valuable content that should also be examined, and some of the items found on it may have updated versions of the DataPower Web page. Although the contents of the CD change occasionally, some examples of what you might find follow:

- **WebGUI User Guide**—This is the most-often used part of the documentation set. It describes the features and usage of the Web administrative console for DataPower, and has a lot of other auxiliary information as well, such as how to interface with IBM DataPower support. Check this document if you're stuck trying to do something with the CLI, as it often explains configuration choices in more depth than the CLI Guide.
- **Example Configurations Guide**—This is the one document that we recommend you read end-to-end. It shows appliance usage and configuration for several example use cases, such as a Human Resources Web Service Portal.
- **CLI Reference Guide**—This is a good reference to keep handy when performing administration from the command line, as it provides detailed information on the command syntax and example executions.
- **Install Guide**—This is a soft-copy of the printed install guide that comes in the box.
- **ITCAM SE for DataPower**—This was described in our first chapter, and we expand on its use later in this book. It is a tool for managing and clustering multiple appliances, and is covered in Chapter 29, "Multiple Device Management Tools."
- **Eclipse/RAD Management Plugin**—This tool is a DataPower management plugin to be installed in the Eclipse (including Rational® Application Developer) development environment. It is useful for developers who want to administer their own devices from within their Eclipse workspace.
- **Eclipse Co-processing Plugin**—This plugin enables XSLT development done on the Eclipse platform to offload transformations to the DataPower device for testing and debugging.
- **XML Spy Plugin**—This achieves the same purpose as the Eclipse co-proc plugin described previously, except it is used for the Altova XMLSpy development product.

The appliance is a 1U rack-mountable device. All devices in the product line have the same physical characteristics. The printed installation manual has the specifics regarding exact size and weight, and the operating environment and power considerations. Because that information is readily accessible on the IBM product Web site, we won't repeat it here. Due to the devices' massive processing power, there is an array of fans to keep them cool. These are variable speed fans and may be somewhat louder at startup or reboot than during normal runtime.

Let's inspect our newly acquired device. Refer to Figure 2-1 and perhaps the actual appliance pictures in our introductory chapter. Both of these show the appliance with the front bezel plate still attached, but this can be removed for easier access to some of the ports. Referring to the letters in the figure, we see the following features:

K: **Console Port**—This is the DB-9 serial port connector used to initially bootstrap the device. It is hard-wired into a command-line administration shell, as you will see when we move on to initialize the appliance. In some high-security environments, this is the only administrative interface enabled, effectively disabling the ability to do remote administration and forcing the administrator to have physical access to the appliance in the datacenter.

A, B, C, D, I, J: **Link/Activity Lights**—These are on each of the four Ethernet interfaces and show you the network speed and when there is network activity. Their function is described in detail in the Install Guide.

E: **Power Indicator**—This should be green under normal conditions—when the device is turned on and connected to an AC power supply. If the device is powered off, there is no AC power supply (perhaps if it has failed or isn't plugged in), or there is an over-temperature condition, so this LED will be off.

F: **Storage**—This green LED will be on when auxiliary is being accessed.

G: **Locate**—This blue LED is activated and deactivated by the DataPower firmware, as described in the Install Guide.

H: **Error Alarm**—This yellow LED is illuminated upon device failures as described in the Install Guide.

L, M, N, O: **Ethernet Connectors**—The four RJ45 Ethernet ports, MGMT, ETH0, ETH2, ETH1 respectively, as described in Chapter 1.

P: **PED Port**—This is a port for connecting a PIN Entry Device for use with the optional Hardware Security Module (HSM)[1] that can be ordered with a DataPower device. This port is not present for non-HSM appliances.

[1] HSMs provide secure, encrypted storage of keys. The appliance's encrypted firmware and key storage features serve the same purpose; however, the HSM is often ordered with the device to comply with IT Security policies or standards, such as FIPS 140-2 Level 2 and 3.

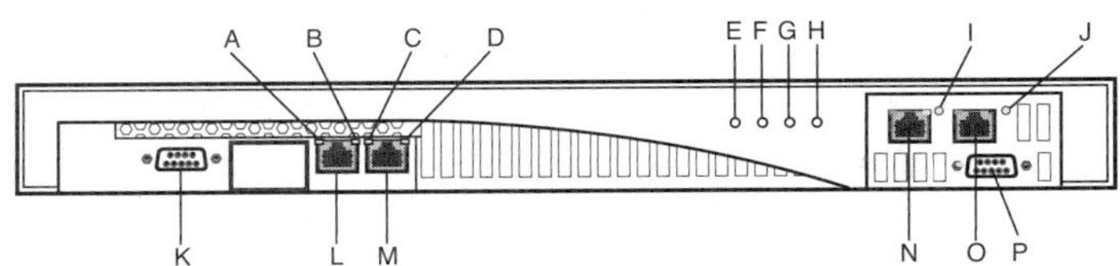

Figure 2-1 Front face of a DataPower appliance.

Let's have a look at the rear of the appliance, as shown in Figure 2-2. The two power supplies are visible here, as well as the power switch and fan trays. There are two power supplies for redundancy and high availability. Should one fail (or not be plugged in), the device will continue to operate on the other (and emit warnings in the device log as to the situation). Care must be taken to not block the fan exhausts, or the device will begin to overheat. The components shown in Figure 2-2 are as follows. Their function is described in detail in the Install Guide.

A, B: **Power Supply LEDs**

C: **LED Diagnostics Panel**

D, E: **Power Supply Modules 1 and 2**

F: **Auxiliary Data Storage**—Either the hard drives or compact flash used for aux storage.

G: **Battery Tray**

H: **Fan Module 2**

I: **Power Switch**

J: **Fan Module 1**

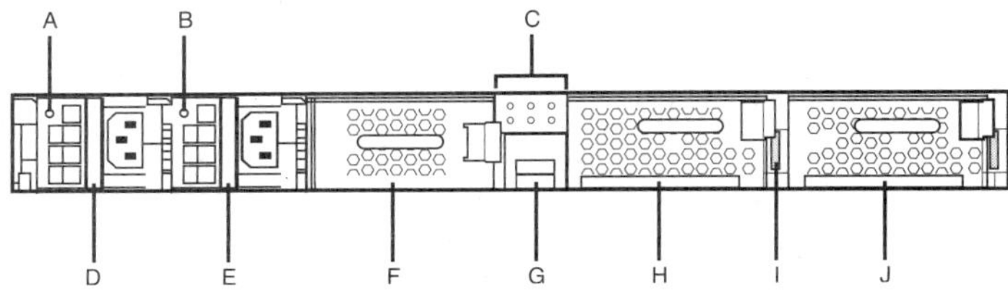

Figure 2-2 Rear of a DataPower appliance.

Important Resources Not in the Box

It's best to be aware of all possible resources when doing any kind of work so that if problems occur, you have places to turn for help. We've already discussed the resources that come with the product. There are also many others you should be aware of, including the following:

- **DataPower Product Home Page**—www.ibm.com/software/integration/datapower is where you find IBM's home base on the Web for the appliance models. There are sub-pages here for the product Library, News, and Support areas. The Support link in particular has important 'Flash" notes plus a wealth of pointers to things like technotes, Redbooks®, FAQs, and troubleshooting guides. A critical link on this page is labeled "Firmware and documentation download" and is where you would go to get updated documentation and the system updates for your particular model. Directions on getting product support are also linked from this page.

- **Redbooks**—www.redbooks.ibm.com has a search box; a query on "DataPower" yields a number of resources, including a Redbook series and other documents related to integration with IBM's other ESB products.
- **developerWorks**—www.ibm.com/developerworks/ also yields an extensive list of articles written about DataPower appliances. Some of these are by the authors of the book you are currently reading.
- **Public Discussion Area**—www.ibm.com/developerworks/forums/forum.jspa?forumID=1198 is the only discussion area officially sanctioned by IBM. Here, you can find members of IBM's technical community (tech sales, support, engineering, and field consultants) answering questions on a continual basis. However, this is not formal product support; questions are answered on an ad-hoc basis.

Next Steps—The Planning Phase

Before moving on to our next step, where you actually configure and enable the device, it is best to have some planning discussions with representatives from various areas of your IT department. For example, the network team should be consulted for placement and integration with other network components, firewall ports that need to be opened, and other topics. You need the network team to assign one or more static IP addresses, depending on how many interfaces on the appliances you plan to enable. You need default gateways, possibly static routes, and other network-related information. If you plan on using SSL for network connections, you may need keys and certificates created by your security team or from outside sources. The application teams may have to describe what types of integration will be necessary for their applications—for example, if Web services endpoints will be looked up in a registry dynamically or LDAP servers need to be read for authentication, then ports may need to be open in the firewalls from DataPower to those servers so that the traffic can flow. Plan carefully!

Next Steps—What You Will Need

To do the initial configuration described in the next section, you need the following items (in addition to what came with the appliance):

- A supported serial terminal emulator; alternatively, a Serial-to-USB cable (discussed in the next section), or serial to RJ-45 adapter if your administration network provides this kind of connectivity

- Network information—one or more IP addresses, default gateways, subnet masks, DNS server info, NTP server IP/hostname, and static routes
- Medium cross-tip (Phillips) screwdriver for rack mounting
- Power source to plug the device into

Connecting and Powering Up

The installation manual has clear instructions and diagrams about the rack-mounting procedure, so we refer you to that document for the hardware installation details. Assuming this has been done, let's get to the good part. Obviously, a good first step might be to connect the power cords. Do not power on the appliance yet.

> **TIP—Power Connections**
>
> Whenever loss of data is a concern, you should have both power cords connected to independent, conditioned power sources. Those redundant power supplies are there for a reason! Failing to do so will result in repeated dire warnings in the DataPower log about a power supply having "failed" when, in fact, the problem is that it is not connected.

At this point, make your serial port connection. The provided null modem cable can be used to connect to a standard ASCII terminal, but frankly those haven't been seen much since the 1980s. The usual procedure is to use a workstation with a serial port or use a USB-to-Serial converter cable and attach it to one end of the serial cable provided with the device and the other end to a USB port on your workstation. A typical converter is shown in Figure 2-3. Of course, the other end of the serial cable should be connected to the serial port on the appliance, as shown in Figure 2-1.

> **TIP—Connect, Then Boot**
>
> On first initialization, you should always connect the serial cable first, and then power up the appliance. This enables you to see the boot sequence and any error messages that might appear.

> **TIP—Don't Forget That Disc!**
>
> If you purchase a USB-serial cable, keep the device driver disc that comes with it in your gear bag with the cable. It's not unusual to have to do this install from other workstations, which may not have the driver for your cable installed. In some high-security environments, there may be no Internet connectivity from the datacenter to download one.

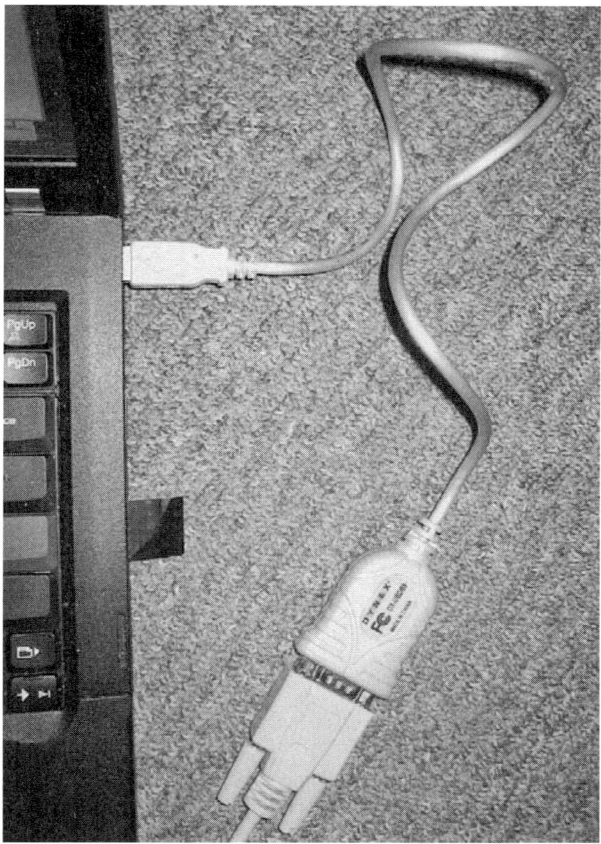

Figure 2-3 USB-to-serial converter cable attachment.

If you are using Windows®, you may want to verify which COM port the USB serial cable is using. To do this, go to Start→My Computer, right-click, and then click on Manage. The Computer Management applet displays. Click on Device Manager and then open the Ports section. You should see your cable listed and the port it is using, as shown in Figure 2-4.

Now it's time to get a terminal session established. Any ASCII terminal emulation software can be used for this, as the requirements are simple. We use the free Windows HyperTerminal utility. It is typically under Start→All Programs→Accessories→Communications, but if you are going to be doing this a lot, we recommend that you create a desktop shortcut. When HyperTerminal runs, it asks for a name for the new connection. You can use whatever value you find reasonable.

Next, you should see a Connect To dialog, and here you want to change the Connect Using drop-down to the COM port that your cable is using, and then click OK. Now you should be at the Port Settings dialog. Enter the values as shown in Figure 2 (although other flow control settings may work as well, and this may depend on the type of serial cable being used) and click OK.

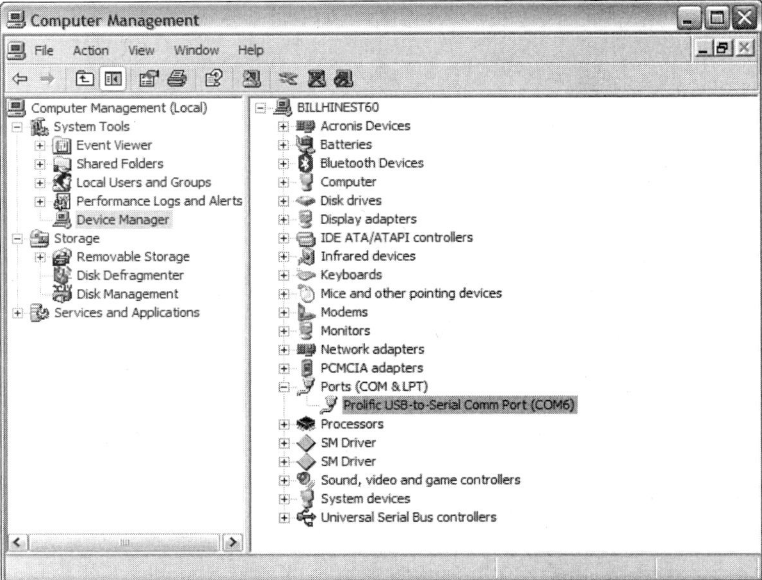

Figure 2-4 Checking the COM port.

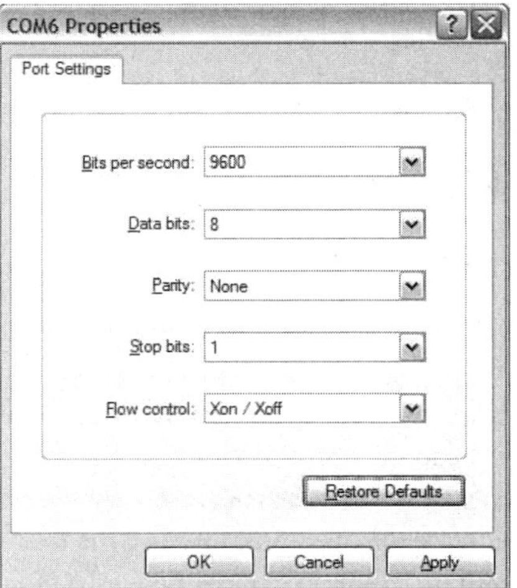

Figure 2-5 HyperTerminal port settings.

You may now fire up the appliance using the power switch on the back. You may notice that initially the fans are quite loud and then decrease in volume as the boot-up sequence progresses. You should now be in the HyperTerminal terminal window. In the lower-left corner, there is a "connected" static string that shows the connection time. If the value there is greater than zero and changing, you are connected. Otherwise, you may have to go to Call→Connect in the menu to establish a connection. When the boot-up sequence finishes, you should be presented with a login prompt. Log in as user admin and provide the password from the instructions included with the device. A license agreement displays; review and accept this if you agree to the terms. Next, you are asked to provide a new password.[2] As we stress in the tip that follows, safeguard this new password and do not lose it! When this is done, you should be at the main prompt, which shows as xi50# for the XI50, as you can see in Figure 2-6.

```
xi50# co
Global configuration mode
xi50(config)# int mgt0
Interface configuration mode (mgt0 )
xi50(config-if[eth4])# ip address 192.168.1.107/24
Operation succeeded
xi50(config-if[eth4])# ip default-gateway 192.168.1.1
Operation succeeded
xi50(config-if[eth4])# exit
xi50(config)# web-mgmt 192.168.1.107 9090
Web management: successfully started
xi50(config)# write mem
Overwrite previously saved configuration [y/n]? y
xi50(config)# exit
xi50# _
Connected 0:50:05    Auto detect    9600 8-N-1    SCROLL  CAPS  NUM  Capture  Print echo
```

Figure 2-6 CLI commands for network setup.

> **TIP—NEVER, NEVER LOSE THE ADMIN PASSWORD!**
>
> The admin password for the device is an important thing. If this password is lost, the only recourse is to send the device back to IBM to be reset. Of course, you may still log on to the device with other accounts that may have been created, but there is only one admin superuser account. Safeguard that password carefully!

Now that you are through the preliminaries, our next objective is to configure one of the network ports and enable the WebGUI so that further administration can be done remotely. We cover the Command Line Interface (CLI) admin model in more detail later in the book, so in this chapter, we show you just enough to accomplish these goals. You may also use the DataPower CLI Command Reference as a guide.

The command sequence is shown in Figure 2-6. We discuss each command in the following list:

- **co**—This is a shortened form of the *configure terminal* command. With CLI, you do not need to enter entire, lengthy commands. You need to enter only enough of the command to uniquely distinguish it from any other command. Notice that after this command is entered, the device responds that it is in Global configuration mode, and the command prompt has changed to xi50(config)# to show the current command context.

[2] If you are using hardware series 9004 or above, you will be prompted to run the Install Wizard. We will demonstrate device setup without this, so as to be compatible with all current models.

- **int mgt0**—This shortened form of *interface* puts the Ethernet interface designated as mgt0 (or the management port as labeled on the front panel of the device) into configuration mode. You can also type eth4, as this is a synonym for mgt0. The other interfaces are referred to as eth0, eth1, and eth2. (There is not an eth3 between eth2 and mgt0/eth4.) Although any interface could be used for administration, for clarity and to avoid confusion you should use the one labeled "MGMT" on the front of the device, which is mgt0. The device responds with a prompt describing the new context.
- **ip address**—With this command, we set the listening IP address for the adapter that we are configuring (mgt0). The dotted quad notation is used, along with a slash and the subnet in CIDR notation. These will be described in Chapter 3, "DataPower as a Network Device," along with more detail on configuring these interfaces. If you don't know CIDR, you can use a dotted quad notation for the subnet as well—for example, ip address 192.168.1.107 255.255.255.0. You would normally obtain an IP address and this other related information from your network team.
- **ip default-gateway**—This command establishes the default gateway for this adapter. In some cases, this is the same address as the IP of the adapter, with a .1 as the last node in the quad. However, it's always best to check with your network team and get this information at the time you obtain an IP address, rather than guess at it.
- **exit**—This command applies any changes that have been made and takes us out of configuration mode for mgt0 and drops us back into global configuration mode.
- **web-mgmt**—This command enables the Web administration console to listen only on the IP address that we have established for mgt0 (see tip that follows) and on the typical port of 9090. Some shops may want to use a port other than the well-known default port, and that can be designated here in place of 9090. The device listens only on SSL for the WebGUI.
- **write mem**—This saves the configuration to the persistent flash memory of the appliance's file system. Until you use this command, the settings will be active only in the running configuration. The settings actually become "live" when you exit out of a particular administration area, as we did with the exit command two commands ago.
- **exit**—This drops us out of global configuration mode. If you are done with the session, enter the exit command one more time to leave the terminal session and go back to the login prompt. This is *very* important for security reasons; you don't want the next person to connect via the serial port to find a conveniently logged in session under your ID. *Always* completely exit the console session!

TIP—Be Sure to Use a Real IP Address

You cannot just guess at an IP address to assign to these interfaces. For example, you might find that your workstation is using 192.168.1.100 and think, "Well, I'll just use 192.168.1.500." IP addresses must conform to strict guidelines and be legitimate values in correlation with their subnet mask values. They must not be within the DHCP range for your network, or the DHCP server may give that same address out to another adapter on the network, causing an outage. You can use DHCP instead of a static IP address so that the appliances get an address dynamically at startup, but this is uncommon for server-type devices.

TIP—Never Use 0.0.0.0

Although many examples you may come across for enabling the WebGUI and other administrative interfaces on the device will show 0.0.0.0 being used as the listening IP address, we strongly urge you not to do this. This means that the appliance will listen on all configured interfaces on the device for administrative traffic. For example, you could access the WebGUI from the adapter designated for client traffic. It is a good security practice to segregate admin traffic from application traffic so that the rest of the world cannot discover your admin interfaces. You could argue that they would still need a password to do anything, but why allow them to get halfway there? Set up a management interface and enforce strictly that all administrative traffic flows through it.

DataPower WebGUI Administrative Console Quick Tour

Now that we have assigned an IP address and default gateway to the management interface and enabled the WebGUI administrative console, we can use the console for further changes. In your favorite Web browser (ours is Mozilla Firefox), go to the address https://<ip_address_of_mgt0>:<port>. Notice that this is https rather than http. You have to use the address and port that you assigned to web-mgmt in the CLI session. The login page is shown in Figure 2-7, although this particular one has been customized a little with some descriptive text. We show you how to do that in a bit.

You will notice that in addition to the typical user and password fields, there is a drop-down called "Domain." The only domain currently is called *default*, as shown in Figure 2-7. Domains are areas of runtime isolation that are somewhat analogous to separate Java Virtual Machines in an application server. They allow your configurations (which are in general proxies to backend applications) to be separated from each other (or grouped together) so that their environments can be independently restarted, backed up, administered, and so on. These are described in more detail in Chapter 12, "Device Administration," where you will also learn how to create additional user and group accounts on the appliances. For now, the only thing important related to domains is that the default domain should be used solely for global device configuration, and not for building application proxies. So, we log in to the default domain and continue our initial configuration. Enter the user admin and the new password that you created earlier, and press the Login button.

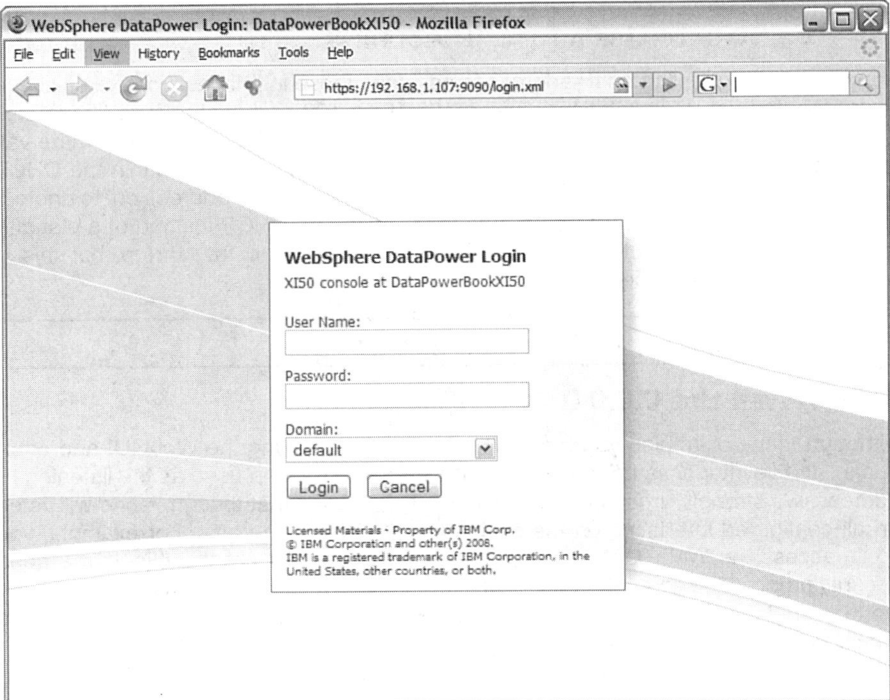

Figure 2-7 DataPower WebGUI console login page.

Essential WebGUI Components

After logging in to the administrative console, the main page displays. This is broken into several main areas, as shown in Figure 2-8. In the upper-right corner, you can see the following:

- **admin@DataPowerBookXI50**—This is a static text string indicating the currently logged in user and device name. Rather than a device name here, your new device may simply show the IP address.
- **Domain**—The domain that the current user is logged in to. You may move between domains simply by selecting another from this drop-down, as long as you have privileges to work in the domain you have selected.
- **Save Config**—As you make changes using the console, they are applied to the running configuration but are not saved to the persistent flash storage until you click this link. This is equivalent to the write mem command that we used from our CLI session when doing the initial config earlier in this chapter.
- **Logout**—This logs the current user out of the console and returns to the login page.

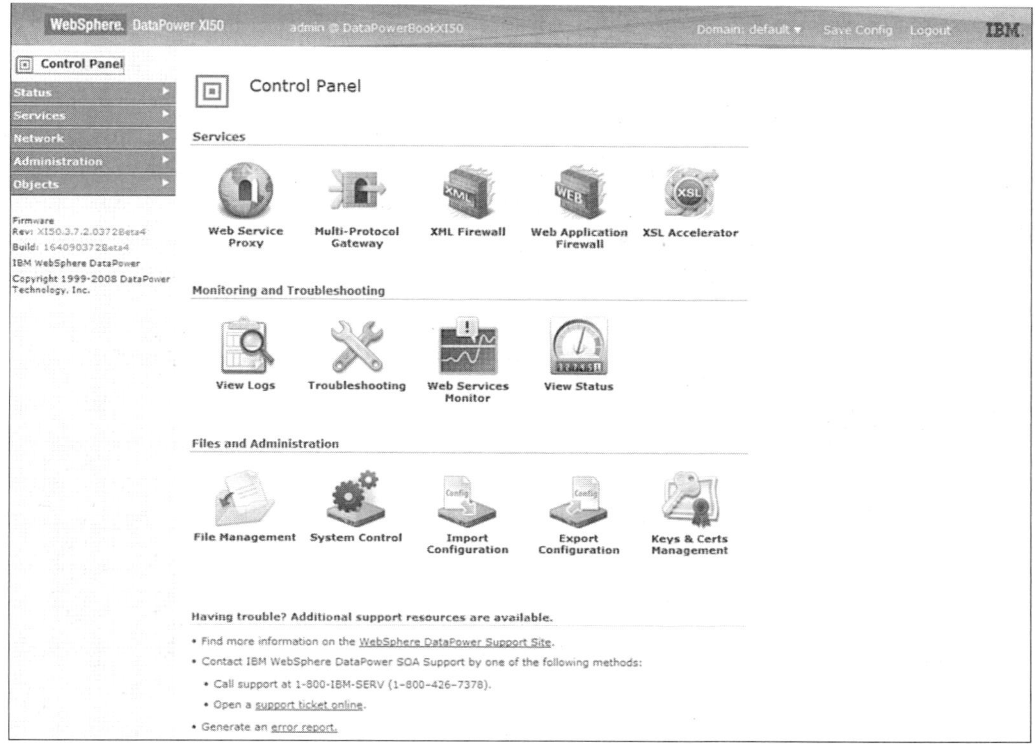

Figure 2-8 WebGUI Control Panel.

> **TIP—ALWAYS REMEMBER TO CLICK SAVE CONFIG**
>
> Configuration changes are not persisted until this button is clicked. If you do not save your changes and the box is recycled for any reason, your changes will be lost.

The bulk of the page is dominated by the Control Panel view, a series of categorized icons. You can see in Figure 2-8 that the icons are broken out into groups for Services (application proxies) that can be built, Monitoring and Troubleshooting tools, and File and Administration tools. To return to the Control Panel at any time, you can click the Control Panel link shown in the upper-left corner, which is present in all pages of the console.

This leaves the final area of the console, which is the left-side Navigation menu. Clicking any of these hyperlinked categories (Status, Services, Network, Administration, or Objects) opens up a contextual sub-menu. There is overlap in functionality between the Navigation menu and Control Panel—for example, you can select and edit a Web Service Proxy through either means; however, while the Control Panel often offers a more streamlined and wizard-like screen flow, the interface exposed by the Navigation menu may offer additional advanced options that are not visible through the Control Panel view of the same object (for example, the capability to enable or disable an object). Note the static text below the Navigation menu in Figure 2-8; this is a quick way to find out what model device and what firmware level the appliance you are currently logged in to is running, and also handily shows the email address for DataPower support.

Let's explore the Navigation menu more. Clicking on the Status link opens up this section to an amazingly long sub-menu. It would be worthwhile to spend a lot of time here to get a feel for the types of things that can be monitored on the device. In most cases, these would be monitored by some external software, using SNMP or SOAP, but it's handy to be able to do a quick check using the WebGUI. In Figure 2-9, we clicked on Fan Sensors and can now see relevant information, such as the speed and status of each fan.

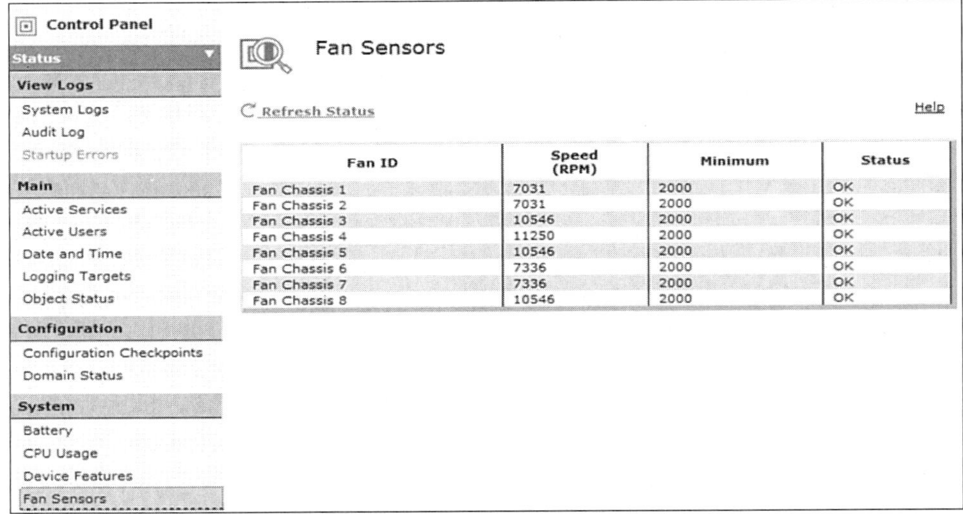

Fan ID	Speed (RPM)	Minimum	Status
Fan Chassis 1	7031	2000	OK
Fan Chassis 2	7031	2000	OK
Fan Chassis 3	10546	2000	OK
Fan Chassis 4	11250	2000	OK
Fan Chassis 5	10546	2000	OK
Fan Chassis 6	7336	2000	OK
Fan Chassis 7	7336	2000	OK
Fan Chassis 8	10546	2000	OK

Figure 2-9 Environmental sensors status.

Two important items in the Status menu are at the top—the System Logs and Audit Log. The system log in the default domain shows logging activity for every domain on the appliance. It can be filtered down to show activity for specific domains, or for specific types of messages (for example, only log messages related to certificate expiry). The audit log shows when things such as maintenance to keys and certs, firmware changes, and device reboots are done and who did them. It shows all historical information until it reaches its maximum size, at which time the oldest records are truncated. See Chapter 14, "Logging and Monitoring," for more details on saving this log for historical data.

TIP—Separate Administrative Accounts

Being able to capture audit log activity is just one of many good reasons to have separate accounts for each person who will be administering the device. Similar to the root account and password for a Unix server, the admin account should rarely be used and the password for it known only to a few select people.

Completing the Configuration

Now that we have completed our initial network configuration and enabled the WebGUI, let's continue. Note that we have only configured one of the Ethernet interfaces available on the appliance. Certainly we will need more than just that one.

Completing the Network Config

We have configured the first management Ethernet interface using CLI; now let's finish the network configuration within the WebGUI. We will enable a second interface for application (client) traffic. The network configuration can be changed only while in the default domain, which is where we still are because we haven't created any other domains. In Figure 2-10, we show the configuration page reached by Network→Interface→Ethernet Interface→eth1. We have entered parameters similar to those we used in the CLI session: the IP address for the interface to listen on and the default gateway. In this screen, we dropped down the Physical Mode list to show the capability to set the speed for a particular interface; in this case we will leave it defaulted to Auto. Keep in mind that when using Auto, the network switch that the device is connected to must also be set to Auto.

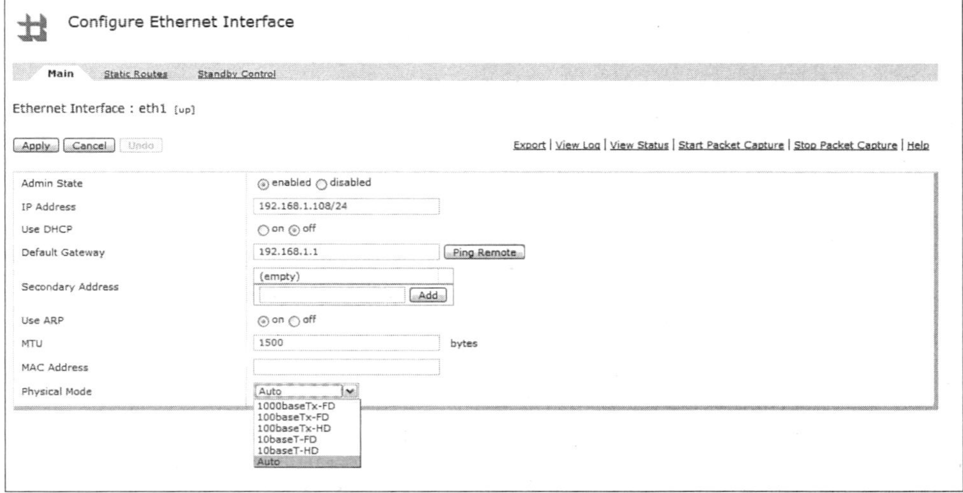

Figure 2-10 Ethernet1 configuration.

The next step in our network setup configures the device for DNS so that hostnames can be resolved. Under Network→Interface→DNS Settings you can see a list of configured servers. Clicking the Add button reveals the entry screen shown in Figure 2-11. We simply need to provide the IP address of a DNS server here and accept the other defaults to add it to the list.

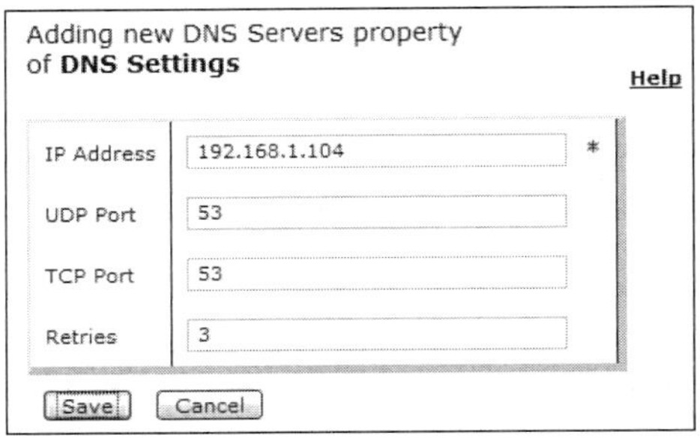

Adding new DNS Servers property
of **DNS Settings**

Help

IP Address	192.168.1.104	*
UDP Port	53	
TCP Port	53	
Retries	3	

Save Cancel

Figure 2-11 DNS server config.

To test the DNS config, you can go back to the Control Panel and choose the Troubleshooting icon; on the resulting page, you see a Ping tool, where you can enter a hostname such as www.google.com and test to see whether it can be resolved and reached by the device.

It is a recommended practice to configure host aliases for the network interfaces on the device. This helps to keep your configurations more portable. We discuss this in more detail in Chapter 15, "Build and Deploy Techniques." Figure 2-12 shows the two host aliases we built by going to Network→Interface→Host Alias.

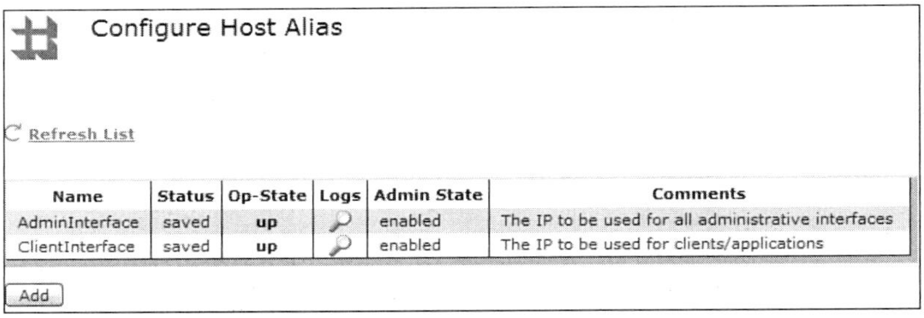

Configure Host Alias

Refresh List

Name	Status	Op-State	Logs	Admin State	Comments
AdminInterface	saved	up		enabled	The IP to be used for all administrative interfaces
ClientInterface	saved	up		enabled	The IP to be used for clients/applications

Add

Figure 2-12 Host Alias configuration.

Let's look at how to take measures to ensure that the system date and time will remain correct. One common way to do this is to set computer systems in the network infrastructure to use NTP to tie them to some common central NTP server for synchronization.

Figure 2-13 shows how to do this by going to Network→Interface→NTP Settings, clicking the radio button to enable the service, providing the hostname or IP address of an NTP server, clicking the Add button, and then committing the changes. You should also go to Administration→Device→Time Settings to set the correct time zone for the geography in which the device will operate.

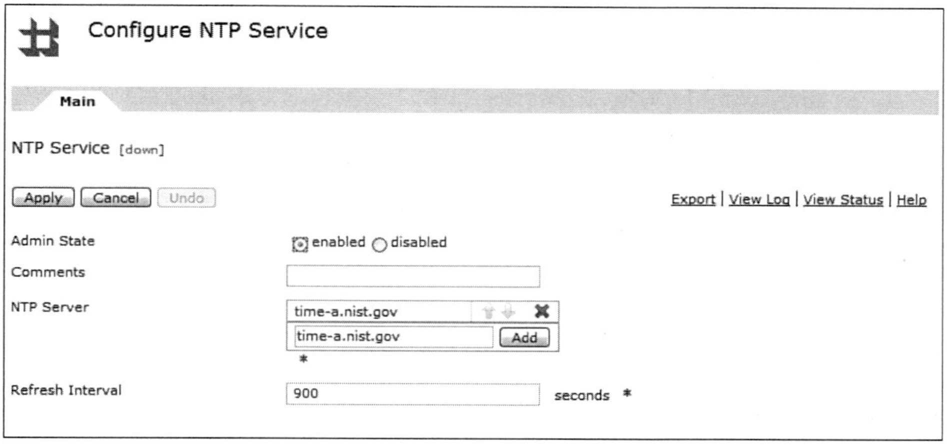

Configure NTP Service

Main

NTP Service [down]

Apply Cancel Undo   Export | View Log | View Status | Help

Admin State   enabled disabled

Comments

NTP Server   time-a.nist.gov

time-a.nist.gov Add

*

Refresh Interval   900 seconds *

Figure 2-13 NTP settings.

Let's continue with the Network menu to turn on the SSH Service so that we can do secure remote command line administration. As shown in Figure 2-14 (reached from Network→Management→SSH Service), we have clicked the Select Alias button to choose the AdminInterface host alias (rather than entering the IP address directly, or worse yet—0.0.0.0!) and then enabled the service with the radio button and clicked the Apply button. Notice in this figure that you can also enter an access control list of client IP addresses that are permitted to connect to the SSH service on the device. This is available for all administrative interfaces.

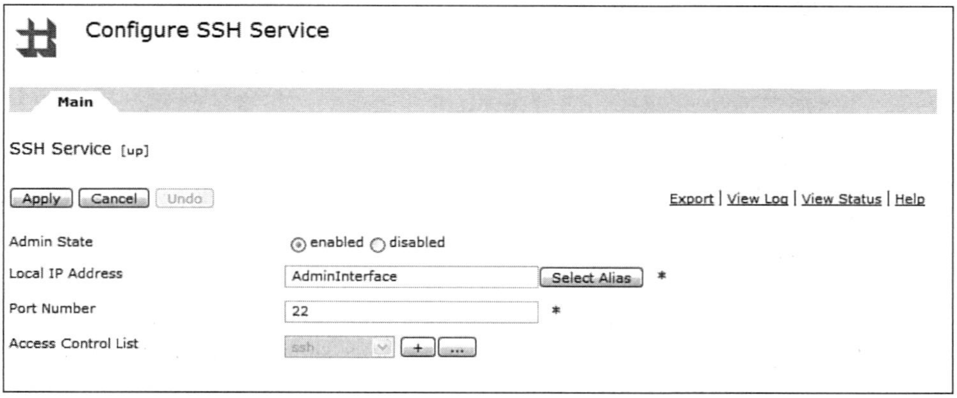

Configure SSH Service

Main

SSH Service [up]

Apply Cancel Undo   Export | View Log | View Status | Help

Admin State   enabled disabled

Local IP Address   AdminInterface Select Alias *

Port Number   22 *

Access Control List   ssh + ...

Figure 2-14 SSH configuration.

Similarly, the WebGUI settings can be tweaked. Figure 2-15 shows this configuration screen, reached from Network→Management→Web Management Service. This was already enabled in our CLI session, but we have switched the hard-coded IP address to our new host alias and extended the timeout value.

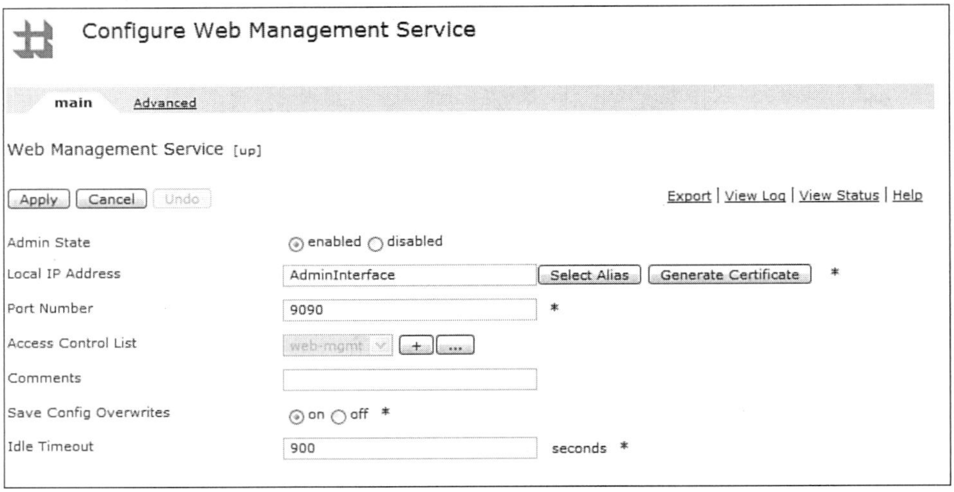

Configure Web Management Service

main Advanced

Web Management Service [up]

Apply Cancel Undo Export | View Log | View Status | Help

Admin State	enabled disabled
Local IP Address	AdminInterface Select Alias Generate Certificate *
Port Number	9090 *
Access Control List	web-mgmt + ...
Comments	
Save Config Overwrites	on off *
Idle Timeout	900 seconds *

Figure 2-15 WebGUI configuration.

TIP—WebGUI Idle Timeout Values

Be careful with this value. The default is 600 seconds, or 10 minutes. Extending this value means you are decreasing security (for example, in the event someone leaves their workstation unlocked while logged in). While extending this may be acceptable in some development environments, we suggest never using the setting of zero, which means no timeout. When a user logs out (or is timed out), resources such as temp file space are freed up on the device for efficiency. As long as it takes for that to happen, those resources will continue to accumulate.

The last stop in the Network menu is to turn on the XML Management Interface (discussed in Chapter 13, "Alternate Management Interfaces.") As you may have guessed by now, this is reached by Network→Management→XML Management Interface. Here, you simply specify the Admin Interface host alias again, and enable the service as we have done for SSH and the WebGUI.

We will do one last bit of housekeeping before we move on. Remember the customized device name (rather than the IP address) that was shown on our login screen in Figure 2-7? Here's how you set that. Figure 2-16 shows the configuration from Administration→Device→System Settings. Now you can see where that customized device name shown on the login page is set.

You may also notice the ability to add a "Custom User Interface File" in Figure 2-16. This feature was added in firmware version 3.7.1. This expands on the capability to add a "welcome message" on the WebGUI page in earlier firmware versions. By editing the custom user interface XML file, you can provide custom text for CLI command prompts and pre-login, post-login, and other appliances messages (for example, "This is the production system; make changes with care!") for both the CLI and the WebGUI, and also color code those messages on the WebGUI. This feature is well documented in the WebGUI Guide, and it is highly recommended to take advantage of it to reduce the chance of administrators making changes to the "wrong" system!

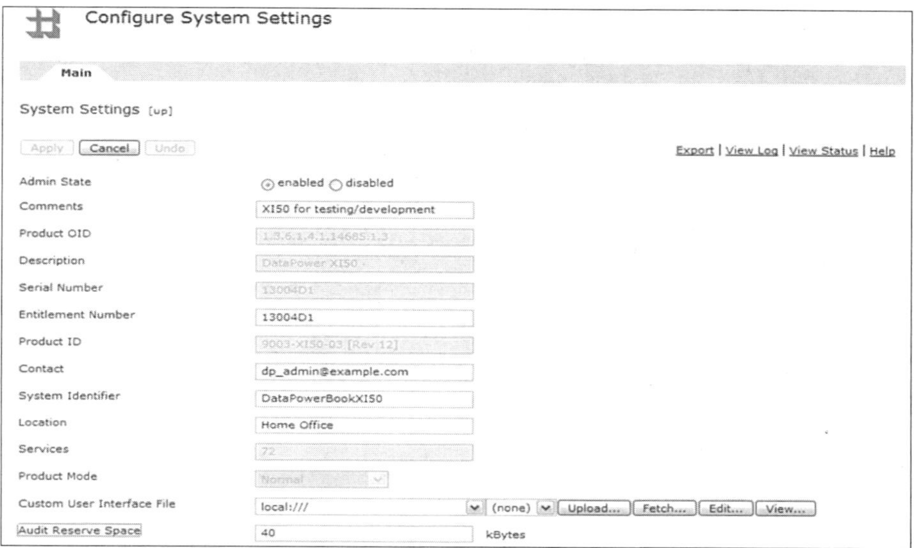

Figure 2-16 Customizing system settings.

Configuring Auxiliary Storage

If you are using hardware series 9004 or above, your system is configured with auxiliary storage, which would be either a compact flash card or dual hard disk RAID array. This auxiliary storage needs to be initialized before it can be used. We will provide the configuration sequence for the hard disk array, as it is more complex than the compact flash, and not entirely straightforward or intuitive.

From the default domain in the WebGUI, navigate using the left-side menu to Administration→Storage Devices→Hard Disk Array. Select the raid0 array, which should be disabled at this point. From the hyperlink menus, select Initialize Hard Disk Array and then press the Confirm button. Next, select the Initialize File System hyperlink, and press the Confirm button (take note of the warning that this will destroy any contents previously on the disks!). This action will take a minute or two. When it is complete, provide a default directory name and then enable the array. The status should show as 'up'. The status of the RAID physical disks and volumes can be checked from the Status→System menu. The new directory for the RAID array should appear for each domain under the local and logstore directories.

Backing Up the System

Before we take our last step (update the firmware), let's back up the system configuration. Even though firmware updates should not affect your configuration in any way, this is always a good idea before making major changes or updates to any computer system. With DataPower, this is simple to do. Figure 2-17 shows that we have gone to Administration→Configuration→Export Configuration and chosen to back up the entire system. Clicking the Next button here takes you to a page that enables you to enter a backup name (this should be something descriptive such as exportFullMyXI50_3613_Init_Config_<date>) and any comments you want to add. DataPower appends the .zip extension to whatever filename you give it, so don't include it in the filename. Clicking the Next button on that page results in a brief pause, and then a page appears with a

Download button to enable you to download the backup zip file to your workstation. For flexibility and redundancy, you may also want to make a separate backup of just the default domain (although this information is included in a full system backup).

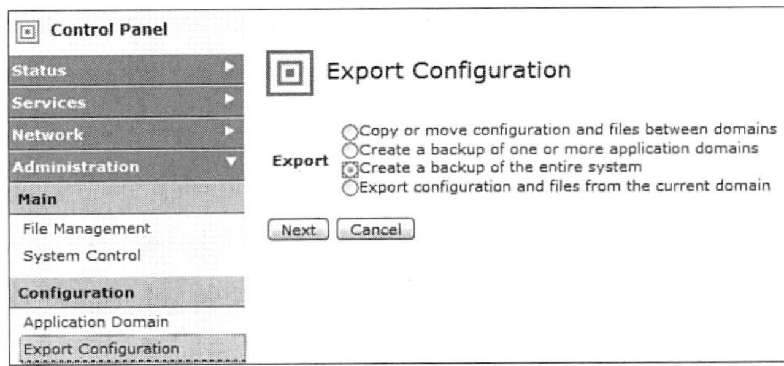

Figure 2-17 Backing up the appliance.

Updating the Appliance Firmware

The final step in the initial configuration of the device is typically to upgrade the firmware from whatever level was installed in the factory to the latest level. First, check to see whether you are already up to date. You saw in Figure 2-8 how to quickly see what version you have. Also, go to Administration→Device→System Settings and take note of your machine type.

Next, you need to go to the IBM DataPower Web site (the link was shown earlier in this chapter) and check the available firmware levels to see whether there are newer ones. If so, download the firmware file that corresponds to the features that you purchased with your appliance. If you aren't sure, you can check by going to Status→System→Device Features, which shows which licenses are *enabled* for this device. Do not confuse this with the similarly named menu choice Status→System→Library Information, which shows which features are actually *installed* on the device firmware. For instance, you may have purchased the TAM feature and have that license enabled on your appliance, but if you install a firmware image without it, then it will not actually be installed. (This can always be fixed by downloading a firmware image with that feature.)

Our particular XI50 appliance used for these examples started at version 3.6.1.3 and has licenses for MQ, ODBC, and TAM. From the download site, we have obtained file xi3711.mq6.odbc52.tam6.scrypt2. The filename begins with "xi", designating that it is for an XI50, then continues with the firmware version (3711 meaning 3.7.1.1), the features included (MQ v6, ODBC v5.2, TAM v6), and then the scrypt2 extension, which designates the firmware generation for firmware versions above 3.5.x.x.

Now that this update is on our workstation, we will move to Administration→Main→System Control in the Control Panel to do the update. First click the Save Configuration button to ensure that any changes we have made thus far are written to the flash.

There are three steps to the firmware upgrade process:

1. Upload the new firmware file.
2. Reload the current firmware. (This is an important step that is often not taken.)
3. Boot the new image.

Figure 2-18 shows the first two steps of this process. In this figure, the Upload button has already been used to bring the firmware file up to the device. It is now shown in the drop-down list. Once that is done, Reload Firmware should be selected in the Shutdown section and the Shutdown button clicked, as shown. There will be a brief pause, and then a page should display saying "Action Completed Successfully." Close that page and you will be returned to the login page. (Click the Control Panel link to get there if you are not.)

Log back in to the device and return to Administration→Main→System Control. Reselect the uploaded firmware image in the Boot Image section, and then press the Boot Image button. You get a Confirm page, and from there it takes a few minutes to actually apply the update. We do mean a few minutes, so be patient!

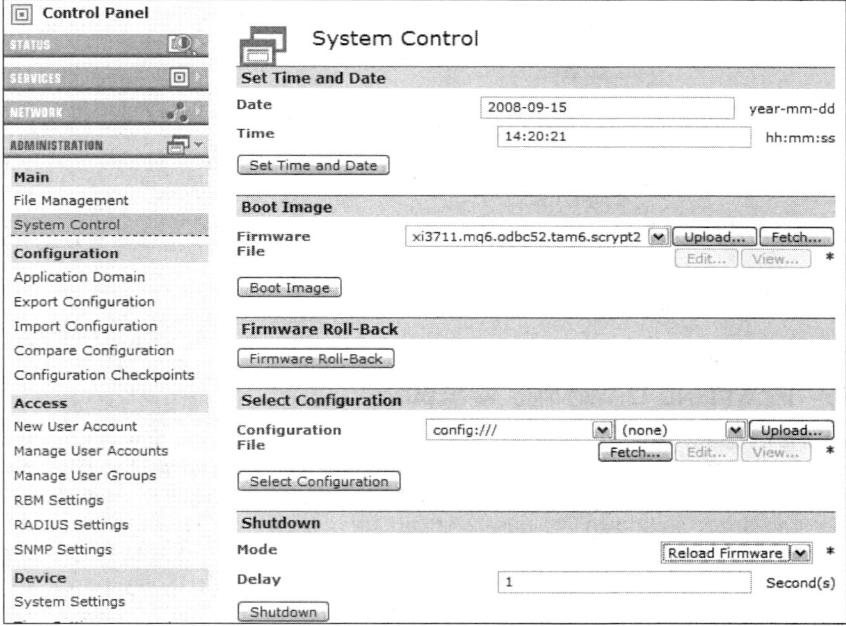

Figure 2-18 Uploading the firmware update file.

While this is typically much faster than a standard server reboot, there is a lot of intensive action going on behind the scenes. Finally, reboot the appliance (you are prompted at these steps to click an OK button) and then you should be able to load the login page again.

We think you will agree—this is much faster and simpler than updating the software on a typical server! Figure 2-19 shows that our appliance has now been updated to version 3.7.1.1. (We later upgraded it to 3.7.2 for you to have the most up-to-date information.) You may also want to capture another backup at this point.

> **ALTERNATE METHODS OF UPDATING FIRMWARE**
>
> It may be preferable to upgrade the firmware from the CLI command shell (which is covered in the Alternate Management Interfaces chapter), as it is an intensive operation for a browser-based interface, and the CLI would provide more feedback during the process. There is a detailed technote available on the DataPower support page with instructions on how to do this. Another approach would be to use ITCAM SE for DataPower. As discussed in Chapter 29, this utility applies firmware updates across a managed set of devices in a controlled manner.

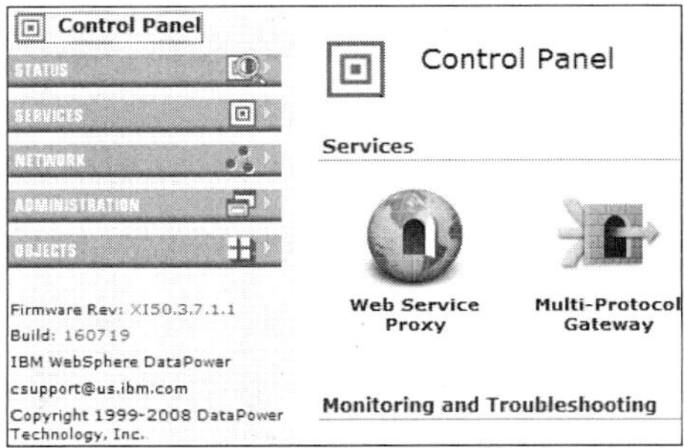

Figure 2-19 Firmware update completed.

> **TIP—POWERING DOWN THE APPLIANCE**
>
> While it is rare, any time you need to power down the appliance, you may be tempted to simply flip the power switch on the back. It is a better practice to bring the system to a graceful halt first. To do this, save your configuration, select "Halt System" from the Mode drop-down, as shown in Figure 2-18, and then click the Shutdown button. When the system responds that this is complete, although you will see no physical changes as the lights are still on and fans still spinning, you may then turn off the power switch on the rear of the device. A major advantage of this approach is that you are warned if there are unsaved configuration changes.

Summary

In this chapter, we have shown you the entire process of unpacking a brand new device all the way through the initial configuration and prep, including a full backup. We have toured the physical characteristics of the appliance, as well as taken a spin through the main functional areas of the Web administration console. We have enabled two Ethernet interfaces for administrative and client use, performed the initial network configuration, and enabled the SSH and XML Management administrative interfaces. Not bad work for our first hands-on chapter! This concludes Part I, "DataPower Introduction." In Part II, "DataPower Networking," we further explore the network capabilities of the device and discuss some common usage patterns in the network.

PART II

DataPower Networking

CHAPTER 3

DataPower as a Network Device

The DataPower appliance is fundamentally a network device; it communicates with other nodes on an IP network. Networking really matters; IP networking settings have to be correct before anything else. Working from the bottom of the stack up, IP connectivity is required for HTTP connections, matching actions, processing policies, and any other interaction with the device to be possible.

If you are already well versed in IP networking, or if you simply need to configure the device using settings provided by your network administrator, this chapter covers the basic configuration of the network stack. Chapter 4, "Advanced DataPower Networking," contains more theory and a more detailed look at advanced scenarios for those who want to learn more about networking and how the device behaves as part of a network.

Interface Configuration

This section discusses how to configure the device's network interfaces. We assign IP addresses and netmasks, show how to control low-level TCP/IP settings, configure the routing table with both static and dynamic routes, and so on. If you don't know what any of these configuration steps mean, don't worry! Remember, this chapter is focused on configuration. Chapter 4 explains the theory and terminology.

DataPower appliances come with four physical network interfaces, referred to as eth0, eth1, eth2, and eth4. The eth4 interface is also referred to as mgmt0 and is often used as a management interface, although it is almost identical to the other three interfaces. The biggest difference is that if you do not explicitly assign an IP address to the Secure Shell (SSH) service, it first attempts to bind to the management interface, and only if this interface has not been explicitly defined will it bind to 0.0.0.0, which means it will listen on all configured interfaces.

Configuration of the network interfaces of the device is carried out in the default domain, by clicking on Network→Interface→Ethernet Interface in the Navigation Bar on the left side (see Figure 3-1).

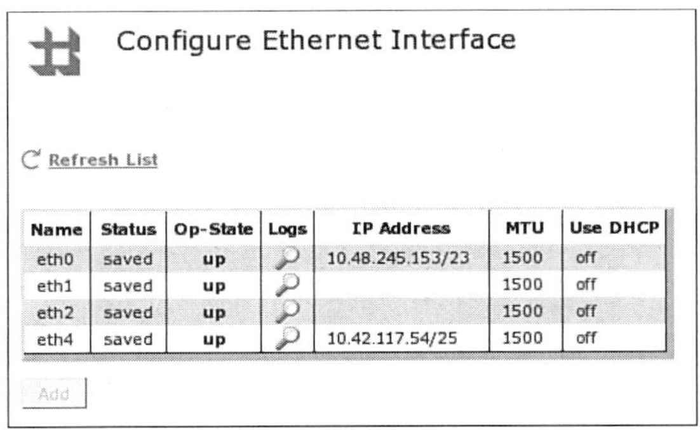

Name	Status	Op-State	Logs	IP Address	MTU	Use DHCP
eth0	saved	up		10.48.245.153/23	1500	off
eth1	saved	up			1500	off
eth2	saved	up			1500	off
eth4	saved	up		10.42.117.54/25	1500	off

Figure 3-1 Network interfaces.

This appliance in Figure 3-1 has two network interfaces configured: eth0 and eth4. The summary page shows the IP address and netmask in CIDR format.

TIP—Drinking CIDR?

CIDR, pronounced "Cider," is a way of expressing variable length subnet masks by simply stating the number of masking bits. It is usually shown by suffixing an IP address with the character / and the number—for instance the 10.48.245.153/23 in Figure 3-1. For more details on subnet masks, see Chapter 4.

Virtual LAN sub-interfaces, utilizing the IEEE 802.1Q tagging protocol, can also be created and configured in a similar manner to Ethernet interfaces, using Network→Interface→VLAN Sub-interface. These sub-interfaces are attached to a physical Ethernet interface, and multiple VLAN sub-interfaces can be created on a single Ethernet interface. More on VLAN sub-interfaces can be found in Chapter 4.

To modify the Ethernet settings, users must have appropriate permissions. The access profile must include access to the Ethernet interface under the Network section for the device. Chapter 12: "Device Administration," shows in detail how to grant these permissions.

Assuming that the user has the correct permissions, clicking the name of an interface leads to the configuration screen for that interface. If you click eth1, you will see the screen displayed in Figure 3-2; it controls the configuration for the interface. The example in Figure 3-2 deals with the configuration of the interface eth1. The settings make changes to the behavior at both the data link layer and the network layer.

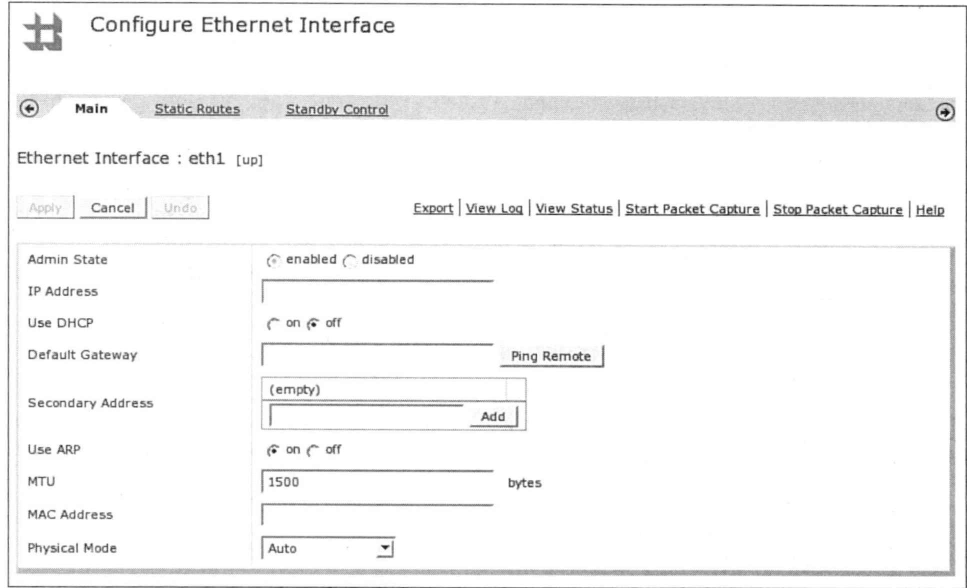

Figure 3-2 Configuration screen for interface eth1.

Each of the settings can be configured on the main interface tab, which is explained in more detail in Table 3-1.

Table 3-1 Explanation of Interface Configuration Settings

Setting	Explanation
IP Address	The main IP address assigned to this interface, followed by the subnet mask. The subnet mask can be in CIDR format (Classless Inter-Domain Routing) as a suffix onto the end of the IP address or in dotted quad format, in which case it must be separated from the IP address with a space.
Use DHCP	This setting determines whether the Dynamic Host Configuration Protocol (DHCP) should be used to configure this interface. Because these are server class appliances, it is unlikely that DHCP would be used, but if it is needed (for instance in an environment where DHCP is mandated and static leases are assigned for accounting purposes), it is available.
Default Gateway	The node that should be the default gateway address for this interface. For the vast majority of configurations, there should only ever be one interface that is configured with a default gateway (also known as default router). Some more complex scenarios, which may necessitate more than one default gateway, are discussed in greater detail in Chapter 4.

(continued)

Table 3-1 Explanation of Interface Configuration Settings ***(continued)***

Setting	Explanation
Secondary Address	This is a list of "secondary addresses" or IP aliases that are assigned to this interface. The appliance responds on this interface to an Address Resolution Protocol request for any IP address configured here. Important: This is different than having more than one interface! This setting configures more than one address on a single interface. IP aliasing is a powerful concept which is often used to have multiple services listening on the same port (e.g. port 80 or port 443); Chapter 4 contains an example of where they might be used.
Use ARP	This setting specifies whether the appliance should respond to Address Resolution Protocol (ARP) requests for this interface. It is likely that this should be left to the default of On. This is discussed in more detail in Chapter 4.
MTU	The Maximum Transmission Unit (MTU) is the size of the largest packet that the Ethernet interface should process. The default of 1500 is the largest allowed by the Ethernet protocol, but there may be valid reasons for reducing this. Only change this setting if told to by your network administrator.
MAC Address	This setting enables you to override the hardware address of the interface. This is discussed further in Chapter 4; it is unlikely that you will need to change this.
Physical Mode	Choose the form of negotiation for the physical link speed of the interface. The default of Auto may be right, but this is the single most commonly changed "advanced" setting on this screen and your network administrator may require it to be explicitly set.

TIP—Physical Modes

Chapter 4 goes into more detail on the Physical layer, but this setting is worth highlighting here. Most times, auto-negotiation will be fine—but when it isn't, things can go wrong!

If you use auto-negotiation, it should be set on both ends. Sometimes, having one side try to auto-negotiate where the other side is set to a fixed speed can end in complete failure to communicate. Also, some specific switches have issues auto-negotiating with newer hardware. If you appear to be getting bad network performance, no link light, packet loss, CRC errors, or the like, this is the setting you should check first!

Static Routes

Network devices maintain an in-memory table of rules that are used to decide how to send traffic to other nodes. These rules are called routes. Many routes are generated dynamically based on the configuration of interfaces, but sometimes there is a need to explicitly add a static entry.

The second tab on the interface configuration settings page is where you define static routes. This Static Routes tab, as depicted in Figure 3-3, enables you to enter for this interface any static routes that your network administrator may have defined. This is an option not to be taken lightly—an incorrect routing configuration can possibly make the device inaccessible from the network, or even worse can create problems with inconsistent symptoms, which are extremely difficult to debug! Chapter 4 goes into more detail on routing configuration and static routes and where they might be useful—for now only add entries to this tab if your network administrator has asked you to, or if you know what you are doing!

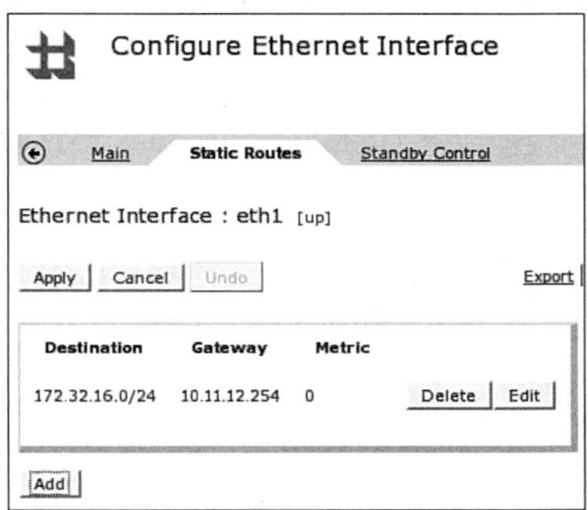

Figure 3-3 Static Routes configuration.

If you do need to add a static route, click the Add button. On the screen that appears, shown in Figure 3-4, type in the destination with subnet mask (either in CIDR format or as dotted quads separated by a space). Also supply the gateway for each static route for this interface.

Adding new Static Routes property
of **Ethernet Interface**

Destination	192.168.47.0/24	*
Gateway	192.168.47.1	*
Metric	0	*

Save Cancel

Figure 3-4 Adding new Static Routes.

The metric field is used to differentiate between routes that match for the same destination; if there are two possible routes to a given destination (as will be explained in Chapter 4), the one with the lowest number is used.

Other Network Settings

This section describes a number of other network settings that can be configured but that are not specific to a given interface. These include general network settings and DNS settings.

General Network Settings

In addition to the interface-specific configuration settings shown earlier, there are also a number of general network configuration settings that are accessed by clicking Network→Interface→Network Settings in the Navigation Bar on the left side of the console. These settings are shown in Figure 3-5.

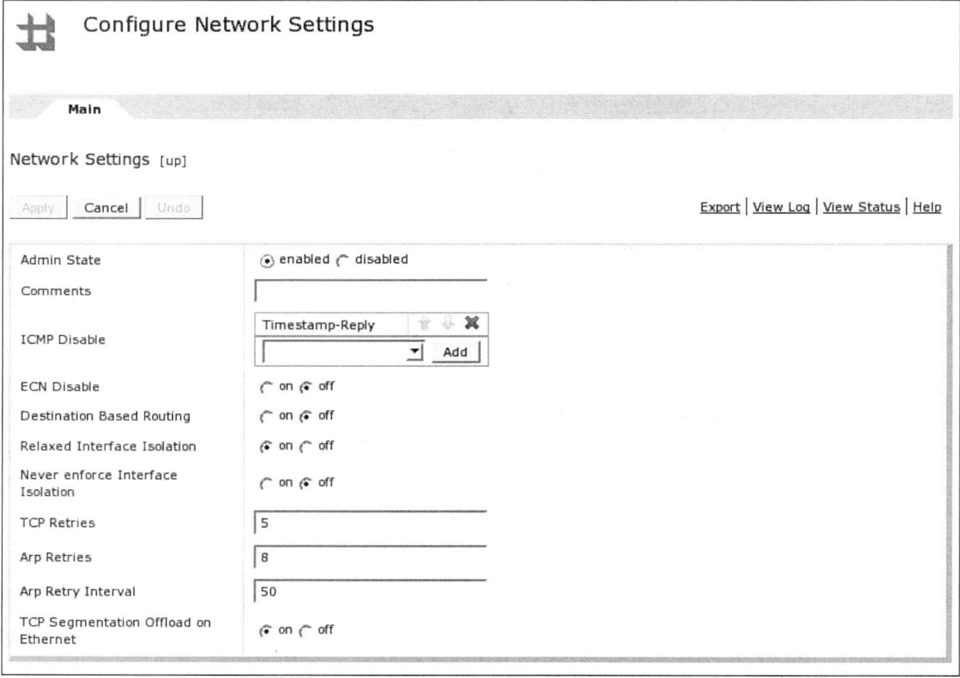

Figure 3-5 General network settings affecting all interfaces.

The settings in this configuration panel are global settings; that is, they affect the behavior of all the interfaces on the device. These settings are more advanced, and it is unlikely that you will need to change any of them. The safest route is to leave them as defaults unless you know exactly what you are doing. Nonetheless, if your network administrator asks whether you are capable of changing the number of TCP retries, you can consult Table 3-2, where each of these settings are explained, and say yes!

Table 3-2 Explanation of General Network Settings

Setting	Explanation
ICMP Disable	This configuration option allows you to stop the device from responding to ICMP (Internet Control Message Protocol) requests of various kinds. For instance, you may want the device to ignore ICMP Echo Requests or "pings," which can be configured here.
ECN Disable	Choose to disable Explicit Congestion Notification TCP sessions. These are used by default, and changing this only affects new TCP sessions because ECN is negotiated at TCP connection establishment during the initial SYN phase. Sometimes network switches and routers have trouble with ECN, although this usually applies to older network hardware; if there are unexplained network problems, try turning on this option, although it should be disabled again if it doesn't fix the problem. It is unlikely that you will need to change the default setting here.
Destination Based Routing	By default, DataPower appliances send responses to incoming requests via the interface to which a given service is bound, or via the interface on which the incoming request was received if the service is bound to multiple addresses. By setting Destination Based Routing to On, we can enable different behavior where outbound packets for responses are sent using the best possible path to a client irrespective of which interface the request was received on. This is a legacy setting which in most cases should not be enabled.
Relaxed Interface Isolation	Generally speaking, packets will only be accepted on an interface if they are addressed to an IP address on that specific interface. Putting this setting to On will relax this isolation, such that the packet will be accepted if the destination IP address is on the same subnet as one of the addresses on the interface. This option is intended for use with the Destination Based Routing option in the previous entry and in most cases should not be enabled.
Never Enforce Interface Isolation	This setting relaxes the interface isolation described in the previous entry even more, such that any packet with the destination MAC address will be accepted irrespective of the IP address set as the target of the packet. Note that the IP stack will still not handle the packet unless the address is configured somewhere on the device. This option could be used to, for instance, have a "hidden" IP address that does not respond to ARP requests but will be accepted if the address is spoofed onto a packet with the correct MAC destination address. In most instances, you will not need to change the default setting here.
TCP Retries	Configure the number of times the device will try to open a new TCP connection with a SYN packet before giving up. The default of 5 is usually fine for most deployments; modifying this setting changes the time required to detect failures at the network layer.
ARP Retries	Configure the number of times the device will try to find the MAC address for a specific IP address using the Address Resolution Protocol (ARP). The default of 8 is usually enough to allow normal network devices to respond and should only be modified where necessary; modifying this setting changes the time required to detect failures at the network layer.
ARP Retry Interval	The amount of time, in milliseconds, to wait before trying an ARP request again; the 50 millisecond default along with the default 8 attempts gives a 400 millisecond default total time to respond, which should be enough for most networks; modifying this setting changes the time required to detect failures at the network layer.
TCP Segmentation Offload on Ethernet	TCP segmentation offloading is a method of improving the performance of large TCP data transfers by allowing the hardware to split the data up into packets as opposed to allowing the application to do so itself. This setting is enabled by default and should only be disabled in response to specific problems. For instance, in some use cases, TCP segmentation offloading might cause interface resets and other network inconsistencies, and in those cases this setting should be disabled.

DNS Settings

The Domain Name Service is a way of resolving hostnames to IP addresses, or vice versa. It is possible to configure the DataPower appliance to utilize one or more DNS servers. This may or may not be needed for your environment. Making the appliance dependent on any external service is always adding an element of risk; if there is no *requirement* for an external DNS server, simply do not configure one. If you choose to configure a DNS server, select Network →DNS Settings from the Navigation Bar on the left side. Doing so brings up the screen shown in Figure 3-6.

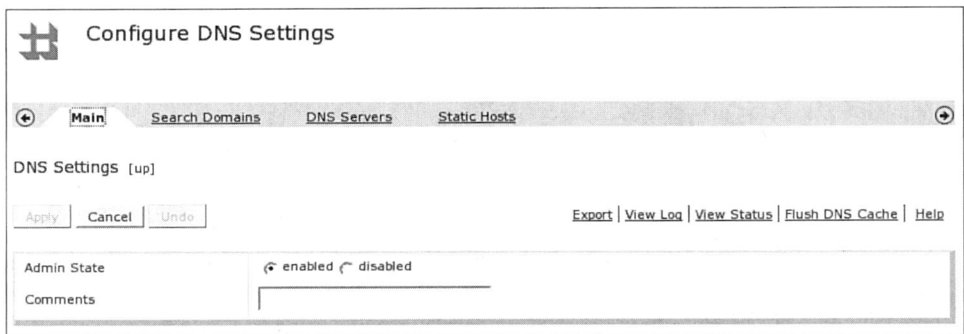

Figure 3-6 DNS configuration.

DNS configuration consists of domain stems, which are automatically added to the search if you search by a hostname, along with DNS server configuration and static hosts information. The search domains, shown in Figure 3-7, are the DNS name stems to add if looking up a hostname without a domain name. In the example, if you are on this particular device to perform a DNS look up for say the hostname "www," this domain name would be appended to make the lookup search for "www.example.com."

Configure DNS Settings

Main **Search Domains** DNS Servers Static Hosts

DNS Settings [up]

Apply Cancel Undo Export | View Log | View Status | Flush DNS Cache | Help

Search Domain

example.com Delete Edit

Add

Figure 3-7 Search domain configuration.

The next tab, depicted in Figure 3-8, defines the actual DNS servers to be used. They are used in the order included on the screen. The configuration consists of the IP address of the server to use, the port for UDP and TCP connection, and the number of times to retry a failed lookup before giving up.

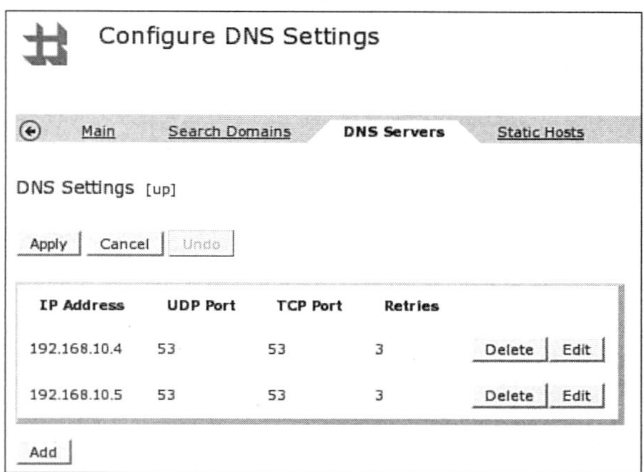

Figure 3-8 DNS server configuration.

The last tab is for defining static hosts. These are the equivalent of entries in a hosts file on a distributed operating system—hostnames that are resolved locally on the device to a fixed IP address. The example in Figure 3-9 shows a single hostname, FTP_Server_IP, which when resolved on the device will always return the IP address 81.146.57.62.

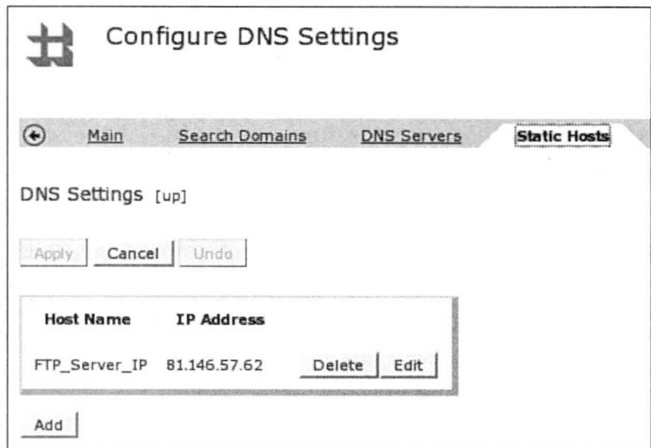

Figure 3-9 Static hosts settings.

There is one more important option on the DNS settings page, located on the right side of each tab: the Flush DNS Cache option, as shown in Figure 3-10. Like the vast majority of DNS clients, the DataPower appliance will cache DNS responses locally, and if it needs to look up the same hostname again, it will retrieve it from cache rather than contacting the DNS server again. You can see this cache information by clicking on Status→DNS Cached Hosts on the Navigation Bar. Sometimes, however, you need to be able to make certain that the next lookup goes to the DNS server—for example, if the entry on the server has been updated. This can be done by clicking Flush DNS Cache.

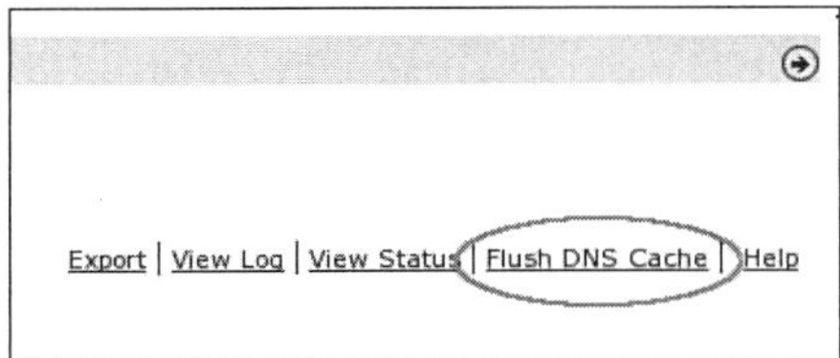

Figure 3-10 Click to flush the DNS cache.

Network Status Information

DataPower SOA appliances can provide a lot of information about the status of the network configuration. This information can be invaluable in debugging network issues. This section lists the key tools available to examine the internal workings of the IP stack. If the concepts in this section are not familiar to you, please see Chapter 4.

Interface Status

If you click on Status→Ethernet Interfaces, you can see information about the way that the interfaces have been configured.

As Figure 3-11 shows, it is possible at a glance to see which interfaces are physically connected, what negotiation mode and speed they have used, IP addresses configured, hardware addresses, received and sent bytes and packets, and so on. One of the chief uses for the interface status page is to debug network errors. Collisions of packets on the network or even packets being dropped can have a serious effect on the function of the device. This behavior may be related to, for instance, a failure to correctly negotiate network speed, as described earlier.

Ethernet Interfaces

Refresh Status

interface	IP address	MAC address	status	negotiate	mode	MTU	RX kbytes	RX packets	RX errors	RX drops	TX kbytes	TX packets	TX errors	TX drops	collisions
eth0	10.48.245.153/23	00:0a:4b:09:c5:10	no-link	auto	10baseT-HD	1500	0	0	0	0	0	0	0	0	0
eth1	0.0.0.0/0	00:0a:4b:09:c5:11	no-link	auto	10baseT-HD	1500	0	0	0	0	0	0	0	0	0
eth2	0.0.0.0/0	00:0a:4b:09:c5:12	no-link	auto	10baseT-HD	1500	0	0	0	0	0	0	0	0	0
mgt0	10.42.117.54/25	00:0a:4b:09:c5:14	ok	auto	100baseTx-FD	1500	17167	141694	0	0	8014	57875	0	0	0

Figure 3-11 A lot of information is available about the state of network interfaces.

> **TIP—DHCP**
>
> While it is unlikely you will use DHCP on this enterprise server class appliance, if you do then the Interface Status page is the only way in the GUI to determine the IP address that has been negotiated via DHCP on an interface.

Routing Table

Network devices such as the DataPower appliance maintain an in-memory routing table; a list of rules that define how packets should be sent based on the destination addresses. The device's routing table can be displayed by clicking Status→Routing Table, as shown in Figure 3-12.

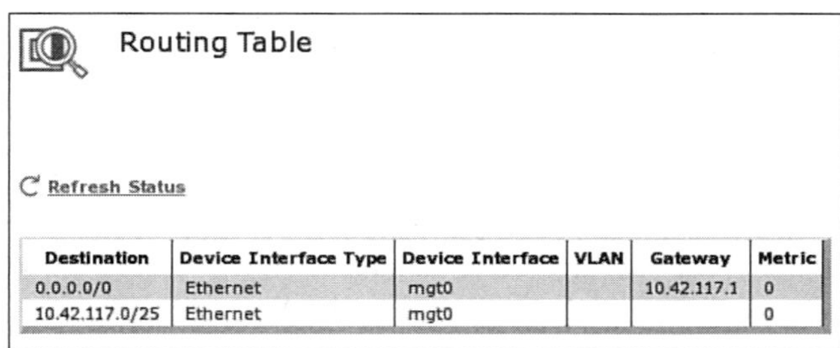

Routing Table
Refresh Status
Destination
Device Interface Type
Device Interface
VLAN
Gateway
Metric
0.0.0.0/0
Ethernet
mgt0
10.42.117.1
0
10.42.117.0/25
Ethernet
mgt0
0

Figure 3-12 The routing table can be displayed.

The information in the routing table includes any specific routes that relate to a given interface, any default routes that have been configured, and any static routes that have been added. More information on routing can be found in Chapter 4.

TCP port Status

Possibly the most-often used network status screen is the TCP Port Status. This is the equivalent of a `netstat -an` on a distributed platform. It lists the TCP sockets on a given device, what state they are in, what the source and destination addresses and ports are, and so on. If you look for just the sockets that are in "listen" state, you can see all the services that are active on a device, which domain they are in, and what port/interface they are bound to. Figure 3-13 demonstrates this extremely useful functionality.

The most important use of this screen is to check which services are listening on which ports. There can only be a single service (such as an XML Firewall or a Front Side Handler) listening on a given IP address and port combination; if due to a misconfiguration or miscommunication, two services have been configured to listen on the same IP address and port, only the first one that tries to bind will be able to start. Using the TCP port status screen, if a service is down we can easily check to see whether another service is using its IP address and port combination, to see whether that is the reason the service didn't start.

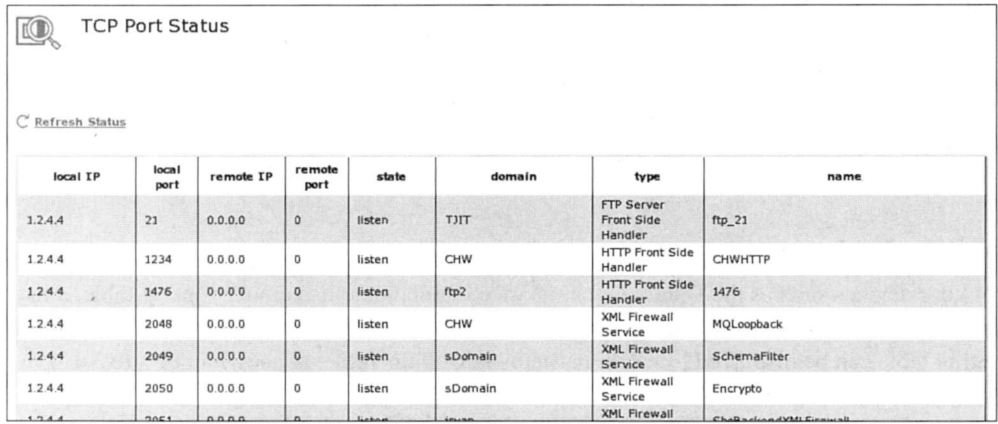

TCP Port Status

Refresh Status

local IP	local port	remote IP	remote port	state	domain	type	name
1.2.4.4	21	0.0.0.0	0	listen	TJIT	FTP Server Front Side Handler	ftp_21
1.2.4.4	1234	0.0.0.0	0	listen	CHW	HTTP Front Side Handler	CHWHTTP
1.2.4.4	1476	0.0.0.0	0	listen	ftp2	HTTP Front Side Handler	1476
1.2.4.4	2048	0.0.0.0	0	listen	CHW	XML Firewall Service	MQLoopback
1.2.4.4	2049	0.0.0.0	0	listen	sDomain	XML Firewall Service	SchemaFilter
1.2.4.4	2050	0.0.0.0	0	listen	sDomain	XML Firewall Service	Encrypto

Figure 3-13 TCP port status.

ARP Table

The Address Resolution Protocol (ARP) resolves IP addresses to physical Ethernet addresses. As with most nodes on an IP network, the device maintains an ARP cache, and you can list the current cache of nodes for which ARP has completed in the ARP table, like `arp -a` on distributed platforms. The ARP table can be displayed using the `show netarp` command in the CLI, as in Listing 3-1.

Listing 3-1 Address Resolution Table

```
xi50# show netarp

 IP address        MAC address        Interface Interface Type VLAN
 ----------        -----------        --------- -------------- ----
 192.168.10.4      00:15:2c:b2:ac:00  eth0      Ethernet
 192.168.10.114    00:1e:37:90:3c:af  eth0      Ethernet

xi50#
```

The device's ARP cache contains the hardware addresses of all the nodes with which the appliance communicates. This particular device contains only two hosts in its ARP cache, because there are only two other nodes currently communicating with it.

Network Configuration Checklist

How should the network interfaces be configured? The following set of starter questions can be asked of your network administrator to provide the basic information required:

- How many of the four network interfaces on my device should I configure? Note that it is common for production servers to have more than one.
- For each interface, what is the IP address and netmask that I should use? Ideally, ask for the netmask in CIDR format—or read the next chapter to find out what that means and how to calculate it!
- What should the default gateway be, and which interface should it use? It is most likely that only one default gateway should be configured.
- Do I need to configure any static routes, and if so what are they?

These four simple questions coupled with the rest of the configuration information in this chapter will give you all the information you need to successfully configure networking on the device.

Summary

This chapter explained the basic use of the administrative console for configuring the main networking features of the DataPower device. Chapter 4 goes into more detail about networking and describes some of the advanced networking configuration that the appliance is capable of.

CHAPTER 4

Advanced DataPower Networking

Chapter 3, "DataPower as a Network Device," presented the basic steps for configuring the DataPower appliance's network stack. But what do all of the steps in Chapter 3 actually mean? If you are new to networking or if you want more detail on how the internals of the device work, this chapter is for you! This is a detailed chapter with a lot of background information, because the complex topics covered cannot be explained without providing a detailed context. Stick with it, and the rewards will be great.

First, Some Theory

Since the dawn of time (which is even earlier than January 1, 1970 at 12:00 a.m., as the UNIX people would have us believe), computers have been networked together. In fact, much like the first UNICS system (the precursor of UNIX), the first "modern network" predates the UNIX zero time point. The creation in 1969 of the ARPANET (named after the U.S. Department of Defense's Advanced Research Projects Agency) was the evolution of the first modern packet switched network, using various types of network protocols before standardizing on the ITU-T X.25 protocol over Network Control Protocol (NCP) at heady speeds of up to 50kbps.

In 1974, NCP was replaced by a more robust protocol called Transmission Control Protocol (TCP), which in 1978 was split into two separate protocols; TCP was redefined as a "higher level" protocol to provide reliable end-to-end communication, while the parts that dealt with packet routing were rolled up into a new protocol called Internet Protocol (IP). It is because of this joint heritage, where both were originally part of a single protocol, that the suite of protocols together is known as TCP/IP—the protocols with which our modern Internet and all devices connected to it communicate.

This chapter provides some detail about how TCP/IP works. It is framed in a context in which the DataPower-specific issues are presented and as a backdrop for the knowledge contained in the other chapters of the book. For a more advanced reference, we suggest readers use the TCP/IP bible, *TCP/IP Illustrated: Volume 1: The Protocols* by Richard Stevens (Boston, MA: Addison-Wesley: 1994).

Terminology

SOA appliances would be fundamentally useless if they could not communicate. DataPower appliances use Ethernet networking and the common networking formats and protocols of the Internet. Figure 4-1 shows two of the network ports of an XI50 device, standard CAT5 RJ45 Ethernet connections. But what does that actually mean?

Figure 4-1 RJ45 CAT5 Ethernet.

The devices are complex in their use of networking, and to be able to properly appreciate and use them to their fullest potential, you must understand some networking technology. To explain the networking concepts, a common terminology and an explanation of the Internet are necessary.

Let's start by defining a few basic concepts. A *packet* is simply a block of data; it is nothing more and nothing less. It makes no judgment on what that data is; there are no "better" or "worse" packets, and there is no inherent specific definition that determines what size a packet should be, where or how it should be processed, or what to do with it. Of course, just as with anything in IT, for packets to be of use, people need to agree on the standards for using them, which we discuss later in this chapter.

These blocks of data are sent between separate *nodes* on a *network*. A network simply refers to a group of nodes that can communicate by sending packets to each other. A node is any device attached to the network that might want to share information; that is, to send and receive packets. A node can be everything from computers to routers to personal digital assistants to mobile telephones and even refrigerators. (It is true that a refrigerator can be a node on a network. Google it to learn more!) The nodes may all be similar or they might be different; there are no set rules, except that they are all nodes and are connected to the same network.

Point-to-Point Connections

Assume that there are two nodes that want to send packets of data to each other. The simplest form of network is a direct link between the two nodes; this is generally referred to as a *point-to-point* connection. This can be as simple as two computers with a null-modem cable joining them or a crossover Ethernet link. As long as the two nodes have agreed on the standards to use and the language they send, they will be able to communicate with each other. Sending data is simple; there are exactly two nodes, so when one node wants to send a packet of data, the only possible target to send it to is the other node (referred to as the "peer"). There doesn't need to be a concept of "addressing"—each node understands only "me" and "the peer."

A point-to-point connection is the technical equivalent of throwing a letter over your next-door neighbor's fence. The letter goes directly to them; it could not have come from anyone but you, and when they want to reply, they just need to throw a letter back over the same fence. (Some people actually have neighbors like this and end up moving.)

The serial link used to connect a workstation to the DataPower device for initial configuration and direct console access, shown in Chapter 2, "DataPower Quick Tour and Setup" and depicted in Figure 4-2, is an example of a point-to-point connection. There is no other node on this connection, and to impersonate one of the nodes, an attacker would have to physically reconnect the link.

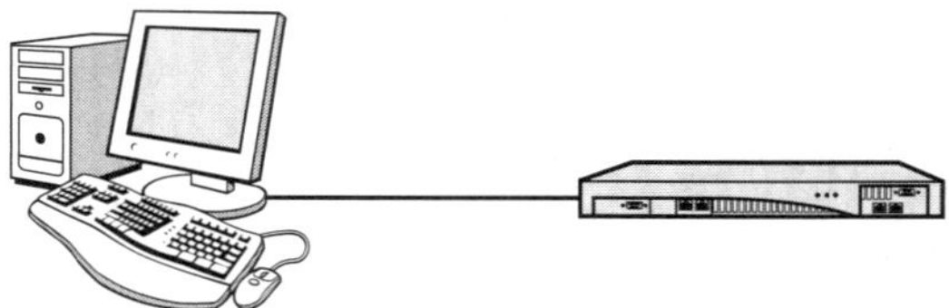

Figure 4-2 A serial link from a workstation to DataPower is a point-to-point connection.

Broadcast Networks

Of course the directly linked network is useful in some ways, but for networking, perhaps it might be of more value for more than two nodes to be involved. The simplest way to do this is to connect all the nodes to the same physical medium and let them communicate, in what is known as a *broadcast network*. An example of a shared physical medium in this context might be a hub to which all nodes are connected. When a node wants to send a packet of data to one of the other nodes, it puts the packet out onto the network. Because the medium is shared, all of the nodes can see all of the packets of data. This means that they now have to agree on a mechanism to be able to explain who the data is meant for; when node A wants to send data to node C, it needs to be able to say "this packet is destined for node C" so that node C knows to pick it up and use it.

An analogy of a broadcast network in the real world would be a system of pigeonholes in a university. These are like a set of open mail boxes, often used in environments around the world where everyone is considered trusted. If a young student, Alice, needs to send a note to her professor, Bob, she goes to the campus post office and places the note in his pigeonhole. Anyone who goes into the post office can see that there is a note for Professor Bob. Indeed, if they were rude, they could take the note, read it, and put it back, and neither Professor Bob nor Alice would ever know that they did. But the note is clearly intended for Professor Bob because it is in his pigeonhole; this is a rudimentary form of addressing.

Figure 4-3 shows an example of a broadcast network; all the nodes are connected to the same physical network, and they all can communicate with each other.

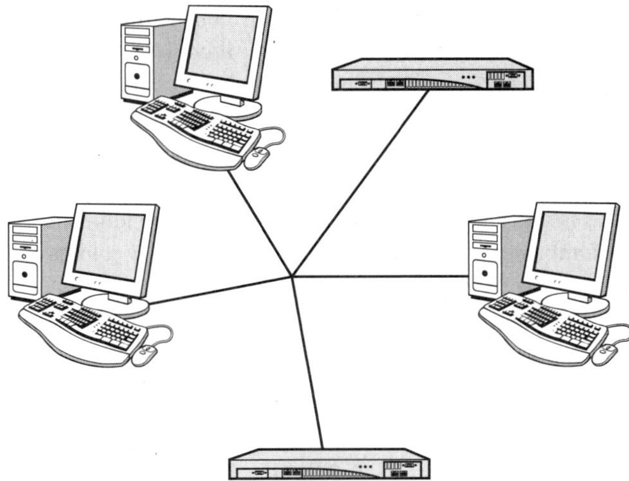

Figure 4-3 A broadcast network with locally connected nodes.

In this example, because all the nodes are linked together, if one of the nodes needs to contact one of the DataPower devices, it would simply send a packet onto the network using various protocols. (These protocols are described later in this chapter.) The key difference between a broadcast network and a point-to-point connection is that in the broadcast network, all other nodes sharing the same physical medium can see the data!

> **TIP—SENSITIVE CONNECTIONS**
>
> Just as the most sensitive of routers do not accept administrative connections directly over their network interfaces, but via some form of secure console device, so can DataPower be configured to share its administrative connections only via its serial port. A point-to-point connection with a trusted device will always be more secure than a management network—the less machines involved in a network, the easier it is to secure them!

Routed Networks

What if you can't physically link all the nodes together? When this is the case, you have to move on to a concept known as *routing*. A given machine on a local broadcast network is given the role of taking packets that are not addressed to a local node and forwarding them to other nodes on other networks until the packets find the right node; this machine is known as a *router*. The packets are passed from one router to another until they reach their destinations.

This is similar to what happens when you mail a letter using the British Royal Mail (and likely, the United States Postal Service). Let's say Professor Bob has to consult about Alice's question with his colleague, Dr. Charlie, who works at another university. That university also has a post office with a pigeonhole system, but it is too much hassle for Professor Bob to drive over to Dr. Charlie's university just to put a note in his pigeonhole! So, he writes the address of Dr. Charlie's university on the letter and makes it clear that the letter is destined for Dr. Charlie. He then puts it in the pigeonhole destined for outgoing mail.

At some point, someone will take the letter out of the pigeonhole and deliver it to the local post office. At the post office, they will see that it is destined for Dr. Charlie's university, and they will load the letter onto a truck or van, along with any other letters and packages that happen to be going in that general direction. In this way, the letter will be passed from one truck to another, until (if it is lucky enough not to be lost), it reaches the post office local to Dr. Charlie's university. There it will be collected together along with any other mail for Dr. Charlie's university and delivered to the campus post office, where eventually someone will sort through the incoming mail and place this one in Dr. Charlie's pigeonhole. The letter will finally have been routed to its destination.

Figure 4-4 shows two discrete physically separate networks connected by a single router; of course, such a network may be made up of many hundreds of networks that are interconnected via routers. The term we use for a complex network such as this is a *packet switched network*; this simply refers to routing discrete blocks of data (packets) from one node to another over data links shared with other traffic.

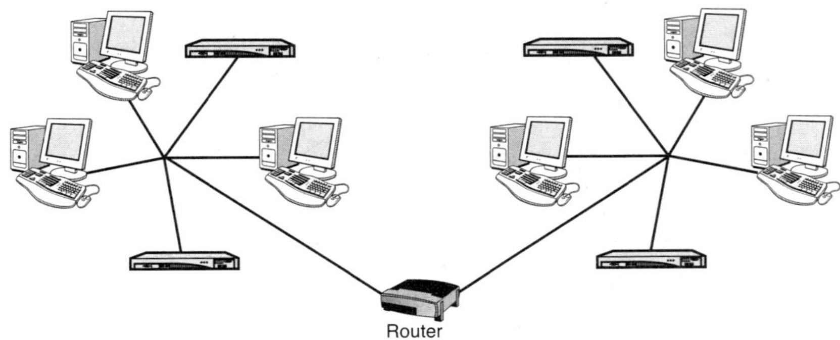

Figure 4-4 Two broadcast networks are connected via a router.

In this routed network, if a node on one of the networks wants to connect to the DataPower appliance on the other side, it has to send the packets to the router, which then relays them on to the final destination. The appliance has an internal routing table, just like any network device, which defines how it will send packets on to routers for forwarding to other nodes; this is a complex subject. Routing is discussed in more detail later in this chapter.

In summary, this is the terminology you should understand. Blocks of data called packets are sent between different nodes on a network, of which there are three main types: point-to-point, which is a direct connection between exactly two nodes; broadcast, which is when two or more nodes send packets to each other via a shared physical medium; and routed, where packets between two or more physically separate broadcast networks are sent between each other via intermediaries named routers.

Abstractions

In order for computers to communicate with each other, it is vital that they agree on a form of protocol, that is, a common language that they can all speak. In the same way as two people from vastly different countries and cultures cannot easily communicate unless they share some form of language or reference point, two computers will be unable to share data unless they both know in advance what the bits and bytes will mean. Standards are required at many levels.

In 1982 the International Standards Organization (ISO), along with many industry players, created something called the Open Systems Interconnection (OSI) initiative. One of the outputs of this initiative was a common model for how to define layers of protocols that clearly describe interoperability between network devices and software.

The OSI model is comprised of seven layers. In this section, we discuss the first four of these, which deal with the network transports themselves; the others are application-level issues and are the subject of the rest of this book. The layers are shown in Table 4-1.

Table 4-1 The OSI Layers

Layer	Name	Function
7	Application	Application service communication
6	Presentation	Data representation; encryption
5	Session	Inter-host communication
4	Transport	End-to-end connections; reliability
3	Network	Logical addressing; routing
2	Data Link	Physical addressing
1	Physical	Physical media; signaling; binary transmission

The first four layers, shown under the thick line in the table, represent the standards and terms agreed on for basic network communications; it is these that DataPower uses as a network device. These are discussed in the following sections.

The Physical Layer

In the physical layer of the OSI model, there are many standards that define exactly how data is sent. These include pinouts, voltages, handshaking, and so on. They define, for instance, what exactly it means for the third pin on a serial connector to be +5v at a given moment. They define which wires in an Ethernet cable are used to send data, and what frequency pulses are sent at. They define when the ring signal should be sent over a 60-volt telephone wire and what frequency range wireless networks should use. Some examples of standards for the physical layer include RS-232 (serial connections), 1000BASE-TX (Gigabit Ethernet physical layer), 802.11b (Wireless Ethernet), and POTS (Plain Old Telephone System).

The physical layer may seem out of scope for a discussion on XML-based SOA appliances—but you must remember that the appliance is still a network device, and the same kinds of issues that can affect any network device using the same technology still do apply. Indeed, the two points that follow *can and do* cause issues that are not easy to diagnose unless you understand how the network stack of the appliance is built!

First, because the appliance's network interfaces are Gigabit Ethernet capable of using the 802.3ab protocol (1000BASE-TX) for high speeds but also able to utilize 802.3u (100BASE-TX) for slower speeds, it is essential that the correct communication parameters are configured. This may seem trivial—doesn't this stuff happen automatically? The answer is that most of the time it does, and the appliance is, by default, configured to auto-negotiate transmission rates and duplex modes as required by 1000BASE-TX. But when communicating with other network devices, it is sometimes necessary to force the interface to use a lower level of negotiation (such as 802.3u) or to not negotiate at all but use a fixed communication. Chapter 3 showed where this can be set.

The second point has to do with the physical layer of the console interface. This uses the RS-232 standard for serial binary data communication with the device, and for successful communication, the parameters on both sides of the interface must be the same. In the past, some SOA appliances have been mistakenly pronounced dead and prepared for return shipment to IBM. In one case, the real culprit was a laptop reboot that had caused its serial port terminal emulation software to revert to a nonstandard setting. In another, a cable was incorrectly connected with voltages on the wrong pins making communication impossible!

The Data Link Layer

On top of the physical layer, whatever it is, lies the data link layer. This layer includes the important concept of device addressing. Physical devices on a network must be addressable in some way so that packets can be addressed to a given device. This is commonly done by agreeing on a size and format for the packet. Certain sections of the packet are given special meaning; for instance, if a standard is adopted that says that bytes 9 through 15 are the destination address for the packet, all nodes can easily see which packets are destined for which nodes. Addressing in the data link layer refers to actual physical addresses of nodes on a network; because of this, it is not suitable for a routed network. It is suitable only for a broadcast network with a shared physical medium. Examples of standards for the data link layer are PPP (Point-to-Point Protocol) for serial or modem connections, 802.3 (Ethernet packet format), and 802.1Q (VLAN).

Many people do not realize that, in the same way as network layer addresses can be configured dynamically at runtime, so can the physical addresses of most devices. In Chapter 3, we showed you how to modify the Ethernet (MAC) address of an interface instead of using the built in MAC address. There are often valid reasons to do this. One example might be when swapping out an appliance that has been physically destroyed or otherwise taken out of service; in this case, it may be prudent to configure the new replacement appliance with the MAC address of the old one so that switches and other network hardware do not consider the swap out to be a security violation, negating the requirement to flush ARP tables and so on at the switch.

> **TIP—HARDWARE ADDRESSES**
>
> The Hardware address for the Ethernet implementation of the data link layer is commonly referred to as a Media Access Control, or MAC, address. You will often see the terms "Hardware address," "Ethernet address," and "MAC address" used interchangeably. This is usually valid. Hardware address is more generic and can be used to refer to any technology's hardware addresses, while MAC address and Ethernet address are only used for Ethernet networks. Whenever we say Hardware address in a DataPower context, we mean the MAC address because this is the networking technology used by DataPower.

The Network Layer

On top of the data link layer lies the network layer. This is where devices can be given an address that is valid for more than just a local broadcast network with a shared physical medium. Of course, the address still has to uniquely identify the node in the network at large. Addressing in the network layer is performed in a similar manner to that of the data layer—all users agree that a certain set of bytes in a specific position in a packet refer to the addresses, and therefore it is obvious where a packet is meant to go. Examples of network layer standards include Internet Protocol (IP), Address Resolution Protocol (ARP), Internet Control Message Protocol (ICMP), and Routing Information Protocol (RIP).

DataPower SOA appliances are an advanced form of network device. As seen in Chapter 3, there is a detailed level of configuration that can control how the appliance behaves, especially with respect to network layer protocols. This includes ways of responding to ICMP requests using ARP, and aliasing multiple IP addresses onto single physical interfaces.

The Transport Layer

Finally, on top of the network layer is the transport layer. The transport layer is responsible for providing an end-to-end connection between two nodes, regardless of where they lie on the network. It may use techniques such as flow and error control, and some more reliable transport protocols will retry packets that fail in order to keep track of connection state. Common standards for transport layer protocols are Transmission Control Protocol (TCP), User Datagram Protocol (UDP), and Point-to-Point Tunneling Protocol (PPTP).

As its primary transport layer protocol, DataPower primarily uses TCP. All administrative connections and the vast majority of client connections will be TCP. The main exceptions are that NFS can use UDP instead of TCP, and both Syslog and SNMP use UDP.

The abstractions we have described show the four layers of the OSI model applicable to DataPower as a network device. A packet that is being sent over a network from one node to another, while being just a set of data, will need to be formatted specifically in a way that all the layers can understand. Each layer is encapsulated in the previous layer; for instance, a data layer packet has some information (such as physical addresses) and some data; that data will contain a network layer packet that has information (such as logical addresses) and some data, which contains a transport layer packet, and so on. In DataPower, these packets are usually TCP packets encapsulated within IP packets encapsulated within Ethernet packets; the next section explores the specific protocols used by the DataPower appliance.

TCP/IP Primer

The DataPower appliance uses a specific set of standards and protocols that are the common standards and protocols of the Internet: Ethernet interfaces, with an IP stack using TCP sockets. (As mentioned earlier, the device also supports UDP for some scenarios where it is relevant to the protocol being used.)

Packet Structure

First, let's look at the specific structure of a TCP packet, as shown in Figure 4-5.

```
-----------------------------------------------
00 01 02 03 04 05 06 07 08 09 0A 0B 0C 0D 0E 0F
-----------------------------------------------
PRE PRE PRE PRE PRE |FR| DST DST DST DST | SRC
 SRC SRC SRC   | LEN |VL|TS| LEN | SEQ |F VER|TL|
PR|CKSUM|SRC SRC SRC|DST DST DST| OPT OPT OPT  |
  SRC SRC SRC SRC SRC   |  DST DST DST DST DST |
SEQ SEQ SEQ SEQ SEQ SEQ SEQ SEQ SEQ SEQ SEQ SEQ|
 OFF | RES RES| FLG FLG|  WIN WIN WIN WIN WIN  |
  CHK CHK CHK CHK CHK   |  PTR PTR PTR PTR PTR |
OPT OPT OPT OPT OPT OPT OPT OPT OPT OPT OPT OPT|
DATA DATA DATA DATA DATA DATA DATA DATA DATA DA
DATA DATA DATA DATA DATA DATA DATA DATA DATA DA
...
DATA DATA DATA DATA DATA DATA DATA |  CRC CRC
```

Figure 4-5 The structure of a TCP packet.

As Figure 4-5 shows, the data that is being sent is encapsulated within a TCP packet, which is encapsulated as data within an IP packet, which is encapsulated as data within an Ethernet packet, which is sent out on the wire. The representation in Figure 4-6 helps make this clearer.

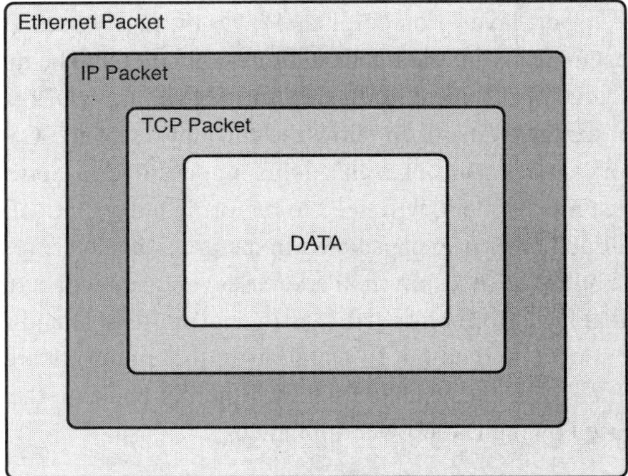

Figure 4-6 Packet encapsulation.

The data is *inside* a TCP packet, which is *inside* an IP packet, which is *inside* an Ethernet packet. Let's start by taking a look at each of the packet headers.

Ethernet Headers

The first sections, from PRE through to LEN, as shown in Figure 4-7, represent the Ethernet headers, which are the data link layer.

```
-----------------------------------------------
00 01 02 03 04 05 06 07 08 09 0A 0B 0C 0D 0E 0F
-----------------------------------------------
PRE PRE PRE PRE PRE |FR| DST DST DST DST | SRC
 SRC SRC SRC   | LEN |DATA DATA DATA DATA DATA DA
...
DATA DATA DATA DATA DATA DATA DATA |  CRC CRC
```

Figure 4-7 The Ethernet headers.

They include a destination address, DST, and a source address, SRC; these are the "hardware" addresses of the nodes on the network. When this packet is sent out onto a broadcastable Ethernet network (such as a hub), all the computers on that network can see which node the packet was sent from and which node it is meant for. In Ethernet terminology, the name for a hardware address is the Media Access Control Address, or MAC address; DST and SRC here represent the MAC addresses of the destination and source machines.

IP Headers

The second part from VL through to OPT, depicted in Figure 4-8, represents the IP headers.

```
-----------------------------------------------
00 01 02 03 04 05 06 07 08 09 0A 0B 0C 0D 0E 0F
-----------------------------------------------
                        |VL|TS| LEN  | SEQ  |F VER|TL|
PR|CKSUM|SRC SRC SRC|DST DST DST| OPT OPT OPT  |
```

Figure 4-8 The IP headers.

These include a destination address, DST, and a source address, SRC. These are the logical or network addresses of the nodes on the network. When this packet is routed through an IP network, the nodes through which it is routed can see which node the packet was sent from and which node it is meant for. The terminology at the network level for IP simply refers to these as IP addresses.

TCP Headers

The third part, as shown in Figure 4-9, from SRC through OPT, represents the TCP headers.

```
-----------------------------------------------
00 01 02 03 04 05 06 07 08 09 0A 0B 0C 0D 0E 0F
-----------------------------------------------
 SRC SRC SRC SRC SRC  |  DST DST DST DST DST  |
SEQ SEQ SEQ SEQ SEQ SEQ SEQ SEQ SEQ SEQ SEQ SEQ|
 OFF  | RES RES| FLG FLG|  WIN WIN WIN WIN WIN  |
 CHK CHK CHK CHK CHK  |  PTR PTR PTR PTR PTR  |
OPT OPT OPT OPT OPT OPT OPT OPT OPT OPT OPT OPT|
```

Figure 4-9 The TCP headers.

The most important fields in the TCP headers are the source port and the destination port, shown as SRC and DST in Figure 4-9. The concept of "port" is a TCP-specific construct for handling sessions between nodes; it provides a metaphor for slots where connections can be made. Each node will have a finite number of TCP ports that can be connected to; the IP address defines the node, and the port defines the connection on that node.

Payload

Finally, the sections marked DATA represent application data—also known as the "payload" of the packet. Anything that needs to be sent over the network is sent inside this part of the packet, with all the headers wrapped around it. It's a lot of work and complexity just to send some data, isn't it?

The payload is what DataPower is all about. TCP is Layer 4 in the OSI model shown previously; the true *raison d'etre* of DataPower is to act as an OSI Layer 7 firewall. That doesn't mean that the lower levels are any less important—indeed DataPower has advanced TCP/IP capabilities that are used to reinforce and strengthen the application layer functionality. It is vital to understand both the methods of configuration and the theory involved, so that the Layer 7 application level traffic can go where it is supposed to go.

Address Resolution

On a broadcast Ethernet IP network, how do nodes determine how to address their packets? Let's say we have two nodes on a network that want to communicate with each other. The first is a Web services client, and the second is a DataPower appliance. The DataPower appliance has IP address 192.168.10.25, and the Web services client has 192.168.10.1. The client wants to send a packet to the DataPower device, to initiate a connection. The packet contains the following information:

- Client Ethernet (MAC) address (source MAC address)
- Client IP address (source IP address)
- DataPower IP address (destination IP address)

However, it does not have the DataPower appliance's Ethernet (MAC) address; it cannot actually create the correct packet to send out onto the network. This is where ARP comes in.

What the client needs to do is send out a special packet called an Address Resolution Protocol (ARP) packet. ARP is a network layer protocol like IP; it is sent out encapsulated in an Ethernet packet. However, it is sent to a special Ethernet destination address, called a broadcast address (for Ethernet, this is FF:FF:FF:FF:FF:FF). This means that every machine on the network should look at the packet to decide whether it should deal with it.

The ARP packet contains a request that effectively says "I am the Web services client with IP address 192.168.10.1, and my Ethernet address is the source address of this packet. I am looking for the device whose IP address is 192.168.10.25. If this is you, please reply to this packet and tell me what your Ethernet address is so that I can communicate with you." When the DataPower device sees the request packet, it picks it up (because it is a broadcast packet, addressed to everyone), and it sees that the Web services client wants to communicate with it. It then sends out an ARP reply packet that is addressed to the Web services client, on its correct Internet and hardware Ethernet address, saying "This is the device with IP address 192.168.10.25. If you want to talk to me, use the source Ethernet (MAC) address of this packet as your destination."

Subnetworks

So, how does a node determine whether another node that it wants to talk to is on the same physical medium? What tells it that it is on the same broadcastable network? To understand this, you need to know how IP addressing works.

An IP address is known as a "dotted quad," because of the most common representation—four numbers separated by periods. Each number ranges from 0–255, which is storable in one byte of data. The IP address uniquely identifies the device on a network. This means that there is a theoretical maximum of 255×255×255×255=4,228,250,625 unique nodes on an IP network such as the Internet as we currently know it. This seems like a lot of nodes! Clearly they are not all plugged in to the same local network; connecting from a Web service client in the UK to a DataPower appliance located physically in Brazil is obviously not a local network connection! But how does the Web service client know that the appliance is not on its local network so that it can send the packet to a router instead of issuing an ARP request for it?

The answer is that we split the networks up by using *subnets*. A subnet is, like it sounds, a separate piece of the overall address space that is configured to tell a node which other nodes are on its own locally broadcastable network. It works as a bitmask—here is an example. Let's take the IP address 192.168.58.31, with a subnet mask (commonly shortened to netmask) of 255.255.255.0. The way we calculate whether a node is on the same network is by performing a binary AND against the netmask. An example is shown in Listing 4-1.

Listing 4-1 Subnet Calculation

```
In binary
IP:        11000000 10101000 00111010 00011111
Netmask:   11111111 11111111 11111111 00000000
Subnet:    11000000 10101000 00111010 00000000
In decimal
IP:        192.168.58.31
Netmask:   255.255.255.0
Subnet:    192.168.58.0
```

Our subnet in this instance is 192.168.58.0. This means that if the node wants to send a packet to any other node that is in the range 192.168.58.[0–255], it simply sends out an ARP request for the address and expects the node to be on the same physical network medium.

While subnets are usually used to group machines that are physically close together, this is not a requirement. Use of a subnet mask is in no way "enforced" on the wire, at any level; rather, subnets are more of a gentleman's agreement. It is perfectly possible for two groups of computers configured with different subnet masks to share the same physical medium. What happens is each computer chooses to look only at packets for the subnet that it is configured to use. Again, this is in no way enforced; subnetting should not be seen as linked to security in any way.

CIDR Format

Another way of referring to the netmask is to use a shorthand called Classless Inter-Domain Routing (CIDR) notation. CIDR is an implementation of variable length subnet masking (VLSM) that exists to work around the limitations of classed networks. (These are explained in the next section.) The CIDR notation is simply a count of the number of 1s in the binary representation of the netmask. In the preceding example, there are twenty-four 1s before we get to zeros—we can write the subnet in CIDR as 192.168.58.0/24.

CIDR is often used by experienced network professionals because it is a compact representation. On the DataPower appliance, CIDR format is the primary method for specifying subnet masks and is used in many fields as the netmask representation. This sometimes confuses people, because they expect to see a separate field in which to specify a subnet mask, as you would in the Windows networking configuration panel (shown in Figure 4-10).

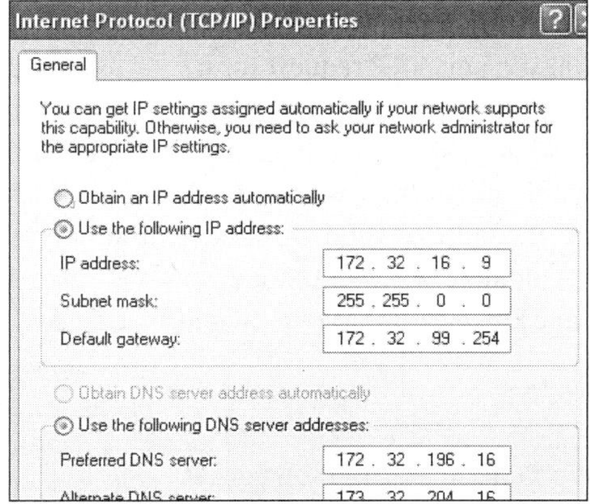

Figure 4-10 The Windows Networking dialog.

However, on the DataPower appliance, it is expected that subnet masks will be specified using CIDR format, and thus there is no subnet mask field on the form, as can be seen in Figure 4-11.

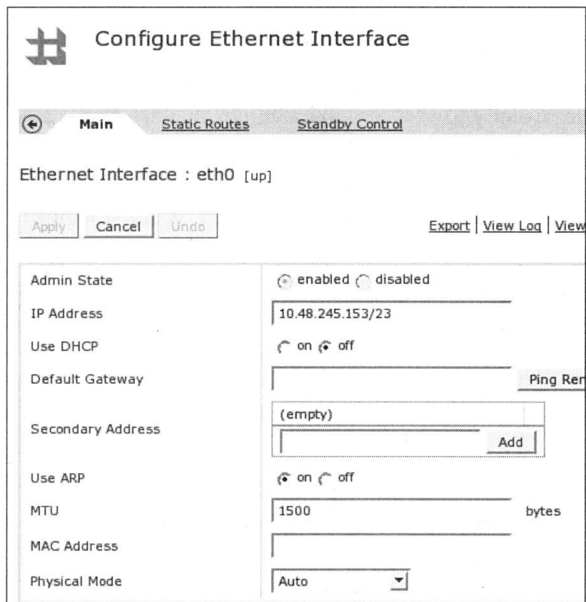

Figure 4-11 Subnet masks are specified in CIDR format.

In fact, it is possible to specify the subnet mask using dotted quad notation by simply leaving a space between the address and the mask, as shown in Figure 4-12.

Figure 4-12 You can also use dotted quad to specify the subnet mask.

Classed Networks

Subnets are commonly described as being broken down into classes. The purpose of classes was, in the early days of the Internet, when things were more structured and there were many less nodes, to allow an allocation of a specific group of IP addresses to a company or an organization. This still holds true to some degree, in that the classes that were allocated cannot be taken away, although the concept of allocating a whole large class to a single organization is falling out of use.

In fact, the concept of classed subnets significantly predates the use of subnets as we know them today on the Internet. It used to only be possible to purchase a whole class—and because these classes are not very granular, this lead to large-scale waste of IP addresses.

The classes are split into A, B, and C. IP addressing uses a 32-bit binary word address space, which is split into four byte-long groups. Each of these classes is an easy- to-use-subnet in that they refer to a one-, two-, or three-byte netmasks. Table 4.2 shows the classes and their subnet masks, in both dotted quad and CIDR format. It also lists the *private* address space relevant to the class; these are addresses that have been pre-allocated for internal use, within private organizations and companies, and are not to be used out on the Internet. Where such networks require Internet access, they commonly use network address translation techniques to achieve this, where a router or firewall maps internal to external addresses dynamically to connect the two networks. Finally, Table 4-2 also contains some real examples of allocated classed networks. This information is publicly available on the Internet via the whois protocol, and most of the examples in the table were chosen at random.

Table 4-2 Classed Networks

Class	Netmask	CIDR	Private	Examples
Class A	255.0.0.0	/8	10.0.0.0/8	9.0.0.0/8—owned by IBM.
				19.0.0.0/8—owned by the Ford Motor Company.
Class B	255.255.0.0	/16	172:32.(16-31).0/16	156.26.0.0/16—owned by Wichita State University. 207.36.0.0/16—owned by Affinity Internet Inc.
Class C	255.255.255.0	/24	192.168.(0-255).0/24	Class C subnets are usually allocated locally by the owner of the encompassing class B network.

Routing

So, how do the packets destined for nodes that are not connected to a single shared physical medium actually get to where they need to go? What will take a letter out of a pigeonhole in one university and deliver it to the other university where it can be placed in the appropriate pigeonhole? The answer is routing—the Internet equivalent of the postal service.

The Internet is a big network that is actually made up of lots of small, interconnected networks. At home, you might have a small local area network of a couple of PCs; at work there maybe a network of hundreds or thousands of nodes. Each of these is a self-contained network in its own right, with a shared physical medium (probably Ethernet), and each is capable of sending traffic to the other machines on its own network. But when you want to access a machine that is not on the same physical network segment, you cannot simply put its hardware address into the destination field of your packets; it will never see your request.

What if we have a general purpose computer and a DataPower appliance that want to communicate, but they are actually on separate physical networks? Let's say our computer is a PC, and it wants to make a Web service call to the DataPower appliance. They too are on separate subnets, because they are separately physically connected to completely different networks. This means that the PC initiating the connection knows that the target IP address it wants to contact is not on its own subnet, so it will not look for the node locally using ARP. Instead it will be configured to send the packet to the hardware address of a machine called a router.

The router's job is to forward on the packet to the target machine. If the router has another interface on the DataPower appliance's subnet, this is as simple as issuing an ARP request for the DataPower appliance and sending the packet to the appropriate Ethernet address. However it may be that the router needs to forward the packet on to another router. Indeed, that other router may in turn need to forward the packet on to yet another router. And so on and so on until the packet finally reaches a router that is local to the DataPower appliance, which uses ARP to find the hardware address and passes on the packet.

Routing Table

So, what does the node do when it realizes that the address it wants to send packets to is not in its subnet? This is what the routing table is for. Every machine on an IP network, be it a Windows PC, a Unix Server, or a DataPower appliance, has a routing table. The routing table tells the machine what to do with packets when they are on different subnets. Listing 4-2 contains an example of a routing table from a DataPower appliance.

Listing 4-2 The Routing Table from a DataPower Appliance

```
xi50# show route
 Destination       Interface Type   Interface VLAN Gateway       Metric
 -----------       --------------   --------- ---- -------       ------
 0.0.0.0/0         Ethernet         mgt0           192.168.58.1  0
 192.168.58.0/24   Ethernet         mgt0                         0
 10.0.0.0/8        Ethernet         eth1           10.24.14.1    0
xi50#
```

This routing table shows first that the machine has more than one physical interface in use; under Device Interface, you can see mgt0 and eth1 as active. This means that the machine is "multihomed"—which simply means that it has more than one interface. Each route is assigned a metric—in this case they are all set to 0, but if needed this could be used to differentiate between two routes that are valid for the same traffic. This routing table says the following:

- If the destination address is on network 192.168.58.0/24, send the packet directly to the node via network interface mgt0. ARP will look for the destination node directly.
- If the destination address is on network 10.0.0.0/8, send the packet to the router 10.24.14.1 via network interface eth1. ARP will look for the router 10.24.14.1 on this interface.
- If the destination address does not match any other route, send the packet to the router 192.168.58.1 via network interface mgt0. ARP looks for the router and sends the packet with the target IP address of the destination node but with the Ethernet address of the router.

The last of these routes is called the default route. The default route must obviously be set to a router that will know how to forward the packet, either directly or via one or more further routers, to the remote network where the remote node is connected.

TIP—Default Routes

The DataPower appliance is perfectly capable of having more than one default route. If you choose to configure the network interfaces and routing table in this way, you need to be aware of the behavior and make a conscious decision to do it.

When outbound traffic has more than one network route available to it, the behavior is undefined; that is, the route chosen (and therefore interface used) will be random. In some instances, this may be appropriate, but it can also lead to some unexpected results!

Consider for instance if one of the "default" routes does not have a valid route to a specific server, but the other does? At random, connections will fail! Or what if there is more than one valid route to a server, but one of them goes over a trusted network and the other routes over an untrusted network? In this case, you'd better hope that you're not sending sensitive data!

The vast majority of configurations should have only a single default route configured on the main interface that is used to process traffic; more specific static routes should likely be used to explicitly define other routes to servers as needed. This is something best discussed with the administrator of your local network.

Virtual LANs

As of the 3.6.1 firmware, DataPower has supported the ability to participate in 802.1Q VLAN trunking. What does that mean?

A Virtual Local Area Network, or VLAN, is a group of hosts that communicate with each other as if they were connected to the same physical network, regardless of whether they are actually physically connected. Everything that you could do on a normal physical network can be done over a VLAN. This includes sending broadcast packets, so ARP works on a VLAN just as it would on a local physical network.

The use of Virtual LANs is a powerful advanced networking configuration. These are fundamentally OSI Layer 2 constructs; by tagging packets as belonging to a specific VLAN, you are effectively plugging in to this virtual transport layer, over which you will send IP traffic. For DataPower, the abstraction provided to encapsulate this is that we can configure a virtual network interface for the VLAN, and to all intents and purposes, we can configure and use that interface as if it were a real physical network interface.

The configuration screen for a VLAN interface (or more properly sub-interface) on the DataPower appliance is shown in Figure 4-13.

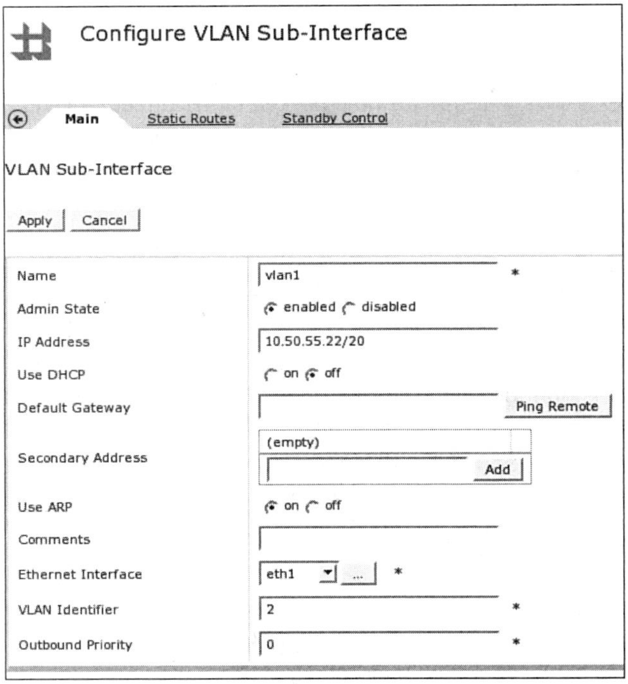

Figure 4-13 Configuring the VLAN interface.

Note that the IP address assigned to this interface is completely different to any of the "real" networks to which the device is connected from earlier configurations. The Virtual LAN uses eth1 as its physical medium, but packets are sent out tagged with a VLAN identifier. (In this case simply 2—note that the identifier 1 should not be used, as switches usually reserve this VLAN for unidentified packets.)

When something on the DataPower appliance tries to contact a server on the subnet served by the VLAN, the appliance sends out packets on eth1 but tagged with the VLAN identifier, and it expects the router or switch to which eth1 is connected will understand this identifier. This is key in using VLANs—if the switch does not understand the tags, the VLAN traffic cannot go anywhere.

DataPower Networking Scenarios

Now that you understand the basic terminology and concepts for networking and routing, at least at a high level, let's go through a number of scenarios of typical appliance network deployments. Chapter 5, "Common DataPower Deployment Patterns," will detail deployment topologies and use cases; this section covers some specific example deployment scenarios explicitly from the point of view of the networking stack. It deliberately does not cover security (other than implied network security issues), performance, availability or any other issues; the idea is to present specific DataPower deployment examples and discuss the issues they raise.

Scenario: External and Internal

This configuration is one of the most common deployment scenarios. The network situation, as depicted in Figure 4-14, has two networks—the first of which is used for incoming client requests and the second to contact backend servers to service those requests. Let's call the incoming network the client network, and the backend network the server network.

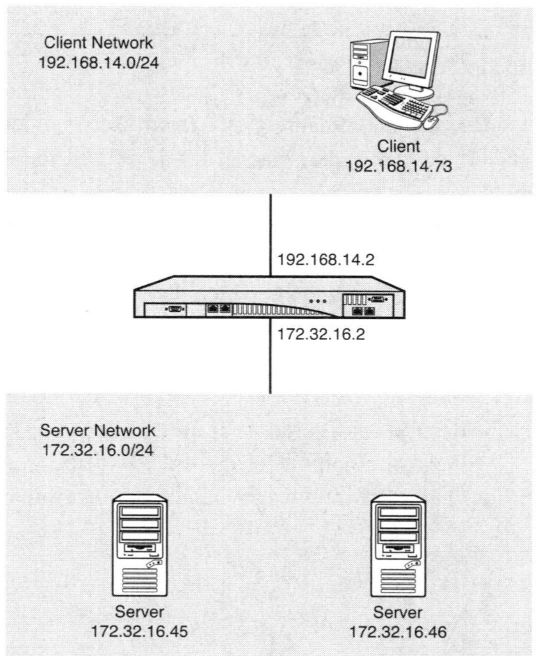

Figure 4-14 External and internal.

Note that this is very different and distinct to linking these networks using a typical packet processing and forwarding device or bridge. With DataPower connecting the networks, the only way that data can make it from one side to the other is if DataPower processes it and explicitly decides to proxy it through.

The client network is configured to be 192.168.14.0/24 and the server network 172.32.16.0/24. The appliance is configured such that one interface is dedicated to the client network, which is 192.168.14.2, and one is dedicated to the server network on 172.32.16.2. It really doesn't matter which interface is configured to which, as long as they are physically plugged into the correct networking infrastructure. For this discussion, let's assume that the client network interface 192.168.14.2 is configured on eth1 and the server network interface 172.32.16.2 is configured on eth2, as shown in Figure 4-15.

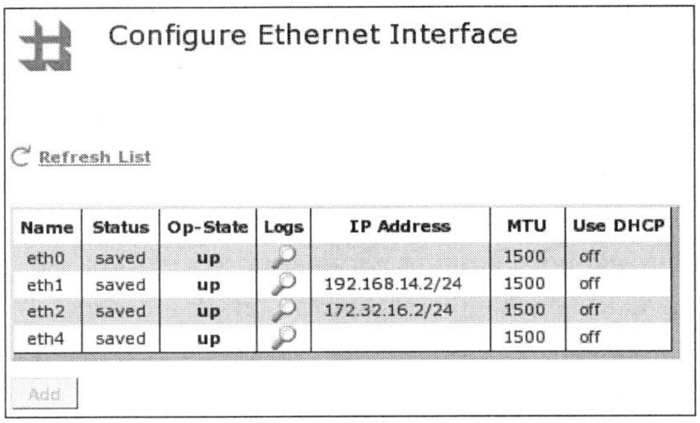

Configure Ethernet Interface

Refresh List

Name	Status	Op-State	Logs	IP Address	MTU	Use DHCP
eth0	saved	up			1500	off
eth1	saved	up		192.168.14.2/24	1500	off
eth2	saved	up		172.32.16.2/24	1500	off
eth4	saved	up			1500	off

Add

Figure 4-15 External and internal interfaces.

The client network accepts incoming requests from Web service clients—in this case, 192.168.14.73 is the Web service client. At a packet level, we call these *ingress* connections—simply meaning incoming. The server network is used to contact backend servers, such as 172.32.16.45 and 172.32.16.46 in the diagram. These are known as *egress* or outgoing connections.

There are two important things to consider in this scenario. First, services (such as Web Service Proxies or Multi-Protocol Gateways), which listen for network connections on the device, should be configured to listen only on the client network. They should be defined such that, when the service is created, its interface setting lists only the host alias that resolves to 192.168.14.2. This means that the service is not accessible by other nodes on the 172.32.16.0/24 network—which is likely the desired configuration. If instead you choose to bind a service to the default of 0.0.0.0, which we always recommend against, it will be available on *both* network interfaces—including the internal interface where it should not be available!

TIP—Host Aliases

Throughout this book, you will notice us telling you to use host aliases. This section uses IP addresses to make it more obvious that routes and subnet masks are applicable to which network traffic; however, in a real configuration, host aliases should always be used to define IP addresses for interfaces, both to make the configuration more portable and to ensure consistency of this vital configuration information.

The second consideration is a routing question—of the two interfaces, which should be the default route for the device? We showed in Chapter 3 how to configure a default route on an interface. However, for most noncomplex configurations, there should be only one default route configured on a single interface on the device. This is the safest way to ensure that "unintended" routing behavior does not occur.

For example, let's configure the default route to be to the client interface, as shown in Listing 4-3.

Listing 4-3 Default Route Configured on the Client Interface

```
xi50# show route
 Destination       Interface Type  Interface VLAN  Gateway       Metric
 -----------       --------------  --------------  -------       ------
 0.0.0.0/0         Ethernet        eth1            192.168.14.1  0
 192.168.14.0/24   Ethernet        eth1                          0
 172.32.16.0/24    Ethernet        eth2                          0
xi50#
```

With this configuration, the only network connections that will be routed onto the server network are those that are explicitly to machines in the subnet 172.32.16.0/24. This is likely to be exactly the desired configuration!

As a matter of fact, some more complex configurations may actually have multiple default routes deliberately. For instance, you may want to have a secondary route available in the event of network congestion. In this instance, for a connection where there is no more specific route, DataPower sends packets randomly over one or other interface. This may or may not be the desired behavior! For static routes, the metric field could be used to specify a preference for sending traffic over a specific link (perhaps one which is less congested or cheaper to use). In the vast majority of cases, it is better to let these kinds of routing decisions be made by dedicated routers, which participate in distributed routing protocols and are best placed to understand how to route traffic appropriately.

Scenario: Management Network

The previous scenario uses two interfaces: one for client and one for server connections. Let's add to this configuration by including a commonly used pattern—a management network. The idea is that a separate network connection should be used for accessing the administrative interfaces (console, SSH, SOAP, and so on) so that this sensitive traffic is not sent over the interfaces that serve customer traffic, to clients or servers. This addition is depicted in Figure 4-16.

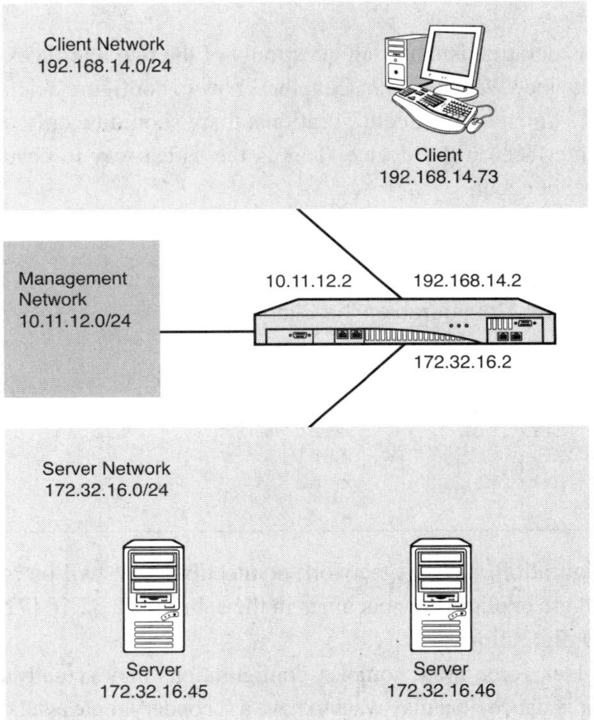

Figure 4-16 Management network.

The management network has an IP range of 10.11.12.0/24, and the DataPower appliance's interface on this network is 10.11.12.2. The updated DataPower configuration is shown in Figure 4-17, where 10.11.12.2 is configured on eth4 (also known as mgt0).

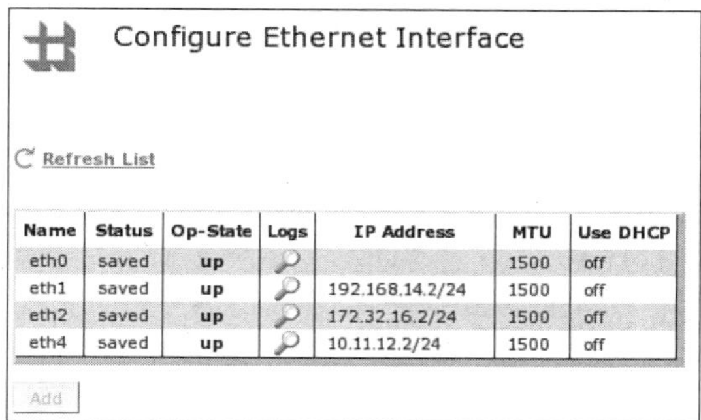

Configure Ethernet Interface

Refresh List

Name	Status	Op-State	Logs	IP Address	MTU	Use DHCP
eth0	saved	up			1500	off
eth1	saved	up		192.168.14.2/24	1500	off
eth2	saved	up		172.32.16.2/24	1500	off
eth4	saved	up		10.11.12.2/24	1500	off

Add

Figure 4-17 Three interfaces, including a management interface.

This configuration has a number of further considerations that must be discussed before implementation.

First, in the same way client services should be made bind-specific and listen only to the client interface, it is important to ensure that the administrative interfaces bind only to the management network. This can be done by specifying the specific IP address (by choosing the host alias tied to that specific IP address) when defining the service—web-mgmt, SSH, and so on as shown in Chapter 2. The listener configuration can be verified by using the TCP Port Status, as described in Chapter 3 and depicted in Figure 4-18.

local IP	local port	remote IP	remote port	state	domain	type	name
0.0.0.0	21	0.0.0.0	0	listen	ITIT	FTP Server Front Side Handler	ftp_21
10.11.12.2/24	9090	0.0.0.0	0	listen	default	Web Management Service	web-mgmt

Figure 4-18 Bind the web-mgmt to the management interface.

The issue of routing is the next important issue. In general, there should be no routes configured over the management network, other than any of those that are explicitly needed to enable the specific traffic to flow. If the machines that are clients are on the same broadcastable subnet (for instance, if a machine was 10.11.12.64 on the management network), ARP is used to contact the server and no routing is required. If, on the other hand, the machines that are used to administer the device are remote but still accessed over the management interface, a specific static route should be added to enable packets to return to that machine.

For instance, traffic coming back to administrative clients on 10.11.72.0/24 would require a static route telling the device how to pass on data for that network, and it would do this by providing a gateway address for that remote network. Listing 4-4 shows the routing table that would provide this configuration; notice that the route to the 10.11.72.0/24 subnet is explicitly being told which router to use, and that router is on the 10.11.12.0/24 subnet accessible via the mgt0 (eth4) interface.

Listing 4-4 Routing with the Management Network

```
xi50# show route
 Destination        Interface Type  Interface VLAN  Gateway        Metric
 -----------        --------------  --------------  -------        ------
 0.0.0.0/0          Ethernet        eth1            192.168.14.1   0
 192.168.14.0/24    Ethernet        eth1                           0
 172.32.16.0/24     Ethernet        eth2                           0
 10.11.12.0/24      Ethernet        mgt0                           0
 10.11.72.0/24      Ethernet        mgt0            10.11.12.1     0
xi50#
```

It is especially important to ensure that no default route is set up for the management network. There is no route with a destination of 0.0.0.0 for mgt0 shown in Listing 4-4, and there should almost never be a need for this. The management network is designed for administering the device; application traffic should in all likelihood never be going onto this network.

Another trap to be aware of is if there is a valid route from the device to another server via its management interface. If the routing table on DataPower is misconfigured, and the other server accepts the traffic over its interface to the management network, customer traffic could go over management network completely unintentionally!

Finally, you should consider whether using a management network is the right thing for you. This is a powerful concept, and is highly recommended, but it is *critical* to configure it correctly. Many people do not consider that when they create a management network, they are creating the perfect platform from which to attack their infrastructure. Often servers have misconfigured management type connections over dedicated management networks—perhaps using default usernames and passwords, and without really thinking about security, because they are considered to be on a "safe" network. However, this "safe" network provides a wonderful back door into systems—a great way for a bad guy to make out-of-band connections to other servers! Configure all nodes on a management network with care, and stay safe.

Scenario: IP Aliases

The DataPower appliance has the capability, as shown in Chapter 3, to add secondary IP addresses or IP aliases to a network interface. Many aliases can be configured on a single interface, and they are all valid IP addresses for that interface. An example is shown in Figure 4-19.

IP aliases have various uses, but one of the most important reasons they are used is so that different frontside handlers can use different SSL certificates. As Chapter 18, "DataPower and SSL," will demonstrate, only one SSL server certificate can be presented over a given IP address and port combination. This is because the SSL handshake has to complete before any application traffic can proceed, so the application level traffic *cannot* choose which SSL certificate is used.

Because of this limitation, which is inherent to the protocol, a configuration such as that presented in Figure 4-19 comes into its own. It can allow four separate HTTPS frontside handlers all listening on the same port but on different IP addresses, on a single network interface.

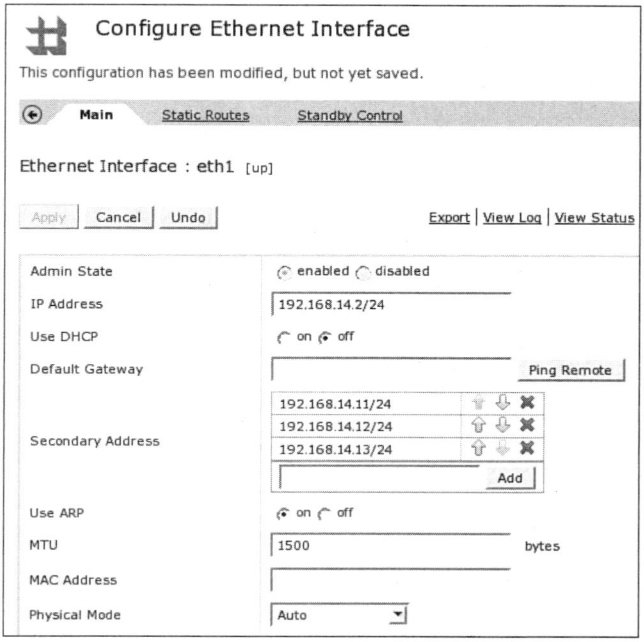

Figure 4-19 IP aliases.

Scenario: Multiple Interfaces on the Same Network

DataPower appliances are high-performance devices. Even though the devices' Ethernet ports are Gigabit Ethernet, the fastest standard in common use today, it is possible that the network speed may become the bottleneck. This might especially be an issue when connecting to older networking hardware—for instance, if the device is plugged into a 100Mb Ethernet port (of which there are still many in use), its available network bandwidth per interface drops by an order of magnitude.

In this situation, it may be desirable to have more than one network interface plugged in to the same network. Consider Figure 4-20.

In this example, there are two network interfaces plugged in to the client network and two network interfaces plugged in to the server network. Clients can connect to either 192.168.14.2 or 192.168.14.3; of course, this needs to somehow be either load balanced or built in to the client logic. Server connections may be initiated from either 172.32.16.2 or 172.32.16.3. The DataPower configuration for this is shown in Figure 4-21.

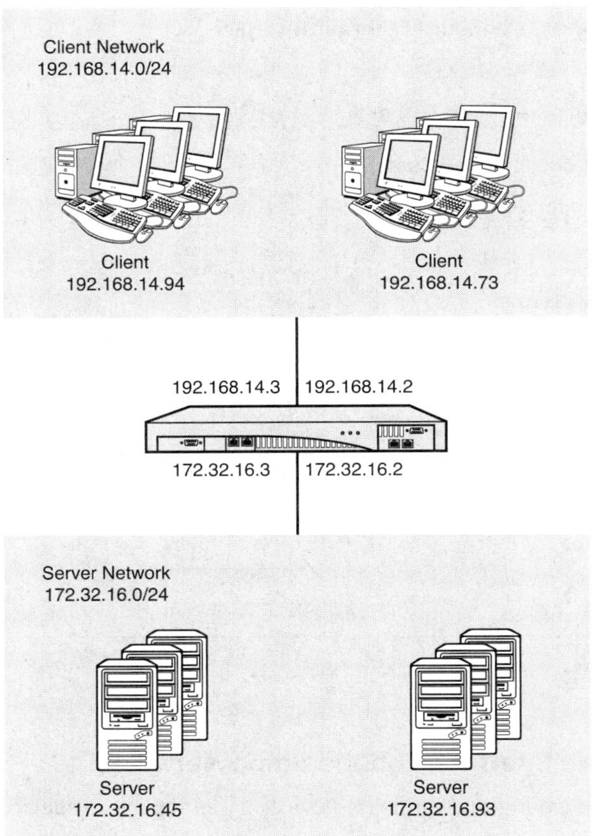

Figure 4-20 Two interfaces per network.

Configure Ethernet Interface

Refresh List

Name	Status	Op-State	Logs	IP Address	MTU	Use DHCP
eth0	saved	up		192.168.14.3/24	1500	off
eth1	saved	up		192.168.14.2/24	1500	off
eth2	saved	up		172.32.16.2/24	1500	off
eth4	saved	up		172.32.16.3/24	1500	off

Add

Figure 4-21 Two network interfaces per network.

In this scenario, we explicitly want to configure the routing table such that there are two equal priority routes on each side. This way, the device will randomly decide which interface to use for both ingress and egress connections. An example of this routing configuration is shown in Listing 4-5.

Listing 4-3 Routing Table for Two Network Interfaces per Network

```
xi50# show route
 Destination       Interface Type  Interface VLAN  Gateway        Metric
 -----------       --------------  --------------  -------        ------
 192.168.14.0/24   Ethernet        eth0                           0
 192.168.14.0/24   Ethernet        eth1                           0
 172.32.16.0/24    Ethernet        eth2                           0
 172.32.16.0/24    Ethernet        mgt0                           0
xi50#
```

In this scenario, there happens to be no default route configured on any of the network interfaces of the appliance. This means that the only networks that are addressable are 172.32.16.0/24 and 192.168.14.0/24; should there be any packets for any reason destined to any other network, they would have no route to use and would fail. Packets that are destined to one of our two valid network targets will be sent out at random from either of the two interfaces configured for the network.

This kind of configuration may be useful in any situation where the gigabit network interface is the limiting factor. These are likely to be few and far between! Possibly when performing fast requests for a high volume of client traffic—on the scale of say an international sporting championship final or a very popular online auction house—the network card may become the bottleneck, at which point this scenario may be useful.

Notice that in this scenario there is no network interface configured for management. This is possibly a valid scenario—but it does not necessarily mean that we have to have the administrative GUI or SSH bound to one of our application traffic interfaces. Especially for high-volume, business-critical, and security-sensitive devices, it is perfectly possible to run the DataPower appliance without running any of the network-based administrative interfaces! After the configuration is uploaded, there may be no need or requirement for network-based administration, and any needed work can always take place via the serial console. Some customers even set up a completely private network where network addressable serial terminal emulators enable highly secure network access to the serial console for remote administration.

Scenario: Different Network Zones

The last example scenario to be presented here is one that some DataPower users have concerns about. It is presented not as a definitive answer or statement saying that this is the best configuration to use; rather we demonstrate it to show how this may be a valid and safe configuration—using the same DataPower appliance in different network zones.

A typical secure middleware deployment with traffic facing an untrusted network such as the Internet might be deployed in three separate network zones. The first of these would likely be a demilitarized zone, or DMZ; the first stop for incoming connections, and a barren, hostile place for an attacker. Behind this may be a server zone, where middleware application servers running business logic would be connected; this zone is also well protected, and can only be accessed via the DMZ. Finally, there may be a backend network area, where Enterprise Systems or databases would run; this is the most protected zone, where actual business data is stored, and only applications running in the server zone can access the backend.

This scenario suggests that it may be safely possible to use a single DataPower appliance to perform services across all these network zones, as in the layout depicted in Figure 4-22.

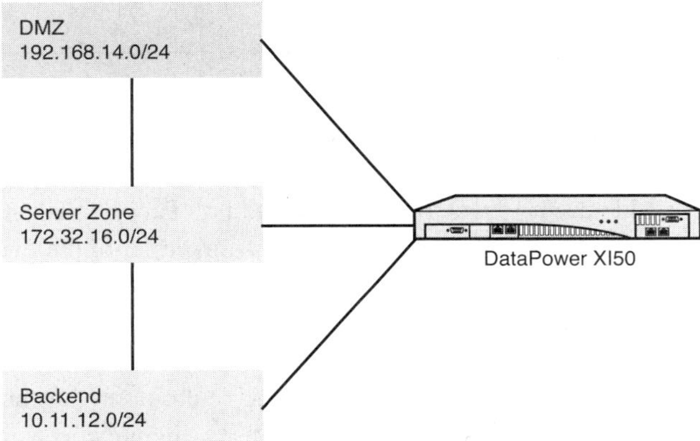

Figure 4-22 One device, three separate network zones!

Don't stop reading just yet! It is true that traditional logic dictates that one should not share servers between different zones. That is certainly true for general purpose servers. But is it also true for appliances? For example, do you actually have separate physical firewalls between your DMZ and your server zone, and between your server zone and your backend network? Why not? Because the firewall is an appliance that is trusted to separate and secure these networks. Why might that same logic not apply to other appliances, especially security hardened appliances?

An oft-asked question from those demilitarized zone DataPower customers who want to deploy the appliance in this manner—especially where the two networks are a DMZ and a server zone as above—is, "Can IBM guarantee that no traffic will be leaked onto the wrong network?" Well, the answer is, "It depends." What is hopefully clear in this chapter is that the flow of packets from and to the device is decided by the routing table. It is, therefore, important to have the routing table well defined and configured such that there is no unexpected behavior.

Before we get into the routing configuration, let's first ask a question: Why would you want to configure the device in this way? Primarily, those who want to do this are interested in saving money. They see a need for the DataPower appliance in each of their zones. For instance, in the DMZ, they want to perform XML Threat Protection and schema validation; in the server zone they are performing routing and mediation as part of an Enterprise Service Bus function; and at the backend, they are carrying out high-speed transformations of data and connectivity to legacy systems. These are all valid use cases for the appliance—indeed it excels at all three. But perhaps the customer doesn't want to (or can't afford, within the scope of a single project) to purchase three separate devices.

Fundamentally, when choosing to save money, there is always a question of saving versus risk. The more you save, the higher the risk grows; this trade-off is well known in IT. The trick is to manage the risk, from both a technical and business perspective, and make informed decisions to try and ensure that you are choosing the best way forward for your company. There will be some level of risk involved in choosing to deploy like this. Let's try to quantify this risk, and then think about how we might mitigate it.

What is the actual risk? This partially depends on how you choose to configure your services. In particular, are you choosing to truly act as if you had three separate devices, with no direct communication from one zone to another through the device, or are you taking shortcuts and in effect bypassing the firewalls? Both of these might be valid deployment decisions, but the implications of each one need to be understood.

The Target Environment

Figure 4-23 shows the same layout as before, but using three separate DataPower appliances—an XS40 and two XI50s. We have also explicitly shown the firewalls between the network zones, to make it clear that there is no direct traffic between the zones that does not go through the firewall. Note how each device is attached to a specific network; it can communicate only with other nodes in that network. If it does want to make a connection to a machine in the server zone, it cannot go directly—it has to go through the firewall that separates the DMZ from the server zone.

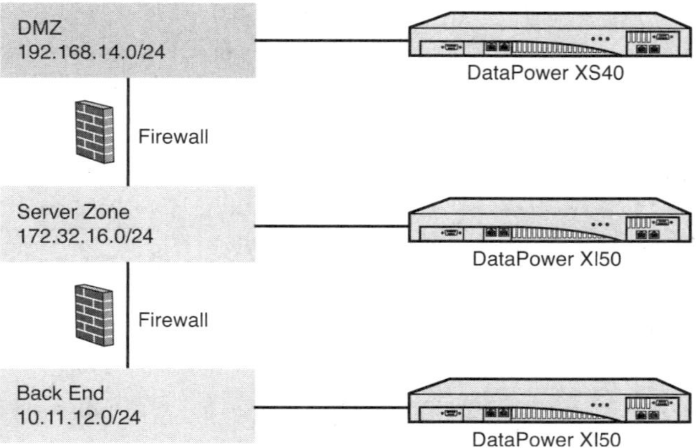

Figure 4-23 Three separate appliances.

This is the safest possible configuration; separate physical devices, and no possible risk of cross contamination between the zones. Everything you do that is less than this is a compromise, balancing the cost of separate devices against the increased complexity of replicating the configuration on a single device.

Using a Single Device

It is possible to replicate this configuration with a single device, using the concept of domains, which will be detailed in Chapter 12, "Device Administration." The device should be split up into three separate domains, one for the DMZ, one for the server zone, and one for the backend. Each domain is administered individually, by separate users, who have no ability to administer the other domains.

Most importantly, an interface needs to be assigned to each network zone, and an agreement has to be made by all administrators that within a given zone, services will *only* be bound to the specific interface for that zone. More than that, the developers for each domain need to agree that they will *not* under any circumstances attempt to make a network connection directly to servers in the other zones, which they theoretically could access.

Finally, what about the valid connections to servers in the other zones? How do you make sure that these go through the firewall? Well, again the answer is complex. The only way to do this is to make sure that the routing table contains a static entry for the specific host, which directs traffic for that host to the router on the correct side of the firewall. Because the device uses source-based routing, this static route entry will not affect connections *from* that host to the device, but it will ensure that any connections from the appliance to the host will use the route through the firewall.

This is a nontrivial area, so let's examine our configuration in more depth, putting specific servers and IP addresses onto the diagram, to understand what the routing table will need to contain. Consider the configuration in Figure 4-24.

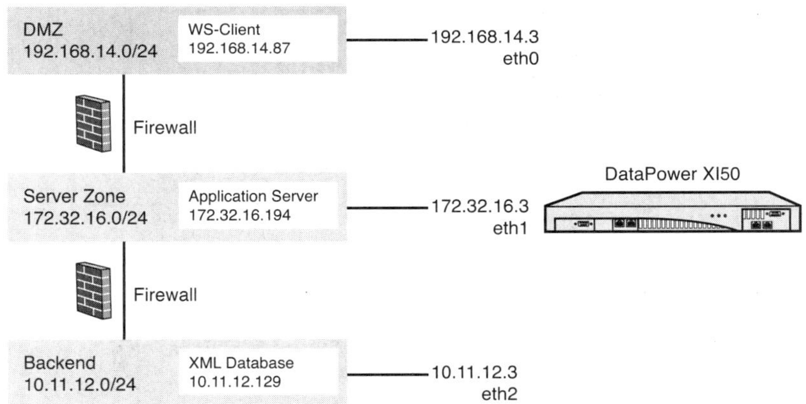

Figure 4-24 A single appliance doing the same job.

The flow of traffic might go from the WS-Client on 192.168.14.87 to a service listening on eth0 of the DataPower device, on 192.168.14.3. This service is a WS-Proxy fronting the application server on 172.32.16.194. In order that outbound traffic from 192.168.14.3 goes to the Application Server via the firewall, we would need to add a static route to 172.32.16.194/32 (that is, to exactly that one host). The application server might then call a Multi-Protocol Gateway listening on eth1, on 172.32.16.3—the response packets for this connection will be sent out back over the same interface rather than using the static route because DataPower's default behavior is to perform source-based routing.

In the same way, the Multi-Protocol Gateway might need to make a call to the XML Database on the backend layer—and so a static route would need to be set to ensure that outbound calls to 10.11.12.129/32 are sent out via eth1 not eth2. The XML database may need to make use of an XML firewall performing complex transformation, running on eth2 10.11.12.3—and response packets back will be sent via eth2, rather than using the static route, because they came in on the eth2 interface.

The routing table to implement such a scenario is shown in Listing 4-6.

Listing 4-1 Routing Table for Two Network Interfaces per Network

```
xi50# show route
 Destination       Interface Type  Interface VLAN  Gateway       Metric
 -- -- -- --       -- -- -- -- --  -- -- -- -- --  -- -- --      -- --
 0.0.0.0/0         Ethernet        eth0            192.168.14.1  0
 192.168.14.0/24   Ethernet        eth0                          0
 172.32.16.0/24    Ethernet        eth1                          0
 10.11.12.0/24     Ethernet        eth2                          0
 172.32.16.194/32  Ethernet        eth0                          0
 10.11.12.129/32   Ethernet        eth1                          0
xi50#
```

The most important routes are highlighted. Our most specific route from the appliance to the Application Server is explicitly directed to eth0, ensuring that this connection will go through the firewall and not straight out through eth1. Likewise, our most specific route to the XML Database is explicitly set to go via eth1 rather than eth2, again making sure that the traffic will be sent via the firewall.

Summary

This chapter has gone into more detail on how the DataPower network stack works and has provided some example deployment scenarios. The terminology included should stand you in good stead for the rest of the book, but the theory has barely touched the surface. We strongly recommend that you explore further, with a dedicated book on networking.

CHAPTER 5

Common DataPower Deployment Patterns

DataPower is often referred to by us in the field as a "Swiss Army knife." You know—the red one with the white cross and a bazillion different blades and appendages. The analogy works because the knife has at least four or five blades capable of performing any given task required of it; some of them might do it faster, some require more brute force or cunning, but they'll all result in the same vital task being satisfactorily completed. In the same way, there are almost always multiple ways that any specific task can be carried out using DataPower. Different services can be used to instigate the same processing—one might be easier to configure based on the inputs available (for instance the WSDL-defined Web Service Proxy [WSP] configuration), while another might be capable of reusing the same processing configuration for multiple inputs (the Multi-Protocol Gateway). Which one you choose depends not only on the task at hand, but on the context within which it is carried out.

There are certain ways to do things that are generally seen as "always correct." However, this doesn't actually mean "always." There is no such thing as a "best" practice, because each and every deployment is different, and there cannot be a single answer that is the best for everyone! There are, however, certain ways of doing things that have been done time and time again, and each time they are done, they have worked because they make sense. In IT, we refer to these as "patterns"—recurring deployment scenarios that can be reused in similar circumstances to give a similar positive result. This chapter describes some common DataPower deployment patterns—things that have worked well for other DataPower customers, and most likely will work just as well for you!

Deployment Topologies

A common DataPower misconception is that appliances have a single use or purpose. This might be true for your common garden-variety kitchen appliances but certainly not for DataPower! Whereas a dishwasher is only good for one thing—washing dishes—a DataPower appliance is adaptable and flexible. If it were a household appliance, it would wash your dishes, launder your clothes, vacuum your carpets, and mow your lawn—and it would do it as well, if not better than your existing appliances!

Okay, DataPower isn't really going to metamorphose into a robot and go trimming your hedges (feel free to submit an Enhancement Request). However, note that each of the tasks mentioned has a completely different setting, depending on the appliance. It would require a single appliance that is just as good in the kitchen as in the garden, in the utility room as in the bedroom. In each area, there are different specific tasks that need to be carried out and carried out well. Imagine if they could all really be carried out by a single appliance that could be easily repurposed or reconfigured to perform whatever task was at hand.

DataPower is an amazingly flexible combination of hardware and firmware in a consumable form that is able to solve many of the extremely difficult SOA problems. It is precisely because of this flexibility that DataPower appliances are often deployed in completely different parts of an enterprise, performing completely separate roles. Deployments cover everything from security protection and application level firewalling to providing interoperability between disparate and incompatible systems to mediation and routing of messages as an Enterprise Service Bus (ESB). These are difficult challenges in the world of SOA that can be solved using a single configurable appliance instead of multiple complex software products that are difficult and expensive to install, deploy, and maintain.

This section describes some of the most common deployment scenarios, although an infinite number of other possibilities exist where DataPower may well be a good fit.

DataPower as Security Gateway

Often the first response that comes to mind when someone asks "so what is this DataPower thing anyway?" is that it is an XML Security Gateway. That term somehow feels like it should have an ® or a ™ somewhere behind it—that it is somehow official, that XML Security Gateway has a deeper meaning and standard behind it. It sounds as official as Firewall, Application Server or Database, and yet only a few years ago no one had heard of the term XML Security Gateway!

So, what is an XML Security Gateway? It is a security hardened proxy that sits at the perimeter of your environment, usually in a network-level DMZ, terminates incoming connections, ensures that the requests are "safe," and passes them on into your infrastructure. An example of an XML Security Gateway deployment pattern is depicted in Figure 5-1.

Figure 5-1 The XML Security Gateway.

Figure 5-1 shows a SOAP request to a server passing straight through IP packet filtering firewalls because those do not work on the application layer at all; this connection can be protected only by using an XML Security Gateway.

As described in Chapter 1, "An Introduction to DataPower SOA Appliances," DataPower is a perfect fit for this type of deployment. The device is designed from the ground up for security and can be deployed into the DMZ without qualms. Moreover, it can ensure that requests are "safe" at multiple levels, including parsing the XML to ensure that there is no malicious or accidentally dangerous content for backend software XML parsers (discussed in Chapter 20, "XML Threats") calling out to external virus scanners and other content checkers via the ICAP protocol (also discussed in Chapter 20) and authenticating, authorizing, and auditing the requests (discussed in Chapter 16, "AAA," and Chapter 17, "Advanced AAA").

This level of protection is unprecedented in security devices. It deals with much more than the packet layer and the protocol layer; it is up at the application layer, OSI levels 5 through 7, dealing with message content. By actually parsing and processing the XML content, DataPower in the role of XML Security Gateway can protect against a class of real and increasingly sophisticated attacks against which to date there has been no real protection. The DataPower XS40 and the DataPower XI50 include functionality to act as an advanced XML Security Gateway.

A typical deployment scenario for DataPower as an XML Security Gateway is shown in Figure 5-2.

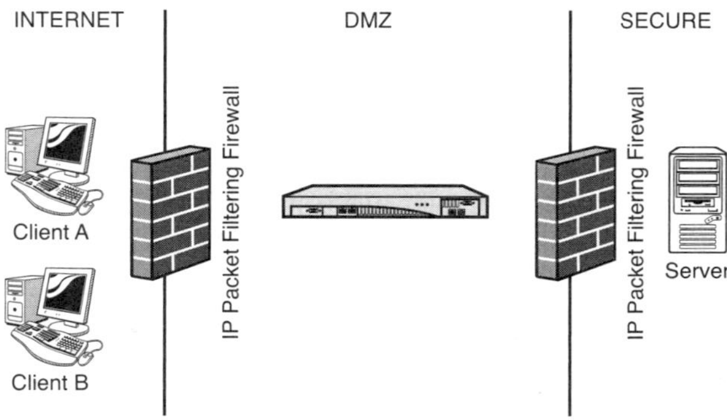

Figure 5-2 DataPower as the XML Security Gateway.

In this instance, the role of the XML Security Gateway is being fulfilled by the DataPower XS40 appliance. The XI50, being a complete superset of the XS40, would also be able to carry out the role of XML Security Gateway.

It's all well talking in abstract terms about generic deployment topologies, but simply saying that DataPower can perform all these roles does not actually demonstrate that it is so. Let's take a slightly deeper look at some of these functions and answer the question: What role does DataPower actually perform when deployed in each of these situations?

SSL Termination

The decision on where to terminate SSL connections is an important decision for any Internet-worked application environment. The SSL endpoint must be a secure hardened box with the capability to process the SSL handshake without detriment to performance and the capability to proxy incoming connections to backend servers. DataPower uses dedicated cryptographic hardware and can do this in an advanced manner, including handling client certificate authentication and specifying which SSL signers to trust, processing all the attributes in an SSL certificate to identify the owner, checking Certificate Revocation Lists and using the Online Certificate Status Protocol, providing specific server certificates depending on the requested IP address and port, specifying which encryption algorithms to use, and more—see Chapter 18, "DataPower and SSL," for details.

SSL termination on DataPower is shown in Figure 5-3.

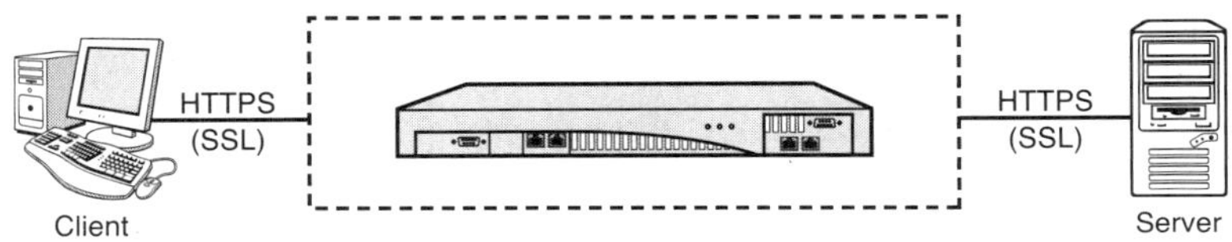

Figure 5-3 DataPower can act as the SSL endpoint.

The inbound HTTPS connection from the client is terminated at DataPower. Messages are then processed on the device, and when an explicit decision is made to do so in a Processing Policy, the messages are sent on to the backend server. Note that the connection to the backend is also over HTTPS—indeed this would likely be mutually authenticated SSL; however, this is a completely separate isolated and independent SSL session to that of the client connection.

Even when SSL is not in use, DataPower still acts as a connection termination point, ensuring that messages can never pass by without being inspected and deliberately routed onward.

Authentication and Authorization

Perimeter security is an increasingly common requirement for complex customer environments. DataPower can authenticate credentials for incoming connections and make authorization decisions based on those credentials and the resources requested. This can be done in many ways, including out of the box integration with big-name enterprise authentication and authorization services and using many different standards. Figure 5-4 shows an example of how DataPower can integrate with an external provider for authentication and authorization.

More information on externalizing authentication and authorization can be found in Chapters 16 and 17.

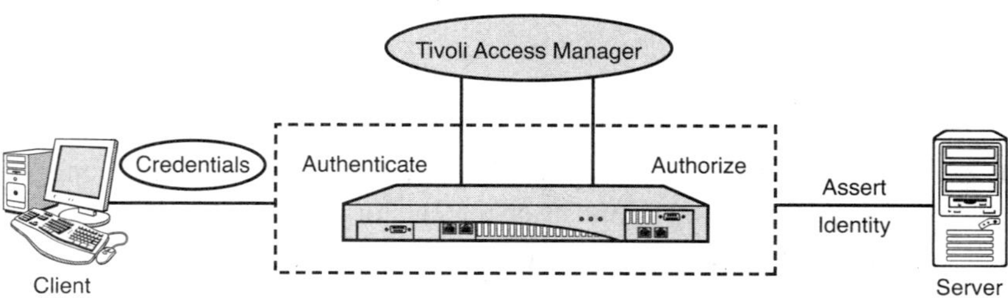

Figure 5-4 Externalized authentication and authorization.

Token Transformation

When Web service consumers authenticate, they do so in a myriad of different ways. There are many different types of tokens in the WS-Security standards, including a custom binary token which might be anything, and then even more possibilities beyond the standards. But what do we do if our Web service consumer wants to provide one type of token, but our Web service provider can only accept another type? Enter DataPower.

DataPower, sometimes in conjunction with another token transformation engine such as Tivoli Federated Identity Manager or other external authentication services, has the capability to mediate in the communication between consumer and provider to map tokens from one kind to the other. The number of types of tokens supported out of the box is impressive, and combined with the advanced cryptographic functionality on the device and the options for customization, the device can truly claim to be able to transform almost any kind of token into any other.

Figure 5-5 shows an example of one possible use case of DataPower performing token transformation.

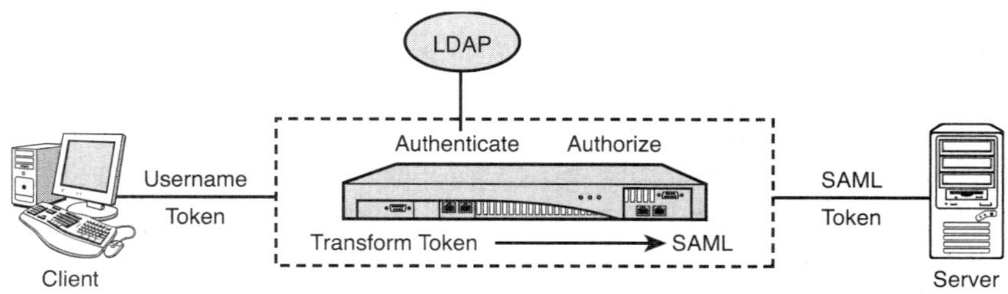

Figure 5-5 Token transformation.

The client sends a request containing a WS-Security Username Token (UNT), however the backend server with which they want to communicate understands only the Security Assertion Markup Language (SAML). DataPower validates the UNT against an LDAP directory, performs an authorization check on the request, and then transforms the token into a SAML authentication assertion—such that the backend server can understand it.

XML Threat Protection

It's a little known fact that even the most modern software XML parsers can be tricked by cleverly but maliciously written well-formed XML into using up significant system resources leading to systems going down or even remote system compromise. The same symptoms can also be induced by simple mistakes in writing input documents or application coding. The problem is that, by their nature, software parsers have to use up a huge amount of resources simply to realize that they are under attack. After they begin to process the XML, it is too late; often the attack has already done its damage.

This is where an XML Security Gateway is required. The security gateway proxies the backend service and processes the XML beforehand, barring malicious or badly written XML from entering the system, as shown in Figure 5-6.

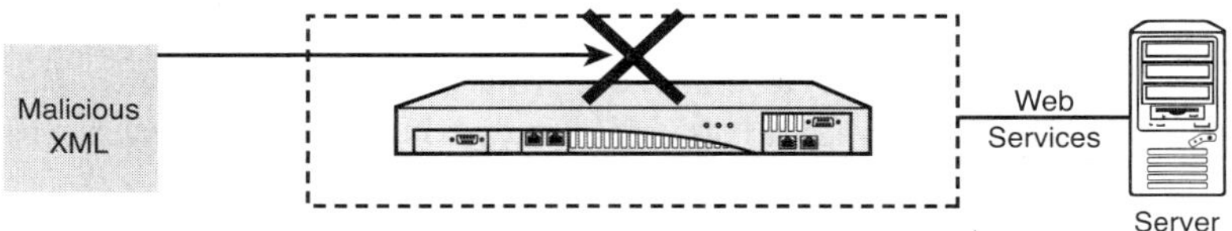

Figure 5-6 Malicious XML can lead to system compromise.

The XML parser in DataPower, described in Chapter 20, is different to these software XML parsers. It is constructed of dedicated custom hardware and a custom written firmware component, which has inherent safeguards built in. It can thus recognize more easily when there is something wrong and prevent such data from reaching the software-based XML parsers in your application servers behind it.

Schema Validation

Schema validation, with a well-written schema that does not use shortcuts like `xs:any` (a way of loosely typing data that makes it much easier to pass through malicious attacks) is a good way of verifying that the input into a Web service request conforms to expected parameters. Unfortunately, in too many cases, schema validation on software-based application servers is disabled, because of the simple fact that performing schema validation is an expensive operation in terms of latency and processing power. Figure 5-7 shows DataPower performing schema validation before allowing a request to continue to an application server, where it is now no longer required and would be significantly more expensive to do.

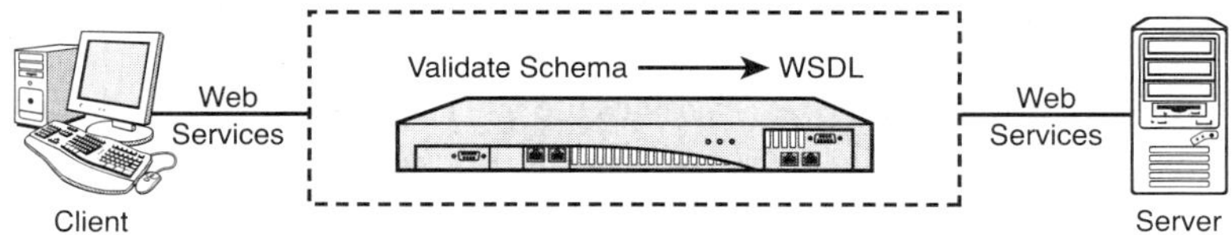

Figure 5-7 Schema validation can be performed inline on DataPower.

DataPower as an XML Security Gateway provides the capability to do lightning-fast schema validation with minimal latency, using a unique patented XML parser that can validate the XML schema while the message streams through the device. This means that there is now no excuse not to perform schema validation on inbound Web services requests.

Resource Masking

When people publish business services on the Web as Web services, they often do not consider what exactly it is they are making available. Thus, a Web service that is automatically generated from some business logic code using a tool designed to simply make processing methods available may actually be giving external users more than was intended. For instance, if a piece of business code provides methods to add and remove money and view the amount that was in an account, but only the view method was intended for external consumption, clearly it is only that view method that should be visible and accessible from the outside. Internal resources can also include URLs and extra parameters on requests; these should not be made visible to external callers where there is no need to do so.

DataPower has facilities to assist with this resource masking. It can rewrite URLs to only allow through specific methods, to change the method names requested, to modify the message format in transit, and in general, to make the frontend service look nothing like that at the backend. Figure 5-8 shows how a resource might be masked using DataPower.

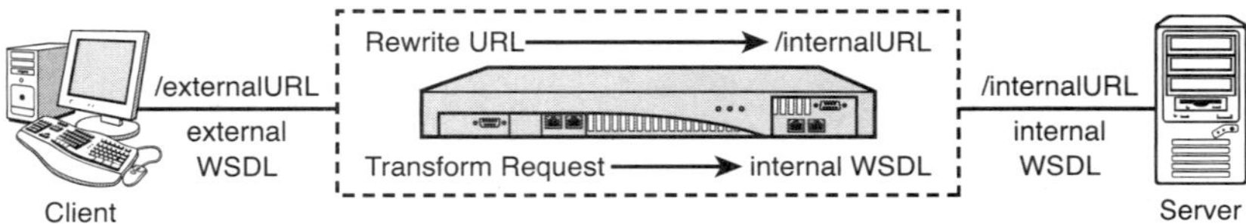

Figure 5-8 DataPower resource masking.

DataPower as Enterprise Service Bus

The Enterprise Service Bus pattern has been described in many books and papers. It is an architectural style, a way of designing intermediary computer systems to process and route data to appropriate backend systems or endpoints in an efficient and secure manner. The ESB pattern is all about service connectivity; in ESB parlance instead of clients and servers, we talk of service consumers and service providers. The ESB acts as a service provider to service consumers and as a service consumer to service providers. Figure 5-9 shows the ESB pattern at a high level.

Two fundamental concepts underlie the ESB style: routing and mediation. Routing in an ESB is much like network routing in concept; a service consumer connects to the bus, and the infrastructure decides which service provider to route the request to. Of course, because the ESB is acting as a service provider to that consumer, it can transparently route the request to any real provider of the service that it wants. It could also respond to the consumer itself, without ever contacting a service provider; it can even contact a number of service providers, aggregate the results, and return them as a single response to the service consumer. Mediation is a slightly more advanced concept that comes into play when service consumers and service providers do not match, when they either do not speak the same wire format, data format, schema, or any other kind of difference. Mediation bridges the differences by transforming data formats, converting transport layers, remapping data structures, and repurposing existing services such that they can fulfill others.

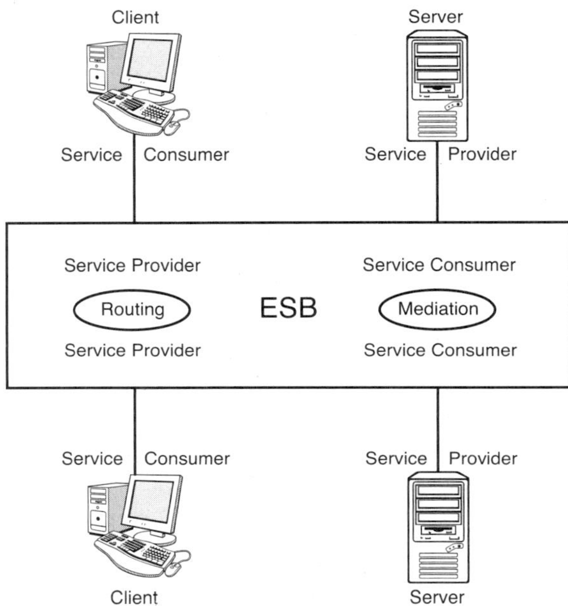

Figure 5-9 The Enterprise Service Bus pattern.

Finally, as an ESB performs its mediation and routing of service requests from consumers to producers and back, it by design adds more value in the form of security enforcement, service-level management and monitoring. A well-designed ESB can perform these functions not just on services or specific providers but on as fine-grained a level as required, even to sections of the individual invocations of specific services. There is a lot of power inherent in the ESB architectural style!

DataPower is a perfect implementation platform for an Enterprise Service Bus, to the extent that IBM has explicitly included it in their ESB strategy and christened the DataPower XI50 appliance the "Hardware ESB." Implementations of routing and mediation are configured, often using processing policies created from out of the box processing actions, to determine appropriate service providers to service specific requests. Where the device shines is in the implementation of the added value features. Performing security enforcement, token transformation, service-level management and monitoring are the bread-and-butter of the appliance, as will become apparent throughout the later chapters of this book.

Figure 5-10 shows a DataPower XI50 deployed as an ESB, in the secure zone and behind another appliance (in this case an XS40) acting as an XML Security Gateway. As discussed in Chapter 4, "Advanced DataPower Networking," the functions could both be served from the same device if security rules on the network are allowed, but often there are hard and fast rules that mandate separate physical devices for these functions.

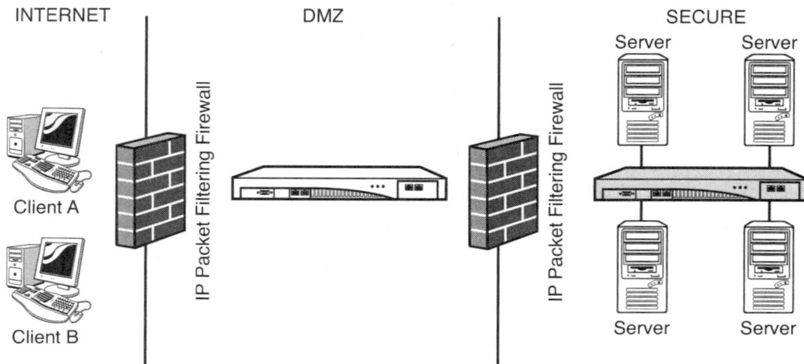

Figure 5-10 DataPower deployed as an ESB.

As an ESB, there are certain "sweet spots"—things that clearly demonstrate that you made the right choice in having DataPower be part of your ESB implementation. This section explores some of those use cases and the role that DataPower plays in them.

Multiple Protocols

One of the chief advantages of DataPower is that it is capable of communicating with many different technologies. Its protocol support covers a number of currently popular transport protocols, including HTTP/HTTPS, FTP/FTPS, WebSphere MQ, NFS, IMS, WebSphere JMS, and Tibco EMS. As will become obvious throughout the book, the device is at home with any of these protocols, and they allow it to communicate with almost any modern Internet-connected system. Figure 5-11 shows an example of DataPower processing multiple protocols.

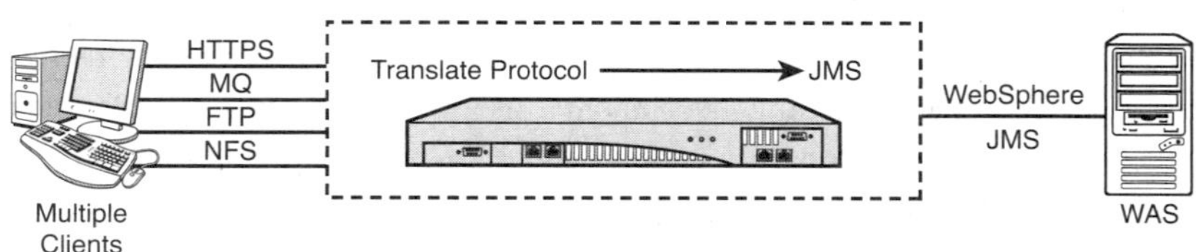

Figure 5-11 DataPower can process multiple protocols.

HTTP and HTTPS are, of course, used for the most-often discussed protocol of the Enterprise Service Bus—Web services. But they are also used for many other forms of communication. Sometimes integration of "traditional" Web applications, designed not for remote system use but for human interaction, is done over HTTP, with the system or bus pretending to be a human user. And, other patterns of stateless or stateful system interaction over HTTP, such as RESTful services, are becoming more and more commonplace. A good ESB must be able to support these.

FTP support is absolutely crucial. There are many "legacy" systems in existence whose main form of communication is files. That is, they accept input files that are put on a file system, and they produce as output other files that are put back onto the file system. To communicate with these systems, we must have a way of processing data from that remote file system; with FTP support, this becomes trivial, because almost every IP-connected system can easily be configured to communicate via FTP! However simply supporting the protocol is not enough; we must be able to support it securely, such that the administrators and owners of these legacy systems are happy allowing us to access them. Thus the DataPower implementation of FTP allows for full AAA processing and for configuration of mutually authenticated SSL over both the control and data channels as required.

Likewise, Network File System (NFS) support is key to integrating with systems that are not quite "up to date" enough to support Web services. Large shared Network Attached Storage (NAS) devices are becoming common in the enterprise and provide a shared platform over which data can be exchanged; DataPower is able to poll and process files from these NAS arrays using NFS and write files to them in response. In addition, DataPower provides an iSCSI Host Bus Adapter (HBA) on some appliances, which can communicate using the iSCSI protocol with iSCSI targets.

Finally, the messaging protocols: WebSphere MQ, WebSphere JMS, and Tibco EMS. Ever since the advent of the IBM Message Queuing protocol, asynchronous queuing has been hugely popular for two reasons. The first is that it provides an asynchronous method of submitting data for processing; that is, you write a message to a queue, and something else will deal with it in its own time. This is a great way of processing large loads at peak efficiency because business systems can draw exactly enough data to process at a time and are short of data to process only if there is no actual work to do; for this reason alone it is vital that an ESB support asynchronous messaging. However there is another reason that applies to WebSphere MQ, and this is that MQ client and server software support is available for an amazing array of platforms. This means that we can use MQ to communicate with everything from a Windows server to a mainframe. Unfortunately, this also often leads to designs that are "less than optimal" from an architectural point of view, where the asynchronous queuing mechanism is used synchronously—clients put a message to one queue and wait for a response on another queue before continuing their processing—but this is of less importance than the fact that they can use the protocol to communicate with a system with which they would otherwise be unable to communicate!

To implement an effective ESB, we must be able to communicate as widely as possible with as many different disparate systems as possible, such that those systems can become consumers of the services we provide and providers of the services we consume. DataPower's protocol support is wide-reaching and covers the core protocols that are popular today.

Multiple Datatypes

Just as we can communicate with many different protocols, the DataPower XI50 is actually capable of processing almost any type of data. What's that I hear you say? Isn't it an XML appliance? Well, yes, it is—much of the internal workings of the appliances is XSLT, and it has hardware XML acceleration to ensure that the performance cost of processing XML at high speed is not an issue. But the creators of DataPower realized that not everything in the world is XML, and that there are a vast amount of systems out there that are not and likely never will be able to communicate using XML. Thus they designed in the capability to work with non-XML data.

Chapter 26, "Transforming Non-XML Data," describes in detail how this functionality can work with non-XML formats—indeed there is a specific example of communicating with a backend using a COBOL Copybook. This extremely powerful functionality in conjunction with the support for different communication protocols means that DataPower is capable of performing integration that in some cases would simply not be possible in any other way without writing significant amounts of application code—so much in fact that it would probably be simpler to rewrite the backend systems! That is the value proposition: Really difficult SOA core work can be completed more easily and mainly using configuration on DataPower.

In addition, it is important not to forget that one of the fundamental core functions of the device is transformation of XML data. XSLT allows for structured and controlled transformations and translations of formats that have absolutely nothing in common with each other except for the fact that they are both expressed in XML.

This ability to perform many transformations is important when dealing with real-life use cases. In the real world, nothing is as simple as it should be. For example, when a system provides a service that is needed, and other systems want to use that service, there is no guarantee that those other systems will in any way be compatible. A typical enterprise might have any number of different clients all performing the same kind of processing, and all doing it with their own definition of what that processing means. Each client and each server may have its own schema and its own understanding of how to process the data, and therefore, the service provider must understand and implement all of them. Figure 5-12 shows this interaction.

Outside of the enterprise there are also many situations in which people do similar things in a similar way, but none of the ways they do things can interoperate with each other. If you look at any given industry, it is highly likely that they will have common industry concepts that anyone performing that kind of business must be able to understand; otherwise, they would be out of business. The more established industries have, over time, defined common standards that everyone adheres to in order to be able to interoperate and communicate. However even those standards are often open to interpretation, or expanded on for commercial advantage, or worse yet competing standards arrive and need to be translated between! The best example of this is the original Web Services standards, which were so noninteroperable that they lead to the creation of the Web Services Interoperability Organization that had to create "Profiles" to explain how to make them interoperate!

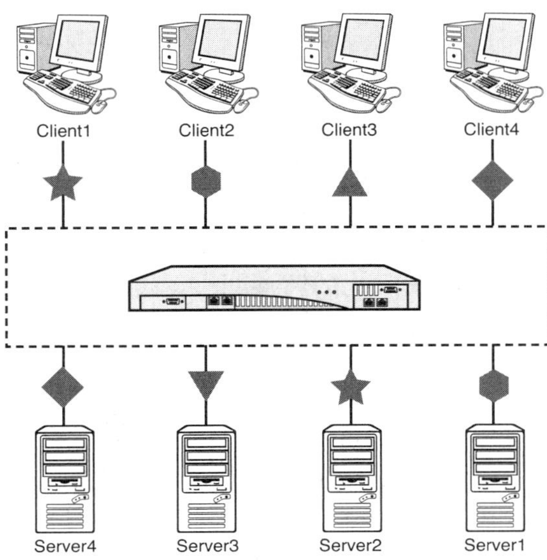

Figure 5-12 Many clients, many servers, many schemas.

Using DataPower, it is possible to process the data for all these scenarios. But what do you do with it once you have it? A useful pattern is to create what is loosely known as a "golden schema." This is a concept where you take all the common points of data and wrap them up into a single definition and representation of that data. Figure 5-13 shows mapping to a golden schema.

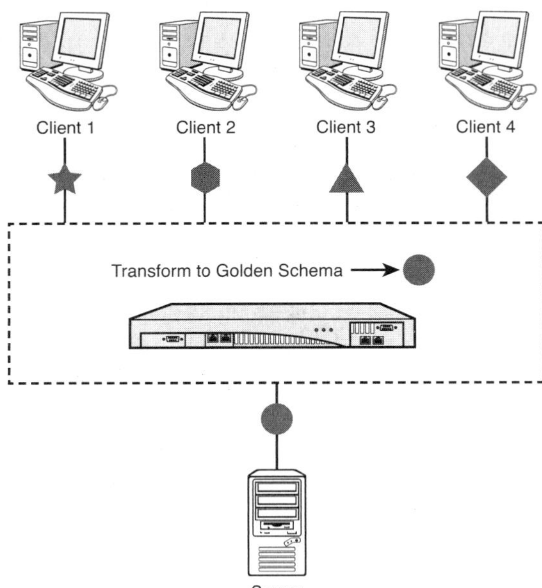

Figure 5-13 The golden schema.

This is hard work, and DataPower will not magically come up with the schema for you! However DataPower provides the frontend to enable mapping of all the disparate data types and formats into this golden schema so that your backend applications can work with this single, united understanding. This leads to a far simpler development process for new applications and with time can be used to provide back to the clients (be they internal clients or industrywide) that such-and-such a definition might be useful because it truly represents the needs of the industry.

Routing and Orchestration

We mentioned earlier that routing and mediation are the two core concepts of an ESB. DataPower is more than capable of implementing both of these; its capability to handle multiple datatypes makes it perfectly placed to mediate between applications. Routing, however, can be extended into a further paradigm known as orchestration.

The primary goal of an ESB is to make it easier to integrate applications and services. Service routing entails taking a request from a service consumer and passing it on to a service provider that will be able to fulfill that request. DataPower can route messages in a myriad of different ways, and even contains an out-of-the-box dynamic "routing" action that can be freely used in a Processing Policy. But what if, rather than simply passing through a request and passing back a response, while potentially transforming the data structure and changing the protocols, we were to take that request and provide a response by building up a number of requests to several services? Would that make DataPower the service provider or just another intermediary? This concept of brokering multiple services into a single combined composite service is known as *orchestration*, which is depicted in Figure 5-14.

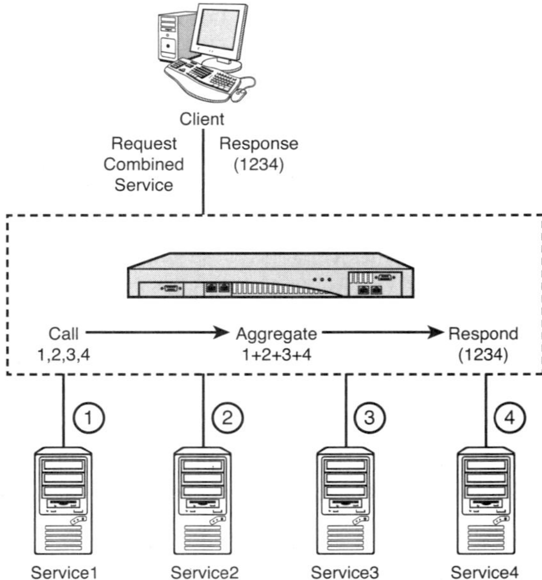

Figure 5-14 Orchestration of multiple services.

The specific orchestration shown in Figure 5-14 is simple; it shows the calling of multiple services in order and aggregating the responses. DataPower's capability to perform orchestration out of the box using simple actions has been extended with the ability to send out multiple asynchronous requests to backend servers and then aggregate the responses in this manner. When using custom processing for orchestration, the device shines because orchestration requires a detailed knowledge of the service to be composed and the services from which it will be formed.

Web Services Management

The third deployment topology that proves more popular with DataPower customers is that of Web Services Management. This use case seems relatively simple at first, but is, in fact, multifaceted and has a lot of detail and complexity hidden within, making it as powerful and compelling a proposition as the first two.

The idea behind Web Services Management is that, for specific services, different consumers of those services may require different levels of service. For instance, if Client A is paying less for a service and Client B is paying more, and there is some kind of a problem that not all requests can be serviced, it seems that Client B, who is paying more for the service, should be given priority over Client A. Of course, Client A would have known up front when choosing the less expensive package that in the event of issues, other clients paying for more expensive packages would be prioritized over him.

How would we implement this on DataPower? Well, DataPower provides a facility called Service Level Monitoring (SLM), which is explored in depth in Chapter 10, "Web Service Proxy." In short, the SLM capability allows for a policy-driven approach to decide with which priority requests are treated. It can throttle or even deny requests that meet certain preset boundaries and conditions, which can be dynamically reallocated at runtime. This is used to enforce policies such as that described previously with different clients paying different fees for the same service but with different Service Level Agreements (SLA), as shown in Figure 5-15.

In the scenario in Figure 5-15, Client A pays less for a service and Client B pays more for the same services. DataPower implements SLM based on the IP address of the client, and because it can identify the client, it can make a decision about whether to allow the traffic through.

SLM can be combined with other capabilities in DataPower to perform more advanced actions. For instance, combining SLM with dynamic routing would allow a variation of the pattern from Figure 5-15, shown in Figure 5-16.

In the scenario in Figure 5-16, there are two backend servers that are capable of providing the service: Slow Server and Fast Server. DataPower again implements SLM based on the IP address of the client (although this could, of course, be based on any of a vast selection of transactional metadata), and this time uses that information to direct requests from Client A to Slow Server and Client B to Fast Server, thus ensuring that Client B gets a better service.

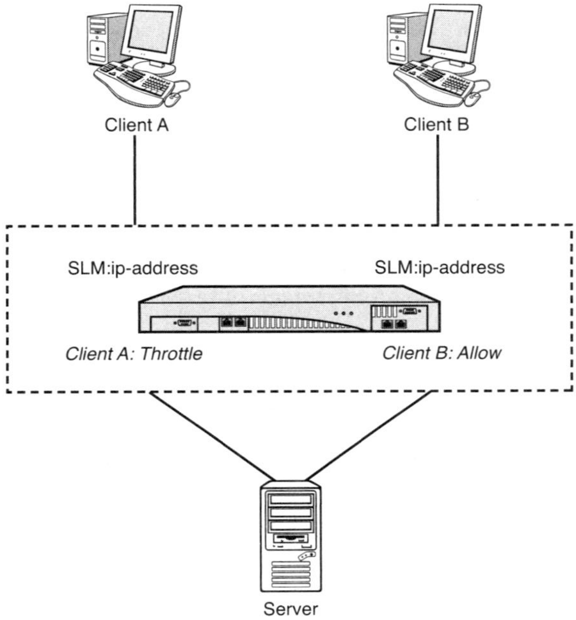

Figure 5-15 Throttle Client A's traffic because he paid less.

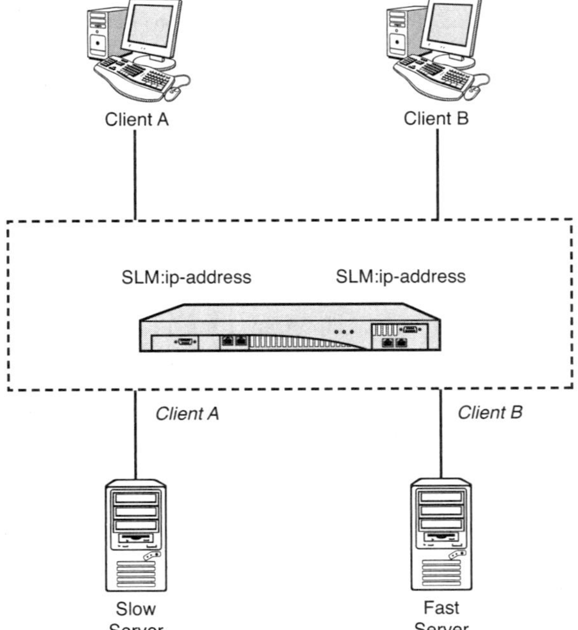

Figure 5-16 Different service levels for different clients sent to different servers.

The SLM functionality can also be used to protect backend application servers from spikes in traffic. Where the capacity of a server or group of servers is known, it is possible to utilize SLM as a traffic management point. where advanced traffic shaping and throttling occurs and requests are queued on the network or in the device up to a limit or until the application server is capable of processing it, or even simply rejected by configuration for specific clients until the traffic situation abates.

Finally, and perhaps most importantly, SLM allows for data to be collected on who is using which backend systems and how. This kind of data is invaluable to enterprises that provide services, because it can become the basis on which to provide usage reports, create cross-charges or chargeback for services used, and monitor the status of services.

Web Services Enablement of Legacy Systems

Another important DataPower deployment topology is that of enabling legacy applications to work in the modern era of Web services. Legacy applications such as CICS® and IMS, usually running on mainframe computers that have been doing their jobs steadily and well for many years, are not significantly different in concept to our modern application servers. They are often designed in a similar idiom to modern form-based Web applications; the user types data into a number of fields, clicks the submit button, and the application processes the input and returns a response. However there are a number of challenges with modernizing these applications.

First of all and most important is the fact that, because these applications have been stable and running for many years, it is very hard in most environments to get a change made to the application. It is possible for implementation of changes to take months or even years! In some cases it is even all but impossible, because the source code to the applications has been lost over the years. Secondly, the applications often use older formats for data and requests, which are not well supported in the age of the Web browser. And finally, the applications are often not capable of communicating via the modern protocols currently in use.

DataPower is a wonderful solution to all these issues. Its support for protocol bridging and data transformation mean that it is possible to configure and front these "legacy" applications with a minimum of fuss, and significantly less effort than would be required with an application coding effort. Moreover it is usually possible to perform this integration without requiring any changes on the mainframe—often turning an impossible project into a realistic one. Figure 5-17 shows DataPower providing a Web services interface for a legacy application.

In addition, there are extra benefits to consider. First, the legacy applications might not have data secured at a granular level of access control. When these applications were written, it was common practice to secure at the level of application access; that is, to provide an identity for a remote application which, after authentication, had access to do whatever it needed to the data. By leveraging DataPower's powerful AAA functionality, we can add more fine-grained security around this data.

Second, DataPower is a high-performance appliance. By processing more of the business logic on the appliance and integrating with the application only at the level of the data to be processed, and by pre-processing wherever possible, it is highly likely that less CPU (measured in MIPS) will be required on the mainframe applications. This may even lead to a reduction in cost for running those applications for some customers!

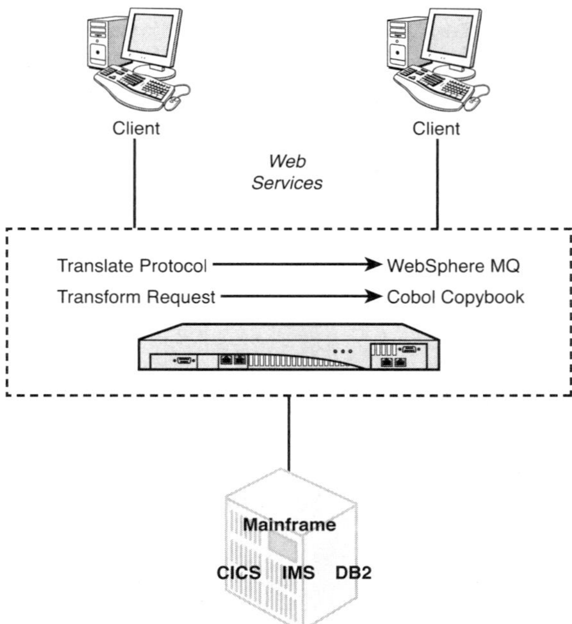

Figure 5-17 Web Service enabling CICS.

Finally, there is the advantage that, by exposing these legacy applications as reusable Web services on an ESB as part of an SOA, we can leverage the existing applications to perform their functions as part of wider processing of newer applications, thus extending the useful life of the legacy services.

Dynamic Content Rendering

The final deployment pattern we discuss is that of dynamic rendering of content. This may seem to be a simple use case, but it is powerful; IBM DataPower clients use the appliances to serve high-traffic Web sites to a multitude of different clients. Moreover, this scenario can be implemented on all the appliances: XA35, XS40, and XI50.

XSLT, the transformation language at the heart of DataPower, was designed to dynamically generate a markup language for the Web—HTML—and this is still a common usage. This usage becomes an order of magnitude more useful when combined with the concept of *transcoding*. If all our content is stored in render-neutral XML, and we create stylesheets to transform it into HTML, we can also write other stylesheets to transform the content into other markup languages, such as Wireless Markup Language (WML). The WML use case is especially interesting, because this is a common format for handheld wireless devices. We could thus dynamically choose whether to render our content for a normal Web browser or a mobile browser—without needing to explicitly modify the content itself.

Performing this translation on DataPower is highly performant as the device itself is capable of processing transformations at extremely high speeds. In addition, DataPower's support for dynamic processing makes it easy for us to render the relevant markup depending on the type of device—for instance, we can recognize the device type based on HTTP headers and run the relevant stylesheet.

To deploy DataPower for dynamic content rendering, it is important to ensure that the device is deployed inline in the processing—that is, clients request the content from DataPower, which then calls back to wherever that content is stored, retrieves it, transforms it, and returns the transformed content back to the requesting client. This pattern for deployment provides much higher performance than "calling out" to DataPower from within another processing flow, and is shown in Figure 5-18.

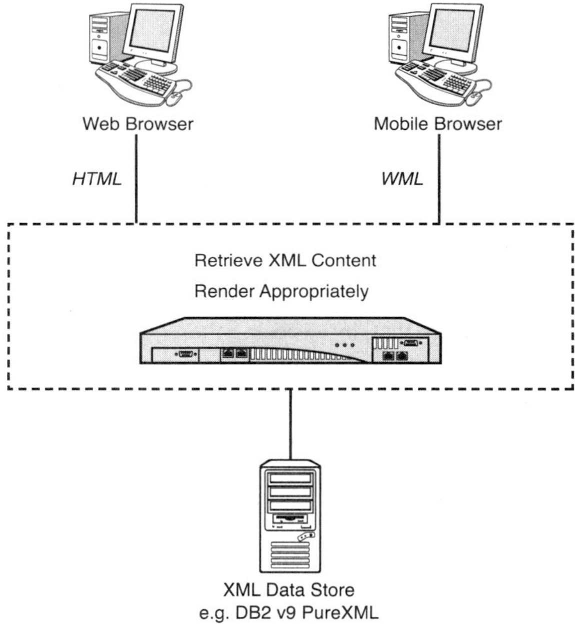

Figure 5-18 Deploying DataPower for dynamic content rendering.

Summary

Choosing how to deploy DataPower is a complex decision process, because there are so many possible ways to do it, and so many places in your infrastructure where it is just a perfect fit to do the job! This chapter presented some common deployment patterns and some ways of deploying the appliance that are known to have worked for other customers and will likely work well for you.

This also brings to a close Part II, "DataPower Networking." Part III, "DataPower Services," goes into more detail for how to configure the device to perform the wonderful things it can do. Onward!

PART III

DataPower Services

CHAPTER 6

Introduction to DataPower Services

So now that you've heard all the great things that the DataPower SOA appliance can do for you, you're probably on the edge of your seat, ready to plug one in and watch it do its magic! Well, there is some assembly required after the appliance is plugged in to your network. Unlike your typical household appliances such as a refrigerator, where you simply plug it in and load all the food, these appliances need to be configured to do precisely what you want them to do. If they are not configured, they will not allow any traffic to pass through them. This is not by mistake, though. The devices are intentionally factory set secure by default, where no traffic is allowed through the device unless it is explicitly configured to accept it. As mentioned in Chapter 1, "An Introduction to DataPower SOA Appliances," it is much more secure to turn on everything you want rather than turn off everything you don't want.

The configurations that you create on the appliances to process and control traffic are called *services*. This chapter describes what a DataPower service is, what components combine to form one, and the different types of services available. After reading this chapter, you should have a general understanding of DataPower services.

What Is a DataPower Service?

DataPower SOA appliances can be configured to perform various types of processing on message requests and responses, such as security, transformation, mediation, and routing. In general, you create proxies for your applications to perform these actions before the messages are sent to them. The proxies created on the appliance to provide these functionalities are called services. For example, you might configure a service type called a Web Service Proxy on DataPower to front the Web service providers on your backend.

In general, a DataPower service is a simple concept; however, it is critical to understand what a service is and how it works as it is the component that is configured to apply any and all processing to incoming and outgoing messages. Without a service configured to listen for and process incoming messages, no traffic can flow though the appliance, assuring that only desired traffic is accepted and providing maximum security.

If you think of a service as a proxy, and understand what a proxy does, you can visualize that there are three high-level processing phases that must be performed for all requests and responses. A service accepts an incoming request on the established front-side connection, processes the request, and passes the request to the backend server over the backend connection. These same phases are also invoked in reverse order on the response from the server back to the client. Figure 6-1 illustrates the three phases of a DataPower service and the order in which they are invoked on a request and response message.

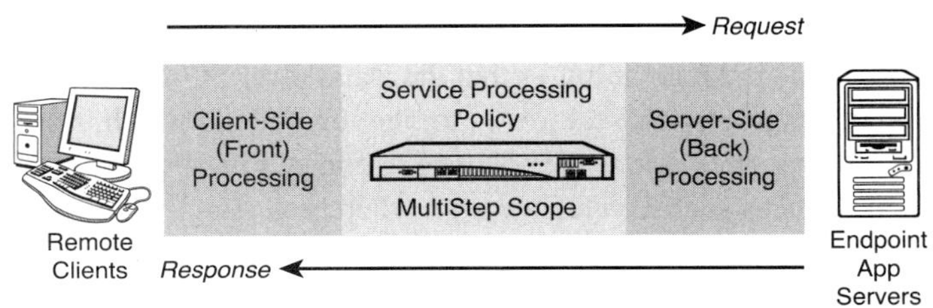

Figure 6-1 DataPower service processing phases.

Client-Side (Front) Processing

As a request is submitted to the DataPower appliance, there could be many different services configured to process incoming messages; however, only one can receive a single request from the client, so there must be something in the configuration that decides which service will handle it. This is determined by the IP address and port combination that the service is configured to listen on. The one exception to this rule is when defining a Web Service Proxy where this can be defined at a more granular level. This will be discussed in detail in Chapter 10, "Web Service Proxy." A service can also be configured to poll for messages, but that is covered in Chapter 9, "Multi-Protocol Gateway." For simplicity, we assume that it is listening on a specific port for incoming requests.

After a service has received the incoming message, there is additional client-side processing that will be applied. If the request is using SSL, this phase will perform the specified level of SSL negotiation and establish the SSL connection, which may include mutual authentication. Transport level decryption of the datastream is also performed for requests sent over SSL.

After the SSL connection has been established and the datastream has been decrypted (if applicable), this phase will apply additional processing on the request such as Service Level Monitoring (SLM), threat protection, attachment processing, message throttles, and URL rewriting. All this processing is configurable within a service and is discussed in Chapter 7, "Introduction to

Services Configuration." For now, it is important to understand that there is a significant amount of processing that occurs in the client-side (front) processing phase before the service even begins to process the message. This phase could reject the message before any message processing is even attempted. Much of this is all that "good stuff" that DataPower provides out of the box such as schema validation and message integrity, while some of it needs to be configured. Again, don't worry about how this all happens for now, just realize that this is where it happens.

Service Processing Policy

This is where all the action is in a service (literally). This phase is also known as multistep processing. After a request to the service is deemed acceptable to the service by passing all threat protection and other client-side (front) processing as described previously, the service can start to perform all the configured processing operations on the message. This is known as the service's Processing Policy. A Processing Policy is a list of rules that contain processing actions that can be applied to a message. Actions are specific processing operations that are applied to a message such as document format transformations, encryption and decryption, message signing, authentication, and so on. As the request message passes through the Processing Policy, the actions are applied to the message in the specified sequence, producing a final message to be passed to the next and final request phase of the service.

Server-Side (Back) Processing

At this point, the request has been accepted and processed by the client-side (front) processing phase, processed by the Service Policy, where all the configured actions were applied and is now ready to be passed to the backend server. Before sending the final message directly to the backend server, there may be some additional steps required. This could include a new SSL connection to the backend server (remember, the frontend client SSL connection is always terminated at the device), setting additional headers in the request, and setting the protocol version that the backend server expects. For example, suppose the incoming request from the client uses HTTP version 1.1 and the backend is a legacy application that supports only HTTP version 1.0. The server-side (back) processing phase would send the request using HTTP version 1.0 as expected by the backend application.

One last and important job of the server-side (back) processing phase is to forward the request to the backend server after it is done being processed by the service. This server location can be defined in one of two different ways. If all requests flowing through the service are always forwarded to the same server, a static backend can be defined in the service configuration. The second method is a powerful feature of a DataPower service that provides the ability to perform dynamic routing. This can be accomplished by defining the backend server as dynamic within the service configuration. It is then the responsibility of the Processing Policy to determine the server location at runtime. This decision can be based on metadata such as protocol headers, URI, or the message content itself.

Response Processing

To this point, the processing phases described have focused on the request from the client to the server. All this processing can also occur on the response back from the server to the client. The backend connection is used to receive the response from the server, the Processing Policy is invoked for response message processing, and finally the frontend connection is used to forward the response to the client. The same types of processing can occur on the response as in the request. The service can be configured to perform the same exact processing as in the request or entirely different processing. For example, if the request is sent in a format that is unrecognizable to the backend application, the service can perform a transformation on the request document to convert it into a format that the backend application can recognize. As the response is sent back from the backend application, the service can perform a similar transformation on the response document that will convert it into a format that the client would recognize.

The three phases described previously show a simplified, conceptual view of a DataPower service. Each of the three phases contains many configuration parameters and options. The available options and parameters may vary by service type. The various service types are discussed later in this chapter; however, the configuration details of the different service types are each covered in separate chapters.

> **TIP—PAY ATTENTION TO THE SEQUENCE OF PROCESSING**
>
> Many man-hours can be wasted looking to do or troubleshoot things in the wrong order.

Anatomy of a DataPower Service

By now you should have a conceptual understanding of what a DataPower service is and what it does, and you're probably ready to dive right in and start creating your services. Not so fast! Before you can create one of your own services, it is important to understand the components of a DataPower service. There are lots of moving parts in a service that can be created, configured, or referenced to provide the end-to-end processing. A DataPower service is object-oriented, so that almost every part of a service is an independent, reusable object. A DataPower service contains a collection of objects that are each configured to perform a specific task. These objects are arranged in a hierarchy with many references and dependencies. Many of these objects will be created automatically for you (depending on how you set up the service), but it is important to know about them even if you never configure them manually. Figure 6-2 shows a top-level object hierarchy of a DataPower service.

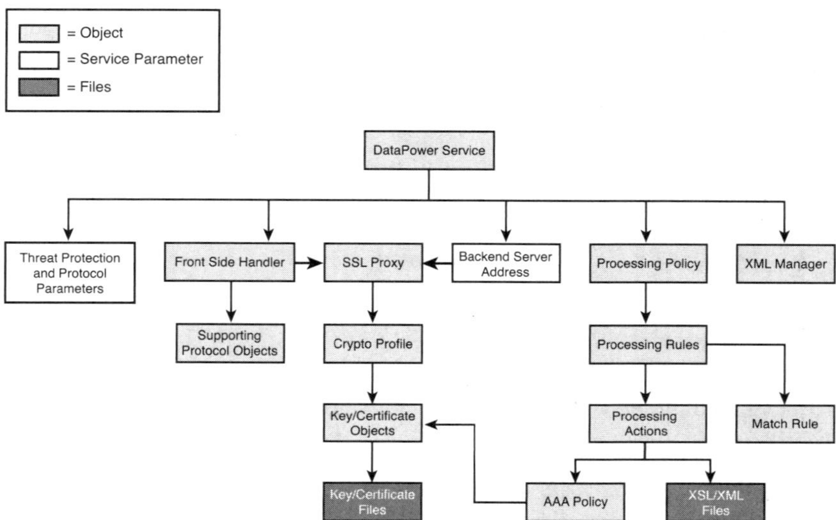

Figure 6-2 DataPower service object hierarchy.

Each of the objects in DataPower services are invoked in one of the three processing phases discussed earlier in the chapter. Figure 6-3 shows the three processing phases, similar to Figure 6-1, but also includes the main service objects in the phase that they are invoked in a request/response transaction.

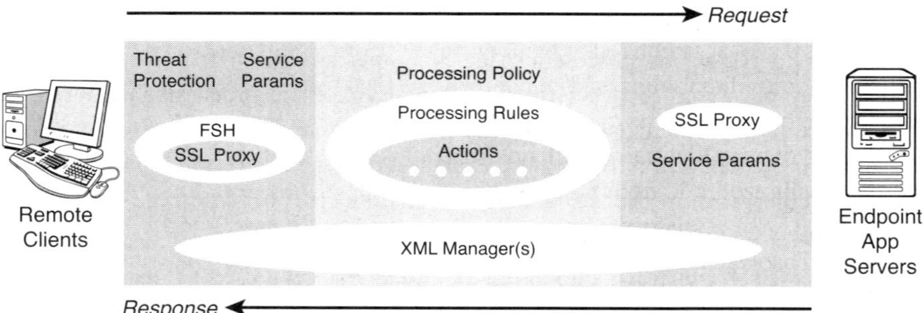

Figure 6-3 Object processing order.

The following list provides a high-level description of each of the main service objects shown in Figure 6-3. A more detailed explanation and the configuration of each object are discussed in future chapters:

- **Front Side Handler**—The Front Side Handler (FSH) object is the first point of entry into the DataPower service. It is kind of like the gatekeeper for your service. It is the object that is configured to listen on a specific IP and port combination for incoming requests (or poll for messages) and perform some level of validation on the request. Most of the validation being performed is protocol-specific, based on the protocol that the FSH object is configured to handle. For example, an HTTP Front Side Handler object can be configured to allow only HTTP 1.1 requests as well as restrict the requests to specific methods such as GET and POST.

  There is a different FSH type that can be configured for each protocol supported on the device. For example, there is an MQ FSH, HTTP FSH, HTTPS FSH, and FTP FSHs. A single service can reference more than one FSH object enabling the service to receive requests on multiple IP address:port combinations or from more than one protocol. The valid protocol types depend on the service type, which is discussed later in this chapter.
- **SSL Proxy**—An SSL Proxy is an object that is configured to handle the SSL communication and negotiation. This object can be referenced by a Front Side Handler object to provide the SSL connection to the client, or it can be used on the backside of the service providing the SSL connection to the backend server. The SSL Proxy determines the SSL version as well as the keys and certificates that are used in the SSL handshake. Basically, everything required to establish SSL communication is defined in this object. This object and its configuration are discussed in detail in Chapter 18, "DataPower and SSL."
- **Processing Policy**—As discussed earlier in this chapter, the Processing Policy is where all the message processing takes place. It is a single object that references processing rules that apply specific processing actions to the request and response messages.
- **Processing Rules**—A processing rule is simply an execution path that a request or response follows as it flows through the service. The processing rule references a sequence of processing actions that perform the actual processing. Separate processing rules can be configured to handle the request and the response. A processing rule can also be configured to execute in the event that an error occurs in the processing of the message.
- **Actions**—Each execution step along the processing rule is called an action. An action can be any type of processing that can be applied to a message. There are many different types of actions that perform different functions. Some of the different types of actions include XSLT transformations, encryption, decryption, signing, logging, and AAA.
- **XML Manager**—The XML Manager is responsible for managing many things across the entire service. There is typically only one XML Manager configured for a service. Some of the responsibilities of the XML Manager are controlling document caching, XML parser options, XSLT compile options, and much more.

DataPower Service Types

Although every DataPower service has the same general characteristics as discussed thus far, there are different types of services that can be created on the DataPower appliance. Each type of DataPower service has built-in features and functionality to handle different types of transactions and protocols for the type of traffic that is to be expected, as well as the type of backend being proxied. The three primary services are the Web Service Proxy, Multi-Protocol Gateway, and XML Firewall.

Figure 6-4 shows the Services section of the Control Panel in the WebGUI, which includes these three service types. Other available service types, such as the two additional services shown in Figure 6-4, are discussed later in this chapter.

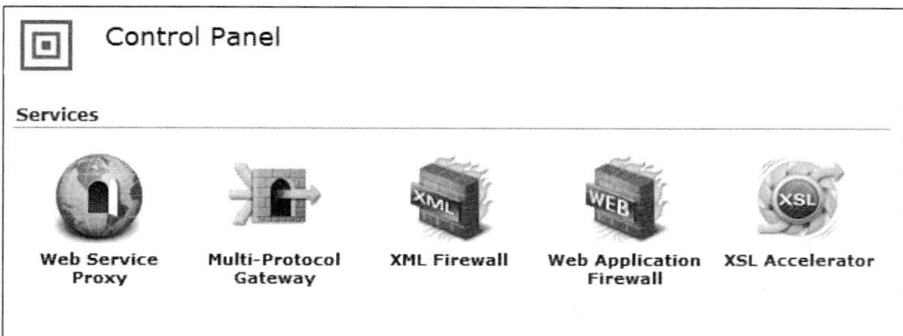

Figure 6-4 DataPower services.

XML Firewall

The XML Firewall (XMLFW) service is designed to process generic XML requests and responses transmitted over the HTTP(S) protocol. It is conceptually one of the simplest services to understand as it can accept messages over one protocol and contains one Processing Policy with a set of request, response, two-way, and error rules providing all the multistep processing capabilities. Unlike the other main service types, the XMLFW does not contain a Front Side Handler object. The listening IP address and port are defined as a service parameter. The XMLFW also provides general threat protection against common XML threats and can be customized to provide the maximum level of threat protection while allowing valid messages to be processed.

Although the XMLFW is designed to process XML documents of all types, including SOAP-formatted messages, it can also accept unprocessed (text/binary) documents. By implementing the multistep processing via a Processing Policy, this service type can apply all the various processing actions to the request or response message regardless of the format. This can include AAA, transformations, schema validation, logging, and cryptographic operations.

Like all other DataPower services, the XMLFW can be configured to proxy backend services by providing a backend URL; however, one of the commonly used features of this service type is the capability to configure it as a loopback firewall. When configured as a loopback firewall, a backend server is not defined. This is because the service itself will generate a response to the client after processing the request message. This is useful when developing, testing, or debugging a service when the backend server is not available.

Because a Multi-Protocol Gateway service (which is another service type discussed later in this chapter) and an XML Firewall can share the same Processing Policy, the XMLFW is often used in loopback mode for testing, allowing easy visibility into message processing without waiting for a valid service backend to be in place and responsive. This loopback capability, as well as tighter integration with its frontend HTTP(S) listener (a tradeoff introduced by its lack of flexibility for protocol mediation) makes the XML firewall a fast, efficient service for development and debugging.

Another use case for a loopback firewall is to provide a standalone service. It may be possible that the DataPower service is capable of generating a response back to the client without ever calling a backend server. Because DataPower has the capability of communicating with many external resources as well as many built-in processing actions, it may be possible to fulfill the client request within the DataPower service itself. This could include a query to a database or an LDAP store based on the incoming message, or a rule that transforms the incoming message and returns the results. All this can be done within a Processing Policy returning the results back to the client without ever calling a backend server. It might be that the client is another DataPower service and the XMLFW is serving as a common "utility" service that can be called by other DataPower services. For example, suppose there is need for many of your DataPower services to perform the same series of LDAP queries to extract information about a user, encrypt some of the data returned, and format it into an XML document. This can be implemented in each DataPower service that requires it, or you can create an XMLFW in loopback mode that will perform these steps based on the user ID passed and return the formatted results.

XMLFW in Loopback Mode

An XMLFW configured in loopback mode is a convenient means for testing services when the backend server is unavailable by using the firewall itself to mimic the backend server.

Web Service Proxy

A Web Service Proxy (WSP) is a DataPower service type used to provide security and abstraction for backend Web services. It is a powerful proxy for the backend Web service. By simply uploading a WSDL[1] document and adding a Front Side Handler to the service, it is created and ready to start receiving requests. This may appear to be a bare bones configuration; however, it is a fully functioning, featured-filled service providing endpoint/URI abstraction, parser-based XML threat protection, XML well-formedness checking, SOAP schema validation, payload schema validation, hooks for monitoring service executions, and a platform for building operation-level rules. All these features are automatically provided as DataPower uses the information provided within the WSDL such as endpoints, schema(s) and operations to configure the service. These few simple steps provide a full-featured service to act as a base for additional configuration required to meet your use case requirements such as AAA, document transformations, message encryption, and so on.

[1] A WSDL file provides critical information about a Web service, including endpoint locations, instructions on binding to those endpoints, and expected message schemas.

In addition to the WSP being capable of uploading or fetching a WSDL, it can also be configured to subscribe to a UDDI registry or a WSRR server to provide automatic updates of the WSDL or dynamically look up the endpoints for the service. Figure 6-5 shows the available methods for acquiring a WSDL file for use by the Web Service Proxy. As you might imagine, this flexibility can be useful for managing WSDLs and receiving updates in your service.

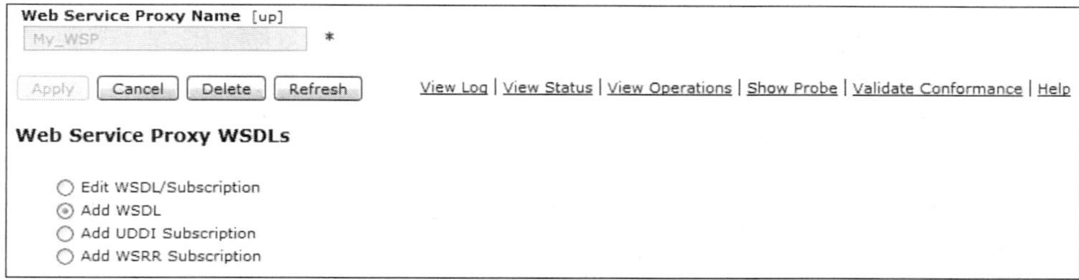

Figure 6-5 Web Service Proxy WSDL options.

DataPower's introspection of the service's WSDL file provides a powerful opportunity to implement rules and actions that are tied closely to that service's natural structure. For example, any of the actions available can be used in a rule and applied to a particular service operation or to every operation in the service. To demonstrate the power and flexibility of this feature, let's take an example Web service that is used for processing online shopping requests. Suppose there is one operation in the Web service for checking out, called checkout, and another for retrieving catalog information, called browseCatalog. It may not be required to authenticate and authorize requests for the browseCatalog operation; however, the checkout operation requires authentication and authorization. Because it is possible to implement a processing rule at the operation level of the WSDL, it is easy to implement this requirement. A processing rule would simply be created to authenticate and authorize the request and applied only to the checkout operation. To illustrate this point, Figure 6-6 shows the Policy configuration screen for a Web Service Proxy. Notice the two operations doGetCachedPage and doGoogleSearch. Each of these two operations implements a different processing rule.

The Web Service Proxy also has some powerful monitoring and logging capabilities. Web service traffic flowing through a WSP can be monitored and logged at the service level or down to the WSDL operation level, providing great flexibility and granularity in the monitoring and logging capabilities. Other features that are provided by the WSP are Service Level Monitoring (SLM) capabilities, WS-ReliableMessaging, WS-Policy, and WS-Addressing.

In summary, a WSP service can be used to proxy Web services by simply importing, referencing, or subscribing to the backend WSDL file. The WSP automatically uses the endpoints contained within the WSDL to expose new, virtualized endpoints. It enforces schema validation based on the contents of the WSDL, providing an extremely powerful and valuable service with minimal configuration. The WSP can also implement all the multistep capabilities that a DataPower service has to offer, while providing many additional Web services features.

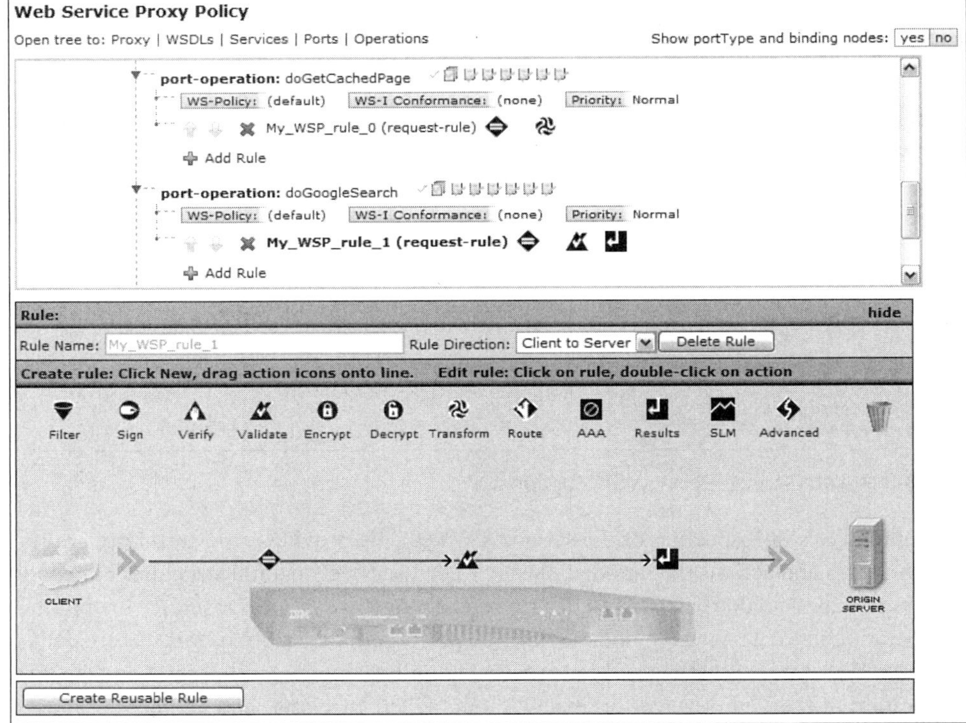

Figure 6-6 Rules applied to the operations.

When configuring a service based on a pre-existing WSDL, you should almost *always* use a Web Service Proxy, as its automatic schema validation and port/binding/operation-level enforcement of policies and service level agreements is unmatched by any of the other service types. In an SOA infrastructure, this service type provides the deepest integration with registry, management, monitoring, and other governance tools.

WSDL = WSP

When configuring a service based on a pre-existing WSDL, you should almost *always* use a Web Service Proxy as it acquires many of the configuration details from the WSDL itself.

Multi-Protocol Gateway

The final service of the three major service types is the Multi-Protocol Gateway (MPGW) and could be called "The Mother of All Services." When you hear of the DataPower appliance being used as an ESB, it is typically the MPGW service that makes this possible. The MPGW is a powerful and versatile service type. In addition to all the threat protection and multistep processing capabilities of the XMLFW, the MPGW is capable of processing requests from/to various protocols. The supported protocols on the XI50 appliance include HTTP, HTTPS, WebSphere MQ, WebSphere JMS, IMS, FTP(S), NFS, and Tibco EMS.

Similar to the XMLFW previously discussed, the MPGW receives incoming requests, processes them within a Processing Policy applying the configured processing actions, and forwards the request to the backend server. In fact, any Processing Policy created in an XML firewall can also be used in a Multi-Protocol Gateway. The service then processes the response similarly, applying the applicable response rule if configured. The big difference is in the multiple protocols that it can communicate with (hence, the name *Multi-Protocol* Gateway). Unlike the XMLFW, the MPGW utilizes a Front Side Handler (FSH) object to establish the connection with the client. FSHs were discussed earlier in this chapter where we mentioned that there is a specific FSH object type for each protocol supported. Leveraging the capabilities of these FSH objects, the MPGW service is capable of communicating with many different protocols.

Because the MPGW service utilizes the FSH object to handle the client connection, it is also possible for the service to have multiple FSH objects listening or polling for requests. This makes it possible to receive requests using different protocols for the same service. For example, a MPGW can have one FSH listening for HTTP requests on a specified IP address and port and another FSH polling an MQ queue for messages. Both FSH objects would forward the incoming message to the service where they can be processed and passed to the backend server.

All the available protocols that the MPGW can receive incoming requests over can also be used on the backend to forward the request to its destination. It is not required that the client side protocol match the backend protocol. It is perfectly valid to receive a request over one protocol such as HTTP and forward the request to a backend URL using an entirely different protocol such as FTP. This is known as protocol bridging and is a key component of an ESB.

Because the MPGW service type features support for many different protocols, you might think that you would use an MPGW only when using mixed protocols or for non-HTTP(s) traffic. The truth of the matter is an MPGW would usually be used for all non-WSDL based backends even where an XMLFW would suffice. Because the XMLFW does not provide any additional functionality over an MPGW (except easily enabled loopback capabilities and perhaps speed of configuration for quick demos and tests) it would be wise to use the MPGW instead of the XMLFW. This provides the flexibility to add additional functionality in the future if needed. For example, after a service has been configured and deployed, a new requirement may dictate that the service listens on more than one IP address and port combination. With an MPGW, this can be easily accomplished by adding an additional FSH object to the already existing service.

In summary, there are three major service types available in the DataPower appliance. Each of the service types provides different functionality and features for proxying different types of backend services and applications. It is important to understand these different service types and what they have to offer when planning for the creation of a new service. A general rule of thumb to guide you through the service type selection is this: If the service is proxying a Web service with an available WSDL, use a Web Service Proxy service. If there is no WSDL provided by the backend application or service, an MPGW is the next best choice. Table 6-1 shows a feature comparison of the three service types discussed.

Table 6-1 Main Services Comparison Chart

Service Type	Loopback Mode	Multiple protocols	Multiple listeners	WSDL Support	SLM
WSP	X*	X	X	X	X
XMLFW	X				
MPGW	X*	X	X		X

* Requires additional configuration within a processing rule

Miscellaneous Services

In addition to the three main services discussed, there are additional, less frequently used service types available on the DataPower appliance. These are discussed in the following sections.

Web Application Firewall (WAF)

The WAF service type is intended to be used to proxy Web applications, providing AAA services as well as cookie encryption, cross-site scripting protection, session timeout management, and name-value input processing/filtering. A common use of the WAF is to provide perimeter authentication for Web applications, asserting the user's identity to the backend application server in a format that can be consumed by the application server. For example, the DataPower WAF can authenticate the user with the credentials passed in the request via HTTP basic authentication and create an LTPA token that can propagate the identity to a backend WebSphere Application Server. This functionality can also be implemented in other service types; however, the WAF provides a wizard for creating the service that will guide you through this configuration as well as the additional features for proxying Web applications mentioned previously.

Although this service type may appear to be the best choice to proxy all Web applications, there may be cases where it is not. It is important to note that the tools available in the WebGUI for configuring the WAF are different than the tools used for configuring all other services. For example, it does not provide any drag-and-drop functionality, such as the policy editor, where the actions can be dragged on the policy line and configured. The terminology used for this service type is also different from other services. For example, a rule in other services is called a map in the WAF. This is discussed in more detail in Chapter 11, "Proxying Web Applications with DataPower."

XSL Accelerator

The XSL Accelerator validates and transforms incoming or outgoing XML documents. An XSL Accelerator service would proxy a backend service, applying all the necessary schema validation and transformations to the incoming document before the message reaches the backend service. Alternatively, it can provide content rendering of outbound messages from XML to other formats (XML, HTML, and WML). This functionality can also be provided by the XMLFW or MPGW. The primary use of this service type is on a DataPower XA35 appliance where other service types are not available.

XSL Coprocessor

Like the XML Accelerator service, the XSL Coprocessor (coproc) provides schema validation and transformations for a backend service. However, the XSL Coprocessor is a loopback service that can only be called by a Java application communicating with the service via the JAXP API. The calling Java application would pass the XSL Coprocessor service the XML document to be validated, parsed, and transformed. The service would then perform the required validation and transformation, returning the results back to the Java application. Although this is a supported service type on the appliance, it is not a recommended practice. The preferred method is to keep the DataPower service inline rather than as a coproc. This provides for much easier configuration of the service, as well as the backend application. This also allows the service to scan the incoming messages for threats before the message reaches the backend application. The XSL Coprocessor service type is utilized by the Eclipse/RAD coproc and the XML Spy plugins.

HTTP Service

An HTTP Service can be configured to serve documents that are stored on the local DataPower appliance to HTTP clients. A service of this type would allow access to certain files on the DataPower file system without requiring a log in to the DataPower appliance. This can be thought of as a mini HTTP/Web server. This functionality is generally superseded by a robust, enterprise-class Web server deployed in your IT architecture; however, it is an available service option. The use of this service type is not a recommended practice as it is not the intent of the appliance and can deplete available memory on the device when storing many or large files on the file system.

Summary

In this chapter, we explained what a DataPower service is, as well as the components and objects that make up a service. We discussed the different types of DataPower services, illustrating the value and key differentiators in each, as well as some general advice on choosing a service type. At this time you should have a good understanding about DataPower services so that you can move forward to subsequent chapters where the configuration of these services is described in depth.

Chapter 7

Introduction to Services Configuration

In the previous chapter, you were introduced to the concept of a *service* in DataPower. We also gave an overview of the types of services available on the appliance; for example, the XML Firewall, Multi-Protocol Gateway, and Web Service Proxy. You were introduced to the three primary phases that messages pass through when being processed by the appliance as the requests or responses. You were introduced to objects such as the Processing Policy, rules, actions, and protocol handlers that are at the heart of what DataPower does. In this chapter, we take you further into the details and inner workings of these concepts.

As you have learned, the services available on DataPower each have their own unique characteristics, such as the Web Service Proxy's capability to leverage the information in a WSDL file to create a proxy in just a few simple steps and the Multi-Protocol Gateway's capability to easily use multiple protocol handlers. Despite that, these services share many common objects and interfaces. So, before we start talking about the services individually, let's learn about these common features and how to use them. Our discussion focuses on the features available in the "big three" services, XML Firewall, Multi-Protocol Gateway, and Web Service Proxy, although much of what you see in this chapter is available on other services such as the XSL Accelerator and Web Application Firewall.

Backend Types

We begin our discussion on the three primary types of backend classifications. By *backend* we mean where the message goes after DataPower has processed it—is the destination known in advance or will it be determined dynamically at runtime? Or perhaps there is none—the appliance returns the response directly to the client. A service can use one of three types of backend destinations:

- **Static Backend**—Statically determined by the configuration of the service

- **Dynamic Backend**—Dynamically determined during runtime
- **Loopback**—None at all, in which case the device returns a response to the client without a backend destination

Every service requires that you specify the type of backend to use. In typical data center environments, these backend server hostnames, ports, URLs, and other attributes might be predefined, such as when DataPower is being set up to proxy applications on a single server. In other circumstances, you might need to make a runtime decision about what server to send the traffic to—perhaps due to current system load or some attribute carried by the messages themselves. Finally, there might be *no* backend server; in this case DataPower will do all processing on the message and send the response to the client.

Static Backends

As the name implies, Static Backends are those whose attributes are known in advance. At configuration time, when you are creating the service on the DataPower appliance, you can simply provide the hostname, port, or other information about the backend server required by your service.

Figure 7-1 shows a typical service configuration for a Static Backend.

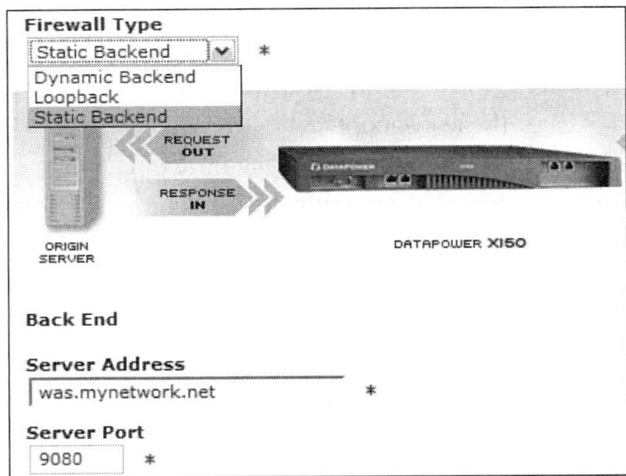

Figure 7-1 Service backend configuration.

In some cases, particularly for stateless operations such as Web services, you might want to send messages to a *group* of backend servers to distribute load and facilitate high availability. This is sometimes referred to as *spraying* or *load balancing* messages. DataPower has some capability to act as a load balancer. In this case, you provide the name of a load-balancer object configuration that you have created for the backend address, rather than a single hostname. We show specific load balancer configurations and discuss this in more detail later in this chapter.

Dynamic Backends

Unfortunately, life isn't always simple. Business always has and always will entail complex scenarios. Often, we come across scenarios where routing decisions must be made by factoring in runtime considerations. The classic example is that of taking the value of a transaction into account—for example, any incoming purchase order with a total value over one million dollars should be routed to a special destination for high-priority handling. Another might be the scenario shown in Figure 7-2. A worldwide bank customer service system routes intercepted messages to an agent with the appropriate linguistic skills to read the message in the language in which it was written. In fact, the dynamic routing and mediation of messages around an enterprise service bus is a principle that is at the core of SOA. Thus, dynamic routing becomes important.

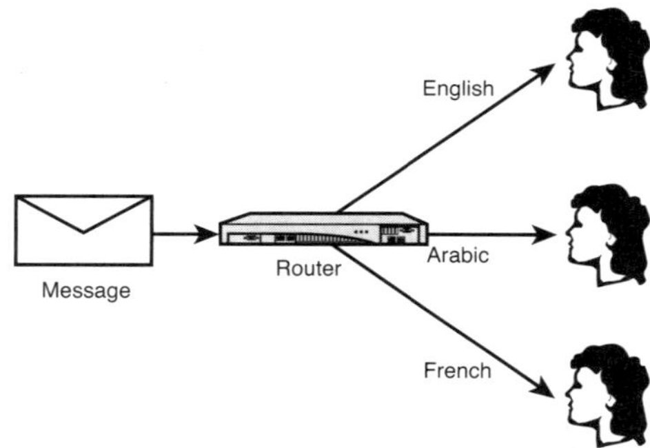

Figure 7-2 Dynamic routing of messages based on language.

Traditionally, dynamic routing has been achieved by placing information in the protocol header, such as a cookie in the HTTP header, or a URL attribute. This has been done because the infrastructure components that must make these content-based routing decisions can only understand data at that layer of the stack. They traditionally cannot look into application-layer data such as SOAP messages. Because of this, we not only must add additional logic to the applications that must be maintained, but we also potentially expose information to those who should not be able to see it. In the networking chapters, you saw how the Ethernet protocol works—message packets are sent to every node on the network, which means such messages can easily be intercepted and read by anyone on the network. This information would be outside the bounds of techniques such as using standards-based encryption for message privacy or digital signatures for message integrity, unless extra steps were taken to encrypt and sign them. In addition, the problem of bloated protocol headers occurs as more and more of this is done.

DataPower appliances can forego these hacks and make routing decisions based on the actual message content. Using XPath, any element or attribute in the XML message can be interrogated to make these decisions. If the routing decision is to be made based on some other data, DataPower has the capability to do so, based on any available information in the message, protocol, or other environmental factors, such as date/time, current backend response time metrics, and so on. In Chapter 8, "XML Firewall," and Chapter 24, "Real World Examples of XSLT Programming," you will see dynamic routing in action.

When choosing this configuration for your service, the entry fields for the backend server address and port are removed from the page because they are at that point unknown, as shown in

Figure 7-3. At some point in the Processing Policy, the routing information must be provided or the transaction will fail. We will show you how to do this as part of the graphical drag-and-drop service policy configuration in Chapter 8, and also how to do it programmatically in Part VI, "DataPower Development."

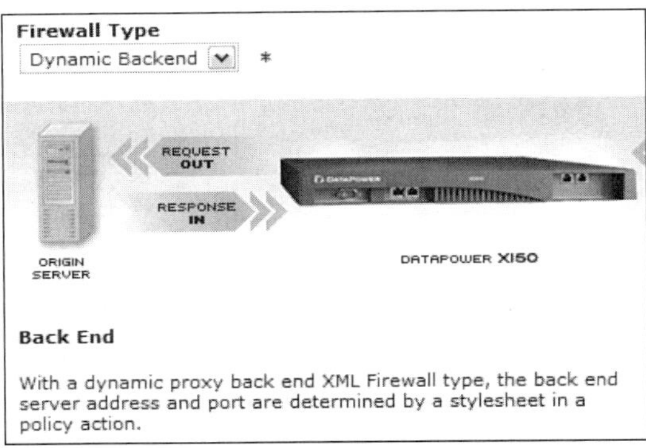

Figure 7-3 XML firewall Dynamic Backend.

Loopback

In some cases, there might not be a backend, particularly given the broad spectrum of use cases for message processing that can be accomplished using the DataPower appliances directly. We discuss the many available processing actions that can be applied to request and response rules later in this chapter, and you can see many of them in use throughout the book.

Another typical use for the loopback configuration is simple testing or development when the backends are not available and when creating utility services on the appliance that are meant solely to provide some capability to other services on a localhost interface.

Of course, when choosing the loopback backend configuration, the server address and port fields will also not appear on the service configuration page.

Supporting Objects

In the Chapter 6, "Introduction to DataPower Services," you were introduced to the three major processing phases that occur as messages move through the device as requests and responses. These were the client/front-side area, Processing Policy (sometimes referred to as multistep), and server/back-side area. The most prominent of these is the Processing Policy, which we discuss in detail later in this chapter. Before we do so, let's look at some of the supporting cast—three objects that can be part of the Processing Policy but also affect what happens in the client or server-side areas.

URL Rewrite Policy

One highly touted feature of DataPower is the capability to virtualize or hide backend implementation details. The URL Rewrite capability provides one more way to do that. There are other uses for this feature, such as to isolate the client from changes in the proxied backend applications, perhaps to preserve their bookmarks. We can also use this capability to provide a more user-friendly URI than what might exist on our backend applications, for example to expose a friendlier URI such as /MyCheckingAccount, to replace a mundane one such as /bankservices/checking. Let's develop that example.

The capability to rewrite URLs shows up in several places throughout the service configuration pages. Figure 7-4 shows where it appears on the XML Firewall main configuration page.

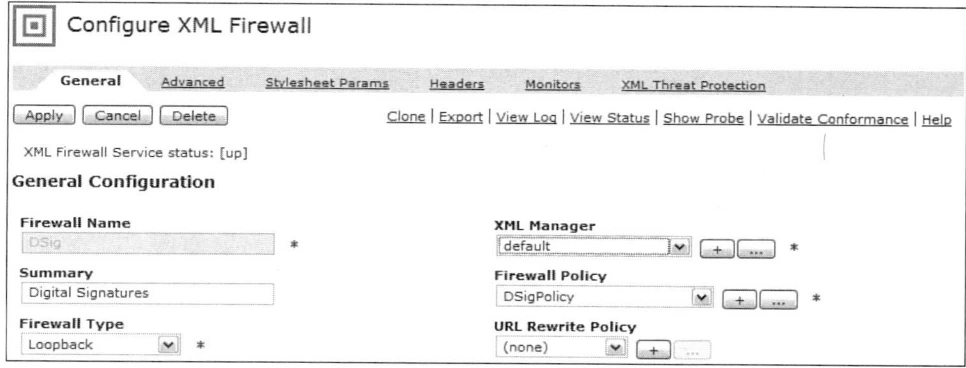

Figure 7-4 URL rewrite policy on the XML Firewall main page.

The URL Rewrite policy has the capability to rewrite all or part of a URL, replace a header value, or even rewrite the HTTP POST body in a message. To demonstrate this feature, we create a new URL Rewrite Policy to modify the incoming request URL. Figure 7-5 shows the base configuration page for the new object (which can be reached by clicking the "Create a new" or "+" button shown in Figure 7-4). Notice that the rewrite policy can be applied to requests, responses, or for both directions.

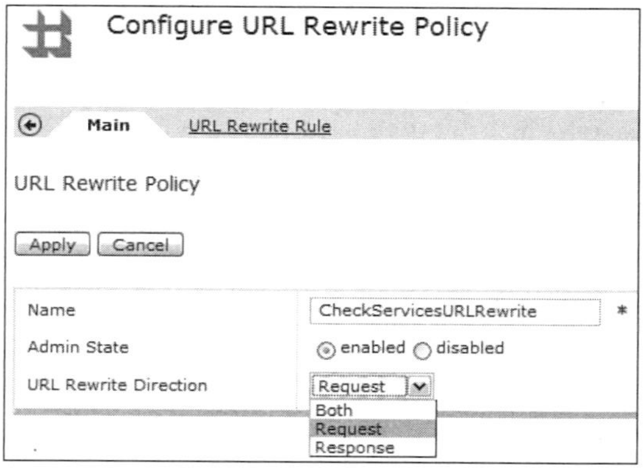

Configure URL Rewrite Policy

Main | URL Rewrite Rule

URL Rewrite Policy

Apply | Cancel

Name: CheckServicesURLRewrite *

Admin State: enabled / disabled

URL Rewrite Direction: Request (Both / Request / Response)

Figure 7-5 Creating a new URL Rewrite Policy.

For requests, these rewrites are applied in the frontside of the processing phases described in Chapter 6, and we describe how that is important when we get to the section on the Processing Policy later in this chapter. This pane simply asks for a name for this new policy, and which direction it should be applied to.

The logic of the policy is on the tab shown next to Main, which is URL Rewrite Rule. Moving there, a list of rules can be configured. Figure 7-6 shows a rule that has been configured using Perl-compatible regular expressions (PCRE) to look for any URL (absolute-rewrite) that contains the string MyCheckingAccount and convert that piece of the URL to /bankservices/checking. We are looking for the user-friendly URI from the client and replacing it with what the backend application expects as part of the request path.

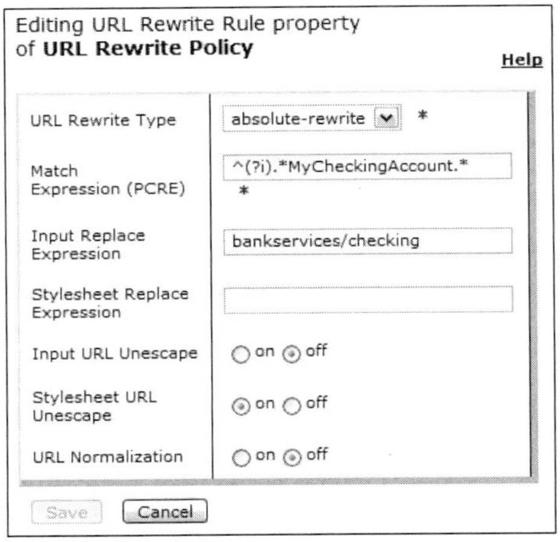

Editing URL Rewrite Rule property
of **URL Rewrite Policy** Help

URL Rewrite Type	absolute-rewrite *
Match Expression (PCRE)	^(?i).*MyCheckingAccount.* *
Input Replace Expression	bankservices/checking
Stylesheet Replace Expression	
Input URL Unescape	on ◉ off
Stylesheet URL Unescape	◉ on off
URL Normalization	on ◉ off

Save Cancel

Figure 7-6 URL rewrite rule.

When a transaction is sent to the device, this policy is enforced whenever the match expression is met. For example, Figure 7-7 shows the log entry for an XML Firewall service that implements our example. Reading the log from the bottom to the top, you can see the incoming transaction has a URI of /MyCheckingAccount and that our URL Rewrite Policy has changed the URI to /bankservices/checking, leaving the rest of the URL intact.

```
xmlfirewall (matchRuleExamples): Latency: 0 0 0 0 27 15 5 27 0 0 0 27 0 0 0 0 [http://ClientInterface:2111/bankservices/checking]
xmlfirewall (matchRuleExamples): rule (matchRuleExamples_Regex): #1 fetch: 'from local:///matchedRegex.xml stored in OUTPUT'
completed ok.
xmlfirewall (matchRuleExamples): Finished parsing local:///matchedRegex.xml
xmlfirewall (matchRuleExamples): Parsing document 'local:///matchedRegex.xml'
xmlfirewall (matchRuleExamples): Finished parsing http://ClientInterface:2111/bankservices/checking
xmlfirewall (matchRuleExamples): Parsing document 'http://ClientInterface:2111/bankservices/checking'
xmlfirewall (matchRuleExamples): Multistep Probe enabled
xmlfirewall (matchRuleExamples): rule (matchRuleExamples_Regex): selected via match 'bankingservices' from processing policy
'matchRuleExamples'
xmlfirewall (matchRuleExamples): New transaction(conn use=1): POST http://192.168.1.108:2111/MyCheckingAccount from 192.168.1.102
```

Figure 7-7 PCRE URL rewrite test.

Another common use of the URL Rewrite Policy is to change the HTTP Content-Type header on-the-fly. Consider a scenario where you receive an XML response from a backend application and transform this into HTML so that it can be rendered in a client's browser. Along with the transform, our policy must also change the Content-Type header or the browser will be confused. Figure 7-8 shows an example URL Rewrite Policy to do that.

Later in this chapter, we show a more granular approach to rewriting URLs.

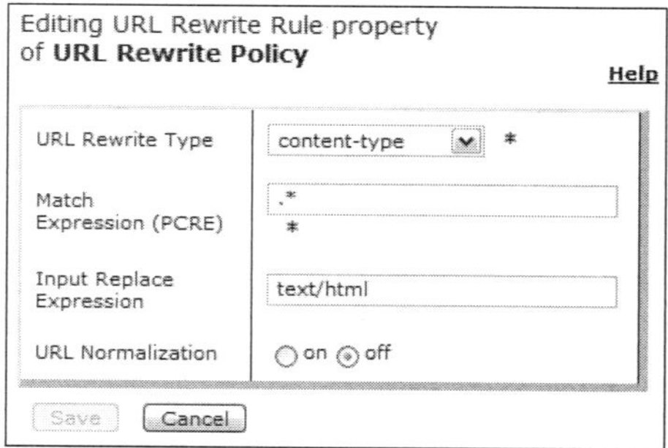

Figure 7-8 Changing the Content-Type header.

XML Manager

Chapter 6 briefly mentioned the capabilities of the XML Manager object. Let's look at the more important features in detail. This object is displayed prominently on the services' configuration pages. In most cases, the default XML Manager is already assigned, but you might want to create derivatives to do things such as cache more aggressively, load balance, or fire scheduled rules. Figure 7-9 shows the main configuration tab of the XML Manager and some of the associated tabs horizontally across the top.

> **TIP—DON'T MODIFY THE DEFAULT XML MANAGER**
>
> It might be tempting to make changes to the default XML Manager, which is normally selected. This object is likely to be shared by other services in the domain, and changing it could unexpectedly modify their behavior as well. Even if there are no other services, some might be added later for which the default behavior is appropriate. Always create a new XML Manager, even if it will be shared across all services in the domain, and give it an appropriate name for the modifications being made (such as AggressiveCacheXMLManager, WASClusterLoadBalanceCacheManager).

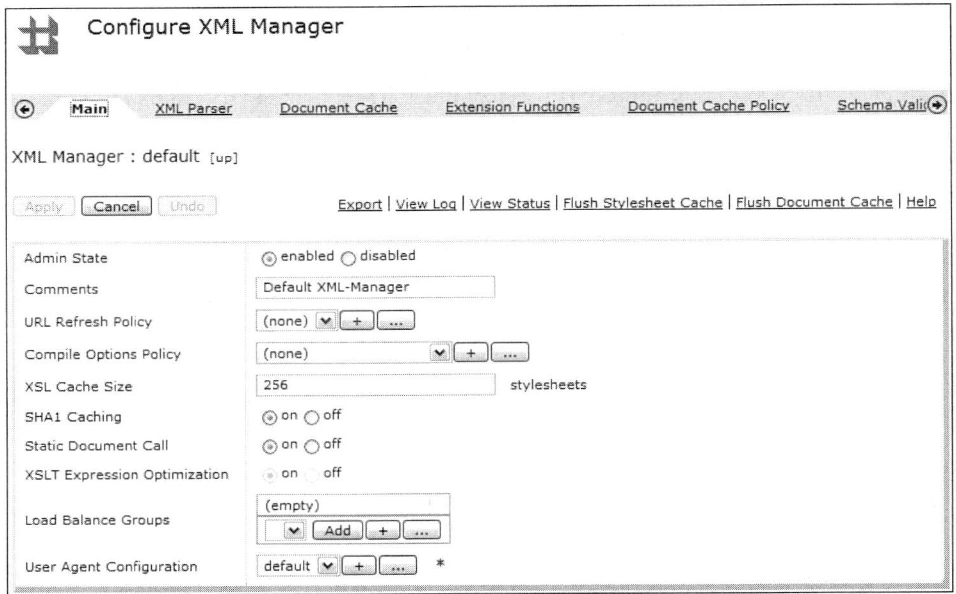

Figure 7-9 The Configure XML Manager page.

Caching Stylesheets

By default, DataPower caches the XSLT stylesheets used by services (and the device itself) whether they exist locally or are pulled in from remote servers. Figure 7-9 shows a field on the main XML Manager page to configure the size of the cache. Take note that this cache is sized in number of stylesheets so that it could become quite large if the stylesheets being cached are large. The cache size should be monitored and sized appropriately as part of the performance and load testing process. The other option is to use SHA1 Caching, also shown in Figure 7-9. Normally stylesheets are cached by their URL, but if the same stylesheet can be pulled in from different URLs, setting this feature to use a SHA1-computed message digest can improve performance in looking up cache entries.

When stylesheets are put into the cache, they remain there until they are pushed out by the policies previously discussed, explicitly flushed (you can see the link to do this in Figure 7-9, or it can be done programmatically), or until the domain or appliance restart. However, what if you would like them to be refreshed on some periodic basis? What if you would like to specify stylesheets that should never be cached or never flushed from the cache? For any of those reasons, you would configure a URL Refresh Policy on the main XML Manager tab. In this area, simple policies can be set up to accomplish those goals based on PCRE expressions and time-based intervals expressed in number of seconds. (Where appropriate, for options like no-cache, you would not supply any time interval.)

Caching XML Documents

The appliance can also cache XML responses to enhance application performance. This feature is application-specific and, therefore, is not active until configured for specific application URLs. Let's take a look at the capabilities for this feature.

The XML Manager Document Cache tab contains fields to tune the cache size—a field for the cache by number of documents and one to set the cache size in bytes. In this case, the byte size takes precedence; so if the cache reaches this configured size, you might not fit the maximum number of documents specified in the other field. Of course, this is related to the Document Cache Policy tab on the XML Manager. Figure 7-10 shows an example policy for caching documents that would be responses from a sporting goods catalog browsing URI. A PCRE expression is used to designate the URLs to be subject to the cache. The Policy Type drop-down designates perhaps that these URLs should have no caching done at all, or perhaps the cache size should be Fixed (in which case you must configure the Time To Live field for the number of seconds each cache entry should stay in the cache), or Protocol-Based.

In this last case, caching is controlled by virtue of several HTTP 1.0 or 1.1 headers such as Last-Modified, Vary, Cache-Control, and Expires. The WebGUI Guide has details for these settings. Finally, the Priority field allows some entries to have a longer life than others should either the maximum number of documents or cache size in bytes be reached. The priority from 1 to 255 may be entered, with lower numbers getting priority to remain. Ties are broken by a First-In First-Out (FIFO) selection. As with the stylesheet cache, this cache can be flushed by the links that appear on any tab in the XML Manager, or programmatically.

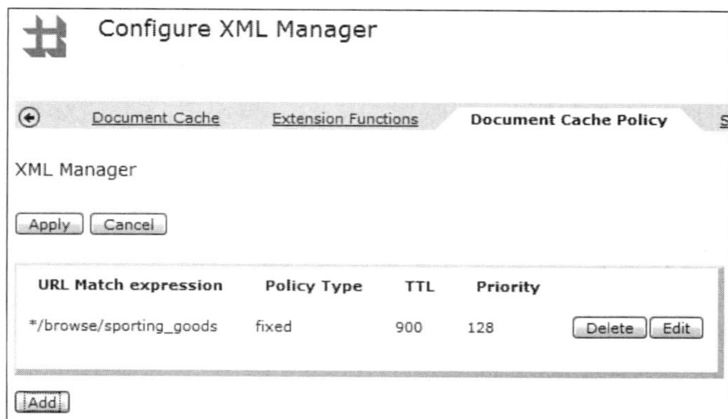

Figure 7-10 XML Manager Document Cache Policy tab.

Load Balancer Groups

In our previous section on backend types, we stated that a Load Balancer Group name could be substituted for a hostname or IP address in a backend configuration or URL. This is normally done in high-availability scenarios to distribute stateless requests over some group of peer servers, or to send requests to standby or secondary servers should the primary server be inactive for some reason. Let's see what's involved with creating a Load Balancer Group.

Our example simulates a cluster of Web service providers. Figure 7-11 shows that we have selected the Least Connections algorithm for our Load Balancer Group. This algorithm forwards the next connection to the server in the group that has the least number of current connections, based on tables held within the appliance's memory. The Round Robin algorithm evenly distributes messages to all members, and the Weighted variant allows you to assign weights to each member, perhaps in accordance with their processing power. The First Alive algorithm is used to primarily send traffic to a main server; it sends traffic to the secondary servers further on down the list only if the primary server(s) above are designated as down.

The Hash algorithm is used to apply stickiness to client messages by keeping a table of hashed IP addresses and which server they have been using. This is typically done when the server has some saved state information for clients, such as in-memory Java EE sessions. Note that this is not a foolproof way of establishing long-term session stickiness because IP addresses can change, and when certain events occur, such as the backend being down, the entire table will be recalculated. DataPower's load balancing capabilities are best used for stateless operations in keeping with the theme of the appliance's design.

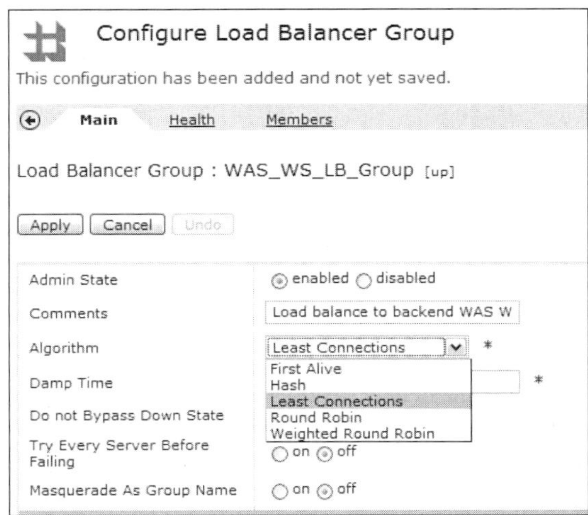

Figure 7-11 Load Balancer Group configuration.

The Masquerade As Group Name setting simply determines whether the Load Balancer Group name will be placed in the message header, or the IP address or hostname of the physical server chosen to receive this message from the Load Balancer Group.

The other settings on this figure relate to the health checking of the members. You may set up a health check policy where each server in the group is occasionally polled to determine whether it is up or down. This is optional, but it would be advisable in order to know that members of the group are inactive before actually sending messages there, if possible.

Figure 7-12 shows the Health tab of the Load Balancer Group. It is off by default. The Standard type of health check shown as selected here is typically used for Web services or Web applications. This sends an HTTP GET (or SOAP message via POST if the Send SOAP Request is turned on) to the remote port and URI defined here. The health checks will be done on the frequency requested, and if a response is not received, the member will be flagged as down.

If you set the Send SOAP Request flag to off, a simple HTTP GET is done, and an HTTP response code of 200 will designate that the server is up. If the Send SOAP Request flag is set to On, a POST will be made using the XML file identified in the SOAP Request Document field. This should be a valid SOAP message. The stylesheet identified in the XSL Health Check Filter is used to check the response using the XPath Expression identified in the corresponding field. The defaults are shown in Figure 7-12—these files already exist on the file system, and you can see that the type of checking done is quite simple—the XPath expression simply looks for a root node in the response. You are free to customize this; in fact, this could be used to do deep health checks, where not only the immediate servers behind DataPower are checked but also layers beyond them. For example, you could do a simple SQL call to see whether a database is up.

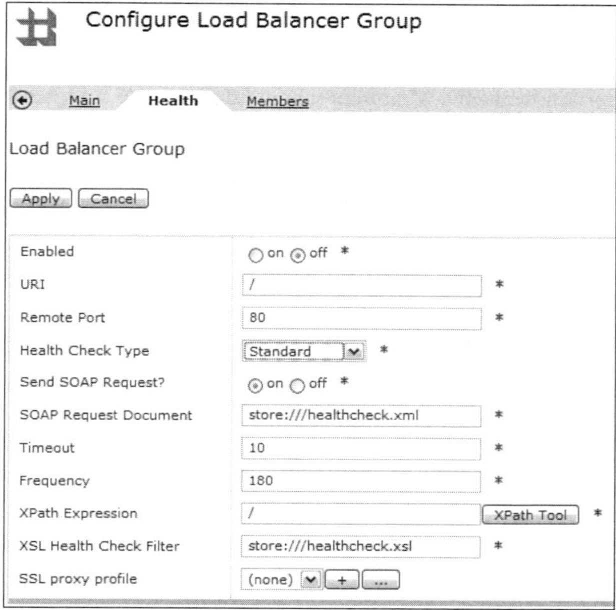

Figure 7-12 Load Balancer Health Check configuration.

The alternatives to the Standard health check type are IMS Connect (anonymous bind to IMS servers) and LDAP (anonymous bind to LDAP servers from the AAA configuration, as we will discuss in Chapter 16, "AAA," rather than from inside the XML Manager).

So what exactly happens when things go wrong? To understand this better, let's first make sure we understand the three possible states of any Load Balancer Group member:

- **Healthy (up)**—The member is considered to be eligible for messages.
- **Convalescent (down)**—If a health check fails, a member is placed in this state. The member is removed from the group and does not receive messages. After the Frequency interval elapses and the health check is done again, if the server is deemed to be back, it will be placed into the up state.
- **Quarantined (softdown)**—A member is placed into this state when a regular transaction/message (as opposed to a health check) fails. When this occurs, the member is quarantined and will not receive any messages until the Damp Time period has elapsed. At this time, the member will be placed back into service (without any checks as to its health), and messages will attempt to be sent to it. It will also be excluded from health checks during this time, so it is truly quarantined!

A few last words on health checks: They can be done over SSL (as indicated by the SSL Proxy Profile setting on Figure 7-12), and the health of any individual member can be set directly using the var://service/lbhealth variable. We will discuss just such a scenario in Chapter 24.

Finally, you might want to know how we add members to a Load Balancer Group. As Figure 7-13 shows, simply move to the Members tab and define each member by clicking the Add button. You can see that in this figure we have added four members, and that each one has the ability to set the weight (if a weighted algorithm was chosen), set a specific port for the transaction to be sent to, and set a specific port for the health check on each member.

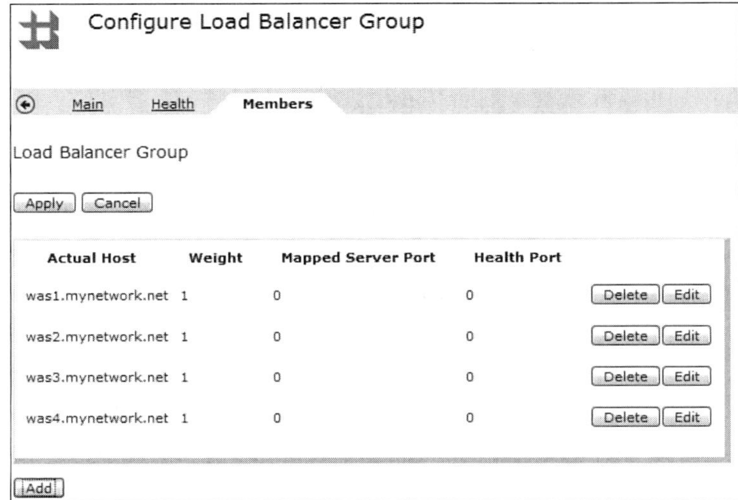

Figure 7-13 Load Balancer Group members.

Scheduled Processing Policy Rules

The Scheduled Processing Policy tab provides a simple-to-configure but powerful capability. Essentially, you can configure any Processing Policy rule (we talk more about this later in the chapter) to be executed on a scheduled interval. These configured rules can provide any processing capability across the entire breadth and depth of the DataPower feature set, making it quite extensible. This means interacting with external resources or triggering some scheduled execution on the appliance itself. Figure 7-14 shows an example of a rule used to execute every 86,400 seconds (or every 24 hours) to fetch a new copy of an onboard properties file, perhaps from an external file system. This might be used at the same time to set the values from that file into global system variables (although these must be carefully used to limit the impact on memory consumption).

> **TIP—EXECUTING RULES ONLY ON STARTUP**
>
> For rules that should execute only on appliance or domain startup, we could set the interval to zero. This would be useful in the previous example if the properties file was static.

Figure 7-14 XML Manager Scheduled Processing Policy rule.

XML Parser Limits

The XML Parser Limits tab of the XML Manager allows for profiling of message characteristics. This is important to protect against XML threats (see Chapter 20, "XML Threats") and just run-away data. Often, despite the absence of bad guys, messages sent by our partners or even our own applications can be well-formed XML or valid SOAP but due to bugs or bad transformations have a negative impact on backend system performance. It is a common usage of the DataPower appliances to catch and filter out such messages before they have a destructive effect. Utilizing the raw horsepower of the appliance for these checks, along with stringent schema validation on request *and* response messages (as well as the result of any transformations done on the device) can prevent these types of problems.

As seen in Figure 7-15, the XML Manager can profile messages by bytes scanned, which includes the parsed message tree and Data Type Definitions (DTDs), maximum nesting depth, size of any nodeset inside a message, and number of attributes. Note that these can be overridden by service-specific settings on the XML Threats Protection tab. We also have the ability on this pane to disable the referencing of external entities such as DTDs and XML Schema Definitions (XSD). Schema-substitution attacks can be thwarted in this manner—the device will look for the files onboard rather than trying to resolve the external reference.

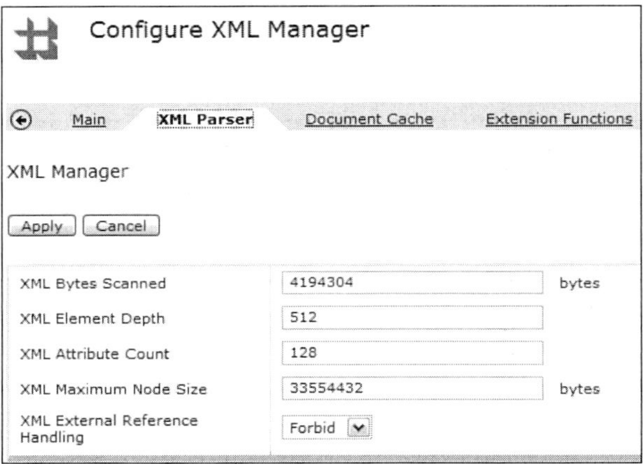

Figure 7-15 XML Manager Parser Limits tab.

Compile Options Policy

The Compile Options Policy object (shown on Figure 7-9) has some powerful capabilities. We can do several things with this object:

- Controlling the compilation of stylesheets by specifying the use of XSLT 1.0, 2.0[1] or having the stylesheet determine the version. (This will be covered in more detail in Part VI, "DataPower Development.") Policies can also be specified here to check the WSDL against conformance with profiles such as WS-I Basic Profile and to skip or use lax or strict validation of SOAP envelopes and faults or SOAP message bodies and headers.
- Measuring the processing times for selected stylesheets and reporting on them (intended only for debugging purposes and the appropriate environments—not for high-traffic production sites).
- Enabling streaming mode processing, which enhances the ability to handle large documents.

[1] XSLT 2.0 and XPath 2.0 support in DataPower is limited to the decimal type. See the WebGUI guide for details.

Refer to Appendix D, "Compile Options Policy Configuration," in the CLI Reference Guide document (not the first place you would guess to look for this type of information) to help with questions.

User Agent

You might have noticed in Figure 7-9 that the User Agent is contained on the XML Manager main configuration page. However, because it is also used in many other scenarios independent of that, and because it is a big and multifaceted object, we cover it in this separate section.

The User Agent can be thought of as a utility object to be used by other higher-level DataPower objects. As you will see, it primarily handles the details for network-related outbound calls from the device. Figure 7-16 shows the main configuration tab—only a few fields exist here, but you can witness the large number of other tabs to perform these operations. The fields on the main page are used to send an HTTP request-header with information about the sending User Agent, to specify the maximum number of redirects to attempt before failing the transaction and to choose an idle timeout value to use before closing the connection. (This is unrelated to connection timeouts related to failed transactions.)

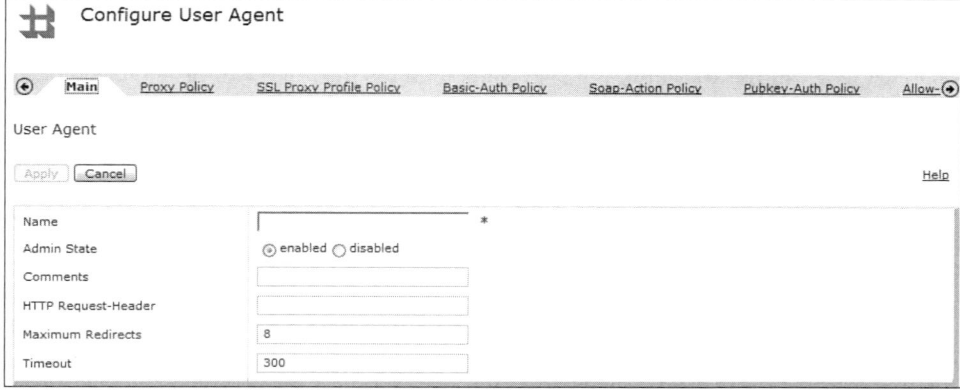

Figure 7-16 User Agent Main Configuration page.

In the following list, we give a brief overview of each tab on the User Agent and its purpose.

- **Proxy Policy**—This tab can be used to have requests forwarded to a HTTP proxy server rather than the host they would otherwise be sent to by the normal service configuration. It is configured by providing a URL match and a hostname and port for the proxy server to receive the requests.

- **SSL Proxy Profile Policy**—This tab is used to automatically initiate SSL client connections from the device for supported protocols. It is configured by providing a URL matching regular expression and a SSL Proxy Profile object (which must set up as either a client or two-way SSL). An example usage here would be to look for URIs that indicate sensitive information might be sent (such as */checkout) and trigger SSL for a secure (encrypted) transport.
- **Basic-Auth Policy**—This tab is used to inject basic authentication (userid and password) into requests. It is configured by providing a URL matching regular expression and a userid and password. Chapter 9, "Multi-Protocol Gateway," shows an example of using this to avoid putting the userid and password on an FTP URL.
- **Soap-Action Policy**—This tab can be used to inject SOAPAction headers into Web service requests. It is configured by providing a URL matching regular expression and a value for the SOAPAction header. (For example, in some cases this must match the Web services operation name for Web services providers that require it, such as those written for .NET.)
- **Pubkey-Auth Policy**—This tab is used to provide a private key that should be used to validate a certificate being presented in a request for authentication. This occurs with certain protocols such as SCP.
- **Allow-Compression Policy**—This tab is used to either allow or disallow compression for certain connections. It is configured by providing a URL matching regular expression and selecting the On or Off radio button for allowing compression. The setting is valid only for protocols that use compression, such as HTTP 1.1.
- **Restrict to HTTP 1.0 Policy**—As its name implies, this tab is used to restrict certain connections to HTTP 1.0, based on the URL. It has a URL matching field and On/Off radio button to restrict or not restrict.
- **Inject Header Policy**—This tab is used to inject or override HTTP headers based on URL matching. In addition to the URL matching field, it has fields for the header name and value.
- **Chunked Uploads Policy**—This tab is similar to the Allow-Compression Policy but is used for HTTP 1.1 chunked uploading.
- **FTP Client Policies**—This tab is used to match FTP URLs with client policies to control options for the outgoing FTP connections. The configurable options and their defaults are shown in Figure 7-17. It is important to note that these can be overridden by URL query parameters, if they are present.

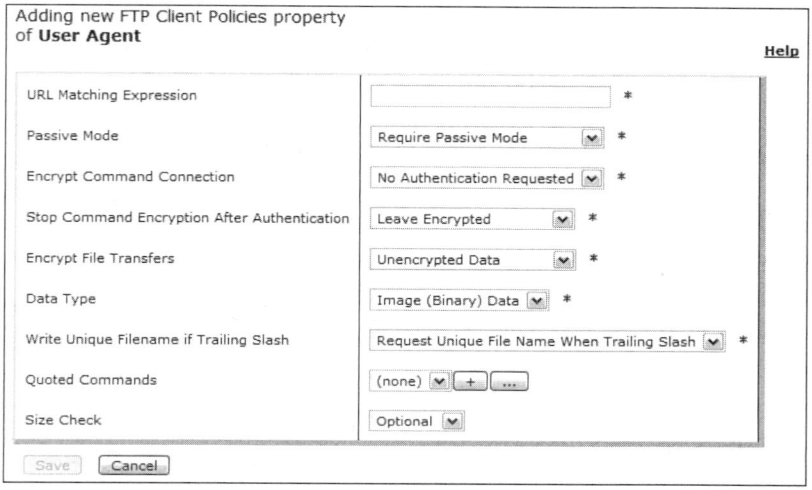

Adding new FTP Client Policies property of **User Agent**

Help

URL Matching Expression	*
Passive Mode	Require Passive Mode *
Encrypt Command Connection	No Authentication Requested *
Stop Command Encryption After Authentication	Leave Encrypted *
Encrypt File Transfers	Unencrypted Data *
Data Type	Image (Binary) Data *
Write Unique Filename if Trailing Slash	Request Unique File Name When Trailing Slash *
Quoted Commands	(none) + ...
Size Check	Optional

Save Cancel

Figure 7-17 User Agent FTP Client Policy configuration.

Protocol Handlers

As you have seen, the User Agent plays a big part in the DataPower appliance's communication with the outside world. However, this part is not as big as the group of objects we discuss in this section. For the services that use them, the protocol handlers are the conduit from the outside world to an appliance. DataPower's mediation capabilities in many areas have been mentioned thus far, and this great array of different protocol handlers will truly bring out the protocol mediation features.

Some services make more extensive use of multiple protocols than others. For example, in Chapter 6 we introduced you to the XML Firewall service, which can have only one front-side protocol and one back side protocol, the choice of which is limited to HTTP or HTTPS for either. Other more complex services such as the Multi-Protocol Gateway and Web Service Proxy allow for multiple protocol handlers. Figure 7-18 shows the default frontend and backend configuration for an XML firewall with a Static Backend, and you can see there is little choice available here—it is either HTTP or HTTPS (by virtue of specifying an SSL Profile).

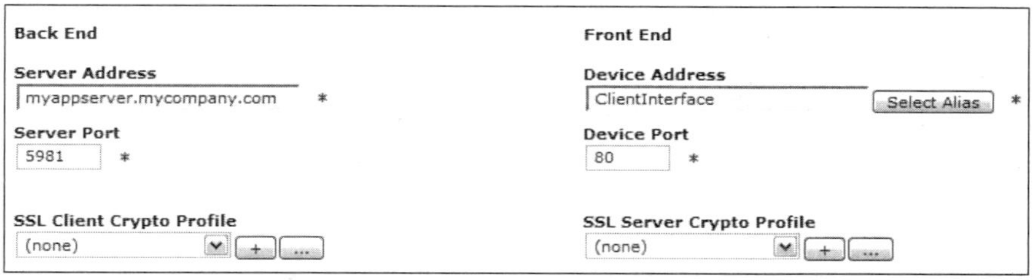

Back End	Front End
Server Address myappserver.mycompany.com *	**Device Address** ClientInterface Select Alias *
Server Port 5981 *	**Device Port** 80 *
SSL Client Crypto Profile (none) + ...	**SSL Server Crypto Profile** (none) + ...

Figure 7-18 XML firewall frontend and backend protocol specification.

In comparison, Figure 7-19 shows the front and back protocol configuration for a Multi-Protocol Gateway—a huge difference in terms of the options available and the ability to add multiple protocol listeners on different ports for a single service instance.

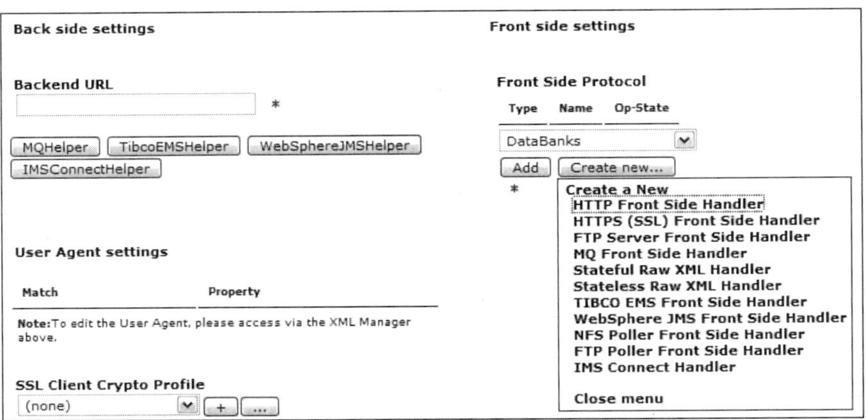

Figure 7-19 Multi-Protocol Gateway frontend and backend protocol specification.

Let's briefly examine the list of available protocols and their typical usages:

- **HTTP**—This one is ubiquitous and by far the most commonly used protocol for application traffic to flow over.
- **HTTPS**—Same as the previous but uses SSL for an encrypted transport to prevent the interception or viewing of message traffic by network listeners.
- **FTP**—The appliances use FTP in several different modes; it can act as an FTP client to poll FTP servers; it can act as an FTP server itself; or it can act as a secure proxy to a true virtualized backend FTP server. However, this feature is not intended to use the appliance as a true FTP server for large files or heavy traffic. It has been implemented as simply another method in which to retrieve messages, perhaps in a scenario where a batch system places them on an FTP server to be consumed by a service running on an appliance. Several FTP scenarios are covered in Chapter 9.
- **MQ (IBM WebSphere MQ)**—The XI50 appliance provides for tight integration for the exchange of messages with MQ Queue Managers using the MQ protocol. This is covered in Chapter 9.
- **Stateful/Stateless RAW XML**—This is a TCP socket level handler used to exchange XML documents. (The only way to know a message has been "sent" is by the closing element for the root of the XML document.)
- **TIBCO EMS**—The XI50 has the capability to exchange messages with TIBCO EMS, if that option is purchased with the device.
- **WebSphere JMS**—The XI50 has the capability to exchange messages with the IBM WebSphere Application Server default messaging provider (Service Integration Bus) over the JMS JFAP protocol. This is covered in Chapter 9.

- **NFS**—The appliances can poll NFS static or dynamic mounts for messages and consume them. This is covered in Chapter 9.
- **IMS Connect**—The XI50 can directly connect to backend IMS instances, avoiding the need for MQ as an intermediary in some enterprise environments.

The DataPower Processing Policy

In Chapter 6, we gave a brief introduction to the Processing Policy Editor, or "multistep," which contains rules for requests, responses, errors, and actions to carry out specific tasks such as encrypting message data. We have stressed several times that this area is truly the heart or control center of what the appliances are all about, so let's take a closer look.

Policy Editor

The Processing Policy is analogous to what might be called a work flow editor or process flow in other products. Figure 7-20 shows an entire Processing Policy that has already been configured to process messages. We'll break down this figure into pieces to describe the various moving parts. However, first let's discuss the major sections (Policy, Rule, and Configured Rules) at a high level, starting at the top.

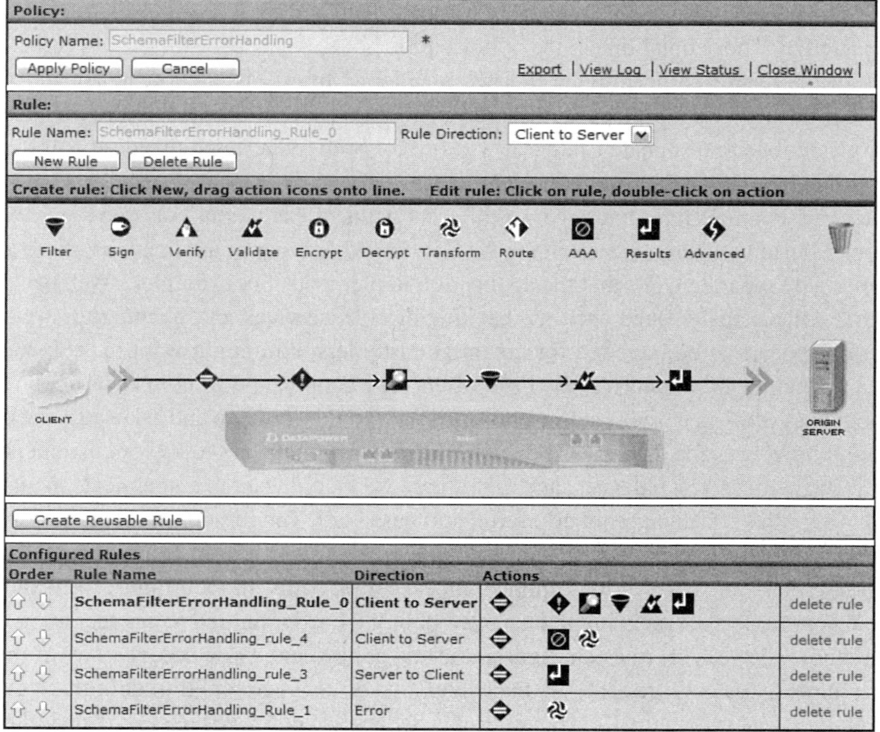

Figure 7-20 Processing Policy editor.

The WebGUI wizards will create a default policy for you. When you are creating a new policy, the Policy Name field at the top will be blank. Think carefully about the name you provide here, because after you enter a value and move the focus away from the field, you can't change it! The Apply Policy button is used like any other Apply button in the DataPower WebGUI, in that it commits changes to the runtime configuration and activates them. However, clicking the Apply button does not close the window here, as it does in many other places. You have to click the Close Window hyperlink in the upper-right corner for that. The other handy links at the top allow you to export the policy, view log messages for this policy, and view the status of the policy and its dependent objects.

Processing Policy Rules

The Rule section (shown in Figure 7-20) shows buttons to create and delete a Rule and designate its direction. So what's a rule? You might think of a rule as a single execution path through the device. This might be a single request message coming through the appliance from a client and on its way to some backend server, or that server's response message flowing through the appliance on its way back to the client. We might want to perform certain actions on these request and response messages; for example, we might decrypt an encrypted request message to save the backend from that heavy lifting and then encrypt it again before it goes back to the client as a response. So a rule represents that request or response path and what *happens* along that path and is represented by a horizontal line in the policy editor.

The Rule Direction drop-down that we mentioned briefly is what designates a rule as a request (Client to Server) or response (Server to Client). There is also a value in the drop-down for Both Directions to designate rules that will fire for both request and response paths, and one with the value Error to create error handling rules, which we will discuss later.

Most applications have a number of different paths of execution. For Web services, this is inherently defined by the operations in the WSDL. For other types of applications, these are typically defined by separate URIs that the application implements. For example, a Web banking site might have URI paths defined such as /banking/browse_services and banking/view_accounts. The former appears to be intended for potential customers who might want to look at rates of return on financial instruments that the bank offers. The bank would want to be as unobtrusive as possible in this case—in a brick-and-mortar store you wouldn't run up and ask a customer browsing through brochures for their ID! The latter URI however, appears to be for customers of that bank to view their account balances, and in this case we would want to authenticate the user, perhaps asking for their account number, userid, and password. The important thing for our discussion is the fact that we often need to have multiple request (two for our example just discussed) and response rules for these various application execution paths. In fact, Figure 7-20 shows two request (Client to Server) rules in the displayed policy. The Configured Rules section at the bottom of Figure 7-20 lists all rules configured for this policy, and by clicking on any of them, the rule with the new focus is brought into the center area of the page for editing. In this figure, you can see that the first rule in the Configured Rules list is selected by virtue of it being bold, so this is also the rule that is displayed in the center editing area.

So, if we have more than one request rule; for example, how do we tell the Processing Policy which to pick for a particular incoming message at runtime? We already know what the determining criterion is for the previous example—it would be the URI. The mechanism by which we match up request and response rules with messages is called the Match Rule and will be discussed shortly.

Processing Actions

The remaining mystery from Figure 7-20 is the icons along the top of the rule editing area. These are referred to as processing actions (or actions as a shortened form). They are dragged down from this horizontal palette and placed within rules to perform certain tasks. For example, in our figure you can see that the last three actions to be performed by this request rule are Filter, Schema Validate, and Send Results. Of course, it's not just drag and drop; you must also configure these actions to do the tasks for which they are intended. For example, if you drag an Encrypt action onto the rule to encrypt messages, you would have to finish the configuration by telling the Encrypt action what certificate to use for the encryption. Shortly, we will show some of these actions and the process of configuring them well, "in action."

Following is a quick list of the available actions and their general purpose:

- **Filter**—This is used to filter messages based on some criteria. There are on-board filters, for example, that look for certain types of threat signatures, such as SQL injection, and reject messages that appear to contain them. You could also create a custom filter by providing your own XSLT stylesheet. This allows you to set your own filter criteria, such as to check for required fields on certain elements in the incoming XML message.
- **Sign**—This action is used to insert digital signatures for entire messages or at the field level to facilitate message integrity and nonrepudiation.
- **Verify**—This action is used to verify digital signatures that might already be in the incoming message.
- **Validate**—This action is used to validate XML message structure against a schema document (XSD).
- **Encrypt**—This action is used to encrypt message data at the message or field level.
- **Decrypt**—This action is used to decrypt messages that have been previously encrypted.
- **Transform**—This is probably the most commonly used action, and it is used to transform message formats using XSLT. Sometimes this action is used to execute XSLT stylesheets that do not do transformation but accomplish some utility-type tasks. It is often used as a container to execute stylesheets written as DataPower custom development, which we will discuss later in the book.
- **Route**—This action is used to set the backend destination for dynamic routing scenarios.
- **AAA**—This action is used to accomplish authentication, authorization, and auditing for security purposes.

- **Results**—This action sends messages to a given destination and either waits for a result or continues without waiting. As discussed, the destination can be the backend server(s) or client, depending on the rule type, or might be a third entity, or auxiliary process.
- **Advanced**—This action is really an abstraction containing a group of advanced actions. When you drag this to the processing rule and double-click to configure it, you are presented with a list of radio buttons for each action within, and must choose one. The choices within the Advanced action follow.
- **Anti-virus**—This action is used to send attachments to a virus scanning server via the ICAP protocol.
- **Call Processing Rule**—This action can call and execute another configured rule in the Processing Policy. This allows you to create an intermediary rule containing more than one action that many other rules in the policy can call, thus eliminating the need to re-create these actions over and over again.
- **Conditional**—This action employs if/then/else processing to select an action, which might be a Call Processing action, to fire within a single action, which makes it quite powerful. The Conditional action allows you to design branching logic in your policy.
- **Convert Query Params to XML**—This action is quite useful in processing HTTP form POSTS and GET query parameters as it will take the HTTP input and convert it to an XML nodeset, which makes the request much easier to process in DataPower!
- **Crypto Binary** —This action is used for crypto operations on non-XML data. For example non-XML data can be encrypted, decrypted, signed, or signature-validated using Public Key Cryptography Standard (PKCS) #7.
- **Event-sink**—This action causes the system to wait for all listed asynchronous actions to complete before proceeding to the next action in the Processing Policy. This is useful to pull together the results of one or more actions that have been processing asynchronously.
- **Extract Using XPath**—This action uses an XPath expression to pull data out of another context (contexts are described later in this chapter) and store it either in another context or a variable.
- **Fetch**—This action can retrieve documents from either the DataPower file system or remote resources, for example a properties file.
- **For-each**—This powerful action executes a looping construct, as named, using counters or expressions.
- **Header Rewrite**—This action has the capability to do rewriting similar to that available on the service configuration page, only at a more granular level—from inside a policy rule.
- **Log**—This action is used to send message content to a remote logging facility. Care should be taken to not expose private information in the message. The log message can be encrypted and/or signed. Note that as this is used from within the Processing Policy, it is typically used for transaction/message logging, rather than event logging. Due to the larger size of these log messages, they are normally sent directly to targets off-device using protocols such as syslog.

- **MQ Header**—This action is used to manipulate MQ MQMD headers for GETs and PUTs.
- **On Error**—This action is used to handle errors that occur within the processing rule. It can abort the transaction and call another rule (typically an error handling rule). It is discussed at the end of this chapter.
- **Results Asynchronous**—This rule can be used to send async or fire and forget results out from the processing rule, for example to write audit log records to a database.
- **Route (Using Variable)**—This action can be used to set the destination URL for a message dynamically.
- **Set Variable**—This action is used to simply set a DataPower variable to some value.
- **SQL**—This action is used to execute SQL commands against a database, if the appliance is licensed to do so. The result can be captured and used for further processing. A typical use is to enrich message content with additional data, or to customize the AAA Policy to read a nonstandard user registry housed in a database.
- **Strip Attachments**—This action can be used to remove attachments from a message.
- **Transform (using Processing Instruction)**—This action transforms the XML based on some processing instructions that are contained within the input document itself.
- **Transform Binary**—This action is used to do non-XML transforms on an XI50 such as EDI to XML or vice versa.

Matching Rules

A Matching Rule is just what it sounds like. It matches request and response messages arriving at the device, and error conditions, with the Processing Policy rules that are meant to handle them. In this next section, we walk through a complete scenario. Before we get to that, let's look at a few sample Matching Rules. Figure 7-21 shows an example that will match on *two* conditions—the incoming message must have a URL that ends with /bankingservices/checking *and* must contain a HTTP header named AccountNumber that must contain a value that begins with 0123. There is a radio button on the Match configuration page titled Boolean Or Combinations that can be used to specify "all must match" or "any can match" behavior for multiple matching conditions listed here.

Many common network components, such as load balancers and proxies, can interrogate HTTP-level data like the URL and header values. What sets the DataPower appliances apart from these is their ability to understand deeper application layer message formats, such as XML and SOAP. Let's look at that in our next example. Figure 7-22 shows how we begin the configuration. XPath has been selected as the Matching Type. This displays the XPath Tool, a feature that you might see in several places when configuring processing policies, such as when signing or encrypting messages at the field level. To find nodes in XML documents, the XPath language is used by this convenient utility, as shown in Figure 7-22.

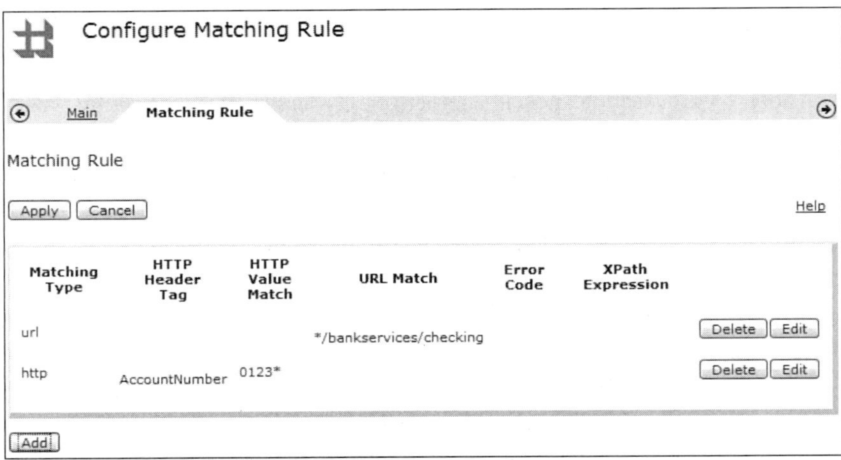

Figure 7-21 Matching Rule for a URL and HTTP header.

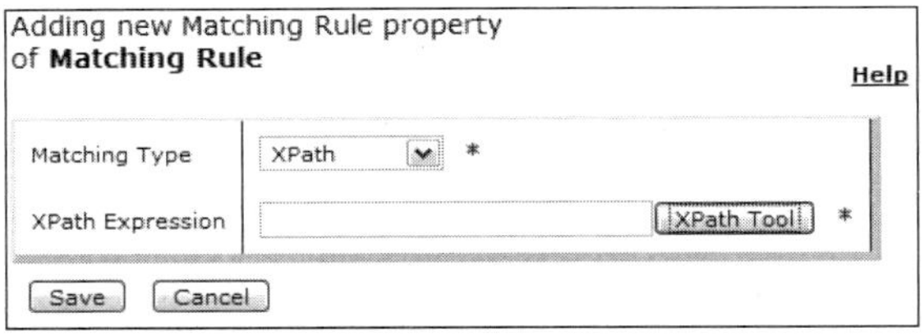

Adding new Matching Rule property
of **Matching Rule**
Help
Matching Type XPath *
XPath Expression XPath Tool *
Save Cancel

Figure 7-22 Configuring an XPath Matching Rule.

This lets us upload a sample input message to the device, and click on the element we are interested in, and DataPower will generate the XPath expression. Figure 7-23 shows the completed page, after we have clicked on the AccountInquiry element in the sample message bankRequest.xml, which was uploaded.

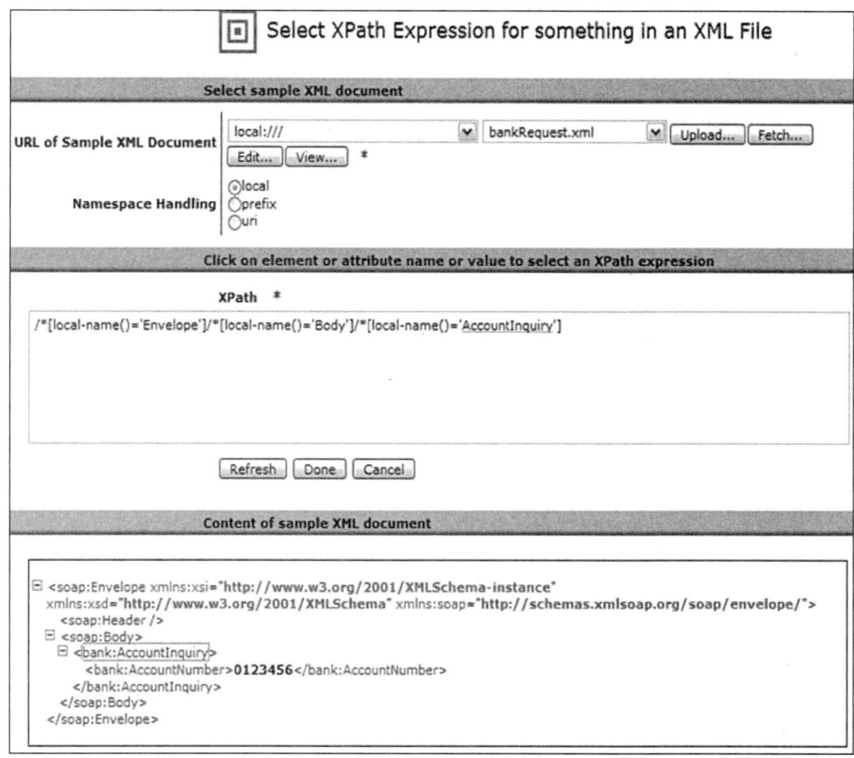

Figure 7-23 Using the XPath Tool.

Figure 7-24 shows the completed XPath Matching Rule. Now that's powerful!

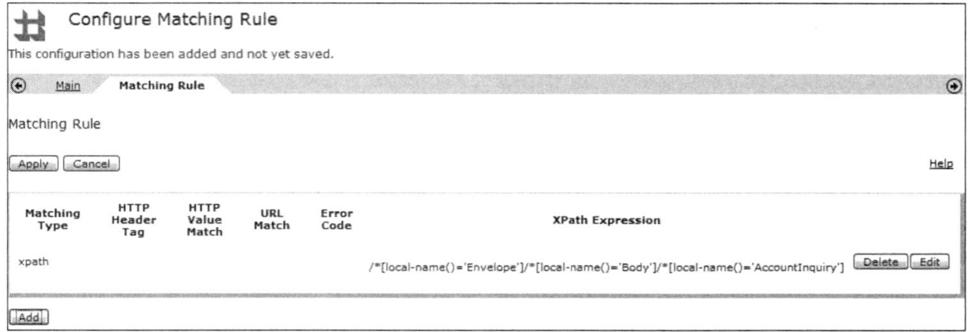

Figure 7-24 Completed XPath Matching Rule.

In addition to the URL, Header, and XPath matches we have shown, Match Rules also allow for matching on error codes. We will demonstrate this in Chapter 24. The other two choices in the Matching Type drop-down, Host and Full URL, should not be used as they are legacy configurations. HTTP and URL should be used instead, respectively.

The terms Matching Rule and Match Action are often used synonymously, however there is a distinction. Referring again to Figure 7-20, you can see that each configured rule has at its start an icon with an equal sign at its center. Looks like an action, doesn't it? Well...it is. This is the Match Action, which does nothing more than house a Match Rule, as you will see.

Creating an Example Processing Policy

To gain a better understanding of what we have discussed thus far, let's create the scenario for one of our banking URIs. Figure 7-25 shows a new policy. (How you get here will be discussed in our upcoming chapters on services.) The TestBankingPolicy Policy Name has been entered, the New Rule button has been clicked, and Client to Server has been selected in the Rule Direction drop-down list. When the New Rule button is pressed, a brand new horizontal rule line is presented in the workspace, and a Match Action is presented on it bordered in yellow highlight, which indicates some configuration is necessary. The system is saying "You have created a new request rule, so now first configure this Match Action on it to tell me when this new request rule should be fired." You can see also that the rule has appeared in the Configured Rules list at the bottom, even though we haven't truly configured it yet.

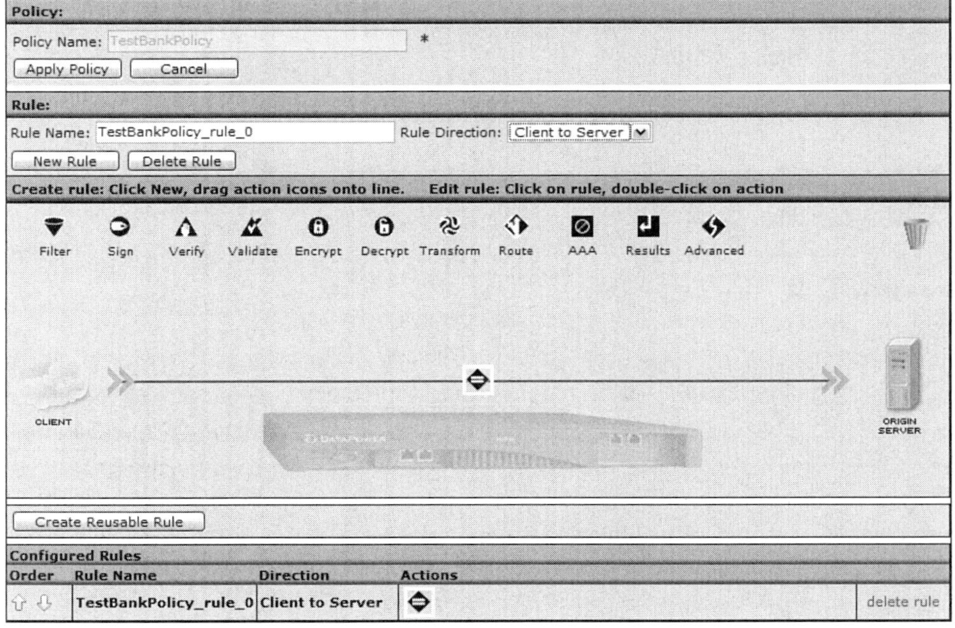

Figure 7-25 New Processing Policy Rule.

So our first course of action would be to double-click the Match Rule to configure it. When this is done, a new page pops up, as shown in Figure 7-26, asking us to configure the Match Action. As you can see, the only thing to configure is a Match Rule embedded inside. This is a simple config page but it allows us to point out something about how the DataPower WebGUI works. Notice that there is no Matching Rule selected in the drop-down, and there are plus (+) and ellipsis (...) buttons next to it. This pattern is seen throughout the DataPower WebGUI for editing objects. The plus button is always used to create a new object, so in this case if we were to click it a new page would pop up letting us configure a new Match Rule. If we had an existing Match Rule selected in the drop-down list, we might want to click the ellipsis button to edit that object. So, plus means create new, and ellipsis means edit existing. Memorize this, because you will see it a lot!

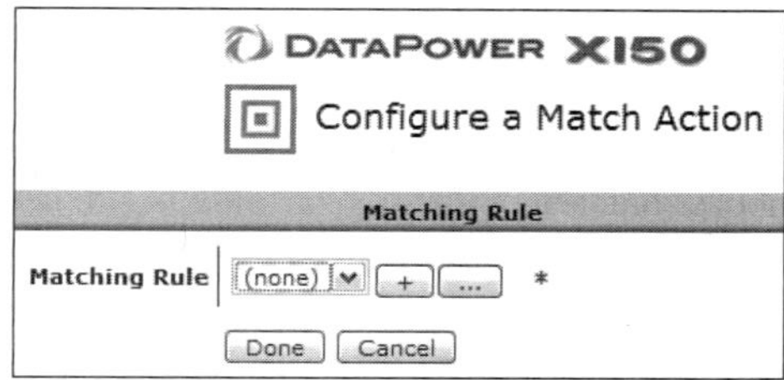

Figure 7-26 Match configuration.

In this example, we are showing how to create the first banking rule scenario, so we have clicked the plus button and entered a Matching Rule name of BrowseBankingServices on the main tab and then moved to the Matching Rule tab and added a new Matching Rule, as shown in Figure 7-27.

Figure 7-27 BrowseBankingServices URL Match.

Notice the format of the URL Match expression; it doesn't look like PCRE, does it? Matching Rules use simple Unix-style matching syntax by default; thus, the star (*) character represents 0 (zero) or more characters of any value, and a question mark (?) represents any one character. The first tab of the Matching Rule configuration page lets you select the match syntax. If you wanted to use PCRE, you could select that syntax instead (in which case, the above URL Match would be expressed as ".*/banking/browse_services").

After pressing the Save, Apply, and Done buttons to get back to the Policy Editor, our Match Action is no longer highlighted, as it has been configured, and hovering over it with the cursor shows a convenient pop-up bubble with the configuration (see Figure 7-28). Notice also how the GUI is showing the request flow graphically from the client cloud to the server.

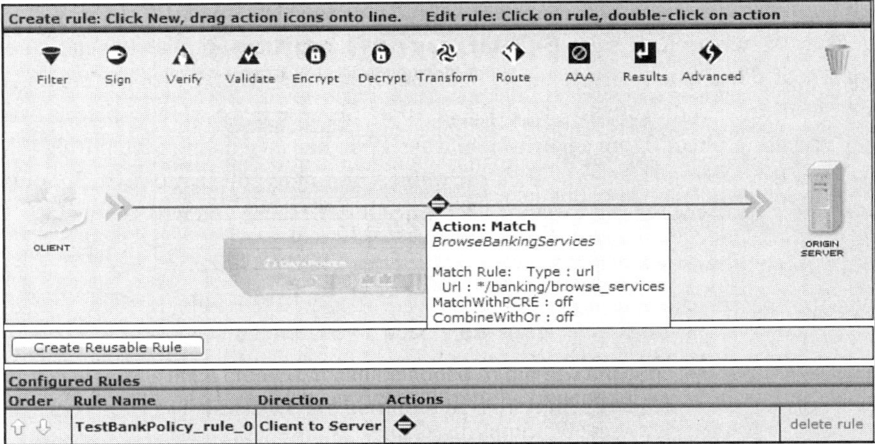

Figure 7-28 Request Rule with Banking match.

Processing Rule Priority

Refer for a moment back to Figure 7-20. Notice that we had two request rules there. Now that we know how to configure Matching Rules, and we know that the appliance uses those to pick the correct rule, how does that happen, exactly? It is important to understand this process, because a failure to do so, or to not pay attention to it, can cause some difficult to debug problems. The process is that the runtime starts at the top of the configured rules and checks each rule for a match until it finds one. This happens for request, response, and error rules. So consider what would happen if the top-most rule had a match on a URL of * and the ones beneath it were more granular, for example /banking/browse_services and /banking/view_accounts.

If you think about this, you will realize that the request rules under the top one will never get fired, because a URL match on broad wildcard such as * consumes each incoming message, as it matches everything. How do we fix this? Notice the column titled Order at the left of the Configurable Rules table. This is where you would use the arrows to move a more loosely defined match to the bottom of the list. Check these carefully as part of your configuration reviews and always consider this issue in your troubleshooting endeavors!

Configuring a Policy Rule

Now let's get back to our example policy rule. Alas, a request rule cannot live by a simple match alone! Well, it could but then it wouldn't accomplish anything. There must be something additional that we want to do on this request rule flow. Let's assume that we want to schema validate the incoming request XML message, transform the incoming XML to a schema more suitable to our backend application, and then send those results to the backend. Of course, we will need actions to accomplish these tasks. You can probably already guess which ones. To begin, we have dragged down the Validate action to the request rule and placed it to the right of the Match. To configure, we double-click and select the radio button to validate with an external schema (XSD) document, which we then upload from our workstation file system, as shown in Figure 7-29. This schema definition file now resides in the local: directory of our domain's file system.

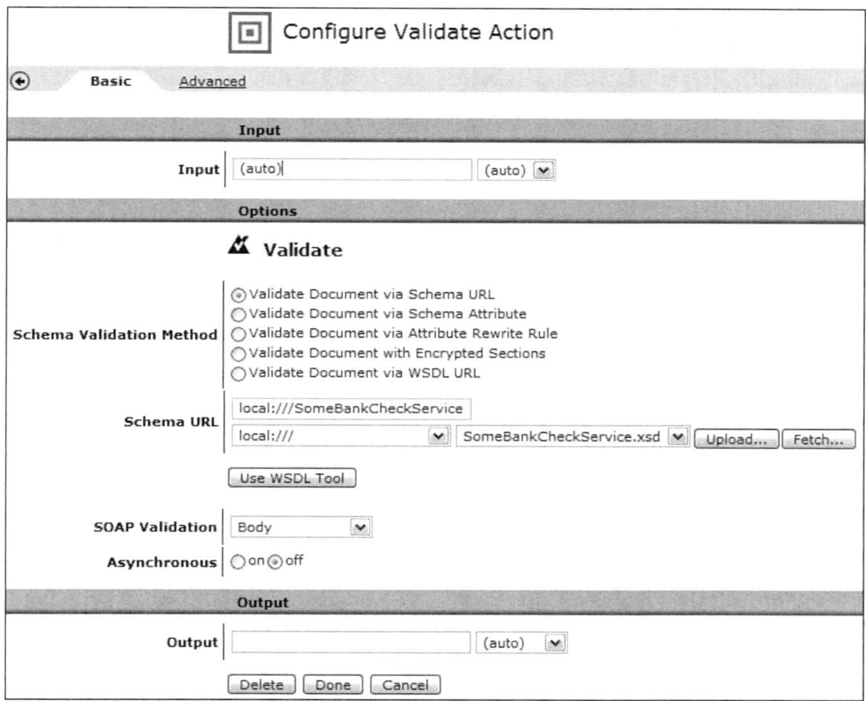

Figure 7-29 Configuring the Validate Action.

After closing the Validate action, we drag a Transform action to the right of it on the processing rule and double-click again to edit. Similar to the Validate, we rely on an external file here—the actual XSLT processing file that contains the transform instructions. Figure 7-30 shows the configuration of this action.

Finally, for completeness, we drag a Results action to the end of the request rule. You might have noticed that one of our request rules in Figure 7-20 had a Results action at the end, and the other request rule did not (it ended in a Transform). This might look quite peculiar and incomplete. The truth of the matter is that certain actions are capable of sending results on their own if they end a processing rule, whereas others cannot and require a Results action to follow. Rather than try to remember which are which, some users might simply insist on always closing a rule with a Results action (in fact, DataPower will add this for you automatically), whereas others might consider this wasteful. Neither approach is wrong. Our completed policy is shown in Figure 7-31.

Configure Transform Action

Basic | Advanced

Input

Input	(auto) (auto)

Options

Transform

Use Document Processing Instructions	◉ Use XSLT specified in this action ◯ Use XSLT specified in XML document processing instructions, if available ◯ Use XSLT specified in this action on a non-XML message
Processing Control File	local:///bankXMLTransform.xsl * local:/// bankXMLTransform.xsl Upload... Fetch... *
URL Rewrite Policy	(none) + ...
Asynchronous	◯ on ◉ off

Output

Output	(auto) (auto)

Delete Done Cancel

Figure 7-30 Configuring the Transform Action.

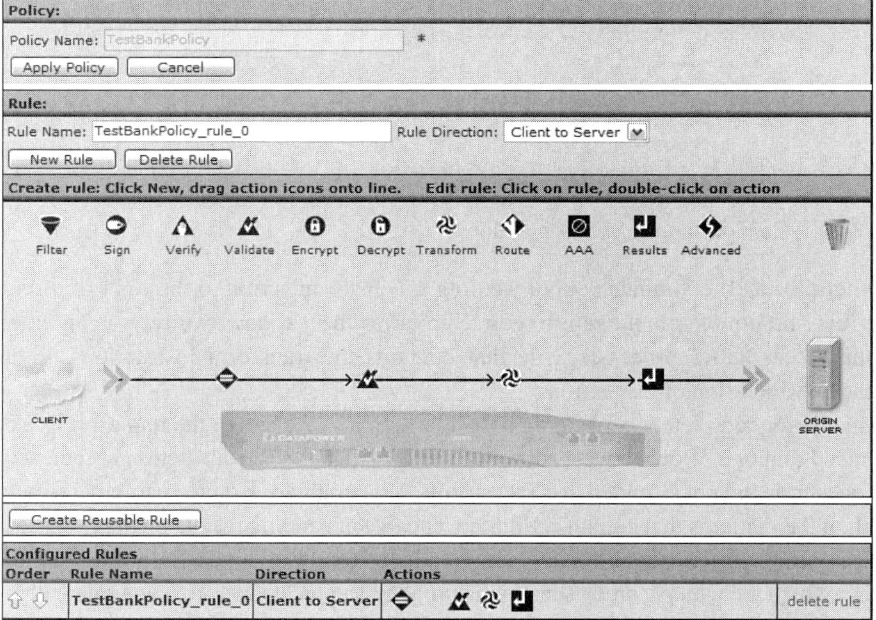

Figure 7-31 Completed Banking Processing Policy.

Contexts

There is more to understand about DataPower Processing Policy rules and actions. An important concept is the context. These are named memory segments in which transient data can be stored as the message moves across our processing rule flow. Two contexts that are created automatically for you are called INPUT and OUTPUT. For a request message, the INPUT context can be referenced by any action that wants a clean copy of the message as it arrived at the Processing Policy. (It might have been altered subsequently in other contexts by transformation and so on.) To get this, the action would have to specify the INPUT context as its input. Refer to Figure 7-30, where we configured our Transform Action. Do you see the input context designation drop-down at the top and the output context designation at the bottom? Right now they are set to Auto, which means the appliance will do its best job to figure this out for you. Our next example shows how well it did. Because this transform was acting on the input message, we could have just selected INPUT from that drop-down and gotten the same results. If our transform were going to pass the newly modified XML to another transform, it would use a temporary variable name in the output context (or PIPE, as discussed next), and this would then be used as the input context for the next Transform action. The OUTPUT context is simply the data to be sent to the backend server in a request rule. For response rules, the INPUT context is what comes from the backend server as a response, and the OUTPUT context is what we would end up responding to the client with.

There are two other reserved context names—PIPE and NULL. PIPE is used in situations such as we just described for Transforms where the output of one action is the input of an adjacent action. PIPE allows this data to be streamed through as it is processed, which is good for performance! There are some restrictions on its use, such as if you are setting variables in the stylesheet housed by this transform. NULL is used as an efficiency construct for actions that do not modify the message content at all.

Let's see how the contexts were set up for us in our sample policy. If you re-create our example and hover the mouse over each of the actions, you will see how the contexts flow together. Note that the user interface has made a "best guess" about what input and output contexts to use for each action in the processing rule. Alas, the best guess is sometimes not the intended behavior. Always double-check your context chain through an entire rule to make sure the desired data gets to each individual action and makes it to the OUTPUT context.

Error Handling

What about when things go wrong? Bad things sometimes happen to good policies. We must be prepared. Let's use our example to facilitate a quick introduction to DataPower Processing Policy error handling. One fast way to handle errors is to simply create an error rule. Figure 7-32 shows that we have done just that. And it was simple. We just clicked the New Rule button, configured the resulting Match on a URL of * (although we could have matched on specific types of errors), and dragged down a Transform action and included a stylesheet of on-error.xsl, which formats an HTML response to the client. (We assume it is a browser.)

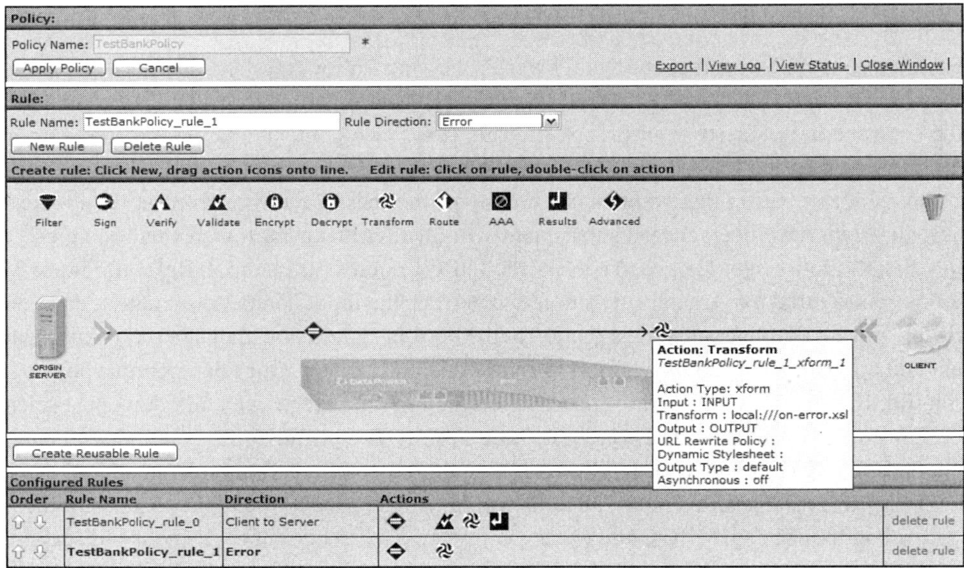

Figure 7-32 Processing policy with error rule.

You are probably searching for some way to determine when this error rule will be invoked. The answer is that it's automatic. When an error condition occurs in a Processing Policy, the appliance searches for any error rules that have been configured by moving down the list from top to bottom, as we discussed earlier with the request and response rules. If it finds one that matches, it will move control there and fire it. This is the fundamental usage of error rules.

However, there is another, more fine-grained approach available. You might remember that earlier in the chapter, we listed the available processing actions, and one of them (under Advanced) was the On Error action. This action can be placed in a Processing Policy to gain control when errors occur. Figure 7-33 shows that we have pulled down an Advanced action just before our schema validation, selected the On Error action from the radio button list, and then configured the action to abort the transaction and call our error rule, should any errors occur. Note that in this case, due to the presence of the error action, DataPower does not comb down through the list of error rules looking for a match. It gives control to the error action in scope, which decides what to do. (The transaction could be allowed to continue, rather than abort.)

As we said previously, when the policy runs into the On Error action during the rule processing from left to right, it puts that action in scope for any errors that might occur from that point forward. However, what if you need to handle transformation errors differently from schema validation errors? As Figure 7-34 shows, you can simply add in a new On Error action. Now, when the second error action is encountered, before the transform, it will fire upon any errors that happen past that point.

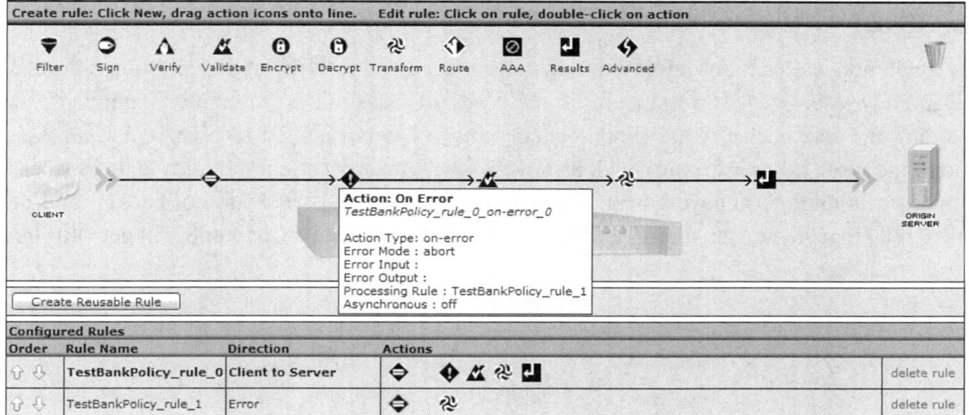

Figure 7-33 On Error action.

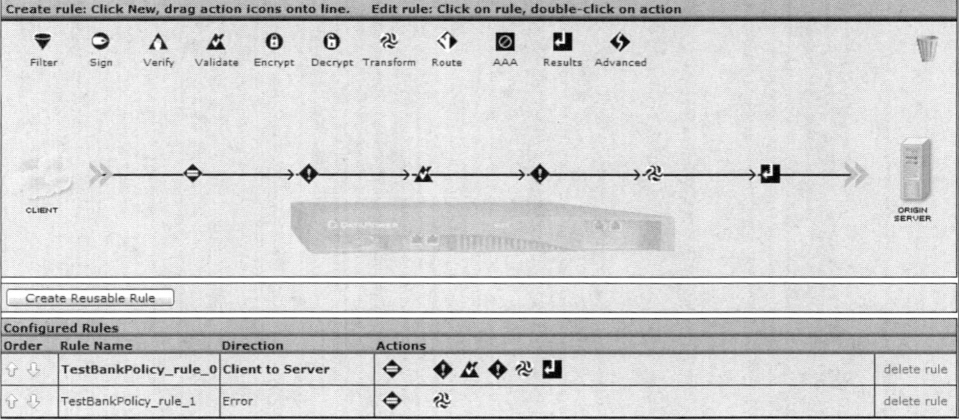

Figure 7-34 Request rule with two On Error actions.

In the preceding example, we took you through the usual business of building a Processing Policy. We intentionally kept this independent of the services that will house the policy, because we don't cover the services until the remaining chapters in this part of the book. We showed a few of the most commonly used actions and listed the rest with a brief overview of each. Many of these will be shown in action in the chapters to come.

Summary

This chapter covered a lot of information that introduced you to many of the common objects used in DataPower services—from the different types of backend configurations utilized (static, dynamic, and loopback) to the fundamental utility objects (XML Manager and User Agent), through the more complex topics such as how to configure processing policies and the rules and actions within them. You have now graduated from the prerequisite section of background information and are ready to start diving into actual DataPower services! Chapter 8 will get you started.

CHAPTER 8

XML Firewall

Now that you have a good understanding of what a DataPower service is and the different service types available, it is time to create our first DataPower service. This chapter takes you step by step through the creation of an XML Firewall service and discusses many of the service parameters and options available. Using simple yet common use cases, these examples give you a good understanding of the capabilities of the XML Firewall service as well as basic configuration of the Processing Policy and actions contained within it.

XML Firewall Overview

An XML Firewall (XMLFW) is a service type that can be used to process XML and non-XML traffic sent over the HTTP(S) protocol. It is considered the simplest of the three main service types to configure because it can have one single IP:port that it can listen on for traffic and can only communicate with the client and the backend server over HTTP(S).[1] Although it is limited to one listening IP address:port and one protocol, it can provide the same level of threat protection and multistep processing capabilities as the Multi-Protocol Gateway service type. The one additional feature that is offered by the XML Firewall is the ability to easily configure it as a loopback proxy.[2] As discussed in Chapter 6, "Introduction to DataPower Services," a loopback proxy does not forward requests to a backend server, but generates and returns the response back to the client itself. As a request enters the XMLFW, it is processed within the service, where a response is also

[1] It is possible to configure the XMLFW to communicate with other protocols by using custom programming, which is discussed in Chapter 23, "Programming within the DataPower Environment."

[2] The Multi-Protocol Gateway and Web Service Proxy services can also act as loopback proxies; however, it is not as easily configured as in the XMLFW service. This is discussed in Chapter 9, "Multi-Protocol Gateway."

generated and sent back to the client. Because of this capability, the XMLFW is often used as a loopback proxy when testing or debugging other services when the backend server is not available. The XMLFW service type is also capable of proxying backend services as it provides threat protection and multistep processing capabilities. We will demonstrate these capabilities in the examples that follow.

Creating an XMLFW

To begin creating the XMLFW service, you must first log in to the DataPower WebGUI as it is the interface used for the creation of the service. Be sure to navigate to the domain in which you want to configure the XMLFW service. Remember, the default domain is only for device and user administration. Never create services within the default domain!

After logging in, you are presented with the home page (Control Panel) that shows three sections: Services, Monitoring and Troubleshooting, and Files and Administration. We are interested in the top section of the main page, labeled Services. To create or modify an XMLFW service, click the XML Firewall icon as shown in Figure 8-1.

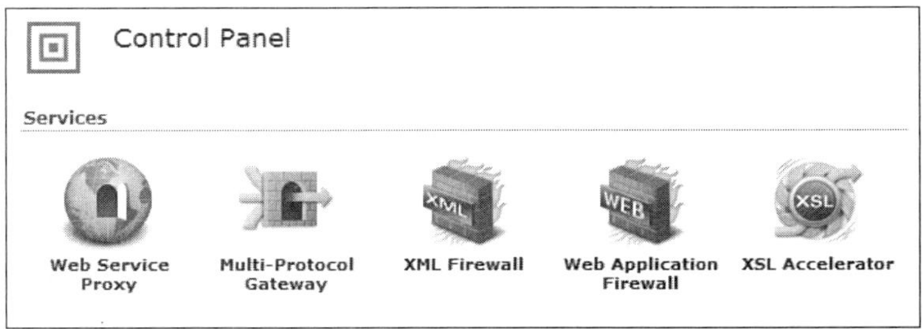

Figure 8-1 Selecting the XMLFW service type from the Control Panel.

When clicking the XML Firewall icon from the Control Panel, a screen is presented showing all XML Firewall services configured within the current domain. Also, notice there is an Add Wizard button on this screen. This option is used to configure a new XMLFW service with the guidance of a wizard. For our first XMLFW service example, we will take advantage of this wizard-driven approach as it guides us through the process of producing a base XMLFW that can be modified after it is created.

The first wizard screen presents a list of options with radio buttons as illustrated in Figure 8-2. This provides a basic starting point for the wizard by indicating the primary function that the service will perform. For example, you can indicate on this screen that the service should only accept XML documents in the request and should schema validate them. Or you can indicate that the request will not be schema validated and might not be XML. This merely gives the wizard some idea of the intent for the service, so it can guide you through its creation. Table 8-1 provides a brief description of each of these options.

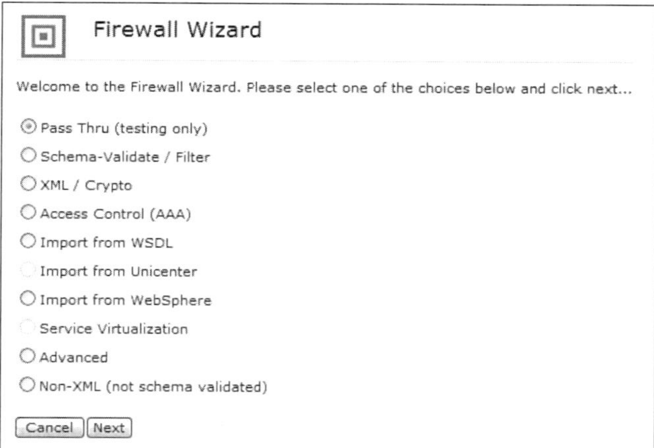

Figure 8-2 Initial XMLFW Wizard screen.

Table 8-1 Initial XMLFW Wizard Screen Options

Option	Description
Pass Thru (testing only)	Creates an XMLFW with a request type of SOAP and a default request (Client to Server) rule consisting of a Match and a Result action. This does not create a rule with a request type of Pass Thru as you might expect.
Schema-Validate/Filter	Creates an XMLFW that contains a request and response processing rule with processing actions to schema validate the request and response messages using the schema file selected in subsequent steps. Optionally, this choice allows the inclusion of a Filter action within the request/response rules.
XML / Crypto	Creates an XMLFW that will verify and/or decrypt request and/or response messages using the certificate specified in the creation of the service
Access Control (AAA)	Creates an XMLFW with a AAA policy that will be used to authenticate, authorize, and audit all requests based on the information provided during the creation of the service
Import from WSDL	Creates an XMLFW using the information provided in a WSDL. This is not a recommended practice as a WSP service type should be used instead.
Import from WebSphere	Creates an XMLFW for a Web service deployed on a WebSphere Application Server (WAS). Three files from WAS are required to be uploaded to the DataPower device to provide the required information—Binding Information file, Extension Information file, and the WSDL.
Advanced	Creates an empty XMLFW, bypassing the wizard. The service created must be configured manually.
Non-XML (not schema validated)	Creates an XMLFW where the request document is not required to be XML, therefore is not schema validated.

A simple example of an XMLFW service might be used to create a service that echoes the request document back to the client in the response. Consider this the Hello World of DataPower services. In this case, because our service simply echoes the request message back to the client in the response, we select the Pass Thru (testing only) option on this screen as shown in Figure 8-2. The second screen presented by the wizard is an easy one. This screen requires a name for the new service we are creating. This should be a descriptive name that has some relevance to what the service does. Because our example simply echoes the request back to the client, we will name this service Echo as shown in Figure 8-3.

TIP—Pass Thru Request Type

Choosing the Pass Thru (testing only) option when configuring an XMLFW via the wizard does not produce a service with a Request Type of Pass Thru. This must be done in the service configuration screen itself. When the Request Type is set to Pass Thru, a Processing Policy is not invoked for requests and no threat protection is provided. Because of this, careful consideration should be given to using an XMLFW service with a request type of Pass Thru.

Create a Pass Thru XML Firewall Service
Help
XML Firewall Service Name
To begin using this wizard, enter the name of the new XML Firewall in the firewall name dialog box.
Firewall Name
Echo *
Cancel Next

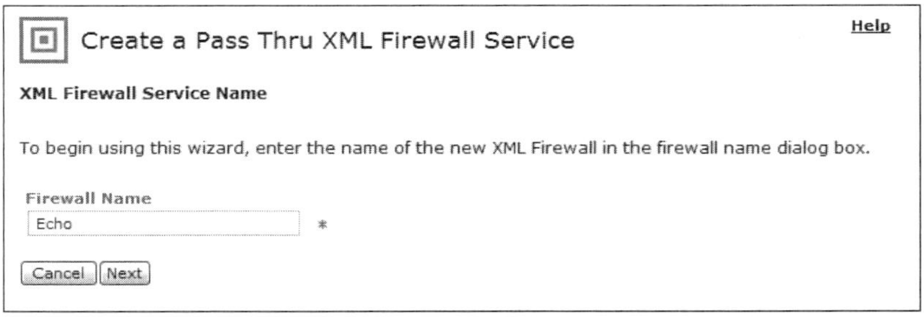

Figure 8-3 Provide a name for the new service.

The next screen asks for the firewall type. This indicates whether the firewall has a static backend server or will act as a loopback proxy. A static backend requires a backend server address that all requests are forwarded to; a loopback-proxy does not require a backend server, as it generates the response within the service itself. Although the XMLFW can have a dynamic backend, this is not an option on this screen. It can be selected only after the service is created; this will be demonstrated in an example later in this chapter. In our example, we create a loopback proxy, so we select the loopback-proxy option from the drop-down for the firewall type as shown in Figure 8-4.

The next, and final, step in creating the service is to assign the IP address and the port that the service listens on. This step requires some careful consideration as the IP:port combination must be unique within the entire device (not just the domain). On this screen, there is a field for the Device Address and a field for the Device Port.

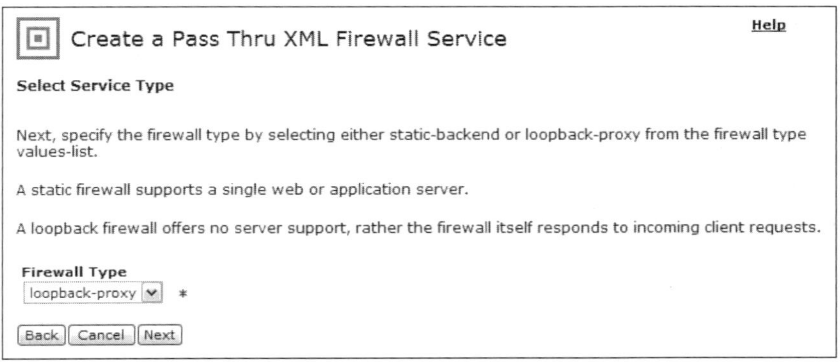
Create a Pass Thru XML Firewall Service
Help
Select Service Type
Next, specify the firewall type by selecting either static-backend or loopback-proxy from the firewall type values-list.
A static firewall supports a single web or application server.
A loopback firewall offers no server support, rather the firewall itself responds to incoming client requests.
Firewall Type
loopback-proxy
*
Back
Cancel
Next

Figure 8-4 Selecting the loopback-proxy option.

The Device Address represents the IP address of an actual Ethernet interface on the device. This can be represented in one of three ways. The first way is the default value that is populated when this screen is presented. Instead of an IP address, there is a series of four zeros separated by periods (0.0.0.0). This indicates that the service can receive requests on any of the configured Ethernet interfaces on the device. This is a highly discouraged practice as the payload traffic should always be segregated from the device management traffic, which should be dedicated to one of the four interfaces.

The second method of entering the IP address that the service listens on is by simply entering the actual IP address of the Ethernet interface. Although this is more acceptable than listening on all interfaces, it hard codes the IP address in the service configuration itself, which presents migration issues when migrating the service from one environment to another (e.g. development environment to test environment). This topic is addressed in detail in Chapter 15, "Build and Deploy Techniques."

The last, and recommended, method for providing the IP address is to use a host alias. A host alias is an abstraction of the IP address of an Ethernet interface and is configured within the default domain. This method provides a more seamless migration from environment to environment as the IP address is not embedded in the service configuration; however it will need to be defined on each device within the default domain. The benefits and configuration of a host alias are discussed in detail in Chapter 2, "DataPower Quick Tour and Setup," and Chapter 15.

For this example we use a host alias that we have configured named PayloadTraffic that resolves to a specific IP address on the device. Clicking the Host Alias button next to the Device Address field presents a list of configured host aliases where we select PayloadTraffic as shown in Figure 8-5.

DATAPOWER

Apply Cancel

select	alias	ip-address	comments
○	DeviceManagement	192.168.1.255	Used for device management
⦿	PayloadTraffic	192.168.1.254	Used for service payload traffic

Figure 8-5 Select a host alias.

Now that we have configured the IP address that the device accepts traffic on, it is also necessary to enter the port that the service listens on. The default port listed is the next available port on the device starting from 2048 and counting up. You can choose to leave the default port here or enter a new port that is not already in use on your device for the same interface. It is important to assign and keep track of all ports being used on the device to avoid port collisions. For our example, we entered port 6000 in this field. Figure 8-6 shows the final Device Address and Device Port configuration for our Echo service. Notice that you can indicate on this screen whether the request will be sent over SSL.

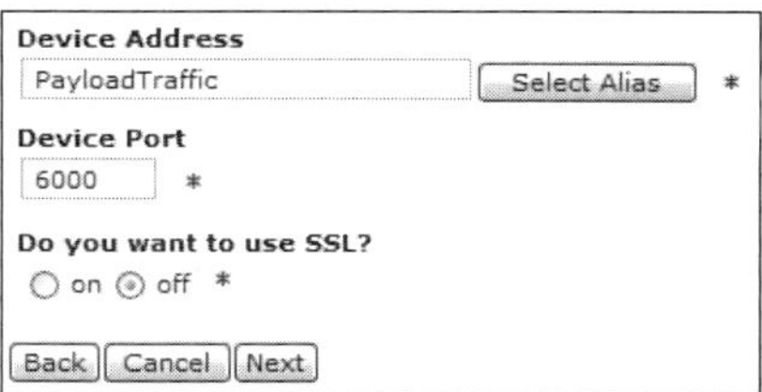

Figure 8-6 Device Address and Port configuration.

Now that all the required information has been entered for our new service, the next, and final screen, presents a summary of the service that will be created. Here we can confirm and commit all our configuration choices. Congratulations! We just created our first DataPower service. You can now see the objects created, as well as their current status as shown in Figure 8-7. All these objects should have a status of up, indicating they are active.

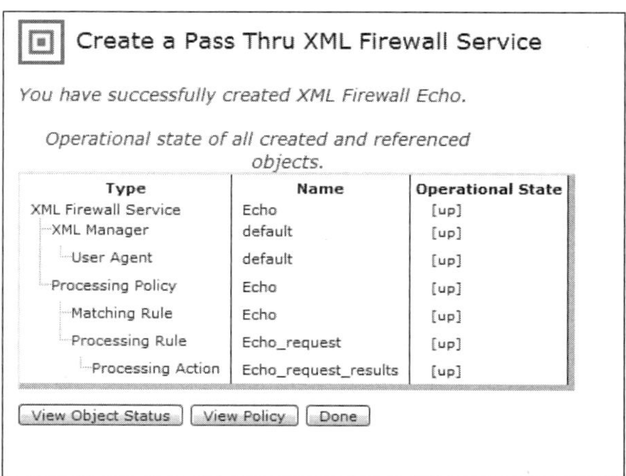

Figure 8-7 Service objects and status.

This section described how to create an XMLFW using the built-in wizard. This was demonstrated by providing a simple example of creating a service that echoes the request document back to the client in the response. Although this simple example was chosen for demonstration purposes, it can be useful when testing and debugging other services by providing this Echo service URL as the backend server where a response is required.

Testing the Service

After creating a DataPower service, it is likely that you will want to test it to be sure that you get the expected results. This test involves sending a request document to the IP address:port combination on which the service is listening. There are several methods and utilities that can be used to accomplish this, which are discussed in Chapter 27, "Problem Determination Using Built-In Tools" and Chapter 28, "Problem Determination Using External Tools." One simple way to do this is to use the built-in testing tool that DataPower provides to send a request document to a service and view the results.

This utility is accessed from the left-side menu of the WebGUI under Administration→Debug→Send a Test Message. Clicking this link brings up a screen that allows you to enter a test message, as well as request headers that you want to send to your service.

Let's utilize this feature to test our Echo XMLFW created in the previous example. At the test message screen, enter the URL of the service to which you will be sending a test message. If we are testing the Echo service, we enter http://<ip address>:<port>, where the IP address is the address that the service is listening on and the port is the port that the service is listening on. In our example, the IP address would be the address mapped to the host alias specified in the service configuration and port 6000.

After entering the URL that the request will be sent to, we can enter the actual request document in the Request Body text box. For our example, we will send the SOAP document shown in Listing 8-1. Because the Echo service does not expect any specific request header, we will leave this section blank.

Listing 8-1 Sample XML Request Document

```
<?xml version='1.0' ?>
<SOAP-ENV:Envelope
xmlns:SOAP-ENV="http://schemas.xmlsoap.org/soap/envelope/">
  <SOAP-ENV:Body>
    <book>
      <name>Moby Dick</name>
      <author>Herman Melville</author>
    </book>
  </SOAP-ENV:Body>
</SOAP-ENV:Envelope>
```

After this information is entered as shown in Figure 8-8, clicking the Make Call button sends the request to the Echo service.

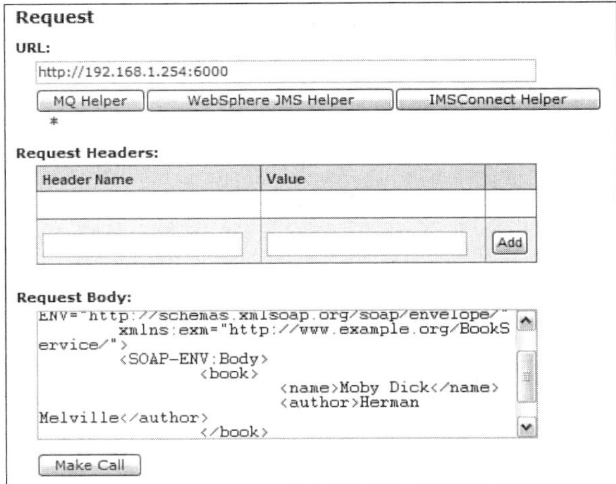

Figure 8-8 Send the test request.

After the request is sent, the response from the Echo service is displayed in the Response section of the screen. Because the Echo service simply echoes the request document back to the client, the request body is identical to the response body as shown in Figure 8-9. In addition to the response body, you will notice that all response headers and the return code are also displayed.

To show that the request actually hit the service and the service generated a response, we can take a look at the DataPower logs. If you were to look at the logs after sending the previous test request, you would most likely not see an entry for this request. This is because by default, DataPower is set only to log messages with a priority/severity of "error" or greater. To see our service generate messages that are written to the DataPower log, we can set the log level to debug. This setting is found at Control Panel→Troubleshooting→Set Log Level. Here we can set the log level to log all messages by selecting debug from the drop-down and clicking the Set Log Level button as shown in Figure 8-10. Note that this level of logging is recommended only in development environments because it logs a significant amount of data that would not be desirable in a production environment.

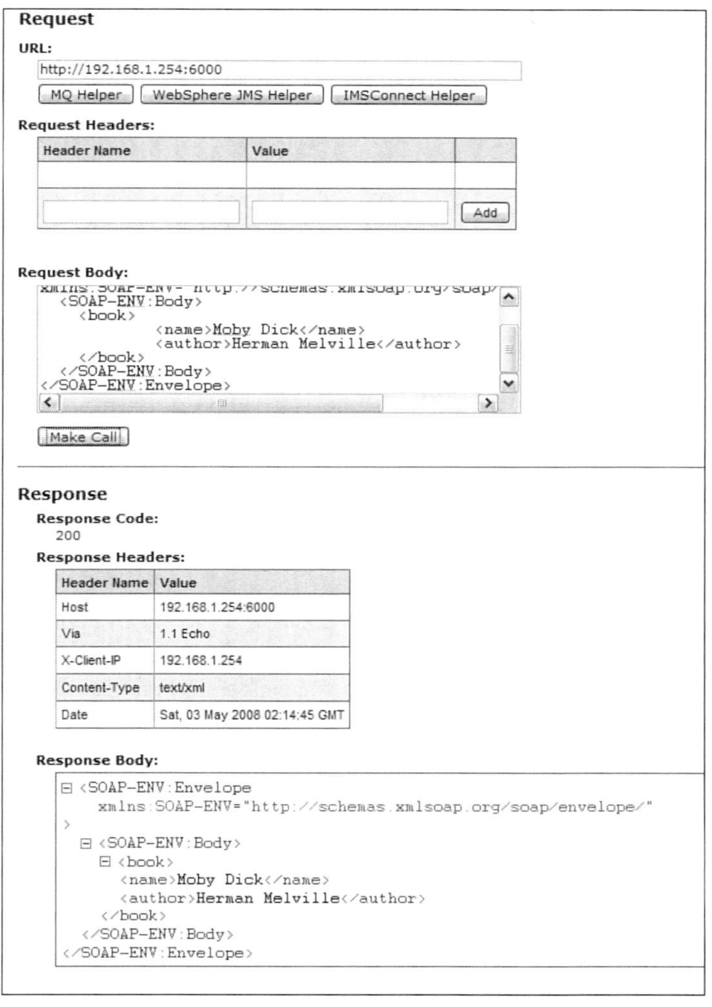

Figure 8-9 Response from Echo service.

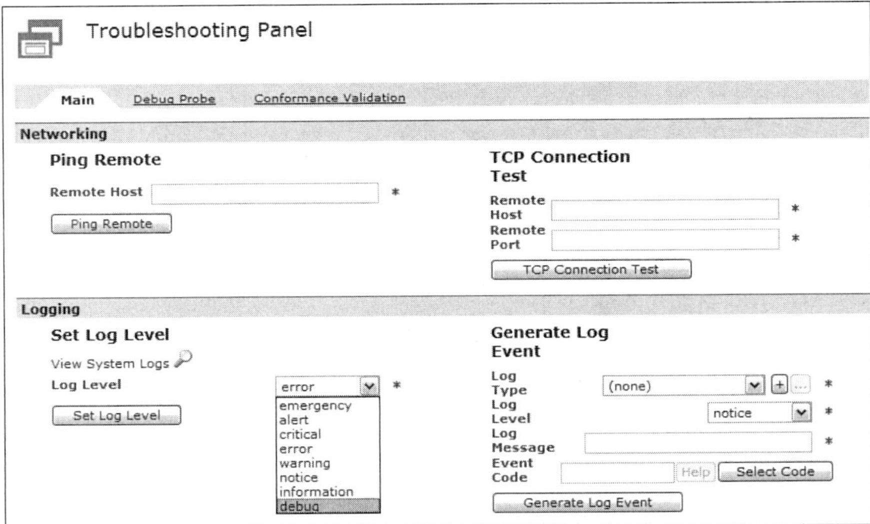

Figure 8-10 Set log level.

After confirming your selection, the log level is now set to log all events within the current domain. We can now submit the test message to our Echo service again and view the logs. The logs can be found at Control Panel→View Logs. You can see in Figure 8-11 that the request did hit our Echo XMLFW.

System Log

Refresh Log Target: default-log Filter: (none) (none)

current time: 22:20:53 on 2008-05-02

time	category	level	tid	dir	client	msgid	message (Show last 50 100 all)
Fri May 02 2008							
22:20:48	latency	info	10931		192.168.1.254	0x80e00073	xmlfirewall (Echo): Latency: 0 0 0 0 0 0 0 0 0 0 0 0 0 0 0 0 [http://192.168.1.254:6000/]
22:20:48	xmlfirewall	debug	10931		192.168.1.254	0x80e00073	xmlfirewall (Echo): Latency: 0 0 0 0 0 0 0 0 0 0 0 0 0 0 0 0 [http://192.168.1.254:6000/]
22:20:48	multistep	info	10931	>	192.168.1.254	0x80c00002	xmlfirewall (Echo): rule (Echo_request): #1 results: 'generated from INPUT' completed ok.
22:20:48	xmlparse	debug	10931	>	192.168.1.254		xmlfirewall (Echo): Finished parsing http://192.168.1.254:6000/
22:20:48	xmlparse	debug	10931	>	192.168.1.254		xmlfirewall (Echo): Parsing document 'http://192.168.1.254:6000/'
22:20:48	schema	debug	10931		192.168.1.254		xmlmgr (default): xsd Compilation Request: Found in cache (store:///schemas/soap-envelope.xsd)
22:20:48	schema	debug	10931		192.168.1.254		xmlmgr (default): xsd Compilation Request: Checking cache for URL store:///schemas/soap-envelope.xsd
22:20:48	multistep	debug	10931	>	192.168.1.254	0x80c00004	xmlfirewall (Echo): Protocol layer did not supply Content-Type
22:20:48	xmlfirewall	info	10931	>	192.168.1.254	0x80e000b4	xmlfirewall (Echo): rule (Echo_request): selected via match 'Echo' from processing policy 'Echo'
22:20:48	xmlfirewall	debug	10931		192.168.1.254		Matching (Echo): Match: Received URL [/] matches rule '*'
22:20:48	xmlfirewall	info	10931	>	192.168.1.254	0x80e00077	xmlfirewall (Echo): New transaction(conn use=1): POST http://192.168.1.254:6000/ from 192.168.1.254

Figure 8-11 Echo service log entries.

A Quick Tour of an XMLFW

In the previous section, we demonstrated how to create an XMLFW service using the built-in wizard as well as how to test it using the built-in test tool. However, what did we actually create here? Because we used the wizard driven approach, we never actually saw what was built and how. We actually created an XMLFW service with many different options and service parameters that can be viewed and edited via the WebGUI. In this section, we will look at the major components and parameters that make up an XMLFW service.

You can access an XMLFW service by navigating to Control Panel→XML Firewall and clicking on the service name. This will bring up the main configuration page for the service as shown in Figure 8-12. You can see that there are several tabs at the top of the page and you are viewing the General tab. As the name suggests, this tab contains all the general information about the XMLFW. You might recognize the XMLFW shown in Figure 8-12 as it is the Echo service we configured in our previous example. Notice the Firewall Type is Loopback and the Device Address and Device Port are as we specified during the creation of the service. All other configuration parameters are set to the default values.

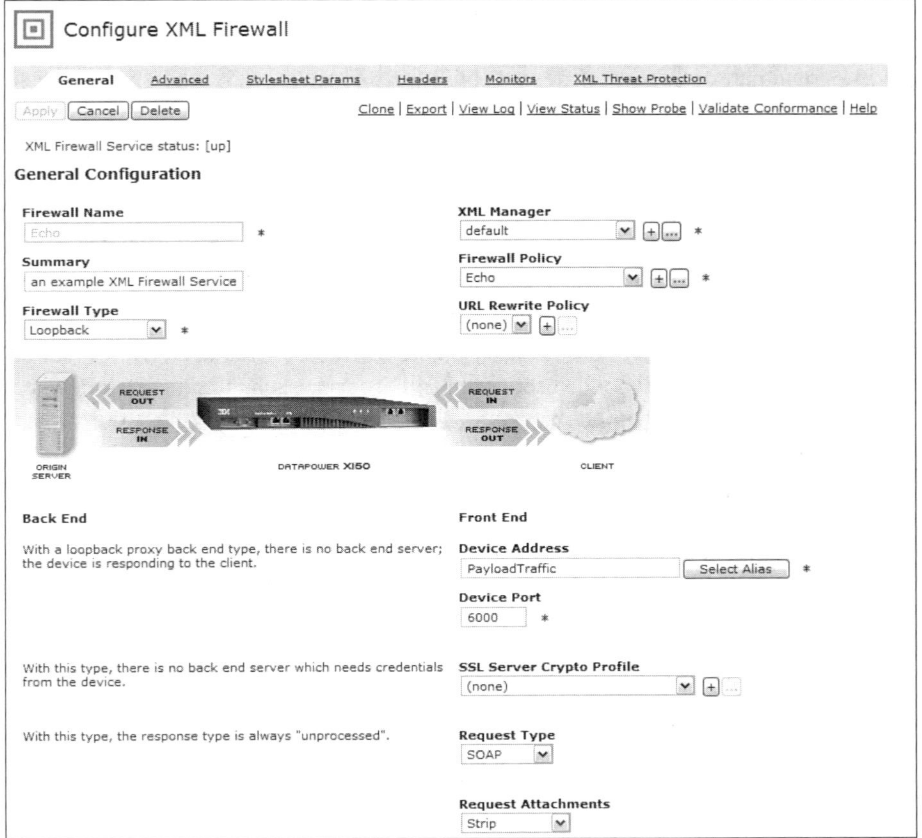

Figure 8-12 Configure XML Firewall—General.

Notice on the bottom half of the screen in this tab, the Front End (bottom right) and Back End (bottom left) parameters are separate. In Figure 8-12, you do not see any Back End parameters as this is our Echo service, which is a loopback firewall type so it will not have a backend server defined. Let's now take a look at the major service configuration parameters found within this General tab:

- **Firewall Type**—Define the type of backend used for this service. Three possible options exist for this parameter:
    - **Loopback**—Used when there is no backend for the service. It is the responsibility of the service to produce a response back to the client.
    - **Static-Backend**—Used when there is a known backend address that all requests will be forwarded to. When this option is selected, a backend URL and port must be provided.
    - **Dynamic-Backend**—Indicates that the backend server address is determined at runtime. When this option is selected, no backend URL is provided in the service configuration. It is then the responsibility of the Processing Policy to assign this at runtime.
- **XML Manager—**The XML manager used for this service. A detailed description of the XML Manager can be found in Chapter 7, "Introduction to Services Configuration."
- **Firewall Policy—**The Processing Policy used for this service. This is perhaps the most important part of the XML Firewall configuration and is likely where you'll spend most of your service development time.
- **URL Rewrite Policy—**The URL Rewrite Policy that is optionally invoked for each request. The URL Rewrite Policy can rewrite all or part of a URL before the Processing Policy processes the incoming request.
- **Device Address**—The IP address on which the service should accept requests. This IP address must be an IP address, or secondary IP address of a physical Ethernet interface on the device. A configured host alias can also be used here to reference a device interface.
- **Device Port**—The port that the service uses to listen for requests. The IP address and port combination must not be used by any other services on the same DataPower device.
- **SSL Server Crypto Profile**—The SSL Crypto Profile used for frontside SSL connections. This object defines all the SSL information required to establish the SSL connection.
- **Request Type**—Defines the type of request documents accepted by this service. The valid values are
    - **SOAP**—All request documents sent to this service must be valid SOAP documents that will be validated against a SOAP schema for well-formedness. This is the default value for an XMLFW.
    - **Non-XML**—The request might or might not be an XML document and is not schema validated.
    - **Pass-Thru**—The request is not validated and is not processed by the Processing Policy defined within the service. No threat protection is provided by the service when this Request Type is selected.
    - **XML**—The request document must be a valid, well formed XML document.

- **Request Attachments**—When the request type is SOAP or XML, this setting determines what action to take if the request contains attachments. The valid values for this parameter are
    - **Strip**—The attachment(s) is stripped from the request and then the request continues to be processed by the service. This is the default setting.
    - **Allow**—The request (and attachment) is accepted and processed by the service. The attachment is also available for processing by the service.
    - **Reject**—The entire request is rejected by the service if an attachment is sent.
    - **Streaming**—Allows the message to be processed in streaming mode where the attachments are available to the service for processing.
    - **Unprocessed**—The request is allowed with the attachments, however the attachments are not available to the service for processing.
- **Backend**—When the Firewall Type is set to Static, parameters for the backend server become visible in this space. These parameters are identical to the Front End parameters; however they are applied to the back end connection. This is discussed and demonstrated later in this chapter.

In addition to the basic configuration parameters found in the General tab, the Advanced tab contains many advanced options and parameters that can be set as shown in Figure 8-13.

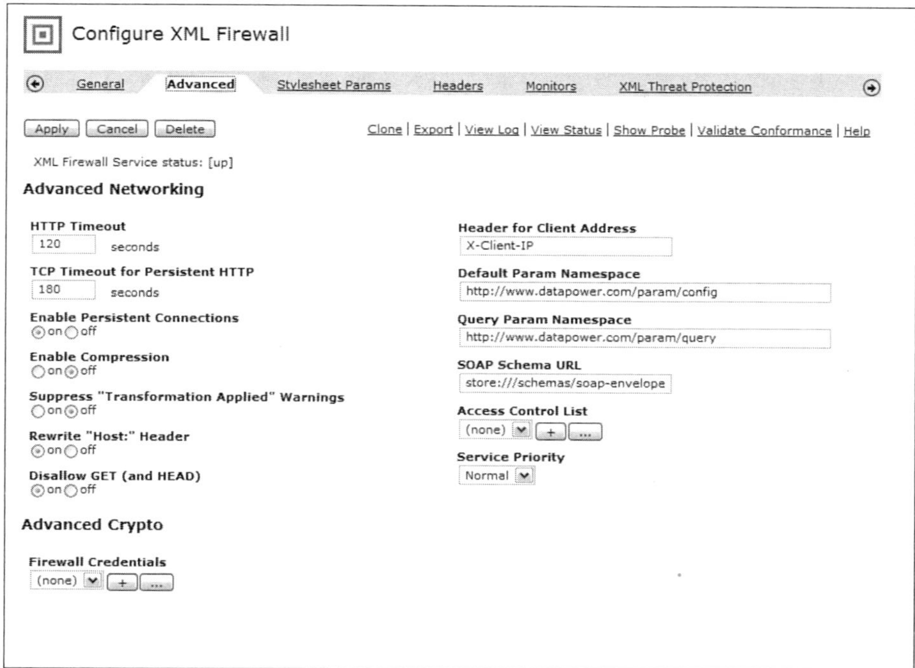

Figure 8-13 Configure XML Firewall—Advanced.

Many of the settings within the Advanced tab will be left at the default values; however it is important to understand what each setting represents and how it can affect the processing within your service in the event that you might need to change the default behavior. Table 8-2 provides a brief description of each of the service configuration parameters found in this tab.

Table 8-2 Advanced XMLFW Configuration Parameters

Parameter Name	Description
HTTP Timeout	Specifies the duration in seconds that the service maintains an idle HTTP connection with a client or server. The number of seconds entered must be between 3 and 7200. The default is 120 seconds.
TCP Timeout for Persistent HTTP	Specifies the duration in seconds that the service maintains an idle TCP connection with a client or server. The number of seconds entered must be between 0 and 7200. The default is 180 seconds.
Enable Persistent Connections	Enables persistent connections to clients and servers that this service communicates with. When this setting is On, the service keeps a single HTTP connection open to a client or server for multiple URL requests. The connection is left open for the duration specified in the TCP Timeout for Persistent HTTP setting. The default for this parameter is On.
Enable Compression	Enables GZIP compression negotiation with an HTTP peer.
Suppress "Transformation Applied" Warnings	As per RFC2616, if the service changes the content coding or media type, a warning header should be sent in the response. If this setting is Off, this warning is sent. If it is On, this warning is suppressed. The default for this setting is Off.
Rewrite "Host" Header	As a request comes into this service, a Host header is sent along with it. This header is set by the client and contains the address and method that the client used to access the service. When this parameter is set to On, the service rewrites this header to reflect the backend address and method that the request is forwarded to by the XMLFW. When set to Off, this header is not rewritten. The default for this parameter is On, indicating the header is rewritten by the service. This might not be desirable when the backend server is responding to the client with a redirect location as the redirect location could be derived using the Host header. This causes the redirect to bypass the DataPower service and go directly to the backend server.
Disallow GET (and HEAD)	When set to On, the service does not allow HTTP GET or HTTP HEAD requests. When set to Off, these requests are allowed. The default for this parameter is On.
Header for Client Address	DataPower inserts an HTTP header in the request containing the client IP Address. This parameter specifies the name of the header.
Default Param Namespace	The default namespace used when passing parameters to a stylesheet via the WebGUI if the parameter is defined without a namespace or without explicitly specifying a null namespace.

Parameter Name	Description
Query Param Namespace	The default namespace used when passing parameters to the service via a URL query string.
SOAP Schema URL	The URL for the schema the service uses to validate SOAP documents.
Access Control List	An access control list that can be created to restrict access to the service by IP address or range.
Service Priority	Assigns a priority to the service of High, Medium, or Low. This priority is used to allocate resources across multiple services.
Firewall Credentials	A list of keys and certificates made available to the service. If none are specified, the service has access to all keys and certificates that are defined within the domain.

TIP—Setting the Rewrite "Host" Header

When the service is proxying a backend server that will respond with redirects and locations to the client, this setting should be set to Off. Because the server may use this header to specify the redirect location, you would not want this header changed to the actual backend address.

All other tabs within the service configuration screen are not specific to the XMLFW service type; therefore they are covered in separate chapters throughout this book.

Processing Policy, Rules, and Actions

Now that we have created our first DataPower service, you might think that it wasn't exciting. That's because we created the simplest type of service that really doesn't do much at all but echo back the request document to the client. You see, the real power in a DataPower service lies in the ability to apply many different types of processing to the request and response messages. This is configured via the Processing Policy within the service. This section discusses and demonstrates the creation of a Processing Policy, processing rules, and actions within an XMLFW service.

As shown in the previous section, the Firewall Policy within an XMLFW can be created or accessed via the General tab on the Configure XML Firewall screen. When an XMLFW is created using the wizard, as in the previous example, a Firewall Policy object is automatically created for you. If you used the Add Advanced option to create your service, you will have to create one yourself. To demonstrate this, let's create another example XMLFW service.

In this example, we will build another XMLFW that acts as a loopback proxy as in the first example; however, this example actually provides a valid response to the request. This service accepts a SOAP request document that provides a book name and book author in the SOAP body and returns information about the book requested.

Because we already know how to use the wizard for creating an XMLFW, let's try to create one using the Add Advanced option. This can be found next to the Add Wizard button after navigating to the Control Panel→XML Firewall screen. After clicking this button, you are taken directly to the XMLFW Configuration screen within the General tab where all the required information must be entered.

You enter the same kind of information here as you did when creating the XMLFW via the wizard; however, you are not prompted with these questions. On the General tab, you enter the Firewall name and summary (optional), the Firewall Type (with backend information if applicable), and all the frontend information.

In this example, let's assume that the real backend service is not yet available, which is why we will create an XMLFW that will generate the response to the client. We named this service BookQueryService. As seen in Figure 8-14, we are creating a service that is a loopback firewall as the service itself provides a response and listens on port 4000 on the PayloadTraffic host alias.

Figure 8-14 BookQueryService configuration.

Now that we have all the information required on the General tab, we can create a Firewall Policy. As with all objects, to edit an existing object you click the ... button next to the Firewall Policy name and to create a new object, you click the + button. Because we do not have a Firewall Policy object already created, we need to click the + to create a new one. This brings us to the policy editor screen. To start, the new policy requires a name. As a general practice, we name our policy with the same name as our service. In this case we name it BookQueryService. We now have a Processing Policy; however it is quite useless unless we add some rules and actions to it.

For our example, let's create a new request (client to server) rule to our new policy. When a new rule is created, a match rule is automatically added to it that needs to be configured. Because this is the only request rule in our policy and it should act on all requests to the service, we create a match rule that matches on all URLs as shown in Figure 8-15.

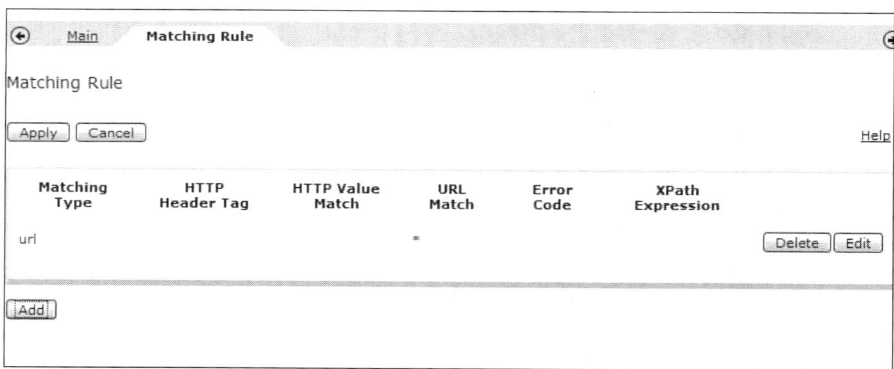

Figure 8-15 Match rule for all URLs.

Because we already know how to work with the Policy editor, let's now take the time to explore two specific actions that can be added to a processing rule.

Fetch Action

The Fetch action can be a useful action because it can fetch a document from a specified location using a URL provided. The URL can reference a remote location or it can reference the DataPower file system itself. This action retrieves the document from the URL specified and outputs this document to the output context specified in its configuration. For example, if the output context is OUTPUT, the document retrieved will be sent to the output of the rule. The output context of the Fetch action can also be the same as the input context of the next action. If this is the case, the document fetched will be passed directly to the next action for processing.

In our example we said that we will return a valid response back to the client. To do this we use the Fetch action to retrieve the response document from the DataPower file system, passing it back to the client in the response.

You might notice when configuring your processing rules that there is no action named Fetch in the array of actions listed above the policy line. As discussed in Chapter 7, "Introduction to

Services Configuration," this, and many other actions, are grouped into a single icon called Advanced in the Policy editor and can be identified by the diamond-shaped icon labeled Advanced. When this action is added to the policy line, it will be outlined in yellow, which means that you are required to configure it. The first step in configuring it is to select the actual action that you want to use or the action type. This is where we select the Fetch action as shown in Figure 8-16.

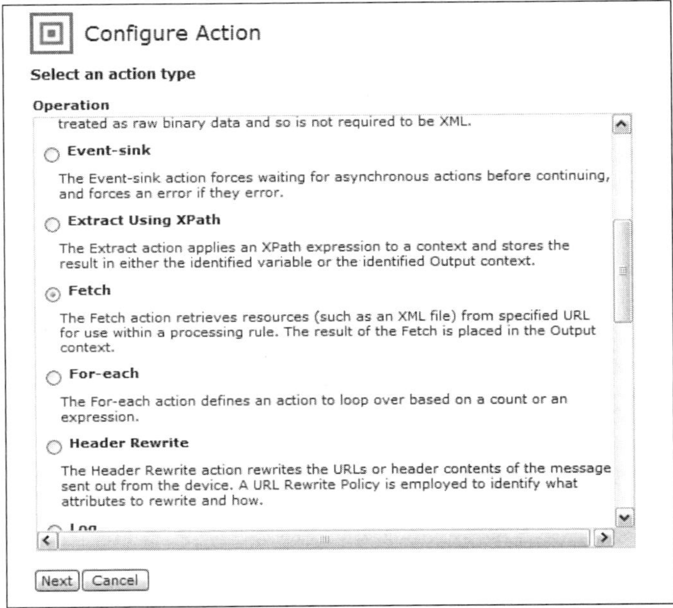

Figure 8-16 Choosing the Fetch action.

After the Fetch action is selected, we are required to enter a URL in the Source field for the location of the document to be fetched. This URL can be constructed to reference any of the supported protocols on the DataPower device by using the applicable URL scheme.

In our example, we reference a document named bookQueryResponse.xml in the local folder on the DataPower file system that was previously uploaded to the local directory on the device file system. Figure 8-17 shows this configured in the Fetch action configuration screen.

The output of this action is the actual document that was fetched from the URL provided. You will notice after configuring this action that the Advanced action icon has been replaced by the Fetch icon on the policy line as shown in Figure 8-18.

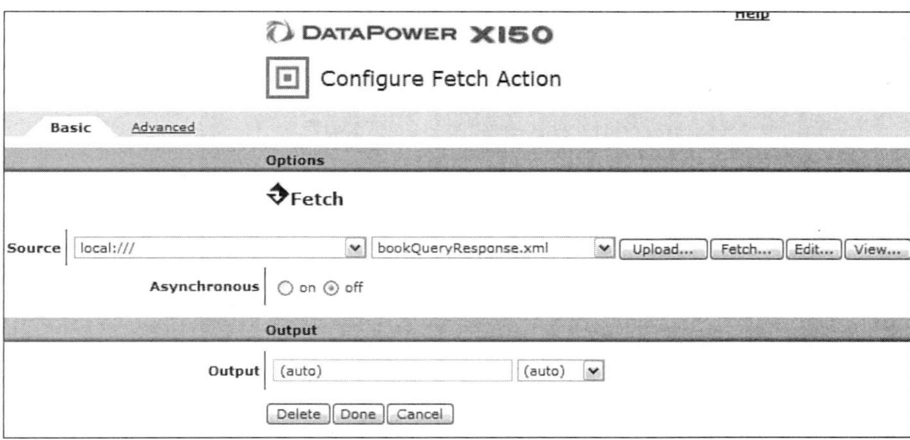

Figure 8-17 Enter URL to fetch.

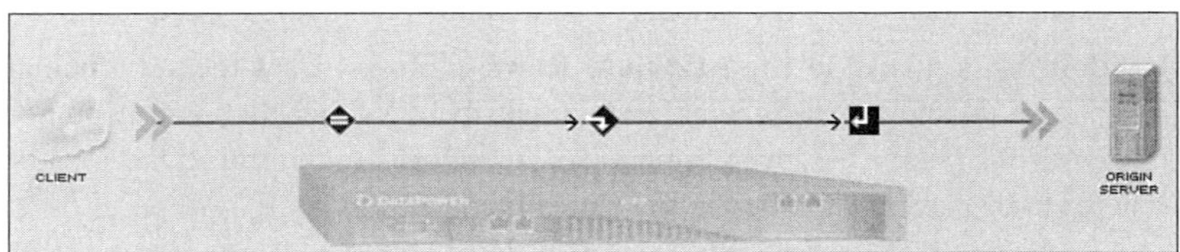

Figure 8-18 The Fetch icon.

Validate Action

In most cases, you will be configuring an XML Firewall to process XML requests and responses. One common and useful function that a DataPower service can perform is not only to ensure that the XML is well formed, but also to validate the request and the response document to ensure that it is compliant with a specific schema. This then ensures that the backend service is receiving only valid, schema-compliant documents, freeing it up from the resource intensive process of validating the document itself.

To accomplish this task, there is a specific action called Validate that validates the input document against a schema that can be specified at configuration time or dynamically determined at runtime by the input document itself.

This action is shown in the actions displayed above the Policy editor and can be identified by the triangle-shaped icon with a check mark labeled Validate.

So, let's say that in BookQueryService we wanted to validate the request against a schema that has been uploaded to the DataPower file system. To do this, you simply add a Validate action to the Request rule created after the Match rule and before the Fetch action, as shown in Figure 8-19.

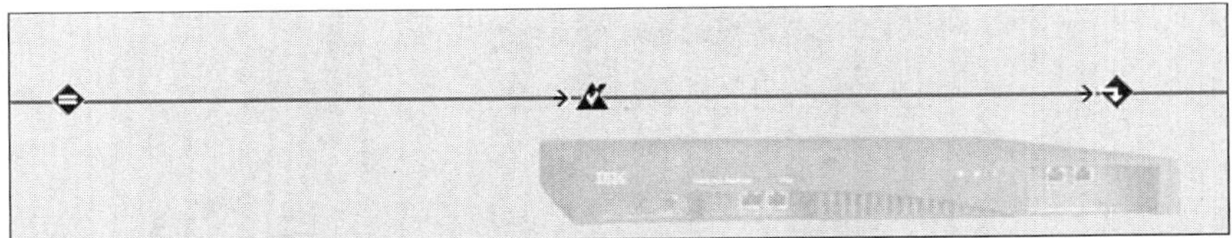

Figure 8-19 BookQueryRequest rule.

After it is added to the policy line, this action must be configured by double-clicking the icon. When configuring this action, you must indicate how the input document will be validated, otherwise known as its schema validation method. The choices are

- **Validate Document via Schema URL**—Uses the URL provided to access the schema that will be used to validate the input document
- **Validate Document via Schema Attribute**—Uses the values of the xsi:schemaLocation and the xsi:noNamespaceSchemaLocation attributes within the input document to determine the location of the schema to be used to validate the input document
- **Validate Document via the Attribute Rewrite Rule**—Uses the xsi:schemaLocation and the xsi:noNamespaceSchemaLocation attributes within the input document after a URL rewrite policy has been applied to the values to determine the location of the schema to be used to validate the input document
- **Validate Document with Encrypted Sections**—Validates the document using a Schema Exception map, where some parts of the document may be encrypted
- **Validate Document via WSDL URL**—Uses the schema within a WSDL specified to validate the input document

Depending on the schema validation method, other fields might be required in the configuration, such as the URL to access the schema or a WSDL file. After the Validate action is configured, it validates the request or response document based on the direction of the rule that it was added to.

For our BookQueryService we know that we have a schema that we want to validate our request document against. In this case we would select the Validate Schema via Schema URL option and provide the URL to the .xsd file in the local file system. It is assumed that the schema file that we will reference for this example has already been uploaded to the device and is called bookQueryRequest.xsd. Figure 8-20 shows this configuration screen with a reference to this schema file.

In addition to specifying the method to use to validate the input document, the Validate action also lets you specify what portion of the document will be validated in the event that the input document is a SOAP document. For example, you can choose only to validate the SOAP Body of the input document, or you can validate the entire SOAP Envelope. This is determined by the SOAP Validation field in the Validate action configuration screen shown in Figure 8-20. The options that can be selected for this field are as follows:

- **Envelope**—Validate the entire input SOAP message, including the SOAP Envelope against the schema specified.
- **Body**—Validate only the Body of the SOAP message against the schema specified. This is the default.
- **Body or Detail**—Validate the Body of the SOAP message against the schema specified or validate the detail element if the document contains a SOAP Fault.
- **Ignore Faults**—If the document contains a SOAP Fault, no validation is performed. If the SOAP document does not contain a SOAP Fault, the SOAP Body is validated.

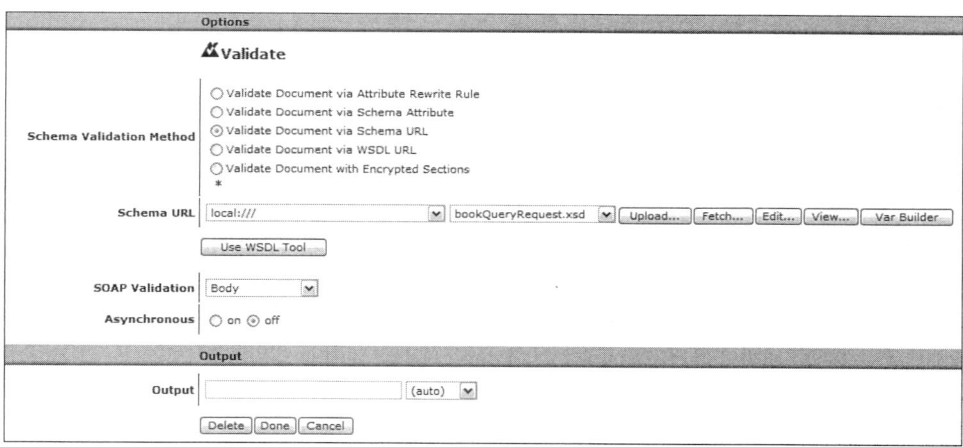

Figure 8-20 Request Validate action configuration.

In our BookQueryService, the schema used to validate the request document does not include the SOAP Envelope so we leave the default as Body for the SOAP Validation parameter and click Done to finish the Validate action configuration. Clicking the Done button on this screen completes the action configuration and returns you to the Policy configuration screen. Clicking the Apply Policy button commits the changes made to the policy.

There you have it! We now have a working service that accepts and schema validates a SOAP request document, fetches a response document, and returns it back to the client in the response. Although this is just an example service to demonstrate the configuration of the Processing Policy and the two actions discussed, this type of service can actually provide a tremendous amount of value in a real-world scenario. As we mentioned earlier, suppose there was actually going to be a service on the backend that would generate the response to the client. Many times the actual service is not available or ready when you are prepared to create your DataPower service. If the schema for the request message is defined, you can create a similar service to perform the validation of the request document and actually generate the response as shown in this example. This can then be used by the actual clients as they test their client code until the real backend service is ready and available.

Testing the BookQueryService

To prove that our service is actually validating the request and response document, we can send a test message to the service using the built-in tool as in the previous example. Listing 8-2 shows a schema-compliant sample request document that we might send to our BookQueryService.

Listing 8-2 Sample BookQueryService Request Document

```
<?xml version='1.0' ?>
<SOAP-ENV:Envelope
xmlns:SOAP-ENV="http://schemas.xmlsoap.org/soap/envelope/">
  <SOAP-ENV:Body>
    <book>
       <name>Moby Dick</name>
       <author>Herman Melville</author>
    </book>
  </SOAP-ENV:Body>
</SOAP-ENV:Envelope>
```

Upon sending the document shown in Listing 8-2, we would expect a valid response from the service as it should have passed the Validate action in the request and generated a response. Figure 8-21 shows the response received after submitting the request document shown in Listing 8-2. Notice that a response code of 200 was returned with the response document that was fetched from the request rule within the service. This would indicate that the request and response were both successful.

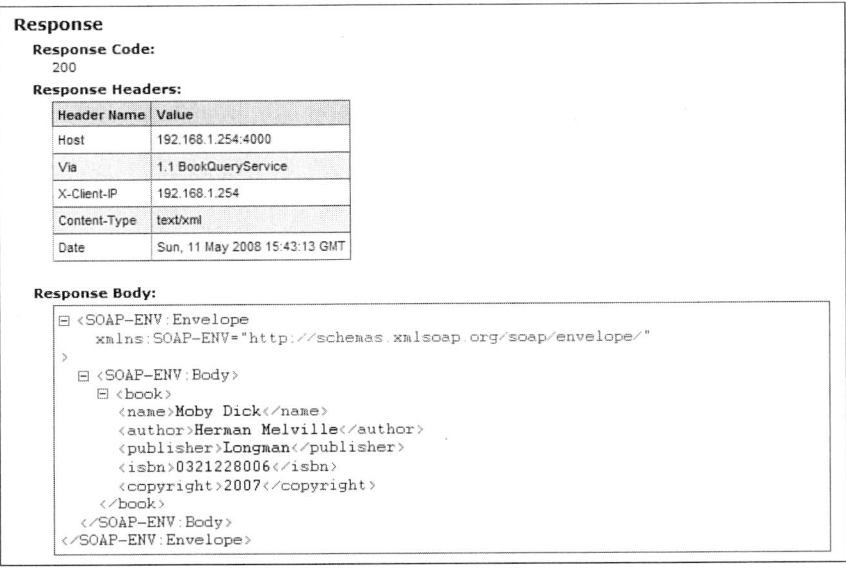

Response

Response Code:
200

Response Headers:

Header Name	Value
Host	192.168.1.254:4000
Via	1.1 BookQueryService
X-Client-IP	192.168.1.254
Content-Type	text/xml
Date	Sun, 11 May 2008 15:43:13 GMT

Response Body:

```
⊟ <SOAP-ENV:Envelope
    xmlns:SOAP-ENV="http://schemas.xmlsoap.org/soap/envelope/"
  >
  ⊟ <SOAP-ENV:Body>
    ⊟ <book>
        <name>Moby Dick</name>
        <author>Herman Melville</author>
        <publisher>Longman</publisher>
        <isbn>0321228006</isbn>
        <copyright>2007</copyright>
      </book>
    </SOAP-ENV:Body>
</SOAP-ENV:Envelope>
```

Figure 8-21 BookQueryService response.

We received a valid response from the service as expected but how can we be sure that the request document was validated against the schema specified in the configuration? We can take a look at the DataPower logs to see that this was accomplished. Figure 8-22 shows a portion of the log from this request. Notice that the input was parsed as SOAP and was validated against the bookQueryRequest.xsd schema.

11:43:13	xmlparse	debug	15377	>	192.168.1.254		xmlfirewall (BookQueryService): Finished parsing local:///bookQueryResponse.xml
11:43:13	xmlparse	debug	15377	>	192.168.1.254		xmlfirewall (BookQueryService): Parsing document 'local:///bookQueryResponse.xml'
11:43:13	multistep	info	15377	>	192.168.1.254	0x80c00002	xmlfirewall (BookQueryService): rule (BookQueryService_rule_0): #1 Parse input as SOAP and validate with local:///bookQueryRequest.xsd, attempt pipeline completed ok.
11:43:13	xmlparse	debug	15377	>	192.168.1.254		xmlfirewall (BookQueryService): Finished parsing http://192.168.1.254:4000/
11:43:13	xmlparse	debug	15377	>	192.168.1.254		xmlfirewall (BookQueryService): Parsing document 'http://192.168.1.254:4000/'

Figure 8-22 BookQueryService request log.

Now we have proven that a valid, schema-compliant SOAP request document will be processed by the XMLFW and return a response SOAP document. Let's see what happens if the request document does not comply with the schema used in the validation step within the service. To do this, we can change our request document so that it no longer conforms to the schema being used to validate it within the service. To accomplish this we add an additional node to the document called <publisher> as shown in Listing 8-3.

Listing 8-3 Invalid BookQueryService Request Document

```
<?xml version='1.0' ?>
<SOAP-ENV:Envelope
xmlns:SOAP-ENV="http://schemas.xmlsoap.org/soap/envelope/">
  <SOAP-ENV:Body>
    <book>
       <name>Moby Dick</name>
       <author>Herman Melville</author>
       <publisher>xyz Publishing</publisher>
    </book>
  </SOAP-ENV:Body>
</SOAP-ENV:Envelope>
```

After submitting this invalid request, you can see in Figure 8-23 that we get a return code of 500 with a SOAP fault returned in the response body.

If we take a look at the log from the request, shown in Figure 8-24, you can see that the request was rejected due to a validation error. It indicates that the service found a node called <publisher> when it expected to find an end element. This can be handy when determining the cause of the validation error.

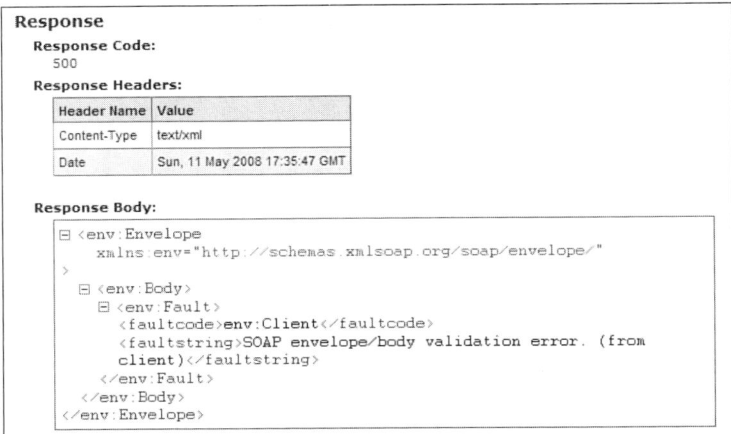

Figure 8-23 Response from Invalid BookQueryService request.

22:14:30	xmlfirewall	error	4162	e	192.168.1.102	0x00d30006	xmlfirewall (BookQueryService): SOAP envelope/body validation error.
22:14:30	xmlfirewall	warn	4162		192.168.1.102	0x80e0007d	xmlfirewall (BookQueryService): Generated error on URL 'http://192.168.1.254:4000/': <?xml version="1.0" encoding="UTF-8"?> <env:Envelope xmlns:env="http://schemas.xmlsoap.org/soap/envelope/"><env:Body><env:Fault><faultcode>env:Client</faultcode><faultstring>SOAP envelope/body validation error. (from client)</faultstring></env:Fault></env:Body></env:Envelope>
22:14:30	multistep	error	4162		192.168.1.102	0x00d30006	xmlfirewall (BookQueryService): SOAP envelope/body validation error.
22:14:30	multistep	error	4162	>	192.168.1.102	0x80c00009	xmlfirewall (BookQueryService): request BookQueryService_rule_0 #1 Parse input as SOAP and validate with local:///bookQueryRequest.xsd, attempt pipeline failed: http://192.168.1.254:4000/:8: cvc-complex-type 2.4: in element book with anonymous type, found <publisher> (in default namespace), but next item should be end-element
22:14:30	xmlparse	error	4162	>	192.168.1.102	0x80e003aa	xmlfirewall (BookQueryService): http://192.168.1.254:4000/:8: cvc-complex-type 2.4: in element book with anonymous type, found <publisher> (in default namespace), but next item should be end-element

Figure 8-24 Invalid BookQueryService Request log.

Configuring the Backend

Up to this point, we have been focusing on the XML Firewall's ability to be configured in loopback mode. It is entirely possible for the XMLFW service to proxy an actual backend application or service providing all the threat protection, schema validation, and multistep processing capabilities that the XMLFW has to offer.

When creating an XMLFW service to proxy an application or a service running on a server, the URL of the server that the service forwards requests to must be defined. In many cases, this server is the same for all requests and can be specified in the XMLFW configuration itself. This is known as a static backend. There might, however, be times where this will be different based on information that can be obtained from the request such as data found in the payload or request headers. This is defined as a dynamic backend within the service configuration.

Defining a Static Backend

When the XMLFW service forwards all requests to one backend server[3], the URL for the backend server can be defined in the service configuration within the General tab of the XML Firewall Configuration screen. Before specifying the actual URL, you must first specify that the service contains a static backend server. This can also be set within the General tab in the XML Firewall Configuration screen by setting the Firewall Type to Static Backend. After this option is selected, the screen redraws, presenting additional fields for defining the backend server address, port, response type, and the SSL Client Crypto Profile to use if the backend connection is using SSL. Figure 8-25 shows the General tab of an XMLFW, where the Firewall Type has been set to Static Backend. Because of this, the configuration parameters used to specify the backend connection information are displayed. Notice that these parameters are similar to those used on the front end connection but are used to establish the connection to the backend server.

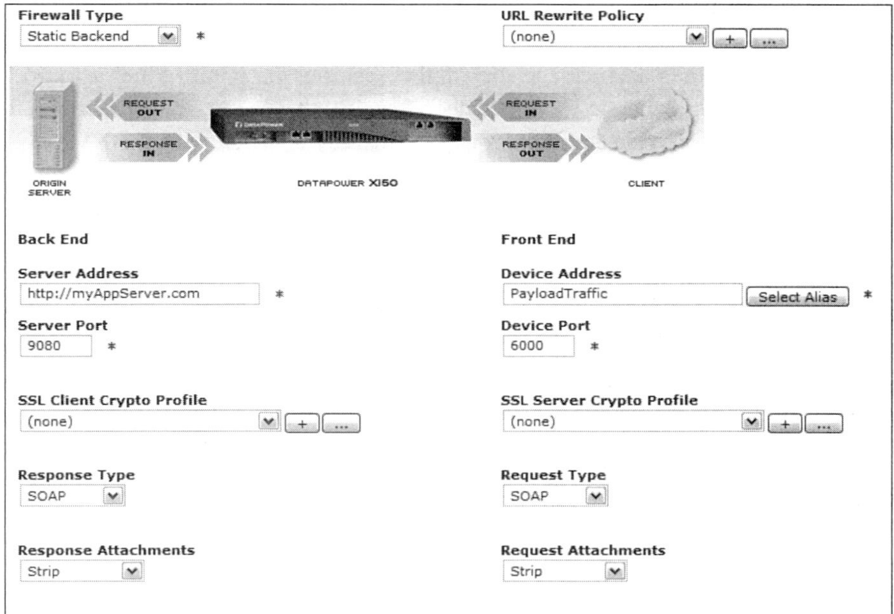

Figure 8-25 Configuring a static backend.

[3] The URL for the backend server can be a URL to one server location or it can reference a Load Balancer Group defined on the device that balances the traffic across multiple servers.

Notice that there is a separate parameter to specify the port that is used as part of the Server Address; therefore, the port is not specified in the URL itself.[4] The Server Address parameter also dictates whether the backend connection uses SSL. If the protocol specified is HTTPS, the backend communication will be over SSL. The service then uses the SSL Client Crypto Profile specified for all the SSL information. Configuring a service to use SSL is covered in detail in Chapter 18, "DataPower and SSL."

Dynamic Backend

You might want to forward requests to differing backend servers based on some information contained in the request. For example, suppose a hotel reservation system was being proxied by an XMLFW service. It might be desirable to send reservation requests to a different server on a different network based on the hotel preferred status of the customer making the reservation. So a customer with platinum preferred status might be sent to a faster network used only to process requests for platinum customers where all other customer requests would go to an entirely different server and network. In this case, the service can make the decision for the backend server at runtime based on the field in the message content that specifies the status of the customer.

To accomplish this dynamic routing scenario, you first need to set the Firewall Type to Dynamic-Backend in the service configuration. Note that if you are creating the XMLFW via the wizard; this option will not be presented. You must first create the service with a different Firewall Type and change it in the service configuration screen. It is most convenient to initially select loopback-proxy in this case because you are not required to enter a backend URL.

After the Firewall Type is set to Dynamic-Backend, it is then the responsibly of the Processing Policy configured to determine the URL for the server that the request will be forwarded to at runtime. This is typically configured by adding a Route action to the request rule(s) of the Processing Policy as shown in Figure 8-26. Note that this must be done for all request rules within the Processing Policy that are expected to forward traffic to a backend location.

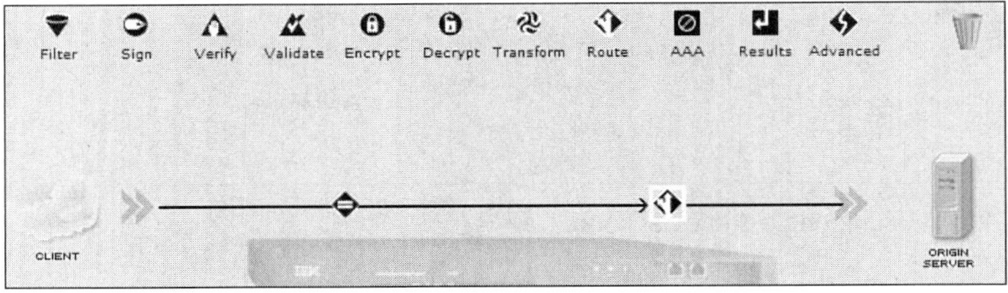

Figure 8-26 Drag the Route action onto the policy line.

[4] If a Load Balancer Group object is specified for the Server Address, the ports specified in the members of the group take precedence over the port specified in the service configuration

After the Route action is added to the request rule, you must configure it to specify how to determine the backend location. The Route action configuration screen provides three methods for setting the backend server as shown in Figure 8-27. These three methods are

- **Use Stylesheet to Select Destination—**Allows you to reference an XSLT stylesheet that determines the backend server.
- **Use XPath to Select Destination—** Executes an XPath expression against the input message to the Route action. If a match is found, the backend is set to the URL specified in the XPath routing map that will need to be configured.
- **Use Variable to Select Destination—**Uses the value of a previously set DataPower variable. It is also possible to hard code the destination URL here.

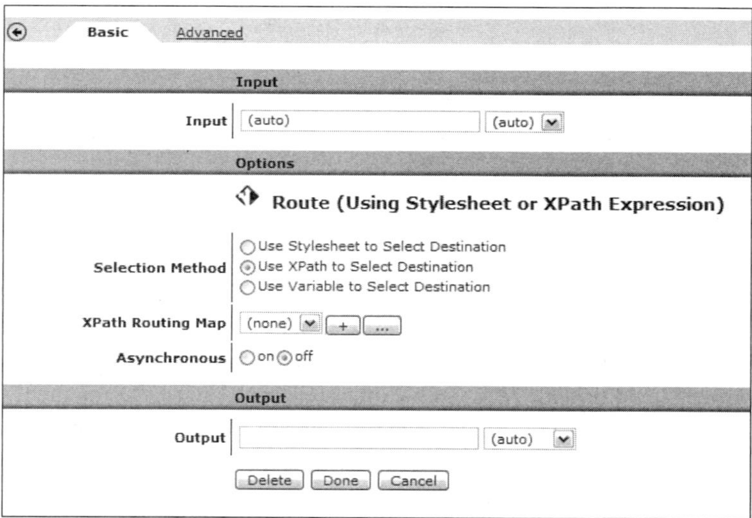

Figure 8-27 Route action configuration screen.

In our hotel reservation example, we will set the backend destination based on the status of the customer making the request. Because this information is contained within the request document, we can use the Use XPath to Select Destination option to make this decision. This allows us to create an XPath routing map that contains XPath expressions and corresponding backend addresses to set the backend destination.

After the Use XPath to Select Destination is selected, you see a field labeled XPath Routing Map appear on the configuration screen. This references an object that contains the XPath expressions and backend addresses. We create a new XPath Routing Map for our example.

The main configuration page of the XPath Routing Map object requires a name for this new object. This name should be reflective of the function that this object performs. We call our

XPath Routing Map HotelStatusRouting for the hotel reservations example. The configuration of the XPath expressions and mappings is done on the Rules tab of the configuration page as shown in Figure 8-28. As you can see by the column headings, this is where each XPath expression maps to a remote host and port.

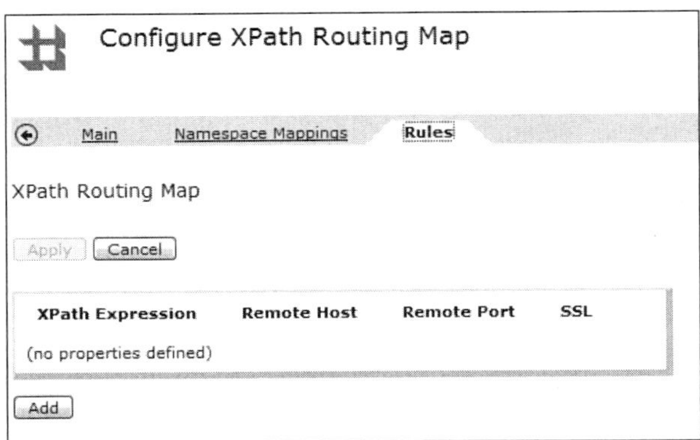

Figure 8-28 XPath routing map rules.

Let's suppose that we wanted to create a routing map rule for setting the remote host and port for our hotel reservation requests that contain a <status> element value of Platinum in the request document. A sample request document that would match this requirement is shown in Listing 8-4. We can click the Add button on the Rules tab to create a new rule for this. We then see the four fields that need to be entered that correspond to the column headings in Figure 8-28. Here is where you would provide the XPath expression that matches the element of interest. In our case, this is an element named <status> with a value of Platinum. You then enter the remote host and port that the request should be routed to if the XPath expression evaluates to true. The last field is a radio button to indicate whether the connection should be over SSL.

Listing 8-4 Hotel Reservation Request Document

```
<?xml version='1.0' ?>
<SOAP-ENV:Envelope
xmlns:SOAP-ENV="http://schemas.xmlsoap.org/soap/envelope/">
  <SOAP-ENV:Body>
    <reservation>
        <name>Joe Traveler</name>
        <checkin-Date>2008-05-12</checkin-Date>
        <checkout-Date>2008-05-16</checkout-Date>
        <status>Platinum</status>
    </reservation>
  </SOAP-ENV:Body>
</SOAP-ENV:Envelope>
```

Of these four fields, three of them should be straightforward and simple to configure. The one that might not be so simple is the actual XPath expression that will be applied to the request document. Luckily, you don't have to be an XPath expert to determine the correct XPath expression to perform the appropriate match. There is a built-in XPath tool that creates the XPath expression for you by simply referencing a sample request XML document in a point-and-click fashion.

Notice next to the XPath Expression field there is a button labeled XPath Tool. Clicking this button brings up this tool. Here is where you reference a sample XML document used for building the XPath expression. Note that this file can be fetched from a remote location or referenced on the DataPower file system. There is a mechanism here to upload the file to the local file system if required. After the file is referenced, the contents of the XML document shows in the bottom of the screen labeled Content of Sample XML Document as shown in Figure 8-29.

Figure 8-29 XPath tool.

After this file is referenced in the URL of Sample XML Document field, you can then specify how to handle the namespaces contained within the document. For example, selecting Local creates an XPath expression that ignores the namespaces within the document when applying the expression. This option should be used if you are sure that there will not be duplicate element names that will need to be namespace qualified. In our hotel reservation example, there is no concern of duplicate names, so there is no need to build an XPath expression that requires the namespace qualified element names; so we will select this option. Doing this also helps to avoid exceeding the XPath string length limit when there are many complex namespaces.

Now that we have specified the sample file and how to handle namespaces, we can build the XPath expression. This can be done by simply clicking the value in the element of interest within the sample XML document at the bottom of the screen. In our example, because we are interested in the value Platinum in the <status> element, we will click the word Platinum in our sample document. The tool will then generate the corresponding XPath expression in the XPath field in the middle of the screen as shown in Figure 8-30. This XPath expression evaluates to true when the <status> element contains a value of Platinum in a similarly formed XML document.

Figure 8-30 XPath expression created.

Clicking the Done button adds this XPath expression to the Rule configuration screen. Here you can specify the remote host and the port that the request should be forwarded to when this XPath expression evaluates to true. In our hotel reservation service, we are sending all requests with a customer status of Platinum to a remote host address platinum.reservations.com on port 9080 as shown in Figure 8-31. Notice that the Remote Host is an actual server address and not a URL. This can be an IP address, a DNS-resolved hostname, or a Load Balancer Group name.

Figure 8-31 Platinum route rule.

Now that we have configured a routing rule for our platinum members, we need to configure a route rule for requests from members that do not have status with the hotel and the <status> element contains a value of None. This is configured the same way we configured the routing rule for platinum status; however, the XPath expression matches on the <status> element that contains None instead of Platinum. This route rule points to the remote host and port for the server that handles these types of requests. Figure 8-32 shows our route rule configuration where this XPath match routes to a remote host with an address of reservations.com on port 9080.

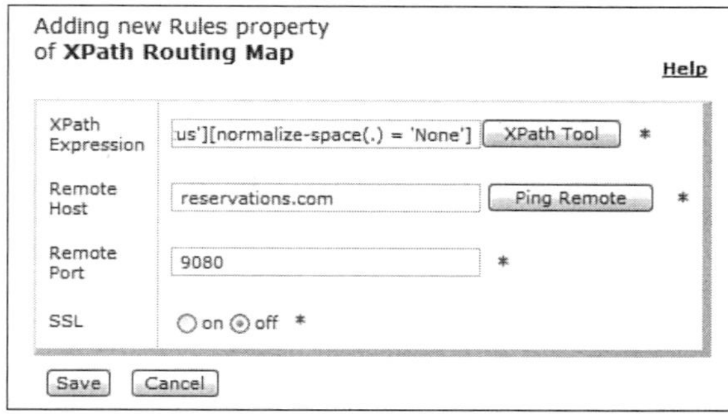

Figure 8-32 No Status route rule.

We have now seen how we can configure route rules within a route map. In our hotel reservations service example, we used two separate XPath expressions to match on the same field but with different values to determine the backend server for the service. Figure 8-33 shows the final hotelRoutingMap configured for this example service. Notice that the XPath expressions are almost identical for each rule with the only difference being the last string in the expression where one is Platinum and the other is None. The corresponding remote host and ports are then listed for each.

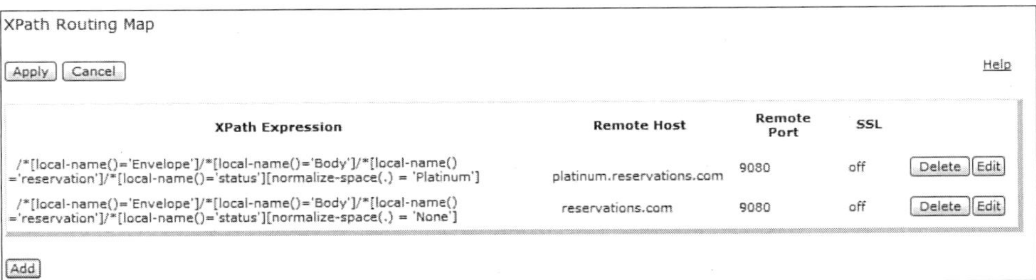

Figure 8-33 HotelRoutingMap.

After you configure your Route action, you can then add additional actions and rules to the policy as required. To demonstrate the Route action, we will not add any additional actions in our example. This service simply routes requests to the appropriate backend server.

To demonstrate this dynamic routing capability in action, we send a request to the hotel reservation service that was configured in the previous example. First, we send a request to the service that has a member status of Platinum as shown in Listing 8-5.

Listing 8-5 Platinum Request

```
<?xml version='1.0' ?>
<SOAP-ENV:Envelope
xmlns:SOAP-ENV="http://schemas.xmlsoap.org/soap/envelope/">
  <SOAP-ENV:Body>
    <reservation>
        <name>Joe Traveler</name>
        <checkin-Date>2008-05-12</checkin-Date>
        <checkout-Date>2008-05-16</checkout-Date>
        <status>Platinum</status>
    </reservation>
  </SOAP-ENV:Body>
</SOAP-ENV:Envelope>
```

After submitting this request, we can look at the log shown in Figure 8-34 to see where the request was forwarded to. Notice that the hotelRoutingMap was used to evaluate the request and set the remote host and remote port. In this case the request was sent with the <status> element containing a value of Platinum, so we see that the server side connection was made to the remote host that was configured to receive requests from platinum hotel members.

20:39:36	xmlfirewall	debug	18515		192.168.1.101	0x80e0006f	xmlfirewall (example-Firewall): Server side connection made for POST http://platinum.reservations.com:9080/ to 192.168.1.254:9080. Obtaining Response
20:39:36	multistep	info	18515	>	192.168.1.101	0x80c00002	xmlfirewall (example-Firewall): rule (HotelReservationService_rule_0): #2 results: 'generated from INPUT' completed ok.
20:39:36	multistep	info	18515	>	192.168.1.101	0x80c00002	xmlfirewall (example-Firewall): rule (HotelReservationService_rule_0): #1 route-action: 'setting route according to context INPUT and stylesheet http://127.0.0.1:63502/XPathRoutingMap.xml?objDomain=DP_book_examples&objName=hotelRoutingMap' completed ok.
20:39:36	xmlfilter	info	18515	>	192.168.1.101	0x80c00036	xmlfirewall (example-Firewall): Accept set.
20:39:36	xsltmsg	info	18515	>	192.168.1.101	0x80000001	XPathRoutingMap (hotelRoutingMap): Document matching XPath "/*[local-name()='Envelope']/*[local-name()='Body']/*[local-name()='reservation']/*[local-name()='status'][normalize-space(.) = 'Platinum']" routed to platinum.reservations.com:9080
20:39:36	xslt	info	18515		192.168.1.101		xmlmgr (default): xslt Compilation Request: Compilation complete of URL http://127.0.0.1:63502/XPathRoutingMap.xml?objDomain=DP_book_examples&objName=hotelRoutingMap

Figure 8-34 Platinum request log.

To demonstrate the routing for requests from customers with a status of None, we send the request document shown in Listing 8-6.

Listing 8-6 No Status (None) Request

```
<?xml version='1.0' ?>
<SOAP-ENV:Envelope
xmlns:SOAP-ENV="http://schemas.xmlsoap.org/soap/envelope/">
  <SOAP-ENV:Body>
    <reservation>
        <name> Joe Traveler</name>
        <checkin-Date>2008-05-12</checkin-Date>
        <checkout-Date>2008-05-16</checkout-Date>
        <status>None</status>
    </reservation>
  </SOAP-ENV:Body>
</SOAP-ENV:Envelope>
```

Notice the logs from this request in Figure 8-35. You see that the same routing map was used; however, the remote server and port were set to the appropriate values that were configured for customers with no status.

20:47:06	xmlfirewall	debug	18611		192.168.1.101	0x80e0006f	xmlfirewall (example-Firewall): Server side connection made for POST http://reservations.com:9080/ to 192.168.1.254:9080. Obtaining Response
20:47:06	multistep	info	18611	>	192.168.1.101	0x80c00002	xmlfirewall (example-Firewall): rule (HotelReservationService_rule_0): #2 results: 'generated from INPUT' completed ok.
20:47:06	multistep	info	18611	>	192.168.1.101	0x80c00002	xmlfirewall (example-Firewall): rule (HotelReservationService_rule_0): #1 route-action: 'setting route according to context INPUT and stylesheet http://127.0.0.1:63502/XPathRoutingMap.xml?objDomain=DP_book_examples&objName=hotelRoutingMap' completed ok.
20:47:06	xmlfilter	info	18611	>	192.168.1.101	0x80c00036	xmlfirewall (example-Firewall): Accept set.
20:47:06	xsltmsg	info	18611	>	192.168.1.101	0x80000001	XPathRoutingMap (hotelRoutingMap): Document matching XPath "/*[local-name()='Envelope']/*[local-name()='Body']/*[local-name()='reservation']/*[local-name()='status'][normalize-space(.) = 'None']" routed to reservations.com:9080
20:47:06	xslt	debug	18611		192.168.1.101		xmlmgr (default): xslt Compilation Request: Found in cache (http://127.0.0.1:63502/XPathRoutingMap.xml?objDomain=DP_book_examples&objName=hotelRoutingMap)

Figure 8-35 No Status Request Log.

This section demonstrated the power and flexibility of dynamic routing. Although our example showed this routing based on the value of an element in the request document, it is entirely possible to perform this routing based on any information that can be obtained from the request itself, such as request header values. This information used to determine the backend server does not need to be in the request at all but can be any information the service has access to. For example, you can perform dynamic routing based on the time of day or day in the month. This is all possible due to the fact that the route determination can be easily configured within the Route action, or it can be customized within an XSLT stylesheet.

We have mentioned several times that a loopback proxy can be handy as a replacement for the actual backend server when the real server is not available. To show how this can be done elegantly without disrupting the service configuration when the server becomes available, let's take a closer look at this hotel reservation example.

In our routing map, we hard-coded two separate backend servers that will be used based on some information in the request document. Suppose these servers were not available and we wanted to use a loopback proxy to emulate these servers until they became available. It would not be very convenient to have to go back to the routing map when we wanted to add our real backend servers as the destination servers. Fortunately, there is a solution. Much like the host alias is used to provide an abstraction for IP address of the DataPower interface that the service will listen on, we can use a static host to define the backend servers that the service will forward requests to. In our hotel reservation example, we forwarded platinum requests to a server address platinum.reservations.com and nonstatus customers to reservations.com. By configuring a static host for these backend servers, as shown in Figure 8-36, we can change the static host entries to the actual backend server addresses when they are available, and the routing map never has to be touched. A static host must be defined in the default domain and can be navigated to from the left navigation menu under Network→DNS Settings→Static Hosts. This topic is discussed in detail in Chapter 15, "Build and Deploy Techniques."

Figure 8-36 Static Host definition.

Summary

This chapter explained, and demonstrated through examples, some common use cases for an XMLFW as well as some basic fundamentals of service configuration. You saw how to create a simple loopback firewall, implement a Fetch action, schema validate a request document, and perform dynamic routing. Many of the lessons learned in this chapter are not only applicable to the XMLFW service type but can also be applied to many of the other service types. This knowledge will prove to be extremely valuable as you build upon it throughout the rest of the chapters in this book.

CHAPTER 9

Multi-Protocol Gateway

This chapter describes the implementation of the Multi-Protocol Gateway Service (MPGW), a service that is available on the DataPower XS40 and XI50. Among its extensive capabilities, the MPGW plays a significant role in the Enterprise Service Bus (ESB), an important part of many distributed and Service Orientated Architectures (SOA). This chapter introduces the concepts of the ESB, and it demonstrates several use cases and their configuration and execution utilizing the MPGW.

Enterprise Service Bus Introduction

As shown in Figure 9-1, the ESB is an architectural pattern that is used as an intermediary and mediation mechanism for service providers and requestors. By supplying interconnectivity to disparate software services, the ESB can provide a virtualization of the interfaces, protocols, and patterns required by individual service providers. It can also act as the mediator between requestor and provider with the benefit of disassociating the requirements of the service from the client. Benefits of this architecture include allowing for many potential service implementations and providers whose protocol and message structure might be unknown to the requestor. For example, the service might receive requests over many protocols, including HTTP, WebSphere MQ, WebSphere JMS, NFS, IMS, or FTP, and integrate with providers over a similar range of protocols with differing message schemas mediated through a Processing Policy.

The MPGW can be considered a superset of the XML Firewall (XMLFW), and although the XMLFW is convenient in many cases for rapid prototyping, the MPGW should be considered the primary vehicle for most non-Web service XML/SOAP use cases. Web service applications can be identified in most cases by the existence of a WSDL document. Therefore, the majority of use cases in which no WSDL is defined should use the MPGW for service implementation.

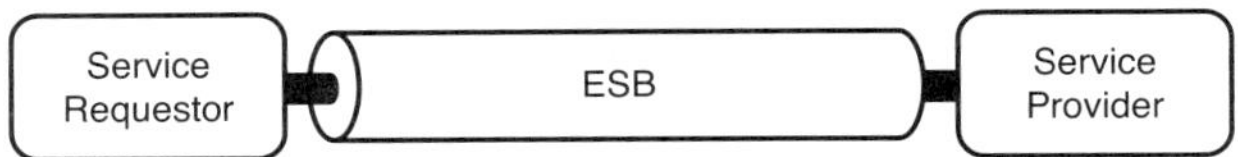

Figure 9-1 Enterprise Service Bus.

In addition to describing the construction of the MPGW service, this discussion encompasses several objects associated with the MPGW, such as the Front Side Handler (FSH), XML Manager, User Agents, AAA Policies, and the building of Backend URLs. You should be familiar with the basic patterns offered by the DataPower services and their basic configurations. If not, you should review Chapter 6, "Introduction to DataPower Services" and Chapter 7, "Introduction to Services Configuration" before proceeding with this chapter.

MPGW Basic Configuration

The MPGW is primarily configured via the WebGUI interface. Configuration via other DataPower options such as the Command Line Interface (CLI) or the XML Management Interface is possible, but not recommended. Figure 9-2 shows the General tab of the MPGW configuration screen. You should be familiar with many of the properties shown on this screen such as Request and Response Type, XML Manager, and the Multi-Protocol Gateway Policy, as the MPGW shares many of these configuration parameters with the other services.

Protocol Control Objects

The MPGW accepts traffic over the FSH and provides support for several protocols. Backend URL strings are utilized for backend communication and can leverage a similar set of protocols. Both front and back side processing can be affected by actions within the Processing Policy. For example, the backend endpoint can be customized and routing information dynamically determined via a Route action, or the MQ Queue on which reply messages are placed can be changed. We see examples of this and front side customization in the examples to follow.

MPGW Front Side Handlers

DataPower provides FSHs targeted to specific protocols. For example, you will find an FSH object specifically targeted to HTTP, another to HTTPS, one for WebSphere MQ, WebSphere JMS, NFS, and so on. You should find an FSH to handle the vast majority of protocols you'll need to receive traffic on. As we will see in the examples to follow, each version of the FSH contains control properties to fine-tune the mediation, for example to handle MQ sync-pointing or the renaming of files fetched via FTP. Not only can the MPGW accept traffic easily over the various FSHs, but a single MPGW can implement more than one, allowing it to accept traffic over many protocols simultaneously. Can you imagine having to write Java code to do this? Table 9-1 lists the supported protocols.

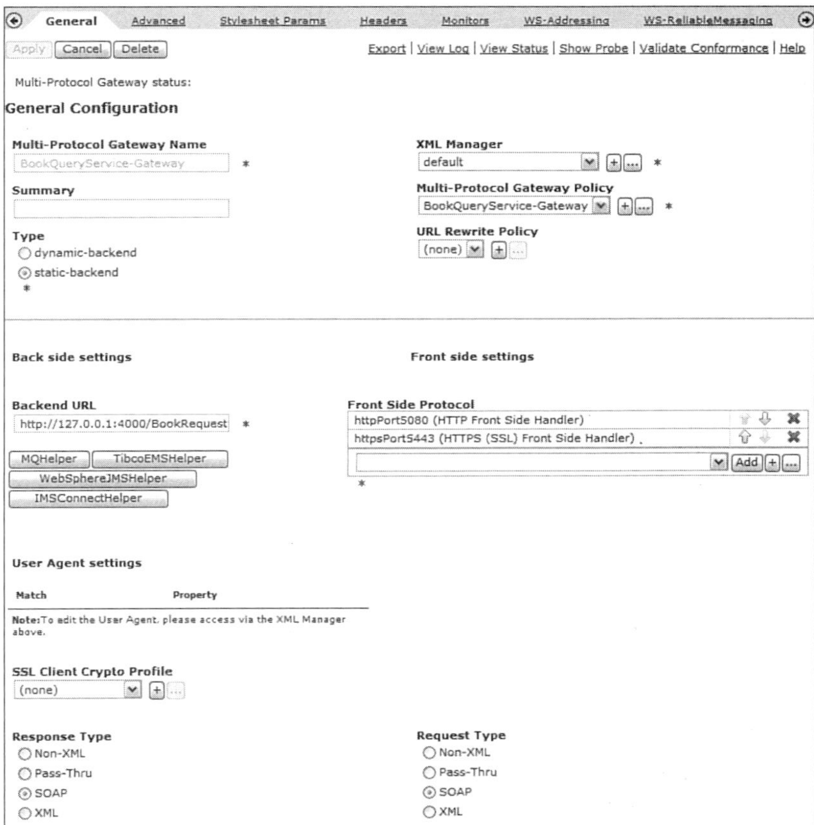

Figure 9-2 Multi-Protocol Gateway Service General tab.

Table 9-1 Front Side Handler protocols

Protocol	Description
FTP	The gateway can act as either an FTP client, polling a remote FTP server for requests, or as an FTP server, accepting incoming FTP connections.
HTTP	Receive requests using unencrypted HTTP.
HTTPS	Receive encrypted requests using HTTP over Secured Sockets Layer.
IMS	The gateway can accept incoming IMS protocol requests and can initiate IMS connections on the back side.
NFS	The gateway can poll an NFS-mounted directory for the presence of new files and place responses on an NFS-mounted directory.
WebSphere MQ	The gateway can use GET and PUT queues to communicate using MQ messages.
TIBCO EMS	Supports TIBCO Enterprise Messaging Service, if licensed.
WebSphere JMS	Supports the default WebSphere JMS server (Service Integration Bus).

Backend URL

While the front side traffic is described by the FSH, the back side of the MPGW is described by the creation of a backend URL string. This URL is constructed in a standard URL format and might include a protocol, hostname, port, URI, and query names and values. The protocol string determines which protocol will be used for the back side connection. In addition, the URL might contain custom parameters such as the name of a queue to place messages on, or the channel to use for connectivity. In fact, the backend URL provides a similar set of features as the FSH in another format.

We describe the various backend URL formats later, but for now we demonstrate some examples in Listing 9-1. You might notice the protocol prefix that designates which protocol that will be used for communication. You will, of course, be familiar with HTTP, but the others beginning with dp may not be familiar. These are DataPower internal URL protocol formats that we will introduce within this chapter.

Listing 9-1 Sample Backend URLs

```
http://someCompany.com:8080/aService/aRequest
https://someCompany.com:4443/aService/aRequest
dpmq://mqQueueManagerObject/uri?RequestQueue=requestQueue
dpnfs://host:23/URI
dptibems://emsServerObject/?RequestQueue=reqQueueName
dpwasjms://jmsServerObject/?RequestQueue=reqQueueName
```

Example Configurations

To demonstrate the capabilities of the MPGW and the use of various types of FSHs and backend URLs, examples are presented to describe typical use cases. Several of these use cases demonstrate advanced features such as header injection, dynamic routing, and queue selection.

Many of these examples use the BookQueryService XML Firewall that was presented in Chapter 8, "XML Firewall." It is used in several instances throughout this chapter to act as a backend server. It receives a request document on port 4000, containing an author and book title, and responds with a response document containing the publisher, ISBN, and copyright for the book. Please refer to Chapter 8 to understand the functionality of this XMLFW. Many of these examples will use Pass-Thru request and response types. The primary objective in these examples is to demonstrate protocol mediation rather than message enrichment, policy enforcement, or other functions typically performed in the processing policy.

Protocol Mediation: HTTPS and HTTP to HTTP

Figure 9-3 demonstrates an architectural perspective of simple protocol mediation. Client applications send requests over HTTP or HTTPS to a MPGW service on the XI50, which then forwards the requests using HTTP to the backend service.

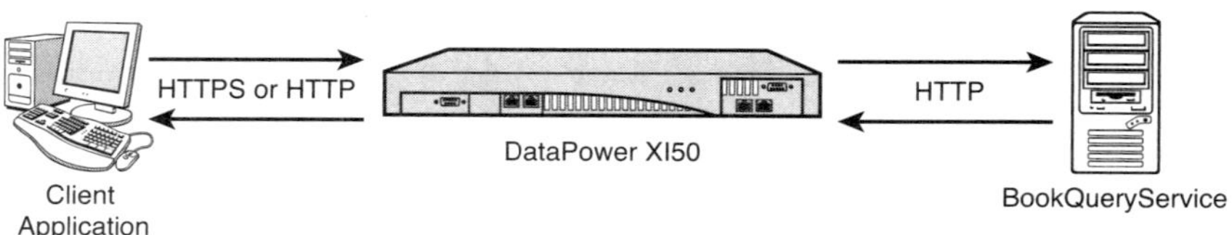

Figure 9-3 Protocol mediation between HTTPS and HTTP.

This example demonstrates a basic implementation of the MPGW. The service is constructed to serve two classes of clients: external clients whose credentials will be validated and transport encrypted over HTTPS, and internal clients whose location will be validated via an Access Control List and will be allowed to communicate over HTTP. In each case, messages are sent to a backend service over HTTP. The use of HTTP should be limited to internal networks if the message is of a sensitive nature because a third party could potentially view it.

This example introduces the fundamental concepts, such as the ability to assign multiple FSHs to a MPGW and the creation of the backend URL. As with all service creation, the entry point is the Control Panel; from there, simply select the Multi-Protocol Gateway icon as shown in Figure 9-4.

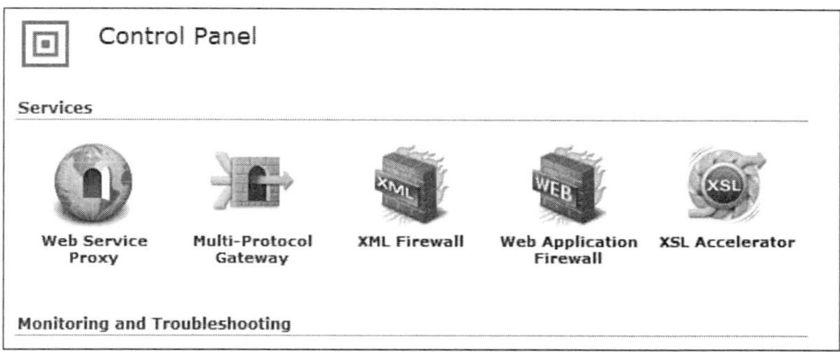

Figure 9-4 Control Panel with the Multi-Protocol Gateway icon.

This brings you to a list of all previously created MPGW objects. From the Multi-Protocol Gateway list screen you can click on any of the existing MPGWs to open them for editing; if you are creating a new MPGW, click the Add button at the bottom of the display.

In this example, a new MPGW is created, it is assigned a name (BookQueryService-Gateway), and a Multi-Protocol Gateway Policy of the same name as seen in Figure 9-5. It is often beneficial to use the same name for the policy and the service to which it is associated. The backend URL is used to designate the URL of the backend connection. In its simplest form the URL is a standard protocol, host, port, and URI designator. We can override the URI components, as will be seen in the later examples. Special query parameters may be used that affect the functionality of the connection and characteristics such as queue names and security settings.

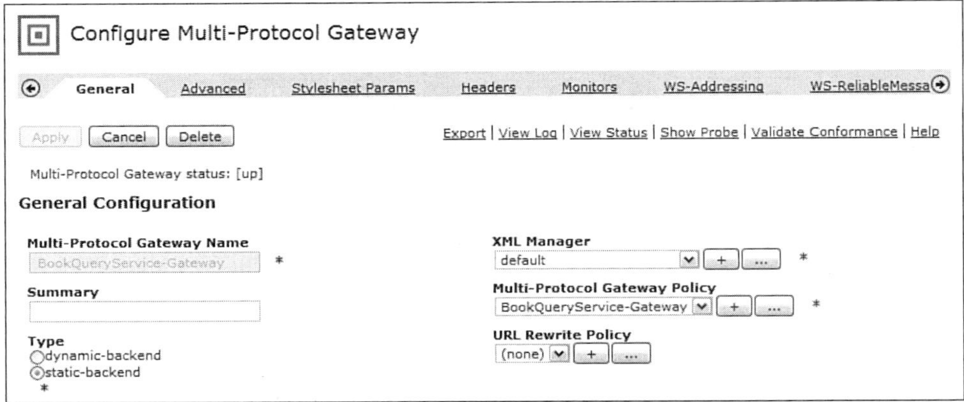

Figure 9-5 MPGW creation.

As our first step, we create a new HTTPS (SSL) FSH. Click the Create new button under the Front Side Protocol (see Figure 9-6) to expose a list of possible Front Side Protocols, and then click HTTPS (SSL) Front Side Handler.

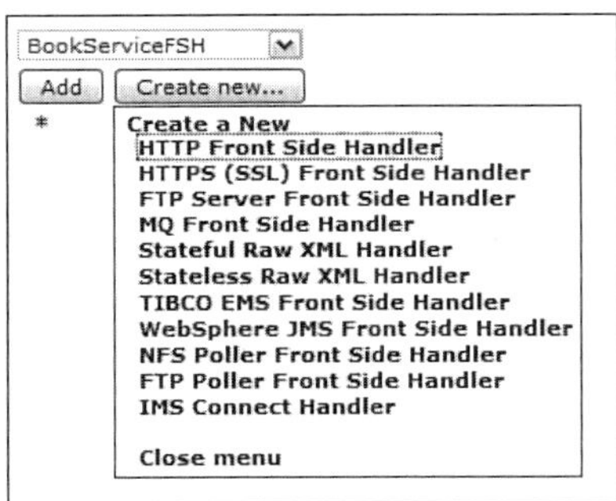

Figure 9-6 MPGW, creating a new HTTPS FSH.

The FSH as seen in Figure 9-7 enables the configuration of several protocol-specific threat protection capabilities. For example, the allowable HTTP(S) request methods may be controlled by the parameters of the FSH. Notice that the GET method is not allowed by default. The MPGW is normally used for PUT/POST method processing; however GET can also be used if this is enabled. Controls are also provided for URL options such as query strings, fragment identifiers, "..", and filenames with .exe extensions. Finally, various lengths may be checked including that of headers, URL, Query Parameters, and so on.

Our example will assign the port of 5433 for use by this HTTPS FSH. Notice that the Local IP Address has been assigned a Host Alias rather than an IP address. This allows a client request and response traffic only on the Ethernet interface assigned to the authenticatedTraffic host alias, thereby assuring that client traffic is from a known subnet. The host alias object is unique to each appliance, allowing for an environment neutral configuration in regard to interface assignment.

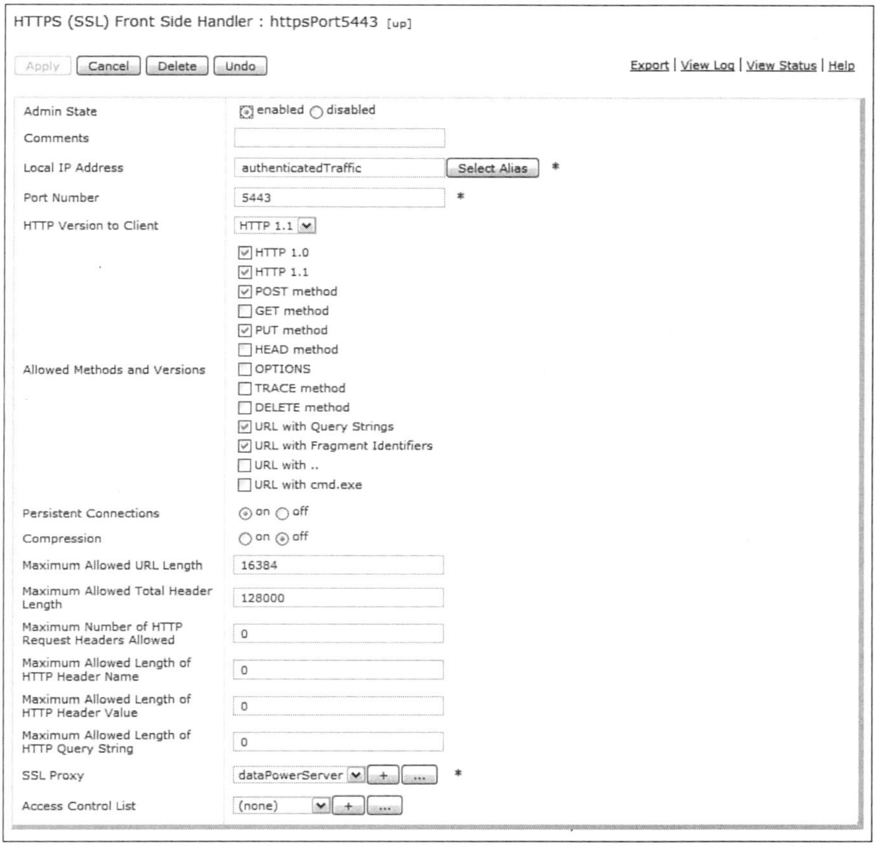

HTTPS (SSL) Front Side Handler : httpsPort5443 [up]

Apply | Cancel | Delete | Undo

Export | View Log | View Status | Help

Admin State	enabled / disabled
Comments	
Local IP Address	authenticatedTraffic [Select Alias] *
Port Number	5443 *
HTTP Version to Client	HTTP 1.1
Allowed Methods and Versions	HTTP 1.0 HTTP 1.1 POST method GET method PUT method HEAD method OPTIONS TRACE method DELETE method URL with Query Strings URL with Fragment Identifiers URL with .. URL with cmd.exe
Persistent Connections	on / off
Compression	on / off
Maximum Allowed URL Length	16384
Maximum Allowed Total Header Length	128000
Maximum Number of HTTP Request Headers Allowed	0
Maximum Allowed Length of HTTP Header Name	0
Maximum Allowed Length of HTTP Header Value	0
Maximum Allowed Length of HTTP Query String	0
SSL Proxy	dataPowerServer *
Access Control List	(none)

Figure 9-7 HTTPS FSH.

As the FSH is using HTTPS, a critical component of this configuration is the SSL Proxy object. This object controls all aspects of the SSL communication to this FSH. It determines which X.509 private key and public certificate are used to initiate the SSL communication and determines whether validation of the client's X.509 public certificate will take place. You can refer to Chapter 18, "DataPower and SSL," for a detailed discussion on the creation and use of the SSL Proxy. After completing the FSH, you need to add it to the MPGW by clicking the Add button.

Having created and added the HTTPS FSH, the same sequence is performed for the HTTP FSH. The methodology is the same: First you need to create the HTTP FSH, and then add it to the MPGW. A distinguishing characteristic of our HTTP FSH use case (only allow local traffic) is the requirement to validate the location of the client. This is done by the creation of an Access Control List (ACL) from the FSH. Please refer to Chapter 7 for more details on ACLs. Figure 9-8 demonstrates the creation of the ACL, in this case only allowing clients with an IP in the 192.168.1.0–192.168.1.255 range to have permission to access the service.

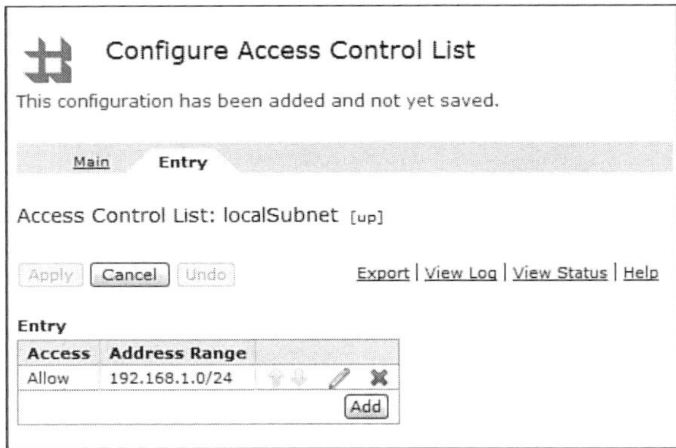

Figure 9-8 ACL.

Now that the ACL has been created, it can be added to the FSH. Figure 9-9 shows the association of the ACL on the HTTP FSH; we are certain that only traffic from the subnet identified by the ACL will be allowed over this particular FSH. We now have a two-factor approach for authenticating traffic. Not only must traffic be received over the interface assigned by the host alias, but traffic utilizing HTTP must be from a known IP address range.

Now that both the HTTP and HTTPS FSHs have been created, they can be added to the MGPW. Figure 9-10 shows the configuration of both. Traffic will be allowed on either of the FSH as long as it is received over the authenticatedTraffic interface, and HTTP traffic will be accepted only from the known IP addresses identified by the ACL.

The Processing Policy

Each MPGW will have a Processing Policy associated with it, which as in all services, will define the actions performed on transaction request and response messages from the backend service. You will remember that the request and response type play a role in policy processing; for instance, a Pass-Thru type will bypass policy execution. In the BookQueryService-Gateway policy, each request and response will be schema validated. Messages that result in schema validation errors will result in transaction failure and a SOAP fault being returned to the client. The policy, as shown in Figure 9-11, contains the request ("Client to Server") and the response ("Server to Client") rules and their Validate actions.

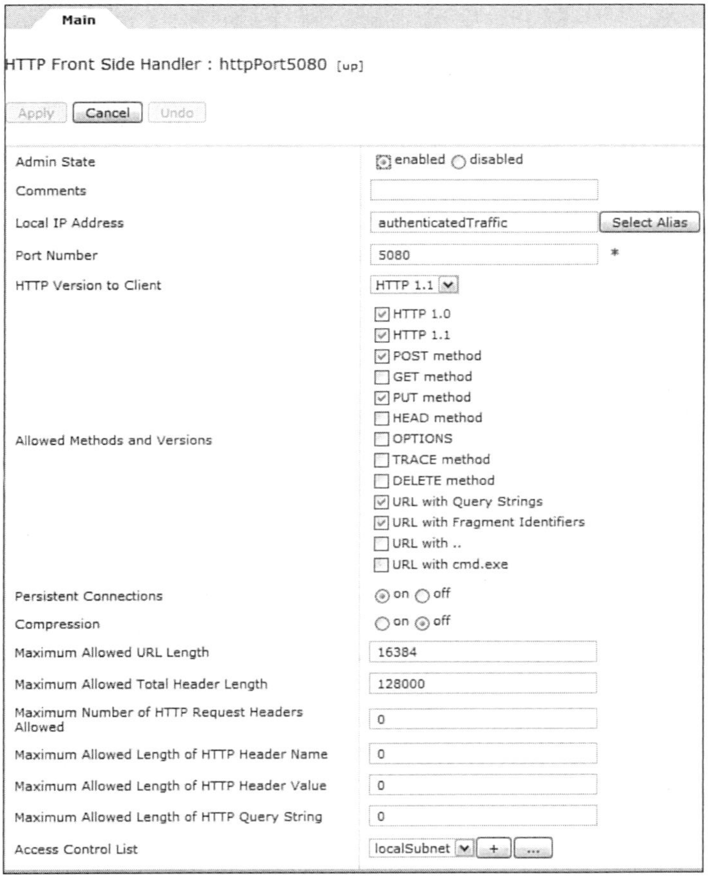

Figure 9-9 HTTP FSH with ACL.

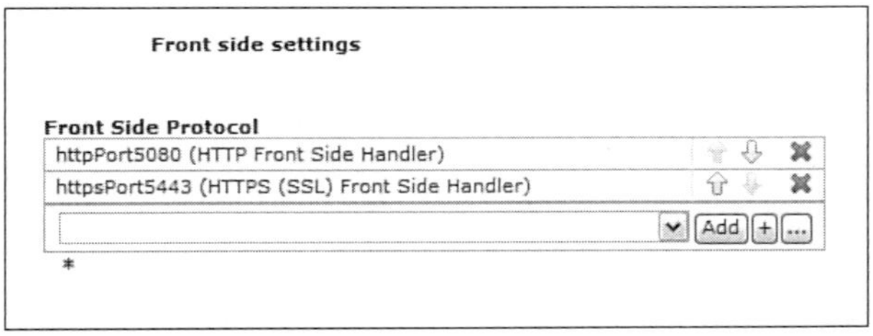

Figure 9-10 MPGW with multiple FSHs.

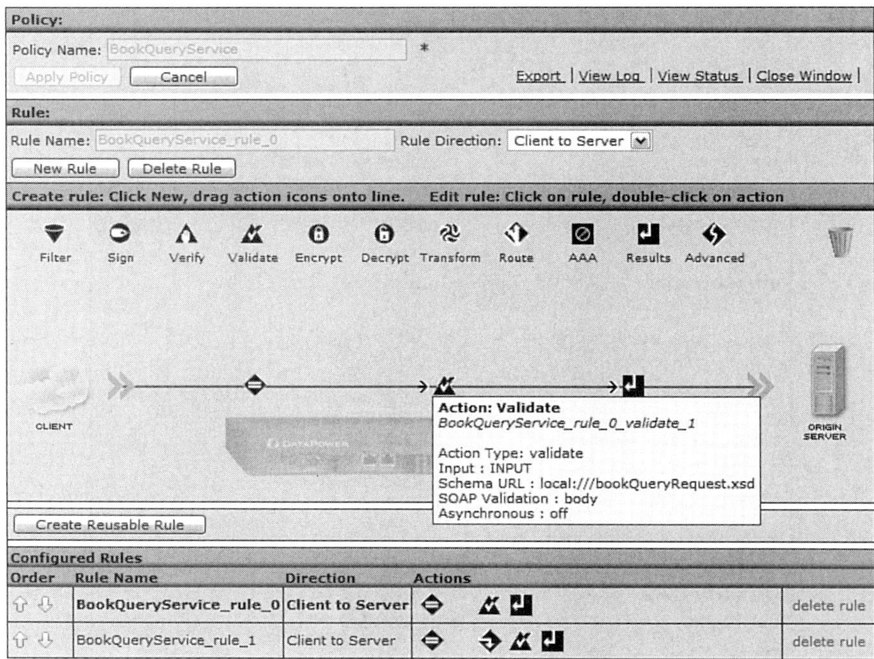

Figure 9-11 BookQueryService Processing Policy.

Testing the Service

The following request sends a sample message to our newly defined MPGW service exposed on port 5433 over SSL. We use cURL, and the -k (insecure) option is used to avoid the server name error that would have been generated by SSL by not validating the server's SSL certificate. You can use the --help option of cURL for further explanation of its options. For more information on cURL, visit http://curl.haxx.se/. In this example (shown in Listing 9-2) the request document is sent to the BookQueryService-Gateway MPGW over SSL on port 5433. It is forwarded to the BookQueryService XMLFW by the MPGW and a response document is returned. Schema validation is performed on both the request and the response to ensure the integrity of the documents.

Listing 9-2 BookQueryService HTTPS Testing

```
curl  -data-binary @bookQueryRequest.xml
https://192.168.1.35:5443/bookQuery -k
<?xml version="1.0" encoding="UTF-8"?>
<SOAP-ENV:Envelope xmlns:SOAP-
ENV="http://schemas.xmlsoap.org/soap/envelope/">
  <SOAP-ENV:Body>
    <book>
            <name>Moby Dick</name>
            <author>Herman Melville</author>
```

```
            <publisher>Longman</publisher>
            <isbn>0321228006</isbn>
            <copyright>2007</copyright>
    </book>
  </SOAP-ENV:Body>
</SOAP-ENV:Envelope>
```

A second request is made over port 5080 to demonstrate the HTTP, local client use case, as seen in Listing 9-3. The request is made from IP address 192.168.1.108, which is within the range specified by the ACL. Had the request been outside that range, the request would have been rejected.

Listing 9-3 BookQueryService HTTP Testing

```
curl  -data-binary @bookQueryRequest.xml http://192.168.1.35:5080/bookQuery
<?xml version="1.0" encoding="UTF-8"?>
<SOAP-ENV:Envelope xmlns:SOAP-
ENV="http://schemas.xmlsoap.org/soap/envelope/">
  <SOAP-ENV:Body>
    <book>
            <name>Moby Dick</name>
            <author>Herman Melville</author>
            <publisher>Longman</publisher>
            <isbn>0321228006</isbn>
            <copyright>2007</copyright>
    </book>
  </SOAP-ENV:Body>
</SOAP-ENV:Envelope>
```

FTP Use Cases

FTP is used to get files from and put files to remote servers. An FTP server uses a default port of 21 for listening to client connections, and creates a secondary connection for the actual transfer of data. Typical use cases involve polling a server for files, and the getting and putting of files onto an actual FTP device.

Within the DataPower appliance, two distinct FSHs can be used to implement FTP. The FTP Poller FSH, as its name implies, retrieves messages through FTP server inquiry. The FTP Server FSH is used to implement the functionality of an FTP server on the appliance or in conjunction with an off device FTP server.

The FTP Poller process and the documents it receives can be associated with and processed by Processing Policy actions. A remote FTP server can be accessed and queried for document availability. After a document is fetched it is processed like any other request. Actions such as message enrichment might be performed, or perhaps the request is authenticated. After the message is processed, it can be sent to a backend resource such as an MQ queue or to an application over HTTP. The point here is that where the message came from is irrelevant; the processing capabilities of the ESB are enacted, and the protocol has been decoupled from the service. The request that we demonstrated over HTTP can be processed by fetching the request from an FTP server just as easily!

The FTP Server FSH acts as a façade and can be used in conjunction with another FTP server that resides off the appliance. It can also use the DataPower device's on-board file system to respond to GET/PUT requests and eliminates the need for an actual off box FTP server. The FTP Server FSH property Filesystem-Type controls this behavior as we see in the examples that follow.

Although front side processing of FTP resources is provided via the FSH, backend FTP resources are accessed via the FTP URL construction, as is the case with other supported backend protocols. We'll see some actual use cases, but for now, an example of the FTP URL is presented in Listing 9-4.

Listing 9-4 Backend URL Example

```
ftp://user:password@host:port/URI?queryParameters
```

We're now going to put this together with three functioning examples of FTP use cases. They are

- **An FTP Poller with User Agent for injection of Username and Password**— This example performs authenticated fetches of requests for the BookQueryService from an FTP server, processes the request, and returns responses to the FTP server.
- **An FTP server with Transparent Filesystem and Password AAA Policy**—This example demonstrates the use of the device as an authentication gateway to an off device FTP server.
- **An FTP server with Virtual Ephemeral Filesystem**—This example demonstrates the use of the device as a virtual FTP server, with the PUTs of BookQueryService requests, processing of the request, and the GETs of BookQueryService responses.

FTP Poller with User Agent for Username and Password

This example demonstrates the extraction of a document from an FTP server via an FTP Poller FSH as seen in Figure 9-12. An XML Manager with an associated User Agent will be utilized to provide credentials to the FTP server. The User Agent is contained as a property of the XML Manager. The XML Manager is defined on the FSH. We'll see exactly how this is done shortly.

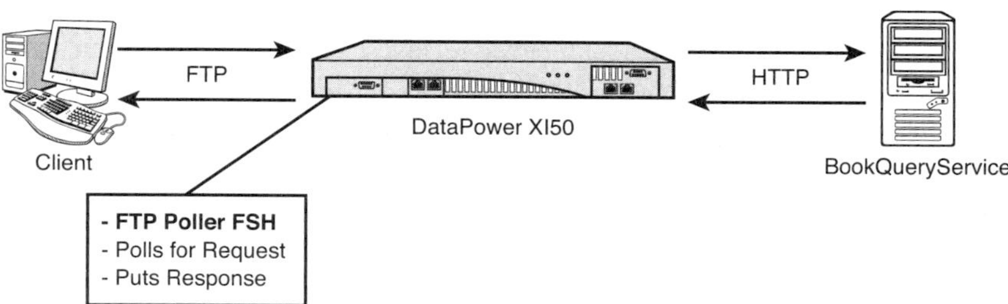

Figure 9-12 FTP Poller with User Agent example.

Front Side Handler

The FTP Poller Front Side Handler can define the access and control the fetching of documents from an external FTP server. In this case, the external FTP server is located at ftp://192.168.1.102/book/ftp/, which is used as the target Directory URL. The default FTP server listening port of 21 is assumed. Documents that match the regular expression "^(.*)(.ftp)" (all documents that end in ftp) in the target directory are fetched from the server.

The FSH can control whether files are deleted or renamed during successful and failed operations. Figure 9-13 shows several of the associated properties. The "$1" in the property values refers to the first component (designated by the first pair of parentheses) of the name of the file that was fetched. So, as the property Success File Renaming Pattern contains $1.processed.ok, the file is renamed with a processed.ok suffix on successful completion. When documents are fetched from the FTP server, they are temporarily renamed so that other clients do not fetch them while they are being processed. This is referred to as the "seize" mechanism. Properties on the FSH can control this behavior, though the default functionality should work in most cases and is used here. The renaming process uses a pattern of filename.serial.domain.poller.timestamp (renamed input file, serial number of the appliance, domain of the polling object, the name of the polling object, timestamp), and with the default case, the filename portion will remain the same as the original request.

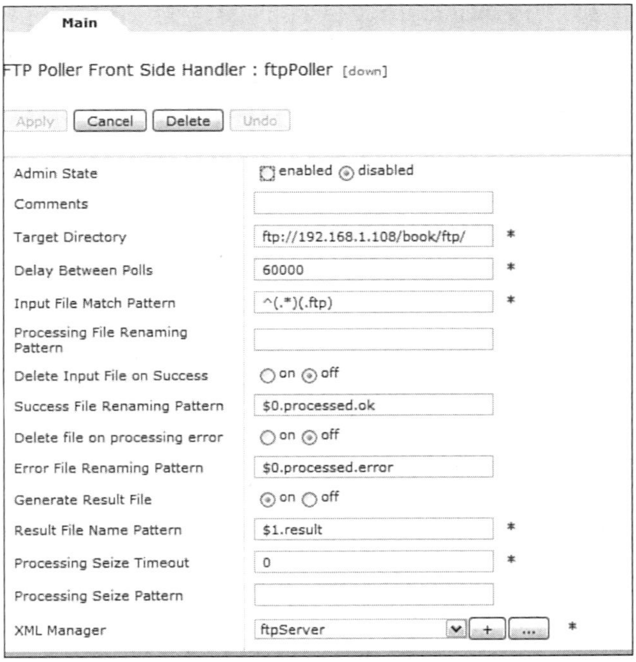

Figure 9-13 FTP Poller FSH with XML Manager defined.

Use of User Agent to Provide Passwords

The particular FTP server in use in these examples requires authenticated access. We could have coded the username and password on the FSH target Directory URL, ftp://user:password@ 192.168.1.102/book/ftp/. However, this would have the undesirable consequence of displaying this potentially sensitive information in log files.

An alternative and more secure method would be to use a User Agent to supply these credentials. A User Agent is defined as an object that makes a request on the behalf of another process.

In this case, as you can see in Figure 9-14, the User Agent is defined on the XML Manager object identified on the FTP Poller FSH. The XML Manager controls a number of other functions, such as caching mechanisms, and can be defined at several other levels in the DataPower configuration. Figure 9-14 shows the XML Manager and the User Agent that have been created.

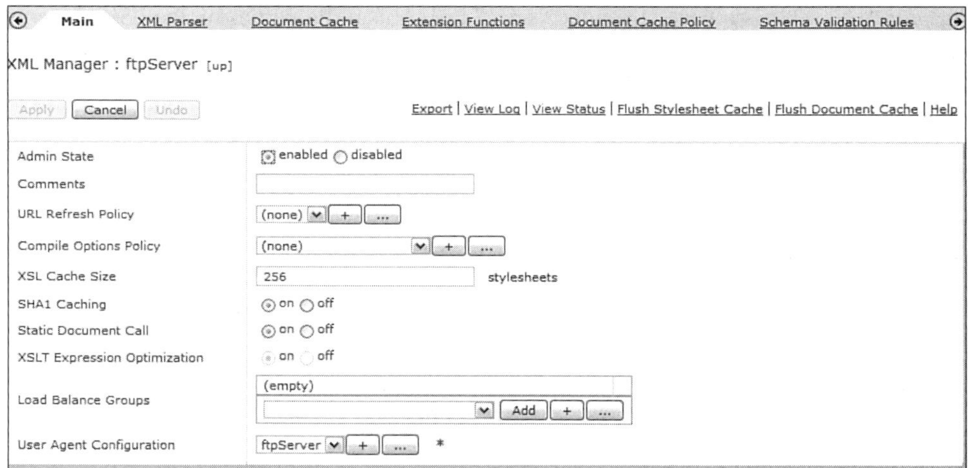

Figure 9-14 XML Manager with User Agent.

In this case, the User Agent Basic-Auth Policy is utilized to inject username and password information. Notice that the wildcard of * has been used in Figure 9-15. Other match expressions could have been configured to provide a fine-grained credential policy. This policy simply replaces the username and password for all requests.

The MPGW Service

Having defined the FSH, XML Manager, and User Agent, the configuration of the MPGW is a straightforward process. The Front Side Protocol list as shown in Figure 9-16 displays all handlers previously created. (We could create additional handlers from this screen.) The backend URL is entered as http://127.0.0.1:4000 (the BookQueryService XMLFW). The 127.0.0.1 IP address is used to identify the local appliance. As this service will be receiving and returning SOAP documents, the Request and Response Types have been set to SOAP.

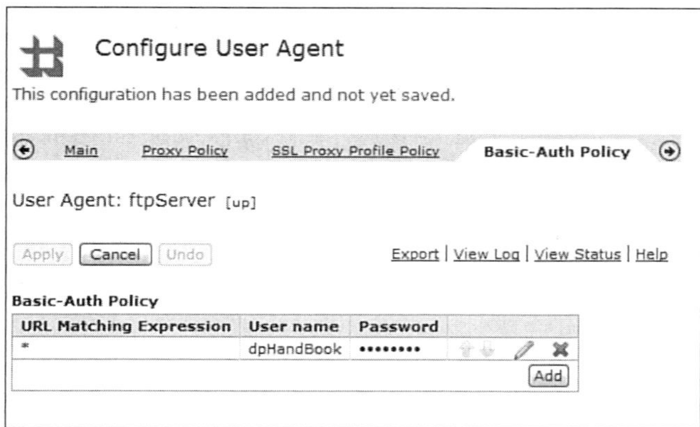

Figure 9-15 User Agent with Basic-Auth Policy.

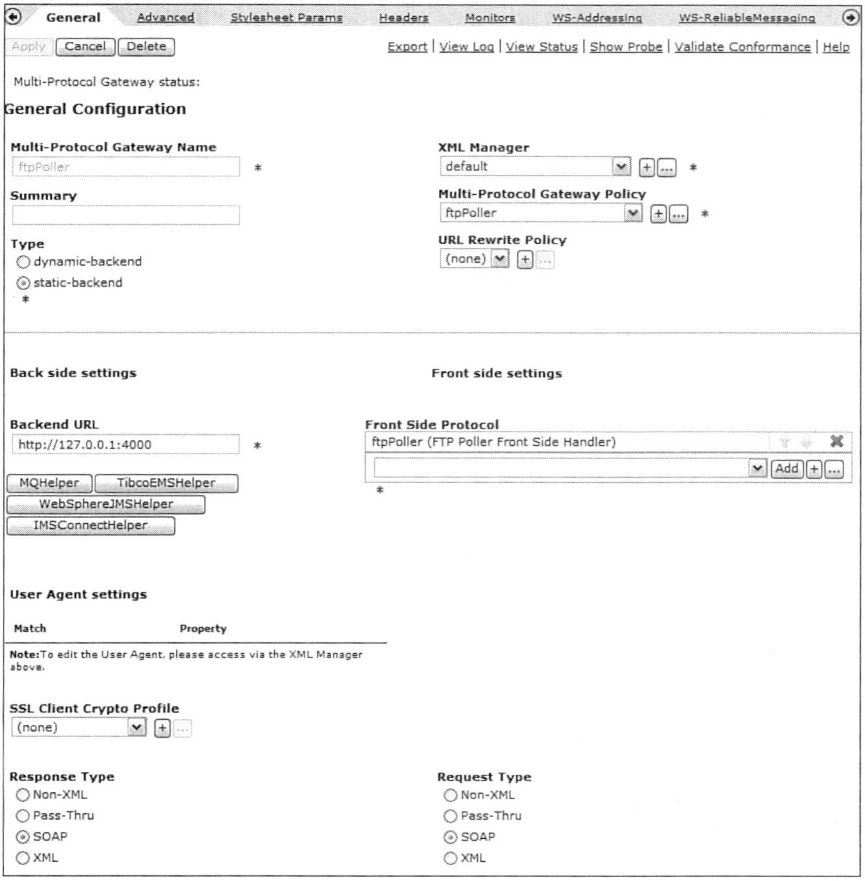

General | Advanced | Stylesheet Params | Headers | Monitors | WS-Addressing | WS-ReliableMessaging

Apply | Cancel | Delete

Export | View Log | View Status | Show Probe | Validate Conformance | Help

Multi-Protocol Gateway status:

General Configuration

Multi-Protocol Gateway Name
ftpPoller *

Summary

Type
dynamic-backend
static-backend
*

XML Manager
default *

Multi-Protocol Gateway Policy
ftpPoller *

URL Rewrite Policy
(none)

Back side settings

Backend URL
http://127.0.0.1:4000 *

MQHelper | TibcoEMSHelper
WebSphereJMSHelper
IMSConnectHelper

Front side settings

Front Side Protocol
ftpPoller (FTP Poller Front Side Handler)
Add
*

User Agent settings

Match | Property

Note:To edit the User Agent, please access via the XML Manager above.

SSL Client Crypto Profile
(none)

Response Type
Non-XML
Pass-Thru
SOAP
XML

Request Type
Non-XML
Pass-Thru
SOAP
XML

Figure 9-16 ftpPoller MPGW.

Testing of FTP Poller MPGW

To test our service, a request document ending in .ftp is placed in the directory identified in the FSH. It is fetched by the FSH from the directory as displayed in Listing 9-5, processed by the MPGW, and submitted to the backend XMLFW. A response document is returned and named according to the Result File Name Pattern specified on the FSH.

Listing 9-5 ftpServer PUT Execution and Resulting File

```
Directory of \ftp
03/11/2008  08:00 AM    <DIR>          .
03/11/2008  08:00 AM    <DIR>          ..
03/06/2008  08:17 PM               401 bookQueryRequest.ftp
               1 File(s)            401 bytes
               2 Dir(s)  14,865,592,320 bytes free
```

After the bookQueryRequest.ftp document is processed, input file and result file processing is determined by the properties selected on the FTP FSH. We have control over the potential deletion or renaming of the input and the naming of results returned. This example specified the properties shown in Table 9-2.

Table 9-2 FSH Document Control Properties

Property Name	Value
Delete Input File on Success	Off
Success File Renaming Pattern	$1.processed.ok
Generate Result File	On
Result File Name Pattern	$1.result
Delete File on Processing Error	Off
Error File Renaming Pattern	$1.processed.error

According to the "Success File Renaming Pattern" property established on the FTP FSH, the client request document is renamed with a .processed.ok suffix. If there has been an error, the input file is not deleted, and if successful, the response document is renamed with a .result suffix. The results of processing of the request are displayed in Listing 9-6 and show that our request was processed successfully!

Listing 9-6 FTP Directory After Poll

```
Directory
03/24/2008  03:36 PM    <DIR>          .
03/24/2008  03:36 PM    <DIR>          ..
03/06/2008  08:17 PM               401 bookQueryRequest.processed.ok
03/24/2008  03:36 PM               630 bookQueryRequest.result
               2 File(s)          1,231 bytes
               2 Dir(s)  11,883,442,176 bytes free
```

Printing of the response document indeed shows that our intended request was received. The request for the BookQueryService was fetched by the FTP Poller FSH, submitted to the backend URL, and the response was put onto the FTP server. Listing 9-7 shows the response from the BookQueryService XMLFW.

Listing 9-7 Display of Response Document from FTP

```
more bookQueryRequest.result
<?xml version='1.0' ?>
<SOAP-ENV:Envelope:SOAP-ENV="http://schemas.xmlsoap.org/soap/envelope/">
 <SOAP-ENV:Body>
   <book>
        <name>Moby Dick</name>
        <author>Herman Melville</author>
        <publisher>Longman</publisher>
        <isbn>0321228006</isbn>
        <copyright>2007</copyright>
   </book>
 </SOAP-ENV:Body>
</SOAP-ENV:Envelope>
```

FTP Server with Transparent File System and Password AAA Policy

In this example, an FTP Server FSH is used to control access to an FTP server residing off the appliance. DataPower acts as a proxy to the FTP server and authenticates requests to it. This is done by using the Password Policy option of the FSH. The client signs on to the FTP Server FSH using a username and password. The FTP FSH uses a AAA Policy for authentication. AAA Polices do much more than authentication, and you can learn more about AAA Policies in Chapter 16, "AAA." However, for our discussion and this example, we match the credentials to an onboard XML document of valid entries. The client supplies a username of dp, and we change that to dpHandBook and send the password that the FTP server expects. Figure 9-17 shows the configured FTP FSH with the Password AAA Policy defined.

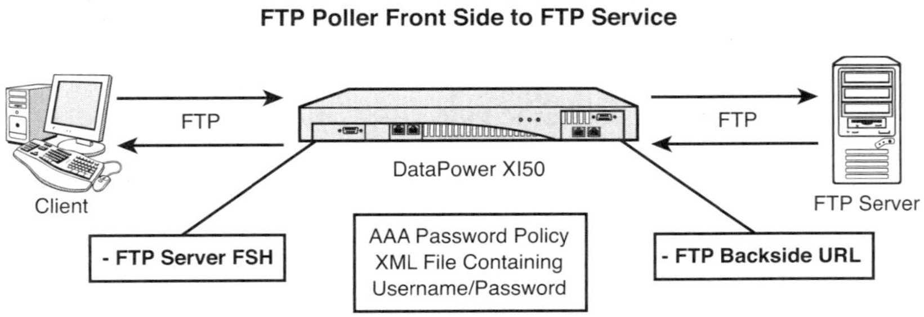

Figure 9-17 FTP Server FSH to HTTP Service.

An important property of the FTP Server FSH is the Filesystem Type. This allows for the utilization of the appliance's file system or the use of an off device FTP server for the completion of FTP requests. In this fashion, the appliance *can* operate as a self-contained FTP server. However, the use of the appliance's file system must be done judiciously. This is a finite resource, and the storing of files for FTP access should be managed as such. Acceptable Filesystem Type values are described in Table 9-3.

Table 9-3 Filesystem Type Values

Filesystem Type	Description
Transparent	The FTP server FSH has a transparent file system. The files and directories shown are those on the backend FTP server of the associated Multi-Protocol Gateway.
Virtual Ephemeral	The FTP server FSH has an ephemeral virtual file system with subdirectories created by configuration. The contents of this file system are private to an individual FTP control connection to the FTP server. The contents of this file system do not persist after this FTP control connection ends.
Virtual Persistent	The FTP server FSH has a persistent virtual file system with subdirectories created by configuration. The contents of this file system are shared by all FTP control connections to this FTP server with the same authenticated user identity.

Figure 9-18 shows an FTP Server FSH with the Filesystem Type set to Transparent. This example is intended to use an actual off device FTP Server, and the transparent setting accomplishes that.

Within the ftpAuthenticate AAA Policy, there are several phases such as Extract Identity, Authenticate, Extract Resource, and Authorize (see Figure 9-19). In the Extract Identity phase, selecting Processing Metadata, and ftp-username-metadata gets the client credentials (the username and password they signed on with) as we require.

In the Authenticate phase, an XML AAA Info File is used for credential matching. We match the username provided with dp, and to assign this username a new value of dpHandBook. The AAA Info entry seen in Figure 9-20 is all that is required. This causes all clients whose username is dp to be assigned the new credential value that is used to authenticate to the actual FTP server. Once again, please refer to Chapter 16 for detailed information on the use of AAA and the XML File in particular.

Putting it all together in the MPGW is again a straightforward process. Figure 9-21 shows the completed MPGW, complete with the XML Manager, backend URL, and FTP Server FSH. Of note here is the use of Pass-Thru on the Request and Response Type settings. As we will be supporting a variety of FTP commands, not all of which may be XML, we will not be parsing the documents. Pass-Thru simply sends the documents to the backend without processing. We could have created a policy by using the Non-XML setting and performed many other functions such as differentiating on the file being requested or posted and performing other authentications based on that information.

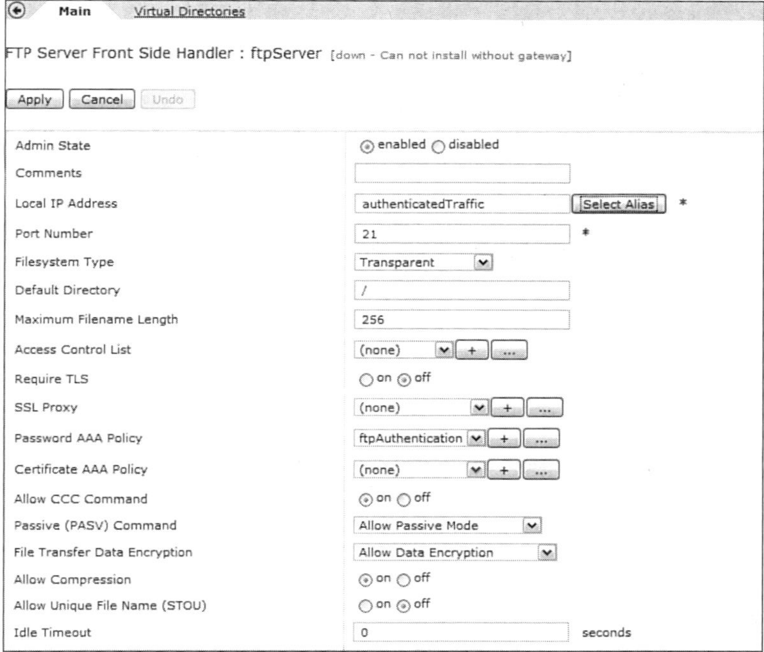

Figure 9-18 FTP Server FSH.

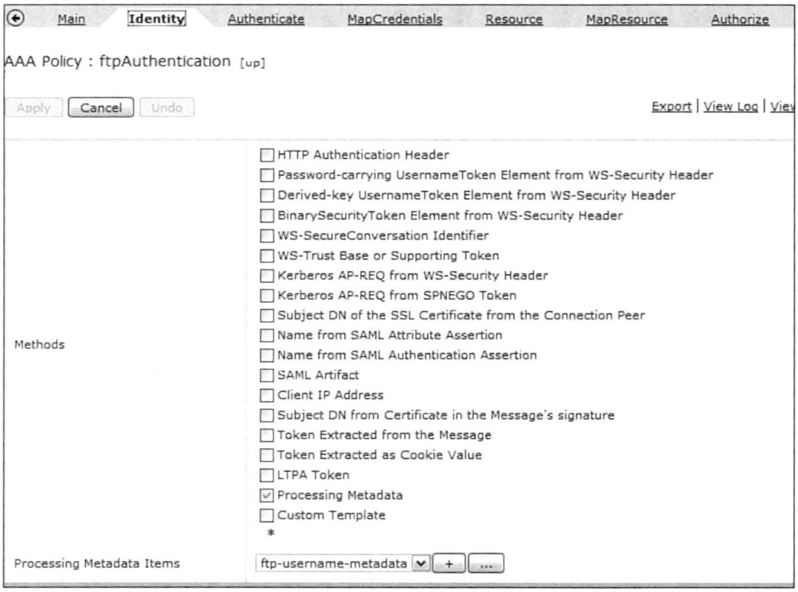

Figure 9-19 AAA identity extraction.

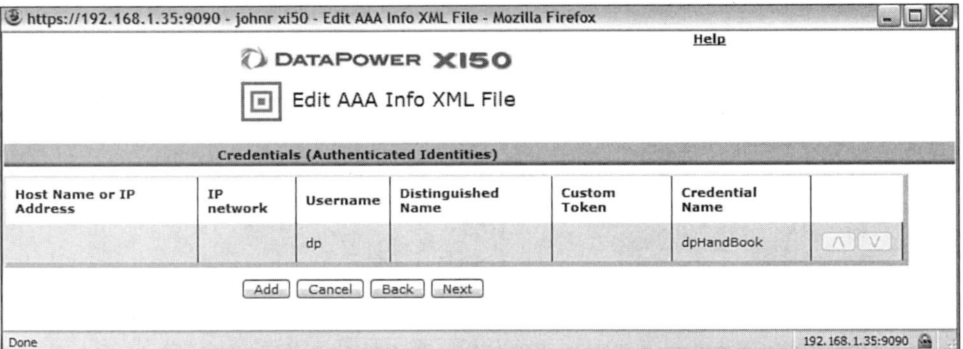

Figure 9-20 AAA Info File.

Figure 9-21 ftpServer MPGW.

Testing the FTP Server Service

To test the service, a client opens an FTP connection to the appliance and then signs on. Having successfully authenticated via the AAA Policy, the client can PUT a file onto the off box FTP server. The FTP session is shown in Listing 9-8. Notice that after the user authenticates and PUTs the file, a dir command is executed. The results of this are of the FTP Server's file system. Again, this is because the filesystem type is transparent.

Listing 9-8 ftpServer PUT Execution and Resulting File

```
ftp 192.168.1.35
Connected to 192.168.1.35.
220 (IBM WebSphere DataPower)
User (192.168.1.35:(none)): dp
331 password please
Password:
230 user logged in
ftp> PUT fo.soap
200 port acceptable
150 starting store
226 write completed successfully
ftp: 322 bytes sent in 0.00Seconds 322000.00Kbytes/sec.
ftp>
dir fo.soap
03/11/2008  02:05 PM                322 fo.soap
               1 File(s)            322 bytes
               0 Dir(s)  11,876,028,416 bytes free
```

Viewing the transaction within the DataPower log, (see Figure 9-22) shows the authentication process. You can see that the user logged in with a username of dp, and notice that the password is masked. As this is the username we matched, it is replaced by dpHandBook when authenticating to the FTP server.

Figure 9-22 Log target showing AAA actions.

Figure 9-23 shows the default log filtered to only show ftp category commands. The FTP process is informative at the debug level, and you can see a great amount of detail from it. You can see the complete interaction from the DataPower device to the FTP server from user sign-on to the store of the file onto the FTP server.

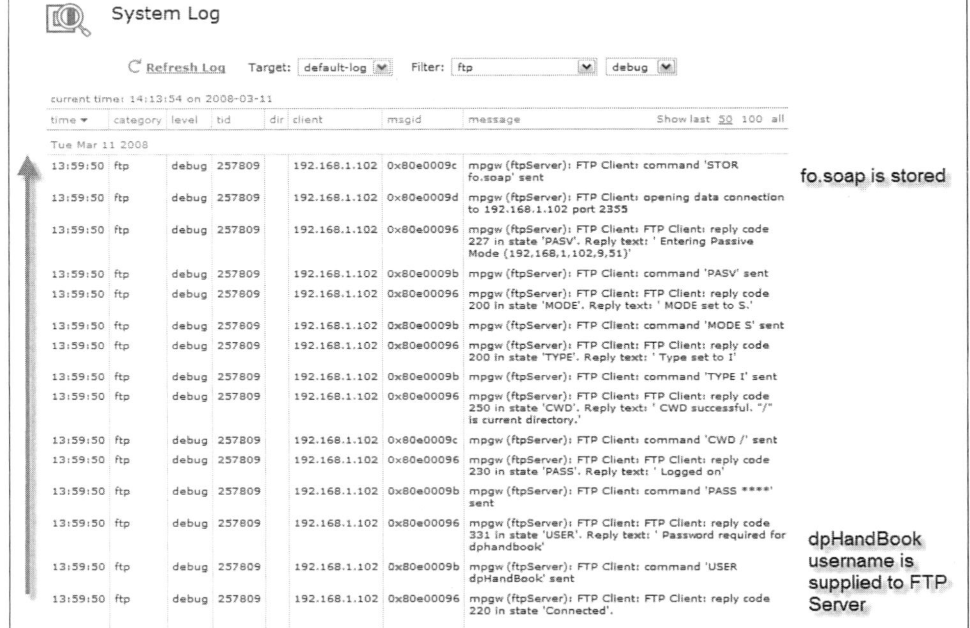

Figure 9-23 FTP Logging data.

FTP Server with Virtual Ephemeral Filesystem

The next example of FTP processing demonstrates the use of the Virtual Ephemeral Filesystem Type. This allows the DataPower appliance to utilize its own file system in the completion of FTP commands from clients. A virtual ephemeral file system is defined as existing only during the period of the client's connection. Virtual persistent, on the other, hand maintains the files beyond the connection period. In either case, files may be PUT to and fetched from the appliance. Remember, persistent files consume resources on the appliance! Files processed by the MPGW are processed by the actions specified within the Processing Policy associated with the MPGW.

In this example, the Processing Policy contains a simple Result action which will submit the request to the backend URL, the BookQueryService XML Firewall (see Figure 9-24). Again, this service will return a response document that will be stored in the virtual file system. To GET the response document, the client will perform a GET FTP command. Figure 9-25 shows the creation of the FTP Server FSH with the Virtual Ephemeral Filesystem selection, and Figure 9-26 shows the creation of the MPGW with the implementation of the FTP Server FSH. Notice the backend URL has been defined as the IP address and port of the BookQueryService XML Firewall service.

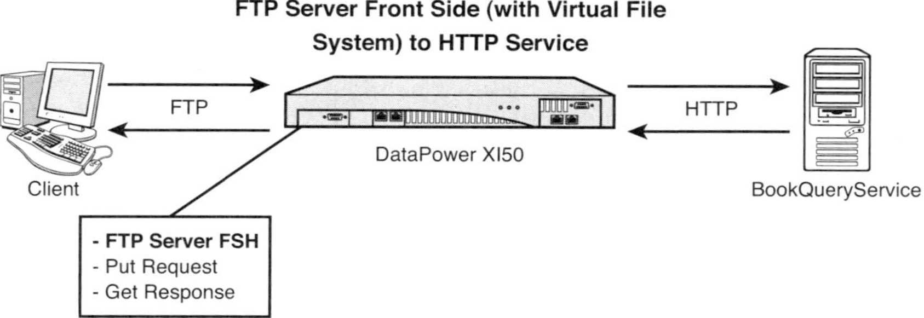

Figure 9-24 FTP server to HTTP.

Main | Virtual Directories

FTP Server Front Side Handler : ftpServerVirtEphem [up]

Apply | Cancel | Delete | Undo

Admin State	(•) enabled ( ) disabled
Comments	
Local IP Address	authenticatedTraffic [Select Alias] *
Port Number	21 *
Filesystem Type	Virtual Ephemeral
Default Directory	/
Maximum Filename Length	256
Access Control List	(none) [+] [...]
Require TLS	( ) on (•) off
SSL Proxy	(none) [+] [...]
Password AAA Policy	(none) [+] [...]
Certificate AAA Policy	(none) [+] [...]
Allow CCC Command	(•) on ( ) off
Passive (PASV) Command	Allow Passive Mode
File Transfer Data Encryption	Allow Data Encryption
Allow Compression	(•) on ( ) off
Allow Unique File Name (STOU)	( ) on (•) off
Idle Timeout	0 seconds
Response Type	Virtual Filesystem
Response Storage	Temporary
Temporary Storage Size	32
Response Suffix	.response

Figure 9-25 FTP server with Virtual Ephemeral File System.

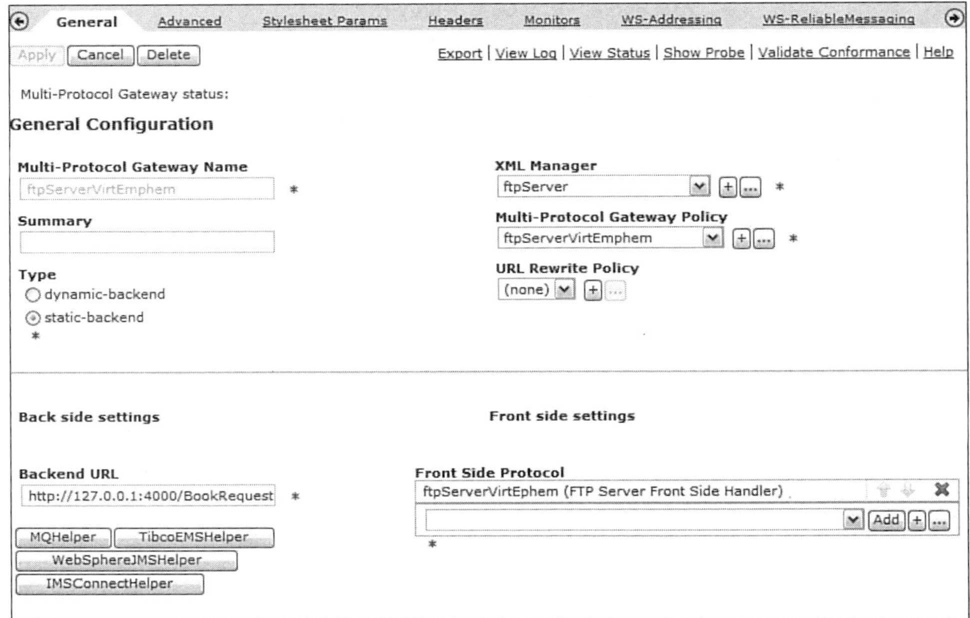

Figure 9-26 MPGW implementing a Virtual Ephemeral FSH.

Testing of the Virtual Ephemeral Filesystem will be done by putting a SOAP request onto the FSH via FTP. This request is processed by the MPGW's Policy, which submits the request to the BookQueryService XML Firewall. This results in the response from the firewall being placed in the virtual file system. To view the response document, a GET is executed by the client to fetch the response. As the file system is virtual, the request and response are deleted from the device when the user ends the FTP session.

Listing 9-9 demonstrates the login, PUT and GET process, and after having quit the FTP session, the response document is displayed. Again, the processing power of the MPGW is demonstrated, this time by acting as an FTP Server!

Listing 9-9 Request PUT, Response GET from Appliance

```
\ftp>ftp 192.168.1.35
Connected to 192.168.1.35.
220 (IBM WebSphere DataPower)
User (192.168.1.35:(none)): dp
331 password please
Password:
230 user logged in
ftp> put bookQueryRequest.xml
200 port acceptable
150 starting store
226 write completed successfully
ftp: 246 bytes sent in 0.00Seconds 246000.00Kbytes/sec.
```

```
ftp> dir
200 port acceptable
150 starting directory listing
-w -w -w-    1 dp       dp            237 May  2 11:44
bookQueryRequest.xml
-r -r -r -   1 dp       dp            253 May  2 11:44
bookQueryRequest.xml.response
226 Directory send OK.
ftp: 165 bytes received in 0.00Seconds 165000.00Kbytes/sec.
ftp> get bookQueryRequest.xml.response
200 port acceptable
150 starting file retrieve
226 response file read successfully
ftp: 261 bytes received in 0.00Seconds 261000.00Kbytes/sec.
ftp> quit
221 goodbye
ftp>more bookQueryRequest.xml.response
<?xml version='1.0' ?>
<SOAP-ENV:Envelope
xmlns:SOAP-ENV="http://schemas.xmlsoap.org/soap/envelope/">
  <SOAP-ENV:Body>
    <book>
        <name>Moby Dick</name>
        <author>Herman Melville</author>
        <publisher>Longman</publisher>
        <isbn>0321228006</isbn>
        <copyright>2007</copyright>
    </book>
  </SOAP-ENV:Body>
</SOAP-ENV:Envelope>
```

WebSphere MQ Examples

The Multi-Protocol Gateway service provides the capability to exchange messages with WebSphere MQ (WMQ) systems by acting as an MQ Client. We see examples of how FSHs and backend URLs are used to GET and PUT messages onto WebSphere MQ Queues. We also introduce a new object, the MQ Queue Manager (QM), which is used to describe the interaction between the appliance and the actual QM. The MQ QM objects are used on the MQ FSH and MQ backend URLs, and we see how they are constructed and utilized in the examples that follow. These examples use a single MQ QM; however, the appliance actually allows for the creation of Queue Manger Groups that can combine multiple QMs in a redundant and highly available architecture. You can read more about QM Groups in the DataPower WebGUI Guide.

As with all other protocol handlers and backend URLs, WebSphere MQ services may be used in conjunction with any of the other supported protocols, and messages traversing a MPGW implementing WMQ may use the standard features of the DataPower Processing Policies to implement message enrichment, security, dynamic routing, logging, orchestration, or any of the other available actions. The examples that follow demonstrate some fundamental features of the DataPower MQ interaction, such as:

- One-way and request-response message patterns
- Transactionality or the implementation of a Unit of Work pattern to control the message behavior in error situations
- Routing or the dynamic selection of MQ QM attributes such as replyToQueue, and the interaction with MQMD Headers in the assigning of these values

Backend MQ resource functionality is implemented in the use of a backend URL. As in the case of other backend URL implementations, various parameters may be utilized to fine-tune the MQ interaction. The following examples illustrate how the MPGW provides a helper function (MQ Builder) that makes the creation of the backend URL a simple process; however, knowing the details helps in understanding the URL. These URLs use the DataPower protocol string dpmq, which is used to designate the DataPower MQ client protocol. The use of parameters controls features such as messaging patterns (one-way, request-response), timeouts, and synchronization. Lower-level MQ features can also be set using the PUT Message Options (PMO) parameter. PMO parameters are used to customize the process of putting messages onto a queue. Examples include forcing the PUT operation to fail if the queue is "quiescing," or closing. You should consult your MQ documentation for a complete list of options.

Listing 9-10 shows an example of a dpmq URL, and Table 9-4 contains an explanation of the possible parameters.

Listing 9-10 Sample dpmq URL

```
dpmq://QueueManager/URI?RequestQueue=PUTQ;ReplyQueue=GETQ;Sync=true;
Model=true;Timeout=1000;PMO=2048
```

Table 9-4 DPMQ URL Structure

URL Component	Description
QueueManager	The name of an MQ QM object defined on the appliance.
RequestQueue	Specifies the required name of the MQ request queue that receives the message.
ReplyQueue	Optionally specifies the name of the MQ reply queue that contains the message the service retrieves as a response.
Optional Query Parameters	
Sync	Insert Sync=true to ensure the transactional nature of backend. The PUT to the Request Queue is committed upon PUT regardless of specification of Reply Queue.
Transactional	Insert Transactional=true to ensure the transactional nature of backend. If there is both a Request Queue and Reply Queue specified, the PUT to the Request Queue is committed when a message is retrieved from Response Queue. If there is only a Request Queue it is committed upon PUT.

URL Component	Description
SetReplyTo	Insert SetReplyTo=true to automatically set the MQMD ReplyToQ to the value specified as the ReplyQueue of the dpmq URL. If disabled, the MQMD ReplyToQ must be manually set via a header injection.
Model	Can be true or false. When true, instructs the DataPower appliance to connect to the RequestQueue indicated and use the dynamic, temporary Model queue defined by the ReplyQueue value to GET the response. When the response is received, the connection to the temporary queue is closed. This advanced option is seldom used. Refer to WebGUI Guide for additional details.
Timeout	Sets a timeout, in milliseconds, for the transaction.
PMO	Optionally sets MQPMO.Options.

While the dpmq protocol string provides the vast majority of features that will be required of MQ message exchanges, you can also construct a dynamic MQ URL. This backend URL format can dynamically define MQ QM attributes. This is not necessary in cases where the backend URL is statically defined on the MPGW service but could conceivably be valuable in dynamic routing situations where the MQ Server is unknown at service definition time, for example, if the destination QM is embedded in the message or needs to be looked up from some other resource. An example of this URL is shown in Listing 9-11, and additional parameters for this protocol are detailed in Table 9-5.

Listing 9-11 Sample mq URL

```
mq://ipAddress:Port/example?Channel=chanName;QueueManager=qmName;
UserName=uName;ChannelLimit=maxChannels;ChannelTimeout=timeout;
RequestQueue=requestQueueName;ReplyQueue=replyQueueName
```

Table 9-5 MQ URL Structure

URL Component	Description
ipAddress	The dotted decimal address or hostname of the MQ server.
Port	The port of the MQ server.
Optional Query Parameters	
Channel	The name of the channel used to access the MQ QM.
QueueManager	The name of the target MQ QM. You can optionally use the name of a QM Group to implement failover.
UserName	The plaintext string used to identify the client to the MQ server.

continues

Table 9-5 MQ URL Structure continued

URL Component	Description
ChannelLimit	An integer within the range 2 to 5000 that specifies the maximum number of open channels allowed between the appliance and MQ QM.
ChannelTimeout	An integer specifying the number of seconds that inactive channels will be cached (remain open)—the dynamic channels will be cached until they timeout—after all channels have timed out, the dynamically defined QM is deleted from the appliance.
RequestQueue	The name of the queue to PUT messages to.
ReplyQueue	The optional name of the queue to GET reply messages from.

Now that we have an understanding of the objects required to GET MQ messages and PUT MQ responses, the mechanics of sending messages to an MQ Queue and the role that the MQ QM object plays in tying together the DataPower appliance's MQ Client with an actual MQ QM, it's time to see some real-world examples:

- **An HTTP to MQ Protocol Bridge**—This example demonstrates the ability to accept a message over HTTP and place it on an MQ queue in a one-way message model.
- **Request Queue fetching and processing with Transactionality**—This example demonstrates the ability to use an MQ FSH to process BookQueryService requests, and the implementation of a Unit of Work to control the removal of messages from the request queue.

HTTP to MQ Pattern

Figure 9-27 demonstrates the architecture of the HTTP to MQ Protocol Bridge. Clients send messages over HTTP to the DataPower MPGW service. The MPGW then delivers the message over MQ to a specific queue.

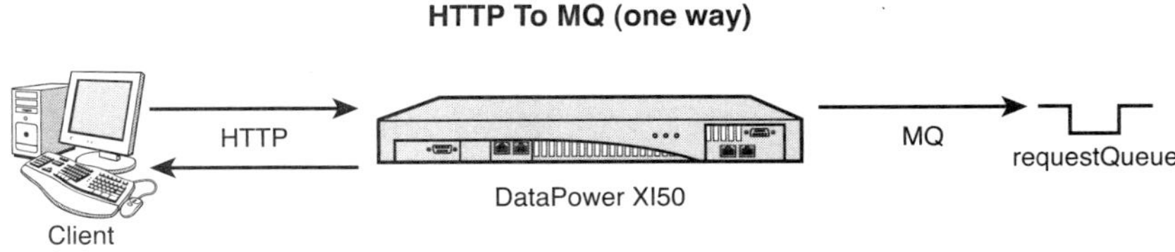

Figure 9-27 HTTP to MQ one-way pattern.

The first step in this use case is to define an HTTP FSH that exposes traffic (we'll use port 4002) to the service. This is straightforward and simple as demonstrated previously. Note that you can create the FSHs before beginning the creation of the MPGW, or in conjunction with the MPGW creation. As previously discussed, threat protection mechanisms can be implemented on the HTTP FSH. Figure 9-28 shows the FSH being created.

Main

HTTP Front Side Handler : httpPort4002 [up]

Apply Cancel Delete Undo

Admin State	enabled disabled
Comments	
Local IP Address	authenticatedTraffic Select Alias *
Port Number	4002 *

Figure 9-28 HTTP FSH on port 4002.

Figure 9-29 shows the FSH drop-down box after httpPort4002 FSH has been added. Notice also the MQHelper button below the backend URL. We use this when we define the backend MQ resource. It will build the dpmq protocol URL required for backend communication.

Back side settings

Backend URL *

MQHelper TibcoEMSHelper WebSphereJMSHelper IMSConnectHelper

Front side settings

Front Side Protocol

httpPort4002 (HTTP Front Side Handler)

Add + ... *

Figure 9-29 FSH being added.

Next, the MQ QM object must be defined. Again, you can build this object in conjunction with the MPGW creation, or you can create it prior to the MPGW. Because this object can be shared across multiple services and FSHs, it is often constructed first to ensure appropriate connectivity. After defining with the correct parameters, it can be reused without modification. It is helpful to create it first, and to ensure that the object is properly enabled prior to beginning the MPGW configuration. This allows you to resolve any network issue, such as an inaccurate IP:port, first.

This service integrates with an actual WebSphere QM that contains three queues, one from which to GET requests (requestQueue), one on which to PUT responses (responseQueue), and one to place undeliverable messages (deadLetterQueue). Figure 9-30 shows the three queues.

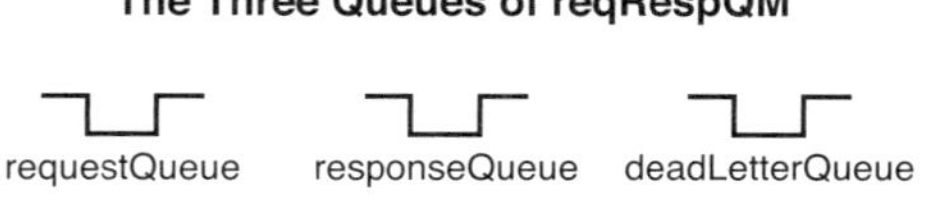

Figure 9-30 ReqRespQM, three queues.

MQ Queue Manager

The QM object is depicted in Figure 9-31, and has only one required field: the hostname or IP address of the WebSphere QM. Notice that the port is assigned within parentheses. If the QM desired is not the default for the host identified, a QM Name can be entered. The default channel SYSTEM.DEF.SVRCONN is used. Among the other parameters are those allowing for the assignment of SSL connection details for accessing MQ over SSL, credential information, and connection limits. We also demonstrate in the second MQ example, the Unit of Work parameter that controls whether transactionality, or the rolling back of messages in the event of transaction failure, is implemented. We see how this QM is associated with Front Side Protocol Handlers and backend URLs to perform MQ message processing.

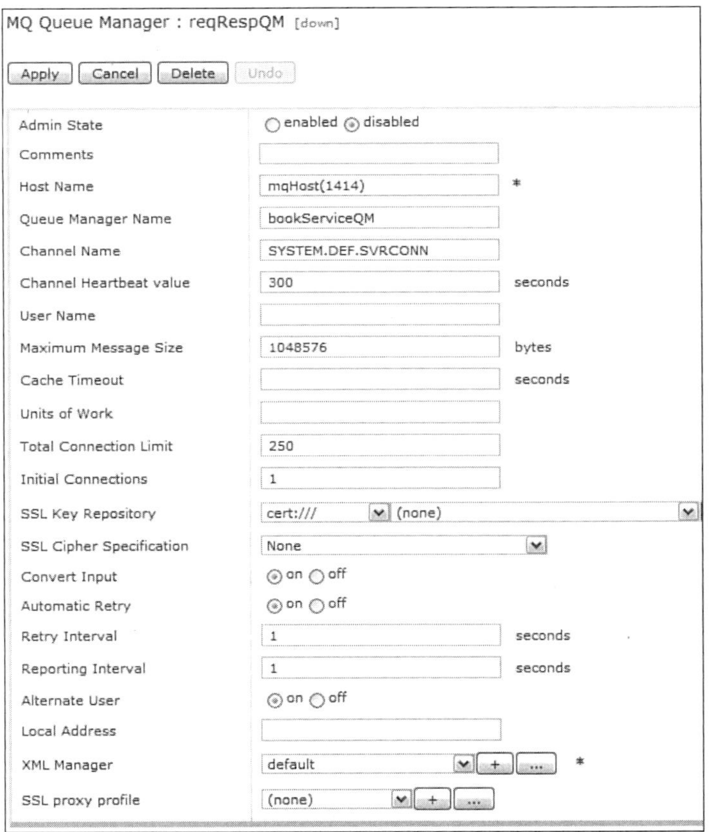

Figure 9-31 Queue Manager object.

Now let's put the FSH and MQ QM to work on the MPGW. We've already discussed how to add the FSH; now let's look at the backend URL. You saw the MQ Helper button in Figure 9-29, and how it makes the job of constructing a dpmq:// URL simpler. We need an MQ backend as our intention is to place a message on an MQ queue. Clicking the MQ Helper button reveals a dialog box, as seen in Figure 9-32, that requests basic information such as the MQ QM to use and the queues to use for request and response. The response queue is optional, and not assigning one is typical of a "fire and forget" one-way message pattern—just what we want!

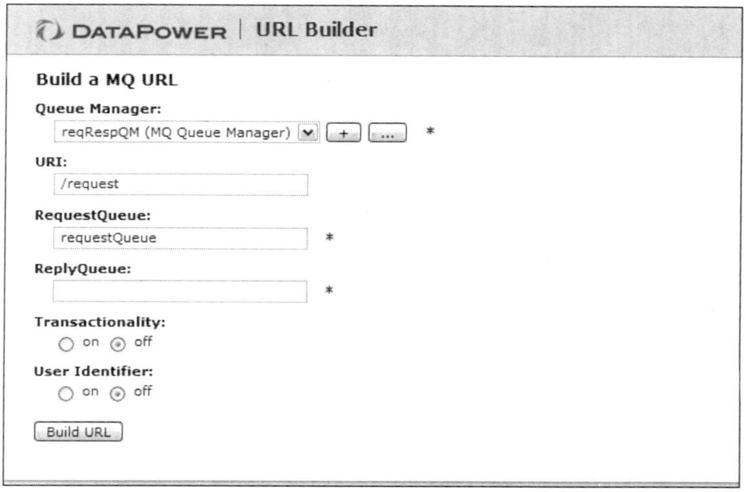

Figure 9-32 DPMQ URL Builder.

Putting all the pieces together on the MPGW completes the creation of the HTTP to MQ Service. SOAP requests are submitted to the MPGW service, which are then forwarded to the MQ Queue, requestQueue. Notice in Figure 9-33 that the request and response types are set to Pass-Thru. It was our stated intention in this example to simply accept messages over HTTP and send them to MQ. No processing of the message is necessary, hence no need to define a Processing Policy (notice that default is selected), and the message can traverse the MPGW without processing. A more robust implementation would include authentication of the client, but this is not our focus here.

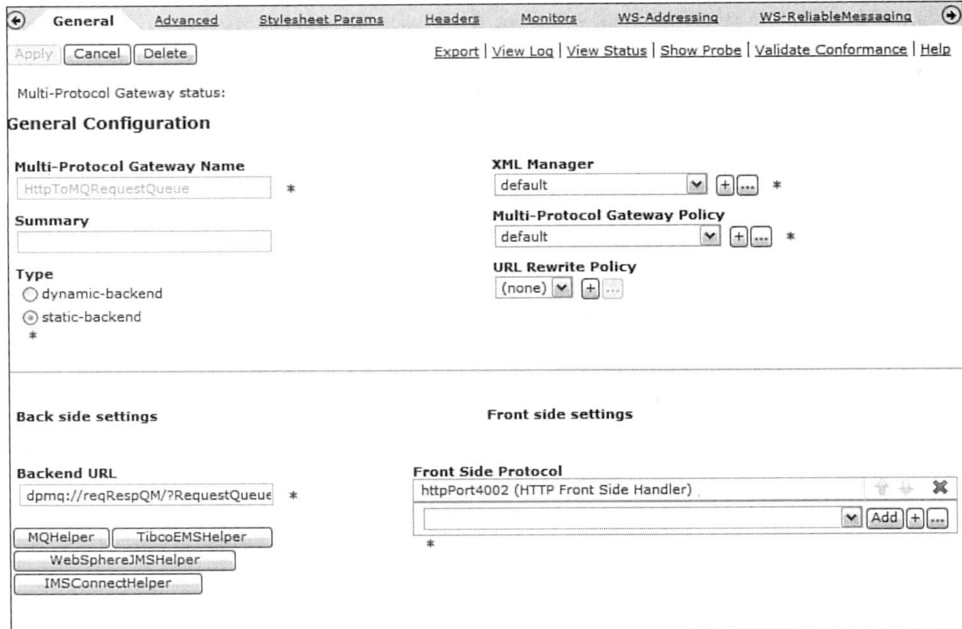

Figure 9-33 HTTP to MQ MPGW.

Testing the HTTP to MQ Service

We can test the newly created service by sending a request SOAP document to the MGPW via the HTTP FSH, as demonstrated in Listing 9-12.

Listing 9-12 Testing HTTP to MQ Service

```
curl  -data-binary @BookQueryRequest.xml http://192.168.1.35:4002 -v
* About to connect() to 192.168.1.35 port 4002 (#0)
*   Trying 192.168.1.35... connected
* Connected to 192.168.1.35 (192.168.1.35) port 4002 (#0)
> POST / HTTP/1.1
> User-Agent: curl/7.16.4 (i586-pc-mingw32msvc) libcurl/7.16.4
OpenSSL/0.9.7e zlib/1.2.2
> Host: 192.168.1.35:4002
> Accept: */*
> Content-Length: 246
> Content-Type: application/x-www-form-urlencoded
>
< HTTP/1.1 200 OK
< X-Backside-Transport: OK OK
< Connection: Keep-Alive
< Transfer-Encoding: chunked
< X-Client-IP: 192.168.1.108
<
* Connection #0 to host 192.168.1.35 left intact
* Closing connection #0
```

No response is returned from the service as it is a one-way message pattern. The MPGW replies with an HTTP Status of 200 and with an empty reply body. This can be verified by using the verbose option of cURL, as is shown in Listing 9-12, with the use of the -v parameter. We can construct a response message if we want. However, by viewing the log for MQ events shown in Figure 9-34, we can see the successful processing of the request. Notice that a filter has been applied to the log display only showing MQ event messages.

Figure 9-34 HTTP to MQ log.

In addition, to ensure that our message was delivered to the MQ Queue, we can use MQ Explorer[2] to browse the messages on the requestQueue. Sure enough, as we can see in Figure 9-35, our SOAP request was placed on the queue.

MQ Request/Response to HTTP Pattern

Figure 9-36 demonstrates the architecture of the MQ Request Response to HTTP pattern. Messages are fetched from the MQ request queue, and then posted over HTTP to the Book Query Service. The response from the Book Query Service then delivers to the MQ reply queue.

The previous example demonstrates a mechanism for the posting of messages onto the MQ queue. Our next example demonstrates a request-response pattern in which an MQ FSH is used to fetch a request message, post it to the BookQueryService XML Firewall, and then if successful, place the response from the XMLFW on the Response queue. In addition, while we can statically assign the reply queue PUT Queue name on the FSH, this example demonstrates a more dynamic methodology of queue name assignment via header injection.

2. MQ Explorer is a product from IBM for browsing an MQ Queue.

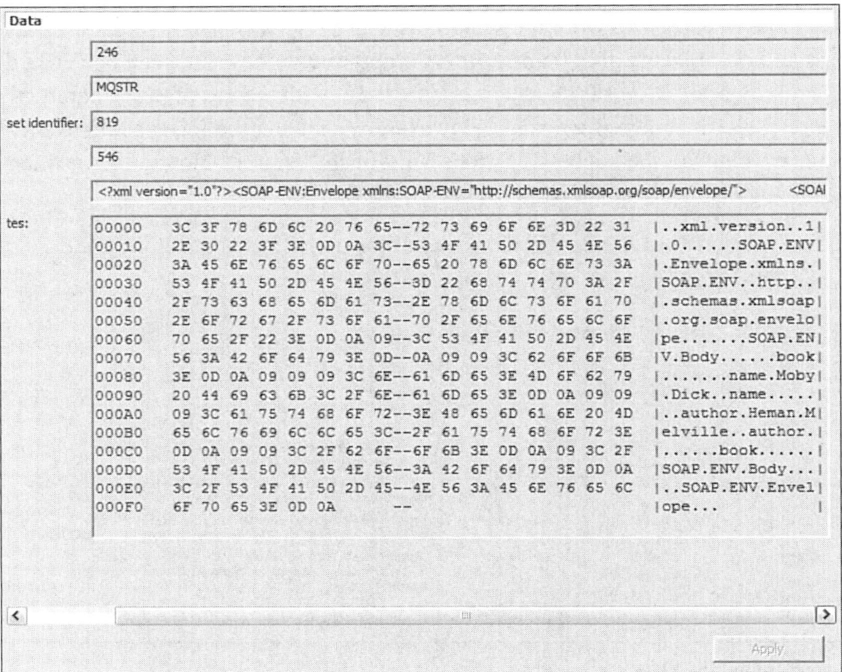

Figure 9-35 MQ Explorer viewing messages.

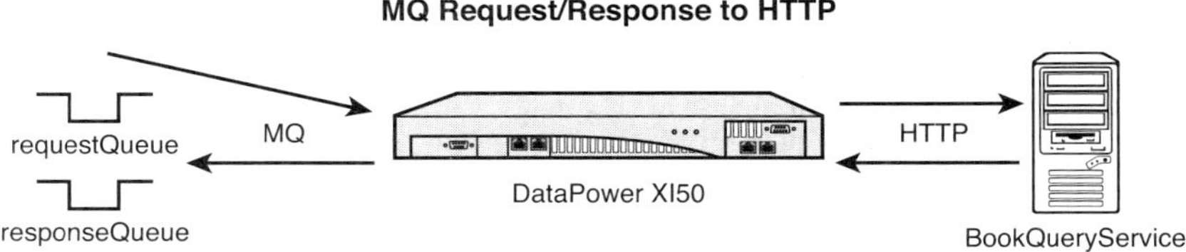

Figure 9-36 MQ Request Response to HTTP.

As you can see in Figure 9-37, our configuration of the MQ FSH does not contain a PUT Queue assignment. It does contain a reference to the DataPower QM object that was previously created. An MQ FSH also contains options for the processing of MQ Headers. Various headers may be included with messages such as Rules and Formatting Headers RFH and RFH2. To have these headers accessible, and not to become part of the message being parsed, the Exclude Message Headers options should be chosen, or the headers will be consumed and parsed as part of the message body.

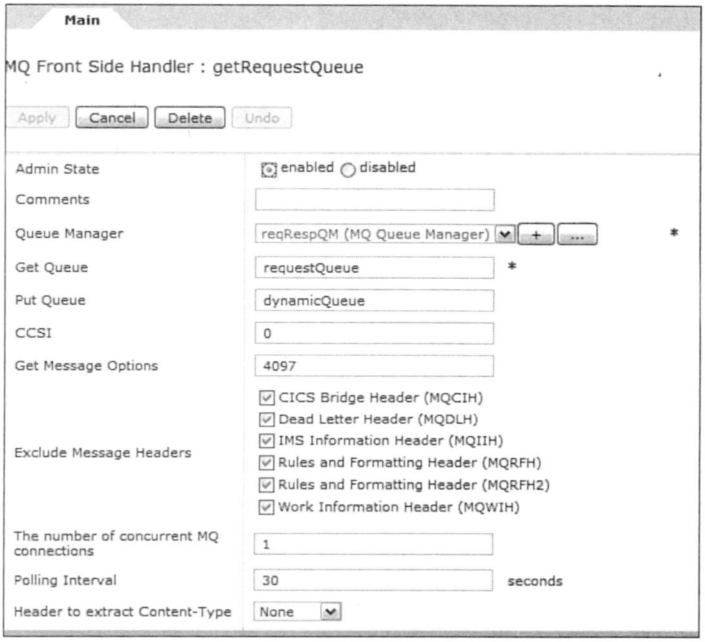

Figure 9-37 MQ FSH.

DataPower provides multiple ways to inject headers into a message stream, including the use of XSLT. We are interested in injecting a ReplyToQ header for the purposes of dynamic queue selection. Although this designation might be better suited to a programmatic XSLT solution in which dynamic queue selection can be performed, this particular example uses the header injection capabilities of the MPGW Header tab. As you can see in Figure 9-38, all that needs to be done is to assign the header name and a value. The direction is specific to either the front (Front Side Handler), or back (the backend URL).

If the SetReplyTo option had been utilized on the backend dpmq URL, any ReplyQueue specified would have been entered automatically into the MQMQ ReplyToQ header. The SetReplyTo parameter and other dpmq options were discussed earlier in Table 9-4, and the use of the MQ URL Builder as was seen in Figure 9-32.

Figure 9-39 shows the completed MPGW with the FSH assigned and the HTTP backend URL for the posting of the message to the XML Firewall. Again, as our intention here is to perform protocol mediation and not to enrich the message or perform other actions upon the request, there is no need to define a Processing Policy. The request and response types can be set to Pass-Thru for maximum efficiency, but as was mentioned previously, this precludes the ability to apply an authentication of the client request and would normally only be valid for a test or production implementation which does not require authentication.

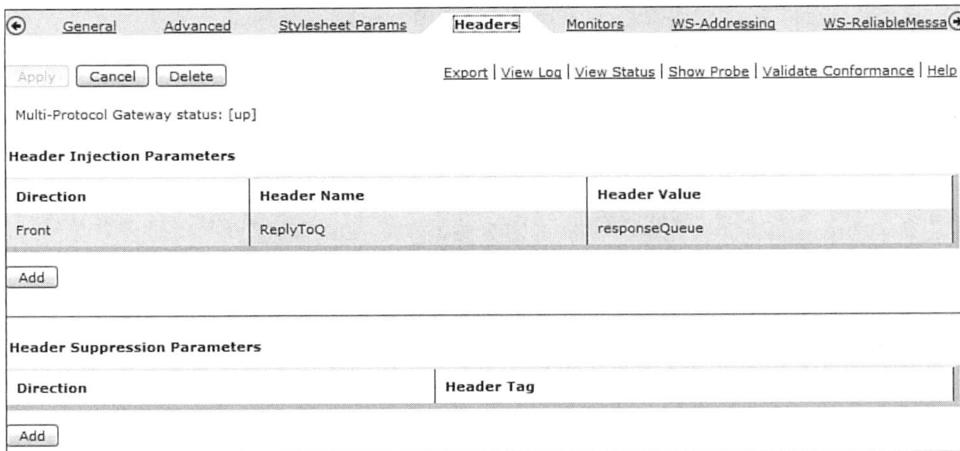

Figure 9-38 Static MQMD header injection.

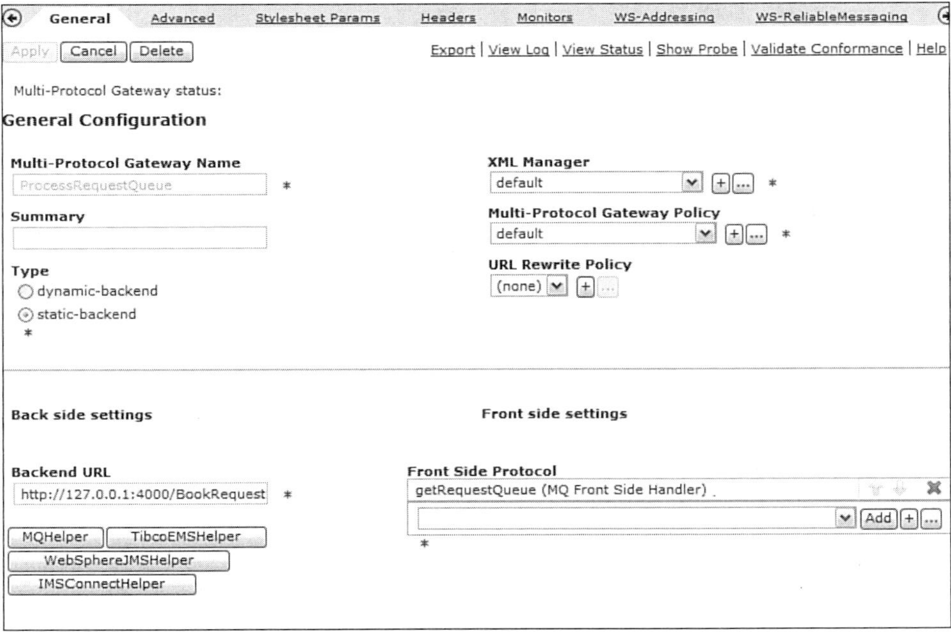

Figure 9-39 ProcessRequestQueue MPGW.

Submitting another request to the HTTP To MQ service HttpToMQRequestQueue places another request message on the request queue. Now the ProcessRequestQueue service fetches the message, submits it over HTTP to the Book Query service, and places the response on the queue as determined by the ReplyToQ header injection. You can refer back to Figure 9-36 if you want a graphical depiction of this process.

Error Processing

The final MQ example raises the subject of error processing. In this scenario we want to control the behavior of the request messages on the request queue such that messages are removed from this queue only when a successful response is received from the backend service. The Book Query XML Firewall is disabled to simulate a failure.

This topic introduces the concept of commitment of MQ GET and PUT operations. When a message is fetched from a queue via a GET, it is not physically removed from that queue until a commit is performed via the MQCOMMIT operation. Similarly, when a message is PUT onto a queue, it is not actually available for another operation to GET until the commit is performed.

The image in Figure 9-40 provides a graphical depiction of a scenario where MQ operations are being performed on both the front side and backend of the MPGW. In this example two Queue Managers are utilized, and while they may in fact be the same QM instance, they could represent two physically independent Queue Managers; in either case, separate connections are utilized.

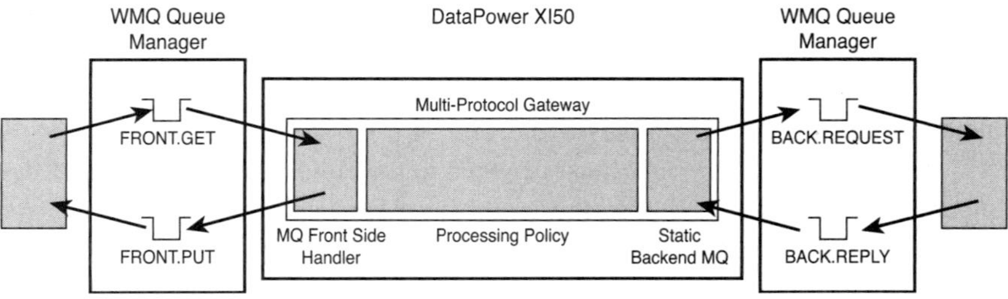

Figure 9-40 MQ Transaction support

The DataPower MQ client library provides transactional support on both sides of the MPGW service. There are three properties that affect MQ transactional characteristics: the Units of Work setting on the DataPower MQ QM object, which controls front side synchronization; and two variations of backend synchronization, which are implemented by the Transactional and Sync parameters of the backend dpmq URL.

The result of synchronization (parameters or MQ properties) is dependant upon the completion each transaction. This is defined as when the response message is delivered to the client. If there is a reply queue specified on the FSH, transaction completion is defined as when a message is processed by the response rule (if specified) and delivered to FRONT.PUT. If there is no front side reply queue (which is typically associated with one-way messaging and no specification of backend reply queue), the transaction is completed when the initial request message is delivered to BACK.REQUEST.

Front side synchronization is managed via the Units of Work (UOW) property of the MQ QM Object associated with the FSH. Messages retrieved via the FSH from FRONT.GET may be synchronized (by setting UOW to '1') with successful delivery to the backend designation BACK.REQUEST and completion of the transaction. Commitment removes the message from FRONT.GET.

Backend synchronization may be managed via two optional parameters of the backend dpmq URL: Transactional=true and Sync=true. Their implementation share similarities, so it's important to understand the nuances.

Transactional=true synchronizes the PUT to BACK.REQUEST with the GET from BACK.REPLY. The GET and PUT are committed upon the GET from BACK.REPLY and completion of the transaction. Hence, if there is no reply queue specified, then the PUT to BACK.REQUEST is committed immediately.

Sync=true is a less restrictive commit of the PUT to BACK.REQUEST. The PUT will be committed immediately upon successful delivery of the message. This allows backend applications to see messages on BACK.REQUEST so that they may GET and process them for potential delivery to BACK.REPLY. Sync=true must be set if there is both a backend request and reply queue. If not set, the backend application will not see the message placed on BACK.REQUEST.

When a transaction fails and a message is left on the FRONT.GET (Front Side Handler's MQ QM UOW property='1'), thought must be given to the effect of leaving this message on the request queue. This results in the message being processed continuously. This is sometimes referred to as a "poison message" and might not be the desired result. In this case, the QM object has three properties to adjust this behavior: Automatic Backout, Backout Threshold, and Backout Queue Name, as seen in Figure 9-41. As the MQ QM object continues to re-GET the message, the backout count increases. After the backout count exceeds the backout threshold, the MQ QM moves the message to the backout queue. If automatic backout is not enabled, the bad message would remain on the GET queue and continue to be reprocessed by the appliance until the QM managing the GET queue removes it or the appliance reroutes the offending message.

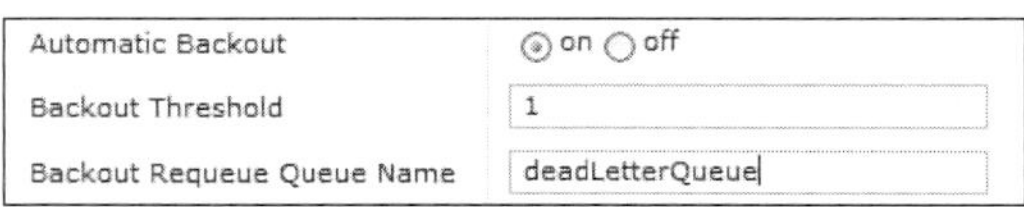

Figure 9-41 FSH setting backout queue.

Now when a request is submitted to the requestQueue, the Backend request fails because we disabled the XMLFW service, the message rollback procedure is initiated, and the message is moved to the deadLetterQueue, as seen in Figure 9-42.

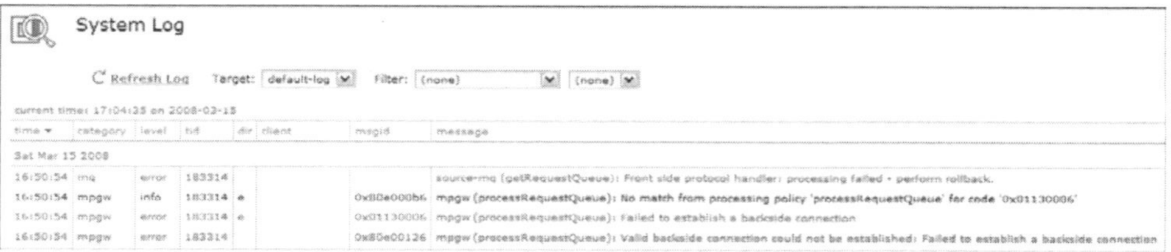

Figure 9-42 Log display showing rollback of request message to request queue.

Advanced Messaging Options

The MPGW fetches messages from request queues, delivers to backend services, and processes messages from response queues in a highly optimized fashion. Depending on the latency of a particular message, the order of processing may not always be serial in nature. This may result in messages being processed by request rules, sent to backend services and subsequently processed by response rules in an order differing from their original order in the source queue.

This processing can be altered to maintain message ordering. The Advanced tab of the MPGW offers three options under Message Processing Modes: Request Rule in Order, Backend in Order, and Response Rule in Order. These options will ensure that each sequence of processing maintains original message order. Any or all of the options may be selected.

These processing modes apply to MQ and JMS message processing.

WebSphere JMS

The DataPower appliance might interact with the default WebSphere JMS providers on the front side and backend of MPGW services. Front Side WebSphere JMS Handlers may be configured to GET and PUT messages on JMS Queues, as well as publish and subscribe to JMS Topics. Backend URLs can be employed to interact with JMS providers on the backend using the dpwasjms protocol string. Support is provided for the WebSphere Default Messaging provider or Service Integration Bus (SIB). JMS Headers may be accessed and set, enabling a mechanism to provide for dynamic queue determination and message correlation, among other JMS options.

Support for front side and backend JMS processing is enabled by the creation of a WebSphere JMS object on the DataPower appliance. This object encapsulates parameters related to the particular instance of a WebSphere Application Server that will be utilized. Connection variables such as hostname, user credentials, and connection properties can be set. Constraints such as maximum message size and connection limits can also be defined. JMS defines five forms of message bodies: text, byte, stream, map, and object; DataPower supports only the text and byte formats, and does not provide Java object serialization support. Text is the default message type, and should be used for XML messages, whereas byte would be used for other use cases. When processing non-XML data, it will be necessary to use a Non-XML or Pass-Thru setting on the MPGW to avoid a parsing error.

The minimal configuration of the WebSphere JMS object (as seen in Figure 9-43) requires only the WebSphere JMS Messaging Bus assignment and endpoint information.

Figure 9-44 shows the WAS endpoint information. The required port value is the SIB_ENDPOINT_ADDRESS port of the bus member. Please refer to the JMS documentation for more information on WebSphere JMS Administration.

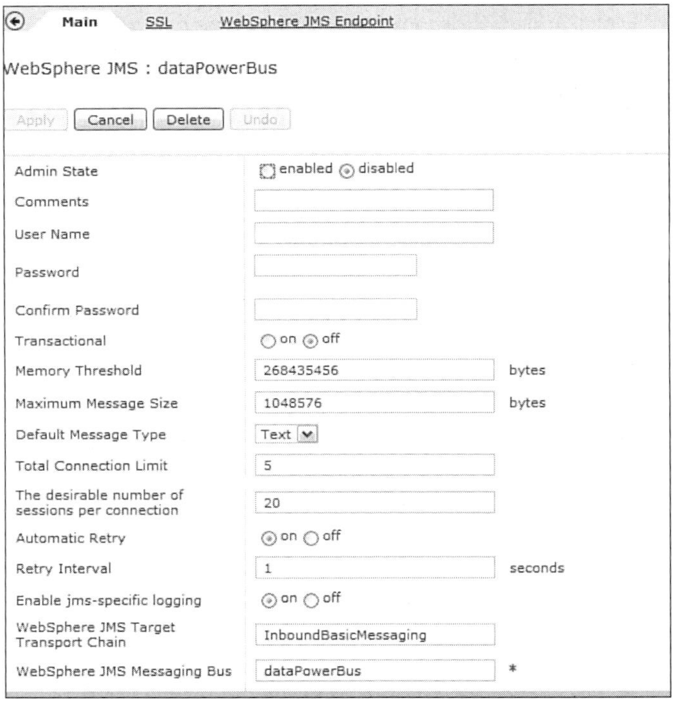

Figure 9-43 WebSphere JMS object.

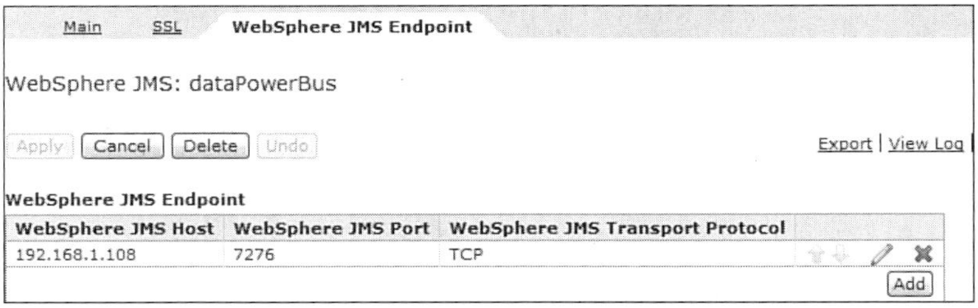

Figure 9-44 WebSphere JMS object endpoint information.

The WebSphere JMS FSH provides the information necessary to interact with JMS queues and topics. As in the case of the MQ FSH, the presence of GET and PUT queues can be an indication of the messaging model. For example, one-way behavior is indicated when no PUT queue is described. However, in the case of dynamic queue selection, the reply to queue (PUT Queue), can be programmatically determined. Dynamic queue selection can be done by injecting a JMS header, JMSReplyTo.

In addition to the standard JMS Headers, three custom DataPower headers are also available as described in Listing 9-13:

Listing 9-13 Custom JMS Headers

```
DP_JMSMessageType - for the selection of message type as sent to WAS
DP_JMSReplyToServer - for the dynamic selection of a reply server
DP_JMSReplyToTopicSpace - for the dynamic selection of a reply to topic
space
```

As is the case with MQ headers, these values might be injected into the message stream via the Header tab of the MPGW service, or via the use of DataPower extension functions such as dp:set-response-header. See Chapter 22, "Introduction to DataPower Development," for more information on programming in XSLT and the use of the extension functions.

It is possible to transport JMS messages over an MQ system. The DataPower appliance views JMS messages over MQ as a JMS body and headers within an MQ body and headers. JMS headers such as MQRFH2 can be accessed and injected just as other headers. It is important to note that constraints exist in the construction of these headers; for example, the MQMD.Format field must contain MQFRH2 when it is followed by an RFH2 header. Readers requiring detailed knowledge of this and other constraints should consult the WebSphere MQ documentation.

The backend URL used to access JMS resources takes the following form shown in Listing 9-14.

Listing 9-14 Sample dpwasjms URL

```
dpwasjms://WebSphereJMS?RequestQueue=QueueOrTopicName;
➥ReplyQueue=QueueOrTopicName;RequestTopicSpace=TopicSpace;
➥ReplyTopicSpace=TopicSpace;Selector=value;TimeOut=value
```

Using the WebSphere JMS URL builder makes construction of this string straightforward. The possible values are shown in Table 9-6.

Table 9-6 WebSphere URL Construction

URL Component	Description
WebSphere JMS	Name of an enabled WebSphere JMS object. The object provides the necessary information to access a remote WebSphere JMS provider.
RequestQueue	Name of the WebSphere JMS request queue.
ReplyQueue	Name of the WebSphere JMS reply queue.
RequestTopicSpace	Name of the JMS request topic space.
ReplyTopicSpace	Name of the JMS reply topic space.
Selector	The message selector provides an SQL-like expression used to select messages from the reply queue. The message selector is a conditional expression based on a subset of SQL92 conditional expression syntax. JMS headers and properties may be used in message selection statements.
TimeOut	Integer that specifies the operational timeout in seconds.

JMS Example

Figure 9-45 demonstrates the architecture of our JMS example. In this use case, a client sends Book Query Requests over HTTP to an MPGW, which then places the request onto a request queue. Another MPGW (assumedly on another device) then fetches the requests from the request queue and makes the HTTP request to the Book Query Service. The response from the Book Query Service is delivered to the JMS reply queue, and then picked up by the originating MPGW and returned to the client.

HTTP To JMS, JMS to HTTP Request Response

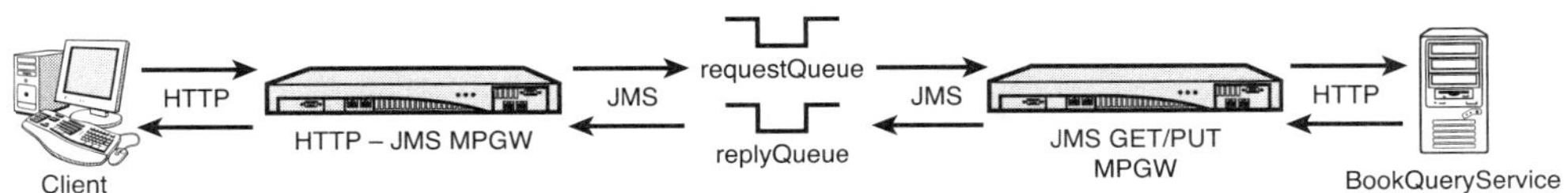

Figure 9-45 HTTP to JMS, JMS to HTTP request response.

The following JMS MPGW demonstrates some fundamental features of an MPGW and JMS. First an HTTP to JMS MPGW takes the sample request and PUTs it to a JMS queue. Usually, the response to a message traversing a queuing system is correlated based on the message-id of the original message. In this case, the message-id is moved to the correlation-id of the message placed on the response queue. We can override this behavior and simply GET any message on the response queue by setting a special header named X-MQMD-GET. We can inject this header, or we can set a system variable to produce the same effect. In this example, we'll demonstrate the latter method.

A second MPGW is configured with a JMS FSH to read the request message from the defined JMS queue and post it to the BookQueryService XML Firewall. It then places the response from this firewall on the response queue. This response is then picked up by the backend URL of the first MPGW and finally returned to the client over HTTP. You can see this flow graphically in Figure 9-45.

Having configured the WebSphere JMS object, the WebSphere JMS Builder is used on the MPGW screen to define the backend JMS resource for the HTTP to JMS MPGW. Just as with WebSphere MQ, you can construct the backend URL manually, or as is usually the case, you can use the helper buttons. Notice in Figure 9-46 that an HTTP FSH has been created to use port 4003, and that the backend URL is populated based on the WebSphere JMS Helper button.

We have stated the goal of fetching any response message from the reply queue. The setting of the correlation ID variable is done in a Set Variable action, as you can see in Figure 9-47, setting var://context/INPUT/_extension/header/X-MQMD-GET, within the Processing Policy.

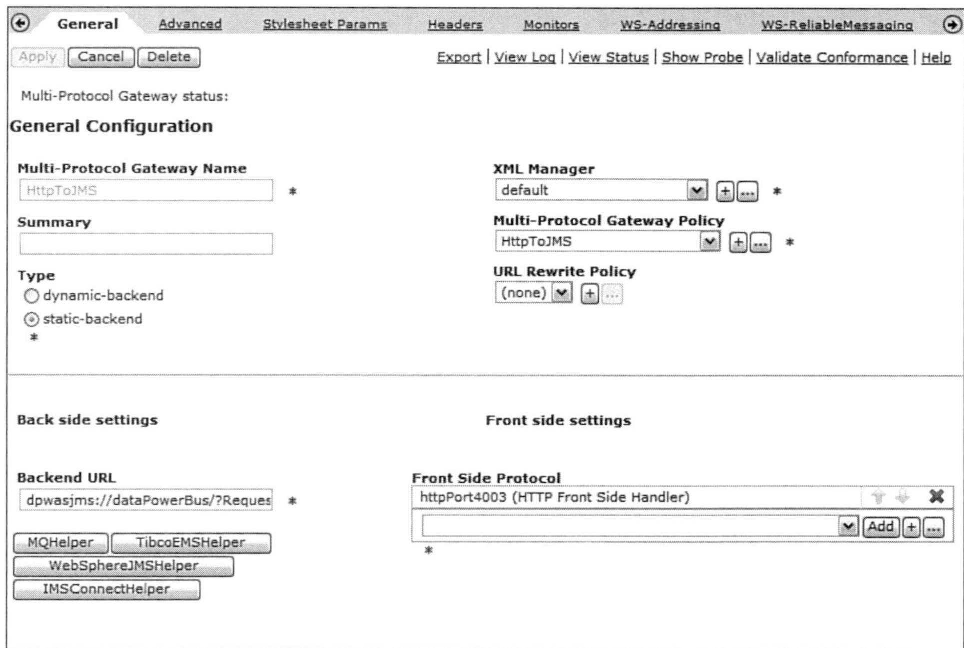

Figure 9-46 HTTP to JMS MPGW front and back settings.

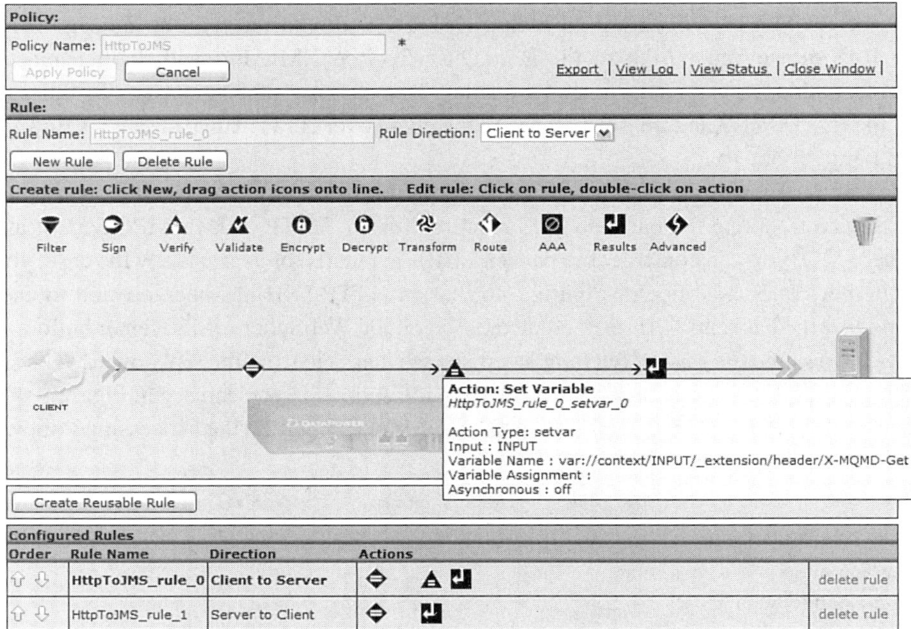

Figure 9-47 JMS SetVar Processing Policy.

The variable var://context/INPUT/_extension/header/X-MQMD-GET is set on the Request or Client to Server processing rule, and is set to a null value, or <MQMD/> as seen in Figure 9-48. This allows for the getting of any message on the reply queue, not just one with a message ID equal to the correlation ID of the request message.

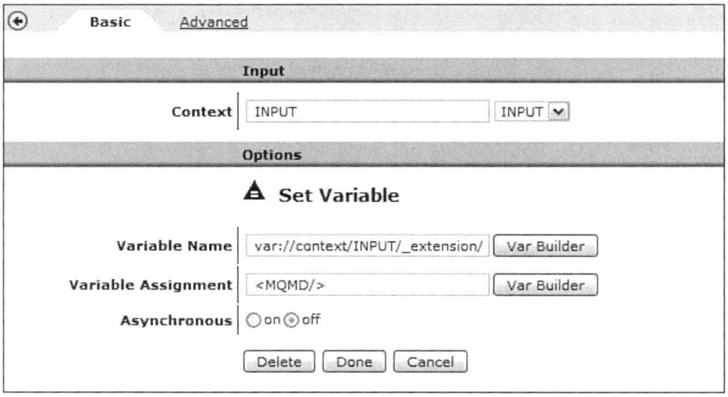

Basic Advanced

Input

Context INPUT INPUT

Options

Set Variable

Variable Name var://context/INPUT/_extension/ Var Builder

Variable Assignment <MQMD/> Var Builder

Asynchronous on off

Delete Done Cancel

Figure 9-48 Setting var://context/INPUT/_extension/header/X-MQMD-GET.

Having constructed an MPGW to accept a message over HTTP and to place it on a JMS queue, the second MPGW will fetch the request message, post it to the backend XML Firewall, and wait for a response. In this case, we dynamically assign the reply-to queue to demonstrate the injection of the JMS header, JMSReplyTo.

This is done on the Header tab of the MPGW (see Figure 9-49). Again, although we use static values, these actions could have been implemented programmatically with a Transform action using XSLT.

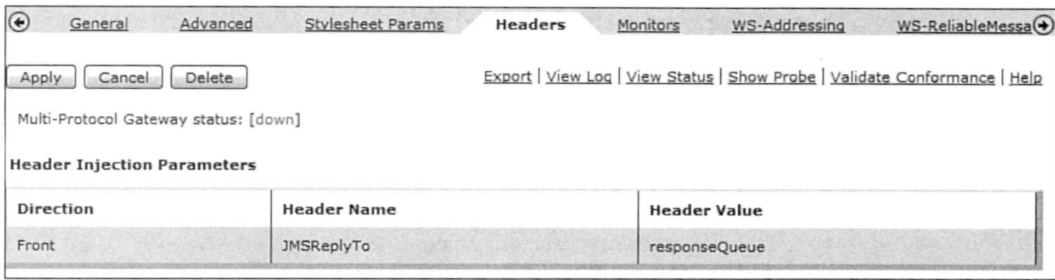

Figure 9-49 Setting Reply-To queue header.

Figure 9-50 shows the completed JMSRequestResponse MPGW. It takes a request from the request queue, sends it over HTTP to the XML Firewall, and waits for a response, which it places on the reply queue. Notice, as was the case for previous examples, this MPGW is not modifying the message, nor performing other actions; there is no need for a Processing Policy. The default policy is selected, and the request and response types have been set to Pass-Thru.

Figure 9-50 JMSRequestResponse MPGW.

Testing the HTTP to JMS MPGW

Submitting the request document to the HTTP to JMS MPGW performs the actions as described in Figure 9-45. Listing 9-15 shows the execution of the request and the response document returned from the MPGW.

Listing 9-15 HTTP to JMS to HTTP Test

```
curl --data-binary @BookQueryRequest.xml http://192.168.1.35:4003
<?xml version="1.0" encoding="UTF-8"?>
<SOAP-ENV:Envelope xmlns:SOAP-
ENV="http://schemas.xmlsoap.org/soap/envelope/">
        <SOAP-ENV:Body>
                <book>
                        <name>Moby Dick</name>
                        <author>Herman Melville</author>
                </book>
        </SOAP-ENV:Body>
</SOAP-ENV:Envelope>
```

It might be helpful to refer back to the diagram in Figure 9-45 to get a better understanding of what is happening on this request. Here are the steps that occur.

1. HTTPtoJMS MPGW receives message from the HTTP client.
2. HTTPtoJMS MPGW places message on request queue.
3. JMSRequestResponse MPGW retrieves message from request queue and posts to BookQueryService XML Firewall.
4. BookQueryService XML Firewall responses with the response document.
5. JMSRequestResponse MPGW places message on reply queue.
6. HTTPtoJMS MPGW retrieves response from reply queue and returns to HTTP Client.

NFS Support Example

Read and write access is provided to NFS remote servers via both the NFS Poller FSH, and a dpnfs: backend protocol URL string. NFS mounts can be statically or dynamically mounted. Dynamic mounts are constructed via a URL in the form of: "dpnfs://hostname/path/file", causing the directory hostname:/path to be automatically mounted by NFS. It remains mounted until it times out due to inactivity. Defining a static mount allows for the referencing of the NFS Static Mount object in the URL and avoids the connection overhead associated with dynamic mounting. In addition to supporting FSHs and backend URLs, mounted NFS file systems are exposed as a folder with the appliance's file system. This allows for NFS endpoints to be utilized in other configuration objects such as the XSLT to be used in a Transform action within a Processing Policy. Keep in mind that if the NFS file system is not highly available, this may not be a good option to use.

> **NFS Endpoints in Transform Actions**
>
> Using NFS endpoints in Transform actions is not advisable in a production environment.
>
> Due to the possibility of an NFS mount not being available, NFS endpoints should not typically be used in a production environment, unless accessibility is guaranteed.

The directory display of an NFS Mounted file system is viewable only from the CLI interface, not the WebGUI. So the only way to view files on an NFS mounted file system is to use the CLI, as demonstrated in Listing 9-16.

Listing 9-16 NFS File System Display via CLI

```
xi50[book](config)# dir nfs-nfsStaticMount:
   File Name                Last Modified               Size
    - - - --                 - - - - - - --              - -
   aaaIdentity.xml          Wed Feb 28 21:26:15 2007   305
   AAAINOUT.txt             Thu Jun 21 16:29:37 2007   13223
```

In Figure 9-51, an NFS Export is statically mounted and a request document is fetched and processed. The request is sent to the BookQueryService XML Firewall, and the response message is placed onto the NFS file system. This procedure requires the creation of an NFS Static Mount, an NFS FSH, and the MPGW Service itself.

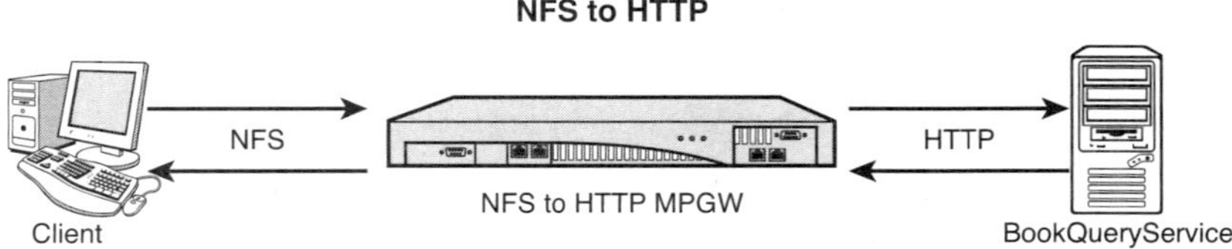

Figure 9-51 NFS to HTTP.

The NFS Static Mount requires only an NFS-exported file system to mount, in the form host:/path (notice only a single slash is used), where host is the DNS name or IP address of the NFS server, and path is the path exported by the host to mount. In Figure 9-52 the IP address and mount point are defined. This object is navigated to via the default domain Objects menu→Network→NFS Static Mount.

The NFS server should be configured to accept requests from the IP address of the DataPower device. This example uses AUTH_SYS authentication, and the NFS server must also be configured to accept that form of authentication. Kerberos could alternately be used for authentication, and it might be a better choice as it provides data integrity and confidentiality if it is supported by the NFS server.

The NFS Front Side Poller shown in Figure 9-53 is similar to the FTP Poller described earlier in this chapter, and requires a target directory in the form dpnfs://{staticMountName}/{directory below export point}. The input file match pattern is using a regular expression and will extract files with the .nfs suffix from the export directory. Response files are placed onto the directory with name suffixed with .ok, or .error in the case of error occurrence. As was the case with an FTP FSH, there are options for the deletion and renaming of input and result files.

Main

NFS Static Mounts : nfsStaticMount

Apply Cancel Delete Undo Expo

Admin State	enabled disabled
Comments	
Remote NFS Export	NFSHost:/Support *
Local Filesystem Access	on off
NFS Version	3
Transport Protocol	TCP
Authentication Protocol	AUTH_SYS
Read-Only	on off
Read Size	4096 bytes
Write Size	4096 bytes
Retransmission Timeout	7 tenths of seconds
Maximum Retransmissions	3

Figure 9-52 Static NFS Mount.

Completing the configuration of the MPGW brings together the NFS Poller FSH, Static Mount, and backend URL construction as seen in Figure 9-54. Again as we are not manipulating the message or performing other actions on the request, there is no need for a Processing Policy and the request and response type has been set to Pass-Thru.

Testing the Service

All that is required to test the service is to place the bookQueryRequest.nfs file in the polled directory. The MPGW picks up the request, submits it to the XML Firewall backend, and places the response, named bookQueryRequest.ok, back on the NFS export directory. Listing 9-17 shows this interaction. First the request is copied into the request directory and then the response document is displayed.

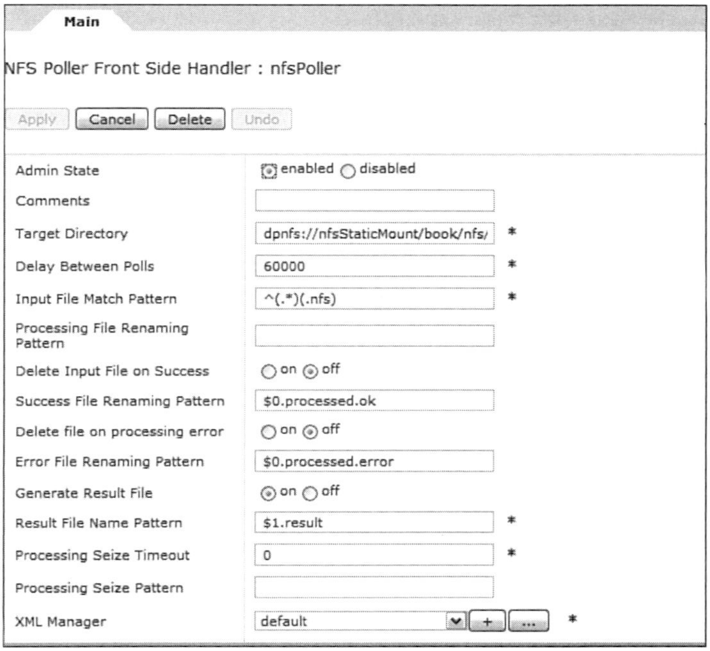

Main

NFS Poller Front Side Handler : nfsPoller

Apply | Cancel | Delete | Undo

Admin State	(•) enabled ( ) disabled
Comments	
Target Directory	dpnfs://nfsStaticMount/book/nfs/ *
Delay Between Polls	60000 *
Input File Match Pattern	^(.*)(.nfs) *
Processing File Renaming Pattern	
Delete Input File on Success	( ) on (•) off
Success File Renaming Pattern	$0.processed.ok
Delete file on processing error	( ) on (•) off
Error File Renaming Pattern	$0.processed.error
Generate Result File	(•) on ( ) off
Result File Name Pattern	$1.result *
Processing Seize Timeout	0 *
Processing Seize Pattern	
XML Manager	default + ... *

Figure 9-53 NFS Front Side Poller.

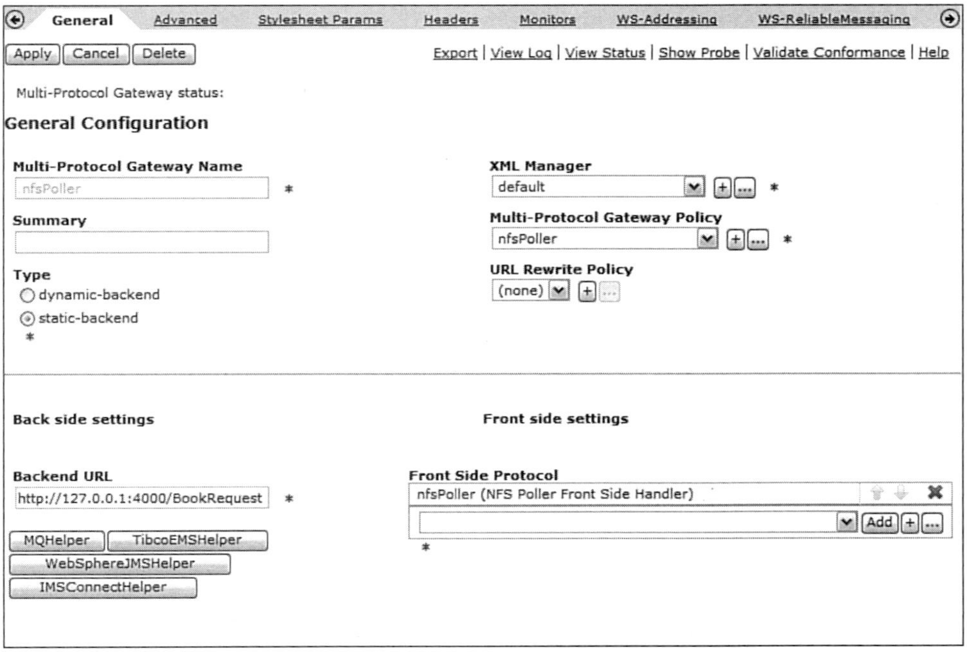

General | Advanced | Stylesheet Params | Headers | Monitors | WS-Addressing | WS-ReliableMessaging

Apply | Cancel | Delete

Export | View Log | View Status | Show Probe | Validate Conformance | Help

Multi-Protocol Gateway status:

General Configuration

Multi-Protocol Gateway Name
nfsPoller *

Summary

Type
( ) dynamic-backend
(•) static-backend
*

XML Manager
default + ... *

Multi-Protocol Gateway Policy
nfsPoller + ... *

URL Rewrite Policy
(none) + ...

Back side settings

Backend URL
http://127.0.0.1:4000/BookRequest *

MQHelper | TibcoEMSHelper
WebSphereJMSHelper
IMSConnectHelper

Front side settings

Front Side Protocol
nfsPoller (NFS Poller Front Side Handler)
Add + ...
*

Figure 9-54 NFS Poller MPGW.

Listing 9-17 Result from NFS Poller MPGW Test

```
nfs>copy ..\ftp\bookQueryRequest.xml bookQueryRequest.nfs
        1 file(s) copied.

more bookQueryRequest.result
<?xml version="1.0" encoding="UTF-8"?>
<SOAP-ENV:Envelope xmlns:SOAP-
ENV="http://schemas.xmlsoap.org/soap/envelope/">
        <SOAP-ENV:Body>
                <book>
                        <name>Moby Dick</name>
                        <author>Herman Melville</author>
                </book>
        </SOAP-ENV:Body>
</SOAP-ENV:Envelope>
```

Summary

The Multi-Protocol Gateway provides many of the functions of an Enterprise Service Bus architecture. Protocol mediation is accomplished via the use of FSHs and backend URL construction. Message mediation is provided via the implementation of Processing Policies and XSLT transformations.

The examples in this chapter demonstrated the ease of implementation of the primary protocols that are supported by the MPGW. We started by demonstrating the simplicity of bridging protocols such as HTTP, HTTPS, and MQ with the BookQueryService. Then we extended these examples by the use of additional protocols such as FTP, NFS, and JMS. In each case, the fundamental nature of the MPGW remained the same. All we did was change the type of Front Side Protocol Handler. Some of the examples were quite complex, with messages being picked up from queues, moved from request to response queue, and submitting requests to the XMLFW service.

Can you imagine writing Java code to do all this? Aren't you glad the Multi-Protocol Gateway made it so easy!

CHAPTER 10

Web Service Proxy

We have discussed two of the three major service types available on a DataPower appliance. We could say that we have saved the best for last but that will be for you to decide. The Web Service Proxy (WSP) is certainly an impressive service type due to its flexibility and ability to "magically" configure itself—so it might appear. The truth of the matter is that the WSP can provide a tremendous amount of value by placing it in front of your Web services, providing most of the features that the other service types have to offer and more at a granular level.

With the growing popularity of Web services and the evolving WS-* specifications, it becomes convenient to enforce the adherence to these specifications in one central place. The WSP service provides this for you as these specifications can be enforced at various levels of granularity within the service. In addition to complying with and enforcing WS-* specifications, this service type can provide additional value by virtualizing service endpoints, deriving many of the configuration details from the Web service WSDL, providing the ability to apply processing rules at a granular level, automatically decrypting request documents and verifying signatures, and much more! All of these benefits and how to configure this service type to take advantage of them are discussed in this chapter.

Web Services

Before diving into configuring a DataPower service to proxy a Web service, it is important to understand what a Web service is. This is not intended to be a comprehensive Web service tutorial, however a brief overview is beneficial.

Today, it seems that everyone is striving to build a Service Oriented Architecture (SOA). SOA can be described as an architecture consisting of a set of independent, reusable assets, or services that can be consumed by other applications in the enterprise. Essentially, that is what a Web service is. It is a self-describing, standalone application that can be consumed by other applications. So what does that really mean? Think of it as a mini application that can be called by many different applications. This application provides a type of functionality that is needed by the calling application. For example, a simple service that returns a real time stock quote for a submitted stock symbol is a common task that may be needed by many applications.

Web services can be developed to run on numerous platforms such as Java EE and Microsoft .NET and requested over many different transport protocols. Part of their power and appeal is that they can be developed on any platform and can be consumed by applications on another platform providing interoperability between disparate systems. Web services can support several different messaging and transport protocols. One common way of calling Web services is using the SOAP messaging format over the HTTP(S) transport protocol.

Web Services Description Language (WSDL)

After a Web service is created and deployed, it is available to all the consumers that have access. The challenge is, "How do those consumers know how to call the service?" There are several details that you must know about the service interface in order to call it. As mentioned previously, Web services are self describing. This self description is provided in a file called a WSDL document.

A WSDL document is an XML document in a specific format that tells the consumer everything he needs to know to call the service. This format, as well as how the information is conveyed within the document, is dictated by an approved W3C specification. You can think of it as the instruction manual for the Web service. There are four primary things that the consumer must know to make this call: the operations available, the message formats, the protocol, and the location of the service.

Before calling a Web service, you must first know the operations that are available within the service. An operation is somewhat analogous to a method or function in other programming languages. Just as other programs can have many different methods or functions, Web services can expose many different operations that can be called to provide different functionality within the service. For example, a banking Web service may have a balanceQuery operation, a withdrawFunds operation, and a depositFunds operation.

After you determine which operation you need to call, you must then know how to format the request message; knowing the response format also helps you prepare to process the returning data. As mentioned before, the request and response messages are SOAP documents. In addition, error messages can also be returned in a SOAP document called a SOAP fault. Because a SOAP document is built on XML, the request, response, and fault formats can be described through an XML schema. These schemas are included (or referenced) in the WSDL document.

Now that you know what operation you want to call and how to build the request message, there are two small details remaining. Because Web services support many different protocols, you must know the protocol to use for the particular operation you are calling. This is known as the *binding information*. The last piece of information you need to know is where to send the request. This is known as the *endpoint*. The endpoint is the complete URL that the request will be sent to. When calling a service over HTTP, this will look like a standard Web URL consisting of the hostname, port, and URI. For example, let's suppose there is a banking Web service that can be accessed via HTTPS at the hostname mybank.com over port 4443 with a URI of bankservice. The endpoint for calling this service would be https://mybank.com:4443/bankservice.

You now know what pieces of information you need and where to find them, but how is this information conveyed in the WSDL document? To be honest, it's not pretty. That is, reading a WSDL document is not like reading the comics section in the Sunday newspaper. When viewed in their raw format (text), they can be difficult to understand. It is sometimes difficult to follow the interaction between the various sections, and to figure out *exactly* what message needs to be sent for a given operation. Fortunately, there are many tools available to help in writing and reading these files. Often a WSDL is comprised of many separate documents that are referenced from within the main document. For example, the schemas for the request and response messages are usually contained in separate documents and referenced within the WSDL. This makes maintenance and reusability for the schemas easier.

Being the technologists that we are, we just can't resist taking a look under the hood and seeing what a WSDL looks like. After all, it is just XML and how bad can that be?

As we mentioned earlier in this section, there are four main pieces of information that you will need to call a Web service. Because a WSDL provides these pieces of information, the document is broken up into multiple sections.

After the root element of the WSDL document <wsdl:definitions>, in the first section, you will see <wsdl:types>. This contains all the schemas for the request, response, and SOAP fault messages for all the operations exposed by the service. These schemas can be coded directly in the WSDL itself or the schema files can be referenced. Listing 10-1 shows the schema for a request message.

Listing 10-1 Request Message Schema Within a WSDL

```
<wsdl:types>
   <xsd:schema targetNamespace="http://www.example.org/BookService/"
        xmlns:xsd="http://www.w3.org/2001/XMLSchema">
      <xsd:element name="BookQuery">
         <xsd:complexType>
            <xsd:sequence>
               <xsd:element name="book">
                  <xsd:complexType>
                     <xsd:sequence>
                        <xsd:element name="name" type="xsd:string" />
                        <xsd:element name="author" type="xsd:string"/>
                     </xsd:sequence>
                  </xsd:complexType>
               </xsd:element>
            </xsd:sequence>
         </xsd:complexType>
      </xsd:element>
```

Because there can be many schemas and elements within the schemas, the WSDL must identify which portion of the schema(s) actually form a request or response message. This is identified in the next section of the WSDL in the <wsdl:message> element. Listing 10-2 shows an example of a message element that has an attribute "name" with a value of "BookQueryRequest." The <part> element in this message identifies the portion of a schema that makes up this message. In this example it refers to the <BookQuery> element, which is in the schema shown in Listing 10-1. We now have a message called BookQueryRequest, and we know that it should conform to the BookQuery element definition in the schema.

Listing 10-2 Linking the BookQueryRequest Message to the Schema

```
<wsdl:message name="BookQueryRequest">
   <wsdl:part element="tns:BookQuery" name="parameters" />
</wsdl:message>
```

The next part of the WSDL describes the operations that are available within the service. This description will provide the operation name, the request message used to call it, and the response message that can be expected. All of the operations listed are enclosed within a <wsdl:portType> element and can be identified by the <wsdl:operation> element within. Just as a port in the networking world describes a connection point to a physical server or device, the portType in the WSDL describes the connection point to the Web service. Listing 10-3 shows an operation named BookQuery. The input message for this operation is the BookQueryRequest message shown in Listing 10-2, which is defined by the schema shown in Listing 10-1.

Listing 10-3 Describing the Operations

```
<wsdl:portType name="BookService">
    <wsdl:operation name="BookQuery">
         <wsdl:input message="tns:BookQueryRequest" name="test"/>
         <wsdl:output message="tns:BookQueryResponse" />
    </wsdl:operation>
</wsdl:portType>
```

We now know all the operations available in the Web service and how they should be formatted. The next section of the WSDL describes the communication protocol that must be used. It is valid for different operations within the same service to be called using different communication protocols. This information is contained within the <wsdl:binding> element. Listing 10-4 shows an example of a binding element for the example WSDL that we have been building. Notice the type attribute of the binding element refers to the portType shown in Listing 10-3. This indicates that all of the binding information specified in this element applies to this portType. Notice the soap:binding element has an attribute named transport. This indicates the transport protocol to be used. In this example it is SOAP over the HTTP protocol.

Listing 10-4 WSDL Binding

```
<wsdl:binding name="BookServiceSOAP" type="tns:BookService">
    <soap:binding style="document"
transport="http://schemas.xmlsoap.org/soap/http" />
    <wsdl:operation name="BookQuery">
        <soap:operation
soapAction="http://www.example.org/BookService/BookQuery" />
        <wsdl:input name="bookQueryRequest">
            <soap:body use="literal" />
        </wsdl:input>
        <wsdl:output>
            <soap:body use="literal" />
        </wsdl:output>
    </wsdl:operation>
</wsdl:binding>
```

You now should have almost every piece of information required to call this Web service. We know what operations are available, the format of the request and response messages, and the transport protocol to use. The one small piece missing from this puzzle is where to send the request. The address, or endpoint of the service is provided in the <wsdl:service> element at the end of the WSDL document. In this element you can specify an address, or endpoint, for each binding specified in the binding section. This information is contained within the <wsdl:port> element, which is a child of the <wsdl:service> element. Listing 10-5 shows an endpoint example. Notice that the port element refers to the BookServiceSOAP binding defined in Listing 10-4. The <soap:address> element provides the actual endpoint where you would send your request.

Listing 10-5 Defining the Endpoint

```
<wsdl:service name="BookService">
    <wsdl:port binding="tns:BookServiceSOAP" name="BookServiceSOAP">
        <soap:address
location="http://www.abcbooks.com/books/query/queryService"/>
    </wsdl:port>
</wsdl:service>
```

So, there you have it! One "simple" document has provided every piece of information required to call a Web service. We did warn you that it isn't a user-friendly document. This is why there are many tools available for creating and viewing WSDL documents. Figure 10-1 shows the same example WSDL that we have been looking at as it is displayed within the Rational Application Developer (RAD) product. This is much easier on the eyes than the raw text!

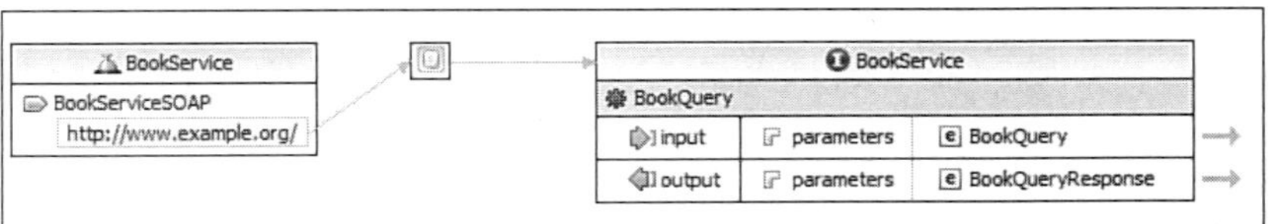

Figure 10-1 Viewing a WSDL in RAD.

Although this was a brief introduction to the WSDL document, it provided enough detail for you to understand how the DataPower WSP service uses this document to determine the full interface definition within the configuration.

Creating a Web Service Proxy (WSP)

We've already seen how DataPower provides the capability to perform many different types of processing on request and response messages such as Authentication, Authorization, and Auditing (AAA), cryptographic functions, message transformations, and dynamic routing. As you might expect, all this is available in a WSP but there is an added benefit provided in this service type. Because a Web Service Proxy uses a WSDL for configuration, it is able to parse the document, determine the hierarchy (WSDL, service, port, binding, operation) inherent in the service, and define these processing rules at any level of that hierarchy. For example, processing rules can be configured for individual operations or portTypes, at the WSDL level, or at the service level. This service also provides all the threat protection that DataPower has to offer. In Chapter 20, "XML Threats," you'll see how Web services, although convenient, are vulnerable to attack.

It is often surprising how easy it is to configure a WSP that provides threat protection, schema validation, and service-level monitoring. All you need to provide to build a service that provides this value is three simple things: a WSDL, a name for your service, and a Front Side Handler (FSH). That is it! Although it might appear as some magic trick, it should come as no surprise how this is accomplished. As we mentioned earlier in this chapter, a Web service is described by a WSDL document that provides all the information required to call the service. So if this is a magic trick, the WSDL is the smoke and mirrors. Now let's take a look at how this is all done.

Much like the other services we have discussed thus far, a WSP can be created by navigating from the Control Panel in the WebGUI to Web Service Proxy and selecting Add. The wizard immediately asks for the first of the three pieces of information required—a name. After a name is provided, clicking the Create Web Service Proxy button prompts for the second piece of information—the WSDL. This can be uploaded to the device's file system or fetched just as you would any other file. Figure 10-2 shows this configuration screen where the BookService.wsdl file has been selected from the DataPower file system in the local directory. Notice the options to upload and fetch the WSDL from a remote location.

You may also notice other available options on this screen such as options to browse UDDI or to add UDDI and WSRR subscriptions. There are other possibilities for referencing a WSDL; we will defer those discussions until later in this chapter. On the bottom of this configuration screen are two options for defining and enforcing WS-Policy sets. WS-Policy is a specification that allows security policies to be defined for a Web service that must be adhered to by the consumers. The WSP provides support for this and is discussed in detail in Chapter 19, "Web Services Security." However, most simple use cases won't require any special WS-Policy action during configuration.

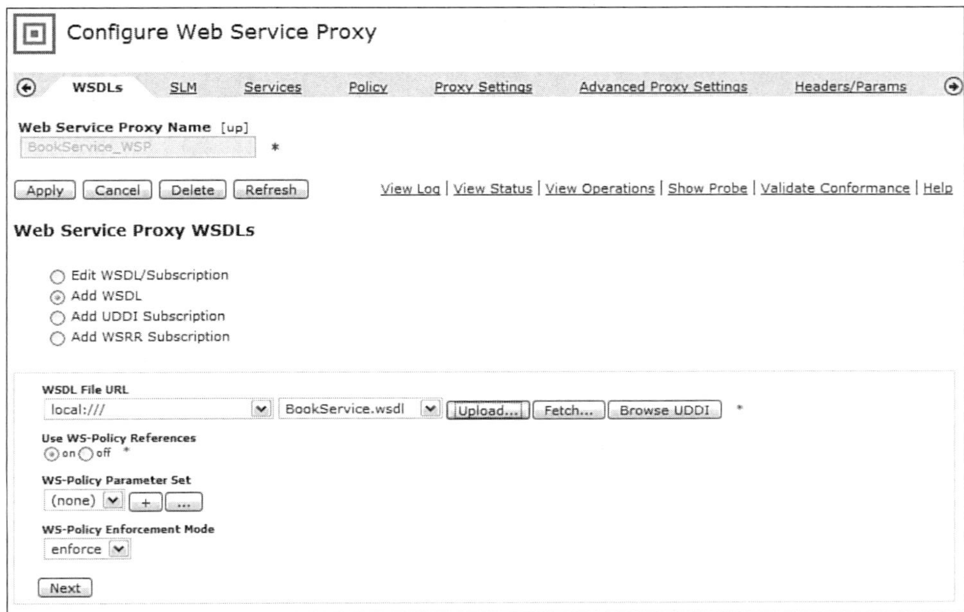

Figure 10-2 Adding a WSDL to the Web Service Proxy.

Clicking the Next button creates a WSP, but there is one critical piece of information missing. That is the FSH that will be configured to listen for requests to be processed by this service. The next screen presented is where this will be configured. This is the WSDLs tab within the service configuration. You will notice three sections here. The top section is labeled "local" and is where you will define the FSH object(s) that will be configured to handle requests. The middle section is labeled "remote" and defines the backend that the request will be sent to. This information is provided within the WSDL, so the service already populates this for you. The bottom section on this screen is labeled "published." This simply defines the endpoint information that is published to the client if DataPower will republish this WSDL such as to an external repository. This is typically configured to "use local," which means that the published WSDL will contain the endpoint information that you will define in the top "local" section of this screen.

Because the WSDL already provided the remote endpoint information for us, the only thing required to be configured on this screen is the FSH object in the local section. Note that any of the remote information can be changed if need be. An existing FSH object can be selected from the drop-down here or a new object can be created by clicking the + button. After creating or selecting a FSH for this configuration, a URI must be associated with it. By default the URI from the endpoint within the WSDL is populated but this can be changed. This URI is required because Web services publish endpoints to the clients that consist of the complete URL, including the URI. This also can abstract the actual URI from the client and provide a shorter, simpler one. Figure 10-3 shows where we are configuring an HTTP FSH object to our service with a URI of /bookService. This is the endpoint that the client uses to call this service.

Notice in this example that the URI we are exposing to the client is much shorter than the actual URI that the backend Web service is expecting. Because the FSH is used in conjunction with the URI defined, it is possible to use the same FSH in more than one configuration. We discuss more about this later in this chapter. After the FSH is configured and the URI is entered, the Add button must be clicked to add this to the configuration.

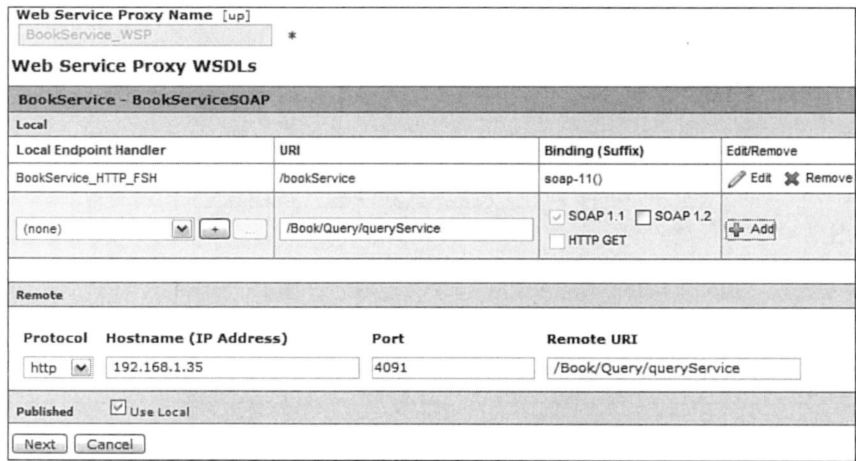

Figure 10-3 Adding an FSH.

TIP—Remember to Click the Add Button!

After creating or selecting an existing FSH Object and specifying a URI to associate with it, you must click the Add button to add it to the configuration. Not clicking Add is a mistake that is easy to make as the FSH appears to have been added to the service when it is visible in the drop-down and the URI is entered in the text box.

Figure 10-3 also shows the Remote configuration for this service. This is the backend definition where all requests will be forwarded. This information has been automatically populated from our WSDL as it is defined in the <service> section.

Clicking the Next button completes the configuration of the WSP and redisplays the WSDL configuration tab. The Endpoint Handler Summary indicates how many endpoints are configured for the WSDL and how many are in the "up" status. In our example, we configured only one so there should be one up and one configured, as shown in Figure 10-4. The WSDL status of "Okay" indicates that the WSDL is valid.

Figure 10-4 WSDL and endpoint status.

In three simple steps, we configured a WSP service. The service created is not just a proxy that knows how to listen to requests and pass them to the backend. As mentioned earlier, this proxy provides a tremendous amount of value by providing threat protection and schema validation. By virtue of the WSDL that you imported, it will allow requests only to the backend Web service that fully complies with the WSDL. Think about how much that frees up the actual service, knowing that it will receive only requests that conform to the WSDL.

To demonstrate this power, let's take a look at what happens when we send a request to the service. Let's assume that the WSDL we imported in our example is the same WSDL we used in our examples in the previous section of this chapter. We know from Listing 10-3 that there is an operation named BookQuery that we can call. We also know from looking at Listing 10-1 how this request should be formatted. So it is safe to say that if we send a SOAP document over HTTP for the BookQuery operation that complies with the request schema, it should be accepted by our DataPower service and passed to the backend Web service. Listing 10-6 shows such a request.

Listing 10-6 Valid BookService SOAP Request

```
<soapenv:Envelope
   xmlns:q0="http://www.example.org/BookService/"
  xmlns:soapenv="http://schemas.xmlsoap.org/soap/envelope/"
  xmlns:xsd="http://www.w3.org/2001/XMLSchema"
  xmlns:xsi="http://www.w3.org/2001/XMLSchema-instance">
  <soapenv:Body>
    <q0:BookQuery>
      <book>
        <name>Moby Dick</name>
        <author>Herman Melville</author>
      </book>
    </q0:BookQuery>
  </soapenv:Body>
</soapenv:Envelope>
```

Now that we have a valid request document, we can send it to our new WSP. As we know, the endpoint that we should send the request to is specified in the WSDL for the service. Because we are using DataPower to proxy this Web service, we cannot use the endpoint listed in this WSDL. We must use the endpoint that is virtualized within our proxy. This is the combination of the FSH object used by the service and the URI configured with it when we added it to our service as shown in Figure 10-3. In this case, we would send our request to the IP:port that the BookService_HTTP_FSH object is listening on with a URI of bookService. For example, if this FSH was listening on IP address 192.168.22.5 and port 3100, we would send this SOAP request document to http://192.168.22.5:3100/bookService.

After sending this valid request, the service would have performed its request schema validation and threat protection, forwarded it to the back-end Web service, and returned the response back to the client. Figure 10-5 shows the DataPower log from this valid request. Notice, reading from the bottom entry up, how DataPower recognized the IP:port and URL combination as being that of an endpoint configuration within the BookService_WSP configuration. Next, you can see how the SOAP Body is looked at for an operation. Finally, DataPower recognizes the BookQuery operation and allows the request to proceed through the service.

20:35:46	ws-proxy	info	7268756		192.168.1.101		source-http (BookService_HTTP_FSH): WS-Proxy selected: 'BookService_WSP'. Operation 'BookQuery' matches all criteria.
20:35:46	xslt	debug	7268756		192.168.1.101		xmlmgr (default): patterns Compilation Request: Found in cache (expr:////*[local-name()='Envelope']/*[local-name()='Body']/*)
20:35:46	xslt	debug	7268756		192.168.1.101		xmlmgr (default): patterns Compilation Request: Checking cache for URL expr:////*[local-name()='Envelope']/*[local-name()='Body']/*
20:35:46	ws-proxy	debug	7268756		192.168.1.101		source-http (BookService_HTTP_FSH): WS-Proxy BookService_WSP operation BookQuery matches address (9.42.117.9:6880) url (/bookService). SOAP operation and Action will be evaluated.

Figure 10-5 DataPower logs from a valid Web service request.

We have seen how a valid request looks within the DataPower logs when sent to our WSP service. Now, to prove that the request document is actually schema validated, let's send an invalid request to this service that does not comply with the schema for the BookQuery request. To do this we will simply reverse the order of the <name> and the <author> elements in the request document. After sending the request, we received a plain SOAP fault with a nondescriptive message. If we were to take a look at the DataPower log, as shown in Figure 10-6, we can see why the request was rejected. Notice that the BookService WSDL was found in the DataPower cache and then the request document was parsed. Immediately after this, the request is rejected. You can see a descriptive message indicating that the element <author> was found but the next item should have been <name>. This is proof that the request document is validated against the appropriate schema within the WSDL. All this happens without having to configure a single processing rule! This is the power of the WSP.

23:43:09	ws-proxy	error	1431441	e	192.168.1.101	0x00230001	wsgw (BookService_WSP): Dynamic Execution Error
23:43:09	multistep	error	1431441	>	192.168.1.101	0x80c00008	wsgw (BookService_WSP): rule (BookService_WSP_default_request-rule): Pipeline beginning at implied action Parse input as SOAP, attempt pipeline failed: http://192.168.1.254:6880/bookService:10: cvc-particle 3.1: in element book with anonymous type, found <author> (in default namespace), but next item should be name
23:43:09	xmlparse	error	1431441	>	192.168.1.101		wsgw (BookService_WSP): http://192.168.1.254:6880/bookService:10: cvc-particle 3.1: in element book with anonymous type, found <author> (in default namespace), but next item should be name
23:43:09	xmlparse	debug	1431441	>	192.168.1.101		wsgw (BookService_WSP): Parsing document 'http://192.168.1.254:6880/bookService'
23:43:09	multistep	debug	1431441	>	192.168.1.101		wsgw (BookService_WSP): Schema URL to compile is 'local:///BookService.wsdl'

Figure 10-6 DataPower logs from an invalid Web service request.

The Processing Policy

Although the simple service configuration described in the previous section produced a powerful proxy for your Web service, you will most likely want to add some other processing capabilities to your service such as AAA, message transformation, or encryption. We already know what a Processing Policy is and how it contains actions to be applied to a request, response, or on error, but this service type offers even more configuration options for the Processing Policy.

Processing Rules

In the first two DataPower service types discussed in the previous chapters, you saw how a Processing Policy is used to configure processing rules to be applied to request or response messages. These rules were applied based on a match condition configured in the match rule and were evaluated for every request/response. The WSP implements the Processing Policy and rules in a slightly different manner. The WSP allows for separate processing rules to be configured at any level of the WSDL. For example, you might want to apply a separate processing rule for each operation within the WSDL. The WSP offers this flexibility at multiple levels of granularity. From the most granular to the least, a processing rule can be configured at the operations level, the port level, the service level, the WSDL level, or the DataPower proxy level. During execution, this processing rule hierarchy is also evaluated and applied in this order. So if there is a request processing rule configured at the operation level and another rule configured at the WSDL level, the rule at the operation level will be evaluated and executed. When a WSP service is created, a default request rule is created at the proxy level that will contain one action. This rule and the action contained within it are discussed later in this chapter.

To illustrate how this rule granularity can be useful, let's take a look at the BookService_WSP that we demonstrated earlier in this chapter. We saw that this service has an operation called BookQuery. Let's suppose there is an additional operation that the service exposes called BookPurchase. As you would expect, this operation would be used to purchase a book. It may be that only registered users should be permitted to purchase books through this service and must first be authenticated. As we know, a DataPower service can provide this authentication and authorization within a processing rule by implementing a AAA policy. We will not discuss the configuration of the AAA policy here as it will be discussed in detail in Chapter 16, "AAA" and Chapter 17, "Advanced AAA." For now we know that it is an action that can be used within a processing rule to perform the authentication and authorization required.

A processing rule within a WSP can be configured by first navigating to the Web Service Proxy configuration page starting from the Control Panel, clicking the Web Service Proxy icon, and finally the Web Service Proxy name. This renders the WSDLs tab in the service configuration screen. Clicking the Policy tab at the top of the screen displays the Web Service Proxy Policy screen. This is where the Processing Policy can be configured by adding rules and actions.

In the main section of this configuration screen is a tree-like structure containing the five different levels of the proxy/WSDL at which rules can be configured. This tree will not be fully expanded, but it can be expanded one branch at a time, or the links above the tree can be utilized to open it to any of the five levels. Figure 10-7 shows this screen for our BookService_WSP service. Notice that the tree is fully expanded to the operations level. You can see that default request and response rules were created for you at the proxy level. The response rule contains only a Match and a Results action. The request rule, on the other hand, has an additional action configured. This is a SLM (Service Level Monitor) action that can be used to monitor the traffic flowing through the service. We discuss this action in detail later in this chapter.

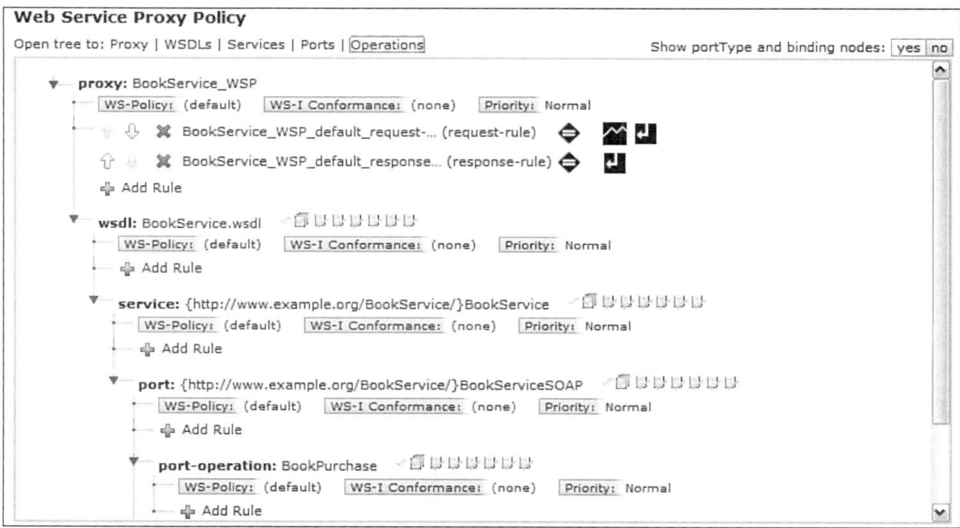

Figure 10-7 Web Service Proxy Policy configuration screen.

At each level of the policy tree is a plus (+) sign and the text Add Rule. This indicates that a processing rule can be configured here. Clicking this link opens up the Processing Policy line where you can configure a processing rule. This portion of the screen should look somewhat familiar as it is identical to the policy editor used in the Multi-Protocol Gateway and XML Firewall policy configuration. Figure 10-8 shows this screen after clicking on the Add Rule link under the BookPurchase operation within our BookService_WSP service.

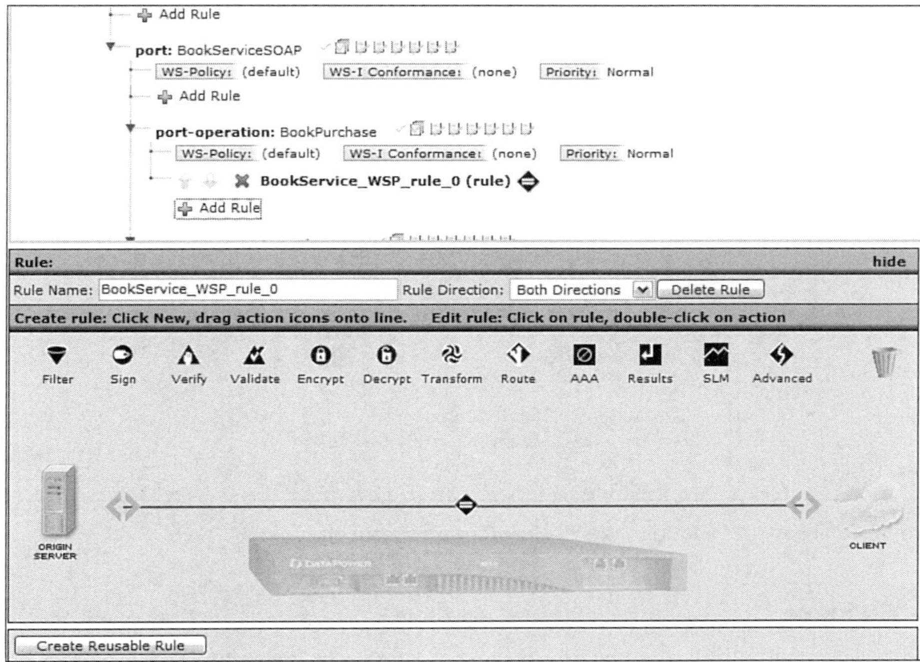

Figure 10-8 Configuring a processing rule.

The processing rule can now be configured by dragging actions onto the policy line and specifying the rule direction. Notice that a match rule is still required within the processing rule. A default match rule is created matching on all URLs; though only messages destined for this service operation will reach this rule, you can further filter the inputs by creating a more specific match rule. After configuring the processing rule and clicking the Apply button, the new rule is added to the service for only the BookPurchase operation. Figure 10-9 shows this new request rule containing a AAA policy action added to the BookPurchase operation. Now only requests for this operation will be authenticated and authorized per the AAA policy configuration contained within this request rule.

We now have in our BookService_WSP two different request rules configured. We have the newly configured request rule at the BookPurchase operation level and the default request rule at the proxy level. Now when a request comes in for the BookPurchase operation, it will execute the rule containing the AAA policy, assuming that the match condition contained within this rule is satisfied. If the match rule was not satisfied, the service would continue to search up the tree until a match was found for the incoming request. Because we do not have a rule specified at the operation, port, or service level for the BookQuery operation, any requests for it will execute the default rule at the proxy level.

Figure 10-9 New rule added to the BookPurchase operation.

User Policy

In addition to configuring processing rules at the various levels of the WSDL, there are also options that can be configured at each level. You will notice a series of icons with check marks just to the right of each level of the Processing Policy tree. Each of these icons represents an option that can be enabled or disabled at that level. This is called the user policy. Figure 10-10 shows options for the BookQuery operation in our BookService_WSP service.

By default, all the options in each of the user policies are enabled as indicated by a green check mark. To modify these options, simply click on the user policy icons and a checklist of all of the options is displayed as shown in Figure 10-10. The option can be selected and deselected as desired.

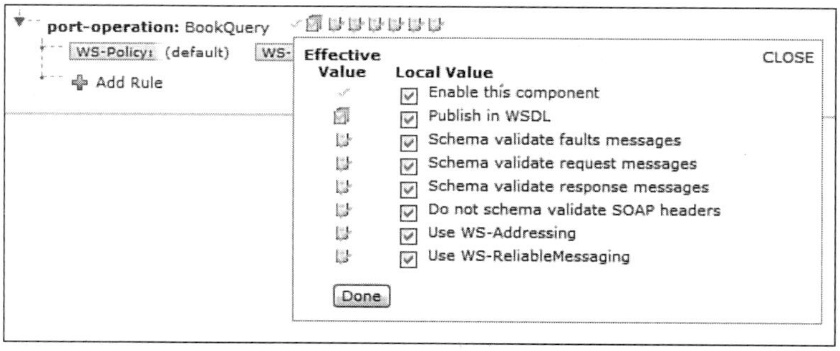

Figure 10-10 User Policy options.

Most of the options shown in Figure 10-10 are self-explanatory; however, two may not be. These are the two WS-* options. These are two of the WS-* specifications that are supported within the WSP service. The first one in the list is WS-Addressing. WS-Addressing is a specification that enables routing information to be carried in the SOAP header. The second WS-* option in this list is WS-ReliableMessaging. In short, this is a specification that allows for messages to be delivered reliably between endpoints. These two specifications and the support for them within a DataPower service are covered in more detail in Chapter 19.

Front Side Handler Configuration (FSH)

We already discussed FSH objects in Chapter 9, "Multi-Protocol Gateway," so you should already know how to configure them. The FSH objects that are configured for a Web Service Proxy are no different than the ones you configured in the Multi-Protocol Gateway (MPGW); however, there are some differences in the way that they are implemented. We already saw in our first WSP example in this chapter how the FSH object is used in conjunction with a specified URI to form an endpoint for the client, so this is one way that it is configured differently. In this section we discuss other ways that this FSH/endpoint configuration is the same and also how it can be different from the MPGW service.

As you already know, there are different types of FSH objects to support different protocols, as shown in Chapter 9; however, the MPGW is not the only service type that can take advantage of different protocols. Even if the backend Web service that your WSP is proxying supports only HTTP(s), your service can also receive requests from MQ. Keep in mind that the request document sent to the service must comply with the WSDL referenced by the WSP service. For example, suppose you had an MQ queue that holds valid Web service requests. You could add an MQ FSH to your Web Service Proxy and pull these requests from the queue, process them as you wish within your Processing Policy, and send them the backend Web service over HTTP(s). Be aware that the Web service will send a response back to the service. This response can be written to a response queue; however, if the response is to be ignored, you must set the ReplyToQ HTTP header to a null value. This can be done in the header injection tab of the service.

Another important thing to remember about configuring the FSH in your WSP is that it can be reused. This is different from any other service you configure, where your FSH must be used by only one service. This is possible because the WSP does not only use the IP:port combination to listen for requests, it also includes the URI specified in the configuration as well as the operation being requested. This means that a FSH can be reused in the same or different Web Service Proxies within a single domain as long as the combination of the IP address, port, URI, and operation are unique. This is a common thing to do when your WSDL contains multiple bindings. This is because an endpoint must be configured for each binding specified in the WSDL. As an example, let's take the BookService WSDL that we used in our BookService_WSP service. We saw that this WSDL specified two different operations, but they were all contained within the same binding within the WSDL as shown in Listing 10-7. This is why when we showed the configuration for the WSP service, we were required to configure only one FSH and URI combination.

Listing 10-7 Two Operations Within the Same Binding

```
<wsdl:binding name="BookServiceSOAP" type="tns:BookService">
   <soap:binding style="document"
transport="http://schemas.xmlsoap.org/soap/http"/>
      <!- ->
   <wsdl:operation name="BookQuery">
      <soap:operation
soapAction="http://www.example.org/BookService/BookQuery"/>
         <wsdl:input name="BookQueryRequest">
            <soap:body use="literal"/>
         </wsdl:input>
         <wsdl:output>
            <soap:body use="literal"/>
         </wsdl:output>
      </wsdl:operation>
      <wsdl:operation name="BookPurchase">
         <soap:operation
soapAction="http://www.example.org/BookService/BookPurchase"/>
            <wsdl:input name="BookPurchaseRequest">
               <soap:body use="literal"/>
            </wsdl:input>
            <wsdl:output>
               <soap:body use="literal"/>
            </wsdl:output>
       </wsdl:operation>
   </wsdl:binding>
```

Let's suppose that this WSDL had the same two operations but they were listed in two separate bindings within the WSDL, such as the example shown in Listing 10-8. Notice that there are two binding elements specified, each containing an operation. This is a common occurrence, so let's take a look at what happens when this is referenced by our BookService_WSP service.

Listing 10-8 Two Binding Elements with Two Operations

```
<wsdl:binding name="BookQuerySOAP" type="tns:BookQuery">
   <soap:binding style="document"
transport="http://schemas.xmlsoap.org/soap/http"/>
    <!- ->
       <wsdl:operation name="BookQuery">
          <soap:operation
soapAction="http://www.example.org/BookService/BookQuery"/>
       <wsdl:input name="BookQueryRequest">
          <soap:body use="literal"/>
       </wsdl:input>
       <wsdl:output>
          <soap:body use="literal"/>
       </wsdl:output>
   </wsdl:operation>
</wsdl:binding>
<!- ->
<wsdl:binding name="BookPurchaseSOAP" type="tns:BookPurchase">
```

```
   <soap:binding style="document"
transport="http://schemas.xmlsoap.org/soap/http"/>
   <wsdl:operation name="BookPurchase">
      <soap:operation
soapAction="http://www.example.org/BookService/BookPurchase"/>
      <wsdl:input name="BookPurchaseRequest">
         <soap:body use="literal"/>
      </wsdl:input>
      <wsdl:output>
         <soap:body use="literal"/>
      </wsdl:output>
   </wsdl:operation>
</wsdl:binding>
```

As the WSDL referenced by our BookService_WSP service is changed to contain the two bindings as shown in Listing 10-8, you will see that instead of one local, remote, published configuration, there are two. Figure 10-11 shows the service with the new BookService WSDL referenced. Notice that we now have two sections to complete, each containing a FSH/URI combination and a remote endpoint configuration. Also notice that we are using the same FSH object for each with a different URI. That could have just as easily been different FSH objects. For example, because the BookPurchase operation may contain sensitive data, you would probably configure an HTTPS FSH for that operation. As you can see, it is also possible to configure different backends, or endpoints, for each operation—so we could also configure this operation to go to the backend Web service over an encrypted transport such as HTTPS.

Because these two operations are separated into two separate bindings, the Processing Policy would reflect that and display two binding sections each with one operation. In this case, you could configure processing rules at the binding level or at the operation level as we saw in the first example.

It is also possible to configure more than one FSH object for the same WSDL and binding. For example, suppose we wanted to provide the ability to call the BookPurchase operation in our BookService_WSP over HTTP or HTTPS. We could add a second HTTPS FSH object to this binding in our configuration as shown in Figure 10-12. A new FSH configuration was added called BookService_HTTPS_FSH to the BookPurchaseSOAP binding. The operations contained within this binding (BookPurchase) can now receive requests by both FSH objects. Although it is not shown in this example, the URI that is used can also be different for this new configuration.

WSDL Source Location	Endpoint Handler Summary	WSDL Status	WS-I BP Status
local:///BookService.wsdl	2 up / 2 configured	Okay	Okay

BookQuery - BookQuerySOAP

Local

Local Endpoint Handler	URI	Binding (Suffix)	Edit/Remove
BookService_HTTP_FSH	/BookQuery	soap-11()	Edit Remove
BookService_HTTP_F + ...	/BookQuery	SOAP 1.1 SOAP 1.2 HTTP GET	Add

Remote

Protocol	Hostname (IP Address)	Port	Remote URI
http	www.books.org	80	books/query/queryService

Published Use Local

BookPurchase - BookPurchaseSOAP

Local

Local Endpoint Handler	URI	Binding (Suffix)	Edit/Remove
BookService_HTTP_FSH	/BookPurchase	soap-11()	Edit Remove
BookService_HTTP_F + ...	/BookPurchase	SOAP 1.1 SOAP 1.2 HTTP GET	Add

Remote

Protocol	Hostname (IP Address)	Port	Remote URI
http	www.books.org	80	books/purchase/purchaseService

Published Use Local

Figure 10-11 Configuring multiple bindings within a WSP.

BookPurchase - BookPurchaseSOAP

Local

Local Endpoint Handler	URI	Binding (Suffix)	Edit/Remove
BookService_HTTP_FSH	/BookPurchase	soap-11()	Edit Remove
BookService_HTTPS_FSH	/BookPurchase	soap-11(0)	Edit Remove
BookService_HTTP_F + ...	/BookPurchase	SOAP 1.1 SOAP 1.2 HTTP GET	Add

Remote

Protocol	Hostname (IP Address)	Port	Remote URI
https	www.books.org	443	books/purchase/purchaseService

Published Use Local

Figure 10-12 Adding a second FSH object.

Now that we have two FSH objects configured for our BookPurchaseSOAP binding, it is important to take a look again at our Processing Policy. This is another area where the WSP service is different from the MPGW service. When we added additional FSH objects to a MPGW, all requests handled by any of these objects would evaluate the same set of processing rules to determine what rule would be executed on the request, response, or error. When multiple FSH objects are added to a WSP, however, this is not the case. You saw what happened to our Processing Policy when we put each of our operations within the WSDL into separate bindings. Another binding was introduced in the policy where rules could be configured. When we add the additional FSH to our service, the same thing happens. This is because adding another listening protocol and port is adding another binding to your service. This is how the DataPower service virtualizes the endpoints. So just because you added another FSH to your service does not mean that the same processing rules will be applied to each even though they are the same operation. Figure 10-13 shows our Processing Policy after this second FSH was added to our BookPurchaseSOAP binding. Notice that the BookPurchaseSOAP binding is still there containing a BookPurchase operation along with the rule that we configured for it. Looking a little closer you will realize that a second binding was created called BookPurchaseSOAP.0. This is the binding for our new HTTPS FSH. So this means that the rule containing the AAA action for our BookPurchase operation will not fire if the request is sent over HTTPS to the new FSH configured. We must configure another rule for this binding.

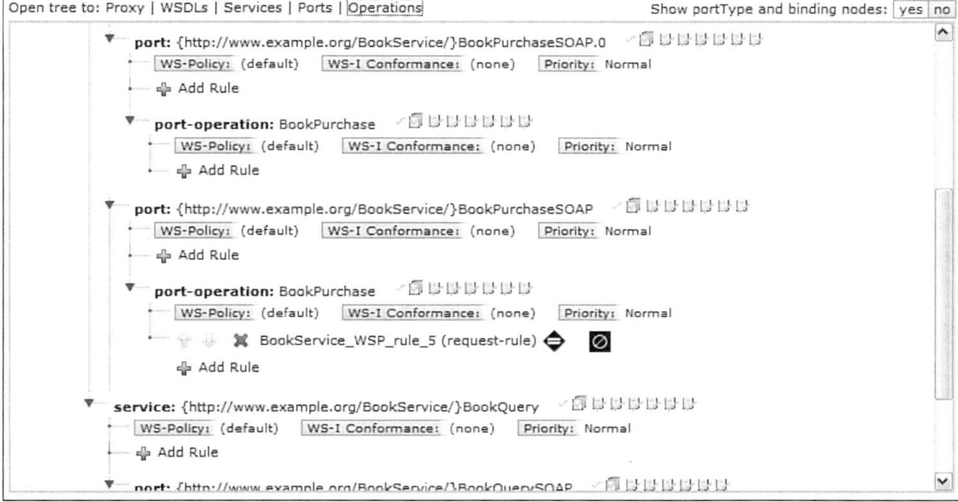

Figure 10-13 Processing policy with multiple FSH objects.

Reusable Rules

Although the concept of reusable rules is not unique to the Web Service Proxy Service, this might be a good place to discuss them, because it can solve the problem we previously discussed when adding multiple FSH objects to a single binding.

A reusable rule is simply a rule, or part of a rule, that can be called from within another rule. After the callable rule is finished, it returns the results back to the calling rule where the rule processing resumes. This call can be made by implementing a call or on-error action in a processing rule. To demonstrate how to configure and call these rules, let's take a look at our previous example in Figure 10-13.

In this example, we demonstrated what happens to a Processing Policy when multiple FSH objects are added to a single binding within a WSDL. In this example, there was only one AAA action in the BookPurchase operation, so it would be easy enough to just add that same AAA policy to the second BookPurchase request rule. This would not be as simple if there were several actions within the request rule for this operation. For example, let's suppose that after the AAA action there were a Transform action and an Encrypt action in this request rule. This would be more difficult to duplicate in the second rule. By making this rule a reusable rule, we could have requests handled by the second FSH object execute the same processing rule by calling it. Let's see how this is done.

To create a reusable rule, you must first start with an existing rule that has already been configured. In our example we have the request rule containing the AAA action, a Transform action, and an Encrypt action for the BookPurchase operation. To begin, the rule must be displayed in the policy editor, which can be done by simply clicking the rule within the Web Service Proxy Policy. After the rule is displayed in the policy editor, clicking the Create Reusable Rule button causes the cursor to change to a crosshair. Left-clicking and dragging the crosshair over the actions that are to be contained in the reusable rule creates a new reusable rule consisting of those actions. The actions to be included are identified by a blue highlighted box. Figure 10-14 shows our request rule for the BookPurchase operation where we have combined all three actions to form a new reusable rule.

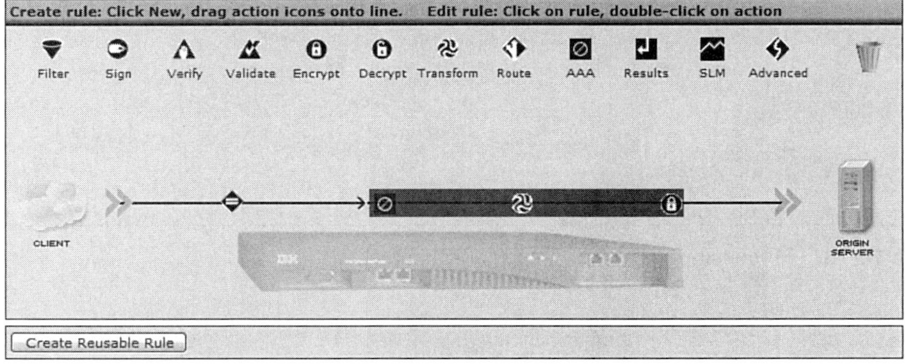

Figure 10-14 Creating a reusable rule.

Now that we have a reusable rule for the BookPurchase operation, we can call it from the second binding that was created when we added our HTTPS FSH to the BookPurchase binding. To do this we added a new request rule to this second BookPurchase operation and added an Advanced action to the rule. We then configured this Advanced action as a Call Processing Rule type, selecting the new callable rule as the processing rule to call, as shown in Figure 10-15. Notice that the name given to the reusable rule when it was created was the name of the actual request rule that it was created from with _callrule_0 appended to it.

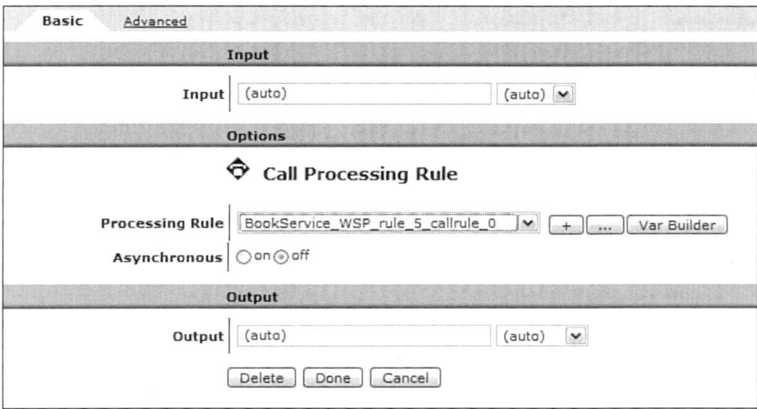

Figure 10-15 Configuring the Call Processing Rule action.

We have now configured the three actions in the BookPurchase operation to be a reusable rule. The second BookPurchase operation that was added for the HTTPS FSH now contains a request rule with a Call Processing Rule action to call this reusable rule. Now any request to the BookPurchase operation will execute the same three actions as desired.

Proxy Settings

As you have seen, the WSDL file referenced by the Web Service Proxy describes many of the details for calling the actual Web service, enabling the proxy to automatically produce a base configuration. There are, however, many configuration options within the service that cannot be derived from the WSDL and that can be set at the proxy level. Many of these configuration options are found in the Proxy Settings tab on the service configuration screen. Figure 10-16 shows this configuration tab with all of the default settings. You should notice the similarities between this configuration screen and the General service configuration screen in the MPGW service.

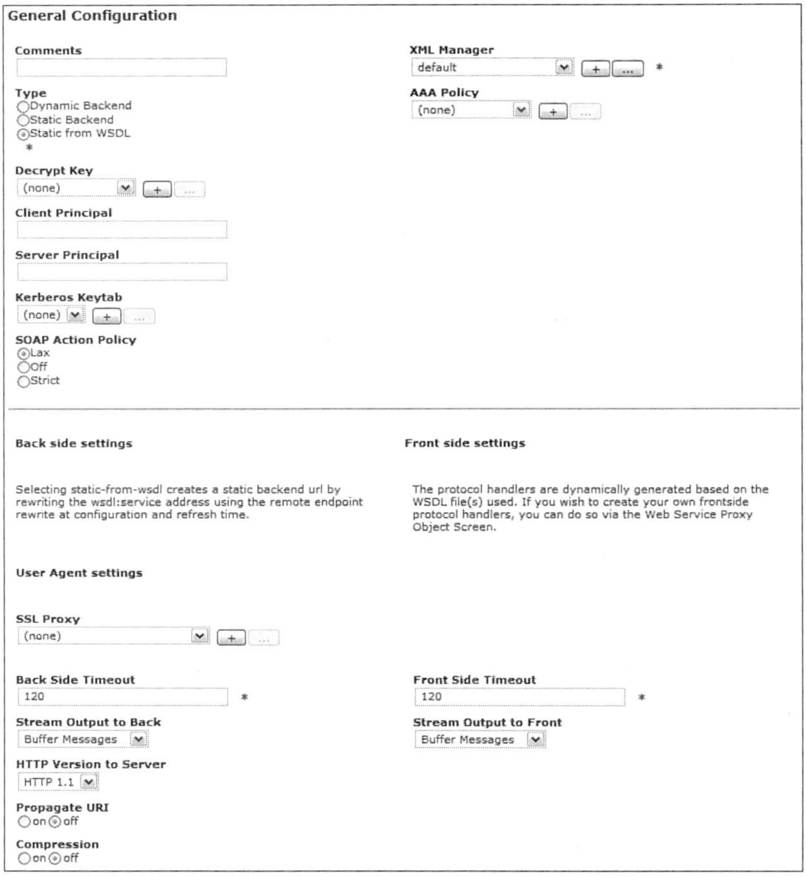

General Configuration

Comments

Type
Dynamic Backend
Static Backend
Static from WSDL
*

Decrypt Key
(none)

Client Principal

Server Principal

Kerberos Keytab
(none)

SOAP Action Policy
Lax
Off
Strict

XML Manager
default *

AAA Policy
(none)

Back side settings

Selecting static-from-wsdl creates a static backend url by rewriting the wsdl:service address using the remote endpoint rewrite at configuration and refresh time.

Front side settings

The protocol handlers are dynamically generated based on the WSDL file(s) used. If you wish to create your own frontside protocol handlers, you can do so via the Web Service Proxy Object Screen.

User Agent settings

SSL Proxy
(none)

Back Side Timeout
120 *

Stream Output to Back
Buffer Messages

HTTP Version to Server
HTTP 1.1

Propagate URI
on off

Compression
on off

Front Side Timeout
120 *

Stream Output to Front
Buffer Messages

Figure 10-16 Proxy Settings tab

Defining the Backend

When the Web Service Proxy is created, the endpoint listed in the WSDL is used to automatically populate the endpoint, or backend, within the service. There are times however, when this is not the actual endpoint that you want your DataPower service to forward requests to. This is when you can utilize the flexibility that the WSP offers when defining the endpoint.

When defining the backend for your Web Service Proxy, there are three different options that you can choose. You can keep the endpoint described in the WSDL, you can provide your own static backend, or you can specify a dynamic backend. The default behavior is to use the endpoint specified in the WSDL, but this can be changed under the Type heading in the Proxy Settings tab.

If you choose not to use the endpoint specified in the WSDL but still want to define a static backend, you can specify the new endpoint in two different ways. The first option is to type directly over the values in the Remote section on the WSDL tab with the new endpoint. This might be the best option if there are multiple endpoint configurations and you want to change only one. But what if you have multiple bindings, each requiring an endpoint definition and you want all requests to go to one single endpoint? This is where you can use the Static Backend option. Figure 10-17 shows this option selected. Notice what happens when the Type is set to Static backend. The Backend URL field is shown where you would specify the backend—but notice the buttons below it. There are buttons for generating the Backend URL for protocols other than HTTP. All the DataPower supported protocol options are available for the backend. In fact, the backend does not even have to be an actual Web service.

Suppose you had many clients on different platforms and programming languages that all needed to send files to an FTP server and you needed them to all be in a specific format. There are a couple of challenges you might face. First, you would need to be sure that they can all communicate over FTP. If they can communicate with your FTP server, you would then be required to provide them with the details for connecting to the server. If this is possible, you will need to communicate the format of the message to each potential client. This could be difficult if the message is not an XML document. Now think about how convenient it would be to generate and publish a WSDL that would represent the message to be sent to the FTP server but in an XML format. You could then create a Web Service Proxy on the DataPower appliance that would reference that WSDL and enforce it on all requests. You could even authenticate and authorize the request before sending to the backend FTP server. Any response codes back from the server can then be converted back into a SOAP response and sent back to the client. In this scenario the clients never know the backend implementation details because they think they are sending a simple Web service request over HTTP(s). Now when the backend server changes the end clients will never have to know.

Figure 10-17 Selecting a Static backend in a WSP.

The last option available for the backend is to have a dynamic backend. As we discussed in Chapter 8, "XML Firewall," a dynamic backend simply indicates that the backend server will be decided within the Processing Policy as each request is processed. This is no different in a WSP service; however, the flexibility of the Processing Policy makes it easier to implement. For example, you might have a different backend for each operation within the Web service. Because the Processing Policy allows for rules to be configured at the operation level, a rule can be configured for each operation containing a Route action. The hierarchy of the WSDL within the Processing Policy can also be taken advantage of when specifying a backend. Suppose you had a Web service with many operations and you wanted requests for all of the operations, except for one, to be forwarded to the same backend address. You could configure a rule at the WSDL level that sets the backend server via a Route action for the majority of the operations. You would then configure a rule with a different Route action for the one operation requiring a different backend.

Decrypt Key

There may be times when the Web service request message being sent is expected to be encrypted by the client. Because the DataPower device supports most of the popular encryption algorithms, these messages can be decrypted within your service. In all other service types, this decryption is performed via a Decrypt action that would be added to a request rule. This is also possible to do in a WSP service; however, it presents some issues. Before the message even gets to the Processing Policy, it is validated for WSDL compliance, which includes schema validation and valid operations being requested. If the request message is encrypted, this would not be possible. This is why the Decrypt key option is available.

Configuring a Decrypt key within the service provides the service the appropriate key to decrypt the request message. This key is used to decrypt the message as it enters the service before it is validated for WSDL compliance. Now the decrypted message can be validated and passed to the Processing Policy.

Creating this Decrypt Key object is simple. Clicking the plus (+) sign next to the Decrypt Key drop-down box on the Proxy Settings tab shown in Figure 10-16 will display the Configure Crypto Key screen. The private key can then be selected that should be used for decrypting the message. More information about key and certificate management can be found in Chapter 18, "DataPower and SSL."

Although the Decrypt Key object provides a way to specify the key that will decrypt the incoming document, it is not always necessary. If the request document contains a Binary Security Token (BST) in the WS-Security header, the WSP will use the certificate within it and attempt to find the corresponding key within a configured Crypto Identification Credential object on the device. If the key is found, it is used to decrypt the message.

SOAP Action Policy

Often a WSDL specifies a soapAction parameter with a URI as its value. This indicates that a soapAction HTTP header with the corresponding value should be sent along with all requests for that particular operation. The purpose of this header is to indicate the intent of the request; however, there are no restrictions on what this value must or must not be as long as it is a URI.

The Web Service Proxy has an option on the Proxy Settings tab shown in Figure 10-16 named SOAP Action Policy. This indicates how strictly this header specified in the WSDL will be enforced. The default value is Lax, which indicates that an empty header is considered a match. The other two options are Strict, which indicates that the request must contain the soapAction header with an exact match, and Off, which does not check the header at all.

WSDL Configuration and Management

As we have stated several times throughout this chapter, the WSDL describes the backend Web service and provides many of the configuration details for the Web Service Proxy. Because the service uses much of the information specified in the WSDL for its configuration, it is important that the DataPower service be notified when it is changed. This section explains the different methods for managing these changes and the different methods for dynamically looking up a WSDL or even combining multiple WSDLs within a single service.

Adding Additional WSDLs

After a Web Service Proxy is created using a single WSDL that describes the backend Web service, it is possible to add additional WSDLs to the service. This would provide the convenience of combining two WSDLs within a single DataPower service. Let's take our BookService_WSP service as an example. Suppose the company providing this service acquired an online music store and can now offer music as well as books. It just so happens that the online music store that was acquired already has a Web service for this. It would be very convenient for our customers to view both of these Web services as one. This is entirely possible using our Web Service Proxy service by simply adding this new WSDL to our service.

Adding multiple WSDLs to an existing service is easy to do. From the WSDL tab in the Web Service Proxy configuration screen, selecting the Add WSDL radio button renders a screen with the familiar Upload and Fetch buttons that can be used to add the new WSDL. This process is the same as the process used to add the first WSDL when the service was initially created. An FSH and URI must be entered in the Local section to reflect the endpoint that the client will use to access the service. As we saw in the previous examples, the Remote information is taken from the WSDL. As we discussed earlier in this chapter, this backend information can be changed in several different ways.

After all the required information for the new WSDL is entered, you will see that the second WSDL has been added to the service. Now, as you can see in Figure 10-18, we have two WSDLs configured within our BookService_WSP. Also, notice the Endpoint Handler Summary for each. The BookService.wsdl indicates 3 up / 3 configured. This is because we have two bindings within that WSDL and we also added one additional FSH to it. The MusicService.wsdl only shows 1 up / 1 configured. This is because there is only one binding within this WSDL and we added only one FSH for it. If we expand the MusicService.wsdl as shown in Figure 10-19, we can see that we configured it to use the same HTTP Front Side Handler object as we did with the BookService.wsdl. You can also see that this new WSDL requires another Remote configuration that provides a new backend protocol, Hostname, port, and URI. This allows us to have separate backends for each of the WSDLs added to the service.

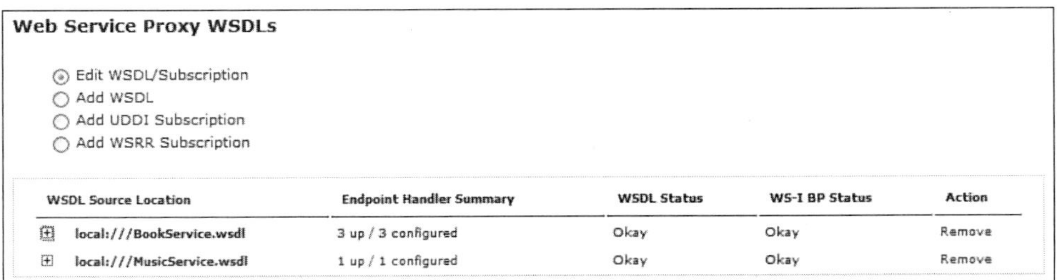

Figure 10-18 Second WSDL added to the Web Service Proxy.

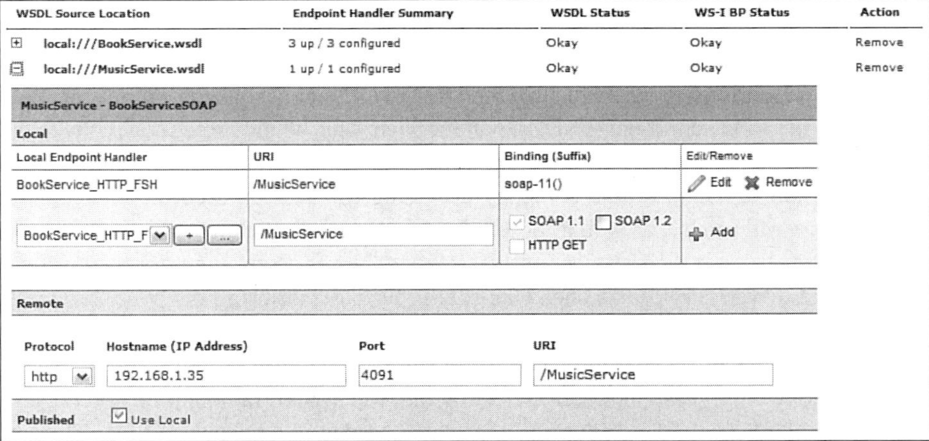

Figure 10-19 MusicService.wsdl endpoint configuration.

Now that we have seen the WSDL configuration for adding additional WSDLs to a service, let's see how the Processing Policy looks. Because the Processing Policy reflects the hierarchy of the WSDL configured with the proxy itself being the highest level, adding a new WSDL adds a new WSDL sub-tree under the proxy within the policy. This enables processing rules to be configured for the new WSDL providing the same level of granularity as the first WSDL added. Figure 10-20 shows the Processing Policy in our example service after adding the MusicService.wsdl. We have expanded only the MusicService level to show the port and operations within it. We now can configure rules for both WSDLs at any level of granularity.

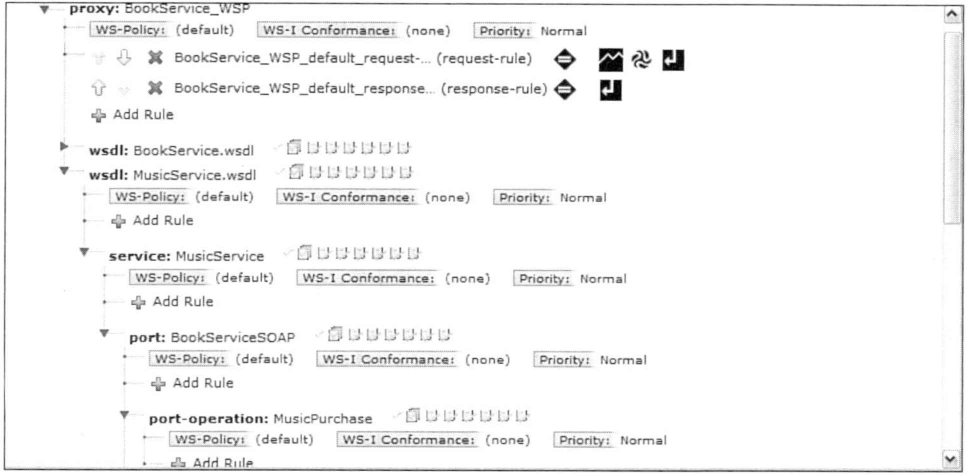

Figure 10-20 Processing Policy with the MusicService.wsdl added.

WSDL Cache Policy

After a service has been configured, it is possible that the WSDL that it is configured to use will change over time. Because the service actually compiles and caches the WSDL, there needs to be some mechanism to tell the service that it has changed and to refresh the cache. To do this, we can configure a WSDL refresh policy within our WSP that dictates how often this cache will be refreshed.

To configure a WSDL cache policy, you must access the Web Service Proxy configuration screen from the left navigation menu; go to Objects→Services→Web Service Proxy, and then select the service you want to configure it for. After the service configuration screen is rendered, the WSDL Cache Policy tab can be selected from the top menu. Note that this link will not be visible at first. Scrolling this top menu to the right is required to access it. Figure 10-21 shows this configuration screen.

Configure Web Service Proxy

This configuration has been modified, but not yet saved.

er Injection | HTTP Header Suppression | Stylesheet Parameter | Probe Triggers | WSDL Cache Policy | WSD

Web Service Proxy : BookService_WSP [up]

Apply | Cancel | Delete | Undo

Export | View Log | View Status | Show Probe | Validate Conformance | Help

URL Match expression	TTL
(no properties defined)	

Add

Figure 10-21 WSDL Cache Policy configuration screen.

From this screen you can now click the Add button to configure a new WSDL cache policy for your service. There are two fields required for each policy. The first field is the URL Match expression. This field enables you to define which WSDLs are refreshed by this policy. This is the URL of the WSDL file which can be a literal representation or a wildcarded URL. For example, if we wanted to just have a refresh policy that applies only to the BookService.wsdl, which resides in the local directory of the DataPower file system, you could add local:///BookService.wsdl in this field. However, if you wanted this policy to be applied to all WSDLs within the service, you simply put an * as a wildcard indicating all. Although our example shows a WSDL cache policy for a WSDL that resides on the local file system, the real benefit of this policy is realized when it is retrieved remotely. In this case the match expression might be something like http://services.mycompany.com/*.wsdl.

The second field you can specify is the TTL (Time to Live) parameter. This specifies how often the WSDL will be refreshed. This is entered in seconds and a default value of 900 seconds is pre-populated. If a new value is entered, it must be an integer between 5 and 86400. Figure 10-22 shows a WSDL cache policy for our BookService_WSP. As you can see, the BookService.wsdl is refreshed only every 1800 seconds, whereas the MusicService.wsdl is refreshed every 900 seconds.

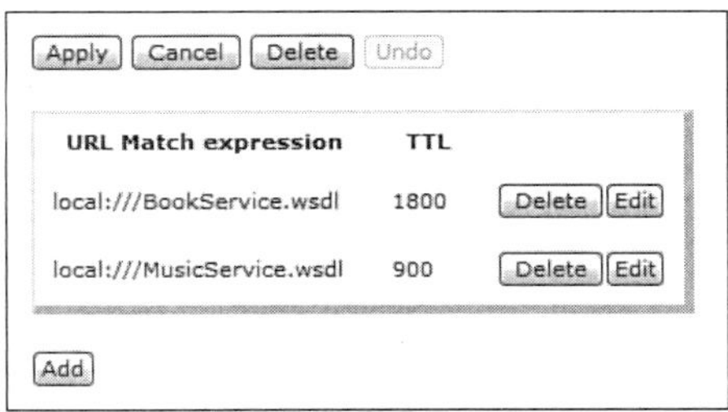

Figure 10-22 WSDL cache policy.

After a WSDL cache policy is created and applied to the service, the WSDLs will be refreshed at the specified intervals. Once it is refreshed it is also reflected in the Web Service Proxy configuration. Although the service configuration is updated automatically, it is important to know what changes are being made to the WSDL and how they can affect the service. For example, if new binding is added to a WSDL and the service is updated to reflect it, you will still need to configure a new endpoint configuration for it.

UDDI

Because many Web services are available to the general public or external business partners, there is a challenge that is presented. We know that a WSDL describes the Web service providing all of the required information to the consumer, but how does the service provider publish this WSDL so people who wish to consume the service can find this Web service and its operations? The open industry initiative called Universal Description Discovery and Integration (UDDI) was created to solve this specific challenge. UDDI is an XML-based registry specification that describes how Web service providers can publish a WSDL and how consumers can find it. This registry can be made available over the Internet or private networks. This can be thought of as a

Yellow Pages for Web services. Consumers of the services can be configured to dynamically look up the WSDL for the services of interest and know exactly how and where to call them.

We have seen when configuring a Web Service Proxy that a WSDL must be referenced to gather the required service information. It is possible to have the DataPower service automatically obtain the WSDL from a UDDI registry or to browse the registry for one when configuring the service. To have DataPower automatically obtain a WSDL from the UDDI registry you must add a UDDI subscription within your service. From the WSDL configuration tab within the service configuration, you will see a radio button labeled Add UDDI Subscription. Selecting this radio button presents the screen for configuring a new UDDI subscription.

A UDDI subscription object provides the information that enables the DataPower service to retrieve the WSDL and also to be notified of any updates to it. The UDDI subscription object defines all of the parameters for subscribing to a particular WSDL; however, it does not define the UDDI registry connection details. This is defined within a UDDI Registry object, which is then referenced by the UDDI subscription object.

As with most objects within DataPower, the UDDI Registry object can be configured from the Objects section in the left navigation menu, or we can configure it by clicking the plus + sign within the UDDI subscription configuration. In either case, the UDDI Registry object is configured via the configuration screen shown in Figure 10-23. When configuring this object, you must supply a name for the object as well as the host and port of the UDDI registry. In addition to these required fields, you can also specify if the connection to the UDDI registry should use SSL for publishing only or for all lookups. In either case a SSL proxy profile must be defined along with the SSL port for the registry. You can also define the URLs used by the registry for inquiries, publishing, and subscribing. This is left as the default in many cases. The last field defines the version of UDDI that will be used.

UDDI Registry

Apply Cancel Help

Name	BookService_UDDIRegistry *
Admin State	enabled disabled
Comments	
Host	192.168.1.101 *
Port	80 *
Use SSL	Publish
Port (SSL)	443
SSL proxy profile	UDDI_SSLProxyProfile (SSL Proxy Profile) + ...
Inquiry URL	/uddi/inquiry
Publish URL	/uddi/publishing
Subscription URL	/uddi/subscription
Security URL	/uddi/security
Version	Version 2

Figure 10-23 UDDI Registry configuration.

After the UDDI Registry object is configured, you can then continue to configure the UDDI subscription object. The remainder of this configuration requires only a few remaining details. As usual, the object requires a name. A username and password are required for connecting to the registry and finally, the Subscription Key(s) are required for locating the WSDL within the registry. This key can be found in the UDDI registry for the WSDL document you are subscribing to. To add a key to this subscription, you must enter the key and click the Add button. Many times there will be more than one key required for locating the particular service. Figure 10-24 shows a completed UDDI subscription object. Once this object is configured within the WSP, it will appear along with the WSDLs within the service requiring the same endpoint configuration as when a WSDL was added locally.

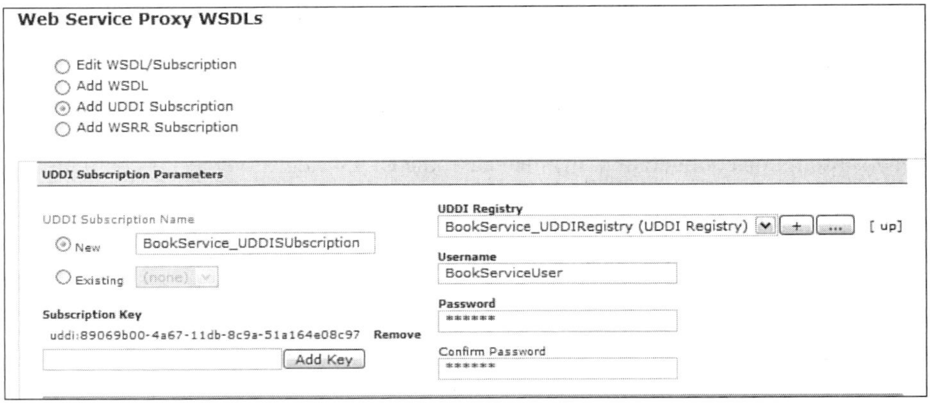

Figure 10-24 Completed UDDI Subscription object.

In addition to DataPower using a WSDL for its service configuration, it can also publish a WSDL to a UDDI registry. When publishing WSDLs to an external registry, DataPower uses the endpoint configuration specified in the Publish section of the service configuration within the WSDL tab. This Publish section can specify a new service endpoint, or it can use the endpoint that is specified in the Local section of the configuration. The Local section represents the actual endpoint that the consumers connect to within the DataPower device, that is, the virtualized endpoints that the service creates consisting of the hostname, listening port from the FSH, and the URI. This will be embedded in the appropriate location in the original WSDL and published by DataPower, so subscribers can consume the Web service(s) proxied by the Web Service Proxy. This can be accomplished from the Services tab in the Web Service Proxy configuration screen as shown in Figure 10-25. As you can see, each binding within each WSDL can be published separately. Clicking the Publish to UDDI button for a particular binding will then prompt you for a UDDI Registry object that must be configured on the device, and subsequently a username and password for authenticating to the registry.

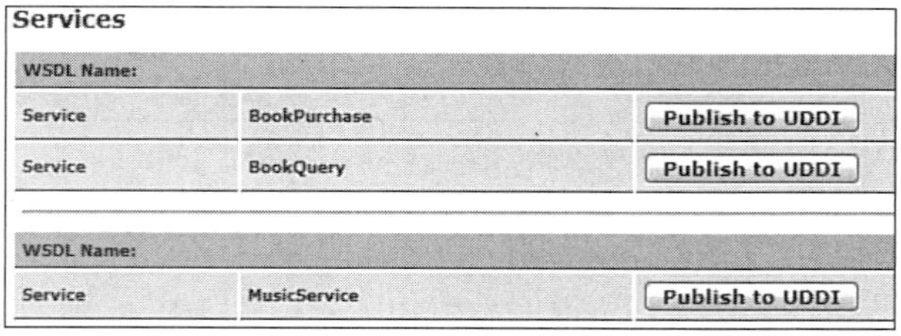

Services

WSDL Name:		
Service	BookPurchase	Publish to UDDI
Service	BookQuery	Publish to UDDI

WSDL Name:		
Service	MusicService	Publish to UDDI

Figure 10-25 Services tab in a WSP Configuration.

After a service is published to the UDDI registry, subscribers to that service can retrieve the WSDL, which will contain the DataPower Web Service Proxy as the endpoint instead of the original service endpoints. This truly reflects the power of the Web Service Proxy to virtualize the Web service endpoints. This virtualizes and hides the actual backend endpoints forcing all the consumers to go through the DataPower Web Service Proxy.

WSRR

Although UDDI provides a solution to Web Service publishing and subscribing, it is a rudimentary approach that may not suit your needs. For more robust requirements, DataPower also supports the IBM WebSphere Service Registry and Repository (WSRR), from which a WSDL can be referenced. WSRR enables you to quickly and easily publish, find, enrich, manage, and govern services and policies within your SOA. We do not discuss all the additional value of WSRR in this book as you can find that information in your WSRR documentation; however we focus on the integration with the product from within a DataPower Web Service Proxy.

Adding a Document to WSRR

Let's start by taking a look the WSRR administration console. WSRR is actually a Java EE application that runs within a WebSphere Application Server (WAS) and can be administered through a Web browser. If you are familiar with the WAS administration console, it may look somewhat familiar because it uses the Integrated Solutions Console that provides a similar look and feel. Although many different types of documents and metadata can be stored within WSRR, we only talk about WSDLs in this chapter.

Before you can do anything with the product, you must first install all the supporting products and WSRR itself. WSRR requires a database (DB2, Oracle, or Cloudscape®) and a WebSphere Application Server to be installed. For complete installation instructions, please refer to the WSRR documentation. Once all of the products are installed and deployed, you can access the administration console through a browser. Once you have logged into WSRR, adding a WSDL is a simple process. From the administration console, you would navigate from the left menu to Service Documents→Load Documents as shown in Figure 10-26.

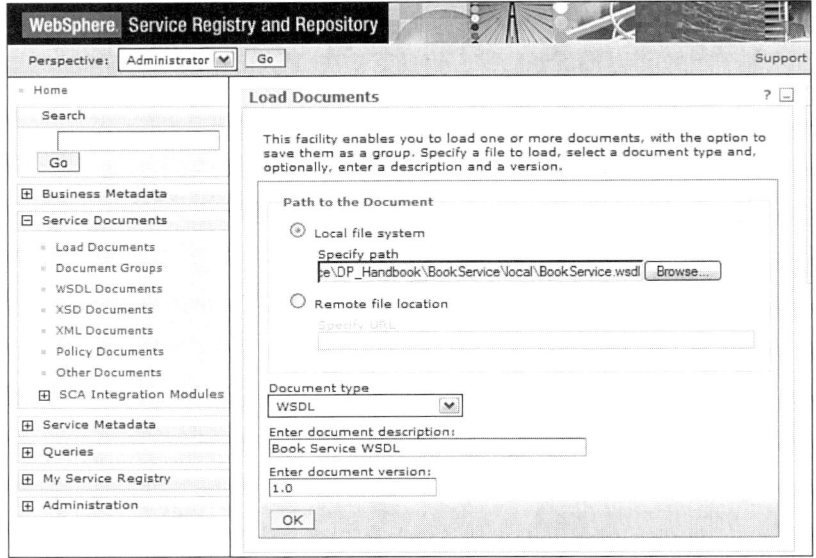

Figure 10-26 Loading a document in WSRR.

As you can see, there are not many fields to be entered on the screen presented. By clicking the Browse button, you can navigate to the WSDL on your local computer. You can also reference a remote location for retrieving the WSDL by providing a URL. You can then optionally add a description and a document version. Notice in Figure 10-26 that we are loading the Book Service.wsdl file and entering a version of 1.0 (version is optional). Clicking OK and Finish loads the WSDL in the repository, and a message is displayed that the document has been loaded successfully as shown in Figure 10-27.

Figure 10-27 WSDL successfully loaded to the repository.

So we said that the WSDL was loaded into the repository but what does that mean to us? Let's take a look at the WSDL within WSRR. Again, through the WSRR administration console, we can navigate to Service Documents→WSDL Documents from the left navigation menu. Or, if you are still on the success screen after loading the document, you can click the filename. In our example we can click the BookService.wsdl shown in Figure 10-27. This displays the details of the document loaded. Figure 10-28 shows the BookService.wsdl details within the WSRR administration console.

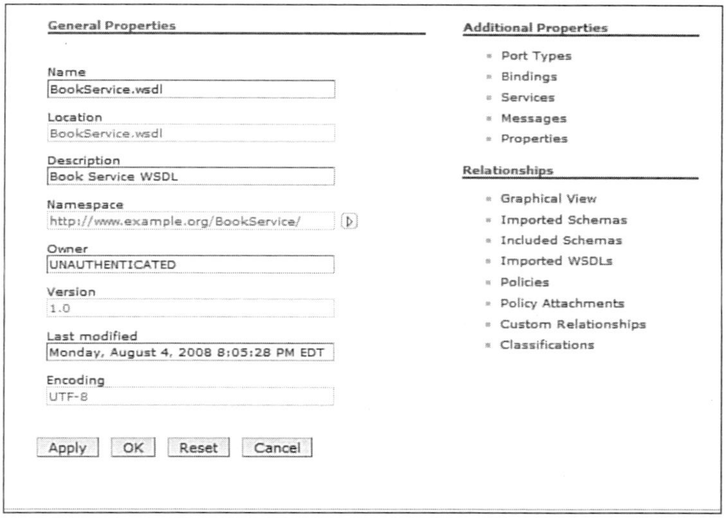

Figure 10-28 BookService.wsdl within WSRR.

There are only a handful of details shown here but there are many links that can display additional details if they are available. Of particular interest to us are the Name and the Namespace on this screen, as this is how we will reference the file from our DataPower service. There is also a Last modified date and time as well as the version number that we had given it when we loaded it.

Some other links from the WSDL document screen shown in Figure 10-28 are under the Additional Properties headings. Most of these links should look somewhat familiar to you as they are the different parts of a WSDL that we discussed earlier in this chapter. These can be selected to view the applicable information for the WSDL document. For example, Figure 10-29 shows the Bindings within our BookService.wsdl file. We see the two bindings that we created for this service. Each binding can also be selected to view information about it. Notice that each entry also has a Name and a Namespace associated with it. This is because individual sections of the WSDL can be retrieved independently from WSRR.

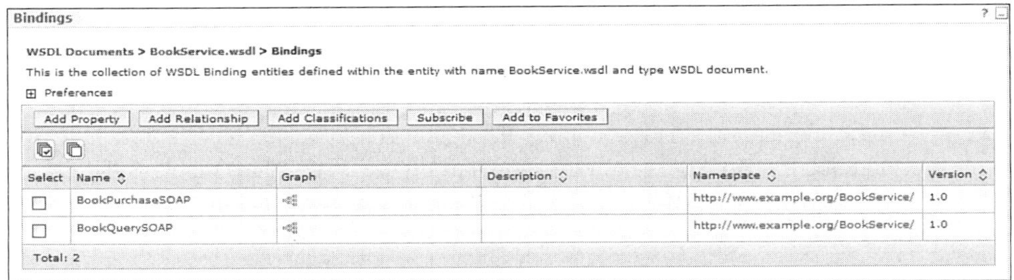
Bindings

WSDL Documents > BookService.wsdl > Bindings

This is the collection of WSDL Binding entities defined within the entity with name BookService.wsdl and type WSDL document.

Preferences

Add Property | Add Relationship | Add Classifications | Subscribe | Add to Favorites

Select	Name	Graph	Description	Namespace	Version
☐	BookPurchaseSOAP			http://www.example.org/BookService/	1.0
☐	BookQuerySOAP			http://www.example.org/BookService/	1.0

Total: 2

Figure 10-29 Bindings within the BookService.wsdl.

Although there is much more that you can do with WSRR, simply adding a WSDL as shown in this section is all that is required for a DataPower service to subscribe to it.

Subscribing to WSRR from a DataPower Service

Now that we have a WSDL loaded into WSRR we can talk about referencing it from a DataPower service. Much like subscribing to a UDDI registry from a DataPower service, a WSRR subscription must also be created. This object references a WSRR Server object that provides all the connection details for connecting to the repository, and then you will need to configure a subscription describing what you want to retrieve from it.

You can begin to configure these required objects from within the WSDL tab of the service configuration screen because you are essentially adding a WSDL to the service. Selecting the Add WSRR Subscription displays the screen for configuring the objects.

On this screen there are few parameters here that need to be supplied. To start, you need to provide a name for this Object. You will then be required to add a WSRR Server object; an existing one can be referenced or edited, or a new object can be created. The configuration screen for this object is shown in Figure 10-30. The only two required fields for this object are a name and a SOAP URL where the WSRR server can be contacted. If you are contacting the WSRR server over HTTPS, you will also need to specify a SSL Proxy Profile object. If your WSRR repository requires authentication, you will need to provide the username and password here as well.

Now that we have a name for our WSRR Subscription object and a WSRR Server Object, we can specify the subscription details for the document that we want to retrieve. To indicate this, we must provide the name of the document, the namespace, and optionally the version. Note that the option to subscribe to a particular version of a document from DataPower is only available in firmware 3.7.1 and later.

If you recall from Figure 10-27 when we loaded the WSDL into the WSRR repository, there was a name, a namespace, and a version specified. For our example document, the name was BookService.wsdl, the corresponding namespace was http://www.example.org/BookService/, and the version was 1.0. This is what we enter in the corresponding fields for our WSRR Subscription object. Before entering the version, the Use WSDL Version radio option must be set to on. Also notice the field labeled Synchronization Method, which indicates how the WSDL will be synchronized with the repository. The options are Poll, where the object will poll the repository at the interval specified in the Refresh Interval field, and Manual, where you would need to manually refresh the WSDL.

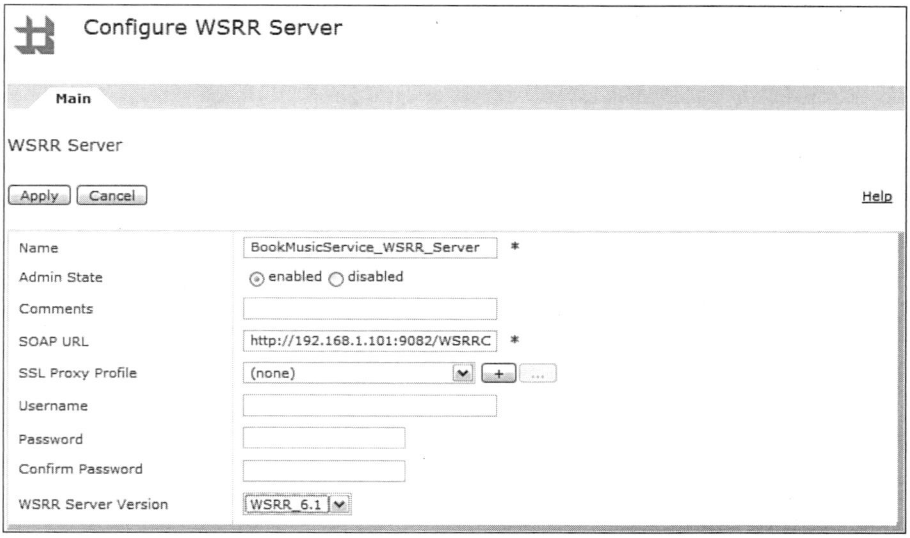

Configure WSRR Server

Main

WSRR Server

Apply Cancel Help

Name	BookMusicService_WSRR_Server *
Admin State	enabled disabled
Comments	
SOAP URL	http://192.168.1.101:9082/WSRRC *
SSL Proxy Profile	(none)
Username	
Password	
Confirm Password	
WSRR Server Version	WSRR_6.1

Figure 10-30 WSRR Server Object configuration screen.

Figure 10-31 shows our completed WSRR Subscription for the BookService.wsdl. Another interesting option available in firmware versions 3.7.1 and later is the Fetch Policy Attachments option in the WSRR subscription. This allows for the DataPower service to retrieve any Web Service policy attachments that are stored in the repository for a given WSDL. Policy attachments are discussed further in Chapter 19.

Clicking Next from this screen completes the WSRR Subscription, but remember, this is still just a WSDL we are adding, and we will need to add an FSH object. You will notice a slight difference when configuring the Local and Remote sections for this WSDL. The fields that are usually populated with information from the WSDL are no longer populated. This is because this information is not yet known by our service as it will retrieve it from the repository. Instead you will see a radio button labeled From WSDL for the information that can be obtained from the WSDL. There is also a radio button that enables you to override this information. Figure 10-32 shows this configuration screen where we added one FSH object for the Local Endpoint handler and left the remaining fields to be obtained from the WSDL.

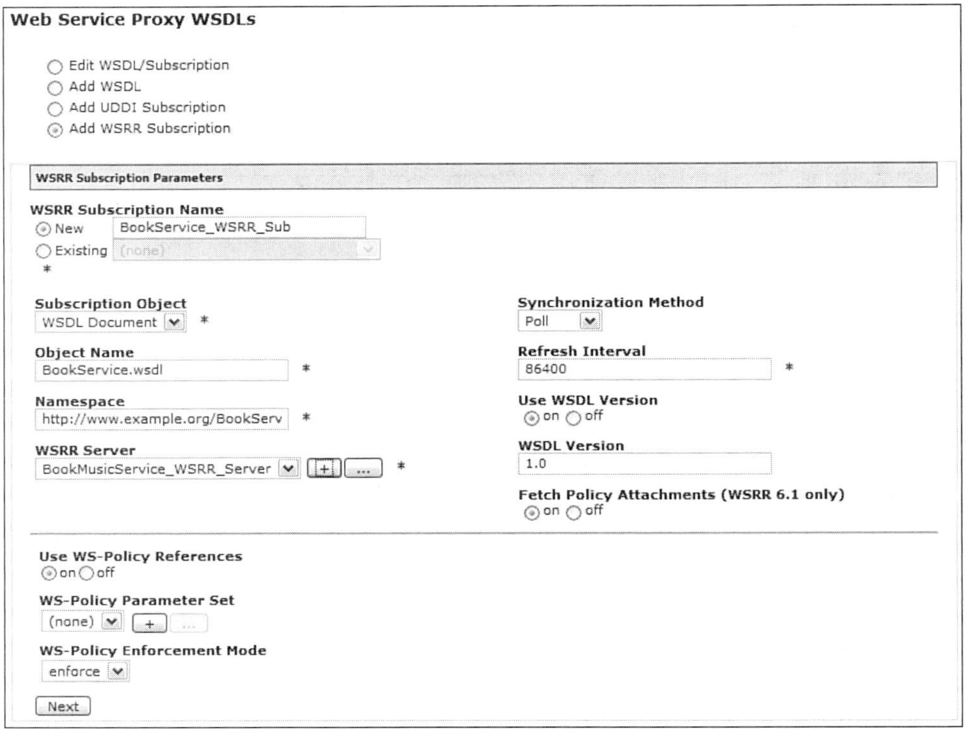

Figure 10-31 Completed WSRR Subscription.

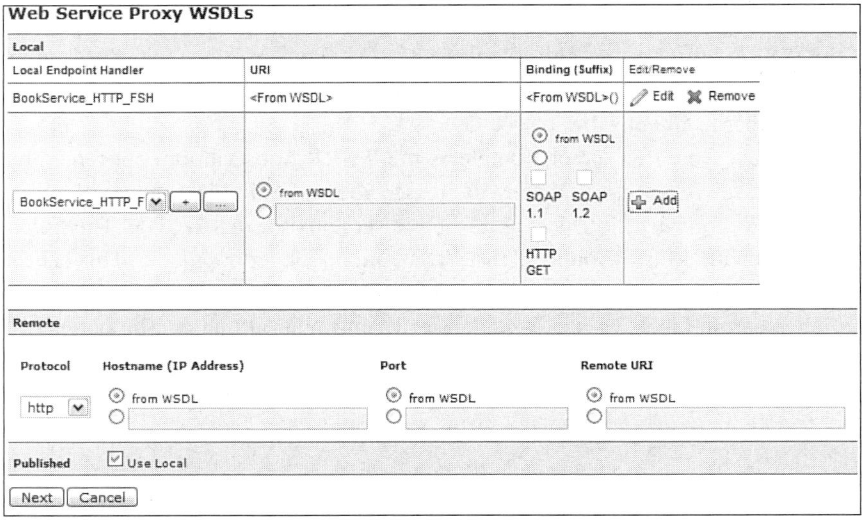

Figure 10-32 Endpoint configuration screen.

After you have created the endpoint configuration and clicked Next, you have completed the subscription. You should now see the name of the WSRR Subscription object where you would normally see the WSDL filename and a status of Okay if everything is configured properly. Figure 10-33 shows our BookService_WSP with the MusicService.wsdl being retrieved from the local file system and the BookService.wsdl being retrieved from WSRR via the BookService_WSRR_Sub object.

Web Service Proxy WSDLs

- ◉ Edit WSDL/Subscription
- ○ Add WSDL
- ○ Add UDDI Subscription
- ○ Add WSRR Subscription

	WSDL Source Location	Endpoint Handler Summary	WSDL Status	WS-I BP Status	Action
⊞	local:///MusicService.wsdl	1 up / 1 configured	Okay	Okay	Remove
⊞	BookService_WSRR_Sub	1 up / 1 configured	Okay		Remove

Figure 10-33 WSDLs added to the service.

As an added checkpoint, the status of the WSRR subscription can be checked by navigating to Status→Web Service→WSRR Subscription Status in the left-side menu. Here the status of each WSRR Subscription created within the working domain can be viewed. The information provided on this screen for each subscription is the status, last refresh date and time, synchronization method, refresh interval, and number of WSDLs. There is also a button labeled Synchronize that enables the manual synchronization, or refresh, of the WSDL(s). Figure 10-34 shows this screen with our newly created WSRR subscription.

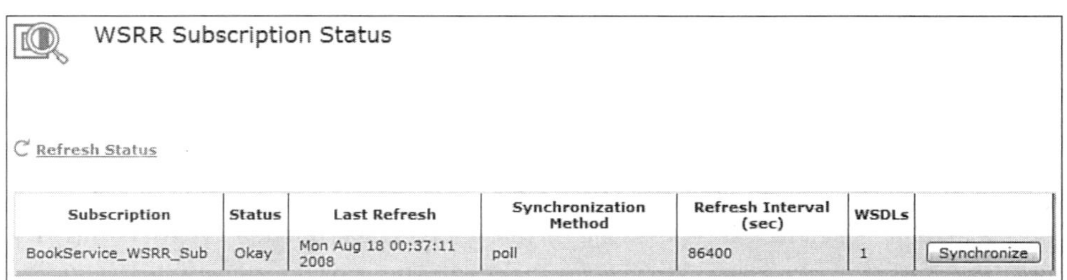

WSRR Subscription Status
Refresh Status
Subscription
Status
Last Refresh
Synchronization Method
Refresh Interval (sec)
WSDLs
BookService_WSRR_Sub
Okay
Mon Aug 18 00:37:11 2008
poll
86400
1
Synchronize

Figure 10-34 WSRR Subscription status.

Because we can't see any details about the BookService.wsdl file within the WSDLs tab of our service, let's take a look at the Policy tab to see what it looks like after adding this new subscription. Figure 10-35 shows our policy after adding the WSRR Subscription for the BookService.wsdl. Notice that all the bindings and operations are shown where rules can be configured, but there is an additional level at the top of this hierarchy. This is the subscription level.

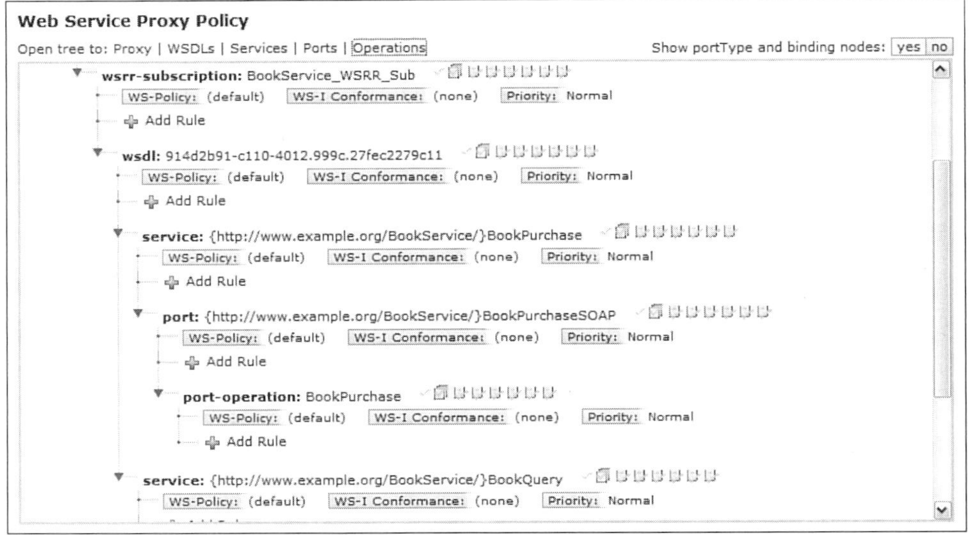

Figure 10-35 Web Service Proxy policy showing a WSRR subscription.

Now that we have a service that is subscribing to a WSRR repository for a WSDL, any time the WSDL changes in the repository, the changes will be reflected in the service at the next scheduled polling interval for the WSRR Subscription. This can be powerful when subscribing to a common service, as you will not need to be notified of the changes. This is only one of the many benefits of using WSRR for document management and governance. For more information on the WebSphere Registry and Repository product, please visit the WebSphere products section of the IBM Web site.

WSRR Concepts

We have seen how to subscribe to a single WSDL within WSRR in the previous example. It was the BookService.wsdl that was retrieved from the repository. Our MusicService.wsdl file was still being stored locally. We would most likely want to add both WSDLs to the repository where we can manage both of them together. It is possible to create a second subscription to retrieve this WSDL, but there is a more convenient and efficient way to do this. This is by utilizing a WSRR concept.

A WSRR concept is an association of related files within WSRR. This association is configured in WSRR and can be subscribed to instead of subscribing to each individual resource. Creating a concept is simple. From within the WSRR administration console, navigate to Service Metadata→Concepts to display all the configured concepts in the repository. There is also a button labeled New that allows you to create a new concept. Much like adding a WSDL file, the configuration screen asks for a name, a description, a namespace, and a version as shown in Figure 10-36.

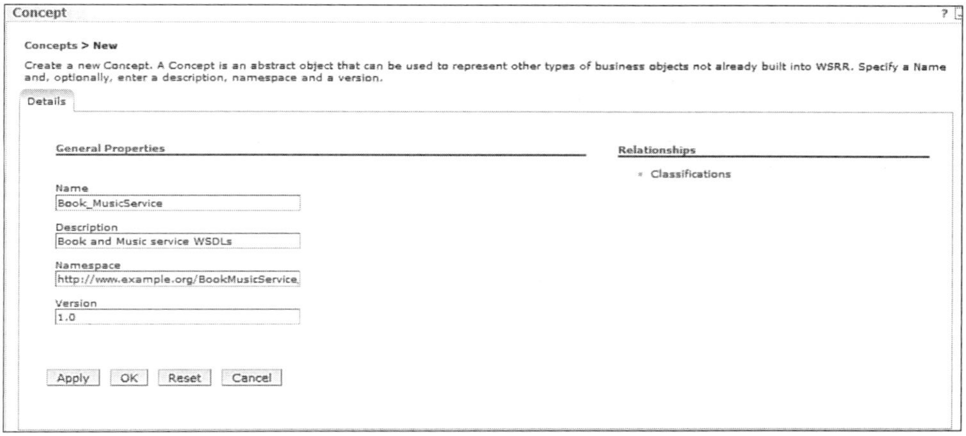

Figure 10-36 Creating a new concept in WSRR.

After the concept is created, the relationships can be added to it; that is, the files that you will want to reference as one entity. From the list of concepts, selecting the concept just created and then clicking the Add Relationship will present the first of five screens for creating these relationships. This simply asks for a relationship name. Figure 10-37 shows that we named our relationship Book_Music_WSDLs.

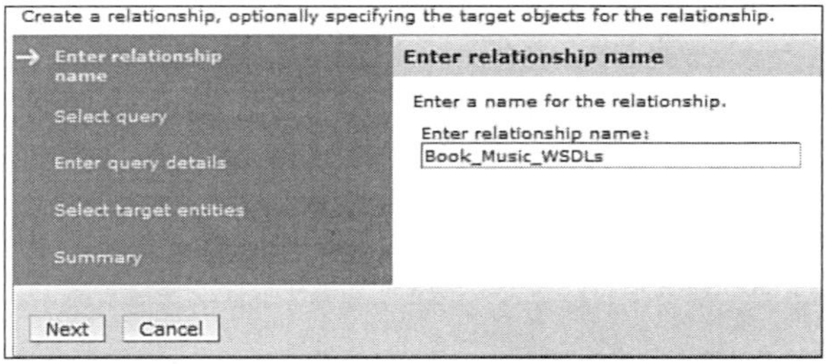

Figure 10-37 Specify a relationship name.

The next screen is the Select query where an entity type is selected. Because many different types of entities can be stored in WSRR, this list is quite long. For our example, we are referencing WSDL Documents, so we choose that option, as shown in Figure 10-38. You may find it interesting to browse through this list to get an idea of what can be stored and referenced in a relationship.

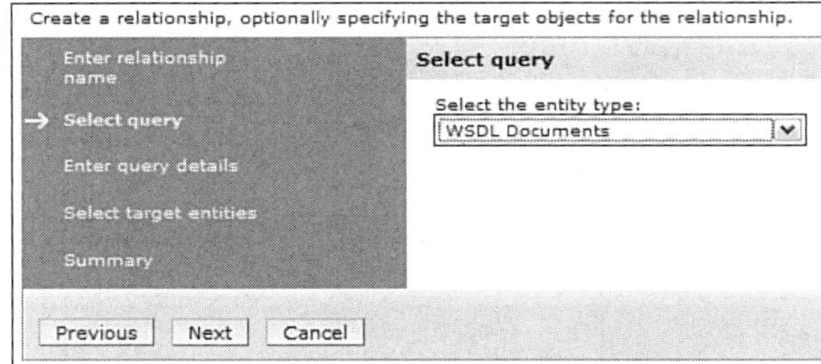

Figure 10-38 Selecting an entity type.

Next the query details can be entered. This is where a query can be created to narrow down, or filter, the list of documents to be selected for the relationship. If there were several hundred or even thousands of documents, this query would come in handy at this point. In our example, we have uploaded only two WSDL documents. This is assuming that the second WSDL has been uploaded. Because we have only two WSDL documents in our repository, we can enter a * in the Name for the query. This returns the list of all WSDL documents in the repository, as shown in Figure 10-39. Here, you can see the two WSDL documents that we are interested in.

Create a relationship, optionally specifying the target objects for the relationship.

Enter relationship name
Select query
Enter query details
Select target entities
Summary

Select target entities

Select the target entities for the relationship.

Select	Name	Description	Namespace	Version
☐	BookService.wsdl	Book Service WSDL	http://www.example.org/BookService/	1.0
☐	MusicService.wsdl		http://www.example.org/BookService/	1.0

Total:2

Previous Next Cancel

Figure 10-39 WSDL Documents in the repository.

Selecting the two WSDLs displayed and clicking Next completes the configuration of our concept. We now have a concept in the WSRR repository that contains both the BookService.wsdl and the MusicService.wsdl documents.

Back in our DataPower service, we can now create a subscription to this new concept. This is identical to creating a WSRR subscription that retrieves a single WSDL; however, instead of selecting WSDL as the Subscription Object, we would select Concept. Figure 10-40 shows our WSRR subscription for the newly created concept.

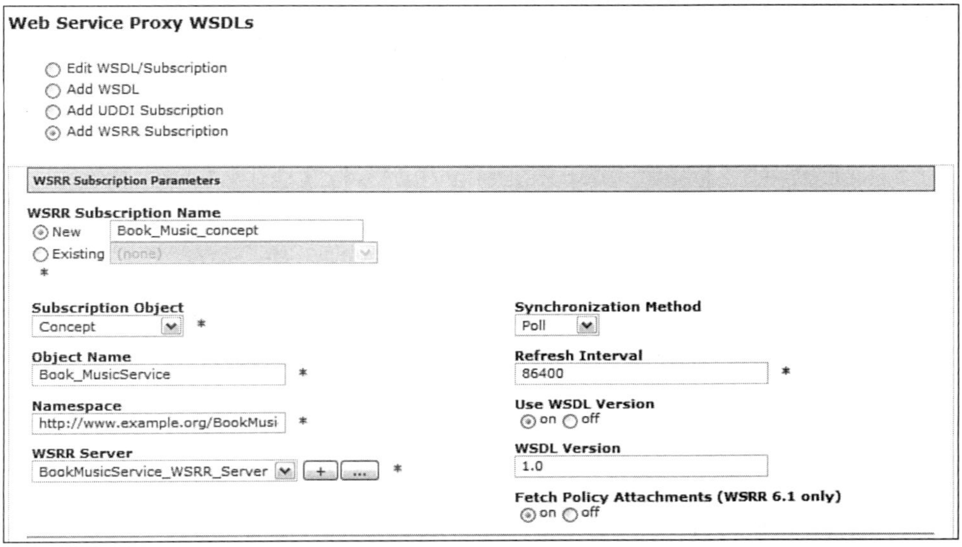

Figure 10-40 Creating a WSRR Subscription for a concept.

After creating this WSRR subscription, an FSH must be configured for it. In this case, we are working with more than one WSDL, so we might want to create a new, common URI to add to our Local configuration, as shown in Figure 10-41. Also notice that we chose to configure one Remote endpoint for this configuration. We could have chosen to select the endpoint from the WSDL as well.

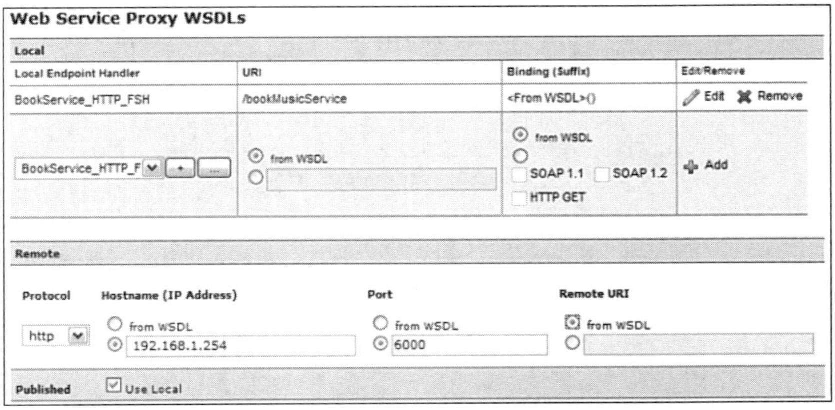

Figure 10-41 Endpoint configuration for the WSRR concept.

We have now created one WSRR subscription for our service that subscribes to a WSRR concept that contains two WSDLs. We no longer need to maintain two WSDLs and endpoint configurations within the WSP as the WSDLs are retrieved from and maintained within the repository. If we wanted to confirm that we are indeed retrieving two WSDL documents from this concept, we can again view the WSDL subscription status. You can see in Figure 10-42 that our new subscription contains two WSDLs as expected.

Subscription	Status	Last Refresh	Synchronization Method	Refresh Interval (sec)	WSDLs	
Book_Music_Concept	Okay	Sun Aug 17 20:51:08 2008	poll	86400	2	Synchronize

Figure 10-42 WSRR subscription status for a concept.

Going back to our WSP, we can now view the new WSRR subscription in our service within the WSDL tab. As shown in Figure 10-43, the subscription shows the three bindings that are identified within the two WSDL documents as well as our endpoint configuration.

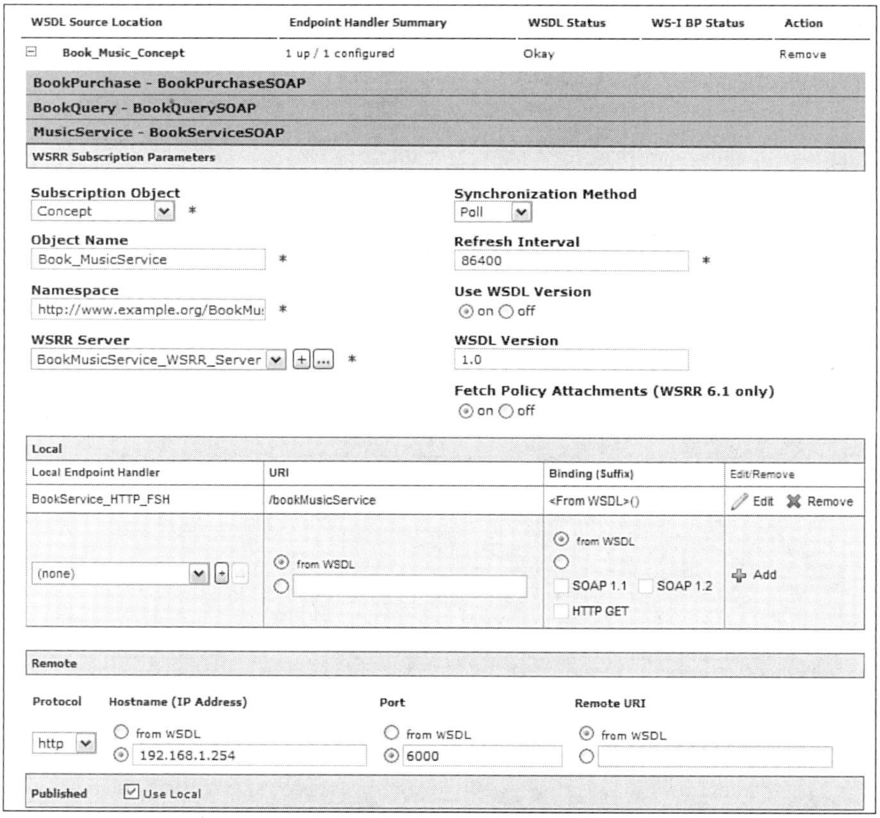

Figure 10-43 Refreshed Book_Music_Concept WSRR subscription.

Throughout the examples in this chapter, we have been combining two different WSDLs. We mentioned that DataPower can publish these WSDLs with the new virtualized endpoints. When multiple WSDLs are added to a service and the WSDLs are published, they are done so as one combined WSDL.

To view how a WSDL will be published, it is possible to retrieve the WSDL through a browser using the endpoint of the service (the virtualized DataPower endpoint) with a ?WSDL appended to it. This will then return the WSDL as DataPower would publish it. Because this is performing an HTTP GET when this request is made, the GET method must be enabled within the FSH object for this request to be accepted. After this is enabled in our FSH object, we can submit the request. For our BookService_WSP, we would enter the URL http://192.168.1.254:6880/bookMusicService?WSDL, which would return one WSDL that contains the combined WSDLs within our service.

Service Level Monitoring (SLM)

We have now configured a WSP, including processing policies and WSDL management. After this service is up and running, you may be interested in monitoring and controlling the traffic to the service. This is made possible by the SLM action that is added to your service by default.

As we showed when we created our first WSP service back in Figure 10-7, a request and a response rule are automatically created for you at the Proxy level. The response rule is just an empty rule with a Match Rule and a Results action, but if you look at the request rule; the request rule contains an SLM action that looks like a simulated line graph and will enable the monitoring of the service.

The nice thing about the default SLM action is that there is really no configuration required for it. The only configuration required for the SLM action is an SLM Policy object. This object is created by default and added to the default SLM action upon WSP creation; it can be configured via the SLM tab in the policy configuration. We will see how this is configured shortly. Figure 10-44 shows the default SLM action configuration for our BookService_WSP service.

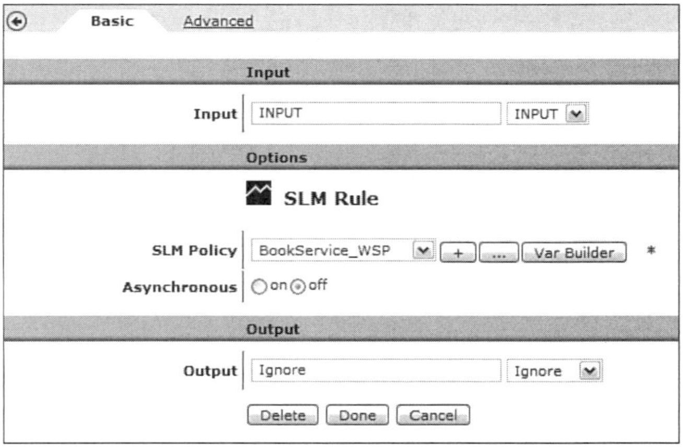

Figure 10-44 Default SLM action configuration.

One very unique feature of this action that was created by default is that it is propagated to all other request rules within the policy behind the scenes. You will not see an SLM action in the request rules that you might configure at the different levels of the hierarchy, but it is always invoked as long as it is not removed from the proxy level. Because of this, you do not have to configure an SLM action for any other rules to have the SLM policy triggered.

The SLM action that was added to the service by default allows for the traffic to the service to be monitored and controlled. Even though the name of the action is Service Level Monitoring, it allows for more than just monitoring the traffic. You can set a limit on how many transactions should be allowed to hit a certain operation, port, WSDL, or service in a specified amount of time. After this maximum threshold is reached, you can then decide if the service should reject subsequent traffic (throttle), queue the traffic for later submission (shape), or generate a log message (notify). When the shape option is chosen, there is a maximum of 2,500 transactions that will be queued. After that limit is reached, all subsequent transactions are dropped. Let's take a look at how this all can be configured.

Within the Web Service Proxy Configuration screen, there is a SLM tab located to the right of the WSDL tab. This tab contains all the SLM information for the service. Figure 10-45 shows the SLM tab for a WSP.

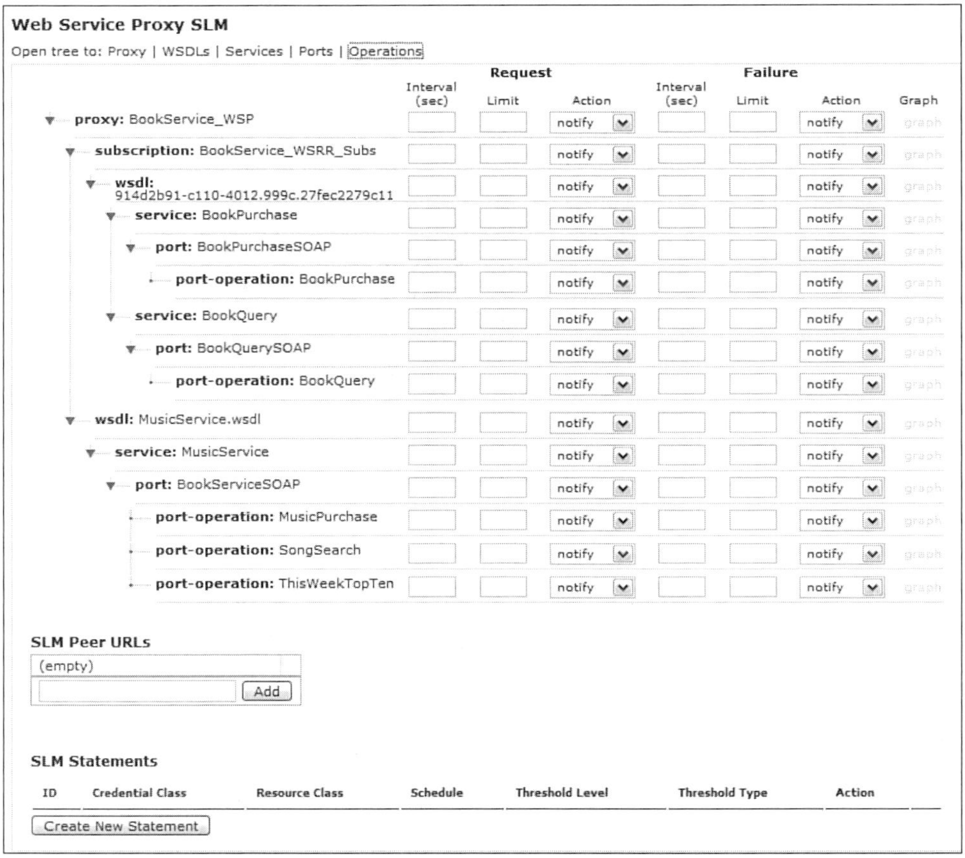

Web Service Proxy SLM

Open tree to: Proxy | WSDLs | Services | Ports | Operations

	Request			Failure			
	Interval (sec)	Limit	Action	Interval (sec)	Limit	Action	Graph
proxy: BookService_WSP			notify			notify	graph
subscription: BookService_WSRR_Subs			notify			notify	graph
wsdl: 914d2b91-c110-4012.999c.27fec2279c11			notify			notify	graph
service: BookPurchase			notify			notify	graph
port: BookPurchaseSOAP			notify			notify	graph
port-operation: BookPurchase			notify			notify	graph
service: BookQuery			notify			notify	graph
port: BookQuerySOAP			notify			notify	graph
port-operation: BookQuery			notify			notify	graph
wsdl: MusicService.wsdl			notify			notify	graph
service: MusicService			notify			notify	graph
port: BookServiceSOAP			notify			notify	graph
port-operation: MusicPurchase			notify			notify	graph
port-operation: SongSearch			notify			notify	graph
port-operation: ThisWeekTopTen			notify			notify	graph

SLM Peer URLs

(empty)

Add

SLM Statements

ID	Credential Class	Resource Class	Schedule	Threshold Level	Threshold Type	Action

Create New Statement

Figure 10-45 SLM tab.

Much like the Policy tab, this screen contains a hierarchy of all the WSDLs within the service down to the operations. Here it is possible to specify the transaction limits and intervals for requests to the service at a granular level. The interval indicates the number of seconds that the transactions will be counted, and the Limit indicates the maximum number of transactions for the number of seconds specified in the Interval field. So if you wanted to limit the number of transactions for a given operation to 5,000 transactions in a three-second span, you would specify 5,000 as the limit and 3 as the interval.

The action can then be set to indicate whether the traffic should be shaped or throttled, or to write a message to the log. Each of these options can be very useful for serving different purposes. The notify action, which will write a message to the log might be used for keeping track of peaks in traffic for future capacity planning. The shape action can be used to protect your backend server from bursts of traffic over a longer period of time. And the throttle action might be used to enforce a maximum number of transactions allowed in a given period of time from a specific consumer. In addition to being able to monitor and control the request traffic to the service, you can also do the same for transactions that fail.

To see how this all works, let's suppose we performed a load test on our Book service and determined that the BookPurchase operation is resource-intensive, and it was determined that the saturation or break point of the operation was reached when it received 100 transactions per second. With this information, we can decide how we will configure our Service Level Monitor. Because we know that it is only the BookPurchase operation that causes the Web service to buckle, we will set our limit for this operation. We must now decide what should happen to the transactions after this limit is reached. Because we know that the holiday season usually brings spikes of traffic to our service, it might be possible to reach this level. Being that this is the purchase operation, we certainly would not want to lose any sales by rejecting transactions. This is where we could set the action to shape. Now when the transaction limit is reached, the subsequent requests will be queued and finally released to the backend at a rate that will not exceed our defined limit. This allows for a spike in traffic to be handled that would otherwise bring down the backend service or server. This seems like a much better alternative.

Figure 10-46 shows how the SLM within our service would be configured in this scenario. As you can see, we set the interval to 1 second and the limit to 100 with an action of shape. This indicates that when the requests to the BookPurchase operation reaches 100 transactions within a one second span, the subsequent requests will begin to be queued for later submission until the spike subsides.

Now that we have set our SLM Policy to shape all requests to the BookPurchase over 100 per second, let's see what happens when this limit is reached. To do this we must send multiple concurrent requests to this operation. This can be accomplished using a load generating tool such as Apachebench. Apachebench is a free tool that allows you send multiple concurrent HTTP requests to a single destination.

Web Service Proxy SLM

Open tree to: Proxy | WSDLs | Services | Ports | Operations

	Request			Failure			
	Interval (sec)	Limit	Action	Interval (sec)	Limit	Action	Graph
proxy: BookService_WSP			notify			notify	graph
wsdl: BookService.wsdl			notify			notify	graph
service: BookPurchase			notify			notify	graph
port: BookPurchaseSOAP			notify			notify	graph
port-operation: BookPurchase	1	100	shape			notify	graph
service: BookQuery			notify			notify	graph
port: BookQuerySOAP			notify			notify	graph
port-operation: BookQuery			notify			notify	graph

Figure 10-46 Setting a SLM for the BookPurchase operation.

After using this tool to submit a total of 5,000 requests to our BookQuery operation, we can take a look at how our SLM affected the requests. Clicking the graph link next to the Book Purchase operation in the SLM tab displays a graph representing the transactions for this operation. Three different types of graphs are available here. The transactions can be viewed by rate, latency, or count. The default graph shown is latency. Figure 10-47 shows this graph after we submitted the 5,000 requests from our Apachebench tool. Notice that all 5,000 requests were sent, but the number of requests within a one-second interval was capped at 100. This was because we set our SLM Policy for this operation to shape the traffic at 100 requests in a one-second time span.

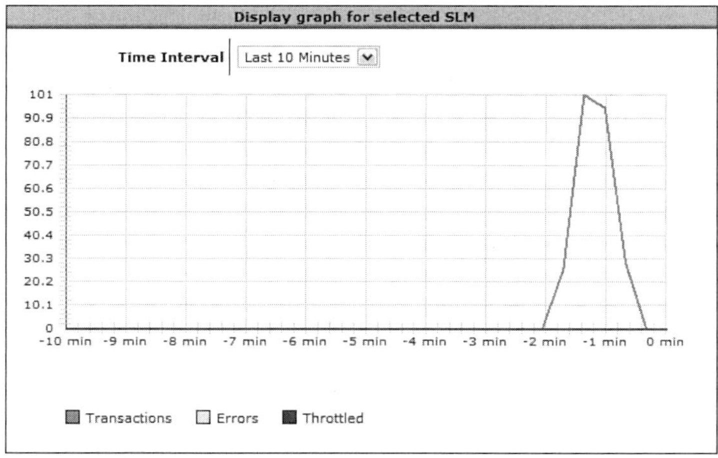

Figure 10-47 Latency graph for BookPurchase transactions.

Our previous SLM example demonstrates that the traffic to the backend Web service can be shaped to accommodate any peaks in traffic without bringing down the backend service or infrastructure. This seems to work fine, and it would if there was only one DataPower device forwarding requests to the backend service. But what if there were multiple devices sitting behind a load balancer, all servicing requests for the same Web service? In our example we knew that we could not send more than 100 transactions to our service per second. If there were multiple devices sending requests to this backend service, then each device would have to know how many requests were being sent by the others in order to start shaping the traffic.

This problem is solved by configuring an SLM Peer Group. An SLM Peer Group allows each SLM policy on these different devices to communicate with each other, providing the number of transactions sent to the backend service. This allows for the aggregation of these transactions, which can then be used to enforce the limit and threshold for the SLM policy. The SLM Peer group can be configured from within the SLM tab of the WSP. Each device must have identical SLM policies with the same SLM Peer group configured. Each peer group on each device must list all the device members, including itself.

A SLM Peer Group can be configured within the SLM tab for a WSP service; however, other service types must first create a Peer Group Object to facilitate this. This object can be created by navigating to Objects→Peer Group from the left navigation menu. Because we are working with WSP services here, we will show how this is accomplished within the SLM tab of the WSP configuration.

Figure 10-48 shows our BookService_WSP SLM tab now with two URLs added to the SLM Peer URLs. The IP address and port specified must be the interface and port that the XML Management Interface is configured to listen on for the DataPower device being added. The default HTTPS port is 5550 and can be changed in the XML Management Interface settings. The XML Management Interface must also be enabled with the SLM Endpoint option selected. One of these URLs in this list must be the local DataPower IP:Port that this service is configured on. All members of the peer group must have identical SLM policies and SLM Peer URLs.

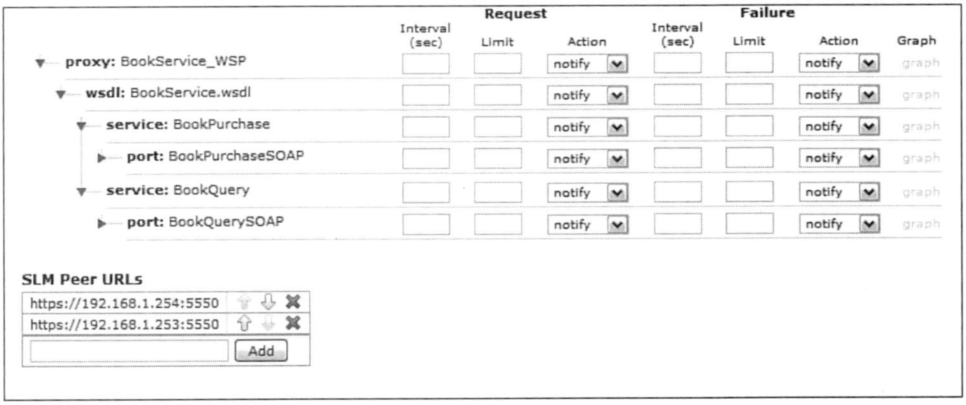

Figure 10-48 SLM Peer group configuration for the BookService_WSP.

With the SLM Peer URLs setup, as shown in Figure 10-48, we can load balance traffic across two DataPower devices for our BookService_WSP service. Now the SLM policy configured for the BookPurchase operation will take into account the requests being sent to the backend service by both devices.

Custom Service Level Monitors

We have demonstrated the flexibility and level of granularity of the SLM configuration within a WSP and, for the most part, this should suffice for your monitoring needs. There may be times, however, when you actually would like to configure an SLM Policy at a more granular level than what is offered here. This could be anything: a specific time of day, a specific user or group, or a specific header within the message itself. There are many possible scenarios that you might come across which is why DataPower offers the option of creating a custom SLM statement.

An SLM statement is a user-defined set of conditions and actions that specify when an SLM Policy will be executed, under what conditions, the action to take, and the thresholds to set. The options within this configuration allow for customization at every level of the policy. The possibilities are endless, so we will walk you through the configuration screen and a sample scenario to give you a feel for what can be accomplished. After that you will be equipped to configure your own custom rules.

Located at the bottom of the SLM tab of the WSP configuration is a section labeled SLM Statements. This is where you will define any custom SLM statements that are to be applied to transactions flowing through the service. Clicking the Create New Statement button opens the configuration screen for the new SLM Statement. The first thing you might notice is that there are many more options and configuration parameters than just the Interval, Limit, and Action that are configured in the standard SLM configuration above it. This should give you your first indication of how specific you can make this statement.

To demonstrate the configuration options and how to configure this statement, let's take another example scenario for our BookService_WSP service. Suppose there was an external company that we know utilizes our service for purchasing books. This company purchases a significant number of books from us; however, they do not submit their purchases as the requests come in to them in real time. They store all their purchases for the week and kick off a batch process at the end of the week to submit them through the BookPurchase operation within our Web service. Our concern in that when this batch process kicks off it will impact the performance of the real time requests being made to our service. This would increase the response time to our other customers. Let's take a look at how this can be solved by adding a SLM Statement to our SLM Policy.

Figure 10-49 shows the SLM Statement configuration screen presented after clicking the Create New Statement button. The first field here is the User Annotation, which is simply a place to enter a comment for this statement. The next field is the Credential class field. This refers to a credential class object that can represent a specific user credential for which this SLM Policy is enforced. An existing Credential Class can be selected or a new one can be created.

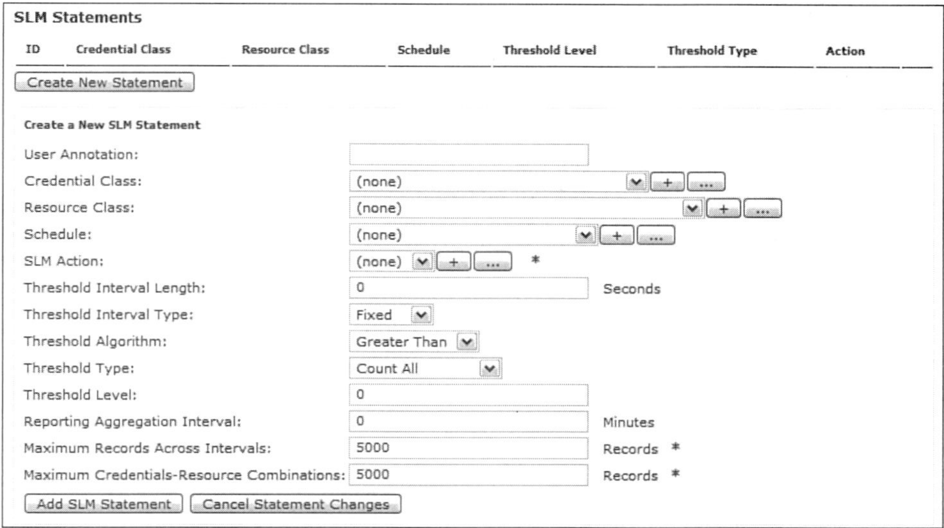

Figure 10-49 SLM Statement configuration screen.

Figure 10-50 shows the configuration screen for the SLM Credential Class. As usual, this object requires a name, and optional comments may be entered. The type of credential to be matched is specified in the Credential Type field. The options here are

- **Mapped Credential**—This credential is the result of the Mapped Credential phase in a AAA policy.
- **Extracted Identity**—This credential is the result of the Extract Identity phase in a AAA policy.
- **Client IP**—The IP of the client making the request.
- **Custom Stylesheet**—Specify a custom XSLT stylesheet to extract the credential.
- **IP From Header**—The IP address specified in the HTTP header.
- **MQ Application**—The MQ application specified in the MQ message.
- **Request Header**—Uses the value of a specified request header.

As you can see, there are quite a few options to choose from when you need to execute an SLM policy based on a credential. In our example we know that the BookPurchase operation contains a AAA policy that will extract the identity of the client making the requests. Because the company making the request will always send the same credentials, we can choose the Extracted Identity for the Credentials Type field.

The next field in this configuration is the Match Type. Here we can specify how we want to match on the credential. Here we can specify that an exact match is required, a regular expression to match with, or to allow DataPower to extract and store each unique credential for the specified type. In our example we know the credential that will be passed, so we will choose Exact for this field. We can now specify the value of the credential that is to be matched. Let's suppose the company that submits this batch process passes a credential that is authenticated within our AAA policy with a username of monsterBooks. Figure 10-50 shows the configuration that we created to match on the Extracted Identity on a credential with the name of monsterBooks. Now when this batch process is submitted, each request will be identified by our SLM Credential Class.

Each of these fields is filtering the set of messages to which this SLM statement will actually apply. By adding a specific credential, we have assured that this statement will be executed *only* on calls submitted by monsterBooks. If we want it to apply to other customers, we would also have to enter their exact credentials. To define unique parameters for each user's requests, you would need to create a new SLM statement for each customer.

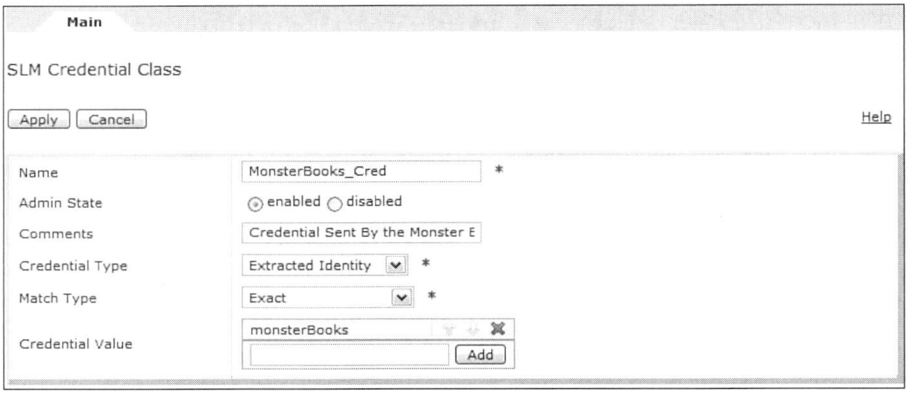

Main

SLM Credential Class

Apply Cancel Help

Name	MonsterBooks_Cred *
Admin State	enabled disabled
Comments	Credential Sent By the Monster E
Credential Type	Extracted Identity *
Match Type	Exact *
Credential Value	monsterBooks Add

Figure 10-50 SLM Credential Class configuration.

Returning to our SLM Statement configuration, the next field we can configure is the Resource Class. This references a Resource Class object that specifies what type of request this SLM statement will apply to. Figure 10-51 shows this object's configuration screen with all the available Resource types. Notice that this is a very exhaustive list to choose from. Because we are concerned with our BookPurchase operation, we chose WSDL operation from this drop-down.

Once the Resource Type is specified, Match Type must be specified just as we did in the SLM Credential Class object. The actual operation name that is recognized by DataPower within each request is a fully namespace qualified name that includes the port as well as the operation. Because of this, we can simple specify that this is a regular expression match and just provide the operation name as we know it. Remember that you must click the Add button to add the value entered for the Resource Value in order for it to be added to the object's configuration. Figure 10-52 shows the completed Resource Class configuration for our example.

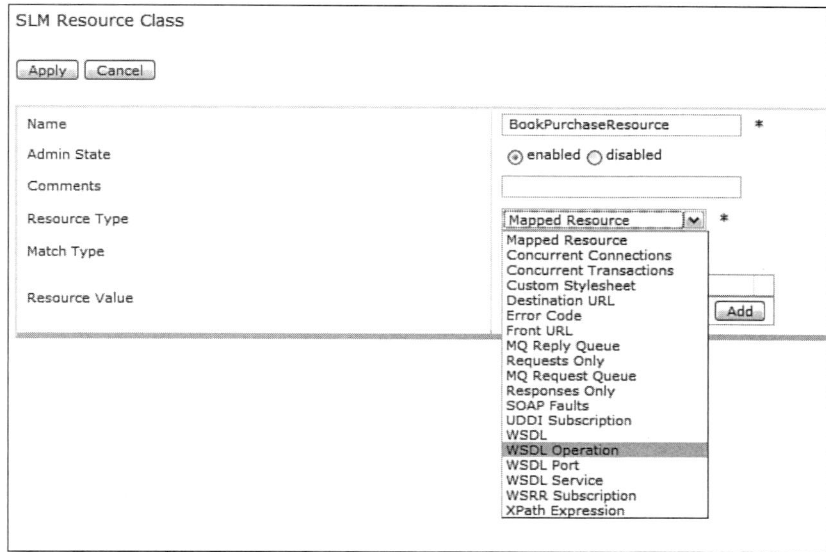

Figure 10-51 Selecting a resource type.

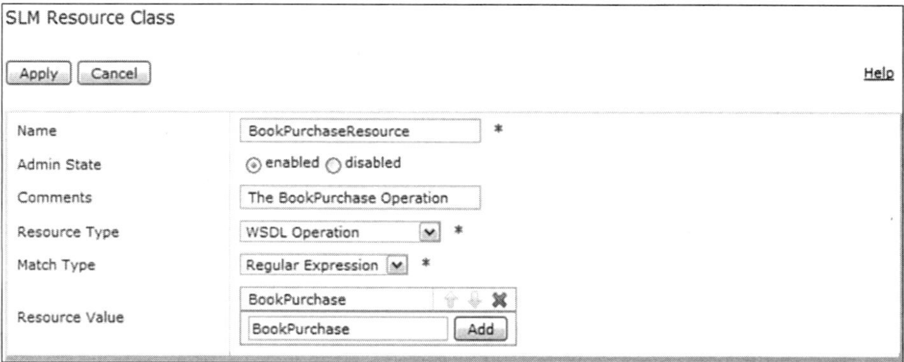

Figure 10-52 Completed SLM Resource Class object.

Now that we specified in our SLM statement that we are looking for a request carrying the monsterBooks credential for the BookPurchase operation, we have narrowed down this statement to the correct requestor and request type. We can narrow this a bit more if we would like to. We know that this company triggers this batch process once a week on a Saturday night at 8:00 PM. In an effort to not restrict any real time requests from this company during the week, we can specify that we only want this statement to apply to requests on this day and time. This can be specified in the SLM statement within the Schedule field. This field references a Schedule object that can be configured. Figure 10-53 shows how we would configure this object to restrict this SLM statement to requests made on Saturdays between 8:00 PM and 10:00 PM.

SLM Schedule	
Apply Cancel	Help
Name	MonsterBooks_batch *
Admin State	enabled disabled
Comments	Schedule for the Monster Books I
Week Days	Sunday Monday Tuesday Wednesday Thursday Friday Saturday *
Start Time	20:00:00 *
Duration	120 minutes *

Figure 10-53 SLM Schedule object configuration.

Now that we have scoped this SLM statement down to the requestor, the operation, and the day and time, we can specify the actual SLM thresholds and actions. In the SLM statement, we can specify the same type of actions as we did in our first SLM policy. That is, what to do when a threshold is exceeded. Because we do not want to reject these batch transactions, we can simply shape this traffic as we did in our first example. Because this is a batch process, we are not as concerned with the response times so we queue these transactions with this option.

We then specify the Threshold Interval Length. This again is the length in seconds that the transactions will be measured. So, if we want to restrict this process to 20 transactions per second, we would specify a 1 here to represent the 1 second. The threshold level would then be set at 20.

Figure 10-54 shows the completed SLM statement. Clicking the Add SLM Statement button adds this statement to the policy. We now have an SLM statement that shapes the traffic to the BookPurchase operation on Saturday nights between the hours of 8:00 PM and 10:00 PM that were submitted with a credential of monsterBooks.

All fields within the SLM statement are optional. By not providing a value for any given field implies that all possible values for that field are accepted for this SLM statement. Supplying values, however, provides additional filtering, lowering the number of potential messages to which this statement could apply.

As you can see, the SLM capabilities within DataPower are extremely flexible when implementing your own SLM statements. We showed only a sample of what the possibilities are for SLM. It is advised that you consult your WebGUI guide for additional options and features within the SLM policy.

SLM Statements

ID	Credential Class	Resource Class	Schedule	Threshold Level	Threshold Type	Action

Create New Statement

Create a New SLM Statement

User Annotation:	SLM Statement for Monster Books	
Credential Class:	MonsterBooks_Cred	
Resource Class:	BookService_WSP_port-operation_BookPurchase	
Schedule:	MonsterBooks_batch	
SLM Action:	shape	*
Threshold Interval Length:	1	Seconds
Threshold Interval Type:	Fixed	
Threshold Algorithm:	Greater Than	
Threshold Type:	Count All	
Threshold Level:	20	
Reporting Aggregation Interval:	0	Minutes
Maximum Records Across Intervals:	5000	Records *
Maximum Credentials-Resource Combinations:	5000	Records *

Add SLM Statement | Cancel Statement Changes

Figure 10-54 Completed SLM statement.

Service Priority

It is nice to think that all things are created equal, but when we are dealing with transactions flowing through our IT systems, this is not likely the case. It is likely that different DataPower services, WSDLs, or even operations within a service will be more critical than others. In this case you might want to prioritize these so that when there is a heavy demand on the DataPower service, the more critical transactions are serviced first. For example, in our BookService_WSP, we have a BookQuery operation and a BookPurchase operation. It is likely that you would want the transactions for purchasing books to have a higher priority to access the DataPower resources. That is, the requests for it will be handled first. This is a very simple configuration option within the service Policy that we can set.

Because this priority is set within the WSP Policy tab, we have the flexibility of setting it for any level of the Policy tree provided. This means that different priorities can be set at an operation, port, WSDL, or service level. At each of these levels within the Policy, there is a button labeled Priority. Clicking this button presents three options to choose from—Low, Normal, and High. As you would have guessed, a setting of Low assigns the lowest priority and a High is the highest priority. Figure 10-55 shows how we set the BookQuery operation to a priority of Low and the BookPurchase operation to High.

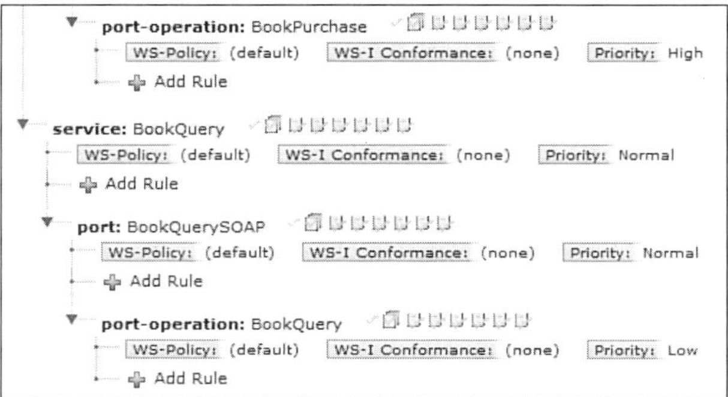

Figure 10-55 Priority set at the operation level.

This is not only convenient for prioritizing operations within a WSP, it can also be configured at the service proxy level, which will provide prioritization of all your services on the same device. Keep in mind that there are only three possible priority values that can be assigned to a given service, so it is likely that some services will be assigned the same priority on a single device.

Viewing the Status of the WSPs

Once the Web Service Proxies have been configured, DataPower provides some very convenient status screens for viewing the status of the parts of the WSP configuration, such as WSDLs, operations, WSRR and UDDI subscriptions, and more. We will briefly take a look at some of these status screens and demonstrate how they can be very handy.

All the status screens for the Web Service Proxies must be accessed from the left navigation menu in the WebGUI and will be under Status→Web Service. The first one that we will take a look at is the Web Services WSDLs screen. This screen, shown in Figure 10-56, shows the status of each WSDL that is configured within a WSP in the current domain. Here, a full status of each WSDL can be viewed along with the WSP that it is configured in, the location of the WSDL, the refresh interval, and when the last refresh occurred.

WSProxy	Identifier	WSDL Source URL	Status	Refresh Interval (sec)	Last Refresh	Processing Log	Policy Execution
BookService_WSP	2	local:///MusicService.wsdl	Okay	0	Sun Aug 17 16:17:42 2008		0
BookService_WSP	3	wsrr://MusicService_WSRR_Server/914d2b91-c110-4012.999c.27fec2279c11/	Okay	0	Sun Aug 17 16:17:42 2008		0

Figure 10-56 Web Services WSDLs screen.

Another handy status screen is the Web Services Operations screen. Here you can view all the operations available within all the WSDLs contained within the WSPs in the current working domain. Figure 10-57 shows this screen. Here, in one single screen, you can see the operations, WSP handling the requests to it, the IP address and port of the FSH listening for requests, the URI, SOAP action and body, the backend address, and the front-side and back-side protocols.

WSProxy	Index	Interface	Port	URL	SOAP Action	SOAP Body	Status	Backend address	Frontside Protocol
BookService_WSP	0	192.168.1.254	6880	/MusicService	http://www.example.org/MusicService/MusicPurchase	{http://www.example.org/BookService/}MusicPurchase	Registered	http://192.168.1.35:4091/MusicService	soap-11
BookService_WSP	1	192.168.1.254	6880	/MusicService	http://www.example.org/MusicService/SongSearch	{http://www.example.org/BookService/}SongSearch	Registered	http://192.168.1.35:4091/MusicService	soap-11
BookService_WSP	2	192.168.1.254	6880	/MusicService	http://www.example.org/MusicService/ThisWeekTopTen	{http://www.example.org/BookService/}ThisWeekTopTen	Registered	http://192.168.1.35:4091/MusicService	soap-11
BookService_WSP	3	192.168.1.254	6880	/bookService	http://www.example.org/BookService/BookPurchase	{http://www.example.org/BookService/}BookPurchase	Registered	http://192.168.1.254:6000/BookPurchase	soap-11
BookService_WSP	4	192.168.1.254	6880	/bookService	http://www.example.org/BookService/BookQuery	{http://www.example.org/BookService/}BookQuery	Registered	http://192.168.1.254:6000/BookQuery	soap-11

Figure 10-57 Web Service Operations status screen.

The last status screen we discuss here is the Web Services Operation Metrics. Shown in Figure 10-58, this screen displays information about the requests and responses that have hit a particular operation. It provides the endpoint, port, and operation along with information about the requests and responses to them. Here you can see the request and response totals, successes, failures, size, and response times. This information can be valuable when identifying the load on each operation and the response times.

Service Endpoint	PortType	Operation	Number of Requests	Number of Failed Requests	Number of Successful Requests	Service Time (msec)	Maximum Response Time (msec)	Last Response Time (msec)	Max Request Size (bytes)	Last Request Size (bytes)	Max Response Size (bytes)	Last Response Size (bytes)
http://192.168.1.254:6880/MusicService	{http://www.example.org/BookService/}MusicService	MusicPurchase	0	0	0	0	0	0	0	0	0	0
http://192.168.1.254:6880/MusicService	{http://www.example.org/BookService/}MusicService	SongSearch	0	0	0	0	0	0	0	0	0	0
http://192.168.1.254:6880/MusicService	{http://www.example.org/BookService/}MusicService	ThisWeekTopTen	0	0	0	0	0	0	0	0	0	0
http://192.168.1.254:6880/bookService	{http://www.example.org/BookService/}BookPurchase	BookPurchase	1567	0	1567	36952	687	3	0	0	429	429
http://192.168.1.254:6880/bookService	{http://www.example.org/BookService/}BookQuery	BookQuery	5001	0	5001	10595	303	2	0	0	429	429

Figure 10-58 Web Service Operation Metrics.

Summary

As the popularity of Web services and SOA continues to grow, so do the challenges around security, governance, integration, and monitoring. We demonstrated throughout this chapter that the DataPower Web Service Proxy provides the ease, flexibility, and power to solve many of these challenges. This service has the capability to secure your Web Services against potential threats, virtualize endpoints, and schema validate requests all by simply importing a WSDL. In addition to this, the service can be configured to provide all the request and response processing that is available within other service types. The ease of use combined with the power, flexibility, and benefits provided make the Web Service Proxy a must-have when exposing Web services.

CHAPTER 11

Proxying Web Applications with DataPower

Throughout this book, we have talked about how valuable DataPower can be when fronting XML-based applications such as Web services, as well as providing an ESB for your infrastructure. Hopefully you have seen that there is no doubting its capability to provide several benefits in these scenarios, such as threat protection, protocol bridging, routing, and so on. What about all the Web applications in your organization that are exposed to external and internal-facing clients? Can DataPower provide some benefit to these? The answer is yes. DataPower can provide a tremendous amount of value to your organization by placing it in front of these applications. What that value is and how you implement it is precisely what we discuss in this chapter. Although the main use case for DataPower in this scenario is to provide AAA functionality, we do not focus on that in this chapter, as it is similar to configuring AAA policies for other backend applications which is discussed in depth later in Chapter 16, "AAA," and Chapter 17, "Advanced AAA."

Web Applications Are "Different"

Now that we have discussed several different types of services, you realize how easy it could be to verify request and response messages in a DataPower service by simply importing a WSDL or referencing a schema. This is simple and effective because WSDL-based applications, or Web services, are basically atomic, stateless applications and usually involve computer-to-computer interaction. This enables a describable and predictable message format and flow. For example, only operations described in the WSDL can be called with the message format described in the schema. A response message schema is also provided in the WSDL, describing the format that the response must be in. Any subsequent request to the Web service by that client is a new transaction with no dependency or ties to the previous transaction(s). Because WSDL files can be added to and referenced from registries such as UDDI or WSRR, the consumer can dynamically construct a Web service call without any human intervention.

Due to the nature of Web applications, things might not be that simple when proxying them because they are extremely different from the Web services model. To start with, Web application clients are usually browser-based, with a human doing the driving rather than computer-to-computer interaction. If there are two things that are unpredictable, they are browsers and humans! There are many variations of browsers, each with their own interpretation of the HTML specification and nuances. Then there are the humans at the other end—there is no telling what they might do. Between the browser's Back and Forward buttons and the application navigation, they can cause all kinds of havoc that is entirely unpredictable.

After we get past the unpredictability of the client, we have to deal with the Web application in the back. Web applications are typically stateful, requiring the backend application to "remember" the client and session data throughout many concurrent requests. Let's take the common shopping cart request scenario. As a person is browsing through the catalog of an online retailer, he might add certain items to a shopping cart. As he proceeds to check out, the application must remember all the items that were added to the shopping cart during the shopping experience.

Humans rarely want a single piece of information in a computer-consumable format; instead, they want a rich, interactive, and often graphical experience. This requires support for multiple message formats; not just HTML, but images, videos, and yes, even structured data. To make these interactions personalized and "pretty," content rendering engines allow JavaScript, cascading stylesheets, and cookies to affect both the information seen by the user and the manner in which it is displayed. This is not even getting into the new possibilities with Ajax and Web 2.0! An attempt to represent any of this interaction in something as simple as a WSDL file would simply be ludicrous.

It should now be obvious that Web applications are different from the other types of services we have been dealing with thus far. This is not intended to scare you off from ever wanting to deal with a Web application again. It is simply to make you aware that there are many things that you need to consider when configuring a DataPower service to front your Web applications. Hopefully, by the end of this chapter, you will have gained the knowledge of how to deal with and overcome these challenges.

Why Use DataPower?

You might be thinking to yourself "My applications are running fine and given all these challenges, why would I introduce DataPower into the picture?" This is a valid question. Let's take a look at why you might want to use a DataPower device to proxy your applications and you might change your mind.

Threat Protection

We have discussed the many different types of threats that can potentially penetrate your Web services and other XML-based applications. Many of these threats are relevant to Web applications as well. It is possible for Web requests to contain data that is formatted as XML, where the backend application must parse and process this data. The same types of XML threats that we have discussed throughout this book apply to these applications. Web applications are also susceptible to other threats such as SQL injection and dictionary attacks. In addition to these common threats, these applications are at risk to cross-site scripting attacks. This is where malicious code is injected into Web pages that will be viewed by other users in an attempt to gain access to sensitive data. DataPower provides protection against all these types of threats with minimal configuration required.

Perimeter Security

It is becoming increasingly popular for organizations to require that all requests to backend applications be authenticated prior to entering the trusted zones in their network. This would mean that the authentication has to take place in the DMZ. This presents a challenge due to the fact that you would never deploy an application server or Java runtime in the DMZ. This means that the application server can no longer perform the authentication for incoming requests. Because the DataPower device is a hardened, DMZ deployable appliance, it is a good candidate to provide this functionality. Because it can accept many different types of credentials, authenticate, and authorize the user using the credentials passed, and assert the identity to the backend application server in many different formats, it can provide perimeter security for various types of applications running on various application servers. This allows the DataPower service to convert one security token to another, which provides integration between application servers consuming different types of tokens. By having the DataPower service provide this AAA functionality, the burden of this resource-intensive task is taken off the application, freeing it up to perform the business logic that it is intended to do. We discuss how to implement this security in a DataPower service later in this chapter.

In addition to the threat protection and perimeter security, the DataPower appliance also provides other benefits, such as SSL termination, encryption services, and URL rewriting.

Choosing a DataPower Service

As we walk through the different DataPower service types that we have to choose from, it may seem fairly obvious which service type to use in what circumstances. For example, when proxying a Web service, you would use a Web Service Proxy. When dealing with multiple protocols, you would use a Multi-Protocol Gateway (MPGW). These scenarios seem straightforward, as the name of the service type indicates its usage. In Chapter 6, "Introduction to DataPower Services," we briefly discussed a service type called a Web Application Firewall (WAF). As with the previously mentioned service types, this name seems to indicate its usage and would tell us that we would use it to proxy Web applications. This may be the case in some instances, but not in all. The WAF service type has some powerful features for proxying Web applications; however, it is not the only service type that can be used.

The Web application firewall provides drop-dead simple integration of transport-layer encryption, threat protection, and standard authentication and authorization mechanisms into an existing Web application. It also provides easy definition and enforcement of security policies regarding commonly used Web application parameters such as cookies, form variables, query strings, and HTTP headers. However, for cases that require significant message structure processing, dynamic routing to various backends, or additional nonsecurity-related features, you may want to use one of the other DataPower service types, such as the MPGW. Let's discuss some of the WAF features more specifically, and then go beyond this service to add some functionality.

Web Application Firewall

As its name implies, the WAF is used to provide a firewall, or proxy, for a backend Web application. It can be configured to perform all the AAA functionality that is found in all other service types as well as other multistep processing. Because it is specifically designed to proxy Web applications, the WAF provides a fast and convenient way to create a service by using a wizard-driven process. This wizard guides you through a step-by-step process to configure the WAF for providing AAA functionality on behalf of the backend application, which is a typical use case for this service type. When the service is created, all the service parameters default to values that would be common for most Web applications. For example, the common HTTP methods used for Web applications, such as GET, POST, and HEAD, are enabled by default. The WAF provides many added features over and above the other service types that are applicable only to Web applications. These features are

- **Session Start and Timeout**—The WAF can set a session timeout value for a user's browser session. When the session expires, the user can be redirected to a login page.
- **Cookie Encryption/Signing**—The WAF can easily encrypt or sign all cookies.
- **Name-Value Input Processing**—The WAF can configure name-value lists for request data such as headers, query parameters, form fields, and cookies. The name-value pairs can be used to filter invalid request data. The names and the values can be regular expressions that will be used to match the incoming request data. For example, if an application has a form that contains a field used for entering a numeric, five-digit ZIP code, a name-value expression can be set up for that form field with a regular expression that dictates that the value must be five characters and numeric.
- **Cross Site Scripting (XXS) Protection**—The WAF can be configured to provide protection against cross-site scripting attacks.

As you can see, the WAF provides some nice features to enhance the threat protection and security benefits offered in other firewall types. A good use case for this service type would be for proxying a Web application providing AAA functionality and form field validation. This ensures all requests are authenticated before reaching the trusted zone in the network. Also, by enforcing this positive security model, which enables only acceptable, properly formatted form field data, the request data is sanitized, reducing the amount of exceptions thrown by the backend application due to bad data.

Before you jump right into configuring a WAF, we should first discuss some differences in the WebGUI from what you have seen thus far with other service types. With WAF, the focus is no longer on message transformation and processing, so the configuration screens are significantly different. They are less graphically driven and tailored more to the quick configuration of multiple text-based security policies. In addition, much of the terminology is specific to Web applications, rather than to generic message processing. To give you some idea of these differences, take a look at Figure 11-1. This is where you configure your request, response, and error rules for your service. This is the equivalent to the Policy Editor in the other service types. The first thing you might notice is that the title of the screen refers to an Application Security Policy rather than a Processing Policy as in other services. It is called a Security Policy, which indicates that the intent of this service type is not necessarily to process the request/response message but to provide security.

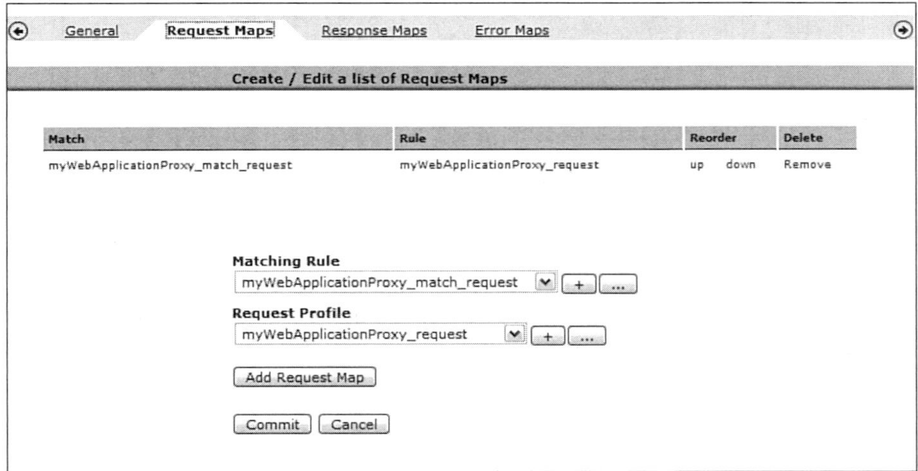

Figure 11-1 WAF Security Policy Editor.

As we know, a Processing Policy (or Application Security Policy) is made up of rules and actions. This is also true within the WAF configuration; however, they are not called rules. Notice in Figure 11-1 that there are several tabs that reference different types of "maps," such as Request Maps, Response Maps, and Error Maps. These are the rules that you are used to configuring in other service types.

Each Request/Response Map in a security policy contains a matching rule and an accompanying profile. The matching rule defines which headers, URLs, or input data will determine the profile that is executed. A profile is simply a collection of policies that will be enforced on the incoming message. These include AAA policies, session policies, protocol restrictions, and various name-value profiles. Figure 11-2 shows an example of a request profile that provides a AAA policy and many other capabilities the WAF has to offer.

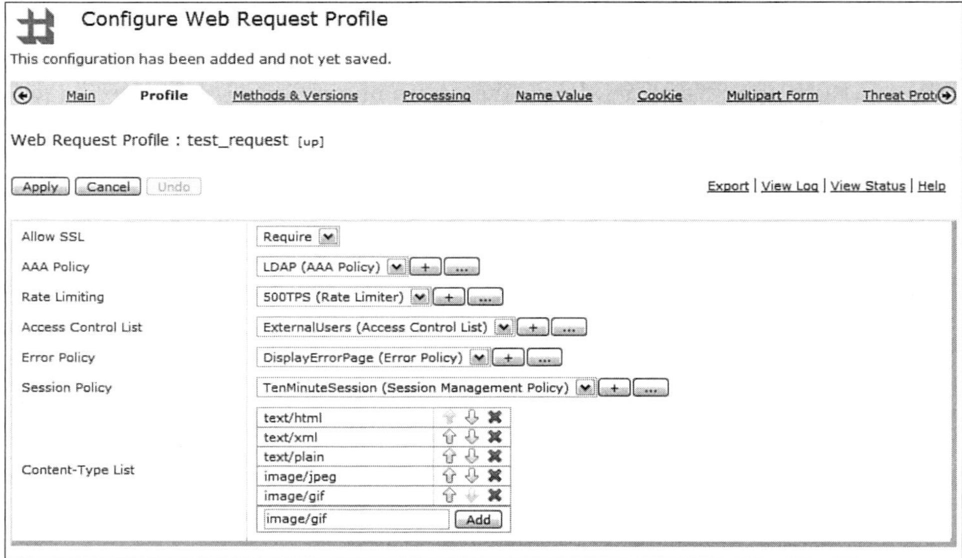

Figure 11-2 Web Request Profile.

There may be a slight learning curve when configuring a WAF for the first time. This should not discourage you from using it as there are several added benefits when using this service type. It is ideal for providing perimeter security, form field validation, and Web-specific threat protection for Web applications.

Another Option

As we saw in the previous section, the WAF service focuses primarily on securing your Web applications by providing threat protection, AAA functionality, form field validation, and so on. There may be times where you need to focus on processing the data in the Web application request and response, such as within a Processing Policy. In this case, you might decide to use an MPGW service type as the Web application proxy. Because the MPGW supports HTTP and HTTPS(s), it can proxy Web applications. The MPGW can provide AAA functionality, dynamic routing, multiple FSHs, header rewriting, and more. If you require that a processing rule executes on each and every transaction, this can be configured as well. Keep in mind that because the MPGW is not specifically designed for Web applications, some default configuration parameters need to be changed. These specific parameters and options are discussed in the next section.

Service Configuration Parameters

Because every Web application is different, it is likely that you will have to change some of the configuration parameters in your service for each application you are proxying. In this section, we discuss some of the most common parameters that you should be aware of in the WAF and the MPGW services.

Methods and Versions

In a DataPower service, you can define which HTTP methods as well as HTTP versions are allowed. It is likely that you will allow only the POST, GET, and HEAD method to your Web application because they are the most commonly used. The WAF is specifically designed to proxy Web applications, so these methods are allowed by default. This can be set at the request profile level for each one configured within the service. If, for some reason, you want to disable these or enable others, this configuration screen can be found in the Methods and Versions tab in the Request Profile, as shown in Figure 11-3.

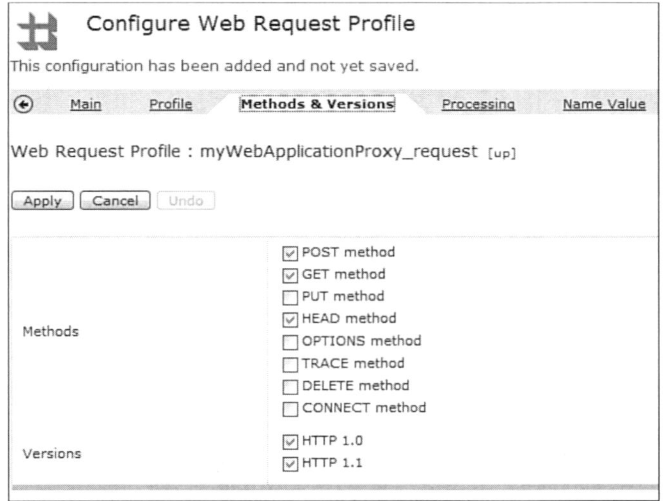

Figure 11-3 WAF methods and versions.

It is not likely that you will have to change these parameters for a WAF service; however, you will need to make a change for an MPGW when proxying Web applications. When an HTTP FSH is configured, it does not allow the GET method by default. This can be changed within the Front Side Handler Object(s) as shown in Figure 11-4.

Request and Response Type

Because the MPGW can accept requests and responses in many different formats, the request and response type must be changed from the default (SOAP) when proxying Web applications to Non-XML. Because the WAF is specifically designed to proxy Web applications, this is not a concern; however, you can specify the allowable content type.

HTTP Front Side Handler

Apply Cancel

Name	myWebApplicationProxyFSH *
Admin State	enabled disabled
Comments	
Local IP Address	ClientInterface Select Alias *
Port Number	80 *
HTTP Version to Client	HTTP 1.1
Allowed Methods and Versions	[x] HTTP 1.0 [x] HTTP 1.1 [x] POST method [x] GET method [x] PUT method [ ] HEAD method [ ] OPTIONS [ ] TRACE method [ ] DELETE method [x] URL with Query Strings [x] URL with Fragment Identifiers [ ] URL with .. [ ] URL with cmd.exe

Figure 11-4 MPGW methods and versions.

Follow Redirects

As a Web application responds to a client request, there are many times that the response will contain a redirect directive in the HTTP header, which indicates that the client should redirect the request to the URL specified. The client browser would act on this directive and automatically send a new request to this location. It is possible to have your DataPower service recognize these redirect responses, make a request to the location specified, and then return the response to the browser. The setting to enable and disable this feature can be found on the HTTP Options tab of the service configuration screen, which can be accessed only through the Navigation menu. For a MPGW service, this can be found via Objects→Multi-Protocol Gateway→Service name→HTTP Options. Similarly, it can be found for a WAF via Objects→Web Application Firewall→Service name→HTTP Options. The default for this parameter is On, which tells the service to follow the redirects for the client.

There are a couple of reasons why you may want to turn this off. The first reason is that the redirect location may not always be accessible from the DataPower device, therefore, it should be requested by the client browser. Also, when the DataPower device performs the redirect, the URL address in the client browser never changes to the new location. This unusual behavior could cause problems if the end user wants to bookmark this address. As a general practice, it is recommended that this be turned off, allowing the browser to follow the redirects as intended.

Rewrite Hostnames When Gatewaying

When a browser sends a request to a Web application, it can automatically add an HTTP header named Host with a value of the host address that it is sending the request to. If the request was sent directly to the application server, this value would be the address of the application server itself. Because the application is being proxied by a DataPower service, the Host header would most likely be the address of the DataPower device, load balancer, or virtual IP that the request was sent to. As the DataPower service receives this request, it has the capability to rewrite this header to the value of the backend server that it is forwarding the request to.

It is common for Web applications to use this header to build a redirect location URL to send back to the client. This is where the problem lies with having DataPower rewrite this Host header. If the DataPower service rewrites this header to the actual value of the backend server, the redirect location would be built pointing to this server and bypassing the DataPower service that proxies the application.

To demonstrate this behavior, look at Figure 11-5, where a client is sending a request to the DataPower device, which is proxying a backend Web application. The service in this scenario is configured to *not* rewrite the Host header. Notice that the Host header sent in the request is the address that the request was sent to (DataPower). As the request is forwarded to the application, this header is not changed. Now when the application uses it to build a redirect location, it will use the Host header, which is the DataPower device. When the browser follows this redirect, it will again go back to the DataPower service that proxies the application.

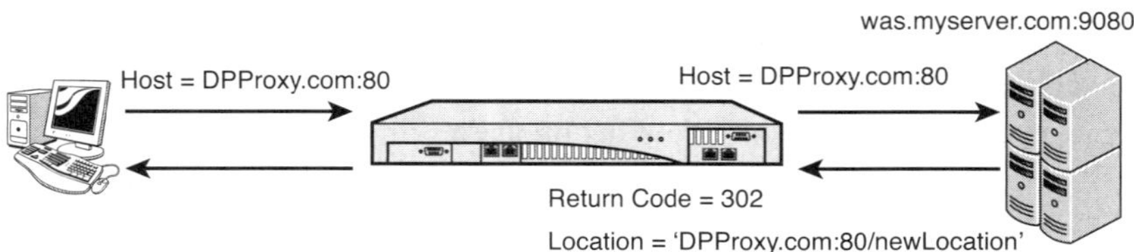

Figure 11-5 Redirect after DataPower does not rewrite the Host header.

Figure 11-6 shows the same example but demonstrates what would happen if the DataPower service rewrote the Host header to be the address of the backend server. Now when the redirect location is set, it is set to the address of the application server itself. This causes the browser to attempt to bypass the DataPower service and access the application directly. This is not the desired behavior.

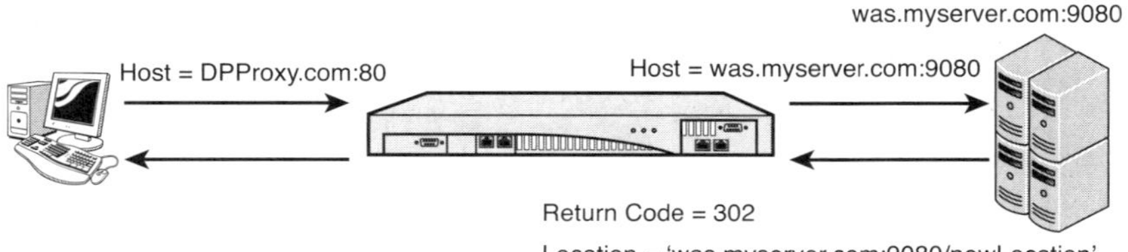

Figure 11-6 Redirect after DataPower rewrites the Host header.

This is why it is recommended you set this parameter to Off in the service configuration. This setting can be found in the HTTP Options tab of the service configuration screen. As mentioned before, this screen must be accessed through the left navigation menu: Object→Multi-Protocol Gateway→Service name →HTTP Options for a MPGW service and Objects→Web Application Firewall→Service name →HTTP Options for a WAF. The default for this parameter is On and should be changed.

Request Processing

As a request is sent to a Web application, it may be desirable to take some action based on data within the request. This might include query parameters, form data, or request headers. This section discusses different techniques that can be used for accessing this data.

Query Parameters and Form Data

Much like XML-based services, there are many cases in which you would be interested in inspecting the payload of the request to a Web application. Instead of an XML document in the payload, Web applications can contain POST data that is submitted from an HTML form. In addition to sending POST data, a request can send name value pairs in the URI, called query parameters. This data can be accessed in a DataPower service to perform tasks such a dynamic routing, logging, or even AAA.

As you might have realized by now, DataPower is optimized for dealing with XML. If you can get this data into an XML nodeset, you can parse it, query it with XPath, transform it, and so on. Fortunately, there is a specific action provided to do just that. This action is called Convert Query Params to XML and is found in the list of actions within the Advanced action. You can simply add it to the Processing Policy, and it will convert the form data or query parameters to a well-formed XML nodeset.

Let's look at an example to demonstrate how this works. Figure 11-7 shows a request rule that consists of a Match Rule, a Convert Query Params to XML action, and then a Transform action. As this rule executes against a request that contains POST data, we would expect the output of the Convert Query Params to XML to be a well-formed XML nodeset containing the POST data fields and values. This would then be the input to the Transform action where it can be evaluated.

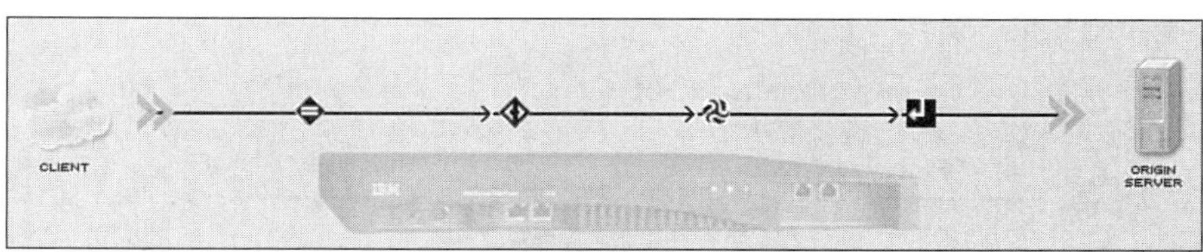

Figure 11-7 Convert Query Params to XML rule.

Listing 11-1 shows a simple HTML document that, when opened with a browser, would present a form as shown in Figure 11-8, where we have entered a first name and a last name, respectively. Notice in the HTML code that there are two fields within this form. One field has a name of firstname and the other lastname.

Listing 11-1 Test Form HTML

```
First name: <input type="text" name="firstname"><br>
Last name: <input type="text" name="lastname">
<input type="submit" value="Submit"> </form>
```

First Name: Bob
Last Name: Jones
Login

Figure 11-8 Test Form within a browser.

If we were to submit this form to the DataPower service where it would be processed by the rule shown in Figure 11-7, we would expect these two fields to be included in an XML node-set that would be created and used as the input to our Transform action. To illustrate this, the probe in Figure 11-9 shows the request as it entered the rule in ASCII format.

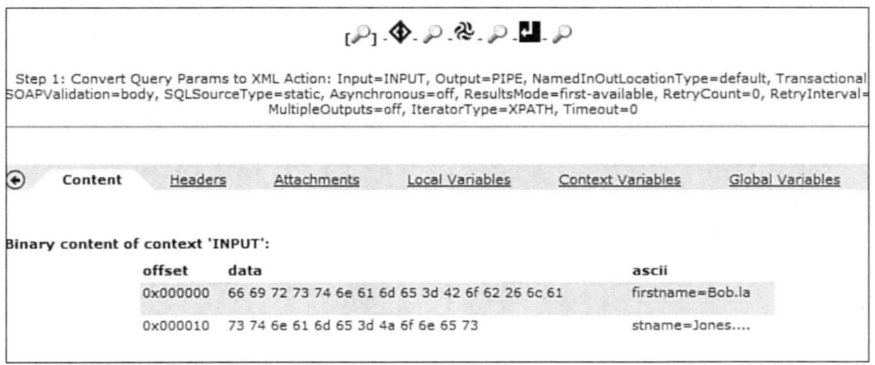

Figure 11-9 Probe before Convert Query Params to XML action.

After the request is processed by the Convert Query Params to XML action, the form data is converted into an XML nodeset. Figure 11-10 shows the probe with the output of this action displayed. You will notice that the output contains an XML nodeset with several elements. You can see within the <args src="body"> element that there are two elements representing the form fields and values of the form that was submitted. This XML can now be parsed and processed by the transformation step.

Step 2: Transform Action: Input=PIPE, Transform=store:///identity.xsl, Output=PIPE, NamedI
OutputType=default, Transactional=off, SOAPValidation=body, SQLSourceType=static,
ResultsMode=first-available, RetryCount=0, RetryInterval=1000, MultipleOutputs=off, Iterator
Content
Headers
Attachments
Local Variables
Context Variables
Content of context 'PIPE':
<request>
<url>/login</url>
<base-url>/login</base-url>
<args src="url" />
<args src="body">
<arg name="firstname">Bob</arg>
<arg name="lastname">Jones</arg>
</args>
</request>
Show unformatted
Send as message

Figure 11-10 Probe after the Convert Query Params action.

Request Headers

Another part of the request that may be of interest is the set of HTTP headers. For example, you may want to view the cookie header to view all the cookies sent within a request. It is also possible to add, remove, and append headers to the HTTP request. These functions are typically performed within an XSLT stylesheet using the DataPower extension functions and elements. The available functions and elements are

- **dp:request-header()**—Used to read a protocol request header
- **<dp:set-request-header>**—Used to set an HTTP request header
- **<dp:append-request-header>**—Used to append to an existing protocol header or add a new header if the one specified does not exist
- **<dp:remove-http-request-header>**—Used to remove the specified HTTP request header

For additional information and implementation details for these extension functions, you can refer to Part VI, "DataPower Development," or the DataPower extension functions document shipped with the device. Also note that there are corresponding extension functions and elements to work with the response headers.

> **WARNING!**
>
> The remainder of this chapter discusses topics that require XSLT knowledge. If you are not familiar with XSLT programming in DataPower, please refer to Chapter 22, "Introduction to DataPower Development," and Chapter 23, "Programming Within the DataPower Environment," before proceeding.
>
> Although XSLT knowledge is not mandatory when proxying Web applications, there may be instances when you will need this flexibility when using an MPGW for the topics that follow.

Response Processing

Within a Web application proxy, you may need to take some action based on the response back from the application. For example, you may want to inspect the response code sent from the application server and take action on it. You may even want to redirect the user to a different location based on the response received from the application. This can all be done within a response rule. In this section, we discuss how to accomplish these tasks.

Response Codes

As the response is sent back from the application, it may be required to take specific action within the DataPower service based on the response code. For example, when the backend application server is experiencing problems or is unavailable, it may send back an HTTP response code 500 with no content. Sent directly to the client, the browser displays a standard error page that is not very informative or visually stimulating. By examining the response code in the response, your DataPower service can take action when this code is returned and either serve a custom error page or redirect the client to a custom error page. This page might have the look and feel of the rest of the application and could provide a more descriptive error message that might include the helpdesk contact information and a unique error ID. This error ID could have been written to a log by the DataPower service prior to sending the redirect and could then be used by the help desk to correlate the problem call with the log entries to gain more insight into the failed transaction.

As the response is returned from the application, the DataPower service sets the response code in an HTTP response header named x-dp-response-code. This value can be retrieved using the DataPower extension function dp:response-header. For example, the following line of XSLT retrieves this response code from the header and stores it in an XSLT variable named http-resp-code:

```
<xsl:variable name="http-resp-code" select="dp:response-header
('x-dp-response-code')"/>
```

This variable can then be used in further processing within the stylesheet. Setting this variable can also be accomplished via the Set Variable action.

It is important to note that retrieving the response code is entirely different if you are executing an error rule. When an error is fired after the response is sent back from the request, the DataPower service stores the response code in a DataPower variable named var://service/error-protocol-response. This variable can be accessed using the DataPower extension function dp:variable(). The following line of XSLT shows how you could read the response code into an XSLT variable from within an error rule:

```
<xsl:variable name="http-resp-code"
select="dp:variable('var://service/error-protocol-response')"/>
```

Redirects

As mentioned earlier, the backend application that your DataPower service is proxying may respond with a redirect directive and a location instructing the client browser to redirect the client to this new location. This redirect directive is indicated by a response code of 3XX along with a Location header indicating to the client agent the new location to send the user request. There are several redirect response codes that can be used for different reasons; however, the most common response code you will see for a redirect is a 302 accompanied by a reason phrase of Found.

So what does all this mean to your DataPower service? Although it is possible to intercept a redirect response from the backend server and take action on it, such as change the Location header, it is more likely that you will be creating a new redirect and sending it back to the client from the service. For example, we discussed previously that you may want to intercept certain response codes, such as a 500, within a response rule and redirect the user to an error page. This is entirely possible by recognizing the response code, setting it to the correct redirect response code, and then setting the Location header with the new URL. Because we already know how to access the response code and how to add response headers, we can accomplish this fairly easily.

Listing 11-2 shows an XSLT code snippet demonstrating how you might perform a redirect based on the return code from the backend server. Notice that we obtain the return code from the DataPower variable x-dp-response-code in the first line. We then check whether the first three characters are equal to 500. If so, we send a redirect back to the client by setting the applicable headers as discussed.

Listing 11-2 XSLT Snippet to Redirect Based on Return Code

```
<xsl:variable name="return_code" select="dp:http-response-header
('x-dp-response-code')"/>
<xsl:if test="substring($return_code,1,3) = '500'">

   <dp:set-http-response-header name="'x-dp-response-code'" value="'302'"/>

   <dp:set-http-response-header name="'Location'"
value="'http://www.myAppServer.com/error.html'"/>
</xsl:if>
```

Listing 11-2 demonstrates how a redirect can be sent back to the client from within a response rule. Remember, this will be different if you are processing the response in an error rule because the return code is obtained and set differently, and the response headers are set differently, too. Listing 11-3 shows the XSLT that would accomplish this. Notice that in addition to setting the response code and the Location header, you must also set one additional header for the reason phrase. The reason phrase for a 302 redirect should be Found as shown. Also notice that the Location header is being set using an XSLT variable that would have been set to contain the location string.

Listing 11-3 Setting a Redirect from an Error Rule

```
<dp:set-variable name="'var://service/error-protocol-response'"
value="'302'"/>
<dp:set-variable  name="'var://service/error-protocol-reason-phrase'"
value="'Found'"/>
<dp:set-variable name="'var://service/set-response-header/Location'"
value="$redir_location"/>
```

If, for some reason, you are proxying your Web application using an XMLFW, this will also be slightly different. When setting the response code, you cannot just set it to 302. It must include the full response code and reason phrase (for example, 302 Found).

Cookies

Like it or not, cookies play a big part in Web applications and are used extensively. If you are not familiar with cookies, they are name:value pairs that are sent by the application and are stored by the browser. These cookies are then sent back to the application server in subsequent requests within one header called Cookie. There are two types of cookies that can be set. The first type of cookie is a persistent cookie. A *persistent cookie* is saved on the client computer with a timeout value. This cookie lives until it has expired and survives browser restarts and computer reboots. This type of cookie should never be used when storing sensitive data. The second type of cookie is a session cookie. A *session cookie* is set with no timeout value, which indicates to the browser that the cookie should be stored within its memory space until the browser session ends. If cookies must be used, session cookies are strongly recommended.

Because cookies are set and sent via request and response headers, your DataPower service can read, change, and create cookies. The only difference here is that there are many cookie name:value pairs within one header. Because we already know how to handle headers within a DataPower service, let's dive into some cookie-specific details.

Match Rules and Cookies

As a request enters your DataPower service, it may be necessary to execute a particular rule in the Processing Policy upon the existence of a cookie within the request. Because all cookies sent by the browser are contained in one request header called Cookie, we can simply match on an HTTP header tag named Cookie. Now that we know we are matching on a header named Cookie, we need to supply the match criteria. We know that cookies are name:value pairs delimited by a semicolon. We may know the name part of the equation but we might not know the value, and we certainly cannot predict where in the sequence of cookies it will be.

For example, let's say we wanted to match on a request that contains a cookie named ltpa. We are not interested in the value of the ltpa cookie at this time because we are just matching on the existence of the cookie. Let's say a request was sent containing a total of three cookies and the ltpa cookie is second in the sequence, which might look something like myName=Joe Public;**ltpa=&356ah6!9*2**;myStatus=gold

Notice that the text ltpa=&356ah6!9*2 is the cookie we are interested in. Because the only thing that we know will be in this string is ltpa=, we can use this string as the match criteria by placing a wildcard character (*) before and after it. Figure 11-11 shows this Match Rule configuration.

Figure 11-11 Match Rule for ltpa cookie.

Reading Cookies

After you have matched on a cookie, you may want to parse the cookie in an XSLT stylesheet and inspect the value. To accomplish this, you can extract the header named Cookie (we know how to do this) and then extract the particular cookie you are interested in. To extract the cookie, use a regular expression. If you are not familiar with regular expressions, please refer to Chapters 22 and 23. Listing 11-4 demonstrates how to accomplish this if you are interested in the value of a cookie called ltpa. This example accomplishes this in four simple steps as follows:

1. Read the entire Cookie header into an XSLT variable.
2. Create a regular expression that matches on the value ltpa= storing the left side of the equal sign (or the cookie name) separate from the right side of the equal sign (the cookie value) but within the same variable in separate indexes.
3. Apply the regular expression to the entire Cookie header extracted.
4. Assign the value of the ltpa cookie (or right side of the equal sign) to an XSLT variable by referencing the $extracted-cookie[2] variable.

The key to extracting the value of this cookie is in the regular expression that we built. In short, this regular expression means this; the \b indicates a word boundary, which is where a letter or number meets anything that is not a letter or number. Next we indicate that this word we are looking for is 'ltpa=' and then all characters except for the semicolon.

Listing 11-4 Extracting a Cookie Within XSLT

```
<xsl:variable name="all-cookies" select="dp:http-request-header('Cookie')" />
    <xsl:variable name="cookie-regexp" select="concat('\b', 'ltpa',
'=([^;]*)')" />

    <xsl:variable name="extracted-cookie" select="regexp:match($all-cookies,
$cookie-regexp)" />

<xsl:variable name="LTPA_Cookie" select="$extracted-cookie[2]"/>
```

Setting Cookies

There may be times when you want to set a cookie in the client browser from within your DataPower service. This cookie can then be referenced in subsequent requests as it will be sent by the browser. Cookies are sent back to the browser in a response header called Set-Cookie. The value of this header will contain the name:value pair for the cookie being set. Because we know how to set response headers within XSLT, we know how to set cookies. There is one caveat here: Because the header that is used to set a cookie is static, what if the backend application is also trying to set a cookie by sending the response header Set-Cookie? If we try to use the same extension function shown previously to set a response header, DataPower overwrites any existing Set-Cookie header. Lucky for us there is an extension function called append-response-header that appends your response header to an existing one of the same name if it exists. If there is no existing response header, a new one is created. Once the appended response header is sent back to the browser, it knows how to parse and set the cookies. For example, we could set a cookie named userName with a value of Bob to be stored by the client with one line of XSLT as follows:

```
<dp:append-response-header name="'Set-Cookie'" value="'userName=Bob;'"/>
```

Notice that when we set the cookie in this example there is no mention of an expiration date. This would cause the cookie to be set as a session cookie and would expire when the client browser session ends. There are many parameters that can be set when setting a cookie, such as indicating that this cookie should only be sent over an SSL connection. This and other parameters can be found in many publications and online reference sites.

Removing Cookies

We have talked about reading and writing these cookies in a DataPower service. What if you wanted to remove one from the client's browser that you have previously set? Maybe it's a cookie that contained a timestamp in the value and your service has decided that it has expired. You can remove it by sending another Set-Cookie response header for the same cookie but this time adding an expiration date in the past. This causes the browser to recognize that the cookie has expired and it removes it from the browser session. Listing 11-5 shows how we could remove the userName cookie from the browser that was set in the previous example.

Listing 11-5 Removing a Cookie from the Browser

```
<dp:append-response-header name="'Set-Cookie'" value="'
userName=Bob;expires=Thu, 10-Jan-2006 16:00:00 GMT;'"/>
```

Form-Based Authentication

In the introduction of this chapter, we mentioned that a primary use case for proxying Web applications is to provide perimeter security by means of DataPower's AAA capabilities. We also mentioned that we will not be covering that in this chapter as it is no different from most other AAA scenarios. There is, however, one exception, and it is a common one. Web clients can be authenticated in several different ways. For example, they can use basic authentication or certificates to provide credentials to the authenticating service. As you will learn in Chapter 16, these two credentials can be parsed and used for authenticating the client natively within a AAA policy. One other very common way of gathering and sending credentials is called form-based authentication.

Form-based authentication provides a means for the application to present a customized login form to the client. This form can be decorated to match the rest of the application screens presented, including company logos and other images. These forms can be customized in any way the developer sees fit; however, the field names that are used within the form for the user name and password must match what the application server expects. When using this form of authentication within a WebSphere Application Server (WAS), these fields must be named j_username for the username field and j_password for the password field. This form will then POST to j_security_check, and the WAS security framework will then know how to extract the username and password from within the POST data.

Because this is a common means of authentication, we should be able to implement this within a DataPower AAA policy—and we can. It might not be an out-of-the box option seen in the AAA policy editor but it is not difficult to implement. From a AAA perspective, the only difference in form-based authentication from basic authorization is how the policy extracts the identity. After that, the authentication and authorization steps are dealing with a username and a password in each case. So once we extract the identity from the form submitted, the rest is business as usual!

Within each step of the AAA policy, there are many options presented to complete the given step, such as extract identity, authenticate, and authorize. If none of the options available suits your needs, there is always a custom option that allows you to take the responsibility of that step within an XSLT stylesheet and pass the results to the next step as expected. Because there is no option in the extract identity phase for form-based authentication, we will have to customize this by extracting the identity via XSLT and pass the username and password to the authentication step as it expects it.

Before we get into the AAA policy, we have to get the form data into a format that can be parsed by an XLST stylesheet. We would use the Convert Query Params to XML action as discussed earlier in this chapter. The output of this action would serve as the input to our AAA action, as shown in Figure 11-12.

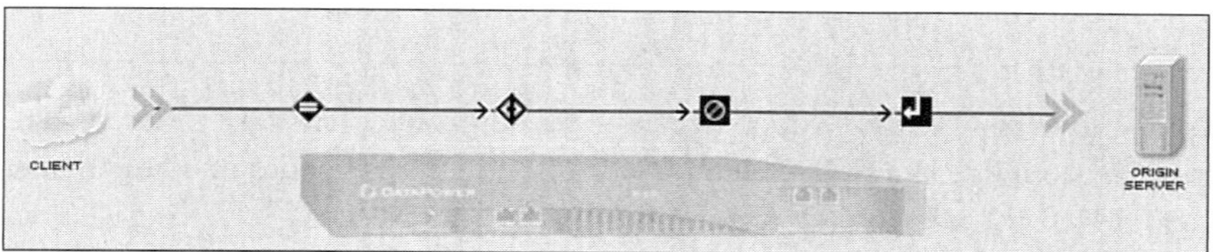

Figure 11-12 Form-based authentication policy.

When configuring the AAA policy, you must select the custom option in the extract identity and provide a stylesheet that does the identity extraction as shown in Figure 11-13.

Define how to extract a user's identity from an incoming request.

Identification Methods

- [ ] HTTP Authentication Header
- [ ] Password-carrying UsernameToken Element from WS-Security Header
- [ ] Derived-key UsernameToken Element from WS-Security Header
- [ ] BinarySecurityToken Element from WS-Security Header
- [ ] WS-SecureConversation Identifier
- [ ] WS-Trust Base or Supporting Token
- [ ] Kerberos AP-REQ from WS-Security Header
- [ ] Kerberos AP-REQ from SPNEGO Token
- [ ] Subject DN of the SSL Certificate from the Connection Peer
- [ ] Name from SAML Attribute Assertion
- [ ] Name from SAML Authentication Assertion
- [ ] SAML Artifact
- [ ] Client IP Address
- [ ] Subject DN from Certificate in the Message's signature
- [ ] Token Extracted from the Message
- [ ] Token Extracted as Cookie Value
- [ ] LTPA Token
- [ ] Processing Metadata
- [x] Custom Template

*

URL local:/// FormBasedAuthExtract.xsl

Upload... Fetch...

Back Next Cancel

Figure 11-13 Custom extract identity.

When choosing the custom option in the extract identity, you take responsibility for extracting the credentials from the request and pass them to the next step in the AAA policy, which is the Authenticate step. The format in which the Authenticate step expects this data is shown in Listing 11-6.

Listing 11-6 Format Passed to the Authentication Step

```
<identity>
    <entry type="custom">
       <username>userid<username>
       <password>password</password>
    </entry>
</identity>
```

To show how this identity extraction can be accomplished, let's take a simple HTML form that accepts the username in a field called j_username and the password in a field named j_password. The HTML for this form is shown in Listing 11-7.

Listing 11-7 Login Form HTML

```
<form method="POST" action="http://myDataPowerDevice.com:6000/login">
  Username: <input type="text"     name="j_username"><br />
  Password: <input type="password" name="j_password"><br />
  <br />
  <input type="submit" value="Login">
  <input type="reset"  value="Reset">
</form>
```

The custom XSLT needs to extract the username and password from this form after it has been converted to XML by the Convert Query Params to XML action. The XML generated from this form when submitted for a user testuser and a password password is shown in Listing 11-8.

Listing 11-8 Login Form Converted to XML

```
<request>
    <url>/login</url>
    <base-url>/login</base-url>
    <args src="url" />
    <args src="body">
          <arg name="j_username">testuser</arg>
          <arg name="j_password">password</arg>
      </args>
</request>
```

The XSLT referenced in our AAA policy must now extract the username and password from this XML nodeset. Because we know the username is in element j_username, and the password is in element j_password, this shouldn't be too difficult. After we extract these fields, we must then build the XML nodeset that is shown in Listing 11-7. The XSLT code to accomplish this is shown in Listing 11-9.

Listing 11-9 Extract Identity XSLT

```
<xsl:variable name="uid">
    <xsl:value-of
select="/request/args[@src='body']/arg[@name='j_username']"/>
</xsl:variable>
<xsl:variable name="password">
    <xsl:value-of
select="/request/args[@src='body']/arg[@name='j_password']"/>
</xsl:variable>
<identity>
    <entry type="custom">
        <username><xsl:value-of select="$uid"/></username>
        <password sanitize="true"><xsl:value-of
select="$password"/></password>
    </entry>
</identity>
```

Now that we have created our policy to convert the form to XML and the custom stylesheet to extract the credentials, the rest of the AAA policy can be configured as usual. The extracted credentials are passed to the Authentication step where they can be authenticated using one of the options available.

There you have it! This is how you would authenticate using the very common form-based authentication method. This may seem like a lot of steps and coding at first, but it is a very common means of authenticating; this AAA policy and stylesheet are reusable for many other Web application proxies.

Can DataPower Replace the WebSphere Application Server Plugin?

Now that you see all the things that DataPower can do for your Web applications, your wheels are probably turning and you are thinking "maybe this can replace other components within my topology such as the WAS plugin." At first this may seem like a suitable replacement. You should give careful thought to this before doing such a thing. Although DataPower is powerful and efficient, it is not built to do some of the things that the WAS plugin can do. For example, the WAS plugin has some powerful caching and work load management (WLM) mechanisms that are difficult to duplicate on the DataPower device. Although the DataPower device can perform load balancing to the multiple backend servers, it is no match for the sophisticated load balancing algorithms and health check capabilities provided by the plugin. The plugin is also "application-smart," which means that it is aware of the backend application URIs with knowledge of the application deployment descriptor. This allows the plugin to gain insight into the application for things such as which resources are protected within the application.

So instead of replacing the WAS plugin with DataPower, you may want to consider moving the Web server with the plugin out of the DMZ and have DataPower placed there where it can complement the Web server and plugin.

Summary

Hopefully this chapter has opened your eyes to the enormous potential the DataPower device has to proxy your Web applications. We have discussed the different types of services that can be used to do this as well as the benefits of each. Many valuable patterns and techniques were discussed that can be added to your tool belt to be used when you are configuring these services, including working with Web application requests, responses, and cookies. We also demonstrated a simple, yet effective way to configure a service to perform form-based authentication for your backend application. Combining these techniques can help you in building flexible, efficient, and powerful Web service proxies for all your Web applications.

Part IV

Managing DataPower

CHAPTER 12

Device Administration

SOA Appliances have the potential to be accessed by a number of groups with varied roles in an enterprise; networking, security, and application development groups can find uses for the appliance functionality. Their cross-departmental appeal is an asset to the organization but can be a headache for a device administrator, who must now define who has access to the appliance and at what granularity. The enforcement of this access will depend heavily on corporate governance policies concerning user access, including passwords and permissions. Fortunately, the architecture is engineered so that every user can have access to an appropriate subset of the appliance's configuration interfaces and features. This chapter provides a device administrator the knowledge necessary to create and manage domains, users, and groups on development, test, and production devices. It explains the built-in user groups and the creation of new groups with custom permission profiles. It also demonstrates administration of device access control using off-device authentication mechanisms for role-based management using existing identity management tools.

Application Domains

DataPower appliances are divided into logical partitions called application domains. Think of them as different virtual machines running in a server for application isolation, or (at a high level) logical partitions (LPAR) defined in a mainframe/iSeries® environment. Domains provide the capability to create services, upload files, and perform other configuration tasks without interfering with the services in any of the other domains. They can be used as collaborative sandboxes, project development spaces, or even as test platforms for single users. Though the precise granularity of a domain and its users is entirely flexible, the most common scenario is to create domains for an application development group or project. When used for an entire development group, domains enable sharing of files and reusable policies such as access control definitions or matching rules. Services can be defined collaboratively, with a security-focused developer creating Web services security configurations while mainframe developers create maps between non-XML and XML formats in a transformation service. When used for a specific development project, a domain can act as a *unit for environment promotion*. When the development work is done, active services from within that domain can be copied onto a QA device for testing. These updates won't affect other services that are already running in other domains, with the possible exception of network-level port conflicts, which we discuss later in this chapter.

Upon initialization of a new device, there is only one predefined domain: default. The default domain is special in that it contains the network and device management operations, such as user creation and Ethernet interface configuration. By isolating these functions from everyday usage, the default domain protects vital resources from normal developers. A device administrator will spend much of his time in the default domain, configuring connections to DNS and time servers, creating additional domains for new projects, and allocating user permissions.

Administration Versus Development Domains

Changes to the default domain should *always* be restricted to device configuration only; separate application domains should be used for any application-specific proxies or configurations.

Please note that although domains are logically separate from a service and file perspective, they do share the same pool of resources (memory, CPU) and network-level connections. On each device, there can be only one listener configured per IP:port combination. Thus, if a service or Front Side Handler in one domain is listening on port 80, no listener in another domain can be configured on the same IP address at port 80. If the architecture requires services to be listening on standard HTTP and HTTPS ports (80 and 443), then secondary IP addresses can be configured for use in different domains; that is, an Ethernet interface can have two IP addresses, each used by listeners in a specific domain. A list of currently active ports can be found by navigating to Status→IP-Network→TCP Port Status from the left-side menu.

Alternatively, a simple pass-through service can be defined to listen on port 80 and route all traffic to the appropriate DataPower service on another port—even if that service is running in a different domain. If a service backend is defined using the localhost IP, 127.0.0.1, DataPower-defined services can be called without exiting to the network stack and running into firewall complications. This works on port 443 for terminating SSL connections as well, but keep in mind that only a single certificate can be presented on any IP:port combination due to the nature of SSL.

Creating Domains

Generally, creating a domain involves only the single step of providing a name, as shown in Figure 12-1, though there are certainly many configuration options that can be tweaked if necessary.

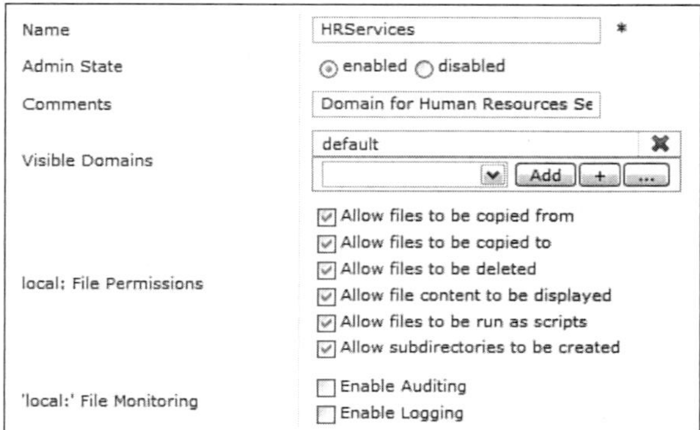

Figure 12-1 Adding a new application domain.

The domain name is the only required field, while the default values for the other fields provide a reasonable level of access for a domain that is currently being used for development. In a domain on a QA or production device, some local: file permissions can be removed for additional security. For enterprises that require an audit trail any time an in-use file is modified, auditing or logging can be enabled on the local: directory as well.

The Visible Domains property provides some level of access to the file system in other domains. The default domain, which includes the store: directory containing commonly used, DataPower-provided files, is always included in a new domain's list, enabling services in this domain to have access to files in the store: directory. Adding other visible domains to this list will create additional links from the File Management screen within the domain being created. If a hypothetical CoreServices domain is added to the list when creating the HRServices domain, then the File Management screen within HRServices will include a CoreServices: directory for design-time copying of shared files. This connectivity is available *only* during the design phase; with the exception of the store: directory, files within these visible domains cannot be referenced during runtime execution.

Remote Domain Configuration

Domain configurations, including the services and objects that have been created within, are generally stored on the local file system (in each domain's config: directory) and loaded at device startup. The Add Domain screen's Configuration tab contains an interesting alternative; domain configurations can be loaded from remote servers at startup. In Figure 12-2, the HRServices domain will be retrieved from a configuration server.

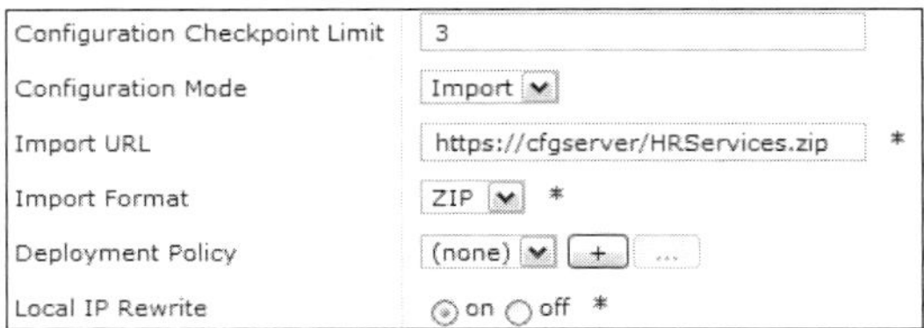

Figure 12-2 Defining a remote domain configuration file.

By choosing Import as the configuration mode and providing the URL of a remote configuration that has been exported from the device, domains can be dynamically generated at startup and shared between multiple devices. Every device in a cluster can point at a single golden exported copy of a domain, perhaps stored in a version control system; updates to that domain on every device would simply require a domain restart or device reboot after modifying the configuration file. Another advantage of this approach is that the limited available space on the DataPower flash memory is conserved. This is a requirement of certain high-security environments, which do not allow configuration files to be stored on the file system of DMZ devices (even highly secure ones).

If you choose this configuration method, there are a few things to keep in mind:

- The domain should be hosted on a highly available server or cluster of servers. If the server is down and the configuration cannot be retrieved, the domain will be down upon device startup. An alert is generated to warn you of this status.
- The server should use mutually authenticated SSL for its communication; this prevents substitution attacks and protects the configuration file in-transit.
- The export should be backed up and stored in a source code repository to make sure that hardware failures and other server problems do not permanently destroy a configuration.
- Keys, certificates, and other files stored in the cert: directory need to be uploaded separately from the configuration, as these files will not be included in the export for security purposes.

Customizing an imported configuration using deployment policies and IP rewriting are discussed in Chapter 15, "Build and Deploy Techniques." Domain configurations can also be "pushed" to a device using ITCAM[1] System Edition for DataPower. In this case, the Configuration Mode field would retain its default value of local.

Managing Domains

Management of domains for environment promotion is discussed in Chapter 15; however, for the purposes of this chapter, you need to know how a device administrator performs basic management tasks, including domain exports, checkpoints, and comparisons.

[1] The IBM Tivoli Composite Application Manager is an external software application that provides device management capabilities; see Chapter 15 for more details.

Configuration Exports

To back up a full domain for insertion into a code repository, simply click the Export Configuration link from the Control Panel. Choosing "Create a backup of one or more application domains" allows you to select any domains subject to continuous development and download them to a local machine. The end result is a .zip file that can be backed up or saved on a local machine for manual import on another device. If exported in this manner and imported on another device, these domains will be created as new.

To export a configuration for hosting on an HTTP server for remote domain configuration, as discussed earlier in this chapter, choose "Export configuration and files from the current domain," and then select All Objects. This results in an appropriately formatted .zip file for dynamic configuration imports. This export method also enables the services to be imported into *any* domain, as the domain itself is not included.

Configuration Checkpoints

While performing day-to-day configuration changes, especially when making modifications that may potentially modify existing behavior, it may be helpful to take a snapshot of the current state without performing a full domain export. To take an on-device snapshot of a domain's current configuration, a checkpoint can be created. From within the domain in question, select Administration→Configuration→Configuration Checkpoints from the left menu. Provide a unique, descriptive checkpoint name and click Save Checkpoint. In Figure 12-3, we created a checkpoint before making modifications to the current configuration.

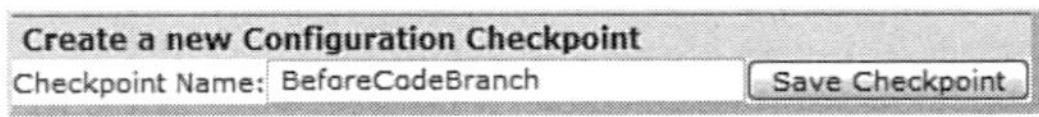

Figure 12-3 Saving a configuration checkpoint.

A saved checkpoint references its name, the time it was taken, and the various operations available, as seen in Figure 12-4.

Figure 12-4 Configuration checkpoint options.

Choosing Rollback reverts the domain configuration to the state saved in the checkpoint. All changes made since the timestamp are lost; be sure the checkpoint names are descriptive enough to confirm appropriate use of the checkpoint you have chosen. Choosing Remove deletes the configuration checkpoint, freeing room for new ones to be created. The number of checkpoints allowed per domain is configurable from within the Application Domain object.

On-device checkpoints are not a replacement for a strong IT backup policy, which should incorporate the backup of your DataPower configurations. There is limited on-board file system space, so don't get carried away with hundreds of checkpoints. If the flash file system or the device itself happens to experience a hardware failure, these checkpoints would not be retrievable. However, this is a helpful feature for taking quick snapshots of configurations during service development.

Configuration Comparisons

Before performing a rollback, saving a currently running domain to the persisted file system, or importing a slightly different version of a domain, it may be helpful to compare two potential configurations. Revealing their differences can help you make choices about saving, rolling back, or importing a domain.

To compare any two domain configurations, including checkpoints, external config files, and the currently running configuration, navigate to Administration→Configuration→Compare Configuration, or click Compare next to a specific checkpoint. This opens the Configuration Comparison screen seen in Figure 12-5.

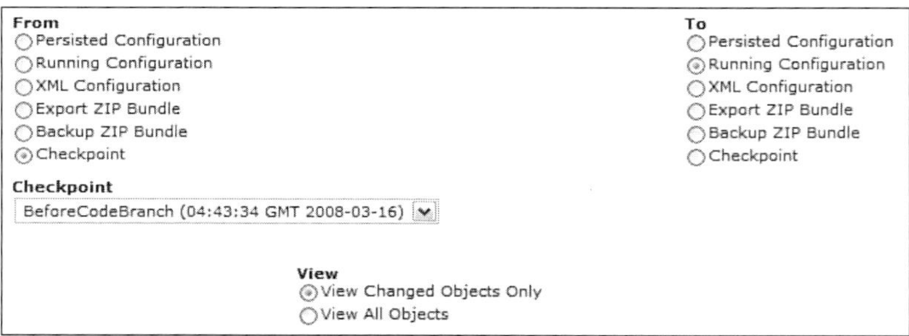

Figure 12-5 Comparing a saved checkpoint to the currently running configuration.

Configuration comparison can determine the modified objects between any two of the following:

- **Persisted Configuration**—The configuration currently saved to the file system for this domain.
- **Running Configuration**—The configuration currently running, including any changes made since the last time the configuration was persisted using the Save Config link.
- **XML Configuration**—A set of objects (or even all objects from a domain) that have been exported as an XML file.
- **Export ZIP Bundle**—A domain or set of objects that has been exported as a zip file.
- **Backup ZIP Bundle**—A set of domains that have been exported as a single zip file.
- **Checkpoint**—A checkpoint that has been saved for the current domain.

Choose a checkpoint or configuration on each side and select whether to compare every object, or only the changed objects. In domains with a large number of services, you should definitely choose View Changed Objects Only to view a more manageable comparison.

Users

Users of DataPower SOA Appliances fall into several categories, from network admins to production support personnel to application developers. Each of these distinct users requires access to different portions of the device, with varying levels of permission to create, read, modify, and delete configuration objects. Keep in mind that these users of the DataPower administration interfaces are very different from application users who might want to execute a service configured on the device.

There is only one user predefined on the appliance at initialization: the admin user. This super user has full control over everything on the device—essentially unlimited permissions. Think of this account as the root user in a *nix system, or an Administrator with full access rights on a Windows server. Initial login using this username is discussed in Chapter 2, "DataPower Quick Tour and Setup," but this point cannot be stressed enough: ***Don't lose the admin password!***[2] There is no password reset for the admin user, and if you lose it, the entire device will need to be shipped to DataPower HQ for a re-initialization.

After you have performed initial setup steps and logged on to the DataPower WebGUI, you can begin creating users that will administer, develop, or view configurations within that device. User definitions can be defined locally, on the device, or remotely, within an external authentication server. External users will be discussed in the "Role-Based Management" section later in this chapter; the following sections apply to local users defined within the appliance.

Admin and Auditing

After initializing a device as the admin user, you should immediately create new users for performing all subsequent administrative tasks. The time and date of any changes saved to the default domain are recorded in a locked audit log. The audit log is available from Status→View Status→Audit Log in the left-side menu. By distributing varied administrative accounts and enforcing login using only those credentials (and not the admin account), you can provide an audit record and change tracking for any modifications made by these users.

Creating Users

To create a new user, browse to Administration→Access→New User Account in the left-side menu. The first question asked is whether the user should be restricted to a particular domain. If so, the user is created with a custom-defined group (set of permissions) called developer_*DomainName*. The user is given full access to define services and other objects within the selected domain, and no access to any other domains (including default). While simply restricting the user

[2] We mean it. Do not lose this password. Shipping an appliance to Massachusetts is a lot of trouble. Just remember the password.

to a domain may be sufficient for simple implementations or on a generic development appliance, many users require higher-level or custom access rights. If the user is *not* restricted to a particular domain, then they must be placed within a user group to fully define their level of access. User groups provide a mapping between a set of users and the administration permissions provided to them, and can be thought of as administrative roles. Figure 12-6 shows the options for built-in user groups unrestricted by domain.

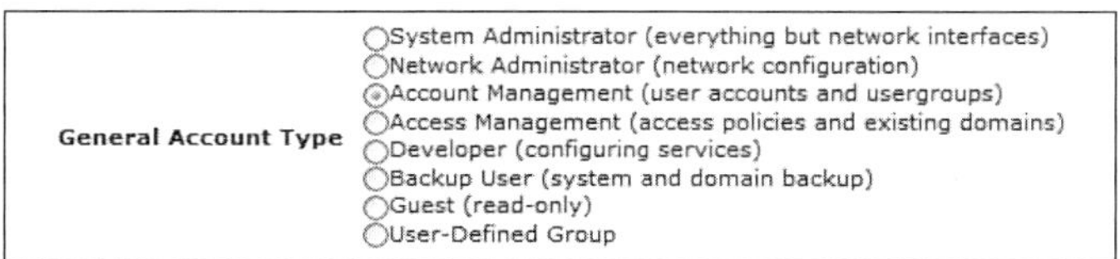

Figure 12-6 Choosing a group for the new user.

After the account type has been defined, you'll need to provide a username and an initial password. Usernames are not case-sensitive, so feel free to use any combination of uppercase and lowercase letters. During the user's first login, they'll have to change their password, so you can pick a random (and secure) string to provide with their username. The default password policy requires them to be at least six characters. You'll need to type it twice for verification, as shown in Figure 12-7.

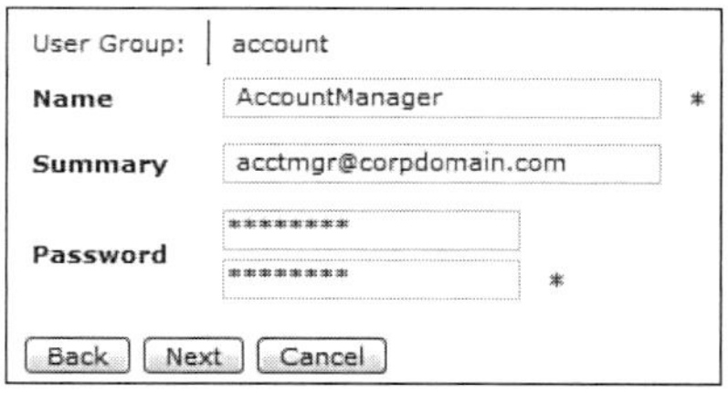

User Group: account
Name AccountManager *
Summary acctmgr@corpdomain.com
Password ******** ******** *
Back Next Cancel

Figure 12-7 Defining a username/password combination.

The summary is a good place to provide a comment about the user, including either a description of their role or contact information for that user. A corporate email address in this field would give device administrators a method for contacting the user if necessary.

Defining a Password Policy

If your enterprise requires a specific password policy for local accounts on internal servers, you can define stricter password requirements by navigating to Administration→Access→RBM Settings and clicking on the Password Policy tab. The password options are shown in Figure 12-8.

Though this should be modified to meet your corporate security policy, the most common updates are requiring mixed case and either a digit or a nonalphanumeric character. Enabling aging enables you to define a maximum password age. Disallowing password reuse retains a user-configurable number of old passwords to check for duplication.

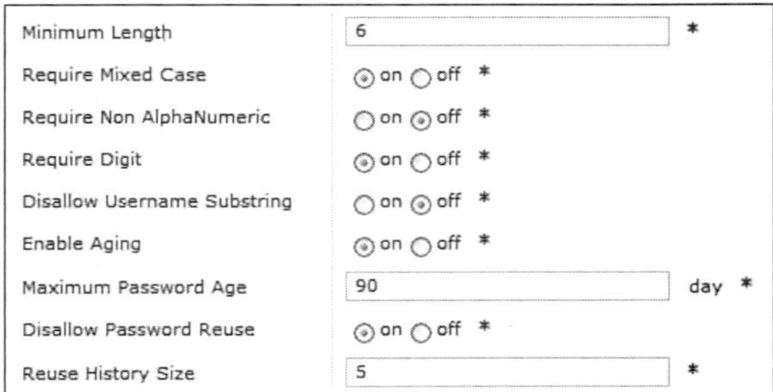

Figure 12-8 Updating the default password policy for local users.

User Groups

User groups provide an easy way to combine individual permissions into a more comprehensive access profile. There are both built-in and user-defined groups, allowing for generic roles or fine-grained object access.

Built-In User Groups

Built-in user groups provide analogs to common roles within an organization so that most users can simply fit in to the category that best describes their job role. Though a brief description is supplied in the WebGUI, how do these map to real-life permissions?

System Administrator

The system administrator can modify everything except network interfaces. The system administrator has these permissions:

- Read-only access to store: directory on file system
- Read-only access to Ethernet interfaces
- Full access to all other objects on the device

Network Administrator

The network administrator can perform the network-level tasks that the system administrator cannot and has these permissions:

- Read-write access to all network-level objects, including Ethernet interfaces, device access points (WebGUI, CLI, SSH, Telnet), DNS and NTP servers, and SNMP configurations
- Read access for all network-related status screens, including routing tables, ARP tables, and server connectivity
- Execute access for network troubleshooting operations such as pings, packet captures, and error reports

Account Management

An account manager can create users and groups on the device and has these permissions:

- Login access to the WebGUI and SSH/Telnet interfaces
- Full access to create users and user groups, with the exception of privileged users
- Execute access for modifying log levels for Role-Based Management

Access Management

An access manager can set up login authentication to use a remote server and has these permissions:

- Read-write access to all interfaces (WebGUI, XML Management, SSH, Telnet) to modify access policies
- Full access to create users and user groups
- Ability to modify Role-Based Management settings to perform login authentication on a remote authentication server

Developer

A developer can create and modify services in all domains and has the following permissions:

- Read-only access to users, domains, network interfaces, and system information
- No access to system control operations such as device shutdown and firmware upgrades
- Full access to all other objects, allowing configuration of services in any domain

Backup User

A backup user can perform operations for configuration management and has the following permissions:

- Execute access to checkpoint operations (save, rollback, remove)
- Execute access to backup operations
- Read access to checkpoint status information

Guest

A guest is limited to purely read operations on all objects and has the following permission:

- Read-only access to entire device

Custom User Groups

In situations when there is no built-in user group that contains the exact set of desired permissions, such as users who are limited to an admin-defined selection of domains, a custom user group can be constructed from granular permission statements. These groups can then be reused for all users that require this particular access policy. To create a new user group, browse to Administration→Access→Manage User Groups in the left-side menu and click Add. This opens the configuration page seen in Figure 12-9.

Figure 12-9 Creating a new user group.

A user group consists of a name and an associated access profile. Access policies are built individually and then added to the list to create a profile. Provide a descriptive name so that other administrators provisioning users will not need to look up the specific permissions within a custom group.

Access Profiles

Access profiles consist of a set of access policies that combine to form a level of access appropriate to members of the group. When a user attempts to perform an operation (read, write, add, delete, or execute) on a resource within DataPower, these policies are checked for the permissions that have been applied to that resource. When more than one policy applies, the most specific policy will be in effect. Thus it is possible to define broad, generic policies that apply to large groups of objects, and more specific statements that will override the generic rule for certain resources.

Click Build within a user group, as demonstrated in Figure 12-9, to open the access policy window shown in Figure 12-10.

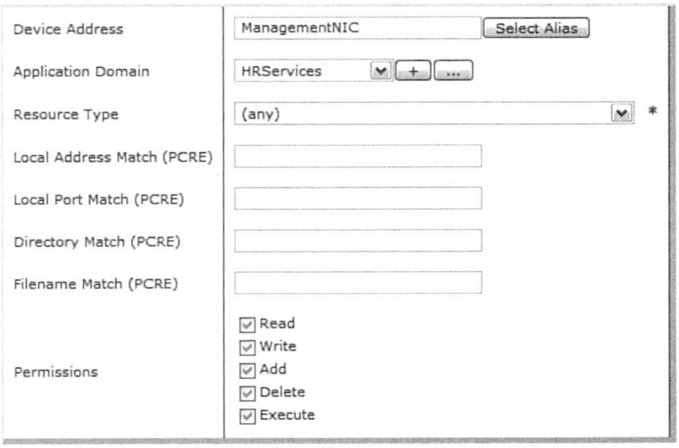

Device Address	ManagementNIC [Select Alias]
Application Domain	HRServices [+] [...]
Resource Type	(any) *
Local Address Match (PCRE)	
Local Port Match (PCRE)	
Directory Match (PCRE)	
Filename Match (PCRE)	
Permissions	Read Write Add Delete Execute

Figure 12-10 Creating an access policy.

Access policies use a top-down approach to defining a resource. In Figure 12-10, you can see the properties, from Device Address to Permissions; these will compose an access policy statement. The syntax for an access policy is *Address/Domain/Resource*?Access=*permissions*[&field=*value*].

- *Address* is the device address on which this resource can be accessed. This can limit a user to logging in for device management via a particular Ethernet interface. It must take the form of a fully specified hostname, an IP address, or a local host alias. For access on all addresses, an asterisk (*) can be used to designate any.
- *Domain* is the application domain containing the resource in question. This must either be the complete name of a domain or an asterisk to represent any domain.
- *Resource* is the type of resource being accessed. Choose from the drop-down list any of the resources on the device; they are divided into categories for easy access. Due to the large number of potential options, it is best to define a generic policy giving the default permissions, and then define a few more specific policies to override the defaults in particular cases. Selecting (all resources) will use an asterisk to designate all resources.
- *Permissions* are the set of operations that a user can perform on this resource. They include read, write, add, delete, and execute. Any combination of these operations can be added to a single access policy, though they don't all apply to every resource. For example, any resource in the status category requires only read access, because these are all read-only objects. Similarly, resources that perform operations such as "change-password" or "rollback-chkpoint" only require execute access. Services and their related objects (handlers, processing policies, rules, and actions) can be added, deleted, read, or modified (write).
- *Fields* available for matching a specific object will depend on the object type. A File resource may have a Directory field and a Name field on which to match, while a Web Service Proxy object will have only a Name field. Any Field/Value pairs provided here serve to limit the object to which this access profile applies. You can see an example of a Name match in the access profiles depicted in Figure 12-11.
- *Values* provided for a given field are PCRE (Perl Compatible Regular Expression) statements that define specific objects or groups of objects. By using wildcards and other PCRE designators, single policy statements can apply to multiple resources.

After filling in the appropriate fields in the access policy, click Save to return to the user group definition. Add the new policy to the list, and then build as many new policy statements as are required to complete the user group's access profile.

Every new user group has a single access policy defined by default. The generic read-only access policy (*/*/*?Access=r) can be removed or modified to provide more privacy for other domains. Choosing a resource type and providing a filter can add specific access to additional objects. In Figure 12-11, this group is given full permissions to all current and future Web Service Proxies with names containing the string "HR" that are defined in the CoreServices domain.

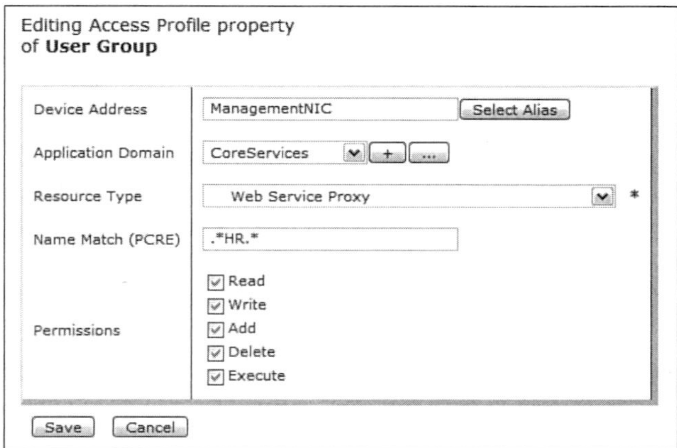

Figure 12-11 Defining a filter on a subset of domain objects.

In the full user group definition shown in Figure 12-12, the HRServicesGroup has read-only access to every domain (Line 1), full access to the HRServices domain (Line 2), and access to a subset of services in the CoreServices domain: those with HR in their name (Line 3). Any Web Service Proxies without HR in their names are subjected to the read-only permissions defined in Line 1.

Figure 12-12 Adding multiple access policies to a custom user group.

Here are a few example policies, from the Network Administrator group:

- `*/*/access/change-password?Access=x` allows the user to change their own password.
- `*/*/config/rollback-chkpoint?Access=x` allows the user to roll back to an earlier configuration checkpoint.
- `*/*/debug/ping?Access=x` allows the user to ping remote hosts to test network connectivity.
- `*/*/mgmt/web-mgmt?Access=rw` allows the user to view and modify the configuration of the WebGUI management interface.
- `*/*/network/interface?Access=rwad` allows modification of the Ethernet interface configurations.

You can get additional samples from any of the built-in user groups defined on the device,[3] Custom roles often need a combination of rights; if an account manager also needs some development rights, you can combine the access policies (by hand) into an appropriate custom role.

Role-Based Management

For devices that will only ever be accessed by a few users, especially in nondevelopment environments that should be locked down to QA/production support teams, the local users and groups defined earlier in this chapter should suffice for user authentication. However, most enterprises have a corporate directory stored in LDAP or another registry and might want to leverage the accounts there, rather than create yet another account ID and password for their employees. This is especially true for development groups with large numbers of potential users of the appliance. In these cases, DataPower's Role-Based Management (RBM) policy can use external authentication servers for user login. Browse to Administration→Access→RBM Settings to modify the login method.

As you read the instructions that follow, keep in mind that any changes made on this screen will take effect immediately upon clicking Apply in the RBM policy. Make sure that your authentication server is available and appropriately configured, or you could be locked out of the WebGUI and need to rely on a fallback user or CLI override. If you have access to the physical device, you can use the following steps to double-check your changes:

1. Perform your RBM modifications.
2. Click Apply to enforce the changes, but do not click Save Config.
3. Verify appropriate access for two users, one affected by the change and one not affected.
4. If access is not as expected, physically restart the device; the configuration (including RBM changes) will be rolled back to the last saved state.

> **Reliance on External Servers**
>
> As with all configuration options that require connectivity to external servers, RBM modifications should be approached with care. High availability and guaranteed connectivity for authentication servers is especially important in this case, as a misconfiguration or network failure could impact your ability to log in to the appliance.

Authenticating Users

The first step of any login process is to authenticate the user. For local users, the RBM settings need not be modified in any way, though you can strengthen the on-device password policies if necessary, as we demonstrated in Figure 12-8. If there is a requirement to check usernames and

[3] Note that these built-in groups are not available from the Manage User Groups screen until at least one user has been assigned to the group. They are only added to the list as necessary to fit your pool of users.

passwords against a remote authentication server such as LDAP, rather than the local device, you can choose from one of the supported server types shown in Figure 12-13.

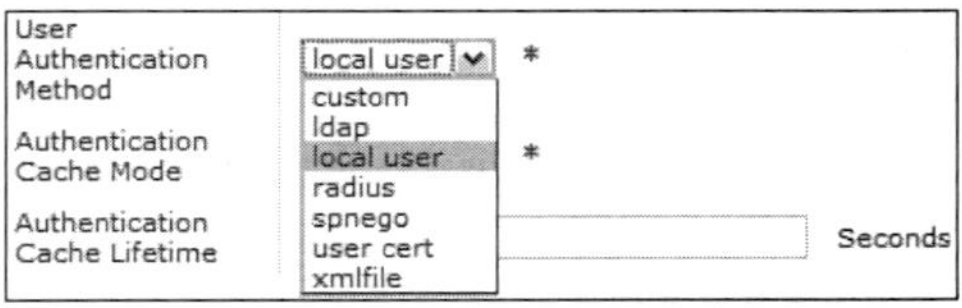

Figure 12-13 Selecting a remote authentication method for RBM.

When using LDAP or RADIUS, the user must still log in from the main DataPower login page. The username and password provided are extracted and sent to the authentication server. Depending on the server type, you'll need to provide various other fields. LDAP servers require a host:port combination, as well as a prefix and suffix to append to the username to create a valid Distinguished Name (DN); DataPower performs a full DN search on the registry using the newly created string. Authentication against a RADIUS server requires a predefined server definition in Administration→Access→RADIUS Settings. SPNEGO access will require a Kerberos keytab for decrypting the incoming ticket. Users can also be defined in an XML file that can be hosted on a remote server and modified by security personnel.

Authentication using LDAP is the most common use case, and requires some additional parameters as described previously. In Figure 12-14, the authentication call uses a load balanced group of LDAP servers for high availability purposes. The full DN is built from the prefix, suffix, and login username. For example, logging in as AUser attempts to authenticate using the following DN: uid=AUser,ou=People,dc=xyco,dc=com. It also is transmitted using SSL, to ensure transport encryption of the submitted username/password.

Comments	Authenticate users using LDAP a
User Authentication Method	ldap *
Authentication Server Host	LDAPServerGroup *
Authentication Server Port	636 *
LDAP Prefix	uid=
LDAP Suffix	ou=People,dc=xyco,dc=com *
LDAP SSL Proxy Profile	LDAPAuthClient (SSL Proxy Profile) + ...
LDAP Version	v3
LDAP Load Balancer Group	LDAPServerGroup (Load Balancer Group) + ...
Authentication Cache Mode	Absolute *
Authentication Cache Lifetime	600 Seconds
Mapping Credentials Method	xmlfile *

Figure 12-14 RBM configuration using an LDAP authentication server.

If the DataPower device cannot contact the remote authentication server due to network or other connectivity problems, all appliance (administrative) login attempts will fail. In order to prevent device lockout, set Local Login As Fallback to either all users or specific users. If set for specific users, define the subset of local users that are allowed to log in using their local credentials, as shown in Figure 12-15. This backup authentication mechanism will only be invoked in the case of network or infrastructure failure preventing access to the primary authentication mechanism.

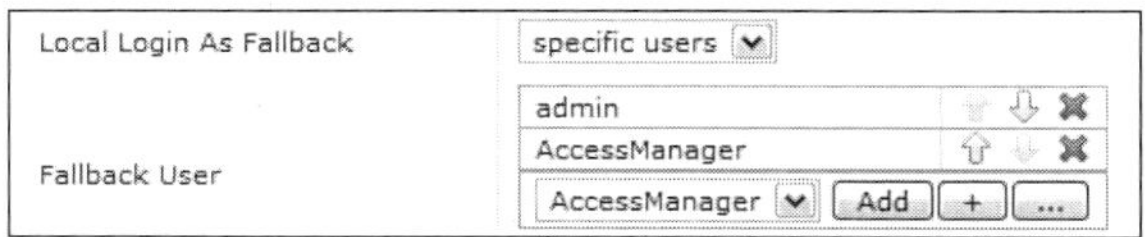

Figure 12-15 Defining specific users for local fallback access.

In addition, for complete administrative access to the device, even when successfully connecting to your backend authentication server, the registry in question must have an entry for the admin user. In most cases, this requires you to add such a user to your LDAP/RADIUS credential store. Make sure to complete this addition before updating your RBM settings.

Mapping User Credentials

An authenticated user must then be mapped to a credential; the credential is then used to determine the authorization status of the user for any particular resource. When employing local access management, the user is assigned to a particular user group, which assigns an access profile that determines authorization. Authentication done using an on-board XML file also allows mapping between an input credential (username) and an output credential (group). When the user is authenticated off-device, you can define both the input→output credential mapping and the mapping of output credential to access profile.

The easiest way to perform these mappings and generate an appropriate access profile is to use the xmlfile method of credential mapping. This requires a Mapping RBM Policy URL, which can reference a local or remote XML file that follows the proper format. If you create a new RBM Policy File from the RBM Settings page (click + next to the Mapping RBM Policy URL), a wizard takes you through each step in the process. Let's walk through each step in the wizard; at the end, you'll have a new XML file that maps user credentials to a set of access policies.

First, you can define a default credential given to unauthenticated users. If you want everyone with network access to the device to have read-only permission to login and view configurations, you could define a "guest" default credential as demonstrated in Figure 12-16. Leaving this blank will simply reject any user that doesn't have an authenticated user credential. Unless you have an overwhelming need for allowing *all* potential users some level of access, the default credential should be left blank.

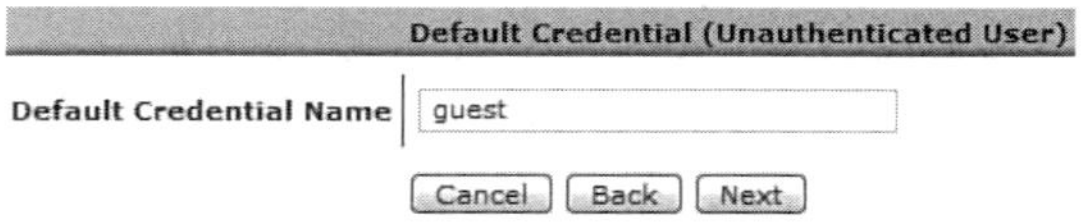

Default Credential (Unauthenticated User)

Default Credential Name | guest

Cancel Back Next

Figure 12-16 Defining a guest credential for unauthenticated access.

In the next wizard screen, map from the username to a credential name. Define your input credential and the output credential that will be created. If your authentication method was LDAP, your username (input credential) will no longer be just a username; it will be the distinguished name that was sent to the authentication server (see Figure 12-17).

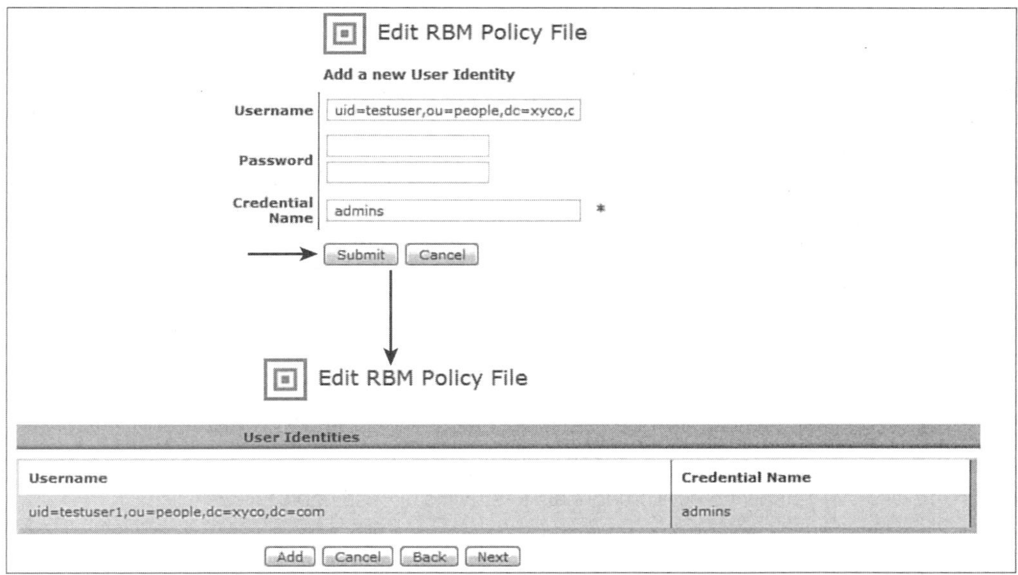

Figure 12-17 Mapping a user identity to an output credential.

Adding the appropriate Username and Credential Name entry in the wizard, as shown in Figure 12-17, will produce a mapping statement in the underlying XML file, as shown in Listing 12-1.

Listing 12-1 Mapping an LDAP DN to an output credential

```
<! - Map credentials to different credentials.  ->
<aaa:MapCredentials>
  <aaa:InputCredential>
    uid=testuser1,ou=people,dc=hr,dc=xyco,dc=com
  </aaa:InputCredential>
  <aaa:OutputCredential>admins</aaa:OutputCredential>
</aaa:MapCredentials>
```

These credential mappings also allow wildcards, so that `uid=.*,ou=people,dc=hr,dc=xyco,dc=com` allows you to map any authenticated credential to an output credential.

The next step in the wizard allows you to map from this output credential to an access profile consisting of one or more permissions statements. In the example in Figure 12-18, the admins are being mapped to a powerful access policy that gives all permissions on all device objects.

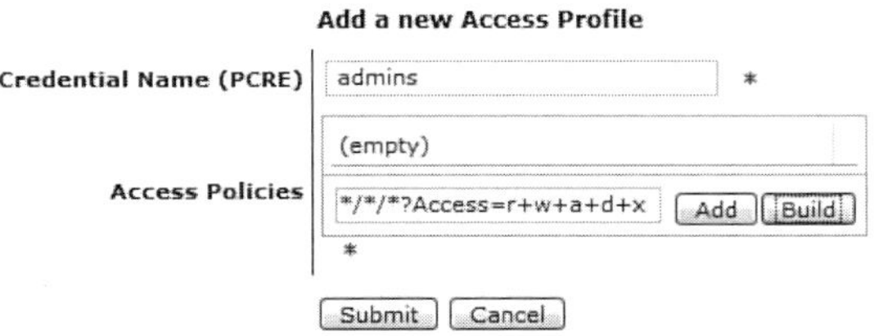

Figure 12-18 Creating an access profile for a mapped credential.

Defining a set of these access profiles for each mapped credential creates a list similar to that in Figure 12-19. When the full list of possible credentials is mapped, the RBM file is complete. Finish the wizard by defining a filename and saving it to the local filesystem. The file can then be exported (if desired), and referenced remotely.

Access Profile Mappings

Credential Name	Access Profile	
admins	*/*/*?Access=r+w+a+d+x	/\ V
guest	*/*/*?Access=r	/\ V

Figure 12-19 Mapping incoming credentials to specific access rights.

Using Access Profiles

Just as they must be defined from their individual access policies for custom user groups, Access Profiles must also be defined on each RBM Output Credential. Figure 12-19 demonstrates an example of this mapping. Access profile basics, more examples, and a complete dissection of the profile string syntax are discussed in detail in their own section earlier in this chapter.

Configuring each step in the wizard produces an XML file that can be named and saved to the local: directory. When used as the RBM Policy Mapping file, this enforces the appropriate permissions for users authenticated using off-device credential stores.

User Authentication Caching

When a user is authenticated using a credential store, either on the device or off, that authentication decision is cached by default. This caching means that the authentication server does not need to be accessed on every request, to reduce network operations for a lookup that will likely change very infrequently. The caching mode and duration can be defined from the RBM Settings page, as shown in Figure 12-20.

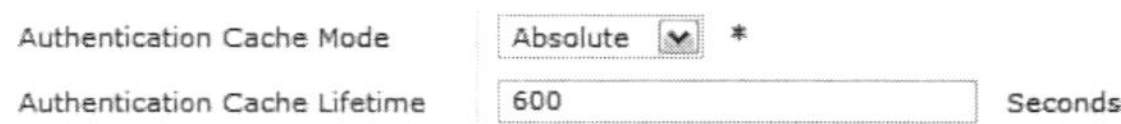

Figure 12-20 Defining a caching policy for authenticated users.

A setting of Absolute always uses the cache lifetime defined below it; the default is 600 seconds, or 10 minutes. By choosing a different cache mode, this caching can be disabled or tied to a TTL (time-to-live) provided by the authentication server, if such a parameter was included in the authentication response. Maximum uses the higher of the two values, between the user-defined cache lifetime and the TTL, while minimum uses the lower of the two values.

If your enterprise has uncharacteristic changes performed on its authentication servers, so that a large number of authentication decisions need to be invalidated and retrieved from scratch, you can require this revalidation from the WebGUI. Along the top of the RBM Settings page are the helpful links shown in Figure 12-21, including Flush RBM Cache.

Figure 12-21 Flushing the authentication cache from the RBM Settings page.

By flushing the cache, each new request checks against the authentication store. The current cache settings are still in effect, so all responses after the flush will be cached as desired.

Access to the Command Line Interface

Management of access to the Command Line Interface (CLI) is a bit more flexible—it can use the same rules that have been defined for WebGUI access, or it can be separately defined in a CLI-specific manner. To define all CLI access to use the exact same policies as the WebGUI, navigate to Administration→Access→RBM Settings. Set the Enforce RBM on CLI option to on. This will override all other CLI permissions settings discussed in the following sections. Because groups of CLI commands can't be delegated to an external registry, administrative access to the CLI is often enforced using the following methods instead.

If the WebGUI login settings are not used for the CLI as well, then there are two steps for determining whether a user will have access to a particular operation within a domain. First, a user group is given access to specific operation categories from the User Group configuration page, as described in the next section. Then our discussion will shift to the following step, where a user is given the rights to a domain from the Application Domain configuration page.

Command Groups

A command group is a group of associated commands that fit within a given category. For example, the File Management command group gives permission for operations on both the local file system and remote file servers, by allowing the definition of NFS mount objects. These groups provide a method for provisioning commands without having to define every specific command that is allowed; however, the granularity should still be small enough that no unnecessary permissions need to be granted.

To give a user group access to a command group, navigate to Administration→Access→Manage User Groups from the left-side menu, and then choose a user group on which to apply CLI permissions. Select the CLI Command Groups tab to expose the drop-down list of potential command groups that can be set for this user group, as seen in Figure 12-22. In this example, the capability to create and modify users and user groups is being added to the list of allowed commands.

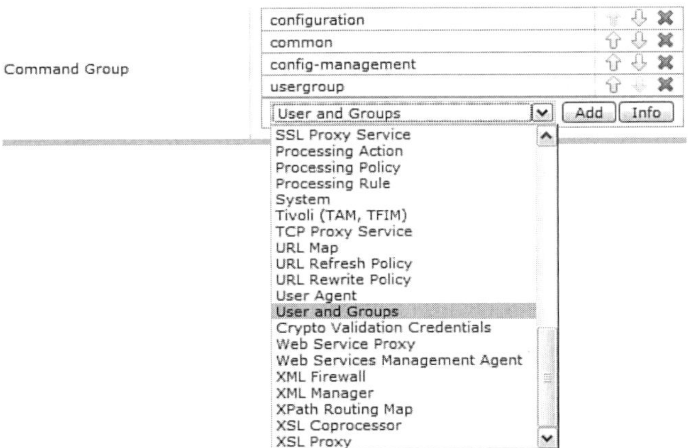

Figure 12-22 Selecting which types of commands can be run by members of this user group.

For each option, you can select it in the drop-down and click Info to get precise information about which options are included in a given category. By combining the appropriate set of commands for a given user group, you can create a comprehensive permission profile between both the WebGUI and CLI. For example, an account manager will likely need permission to the Users and Groups and RBM command groups.

Domain-Based CLI User Access

Once general categories of commands have been applied to a given user group, specific users within that group can be given access to a set of application domains in which to perform those operations. Navigate to Administration→Configuration→Application Domain to modify these settings. Choose a domain and click the CLI Access tab to begin the process of adding users.

Select local users from the drop-down list, and click Add to allow those users to run CLI operations in this domain. Figure 12-23 shows a group of users that have been given access. These users will *only* be able to run the commands granted to them by the command groups in the previous section.

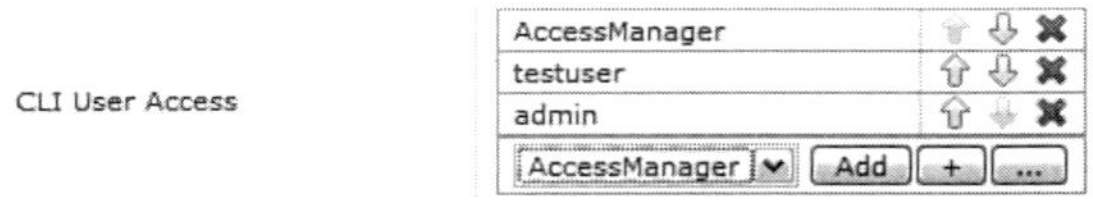

Figure 12-23 Defining the users who can access this domain from the command line (CLI).

Summary

The device administrator's job is now largely complete from a management perspective, after defining the domain structure on the device and creating users with appropriate permissions to act on services within those domains. From this point on, additional administrative tasks such as network configuration, setup of logging/monitoring, backup and deployment of environments, and service development can all be delegated to their responsible parties. The permissions granted to those users, whether they are from the networking, security, production management, or development teams, will allow them to log in to the device, perform operations specific to their bailiwick, and not interfere with any other users, all while staying within the boundaries of predefined corporate governance policies.

CHAPTER 13

Alternate Management Interfaces

Though the majority of users spend most of their time developing services and administering DataPower appliances from within the graphical WebGUI, there are a number of ways to access the device using nongraphical interfaces. The preferred method of interaction usually depends on the user's past experience and current job description; many network administrators simply feel more comfortable using a Command Line Interface (CLI), whereas deployment engineers may want to script device interaction as a series of SOAP calls to the XML Management Interface, a secure listener for retrieving data or executing commands in an automated fashion. Retrieving a quick, interactive status update or running a series of batched, aliased commands using Secure Shell (SSH) may be easiest from the CLI, while the XML Management Interface lends itself to pushing configurations to large numbers of devices using HTTPS. These are both perfectly valid approaches, and this chapter focuses on the power of using these alternate management interfaces on the appliances. We discuss how to access these interfaces and how to employ the most common and helpful commands. Though these alternate methods of access provide nearly the complete functionality enabled by the WebGUI, this chapter focuses mainly on interactive monitoring and management. Less interactive methods for long-term logging and configuration management are discussed in Chapter 14, "Logging and Monitoring," and Chapter 15, "Build and Deploy Techniques." With that, let's begin exploring our options.

Command Line Interface

The CLI provides nearly all the same capabilities as the WebGUI interface, as well as some CLI-only features. You can create a Web Service Proxy, define a Processing Policy, and configure actions to act upon messages flowing through the device, all using text-based commands typed into a shell communicating to the device over SSH—but why would you want to? In the DataPower Services portion of this book, you learned how easy it is to drag and drop actions into a Processing

Policy, configure a listener, and create a service using DataPower's award-winning graphical interface; though entirely possible, there's no need to investigate the syntax of each obscure CLI command to accomplish the same end goal. Instead, let's focus on the strengths of the appliance's CLI: quick access to extensive status information, easy debugging and modification of network configurations, manipulation/transfer of files to/from the appliance to various external servers, and configuration and firmware management.

Accessing the CLI

There are three different ways to get to the device's CLI. The first comes into play immediately upon receiving the appliance; in order to initialize the device after racking it in a datacenter, you must connect to it via serial cable and use the CLI in a terminal session to assign an Ethernet interface and enable the WebGUI. The other two connection methods, telnet and SSH, need to be enabled from either the serial interface or the WebGUI, as they are disabled by default. Telnet is included for backward compatibility and is not recommended due its unencrypted nature. To ensure an encrypted connection and verify the cryptographic authenticity of the server, SSH is the more secure choice.

From the initial login prompt, you need to enter configuration mode, a context that provides commands for device-level functionality. Type `co`, an abbreviation of `configure terminal`, at the login prompt to enter this mode. To enable SSH from the serial interface while in configuration mode, run the commands in Listing 13-1 .

Listing 13-1 Enabling SSH from the Command Line Interface

```
xi50# co
Global configuration mode
xi50(config)# ssh 192.168.1.199 22
%       Pending
SSH service listener enabled
xi50(config)# write mem
Overwrite previously saved configuration [y/n]? y
xi50(config)# exit
xi50# exit
```

Running this command without a host or port specified attempts to bind SSH to the management Ethernet interface (mgmt). If no management interface has been defined, SSH will listen on all configured interfaces; be sure to define a specific address to isolate management traffic from application data traffic. In each case, SSH listens to the canonical port (22) unless otherwise specified. To turn off the SSH interface, `no ssh` is the appropriate command.

To save these changes to the persisted file system and exit configuration mode, follow the command with a write mem and an exit command.

Configuration Modes

The CLI is segmented into configuration modes that represent the context in which your commands are executed. You were introduced to the global configuration mode in Listing 13-1, and you'll see more options (Action Configuration Mode, Flash Configuration Mode) as we delve deeper into the command line. In every case, you'll enter the mode by typing its name or a unique abbreviation of that name (co, action, flash); you'll exit and apply your changes by typing `exit` at the prompt.

Navigating the CLI

After SSH is enabled on an appliance, the CLI can be accessed remotely. You'll need to connect to the port you defined previously using a client that supports SSH, such as PuTTY on Windows or the shell application ssh on most UNIX/Linux distributions. You will be prompted for a login and password, as shown in Listing 13-2.

Listing 13-2 Logging into an Appliance Through the CLI

```
Unauthorized access prohibited.
login: admin
Password: ******
Welcome to DataPower XI50 console configuration.
(C) 1999-2007 by DataPower Technology, Inc.
Version: XI50.3.6.1.4 build 154519 on 2008/03/14 13:10:30
Serial number: 2703063Z
xi50#
```

Login via SSH

Many traditional servers use password authentication for SSH login. However, DataPower requires a keyboard-interactive process to protect your credential information from potentially being sniffed or stolen during the cryptographic handshake. The device initiates a secure channel automatically, and then provides an encrypted login process. As a side effect of the initial connection, and depending on your client, you may see an extraneous login as: prompt; simply press Enter at this point. You are warned that Unauthorized access is prohibited and then presented with the prompt shown in Listing 13-2.

CLI permissions depend on either the access policies defined for your user group or on a combination of command groups and specifically provisioned users. See Chapter 12, "Device Administration," for more details. If granted access to the CLI with your username and password, you'll find a prompt consisting of the device type (xa35, xs40, or xi50) followed by the pound sign (#). From this initial prompt, there are some initial, top-level commands that can be run, or you can enter the global configuration mode to make additional commands available. Enter global configuration mode by typing `configure terminal` (or `co` as a shortcut) at the CLI.

Notice the shortcut that just saved you sixteen keystrokes (configure terminal→co). CLI commands can always be abbreviated to the shortest unique string that identifies them; as you grow more comfortable with the range of commands available to you, try your hand at shortening them to save time.

> **GLOBAL CONFIGURATION MODE**
>
> Aside from a few high-level commands that act on the appliance as a whole, most of your CLI time will be spent configuring or querying objects or status information on the device. These usually require you to be in a configuration mode. If your prompt does not contain some form of (config) and you're having trouble with your commands not being recognized, enter global configuration mode by typing `co` at the prompt. The prompt changes to indicate you are in configuration mode. CLI commands can have various effects, depending on the context (configuration mode) in which they are executed. A full list of every available command in every configuration mode is available in the Reference Guide provided with the Resource CD that accompanies the DataPower appliances; this file can also be downloaded from the IBM support site. See Chapter 2, "DataPower Quick Tour and Setup," for more information. While we generally suggest that everyone RTFM (Read The Fantastic Manuals), this interface should generally feel familiar to anyone used to dealing with other datacenter hardware, such as routers and load balancers. This familiarity combined with powerful context-sensitive help should make CLI navigation relatively self-explanatory. When in doubt, let's see how to get help.

Help Is Your Friend

Perhaps the most useful command available from the CLI is the help command. This provides context-based information about the commands available to you at any given point in CLI navigation. If you have just logged in, help displays the high-level commands that can be run. In configuration mode, help displays a long list of available commands to enter other modes, perform operations, and so on. When in a more specific mode such as Web Service Proxy (WSP) configuration mode, help shows you the available options for modifying the WSP in question. In addition, you can execute the help command on any of the commands available to you to get more information about parameters and syntax. Let's take a look at a couple of examples in Listing 13-3.

Listing 13-3 Using Context-Sensitive Help in the CLI

```
xi50# help
clock                  Sets the date or time
configure terminal     Enters Global Configuration Mode
disable                Enters User Mode
disconnect             Terminates a user session
echo                   Echoes text to the console
exec                   Executes a configuration script
exit                   Terminates the CLI connection
help                   Displays general or command-specific help
```

```
login                  Logs in as a specific user
ntp                    Identifies a network time server
ping                   Sends an ICMP echo request
show                   Displays statistical or configuration data
shutdown               Shuts down or restarts the system
switch domain          Moves to a different application domain
test tcp-connection    Test TCP reachability
top                    Returns to initial login mode
traceroute             Displays the route to a host
xi50# help show
show [what]
 Displays configuration or status information relevant to the provided
argument. If no argument is provided, a list of available options is
displayed.
```

An initial execution of help shows the commands available. By executing help again and referencing one of these possible commands, we get more information about that command's syntax and purpose. In this case, the command we learned about is one of the most useful: the show command.

"Show" Me the Money

We've learned how to get help; let's talk about one additional command that is useful in just about every context: the show command. Show provides the current status or configuration of any object on the appliance. If there's a status page for the object in the WebGUI, there's a show command for it in the CLI. Similarly, if there's a configuration page for an object, we can view that configuration with a show command. We'll see a lot of examples in the following sections—this command is ubiquitous. Along with show commands, we'll also discuss commands used for network configuration and troubleshooting, device information and health retrieval, object modification, and file system operations. Let's dive right into some helpful command examples.

Network Configuration Commands

Upon receipt of an appliance, the device administrator used a serial cable and the CLI to assign an IP address and default gateway, and turn on the Web management interface. It's likely that all further network configuration—including DNS (for hostname resolution), NTP (for time synchronization), and additional interface enablement—was done from the WebGUI. This is perfectly reasonable, but sometimes you need to perform these operations from the CLI as well. Let's walk through some of the more common network commands.

We'll start from the beginning and see what's already been done using Chapter 2. First, an IP address was assigned to at least one Ethernet interface. We can use the show interface command (shortened to show int) to display the current status of each interface, including configured IP addresses and transferred data, as shown in Listing 13-4.

Listing 13-4 Displaying the Current Ethernet Interface Configuration

```
xi50(config)# show int
 interface    IP Address           RX (kb/pkts/errs)   TX (kb/pkts/errs)
 ---------    ----------           -----------------   -----------------
 eth1         10.32.40.80/32       0/0/0               0/0/0
 eth2         172.18.206.210/23    0/0/0               0/0/0
 eth4         192.168.1.199/24     2425/14535/0        14954/17314/0
 eth0         0.0.0.0/0            0/0/0               0/0/0
```

For more specific information about the configuration of one Ethernet interface in particular, we can expand our show int command to include the name of an interface. The management interface (mgt0) is listed as eth4 in the previous example; the names are synonymous when referencing this object. The more granular show command executed in Listing 13-5 provides us information about the MAC address, status, and interface mode.

Listing 13-5 Retrieving More Information About an Ethernet Interface

```
xi50(config)# show int mgt0
  interface: mgt0
 IP address: 192.168.1.199/24
MAC address: 00:0a:4b:80:06:54
     status: ok
  negotiate: auto
       mode: 1000baseTx-FD
        MTU: 1500
  RX kbytes: 2433
 RX packets: 14624
  RX errors: 0
   RX drops: 0
  TX kbytes: 14960
 TX packets: 17383
  TX errors: 0
   TX drops: 0
 collisions: 0
```

The next setup step is to enable the Web Management Interface. We can check to see which IP:port is assigned for the WebGUI and modify this if it needs to be changed. The show web-mgmt command displays the current settings; `web-mgmt` *`ip-address port timeout`* sets the new values, as shown in Listing 13-6.

Listing 13-6 Viewing and Modifying the Web Management Interface Listener

```
xi50(config)# show web-mgmt
web-mgmt [up] (modified)
--------
 admin-state enabled
 ip-address 0.0.0.0
 port 9090
 save-config-overwrite on
```

```
 idle-timeout 600 seconds
 acl web-mgmt  [up]
xi50(config)# web-mgmt 192.168.1.199 9090 3600
Web management: successfully started
```

In this example, the WebGUI was configured to listen on every enabled Ethernet interface. To restrict access to just the management interface, we set it to listen on a specific IP (192.168.1.199). We also raise the WebGUI idle timeout value from the default (600 seconds = 10 minutes) to 3600 seconds, or one hour. This enables DataPower users to pause during development without being timed out in the middle of a task. WebGUI timeouts should be set based on your internal security requirements (How long does it take your workstation to go to a locked screen-saver?) and common sense. Turning off the timeout entirely by setting a value of 0 creates a potential security risk in the case of an unlocked workstation, and allows for orphaned browser sessions that consume device resources. For these reasons, removing the idle timeout is *not* recommended.

The next piece of network configuration is the selection of DNS servers for hostname resolution. While this will likely be done using the WebGUI, we can view the configuration with our handy show command, as seen in Listing 13-7.

Listing 13-7 Viewing Current DNS Settings

```
xi50(config)# show dns
dns [up]
--
 admin-state enabled
 search-domain xyco.com
 search-domain xycorp.com
 name-server 172.20.135.156 53 53 3
 name-server 172.21.135.156 53 53 3
```

The DNS search domains have been defined to match our internal domain names, so a remote device referenced as server1 is looked up using server1.xyco.com and server1.xycorp.com. Having multiple DNS servers ensures that a single server failure is not the cause of network issues. The values after the IP addresses represent the UDP port, TCP port, and number of retries before failure.

Now that DNS has been configured, we can reference hostnames in any additional configuration objects. For example, we can set up our NTP server connectivity with a simple reference (`ntp time.nist.gov`) to a time server.

Network Troubleshooting Commands

Now that we've defined network connectivity options (Ethernet interfaces, management interfaces, DNS servers), we should test to make sure that the appliance can connect to other nodes in the network, including backend application servers, authentication/authorization servers, and any supporting Web servers. This can be done from the WebGUI as well, but there are often restrictions on having active Web interfaces in the Demilitarized Zone (DMZ). Let's walk through some example commands that might be useful under these circumstances. Some of these will also be discussed in Chapter 27, "Problem Determination Using Built-In Tools," but they're worth noting here as well.

If there appears to be an issue in routing to the appropriate remote network, traceroute will display each hop to the targeted server. A failure to find the remote server indicates network inaccessibility, and the last successful gateway should give you an indication of where the problem lies. In Listing 13-8, we can see the full path to Google.

Listing 13-8 Determining a Network Path to a Server

```
xi50# traceroute www.google.com
Traceroute www.google.com (64.233.167.147)
 1:       192.168.1.1  rtt= 0 ms
 2:      76.176.224.1  rtt= 1 ms
 3:       76.176.0.25  rtt= 0 ms
 4:       76.176.0.13  rtt=11 ms
 5:         4.79.36.9  rtt=52 ms
 6:       4.68.113.69  rtt=43 ms
 7:       4.68.101.34  rtt=59 ms
 8:       4.79.208.18  rtt=58 ms
 9:      72.14.232.53  rtt=57 ms
10:     64.233.175.42  rtt=61 ms
11:    64.233.167.147  rtt=50 ms
```

To test general connectivity, you can ping a remote host or IP address, as shown in Listing 13-9. A failure to ping usually represents either host inaccessibility, network firewall misconfiguration, or simply that ICMP echo requests (the utility used by ping) have been disabled on the target server. Keep this last possibility in mind—do not assume that a failed ping means no addressability. Perform a similar ping test from another server/workstation in the same network with demonstrated connectivity. If that test is successful but DataPower is not, it's likely a firewall/Access Control List (ACL) issue.

Listing 13-9 Ensuring Network Connectivity to a Remote Server

```
xi50(config)# ping 192.168.1.103
PING 192.168.1.103 (192.168.1.103) with 56 data bytes of data
64 bytes from 192.168.1.103: seq=0, ttl=128, rtt=0.0 ms
64 bytes from 192.168.1.103: seq=1, ttl=128, rtt=0.0 ms
64 bytes from 192.168.1.103: seq=2, ttl=128, rtt=0.0 ms
3 packets transmitted, 3 received, 0% loss, time 6001ms
xi50(config)#
```

After basic connectivity has been established, you may want to verify a listener on a specific TCP port. This IP:port combination could represent a backend application or an authentication server, such as the attempt to verify an LDAP installation shown in Listing 13-10. You may have performed this sort of test before using telnet from a server or workstation command shell.

Listing 13-10 Testing for a Listener on a Specific TCP Port

```
xi50# test tcp-connection 192.168.1.198 389
TCP connection successful
```

If any of the preceding commands fail, check whether the appropriate ports are open on any internal firewalls, and whether the appliance's IP addresses are whitelisted in any server-side ACL. If they all succeed and there is still a connectivity problem, check for SSL communication issues and/or application-layer access control.

System Information Commands

There are a few times when it becomes necessary to retrieve system information from an appliance, including that unit's hardware type, serial number, firmware version, and applicable license data. One of these moments is when upgrading the firmware; the other is when contacting IBM for DataPower support. In each of these cases, there are a series of CLI commands that become especially useful.

The support contract for DataPower appliances is tied to the device's serial number, so this will be one of the first things that Customer Support asks for when opening a support ticket with IBM. This can be retrieved with the show system command, as seen in Listing 13-11. The description tells you the model number (9002/3/4), and the Product ID field contains information about the hardware type (9003 in this example). These are both necessary pieces of information when selecting a firmware file for upgrading an appliance.

Listing 13-11 Discovering an Appliance Serial Number

```
xi50(config)# show system
  description: DataPower XI50
serial number: 2703063Z
   product id: 9003-XI50-03 [Rev 16]
          OID: 1.3.6.1.4.1.1468.1.3
       uptime: 0 days 01:57:23
      contact: deviceadmin@xyco.com
         name: John Smith
     location: Peoria, IL
     services: 72
login-message: Welcome to XMLGateway12
```

Determining the current version of the firmware is often useful when checking for updates that may provide some new functionality. The show version command seen in Listing 13-12 displays the current firmware version and the versions of additional libraries used by the device. You will likely want these library versions to remain the same in the new firmware image. For instance, if the Tivoli Access Manager (TAM) version is listed as 6.0, be sure to download the firmware image that includes TAM6.

Listing 13-12 Querying for Firmware and Library Versions

```
xi50(config)# show version
          Serial: 2703063Z
         Version: XI50.3.6.1.4
           Build: 154519
      Build Date: 2008/03/14 13:10:30
  Watchdog Build: XI50.3.6.1.4
  Installed DPOS: XI50.3.6.1.4
    Running DPOS: XI50.3.6.1.4
 XML accelerator: xg3
  Coproc library: 1.2
              MQ: 6.0.0-0
            ODBC: 5.2
             TAM: 6.0
       Tibco EMS: 4.4.0
   WebSphere JMS: 1.2.3
```

To see a full list of options for which the appliance is licensed, use the show license command as seen in Listing 13-13. If the feature is listed and marked as Enabled, this appliance can use that functionality; if the feature is not in the list, this appliance will not execute that functionality. Attempting to upgrade a firmware image containing unlicensed options will cause the update to fail. This has no negative side effects, but the firmware is not upgraded as desired.

Listing 13-13 Gathering a List of Licensed Options

```
xi50(config)# show license
 Feature              Enabled
  - - --               - - --
 MQ                   Yes
 TAM                  Yes
 DataGlue             Yes
 JAXP-API             Yes
 PKCS7-SMIME          Yes
 SQL-ODBC             Yes
 Tibco-EMS            Yes
 WebSphere-JMS        Yes
```

Some features are included with every firmware image; for example, DataGlue is licensed and installed on every XI50 appliance. These features do not require a firmware image that specifically includes them in the filename. For those options that *do* require special firmware (including MQ, TAM, Tibco, and ODBC), make sure you download the appropriate image.

From the device information returned by the three previous commands, we can determine that this appliance is an XI50 running on 9003 hardware and 3.6.1.4 firmware, and licensed for MQ, Tibco, ODBC, and TAM (Version 6). To upgrade this device to the next firmware release, the image filename should look like the following: `xi3615.9003.mq6.odbc52.tam6.tibco.scrypt2`.

Appliance Load and Health Monitoring Commands

Monitoring the current health of the DataPower appliance is generally handled by a network operations/monitoring team using standards such as SNMP and syslog. Setup of these interactions is thoroughly discussed in Chapter 14, "Logging and Monitoring." It is also sometimes helpful for an administrator to be able to submit a real-time request for hardware status.

First let's focus on indicators of processing load. Fittingly enough, the best metric to use for overall device status is the show load command shown in Listing 13-14. This command, called System Usage in the WebGUI status menu, takes into account the current CPU, memory, and connection information to provide a single value (load %).

Listing 13-14 Checking Load Provides a Good Indication of Device Usage

```
xi50(config)# show load
 interval: 1000 msec
     load: 1 %
work list: 24
```

While system usage is the best overall indicator of device workload, many enterprises also desire measurements for common server characteristics, such as memory and CPU. Keep in mind that the CPU or memory usage may be temporarily high, even under low device load, due to optimization of message processing. Though they should not be used to trigger alerts or device health concerns, these statistics are available through the CLI as well. In Listing 13-15, the memory usage is shown as a percentage, along with specific byte counts. CPU usage percentage is shown at several intervals, demonstrating trends that may occur over a larger time period.

Listing 13-15 Assessing the Device Memory and CPU Usage

```
xi50(config)# show mem
    Memory Usage: 12 %
    Total Memory: 4150124 kbytes
     Used Memory: 515859 kbytes
     Free Memory: 3634265 kbytes
Requested Memory: 652800 kbytes
xi50(config)# show cpu
                 10 sec    1 min   10 min   1 hour    1 day
cpu usage (%):        3        3       15       15       15
```

While file system usage statistics have no impact on workload or current processing, they also represent commonly tracked metrics. If the file system becomes full, it could have an impact on on-device logging and other activities that use either the encrypted file store or the temporary file system loaded in memory. Using the CLI to check the file system space available, as shown in Listing 13-16, is an easy way to figure out how much of an impact file system operations (copying files on/off of the device, deleting files) have had on the free space. The encrypted space metrics refer to long-term directories such as local, store, and cert, while temporary space refers to directories that are cleared on device restart, such as temporary and logtemp.

Listing 13-16 Checking for Free Space on the Device File System

```
xi50(config)# show filesystem
 Free Encrypted Space: 245 Mbytes
Total Encrypted Space: 475 Mbytes
 Free Temporary Space: 234 Mbytes
Total Temporary Space: 242 Mbytes
```

Digging even deeper into actual hardware statistics, the show sensors and show sensors-fans commands provide information from internal environmental sensors. These include temperatures, fan speeds, voltages, power supply status, and intrusion detection sensor status. As seen in Listing 13-17, each CPU has its own temperature measurement and each fan has its own individual speed information.

Listing 13-17 Monitoring the Internal Environmental and Hardware Sensors

```
xi50(config)# show sensors
      Ambient Temperature: 24 C
        CPU 1 Temperature: 34 C
        CPU 2 Temperature: 36 C
          CPU 1 Fan speed: 7031 RPM
          CPU 2 Fan speed: 6750 RPM
      Chassis Fan 1 speed: 11250 RPM
      Chassis Fan 2 speed: 9926 RPM
      Chassis Fan 3 speed: 10546 RPM
       Intrusion Detected: no
              3.3 Voltage: 3.29 V
                5 Voltage: 4.91 V
               12 Voltage: 12.00 V
      Power supply status: ok
Battery installation date: Mon Aug  6 09:54:20 2007
xi50(config)# show sensors-fans
 Fan ID     Speed
 ------     -----
 chassis-1  7031
 chassis-2  6750
 chassis-3  11250
 chassis-4  10546
 chassis-5  10546
 chassis-6  6750
 chassis-7  7031
 chassis-8  9926
```

Note that some of the monitoring and statistics commands require that you first enable the gathering of statistics on the device. This is particularly true of those commands that output values over time (1 second, 1 minute, 1 hour, etc.). Enter Global Configuration mode in the CLI (`co`) and then type `statistics` to enable statistics.

Object Modification Commands

As we've mentioned, the command line interface is tailored very well to some tasks—namely, retrieving real-time status information, making quick changes to network and device configurations, and performing file system operations to move firmware, configurations, and files to and from the appliance. That said, the CLI can also be used to create and modify higher-level objects such as services, policies, and actions. Due to the large numbers of configuration fields and compatibility options, defining a service and all its supporting objects is generally not practical, but making small changes and creating simple objects is common, and all the commands are there if more is necessary. In this case, the Reference Guide and context-sensitive CLI help are the best places to look for the syntax and field defaults for each object; there are simply too many to cover here. However, we can give you some insight into the general methodology for making these modifications.

When you first log in to the CLI, you enter into an initial login mode that contains only a few available commands that act on the device as a whole. By switching into global configuration mode with the configure terminal command, you can open a whole new world of options—over two hundred of them! Try not to be overwhelmed; just be very specific about what you want to create/edit, and then navigate to that object's configuration mode. For instance, let's edit a Filter action that we've defined within a service's Processing Policy.

If you've followed our suggestions, there won't be any services defined in the default domain. Those will be restricted to an application domain that has been created for the project or for the development group that's working on that service. So, your first step to tracking down the action to edit is to move into the appropriate domain. The switch domain command takes you there. In Listing 13-18, we change our context from the default domain (no domain designation) into the HRServices domain, and the cursor changes to reflect our current position. You would have to execute the command switch domain default to get back into the default domain.

Listing 13-18 Navigating to a Particular Domain with the Switch Domain Command

```
xi50(config)# switch domain HRServices
xi50[HRServices](config)#
```

CLI Permissions

To this point, we've been executing device-level commands in the default domain. These have required admin-level access to administrative commands. Now that we're switching domains and focusing on configuration objects, you'll have to make sure your user has CLI access to the domain; you may also need permission to additional commands. Talk to your device administrator about whether Role-Based Management is being enforced on the CLI (in which case you likely have all the permissions you're going to get; use `show rbm` to see whether RBM for CLI is active), or whether additional permissions need to be provided to your user group or domain. See Chapter 12 for more information.

Now that we're in a particular domain, let's track down the action we want to modify. A simple show action command lists all the actions in the domain; depending on the extent of development, this can be a long list! Narrow it down by adding an action name to retrieve only the configuration information for that action. In Listing 13-19, we see all the configuration options that can be set for a Filter action—we warned you this was easier from the WebGUI.

Listing 13-19 Reviewing the Configuration for a Particular Action

```
xi50[HRServices](config)# show action HRService_response_Filter
action: HRService_response_Filter [up]
 - - - - - - - - - - - - - - - - - - --
 admin-state enabled
 type filter
 input tempvar2
 transform local:///HRService.xsl
 named-inouts default
 transactional off
 soap-validation body
 sql-source-type static
 asynchronous off
 results-mode first-available
 retry-count 0
 retry-interval 1000 msec
 multiple-outputs off
 iterator-type XPATH
 timeout 0 msec
```

To edit the action, we need to switch to the action configuration mode. Navigating to the configuration mode of any object is usually just a matter of combining its type and its name. If you want to create a new object, just use a new, unique name. In this case, action HRService_response_Filter gets us to where we want to be, as seen in the first line of Listing 13-20; the prompt changes to display both the domain (HRServices) and the current context (config action HRService_response_Filter). Now that we're editing the action, we need to find the appropriate command to change a property. Using the help command to get additional information provides us with a long list of possible options; in fact, it provides every command for every type of processing action, not just the Filter Actions. However, at the end of the list are some commands that are common to all object configuration menus, as shown in Listing 13-20.

Listing 13-20 Getting Help on Common Object Configuration Commands

```
xi50[HRServices](config)# action HRService_response_Filter
Modify Processing Action configuration
xi50[HRServices](config action HRService_response_Filter)# help
     *** Full list of commands snipped here ***
admin-state                 Administratively enables or disables the object.
cancel                      Exits the current mode (no changes applied)
disconnect                  Terminates a user session
```

```
echo                      Echoes text to the console
exit                      Applies properties and exits
help                      Displays general or command-specific help
ping                      Sends an ICMP echo request
reset                     Exits the current mode (default values applied)
show                      Displays statistical or configuration data
test tcp-connection       Test TCP reachability
traceroute                Displays the route to a host
xi50[HRServices](config action HRService_response_Filter)#
```

One command that is common to all objects and often useful for taking quick action is the admin-state property. This enables or disables the object. Disabling an object (admin-state disabled) removes it from the possibility of execution without deleting or changing it in any other way. Enabling the object again (admin-state enabled) brings it back. As with all modification commands executed within configuration modes, this enable/disable change applies as soon as you exit the object configuration.

ADMIN-STATE

The admin-state command sets an object to be enabled or disabled. While this is one method of removing an object (domain, policy, rule) from service, keep in mind that any objects dependent on a newly disabled object are impacted. If an action is disabled, all rules that reference the action are also down. This affects policies that reference the rule and services that reference those policies. Make sure this ripple effect is intended before changing the administrative state of any object.

Other common object commands tend to be meta-commands, in that they act on the other changes you have already made. The exit command applies the changes you have made to the object. If you change your mind, the cancel command exits the object configuration mode without applying the changes. The reset command also exits the current mode, but not before applying the *default* values to the object; this essentially sets the object back to factory settings.

Before we can decide whether we want to save or discard our changes, we have to actually modify the object. We've been dealing with a Filter action that uses a stylesheet (local:///HRService.xsl) to perform its filtering duties. This is evident from the line that says transform local:///HRService.xsl in Listing 13-19. To change the execution to a new version of the stylesheet, just replace the line by referencing the transform parameter, as shown in Listing 13-21. The show command, executed within the action configuration mode, then provides a nice contextual display of the parameter values, including the new stylesheet name.

Listing 13-21 Setting a New Transform, and then Checking Our Work

```
xi50[HRServices](config action HRService_response_Filter)# transform
local:///hrservice2.xsl
xi50[HRServices](config action HRService_response_Filter)# show
 admin-state enabled
 type filter
 input tempvar2
 transform local:///hrservice2.xsl
    *** Lines snipped for brevity ***
```

All changes that affect the configuration of objects on the appliance should be applied and then saved to the persistent configuration using the write mem command. This command can be executed only in the global configuration mode—it will not work from object configuration modes. Use the exit command to move out of the configuration contexts, saving changes as you progress. Save the configuration, and then exit the entire CLI when you've completed your work.

Exiting the CLI is an important step—there is no predefined idle timeout as there is in the WebGUI. If your workstation is not locked, anyone can walk up and administer the device using your permissions.

File and Configuration Management Commands

Another common use case of the CLI is the execution of commands that have an effect on the entire device at once. Backing up a configuration, upgrading the firmware, and rebooting the device are all simple. They also require some file management, to move files onto and off of the device. Let's walk through the process of backing up specific domains, copying the backup file off of the appliance, copying a firmware image onto the device, and then upgrading the firmware by booting to the new image.

The backup command combines domains into a single ZIP configuration file for moving off the device to a source control or backup/archive server. There are three commands shown in Listing 13-22. First, the backup command takes a filename, followed by a list of domains to include in the backup. Next, the dir command provides a simple directory listing; all domain exports are placed in the export: directory. Finally, the copy command copies the file from the export: directory to a remote configuration server.

Listing 13-22 Exporting and Offloading a Backup File from the Appliance

```
xi50(config)# backup AllHRServices.zip HRServices CoreServices
Backup to 'AllHRServices.zip' scheduled (may take a few minutes to
complete).
Backup is complete.
xi50(config)# dir export:
   File Name               Last Modified               Size
    - - - - --              - - - - - - --              - -
   CoreServices/           Tue Apr  8 00:33:53 2008    1024
   HRServices/             Tue Apr  8 00:33:53 2008    1024
   AllHRServices.zip       Tue Apr  8 02:40:57 2008    1112948
   233.1 MB available to export:
```

```
xi50(config)# copy export:///AllHRServices.zip
scp://jsmith@cfgserver.xyco.com/AllHRServices.zip
Password: *******
File copy success
```

The copy command is powerful, as it can copy files on and off the appliance using several different protocols, including http, https, scp, sftp, and smtp. Local URLs are referred to using a *directory:///filename* syntax; notice the *three* slashes in every on-device directory URL. The syntax for remote URLs depends on the protocol. See the help copy command and the Reference Guide for the complete syntax descriptions. To see another example and segue into firmware management, let's copy a new image to the device and then upgrade the firmware.

Listing 13-23 uses the copy command to retrieve a file from a remote server and the dir command to display a directory listing for file verification; firmware upgrades should always be placed in the image: directory. The flash command then switches the context to flash configuration mode, where the device is booted using the new image. This boot image command produces a string of status indicators, after which the new firmware has been successfully installed and the device will reboot.

Listing 13-23 Upgrading Using a New Firmware Image

```
xi50(config)# copy https://cfgserver/xi3614.9003.mq6.tam6.scrypt2
image:///xi3614.9003.mq6.tam6.scrypt2
File copy success (49725285 bytes copied)
xi50(config)# dir image:
   File Name                 Last Modified                  Size
   ---------                 -------------                  ----
   xi3614.9003.mq6.tam6.scrypt2 Tue Apr  8 03:21:08 2008   49725285
   185.5 MB available to image:
xi50(config)# flash
Flash configuration mode
xi50(config-flash)# boot image xi3614.9003.mq6.tam6.scrypt2
```

To be assured of a successful firmware upgrade process, you should upload the firmware, reload the currently-running firmware as shown in Listing 13-24, and then boot to the new firmware image. Reloading the firmware clears out any unneeded temporary files from the file system.

The appliance always reboots after a successful firmware upgrade. However, there are times when you may want to shut down or reboot the device manually. You can also reload the firmware on the device, which takes only a few seconds and doesn't require a full reboot; it doesn't even reboot the domains! These commands all allow for a timer countdown, in order to delay the actual shutdown/reboot. In Listing 13-24, each of the commands would execute ten seconds after responding affirmatively (y) to the prompt.

Listing 13-24 Evaluating the Appliance Shutdown Options

```
xi50# shutdown reboot 10
You have requested a system shutdown reboot. Do you want to continue?
[y/n]: n
xi50# shutdown halt 10
You have requested a system shutdown. Do you want to continue? [y/n]: n
xi50# shutdown reload 10
You have requested a system shutdown reload. Do you want to continue?
[y/n]: n
```

Aliases

Executing individual CLI commands is useful, but putting them together into batches is even more powerful. To enable this type of batch processing, use the alias command, which creates aliases comprised of a series of individual commands. These aliases can represent commonly used tasks, such as those demonstrated earlier in this chapter. In Listing 13-25, we've created two aliases called disableHRService and enableHRService, which do exactly what their names imply. The alias command creates the sequence of commands, which are then executed using the alias name. In this case, the disableHRService alias switches to the HRServices domain, opens the WS-Proxy called HRService for modification, sets the service's admin-state to disabled, exits to apply the changes, and then switches back to the default domain to wait for the next command. The full interaction with the CLI isn't displayed by the alias execution, but the end result is that the Web Service Proxy is disabled.

Listing 13-25 Defining and Executing a Command Alias

```
xi50(config)# alias disableHRService "switch domain HRServices; wsgw
HRService; admin-state disabled; exit; switch domain default"
Alias update successful
xi50(config)# alias enableHRService "switch domain HRServices; wsgw
HRService; admin-state enabled; exit; switch domain default"
Alias update successful
xi50(config)# show alias
  Alias Name           Command
  ----------           -------
  disableHRService     switch domain HRServices; wsgw HRService;
                       admin-state disabled; exit; switch domain default
  enableHRService      switch domain HRServices; wsgw HRService;
                       admin-state enabled; exit; switch domain default
xi50(config)# disableHRService
Modify Web Service Proxy configuration[1]
xi50(config)#
```

[1] This text is a side effect of the alias execution. Even though the rest of the commands and CLI prompts aren't shown, rest assured that the modifications have taken place.

We have now used the CLI from appliance initialization all the way to shutdown. In between, we used the CLI to set up DNS and management listeners, verify network connectivity, retrieve device information and health statistics, modify object configurations, move files to and from the file system, back up configurations, and upgrade the firmware. We've also combined these commands into a series of processing tasks using the alias command. These are the most common and useful CLI commands that are available and should be of great use to network personnel, device administrators, and configuration management experts.

XML Management Interface

The XML Management Interface presents an interface to retrieve status information, modify configurations, and perform operations on the device by sending SOAP-formatted Web service calls to a user-defined address and port on the device. The same full range of configuration options and status gathering operations offered by the WebGUI are available through the XML Management Interface. This method of management will be referred to as SOAP management in the sections to follow. The XML Management interface is defined to listen on a device IP and port using SSL. This listener also supports other standards for automated device interaction, such as WSDM[2], WS-Management, and AMP[3], some of which are discussed in Chapter 14. For this discussion, we focus on just the SOAP management requests, which are sent to the XML management interface using HTTP Basic Authentication as a credential mechanism. Once received, these SOAP management calls will execute the desired operations on the appliance and will be subject to all the same permissions given to the user for WebGUI administration.

Enabling the SOAP Management Interface

To enable the SOAP listener, navigate in the WebGUI to Network→Management→XML Management Interface in the menu on the left. As shown in Figure 13-1, the service must be enabled and configured with an interface and port for the listener. Selecting the enabled services will allow for various requests to this interface. The SOAP-prefixed options are important for SOAP Management. For instance, the SOAP Configuration Management service listens on a URI of /service/mgmt/current and reflects the latest API. The option appended with (v2004) is available for legacy purposes and should not be used unless there are existing applications connecting to this interface using a legacy API. The SOAP Management URI option allows messages to be received on any URI. This is also for legacy purposes and should be enabled only if you have existing applications that connect to a URI other than those specifically defined. As always, administrative listeners (WebGUI, SSH, XML management) should be locked down to an Ethernet management interface for maximum security.

---

[2] Web Services Distributed Management (WSDM) is an OASIS specification dealing with the automated monitoring and management of Web services. On DataPower, this functionality is used to interact with ITCAM for SOA, which will be discussed in later chapters.

[3] AMP is a proprietary management interface protocol used to communicate between appliances.

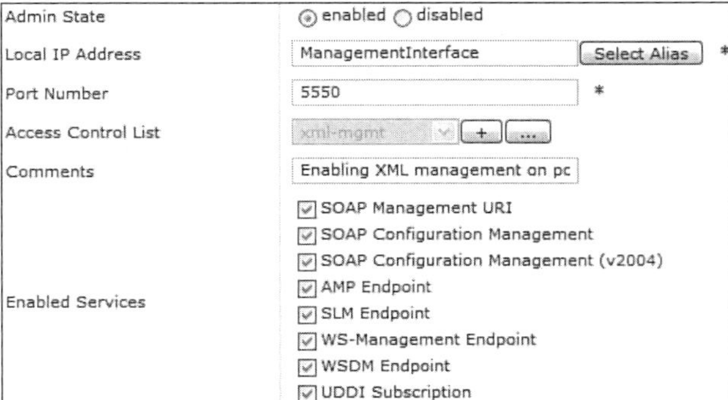

Figure 13-1 Turning on the XML Management listener on port 5550.

Submitting SOAP Management Requests

Because this is a Web service interface, valid requests must be POSTed to the SOAP management URL, using the appropriate URI, and contain an HTTP Basic Authentication header containing the user's credentials. This can be accomplished using a simple Web services client, including cURL, SoapUI, XMLSpy, or any application platform with a Web service stack (.Net, J2EE, and so forth). The listener uses SSL by default; therefore, you may need a copy of the public certificate that will be sent during the SSL handshake. This file is named `root-ca-cert.pem` and is available for download from the DataPower Appliance Firmware site, or from the Resource CD that came with the appliance. Alternatively, a new SSL profile can be defined from the XML Management configuration page in the WebGUI.

A sample SOAP management request could be submitted using curl[4] with the following syntax:

```
curl  -data-binary @GetSystemUsage.xml -u jsmith:passwd
https://xmlgw01:5550/service/mgmt/current
```

Defining the Management Service API

The SOAP management Web service listening on the XML management interface is defined by a WSDL that is stored on the device. The WSDL and supporting schema documents are in the store: directory and can be downloaded from the File Management area in the WebGUI.

- `xml-mgmt.wsdl` is the WSDL file that describes the services available from the XML Management interface.
- `xml-mgmt-ops.xsd` is the schema file that lists the operations available for execution. Operations include get-file, get-log, do-backup, do-action, modify-config, and many more. See the Reference Guide for an explanation of each and this schema file for the operation syntax.

[4] cURL is a simple command-line application that can used to POST input messages to the appliance. It can be downloaded from `http://curl.haxx.se/`.

- `xml-mgmt.xsd` is the schema file that defines the syntax for DataPower objects to be acted on. This includes high-level objects such as XMLFirewallService, low-level objects such as FilterAction, and even device-level objects such as Domain and TimeStatus.
- `xml-mgmt-base.xsd` is the schema file that defines the primitive types used in xml-mgmt.xsd. These include text and numerical data types that map to XML Schema primitive types.

These four files provide the basis for every SOAP configuration call that can be made to the appliance. For a full understanding of the message structure, download and review the files.

Request Message Structure

Every request message has the same general structure, as seen in Listing 13-26. The SOAP body contains a request element in the dp: DataPower management namespace. That request element then contains the operation element, which in turn contains its own parameters. The only optional modification to this structure is the addition of a domain=*domainName* attribute on the dp:request element. This restricts the effects of the call to a single domain.

Listing 13-26 Defining the SOAP Structure for SOAP Management Requests

```
<?xml version="1.0" encoding="UTF-8"?>
<env:Envelope xmlns:env="http://www.w3.org/2001/12/soap-envelope">
  <env:Body>
    <dp:request xmlns:dp="http://www.datapower.com/schemas/management">
      ...
    </dp:request>
  </env:Body>
</env:Envelope>
```

Response Message Structure

Every response message also has the same general structure, as seen in Listing 13-27. The SOAP body contains a response element in the DataPower management namespace. That response element then contains a timestamp element, which defines the moment at which the command was executed, followed by a response from the operation.

Listing 13-27 Demonstrating the Response Structure from SOAP Management Requests

```
<?xml version="1.0" encoding="UTF-8"?>
<env:Envelope xmlns:env="http://schemas.xmlsoap.org/soap/envelope/">
  <env:Body>
    <dp:response
      xmlns:dp="http://www.datapower.com/schemas/management">
      <dp:timestamp>2008-04-10T15:59:16-07:00</dp:timestamp>
      ...
    </dp:response>
  </env:Body>
</env:Envelope>
```

Common SOAP Management Operations

Though the XML management interface provides the full range of configuration options, some tasks are often better suited for other interfaces. For example, comparing configurations is much easier when viewing the graphical interface in the WebGUI. Similarly, copying files on and off the device is best suited to the CLI; performing the same operation using SOAP requires base64-encoding the file so that it can be embedded in the SOAP body. The Reference Guide and SOAP management schemas provide more information if you want to implement these use cases, but we're going to focus on some more common use cases.

get-status

The get-status operation is used for real-time retrieval of status information about an object configured on the appliance, statistics gathered by the device, or the health of the appliance itself. Sending the get-status operation with no domain limitations and no parameters retrieves every status object on the device. For a more manageable response message, define the class of status information desired, as shown in Listing 13-28. By requesting only the SystemUsage status, we get a single response with the current device load; this is equivalent to Status→System→System Usage from the WebGUI, or the show load command from the CLI.

Listing 13-28 Requesting SystemUsage Status Using the get-status Operation

```
<env:Envelope xmlns:env="http://schemas.xmlsoap.org/soap/envelope/">
  <env:Body>
    <dp:request
      xmlns:dp="http://www.datapower.com/schemas/management">
      <dp:get-status class="SystemUsage"/>
    </dp:request>
  </env:Body>
</env:Envelope>
<?xml version="1.0" encoding="UTF-8"?>
<env:Envelope xmlns:env="http://schemas.xmlsoap.org/soap/envelope/">
  <env:Body>
    <dp:response
      xmlns:dp="http://www.datapower.com/schemas/management">
      <dp:timestamp>2008-04-10T15:59:16-07:00</dp:timestamp>
      <dp:status>
        <SystemUsage>
          <Interval>5000</Interval>
          <Load>3</Load>
          <WorkList>0</WorkList>
        </SystemUsage>
      </dp:status>
    </dp:response>
  </env:Body>
</env:Envelope>
```

A simple modification of the class retrieves other important device information. A full list of status reports that can be retrieved is enumerated in xml-mgmt.xsd as the StatusEnum type; some of the *most common* device-level status requests are as follows:

- **ActiveUsers**—A list of users currently logged into the device
- **DateTimeStatus**—The current time, according to the appliance clock
- **Version**—The device serial number, currently running firmware version, and installed library (TAM, MQ, ODBC) versions
- **MemoryStatus**—Returns the total, used, and free memory allocations
- **FilesystemStatus**—The available free memory on the encrypted and temporary file systems
- **EnvironmentalSensors**—A list of CPU temperatures and fan speeds
- **CPUUsage**—A historical view of CPU percentages over time
- **TCPTable**—A list of active ports and the services/listeners that are using them
- **HTTPConnections**—A list of active HTTP connections and their current status
- **DomainStatus**—A list of all domains, whether they have been modified, and whether their debug log or probe settings are enabled

It is also helpful to have some insight into the services and objects that have been defined within a particular domain. By adding the domain attribute to the dp:request element, we can restrict the following types of status queries to a named domain:

- **StylesheetStatus**—The stylesheets cached by each XML manager, including any compilation warnings or errors
- **DocumentStatus**—The XML documents cached by each XML manager, including any compilation warnings or errors
- **LoadBalancerStatus**—The current status of members in each configured load balancer object
- **SLMSummaryStatus**—A list of Service Level Management statements and the number of matching requests received
- **WSOperationMetrics**—Statistics gathered about services being executed in this domain

do-action

The do-action operation is used for dynamic execution of remote commands on an appliance. These commands can act on the device itself (Shutdown), on a high-level object (RestartDomain), or on a low-level object (RefreshStylesheet). These operations can be selectively called within a particular domain (when appropriate) by adding the domain attribute. Within dp:request is a dp:action element containing the specific action being called. Additionally, the action taken may require more information about the object it is acting on or the parameters for execution. In Listing 13-29, the FlushStylesheetCache command takes a single argument, an XMLManager element containing the name of an XML Manager (LongTermCache) within the specified domain. Actions such as these can be automated for use in a build process; as stylesheets are modified, the cached version can be flushed from the XML management interface.

Listing 13-29 Flushing a Designated Stylesheet Cache Within a Domain

```
<env:Envelope xmlns:env="http://schemas.xmlsoap.org/soap/envelope/">
  <env:Body>
    <dp:request
      xmlns:dp="http://www.datapower.com/schemas/management"
      domain="HRServices">
      <dp:do-action>
        <FlushStylesheetCache>
          <XMLManager>LongTermCache</XMLManager>
        </FlushStylesheetCache>
      </dp:do-action>
    </dp:request>
  </env:Body>
</env:Envelope>
<?xml version="1.0" encoding="UTF-8"?>
<env:Envelope xmlns:env="http://schemas.xmlsoap.org/soap/envelope/">
  <env:Body>
    <dp:response
      xmlns:dp="http://www.datapower.com/schemas/management">
      <dp:timestamp>2008-04-10T17:18:48-07:00</dp:timestamp>
      <dp:result>OK</dp:result>
    </dp:response>
  </env:Body>
</env:Envelope>
```

Successful do-action commands always return a dp:result node with the value OK. Failed requests either reference an authentication error, meaning something is wrong with the credentials being passed to DataPower using HTTP Basic Authentication, or an Internal Error, which likely means an error in the syntax of the request document.

The syntax for each command is defined in the XML schema files we discussed earlier; these are the definitive sources for the exact formats required. All the do-action commands are enumerated in xml-mgmt.xsd as the ActionEnum type; some of the *most common* commands are as follows:

- **FlushStylesheetCache**—Clears a domain's stylesheet cache of all files
- **FlushDocumentCache**—Clears a domain's document cache of all documents
- **RefreshStylesheet**—Recompiles a specific stylesheet (or group of stylesheets) without affecting the rest of the cache
- **FlushAAACache**—Clears an access control policy's cache to require upcoming requests to re-authenticate and re-authorize

- **Shutdown**—Causes the appliance to reboot, reload, or halt
- **SetTimeAndDate**—Sets the appliances time and date
- **Ping**—Executes a ping command for network troubleshooting
- **TCPConnectionTest**—Attempts to connect to a remote TCP port for network troubleshooting
- **Keygen**—Generates a private key and self-signed certificate on the appliance
- **SetLogLevel**—Sets the log level for a domain; useful for quickly modifying the level while troubleshooting
- **SendLogEvent**—Creates a user-defined log event in a specified category at a given priority
- **SaveConfig**—Saves the currently running configuration, including any changes made through the XML management interface, to the file system for persistence

get-config

The get-config operation is used for the retrieval of current configuration parameters for a given object. These objects can be at a device level or within a domain (referenced with the domain attribute). Within dp:request is a dp:get-config element; this element can take class and name attributes to further narrow the selection to a smaller number of objects. In Listing 13-30, the request is not limited to a domain, as User Groups are a device-level object. We do, however, select by object type (UserGroup) and by the name of the object (sysadmin). Because names are unique among objects of the same type, we know that we will retrieve only one response, the full configuration of the sysadmin user group.

Listing 13-30 Viewing a Specific User Group Configuration from a SOAP Management Call

```
<soapenv:Envelope
xmlns:soapenv="http://schemas.xmlsoap.org/soap/envelope/">
  <soapenv:Body>
    <dp:request
      xmlns:dp="http://www.datapower.com/schemas/management">
      <dp:get-config class="UserGroup" name="sysadmin"/>
    </dp:request>
  </soapenv:Body>
</soapenv:Envelope
<?xml version="1.0" encoding="UTF-8"?>
<env:Envelope xmlns:env="http://schemas.xmlsoap.org/soap/envelope/">
  <env:Body>
    <dp:response xmlns:dp="http://www.datapower.com/schemas/management">
      <dp:timestamp>2008-04-10T17:58:06-07:00</dp:timestamp>
      <dp:config>
        <UserGroup name="sysadmin">
          <mAdminState>enabled</mAdminState>
          <UserSummary>System Administrator</UserSummary>
```

```
          <AccessPolicies>*/*/*?Access=rwadx</AccessPolicies>
          <AccessPolicies>*/*/file/store?Access=r</AccessPolicies>
          <CommandGroup>configuration</CommandGroup>
          <CommandGroup>crypto</CommandGroup>
        </UserGroup>
      </dp:config>
    </dp:response>
  </env:Body>
</env:Envelope>
```

All the objects on which get-config can act are defined in xml-mgmt.xsd as the ConfigEnum type.

set-config

Because get-config retrieves static information (the defined configuration), it is often useful only when combined with modify-config or set-config. These two commands act similarly; each takes an object either retrieved from a get-config or built from scratch, and updates or creates the configuration on the appliance. Use set-config for a new object and use modify-config for an existing object. Multiple objects can also be combined into a single set-config request; each section of the request payload will create a new object. Let's see how this works in a real situation. Consider the need to build out new development domains for users who are joining a project. We need a new domain, but we also need a new developer account and a user group that restricts that user to his new domain. We can create a domain, user, and user group in a single call to the appliance using the XML management interface, as shown in Listing 13-31.

Listing 13-31 Creating a Domain, User, and User Group with a Single Set-Config Command

```
<soapenv:Envelope
xmlns:soapenv="http://schemas.xmlsoap.org/soap/envelope/">
  <soapenv:Body>
    <dp:request
      xmlns:dp="http://www.datapower.com/schemas/management">
      <dp:set-config>
        <Domain name="JohnSmith">
          <UserSummary>Sandbox domain for John Smith</UserSummary>
          <NeighborDomain class="Domain">default</NeighborDomain>
        </Domain>
        <UserGroup name="JohnSmithGroup">
          <UserSummary>Developers in JohnSmith domain</UserSummary>
          <AccessPolicies>*/JohnSmith/*?Access=rwadx</AccessPolicies>
        </UserGroup>
        <User name="jsmith">
          <Password>newuser97</Password>
          <GroupName>JohnSmithGroup</GroupName>
          <AccessLevel>group-defined</AccessLevel>
          <UserSummary>jsmith@xyco.com</UserSummary>
```

```
        </User>
      </dp:set-config>
    </dp:request>
  </soapenv:Body>
</soapenv:Envelope>

<?xml version="1.0" encoding="UTF-8"?>
<env:Envelope xmlns:env="http://schemas.xmlsoap.org/soap/envelope/">
  <env:Body>
    <dp:response
      xmlns:dp="http://www.datapower.com/schemas/management">
      <dp:timestamp>2008-04-10T18:30:57-07:00</dp:timestamp>
      <dp:result>OK</dp:result>
      <dp:result>OK</dp:result>
      <dp:result>OK</dp:result>
    </dp:response>
  </env:Body>
</env:Envelope>
```

The response from our set-config request contains three dp:result elements, one for each object that was created. This call has created a new domain called JohnSmith, a user group called JohnSmithGroup, with full permission to that domain and no others, and a user called jsmith, whose permissions are defined by the JohnSmithGroup. If we now send a do-action command with a SaveConfig action, the new configuration will be persisted.

We have now used the XML management interface for retrieving status, performing device-level operations, viewing existing configurations, and creating new objects, all without ever logging into the WebGUI. The GUI is generally preferable for interactive development of complex services—you'd have to dig through a lot of XML schema definitions to define every object within a Web Service Proxy or Multi-Protocol Gateway to create them with a SOAP management call. However, for scripted or batch processing of commonly used commands or for creating multiple configurations that each require only a minor change, the SOAP management interface provides a valuable method of interaction.

As the previous example demonstrated, the SOAP management interface presents an effective means for performing repetitive tasks with some degree of complexity. Such a request executed three different changes, much like the CLI alias command, but with only one call to the device. Because the interface employs an interface well-defined by a machine-readable schema, it is possible to create very powerful device configuration and management utilities that do not require access to either the CLI or the WebGUI. This means that some tasks can be completely automated by external hosts executing calls on a regular timetable.

Similarly, once a set of requests for any given single device works, this same request can then be easily sent to other devices in the datacenter, thus keeping all devices synchronized with little effort. You can see that the SOAP management interface rocks!

Summary

The DataPower Web interface gets the vast majority of attention from users, as its point-and-click configuration of complex functionality is unrivaled. This attention is well-deserved, but should not completely overshadow the power and flexibility inherent in alternate management interfaces. As the savvy network analyst, appliance administrator, and deployment engineer know, when used correctly, the CLI and XML management interface are potent instruments for efficient, stable, and repeatable configuration and administration.

CHAPTER 14

Logging and Monitoring

Care and responsibility for DataPower SOA Appliances tend to cross operational boundaries, as they function at a network level, but perform security and application-specific roles. This separation of concerns is most prominent in the logging and monitoring configurations, as various enterprise teams require vastly different information about device health, processing actions, and performance metrics. This chapter discusses various options for both logging and monitoring schemes. We discuss the power of a publish-subscribe logging system, the configuration of various log delivery methods, and some common delineations between hardware-level and application-level events. This includes both shortcuts for common notifications and the creation of custom log categories and messages for maximum flexibility. On the monitoring side, we discuss the configuration of SNMP-based monitoring tools for maximum device visibility, suggested items for polling, and options for Web Services monitoring.

The power of each of these systems allows for some amazing opportunities for real-time modification of running configurations and error remediation. Log recipients can send SOAP messages to update a service level agreement based on current conditions, dynamically provision new backend servers to a load balancer configuration, and enable or disable entire services. Monitoring stations can gather real-time Web service metrics to identify troublesome servers before they compromise guaranteed service levels, notify an operations team at the first sign of a bottleneck, and provide detailed chargeback statistics.

Anatomy of a Log Message

We'll get to the fun stuff—the capabilities of a flexible publish-subscribe logging system—shortly, but first we should discuss the anatomy of a log message. No matter which system generates a message, which protocol delivers it, or where it is read, each message has very similar fields. The first place you're likely to see these fields is in the default log, which we discuss in detail later; for now, you can see some of the fields defined across the top, as shown in Figure 14-1.

current time: 21:48:14 on 2008-05-04

time ▾	category	level	tid	dir	client	msgid	message
Sun May 04 2008							
21:47:59	latency	info	7857		192.168.1.198	0x80e00073	wsgw (HRServices): Latency: 0 1 0 1 1 1 [http://192.168.1.199:8050/HRService]

Figure 14-1 Viewing the fields available to a log message.

Domain

The domain field represents the application domain from which the log message originated. Depending on your domain usage strategy, this can narrow down the event to a particular project team, application, or even user. On devices with multiple development environments (development, QA, pre-production), this field will likely specify the environment as well. This field is not visible in the figure; when not present, the message came from the current working domain.

Timestamp

The event timestamp is used for sorting and correlation of log events. Each event is recorded as it enters the log subsystem and receives a timestamp. Depending on the configuration, this can be expressed in a syslog timestamp format, which provides only the date and time expressed to the second, or in a numeric format that is expressed as milliseconds since the January 1, 1970 (known as the epoch). The latter is obviously more precise, but is not supported by syslog and syslog-ng logging servers, nor is it available on the default log.

Type

The event type signifies the category of message. These categories are preconfigured on the device but can be extended through the use of custom log categories, which we discuss later in this chapter. Some message types include aaa, which represents events dealing with authentication, authorization, and auditing decisions; mq, which deals with WebSphere MQ interaction; and wsrr, which notes interactions between DataPower and the WebSphere Services Registry and Repository. High-level services have their own categories (xmlfirewall, ws-proxy, and mpgw), as do low-level system operations (crypto, system, and xmlparse).

Class

If the event originates with a configuration object on the device, the class field represents the type of object that creates the log message. This can be similar to the type, but it is limited to objects; if the message is logged by the system itself (for a hardware issue or something similar), this field will not be present. Example values for this field include wsgw (for a Web Service Proxy), xmlfirewall, xmlmgr (for an XML manager), and source-http (for an HTTP front-side handler).

Object

Every object created on the device has a name, and this name populates the object field if it has sent a message to the log system. This is closely tied to the class field, as the name refers to an object of that type. For instance, there may be a domain, a Web Service Proxy, and a Processing Policy, and all of them are called HRServices. However, if the log entry contains wsgw (HRServices), then you know the message is from the Web Service Proxy.

Priority

Priority is a particularly important log field, as this is the one most commonly used for message filtering. This is also sometimes called severity, and the eight possible values correspond closely to those defined by the syslog specification. In ascending order of severity, the levels are debug, information, notice, warning, error, critical, alert, and emergency. These priorities are relatively self-explanatory; some examples are Power Supply Failure at a critical level, File Downloaded at a notice level, and Unable to open URL http://badurl/ at an error level.

Transaction Type

The transaction type represents the current processing mode when the log message is created. If a service is currently processing a response rule, the transaction type would be response. Possible options are request, response, and error. If the event occurred outside the scope of a Processing Policy, this field will be absent.

Transaction

Each execution of a service is assigned a transaction identifier (ID), as are some internal processes. This ID is unique to the device and can be used for event correlation, as every log message generated during an execution will share the same transaction ID. The transaction field contains this value. Please note that these identifiers are not simply incremented by one for each transaction, nor are they necessarily sequential.

> **TRANSACTION IDENTIFIERS**
>
> It is important to note that transaction identifiers are not sequential, nor are they unique across device reboots. Log correlation should also depend on additional fields such as timestamps.

Client IP

This field contains the IP address of the client that initiated the transaction. Though IP is not necessarily a sure indicator of a unique user, especially when segmented at an ISP level, the subnets in use can often provide some additional information about the caller and can usually differentiate one client from the next.

Event Code

The event code is a unique identifier for a particular error message. There can be many instances of this message, but the event itself is the same. For instance, event code 0x00e4000a represents the error message No NTP servers are configured. These event codes can be viewed directly from the WebGUI by navigating to Administration→Debug→View List of Event Codes in the left-side menu. They are also grouped by category so that you can use filters with wildcard values to select whole ranges of events. For example, all the MQ-related event codes contain the prefix 0x0133.

Message

Last but not least, the text of the message itself is included in the message field. This might be generic, such as Power Supply #1 Failed, or it might be specific to a particular processing action, such as Schema validation failed: cvc-simple-type 1: element product-id value '1234' is not a valid instance of the element type. This is the least structured of the fields and can contain any text, including messages custom-defined during development.

Log Message Example

Here is an example log message with each of the preceding fields defined:

```
Sun May 04 2008 15:55:35 [HRServices][multistep][info] wsgw(HRServices):
tid(20018)[request][192.168.1.198]: rule (HRServices_default_request-rule):
#2 results: 'generated from INPUT results stored in OUTPUT' completed ok.
```

Each field can be separated out for explanation, as seen in Table 14-1.

Table 14-1 Parsing a Log Message into Its Component Fields

Field	Value
Timestamp	Sun May 04 2008 15:55:35
Domain	HRServices
Type	multistep
Priority	info
Class	wsgw
Object	HRServices
Transaction	20018
Transaction Type	request
Client IP	192.168.1.198
Message	rule (HRServices_default_request-rule): #2 results: 'generated from INPUT results stored in OUTPUT' completed ok.

Default Logs

Each domain has a default log defined that provides event information from the WebGUI. To access the current log, click on the View Logs link from the Control Panel, as seen in Figure 14-2, or navigate to Status→View Logs→System Logs from the left-side panel.

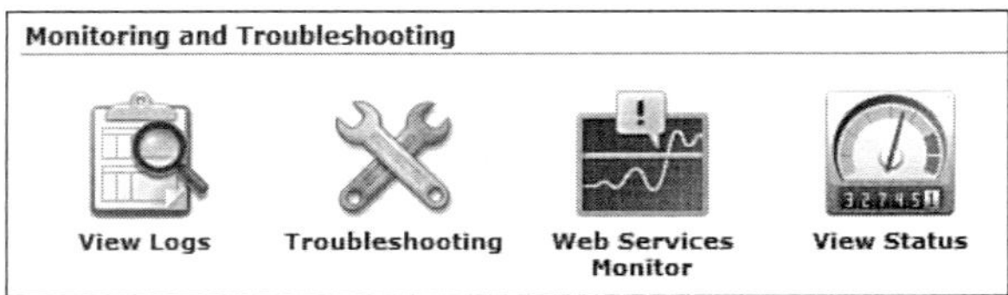

Figure 14-2 Accessing the default log from the Control Panel.

Either method of navigation takes you to the system log page, which by default shows the last 50 entries in the default log. The interface enables you to filter the entries by category and/or priority, in order to limit the number of lines. These options are available from the drop-down menus at the top of the screen, as shown in Figure 14-3.

Refresh Log Target: default-log Filter: (none) (none)

current time: 21:48:14 on 2008-05-04

time	category	level	tid	dir	client	msgid	message (Show last 50 100 all)
Sun May 04 2008							
21:47:59	latency	info	7857		192.168.1.198	0x80e00073	wsgw (HRServices): Latency: 0 1 0 1 1 1 0 2 3 2 3 3 3 3 1 1 [http://192.168.1.199:8050/HRService]
21:47:59	ws-proxy	debug	7857		192.168.1.198	0x80e00073	wsgw (HRServices): Latency: 0 1 0 1 1 1 0 2 3 2 3 3 3 3 1 1 [http://192.168.1.199:8050/HRService]
21:47:59	multistep	info	7857	<	192.168.1.198	0x80c00002	wsgw (HRServices): rule (HRServices_default_response-rule): #1 results: 'generated from INPUT results stored in OUTPUT' completed ok.
21:47:59	xmlparse	debug	7857	<	192.168.1.198		wsgw (HRServices): Finished parsing http://192.168.1.199:8050/HRService
21:47:59	xmlparse	debug	7857	<	192.168.1.198		wsgw (HRServices): Parsing document 'http://192.168.1.199:8050/HRService'
21:47:59	ws-proxy	debug	7857		192.168.1.198		xmlmgr (default): wsdl Compilation Request: Found in cache (http://server1:5005/xycohr.wsdl)
21:47:59	ws-proxy	debug	7857		192.168.1.198		xmlmgr (default): wsdl Compilation Request: Checking cache for URL http://server1:5005/xycohr.wsdl
21:47:59	multistep	debug	7857	<	192.168.1.198		wsgw (HRServices): Schema URL to compile is 'http://server1:5005/xycohr.wsdl'
21:47:59	ws-proxy	info	7857	<	192.168.1.198	0x80e000b4	wsgw (HRServices): rule (HRServices_default_response-rule): selected via match 'HRServices_match_all' from processing policy 'HRServices'
21:47:59	http	debug	7857		192.168.1.198		Matching (HRServices_match_all): Match: Received URL [/] matches rule '*'

Figure 14-3 Viewing the default log.

For additional filtering, you can click a transaction number, client IP address, or event code. Each of these opens a new window with messages related to the selected value; for example, clicking a transaction ID displays only messages from that transaction. To view more entries on a single page, you can choose to show the last 100 entries or to show all entries since the last log rotation. Click one of these options in the upper-right to see more; just because you don't see a message in the last 50 entries doesn't mean it is gone.

The priority of messages gathered by the default log can be modified from the Troubleshooting screen. From the Control Panel, click the Troubleshooting icon seen in Figure 14-2. From the Logging section shown in Figure 14-4, choose a new priority level and click Set Log Level. In development environments, it is fine to go all the way down to debug-level logging; in production environments, however, default logging should be set to a warning or error level to avoid any impact on performance.

Figure 14-4 Changing the default log level.

During development or while attempting to debug a series of transactions, it is often helpful to click the View System Logs link from this page. As opposed to viewing the log from the Troubleshooting page or Navigation menu, this opens the log page in a new window, enabling you to modify configurations in one window and refresh the logs in another. This log is also available from the file system; the logtemp: directory contains the default log in both text and XML formats.

All services and many other objects have a View Log link at the top of their configuration screen. Each of these links is a simple filter of the same default log file, extracting only messages that pertain to that object.

System Logs in the Default Domain

Log configuration in the default domain is somewhat omniscient, in that the messages logged there are gathered from all domains on the device as well as device-specific events. For example, if the log is configured to record all information level events, then events occurring at that level (or higher) in all domains will be inserted into the default log.

The default domain often captures log events for other domains that are not in the logs for that domain. These are usually low-level network events, such as SSL failures and Tivoli Access Manager configuration messages.

In the end, the default system log is special only in that it is predefined and its behavior (aside from filtering on priority) cannot be modified. In reality, it is just one of many possible targets for log messages on (or off) the device. We continue with a discussion of how to enable additional log destinations.

Log Targets

The logging subsystem on DataPower SOA Appliances is based on a publish-subscribe concept that enables distribution of selected messages to various protocols and destinations; message selection is a user-configurable process that can select broad message categories and priorities but can also be very granular if necessary. Event messages can be generated by anything on the appliance, including a hardware-level device monitor, a service processing an application transaction, or a stylesheet logging a custom error message. Obviously, some of these items are more critical than others, and some may only be of interest to a select group of users; some messages may not be of any interest at all. The goal of a reasonable logging configuration is to make sure that appropriate events are being received by the team that would be interested in those messages, are being delivered using the most suitable protocol, and are not impacting the flow of production traffic. Get those messages to the people that need to see them! This can initiate active configuration management or error remediation, depending upon what information is being delivered.

Target Fields

Directing a subset of all log messages to a particular destination/protocol is accomplished through the use of log targets. A log target describes both the endpoint to which the logs will be sent and the events that should be selected for sending. They include both protocol-level specifications (hostnames for remote log servers) and subscriptions to events in certain categories at user-defined levels. These subscriptions can also include filters for granular selection of events logged by specific objects.

To create a new log target in a domain, navigate to Administration→Miscellaneous→Manage Log Targets in the left-side menu. You'll notice there is always one predefined log target (default-log) that populates the system log; this target can be modified only in terms of the priority of events gathered. Click Add to configure a new log target, resulting in the log target configuration page seen in Figure 14-5.

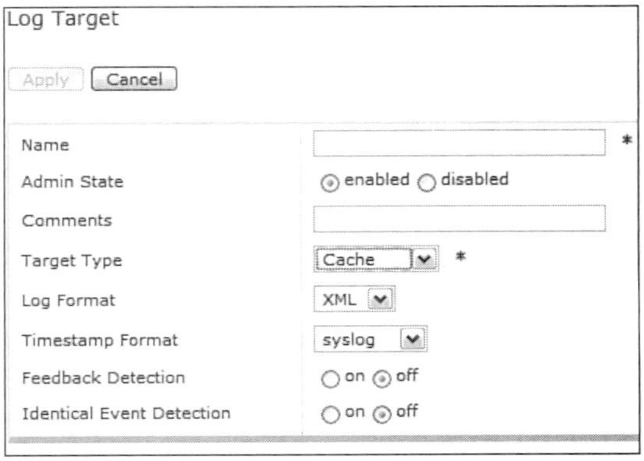

Log Target

Apply Cancel

Name	*
Admin State	enabled disabled
Comments	
Target Type	Cache *
Log Format	XML
Timestamp Format	syslog
Feedback Detection	on off
Identical Event Detection	on off

Figure 14-5 Defining a new log target.

We'll soon define the events that will be subscribed to by this log target, but first we need to make some basic format choices and define a destination. Choose a log format from the drop-down menu; some target types require a particular format (XML for a SOAP target), but many targets (File, for instance) will accept various formats.

Log Formats

The default log format, XML, places each log entry into an <entry/> node containing elements and attributes with all the log data. The CSV (comma separated values) format is similar but uses commas as delimiters between each field. The text format outputs each entry in a one-line string of text without any delimiting structure. The CBE (Common Base Event) format is a specification-defined XML standard designed to be common across various hardware and software products. Lastly, the Raw format outputs the message field in each entry without any of the other fields (timestamp, category, priority, and so on).

Common Fields

The timestamp format (syslog or numeric) defines the version of the timestamp used for each message; you must choose syslog for a remote syslog or syslog-ng server, and can use numeric for all others. Feedback detection prevents any loops caused by messages from the log system by suppressing all events related to the logs, while identical event detection prevents an identical event from occurring for a user-defined time period. Some target types also allow a backup log; if the logs cannot reach their intended destination, the backup target will receive any ensuing messages.

Target Types

Every target requires a name and a type. The type represents the log storage format or protocol over which events are sent; choose one from the drop-down menu. Depending on the target chosen, additional options are provided. This is an opportunity to integrate DataPower with the logging infrastructure chosen by your enterprise, be it syslog, SNMP, or a remote drive mounted using NFS. The following sections discuss the details of each option.

Cache Target

The cache option is used for short-term viewing of logs on the device. Upon creation of the log target, as shown in Figure 14-6, entries are collected in memory.

Name	HRServicesCacheLog *
Admin State	enabled disabled
Comments	Cache log for HR Services
Target Type	Cache *
Log Format	XML
Timestamp Format	syslog
Feedback Detection	on off
Identical Event Detection	on off

Figure 14-6 Creating a cache-based log target.

The messages gathered by a cache-based log target are available for viewing from the system logs page. Click View Logs from the Control Panel and then choose the target name from the drop-down menu, as seen in Figure 14-7.

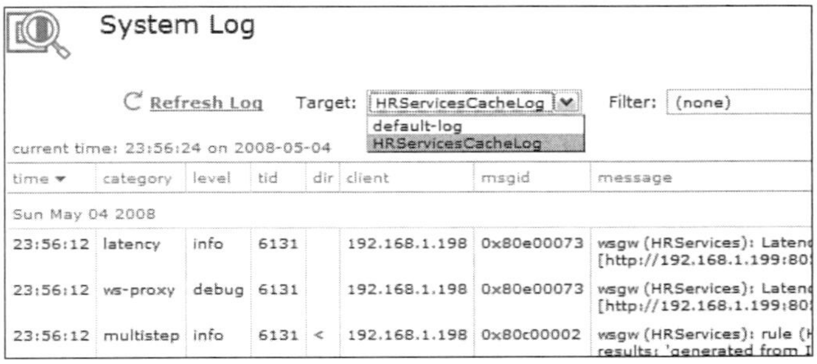

Figure 14-7 Viewing a cache log target.

After you view the messages from the log page, the cache on those messages expires. That is, the next time you open this page, these events no longer appear. Even clicking Refresh Log makes the displayed events disappear. For this reason, the cache target should only be used for quick peeks at short-term events.

Console Target

The console log type is for short-term viewing, similar to the cache target, but messages are written to the Command Line Interface (CLI), rather than to an in-memory cache. To view the messages generated by this target type, you must use SSH (or TELNET) to log in to the CLI for the device. Switch to the domain in which the target is defined; any applicable log messages will flow across the screen as traffic flows through the device.

File Target

A file log target keeps event messages in a file on the local device. This file grows as log messages are added. When the file size reaches a user-defined threshold, it is either rotated or uploaded to a remote server, as defined by an administrator. Figure 14-8 shows the full configuration; depending on the options chosen, additional fields need to be completed.

File targets require a name and location for the local file. These files can be stored in either the logtemp: or logstore: directories. Logtemp files are available from the file system but are technically stored in volatile memory and will not persist during a device reboot; logstore files will stay on the device even after it is rebooted. Files written to the hard drive or flash drive on devices with persistent storage will also survive a reboot.

Name	HRServicesFileLog *
Admin State	(•) enabled ( ) disabled
Comments	File Target for HR Services
Target Type	File *
Log Format	XML
Timestamp Format	Numeric
Log Size (in KB)	500 *
File Name	logtemp:///HRServicesLog.log *
Archive Mode	Upload *
Upload Method	SFTP *
Remote Host	logserver.xyco.com [Ping Remote] *
Remote Login	ftpadmin *
Remote Password	********
Confirm Remote Password	********
Remote Directory	/DataPower/logs/
Signing Mode	(•) on ( ) off
Signing Algorithm	S/MIME *
Crypto Identification Credentials	LogKeypair (Crypto Identification Credentials) [+] [...] *
Encryption Mode	( ) on (•) off
Feedback Detection	( ) on (•) off
Identical Event Detection	( ) on (•) off
Backup Log	HRServicesCacheLog [+] [...]

Figure 14-8 Defining a local file for log messages.

These targets also require a size at which the file will be acted upon; the default is 500KB, but it can range from 100KB to 5MB. When the log file reaches the configured size, it will be archived by either rotating to a new file or being uploaded to a remote server. Choosing rotate allows you to specify how many times the file rotates to an archived version (in the same directory) before the oldest files begin to be deleted. Choosing upload asks for additional protocol details.

Log file uploading can be accomplished through a number of different protocols. The FTP and Secure FTP (SFTP) options require a remote FTP host, login, password, and directory. The Secure Copy (SCP) option requires the same fields and uses SSH as the underlying protocol to copy files remotely. The SMTP server takes sender and destination email addresses, and an SMTP server and client domain.

Before logs are uploaded from the device, they can be signed and/or encrypted. Turn on Signing Mode or Encryption Mode to enable these options; they each require a signing algorithm and cryptographic material. The example in Figure 14-8 shows the identification credentials used for file signing.

NFS Target

An NFS target writes log events to a file on a remotely hosted NFS mount. These targets work similarly to file targets, including the option to rotate or upload files when they reach a size threshold. Instead of a local directory, this target requires a static NFS mount to be defined. Because NFS requires a network connection and may introduce some latency, it also allows a Rate Limit to restrict the number of transferred events per second.

SMTP Target

The SMTP target allows an email to be sent with each log message. This obviously requires significant overhead and could produce a large number of emails when used more than sparingly. However, this option is commonly used for critical events that require on-call personnel to be immediately notified. Email targets require an SMTP server and client domain, as well as sender and receiver email addresses.

SNMP Target

An SNMP target uses preconfigured SNMP settings to deliver log events as Notification traps. An SNMP server such as HP OpenView or Tivoli NetView® can configure a trap listener to receive these notifications. For access to the appliance MIBs and assistance in configuring the SNMP settings, see the "Device Monitoring" section later in this chapter.

SOAP Target

System logs can be sent to a remote log server using a predefined SOAP interface. The example in Figure 14-9 shows events being routed to an HTTPS URL and includes an SSL proxy profile for securing the transport.

Name	HRServicesSoapLog *
Admin State	enabled disabled
Comments	SOAP log for HR Services
Target Type	SOAP *
SOAP version	SOAP 1.1
Log Format	XML
Timestamp Format	syslog
URL	https://logserver.xyco.com/loglis *
SSL Proxy Profile	LogClient (SSL Proxy Profile) + ...
Local IP Address	ManagementInterface Select Alias
Rate Limit	500 events/second
Feedback Detection	on off
Identical Event Detection	on off

Figure 14-9 Configuring a SOAP log target.

In order to make creation of a SOAP listener as easy as possible, DataPower provides a WSDL file that describes the service interface and a schema file that describes the log structure. Both of these files (log-soap.wsdl and log-soap.xsd) are available from the store: directory.

Syslog/Syslog-ng Targets

The most common integration between DataPower and a logging infrastructure is the use of syslog or syslog-ng to deliver application-level messages to a common logging server, where events from multiple systems are parsed, correlated, and filtered for importance. Syslog uses the UDP protocol for fast, efficient delivery of messages, while syslog-ng uses TCP for reliability; this allows syslog-ng to use SSL for secure transport.

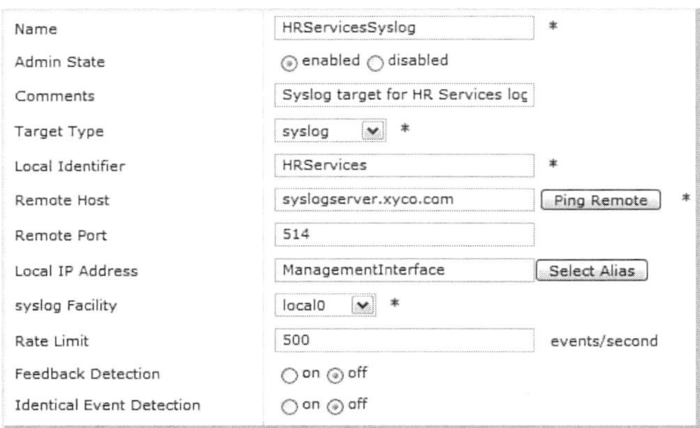

Figure 14-10 Configuring a syslog target.

The example in Figure 14-10 shows the definition of a syslog target that delivers event messages to a remote server.

Event Subscriptions

Log targets have only two requirements: a fully configured target (on the Main tab) and at least one subscription (on the Event Subscriptions tab). Now that we've defined a target protocol and destination for the delivery of log messages, we need to configure DataPower to select the appropriate messages for that target. The Event Subscriptions tab defines all messages that will be initially selected for delivery; these events can later be filtered using the other tabs. By default, there are no subscriptions defined; click Add to create a new subscription. In the pop-up that appears, select an event category and a minimum event priority, as shown in Figure 14-11. In this example, all system events at a critical level or above are gathered by this log target.

Figure 14-11 Subscribing to all critical system events.

Each saved event subscription will be added to the list so that the end result is the union of all applicable messages. In Figure 14-12, multiple subscriptions create a policy that might be used for an operations team monitoring device-level errors. For a more generic log, the event category all can be used to retrieve all messages at a given priority.

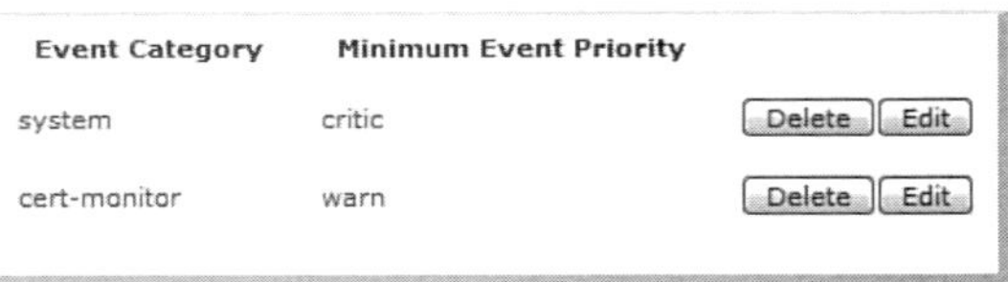

Figure 14-12 Compiling multiple subscriptions.

Now that we've defined the categories and priorities for subscription, we may want to filter these messages to a more specific set. Depending on the options chosen, these targets may produce a large number of error messages, many of which are of no interest to the team that is monitoring the destination log server.

> **SUBSCRIPTIONS ARE REQUIRED**
>
> Though the categories and priorities chosen for a particular logging mechanism can be modest, there *must* be at least one subscription defined for each target. This is a required field, and you will receive zero messages at your log server if no subscriptions have been created. There is no WebGUI warning for an empty subscription list, so keep this in mind if your log is unexpectedly empty.

Object Filters

Messages selected by a log target subscription can be filtered by the objects that created them; for example, you can select only events from a Multi-Protocol Gateway named MarketingService. Click the Object Filters tab to begin configuring the objects you care to receive information about. Click Add to create a new filter selection. Objects are categorized by type; you can filter on high-level objects such as XML Firewalls and Web service proxies, or low-level objects, such as a particular AAA policy. Choose the type of object and type the name of the particular object on which to filter. If you choose a category and leave the object name blank, all objects of that type will be selected. Keep in mind that many messages written to the logs for a given service are actually generated by lower-level objects contained within those services. If you turn on Add Referenced Objects, every lower-level object referenced by the named object will also be included in log collection. In the example shown in Figure 14-13, log messages are limited to those generated by the HRServices Web Service Proxy or objects referenced by that proxy. This log target may be useful for the application development team that created this particular service.

Figure 14-13 Filtering on a specific object.

Object filters are entirely optional and limit the messages being collected. For a broader range of log events, leave the object filters tab empty.

Event Filters

For the ultimate in log granularity, messages can be filtered by their event codes. This filtering can be either negative or positive; that is, you can select which codes you would like to see, or you can select which codes you would like to suppress. Click the Event Filters tab to view the current filters. To add an event code to the list, click Select Code to view a sortable/selectable list of codes that can be added to the filter. Often, the easiest way to choose the actual codes generated by your service configurations is to view the default system log at a debug level and select which events are important. Copy and paste the event code from the log to the filter to prevent any potential typographical errors. In the example in Figure 14-14, MQ connectivity errors are being selected for a log target that may be appropriate for MQ administrators. Alternatively, you could specify the single filter 0x0133*, where the asterisk acts as a wildcard to match all MQ events at once.

Event Subscription Filter	0x01330005 (could not send request) 0x01330006 (could not receive response) 0x01330007 (could not connect to the back QM) Add Help Select Code
Event Suppression Filter	(empty) Add Help Select Code

0x01330003	mq	error	request multistep processing failure	select | help
0x01330004	mq	error	response multistep processing failure	select | help
0x01330005	mq	error	could not send request	select | help
0x01330006	mq	error	could not receive response	select | help
0x01330007	mq	error	could not connect to the back QM	select | help
0x01330008	mq	error	could not enable listener (client port not set)	select | help

Figure 14-14 Selecting specific event codes for a log target.

The need to suppress events is readily apparent if there are too many log messages of one particular type. These events may be repetitive due to constant polling, such as an error that an MQ queue manager is down in a development environment. The event selection process is exactly the same; click Select Code and choose your events, or copy the event codes from an existing set of logs. Keep in mind that event suppression may complicate problem determination and should be used judiciously; consider using Identical Event Detection (on the Main tab) instead.

Selective Suppression

One event that is commonly suppressed in development environments is the message that "Power supply #2 has failed." This message can be caused by the second power supply being unplugged for cost savings or simple oversight. However, even a development box is important, and physical access to the device (often in a remote datacenter) is hard to come by. Instead of suppressing this message, just plug in the second power supply.

Special Log Objects

There are a few special log objects that simplify selection and delivery of important messages. They are configured using wizards to define the message destinations.

Email Pager

An email pager is specifically configured to send all domain events (or device events if created in the default domain) that have a priority defined as critical or above (critical, alert, and emergency) to an email address. Navigate to the email pager configuration at Administration→Miscellaneous→New Email Pager in the left menu. The simple wizard asks for a log target name, some optional comments, an SMTP server hostname, and a destination email address. This wizard generates a new log target subscribing to all critical events in this domain and delivering them to the defined email address.

Failure Notification

A failure notification is generated when a device experiences an unscheduled outage. As the device obviously cannot send a notification while it is down, the message (if configured) is sent via email upon resumption of service. Power failures (affecting both power supplies), device throttle/reboots due to memory thresholds, and accidental power-downs are examples of potential notification triggers. Failure notification must be configured in the default domain, as it deals with a system-level problem. Navigate to Objects→System→Failure Notification to configure the notification destination. Fill in the appropriate email address and server for failure notification, as seen in Figure 14-15.

Admin State	enabled / disabled
Comments	Failure notification for XML Gatev
Location	XmlGwDMZ01
SMTP Server	smtp.xyco.com
Email Address	OpsTeam@xyco.com
Include Internal State	on / off
Always On Startup	on / off

Figure 14-15 Defining a failure notification.

The location field defines the device in question and is inserted into the subject line of the outgoing email. You can also include an email report of the current state of the device or choose to send a notification on every startup (even during planned reboots) by selecting the appropriate radio buttons.

Custom Log Categories

To this point, all the log categories and event priorities we've discussed have been enumerated by DataPower and have correlated directly with syslog-style severities and built-in objects/processes on the device. However, you may want to institute custom log categories for easier filtering or for correlation of device logs with application logs. These custom categories are often created for custom logging within a service defined for a particular application, which we discuss shortly. To create a new custom log category, navigate to Administration→Miscellaneous→Configure Log Categories in the left menu. Click on Add to create a new category, and then provide a name as shown in Figure 14-16.

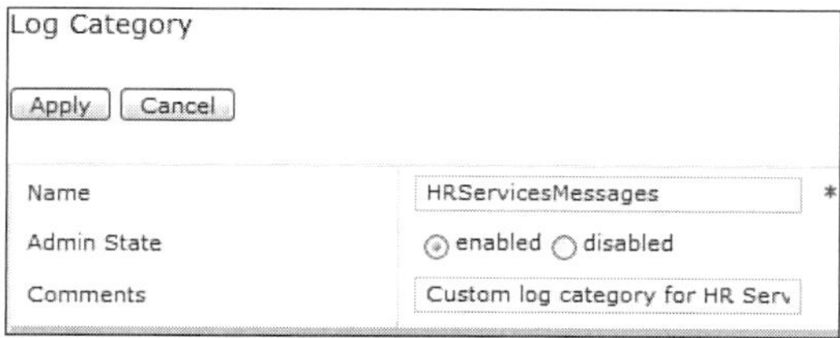

Figure 14-16 Defining a custom log category.

There are a couple of caveats to be aware of when using custom log categories. A custom log category is available only within the domain in which it is created, and that same category name cannot be used in another domain. That means that custom category names must be unique across the entire device.

The example in Figure 14-17 shows the categories for an HRServices domain, along with the new custom category HRServicesMessages.

Name	Status	Op-State	Logs	Comments
aaa	saved	up		AAA Policy
all	saved	up		All Categories
auth	saved	up		Authentication
cert-monitor	saved	up		Crypto Certificate Monitor
cli	saved	up		CLI Trace
crypto	saved	up		Crypto Subsystem
file	saved	up		File Management
file-capture	saved	up		XML File Capture
file-poller	saved	up		File Poller
ftp	saved	up		FTP Message Exchange
HRServicesMessages	new	up		Custom log category for HR Services
http	saved	up		HTTP Proxy
http-convert	saved	up		HTTP to XML Converter
kerberos	saved	up		Kerberos Access

Figure 14-17 Viewing built-in and custom log categories.

If all events generated by the device are already within a given category, why bother defining a custom category? You may want to have log messages that reference application data specific to the transaction, rather than simply listing DataPower processing steps/errors. In the next section, we discuss how to define those custom log messages.

Custom Log Messages

Most information regarding DataPower custom development is discussed in Part VI, "DataPower Development." However, one point bears repeating, as creation of custom log messages requires a stylesheet that takes advantage of the appliance's XSLT extension functions.

DataPower has overloaded the xsl:message element to take additional attributes. As seen in Listing 14-1, dp:type chooses a log category and dp:priority adds a message severity. In the example, a date is written to a custom log message at an information priority in the HRServicesMessages category.

Listing 14-1 Using Extension Elements to Define a Custom Log Message

```
<xsl:message dp:type="HRServicesMessages" dp:priority="info">
 Requested holiday: <xsl:value-of select="//requestedDate"/>
</xsl:message>
```

These log messages do not have to use custom log categories or user-defined priorities; any xsl:message elements are written to the DataPower logs anyway, but the customization is powerful. Both attributes (if used) must be defined in the DataPower namespace (http://www.datapower.com/extensions). More information on programming in a DataPower environment is provided in Part VI.

Separation of Concerns (Division of Log Traffic)

Now that you've seen the various options for configuring new log targets, let's put that knowledge to work. First, you need to define various targets for the disparate enterprise groups that may need to receive information from production devices. Each group should review the log categories, event codes, and delivery protocol options that are available, as well as the logs generated during development and QA. Customize the following suggestions with your own additions; for example, if your services require connectivity to a messaging system (such as MQ, Tibco EMS, or WebSphere JMS), your networking and/or messaging administrators may desire additional logs in those areas. Keep in mind that any target defined in the default directory gathers subscriptions (appropriately filtered) from all the other domains; targets defined within domains are restricted to that domain's messages.

Operations Targets

Log targets created for a production operations department generally deal with the health of the device from a hardware perspective. These departments often have 24/7 device/server monitoring, so these issues are most likely to be noticed immediately and escalated to internal teams or IBM support. The targets are usually located in the default domain and often contain some version of the following:

- SNMP target subscribing to all events at a critical level
- SNMP target subscribing to network events at an error level (optional)
- SMTP target subscribing to all events at a critical level
- Failure notification (SMTP) with internal state and "Always on Startup" turned on

The critical event threshold also gathers alert and emergency messages for complete "serious problem" coverage. The network-focused target is generally applicable only when the operations team is also in charge of network monitoring, rather than being solely hardware-focused. If this is required, it can be added as an additional subscription to the all-critical target. The identical SMTP target is used as a backup, in case there are SNMP connectivity issues. The SMTP failure notification provides coverage for unexpected outages (for which there will obviously be no warning).

Application Targets

Logs directed at application development/administrative groups are often the most disparate, as they depend considerably on the processing requirements of each application. These are usually defined at a domain level to gather information only about a set of services within a project deployment. The vast majority of application level log targets are either syslog/syslog-ng targets for real-time collection or file-based targets for delayed upload via ftp or scp. A sample set of targets could include the following:

- Syslog-ng target using SSL transport and subscribing to all events at an error level
- Individual file targets uploaded via ftp and subscribing to error events filtered on a specific service

- SMTP target subscribing to error level events and filtered to event codes signifying loss of connectivity to a critical business system (queue manager, SQL data source, and so on).

If your enterprise doesn't have a syslog server in place, the first target can be replaced by a file target being uploaded to a central log repository, or a SOAP target that can send real-time logs to a remote listener that logs to a file or database. The individual file targets can be uploaded to the server hosting a backend application (service), to be used for later log correlation. These individual targets can be customized to include additional subscriptions (at perhaps a warning or information level) in specific log categories. It also enables custom messages in user-defined log categories to be logged separately from device-generated messages.

Security Targets

Security is a broad category, as application security policies may be different from IT security policies. Desired log messages for an enterprise security group can vary widely depending on the sphere of influence of the team. The method of delivery is also less well-defined than for other groups, as security monitoring is less often standardized to syslog or SNMP. The exact definition of event subscriptions and log destinations is entirely up to you, but some common realms of interest include the following:

- SOAP target to an intrusion detection server (IDS), subscribing to error events and filtered by IDS-related event codes
- Syslog target subscribing to AAA events at a warning level
- SMTP target subscribing to cert-monitor objects at a warning level
- File target signed and uploaded via FTP, subscribing to auth, cli, and file events at an information level

The first two targets check for intrusions or invalid service authentication or authorization. The cert-monitor target alerts an administrator by email when a certificate on the device is moving toward expiration; configuration of how often and how early these expirations are checked is available from the Objects→Crypto→Crypto Certificate Monitor in the left-side menu. Last, the file target becomes an audit log for a particular domain, so that administrative modifications will generate a record for nonrepudiation purposes. It is important to create separate administrative user accounts to ensure useful audit information; don't share the admin account or you'll lose your oversight!

Transaction Logging

To this point we have been discussing only event logging—that is, events that happen on the device either during processing or because of some internal process or hardware status change. This is very different from transaction logging, which takes a copy of a particular message payload and sends it to a log destination for audit purposes. Adding transaction logging mechanisms can double the amount of network traffic, as each message flows to the backend as well as to the log; keep this in mind when defining your logging requirements. There are several different methods for performing transaction logging, all of which operate on an existing Processing Policy within a service. For a full explanation of how actions are added to processing rules and configured, see Part III, "DataPower Services." For now, we can discuss the various logging options.

> **PRIVACY CONCERNS**
>
> When undertaking any form of transaction logging, be aware of what sort of personal data will be recorded. Depending on the privacy and security laws surrounding your particular industry and the contents of incoming messages, persisting this information may result in lawsuits or significant fines. Check the HIPAA, SOx, PCI[1], or other compliance regulations before configuring this type of logging.

Log Action

The Log action is available from the Advanced Action icon. This action requires a destination URL and will send the input context to the defined endpoint. The message is wrapped in the same schema used for the SOAP log target; it contains all the standard log metadata fields (timestamp, category, client IP, and so on), and the payload is inserted into the message field. The category and priority applied are configurable from the Log action interface. The URL must be an HTTP or HTTPS endpoint.

Results Action

The Results and Results-Async actions, when inserted within a processing rule and defined with a URL, send the current message payload to a defined URL. These actions, as opposed to the Log action, have no wrappers or additional metadata (SOAP envelope, timestamp, and so on) and simply pass the entire message. The URL can use any of the protocols supported by DataPower (such as HTTPS, MQ, JMS); more information on generating these URLs is available in Chapter 9, "Multi-Protocol Gateway." The Results-Async action performs an asynchronous fire-and-forget to the endpoint, while the Results action wait for a valid response.

Using the Results action with a destination for logging is different from the common practice of ending a processing rule with an empty Results action. In the latter case, the action simply provides a method for getting the expected output into the OUTPUT context for delivery to the service backend (on a request) or client (on a response). As this is the most common appearance of the Results action, it is sometimes disconcerting (but perfectly reasonable) to have multiple Results actions spread throughout the processing rule, each sending its current context to a remote destination. They can even be adjacent to one another, stacked to send to multiple targets.

[1] HIPAA, Sarbanes-Oxley, and PCI are regulations for the healthcare, public corporation, and credit card industries.

Custom Transaction Log

A custom transaction log consists of an XSL stylesheet that gathers transaction variables and payload information and creates a message for delivery to a log server. Using DataPower extension functions to write custom stylesheets will be discussed in the development chapters; building a transaction log payload is as simple as assembling an XML message containing the desired data. This can contain the transaction ID, client IP, client credentials, service/operation being called, incoming URLs, and many other pieces of metadata—this provides the most flexibility in defining your own logging schema to match your current infrastructure.

Once the transaction log message has been defined, there are a few options for message delivery. From within the custom stylesheet, you can use the dp:url-open extension element to open a connection to a logging server via any supported protocol. Examples of using dp:url-open are provided in the DataPower development chapters. Similarly, you can output the message to the next step in the processing rule, and then use a Results or Results-Async action to perform the same sort of delivery. If you require more information than the standard event log metadata but would like some portion of the payload delivered through a log target, a custom stylesheet can be used to reduce the message to a size that is suitable for an event log; the entire log message must be less than 2KB. Use the "Custom Log Messages" section earlier in this chapter to submit the custom message to the logging system.

Device Monitoring

In earlier chapters, we've discussed a few different ways to retrieve data from the appliance using common interfaces. In the WebGUI, the Status menu contains most of the information that would be used for monitoring; in the CLI and the XML Management Interface, the show command and the get-status operation provide the same information. However, most common enterprise monitoring solutions use the SNMP[2] standard to retrieve information from network devices. DataPower appliances provide an SNMP interface that can be used to poll the device for data or receive traps generated by the device. Any event message on the device can be sent to an SNMP listener via a log target.

At a high level, monitoring tools that support SNMP poll the appliance (and other devices on the network) for key indicators of health using strictly defined GET[3] requests. Potential status data points are referenced using a complex object identifier (OID); DataPower will recognize incoming OID requests and respond with the appropriate values. As a corollary, enterprise monitoring tools can also listen for "traps," which are messages that can be arbitrarily sent by devices to provide additional information; these traps can be filtered and acted on.

Precise configuration depends upon the SNMP versions supported by your enterprise monitoring tools. DataPower supports all major versions, including v1, v2c, and v3.

---

[2] Simple Network Management Protocol, a polling/trapping standard for monitoring network-accessible devices.

[3] SNMP GET requests should not be confused with GETs for any other protocol (MQ, etc.). The SNMP specification defines both the format and use of these commands.

Where Are the MIBs?

This is likely the first question that will be asked by any operations personnel trying to monitor the appliances. To download the MIB[4] files and perform all other SNMP configuration, navigate to Administration→Access→SNMP Settings from the left menu. The second tab contains the three device MIBs, which can be downloaded by right-clicking on the filenames and saving them to a local machine. They can then be uploaded to a monitoring console such as Tivoli NetView, HP OpenView, or BMC PATROL, which will understand the available monitoring points and can display them to the administrator for selection in various formats. Each of the three files represents a different mode of SNMP interaction:

- drConfigMIB.txt describes a method for retrieving the configuration via SNMP.
- drStatusMIB.txt provides the interface for current status retrieval.
- drNotificationMIB.txt describes the traps sent by log targets on the device.

Configuring SNMP Polling of the Device

The Main tab on the SNMP Settings page defines how a monitoring server can connect to the appliance for polling. Define a local IP (or host alias) and SNMP port on the device, as seen in Figure 14-18; the default port is 161. Turn on the listener for this port by choosing the enabled radio button and clicking Apply.

Figure 14-18 Enabling SNMP polling of the device.

If you'll be using SNMPv3, you can also define users, a security level, and an access level, depending on the permissions you want the poller to have. For version 3, you'll also have to switch to the SNMPv3 Contexts tab and map between contexts and application domains.

For SNMP version 1 or 2c, you'll have to define communities that have access to certain information through polling. A community is defined in external SNMP tooling as a group that sends or receives SNMP traps; the names chosen in DataPower have to match those defined in

[4] A Management Information Base (MIB) file describes the database of objects (and their OIDs) that can be monitored by a network management system via SNMP. Each product that allows SNMP monitoring comes with a MIB file to explain its interfaces to any monitoring product.

your monitoring tools. Switch to the SNMPv1/v2c Communities tab and click Add to define a new community as shown in Figure 14-19.

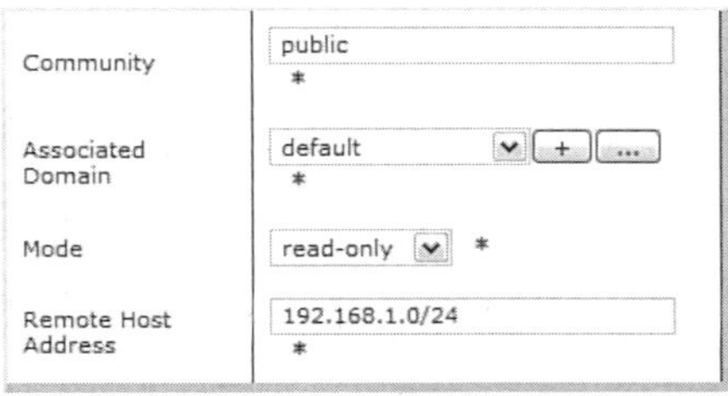

Figure 14-19 Defining a new SNMP community.

Adding a community for a domain allows members of that community to poll for information from that domain. For device-level status information, select the default domain. You also need to define a range of IP addresses that are allowable as device pollers. Using a class C address as shown in the first entry in Figure 14-20 allows a range of IPs, while the distinguished IP shown in the second entry limits access to a single poller.

Community	Associated Domain	Mode	Remote Host Address	
public	default	read-only	192.168.1.0/24	Delete Edit
config	HRServices	read-only	192.168.1.198/32	Delete Edit

Figure 14-20 Viewing multiple defined communities.

After communities have been defined and polling has been enabled, you can begin to poll the device from your monitoring server. Some suggested status parameters to monitor include

- **dpStatusEthernetInterfaceStatusStatus**—Shows the current state of each Ethernet interface. (OK means a successful connection and no-link means a lost connection.)
- **dpStatusSystemStatusLoad**—Shows the current device load percentage; this is the best measure of overall system usage.
- **dpStatusFilesystemStatusFreeEncrypted**—Shows the available space on the file system.
- **dpStatusMemoryStatusFreeMemory**—Shows the available memory available for processing.
- **dpStatusCPUUsagetenSeconds**—Shows the CPU usage percentage for the last ten seconds.

These values can be polled in several different ways; you can retrieve individual values at certain intervals for auditing purposes, graph the numbers over time, or create tables of parameter values. These values should be monitored and the appropriate team should be alerted if these values are out of your acceptable ranges. In Figure 14-21, you can see a graph of system load over time and a table with the current Ethernet interface status.

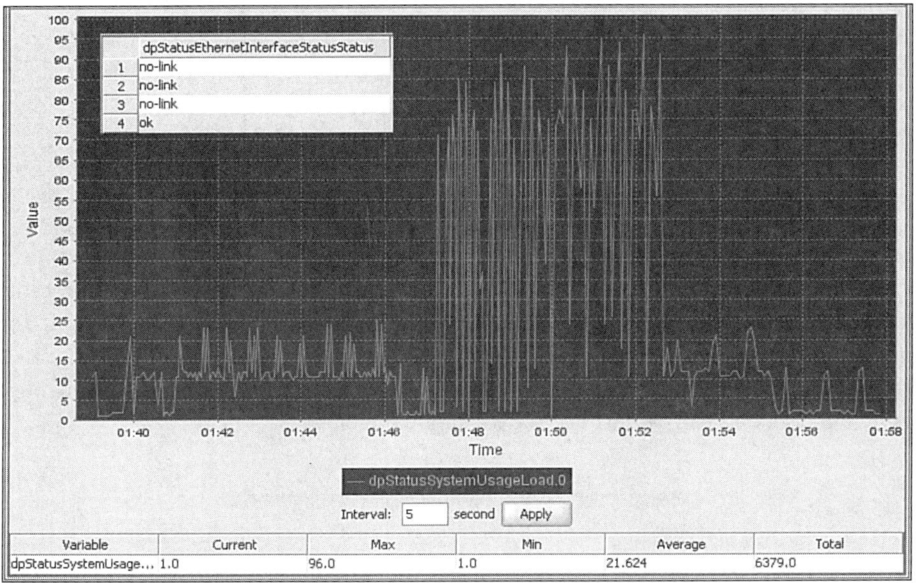

Figure 14-21 Viewing various status parameters using SNMP.

Configuring Sending of SNMP Traps

Aside from proactive polling for device health, monitoring solutions can also receive SNMP traps from the DataPower appliance. This functionality is enabled from the SNMP Settings page; the Trap and Notification Targets tab enables you to define the off-device trap listeners. Choose the IP and port of the remote listener and choose a version and community that will be supported by the monitoring server, as shown in Figure 14-22.

Remote Host Address	192.168.1.198 *
Remote Port	162 *
Community	public
Version	1

Figure 14-22 Defining an off-device trap listener.

Add the listeners that will receive each log message that has been defined to send to an SNMP target. As a shortcut to send specific events, you can select the Trap Event Subscriptions tab and define events that will always send messages to the defined trap targets. For more flexible trap definitions, define an SNMP log target as described earlier in this chapter. A log target gives you the flexibility of subscribing to whole categories of events, filtering on objects that created those events, and selecting specific event codes to include or suppress.

Service Monitoring

Device monitoring is all about device health; service monitoring, on the other hand, is all about gathering operational metrics for the Web services that are present within an infrastructure. Because DataPower acts as a proxy to all Web services traffic, it represents an ideal location in which to gather statistical information about the execution of those services. However, DataPower is not suited to graphing or reporting on those statistics, aside from simple SLM graphs and basic execution numbers. For a full monitoring solution, products such as ITCAM for SOA will correlate service executions, produce graphs, and monitor the entire lifecycle of a service transaction. DataPower can interoperate with ITCAM for SOA using the WSDM standard for exchanging data. This data can be aggregated across domains and appliances, or can be split to see the performance of individual devices. It can also contain information about service clients and can serve as the basis for dynamic distribution of future requests.

For retrieval of simpler statistics that may not need additional processing and multi-dimensional analysis, we have already discussed several methods for status retrieval. Most recently, we demonstrated monitoring of the appliance using SNMP polling; these status parameters include Web service and SLM metrics. From the CLI the show command works on Web services statistics, as does the get-status operation on the SOAP management interface.

Summary

We have seen that there are many different ways to gather information from a DataPower SOA Appliance. Information can be gathered on the device and offloaded at regular intervals, polled from the device using a standards-based monitoring console, and pushed from the device to various targets in a real-time environment. At every opportunity, the appliances will integrate with the best-of-breed tools that have become standard in the enterprise, including tight integration to IBM's monitoring and logging products. The flexibility and granularity provided by the logging system on the device allows for separation of concerns, so that each group receives only the information to which they have subscribed. This allows for complete integration into the enterprise, similar to any other network device.

CHAPTER 15

Build and Deploy Techniques

If you've read the preceding chapters, you are now familiar with some of the capabilities of the DataPower device. You should now understand the techniques required to configure XML Firewall services from the device's WebGUI interface. You might have also read Chapter 13, "Alternate Management Interfaces" and discovered other configuration methodologies such as the command-line interface (CLI) and the XML Management Interface and found that these facilities, while typically not primary service configuration tools, can be used for the modification and ongoing maintenance of services.

This chapter takes a look at DataPower configuration from another angle. In this chapter, we look at the details of how configurations are defined and managed on the device, and we look at the migration of configurations across the spectrum of environments—from initial coding to testing, acceptance, and production.

Goals and Objectives of Configuration, Build, and Deployment

In order to meet our objectives, we present configuration methods, including WebGUI, CLI, and XML Management Interface. We describe the use of DataPower configuration options for migration issue mediation, including externalizing static data, and the modification of configuration parameters. Techniques that ensure that DataPower devices are managed in a consistent and controlled manner in a multi-device and highly available configuration are also presented. This investigation leads to a sample configuration architecture and a demonstration of the migration of configuration settings from development through production.

Finally, the use of supporting products such as IBM Tivoli Composite Application Manager System Edition for DataPower (ITCAMSEDP) and the Integrated Solutions Console (ISC) are introduced as facilitators of multi-device management platforms.

DataPower Configuration Fundamentals

Before we get too deep into our discussion, let's briefly review the associated topics that will play into the methodologies we demonstrate. Some of these topics are addressed in Chapter 12, "Device Administration," so we'll just cover enough to refresh your memory.

File System

The DataPower file system is an encrypted data source separated into several named directories. Directories are used to host configuration data, store XSLT stylesheets, capture logging events, manage cryptographic certificates and keys, and control other system functions.

Each device contains one or more configuration files that describe the details of all services and objects. We look closely at these files shortly. Configuration files are stored in the config: directory, while custom data maintained by the user is stored in the local: directory. The device stores most of its required files in a system directory called store:. You'll find a complete description of the file system in the WebGUI Guide for your device. Figure 15-1 shows a typical directory structure.

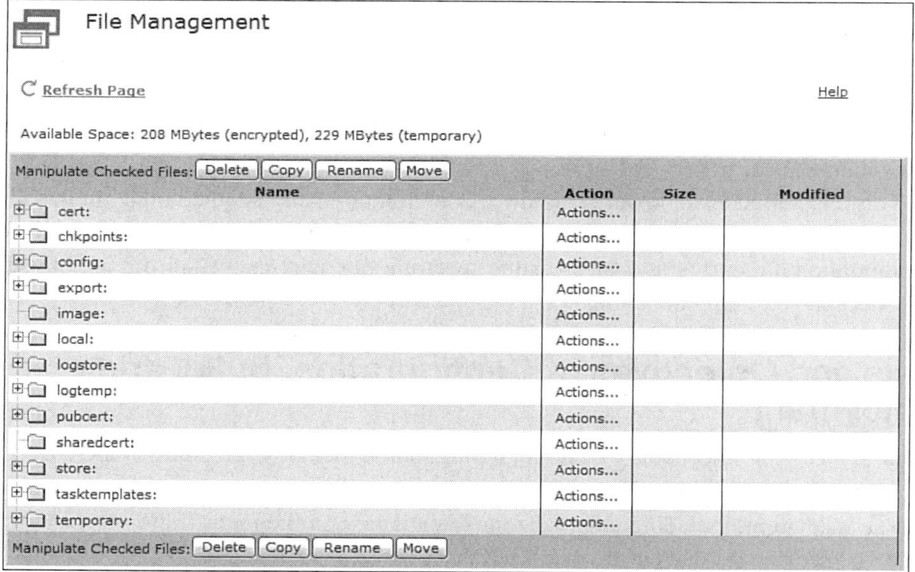

Figure 15-1 DataPower file system.

Application Domains

The DataPower file system is initially booted with a single domain labeled "default." The file system may be further segmented with the creation of application domains. You can read about domains in Chapter 12; however, for our discussion you should know that a newly created domain is provided with its own local: and config: directories and will be configured for read access to files in the store: directory of the default domain. Access to other application domains may also be granted.

Subdirectories may be created. For example, each application domain's configuration is hosted in the default domain in a file (with .cfg suffix) and subdirectory of the same name. Figure 15-2 shows the book and BookService subdirectories, and the BookService.cfg configuration file.

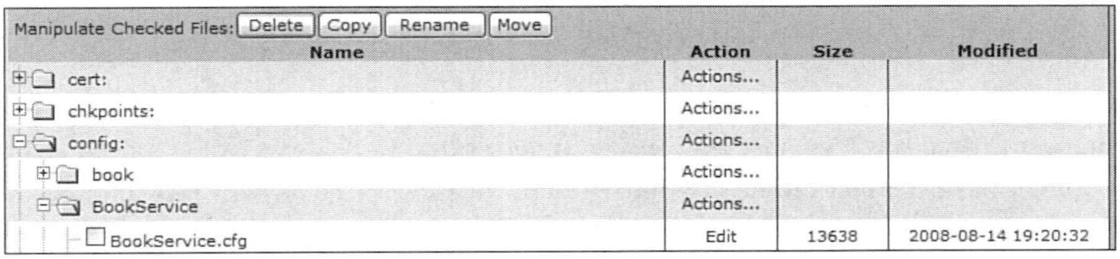

Manipulate Checked Files: Delete Copy Rename Move

Name	Action	Size	Modified
cert:	Actions...		
chkpoints:	Actions...		
config:	Actions...		
book	Actions...		
BookService	Actions...		
BookService.cfg	Edit	13638	2008-08-14 19:20:32

Figure 15-2 Config subdirectory from within default domain.

The BookService subdirectory is also accessible from within the application domain itself, without the default domain hierarchy. Figure 15-3 shows the same configuration file (BookService.cfg), now accessible from within the config: directory of the BookService domain.

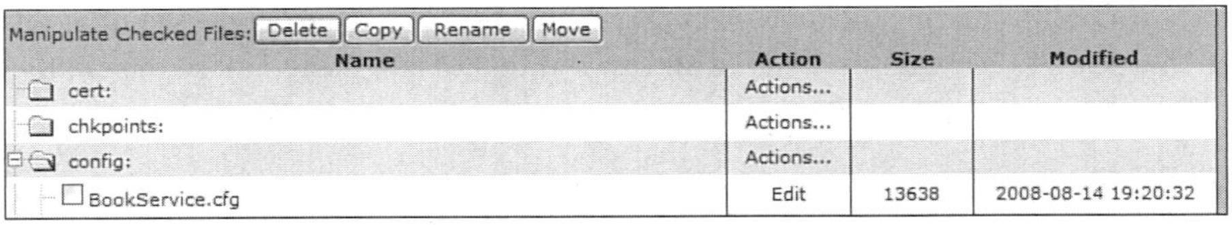

Manipulate Checked Files: Delete Copy Rename Move

Name	Action	Size	Modified
cert:	Actions...		
chkpoints:	Actions...		
config:	Actions...		
BookService.cfg	Edit	13638	2008-08-14 19:20:32

Figure 15-3 Config subdirectory from within application domain.

Devices and Environments

Each DataPower device may participate as a member of a peer group that provides services and shares management information such as Service Level Management (SLM) data with other members of the group. For the purpose of our discussion, a shared environment of devices refers to the group of devices servicing Software Development Life Cycle (SDLC) areas such as development, test, acceptance, or production. Migrating configuration information to an environment refers to the entire group of devices in that environment.

Using a single device to host multiple SDLC environments such as test and acceptance complicates SDLC migration as certain objects such as DNS Static Hosts (which we will discuss later) are defined at the device level and sharing them across life cycle environments breaks their functionality.

> **TIP—AVOID USING A DEVICE FOR MULTIPLE APPLICATION LIFE CYCLE ENVIRONMENTS**
>
> Using a single device for more than one SDLC environment is unwise. Sharing a production device is foolhardy and risks disrupting production activities.

Load Balancers

It is often the case that groups of devices, or perhaps an entire environment, will reside behind a load balancer that acts as a façade, exposing a single Virtual IP Address (VIP) for request traffic. This topology has no effect on the configuration of the device. There will be no device affinity (unless it has been specified at the load balancer itself) as each transaction can be processed by any of the devices in the load balanced group. Service level data is shared by devices via peer group registration, and all transactions participate in service level management. You can read more about SLM in Chapter 10, "Web Service Proxy."

Configuration Persistence

Regardless of which configuration method was used to create DataPower objects, the end result is an entry (in CLI format) in an onboard configuration file within the device's config: directory. Listing 15-1 shows the result of creating an application domain using any of the configuration methods as it is written to the configuration file.

Listing 15-1 Application Domain Configuration Detail

```
domain "BookService"
  base-dir BookService:
  base-dir local:
  config-file BookService.cfg
  visible-domain default
  url-permissions http+https+snmp+ftp+mailto+mq
  file-permissions CopyFrom+CopyTo+Delete+Display+Exec+Subdir
  config-mode import
  import-url "http://192.168.1.35:9099/BookServiceExport.zip"
exit
```

Configuration changes are not persisted until a save configuration action is invoked, either from the WebGUI's Save Config link, the CLI write memory command, or XML Management's SaveConfig action. Changes may be saved for a single domain or all domains. Until this is done, the changes are only part of the running configuration.

When the save action is initiated, the default domain configuration is persisted in a file named autoconfig.cfg, while application domain configuration is persisted in the configuration file defined in the application domain object. This name defaults (as has been seen in the previous file system discussion) to the name of the domain itself.

You may have more than one configuration file on the device at a time, although only one is the active configuration. This allows for the device to be booted into one of several different boot profiles depending on your needs. For example, on a testing device, you might have configuration files for several different services and boot the device with one or the other depending on your testing needs. Figure 15-4 shows the ability to select which configuration file to boot the device with. This is available from the Administration→System Control screen and is only available in the default domain. Restarting the device utilizes the selected configuration.

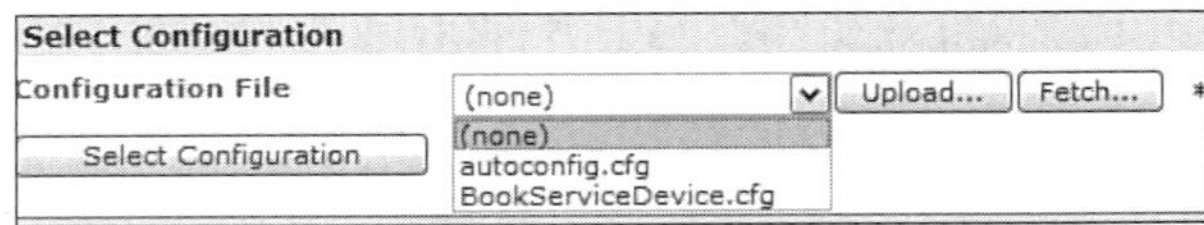

Figure 15-4 Select configuration showing multiple configuration files.

Configuring for Migration

Before configuring a service, it is important to understand the methods, objects, and properties that will best provide for eventual migration to another environment. You will see how the proper use of network objects such as DNS Servers, DNS Static Hosts, and Host Aliases, and the avoidance of static endpoint information in XSLT will greatly ease migration issues and preclude having to modify configurations to fit the targeted environment.

Network Objects

The fundamental problem encountered during migration is the creation of environmental affinities within device configurations. This is often a result of the designation of off box services via dot decimal IP addresses, or the use of environment-specific DNS names. Other affinities can also be created with non-IP-related properties such as ports, MQ queue names, or channels. The following network objects (defined in the default domain) will assist in avoiding these affinities. You may also want to refer to Chapter 4, "Advanced DataPower Networking" for a more thorough investigation of these subjects.

Host Alias

Host Aliases are used to provide abstract names for the Ethernet interfaces on the device. When using services such as the XML Firewall, Web Service Proxy or Multi-Protocol Gateway, where incoming requests may be bound to particular interfaces on the DataPower device, the use of host alias objects in place of the numeric addresses of those interfaces can alleviate migration issues. A host alias is simply a reference to an IP address on an interface of the device. In this fashion requests can also be restricted to a particular interface, furthering the security of the service by restricting access to particular subnets. Figure 15-5 shows the simple definition of a host alias.

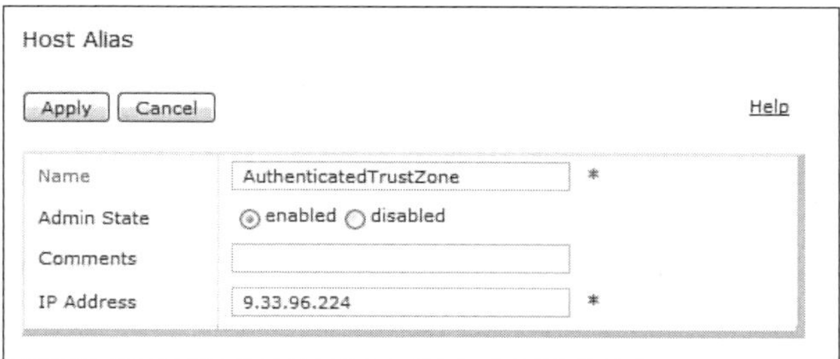

Figure 15-5 Host Alias configuration.

> ### TIP—SDLC Environments and Alias Objects
>
> It is recommended that all SDLC environments contain like-named host alias objects. Each environment's host aliases define addresses specific to its network infrastructure. Furthermore, the host alias names should be self-descriptive, such as those describing the interfaces' trust characteristics: InternetFacingInterface or AuthenticatedTrustZone.
>
> As services are migrated, the host aliases are not moved to the target, and as the names are equivalent, the services will automatically utilize the target's host alias.

All services can use host aliases. The XML Firewall, for example, uses it on the Front End Device Address definition, while services utilizing Front Side Handler (FSH) objects implement host aliases there. Figure 15-6 shows the association of the host alias with an FSH.

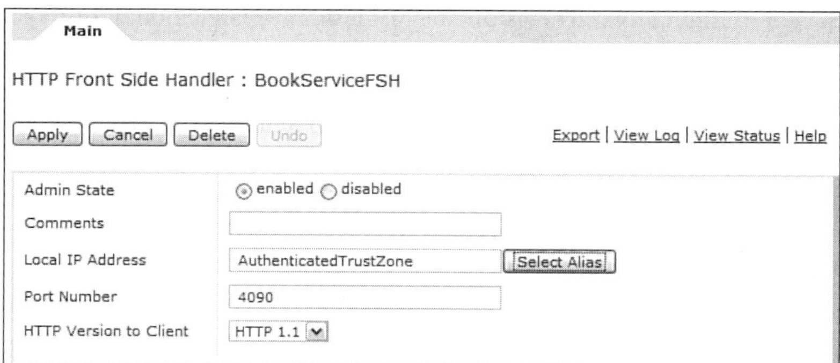

Figure 15-6 FSH with host alias in place of hard-coded interface address.

> ### TIP—Use Hosts Alias Objects Only for IP Addresses
>
> Host aliases are for interface definitions only! Do not use them for any addresses off the box. Host aliases are selected from the service definition Select Host Alias button and only device addresses are appropriate here.

DNS

The DNS Settings object provides for the designation of device-specific DNS servers and DNS Static Host settings that may be used to extend the DNS services. DNS static hosts provide a powerful aliasing capability that will greatly assist in configuration migration. Using literal names such as highPriorityBookHost.books.net as apposed to a dot decimal address also provides a more streamlined configuration migration.

Most objects such as services, log targets, load balancer group members, and even extension functions, can accept a literal name (DNS or DNS static host) in place of a dot decimal address. Figure 15-7 shows the definition of DNS servers available from the Network→DNS Settings menu.

DNS settings are similar to the host alias objects in that they are defined in the default domain, and are not migrated with services. Therefore, when services move to a target environment, they can immediately utilize the DNS settings defined there.

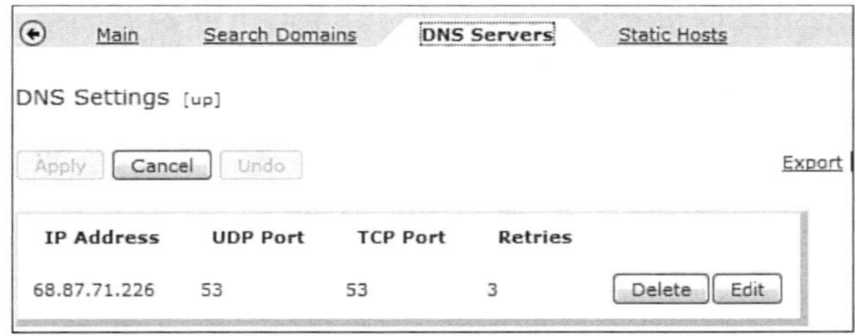

Figure 15-7 DNS Server added to DNS Object.

DNS Static Hosts

Although the DNS server under most circumstances provides address resolution, DataPower also provides for an additional layer of abstraction. The DNS Static Host might be used to define specific DNS name/address resolution. This is similar to the use of the /etc/hosts file, which also provides an extension of DNS services.

This technique can be employed as a migration assistance methodology. In this case, DNS static host entries in the production environment would contain different addresses than the test environment DNS static host entries. Figure 15-8 shows the addition of a DNS static host entry to the DNS Settings object.

Editing Static Hosts property
of **DNS Settings**

Host Name	highPriorityBookHost.books.net	*
IP Address	192.168.1.35	*

Figure 15-8 DNS Static Host entry added to DNS Object.

> **TIP—DNS STATIC HOST SETTINGS**
>
> Use DNS static host settings when environment-specific DNS is not available.
>
> DNS servers should be used as the primary source for address resolution. DNS static host settings may be used for additional address resolution, but caution must be taken to avoid overriding DNS server settings.

XSLT Issues

One area that is often a cause for concern is the use of hard-coded, unnamed numerical constants or *"magic numbers"* in custom XSLT code. Those experienced with DataPower extension functions may be familiar with the possible use of dot decimal addresses or port numbers in routing statements and other extension functions. The use of these hard-coded addresses causes an affinity with the environment. This problem may be easily resolved by externalizing this static data.

This topic introduces the *identity document.* This is a simple XML Document that can be shared by devices within an environment. It can be resident on the device or fetched from a central location such as a Software Configuration Management (SCM) system. We demonstrate its utility for the externalizing and centralizing of aliased configuration details. The example examines the incoming URL, and when it contains a special character string (Purchase), we will route the request to a high-priority server whose address will be fetched from the identity document.

Listing 15-2 shows a sample of an identity document. The XSLT uses the identity document to externalize IP information. This technique could be used for any instance when static data is used with XSLT.

Listing 15-2 XML Identity Document with Externalized Routing Information

```
<?xml version="1.0" encoding="UTF-8"?>
<! -  ->
<! - This document is used to :  ->
<! - Externalize all ip/port information for routing purposes  ->
<! -  ->
<identityDocument>
    <! -  ->
    <! - Routing info for bookService  ->
    <! -  ->
    <service name="bookService">
        <! -  ->
        <! - These addresses will be fetched from within XSLT via xPath  ->
        <! -  ->
        <endPoints>
            <BookServiceHost1>
                <ip>highPriorityBookHost.books.net</ip>
                <port>2129</port>
            </BookServiceHost1>
            <BookServiceHost2>
```

```
                <ip>bookHost.books.net</ip>
                <port>2130</port>
            </BookServiceHost2>
        </endPoints>
    </service>
</identityDocument>
```

In the XSLT that does the actual routing, all that needs to be done is to reference the endpoints within the identity document. The imported identity document is fetched and cached at compilation time, and results in no overhead at execution time. Remember, in many instances routing could have been performed without the use of XSLT; this example uses this technique to demonstrate the identity document principle.

In the XSLT shown in Listing 15-3, the first step is to parse the identity document from the local: directory via the document() function; this creates a parseable document from which we can use XPath to extract values. Refer to Chapter 22, "Introduction to DataPower Development" and Chapter 23, "Programming Within the DataPower Environment" if you need a refresher on XSLT programming within DataPower.

The document() function actually uses an appended XPath to get only the endpoints. That's all we are interested in here and will make the following XPath statements a bit simpler. The resultant nodeset is stored in the endPoints XSL variable.

We check the incoming URL via the system variable var://service/URL-in, and when it contains the Purchase identifier, we route to the host identified in BookServiceHost1 using the xset-target extension element. That is a faster server, and we want to ensure those purchases go through!

Listing 15-3 BookServiceRouter.xsl with Inclusion and Reference to Identity Document

```
<?xml version="1.0" encoding="UTF-8"?>
<xsl:stylesheet version="1.0"
xmlns:xsl="http://www.w3.org/1999/XSL/Transform"
xmlns:dp="http://www.datapower.com/extensions" extension-element-
prefixes="dp">
<!-- -->
<!-- This stylesheet is used to establish routing -->
<!-- Identity Document, identityDocument.xml, is used for ip/port
resolution -->
<!-- -->
<xsl:variable name="endPoints"
select="document('local:///identityDocument.xml')//identityDocument/service
[@name='bookService']/endPoints"/>
<!-- -->
<xsl:template match="/">
    <!-- -->
    <xsl:variable name="urlIn" select="dp:variable('var://service/URL-
in')"/>
    <!-- -->
    <!-- Check the incoming URL, set Route -->
    <!-- -->
```

```
    <xsl:choose>
        <! -  ->
        <! - BookService routing  ->
        <! -  ->
        <xsl:when test="contains($urlIn, 'Purchase')">
            <!-- -->
            <!-- Set routing for Purchases -->
            <!-- -->
            <dp:xset-target host="$endPoints/BookServiceHost1/ip/text()"
port="$endPoints/BookServiceHost1/port/text()" ssl="false()"/>
            <xsl:message dp:priority="'info'">
                <xsl:value-of select="concat('Found ', $urlIn, ', Setting
routing to ',
                $endPoints/BookServiceHost1/ip/text(), ':',
$endPoints/BookServiceHost1/port/text())"/>
            </xsl:message>
        </xsl:when>
        <xsl:when test="contains($urlIn, 'Query')">
            <! -  ->
            <! - Set routing for Query  ->
            <! -  ->
            <dp:xset-target host="$endPoints/BookServiceHost2/ip/text()"
port="$endPoints/BookServiceHost2/port/text()" ssl="false()"/>
            <xsl:message dp:priority="'info'">
                <xsl:value-of select="concat('Found ', $urlIn, ', Setting
routing to ',
                $endPoints/BookServiceHost2/ip/text(), ':',
$endPoints/BookServiceHost2/port/text())"/>
            </xsl:message>
        </xsl:when>
        <xsl:otherwise>
            <xsl:message dp:priority="'error'">
                <xsl:value-of select="concat('Unknown routing based on URL
', $urlIn)"/>
            </xsl:message>
        </xsl:otherwise>
        <! -  ->
    </xsl:choose>
    <! -  ->
</xsl:template>
</xsl:stylesheet>
```

Figure 15-9 shows the results of our routing. The messages we produced are written to the log, and the routing determination is made. Again, the purpose of this example is not so much to present routing as there are many ways to do that (such as using a Route Action) but to demonstrate a simple and effective way to externalize static information from within an XSLT stylesheet. In this manner, the stylesheet could be moved to another environment that contains its own version of the identity document, with different endpoints, and the XSLT will work without change! No environment affinities, no "magic numbers!"

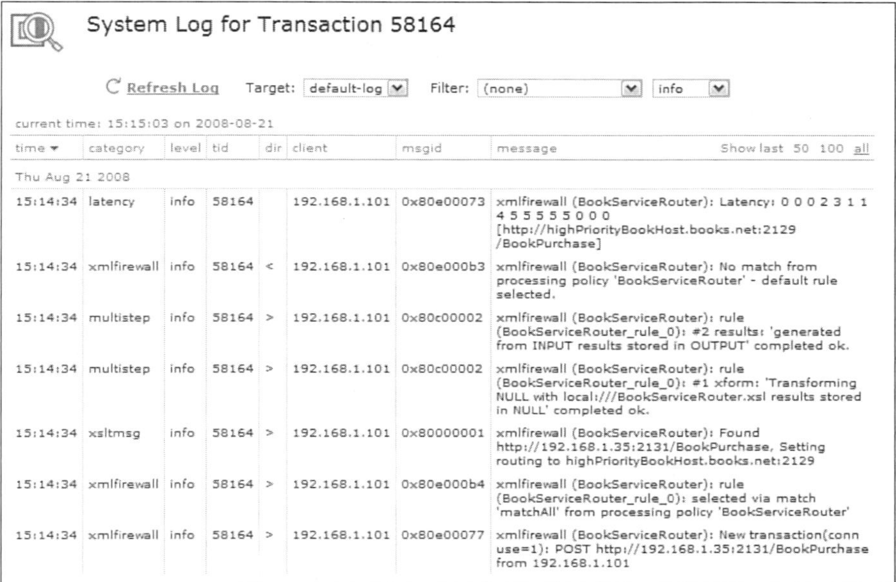

System Log for Transaction 58164

Refresh Log Target: default-log Filter: (none) info

current time: 15:15:03 on 2008-08-21

time	category	level	tid	dir	client	msgid	message
Thu Aug 21 2008							
15:14:34	latency	info	58164		192.168.1.101	0x80e00073	xmlfirewall (BookServiceRouter): Latency: 0 0 0 2 3 1 1 4 5 5 5 5 5 0 0 0 [http://highPriorityBookHost.books.net:2129 /BookPurchase]
15:14:34	xmlfirewall	info	58164	<	192.168.1.101	0x80e000b3	xmlfirewall (BookServiceRouter): No match from processing policy 'BookServiceRouter' - default rule selected.
15:14:34	multistep	info	58164	>	192.168.1.101	0x80c00002	xmlfirewall (BookServiceRouter): rule (BookServiceRouter_rule_0): #2 results: 'generated from INPUT results stored in OUTPUT' completed ok.
15:14:34	multistep	info	58164	>	192.168.1.101	0x80c00002	xmlfirewall (BookServiceRouter): rule (BookServiceRouter_rule_0): #1 xform: 'Transforming NULL with local:///BookServiceRouter.xsl results stored in NULL' completed ok.
15:14:34	xsltmsg	info	58164	>	192.168.1.101	0x80000001	xmlfirewall (BookServiceRouter): Found http://192.168.1.35:2131/BookPurchase, Setting routing to highPriorityBookHost.books.net:2129
15:14:34	xmlfirewall	info	58164	>	192.168.1.101	0x80e000b4	xmlfirewall (BookServiceRouter): rule (BookServiceRouter_rule_0): selected via match 'matchAll' from processing policy 'BookServiceRouter'
15:14:34	xmlfirewall	info	58164	>	192.168.1.101	0x80e00077	xmlfirewall (BookServiceRouter): New transaction(conn use=1): POST http://192.168.1.35:2131/BookPurchase from 192.168.1.101

Show last 50 100 all

Figure 15-9 Identity document routing log results.

> ### TIP—Do Not Use Magic Numbers (Static Data) in XSLT
>
> The use of the identity document principle allows for the construction of environment neutral XSLT. Static data within XSLT forces an affinity to the environment and complicates migration of services.

Configuring for Migration Summary

We have seen how the use of configuration options such as host aliases, DNS static hosts, environment-specific DNS servers, and externalizing magic numbers in XSLT can be effective in easing the issues of configuration migration. Some objects have to be hand-edited when initially establishing a device. For example, each device must have specific Ethernet Interface definitions.

However, after a device is established, the need for maintaining these objects is minimal. Your goal in configuration is to not establish an affinity to an environment within service definitions.

Configuration Migration Tools

You've spent time configuring your Web Service Proxy and your XML Firewall services. You're certainly not going to repeat the key strokes on another device. As you might already know, DataPower provides several ways to move configuration data between devices. All three primary configuration methods, WebGUI, CLI, and XML Management, provide options for you. We look at some of the capabilities.

The following examples utilize a sample domain named BookService, which contains the XML Firewall services shown in Figure 15-10, and the Web Service Proxy shown in Figure 15-11.

XML Firewall Name	Op-State	Logs	Req-Type	Local Address	Port	Resp-Type	Remote Address	Port
BookService1	up		soap	AuthenticatedTrustZone	2129	unprocessed		
BookService2	up		soap	AuthenticatedTrustZone	2130	unprocessed		
BookServiceRouter	up		soap	AuthenticatedTrustZone	2131	unprocessed		

Figure 15-10 BookService domain XML Firewall listing.

Web Service Proxy Name	Op-State	Logs	Type	Req-Type	Back Side URL	Resp-Type
BookService	up		static-from-wsdl	soap	NA	soap

Figure 15-11 BookService domain Web Service Proxy listing.

Package Importing and Exporting

There are several methods for exporting and importing configuration details. In addition to the primary configuration methods, configuration modification can be performed by editing the configuration files on the device (with caution), as we will discuss. The on board configuration files located in the config: directory contains a sequential list of CLI commands.

The methods may well be used in conjunction in a complete configuration migration strategy. For example, an export created by the WebGUI may be referenced by an invocation of the CLI or the XML Management Interface.

WebGUI Methods

The simplest way to move configuration between environments is to use the Import/Export Utilities of the WebGUI. This tool allows for the export of configuration details, and allows for the convenient automatic fetching of subordinate objects. For example, if a Web Service Proxy (WSP) is exported and referenced objects are selected, match rules, style policy rules and actions, XML managers, and other supporting objects used by the WSP are exported as well. This technique even fetches XSLT that is identified within actions.

However, be aware that this does not pick up XSLT and XML files located on the device's file system that are included (either by xsl:include, xsl:import or document() functions) by the action's XSLT. Simply moving local files to a SCM system and fetching from actions or within XSLT eliminates this problem. We address the local file system issue when we talk about configuration architectures, but you need to be aware of it.

> **TIP—XSLT and XML Included by XSLT Are Not Automatically Included in Referenced Objects**
>
> If you have an action that uses an XSLT and that stylesheet includes other XSLT or XML documents, they are not automatically included among the referenced objects of an export. You must either fetch them from off box repositories or copy them onto the device.

Figure 15-12 shows the options available from the WebGUI export configuration screen. You can create backups of entire application domains, export configuration from the current domain, copy or move configuration between domains, or back up the entire system.

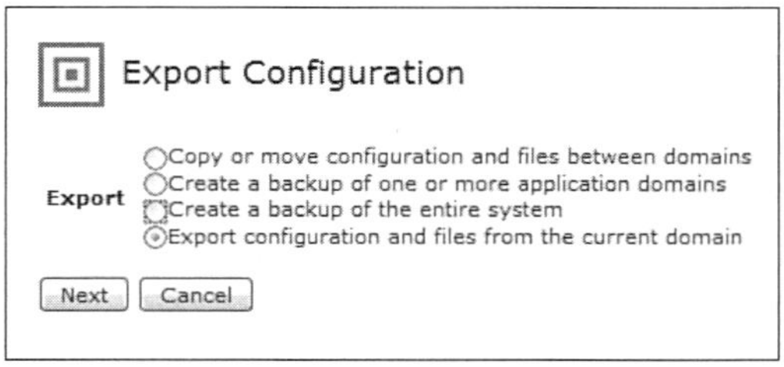

Figure 15-12 Export configuration options.

Let's look at what is actually exported when we do an export of the aforementioned XML FWs and WSPs. Figure 15-13 shows the export screen after having selected the XML Firewall Service and Web Service Proxy objects. Notice that the Export File Name has been entered (rather than accepting the default export filename), and the To property has been set to ZIP Bundle. This will produce a ZIP document containing the exported objects and files. The XML Config option produces an XML document containing the configuration and exported files in base64 format within XML Elements. Their use is quite similar though the ZIP bundle is compressed.

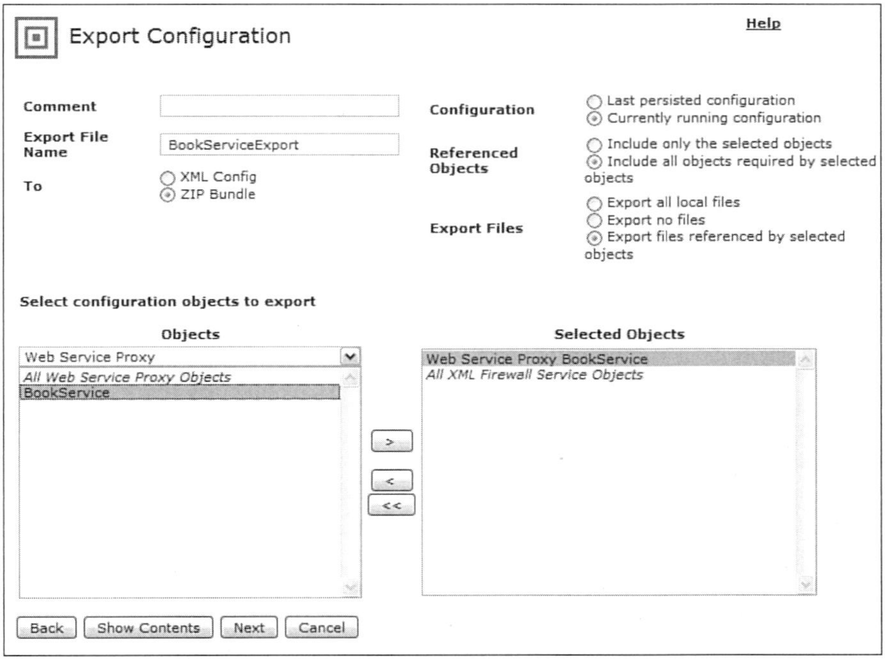

Figure 15-13 Export of BookService domain services using ZIP formatted configuration file.

As we said earlier, the Export files referenced by the selected objects option does a good job of finding all the objects required by the services. In fact if you want to know ahead of time which objects are to be selected, all you have to do is use the Show Contents button. Figure 15-14 shows the objects associated with our services. Some are obvious, such as the Processing Policy; some are not so obvious, such as the WS-Proxy Endpoint Rewrite rules. These are hidden children of the WSP, and ones that you might not even be aware of. They are associated with the remote and local properties of WSP endpoints. The point here is that you cannot just assume that an object lives by itself, the objects have subordinates and some are not readily apparent.

Objects selected for export:
User Agent default
XML Manager default
HTTP Front Side Handler BookServiceFSH
WS-Proxy Endpoint Rewrite BookService
Matching Rule BookService_match_all
SLM Policy BookService
Processing Action BookService_default_request-rule_defaultaction_slm
Processing Action BookService_default_request-rule_defaultaction_result
WS-Proxy Processing Rule BookService_default_request-rule
Processing Action BookService_default_response-rule_defaultaction_result
WS-Proxy Processing Rule BookService_default_response-rule
Processing Action BookService_rule_0_results_output_0
WS-Proxy Processing Rule BookService_rule_0
WS-Proxy Processing Policy BookService
Policy Attachment BookService_BookService.wsdl
Crypto Certificate BookServiceClient
Crypto Key BookService
Policy Parameters Encrypted
Web Service Proxy BookService
Matching Rule matchBookQuery
Processing Action BookService_rule_0_fetch_0
Processing Rule BookService_rule_0
Matching Rule matchBookPurchase
Processing Action BookService_rule_1_fetch_0
Processing Rule BookService_rule_1
Processing Policy BookService
XML Firewall Service BookService1
XML Firewall Service BookService2
Matching Rule matchAll
Processing Action BookServiceRouter_rule_0_xform_0
Processing Action BookServiceRouter_rule_0_results_0
Processing Rule BookServiceRouter_rule_0
Processing Policy BookServiceRouter
XML Firewall Service BookServiceRouter
Dependent files selected for export:
store:///policies/templates/wsp-sp-1-2-encrypted-parts-body.xml
cert:///BookServiceClient-sscert.pem (private key: not exported)
cert:///BookService-privkey.pem (private key: not exported)
local:///BookService.wsdl
local:///bookQueryResponse.xml
local:///bookPurchaseResponse.xml
local:///BookServiceRouter.xsl

Figure 15-14 Manifest of objects selected for export.

Also notice that the private keys are identified as dependents of the services but are not exported. This is a fundamental feature of the appliance. It will not release a private key or certificate from the certificate (cert:) directory; this is a valuable security attribute. If you have read Chapter 18, "DataPower and SSL," then you understand that when you create keys and certificates on the device (using Crypto Tools), you are given a one-time opportunity to save off the keys in the temporary: directory. They may be copied off the device at this time. Be forewarned though, the temporary: directory is cleared on every device reboot, though not on a domain restart or firmware reload.

Importing packages via the WebGUI is a simple and straightforward process as seen in Figure 15-15. Simply use the Import facility, and select the exported ZIP or XML bundle. You'll notice a couple of options here also.

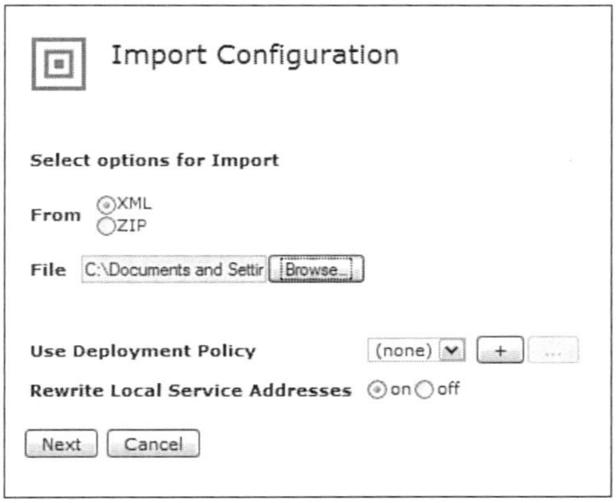

Import Configuration

Select options for Import

From	(•) XML ( ) ZIP
File	C:\Documents and Settir [Browse...]
Use Deployment Policy	(none) [+] [...]
Rewrite Local Service Addresses	(•) on ( ) off

[Next] [Cancel]

Figure 15-15 Import configuration with configuration modification options.

The first option is Use Deployment Policy. We explore this feature shortly; it allows us to build a powerful filtering and selection mechanism to determine which objects from the export bundle are actually imported. It enables us to dynamically change some of the values of properties as they are imported.

The next option is Rewrite Local Service Addresses. This option works with the Ethernet addresses assigned to objects such as XML Firewall and FSHs. Remember we have stressed in most cases it is a best practice to use host alias objects and not the actual address of an interface. If you need to refresh your understanding of interfaces on DataPower, you can refer to Chapter 4.

This feature works only on raw physical addresses. If you had assigned the address of eth1 (whatever the dot decimal IP address is) to an XMLFW, this feature would change that value to the dot decimal of eth1 on the destination device.

If the export contained multiple domains, you would be given the choice of which domains to import. If you attempt to import a configuration exported from a domain into the default domain, you would be warned as application domains are normally imported into application domains. Figure 15-16 shows the selection of the BookService domain configuration

TIP—Avoid Domain Exports When Migrating Services from Development Domains

When migrating services from a development domain where many unrelated configuration objects may exist, it is better to export the individual service objects and their referenced objects rather than the entire domain. In this manner, you have greater control over which objects are actually exported and eventually imported into the target domain.

Details of Configuration to Import

Domain Name:	default
Comment:	
User Name:	admin
Device Name:	
Firmware Version:	XI50.3.6.1.8
Export Timestamp:	2008-08-14 18:55:22 EDT

Domains contained in this Package: Select: All | None

☑ BookService

Back Next Restore Cancel

Figure 15-16 Import domain selection.

Figure 15-17 shows all the objects that were exported from the source platform. You can selectively import individual objects from the list if you desire by checking or unchecking the box next to the object. You will be alerted if the objects are already on the target platform, or if they are identical to the objects on the target platform. Notice that the keys and certificates are identified, but no option to import is provided. A file from the store: directory is also identified without an import option. Recall from the device administration discussions that you may not modify the contents of the store: directory unless you are the device administrator and you are importing into the default domain.

Finally, the success or failure of the importation process is described. Any errors would be presented. As you can see in Figure 15-18, all is well.

We have now completed our task. We imported the three XML Firewalls, the Web Service Proxy, and their supporting objects onto the destination device. We are ready to utilize our imported configuration. Or are we? We need to look at the services on the target device and make sure they are up and enabled.

Figure 15-19 shows the status of the Firewalls. Notice that they are in Op-State down! How could that be, when we received success messages on the import?

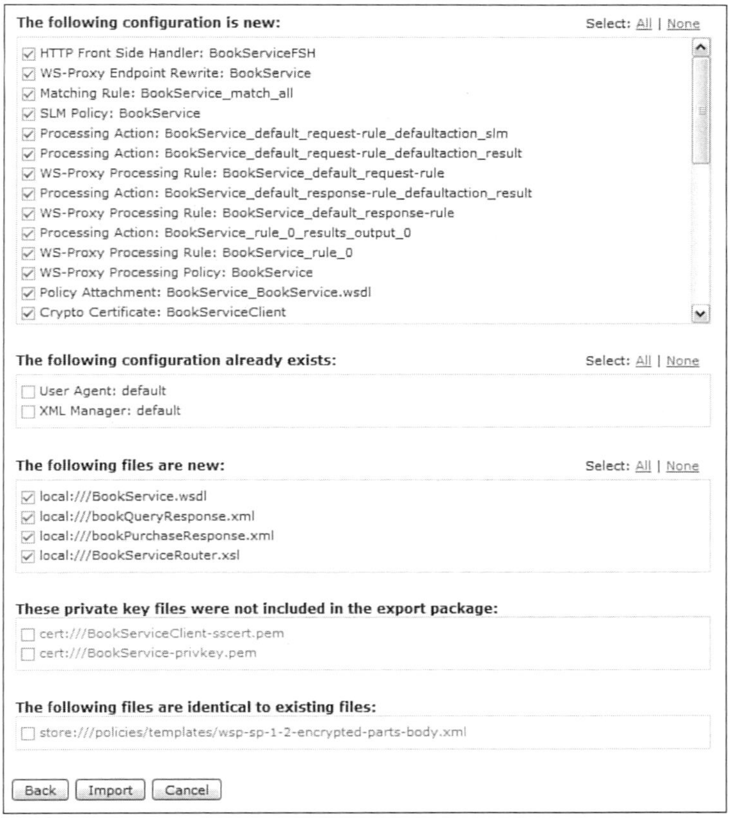

The following configuration is new: Select: All | None

- [x] HTTP Front Side Handler: BookServiceFSH
- [x] WS-Proxy Endpoint Rewrite: BookService
- [x] Matching Rule: BookService_match_all
- [x] SLM Policy: BookService
- [x] Processing Action: BookService_default_request-rule_defaultaction_slm
- [x] Processing Action: BookService_default_request-rule_defaultaction_result
- [x] WS-Proxy Processing Rule: BookService_default_request-rule
- [x] Processing Action: BookService_default_response-rule_defaultaction_result
- [x] WS-Proxy Processing Rule: BookService_default_response-rule
- [x] Processing Action: BookService_rule_0_results_output_0
- [x] WS-Proxy Processing Rule: BookService_rule_0
- [x] WS-Proxy Processing Policy: BookService
- [x] Policy Attachment: BookService_BookService.wsdl
- [x] Crypto Certificate: BookServiceClient

The following configuration already exists: Select: All | None

- [ ] User Agent: default
- [ ] XML Manager: default

The following files are new: Select: All | None

- [x] local:///BookService.wsdl
- [x] local:///bookQueryResponse.xml
- [x] local:///bookPurchaseResponse.xml
- [x] local:///BookServiceRouter.xsl

These private key files were not included in the export package:

- [ ] cert:///BookServiceClient-sscert.pem
- [ ] cert:///BookService-privkey.pem

The following files are identical to existing files:

- [ ] store:///policies/templates/wsp-sp-1-2-encrypted-parts-body.xml

[Back] [Import] [Cancel]

Figure 15-17 Import configuration detail with optional and unexported objects.

Object Import Results

- HTTP Front Side Handler: BookServiceFSH
- WS-Proxy Endpoint Rewrite: BookService
- Matching Rule: BookService_match_all
- SLM Policy: BookService
- Processing Action: BookService_default_request-rule_defaultaction_slm
- Processing Action: BookService_default_request-rule_defaultaction_result
- WS-Proxy Processing Rule: BookService_default_request-rule
- Processing Action: BookService_default_response-rule_defaultaction_result
- WS-Proxy Processing Rule: BookService_default_response-rule
- Processing Action: BookService_rule_0_results_output_0

File Import Results

- local:///BookService.wsdl: OK
- local:///bookQueryResponse.xml: OK
- local:///bookPurchaseResponse.xml: OK
- local:///BookServiceRouter.xsl: OK

[Done]

Figure 15-18 Import results.

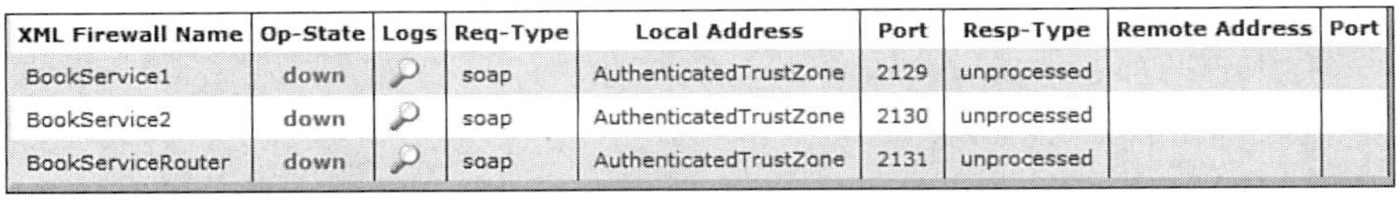

XML Firewall Name	Op-State	Logs	Req-Type	Local Address	Port	Resp-Type	Remote Address	Port
BookService1	down		soap	AuthenticatedTrustZone	2129	unprocessed		
BookService2	down		soap	AuthenticatedTrustZone	2130	unprocessed		
BookServiceRouter	down		soap	AuthenticatedTrustZone	2131	unprocessed		

Figure 15-19 XML Firewalls in down op-state after import of configuration.

Looking closer at the service's status from Status→Object Status shows that they have failed to install on the port; you can see that in Figure 15-20. This is typically caused when another service is already assigned the port the service is attempting to use. This problem is encountered when environments do not share network details. We will see shortly how this problem can be addressed quite easily.

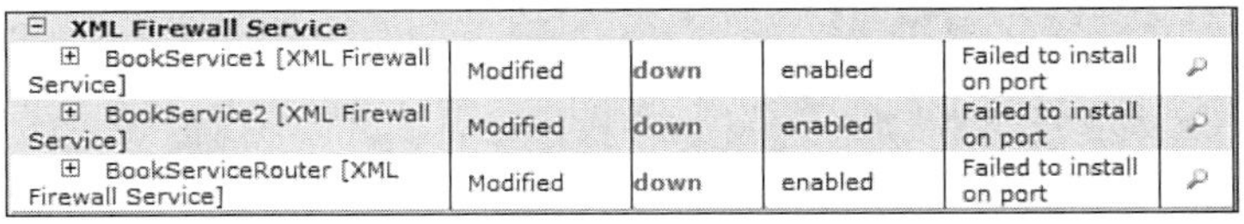

⊟ XML Firewall Service					
⊞ BookService1 [XML Firewall Service]	Modified	down	enabled	Failed to install on port	
⊞ BookService2 [XML Firewall Service]	Modified	down	enabled	Failed to install on port	
⊞ BookServiceRouter [XML Firewall Service]	Modified	down	enabled	Failed to install on port	

Figure 15-20 XML Firewalls object status.

We have seen that although the majority of configuration details can be easily and confidently copied across devices, there are certain properties that require a little more attention. As in our example, the ports used in a test environment might be different from those used in a production environment.

Fortunately, the Deployment Policy can be used to filter which objects are allowed to be imported, and it can change properties of objects that are imported. Let's look at how it works. First, Figure 15-21 shows the use of the deployment policy on the Import Configuration screen.

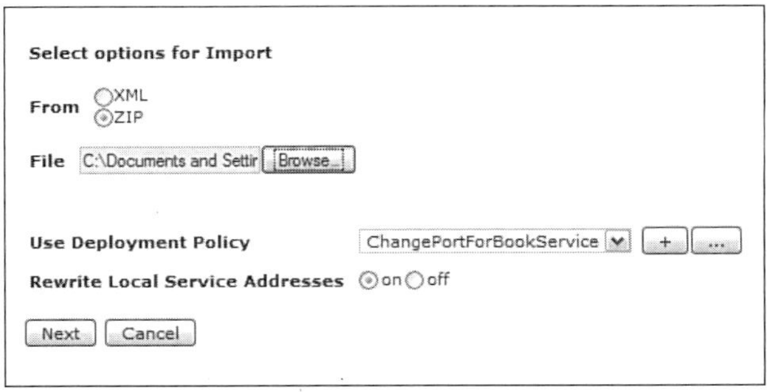

Select options for Import

From ○XML ⦿ZIP

File C:\Documents and Settir [Browse...]

Use Deployment Policy ChangePortForBookService [+] [...]

Rewrite Local Service Addresses ⦿on ○off

[Next] [Cancel]

Figure 15-21 Designation of deployment policy on the import of a configuration.

Opening up the deployment policy object (as always via the ... button), shows some of the configuration options. The deployment policy has two primary objectives.

The first is to select which objects are allowed into the target device. This is done by the definition of a white-list (acceptable objects) and a black-list (filtered objects). These define a fine-grained selection list. The white-list could be all XMLFW objects while the black-list could be a single XMLFW named dont-import-me. The white-list is not required and if not used, all objects will be accepted unless they are contained within the white-list specification. The black-list is not required, and only those objects within the while-list range that are not to be imported need be identified.

The second objective is to modify properties of certain objects. You define the selection criteria and the properties to modify. You can add new values, change values, and remove them.

Our example is just accepting anything that came from the BookService domain. Figure 15-22 shows the configuration. Multiple URIs could have been entered allowing for an expanded white-list, and we could have also configured Filtered Configurations.

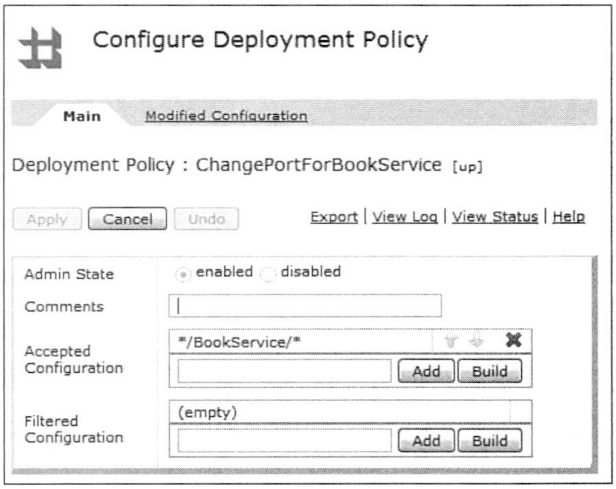

Configure Deployment Policy

Main | Modified Configuration

Deployment Policy : ChangePortForBookService [up]

Apply | Cancel | Undo — Export | View Log | View Status | Help

Admin State	enabled disabled
Comments	
Accepted Configuration	*/BookService/* — Add Build
Filtered Configuration	(empty) — Add Build

Figure 15-22 Deployment Policy accepted configuration.

The Build button allows for the easy creation of the acceptance and filter configuration strings. As you can see in Figure 15-23, selection can be based on a variety of properties such as the original device address and domain, resource type and name, and even the value of a particular property the object might contain. Again, here we are just allowing any object from the BookService domain.

Editing Accepted Configuration property of **Deployment Policy**

Device Address	* — Select Alias
Application Domain	BookService
Resource Type	(all resources)
Name Match (PCRE)	
Configuration Property	
Configuration Value Match (PCRE)	

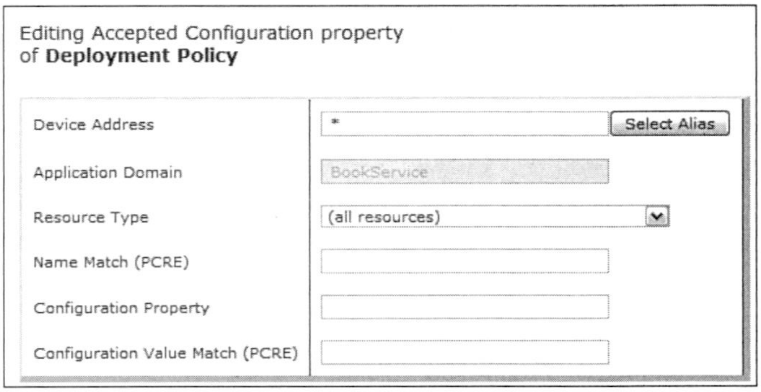

Figure 15-23 Deployment Policy accepted configuration build.

Now that we have identified the objects to allow, it's time to get to what we are really after, modifying properties as they are imported. This detail is defined within the Modified Configuration tab.

As you can see in Figure 15-24, it allows multiple entries, each identifying a particular property to be modified. You can use a wide brush via wildcards, or be selective and just identify a particular object. Some of the properties (Name Match, for example) accept PCRE expressions such as '.*', whereas others (such as Application Domain) accept '*' as the wildcard specification. The build button makes these uses clear.

We'll look at the details shortly, but these entries will select any XML Firewall with a name of BookService1, BookService2, and BookServiceRouter that has a LocalPort property of any value (.*), and then selectively change the firewall's port. This allows us to just change the individual properties that vary between the export and import environments.

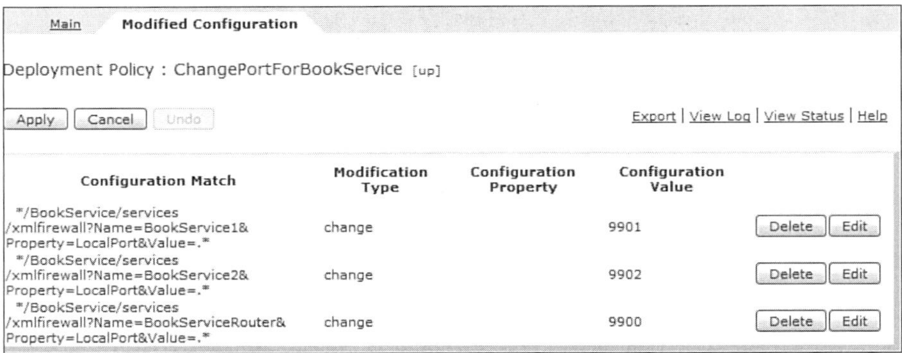

Figure 15-24 Deployment Policy modified configuration.

Each entry within the Modified Configuration contains the Configuration Match (again identifying the object and property), and a Modification Type that allows you to change the value, add additional values, or remove the matched value. Finally, the Configuration Value contains (in this case, as it's a change) the new property value to use. Figure 15-25 shows the completed configuration property assigning a new port value of 9901 to BookService1. (This is at the end of the string and not visible in this display, but was shown in Figure 15-24.)

You may have been intimidated by the URI string, but fear not, the Build button (seen in Figure 15-25) allows for easy creation, just as with the accepted and filtered configuration URI strings. All you have to do is identify the resource—there's even a drop-down box for the resource type (objects), and you can use PCRE (PERL compatible regular expressions) to match multiple objects with a single string. In Figure 15-26, the XML Firewall Service objects named BookService1 from the BookService domain that have a LocalPort property (with any value) are selected.

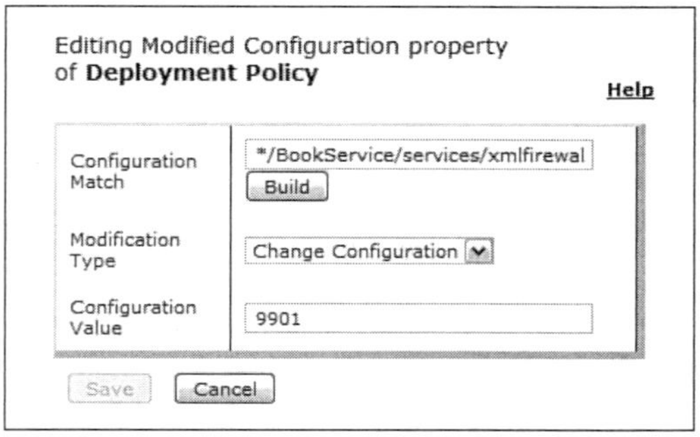

Figure 15-25 Deployment Policy change value.

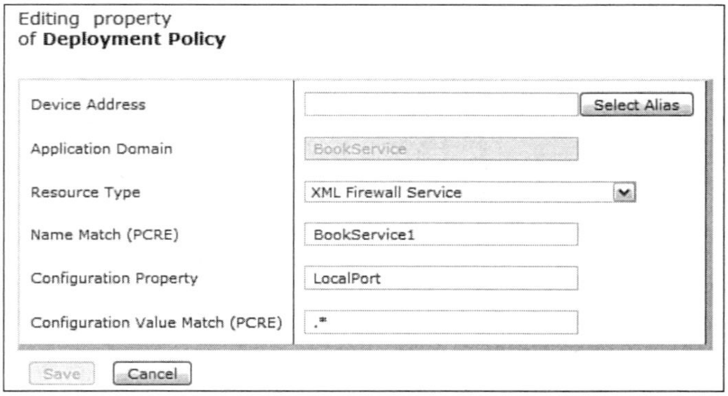

Figure 15-26 Deployment Policy URL builder.

Now the cautious reader might ask, "How did you know the property name was LocalPort?" That is a good question, because there is no documented listing of property names. To find the name of the property requires investigation. Remember when we exported the BookService services to a zip file named BookServiceExport.ZIP? Well, it contains an XML File named export.xml that has all the details of the export. As you can see in Figure 15-27, each of the exported objects is contained within. In fact the two firewalls are clearly shown.

Listing 15-4 is an expanded view of the configuration for BookService1. Only the first few elements are displayed. However, as you can see, the LocalPort is shown as containing the value of 2129. Now the reality is that you will not be changing many properties, and after you do this once or twice, you will be comfortable with it.

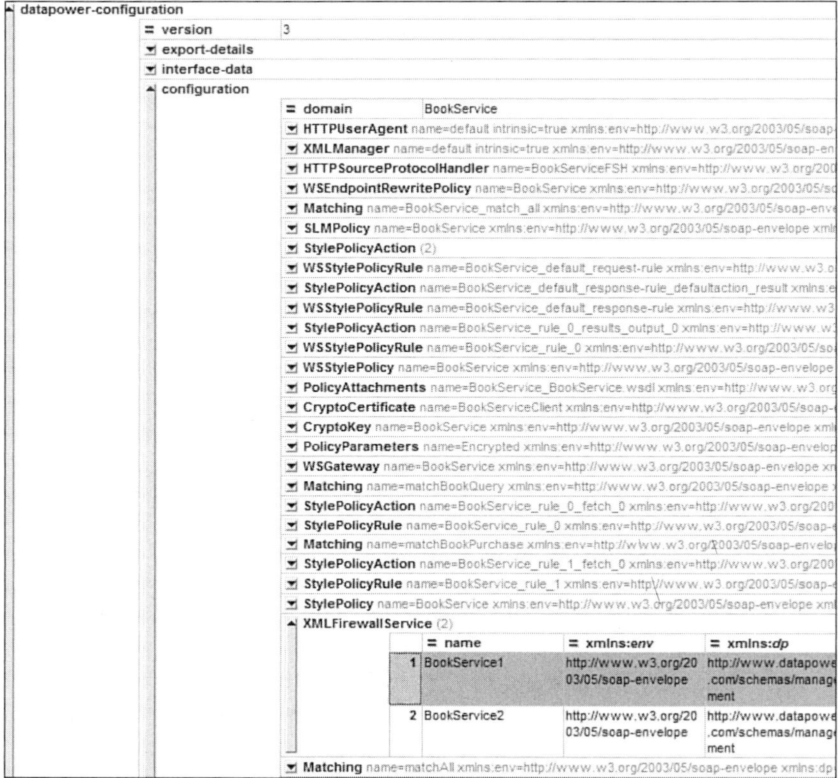

Figure 15-27 XML details of a configuration export.

Listing 15-4 XML Details of Exported XML Firewall Configuration with LocalPort Highlighted

```
<XMLFirewallService name="BookService1"
xmlns:env="http://www.w3.org/2003/05/soap-envelope"
xmlns:dp="http://www.datapower.com/schemas/management">
    <mAdminState>enabled</mAdminState>
    <LocalAddress>InternalTraffic</LocalAddress>
    <UserSummary>an example XML Firewall Service</UserSummary>
    <Priority>normal</Priority>
    <LocalPort>2129</LocalPort>
    <HTTPTimeout>120</HTTPTimeout>
```

Executing the import now with the deployment policy performs the changes we desired. The ports have been changed. This is just what we wanted! Figure 15-28 shows the objects in the up Op-State.

XML Firewall Name	Op-State	Logs	Req-Type	Local Address	Port	Resp-Type	Remote Address	Port
BookService1	up		soap	AuthenticatedTrustZone	9901	unprocessed		
BookService2	up		soap	AuthenticatedTrustZone	9902	unprocessed		
BookServiceRouter	up		soap	AuthenticatedTrustZone	9900	unprocessed		

Figure 15-28 Firewalls in up op-state after importing with deployment policy.

CLI Methods

The CLI has the advantage of providing for automated, scripted execution of Import/Export functions. Importantly though, not all the functionality of the WebGUI is supported. However, the CLI has a special place in the pantheon of configuration methodologies. It is the format of the on-board configuration file as was seen earlier in our discussion of the configuration file format and in the example of application domain definition (way back in Listing 15-1).

We'll be especially interested in CLI functionality that leverages the more-advanced features of the other methods such as creating a selective export of services via the WebGUI. This is important, because as you will see, we can use these commands within the device's configuration file to fetch configurations and files and to import previously exported packages.

Including Configuration

There is no need to have the device's entire configuration details resident on the device. In fact, fetching and sharing configuration resources with other devices is a key component of modular configuration design. The CLI can be used to include source configuration from its file system or external sources using protocols such as HTTP, HTTPS, FTP, or NFS. Secured protocols such as HTTPS should be used in unsecured environments to protect configurations while in transit.

The CLI Exec command is used for this purpose, as seen in Listing 15-5; this causes the included configuration to be executed as if it were originally written in the configuration file. This command could be executed from an interactive CLI session, but it is even more useful when it is part of the device's boot configuration file, and by virtue of its execution, the startup configuration fetches modularized configuration components.

Listing 15-5 Inclusion of External Configuration via "exec" Command

```
exec http://192.168.1.35:8080/SharedBookService.cfg
```

Exporting Configuration

The CLI export functions are performed via the backup command. This functionality is equivalent to the backup entire domain capability of the WebGUI and does not support the selective filtering of objects. However as will be seen shortly, the CLI can be used to import a selective export created by the WebGUI or XML Management Interface.

When executed within the default domain, the Backup command can select which domain to backup via an optional domain argument. When executed in an application domain, only the current domain is exported.

Listing 15-6 shows the execution of the Backup command. Notice that the provided filename (which is the same as the domain name in this example) is appended with the .zip suffix. The XML format is not available here.

Listing 15-6 Backup with Domain

```
xi50[BookService](config)# backup BookService
Backup to 'BookService.zip' scheduled (may take a few minutes to complete).
Backup is complete.
```

Importing Packages

The CLI supports importing of packages created by all export methods. This process is performed by first creating an Import Package describing the export and defining import options. The package is then processed or executed to invoke the import package process.

Several options such as turning on/off overwriting of files and objects are supported, as is automatically performing the import at device startup via the auto-execute property. Deployment policies can also be associated with the package so that when they are imported, all the changes described in the policy will be made.

The import-exec command is used to perform an import of a previously exported configuration package. Listing 15-7 shows the import-package configuration. This is the CLI command structure used to define the import-package.

Listing 15-7 Import Package Configuration with Deployment Policy

```
import-package "bookService"
  source-url "https://9.33.96.224:8080/BookServiceExport.zip"
  deployment-policy ChangePortForBookService
  no auto-execute
exit
```

Listing 15-8 shows two command line CLI executions. The first does a show command to list out the bookService package. This allows for the confirmation of option defaults which were not set in the package creation. You can see that the overwrite and rewrite local IP options are set to on.

The second command, import-exec, demonstrates the actual execution of the import process. As with the previous exec command, the creation of the import package and the import-exec command can be performed in an interactive CLI session as in the example in Listing 15-8. They could also be part of the device's boot configuration.

Listing 15-8 Details of Import-Package Configuration Object and Execution of Package

```
xi50[BookService](config)# show import-package bookService
import-package: bookService [up]
 - - - - - - - - - - - - - - --
 admin-state enabled
 source-url https://9.33.96.224:8080/BookServiceExport.zip
```

```
 import-format ZIP
 overwrite-files on
 overwrite-objects on
 deployment-policy ChangePortForBookService  [up]
 local-ip-rewrite on
 auto-execute off
xi50[BookService](config)#
xi50[BookService](config)# import-exec bookService
Loading import-package 'bookService'.
Import package is complete.
```

Including Files

Although the previous discussion has dealt with configuration packages, there might be instances where individual files (XSLT or XML) need to be imported into the device at startup. Recall when we originally brought this subject up; this is unnecessary if you fetch files from external sources such as an SCM repository.

In either case, this is easily performed with the copy command. Listing 15-9 demonstrates the copy command format. The -f option forces a rewrite if the file already exists on the target platform. Again, all supported protocols can be used, and you should use secured protocols in a production environment. As with all CLI commands we have seen, the copy command can be executed interactively or as part of the boot configuration. This technique may also be used to import key and certificate files from the SCM into the cert: directory of a domain.

Listing 15-9 Execution of Copy Command to Fetch External File

```
copy -f https://9.33.96.224:8080/IdentityDocument.xml
local:///IdentityDocument.xml;
```

XML Management Methods

The XML Management interface is a valuable tool in the management of configurations. It supports a similar set of commands as the WebGUI and CLI. Packages can be exported, imported with deployment polices, configuration files can be loaded onto the device, and the device can be restarted.

Listing 15-10 shows the formatting of a do-import command. This is analogous to the CLI's import-exec command, or the Import feature of the WebGUI. Notice that a deployment policy is defined via an attribute on the dp:do-import element, and that the dp:input-file element contains the actual import package. It needs to be base64 encoded first, and the actual data has been truncated from this display for brevity. Tools such as OpenSSL (www.openssl.org) can be used to perform the base64 encoding, or if you are writing XSLT, you can use the DataPower encode() function.

Listing 15-10 XML Management Do-Import

```
<?xml version="1.0" encoding="UTF-8"?>
<env:Envelope xmlns:env="http://schemas.xmlsoap.org/soap/envelope/">
    <env:Body>
        <dp:request domain="bookService"
xmlns:dp="http://www.datapower.com/schemas/management">
            <dp:do-import source-type="ZIP" deployment-
policy="changeHostAliasAndIPAddress">
                <dp:input-file>
                    {base64 input}
                </dp:input-file>
            </dp:do-import>
        </dp:request>
    </env:Body>
</env:Envelope>
```

As we will see, the XML Management interface will play an important role in device management. Among the primary reasons is the ability to script its execution using tools such as ANT. Doing so provides a platform for configuration modification, migration, execution, and device administration.

You should read the WebGUI product guide for definitive information on XML Management request structure and execution.

Configuration Structure for High Availability and Consistency

Now that we have discussed configuration best practices and methods for exporting and importing configuration details, we can demonstrate methods for their utilization in DataPower device configuration management. This configuration will utilize a three-tiered approach to device management: a device specific fixed component, a component which is shared across devices within an environment, and the support for application domains. The objectives are as follows:

- Provide for a consistent configuration across devices within an environment.
- Provide for a consistent configuration through device restart.
- Utilize Source Control for configurations.
- Segregate environment-specific from shared and application domain configurations.
- Provide a platform for service configuration migration and promotion.

Device Configuration

Each device contains a section of its configuration that is unique from all other devices. At a minimum this is the definition of its Ethernet Interfaces but may contain other objects such as host aliases. No other configuration can be fetched from external resources without first configuring the interfaces!

Each device shares many configuration details with other devices in its environment. DNS and Network Time Protocol (NTP) servers, for example, are all used with similar configuration details. Administrative objects such as user-groups, logging targets, access control lists, and document caching policies will also typically be shared across all devices in an environment. In addition, the application domains are configured in the default domain and are shared across devices.

Services should always be configured in application domains. Services consist of the services themselves and their supporting style policies, rules, actions, AAA policies, match rules, and XSLT, among other objects. It is the services that will bear the majority of ongoing maintenance and, as such, we need to make special provisions for their definition.

TIP—Always Configure Services in Application Domains

Configuring services in application domains (rather than the default domain) provides far greater control in access and management. Access privileges may be limited by domain providing administrative restrictions, and many device configuration options are designed to leverage the domain architecture. The default domain should only be used for device configuration.

Rather than having the service configuration reside on the device, it is desirous that it be fetched from an external source, and furthermore that this resource be under the control of an SCM. Figure 15-29 demonstrates graphically the concept of configuration fetch.

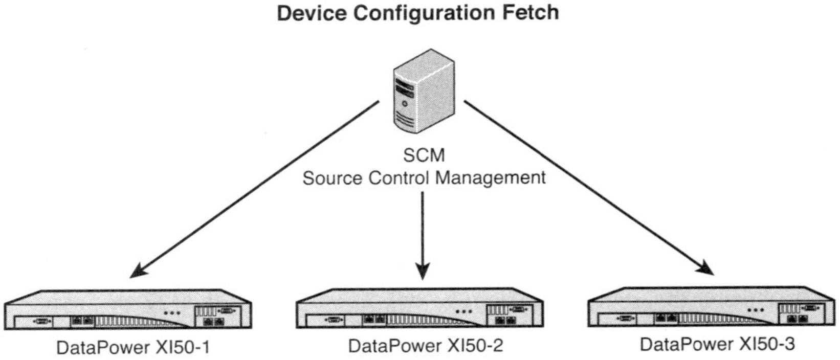

Figure 15-29 Configuration fetch from SCM.

In the following examples, techniques that can be employed to achieve this goal are demonstrated. By using these techniques, the device refreshes itself to a known good configuration at each controlled restart, or even in the event of an uncontrolled restart.

The example in Figure 15-30 illustrates fetching application domain configuration details. The Import URL represents an SCM location of a previously exported configuration. Notice that the deployment policy is also supported here.

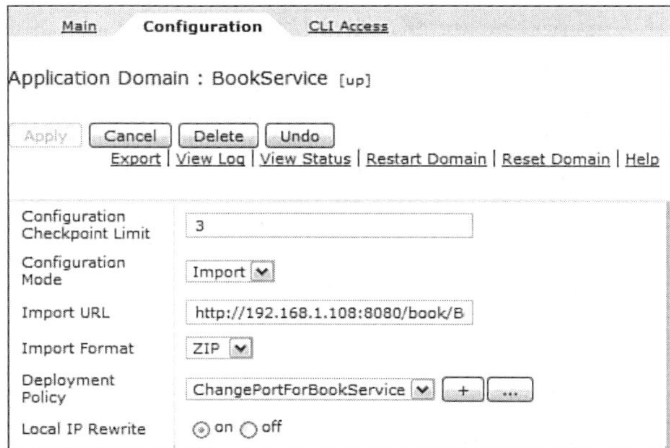

Figure 15-30 Domain configuration with imported configuration and deployment policy.

> **TIP—Always Use Secured Protocols for Fetching Configuration Data**
>
> Although the examples shown in Figure 15-30 show the use of HTTP, any production system should always use secured protocols such as HTTPS to protect configuration details from unscrupulous intermediaries.

Sample Device Configuration

There is no definitive methodology for configuration architecture. Figure 15-31 expands on our configuration fetch graphic of Figure 15-30 by demonstrating an option that provides for several desirable features. First, by relying on an SCM system as the repository for configuration, control and audit are provided. Second, modularity of the configuration is enhanced by separating device specific data from shared and service specific details.

In this scenario, each device contains a unique autoconfig.cfg configuration file. It defines the device specific properties and then fetches the shared configuration which itself contains (among other objects) the application domain definitions which then fetch their configuration from the SCM!

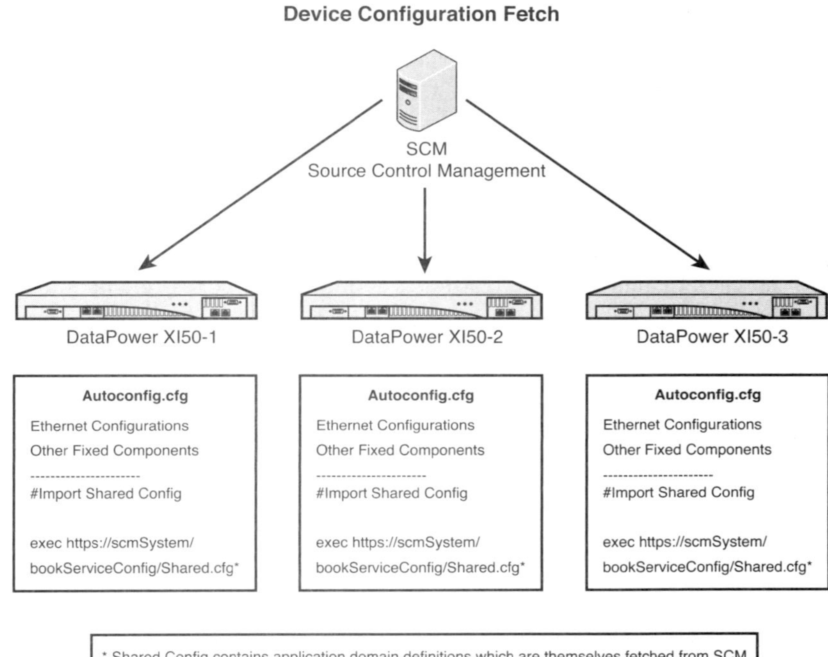

Figure 15-31 Configuration architecture with autoconfig.cfg.

Caution When Editing Device Configuration File

Care must be exercised when directly editing the onboard device configuration file. Specifically, you want to make sure you maintain the Ethernet interfaces. If you do not configure the interfaces, you will have no TCP access to the device! Similarly, make sure you define the WebGUI, SSH, XML Management Interface, and other configuration methods you intend to use. You can always get the current configuration by viewing or downloading the autoconfig.cfg file from the config: directory of the default domain. If you do not define the Ethernet interfaces, you can still get access to the device via the serial port. Please refer to the WebGUI Guide for your device for additional information.

> **Warning—Use Caution When Directly Editing Device Configuration Files!**
>
> You should have serial cable access as a backup. This does not require TCP access and can be used to access an unconfigured (or incorrectly configured) device.

Before you maintain the device configuration file you should

- Make an entire device backup via the WebGUI Export Utility.
- Copy the current autoconfig.cfg to another file in the device's config: directory.
- Have a serial cable and physical access to the device as a fail-safe plan for device access.

Fixed Component of config:///autoconfig.cfg

The example shown in Listing 15-11 demonstrates a sample bare-bones default domain configuration file, which could be uploaded to the config: directory of the device and identified as the boot config on the System Control Panel. It defines the Ethernet interface, host aliases, system contact info, and the WebGUI and the XML Management Interfaces.

It is important to note this represents an example of a fixed configuration file. Your implementation should be based on your particular requirements. The easiest way to define this configuration is to create the necessary objects via the WebGUI and to download the autoconfig.cfg file, make the necessary changes, and to then upload the file back onto the config: directory.

The configuration executes (via exec command) an off box configuration that contains configuration information shared by all devices in the environment. This shared configuration (shown shortly) contains the Application Domain definitions.

Listing 15-11 Sample Default Domain Fixed Config

```
configure terminal
# This is the fixed component of the 'Default' Domain for DataPower device
interface "eth0"
  ip address 192.168.1.35/24
  mtu 1500
  ip default-gateway 192.168.0.1
  arp
  mode 1000baseTx-FD
exit
interface "eth1"
  ip address 192.168.1.36/24
  mtu 1500
  ip default-gateway 192.168.0.1
  arp
  mode 1000baseTx-FD
exit
system
  contact "bookservice admin"
  name "prod bookservice Alpha"
  location "4th Floor Networking"
exit
host-alias "AuthenticatedTrustZone"
  reset
  ip-address 192.168.1.35
exit
```

```
host-alias "AuthenticatedAdminZone"
  reset
  ip-address 192.168.1.36
exit
# Web and XML-MGMT Interfaces can be restricted to a INT, # so put them in
Fixed Config
web-mgmt
  admin-state enabled
  local-address AuthenticatedAdminZone 9090
  idle-timeout 6000
exit
xml-mgmt
  admin-state enabled
  local-address AuthenticatedAdminZone 5050
  mode any+soma+v2004+amp+slm
exit
# Now pull in the variable part of the configuration,
# this is the same for all
# devices in this environment, i.e. Dev/Test/Prod
# This contains the application domain definitions
exec https://192.168.1.35:8080/SharedBookService.cfg
```

Shared Default Domain Configuration, Including Application Domain Definitions

The next example, shown in Listing 15-12, demonstrates a sample variable component of the default domain. It configures objects such as DNS, Simple Network Management Protocol (SNMP), and NTP that are shared by all devices in the environment. It also contains the definition of the bookService application domain that itself identifies an off-box location for its configuration and uses a Deployment Policy.

It is important to note this represents an example of a shared configuration file. Your implementation should be based on your particular requirements. The easiest way to define this configuration is to extract the shared components out of the autoconfig.cfg file downloaded from the config: directory.

Listing 15-12 Sample Default Domain Shared Config

```
# This is the variable component of the 'Default' Domain
# for all DataPower devices in an environment
dns
  admin-state enabled
  search-domain "some.com"
  name-server 152.155.21.10 53 53 0 3
  name-server 152.155.21.60 53 53 0 3
exit
alias "reload" "flash;boot config autoconfig.cfg;shutdown reload"
ntp-service
  admin-state disabled
  remote-server 152.159.20.10
```

```
  remote-server 152.159.20.60
exit
timezone EST5EDT
snmp
  admin-state enabled
  ip-address 192.168.0.52
  community "public" "default" "read-only" "AuthenticatedTrustZone"
exit
ssh AuthenticatedAdminZone 22
save-config overwrite
usergroup "BookService"
  summary "Book Service Admin"
  access-policy */BookService/*?Access=r+w+a+d+x
  access-policy */default/*?Access=r
exit
deployment-policy "ChangePortForBookService"
  accept */BookService/*
  modify
"*/BookService/services/xmlfirewall?Name=BookService1&Property=LocalPort
&Value=.*" "change" "LocalPort" "9901"
  modify
"*/BookService/services/xmlfirewall?Name=BookService2&Property=LocalPort
&Value=.*" "change" "LocalPort" "9902"
  modify
"*/BookService/services/xmlfirewall?Name=BookServiceRouter&Property=
LocalPort&Value=.*" "change" "LocalPort" "9900"
exit
domain "BookService"
  base-dir BookService:
  base-dir local:
  config-file BookService.cfg
  visible-domain default
  url-permissions "http+https+snmp+ftp+mailto+mq"
  file-permissions "CopyFrom+CopyTo+Delete+Display+Exec+Subdir"
  file-monitoring ""
  config-mode import
  import-url "https://192.168.1.09:8080/BookService.zip"
  deployment-policy changePortForBookService
exit
```

Service Promotion

Service promotion describes the migration of newly developed configuration specifications (typically services) through the Software Development Life Cycle (SDLC). This topic is vital for the control of configuration assets and availability of production systems. Changes to configuration must not cause service interruptions, and the configuration architecture must provide for a resilient, failsafe platform that is able to reconstruct itself to a known good synchronization point in the event of unexpected system restarts.

The Environments

The development environment is a no-holds-barred arena where new ideas may be developed and tested without the risk of hindering production systems or the functionality of other services. In the DataPower environment, domains may be created for special purposes, and individual services may be altered and their functionality unit tested without respect to other services that may exist on the device. In this environment, unfortunately often little attention is given to security restriction within the application domains because doing so may hinder creativity and productivity.

The test environment is a more stable arena. Its purpose is to validate configurations. This includes established, as well as newly modified, services because a change to one service may have an unintended effect on another. A testing mechanism includes a collection of scripted service interactions that validate all methods practical and compare those results to a collection of expected results. Many testing methodologies exist, and they may range from simple batch files with request and result compares, to the implementation of complex testing packages. In the test environment, security is critical. No one should be able to modify service configurations once they are established within the test environment so that the testing mechanism itself doesn't become compromised.

The acceptance environment serves two purposes. First, it serves as a validation mechanism across the entire device. Here all services are tested and validated. This ensures that not only are all the services within a domain functioning as required, but that no cross-domain dependencies have been affected. However, the acceptance environment's utility is truly in the validation of the mechanism in which the production system will ultimately be configured, and how it will fetch its configuration and respond to system events. As with the test environment, no one should be able to modify service configurations once they are established within the acceptance environment.

The production environment is of course why all the previous environments exist. The configuration method must ensure that the previously validated domain configurations are properly reconstructed in the event of a system event. This may be performed by utilizing DataPower configuration techniques, such as application domain definitions which fetch their configuration from external sources at startup, and inclusion of external configuration. Of course, no one should make application domain-level configuration changes on a production device.

Environmental Differences

In an ideal infrastructure, there would be no differences in the configuration of services across the SDLC environments. For example, the IP address of backend applications and identification repositories would be the same, queue names and other aspects of MQ topography would be consistent, and ports used for front side service requests would be consistent. Fortunately, DataPower has provided many mediating strategies to alleviate these differences. We have presented Host Aliases, Static Hosts, DNS, and other techniques that make these differences manageable. And we have also discussed the Deployment Policy and how it can be used to change configuration details during the configuration import process. Using these tools in conjunction with the export and import capabilities inherent in the device should make the vast majority of environmental differences manageable.

Application Promotion in Detail

Figure 15-32 demonstrates a complete promotion strategy from development through production. The Software Configuration Management (SCM) System plays an integral part in the facilitation of a secured and auditable configuration repository.

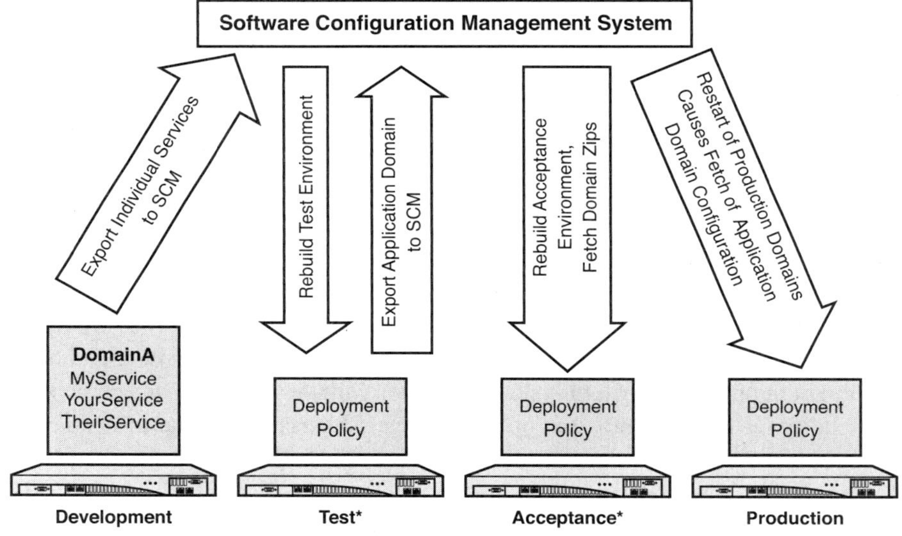

Figure 15-32 Application life cycle utilizing SCM and deployment policies for affinity resolution.

In the development environment, individual services are exported to the SCM upon successful completion of unit testing. This migration could be performed by the developer through the WebGUI export utility, or it may be part of an automated, scripted process that utilizes the XML-Management interface. In either case, the end result is an export that will be stored within the SCM. This technique serves two necessary functions; not only is an archival recording of the service configuration maintained, but the export of the individual service avoids the potential problem of exporting orphaned objects and other unnecessary configuration details that may be resident in the development domains. Had the entire domain been exported, these ancillary objects would have been part of the export, potentially corrupting the test, acceptance, and production environments.

Preparation for testing within the test environment is an automated, scripted process. First, the target domain is deleted from the device. This ensures that no residual objects remain that may effect testing either in a false positive or negative fashion. Second, all services associated with the target domain are imported from the SCM. These are the individual exports that the developers created from the development environment. This process will utilize a domain manifest that describes the individual services comprising a domain. Deployment policies are utilized to manage environmental differences. Upon completion of the domain-wide tests, the entire domain is exported to the SCM. There is no fear of orphaned objects in this export. This is a fresh domain that contains only the services that are required.

The acceptance environment is now established for complete device-level testing and production promotion validation. Once again, the domain is reconstructed via the scripted XML-Management interface, establishing a remote configuration with an Import URL pointing to the domain export that was created from the test environment. A deployment policy is established and utilized to address environmental differences. A restart of the domain causes the device to fetch the domain configuration from the SCM, and the domain is ready for acceptance testing.

Promotion to production is similar to that of acceptance. The domain is reconstructed and refreshed from the remote SCM repository, and deployment policies are used to address environmental differences. It is important to note that post-production verification must be performed to ensure that all went well before releasing the newly configured device.

The reader is encouraged to refer to a two-part IBM developerWorks article related to these topics: "Managing WebSphere DataPower SOA Appliance Configurations for High Availability, Consistency, and Control." Part one contains information relevant to the topics presented in this chapter. In addition, part two contains an example configuration complete with ANT scripts and executions of the XML-Management features required for an automated application promotion methodology.

Use of External Tools in Configuration Management

IBM provides several tools that assist in device management. For example, WAS version 7.0 manages multiple devices simultaneously. A single device can be managed to act as the configuration master for other devices. The methods we've discussed here still apply. However, these tools then distribute the configuration across the dependent devices. Please see Chapter 29, "Multiple Device Management Tools" for more information on the use of these tools.

Summary

There are many way to manage the configuration of the DataPower device. We demonstrated some basic principles that provide for a consistent configuration across device restarts and allow for a service promotion methodology. However, just as importantly, we discussed the significance of configuring a device in an environment neutral fashion, thereby avoiding problems that might be encountered during migration. Adherence to these principles will save you from having to address these issues later.

PART V

DataPower Security

CHAPTER 16

AAA

Now at last we focus on security. Somehow, it seems that this is always the way—security is an afterthought, that thing that is added two weeks before production in order to keep the auditors happy. And yet, DataPower is somehow different. These devices are built from the ground up with security in mind; at every level, security underlies everything you do with the appliance. It should come as no surprise, then, that there is very powerful out-of-the-box functionality to perform complex Authentication, Authorization, and Auditing, all with a few mouse clicks. This chapter examines those mouse clicks in more detail, exploring the powerful and flexible AAA framework and explaining how you can make it integrate into your particular environment.

AAA: The American Automobile Association?

In computer security, the term AAA (usually said as "triple A") is used to refer to the tripartite interaction pattern of user or entity security:

- **Authentication**—Ascertaining who the entity is
- **Authorization**—Determining what the entity can do
- **Accounting**—Tracking what a given entity has done

These concepts brought together are commonly referred to as Access Control. In DataPower, there is a strong framework for implementing this user interaction pattern, called the AAA framework.

Authentication

Authentication is the process of ascertaining who the user is. In order for a user or other entity to authenticate to the appliance, they must present some form of credential—be that a token, a username and password, a digital certificate, or any of the multitude of credential formats that DataPower supports (and DataPower can be extended to support more, as demonstrated in Chapter 17, "Advanced AAA"). On their own, such credentials are nothing more than an assertion—the equivalent of someone saying "I am Bob." In order for authentication to be trusted, the credentials presented have to be validated—perhaps the person claiming to be Bob could give you his passport, where the government of his home country certifies to you that he is Bob.

Credentials in the digital world are checked against a form of identity repository, and a decision needs to be made as to whether the credentials are valid. This might be as simple as checking a username and password combination against a list of valid usernames and passwords, or as complex as verifying the digital signature of a piece of signed XML, transforming the XML into a completely different credential format, and then passing that credential to an external authentication engine that will make the decision.

Authorization

After we know who the user is, we look at the resource the user is trying to access, and decide whether he is allowed or authorized to access it. DataPower is flexible enough to make authorization decisions in many different ways. It might be as simple as allowing any client who has successfully authenticated. (This is a valid authorization decision—different from simply allowing any request, for which there may also be a valid use case.) It might involve examining a list of users from a file, or checking for membership in an LDAP group, or using more sophisticated methods such as delegating the entire authorization decision to an external service.

Audit

After we know who the user is and what he can do, there are important actions that need to be taken in terms of monitoring and logging what happens during the AAA policy. This includes functionality to log successful and unsuccessful requests, and to maintain a counter of authorized and rejected requests, which can later be used as an input into more advanced accounting.

The Accounting stage is referred to in the context of a DataPower AAA policy as Audit. This makes sense in a DataPower context—the Accounting capabilities of the appliance go far beyond security. DataPower's accounting capabilities include fine-grained usage logging if desired, prioritization of services, dynamic service level management (SLM), and throttling responses based on many trigger points, including consumption of resources. The AAA framework in DataPower focuses only on the security specific Accounting capabilities, such as monitoring and logging issues relating to the earlier AAA steps. It is explicitly to differentiate this from all the other powerful Accounting functionality on the device that the AAA-specific accounting is known in the AAA framework as Audit.

Post Processing

Post Processing (PP) doesn't begin with an A? Perhaps the framework should be named AAAPP, because this final step in the DataPower AAA framework is one of the most important. PP enables DataPower, after it has completed its verification of who the user is and whether he is allowed to access the resource he tried to access, to perform any other relevant processing of the request, the contents, the tokens, the credentials, the identity, or anything else, such that it integrates into your environment and works within the enterprise security idiom of your organization. Out of the box, the PP stage can perform powerful actions such as generating a SAML assertion or calling out to Tivoli Federated Identity Manager (TFIM); by using XSLT you can perform almost any action imaginable.

Clearly, there is much more to security than AAA. Other chapters in this book focus on aspects of security, including network security (Chapter 4, "Advanced DataPower Networking"), SSL (Chapter 18, "DataPower and SSL"), Web Services Security (Chapter 19, "Web Services Security"), XML threats (Chapter 20, "XML Threats"), and Security Integration with WebSphere Application Server (Chapter 21, "Security Integration with WebSphere Application Server"). These other chapters discuss transport and message processing, which are important parts of the appliance's functionality. This chapter and Chapter 17 focus explicitly on access control and the AAA framework.

AAA Policy Stages

The AAA framework actually does substantially more than "just" authentication, authorization, and audit. The process is broken up into a number of sequential stages, with the output of each stage feeding in to the input of the next. Every stage of the process is fully customizable, both with multiple out of the box options for each stage selectable with a simple mouse click and parameters, and by writing custom XSLT (we cover this in Chapter 17).

Figure 16-1 shows a flow diagram of the way a AAA policy works.

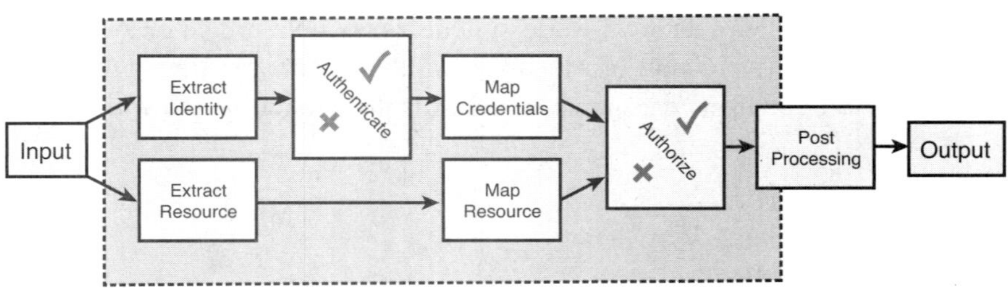

Figure 16-1 Processing phases of a AAA Policy.

The various stages are shown with the order in which they are called. This section examines each stage in depth. Each stage is also referred to by an abbreviation, which is shown in the section headings; for example, Extract Identity is abbreviated to EI, and the authentication stage is commonly abbreviated to AU (in contrast with the authorization stage, which is shortened to AZ).

Extract Identity (EI)

To perform authentication, the entity wanting to authenticate needs to provide a form of credentials. For the vast majority of Internet-facing network servers, this is a static concept. The server is configured so that it accepts one or more specific forms of authentication. In DataPower, however, we can explicitly choose what part of the incoming message we will use as the identity. This stage is known as Identity Extraction, and is commonly referred to as the EI (Extract Identity) phase.

Because a AAA policy is usually deployed as part of an overall Processing Policy, which is started with a match action, we can make a dynamic runtime decision about what we use for the identity, based on the request itself. This gives us a huge amount of flexibility; the result of the match action can determine the type of credentials we decide to use. For example, imagine a business requirement where we have to accept either a Kerberos AP-REQ[1] via SPNEGO (from an internal network where people must be authenticated to a Kerberos KDC), or a specific SSL certificate (for connections that are not expected to be authenticated via Kerberos). The selection might be based on the IP address of the incoming request, a specific HTTP header signed by a reverse proxy, or any other kind of match, which can be specified within the scope of a Processing Policy. In addition, a single AAA policy can actually support multiple methods of identity extraction, although this will have implications on later stages if those stages cannot support one or other of the methods desired!

In the example in Figure 16-2, the AAA policy is set up to extract identity from either:

- **HTTP Basic Authentication**—This is a special HTTP header containing a base-64 encoded username/password combination.
- **A UserNameToken (UNT) in the WS-Security Header**—This also contains a username and password, albeit in an XML token format.

In this instance, the appliance extracts any of these that are available and passes it on to the next stage, Authentication.

There are many options available out of the box. Don't get overwhelmed by all the options! This is going to be a common pattern; all the stages have many possible configurations out of the box, and more with customization. IBM tries to interoperate with as many standards, large market share proprietary solutions, and real-world systems as possible, which means that there will be a lot of choices at each step, most of which you will likely not use. Simply think about your specific infrastructure, and then concentrate on the parts that are relevant to you, and you won't go wrong!

[1] Kerberos is an established trusted third-party security system, and SPNEGO is a protocol for passing a Kerberos token as part of a negotiation over HTTP. More information on these excellent security protocols is available in product documentation, especially in Appendix D of the WebGUI Guide for firmware versions 3.6.1 and above.

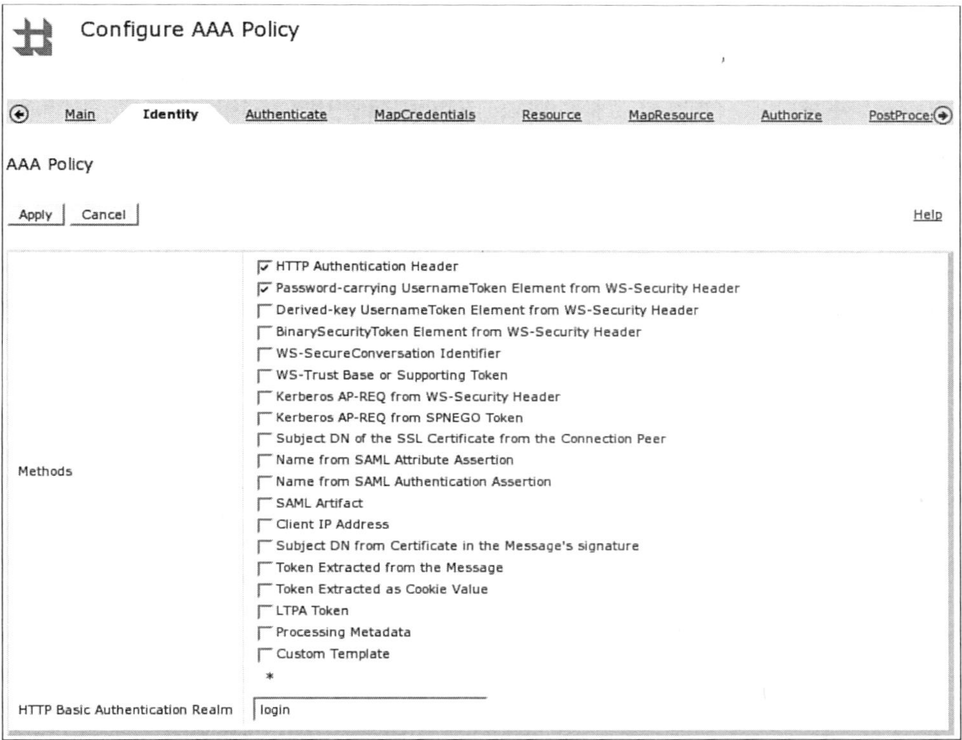

Figure 16-2 Identity Extraction options.

Authentication (AU)

The Authenticate stage takes as its input the output of the identity extraction stage, and defines the method used to authenticate the credentials provided. The number of methods available out of the box is staggering; a list is shown in Figure 16-3.

Different configuration options display on the screen depending on the method chosen from the drop-down list. The options include sending the credentials to a variety of supported external servers including Tivoli Access Manager, Siteminder, ClearTrust, and RADIUS, processing them directly by validating digital signatures or other tokens, using a custom AAA Info file that will be explained later in this chapter, and even simply passing the credentials as-is to the authorize step.

The result of authentication is either an authenticated identity or, in the case of a failure, a lack of identity; the identity is successfully authenticated or it isn't. However, processing continues irrespective of whether authentication is successful. This is because there might be some specific processing that needs to be done even for unsuccessful authentication. For instance, we might want to write an audit record, or create a generic "guest" credential, or redirect to a different service that provides a more detailed form of login.

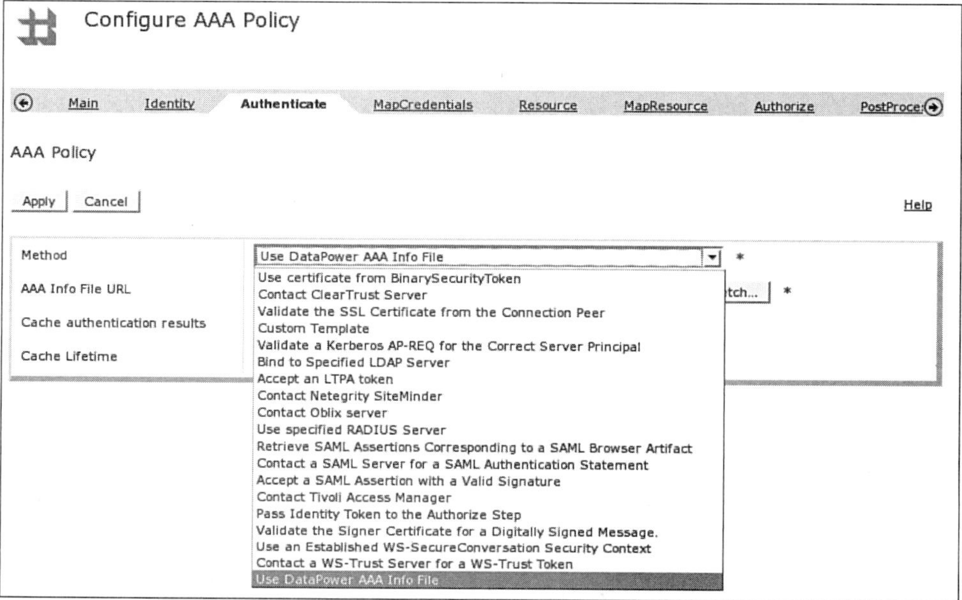

Figure 16-3 Available authentication methods.

After the identity is authenticated, a credential is output and passed to the next step, for credential mapping.

Map Credentials (MC)

The next stage, Map Credentials (MC), is optional; many AAA policies will not use a map credentials step at all. The purpose of the map credentials step is to take the credentials that have been validated in the authentication step and map them to a different format by performing some kind of processing on them.

An example use of this might be where the authentication step is done against one kind of external service, but the authorization stage is against another. For example, the original authentication might be done using a custom signed token, which is then needed to be mapped into a specific distinguished name so that an authorization service based on LDAP could be used to determine group memberships.

The credential mapping options available are shown in Figure 16-4. The number of possible transformations and mappings is immense and can be used for everything from mapping external users to internal users, to transformation of token types such that a different authorization system can understand them. Some credential mapping implementations will of necessity use custom stylesheets or an XPath expression to map the credentials according to an implementation-specific algorithm. For simpler requirements, it is also possible to use a AAA-Info file as described later in this chapter to provide a simple static mapping.

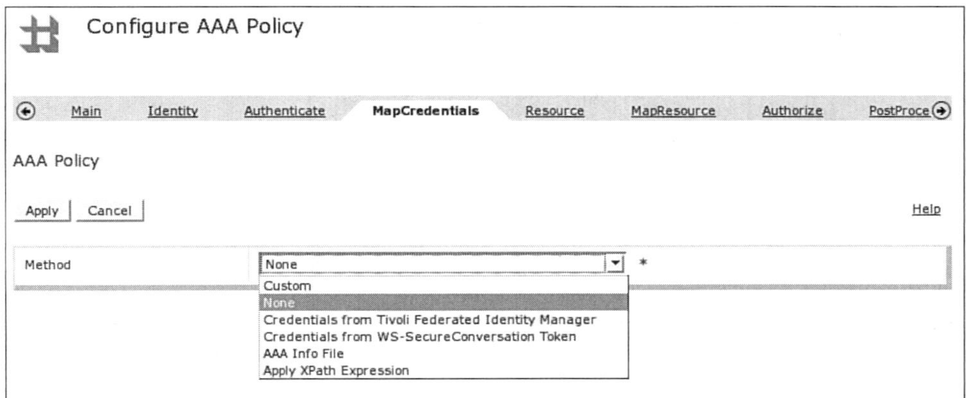

Figure 16-4 Available credential mapping methods.

There are two special cases for credential mapping that are worthy of note. The first of these has to do with the WS-SecureConversation specification. A part of that specification, WS-Trust, can contain a "context token," which is the token representing the user or entity carrying out the conversation. The map credentials step has out-of-the-box functionality to use this context token as the identity. More information on WS-SecureConversation can be found in Chapter 19.

The second special case is that of TFIM, which can be used to perform external token transformation; DataPower will pass the incoming credentials to the TFIM trust service, and it in turn will return appropriate credentials to be used further.

Extract Resource (ER)

The next step identifies the resource upon which an authorization decision should be made. As with identity extraction, DataPower is far more flexible with this than the majority of "normal" servers. For example, typical Web application servers perform authorization based on the URL that the client requests. DataPower can do the same, or it can base the resource on any part of the incoming request. This can include HTTP headers, the type of operation or method (HTTP GET or HTTP POST), or even an XPath expression representing a value within the incoming structure. The options available are shown in Figure 16-5.

For Web Services traffic, by far the most common Web service resource to specify is the one named "Local Name of the Request Element." This will usually refer to the operation name in the Web service, which allows for granular authorization of a particular operation.

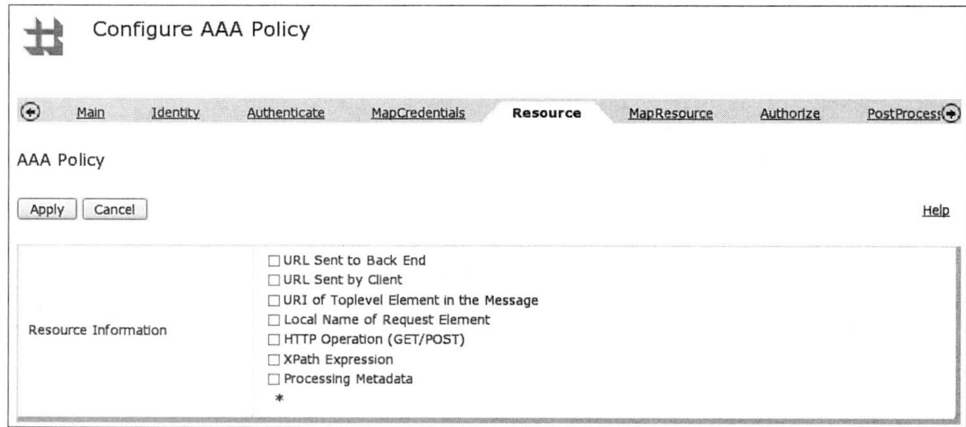

Figure 16-5 Available resource identification methods.

Of particular interest here are the HTTP Operation and Processing Metadata options. HTTP Operation actually refers to the HTTP protocol request method invoked by the client. By choosing the HTTP Operation as the resource, it is possible to authorize a read operation differently than a write operation; this is a relatively common requirement in some situations. An HTTP GET is always a read operation, and an HTTP POST is always a write operation. Note that HTTP GET is not common with Web services, and indeed is disabled by default on the DataPower HTTP FSH, but is often used in other XML remote procedure call implementations such as REST, as well as in plain Web traffic. In addition, this option can be used on the XI50 for non-HTTP traffic; for instance, with an FTP Server FSH choosing the HTTP Operation for the resource allows authorization of FTP uploads differently (PUT) than FTP downloads (GET).

The Processing Metadata option allows for the resource to be defined based on what is known as "transport metadata." This metadata, also available for the identity extraction step, is simply a set of preconfigured medium-specific fields, which might be interesting for processing requests of that type. These can include information extracted from the incoming message, such as header values specific to the protocol used, or internal information from the appliance processing scope, such as system variables.

This is a powerful concept. For instance, let's say that we want to choose as our resource a specific HTTP header in the request, the Content-Type header. The rationale for this might be that, if a client is requesting a double-byte character set (DBCS) content type, we want to perform authorization differently. To extract this resource, we can write a complicated XPath expression or XSLT to identify the specific value from the request, or we can configure a processing metadata item as shown in Figure 16-6.

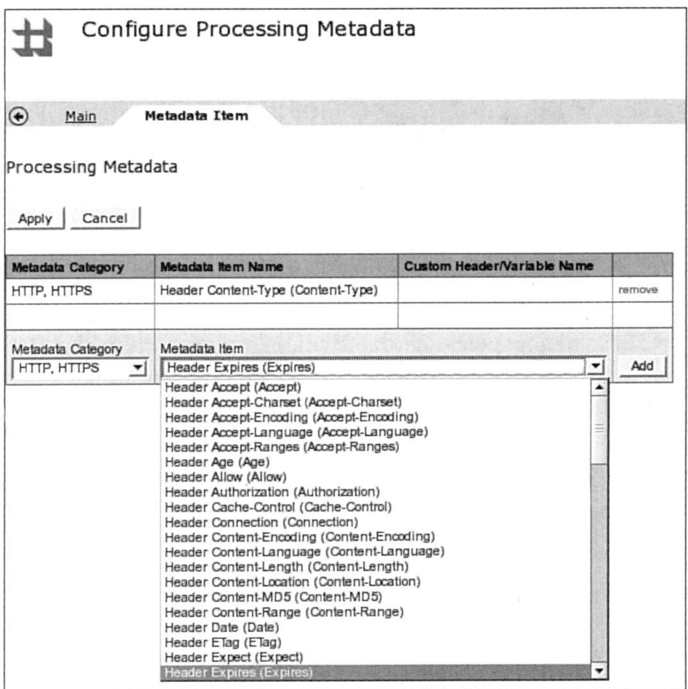

Figure 16-6 Processing metadata.

This metadata item is preconfigured to extract the exact header we need, specific to the protocol. It could just as easily be configured to extract a WebSphere MQ header, as shown in Figure 16-7.

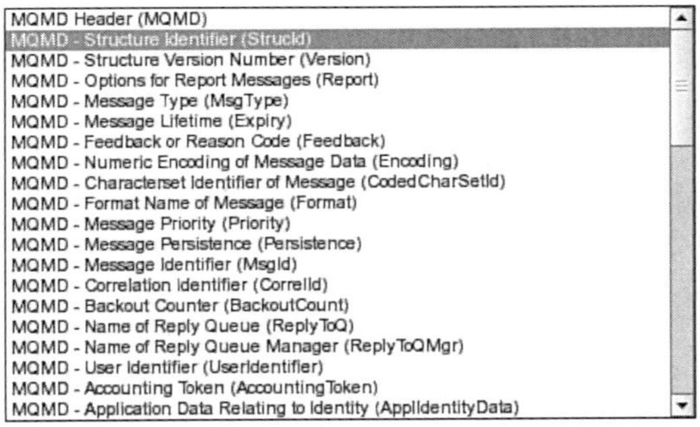

MQMD Header (MQMD)
MQMD - Structure Identifier (StrucId)
MQMD - Structure Version Number (Version)
MQMD - Options for Report Messages (Report)
MQMD - Message Type (MsgType)
MQMD - Message Lifetime (Expiry)
MQMD - Feedback or Reason Code (Feedback)
MQMD - Numeric Encoding of Message Data (Encoding)
MQMD - Characterset Identifier of Message (CodedCharSetId)
MQMD - Format Name of Message (Format)
MQMD - Message Priority (Priority)
MQMD - Message Persistence (Persistence)
MQMD - Message Identifier (MsgId)
MQMD - Correlation Identifier (CorrelId)
MQMD - Backout Counter (BackoutCount)
MQMD - Name of Reply Queue (ReplyToQ)
MQMD - Name of Reply Queue Manager (ReplyToQMgr)
MQMD - User Identifier (UserIdentifier)
MQMD - Accounting Token (AccountingToken)
MQMD - Application Data Relating to Identity (ApplIdentityData)

Figure 16-7 MQ options for processing metadata.

Other options include a Tibco EMS header, a WebSphere JMS header, and many other kinds of information about the incoming request. For instance, we could specify the specific Frontside Service Address over which the request came, allowing us to authorize differently based on the Ethernet interface over which the request was retrieved. We encourage you to explore this useful and powerful functionality.

Map Resource (MR)

In addition to extracting resources in several ways, DataPower can further refine the input into the authorization step. The resource mapping stage allows you to examine the existing resources for a pattern and map multiple different, yet similar, resources into a single logical resource, such that you can then perform a more coarse-grained authorization based on that logical resource.

For example, let's say that we have extracted the simplest type of resource for an inbound Web service—the URL sent by the client. This is a common use case when integrating with external security systems that perform access control based on URL, of which there are many. In this instance, we know that the URLs will represent the required action, because our application happens to follow the same pattern for all URLs. The URL pattern is `/Brand/AccountType/Operation,` such that all the URLs shown in Listing 16-1 are effectively the `apply` operation.

Listing 16-1 URL Patterns to Process

```
/redbank/premium/apply
/redbank/standard/apply
/bluebank/premium/apply
/bluebank/standard/apply
```

The map resource step could be used to translate all these URLs into a single resource identifier—perhaps simply the word `APPLY`—which will then be much easier to perform authorization against. How do we actually do this? The options are shown in Figure 16-8.

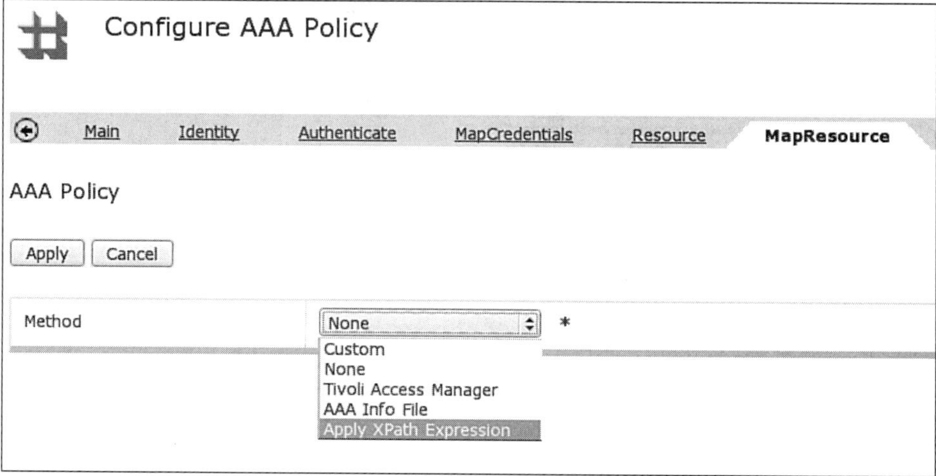

Figure 16-8 Resource mapping options.

We could write a stylesheet to perform the resource mapping and specify that stylesheet using the Custom method. Or we could use XPath to point at the specific information we need. The resource mapping could be externalized to Tivoli Access Manager, where it performs a mapping to add the resource into the TAM Object Space (or TAMBI or TFIM) such that subsequent authorization against TAM is possible. Or the AAA Info File provides an internal method of performing resource mapping—this last option is shown in Figure 16-9.

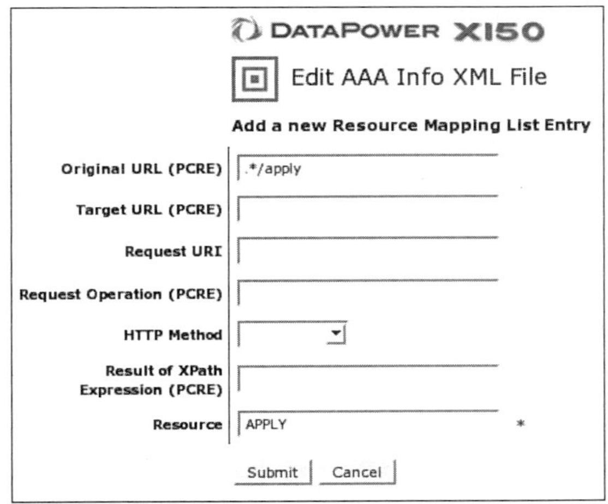

Figure 16-9 Resource mapping using AAA info.

Authorization (AZ)

Now that we finally have an identity (which has been extracted from the incoming message, has either passed or failed authentication, and has optionally been mapped to a more meaningful credential) and a resource (which has been identified flexibly from within the incoming message and optionally mapped to a coarser grained resource), we can make an authorization decision. The decision is relatively simple: Can this specific identity access this specific resource, yes or no? The process by which the decision is reached can be implemented in many ways. Figure 16-10 shows the options available.

The simplest option is Allow Any Authenticated Client. This means that if the request has successfully passed the Authenticate stage, it will automatically be allowed through irrespective of which resource it is trying to access. This is a valid use case for surprisingly many scenarios—quite often, simply authenticating an incoming request is considered to be "enough" at this level. (Although this is usually combined with more fine-grained authorization later down the line on a backend server.)

Figure 16-10 Authorization options.

Note that this option is very different from the option named Always Allow. The difference might not be clear at first, but the subtlety is that if you select Always Allow, all requests will be allowed through, even those that failed authentication. It is possible that there are some valid use cases for this, but it is likely not to be what you want. After all, if you intend to allow all connections through, why put in a AAA policy at all? One possible scenario might be where user identity is used for personalization and not access control—if we know who the user is, we can give them personalized content, but if not then they simply get a generic page.

A number of the authorization methods allow for externalizing the authorization decision. That is, rather than making the decision on the device itself, the information about the authenticated user and the resource they are trying to access is sent to an external server, which then makes the decision. External servers supported out of the box in this manner are Tivoli Access Manager, ClearTrust, and SiteMinder.

Other common methods of making an authorization decision based on external input are also supported out of the box. For example, we can simply check for membership in a specific LDAP group. This works by looking up the specific group that users must be a member of in the LDAP server, retrieving a list of all the members of that group, and checking whether the authenticated user is included in that list. This is not quite the same as externalization, since the appliance makes the authorization decision itself based on input from the external server, rather than relying on the external server to make the decision. We can also use SAML to make an authorization or attribute query, and we can make a call to an external XACML PDP (XML Access Control Markup Language Policy Decision Point).

If the preceding isn't enough, we can also make the authorization decision on box, including using a AAA Info file, a local XACML PDP, or even a custom piece of XSLT, which can do almost anything we need it to do (including make calls out to external services if required).

Although authorization is a simple yes or no decision, DataPower offers substantial integration options and flexibility to enable the decision to be made based on whatever is meaningful to your specific situation.

Post Processing (PP)

The final stage, Post Processing (PP), is optional, but at the same time is possibly the most important value-add from the AAA processing in DataPower. PP can be used to perform any required action after the AAA Policy has completed. Most commonly this involves creating credentials, which will be used on the call to the backend server. In these use cases, DataPower acts as a simple token changer, exchanging one set of frontend credentials for an entirely new backend credential supported by the backend server. This allows us to use a frontend credential mechanism of our choice while integrating with various standard credential mechanisms on the backend—out of the box for many standards!

Out of the box, IBM provides a number of options for creating backend credentials. These are shown in Figure 16-11.

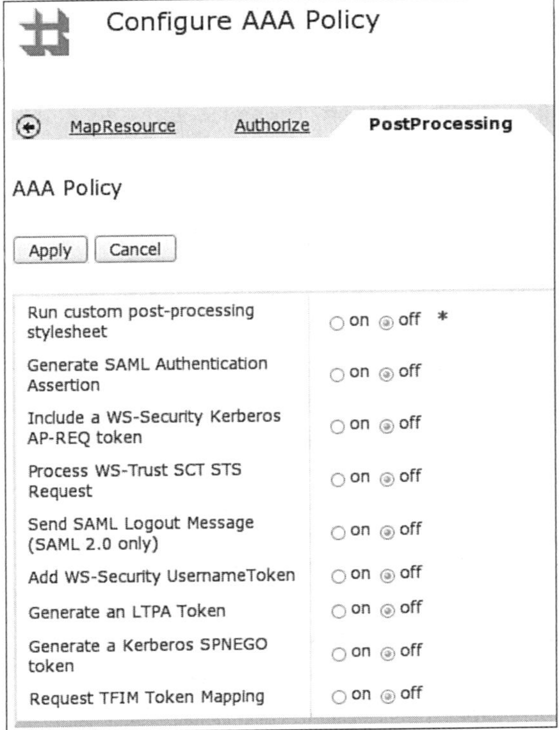

Figure 16-11 PP options.

Some of these options exist to propagate the authenticated credentials to the backend server. For example, the Add WS-Security UsernameToken generates a UNT, which contains the username and password output from the Map Credentials stage. In the same way, Generate an LTPA Token creates a Lightweight Third-Party Authentication (LTPA) token for the authenticated user, and Generate a SAML Authentication Assertion provides an assertion in SAML format to state who the authenticated user is.

The Kerberos options (AP-REQ token and SPNEGO) provide a modicum of extra security by passing a static credential for the backend to consume, potentially providing a level of trust between DataPower and the backend. These options are only capable of creating Kerberos credentials for a specific user whose keytab is contained on the appliance. This has to do with the way Kerberos works—it is impossible to generate a Kerberos credential for a user whose password or keytab we do not have, and we might not have it depending on how they authenticated to us! Thus, this use of Kerberos is to represent the appliance as a system user, rather than propagating actual user credentials. (Although this identity might be used to establish trust over which actual user credentials might be asserted, for instance.)

Other options include participating in a WS-SecureConversation by processing a SecurityContextToken request and acting as a WS-Trust Secure Token Service, and requesting a token mapping from Tivoli Federated Identity Manager.

Finally, as with all the other stages of AAA processing, we can run our own custom XSLT to perform any processing we choose. This processing has access to all the outputs of the previous stages, and with some assembly required, enough work can be used to provide almost any form of backend integration required.

Configuring AAA in DataPower

DataPower's AAA framework is built around one main configuration object called the AAA Policy. This policy is used in many contexts to provide a common configuration idiom for AAA functionality—it can be run as an action in a Processing Policy, attached directly to specific FSHs, and even specified in the profiles of a Web Application Firewall. This common configuration object means that often there are many fields that are not specified, because they are not relevant for a specific configuration, but it also means that the entire required configuration is easy to find irrespective of the deployment context.

There are two ways to create a AAA policy object via the WebGUI: using a sequential wizard, which allows for context-sensitive creation of policies that support the majority of use cases, or by using the object page, which gives access to configuration options not available via the wizard.

An often asked question is: Which of these methods should be used? In most cases, when prototyping, creating processing policies, and generally developing configurations, the wizard is used. It is there when needed, and enables you to quickly create a AAA policy without leaving the context of what you are doing in the GUI. This functionality is valuable. However, there is also much to be said for developing the AAA policy independently of the surrounding configuration, by using the object page. This approach allows for a more considered design of AAA policy, and more often leads to creation of policies that are reused in multiple configurations where the authentication and authorization processes are the same. Thus there are advantages to both methods.

The AAA Policy Object Menu

The previous figures in this chapter all show the AAA Policy Object. To use this for creating a AAA policy, go directly to the object page, using Objects→XML Processing→AAA Policy in the left-side menu. This option gives access to all possible configuration settings, but provides a far more complex configuration screen with multiple tabs and many more options on each tab. The AAA policy object page is shown in Figure 16-12.

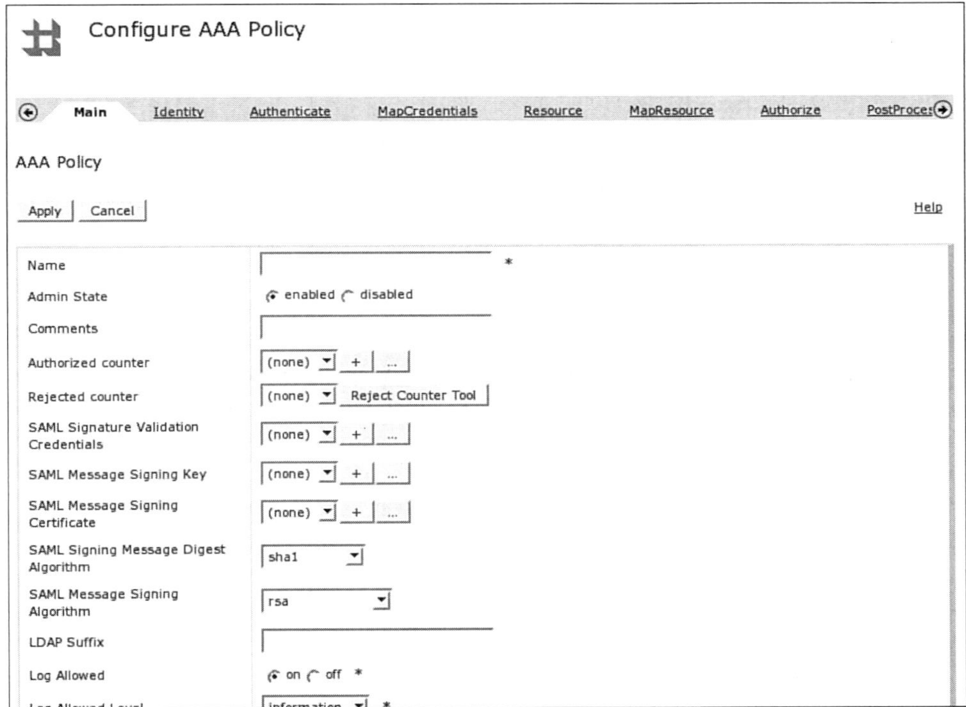

Figure 16-12 A AAA Policy can also be configured directly from the objects page.

The majority of settings can also be configured from within the wizard, and which method you use ends up to be a mixture of personal preference and the order in which you configure the various objects on the device. Many sites will mix the two, perhaps using the wizard for initial configuration followed by manual changes on the object page.

The AAA Policy Wizard

Wherever a AAA policy is required, there is the typical drop-down list of existing policies, and a plus sign or ellipsis button that can be clicked on to launch a wizard. For example, when adding a AAA action to a Processing Policy, the option shown in Figure 16-13 appears; clicking on the plus sign launches the wizard to add the AAA action, which takes you through a configuration process.

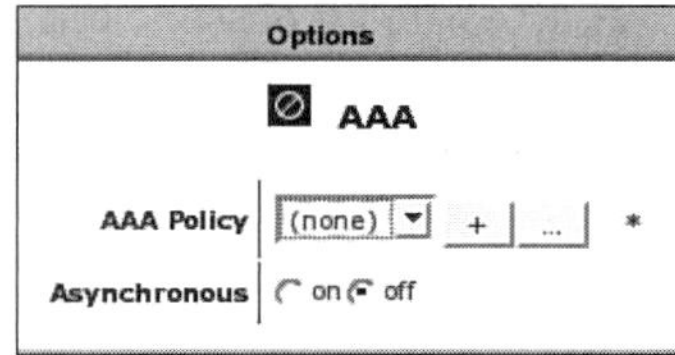

Figure 16-13 The AAA Policy wizard can be launched from anywhere a AAA policy is needed.

The wizard provides a step-by-step process for configuring a AAA policy. This is a less complicated configuration method, as can be expected from a wizard. Some advanced options that are perhaps less common are not shown in the wizard, in order to present a simpler view, which covers the majority of use cases. In addition, because the wizard is sequential, it encourages the user to think about each step of AAA separately.

Let's look at the creation of a simple AAA policy using the wizard. For now, we will shoot through and examine the process; the rest of the chapter will go into the details of what the options mean. It is vital at this stage not to be overwhelmed with the number of options available! In all likelihood you will use only a small subset of them, but because the appliance supports so many options out of the box, you are probably in the nice position that the specific subset applicable to your particular configuration is supported simply on the device.

Let's say we want to create a simple policy to protect access to specific URLs. We enforce security through the use of HTTP Basic Authentication, with a set of usernames and passwords that we can define in a file, along with a list of which user is allowed to access which URL. This simple requirement can easily be implemented by clicking a few buttons in the wizard.

Start with clicking the plus sign (see Figure 16-13) to start the wizard. The first screen of the wizard asks for a name for the policy; after this is supplied, the next screen pops up and asks you how you would like to identify the users, as shown in Figure 16-14.

To enforce the use of HTTP Basic Authentication, we have selected "HTTP Authentication Header" from the wizard. Ignore the other options for now; we will get to them in time.

TIP—Online Help

The online help for AAA is particularly useful. By clicking the Identification Methods hotlink shown on the left side of Figure 16-14, we are taken to a screen that explains each of the methods in turn—the same is true for all the stages in the wizard.

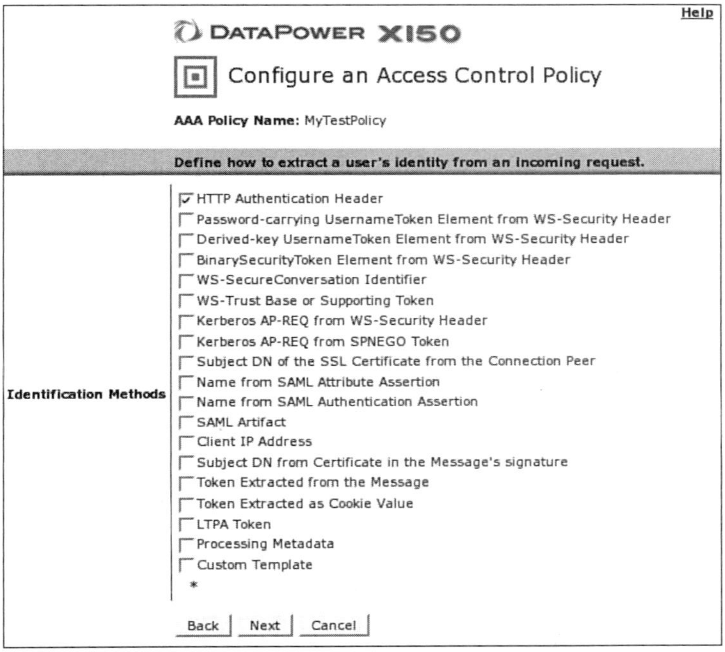

Figure 16-14 How do I identify my clients?

Clicking on Next takes us to the third wizard screen, where we decide how to perform authentication. In this case, we want to specify a simple set of users with passwords and create rules about which URLs each of them can access. The rules we define are shown in Table 16-1.

Table 16-1 Users, Passwords, and Access Rights

User	Password	/public	/private	/secret
Alice	password1	Yes	No	No
Bob	password2	Yes	Yes	No
Charlie	password3	Yes	Yes	Yes

These rules are simple and are designed only to demonstrate the functionality; obviously no organization's access control would be this simplistic! Likewise, we use HTTP Basic Auth for simplicity here; it is rarely used for direct user access to applications, where a login form and form parameters would more likely be presented to users.

Figure 16-15 shows the third screen.

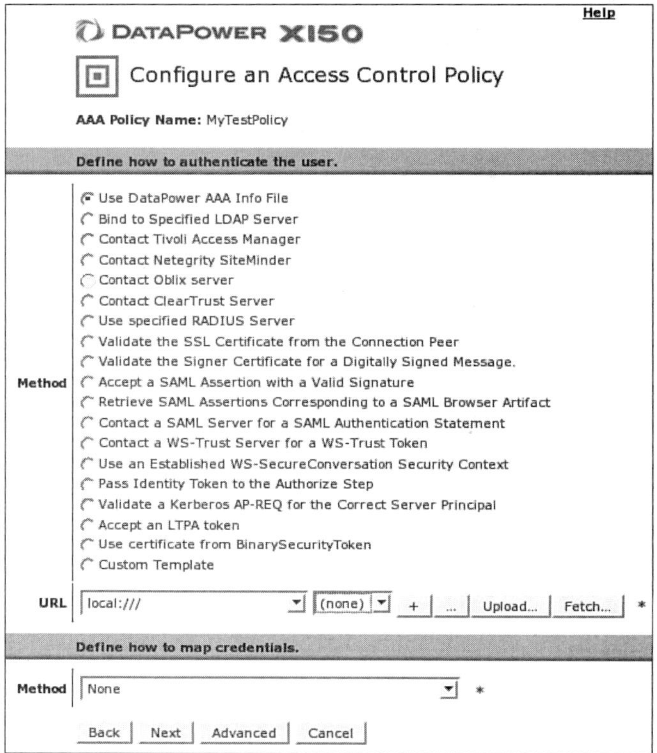

Figure 16-15 How do I authenticate my users?

Note that the option "Use DataPower AAA Info File" is selected. This is an on-device file format, which allows us to provide input into a AAA policy—a simple place to store information such as that shown in Table 16-1. More detail of the structure of the AAA Info file is provided later, but for now we simply use the helpful wizard to create one. At the bottom, under "URL," is where we specify the file to use; we can click on the + sign to create a new file.

The first page of the AAA Info wizard is shown in Figure 16-16.

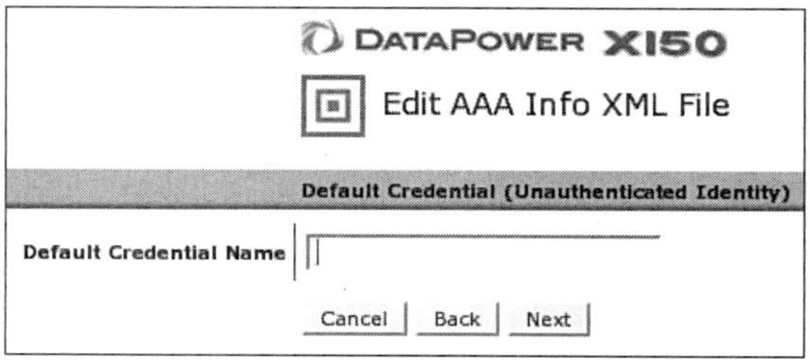

Figure 16-16 Default credential name.

Default Credential is the name used to identify people who try to access protected resources but do not provide a valid credential. This can be a powerful concept; it allows you to explicitly supply a username, which can later be used for making authorization decisions. By leaving it blank, we will state that any requests that do not provide valid credentials should not have any credential passed to the authorization step, and thus should likely be denied.

The next page of the AAA Info wizard shows our list of authenticated identities. These must be populated by clicking the Add button. Figure 16-17 shows us adding the entry for our first user, Alice.

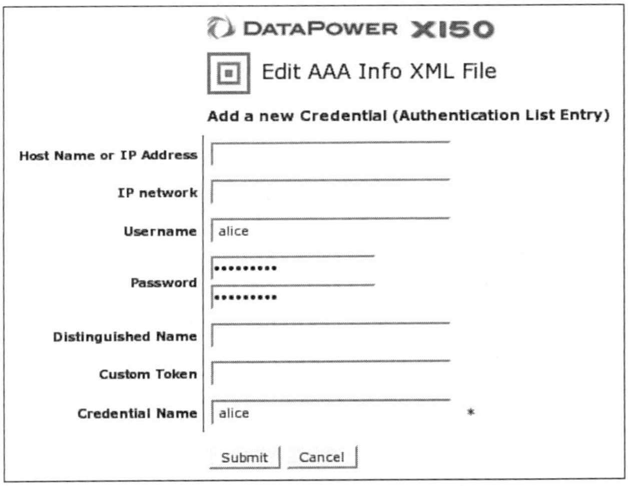

Figure 16-17 Add a new credential.

Note that we have put the word alice twice into Figure 16-17: first as the username, and second as the credential. The username is the name that alice must actually type in for HTTP basic authentication to work; the credential is what the appliance uses to identify her after the authentication has been checked. In our example, we use the same word, but the credential name is arbitrary. We could also specify a number of users with the same "credential" to write access control rules for them all at once—for instance, credentials called "validuser" and "superuser" might be used to define two different groups of users, for whom we can then write specific access control rules. Figure 16-18 shows the final list of users and the credentials they will use.

After clicking next, we get to the next page of the wizard, which is used for mapping credentials; we will not use this page for our sample. Following this is another page we will not use for the sample, regarding mapping of resources. The next page is used for authorization of access to resources. This is where we specify our actual access control rules: which user can access what URL. Again rules must be specified individually, so click Add to see how to add these, as shown in Figure 16-19.

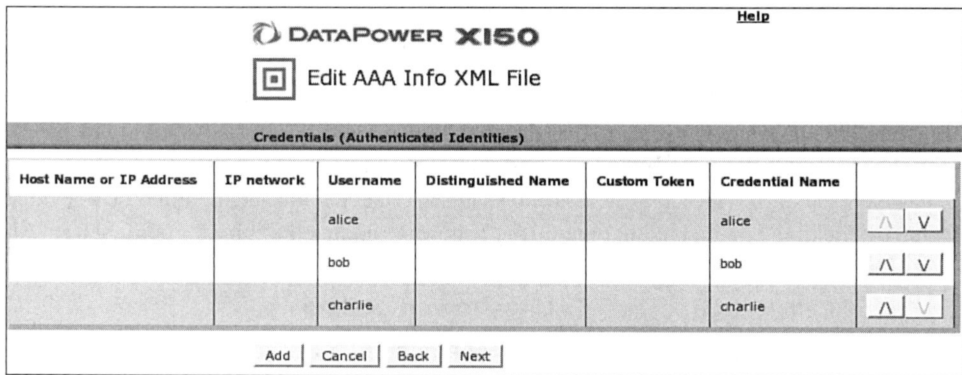

Figure 16-18 All users and their credentials.

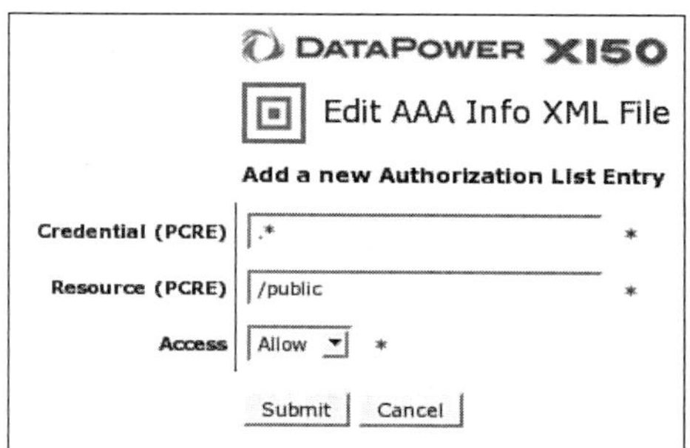

Figure 16-19 Adding an access control rule for /public.

Figure 16-19 shows the adding of a rule for the resource `/public`. This rule is somewhat special, in that the credential required to access public is defined as the Perl Compatible Regular Expression `.*`, which matches anything. Thus, all users can access the URL `/public`. The final list of access control rules is shown in Figure 16-20.

> ### TIP—Removing Entries
>
> To remove an entry from the list, click the credential, resource, or access level to enter the edit screen for that entry, from which you can subsequently remove it by clicking the Delete button. The Delete button is available only on the edit screen, not on the original entry screen!

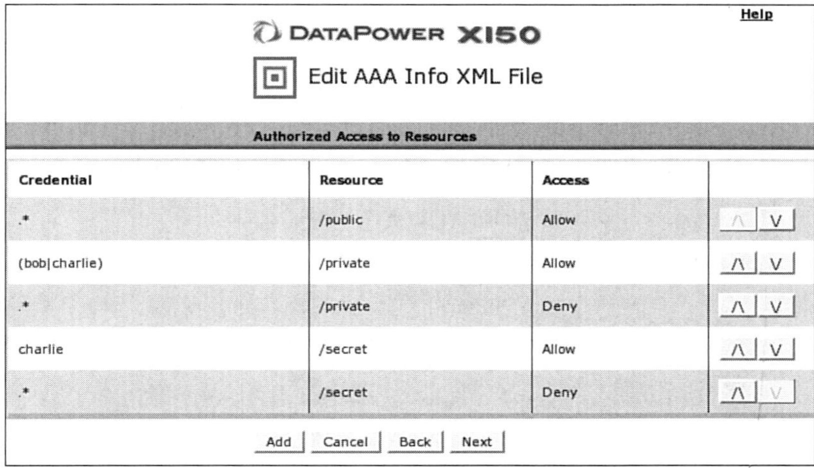

Figure 16-20 Access control rules.

Note again the use of Perl Compatible Regular Expressions to specify two credentials in a single line, with `(bob|charlie)`. Note also that we have explicitly put in a line denying all credentials other than those that have been explicitly allowed. This is not strictly speaking required (if a credential has no Allow entry it will default to Deny), but does not hurt, and it is a good general practice to explicitly deny.

Now that we have our definitions of users and credentials and access control rules, we can click next and specify where on the device to save the resulting file, as depicted in Figure 16-21.

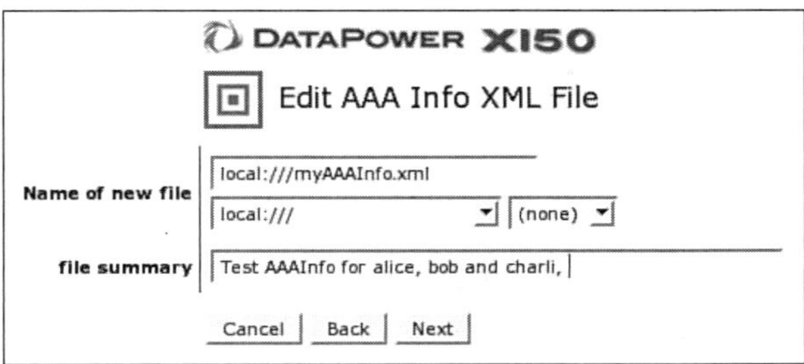

Figure 16-21 Save the file to the device.

After it is saved, we return to the original AAA Policy wizard, where the new AAA Info file is now selected in the URL field at the bottom of the window as shown in Figure 16-22.

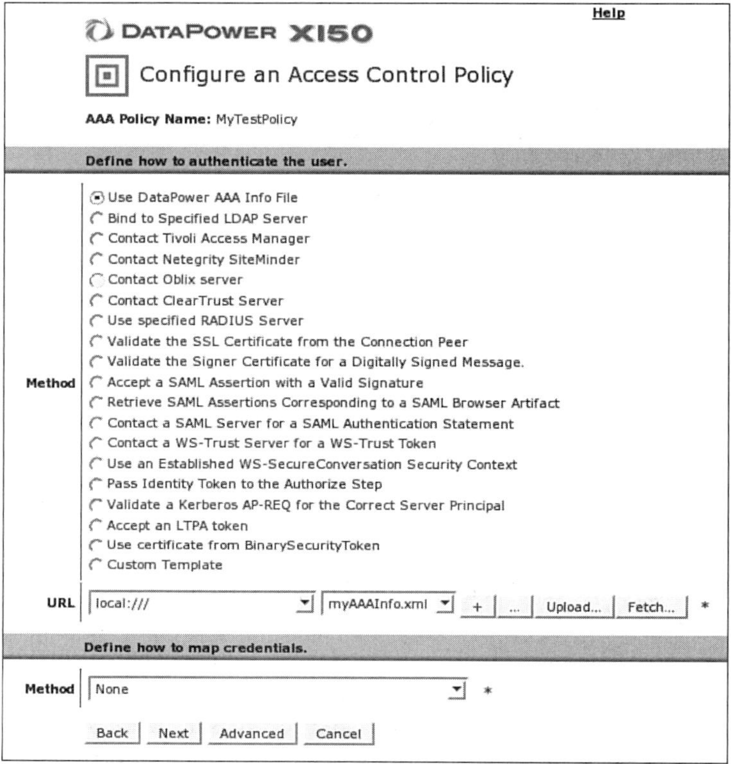

Figure 16-22 Back to the AAA Policy wizard.

For this example, we leave the Map Credentials method at the bottom as None; this step is described in more detail later in the chapter. Clicking on Next goes to the Resource Extraction Methods screen, shown in Figure 16-23.

For our example, the resource we want to protect is the URL that the client requests, as per our definition in Table 16-1. We select URL Sent by Client because this function is available out of the box. Leave the map resources method as "None," and click Next to access the authorization page of the wizard, as shown in Figure 16-24.

Note that we selected the same AAA Info file that we created earlier. Although the whole file was created in one step with the easy-to-use wizard, the various parts of it match with the stages of the AAA policy; it is at this authorization stage that we actually implement checking of the access control rules for the resources we have defined.

Clicking Next leads to the final screen of the wizard, as depicted in Figure 16-25.

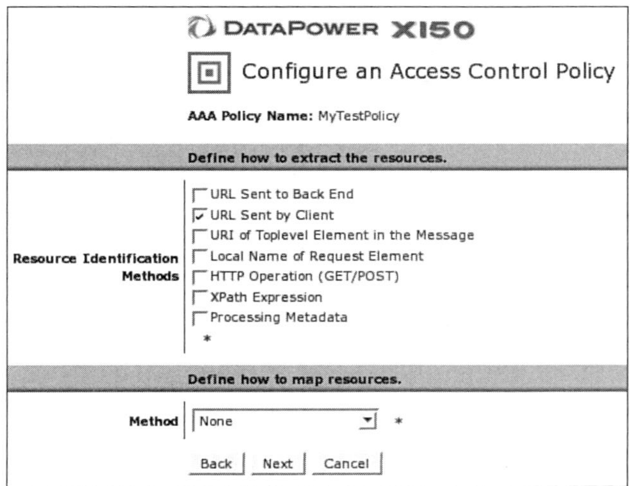

Figure 16-23 Resource identification methods.

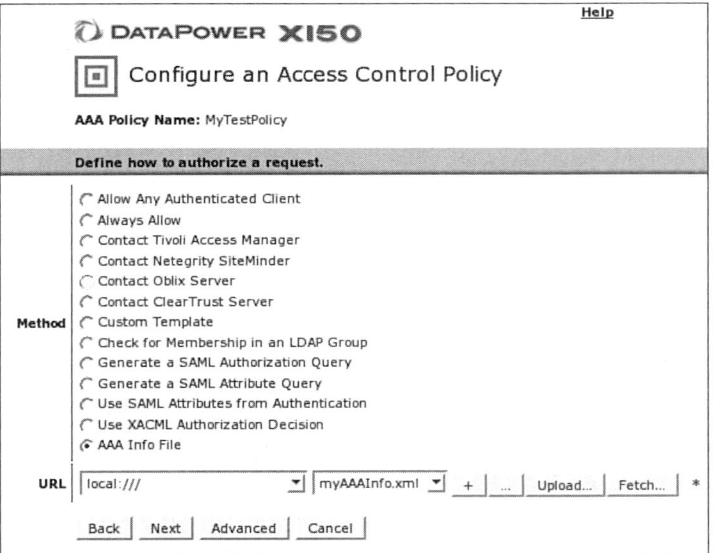

Figure 16-24 Authorization page of the wizard.

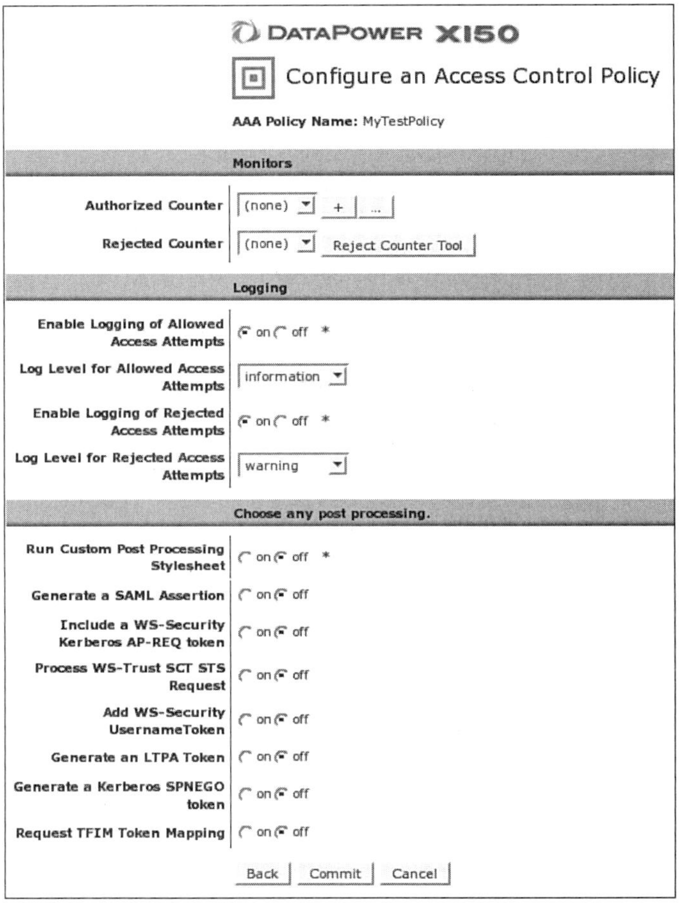

Figure 16-25 Audit and post processing.

This last page allows for setting of counters for successful and failed attempts to access the resources protected by the policy, which can later be used for service level management; definition of logging configuration where successful and failed access attempts can be (and be default are) logged to the DataPower logging infrastructure; and post processing actions, that enable modifying the security aspects of the request before it is passed to the backend. The last of these, post processing, is powerful and important; for instance, it allows generation of tokens to propagate authenticated credentials to the backend. Nonetheless for our simple scenario, nothing except the defaults are needed on this page of the wizard.

And that's it! Clicking Commit on the final page of the wizard creates a fully functional access control policy that can now be used to restrict user access to specific URLs.

Example Scenarios

This section walks you through a number of basic AAA scenarios and explains the configuration required to implement them.

Simple On-Box Authentication/Authorization with AAA Info

Many of the previous stages have mentioned and referenced a file format called AAA Info (pronounced "triple-A info"). This is an on-box custom simple file format for storing information required for AAA processing. An example AAA Info file is shown in Listing 16-2.

Listing 16-2 AAAInfo.xml

```
<?xml version="1.0"?>
<aaa:AAAInfo xmlns:dpfunc="http://www.datapower.com/extensions/functions"
xmlns:aaa="http://www.datapower.com/AAAInfo">
    <aaa:FormatVersion>1</aaa:FormatVersion>
    <aaa:Filename>local:///AAAInfo.xml</aaa:Filename>
    <aaa:Summary/>
    <aaa:Authenticate>
        <aaa:Username>bob</aaa:Username>
        <aaa:Password>passw0rd</aaa:Password>
        <aaa:OutputCredential>bob</aaa:OutputCredential>
    </aaa:Authenticate>
    <aaa:Authenticate>
        <aaa:DN>CN=Bob,OU=Workers,DC=SomeCompany,DC=com</aaa:DN>
        <aaa:OutputCredential>bob</aaa:OutputCredential>
    </aaa:Authenticate>
    <aaa:Authenticate>
        <aaa:Username>alice</aaa:Username>
        <aaa:Password>pa55word</aaa:Password>
        <aaa:OutputCredential>alice</aaa:OutputCredential>
    </aaa:Authenticate>
    <aaa:Authenticate>
        <aaa:Any/>
        <aaa:OutputCredential>guest</aaa:OutputCredential>
    </aaa:Authenticate>
    <aaa:MapCredentials>
        <aaa:InputCredential>bob</aaa:InputCredential>
        <aaa:OutputCredential>VALIDUSERS</aaa:OutputCredential>
    </aaa:MapCredentials>
    <aaa:MapCredentials>
        <aaa:InputCredential>alice</aaa:InputCredential>
        <aaa:OutputCredential>VALIDUSERS</aaa:OutputCredential>
    </aaa:MapCredentials>
    <aaa:MapResource>
        <aaa:OriginalURL>/app3/.*/private</aaa:OriginalURL>
        <aaa:OutputResource>PRIVATE</aaa:OutputResource>
    </aaa:MapResource>
    <aaa:MapResource>
        <aaa:OriginalURL>/private/.*</aaa:OriginalURL>
        <aaa:OutputResource>PRIVATE</aaa:OutputResource>
```

```
    </aaa:MapResource>
    <aaa:Authorize>
        <aaa:InputCredential>VALIDUSERS</aaa:InputCredential>
        <aaa:InputResource>PRIVATE</aaa:InputResource>
        <aaa:Access>allow</aaa:Access>
    </aaa:Authorize>
    <aaa:Authorize>
        <aaa:InputCredential>guest</aaa:InputCredential>
        <aaa:InputResource>PRIVATE</aaa:InputResource>
        <aaa:Access>deny</aaa:Access>
    </aaa:Authorize>
</aaa:AAAInfo>
```

This file contains several entries that relate to the various stages. We explore each of them in the following sections.

Authentication

First, we have the authenticate stage. This works by providing authenticate statements, which contain the credentials to be presented, and the output credential, which is to be the authenticated credential from this stage. In this instance, we have four authenticate entries, as shown in Listing 16-3.

Listing 16-3 Authentication in AAA Info

```
<aaa:Authenticate>
    <aaa:Username>bob</aaa:Username>
    <aaa:Password>passw0rd</aaa:Password>
    <aaa:OutputCredential>bob</aaa:OutputCredential>
</aaa:Authenticate>
<aaa:Authenticate>
    <aaa:DN>CN=Bob,OU=Workers,DC=SomeCompany,DC=com</aaa:DN>
    <aaa:OutputCredential>bob</aaa:OutputCredential>
</aaa:Authenticate>
<aaa:Authenticate>
    <aaa:Username>alice</aaa:Username>
    <aaa:Password>pa55word</aaa:Password>
    <aaa:OutputCredential>alice</aaa:OutputCredential>
</aaa:Authenticate>
<aaa:Authenticate>
    <aaa:Any/>
    <aaa:OutputCredential>guest</aaa:OutputCredential>
</aaa:Authenticate>
```

There are two entries for the user bob, one entry for the user alice, and one entry with no required credentials. The bob entries are especially interesting—there are clearly two separate authenticate sections, with both providing the same output credential. This is because the user bob is allowed to authenticate using one of two methods—either by providing a username and password as shown, or by presenting a client SSL certificate with the distinguished name as shown. Note that the client certificate will have been cryptographically validated using Validation Credentials (which are described in Chapter 18), so we can rely on the value to be correct.

The Any entry, which has no required credentials but provides an output credential of guest, is a simple statement saying that authentication should succeed even for users who do not provide credentials to authenticate with, but that they should be assigned a credential of guest. There is nothing special in the term guest here; this is simply the name we have assigned for use later in the Processing Policy where we decide what the guest user (unauthenticated users) is allowed to do.

Map Credentials

The next stage to which we apply our AAA Info file is credential mapping. Here we map all our actual valid users to a single output credential enabling us to make a more coarse-grained authorization decision. The relevant part of the AAA Info file is shown in Listing 16-4.

Listing 16-4 Credential Mapping in AAA Info

```
<aaa:MapCredentials>
    <aaa:InputCredential>bob</aaa:InputCredential>
    <aaa:OutputCredential>VALIDUSERS</aaa:OutputCredential>
</aaa:MapCredentials>
<aaa:MapCredentials>
    <aaa:InputCredential>alice</aaa:InputCredential>
    <aaa:OutputCredential>VALIDUSERS</aaa:OutputCredential>
</aaa:MapCredentials>
```

Notice how both bob and alice as input credentials are mapped to the same output credential, VALIDUSERS. This credential is used later to make authorization decisions where all valid users should be allowed to access. Because we plan to use it in this way, the term VALIDUSERS is appropriate, but this can be any valid string. Notice also that we do not map the guest user, because there is only one of him defined, mapping his credentials would provide no value.

Map Resource

The next part of the file is related to the Map Resource stage. At this point we have two entries as shown in Listing 16-5.

Listing 16-5 Resource Mapping in AAA Info

```
<aaa:MapResource>
    <aaa:OriginalURL>/app3/.*/private</aaa:OriginalURL>
    <aaa:OutputResource>PRIVATE</aaa:OutputResource>
</aaa:MapResource>
<aaa:MapResource>
    <aaa:OriginalURL>/private/.*</aaa:OriginalURL>
    <aaa:OutputResource>PRIVATE</aaa:OutputResource>
</aaa:MapResource>
```

This entry maps all URLs that match either of the specified regular expressions to the specific output resource PRIVATE. This resource is used in the authorization stage.

Authorization

Finally, we come to the authorization stage. At this point, we have already defined our users to be specific mapped credentials, and we have identified and mapped our resources such that they cover the URLs required. We can now make some authorization decisions, as shown in Listing 16-6.

Listing 16-6 Authorization in AAA Info

```
<aaa:Authorize>
    <aaa:InputCredential>VALIDUSERS</aaa:InputCredential>
    <aaa:InputResource>PRIVATE</aaa:InputResource>
    <aaa:Access>allow</aaa:Access>
</aaa:Authorize>
<aaa:Authorize>
    <aaa:InputCredential>guest</aaa:InputCredential>
    <aaa:InputResource>PRIVATE</aaa:InputResource>
    <aaa:Access>deny</aaa:Access>
</aaa:Authorize>
```

From this snippet it is clear that valid users (remember this is someone who has authenticated as either bob, using his username and password or an SSL certificate, or as alice using her username and password, and has therefore been mapped to the VALIDUSERS credential) can access PRIVATE resources (remember these are anything that match the private URL statements earlier), and that guest users (which is anyone who has not authenticated) are explicitly denied access to PRIVATE resources.

AAA Info is a simple yet powerful way to implement a number of the stages of AAA processing. When used with care, it can be an important tool. However, remember that it has limitations. Chief among these is that the file itself must be maintained, distributed to all appliances where it will be used, updated manually, and so on. It also becomes unwieldy when dealing with large numbers of users—although performance is not a problem. (After all DataPower is good at processing XML quickly!)

Because of these limitations, AAA Info should likely not be used for user authentication for large-scale production use at enterprise class customers. Such customers are likely to have a real enterprise directory service or single sign-on solution, and they should work to integrate with these. AAA Info can be used in these environments for learning about the AAA process, and it can be a good beginning to enable quick deployments, with a longer term goal of slowly migrating in part or in whole to integrate with the external enterprise-wide security systems as and when required. In addition, the credential mapping and resource mapping functionality can be used to invoke the powerful matching engine in DataPower for dynamic regular-expression based mapping, which is a relatively common scenario.

AAA Info is also invaluable in scenarios where the access control required is not end user access control, but rather authentication and authorization of system-to-system calls. In this kind of scenario, the capability to quickly and efficiently define required security credentials for a limited number of known other systems can be extremely useful.

Integration with LDAP

The Authentication and Authorization stages can utilize LDAP—which is a common requirement. The Lightweight Directory Access Protocol has been in use in distributed computing for quite some time, and many enterprises already have such a directory, which contains all their user data. Using that directory makes a lot of sense!

Authentication

Figure 16-26 shows an example of configuring an LDAP server for the authentication stage.

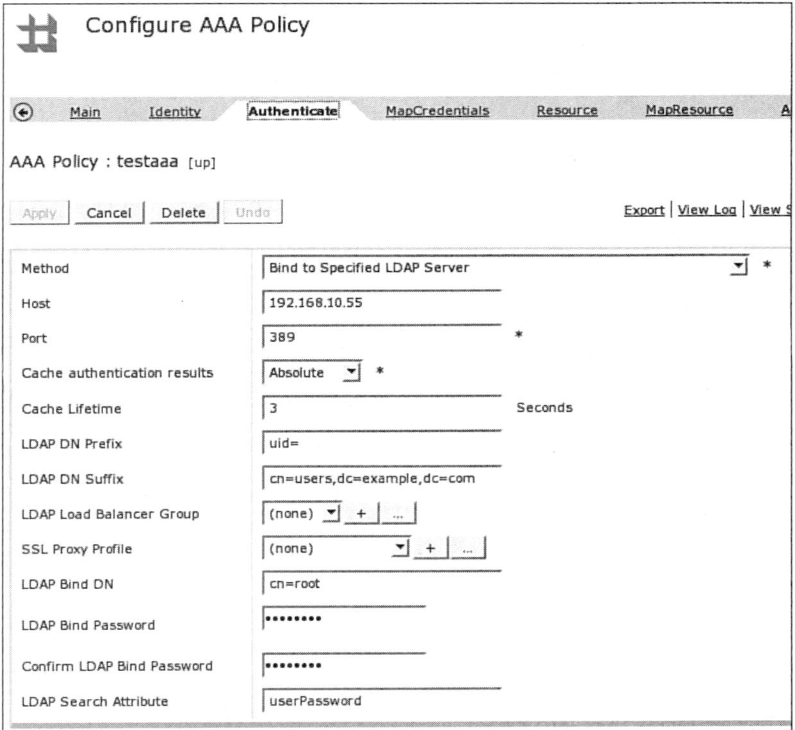

Figure 16-26 LDAP for authentication.

The LDAP DN Prefix and LDAP DN Suffix fields are used to build up a "template" for what the user lookup should look like. The username input from the EI phase will be included in the template, and the resulting distinguished name will be used along with the password from the EI phase. For example, if the username provided was bob, it would create a DN of `uid=bob,cn=users,dc=example,dc=com`. An LDAP bind will be attempted to the server using this distinguished name and the password provided, and if the bind is successful, then the user will be deemed to have authenticated successfully. Otherwise authentication will be deemed to have failed.

The final four fields, the Bind DN and Password and the LDAP Search Attribute fields, are used only in the special circumstance when the password from the Extract Identity stage happened to be a WS-Security UsernameToken PasswordDigest. In that specific case, this specified DN and password are used to bind to the LDAP server so that it can search for a digest, as specified in the LDAP Search Attribute field, to compare the provided digest against. This enables LDAP authentication even when the password is a hash of the plain-text password, which is a common use case in WS-Security.

Authorization

Figure 16-27 shows an example of configuring the same LDAP server as before, but this time for the authorization stage.

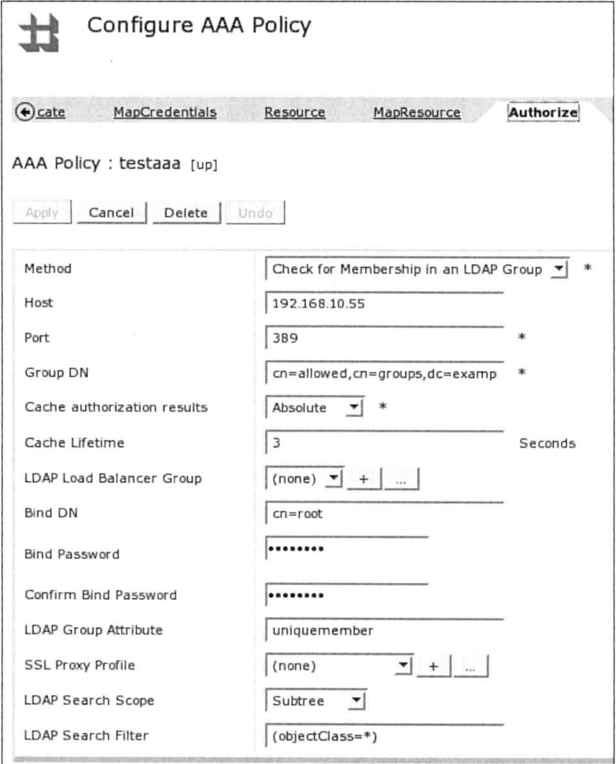

Figure 16-27 LDAP for authorization.

The built-in LDAP authorization is relatively simple. It allows for searching the LDAP server for membership of a specific group. That group is specified in the Group DN field. To perform the search, an authenticated bind is made to the LDAP server using the Bind DN and Bind Password provided. The search is then carried out using the LDAP Search Filter and the LDAP Group Attribute. If the authenticated user is found to be a member of the specified group, authorization is deemed to have been successful; if not, then it has failed.

Under the Covers

Let's examine how the authentication and authorization work here in a little more detail. We have configured a AAA policy, which contains the previous LDAP authentication and authorization stages, and we put it inside a AAA action in the Processing Policy of a simple XML firewall. The AAA policy extracts identity using basic authentication by processing an incoming "Authorization: Basic" HTTP header, and passes the username and password into the LDAP processing stages. Figure 16-28 shows a snippet of the processing log when this policy is run.

```
xmlfirewall (aaatest): Policy(testaaa): Message allowed
xmlfirewall (aaatest): Policy(testaaa): ldap authorization succeeded with credential 'uid=bob,cn=users,dc=example,dc=com' for resource '/'
xmlfirewall (aaatest): Policy(testaaa): Cached Authorize entry
xmlfirewall (aaatest): Policy(testaaa): Authorizing with "ldap"
xmlfirewall (aaatest): Policy(testaaa): Authorize cache check with key="authz<?xml version="1.0" encoding="UTF-8"?> <container><mapped-credentials type="none"
au-success="true"><entry type="ldap">uid=bob,cn=users,dc=example,dc=com</entry></mapped-credentials><mapped-resource type="none"><resource><item
type="original-url">/</item></resource></mapped-resource><identity><entry type="http-basic-auth"><username>bob</username><password
sanitize="true">*****</password><configured-realm>login</configured-realm></entry></identity><au-ancillary-info/><az-ancillary-info/></container>authzldap"
xmlfirewall (aaatest): Policy(testaaa): Authorize Caching is on: absolute
xmlfirewall (aaatest): Policy(testaaa): Mapping resources using none
xmlfirewall (aaatest): Policy(testaaa): Mapping credentials using none
xmlfirewall (aaatest): Policy(testaaa): ldap authentication succeeded with (http-basic-auth, username='bob' password='********'configured-realm='login' )
xmlfirewall (aaatest): Policy(testaaa): Cached Authenticate entry
xmlfirewall (aaatest): Policy(testaaa): Authenticating with "ldap"
xmlfirewall (aaatest): Policy(testaaa): Authenticate cache check with key="policyname<?xml version="1.0" encoding="UTF-8"?> <identity><entry
type="http-basic-auth"><username>bob</username><password
sanitize="true">*****</password><configured-realm>login</configured-realm></entry></identity><?xml version="1.0" encoding="UTF-8"?>
<au-ancillary-info/>ldap"
xmlfirewall (aaatest): Policy(testaaa): Authenticate Caching is on: true
xmlfirewall (aaatest): Policy(testaaa): Resource "/"
xmlfirewall (aaatest): Policy(testaaa): Extracting resources using "original-url"
xmlfirewall (aaatest): Policy(testaaa): Extracting identity using "http-basic-auth"
```

Figure 16-28 Relevant snippet of log.

We can see the processing extract the identity using http-basic-auth, and the resource using "original-url." We then see a search in the authentication cache to see whether we already have a cached authentication entry for these credentials. Because we do not, a new call is made to the LDAP server, which succeeds, and the result is stored in the cache. (So that if this call is repeated within the cache validity lifetime, by default three seconds, a new call to LDAP will not be performed for authentication.)

No mapping of credentials or resources is required, so we check our authorization cache to see if it contains an entry for this user accessing this specific resource. Because again it does not, we call LDAP and check to see whether the user is in the specific group required, and because he is, we deem the authorization to be successful and the message is allowed.

These logs are useful at a high level, but to gain more insight as to what actually happens under the covers, we need to look into the probe. There are two main areas where more information about the LDAP call can be obtained: in the extension trace for the AAA action, and in context variables that specifically exist for debugging purposes when the probe is enabled.

Figure 16-29 shows the extension trace for the AAA action in our Processing Policy.

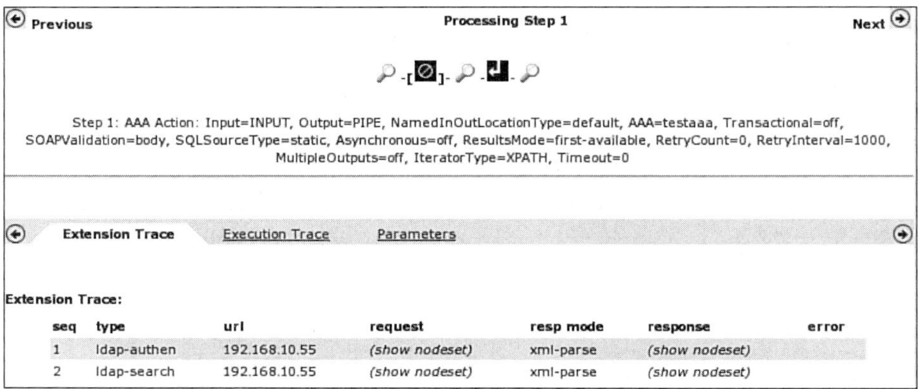

Figure 16-29 AAA action extension trace.

We can see from the extension trace that two LDAP calls are made during this AAA action. The first is an authenticate call; that is, DataPower attempted to bind to the LDAP server as a specific user, specifying his password. The second is an LDAP search; that is, DataPower bound as a user authorized to perform searches and ran an LDAP search (in this case, to see whether our user is in a specific group).

By clicking show nodeset, we can see the parameters used by DataPower for the request and the return of the extension function call in the response. The request for the authentication call is shown in Figure 16-30.

Content of Request:

```
<parameter>
  <bindDN>uid=bob,cn=users,dc=example,dc=com</bindDN>
  <bindPassword>password</bindPassword>
  <lookupDN />
  <lookupAttribute />
  <filter />
</parameter>
```

Show unformatted

Figure 16-30 Request parameters used for LDAP authentication call.

It is clear from the probe that DataPower tried to bind with a DN of `uid=bob,cn=users,dc=example,dc=com`, and a password of password. This information is made up of the LDAP DN Prefix `uid` and LDAP DN Suffix `cn=users,dc=example,dc=com`, shown previously in Figure 16-26, along with the username and password provided in basic auth (user of `bob`, with a password of `password`). The response to this call is shown in Figure 16-31.

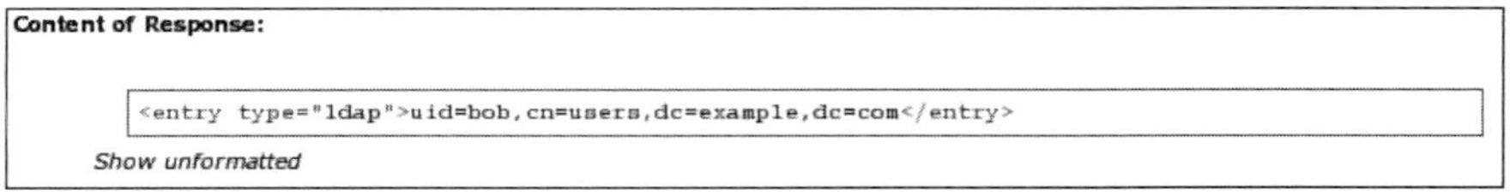

Content of Response:

```
<entry type="ldap">uid=bob,cn=users,dc=example,dc=com</entry>
```

Show unformatted

Figure 16-31 Response from LDAP authentication call.

The response shows the whole LDAP distinguished name for the user that DataPower was able to bind as; this becomes the output credential.

Likewise, we can see the details of the call to the LDAP server for authorization. This is shown in Figure 16-32.

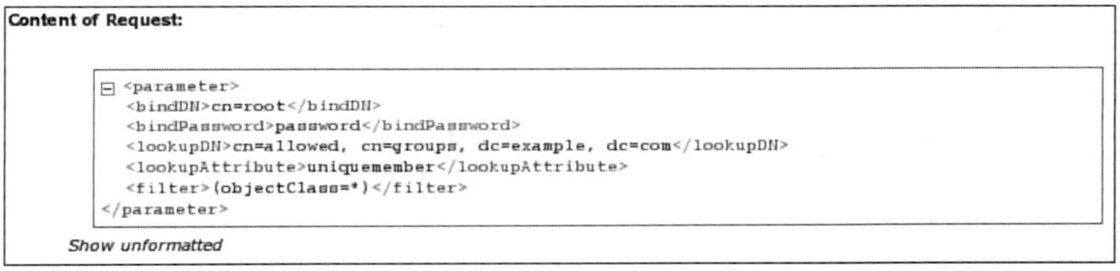

Content of Request:

```
<parameter>
  <bindDN>cn=root</bindDN>
  <bindPassword>password</bindPassword>
  <lookupDN>cn=allowed, cn=groups, dc=example, dc=com</lookupDN>
  <lookupAttribute>uniquemember</lookupAttribute>
  <filter>(objectClass=*)</filter>
</parameter>
```

Show unformatted

Figure 16-32 Request for LDAP authorization.

The request here is made up of the Bind DN, Bind Password, Group DN, LDAP Group Attribute, and LDAP Search Filter parameters from Figure 16-27. DataPower binds as the user specified in the Bind DN, providing the Bind Password, and then performs a search using the other parameters to ensure that the distinguished name, which was the result of the authentication stage (or the map credential stage if one was defined), is a member of the specified group.

The information from the AAA action extension trace is very useful. Sometimes, however, your chosen authentication or authorization mechanism might not provide any extension trace. In those instances, similar information is also available via specific debug variables in the probe.

Note that these variables *are* normal DataPower variables, and could theoretically be manipulated programmatically if desired. However, the variables exist *only* when the probe is enabled. Because the probe should never be enabled in a production environment, this means that the variables are unlikely to be of use programmatically for anything other than debugging specific issues. Because they are directly viewable in the probe itself, it is unlikely that there is any value in accessing the variables from a stylesheet. The variables as displayed in the probe are shown in Figure 16-33.

Inside these variables is fundamentally the same data as shown in the previous extension trace. However, the variables show the actual structure of how DataPower passes the information around between the various stages. For instance, the AU stage is shown in Figure 16-34.

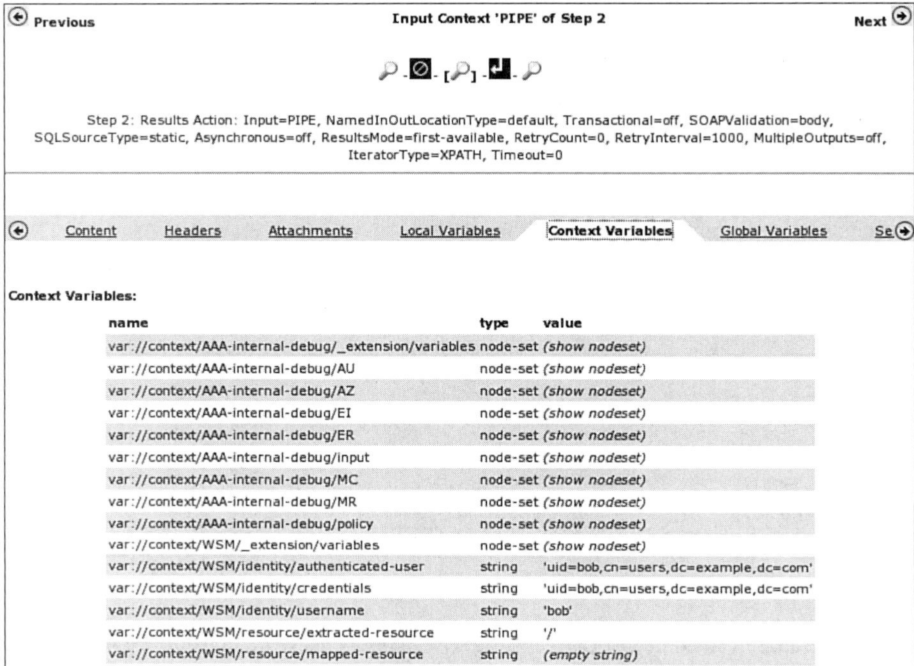

Figure 16-33 AAA internal debugging variables.

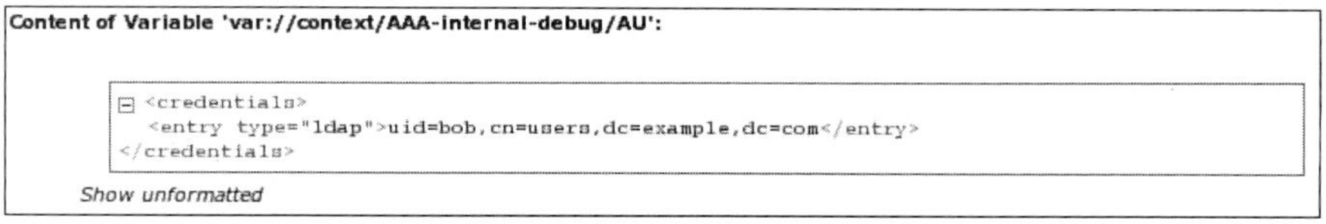

Content of Variable 'var://context/AAA-internal-debug/AU':

```
<credentials>
  <entry type="ldap">uid=bob,cn=users,dc=example,dc=com</entry>
</credentials>
```

Show unformatted

Figure 16-34 The AU internal debugging variable.

This shows the identity that was obtained in the authentication stage, but it is wrapped in a <credentials/> tag. This structure is used as the input to the next stage, Map Credentials. Likewise the EI variable is shown in Figure 16-35.

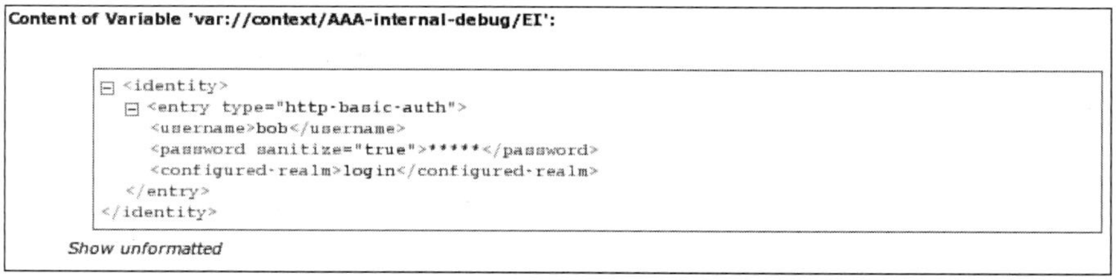

Content of Variable 'var://context/AAA-internal-debug/EI':

```
<identity>
  <entry type="http-basic-auth">
    <username>bob</username>
    <password sanitize="true">*****</password>
    <configured-realm>login</configured-realm>
  </entry>
</identity>
```

Show unformatted

Figure 16-35 The EI internal debugging variable.

This variable shows the extracted identity as an <entry/> inside an <identity/> tag. This structure is used because there can actually be more than one extracted identity, so multiple entries are required, with each entry containing information relevant to the specific type of identity extracted. (For example the realm used for basic auth is given alongside the username and password.)

This information is invaluable when customizing the AAA process using XSLT. An example of customizing with XSLT is given in Chapter 17, which demonstrates how useful the variables are.

Real-World Policy

The final example for this chapter presents a AAA policy, which is representative of the kind of complexity that might be found in real-world situations. At a high level, the policy can be described as follows:

- Extract identity based on a combination of a specific SSL Certificate and a WS-Security Username Token.
- Authenticate the identity using an on-box AAA Info file, to enforce the multiple identities as extracted.
- Identify the resource based on an XPath expression that extracts application specific routing metadata.
- Authorize the connection with an XACML document using the on-box Policy Decision Point.
- Generate a SAML token for the connection to the back end to propagate the credentials to a SAML capable service. (The backend is assumed in this scenario to explicitly trust the DataPower appliance, with that trust built using a mutually authenticated SSL tunnel; this technique will be described in Chapter 18.)

Each of these is described in the following sections.

Identity Extraction

The configuration of identity extraction is done by simply selecting from the WebGUI. However in this case, we actually select more than one method, as shown in Figure 16-36.

By selecting more than one method, we are configuring the policy to extract one or both of the identities if they are present; there is no statement here that one or the other is compulsory. (This comes in the authentication stage.)

Authentication

The authentication stage is where we enforce the specific identities required. For this example, the AAA Info file is useful, because it can enforce multiple required credentials in a single authenticate stanza, as shown in Listing 16-7.

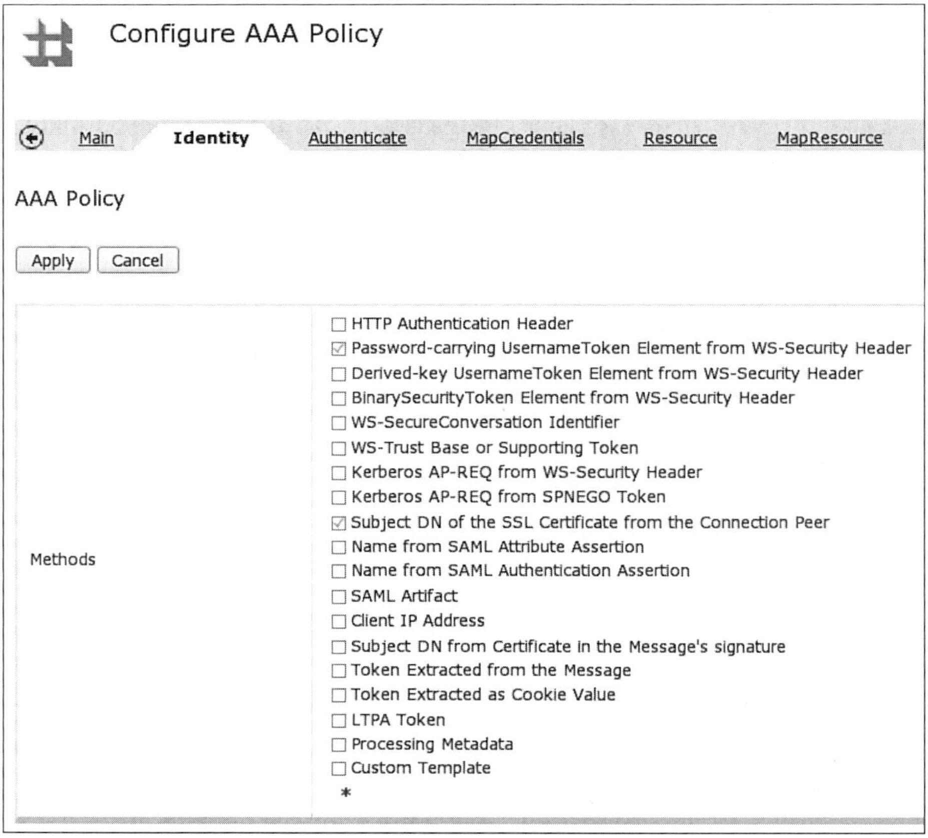

Configure AAA Policy

Main | **Identity** | Authenticate | MapCredentials | Resource | MapResource

AAA Policy

Apply | Cancel

Methods

- [ ] HTTP Authentication Header
- [x] Password-carrying UsernameToken Element from WS-Security Header
- [ ] Derived-key UsernameToken Element from WS-Security Header
- [ ] BinarySecurityToken Element from WS-Security Header
- [ ] WS-SecureConversation Identifier
- [ ] WS-Trust Base or Supporting Token
- [ ] Kerberos AP-REQ from WS-Security Header
- [ ] Kerberos AP-REQ from SPNEGO Token
- [x] Subject DN of the SSL Certificate from the Connection Peer
- [ ] Name from SAML Attribute Assertion
- [ ] Name from SAML Authentication Assertion
- [ ] SAML Artifact
- [ ] Client IP Address
- [ ] Subject DN from Certificate in the Message's signature
- [ ] Token Extracted from the Message
- [ ] Token Extracted as Cookie Value
- [ ] LTPA Token
- [ ] Processing Metadata
- [ ] Custom Template

*

Figure 16-36 Multiple methods of identity extraction.

Listing 16-7 Multiple Credentials

```
<aaa:Authenticate>
     <aaa:Username>bob</aaa:Username>
     <aaa:Password>passw0rd</aaa:Password>
     <aaa:DN>CN=Bob,OU=Workers,DC=SomeCompany,DC=com</aaa:DN>
     <aaa:OutputCredential>bob</aaa:OutputCredential>
</aaa:Authenticate>
```

This stanza is different from those presented earlier. What it says is that to authenticate as the user bob, specified as the OutputCredential, the user must present *both* the username and password *and* the distinguished name from the certificate. Presenting only one or the other of these is not enough. The AAA Info file is the only authentication method that, out of the box, can enforce that more than one type of credential must be present for a single user within a single AAA Policy. To perform similar functionality for other authentication methods, we would have to either have multiple AAA policies or use custom XSLT.

Authorization

After our user has been authenticated, we need to make an authorization decision. To provide a common way of specifying authorization constraints, the company has decided to specify them in an XACML policy file.

The eXtensible Access Control Markup Language (XACML) is a language that enables generic XML declarations of access control policies. DataPower acts as a Policy Enforcement Point for XACML policies; that is, it is able to take the requests it receives and transform them into XACML requests for access to specific resources. It is also capable of acting as a Policy Decision Point, and actually deciding whether access should be granted by interpreting the declared policies and applying them as relevant to the requests it receives. The on-box PDP functionality is capable of using an XACML policy file, and for this scenario that is enough.

Listing 16-8 XACML Policy

```
<Policy PolicyId="LoginPolicy"
 RuleCombiningAlgId="urn:oasis:names:tc:xacml:1.0:
 rule-combining- algorithm:permit-overrides">
<Rule RuleId="LoginRule" Effect="Permit">
<Target>
 <Subjects>
  <Attribute
   AttributeId="urn:oasis:names:tc:xacml:1.0:subject:subject-id"
   DataType="http://www.w3.org/2001/XMLSchema#string">
   <AttributeValue>
    bob
   </AttributeValue>
  </Attribute>
 </Subjects>
 <Resources>
  <ResourceMatch
   MatchId="urn:oasis:names:tc:xacml:1.0:function:string-equal">
   <AttributeValue
   DataType="http://www.w3.org/2001/XMLSchema#string">
    /target/url
   </AttributeValue>
   <ResourceAttributeDesignator
   DataType="http://www.w3.org/2001/XMLSchema#string"
   AttributeId="urn:oasis:names:tc:xacml:1.0:resource:resource-id"/>
  </ResourceMatch>
 </Resources>
</Target>
</Rule>
<Rule RuleId="FinalRule" Effect="Deny"/>
</Policy>
```

Listing 16-9 XACML Request

```
<Request>
 <Subject>
  <Attribute
   AttributeId="urn:oasis:names:tc:xacml:1.0:subject:subject-id"
   DataType="http://www.w3.org/2001/XMLSchema#string">
   <AttributeValue>
    bob
   </AttributeValue>
  </Attribute>
 </Subject>
 <Resource>
  <Attribute
   AttributeId="urn:oasis:names:tc:xacml:1.0:resource:resource-id"
   DataType="http://www.w3.org/2001/XMLSchema#string">
   <AttributeValue>
    /target/url
   </AttributeValue>
  </Attribute>
 </Resource>
</Request>
```

Chapter 17 goes into more detail about how to actually write XSLT to customize the AAA processing. Meanwhile, the configuration needs to be put together under the Authorize tab, as shown in Figure 16-37.

After this is done, the output of the Resource and the Authenticate stages is converted to a XACML request using the CreateXACMLRequest.xsl stylesheet, and then passed to the SimplePDP on-box Policy Decision Point, which contains the policy shown in Listing 16-8.

Post Processing

Finally, after we have authenticated our request, defined our resource, and authorized the entity to access the resource, we need to propagate that request to the backend. Recall that our backend is capable of understanding SAML, and we want to propagate identity using a SAML assertion. The configuration for this is shown in Figure 16-38.

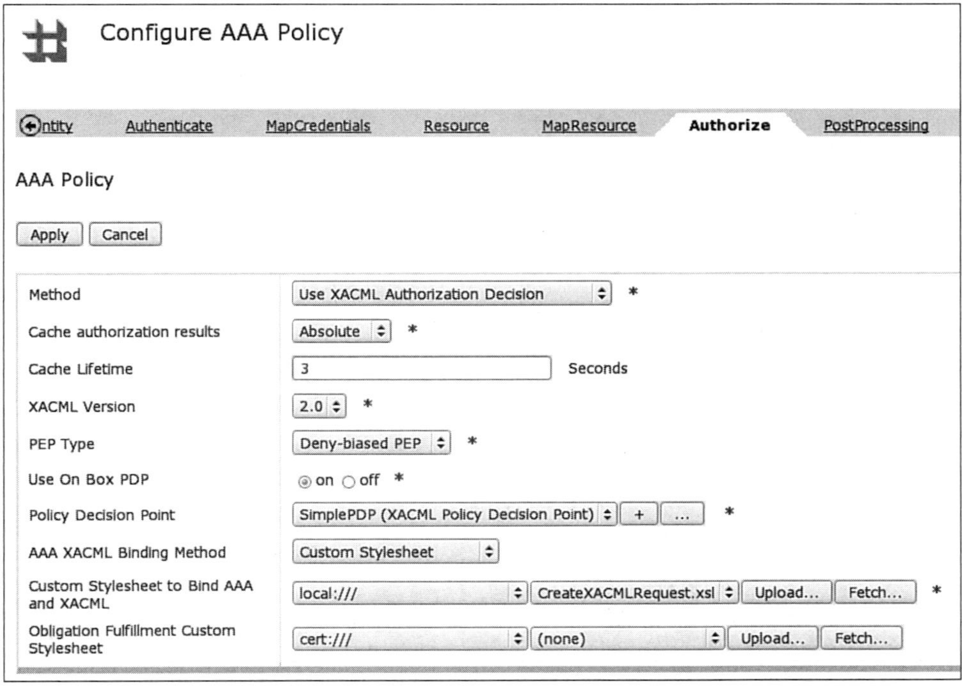

Figure 16-37 The XACML on-box configuration.

The issuer of the assertion is configured as DataPower and the assertion is valid for seven seconds with a possible skew of four seconds. (The skew is to allow for possible latencies in date and time settings on different servers.) For short-lived assertions, which are designed to be processed immediately, this should be enough. SAML is covered in more depth in Chapter 19.

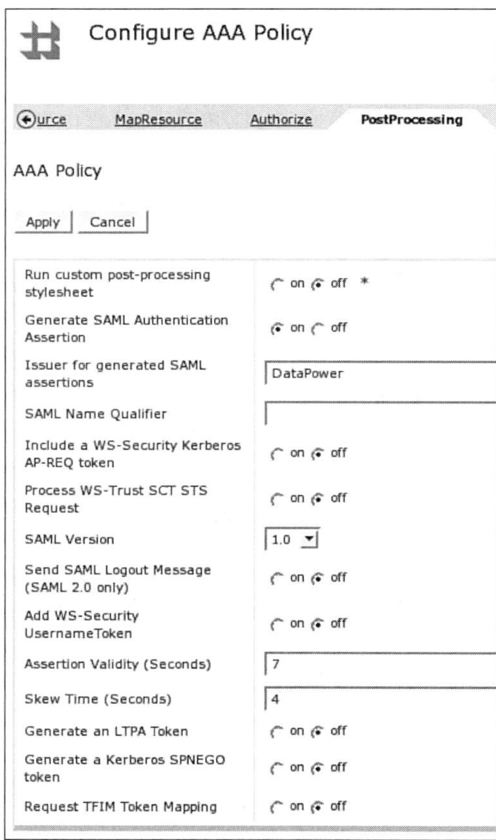

Figure 16-38 Generation of a SAML assertion.

Summary

This chapter provided an introduction into the DataPower AAA framework. We have shown how flexible and powerful it is, allowing you to customize access control to unprecedented levels and integrate with almost any other security system. Chapter 17 goes through some of the deeper levels of customization, explaining exactly how custom XSLT can be used to have complete control over exactly who can do what with your services. You ain't seen nothin' yet!

CHAPTER 17

Advanced AAA

As Chapter 16, "AAA," shows, the DataPower AAA framework is flexible and powerful, allowing you unparalleled control over which users or systems can access your services. This chapter goes through some examples of this at work, including customization of the framework and integration with IBM Tivoli Access Manager (TAM).

Customization is an inherent part of the DataPower device and isn't something to be afraid of. While there are many out-of-the-box options that cover the vast majority of customer requirements, especially in a complex area such as security, there is no way that everything can be covered. The AAA framework enables you to customize to a granular level to integrate with even the most complex of solutions and fulfill even the most difficult requirements.

Customizing the AAA Runtime Process

The AAA runtime described in Chapter 16 can be customized at almost every step. (The exception is resource extraction, but this can be fixed by a subsequent customized resource mapping step.) The steps of the AAA flow are summarized in Figure 17-1. To write a AAA customization stylesheet, you need to know what the inputs and outputs of each stage need to look like.

XML in the AAA Flow

The AAA flow works by passing an XML tree from one step to the next; the XML tree contains information about what happened in the earlier stages. It is built automatically by the out-of-the-box AAA methods; some of these XML trees were shown in Chapter 16 as the contents of the debug variables for the various stages of AAA processing.

When customizing the AAA flow, our own stylesheets need to work with this XML tree and create the relevant output for the next stage. This may seem somewhat complex, but in truth is no different to writing any other XSL; our processing must simply transform the input tree from one stage to the output tree of another, and by doing so, it communicates decisions to DataPower regarding authentication, authorization, and so on.

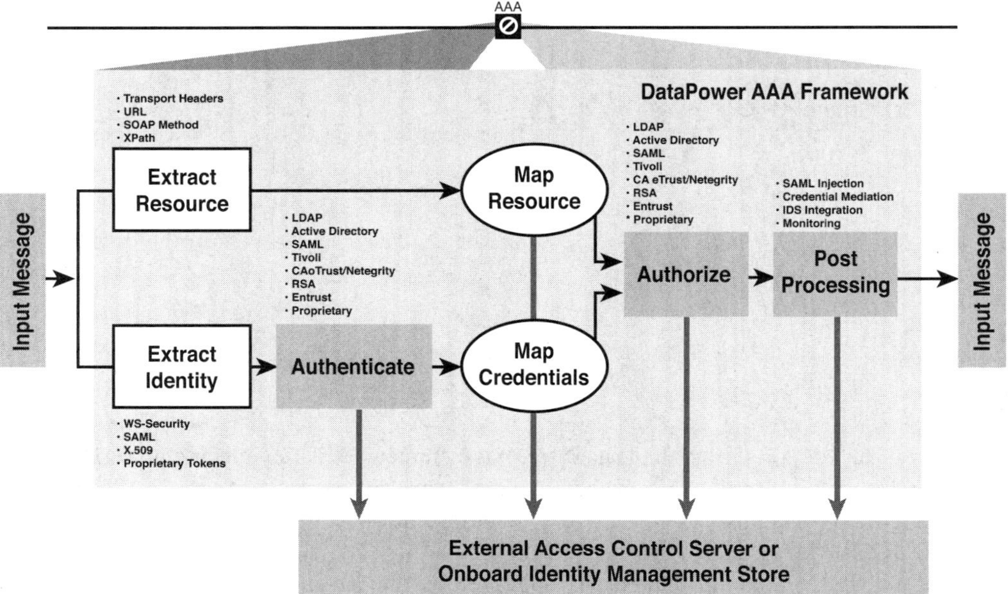

Figure 17-1 AAA flow summary.

This processing is best demonstrated by example, so we will walk you through each stage and show an example of processing at each level. It is highly likely that when you do need to customize the AAA process, you will have to customize only one or two stages; our approach, therefore, enables you to pick the pieces you need to use to customize in your specific environment.

EI—Extract Identity

The EI stage has many out-of-the-box options that cover the vast majority of user requirements. Indeed, it is difficult to think of a realistic requirement that is not already covered! Of course there are real-world requirements, but they do not make for an easy demonstration of the functionality, so this example may appear somewhat contrived; we can only apologize for the huge array of supported out-of-the-box use cases!

The example we use is that of an XML document that contains a username and a password in a specific node. For most similar use cases, we would use the out of the box processing called Token Extracted from the Message, which allows you to specify an XPath expression to extract the required string. However, in this instance the username field needs to be modified before passing to the authenticate step, and therefore, we need to use custom processing.

The input for the EI stage custom processing is the entire XML message passed from the input context to the AAA action. The entire request is available, including protocol headers, through DataPower extension functions. It may be that other processing has taken place before the AAA action; for instance, the client XML message may be encrypted and a Decrypt action was needed, or perhaps form-based login was used in a Web application and a transformation was required to convert it from HTTP to XML. For our example, however, no previous processing has taken place, and the request document appears as shown in Listing 17-1.

Listing 17-1 Request Document

```
<?xml version="1.0"?>
<getAmount>
    <authentication>
        <username>alice</username>
        <password>mysecret</password>
    </authentication>
    <data>
        <values/>
    </data>
</getAmount>
```

Clearly the username and password need to be extracted from the request; however, in this instance, this is not enough, because our authentication server requires usernames to be in the form of an email address to uniquely identify specific users. (There is more than one alice in the world, for example.) The domain part of the username is passed in using an HTTP header, AuthDomain, the value of which needs to be appended to the supplied username in order to form an email address.

This is accomplished using the stylesheet shown in Listing 17-2. If you are not familiar with XSLT, a wealth of information about developing custom stylesheets can be found in Part VI of this book, "DataPower Development."

Listing 17-2 Identity Extraction Stylesheet—IE.xsl

```
<?xml version="1.0" encoding="utf-8"?>
<xsl:stylesheet version="1.0"
        xmlns:xsl="http://www.w3.org/1999/XSL/Transform"
        xmlns:dp="http://www.datapower.com/extensions"
        exclude-result-prefixes="dp">
  <xsl:output method="xml"/>
  <xsl:template match="/">
    <! - Use /*/ to match various requests  ->
    <xsl:variable name="username"
      select="/*/authentication/username/text()"/>
    <xsl:variable name="password"
      select="/*/authentication/password/text()"/>
    <xsl:variable name="domain"
      select="dp:request-header('AuthDomain')"/>
    <username><xsl:value-of
      select="concat($username,'@',$domain)"/></username>
    <password sanitize="true"><xsl:value-of
      select="$password"/></password>
  </xsl:template>
</xsl:stylesheet>
```

This stylesheet processes the input document directly, searching for the username and password fields. It also retrieves the value of the AuthDomain HTTP header. Finally, it outputs an XML structure containing username and password elements with the relevant values for authentication. This choice of output is not accidental; the expected output in this instance is two XML nodes—username and password—with no wrapper element.

The stylesheet is configured in the EI step of a AAA policy, as shown in Figure 17-2.

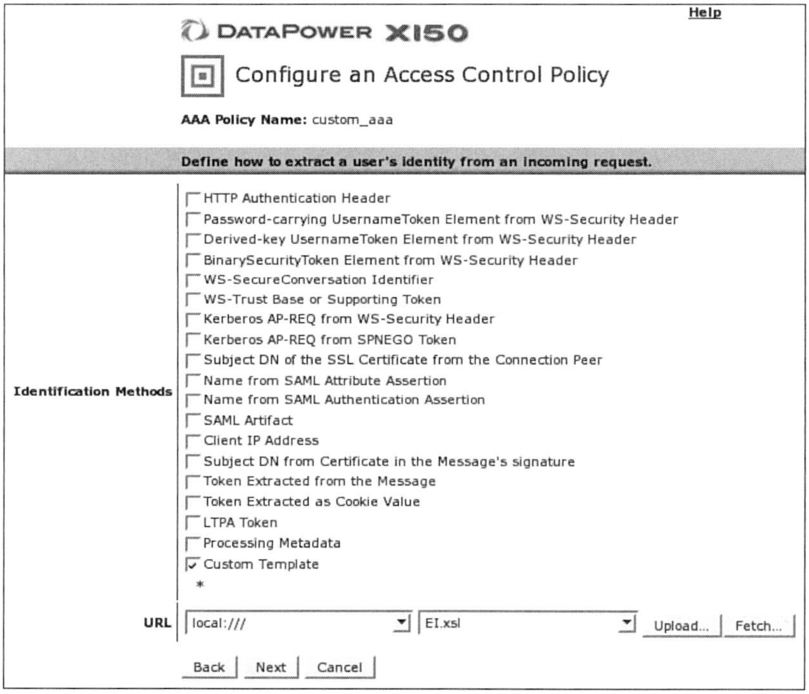

Figure 17-2 Select a custom template and provide the XSL file.

We can use the Probe as described in Chapter 16 to examine the execution trace of the AAA action and see the XML nodeset on the input and output of each custom transformation. If we enable a Probe, submit a transaction, refresh the Probe, and click on that transaction, we are shown a step-by-step representation of the various stages of processing that the request went through. We can click on each stage, in turn, to get details; if we click on the AAA action in the policy, the first tab titled Extension Trace gives details of the custom processing in the AAA policy. As shown in Figure 17-3, each stage has a request and a response nodeset. We can click on the link next to each one to get details of the input or output nodeset for the next part of the processing.

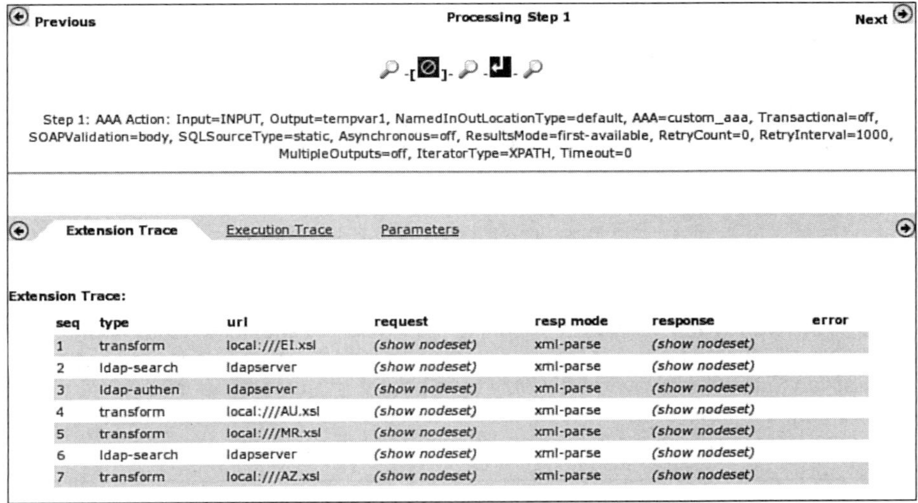

Previous
Processing Step 1
Next
Step 1: AAA Action: Input=INPUT, Output=tempvar1, NamedInOutLocationType=default, AAA=custom_aaa, Transactional=off, SOAPValidation=body, SQLSourceType=static, Asynchronous=off, ResultsMode=first-available, RetryCount=0, RetryInterval=1000, MultipleOutputs=off, IteratorType=XPATH, Timeout=0
Extension Trace
Execution Trace
Parameters
Extension Trace:
seq type url request resp mode response error
1 transform local:///EI.xsl (show nodeset) xml-parse (show nodeset)
2 ldap-search ldapserver (show nodeset) xml-parse (show nodeset)
3 ldap-authen ldapserver (show nodeset) xml-parse (show nodeset)
4 transform local:///AU.xsl (show nodeset) xml-parse (show nodeset)
5 transform local:///MR.xsl (show nodeset) xml-parse (show nodeset)
6 ldap-search ldapserver (show nodeset) xml-parse (show nodeset)
7 transform local:///AZ.xsl (show nodeset) xml-parse (show nodeset)

Figure 17-3 The processing as seen in the Probe.

For instance, Figure 17-4 shows the input into the EI step in the Probe, retrieved by clicking the (show nodeset) link in the request column, which confirms that the input to the EI step is the full submitted XML message.

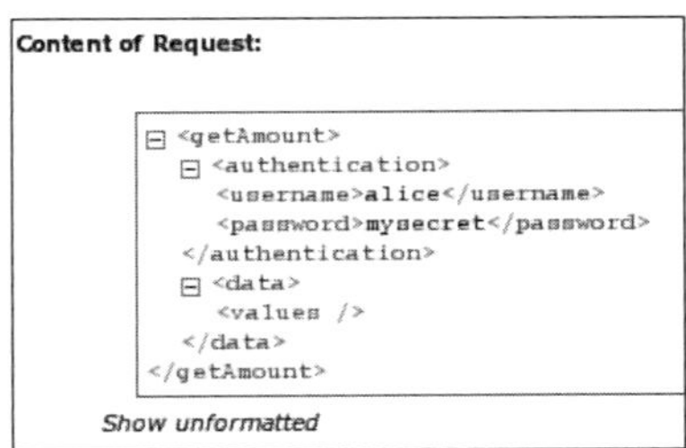

Figure 17-4 Input into the EI step.

This is then transformed by our stylesheet, which also includes the value of the HTTP header AuthDomain, and the output is shown in Figure 17-5.

Content of Response:

```
<username>alice@example.com</username>
<password sanitize="true">mysecret</password>
```

Show unformatted

Figure 17-5 Output from the EI step.

The output from our custom processing presents simply the extracted identity, which Data-Power wraps in an XML structure and passes to the next step.

TIP—SANITIZE PASSWORDS

The previous example shows a construct containing the password, and an attribute has been added to the password node, sanitize="true". By adding this special attribute, we are telling the appliance that the text contents of this node should be masked in any log messages that the device happens to display. For instance, even with debug level AAA logging enabled, the device replaces the actual password supplied with asterisks. This ensures that, when the logs are stored "off box" in a persistent manner (as they always should be in a production environment), the password information is not stored in an insecure location that is not directly under the access control of the device.

Note that this sanitization does not apply to the Probe, as should be clear from Figure 17-2. This should not be cause for concern because the Probe can only be enabled on the appliance itself, and even then only by a user with authority to modify the object being probed. In addition, the Probe should not be used in production (as the warning on the administrative panel when enabling the Probe states clearly).

The XML output from our EI stylesheet is used as the input to the AU step, so the exact content of the response is passed as the input. DataPower automatically wraps this in an XML structure identifying it as an `entry` inside an `identity`, and the entry has an attribute called `type` with the value `custom` and a second attribute called `url` showing where the custom stylesheet is stored. This information is shown in Figure 17-6, which shows the input into the AU step, again taken from the extension trace in the Probe.

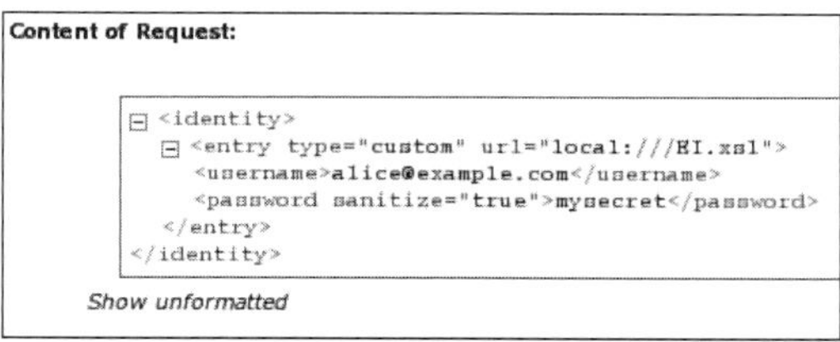
Content of Request:
<identity>
<entry type="custom" url="local:///EI.xsl">
<username>alice@example.com</username>
<password sanitize="true">mysecret</password>
</entry>
</identity>
Show unformatted

Figure 17-6 Output from EI is also input to AU.

The identity XML tree can have more than one entry node, depending on how many options were selected when defining the policy. Thus, if we were to select IP address as well as custom, we would have two entry nodes added by DataPower: one of type custom and the second of type client-ip-address, as shown in Figure 17-7.

Content of Request:

```
<identity>
  <entry type="custom" url="local:///EI.xsl">
    <username>alice@example.com</username>
    <password sanitize="true">mysecret</password>
  </entry>
  <entry type="client-ip-address">
    <ip-address>192.168.10.140</ip-address>
  </entry>
</identity>
```

Show unformatted

Figure 17-7 It is possible to have more than one entry as the output from EI.

However, be aware that the contents can conflict with each other and lead to unexpected results. For instance, because we have created a username and password node, it is likely that our next step, AU, will be configured to use that username and password node to authenticate the user. If we were to *also* select HTTP basic authentication for EI, things would work just fine as long as *either* the custom stylesheet *or* the basic authentication header contained a valid username and password combination. However, if the user then provided *both* a HTTP basic authentication header *and* a username/password for our custom XSL to extract identity from, there would be two sets of username and password nodes. In that situation, because there is no way to tell which set to use, the device will use neither and simply deny the request, as shown in Figure 17-8 (taken from the DataPower log).

```
xmlfirewall (custom_aaa): Rejected by filter; SOAP fault sent
xmlfirewall (custom_aaa): request custom_aaa_request #1 aaa: 'INPUT custom_aaa stored in tempvar1' failed: Username mismatch in input
xmlfirewall (custom_aaa): Execution of 'store:///dp/aaapolicy.xsl' aborted: Username mismatch in input
xmlfirewall (custom_aaa): Policy(custom_aaa): Message rejected
xmlfirewall (custom_aaa): Reject set: Username mismatch in input
xmlfirewall (custom_aaa): Policy(custom_aaa): Username mismatch in input
xmlmgr (default): xslt Compilation Request: Found in cache (local:///EI.xsl)
xmlmgr (default): xslt Compilation Request: Checking cache for URL local:///EI.xsl
xmlfirewall (custom_aaa): Policy(custom_aaa): Extracting identity using "http-basic-auth+custom"
xmlmgr (default): xslt Compilation Request: Found in cache (store:///dp/aaapolicy.xsl)
```

Figure 17-8 Supplying identical identity nodes with two types will fail.

Incidentally, if the usernames are the same, at least processing continues to the next stage, although this may not be what you want, especially if a different password is specified for each!

AU—Authenticate

The AU stage takes the input of the EI stage and processes the extracted identity such as to authenticate it; that is, to ensure in some manner that a valid set of credentials have been presented to prove that the peer entity supplying the credentials actually is the identity they claim to be.

Warning—Security Programming Is Hard

It is easy to accidentally write an AU stylesheet that works and yet is completely insecure. Customization of the AAA process needs to be done with care and attention because this is security code that defines fundamental access control for your system, but, in particular, the AU stylesheet is easy to write badly and should be reviewed and validated many times.

At the AU stage, your stylesheet must decide a basis on which to either trust or not trust the supplied credentials. If this trust is too weak, people will be able to abuse the trust to access resources they should not be able to access. For example, if the stylesheet simply looks at an HTTP header to determine whether the request comes from a specific trusted server, a malicious client could simply spoof this header and become authenticated. If on the other hand the header contains an encrypted signed short lifetime token containing a username, malicious clients would find it much harder to compromise.

An important point for authentication in particular is that successful authentication is signified from an AU stylesheet by outputting any valid XML. Failed authentication is shown by outputting *no* XML at all. It is key to understand this; if your stylesheet outputs any valid XML, authentication is considered to have succeeded, even if the node set looks like this:

```
<authentication>
    <status>FAILED</status>
</authentication>
```

This XML would actually be seen as successful authentication if output by a custom AU stylesheet! To signify authentication failure, you must output nothing.

So, let's take a look at an example AU stylesheet. This stylesheet takes as its input the username and password from the previous example. Recall that the username was made up in the form of an email address, and the domain of the email address was referred to as an authentication domain. Our goal in this AU stylesheet is to authenticate this user to an LDAP server, using a different base distinguished name depending on the domain provided.

The LDAP server works by looking up the email address provided by the client and resolving that into a specific distinguished name; that distinguished name is then used to bind to validate that the password is correct. The AU.xsl stylesheet that performs this interaction with LDAP is shown in Listing 17-3.

Listing 17-3 AU Stylesheet Communicating with LDAP—AU.xsl

```
<?xml version="1.0" encoding="utf-8"?>
<xsl:stylesheet version="1.0"
        xmlns:xsl="http://www.w3.org/1999/XSL/Transform"
        xmlns:dp="http://www.datapower.com/extensions"
        exclude-result-prefixes="dp">
<xsl:output method="xml"/>
```

```
<xsl:template match="/">
<! - Take the username password and domain from the incoming nodeset  ->
<xsl:variable name="username"
  select="/identity/entry[@type='custom']/username/text()"/>
<xsl:variable name="password"
  select="/identity/entry[@type='custom']/password/text()"/>
<xsl:variable name="domain"
  select="substring-after($username,'@')"/>
<xsl:choose>
  <xsl:when test="$domain=('example.com' or 'somewhere.com')">
    <xsl:variable name="SearchFilter"
      select="concat('(&amp;(objectClass=ePerson)(emailAddress=',
      $username,'))')"/>
    <! - make a SUB search for our email address to find the DN  ->
    <xsl:variable name="userid"
      select="dp:ldap-search('ldapserver','389','','',
      concat('o=',$domain),'dn',$SearchFilter,'SUB','','')"/>
    <! - if the search returned a distinguished name…  ->
    <xsl:if test="$userid/LDAP-search-results/result/DN/text()">
      <! - …then try and bind as that distinguished name  ->
      <xsl:if test="dp:ldap-authen(
        $userid/LDAP-search-results/result/DN/text(),
        $password,'ldapserver:389')">
        <! - output XML if successful  ->
        <authenticated>yes</authenticated>
      </xsl:if>
    </xsl:if>
  </xsl:when>
  <xsl:otherwise>
    <! - OUTPUT NOTHING - AU fails  ->
  </xsl:otherwise>
</xsl:choose>
</xsl:template>
</xsl:stylesheet>
```

Let's examine this processing in slightly more depth. This is an LDAP server with two base distinguished names: example.com and somewhere.com. To perform the initial search, we first build an RFC2254-compliant LDAP filter string that looks for an LDAP object with objectClass of ePerson (a common object class representing a user) and an email address equal to that supplied (which was built, recall, by adding the username to the AuthDomain HTTP header). This search filter is then used in an ldap-search extension function call, to contact the server at hostname ldapserver on port 389, and perform an LDAP search for a subset of the relevant base Distinguished Name and extract the DN field specific to that user. Figure 17-9 shows the input into the ldap-search call, again taken from the extension trace in the Probe.

Content of Request:

```
<parameter>
  <bindDN />
  <bindPassword />
  <lookupDN>o=example.com</lookupDN>
  <lookupAttribute>dn</lookupAttribute>
  <filter>(&(objectClass=ePerson)(emailAddress=alice@example.com))</filter>
</parameter>
```

Show unformatted

Figure 17-9 The input nodeset to the ldap-search call.

This nodeset is built automatically by DataPower as a result of running the ldap-search extension function. As is clear from Figure 17-9, the actual connection to LDAP for the search is anonymous. If the server did not support anonymous binds for searching, we could specify a DN and password to use in the ldap-search function call. The search does not authenticate the user at all; rather it finds the attribute in the lookupAttribute node, in this case the DN, shown in Figure 17-10.

Content of Response:

```
<LDAP-search-results>
  <result>
    <DN>uid=alice.smith,c=gb,ou=sales,o=example.com</DN>
  </result>
</LDAP-search-results>
```

Show unformatted

Figure 17-10 The nodeset containing the result of the LDAP search.

After we have the distinguished name, we then attempt to bind as that user with the password provided, by using the ldap-authen function call. The ldap-authen input parameters in this instance are shown in Figure 17-11.

Content of Request:

```
<parameter>
  <bindDN>uid=alice.smith,c=gb,ou=sales,o=example.com</bindDN>
  <bindPassword>mysecret</bindPassword>
  <lookupDN />
  <lookupAttribute />
  <filter />
</parameter>
```

Show unformatted

Figure 17-11 The nodeset built by ldap-authen.

Again, this nodeset is automatically built by the ldap-authen function call. If this bind fails, the ldap-authen call returns no XML nodeset. If the bind is successful, however, the response of the ldap-authen call will contain the DN that was authenticated, depicted in Figure 17-12.

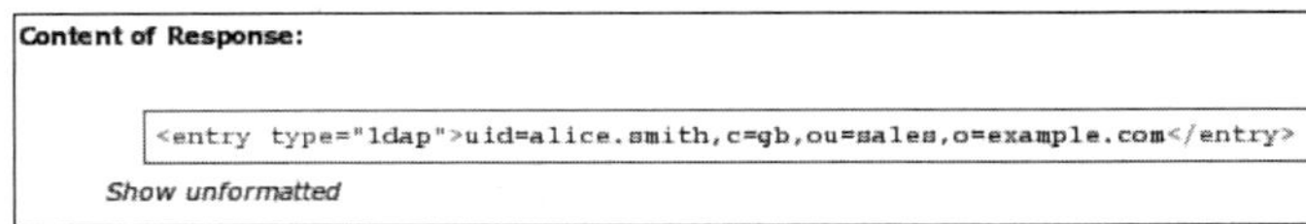
Content of Response:
<entry type="ldap">uid=alice.smith,c=gb,ou=sales,o=example.com</entry>
Show unformatted

Figure 17-12 The response nodeset from the ldap-authen call.

Our stylesheet simply needs to output any valid XML in order for authentication to have been deemed "successful." However, it is often useful to be able to pass on a credential of some sort to the rest of the AAA policy, such that it can make authorization decisions based on that credential. The output of the AU phase, whatever we include, will be made available to later phases in AAA processing, so we can choose to, for instance, pass in the DN that was authenticated. The structure we create can be seen in the Probe either as the output nodeset of our XSLT or by examining the AU debug context variable as shown in Figure 17-13.

Content of Variable 'var://context/AAA-internal-debug/AU':

```
<credentials>
  <entry type="custom" url="local:///AU.xsl">
    <authenticated>
    <entry type="ldap">uid=alice.smith,c=gb,ou=sales,o=example.com</entry>
    </authenticated>
  </entry>
</credentials>
```

Show unformatted

Figure 17-13 The final output of our AU stylesheet.

This XML structure has been generated by DataPower to wrap the output of our stylesheet, and it will be passed to the Map Credentials step.

Because Web services are inherently stateless, there likely will be multiple inbound requests with the same credentials. For performance reasons, the results of the authentication step, as well as the authorization step, will by default be cached for three seconds. Caching can be just as useful for a custom AAA step, because it will lower the load of any backend systems that the AAA step connects with. However, care should be taken that this caching does not cause undesired effects. For instance, if your custom AU stylesheet connects to a service that maintains an audit log intended to record all authentications, caching would mean that some cached requests would not be recorded, and thus caching should likely be disabled. The cache lifetime is configurable within the definition of the AAA policy, and it can be completely disabled if required.

WARNING—DO NOT RELY ON THE PROBE DEBUG VARIABLES

Figure 17-13 shows the content of the internal Probe variable var://context/AAA-internal-debug/AU, instead of using the extension trace as previous examples have. This is deliberate in order to raise this important point: Although these variables are extremely useful for debugging, they should *not* be relied upon in your XSLT!

These variables exist only when the Probe is enabled. This means that, if in your XSLT you read the contents of this or any other of the AAA-internal-debug variables, and make processing decisions based on them, your code will not work when the Probe is disabled.

The Probe should always be disabled in production environments, which means that testing must be carried out much earlier with the Probe disabled, just to make sure that nothing you are doing is affected by the Probe.

MC—Map Credentials

The Map Credentials (MC) step, as discussed in Chapter 16, enables you to modify the output of the authenticate step using a number of methods; one of those methods is to run a custom stylesheet. Of course, when the previous step of authentication was carried out using a stylesheet, in which we were able to present the output of the AU step in any way we chose, there is little value in further modifying it using a second stylesheet in the MC step! Thus, in most instances when AU uses a stylesheet, MC will not.

If authentication was performed using an out-of-the-box method, however, it can often be beneficial to use a custom stylesheet to perform credential mapping. This is also a nice way of performing further authentication over and above what the out-of-the-box authentication methods provide. For instance, if AU was used to simply bind a DN and password to verify that it is valid (a common use case), the MC step could take these credentials and perform further validation (for instance ensure that the user is not on a specific list of users who should be barred from logging in) or enrichment (such as pulling data out of a database for the specific user which will be used during a later phase such as authorization) or token exchange (for instance via a call out to Tivoli Federated Identity Manager).

One specific example of a credential mapping step that is often required is to map a distinguished name from x.509 format, as may often be found in a digital certificate, to the format more commonly found in LDAP servers. For example, the distinguished name `uid=user1, ou=research,o=example.com` would likely be presented in a certificate in x.509 format as `o=example.com/ou=research/uid=user1`—that is, slashes are used instead of commas and the order is reversed. To use this DN to check against an LDAP server, we would need to map the entries into the reverse order; a stylesheet to perform this mapping is shown in Listing 17-4.

Listing 17-4 MC Stylesheet to Map Distinguished Names—MC.xsl

```
<?xml version="1.0" encoding="utf-8"?>
<xsl:stylesheet xmlns:xsl="http://www.w3.org/1999/XSL/Transform"
  xmlns:dp="http://www.datapower.com/extensions"
  xmlns:fn="http://www.w3.org/2005/02/xpath-functions"
  xmlns:str="http://exslt.org/strings"
  extension-element-prefixes="dp" exclude-result-prefixes="dp"
  version="1.0">
  <xsl:output method="xml" />
  <xsl:template match="/">
    <xsl:variable name="originalDN"
      select="/credentials/entry[@type='validate-signer']
      /CertificateDetails/Subject/text()"/>
    <xsl:variable name="splitDN">
      <xsl:copy-of select="str:split($originalDN,'/')"/>
    </xsl:variable>
    <xsl:variable name="newSplitDN">
      <xsl:for-each select="$splitDN/token">
        <xsl:sort order="descending" data-type="number"
          select="position()"/>
        <xsl:variable name="this"
          select="normalize-space(.)"/>
        <xsl:value-of select="concat(',',$this)"/>
      </xsl:for-each>
    </xsl:variable>
    <xsl:variable name="newDN"
      select="substring-after($newSplitDN,',')"/>
    <entry type='custom'>
      <dn><xsl:value-of select="$newDN"/></dn>
    </entry>
  </xsl:template>
</xsl:stylesheet>
```

If the MC stage returns no credentials, the authorization step is likely to fail. Of course, whether or not it does is customizable! The default authorization processes consider authentication to have passed only if credentials are returned by the MC stage; in particular, this is true for the "any authenticated" authorization option, which is perhaps not obvious.

Read that again. The default authorization processes consider authentication to have passed only if credentials are passed to them. What this means is that, if your MC stage changes your authentication, strange and unexpected things can happen. An especially bad case might be if authentication fails, but your credential mapping still outputs a credential; in this case, a user could pass authorization and be allowed to access the protected resource they are trying to, even though authentication failed! Of course, this would likely be due to a bug in your stylesheet, but that is scant comfort when the villains are making off with the swag.

There may however be good use cases for changing the credentials to be valid after a failed authentication. For example, it is possible that if someone fails authentication, we might still want to allow them access to the system but as a guest user with limited privileges.

ER—Extract Resources

The ER stage is unique among the AAA stages in that it is the only one that cannot be replaced with a custom stylesheet. The output of the ER stage can, however, be modified or even completely removed by using a custom stylesheet in the MR stage which is next.

Resource extraction can be flexible. It can include processing metadata, the power of which was shown in Chapter 16, an XPath expression to extract any specific piece of the incoming XML message, and a number of other options as shown in Figure 17-14.

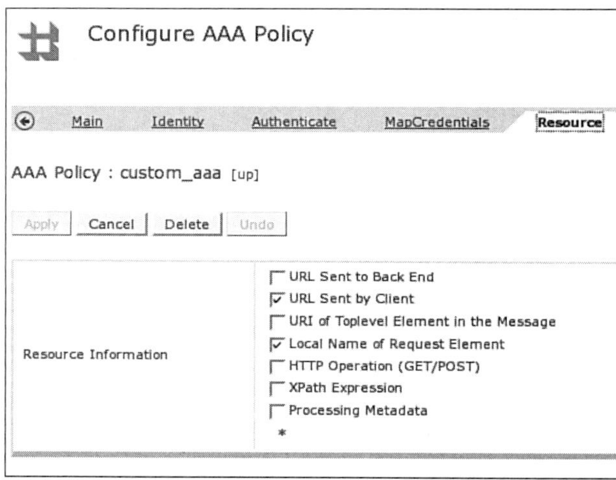

Figure 17-14 Resource extraction can be flexible.

A node tree is output by the ER stage that is used as the input to the MR stage that follows. For the example shown in Figure 17-14, with two types of resources extracted, this node tree looks like Figure 17-15.

Content of Request:

```
<resource>
  <item type="original-url">/bluebank/richpeople/currentAccount</item>
  <item type="request-opname">getAmount</item>
</resource>
```

Show unformatted

Figure 17-15 Multiple resources.

MR—Map Resources

The Map Resources stage modifies the extracted resource. Why would we want to do that? The most common use is to add together different resources of different types into a single resource of a specific type that an external authorization system will be able to understand.

Let's say that our external authorization system, as many do, works by protecting URLs. It can express an authorization constraint in terms of URL pattern matching; for instance, it would be able to protect the following:

```
/bluebank/richpeople/currentaccount
```

This happens to be the URI of a Web service served on a backend application server. Our external authorization system can state a constraint that, in order to access this URL, you have to have authenticated. However, as far as the external authorization system is concerned, this is only a URL; it has no concept of Web services.

This is unfortunate, because under the current account Web service URL shown, our backend application server provides a number of different Web service operations. It has an addMoney operation, a removeMoney operation, and a getAmount operation. What if we want to give one group of users the ability to run just the getAmount operation, and another group of users the ability to addMoney and removeMoney? Or, for instance, what if we require one level of authentication to getAmount, but require extra authentication to addMoney and removeMoney? These are real requirements; authorization at the operation level is a common thing to want to do.

DataPower, of course, is flexible and can easily protect at the Web service operation level. But if the external authorization system cannot understand Web service operations, how can we even ask it who should be allowed to call which operation? That's where the Map Resources step shines. The stylesheet in Listing 17-5 can perform this mapping.

Listing 17-5 MR Stylesheet—MR.xsl

```
<?xml version="1.0" encoding="UTF-8"?>
<xsl:stylesheet xmlns:xsl="http://www.w3.org/1999/XSL/Transform"
  xmlns:dp="http://www.datapower.com/extensions"
  extension-element-prefixes="dp" exclude-result-prefixes="dp"
  version="1.0">
  <xsl:output method="xml" />
  <xsl:template match="/">
    <! - take the url and operation name from the ER output  ->
    <xsl:variable name="url"
      select="resource/item[@type='original-url'][1]/text()"/>
    <xsl:variable name="opname"
      select="resource/item[@type='request-opname'][1]/text()"/>
    <xsl:variable name="resource"
      select="concat($url,'/',$opname,)"/>
    <resource>
      <item type="custom">
        <xsl:value-of select="$resource"/>
      </item>
    </resource>
  </xsl:template>
</xsl:stylesheet>
```

The 'request-opname' entry used is the result of selecting Local Name of Request Element in the resource extraction stage. This simple stylesheet concatenates the name of the operation to the URL that the client requested. Now we have a way of expressing the constraint in the external authorization system, by protecting the fictional URLs:

```
/bluebank/richpeople/currentaccount/getAmount
/bluebank/richpeople/currentaccount/addMoney
/bluebank/richpeople/currentaccount/removeMoney
```

Each of these "URLs" can then be given different authorization constraints in the external authorization system, and the AZ step acts as though the client requested the modified URL.

AZ—Authorization

The authorization step receives a large structure as its input. This node tree contains the output of the EI, MC, and MR steps, such that AZ can make a decision based on whether a given authenticated identity (EI and MC) can access a given resource (MR).

Many out-of-the-box authorization options already exist, and are often a perfect match to customer requirements for authorization. Sometimes, however, there is a need to go beyond these out-of-the-box options, either for integration with a custom external authorization system other than those directly supported, or to expand upon the built-in capabilities. An example of the latter is presented here.

Out-of-the-box integration with LDAP for authorization is implemented as one of the most common use cases—checking for membership of a specific LDAP group. This works by searching the LDAP server for the list of members in that group, and then comparing the output of the MC stage to that list. If the mapped credential is found, authorization succeeds; if not, then it fails. But what if we want to do more than checking for a single group membership? For instance, we might have a number of possible URLs (or Web service methods as demonstrated under MR earlier) and we would like to authorize different groups for each of the URLs, but without having to call out to an external authorization system. This may be an acceptable solution for a small number of static URLs, and would probably be easy to migrate later to a more robust enterprise authorization solution such as TAM.

One way that we might express such a set of authorization constraints would be to create a file that contains an XML nodeset, where the constraints are stated in a way that they can easily be retrieved using XPath. Listing 17-6 shows such a file.

Listing 17-6 One Way in Which Authorization Constraints Could Be Expressed

```
<?xml version="1.0" encoding="UTF-8"?>
<RESOURCES>
  <RESOURCE>
    <URL>/bluebank/richpeople/currentaccount/getAmount</URL>
    <GROUP>cn=workers,ou=groups,ou=example.com</GROUP>
  </RESOURCE>
  <RESOURCE>
    <URL>/bluebank/richpeople/currentaccount/addMoney</URL>
```

```
    <URL>/bluebank/richpeople/currentaccount/removeMoney</URL>
    <GROUP>cn=managers,ou=groups,ou=example.com</GROUP>
  </RESOURCE>
</RESOURCES>
</xsl:stylesheet>
```

This file would be written to the local file system (in this case to the file named local:///AZresources.xml) and will be called from the stylesheet; it could also be loaded from a remote server.

To process these constraints, our AU stylesheet must take the inputs from the MR step and know which resource the user is trying to access, take the input from the MC step and discover what groups the user is in, and then compare them to the expressed authorization constraints and make an authorization decision. The input to the AU stylesheet is shown in Figure 17-16.

Content of Request:

```
⊟ <container>
  ⊟ <mapped-credentials type="none" au-success="true">
    ⊟ <entry type="custom" url="local:///AU.xsl">
      ⊟ <authenticated>
          <entry type="ldap">uid=alice.smith,c=gb,ou=sales,ou=example.com</entry>
        </authenticated>
      </entry>
  </mapped-credentials>
  ⊟ <mapped-resource type="stylesheet" url="local:///MR.xsl">
    ⊟ <resource>
        <item type="custom">/bluebank/richpeople/currentAccount/getAmount</item>
      </resource>
  </mapped-resource>
  ⊟ <identity>
    ⊟ <entry type="custom" url="local:///EI.xsl">
        <username>alice@example.com</username>
        <password sanitize="true">mysecret</password>
      </entry>
  </identity>
  <au-ancillary-info />
  <az-ancillary-info />
</container>
```

Show unformatted

Figure 17-16 The information from previous steps is available for authorization decisions.

To further complicate matters, real world LDAP structures are rarely simple and can sometimes require quite complicated interactions! The example in Listing 17-7 demonstrates an example of the kind of interaction with LDAP that is sometimes needed to determine group memberships and uses the authorization constraints stated in Listing 17-6 to make an authorization decision.

Listing 17-7 Custom Authorization Example

```
<?xml version="1.0" encoding="UTF-8"?>
<xsl:stylesheet xmlns:xsl="http://www.w3.org/1999/XSL/Transform"
  xmlns:dp="http://www.datapower.com/extensions"
  extension-element-prefixes="dp" exclude-result-prefixes="dp"
  version="1.0">
  <xsl:output method="xml" />
  <xsl:template match="/">
```

```
    <xsl:variable name="perms"
      select="document('local:///AZresources.xml')"/>
    <xsl:variable name="resource"
      select="/container/mapped-resource/resource/item/text()"/>
    <xsl:variable name="DN" select="/container/mapped-credentials/
      entry[@type='custom']/authenticated/
      entry[@type='ldap']/text()"/>
    <xsl:variable name="groups" select="dp:ldap-search(
      'ldapserver','389','','',$DN,'ibm-allGroups','',
      'BASE','','')"/>
    <xsl:for-each select="$groups/LDAP-search-results/
      result/attribute-value[@name='ibm-allGroups']">
      <xsl:variable name="group" select="."/>
      <xsl:for-each select="$perms/RESOURCES/
        RESOURCE[URL=$resource]/GROUP">
        <xsl:if test=".=$group"><approved/></xsl:if>
      </xsl:for-each>
    </xsl:for-each>
  </xsl:template>
</xsl:stylesheet>
```

The stylesheet makes an LDAP call to search for a specific attribute of the authenticated user. In this case, we use the IBM Directory Server, and that attribute, `ibm-allGroups`, is a special attribute of the directory server in use. The attribute returns a list of all the groups that a particular entity is a member of. We then go through the list of groups and search for one that matches any of the group entries in the permissions file for the requested resource. If we find a match, an XML node `<approved/>` is emitted and authorization succeeds; if not, no output is emitted, which results in an authorization failure. Indeed, any node set apart from `<approved>` will also be treated as authorization failure; the DataPower runtime is expecting to see an `<approved>` node.

TIP—LDAP OPTIMIZATION

While not part of the LDAP specification itself, many LDAP servers have a "special" attribute that returns a list of the groups for a given user. For the IBM Directory Server, this is `ibm-allGroups`, for Active Directory, it is `memberOf`, and so on. Using this attribute requests that the directory server itself calculate which groups the user is a member of; this is often significantly faster than going through a list of all of the members of a group and comparing them locally.

This is because in a typical directory server a given user will be a member of some relatively small number of groups; however, a group may have a very large number of members, so enumerating all of the members for comparison is much more expensive in terms of computation and network bandwidth than asking the directory server to do it for us.

PP—Post Processing

Finally, the Post Processing stage comes at the end and enables you to do literally anything based on the output of all the other stages. The post processing input includes

- Identity
- Credentials
- Mapped-credentials
- Resource
- Mapped-resource
- The original message

The default Post Processing options cover many scenarios. DataPower can generate an LTPA token, which is discussed in Chapter 21, "Security Integration with WebSphere Application Server." It can generate an SAML assertion, a WS-Security UserNameToken, a WS-Security Kerberos token, or a SPNEGO token. It can call out to Tivoli Federated Identity Manager for token mapping. It can run some of the built-in post processing stylesheets such as strip-wssec-header.xsl to strip off WS-Security headers. Or it can execute a custom PP stylesheet to perform any action you want.

> **TIP—CREDENTIAL TRIMMING**
>
> When DataPower is processing incoming credentials and enforcing your security policies by performing authentication, authorization, and audit, it is likely that the credentials will not be required by the systems DataPower is proxying. If that is the case, they should be removed from the request before passing it on. This is best done in the PP stage with a simple custom stylesheet.

Working with Tivoli Security

Tivoli's Access Manager (TAM) and Federated Identity Manager products (TFIM) are the IBM solutions for externalized authentication and authorization (TAM) and federated identity management (TFIM). These powerful products enable enterprisewide definition of policies for who is allowed to do what in the enterprise, and those policies can be enforced at policy enforcement points, such as DataPower.

Because the focus of this book is DataPower and not the Tivoli product set, the discussion in this section builds on existing work by the Tivoli DataPower integration team published in the TFIM documentation.

That documentation shows how to configure integration with the TAM and TFIM products; this chapter explores the configuration of TAM integration.

Integration with TAM

In order for a DataPower appliance to integrate with TAM, it must have two things: a TAM license on the device and the correct TAM libraries installed in the currently running version of firmware. The firmware contains a built-in configurable TAM client, able to communicate with and externalize authentication and authorization to a specific version of the TAM server. The place to check this is under Status→System→Device Features, where the feature TAM should appear and be set to Enabled, and under Status→System→Library Information, where the library TAM should appear with the correct version. At time of writing, supported TAM versions are version 5 and version 6, and you should use the version of firmware that contains the relevant client version for your TAM server.

Initial Configuration

Before any security integration with TAM can take place, the TAM client must be configured. The configuration process on DataPower works by completing a form to create some configuration files required for TAM integration. This can be found on the TAM configuration object page, which is under Objects→Access→IBM Tivoli Access Manager, as shown in Figure 17-17.

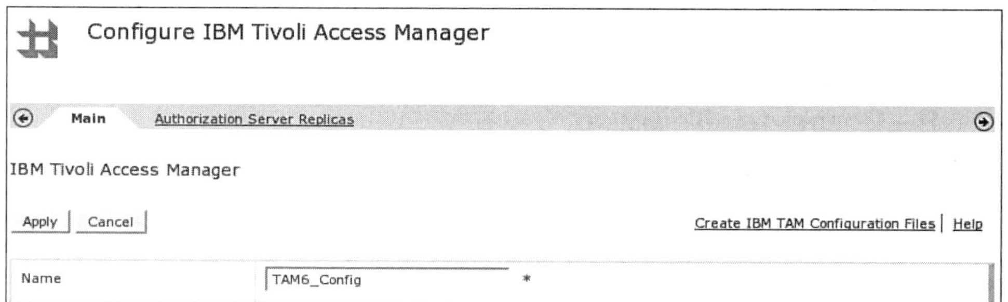

Figure 17-17 From the TAM Object Page, there is a link to create TAM configuration.

Clicking the Create IBM TAM Configuration Files link opens up a new window that determines how the files are to be generated. The window is shown in Figure 17-18. Note that in this example we have used static hosts defined on the DataPower device, for the hostname of the TAM Policy Server and of the LDAP Server, although this may use DNS.

After we click the Create IBM Tivoli Access Manager Configuration button shown in Figure 17-18, the appliance begins the file creation process. It makes a call out to the TAM policy server, authenticates to it using the credentials you have supplied, and asks the Policy server to register it as a valid server for sending authentication and authorization requests. As part of this process, TAM creates a new account for the DataPower appliance that it uses to bind to the LDAP server to perform queries as required. It provides the TAM CA certificate to the DataPower appliance such that SSL connections can be authenticated and trusted. Finally all the TAM configuration files are saved to the relevant areas on the DataPower file system. The DataPower logs of this process are shown in Figure 17-19.

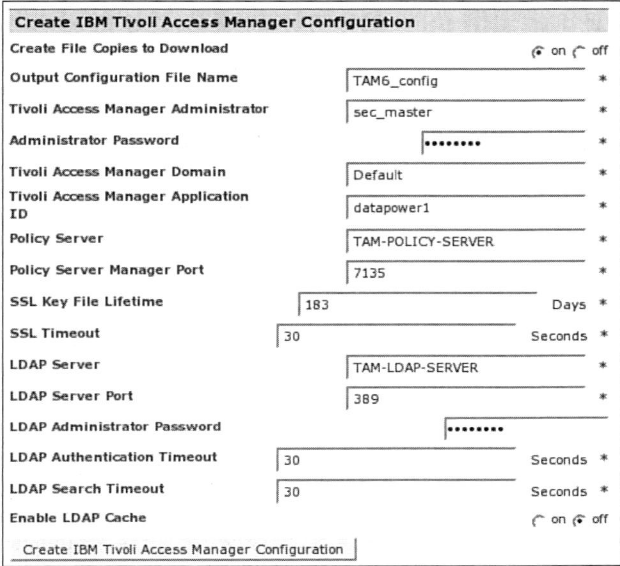

Figure 17-18 TAM configuration.

msgid	message Show last 50 100 all
0x81a0001f	Created Tivoli Access Manager LDAP user registry configuration file
0x81a00031	Starting LDAP registry file creation
0x81a0001f	Created Tivoli Access Manager host runtime configuration file
0x81a0001f	Created Tivoli Access Manager key database and key stash configuration file
0x81a00028	Generating Tivoli Access Manager host config succeeded
0x81a00020	Tivoli Access Manager server CA certificate was successfully retrieved as part of client configuration
0x81a00026	Starting Tivoli Access Manager file creation process
0x81a0000d	Signaling Tivoli Access Manager client file creation

Figure 17-19 TAM configuration logs.

The TAM configuration files that are created consist of four separate files:

1. A text file with a suffix of .conf, which contains specific information obtained from the TAM server about the TAM configuration.
2. A binary file with a suffix of .conf.obf, which contains the same information as the .conf file but in an obfuscated file, and can be used instead of the conf file if there is a need for the passwords used to connect to the LDAP server and TAM to not be stored in plain text.
3. A key database file with a suffix of .kdb, which contains the SSL certificates used to validate the SSL connection with the TAM policy server.
4. A stash file with a suffix of .sth, which contains the stashed password to the key database file.

The names of the files are determined by the Output Configuration File Name option in the configuration screen; in our example from Figure 17-18, the files would be called TAM6_config.conf, TAM6_config.kdb, and so on. Note that the key database file and related stash file are, by default, created only in the `cert://` file system, from which they cannot be exported. If you have a need to export these files (for instance for backup purposes), the Create File Copies to Download option should be selected when creating the configuration; they will then be copied to the `temporary://` file system from which they can be downloaded. The other two files are stored to the `local://` file system of the domain.

Application ID

One of the fields shown in Figure 17-18 is called the "Tivoli Access Manager Application ID." This field is used to create a server definition for this specific DataPower appliance in the TAM database and a server account in the LDAP server used as its repository.

The server definition and account that is created uses both the application ID and the System ID of the DataPower appliance. The System Identity of the DataPower device is configured at an appliance level in the Default domain, by navigating to Administration→Device→System Settings and filling in the System Identifier field. Crucially, whatever is put in here must be resolvable on the TAM server, and must resolve to the DataPower appliance, otherwise the configuration will fail. This can be done by modifying the hosts file on the TAM server, or by specifying a resolvable fully qualified DNS name as the System Identifier. In our example, we used the Application ID `datapower1` and a System ID of `DataPowerBookXI50` (and DataPowerBookXI50 was added to the hosts file of the TAM server), thus the server definition is `datapower1-DataPowerBookXI50` and the account principal is `datapower1/DataPowerBookXI50`.

The Application ID is used in TAM for application-specific authorization purposes. Thus two DataPower devices that serve the same "application" (for instance which both proxy the same Web service and have a Load Balancer in front of them) should use the same Application ID. Their entries in the TAM namespace differ because of the different System ID's with which they should be configured.

If you have a need to configure TAM multiple times on the same appliance, the application ID's used *must* be different. For instance, you may want to have multiple domains all integrating with TAM for development or testing purposes. Because the System ID is a device-level setting configured in the Default domain, no two DataPower domains on the same device should ever use the same Application ID when connecting to the same TAM server.

System Identifier

The System ID of the DataPower appliance must be set for a TAM configuration to work correctly. If you do not set this on your device, the TAM client will still connect and configure itself, however rather than using the System ID for the creation of the server definition and the account principal, it will use the value entered for the TAM policy server on the configuration screen. Things appear to work, but you have incorrect configuration on the TAM server, and this may cause serious problems later. It is strongly recommended that DataPower appliances using TAM should have correctly configured System IDs.

Configuration Failures

If the TAM configuration fails, this will be clear from the logs in the domain. The failure message likely contain a TAM error; these can be decoded by looking at the TAM documentation, or by asking a friendly TAM administrator. The most likely causes of TAM configuration failure are

- Lack of network connectivity. There must be network connectivity between DataPower and the TAM server, not just at runtime but also during configuration. As mentioned, the configuration process involves connecting to and registering with the TAM policy server, and if this is not possible, it will result in a failed configuration.
- Incorrect policy server port. Most TAM policy servers run on the default ports of 7135 and 7136, but this is configurable, and some TAM administrators may have chosen to use a different port.
- Incorrect username or password used for connection to the TAM server or the LDAP server.
- An account for the specific application ID for a given appliance with a given system identifier already exists in this TAM server, perhaps from a prior configuration attempt.
- Incompatible version of TAM client. For instance using a TAM5 DataPower firmware will not work with a TAM6 Server if that TAM6 server is configured in FIPS mode.

Any issues with the TAM configuration must be resolved before continuing. Do not go on to creation of TAM configuration objects until the TAM configuration has completed successfully and been verified in the logs.

Unconfiguration

If the configuration partially succeeds, or if you need to remove an existing configuration, it is not as simple as just removing the files that are created on the DataPower appliance. Because the configuration process connects to the Access Manager server and makes configuration changes, those must also be removed. This is especially important if you intend to use the same application identity, because the configuration will simply fail.

The DataPower TAM client does not include a utility to remove the TAM configuration. Thus removing the entries from the TAM database and LDAP server must be done on the server itself. TAM provides a command, `svrsslcfg`, which is used to manually add and remove server configuration from the database and LDAP server. This command requires a configuration file, an application ID, and a hostname. For removal, it is possible to simply use an empty configuration file; the application id (-n) and the hostname (-h) are the parameters that decide the server definition to be removed. The `touch` command can be used to create an empty configuration file, which is then passed to the `svrsslcfg` command. This process is shown in Listing 17-8.

Listing 17-8 Unconfiguring a DataPower Appliance from TAM

```
tam-server:~ # pdadmin -a sec_master
Enter Password: ********
pdadmin sec_master> server list
  ivacld-tam-server
  datapower1-DataPowerBookXI50
pdadmin sec_master> quit
tam-server:~ # touch dummy.conf
tam-server:~ # svrsslcfg -unconfig -f dummy.conf -n datapower1 -h
DataPowerBookXI50
Enter the password for sec_master:
********
Unconfiguration of application "datapower1" for host "DataPowerBookXI50" is
in progress.
This might take several minutes.
SSL unconfiguration for application "datapower1" has completed
successfully.
tam-server:~ # pdadmin -a sec_master
Enter Password:
pdadmin sec_master> server list
  ivacld-tam-server
pdadmin sec_master> quit
tam-server:~ #
```

Object Creation

After the four configuration files are successfully created, we can go ahead and create a TAM configuration object referencing those files, as shown in Figure 17-20.

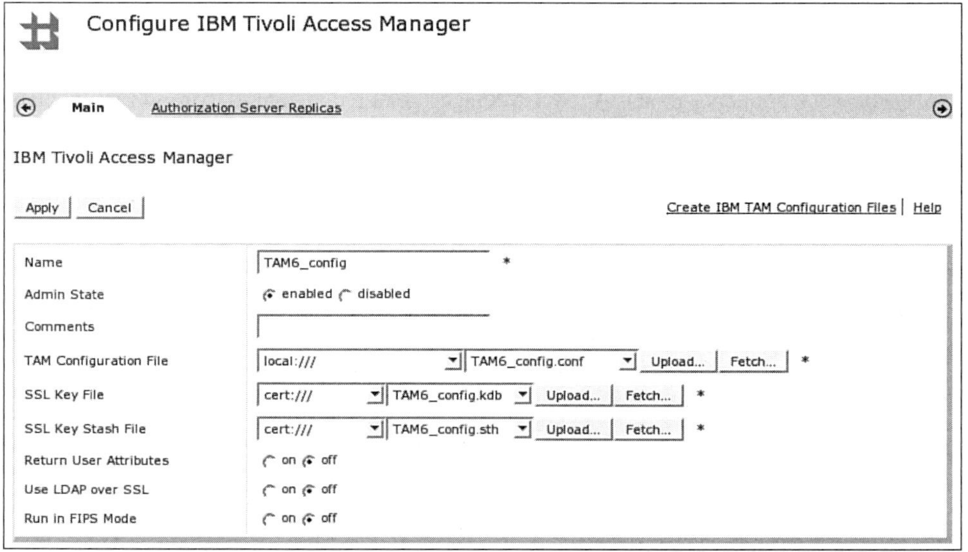

Figure 17-20 TAM configuration.

One of the most important fields on Figure 17-20 is the Run in FIPS Mode field. The Federal Information Processing Standard (FIPS) standard specifies explicitly the types of encryption that can be used. If you are working with a TAM server that uses FIPS-compliant encryption, you will be able to communicate with it *only* if this button is selected. FIPS mode is configured in the SSL stanza of the TAM policy server's pd.conf file—if there is an entry like `ssl-enable-fips = yes` then the Run in FIPS Mode button must be set to on, otherwise you will see in the logs the error shown in Figure 17-21.

```
tam (TAM6_config): Tivoli Access Manager authorization client
log message: TAM server error: azn_initialize : HPDBA0234E
The SSL communications could not be completed. The socket
was closed.
```

Figure 17-21 Incorrect FIPS settings will result in an SSL error.

The second tab of the object screen also needs to be configured with at least one Authorization server replica. (Of course, if there are more we could specify them all here.) In many instances the main authorization server replica resides on the policy server, as it does for our example environment, so we have used the same host alias as before in Figure 17-22. (Note that this is a different port to the manager port shown in Figure 17-18—the default authorization port is 7136, and specifying the wrong port here can be very hard to debug!)

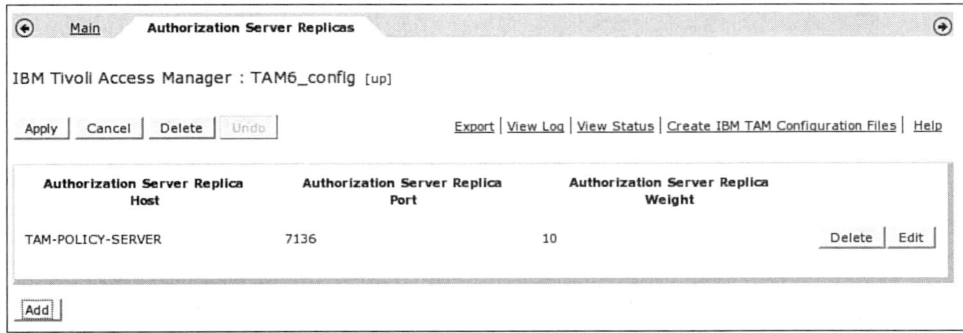

Figure 17-22 At least one Authorization Server replica is required.

After clicking Apply on the TAM object configuration screen, we see the object initially go into a red Pending state, shown in Figure 17-23.

Name	Status	Op-State	Logs	Admin State	TAM Configuration File	SSL Key File	SSL Key Stash File
TAM6_config	new	Pending		enabled	local:///TAM6_config.conf	cert:///TAM6_config.kdb	cert:///TAM6_config.sth

Figure 17-23 Initial Pending state.

This is not a cause for alarm—this is simply the state it goes into when the initial configuration is being verified, because it takes a couple of seconds for everything to fall into place. The logs are shown in Figure 17-24.

08:45:09	mgmt	notice	59088065			0x00350014	tam (TAM6_config): Operational state up
08:45:09	tam	notice				0x81a0001d	tam (TAM6_config): Tivoli Access Manager client successfully enabled
08:45:07	tam	info				0x81a00038	tam (TAM6_config): The Tivoli Access Manager object has been configured; attempting to start client authorization endpoint
08:45:07	mgmt	info	59088065			0x00360001	tam (TAM6_config): Pending
08:45:07	mgmt	notice	59088065			0x00350015	tam (TAM6_config): Operational state down
08:45:07	tam	info	59088065				tam (TAM6_config): starting tam thread
08:45:07	tam	debug	59088065			0x81a0003b	tam (TAM6_config): Successfully added replica to Tivoli Access Manager configuration - hostname 'TAM-POLICY-SERVER', port 7136, weight 10
08:45:06	tam	debug	59088065			0x81a00036	tam (TAM6_config): 1 authorization replica configured
08:45:06	tam	debug	59088065			0x81a00033	tam (TAM6_config): Created LDAP registry file

Figure 17-24 A successful configuration.

The object creation is now complete and can be used in AAA processing policies.

AAA Processing

Once the TAM configuration is complete and the TAM objects exist, configuring for AAA authentication is as easy as selecting the option and pointing it at the TAM configuration. Figure 17-25 shows the configuration for AAA authentication.

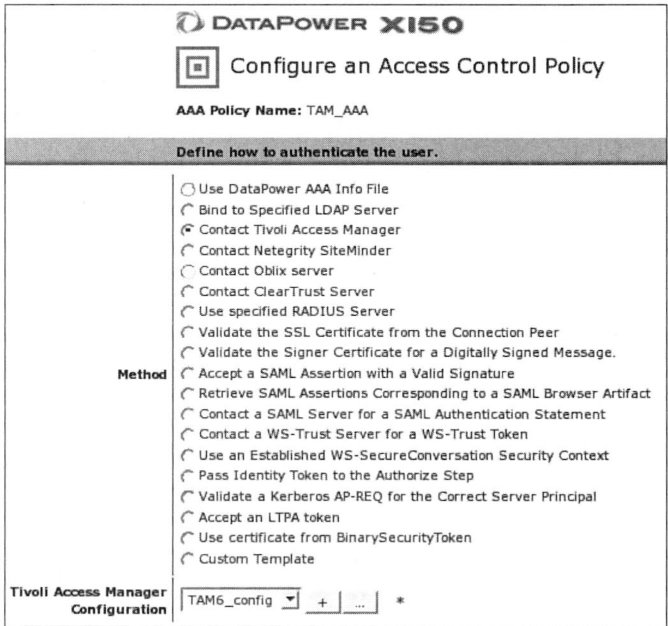

Figure 17-25 AAA Authentication with TAM.

Authorization, however, is rather more involved. TAM authorization has many aspects, and permissions can be granted at many different levels. Because the TAM runtime is very flexible, there are many possible ways that access control can be configured, and it is beyond the scope of this book to examine them in detail. Instead we will show a specific example of configuration to demonstrate the flexibility and power of the combination of TAM and DataPower.

The AZ step to communicate with TAM takes three inputs, which can be seen in Figure 17-26, which displays the Probe extension trace of the input into a TAM AZ step.

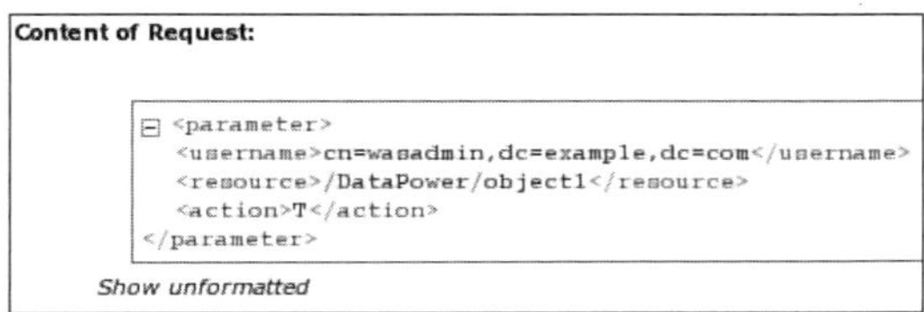

Figure 17-26 Inputs to the TAM AZ step.

The inputs are the authenticated username (which in this instance came directly from a TAM AU step, but could of course have come from a custom AU step or an MC step), the resource being requested (which in this case came from the URL sent by the client, but could of course have come from any other ER or MR step), and the action that DataPower believes the client is trying to perform. The resource and the action here require more explanation.

First, we will examine the resource. In order to understand how TAM makes authorization decisions, we have to look briefly at the TAM object space. This object space is just a hierarchical listing of objects that can have access control lists (ACL) attached to them. When TAM receives a request for authorization of a resource, that resource is mapped directly to the object space. To demonstrate this, we set up an object space with a very simple resource structure. At the top level is the object `/DataPower`, and underneath it are three separate objects: `object1`, `object2`, and `object3`. We have chosen this object space to be a simple representation such that we can easily map it to URLs, which is protected by the object space. The URLs to be protected are shown in Listing 17-9.

Listing 17-9 The URL Structure to Protect

```
http://datapower-ip-address/DataPower/object1
http://datapower-ip-address/DataPower/object2
http://datapower-ip-address/DataPower/object3
```

Listing 17-10 shows the object space of these specific objects in our TAM server and a description of one of the objects.

Listing 17-10 TAM Object Space Configured to Protect Our Simple URL Structure

```
pdadmin sec_master> object list /DataPower
  /DataPower/object1
  /DataPower/object2
  /DataPower/object3
pdadmin sec_master> object show /DataPower/object1
  Name: /DataPower/object1
    Description: Test object 1
    Type: 14 (Application Container Object)
    Is Policy Attachable: Yes
    Extended Attributes:
    Attached ACL: DataPower-acl1
    Attached POP:
    Attached AuthzRule:

    Effective Extended Attributes:
    Effective ACL: DataPower-acl1
    Effective POP:
    Effective AuthzRule:
pdadmin sec_master>
```

The objects in the TAM namespace have an attached Access Control List (ACL). This is similar to, but far more advanced than, a UNIX© file permission. The ACL attached to our objects is shown in Listing 17-11.

Listing 17-11 The ACL Attached to Our Objects

```
pdadmin sec_master> acl show DataPower-acl1
  ACL Name: DataPower-acl1
  Description:
  Entries:
    Any-other T
    User wasadmin Tr
pdadmin sec_master>
```

This ACL is the list of permissions that a specific user has on the object. In this case all authenticated users have the T permission, and the user called wasadmin has both the T and r permissions. T stands for Traverse, while r stands for read. The T permission is required to Traverse the tree; if a user does not have Traverse permission on the object `/DataPower`, they cannot access anything under it such as `/DataPower/object1`. The r permission seems like it should mean that the user can read the resource. However, what that actually means is specific to the application that is mapping the resource.

Back in Figure 17-23, we showed the input into the TAM AZ step, which included an authenticated user, a resource, and an action. The action in Figure 17-23 was T; that is, DataPower was asking TAM "Does this user have the T permission on this resource?" The reason it asked about T permission was because this is how the default AZ action is configured. Figure 17-27 shows the TAM AZ configuration.

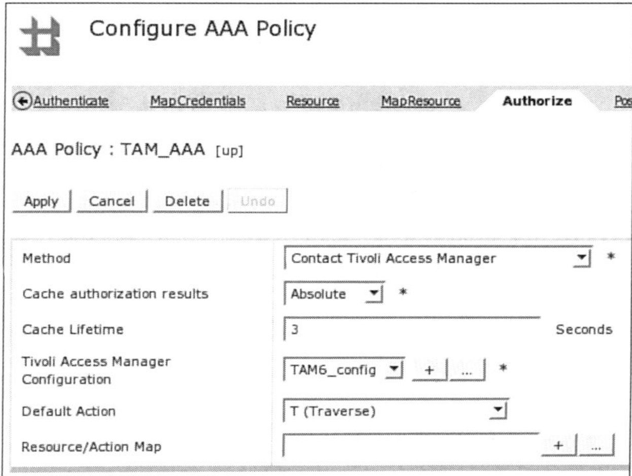

Figure 17-27 The TAM AZ step.

The Default action field defines what permission bit we will be asking TAM for when making the authorization call. Because it is set to T, anyone with T permission on the object that matches the resource will be successfully authorized. Our ACL stated that all users have T permission on the object, so anyone who authenticates can access this object. If however we change this to r, only the user named wasadmin, as the only one with r permission listed in the ACL, will be able to access the object.

Finally, we can create a construct called a Resource/Action map, which allows you to dynamically map an operation such as a URL to a required permission bit based on a simple matching, as shown in Figure 17-28.

Help

DATAPOWER XI50

Edit TAM AAA Authorization Resource/Action Map

TAM authorization Resource/Action mappings

Resource Pattern	TAM Action	WebSEAL Conformance	
getAmount	r (Read)		/\ V
addMoney	x (Execute)		/\ V

Add Cancel Back Next

Figure 17-28 The Resource/Action map.

Summary

This chapter has provided an in-depth look at customizing the AAA process, which is extremely flexible and powerful and enables integration with any form of AAA processing imaginable. We have also gone through externalizing of authentication and authorization to IBM's Tivoli Access Manager, the IBM solution to Enterprise Class centralized Access Control. And yet this knowledge has barely scraped the surface of what is possible with the AAA runtime; you can now go and explore to create the AAA processing that suits your specific requirements and needs!

CHAPTER 18

DataPower and SSL

Cryptography is one of the most powerful security measures we have at our disposal, and DataPower has powerful cryptographic capabilities. The custom cryptographic hardware on the appliance accelerates cryptographic operations, and the ease with which complex cryptography can be utilized is astounding. This chapter explores how DataPower uses the well-known Secure Sockets Layer (SSL) to provide privacy and integrity for incoming and outgoing connections.

The Secure Sockets Layer

SSL is a standardized method of encrypting traffic on TCP/IP networks such as the Internet. The most common use is to protect Web pages. Whenever you see `https://` at the front of a URL, this means that the connection is passed over SSL and requests and responses sent through it will be encrypted. However, SSL is far more general purpose, and is commonly used for much more than encrypting Web traffic using HTTP—and indeed for more than encryption. Authentication based on cryptographic trust is a fundamental part of the SSL protocol, verifying the identity of either just the server side (the entity connected *to*) or indeed authentication of both ends of the connection (known as *mutual authentication*). SSL has been used in the wild for such obscure tasks as encrypting raw ODBC database connections when the database does not support native encryption, and providing a mutually authenticated link between servers that have no other means of authenticating each other. Indeed, general-purpose tunneling[1] software exists to create an SSL tunnel over which any TCP protocol can be passed.

[1] The term tunneling refers to the encapsulation of one protocol within another. HTTPS is in fact two protocols—HTTP is the payload protocol, and it is encapsulated or tunneled within the delivery protocol SSL. Generally, the delivery protocol is more secure than the payload protocol, and it is tunneled to provide a secure path through a less trusted network.

Cryptography

To understand SSL, it is important to have at least a basic understanding of cryptography. Cryptography can be used to solve three fundamental problems:

- **Privacy**—(Also known as confidentiality). How do I ensure that no one other than the intended parties can see what I am sending?
- **Integrity**—How can I be sure that no one has intercepted and tampered with my data?
- **Impersonation**—(Sometimes referred to as nonrepudiation). How can I be sure that I am communicating with whomever I think I am?

Each of these problems can be solved cryptographically using techniques, such as keys, certificates, signatures, and digests. We introduce these in this section.

Privacy: Algorithms and Keys, Encryption and Decryption

For the majority of people, when they think of cryptographic techniques, they think of encryption and decryption of data. In modern cryptography, this is done using cryptographic algorithms and cryptographic keys.

The cryptographic algorithm is usually published and well known. It defines a method for how to take the plain unencrypted data (usually referred to as plain text, even when it is not actually text) and turn it into encrypted data (often known as ciphertext). The key, on the other hand, must be kept secret at all costs. It is a piece of data used to alter how the algorithm behaves, in a unique way. For instance, it can work so that data encrypted with a given key and algorithm can only be decrypted by that same key and algorithm. This kind of encryption, where the same key is used to both encrypt and decrypt, is called *symmetric key encryption.*

Symmetric key encryption has one large advantage. Cryptographically speaking, it is the fastest form of encryption or decryption; the processing cost in terms of CPU and elapsed time is relatively small. However, there are also certain challenges with symmetric key encryption. Most importantly, because the same secret key is used to both encrypt and decrypt, for the encryption to be useful in communication, we need to ensure that both the sender and receiver have the same key. This might be okay for a single point-to-point connection; however, imagine trying to share many different unique keys with many different users; it is obvious that this would not scale.

Figure 18-1 shows the encryption and decryption process with a symmetric key; the same key is used to encrypt and then subsequently to decrypt the text.

Figure 18-1 Encryption using a symmetric key.

Another form of encryption uses two separate keys that have a complex mathematical relationship with each other. The relationship is such that anything encrypted with one of the keys can be decrypted only with the other (and vice versa). Most important, there is no way[2] to derive one key from the other; in order to encrypt and subsequently decrypt both keys are required. This makes it perfect for exchanging encrypted messages with other people; if you have one key and another person has the related key, that person can decrypt your messages and you can decrypt his messages. Encryption using these kinds of keys is called *asymmetric key encryption.*

Keys used for asymmetric key encryption are used in a concept fundamental to SSL known as Public Key Cryptography (referred to also as Public Key Infrastructure [PKI]). One of the keys is designated as "public" meaning that it is freely shared with others, and the other key is designated as "private" and is kept secret. Because the private key cannot be derived from the public key, it is safe to share the public key with all and sundry.

Figure 18-2 shows the encryption/decryption process with a pair of keys.

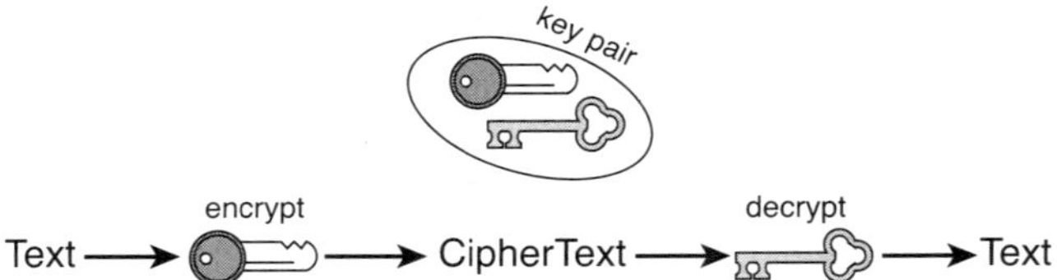

Figure 18-2 Encryption using an asymmetric key pair.

Using PKI, the problem with distribution of keys is solved. We simply share the public key and keep the private key private. Anyone who has the public key can encrypt a message and the only person who will be able to decrypt it is the holder of the private key. The only real disadvantage to using asymmetric key encryption is that it is significantly more computationally expensive than symmetric key encryption. Thus, symmetric key encryption should generally be preferred where extremely high performance is a requirement. (Although with the DataPower appliance this would have to be a *very* extreme performance requirement!)

Integrity: Cryptographic Hashes and Digests

Cryptography can also be used to solve the problem of integrity and answer the question: How can I be sure that no one has tampered with and modified my data? This is done using a different kind of cryptographic algorithm called a cryptographic hash function. The hash function takes an input and turns it into a fixed-length string called a digest (also known as a hash value).

Given the same input data, a cryptographic hash function will always produce the same digest. Moreover, the number of other input values that will produce an identical digest is extraordinarily small, and practically impossible to compute. More importantly, the chance of producing *meaningful* data that will generate an identical digest is even smaller. So, in order to guarantee the

[2] "No way" is of course a point in time statement. Cryptography with asymmetric keys fundamentally relies on the fact that current computing power is not enough to reasonably derive one key from the other. If someone suddenly discovers a computer that is significantly faster (by many orders of magnitude), all our existing asymmetric cryptography will be rendered insecure. With the advent of the quantum computer, this might not be as far away as you think!

integrity of a message, simply compute a digest and send it along with the message. Then, when the receiver receives the message, he can compute the digest himself and see if it matches the one you sent. If the digests do not match, clearly the message has been tampered with.

Keep in mind that cryptographic hashes are only as secure as the hash algorithms which are used to calculate the digests. For instance, a number of years ago a hash function called "MD5" was considered to be strong; it was thought that it would be extremely difficult to create a modified message that has the same digest. However, at the time of writing, it is possible to break an MD5 hash (produce a different message resulting in the same digest) in less than 20 minutes using a typical desktop computer! There are also currently concerns about the replacement for MD5, called SHA-1; we'll see what the future holds with its superfast computers and advanced mathematics!

Impersonation: Digital Signatures

Finally, cryptography can be used to solve the fundamental problem of impersonation[3] and answer the question: How do I know that the person sending me a message or otherwise communicating with me is who she says she is? This is done using digital signatures.

A digital signature is a technique that uses asymmetric key encryption and cryptographic hash functions to cryptographically "sign" a message, such that it could only have been signed by the person who holds the private key used to sign the message. This is an extremely powerful technique, because anyone who has access to the corresponding public key can verify that the signature is real.

The technique works by first calculating a digest for the message to be sent, and then encrypting that digest with the sender's private key. The message is then sent to the receiver along with the encrypted digest. The receiver does two things. First, using the same hash algorithm as the sender, he calculates a digest of the message (without the signature); recall that the same message will always produce the same hash digest, so this should be the same as the original digest unless the message has been modified. Secondly, the receiver will decrypt the original digest using the public key of the sender; the fact that it can be decrypted by the public key means that it was encrypted with the private key. Finally, the receiver will compare the digest he calculated with the decrypted one from the message. If both digests are equal, the message has not been tampered with and only the holder of the private key could have signed it.

The flow of message digests is shown in Figure 18-3.

[3] People sometimes refer to the solution of the impersonation problem as "non-repudiation." This is a confusing and misleading term when applied to digital signatures, because it strongly implies that "someone" is behind a specific action. As will become clear, a digital signature is simply a cryptographic proof that a specific signed message was signed by a specific private key. The signature makes no claims about who currently holds that private key, or about who specifically carried out the signing. In the same way that a traditional paper signature can be repudiated by the signatory claiming that the signature is forged or was signed under coercion, a digital signature can be repudiated by the signer stating that his private key was stolen or otherwise compromised.

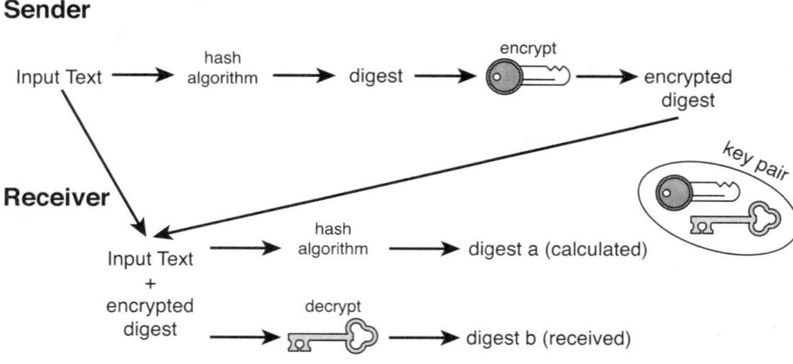

Figure 18-3 Digital signatures use hash algorithms and encryption.

Digital Certificates

The three solutions described are extremely powerful cryptographic techniques. However, none of them actually identify specific servers or people. If a message is encrypted or signed using a specific private key, you can decrypt or verify the signature using the corresponding public key. However, how does that actually help in a practical way? This is why digital certificates exist.

A digital certificate is a special way of sharing a public key with others. It contains information about the person or server to whom the certificate is assigned—perhaps a human name or a server's hostname. It also contains a serial number and expiration date, so that it can be identified by the serial number and is valid only for a certain amount of time. Most importantly, it contains the following cryptographic information:

- A copy of the certificate holder's public key
- A digital signature, signed by a third party (usually *not* the certificate holder)
- Information about who signed the certificate

The signer of the certificate, the trusted third party, is usually referred to as a Certificate Authority (CA). The CA is an institution that exists to sign certificates for people. It will also make *its* public key easily available, so that anyone wishing to verify that a certificate was indeed signed by that CA can do so. Note that the certificate explicitly does not include the private key, either of the certificate holder or the certificate authority—if it did, it would be useless! The private key of the certificate owner is held secretly by the owner of the certificate and is used for encryption and signing. The private key of the CA is held secretly by that CA and is used only for signing certificates. The certificate itself exists only to freely share the certificate owner's public key with others and to "vouch for" who they are.

The role of the CA, and indeed the reason that we choose to trust them, is that it promises to verify that the person or entity requesting that a certificate be signed is indeed who they say they are. The procedure for doing so is usually based on submitting some form of proof of identity; for instance, if you want a public CA to sign a certificate for a specific domain, you need to provide evidence that you actually own that domain.

SSL and Cryptography

The SSL protocol uses all the previous cryptographic techniques to provide privacy and integrity along with optional mutual authentication. It enables privacy using both asymmetric and symmetric key encryption; an initial handshake with asymmetric keys and certificates is used to establish communication, and during that handshake, a symmetric key is shared between both sides, which is later used for all encryption. It provides for message integrity by using the shared secret key along with cryptographic hash functions to ensure that the content of messages sent along an SSL connection is not altered. Finally, it provides mutual authentication by using signed digital certificates to authenticate both sides to each other during the handshake.

Client and Server Roles

As with most TCP protocols, in an SSL conversation, the side that initiates the connection is referred to as the Client, and the side that accepts the connection is called the Server. In the Web browser case, it is obvious which is the Client (the Web browser) and which is the Server (the Web server). However SSL, and in particular HTTP, is often used in server-to-server communications, and in those instances, it is perfectly possible for two "server class" nodes to play either the Client or the Server role.

SSL Authentication and Mutual Authentication

The SSL protocol provides for one or both sides of a conversation to authenticate to each other. The entity in the role of the Server must always authenticate itself; that is, as part of the negotiation for an SSL connection, it always presents a signed certificate as its identity. The Client can also *optionally* authenticate itself with a signed certificate, but this is not a mandatory part of the protocol. When both sides authenticate, the connection is said to be "mutually authenticated."

The SSL Handshake

Enough theory! Let's take a scenario where two DataPower appliances need to communicate with each other, where they need to authenticate each other, be certain that data is not intercepted, and be sure that the data they are sending and receiving has not been modified in transit. Let's explore how the concepts described previously are used in SSL.

The scenario we use is comprised of two DataPower appliances, one deployed in the De-Militarized Zone (DMZ) as a security gateway, and the other deployed in a backend server zone performing the function of an Enterprise Service Bus (ESB). Let's call them DMZDP and ESBDP. The connection between the two needs to be encrypted (to ensure that, if for some reason network security is compromised, data cannot be simply sniffed over the wire by a third party) and mutually authenticated (such that DMZDP can be sure that it is actually connecting to ESBDP, and also that ESBDP can be sure that only DMZDP can connect to it). The scenario is depicted in Figure 18-4.

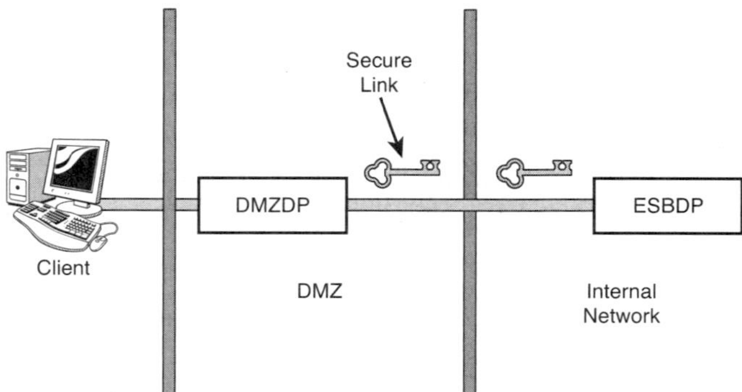

Figure 18-4 Communication between the DMZ and the ESB on the internal network.

This section presents a simplified explanation of the SSL handshake between the two devices, covering the points that are directly relevant to the usage inside DataPower. Significantly more detail can be found in RFC2246 and from many other online sources if required.

The Hello Message

Let's say that DMZDP initiates the SSL connection to ESBDP, thus making DMZDP the "client" and ESBDP the "server." DMZDP opens up a TCP socket, and when that is connected, it sends an SSL "hello" message. Inside that hello message is a list of ciphers (hash functions and encryption algorithms) that DMZDP is capable of using. These are configurable on DataPower as shown later in the chapter.

ESBDP receives the "hello" message and chooses which of the ciphers it wants to use from the ones that DMZDP has sent. If you configure two devices to communicate using SSL, both of them must be configured so that they have at least one set of ciphers (hash functions and encryption algorithms) in common! ESBDP sends back its own "hello" message, which contains the cipher that it has chosen to use for this SSL session.

ESBDP's "hello" message also includes a signed digital certificate. This is the certificate that ESBDP uses to identify itself. The digital certificate contains a public key, and ESBDP holds the corresponding private key in secure storage on the appliance. Who is the certificate signed by? Well, a trusted third party, of course!

DMZDP receives the "hello" message from ESBDP and looks at the certificate. The first thing it does is check whether the certificate is expired. If it is, DMZDP refuses to communicate and closes the connection. Next, DMZDP will validate the signature of the certificate. This means that DMZDP must know where to find the public key of the trusted third party that signed it. To trust ESBDP's certificate, DMZDP must have been preconfigured either with the public key of the signer of ESBDP's certificate or with a copy of the certificate itself. After the signature on the certificate has been validated, DMZDP retrieves ESBDP's public key from the certificate.

This interaction is shown more clearly in Figure 18-5.

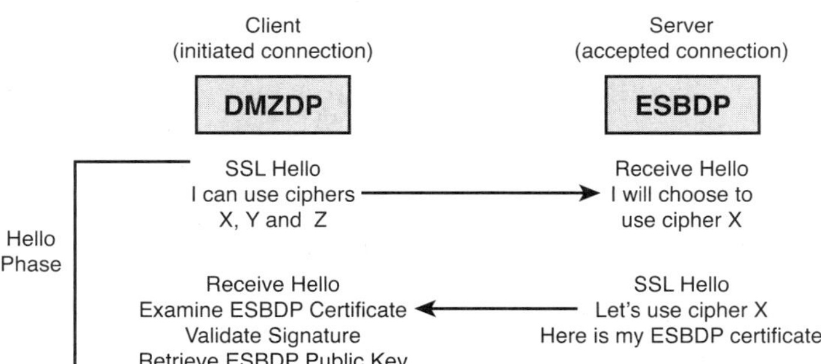

Figure 18-5 The hello phase.

Key Exchange

Recall that asymmetric key encryption is relatively expensive, and should be used sparingly. The SSL protocol recognizes this, and only uses it for the initial handshake; all further communication is done using symmetric key encryption. Thus the next stage for DMZDP is to generate a secret key that is used for symmetric key encryption. To send this secret key securely to ESBDP, DMZDP encrypts it using the public key retrieved from ESBDP's certificate, ensuring that only the holder of the corresponding private key (ESBDP) can decrypt it. Finally, because we are using mutual authentication here, DMZDP sends its own certificate (also signed by a trusted third party) to ESBDP.

ESBDP retrieves the message containing the secret key and DMZDP's certificate, and starts by examining the certificate. First, it checks to see whether the certificate is expired; if it is, ESBDP refuses to communicate further and terminates the connection. Next, ESBDP validates the signer of the certificate—clearly ESBDP must have been preconfigured with the public key of the signer of DMZDP's certificate or the certificate itself.

After the signature on DMZDP's certificate has been validated, ESBDP retrieves the secret key that was sent along with the message and decrypts it using its private key. It then sends a "finish handshake" message back to DMZDP—but this time the message is encrypted using the secret key.

DMZDP receives the "finish handshake" message and decrypts it using the secret key. The fact that it is able to decrypt it means that ESBDP must have held the private key corresponding to the public key of the certificate it had presented earlier. Both sides have now authenticated each other, and both sides now have access to a shared secret key. They can now communicate with each other using the shared secret key for symmetric key encryption; this key is used for the rest of the SSL session.

The full SSL handshake as described is depicted in Figure 18-6.

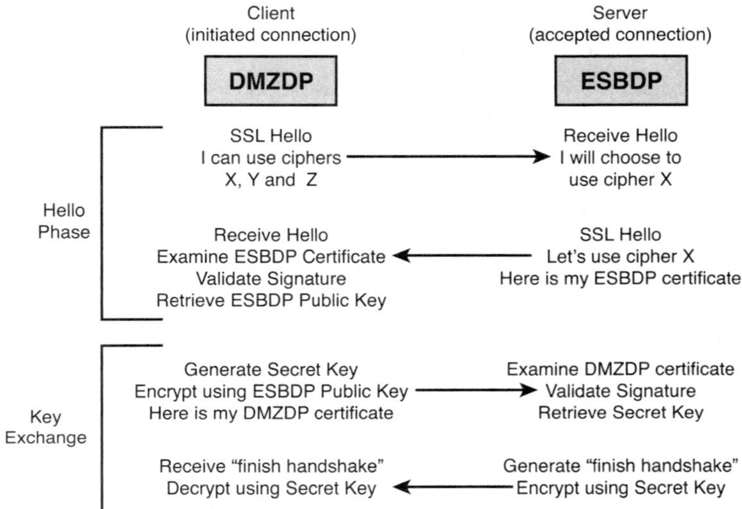

Figure 18-6 The SSL handshake.

Whew—I bet you never guessed so much was happening behind the scenes when you enter `https://` in your browser! It seems complicated, and because of that many people believe that SSL is a drag on performance. That certainly used to be the case, but with the speed of today's modern networks and computers, if things are configured properly you should not fear SSL (and certainly not forego it) for performance reasons.

SSL ID Caching

One extremely important aspect of the previously described handshake is that if it can be helped, we do not want to repeat it. It is a relatively expensive operation. The SSL protocol allows for caching of the secret keys, which is a configurable option. If caching is enabled, as it is by default, when DMZDP wants to initiate a new SSL connection to ESBDP, rather than renegotiating and agreeing a new session key, they can simply agree to use the already existing shared secret key. Because they previously negotiated the key, and they are the only two nodes that have access to it, it is a fair assumption that reusing the same key will be safe. It also means that they do not have to go through all those computationally expensive asymmetric key operations. This directly affects performance of SSL.

By implication, this means that when load balancing SSL over a number of servers, it is extremely important to send a client back to the same server if at all possible, because that server will have the cached secret session key and will be able to reuse it.

> **TIP—Load Balancing SSL**
>
> If SSL connections are load balanced, the load balancer should always endeavor to maintain affinity, otherwise performance will be directly impacted.

Configuring SSL in DataPower

SSL configuration in DataPower often appears complicated at first glance. It requires a number of configuration objects to be created, and the relationship between these objects is sometimes hard to understand. We will examine and define those objects, show where they are used and what the relationships are between them, and show how they can be easily attached to services to allow for strongly defined incoming and dynamic outgoing SSL configurations.

Configuration Objects

This section defines the configuration objects specific to SSL, and shows where they are configured and how they are used. The cryptographic configuration objects can be accessed using the left menu bar as with all objects, but there is also a dedicated Keys and Certificates Management button on the Control Panel, which leads to the page shown in Figure 18-7.

Figure 18-7 The keys and certificates management page.

Figure 18-8 contains a diagram of the relationship between the objects required when configuring the use of SSL in DataPower.

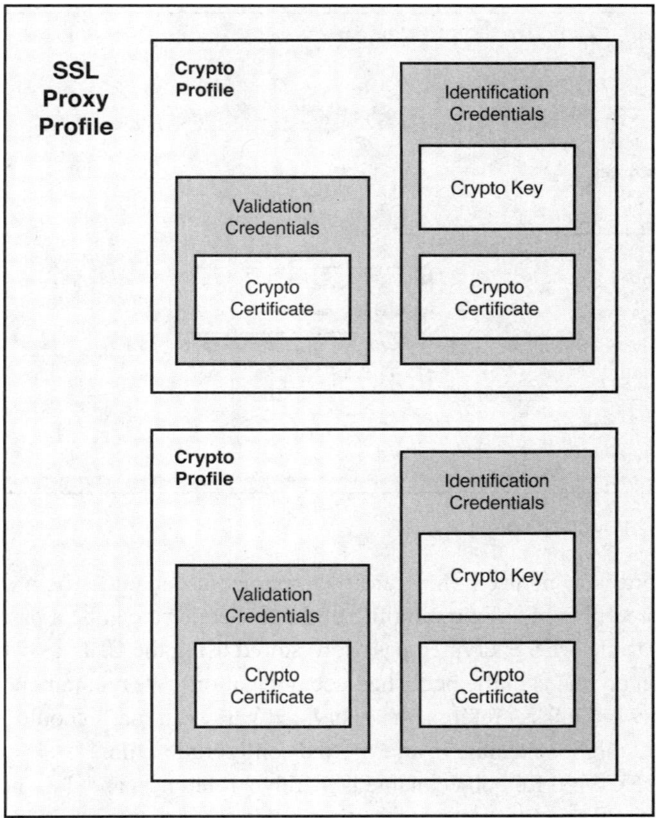

Figure 18-8 The relationships between the configuration objects.

Each of these objects is explained in turn.

The Crypto Key Object—Private Keys

The simplest DataPower object used for SSL communication is the Crypto Key object, shown in Figure 18-9. The Crypto Key object is an abstraction that contains a reference to a file stored on the DataPower directory that contains a private key. The file is stored in the secure cert: directory, and after it is uploaded to the device, it can only be used by the device itself; it cannot be retrieved or copied off the device in any way, including for backup purposes. A Crypto Key object can contain a password, which is used by the system to access the key. This is sometimes required by local security policies, which do not take into account the fact that the key is already stored on the appliance's secure file system and cannot be copied off the device.

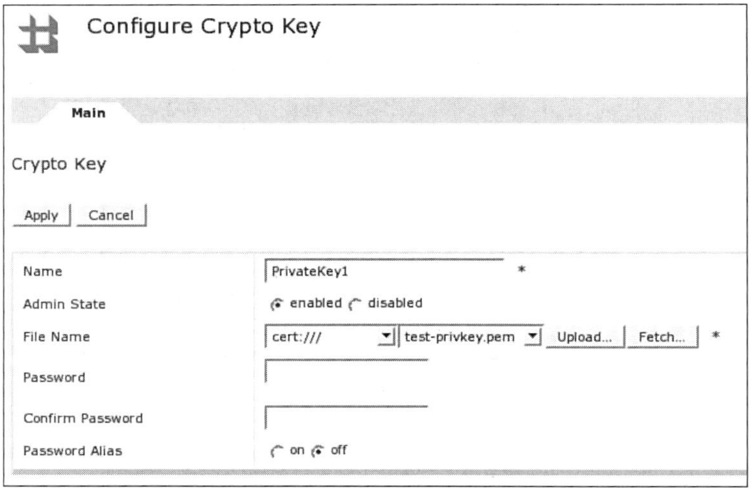

Figure 18-9 A Crypto Key object.

If a password is to be used, there are two options; it can either be a plaintext password, which will be stored in the configuration file of the device, or it can be a password alias, which then references a triple-DES encrypted password stored using the CLI password-map command (more information on this is in the published documentation). We recommend that, if passwords are required, password aliases referencing encrypted password maps should be used, because a plaintext password might be visible in an exported configuration file.

Note that the Crypto Key object name is merely a reference, and does not have to match or in any way relate to the key filename. Abstracting in this manner stands you in good stead for promotion of configuration through different environments, as discussed in Chapter 15, "Build and Deploy Techniques."

The Crypto Certificate Object—Digital Certificates

Just as a Crypto Key object is a reference to a file containing a private key, similarly the Crypto Certificate object is a reference to a file stored on the DataPower directory that contains a digital certificate. A Crypto Certificate object is shown in Figure 18-10.

Again, if required by local policy, a Crypto Certificate can be protected using a plaintext password or a password alias; the password alias should be used in preference. The function to use a password is usually used only when both the certificate and the respective private key are stored in the same file. A Crypto Certificate object also has an additional configuration parameter, called Ignore Expiration Dates. As it sounds, this parameter allows usage of certificates that are out of date.

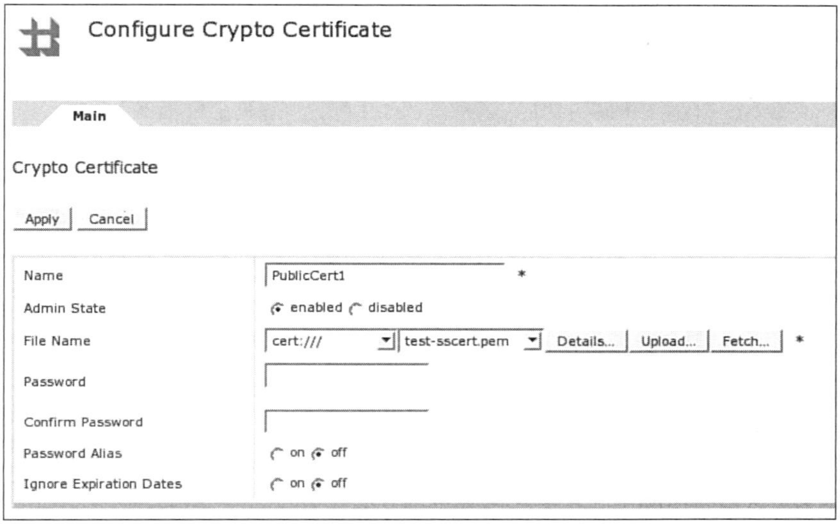

Figure 18-10 A Crypto Certificate object.

By default, the Ignore Expiration Date parameter is disabled. In this default state, that means that any object which references this Crypto Certificate object will be marked as down and unusable if the Crypto Certificate object becomes marked down because the certificate it represents is out of date. If you choose to set Ignore Expiration Date to enabled, this will not happen; certificates will be used irrespective of the dates in the certificate, and objects which reference the Crypto Certificate object will remain available for use, which might have unexpected consequences. Of course, this is a bad idea! Making cryptographic certificates be accepted after their expiration date increases the potential attack surface; the time limitation and expiration is a security feature and should be treated as such.

Certificates exist in the wild in a number of file formats, including PEM, DER, CER, PFX, and P12. If a certificate is expected to be run on DataPower but is not in a format that DataPower understands, the external open source tool OpenSSL can be used to convert between the formats to arrive at an acceptable format for DataPower.

The Crypto Key and Crypto Certificate objects can be used for more than SSL authentication; they are a general abstraction that can also be used for encryption and decryption of documents in addition to performing digital signatures. The SSL use case is only one of many that use this configuration object; for other examples, see Chapter 19, "Web Services Security."

Crypto Identification Credentials—Who Am I?

The Crypto Identification Credentials object is a configuration object that represents an "identity" for a service on the DataPower appliance. It consists of a Crypto Key object and a Crypto Certificate object; that is, a public/private key pair. A Crypto Identification Credentials object is shown in Figure 18-11.

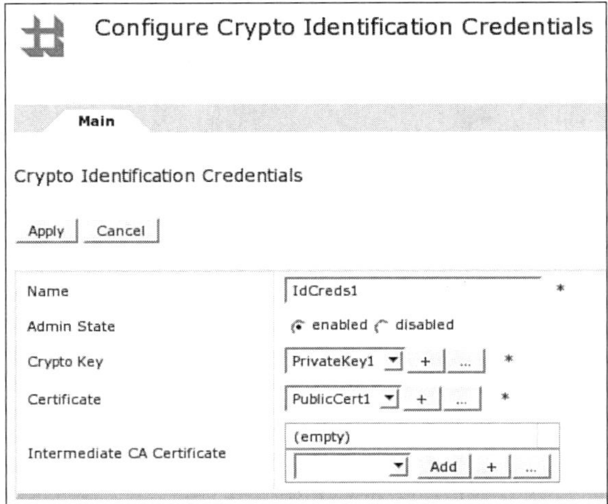

Figure 18-11 A Crypto Identification Credentials object.

A Crypto Identification Credentials object can include an intermediate CA certificate. This is the certificate that has been used to sign the server's certificate, but it, in turn, is signed by a trusted third party; this is known as a trust chain. If this intermediate certificate is provided, it will be sent along with the server certificate as part of the SSL handshake, in order for the client to validate the intermediate certificate while validating the actual server certificate.

The identification credentials can be used both when acting as a server, where the Crypto Certificate object contains a pointer to the certificate that is presented as the server certificate, and when acting as an SSL client, where the Crypto Certificate object contains a pointer to the certificate to be used as the client certificate. In a configuration where DataPower is acting solely as an SSL client and mutual authentication is not required, no identification credentials object is required.

Crypto Validation Credentials—Whom Do I trust?

A Crypto Validation Credentials object, as shown in Figure 18-12, consists of a list of Crypto Certificate objects. These are the "trusted third party" certificate objects we choose to use when deciding whether to trust a signed certificate.

Validation Credentials are often known as the "trust store" in other products. They can contain the public certificates of signers, which are used to validate, or they can contain copies of the certificates themselves (of course without the corresponding private keys).

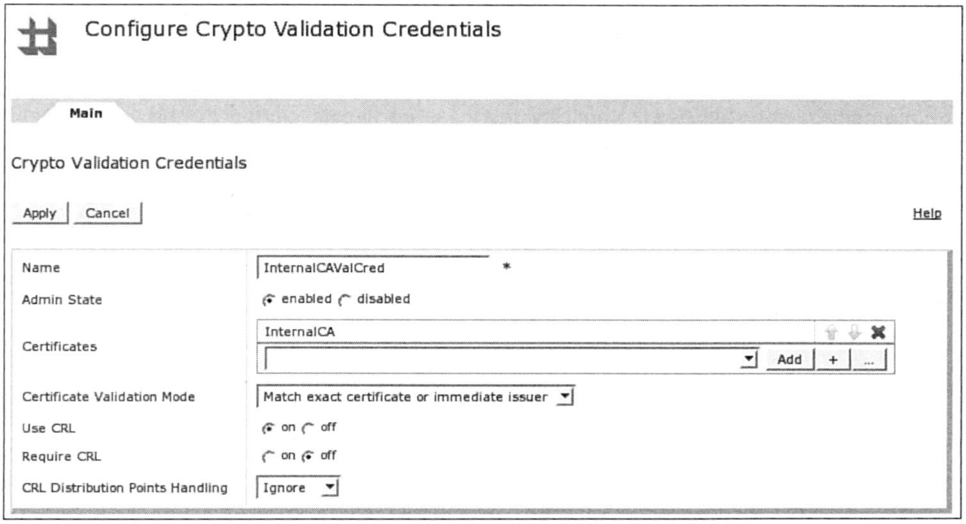

Figure 18-12 A Crypto Validation Credentials object.

TIP—POPULATING THE VALIDATION CREDENTIALS

One of the options to successfully trust an incoming client certificate is to have a copy of that certificate itself in your validation credentials (rather than the certificate of the signer, which would be more common). However in order to connect to an arbitrary SSL service, it might not always be easy to get hold of the certificate so that we can import it into DataPower.

Well, remember that as part of the SSL handshake, the server actually sends over a copy of its signed certificate. Thus all you need to do is to initiate an SSL handshake with a suitable tool, and keep hold of the certificate once it has been sent over the wire. The easiest tool to use for this job is your desktop Web browser—simply accept the certificate into your browser's trust store, and then export it from there for an instant copy!

In fact, because the SSL handshake is complete before any application data is ever sent over the wire, this trick can be used to retrieve the public certificate for any SSL enabled service, not just HTTPS. This is extremely useful if, say, you need to create a validation credential to connect to say an LDAP server over SSL.

The Crypto Validation Credentials object can be set to automatically contain all the certificates in the pubcert: directory on the appliance by clicking the Create Validation Credential from pubcert button. Alternatively, to not trust all the well-known signers, or to only trust specific internal ones, individual certificate objects can be added to the list. This list is the definitive list of trusted signers for any SSL configuration that uses this object.

TIP—Whom Should I Trust?

By including a signer certificate in a validation credential, you are making an explicit statement saying that "I will implicitly trust any certificate signed by this certificate authority." This might not always be what you want!

For example if you include a well-known signer inside a validation credential, and use mutually authenticated SSL, the SSL handshake will successfully complete with any certificate signed by that well-known signer. This includes the ubiquitous J.R. Hacker who applied last week with some photocopied paperwork to prove his identity.

There are two special options for Crypto Validation Credentials objects that define how the certificates are used to validate signatures of peer certificates. The first option, the default, to match the exact certificate or immediate issuer, does exactly that—it validates only the signature if the certificate presented exactly matches one of the certificates in the list of validation credentials, or is signed directly by one of them. The second option performs full chain checking so that any issuer certificates presented must also match; this generally isn't necessary when dealing with trusted business partners who have shared their certificates with you, but might be needed when accepting connections from the general public.

Certificate Directories

There are three directories on the DataPower appliance that are commonly used to store certificates. These are the cert:, sharedcert:, and pubcert: directories. Although all three are identical, and in theory certificates can be stored in any of them, each exists to maintain a convention, and following the convention will help avoid confusion.

- **Cert**—This directory should contain certificates that have been uploaded (or generated on the appliance) and are destined to be used for a particular application. These are not shared among domains.
- **Pubcert**—This directory includes the common root certificate authorities that would usually be found in most common Web browsers.
- **Sharedcert**—This directory should contain certificates that have been uploaded to or generated on the device, which are intended to be shared across all domains. This might be a good place to store an internal root certificate authority's certificate.

Although these are indeed only a convention, mixing the certificates by putting them in the wrong directory can really confuse matters and should be avoided. Finally, note that certificates, keys, or any other such sensitive material should not be stored on the local: directory. The certificate directories are there for a reason—use them!

Crypto Profiles—Wrapping It all Together

A Crypto Profile puts together a set of configuration objects used in SSL communications. This is the basic unit of SSL configuration in DataPower. A Crypto Profile object is shown in Figure 18-13.

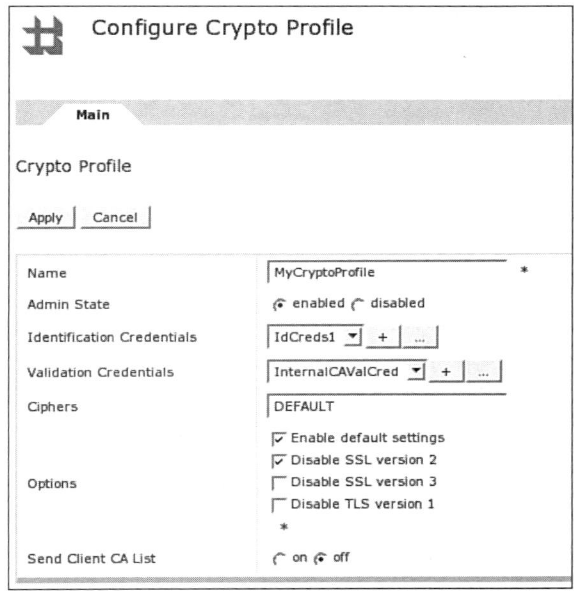

Figure 18-13 A Crypto Profile object.

A Crypto Profile contains a crypto identification credential if one is used in this Crypto Profile (for instance if acting as an SSL server, or if we are an SSL client and we want to use client authentication). It also contains a crypto validation credential if one is used in this Crypto Profile (for instance if acting as an SSL client, or if acting as an SSL server and wanting to accept client authentication).

In addition, a Crypto Profile contains a number of options for deciding which algorithms and which version of the SSL protocol to use. These options are detailed in the documentation; in all likelihood the defaults will suffice, but if you have specific requirements these can be configured.

The SSL Proxy Profile—Using SSL for Proxy Communication

The SSL Proxy Profile is a further level of abstraction for configuring some services on DataPower to use SSL. An example of an SSL Proxy Profile is shown in Figure 18-14.

SSL Proxy Profiles can be either "forward," meaning that they are used when DataPower is an SSL client, "reverse," used for DataPower as an SSL server, or "two-way," where the proxy will be acting as both client and server (usually this means client to appliance and appliance to back end server). The direction here is simply a description of the deployment pattern; that is, how is SSL going to be used.

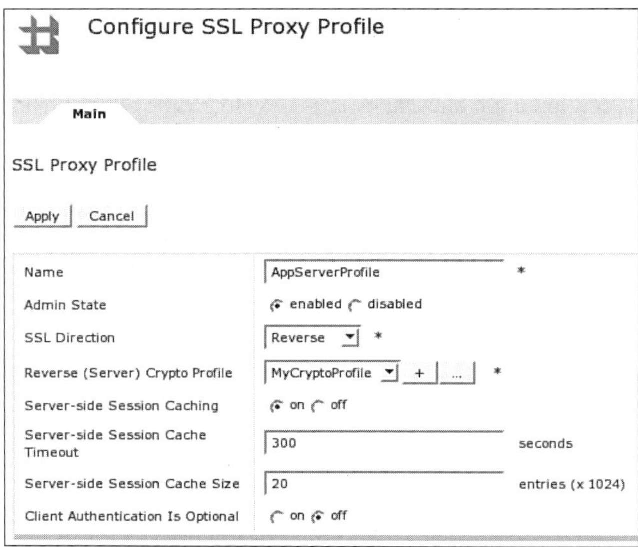

Figure 18-14 An SSL Proxy Profile object.

- When DataPower acts as an SSL client, a validation credential is usually needed (if no validation credential is present we will validate using the certificates in the pubcert: directory) and an identification credential is required if mutual authentication is in use. The SSL direction would be set to Forward, and a "forward" Crypto Profile would be defined.
- When DataPower acts as an SSL server, an identification credential is required, and also a validation credential if mutual authentication is in use. The SSL direction would be set to Reverse, and a "reverse" Crypto Profile would be defined.
- When DataPower is acting as both an SSL server (receiving an SSL connection from an external client) and an SSL client (connecting over SSL to a back end server), *two* sets of identification and validation credentials are required, one for each connection. The SSL direction would be set to "two-way" and *both* a "reverse" and a "forward" Crypto Profile would be defined.

This is really the raison d'etre of the SSL Proxy profile. The SSL Proxy Profile gives us a way of grouping the required validation credential and identification credential objects that are relevant to the required deployment pattern. A Crypto Profile is assigned to the "Forward Crypto Profile," the "Reverse Crypto Profile," or both, depending on the intended usage. These Crypto Profiles contain the entire cryptographic configuration needed by the SSL Proxy Profile.

Settings specific to the usage of caching of SSL in this configuration are also set here. These include server and client side SSL caching, which is on by default, and the cache sizes and timeouts for both server and client side.

Finally, the SSL Proxy Profile has a configuration option called "Client Authentication Is Optional." Client authentication is the component of the mutually authenticated handshake where the client authenticates itself to the server. By default, this option is "Off"—meaning that by default, client authentication is mandatory if a validation credential has been configured. However, authenticating the client is not a mandatory part of the SSL specification. Most Web traffic (requests for HTML pages) that use SSL usually do not enforce client authentication; they mainly require encryption, and use other mechanisms to authenticate their clients. For Web services traffic, there are also valid use cases where encryption and authentication of the server certificate are enough, and, therefore, we do not need to use client authentication. In that case, this option may be disabled.

Creating Targeted Crypto Profiles

Crypto Profiles can be created using the Crypto Profile object page. However, there is also a useful wizard that is accessible anywhere that a Crypto Profile might be required, and this wizard provides a single page that allows you to configure everything the Crypto Profile needs.

The wizard, which in this instance is accessed by clicking the + sign next to the SSL Server Crypto Profile in an XML firewall configuration, is shown in Figure 18-15.

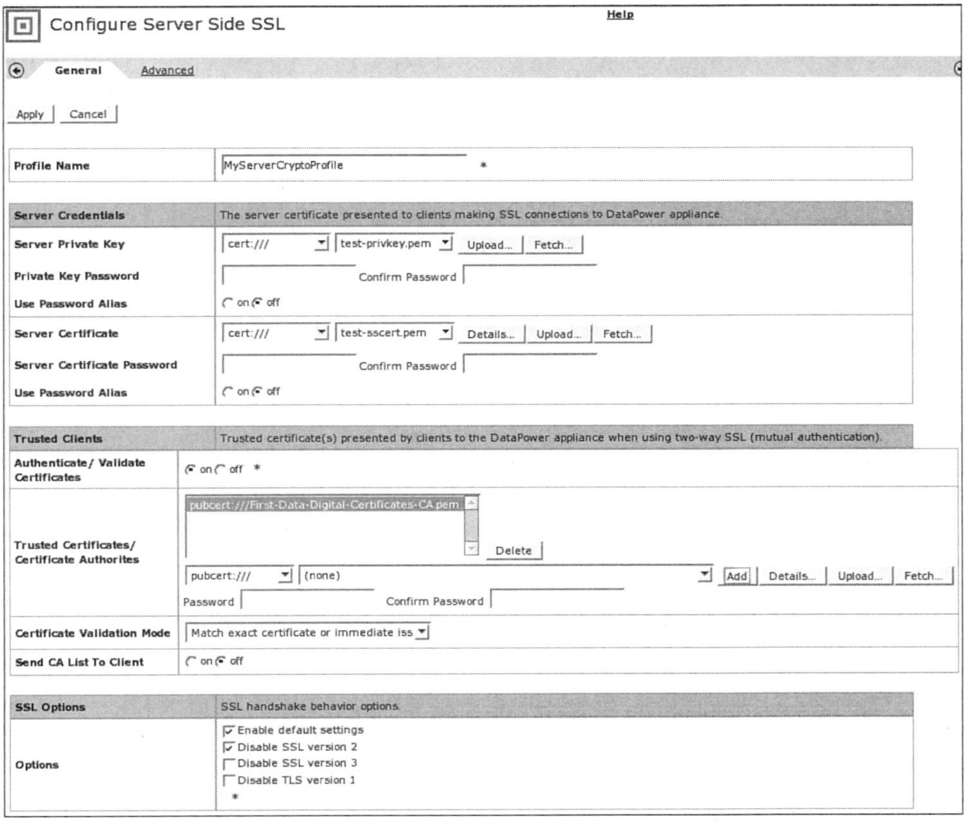

Figure 18-15 The Crypto Profile creation wizard for a Server Crypto Profile.

The wizard creates an identity credential (here referred to as a "server credential") and a validation credential (here referred to as "trusted clients"). It also allows setting of the relevant options regarding version, and on the Advanced tab the ciphers to use, and so on.

SSL Usage Pattern in DataPower

The most common usage pattern of the DataPower appliance is that of a proxy. That is, it accepts a connection over the network, adds value in the form of transformation, AAA, routing, and so on, and then initiates a separate new connection to a backend server to send it the request and receive the response, which it then sends to the client over the original connection on that side. It is, therefore, possible to use SSL on both of these connections—the inbound and the outbound.

Due to the nature of SSL, it is impossible to simply pass the connection on to the backend "transparently." It is impossible for one node to pretend to be another, because they do not possess the private key associated with that other node's certificate. This means that, in the proxy pattern, there is not and cannot be any direct relationship between the incoming and outgoing SSL connections; they are two separated and isolated connections. Of course, it is possible to explicitly share the private keys between the backend and DataPower, so that DataPower can act as if it were the backend server; indeed the two-way Crypto Profile makes this configuration easy to implement. However in most cases there would be no need to share. DataPower would simply *become* the main SSL endpoint, and it would have the only copy of the private key.

Of course, there is no absolute requirement to use SSL both on the inbound and outbound configuration. There may be valid use cases for a service to use SSL on its inbound connection, but to make a plain unencrypted connection to the backend. (Of course this assumes that you trust everyone on your internal network, which is likely a bad idea; a large percentage of real-world attacks are internal, and internal networks are almost never secured as well as they should be, not to mention that there may be privacy laws that you would have to ensure that you respect.) More rarely there might be a use case for going the other way—taking an unencrypted connection inbound, and making an outbound connection with SSL.

Whichever pattern is used, the SSL configuration as defined previously must be attached to a service for inbound connections, or configured for use as an outbound connection. Doing so is a simple matter—a relief after the somewhat complex procedure for configuring the abstractions in the first place! It is when you see how easy it is to attach the configurations that the power of the abstraction becomes obvious.

Using SSL—Inbound Configuration

After an SSL configuration has been created, it is easy to add that configuration to a service. For instance, a specific Crypto Profile can be reused among multiple XML Firewalls within the same domain, and as part of one or more SSL Proxy Profiles. The same SSL Proxy Profile can be added to multiple services of different types, such as HTTPS or FTP Server FSHs for attaching to Web Service Proxies or Multi-Protocol Gateways, or any other type of service requiring SSL.

To attach an SSL Crypto Profile to an XML Firewall object, simply select it as the SSL Server Crypto Profile when defining the firewall, as shown in Figure 18-16.

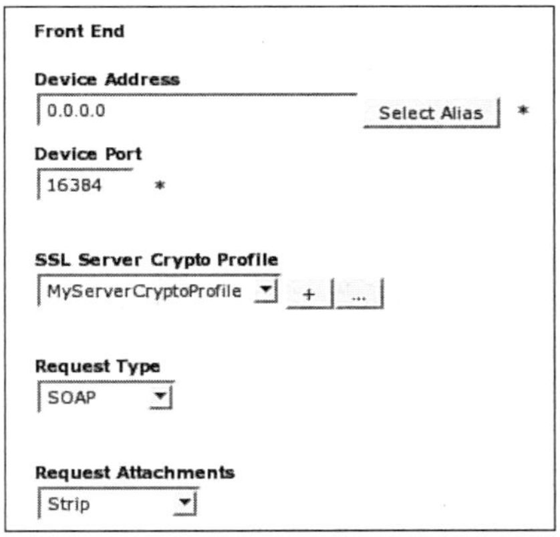

Figure 18-16 SSL Server Crypto Profile configured on an XML Firewall service.

Keep in mind that when you update an XML Firewall to use HTTPS, the HTTP listener will no longer be available, so all your clients will need to change their URLs to use HTTPS.

The same Crypto Profile might be part of an SSL Proxy Profile, as shown in Figure 18-17, which can then be attached to an HTTPS FSH object or an FTP Server FSH object or anywhere else an SSL Proxy Profile can be used.

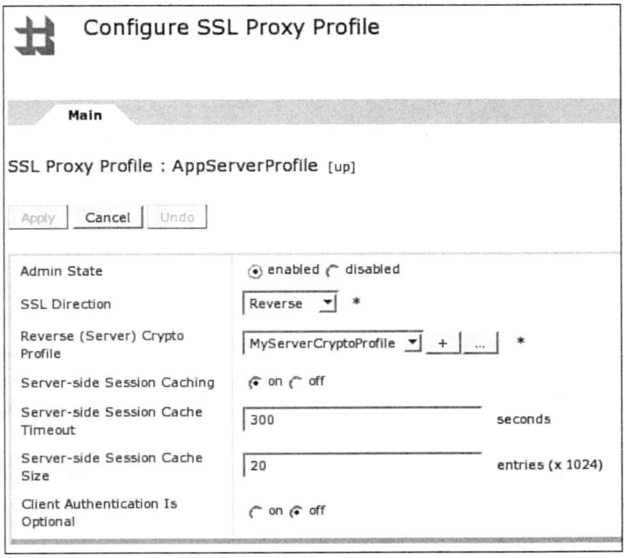

Figure 18-17 The same Crypto Profile configured on an SSL Proxy Profile.

The FTP Server FSH usage of the proxy profile is more complicated, as described later in this chapter, but the fundamental principle holds true: Assigning an SSL configuration (in this case in the form of an SSL Proxy Profile) to a service is trivial, after all the cryptographic configuration is complete.

Using SSL—Outbound Configuration

Outbound SSL connections from DataPower are configured in different ways, depending on the kind of connection being made: a simple backend SSL connection, or a dynamically specified connection to a URL either as a dynamic backend or for SSL connections initiated from XSLT.

Simple Backend Connections

For simple connections to the backend, a Crypto Profile is specified that contains all the SSL configuration information required. This Crypto Profile is specified slightly differently depending on the type of service. For instance, the XML Firewall uses a Crypto Profile object for connections to the backend known as the "SSL Client Crypto Profile," as shown in Figure 18-18.

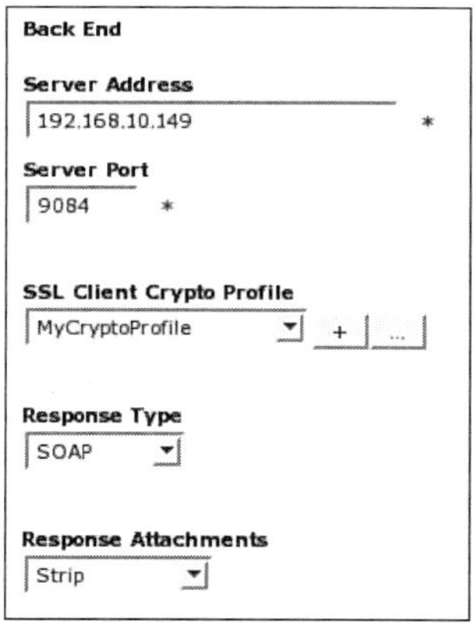

Figure 18-18 SSL Client Crypto Profile.

Recall that because the XML Firewall initiates the connection, it is the SSL client, and that is why the object is called an "SSL Client Crypto Profile." At first, it might seem backward to call the connection to the backend the "Client Profile," but it's correct!

Because an XML Firewall configuration can use only HTTP or HTTPS and only the server hostname or IP address is specified, this Crypto Profile is used when connecting to the backend server, and the definition of this Crypto Profile results in the call being made using HTTPS instead of plain HTTP.

In the Multi-Protocol Gateway, outbound calls are also controlled by specifying a Crypto Profile; this time under the "Back side settings" for the proxy. This configuration is slightly different for each of the services. The configuration for the Multi-Protocol Gateway is shown in Figure 18-19.

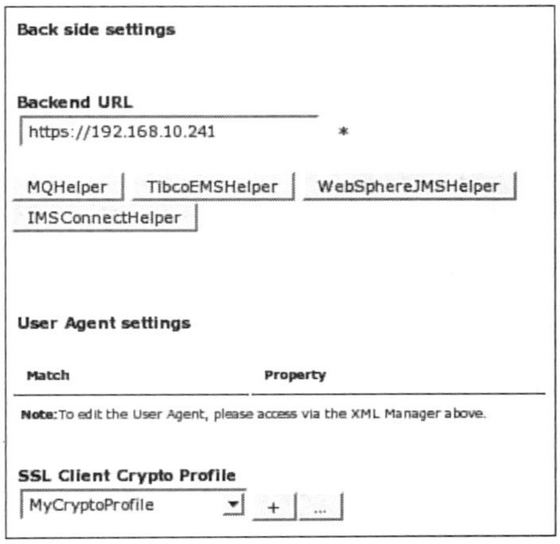

Back side settings

Backend URL

https://192.168.10.241 *

MQHelper | TibcoEMSHelper | WebSphereJMSHelper | IMSConnectHelper

User Agent settings

Match | Property

Note: To edit the User Agent, please access via the XML Manager above.

SSL Client Crypto Profile

MyCryptoProfile

Figure 18-19 SSL Client Crypto Profile for the Multi-Protocol Gateway.

Here, although the connection can use a number of protocols, the SSL Client Crypto Profile is only used if the backend URL is explicitly specified as https. (SSL for MQ is defined separately, as shown later in this chapter.)

For the Web Service Proxy, the definition is similarly under "Back side settings," except that here it uses an SSL Proxy profile, as shown in Figure 18-20.

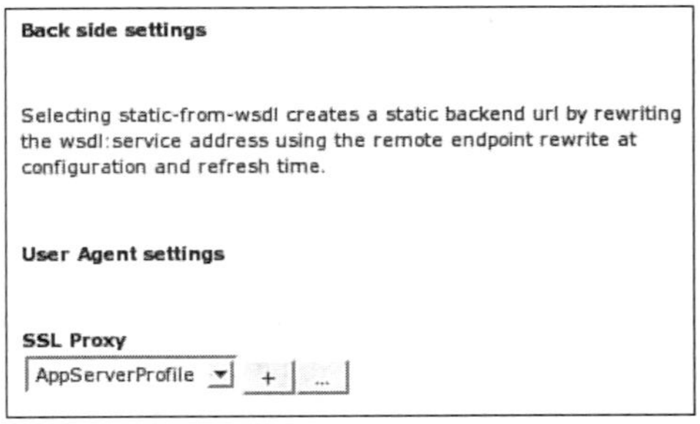

Back side settings

Selecting static-from-wsdl creates a static backend url by rewriting the wsdl:service address using the remote endpoint rewrite at configuration and refresh time.

User Agent settings

SSL Proxy

AppServerProfile

Figure 18-20 SSL Proxy Profile for the back side of a Web Service Proxy.

The SSL Proxy Profile specified is used only for outbound connections to the backend, so it is enough for it to only specify a forward or client Crypto Profile, unless that connection will require a client certificate for mutual authentication.

Dynamically Allocated Outbound SSL Connections

In all configurations, it is also possible to specify an SSL configuration using the User Agent in the XML Manager. The User Agent contains a special policy, called an SSL Proxy Profile Policy, where specific SSL Proxy Profiles can be configured to match specific URLs for outgoing connections. This is a powerful facility—different outbound calls from the same service could potentially use different SSL Proxy Profiles depending on where they are calling to. For instance, consider the configuration shown in Figure 18-21.

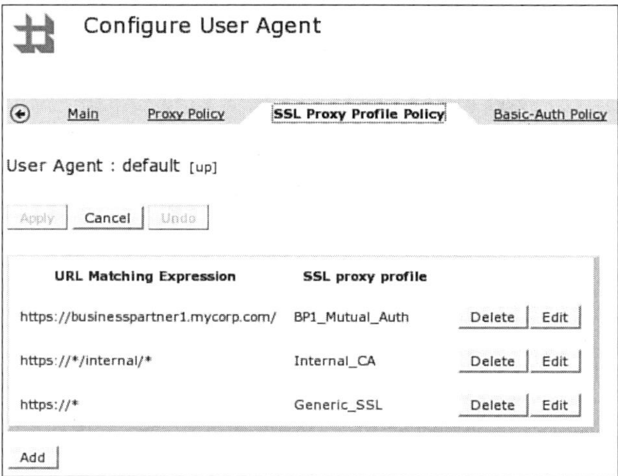

Figure 18-21 SSL Proxy Profile Policy within the User Agent.

Figure 18-21 shows three different SSL Proxy Profiles, which will be used depending on the outgoing URL. If the connection is made to https://businesspartner1.mycorp.com, the proxy profile called BP1_Mutual_Auth will be used. This profile is likely configured to provide a client certificate to authenticate to the business partner. If the connection is made to any URL where the URL stem (or URI) begins with /internal/*, it will use the SSL Proxy Profile called Internal_CA. It is likely that this profile contains a validation credential that trusts an internal certificate authority of some sort. Finally, all remaining connections use the SSL Proxy Profile called Generic_SSL, which likely contains some well-known trusted signers.

Certificate Revocation Lists

One of the problems with certificates is that, once a certificate is issued, it is very hard to take it away again. Since the certificate is signed by the signer, and validation of the certificate is based on the cryptographic principles described in this chapter, the validation will always succeed if the signature is valid. If a CA has mistakenly issued a certificate, there is no way for it to "un-sign" it. This is why CAs publish Certificate Revocation Lists (CRLs).

A CRL is simply a list of specific certificates that should no longer be considered valid, published in a format defined in RFC3280. DataPower can be configured to retrieve and use these CRLs. To create a policy for retrieving CRLs, click Objects→Crypto→CRL Retrieval. DataPower supports retrieving the CRLs using HTTP and LDAP, optionally encrypting the connection to the CRL server using SSL. Figure 18-22 shows an example of retrieving a CRL every four hours over HTTP from a server called internal-crl-server.

The validation credentials shown in Figure 18-22 are used to validate the signature of the CRL itself, thus ensuring that only a trusted CRL will be used.

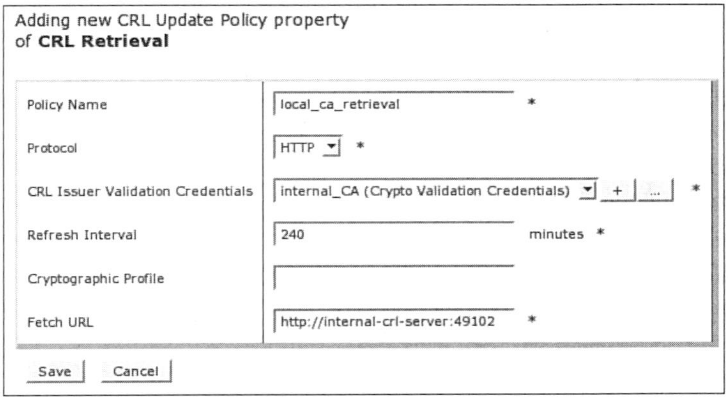

Adding new CRL Update Policy property
of **CRL Retrieval**

Policy Name	local_ca_retrieval *
Protocol	HTTP *
CRL Issuer Validation Credentials	internal_CA (Crypto Validation Credentials) + ... *
Refresh Interval	240 minutes *
Cryptographic Profile	
Fetch URL	http://internal-crl-server:49102 *

Save Cancel

Figure 18-22 CRL retrieval using HTTP.

Device Certificate

Each DataPower appliance has an SSL certificate used for encrypting access to the device over the Web management and XML management ports (ssh uses a different type of key). By default, every appliance uses the same certificate, which is shipped with the appliance. This certificate is signed by a DataPower SSL CA which, in turn, is signed by a DataPower Root CA. However, this certificate should not be used for production systems. The same certificate, and corresponding private key, ship with *every single DataPower appliance*. This means that the private key for the certificate is not very private at all!

Every DataPower customer should use their own SSL certificate for the appliance. This can be done in the default domain, by selecting System Control from the Control Panel in the WebGUI, and scrolling down to the section entitled "Generate Device Certificate," shown in Figure 18-23.

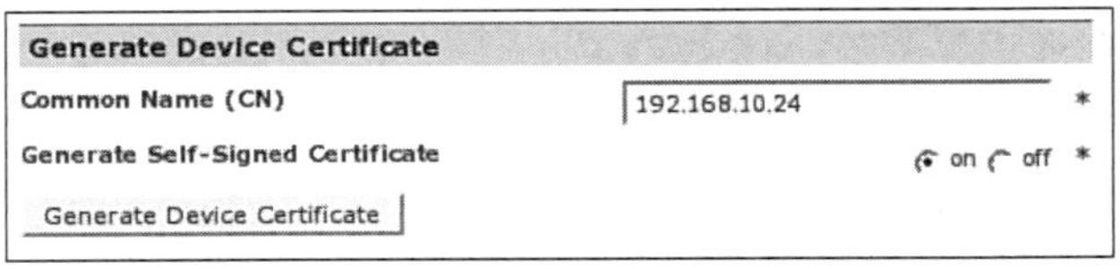

Generate Device Certificate

Common Name (CN)	192.168.10.24 *
Generate Self-Signed Certificate	on off *

Generate Device Certificate

Figure 18-23 Generating the Device Certificate.

Figure 18-23 shows the use of a self-signed SSL certificate; the device generates one with the requested common name, and creates an SSL proxy profile containing the certificate. This SSL proxy profile can then be set on the Web management, under Network→Management→Web Management Service, on the advanced tab, under Custom SSL Proxy Profile (likewise for XML management).

If you choose not to generate a self-signed SSL certificate, instead a private key and a Certificate Signing Request (CSR) will be generated to send to your CA for signing. These are saved to the temporary directory.

TIP—CAREFUL WITH DEVICE CERTIFICATES!

The two most important things about the device certificate are that you should not use the default certificate that ships on the device itself, and that you should be careful when changing it! If you mistakenly select an SSL proxy profile that is incorrectly configured, it is possible to lock yourself out of the Web management GUI entirely. In this situation, you would have to use the CLI to rectify the problem.

Advanced SSL Usage

The previous parts of this chapter gave enough theory and practical instructions to configure SSL for the majority of DataPower SSL use cases. This section goes into some of the more advanced functionality available.

Crypto Tools

The DataPower appliance ships with a set of crypto tools that allow you to generate keys and certificates right on the box itself. The crypto tools can also import and export crypto objects such as certificates (although it cannot export a copy of the private keys, unless your appliance is equipped with a Hardware Security Module (HSM), in which case it can export the private keys in a special HSM encrypted format which can later be imported). The crypto tools key generation page is shown in Figure 18-24.

This allows you to generate a public/private key pair along with a certificate signing request containing the public key. The certificate signing request can then be sent off to an internal or external (such as Verisign) certificate authority for signing. Alternatively, the crypto tools can generate a self-signed certificate, where the private key of the pair is used to sign the certificate, which can be useful.

The tools can also automatically create configuration objects for the key and certificates they generate, saving you the trouble of having to manually create these objects.

TIP—EXPORT THE PRIVATE KEYS!

When you generate your public-private key pair, make sure to export the private key, either to the temporary directory of the device (from which you should remove it and store it somewhere securely offline) or via the HSM if your appliance is equipped with one.

When you do export the keys, it is vital that there is a standard secure process defined for doing so, and that they are kept track of properly, with an audit trail. These keys are the keys to the kingdom—if someone gets hold of them, they can pretend to be your server! Above all else, avoid using methods such as an employee or a consultant putting the private key on a USB memory stick to move it from one computer to another—chances are that it will not be removed, and their child will take the memory stick to school because it also contains her homework, and then the school's geek squad will get hold of it....

If you do not export the private key at this time, you will be unable to retrieve it from the appliance in the future—the only solution will be to delete and re-create it, which means you would need to re-create the corresponding public key and get the new certificate signed, and so on. This could be very bad if you need to replace the appliance, or share the private keys in future for load balancing purposes!

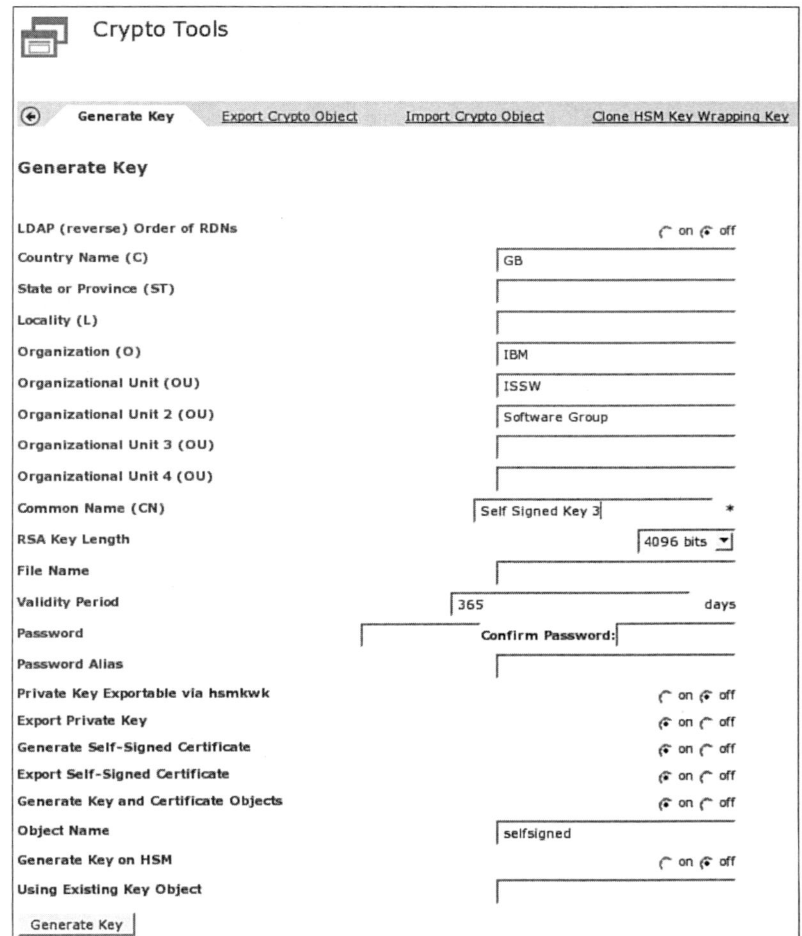

Figure 18-24 Crypto tools key generation.

SSL and FTP

The specification for using SSL with FTP is somewhat more complicated than with other protocols. This is in part because the FTP protocol itself is more complicated—it uses multiple TCP sockets, with a single long-lived "control connection" used for authentication and sending commands, and many "data connections" to actually send data such as directory listings and actual files. RFC4217 describes how SSL should be used with FTP, and DataPower implements this RFC.

Note that this discussion is explicitly about FTPS—FTP over SSL—and not "SFTP" with which it is commonly confused. SFTP is an "FTP-like" protocol that uses Secure Shell (SSH) to transfer files.

One of the big differences between FTPS and HTTPS is that SSL with FTPS is explicit. That is, with HTTP you simply specify the URL to be "https" and the client will automatically (implicitly) know to negotiate SSL, whereas with FTP, you establish a TCP socket without encryption and then you send a command to ask for negotiation of SSL. Furthermore, because SSL works at the socket level, data connections will need to be negotiated separately.

Figure 18-25 shows the configuration page for an FTP Server FSH.

Configure FTP Server Front Side Handler

Main | Virtual Directories

FTP Server Front Side Handler

Apply | Cancel

Name	FTPS_FSH *
Admin State	enabled / disabled
Comments	
Local IP Address	0.0.0.0 Select Alias *
Port Number	21 *
Filesystem Type	Virtual Ephemeral
Default Directory	/
Maximum Filename Length	256
Access Control List	(none) + ...
Require TLS	on / off
SSL Proxy	Generic_SSL + ...
Password AAA Policy	(none) + ...
Certificate AAA Policy	(none) + ...
Allow CCC Command	on / off
Passive (PASV) Command	Require Passive Mode
File Transfer Data Encryption	Require Data Encryption
Allow Compression	on / off
Allow Unique File Name (STOU)	on / off
Idle Timeout	0 seconds
Response Type	No Response
Temporary Storage Size	32

Figure 18-25 FTP Server FSH.

On this configuration page, there are a number of SSL-related settings and we will cover them from top to bottom. The first of these is "Require TLS."[4] If this option is set to on, no FTP

[4] TLS stands for Transport Layer Security and is the new name of the SSL protocol. TLS 1.0 was based on SSL 3.0, and the current version of TLS is 1.1. However, many people still refer to TLS as SSL, and the two can be reasonably interchanged in most contexts. RFC4346 provides a list of the differences between TLS1.0/SSL3.0 and TLS1.1, which consist of some minor security improvements and small clarifications of the specification.

commands will be accepted over a non-SSL connection except the FTP AUTH TLS command used to initiate an SSL negotiation. This will ensure that SSL is used for all FTP command data. The SSL Proxy setting chooses which SSL Proxy Profile will be used with this FSH. The setting to Allow CCC Command determines whether clients, after they have negotiated an SSL connection, will be allowed to fall back to clear text for the control connection (CCC stands for Clear Control Connection). Finally, the File Transfer Data Encryption option can be set to allow, disallow, or require encryption of the data connections as well as the control connection. Using these configuration options, it is possible to ensure that 100 percent of the FTP traffic to and from the appliance goes over SSL.

In a similar manner, Figure 18-26 shows the FTP Client Policies tab of the user agent.

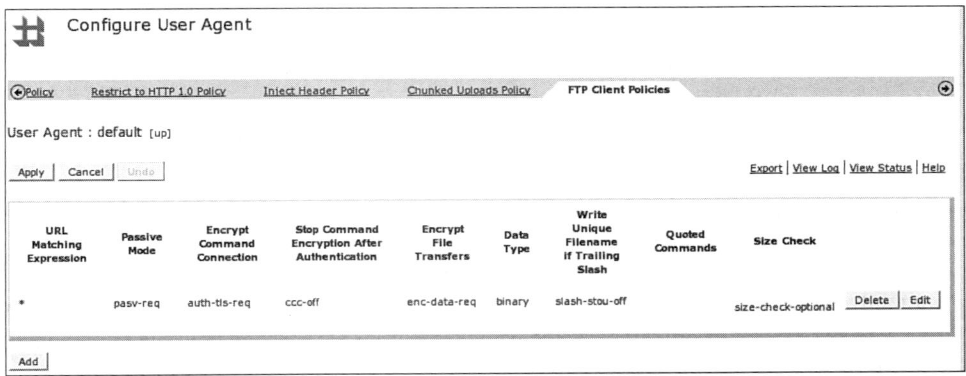

Figure 18-26 FTP client policies.

The FTP client policies control outbound FTP connections, and enable the configuring of exactly the same SSL functionality as on the server side, although the names used are slightly different.

When using SSL with FTP, you should always consider two things. First, because the FTP protocol uses multiple sockets for data, whether file listings or files themselves, each data connection requires a separate SSL handshake. Because of this, it is absolutely vital to use both client and server side SSL session identifier caching. Otherwise each and every socket will entail a full PKI handshake, which will not be good for performance as things scale up!

Secondly, using SSL for FTP will of necessity break the support that some firewalls have for FTP. These stateful packet filtering firewalls have explicit support for FTP, whereby they will monitor the control connection and dynamically open ports in the firewall for data connections as needed. This will not work if the data connection is encrypted, because the firewall will not have the key to decrypt the traffic! For this reason, it is sometimes useful to allow the CCC command so that a client can negotiate the initial SSL session to perform cryptographic authentication, and can still encrypt all data connections, but can use the session long control connection in plain text so that the firewall will be able to dynamically open ports.

SSL and MQ

SSL is used with MQ as a standard method for performing encryption of traffic and cryptographic authentication at a server level. However, configuration of SSL for MQ on DataPower is slightly more complex and requires further explanation.

Figure 18-27 shows part of the definition of an MQ queue manager object.

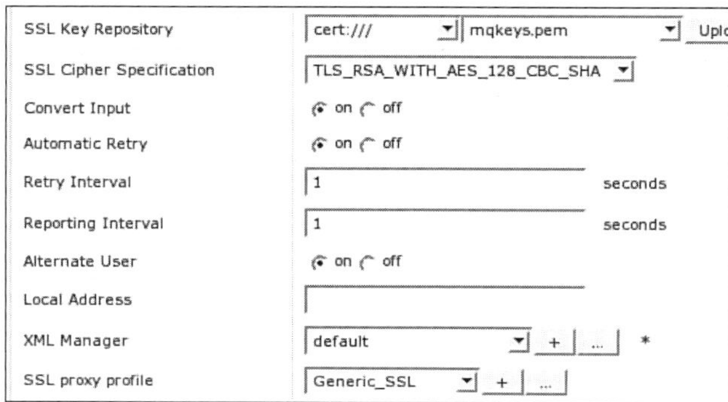

Figure 18-27 An MQ Queue Manager object.

This object has two separate sets of SSL configuration: the SSL Proxy Profile field we know already, and a the slightly older concept of an SSL Key Repository and SSL Cipher Specification. This is because the behavior of the MQ connection depends on how the queue manager object is used.

If the queue manager definition is called by a service that uses an MQ URL to designate its remote destination, the specified SSL Proxy Profile will be used and everything will work exactly as expected. This is the case, for instance, with a Multi-Protocol Gateway. If on the other hand the queue manager object is used by any other type of service (such as the older MQ Gateway or MQ Proxy objects), they will instead use the defined key repository on the queue manager object definition; although these services are rarely used nowadays, and in most cases the configuration should be as simple as shown.

The SSL key repository is a pointer to a key database file and corresponding stash file that must be uploaded to the device. Moreover the stash file must be named exactly the same as the actual key database except that the file extension must be .sth. If the name of the stash file is not the same in this way, the key database will not be able to be opened.

Whether the SSL configuration is specified as an SSL Proxy Profile or as an MQ-specific key repository, it is absolutely critical that the cipher specification and SSL options are compatible with the SSL configuration on the MQ side. For reference, Table 18-1 contains a mapping between the MQ SSL ciphers and DataPower Crypto Profile options.

Table 18-1 Mapping of MQ SSL Ciphers to DataPower Crypto Profile Options

MQ SSL Cipher	SSL Cipher Specification	SSL Options
NULL_MD5	NULL-MD5	OpenSSL-default+Disable-TLSv1
NULL_SHA	NULL-SHA	OpenSSL-default+Disable-TLSv1
RC4_MD5_EXPORT	EXP-RC4-MD5	OpenSSL-default+Disable-TLSv1
RC4_MD5_US	RC4-MD5	OpenSSL-default+Disable-TLSv1
RC4_SHA_US	RC4-SHA	OpenSSL-default+Disable-TLSv1
RC2_MD5_EXPORT	EXP-RC2-CBC-MD5	OpenSSL-default+Disable-TLSv1
DES_SHA_EXPORT	DES-CBC-SHA	OpenSSL-default+Disable-TLSv1
RC4_56_SHA_EXPORT1024	EXP1024-RC4-SHA	OpenSSL-default+Disable-TLSv1
DES_SHA_EXPORT1024	EXP1024-DES-CBC-SHA	OpenSSL-default+Disable-TLSv1
TRIPLE_DES_SHA_US	DES-CBC3-SHA	OpenSSL-default+Disable-TLSv1
TLS_RSA_WITH_AES_128_CBC_SHA	AES128-SHA	OpenSSL-default
TLS_RSA_WITH_AES_256_CBC_SHA	AES256-SHA	OpenSSL-default
AES_SHA_US	AES128-SHA	OpenSSL-default

When Signing Isn't Enough

Recall that with SSL, trust is established by checking whether the digital signature of a certificate is signed by a trusted third party that we have chosen to trust. Under DataPower we configure who we trust by creating a validation credential object.

What happens if this is not fine-grained enough? For instance, what if we want to confirm that not only does the peer have a certificate that is signed by someone we trust, but also that the signed information contains some values that are relevant and important to us? Well, because security is part and parcel of the DataPower appliance, we can examine the signed data and make our decision based on this.

As described in Chapter 16, "AAA," it is possible as part of a AAA policy to choose as an identification method the "Subject DN of the SSL Certificate from the Connection Peer." What does this mean? Well, it means that, after the SSL handshake has been negotiated and session established, based on cryptographic trust, we can then look at the data in the signed certificate and make our decision based on whether or not the distinguished name or DN of the certificate is one we want to allow. Alternatively, we could use the techniques shown in Chapter 17, "Advanced AAA," to make our identity extraction use a custom stylesheet and examine any of the signed data that we so choose.

The SSL Proxy Service

What's that? Haven't we already talked about SSL Proxies? Well, no—earlier we discussed SSL Proxy *Profiles*, but the SSL Proxy *Service* is a completely separate kind of service that deserves mention. Figure 18-28 shows an SSL Proxy Service configuration.

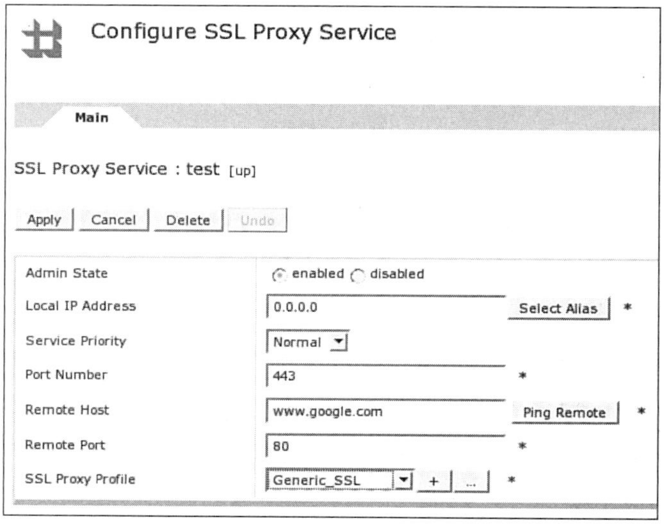

Figure 18-28 The SSL Proxy Service.

The SSL Proxy Service is used to provide a form of tunnel through which connections can be made to a backend server. At its simplest level, this service can provide SSL forwarding; that is, if you connect via SSL to this service, it will connect via SSL to its remote host and any data that you send over your connection to the proxy service will be sent on to the remote host. This in and of itself is likely not all that useful. A rare but valid use case for this might be if the connecting server was unable to support client certificates, so we could add client certificate authentication on the outbound connection to the backend of the proxy.

A more powerful use of the SSL Proxy Service is the fact that the connections do not *have* to utilize SSL. Of course if you use no SSL at all, you should simply use the TCP proxy service, but if you want *either* the incoming *or* the outgoing connection to use SSL, the SSL Proxy Service is perfect. This functionality is similar to the acclaimed open source `stunnel` tool.

The two use-cases are therefore

1. To proxy an inbound SSL connection to an outbound TCP connection, allowing transparent addition of SSL capabilities to a non-SSL service
2. To proxy an inbound TCP connection to an outbound SSL connection, allowing encryption of a call to a backend service where the client is not capable of SSL

Use case 1 is a simple way to quickly upgrade an existing HTTP service to work as HTTPs. Of course, hard-coded links to `http://` URLs will not work, meaning that this service is not really suitable for proxying complex Web applications, but if the requirement is simply to add an SSL frontend, then this is possible. Indeed, this could be used for more than just HTTP—any plain TCP service could be fronted with SSL, so for instance you could enable your LDAP server to work as LDAPs even if it does not support this natively.

To configure use case 1, you would configure the SSL Proxy Profile with an SSL Direction of Reverse and add the certificate you want the service to use as an identification credential in the associated Crypto Profile. Of course, you could also configure the profile with validation credentials and support or enforce mutually authenticated SSL should you desire.

Use case 2, on the other hand, provides a powerful mechanism to encrypt connections to servers where the client is not capable of SSL. For example, imagine you have an LDAP server that accepts only connections using LDAPs, but one of your legacy applications is unable to use SSL for its LDAP client connections. Rather than modifying the legacy application, you could use an SSL proxy service on the DataPower appliance, and point the LDAP client at the port on the appliance, which would then proxy the connection to the backend using SSL.

To implement use case 2, the SSL Proxy Profile would need to be set with an SSL Direction of Forward. A validation credential could be configured to validate the certificate of the backend server. Again, this connection could be made to use mutual authentication.

The Mutually Authenticated Self-Signed SSL Tunnel

Finally, we examine and describe a very important usage pattern that is an extension of that described earlier in the "The SSL Handshake" section.

The scenario is this: We have two DataPower appliances that want to communicate with each other securely. These appliances use a mutually authenticated SSL connection to ensure that all traffic is encrypted and that each appliance can be certain of the identity of the other appliance. To severely limit the number of other nodes that are considered "trusted," we use two separate self-signed certificates.

The advantage of using a self-signed certificate in this manner is that, with a self-signed certificate, there is exactly one, and only one, certificate that has been signed by the signer—and that is the certificate itself. If our validation credential on either side contains no certificates apart from the self-signed certificate of the peer, no one can complete an SSL handshake with us unless they hold the private key to that exact certificate. Because DataPower sensibly does not include any certificates into a validation credential by default, there should not be as much room for error as there is when configuring this pattern on other systems!

Figure 18-29 shows the configuration used here.

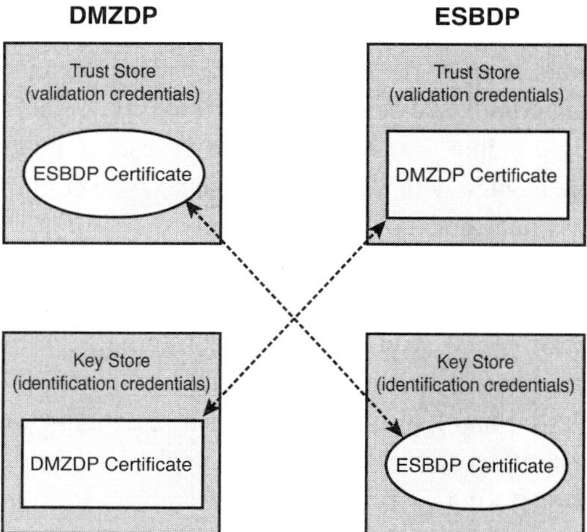

Figure 18-29 The mutually authenticated self-signed SSL tunnel.

As you can see from Figure 18-29, the validation credentials for DMZDP contain exactly one certificate, which is the self-signed certificate of ESBDP, and vice versa—the validation credentials for ESBDP contain exactly one certificate, which is the self-signed certificate of DMZDP. Note that, although the certificate itself is shared, the private key relating to the certificate remains private—only DMZDP has DMZDP's private key, and only ESBDP has ESBDP's private key. Because of this, even if someone else were to somehow get hold of the certificate, he would still be unable to connect because he would not have the corresponding private key.

This powerful technique allows us to link two arbitrary nodes in such a way that we can have absolute cryptographic trust that there is exactly one, and only one, node which will be able to communicate—and that is the configured SSL peer. Indeed this same pattern could be extended by sharing the certificates with a number of nodes, all of whom would be allowed to connect; possession of the private key to the client SSL certificate itself becomes the token by which authorized nodes prove that they should be allowed to connect.

TIP—Point-to-Point Security

People often get excited by the idea of using WS-Security. There is a lot of value in using parts of the specification, and DataPower contains one of the most advanced and current implementations of the specifications available at time of writing. However, if your goal is to simply secure a point-to-point connection between client and server, with no untrusted intermediaries, and provide privacy and integrity for the messages sent over that connection—a mutually authenticated SSL tunnel with a very limited trust domain is a superb way to implement this!

Of course, if your requirements are such that you are routing messages through multiple untrusted intermediaries and have actual requirements for message level encryption and signatures, you may have a valid WS-Security use case, in which case you should read Chapter 19.

Troubleshooting SSL

As this chapter so far has shown, SSL is a powerful mechanism for encryption and cryptographic authentication. However, what happens when things go wrong? How can we diagnose, debug, and repair SSL problems on DataPower?

What Can Go Wrong?

SSL is powerful, but like most powerful concepts, it is complex and thus configuration becomes error prone. This section presents a number of common pitfalls.

Client Authentication Is Optional

The option to say that client authentication is optional is a specific form of double negative. If you say yes, meaning that you want client authentication to be optional, this will mean that clients will *not* have to authenticate (provide a client SSL certificate) to connect. This might seem like a simple problem, but the tricky thing here is that if this is set incorrectly, the connection will *still work*! This is a good example of the general problem that it is not enough to configure something such that it works—you have to configure it explicitly to be secure. In this instance, if the client is configured to use an SSL certificate, it will be requested as part of the SSL handshake and will be sent and used, but if the client does not have an SSL certificate, it still can connect and the user will see no difference.

Incorrect Cipher Suites

Recall that as part of the SSL handshake, the peer that initiates the connection (and thereby becomes known as the client) sends a list of ciphers that it supports, and the server side then chooses which of those ciphers to use. Although the majority of SSL clients and servers are configured correctly, it is still possible that you will connect to a server or client that will choose a completely inappropriate cipher to use. It is, therefore, important to decide what cipher suites are acceptable to your business, and only specify those on the configuration. If you do not, it is possible that while your system will work, it will not be as secure as you believe.

This specific issue was hit unknowingly by many consumers a few years back, when a well-known Internet browser contained a bug causing it to use only weak export quality encryption. Web sites that had been correctly configured to use only strong encryption "broke" in that the browser was unable to communicate with them because they refused to accept weak encryption. However, a large number of public sites were still accessible over HTTPS, because they had never been configured to use only the high-quality encryption and, therefore, graciously stepped down to the low-quality weak encryption!

Certificates for Proxy

Recall that in a proxy scenario, which is the most common form of DataPower deployment, there are two SSL connections: one from the client to the proxy, and a second one from the proxy to the backend server. It is easy to misunderstand which certificate should be placed where. In a proxy scenario, the certificate that would usually have been used by the Web server, or whatever the backend server happens to be, needs to be moved over to the DataPower appliance, along with its private key so that it can be used for encryption. This means that for the original backend server, a new certificate should usually be generated; it is not a good practice to use the same certificate at two layers. Moreover the hostname that was originally used for the certificate should be changed to point to the DataPower appliance, so that it can truly proxy (pretend to be the original server).

Debugging SSL

When things do go wrong, how can you go about working out exactly what is wrong in order to fix it?

Debug Logs

Because the SSL handshake happens before any actual application level traffic is sent over the socket, the Probe cannot be used to debug problems with SSL. However, if you turn on a high level of debug log messages, this will show any errors encountered in the SSL configuration. These debug messages can be extremely helpful in not only showing that the SSL handshake has failed, for instance, but also explaining why exactly it failed and what should be done to rectify the problem.

Packet Capture

If there is a problem with the SSL handshake, one of the most useful ways to debug this is to take a packet capture of the beginning of the handshake. When fed through a high-quality packet capture interpretation tool, such as the excellent freeware Wireshark, the packet capture shows the SSL handshake as it happens, right up until the moment of first encryption. (It is possible to decrypt more if you have the private key, of course, although that is out of scope of this book.)

Client Side Debugging

Many SSL clients have various facilities for SSL debugging. Of note, the cURL utility is capable of producing an extremely detailed debug log showing the various stages of the handshake, the certificates used, and so on. In order to enable SSL debugging in cURL, you can use the `-v` parameter to request verbose messages; this will display the full SSL handshake.

An example of the level of debugging is shown in Listing 18-1. This is the output of the cURL tool being run with `-v` to connect over SSL to the IBM home page, www.ibm.com.

Listing 18-1 Curl Provides Detailed SSL Debugging Information

```
[user@laptop SSL]$ curl -v https://www.ibm.com
* About to connect() to www.ibm.com port 443
*   Trying 129.42.60.216... connected
* Connected to www.ibm.com (129.42.60.216) port 443
* successfully set certificate verify locations:
*   CAfile: /etc/pki/tls/certs/ca-bundle.crt
  CApath: none
* SSLv2, Client hello (1):
SSLv3, TLS handshake, Server hello (2):
SSLv3, TLS handshake, CERT (11):
SSLv3, TLS handshake, Server finished (14):
SSLv3, TLS handshake, Client key exchange (16):
SSLv3, TLS change cipher, Client hello (1):
SSLv3, TLS handshake, Finished (20):
SSLv3, TLS change cipher, Client hello (1):
SSLv3, TLS handshake, Finished (20):
SSL connection using RC4-MD5
* Server certificate:
*        subject: /C=US/ST=North Carolina/L=Research Triangle
Park/O=IBM/OU=Events and ibm.com infrastructure/CN=www.ibm.com
*        start date: 2008-02-20 00:28:07 GMT
*        expire date: 2009-05-21 23:28:07 GMT
*        common name: www.ibm.com (matched)
*        issuer: /C=US/O=Equifax/OU=Equifax Secure Certificate Authority
* SSL certificate verify ok.
> GET / HTTP/1.1
> User-Agent: curl/7.15.5 (i686-redhat-linux-gnu) libcurl/7.15.5
OpenSSL/0.9.8b zlib/1.2.3 libidn/0.6.5
> Host: www.ibm.com
> Accept: */*
>
< HTTP/1.1 302 Found
< Date: Sun, 15 Jun 2008 03:31:27 GMT
< Server: IBM_HTTP_Server
< Location: http://www.ibm.com/
< Content-Length: 203
< Content-Type: text/html
<!DOCTYPE HTML PUBLIC "-//IETF//DTD HTML 2.0//EN">
<html><head>
<title>302 Found</title>
</head><body>
<h1>Found</h1>
<p>The document has moved <a href="http://www.ibm.com/">here</a>.</p>
</body></html>
* Connection #0 to host www.ibm.com left intact
* Closing connection #0
* SSLv3, TLS alert, Client hello (1):
[user@laptop SSL]$
```

Note how each step of the handshake is shown, and then the details of the server's certificate and its signer are displayed. Note also this graphic example of the SSL handshake and connection being completed *before* any application traffic (the HTTP request and response) are ever sent over the wire.

Summary

In this chapter, we examined SSL in depth, exploring its configuration on the DataPower appliance and how extremely valuable and critical it is to the basic function of not just DataPower, but all Internet traffic.

The general cryptographic concepts presented will serve as a base for the equally valuable information in the next chapter, which discusses Web Services security.

CHAPTER 19

Web Services Security

Today's application environment is a complex web of networks, servers, routing, and processing intermediaries. More than ever, concern must be taken for the protection of critical data. An organization might be legally bound to protect the confidentiality of its customers' private information, and might need to ensure the integrity and origin of data that it receives. This chapter will introduce the core of Data Power's cryptographic capabilities. We will describe the vulnerabilities of distributed applications and offer solutions to protect valuable assets both within the application and the client environments.

Web Services Security

We can assume that because you are a reader of this book, you have more than a passing interest in the world of Web services and security. You might have heard of the WS-Security specification and may, in fact, assume that WS-Security is synonymous with Web services security. This is not the case! The remainder of this chapter makes this clear.

Security of Web services may be thought of as existing on two primary axes; first there is the transport level where point-to-point security is offered. Secondly there is the end-to-end security offered by cryptographic techniques such as digital signatures and encryption. There will be situations where either or both of these techniques will provide the security that is required for your application and other situations where you will be required to use a specific technique either due to policy or practical issues of data protection. The technique you use will affect not only the integrity and confidentiality of your data, but could also have performance implications. We will see how DataPower addresses these concerns.

The following sections present some fundamental information regarding message vulnerabilities, security goals, terms and basic definitions, and the relative strengths and weaknesses of various Web services security technologies and WS-Security in detail. Examples will be presented to demonstrate these principles on the DataPower device.

Message Exchange and Vulnerabilities

Common application message exchange (particularly within distributed systems) involves the transmission of data through many intermediaries. Often these intermediaries are unknown or are out of the control of the sender or recipient. A client might enter data within a web browser for consumption by an application server, or a business might transmit a well-formed XML document to a subsidiary outside of the control of its internal network. Often complex network infrastructures require the routing of application traffic via dynamic paths, further complicating the determination of where message data will travel. In either case, this transmission could potentially expose the data to inspection and potential manipulation by unscrupulous parties.

As the saying goes, "The best-laid plans of mice and men often go awry" and IT technologies are not going to do a bit of good if they are not backed up with qualified processes. So, before we jump into the world of security, let us remind ourselves that no implementation of DataPower security functionality is going to solve your problems if it is not backed up by a secured IT infrastructure. All the cryptography in the world will do you no good if you leave the administrative password unchanged. You have no chance of protecting yourselves from exploitation if you do not perform reviews and audits of configuration changes and do not administer the audit log that the device produces. There's information on these topics in other chapters, such as Chapter 12, "Device Administration," Chapter 14, "Logging and Monitoring," and Chapter 15, "Build and Deploy Techniques." However, you must understand that security is not a topic that exists in a vacuum; it is affected by outside influences that you must prepare for and protect against holistically.

Integrity

When a message is sent using the postal system, the contents are typically enclosed within a sealed envelope. The recipient of that message makes the assumption that the message was not exposed or altered during transit. This might, of course, be a misguided assumption because there is no guarantee that the letter was not intercepted and its contents altered prior to its delivery. Message integrity has the goal of providing that guarantee. Integrity's goal in the world of digital data transmission is to provide a mechanism and process such that the recipient might validate that the message has not been changed since it was sent by its creator. This goal does not guarantee that the message was kept private; simply that it was not altered.

Confidentiality

Referring again to our postal system example, the recipient has no guarantee that the message contained within the envelope delivered to her has not been altered. Furthermore, it is equally obvious that she has no guarantee that the message has not been viewed. Perhaps an unscrupulous intermediary has gone to her mailbox, opened the envelope, read the enclosed message, and resealed the envelope or replaced it with another envelope entirely. Who's to know? The most typical and oldest methods of ensuring that the enclosed message remains private is to either keep it out of the reach of all but intended parties (certainly unlikely in our mail or network examples) or to transform the message into an encrypted format that is unreadable by all but the intended party.

With modern multiply-connected systems, you might want to pass information through one party to another, and keep some of the content confidential from the first party. Consider a situation where a customer is ordering something from an online store and needs to pass his credit card information. The online store does not need to know any of the credit card data; the store just needs to pass it to a bank to verify that the charge is authorized. Passing information such as this through one party to be read only by another party is part of the confidentiality capability of Web services security.

Nonrepudiation

We are all familiar with the significance and intent of a handwritten signature. It implies that the signatory has placed his oath of compliance on the document to which it is bound. One might, in fact, be held to account for this signature in a court of law and be compelled to abide to its intended obligations unless the signature is proven to be illegitimate. For example, it may be illegitimate if it was forged or forced. The goal of nonrepudiation in the digital world is the same; the recipient of a message might need to ascertain with a high degree of reliability that the message came from the indicated originator and have a mechanism to assert that origin.

Authentication, Authorization, and Auditing

When someone asks you for something you possess, you might take quite different actions based on who is making the request, and what she asks for. If while standing on a subway platform, a stranger asks you for the time, you would most likely provide her with a response if you had the capacity, such as you have a watch and you speak the same language. However, if the same individual asked for your Social Security number, you would hopefully respond quite differently.

The goal of Authentication, Authorization, and Auditing (AAA) is, of course, to identify requestors, the resources they desire, deciding whether they are entitled to it, and recording the exchange. You can read all about this subject in Chapter 16, "AAA," and Chapter 17, "Advanced AAA," but for the purposes of our Web services security discussion, we will be interested in how this identity and other meta-data is transmitted from requestor to provider.

Cryptographic Terminology, Basic Definitions

The encryption of messages has been around for a long time. It is said that in the fifth century BCE, secured messages were tattooed onto the scalp of the messenger and only sent when the hair had regrown. Certainly an inadequate timeframe for today's millisecond commerce! The discussion to follow references key elements of cryptography. There is a close relationship between this discussion and the discussion presented in Chapter 18, "DataPower and SSL," as the technologies share many key components. The terminology introductions here will be brief and you might want to revisit the Secured Sockets Layer (SSL) discussion for a more in-depth analysis.

Public Key Infrastructure

In the digital world, public and private keys are often employed to perform cryptographic operations, such as encryption of message data. The use of key pairs (public/private) is known as asymmetric encryption. It is vital that the private key is protected, while its public counterpart, the public key (often carried in a certificate), can be freely distributed. Certificates are typically validated by a Certificate Authority, and that authority might revoke a previously distributed certificate.

Symmetric encryption requires that a shared secret key is possessed by both parties. Asymmetric encryption utilizes public and private key pairs that do not require predistribution. Although symmetric encryption requires the distribution of the shared key prior to message encryption or decryption, it is far more efficient than asymmetric encryption.

Chapters 12 and 18 discuss some of the aspects of key distribution within the DataPower environment. Revocation lists may be maintained so that when certificates are revoked, you are aware of it, and you no longer accept them. Additionally, when you produce or request certificates, you need to ensure that the validity period is not too excessive and that the cipher strengths meet your security policies.

Canonicalization

XML is flexible in the authoring of documents; it is possible for a given XML document to be represented in multiple physical structures. As seen in Listing 19-1, the two documents while written in differing formats (attributes ordered differently, whitespaces differ) are equivalent in their XML representation. That is to say that when consumed by the XML Path Language (XPath) or XML parsers, they are processed similarly, and client code would be unable to distinguish between them.

Listing 19-1 Structurally Unique yet Logically Equivalent XML Documents

```
<?xml version="1.0" encoding="UTF-8"?>
<doc>
    <fee name="fee" type="element">fee</fee>
</doc>
- - - - - - - - - - - - - - - - - - - - - - - - - - - - - - -
<?xml version="1.0" encoding="UTF-8"?>
<doc>
    <fee type="element" name="fee" >fee</fee>
</ doc>
```

If these two documents were processed in the textual representation presented in Listing 19-1 by cryptographic algorithms, the results would be quite different. To get around this potential problem, a transformation of the original document, known as canonicalization, is performed. Canonicalization (a subject in its own right) basically describes the transformations necessary to normalize documents into a standardized format. With XML documents, this process describes the ordering of attributes, the handling of whitespace, the representation of empty elements, and other characteristics of XML documents that might account for differing physical representation of logically equivalent documents. Prior to performing the hash calculation, an XML document is typically formatted by the canonicalization method to avoid structural issues that would cause document integrity checking to fail.

Digital Signatures

Digital Signatures can ensure the integrity of messages by attaching a cryptographically generated hash of the original message (or parts thereof) to the document. Public and private keys are often used for this process. XML Digital Signatures (XMLDSIG), a joint effort of the World Wide Web Consortium (W3C) and the Internet Engineering Task Force (IETF), provides the specification for the implementation of digital signatures and the structure of the resultant XML document format. OASIS (Organization for the Advancement of Structured Information Standards) provides similar specifications for WS-Security in conjunction with SOAP documents. XMLDSIG can be used to sign entire XML documents, selected XML elements, as well as other types such as binary images or Multipurpose Internet Mail Extensions (MIME) attachments. All document types result in similar encapsulations. XMLDSIG also plays an important role in many other security techniques and is vital in the integrity processing of these protocols.

By associating a digital signature with a document, the intent is that the holder of the private key used to generate the signature has placed its mark on the origin of the document. The verification of this signature proves that the signature was generated by the holder of the private key and (assuming it has not been stolen or otherwise compromised), its origin may not be repudiated. Similar to the handwritten signature, a digital signature might also be enforced under certain conditions in a court of law and might be held to similar legal standards such as whether the signer intended to sign the document and had the right to sign it.

The reader may want to consult the XMLDSIG protocol for definitive implementation information, but the following discussion describes the basis for XMLDSIG generation and validation.

Typically a hash (digest of canonicalization result) is calculated representing the signature target (be it an XML Document, XML Node, attachment, image, binary data, or combination thereof). This creates a value that corresponds to the original content and is unique to that content. A hash mechanism such as the Secured Hash Algorithm (SHA1) is processed against the byte stream and produces a fixed length string (20 bytes in the case of SHA1.) This provides a more condensed basis for further cryptographic processing. It is computationally infeasible for the message to be reproduced from the resultant string, and no two messages *should* produce the same digest value. There exist arguments exposing potential rebuttals to these assumptions for certain hashing algorithms; however, given constraints such as validity periods (limiting the lifetime of the signature) the computationally infeasible argument has significant merit.

Having produced the digest value, it is encrypted using one of the public/private key pairs. In the case of XMLDSIG, the private key of the sender is used, allowing verification of the signature via the freely available public key.

The validation process involves the recipient producing a digest value of its own using the same hash algorithm as the sender. If it is equivalent to the sender's version, the message has not been modified in transit. Decrypting the encrypted version of the digest using the sender's public key, and validating that key using the Public key infrastructure (PKI) mechanisms ensures that the identity of the sender is validated.

Encryption

Encryption ensures the confidentiality of messages (plaintext) through the implementation of a reversible transformation algorithm to produce encrypted ciphertext. If the message is intercepted prior to its ultimate destination, the contents of the message will not be exposed. However, this methodology does not preclude a man in the middle from changing the contents of the message, encrypted or not. For this reason, it is advisable to combine signatures with encrypted messages to ensure that even though the original contents are not exposed, the message was not altered in transit.

> **TIP—FOR ADDED SECURITY, FIRST SIGN THE MESSAGE, AND THEN ENCRYPT**
>
> Signing the message ensures the integrity of the original message content. Encryption ensures confidentiality and the integrity of the signature metadata.

As has been discussed, two primary types of encryption algorithms exist: symmetric, where a single, shared secret key is used for both the encryption and decryption operations, and asymmetric, in which a public/private key pair is utilized. Symmetric encryption is orders of magnitude faster than asymmetric; however, the difficulty lies in the management of the keys. Symmetric keys must be shared out of band prior to the decryption process. Asymmetric cryptography resolves key management by the free distribution of public keys.

Encryption is performed using the public key of the intended recipient. This ensures that only the holder of the private key can decrypt it. DataPower (as will be examined later in this chapter) enforces the proper use of keys in all encryption and decryption operations, and digital signatures for that matter. In an effort to ameliorate the asymmetric performance problems, encryption systems typically employ the public/private key pair for asymmetric encryption of a dynamically generated shared secret symmetric key (session key) that is used in the actual message encryption process. This is quite similar to the ephemeral key generation processed used in SSL, you might want to again refer to Chapter 18 for a description of this process.

The XML Encryption (XMLENC) protocol specification is defined by the World Wide Web Consortium (W3C). It defines the XML structure that results from the encryption process and describes the algorithms and keys that are used. XMLENC can be used to encrypt any type of document such as XML, binary images or attachments that all result in similar encapsulations. Individual fields can be encrypted or the entire document can be encrypted, and multipass cryptography (super encryption) may be employed.

You might want to consult the XMLENC protocol for definitive implementation information, but the following describes the basis for XMLENC generation and validation.

As was the case with Digital Signature generation, the first step in encryption is the canonicalization of the target data. A canonicalization transformation converts the plaintext into a consistent physical structure and normalizes elements (in the case of XML), whitespace, and other structurally variable document components. The resulting byte stream is then encrypted with a symmetric (session) key. The symmetric key used is then encrypted with the public key from the intended recipient. Decryption is simply the reverse; the session key is decrypted using the recipient's private key and then used to decrypt the ciphertext into plaintext.

SSL/TLS (HTTPS) Use and Vulnerabilities

SSL and associated protocols, such as Transaction Layer Security (TLS), provide transport layer security and are often employed to facilitate the goals of integrity and confidentiality. As is discussed in Chapter 18, HTTPS (SSL over HTTP) is employed for these purposes. SSL employs a combination of asymmetric and symmetric cryptography. Public/private key pairs are used to asymmetrically encrypt a dynamically generated session (ephemeral) key that is used for the communication's data encryption. By validating the public keys of the SSL communication peer (the client or server), the identity of the peer can be determined, and the message can be encrypted and protected from third-party exposure.

However SSL/TLS is not always sufficient for complete data protection because it is only effective point-to-point (between communication endpoints.) If, for example, an SSL terminator is used in a network prior to the delivery of the message to its intended recipient, the message is decrypted into plaintext. This might expose vulnerabilities is several ways; log messages might print the data to external devices (with private information), and importantly, the data is transmitted between these endpoints (and potentially others) in its original form and exposed to network sniffers and other unscrupulous methods of inspection. Similar vulnerabilities exist when messages are transmitted across trust zones where they could be intercepted by unintended intermediaries.

Partial message encryption is also unavailable with SSL because it encrypts the entire message and cannot encrypt only certain parts. There might be occasions when the routing of a message is dependent on an element within the message body. Exposing the routing information necessitates decrypting and exposing the entire message body. Or for example, a credit card number might be part of a request sent over the Internet, and might only be intended to be decrypted by a credit card processing service, while address information may be viewable by others. It would be beneficial in this instance to be able to decrypt only those message components that a particular intermediary requires and leave the remainder of the message protected.

There are many instances when SSL will meet the needs of a particular application, and in those cases it is all that is required. SSL is easily established in most environments. Applications hosted on WebSphere Application Server for example may be configured to utilize SSL with ease. The DataPower devices are also, of course, well suited to receive SSL and to validate either SSL clients or servers.

Web Services Security

Web Services security might be thought of as transport layer security plus additional techniques and methodologies. It's not a standard, but more of a concept. The goals of Web Services security are the core group of features we've discussed; confidentiality, integrity, nonrepudiation and authentication and authorization for resource access. Protocol headers (such as those used for basic authentication) are frequently used to convey identity information. However the lack of confidentiality with these techniques requires the concurrent use of transport layer security. This problem has been addressed with proprietary solutions such as the encrypted Lightweight Third-Party Authentication (LTPA) token utilized by applications within the WebSphere environment; however, this does restrict their usage to supporting environments.

Web Services security is lighter weight than WS-Security with its greater emphasis on extensibility protocols and heavy use of XML for policy definition. And many times the more traditional Web Services security might be all that is required.

Transport level security provides not only point-to-point security and the ability to encrypt traffic but can also authenticate (though not authorize to the resource level) the endpoints, or peer via the inspection of the clients' certificate. XMLDSIG and XMLENC can be used to provide integrity checking and confidentiality.

Additional techniques such as Access Control Lists (ACLs) can also be used to assist in secured client access. However, with the use of Dynamic Host Configuration Protocol (DHCP) this technique might be limited to consistently addressed endpoints such as in-house resources.

DataPower Web Service Security Features

DataPower supports a wide range of traditional security features. SSL/TLS is fully supported. Encryption and signature support is available for raw XML and SOAP document as are ACLs. The AAA functionality described in Chapter 16 and Chapter 17 describes methods to extract SSL credentials from SSL certificates and provides extensive token translation support. Of particular interest to users of WebSphere is the ability to create LTPA tokens for SSO across an application cell. This is presented in Chapter 21, "Security Integration with WebSphere Application Server." Support for the Security Assertion Markup Language (SAML) is also provided (as discussed in Chapter 16) extending the trust domain across organization boundaries and providing the implementation of Single Sign On (SSO) solutions.

WS-Security

WS-Security is not a protocol or specification in and of itself. Rather it was initiated to solve more complex problems than that offered by the point-to-point solutions of Web services and transport layer security, by leveraging existing standards and protocols. Messages may be sent over unanticipated protocols and across trust domains with requirements such as preserving identity information. Multiple encryption and decryption destinations might be required to individually expose message data to only the intended recipient.

WS-Security facilitates these goals by utilizing a SOAP Header to carry security-related information. For example, if XMLDSIG is used to generate a signature, or XMLENC to encrypt an element, the SOAP Header is used to carry the key and algorithm information.

WS-Security also identifies a mechanism for communicating identity information. The Username Token profile stores this data within the SOAP Header, and the Binary Security Token profile defines a mechanism for carrying crypto tokens such as Kerberos tickets or X.509 certificates. You can read more about these specifications on the Organization for the Advancement of Structured Information Standards (OASIS) Web site, and in Chapter 16 and Chapter 17.

WS-Security is not an island, and this framework is constantly being enhanced with additional supporting specifications. We'll talk about WS-Policy (which is used to define the requirements of a Web service) later in this chapter, but there are many others such as WS-Trust for the definition of trust relationships across domains, WS-SecureConversation for dynamic security decisions, WS-ReliableMessaging for the assured delivery of message data, WS-Addressing for dissemination of routing information, WS-Interoperability and WS-Basic Profile for the definition of standards for the sharing of information describing Web Services and how they should interoperate, and WS-Federation for the federation of identity information between parties involved in multisite transactions. Again, you can read about the latest WS-Security specifications (often referred to as WS-*) on the OASIS Web site.

DataPower WS-Security Features

One of the criticisms of WS-Security is the performance hit and complication involved in its implementation. That is where DataPower really shines. Not only does it provide support for an ever expanding list of specifications, but through the use of its purpose built firmware and cryptographic hardware accelerators, it does so at a speed and efficiency of configuration that makes their implementation viable and effective. We'll see an example of WS-Policy implementation on DataPower later in this chapter; you'll see how specifications such as WS-SecureConversation are implemented along with more typical security patterns. DataPower also provides support for WS-Addressing and WS-ReliableMessaging through the Multi-Protocol Gateway and Web Service Proxy Services, and WS-Trust through AAA policies.

DataPower also provides built-in Replay filters that may be added to the multistep policy via the Filter action to check for the repeated submission of like messages (Replay Attacks). This comparison can be performed using the WS-Security Password Digest Nonce or the WS-Addressing Message ID. These selections are made from the advanced screen. The filter will reject subsequent messages with similar characteristics within the time frame specified.

WS-Policy and Policy Governance

If you have read Chapter 10, "Web Service Proxy," or have worked with Web services and WSDL definitions, you understand the power of the WSDL to communicate the structural and networking requirements of a Web service. By consuming the WSDL, the client can develop messages (either automatically or via visual inspection) and understand where and how to send them to invoke the service.

WS-Policy takes the same approach in the specification of Web service interoperability, defining how Web services must be secured, whether requests must be submitted over particular protocols, or whether the request must be part of a transaction. The WS-Policy Framework and WS-Policy Attachment specifications define the metadata describing these requirements, which (in a similar fashion to the WSDL) might be automatically consumed or visually inspected by clients for the proper delivery of service requests.

Assertions are used to define domains such as security, messaging, transaction control, and reliability. Through the definition of collections of assertions (patterns) within these domains, policies may be defined describing the restrictions required for a particular service. There are several existing policy domains such as Web Service Security Policy, Web Service Reliable Messaging Policy, and Web Service Atomic Transaction. These policies may be authored within the WSDL document itself or published in repositories such as Universal Description Discovery and Integration (UDDI) or WebSphere Service Registry and Repository (WSRR). Listing 19-2 demonstrates a policy expression containing two policy assertions that defines the requirements of the signing and encrypting of the message body.

Listing 19-2 Sample Policy Expression and Assertions

```
<wsp:Policy wsu:Id="sign-before-encrypt-1">
     <wsp:ExactlyOne>
         <wsp:All>
             <sp:SignedParts>
                 <sp:Body/>
             </sp:SignedParts>
             <sp:EncryptedParts>
                 <sp:Body/>
             </sp:EncryptedParts>
         </wsp:All>
     </wsp:ExactlyOne>
</wsp:Policy>
```

DataPower WS-Policy Features

DataPower supports the utilization of WS-Policy assertions within the definition of policy configuration. External Policy (not from the WSDL) may be attached at various levels within the WSDL policy definition of the WSP (Web Service Proxy), and policy that has been authored within the WSDL may be attached as well. DataPower has encapsulated many of the aforementioned domain patterns within the /store/policy/templates directory of its file system for ease of implementation.

Policy assertions contain the requirements of a service such as dictating the use of HTTPS in a Transport Binding assertion, but do not define the keys and certificates this protocol would use. DataPower defines Parameter Set for this purpose, and provides screens for their assignment to bindings. We demonstrate the implementation of WS-Policy later in this chapter.

Digital Signatures on DataPower

Having described the reasons for implementing digital signatures, we turn our attention to their implementation on the DataPower device. DataPower provides a simple mechanism for the signing and verification of message data. The multistep policy editor provides Sign and Verify Action icons, which might be placed onto the policy in any location. Standard use cases are typically handled with little effort other than assignment of key information, whereas more atypical requirements can be managed through fine-grained parameter assignment available via the Advanced tab of the Sign action. DataPower can be used to sign and verify signatures of various types of data such as XML documents, SOAP documents, as well as attachments such as MIME and Direct Internet Message Encapsulation (DIME). The following examples demonstrate three typical uses: document level signing of a SOAP document, selective field level signing, and the signing of a MIME attachment.

Document Level Signing

Signing an entire document is easily performed using the Sign action. As can be seen in Figure 19-1, the only configuration detail required is the key and certificate to be used. The signer's private key is used to generate the signature via the encryption of the digest produced by the message target. The public key is specified on this action so that the recipient can verify the signature within after verifying the validity of its public key via their PKI infrastructure.

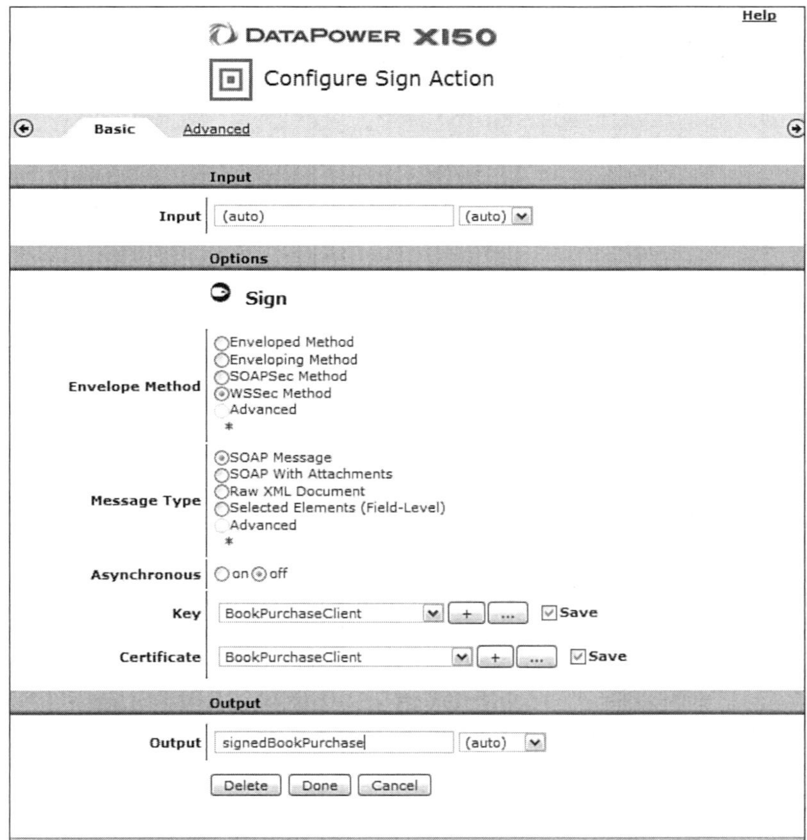

Figure 19-1 Sign action with WS-Security (WSSEC) method and SOAP Document type selected.

There are four different envelope methods available on the Sign action that determine how the signature is carried within the resulting message. Two options may be used with raw XML without a SOAP envelope. Enveloped and enveloping describe the placement of the signature and elements used to contain it. The more common use case (especially with Web services) is the use of the WS-Security (WSSec) or the SOAPSec methods. You should refer to the XMLDSIG Core specification for definitive information on signature encoding. In our first example, a SOAPSec method has been chosen.

Listing 19-3 shows the sample SOAP document used for the following examples. This is a simple book purchase request, and it contains some information such as credit card data that should be considered sensitive.

Listing 19-3 Sample SOAP Document

```
<?xml version="1.0"?>
<SOAP-ENV:Envelope xmlns:SOAP-
ENV="http://schemas.xmlsoap.org/soap/envelope/"
xmlns:exm="http://www.example.org/BookService/">
    <SOAP-ENV:Body>
        <exm:BookPurchase>
            <isbn>0321228006</isbn>
            <price>19.95</price>
            <creditCardInfo>1234567890121234-0808</creditCardInfo>
            <cardHolderName>Ishmael</cardHolderName>
            <address>Sailing Vessel Pequod, Old Harbor, Gloucester MA
01111</address>
        </exm:BookPurchase>
    </SOAP-ENV:Body>
</SOAP-ENV:Envelope>
```

Listing 19-4 shows the results of the signing action. Several of the cryptographic fields such as digest values and X.509 certificates have been truncated for brevity. There are many new fields added that describe the processes required to generate and to verify the signature.

First a SOAP-SEC:Signature header was added to the SOAP:Header. All the details of the procedure are carried within the Signature element. The actual signature is contained within the SignatureValue in Base64-encoded format.

To determine how the signature was created, you need to understand the details of the SignedInfo element. It contains the canonicalization method used to create the byte stream from the original message, and the signature method (for example Kerberos or the RSA algorithm) used to create the signature.

The XMLDSIG specification allows for the signing of multiple fields, and the Reference element is used to describe each occurrence. In our document level signature example there is only one. Each of the potentially multiple entries contains a pointer to the signed content that could not only reference an element within the current document, but a URL reference to any network accessible data. Here we indicate that the body of the SOAP envelope has been signed. The Reference element also contains a digest of the content, how the digest was calculated, and transformations that are required prior to generating the digest, which in our example is XML canonicalization.

Finally, the public certificate of the signer is carried within the KeyInfo element; it will be extracted and validated by the recipient and used for signature verification. It is assumed that this certificate will be validated by the recipient to maintain the chain of trust.

Listing 19-4 Signed XML Document

```
<?xml version="1.0" encoding="UTF-8"?>
<SOAP-ENV:Envelope xmlns:SOAP-
ENV="http://schemas.xmlsoap.org/soap/envelope/"
xmlns:exm="http://www.example.org/BookService/">
  <SOAP:Header xmlns:SOAP-
SEC="http://schemas.xmlsoap.org/soap/security/2000-12"
xmlns:SOAP="http://schemas.xmlsoap.org/soap/envelope/">
    <SOAP-SEC:Signature SOAP:mustUnderstand="1">
      <Signature xmlns="http://www.w3.org/2000/09/xmldsig#">
        <SignedInfo>
          <CanonicalizationMethod Algorithm="http://www.w3.org/TR/2001/REC-
xml-c14n-20010315"/>
          <SignatureMethod
Algorithm="http://www.w3.org/2000/09/xmldsig#rsa-sha1"/>
          <Reference URI="#Body">
             <Transforms>
               <Transform Algorithm="http://www.w3.org/TR/2001/REC-xml-
c14n-20010315"/>
             </Transforms>
             <DigestMethod
Algorithm="http://www.w3.org/2000/09/xmldsig#sha1"/>
                <DigestValue>(Truncated)</DigestValue>
          </Reference>
        </SignedInfo>
          <SignatureValue>(Truncated)</SignatureValue>
            <KeyInfo>
              <X509Data>
                <X509Certificate>(Truncated)</X509Certificate>
                <X509IssuerSerial>
                  <X509IssuerName>CN=BookPurchaseClient</X509IssuerName>
                  <X509SerialNumber>1737560841</X509SerialNumber>
                </X509IssuerSerial>
              <X509Data>
            </KeyInfo>
      </Signature>
    </SOAP-SEC:Signature>
  </SOAP:Header>
  <SOAP-ENV:Body id="Body">
    <exm:BookPurchase>
      <isbn>0321228006</isbn>
      <price>19.95</price>
      <creditCardInfo>1234567890121234-0808</creditCardInfo>
      <cardHolderName>Ishmael</cardHolderName>
      <address>Sailing Vessel Pequod, Old Harbor, Gloucester MA
01111</address>
    </exm:BookPurchase>
  </SOAP-ENV:Body>
</SOAP-ENV:Envelope>
```

Field Level Signing

The next example demonstrates field level signing, that is signing of multiple fields using the same key. This could be useful in many instances. For example, if only one or two elements within a large document contain sensitive information, there is no need to incur the overhead of signing the entire document. A more practical reason might be that multiple signatures are required for request processing, perhaps the purchasing department signs the order date, while shipping signs the shipping date.

Again, the DataPower Sign action is used but a new object, the Document Crypto Map, is added to describe the fields to be signed. This association can be seen in Figure 19-2. Notice also that the Selected Elements radio button has been selected as has the WS-Security (WSSec) Method. Field level signing is available only with the WS-Security Envelope method.

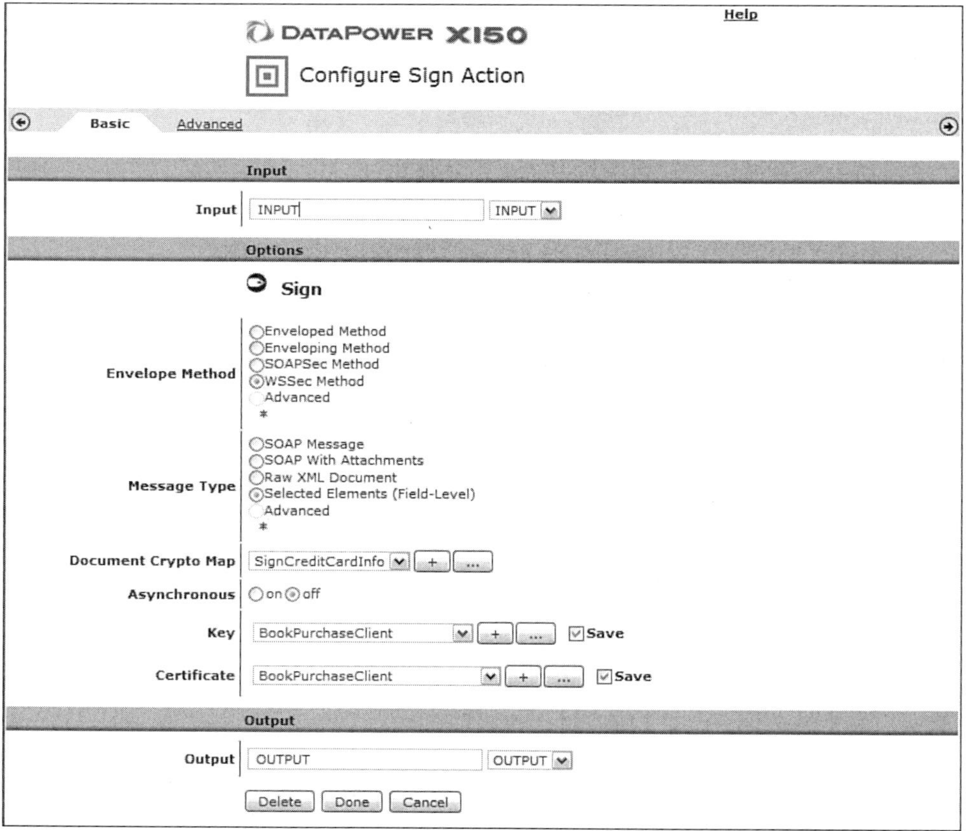

Figure 19-2 Sign action with document crypto map for field level selection.

Figure 19-3 shows the details of the Document Crypto Map with two XPath statements having been added. Any number of individual XPath statements can be added (identifying single or sets of elements), allowing for many elements to be individually signed. The XPath Tool can be used to automatically generate the XPath statement from the anticipated request message.

Figure 19-3 Document Crypto Map.

Submitting the SOAP document previously shown in Listing 19-5 provides an example of field level signing. As per the XPath statements entered in the Document Crypto Map, the card-HolderName and creditCardInfo elements have been signed. The construction of the Signature element and its contents is similar to the document level example previously described. However, in this case we now have multiple Reference elements, each of which describes the element signed and as described previously, the digest value and its calculation methodology.

The careful observer might note the Reference URI attributes pointing to the cardHolder-Name and cardHolderName elements, but you might wonder why there is an extra Reference node. In this example, a Timestamp has been added to the wsse:Security header. This allows for a mechanism to control the period in which the signature is valid. Perhaps you are authorizing a purchase, but you do not want to be locked into the content and price indefinitely. This header (created automatically by the WSSec method) ensures that an unscrupulous intermediary does not change that time period.

Listing 19-5 Sample Field Level Signing

```
<wsse:Security xmlns:wsse="http://docs.oasis-open.org/wss/2004/01/oasis-
200401-wss-WS-Security-secext-1.0.xsd" soapenv:mustUnderstand="1">
    <wsu:Timestamp wsu:Id="Timestamp-7e1b0b40-b9fd-409c-bad4-697a56c02a2f"
xmlns:wsu="http://docs.oasis-open.org/wss/2004/01/oasis-200401-wss-WS-
Security-utility-1.0.xsd">
        <wsu:Created>2008-07-21T16:36:54Z</wsu:Created>
        <wsu:Expires>2008-07-21T16:41:54Z</wsu:Expires>
    </wsu:Timestamp>

    <wsse:BinarySecurityToken (Truncated)/>
        <SignedInfo>
            <CanonicalizationMethod
Algorithm="http://www.w3.org/2001/10/xml-exc-c14n#"/>
            <SignatureMethod
Algorithm="http://www.w3.org/2000/09/xmldsig#rsa-sha1"/>
            <Reference URI="#Id-f16b389e-5193-4cbd-a5d5-92ac55c139c0">
                <Transforms>
                    <Transform Algorithm="http://www.w3.org/2001/10/xml-
exc-c14n#"/>
                </Transforms>
                <DigestMethod
Algorithm="http://www.w3.org/2000/09/xmldsig#sha1"/>
                <DigestValue>uCpOLDKEDz11IwBwyXvfXgnE1cU=</DigestValue>
            </Reference>
            <Reference URI="#Id-cac033a5-42c4-4aa5-83d2-8d4424a4783b">
                <Transforms>
                    <Transform Algorithm="http://www.w3.org/2001/10/xml-
exc-c14n#"/>
                </Transforms>
                <DigestMethod
Algorithm="http://www.w3.org/2000/09/xmldsig#sha1"/>
                <DigestValue>yxXcIJpMuyEwTQaooNlmtlfd27E=</DigestValue>
            </Reference>
            <Reference URI="#Timestamp-7e1b0b40-b9fd-409c-bad4-
697a56c02a2f">
                <Transforms>
                    <Transform Algorithm="http://www.w3.org/2001/10/xml-
exc-c14n#"/>
                </Transforms>
                <DigestMethod
Algorithm="http://www.w3.org/2000/09/xmldsig#sha1"/>
                <DigestValue>WZzZoH+Ls6wbPKDVEkuwlidr3CQ=</DigestValue>
            </Reference>
        </SignedInfo>
        <SignatureValue>RlV(Truncated)</SignatureValue>
    ...(Truncated)...
</wsse:Security>
```

Listing 19-6 shows the body of the signed SOAP envelope. Each signed element has been modified by adding a wsu:Id attribute that links the element to one of the Reference URI attributes contained in the wsse:Security header that describes the signature and generation methodology.

Listing 19-6 Sample Field Level Signing

```
<SOAP-ENV:Body>
    <exm:BookPurchase>
        <isbn>0321228006</isbn>
        <price>19.95</price>
        <creditCardInfo wsu:Id="Id-f16b389e-5193-4cbd-a5d5-92ac55c139c0"
xmlns:wsu="http://docs.oasis-open.org/wss/2004/01/oasis-200401-wss-WS-
Security-utility-1.0.xsd">1234567890121234-0808</creditCardInfo>
        <cardHolderName wsu:Id="Id-cac033a5-42c4-4aa5-83d2-8d4424a4783b"
xmlns:wsu="http://docs.oasis-open.org/wss/2004/01/oasis-200401-wss-WS-
Security-utility-1.0.xsd">Ishmael</cardHolderName>
        <address>Sailing Vessel Pequod, Old Harbor, Gloucester MA
01111</address>
    </exm:BookPurchase>
</SOAP-ENV:Body>
```

Attachment Signing

XMLDSIG allows for the signing of binary data such as images and MIME attachments, as well as XML documents. DataPower also supports this functionality. Again the signing is done via the Sign action, as can be seen in Figure 19-4. The SOAP With Attachments option is selected and the Attachment Handling option has been set to Attachments Only. It is also possible to sign both the root XML document as well as the attachment.

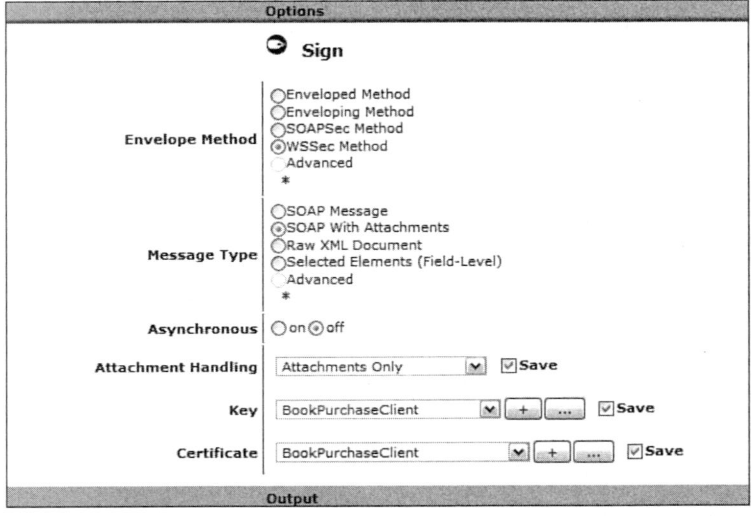

Figure 19-4 Attachment signing.

Listing 19-7 shows some of the interesting elements produced when signing MIME packages. Again, several fields are truncated for brevity. Of note is the Reference element that contains a URI reference to the Content-ID of the attachment. In addition the Transform element now contains an attachment canonicalization not an XML canonicalization method.

Listing 19-7 Attachment Signing

```
<Signature xmlns="http://www.w3.org/2000/09/xmldsig#">
    <SignedInfo>
        <CanonicalizationMethod Algorithm="http://www.w3.org/2001/10/xml-
exc-c14n#"/>
        <SignatureMethod Algorithm="http://www.w3.org/2000/09/xmldsig#rsa-
sha1"/>
        <Reference URI="cid:xml2@bookPurchaseRequest.ibm.com">
            <Transforms>
                <Transform Algorithm="http://docs.oasis-
open.org/wss/2004/XX/oasis-2004XX-wss-swa-profile-1.0#Attachment-Content-
Only-Transform"/>
            </Transforms>
            <DigestMethod
Algorithm="http://www.w3.org/2000/09/xmldsig#sha1"/>
            <DigestValue>xe3pYnsXqkITHdw0UMgJLudCn7o=</DigestValue>
        </Reference>
    </SignedInfo>
<SignatureValue>(Truncated)</SignatureValue>
    <KeyInfo>
        <wsse:SecurityTokenReference xmlns="">
            <wsse:Reference URI="#SecurityToken-4ba7a5c7-5f5c-45bb-aab4-
297aceed3024" ValueType="http://docs.oasis-open.org/wss/2004/01/oasis-
200401-wss-x509-token-profile-1.0#X509v3"/>
        </wsse:SecurityTokenReference>
    </KeyInfo>
</Signature>
 -MIME_boundary
Content-Type: text/xml; charset=UTF-8
Content-Transfer-Encoding: 8bit
Content-ID: <xml2@bookPurchaseRequest.ibm.com>
<?xml version="1.0"?>
<SOAP-ENV:Envelope xmlns:SOAP-
ENV="http://schemas.xmlsoap.org/soap/envelope/">
    <SOAP-ENV:Body>
        <bookPurchase>
            <isbn>0321228006</isbn>
            <price>19.95</price>
            <creditCardInfo>1234567890121234-0808</creditCardInfo>
            <cardHolderName>Ishmael</cardHolderName>
            <address>Sailing Vessel Pequod, Old Harbor, Gloucester MA
01111</address>
        </bookPurchase>
    </SOAP-ENV:Body>
</SOAP-ENV:Envelope>
```

Signing Advanced Options

The advanced tab of the Sign action exposes many parameters you can customize. Figure 19-5 demonstrates a partial list, and the options depend on which signature method is being employed. WS-Security (WSS) allows for more than SOAP Security or the Raw XML signatures that are available for XML without the SOAP envelope structure. These options allow for control over the digest and signature methods, timestamps, and other DSIG characteristics.

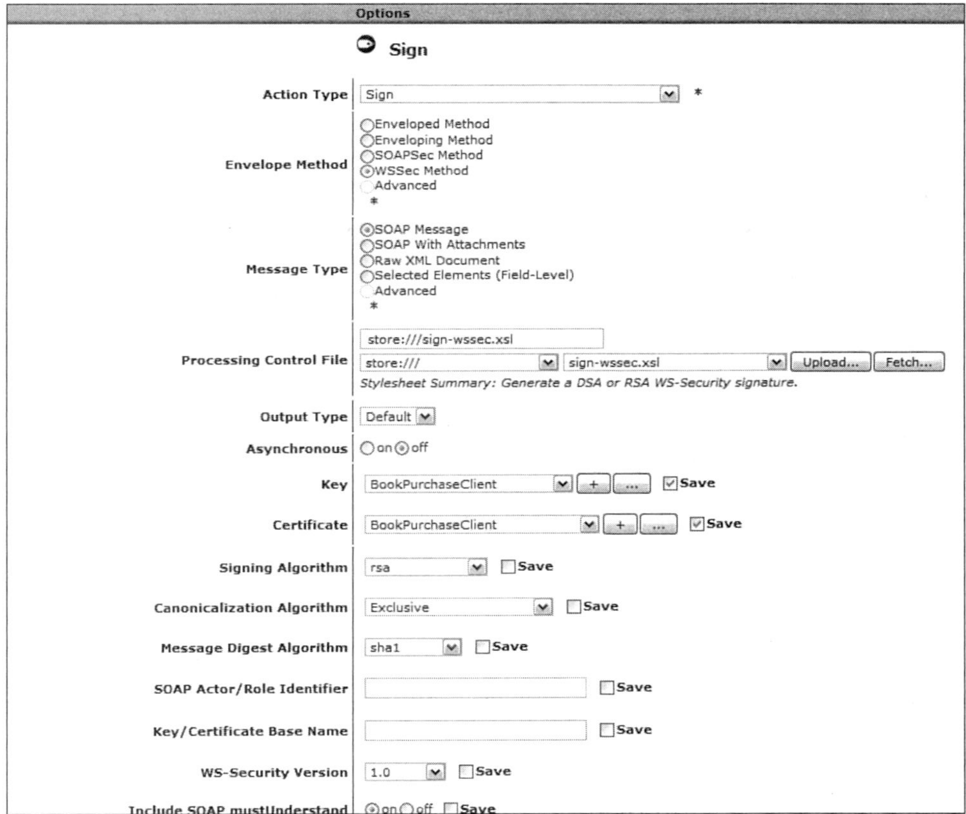

Figure 19-5 Signing advanced options.

Signature Verification

Signature verification is a fairly straightforward process. The multistep policy provides a Verify action for this purpose, and it can be dropped onto the policy at any point. Conveniently a Verify action can be used to authenticate multiple (field level) signatures, document level signatures, and attachment signatures using a single methodology. As was demonstrated in the signature discussion (see "Digital Signatures on DataPower" earlier in this chapter), the public certificate used for validation is often carried within the KeyInfo element of the DSIG message. The most typical method (we see others later in the chapter) of validating a signature is by creating a list of public certificates that match this KeyInfo value. The Validation Credential (ValCred) object is used for this purpose, and as can be seen in Figure 19-6, its use completes the Verification action.

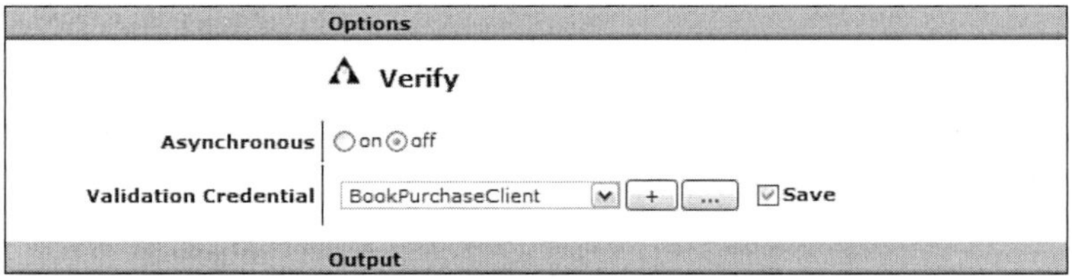

Options

Verify

Asynchronous ○ on ◉ off

Validation Credential BookPurchaseClient [+] [...] ☑ Save

Output

Figure 19-6 Verify action.

Figure 19-7 shows the details of the ValCred object. It contains a reference to the BookPurchaseClient Certificate object that successfully verifies signatures generated by the holder of its private key pair. In fact several certificates could have been added here to facilitate verification of additional signatures. Although this exact match mode is the most typical and efficient method available, an alternative method of verification is provided. Full certificate chain checking (PKIX) requires validation all the way up to the root certificate. This is a resource intensive operation and should only be done when a copy of the public certificate cannot be obtained and placed in the ValCred object.

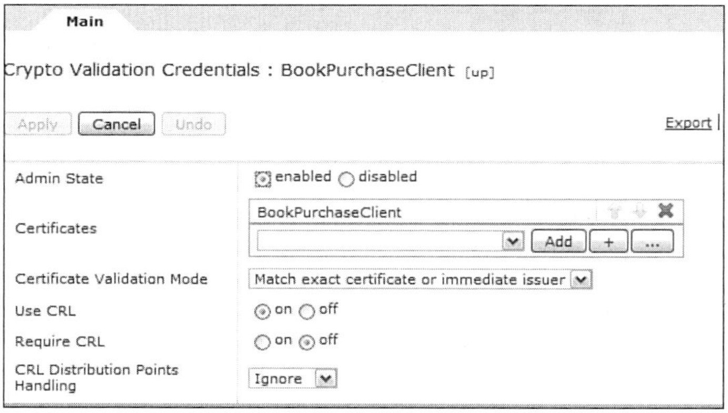

Main

Crypto Validation Credentials : BookPurchaseClient [up]

Apply Cancel Undo Export

Admin State	◉ enabled ○ disabled
Certificates	BookPurchaseClient [Add] [+] [...]
Certificate Validation Mode	Match exact certificate or immediate issuer
Use CRL	◉ on ○ off
Require CRL	○ on ◉ off
CRL Distribution Points Handling	Ignore

Figure 19-7 Validation credentials.

DataPower provides many optional configuration methodologies and signature verification, which in the vast majority of cases will be handled by the use of certificates, and the ValCred object is no exception. As Figure 19-8 shows, there are several parameters available from the advanced screen that may be used to fine-tune the verification process. Specifically, the ValCred can be entered in the Validation Credential field, or a variation called Signer Certificate can be used to directly identify the Certificate object. Other options may be used to turn off timestamp checking as well as restricting what algorithms are acceptable and other verification particulars.

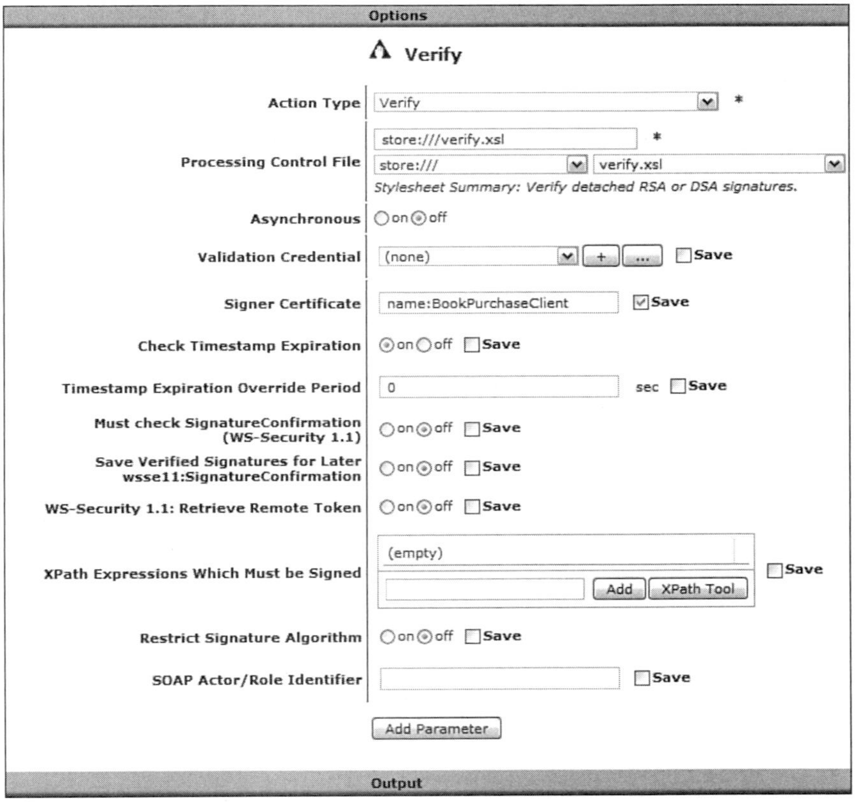

Options

Verify

Action Type: Verify *

Processing Control File: store:///verify.xsl *
store:/// verify.xsl
Stylesheet Summary: Verify detached RSA or DSA signatures.

Asynchronous: on off

Validation Credential: (none) + ... Save

Signer Certificate: name:BookPurchaseClient Save

Check Timestamp Expiration: on off Save

Timestamp Expiration Override Period: 0 sec Save

Must check SignatureConfirmation (WS-Security 1.1): on off Save

Save Verified Signatures for Later wsse11:SignatureConfirmation: on off Save

WS-Security 1.1: Retrieve Remote Token: on off Save

XPath Expressions Which Must be Signed: (empty) Add XPath Tool Save

Restrict Signature Algorithm: on off Save

SOAP Actor/Role Identifier: Save

Add Parameter

Output

Figure 19-8 Validation advanced options.

Digital Signature Verification in DataPower Services

Most of the DataPower services can utilize the Verify action. However, the Web Service Proxy has the additional feature of automatic document level signature verification. The public certificate must exist in a Crypto Validation Credential object. If not, the signature verification will fail with an untrusted certificate error. You can read more about WSP configuration in Chapter 10.

Encryption and Decryption on DataPower

The previous section discussed DataPower configurations to verify the integrity of messages it receives by virtue of their digital signatures. To provide for confidentiality, DataPower provides a simple mechanism for the encryption and decryption of message data. The multistep policy editor provides Encrypt and Decrypt action icons that can be placed onto the policy in any location. Standard use cases are typically handled with little effort other than assignment of key information; although less often encountered, use cases can be managed through fine-tuned advanced parameter assignment. The following sections demonstrate the encryption of an entire document, field level encryption, and the decryption of each.

Document Level Encryption

We'll use the sample book purchase request document presented in Listing 19-3 for the encryption and decryption examples. You might want to refer back to that listing.

The XMLENC specification allows for the encryption of individual elements or combinations of elements within the XML payload. This example will demonstrate document-level encryption using the standard XML encryption mechanism. This Envelope Method (Standard XML Encryption) does not make use of the WS-Security headers and may be used against raw XML Documents, though we are using a SOAP document in this example.

Figure 19-9 shows the completed Encrypt action. All that is required is the recipient's certificate that will be used in the encryption process. The recipient will use their private key to decrypt the message.

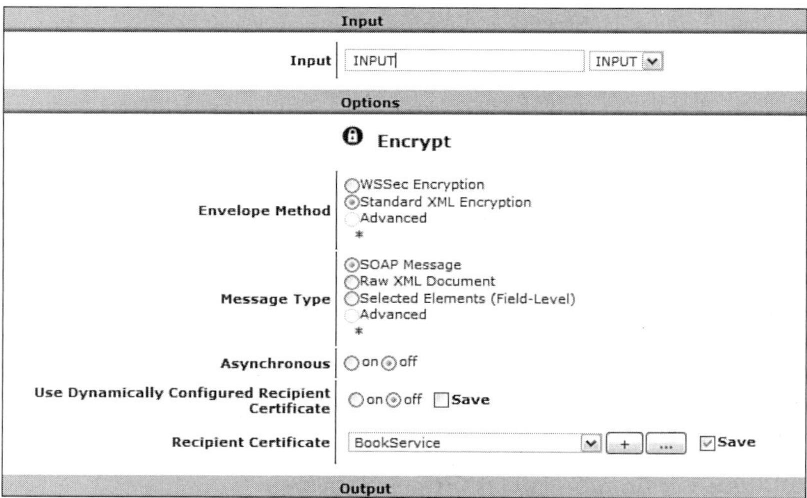

Figure 19-9 Document-level encryption.

Listing 19-8 shows the results of the encryption process. As we've chosen standard XML Encryption, the encryption details are contained within the body of the message (SOAP Body in this case) within a xenc:EncryptedData element. Recall our earlier discussion of asymmetric encryption; we discussed how the inefficiencies of asymmetric encryption are ameliorated by the creation of an ephemeral symmetric session key that is actually used in the encryption of the message data.

The session key is described in the KeyInfo element while the encrypted message is contained within the xenc:CipherData. The cipherdata is decrypted by the recipient who first decrypts the session key using their private key (the asymmetric key), identified in this case by the dsig:KeyName element.

Notice again that the CipherValue element has been truncated to condense the listing; they contain lengthy Base64 data that does not add to the discussion.

Listing 19-8 Encrypted Document

```
<?xml version="1.0" encoding="UTF-8"?>
<SOAP-ENV:Envelope xmlns:SOAP-
ENV="http://schemas.xmlsoap.org/soap/envelope/"
xmlns:exm="http://www.example.org/BookService/">
  <SOAP-ENV:Body>
    <xenc:EncryptedData Type="http://www.w3.org/2001/04/xmlenc#Element"
xmlns:xenc="http://www.w3.org/2001/04/xmlenc#">
        <xenc:EncryptionMethod
Algorithm="http://www.w3.org/2001/04/xmlenc#tripledes-cbc"/>
        <dsig:KeyInfo xmlns:dsig="http://www.w3.org/2000/09/xmldsig#">
          <xenc:EncryptedKey Recipient="name:BookService">
            <xenc:EncryptionMethod
Algorithm="http://www.w3.org/2001/04/xmlenc#rsa-1_5"/>
            <dsig:KeyInfo>
              <dsig:KeyName>BookService</dsig:KeyName>
            </dsig:KeyInfo>
            <xenc:CipherData>
             <xenc:CipherValue>(Truncated)</xenc:CipherValue>
            </xenc:CipherData>
          </xenc:EncryptedKey>
        </dsig:KeyInfo>
        <xenc:CipherData>
            <xenc:CipherValue>(Truncated)</xenc:CipherValue>
        </xenc:CipherData>
      </xenc:EncryptedData>
  </SOAP-ENV:Body>
</SOAP-ENV:Envelope>
```

Field Level Encryption

Our next example demonstrates field level encryption. This is a useful methodology as was previously discussed in the encryption introduction section. We will be encrypting the sensitive credit card information, while leaving the remainder of the message in plaintext and accessible to services that may need it for service routing or other tasks.

Figure 19-10 shows the Encrypt action required to implement field level encryption. The WS-Security (WSSec) Method has been selected, and this results in XMLENC information being placed in the WS-Security SOAP Header element. The Message Type has been set to Selected Elements. This example uses the default option of decrypting element and data, though the Encryption Type option (on advanced screen) does allow for data only encryption.

The encryption of selective elements (as with signing) requires the assignment of a Document Crypto Map. Figure 19-11 shows the details of the Document Crypto Map with two XPath statements added. Any number of individual XPath statements can be added, each indentifying a node within the document to encrypt thus allowing for many elements to be individually encrypted. The XPath Tool can be used to automatically generate the XPath statement from the sample request message.

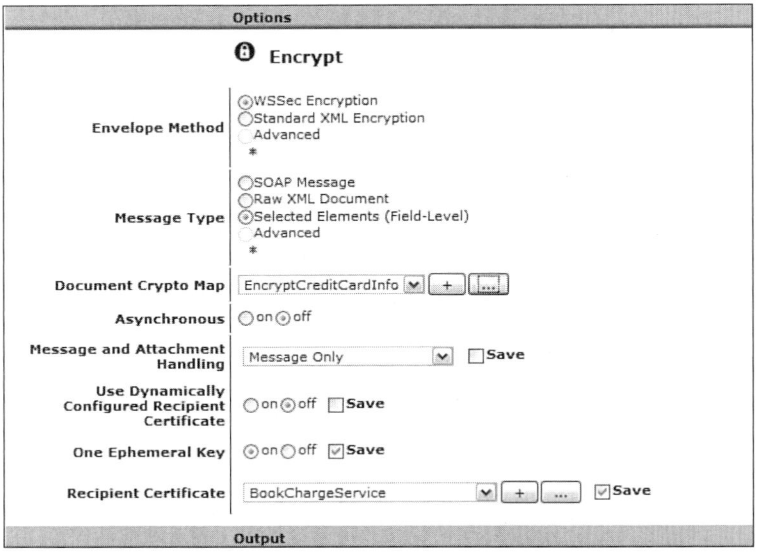

Figure 19-10 Field-level encryption.

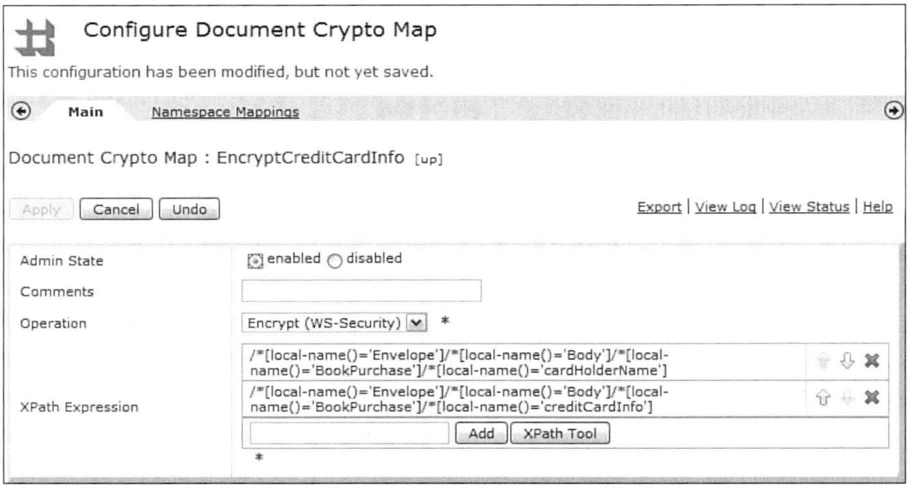

Figure 19-11 Document Crypto Map.

Encrypting the SOAP document in Listing 19-3 provides an example of field-level encryption. As per the XPath statements entered in the Document Crypto Map, the cardHolderName and creditCardInfo elements will be encrypted. The BookService public key will be used in the encryption of the ephemeral session key.

Listing 19-9 shows the soapenv:Header/wsse:Security contents (with truncated data) that results from the encryption process. There are many new fields added to the document that describe exactly the process that was required to encrypt the various elements.

Each field to be encrypted results in the inclusion of a xenc:EncryptedKey element as a child of the wsse:Security element. They are used to transport the session keys (and information about the asymmetric encryption applied to it) between the sender and recipient.

The xenc:ReferenceList element is used to contain a reference (pointer) to the data element that was encrypted using this key. And each encrypted element contains a cipher value and encryption method that can be decrypted using the xenc:EncryptedKey after it has been decrypted using the target's private key. Again the lengthy CipherValues have been truncated out of this display for brevity.

Listing 19-9 Field Level Encrypted Document

```
<xenc:EncryptedKey xmlns:xenc="http://www.w3.org/2001/04/xmlenc#">
    <xenc:EncryptionMethod Algorithm="http://www.w3.org/2001/04/xmlenc#rsa-
1_5" xmlns:dsig="http://www.w3.org/2000/09/xmldsig#"/>
    <dsig:KeyInfo xmlns:dsig="http://www.w3.org/2000/09/xmldsig#">
        <wsse:SecurityTokenReference>
            <wsse:KeyIdentifier ValueType="http://docs.oasis-
open.org/wss/2004/01/oasis-200401-wss-x509-token-profile-
1.0#X509SubjectKeyIdentifier"
EncodingType="http://docs.oasis-open.org/wss/2004/01/oasis-200401-wss-soap-
message-security-
1.0#Base64Binary">FLKVnJ2gyQw1ZdYm+rVIRYGkzFw=</wsse:KeyIdentifier>
        </wsse:SecurityTokenReference>
    </dsig:KeyInfo>
    <xenc:CipherData xmlns:dsig="http://www.w3.org/2000/09/xmldsig#">
        <xenc:CipherValue>(Truncated)</xenc:CipherValue>
    </xenc:CipherData>
    <xenc:ReferenceList>
        <xenc:DataReference URI="#G90e6b258-eD"/>
    </xenc:ReferenceList>
</xenc:EncryptedKey>
<xenc:EncryptedKey xmlns:xenc="http://www.w3.org/2001/04/xmlenc#">
    <xenc:EncryptionMethod Algorithm="http://www.w3.org/2001/04/xmlenc#rsa-
1_5" xmlns:dsig="http://www.w3.org/2000/09/xmldsig#"/>
    <dsig:KeyInfo xmlns:dsig="http://www.w3.org/2000/09/xmldsig#">
        <wsse:SecurityTokenReference>
            <wsse:KeyIdentifier ValueType="http://docs.oasis-
open.org/wss/2004/01/oasis-200401-wss-x509-token-profile-
1.0#X509SubjectKeyIdentifier"
EncodingType="http://docs.oasis-open.org/wss/2004/01/oasis-200401-wss-soap-
message-security-
1.0#Base64Binary">FLKVnJ2gyQw1ZdYm+rVIRYGkzFw=</wsse:KeyIdentifier>
        </wsse:SecurityTokenReference>
    </dsig:KeyInfo>
    <xenc:CipherData xmlns:dsig="http://www.w3.org/2000/09/xmldsig#">
        <xenc:CipherValue>(Truncated)</xenc:CipherValue>
    </xenc:CipherData>
    <xenc:ReferenceList>
        <xenc:DataReference URI="#G90e6b300-11D"/>
    </xenc:ReferenceList>
</xenc:EncryptedKey>
```

Listing 19-10 shows the encrypted SOAP Body. Some of the elements are in the clear (plaintext), while those identified by the Document Crypto Map have been encrypted. Notice that the encrypted elements have been replaced by xenc:EncryptedData elements, and each of these has an Id attribute that points to a xenc:DataReference URI attribute thus providing the information required for decryption.

Listing 19-10 Field Level Encrypted SOAP Body

```
<SOAP-ENV:Body>
    <exm:BookPurchase>
        <isbn>0321228006</isbn>
        <price>19.95</price>
        <xenc:EncryptedData xmlns:xenc="http://www.w3.org/2001/04/xmlenc#"
Id="G90e6b258-eD" Type="http://www.w3.org/2001/04/xmlenc#Element">
            <xenc:EncryptionMethod
Algorithm="http://www.w3.org/2001/04/xmlenc#tripledes-cbc"/>
            <xenc:CipherData>
                <xenc:CipherValue>(Truncated)</xenc:CipherValue>
            </xenc:CipherData>
        </xenc:EncryptedData>
        <xenc:EncryptedData xmlns:xenc="http://www.w3.org/2001/04/xmlenc#"
Id="G90e6b300-11D" Type="http://www.w3.org/2001/04/xmlenc#Element">
            <xenc:EncryptionMethod
Algorithm="http://www.w3.org/2001/04/xmlenc#tripledes-cbc"/>
            <xenc:CipherData>
                <xenc:CipherValue>(Truncated)</xenc:CipherValue>
            </xenc:CipherData>
        </xenc:EncryptedData>
        <address>Sailing Vessel Pequod, Old Harbor, Gloucester MA
01111</address>
    </exm:BookPurchase>
</SOAP-ENV:Body>
```

Options for encryption are available on the Advanced tab of the Encrypt action. Figure 19-12 shows a partial display of the parameters and demonstrates the fine level of control available. You can, for example, select the symmetric and key transport algorithms. Referring back to Listing 19-7, we discussed the creation of individual xenc:EncryptedKey elements for each field that was to be encrypted. In our example there were two, but what if there were dozens, or hundreds? This could become computationally expensive to generate and then to asymmetrically encrypt the symmetric session keys.

By selecting Use Single Ephemeral Key, this process can be reduced to a single session key used for all fields. The Dynamically Configured Recipient Certificate option allows for the dynamic assignment of a public key by the storing of key information in a system variable named "var://context/transaction/encrypting-cert". This could allow for the assignment via XSLT and made conditional at execution time. This advanced option may leverage unique cases where the decryption key must be dynamically assigned, again using XSLT.

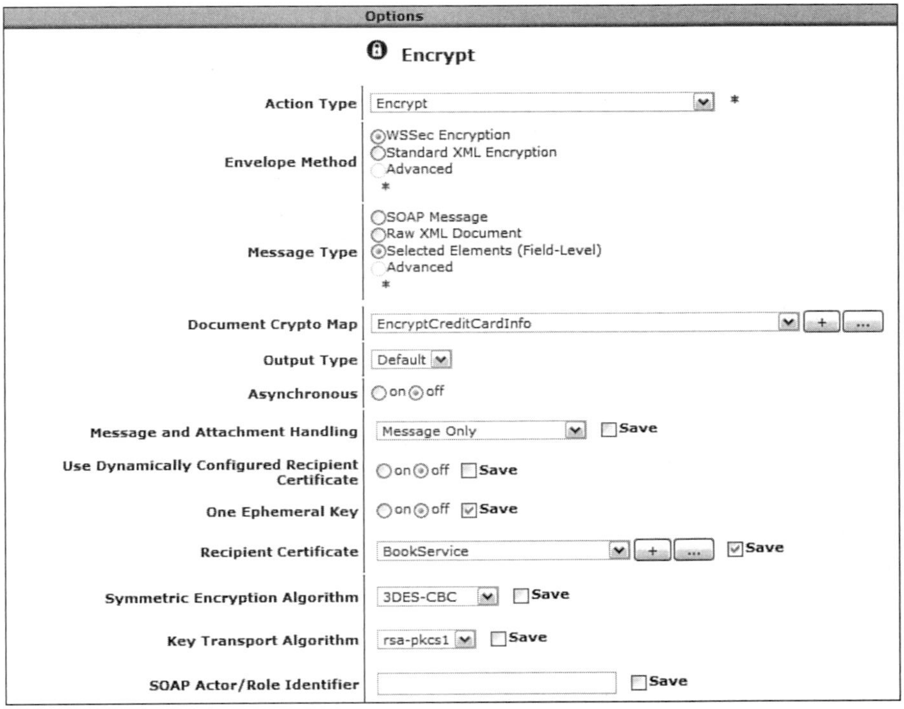

Figure 19-12 Advanced encryption options.

Decryption

Decryption is a straightforward process. The Decrypt action is utilized to specify the decryption key (the private key paired to the public key used for encryption). This results in all the encrypted elements in the document being decrypted. Figure 19-13 shows the complete Decrypt action.

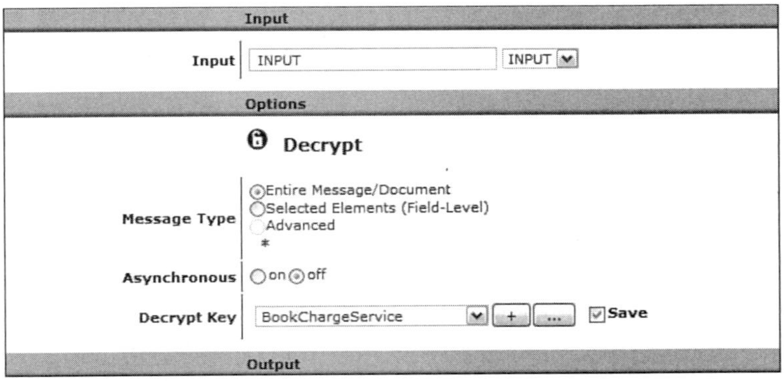

Figure 19-13 Decryption action with decrypt key specified.

Selective Decryption

It is possible to decrypt only selective fields from a document with multiple elements encrypted within it. Again a Document Crypto Map is the tool to use. However, in this case we are dealing not with the plaintext document, but rather the encrypted version. This makes the creation of XPath statements a little trickier. Had the Encryption Type (on advanced screen) been set to "Content," the element name would not have been encrypted. Figure 19-14 shows a version of a Document Crypto Map XPath expression that selects the cardHolderName for decryption. However this is only possible as we know that cardHolderName is the second encrypted element. Another possible XPath statement would be //*[local-name()='BookPurchase']/price/following::*[1]; this would select the element after (following) price, in this case creditCardInfo. The one you use depends on your preferences of XPath notation and the dependability of the encrypted data structure.

Individual field decryption with encrypted element names is possible, though not quite as straightforward as individual field encryption. An alternative technique would be targeted encryption based on the intermediary's public key (as used for decryption) and perhaps the use of the SOAP Actor/Role attribute. This way the intermediary can only decrypt what is intended for them without having to address the field level issues of the Document Crypto Map.

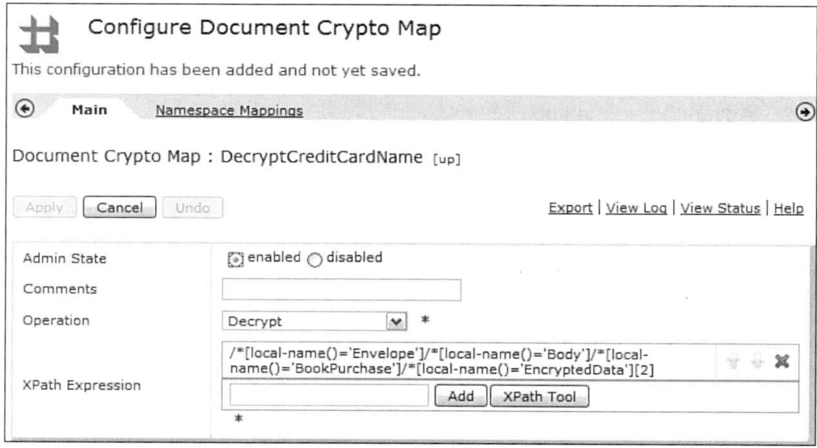

Figure 19-14 Selective Decryption Document Crypto Map.

Decryption in DataPower Services

The DataPower XML Firewall, Multi-Protocol Gateway, and Web Service Proxy services can utilize the Decrypt action. However, the Web Service Proxy has the additional feature of automatic decryption when the entire message or the first child of the SOAP body is encrypted. The private certificate must exist in a Crypto Identification Credential object, or by identification via the Decrypt Key property of the WSP that is found on the Proxy Settings tab within the WebGUI.

Putting It All Together

Now that we have presented the tools for the implementation of Web services security, we can present and implement an architecture that employs mechanisms necessary to leverage some of the techniques we have discussed.

This example demonstrates a client for a book query and purchase service that uses an XML Firewall to encrypt requests as required by a book service Web Service Proxy that uses WS-Policy for policy enforcement. This example uses the option of the client utilizing a DataPower device; however this is not a requirement. The only requirement is that the client encrypts the message using the correct keys and certificates to conform to the WS-Policy specification.

Figure 19-15 shows the architecture, and describes the configured security actions of the client and automatic processing invoked by the WSP.

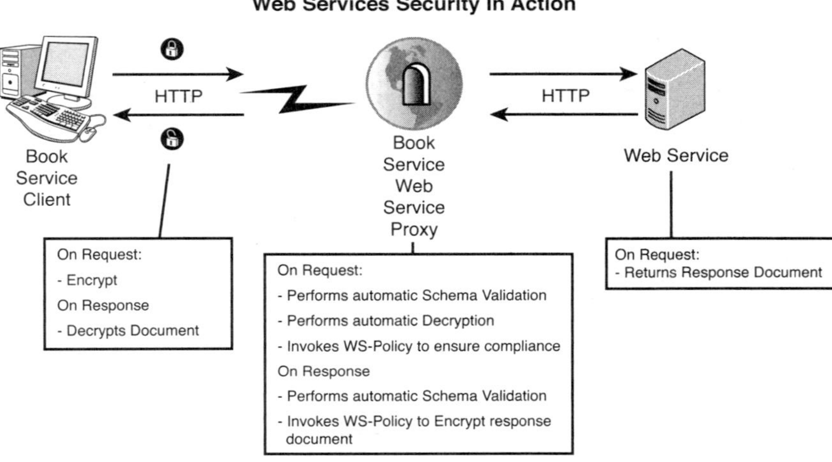

Figure 19-15 Web Services Security.

Figure 19-16 shows the multistep policy required for the book service client. An Encrypt action is used on the request rule with the BookService public certificate, and a Decrypt action is used on the response with the BookServiceClient private key.

The Web Service Proxy is capable of nearly automatic configuration by consuming a WSDL, and exposes the WSDL's service, port, and operations for fine-grained policy configuration. You can read more about WSP configuration in Chapter 10.

Having defined the WSDL and assigned the Front Side Handlers, the WSP is ready to begin receiving traffic. All the automatic features are in place. Schema validation of requests and responses, signature validation, and message decryption (if required) are all enabled.

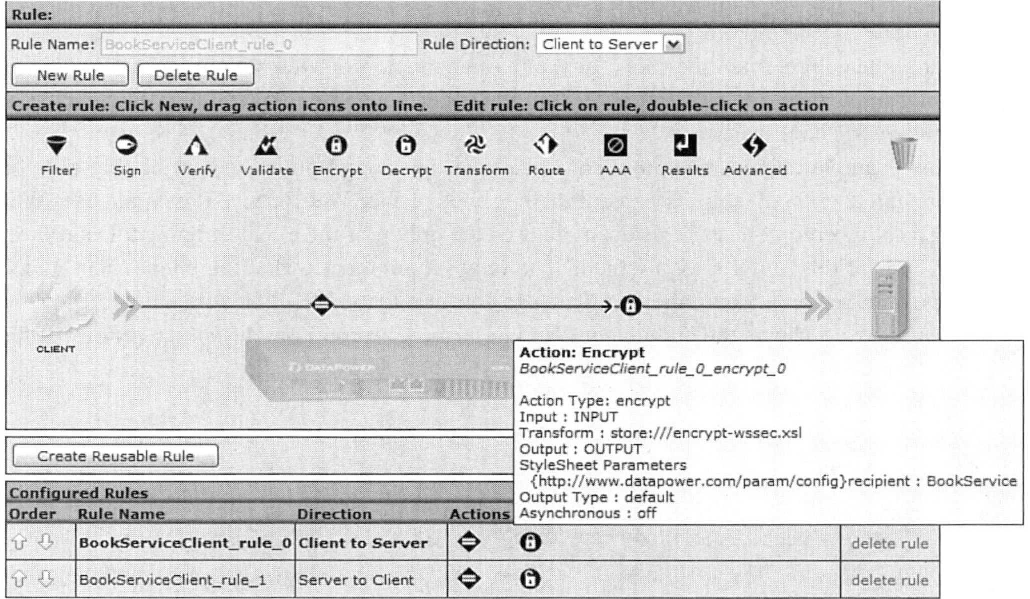

Figure 19-16 Policy with Encrypt action.

Additional processing can be assigned via the multistep policy, and Figure 19-17 shows the Policy screen. Notice that the WSDL has been exposed to allocate rules at multiple levels. Also notice that WS-Policy definitions may be assigned at various levels. As with multistep policy rules, the policy screen allows for the assignment of WS-Policy governance for the entire service, or at a more granular basis such as the operation.

In this example, notice that an external policy attachment has been defined at the port level of the BookPurchase service. External policy attachments are frequently used when the original WSDL was not authored with WS-Policy definitions. This is the WS-Policy association we desire, and we'll look at the details of its definition shortly.

We want to define a policy to enforce that messages must be encrypted. This policy will be enforced at the port level for the BookPurchase service rather than by using WSDL authoring. We will leverage the templates that DataPower provides in the store:///policies/templates/ directory. These templates are based on WS-Policy version 1.1 and 1.2, and contain a number of sample implementations such as wsp-sp-1-2-encrypted-parts-body.xml that provides the encrypt functionality we are interested in. Listing 19-11 shows the wsp-sp-1-2-sign-encrypt-order.xml template.

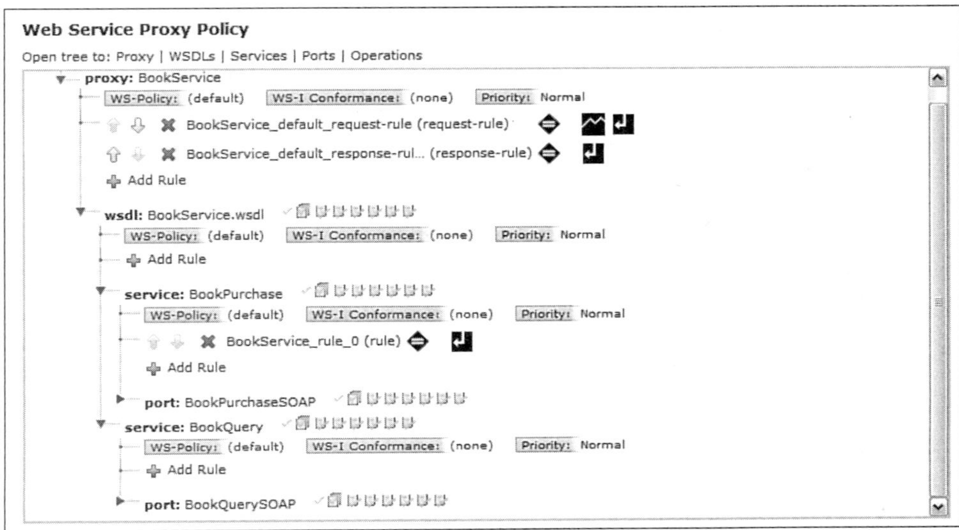

Figure 19-17 Web Service Proxy.

Listing 19-11 wsp-sp-1-2-encrypted-parts-body.xml

```
<wsp:Policy xmlns:wsp="http://www.w3.org/ns/ws-policy"
            xmlns:sp="http://docs.oasis-open.org/ws-sx/WS-
Securitypolicy/200702">
  <dpe:summary xmlns="" xmlns:dpe="http://www.datapower.com/extensions">
    <dppolicy:domain xmlns:dppolicy="http://www.datapower.com/policy">
      http://docs.oasis-open.org/ws-sx/WS-Securitypolicy/200702
    </dppolicy:domain>
    <description>
      Implements WS Security Policy 1.2 - support EncryptedParts
    </description>
  </dpe:summary>
  <wsp:ExactlyOne>
    <wsp:All>
      <sp:EncryptedParts>
        <sp:Body/>
      </sp:EncryptedParts>
    </wsp:All>
  </wsp:ExactlyOne>
</wsp:Policy>
```

Clicking the WS-Policy button (below BookPurchaseSOAP) exposes the WS-Policy definition screen. The first step is to define a Policy Parameter Set. As we discussed earlier, the policy does not contain the implementation specific details such as keys and certificates. The Policy Parameters set allow us to assign the information necessary to perform the cryptographic operations. Figure 19-18 shows the WS-Policy screen.

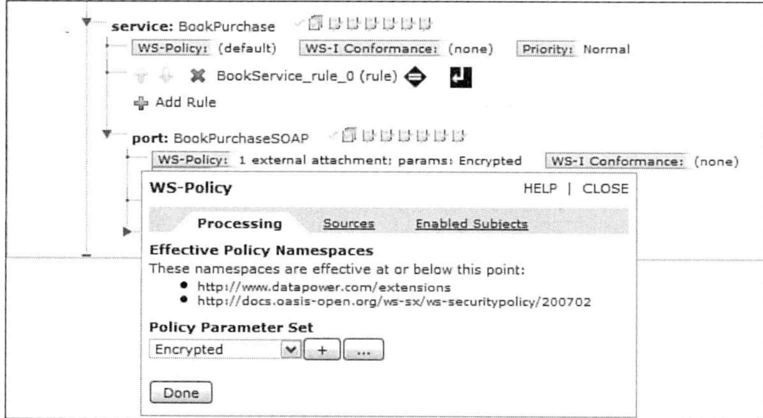

Figure 19-18 WS-Policy definition.

Figure 19-19 shows the definition of the Policy Parameters. First a Policy Domain is selected (http://docs.oasis-open.org/ws-sx/ws-securitypolicy/200702). Then the Assertion Filter is utilized to define parameters required for the policy. In our case, we require EncryptedParts. (You might want to refer back to the policy assertion in Listing 19-11.) Each of these filters exposes several parameters that are listed in the drop-down box below the Parameter Name column. Some of the parameters within assertions are optional, and you can refer to the Security Policy specification for definitive instruction.

DATAPOWER | Policy Parameters

Name: Encrypted

Policy Domain	Parameter Name	Parameter Value	
http://docs.oasis-open.org/ws-sx/ws-securitypolicy/200702	Decryption Key	BookService	Remove
http://docs.oasis-open.org/ws-sx/ws-securitypolicy/200702	Encryption Certificate	BookServiceClient	Remove
http://docs.oasis-open.org/ws-sx/ws-securitypolicy/200702 Assertion Filter: EncryptedParts	Encryption Certificate		Add

Submit Cancel

Figure 19-19 WS-Policy Policy Parameters.

Having defined the parameters necessary for the particular policy domain and assertions used, the final step in WS-Policy configuration is to define the Sources. You can do this first. In our example, the template identified previously (wsp-sp-1-2-encrypted-parts-body.xml) contains the policy we are interested in. Some templates contain multiple polices, and in those cases, they would be identified by their unique wsu:Id. Figure 19-20 shows the configured source.

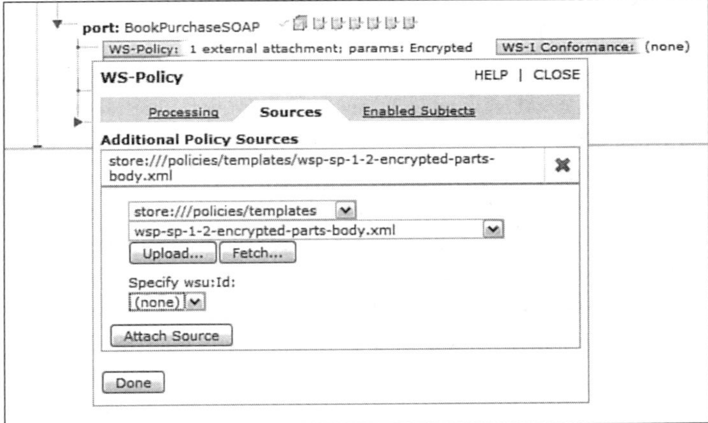

Figure 19-20 WS-Policy policy sources.

WS-Policy configuration is complete. Again, the WSP enforces the governance model that has been described. Without having to configure any multistep actions, the WSP ensures that messages are encrypted and encrypts messages on the response back to the client. Using the WSDL for policy definition affords a centralized governance policy mechanism, and any WSP service utilizing the WS-Policy conforms to the WS-Policy policies.

In addition to the WS-Policy compliance, the WSP has performed automatic schema validation. These powerful features come with minimal configuration requirements, especially when importing WSDLs complete with WS-Policy.

Listing 19-12 shows the submission of a request (again the request is in Listing 19-3) to the book service client. It encrypted the message and sent it along to the WSP. The WSP replied with an encrypted response that the book service client simply decrypted. We could have looked at the Probe and followed the encryption and decryption process through the WSP if we wanted to.

Listing 19-12 BookPurchase Request

```
curl  -data-binary @bookPurchaseRequest.xml
http://192.168.1.35:4089/BookPurchase
<?xml version="1.0" encoding="UTF-8"?>
<SOAP-ENV:Envelope xmlns:exm="http://www.example.org/BookService/"
xmlns:SOAP-ENV="http://schemas.xmlsoap.org/soap/envelope/">
<soapenv:Header xmlns:soapenv="http://schemas.xmlsoap.
org/soap/envelope/"><wsse:Security xmlns:wsse="http://docs.oasis-
open.org/wss/2004/01/oasis-200401-wss-WS-Security-secext-1.0.xsd"
soapenv:mustUnderstand="1"/></soapenv:Header>
<SOAP-ENV:Body>
     <exm:BookPurchaseResponse>
        <response>OK</response>
     </exm:BookPurchaseResponse>
</SOAP-ENV:Body></SOAP-ENV:Envelope>
```

Summary

This chapter has exposed some of the vulnerabilities of modern-day distributed communications. We've discussed the fundamental aspects of IT security, some of which had little to do with technology, and more to do with procedures and process management. Remember, "The best-laid plans of mice and men often go awry." And the same applies to Web Security. On a more technical note, we presented some of the differences between point-to-point security such as that found in SSL/TLS and end-to-end security found in WS-Security and supporting protocols. We dove into the details of digital signatures and encryption and their implantation on DataPower. Finally, we demonstrated a complete architecture of a Web Service Proxy utilizing WS-Policy for the enforcement of policy governance. Using these tools and techniques in a controlled and secured manner will afford you the maximum opportunities to protect organizational and client resources.

CHAPTER 20

XML Threats

Much like HTML, in its earlier incarnations, XML was viewed as a simple and harmless markup language that grew in sophistication until "really bad things" could be done to computing systems using it. Note: XML does not harm computers; humans harm computers. This chapter discusses why XML-based platforms (including Web services and SOA) are being targeted, what types of attacks can be mounted, and how you can protect against them using DataPower.

The New Frontier

When we think of computer-based attacks, the Internet-based worms and viruses that have wreaked so much havoc in the past come to mind. These attacks have typically been mounted against Windows-based computers, primarily due to that particular operating system being "interesting," as it runs on a large percentage of systems, and also because it has had plenty of vulnerabilities to exploit (particularly in earlier versions). However, these attacks seem to have died down in recent years, and this is for several reasons.

Like any technology, Windows has become more mature over time. Mature technologies are much more difficult to attack. Consider the changes in another product—IBM WebSphere Application Server (WAS). While the earliest versions had little security (in part due to the J2EE specification having little security itself), the newest versions are secure by default, with a sophisticated security model (again, partly due to the underlying Java EE specification now having a more robust security model).

Many products have been created as a means of defense against such attacks—such as antivirus products that are constantly updated over the Internet for new attack profiles. Incoming email is scanned for viruses at the mail server before it is forwarded on to client inboxes. We can barely get through the work day without being bothered by our workstations downloading large operating system patches, wanting to install them and reboot our systems.

Attacking Windows-based systems is not the "badge of honor" it used to be. There are wizards and toolkits that can be downloaded to create viruses and worms, so this is not the proud technical achievement it once was. The sophisticated hackers have moved on to more interesting platforms and challenges.

The Technology Adoption Curve

The cycle of technology is repetitive. When new technologies appear on the radar, they are usually raw in terms of bugs, security, performance, and stability. For these reasons, businesses are reluctant to use them in production environments. As they mature, more confidence is gained and eventually they make it to the adoption phase and begin to appear in "interesting" production systems, even though they may not have a developed or well-tested security infrastructure.

By this time, even though the technology may have matured enough for businesses to have confidence in their viability, the staff may be inexperienced and make mistakes in the install or configuration that create vulnerabilities. This creates the "sweet spot" for attackers—interesting targets that have exploitable attack surfaces due to bugs or misconfiguration. As an example, consider Web services—a technology that has been around for quite some time. It seems that the WS-Security specification has taken forever to develop, having spent significant time in draft-12 and draft-13, and even version 1.0 had some problems. When specifications mature, it takes time for the products that are built based on them to appear with those new spec levels, and initially it is common to see bugs, as these specifications are typically complex and ambiguous in areas and, hence, hard to implement.

Although Web services have been around a long time, we are just now seeing common production implementations, now that a more fleshed out WS-Security 1.1 specification is found in the most popular Java EE runtime platforms. SOA and ESB-based systems are newer and have a lower position in the curve, but are also now quite common in production. All these XML-based platforms are now in that "sweet spot" for those wanting to compromise the systems that are running them.

Even newer technologies such as Web 2.0 and AJAX, which make for impressive demos, are frightening from a security perspective. As you might imagine, these are currently at the bottom of the technology adoption curve.

But, I Thought XML Was Our Friend!

Let's go back to the early days of the World Wide Web, when all the amazing Internet technology we know today was in its infancy. HTML was born in order to display information delivered via the Internet over HTTP. For much of the early period of the Web, HTML was viewed as a harmless, innocuous text-based markup language. How could this possibly be harmful? In those friendlier days, it was inconceivable that anyone would or could use this fantastic technology to hurt others. As the need to display more interactive content grew and technicians (as they are wont to do) became more inventive, HTML grew from its simple beginnings to a complex and sophisticated technology. And, the more sophisticated and complex a technology is, the more opportunity there is for building attacks and exploits. With the addition of scripting add-ons such as JavaScript, the potential to do "bad" things with HTML grew.

History has repeated itself with another markup language, XML, which began as a simple markup language to enable self-describing data. As the technology moved up the adoption curve, the specification grew and became more and more complex to accommodate more sophisticated use cases. XML now contains tags to cause parsers to do programmatic operations such as recursion. And where we have recursion, we know that we can do fun things like infinite looping, which are not much fun for computer systems! XML-related languages such as XPath and XSLT allow for even more mischief.

Dirty Little Secrets

It is primarily for these reasons that industry pundits have predicted an explosion of XML-based attacks, and in fact this has already begun to occur. It's easy to dismiss the dire warnings about these types of attacks as hype simply meant to "sell products" because, after all, how many of these attacks has anyone heard of?

The truth of the matter is that by their nature, these types of attacks can conveniently be kept quiet. The earlier Internet attacks were mostly worms and viruses that targeted desktop computers through email. This means that the attacks affected everyone—computers at home, computers at work, computers at media outlets, computers in government—and so they are public. However, the "new frontier" attacks are specifically targeted at XML-based technologies—corporate Web services, ESB, and SOA runtime platforms. When a corporation is compromised by such an attack, it is usually a "targeted hit" on them alone, and thus, it is easier for them to keep quiet. They also have much incentive to do so—if a security compromise of a company in the competitive financial services or banking industry became public, it could cause them to rapidly lose the confidence (and business) of customers and shareholders.

Old Friends, Old Nemeses

These new types of attacks present some problems for the network topologies that have been stable and reliable for so long. Our old friends sitting out in the DMZ (the load balancers, proxies, and Web servers) that have always been the first line of defense and protected us can no longer help much against these attacks.

For example, Denial of Service (DoS) tactics have been a common way to mount attacks on networks. As these became popular, DMZ products were built to be smarter, for example, to monitor network traffic rates and take some action if the traffic profile fell into that suspected of being an attempted DoS. This would usually be something on the order of thousands of messages per second. The messages used for DoS often take the form of HTTP HEAD requests, which are small but deadly in the resources they consume in terms of connections used. The most effective and common way to deal with DoS has been simply to build a massive infrastructure, such as clusters consisting of many replicated, identical back-end runtimes. However, the XML-based attacks we discuss in this chapter go deeper into the application layer of the network stack than simple HEAD messages, to leverage things specifically inside the application messages themselves. This is far outside the radar of traditional network products, which don't understand application message formats such as XML and SOAP.

You will see in this chapter that many of our old nemeses through the short history of computer attacks have come back to haunt us in new forms to take advantage of these more modern XML-based technologies. For example, the DoS attack we discussed in the previous paragraph can now be mounted using far fewer messages with even deadlier consequences. Each message, rather than an innocuous HTTP HEAD, is a small XML file that will by itself take down a single server in a cluster. So if you have a lot of computing power, say a cluster of 20 application servers, this chapter shows how an attacker would need only 20 messages to take down the entire system, rather than many thousands used in a traditional DoS attack.

There are other products designed specifically to help prevent XML-based attacks—but some of them are built on complex runtimes, such as Java Runtime Environment (JRE) or Java EE, which are not suitable for DMZ deployment due to their large attack surface. This means they must be deployed *behind* the DMZ, as shown in Figure 20-1, and your message traffic then incurs yet another hop before reaching its destination. Of course, this is also unfortunate as it would be optimal to detect and repel any attack in the DMZ, as that is its purpose. It is a frightening thought to allow any potentially malicious message into the private/trusted zone. DataPower can replace both the Web and XML Sentry servers and accomplish the goal of heading off threats in the DMZ.

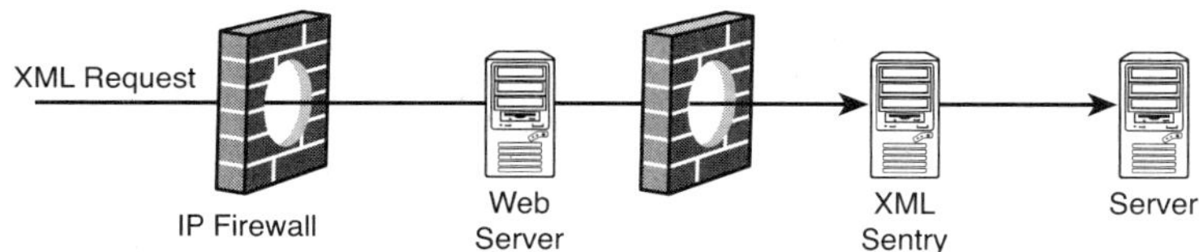

Figure 20-1 Excessive network hop due to the software-based XML security tool.

XML Threat Categories and Examples

We started this chapter with a lot of strong talk. Let's drill down into the specific details and show some examples.

Four Categories of XML Threats

Although there are a lot of blurred lines and gray areas, XML-based threats can generally be broken out into four major categories:

- **XML Denial of Service (xDOS)**—These attacks are meant to slow down or disable an XML-based system so that valid service requests are slowed or fail. This category can be broken down even further into single and multiple message XML-DoS.
- **Unauthorized Access**—These stealth attacks are designed to gain unauthorized access to a backend service or its data.

- **Data Integrity/Confidentiality**—These attacks strike at data integrity of XML-based responses, requests, or underlying data repositories.
- **System Compromise**—These attacks corrupt or attempt to gain control of backend systems.

Some of the threats that we discuss fit into more than one of these categories. In general, some of them are stealthy, "sneak" attacks where the attacker does not want to be detected, while others are quite obvious.

Single-Message Denial of Service Attacks

Single-message attacks can be mounted in several ways. As we discussed earlier, some of these attacks are so potent that a single message can wreak havoc. Let's look at a few examples.

Jumbo Payload Attacks

XML, by its nature, is resource-intensive to process. It was designed to make data easier to understand for humans and computers. Prior to XML and other self-describing data formats, text or binary data would typically be formatted in large blocks and one would need a separate template, or roadmap, that would outline where the different fields and records began and ended. Those more experienced among our readers may remember poring over long sheets of green-bar paper, pencil in hand, delineating each field in a hex dump to look for problems. "Let's see—I believe the street address should begin here, in position forty-two, but it looks like we're off by one...." With XML, this is no longer necessary, as the file itself contains the metadata to delineate and describe each field in the document via its tag name. This approach has many advantages; among them is the ease with which humans and computers can find, validate, and work with the data in the message.

However, this convenience comes at a cost. XML documents are read into memory in a process called *parsing*, which also serves to create a document object model of addressable nodes. The larger or more complex the document, the more intensive this parsing process is on the host system. Parsing is not overly CPU-intensive—the real hit comes in memory utilization. The in-memory representation of an XML document is normally expanded due to additional "leaves" in the parsed tree representation being created as part of the process, and as a result of processing instructions that might be in the XML document and can lead to great expansion during the parsing process. (We discuss this later in this chapter.)

All this is bad enough as far as the effects on a computer system. Now imagine the consequences of parsing huge XML files. In fact, some application XML message schemas are designed with full knowledge that the resulting XML files will be enormous—we've seen examples measured in *gigabytes*. We call these "self-inflicted wounds!"

Hackers know this, too, which is why one of the simplest forms of attack is to send large XML payloads. There are many forms of jumbo payload attacks, from the XML markup itself to large SOAP attachments. You might say, "Well, the payload has to be valid—this is what we have schema validation for," but we would counter that the XML input must be parsed *before* it can be validated in most cases, and many of these are parser-based attacks. As for the many systems we've seen where schema validation is not done for performance or other reasons, well let's not go there!

Recursion Attacks

As we mentioned earlier, XML has grown in complexity and sophistication, moving from a simple, static markup language to a dynamic, full-blown programming model (as implemented in XSLT). One of the programming constructs supported is recursion. And where we can have recursion, we can have infinite or long-lived looping constructs, which are ideal for consuming processing power or resources in the form of memory and file system space. As an example, review Listing 20-1, which is a small XML file. (The listing has been abbreviated for conciseness.)

Listing 20-1 Billion Laughs Recursion Attack

```
<?xml version="1.0"?>
<!DOCTYPE billion [
<!ELEMENT billion (#PCDATA)>
<!ENTITY laugh0 "ha!">
<!ENTITY laugh1 "&laugh0;&laugh0;">
<!ENTITY laugh2 "&laugh1;&laugh1;">
...
<!ENTITY laugh127 "&laugh126;&laugh126;">
]>
<billion>&laugh127;</billion>
```

This is called the "Billion Laughs" attack—without going too far into the nuances of XML trickery, you can see that this file has a series of ENTITY entries, each of which references and expands to the ones above it. So the file grows exponentially in memory when it is parsed, consumes CPU cycles, and mushrooms in size to eat up the memory space of its host computer, particularly Java heaps. The resulting XML file (again abbreviated) is shown in Listing 20-2.

Listing 20-2 Billion Laughs Output

```
<billion>
ha!ha!ha!ha!ha!ha!ha!ha!ha!ha!ha!ha!ha!ha!ha!ha!ha!ha!ha!ha!
ha!ha!ha!ha!ha!ha!ha!ha!ha!ha!ha!ha!ha!ha!ha!ha!ha!ha!ha!ha!
ha!ha!ha!ha!ha!ha!ha!ha!ha!ha!ha!ha!ha!ha!ha!ha!ha!ha!ha!ha!
ha!ha!ha!ha!ha!ha!ha!ha!ha!ha!ha!ha!ha!ha!ha!ha!ha!ha!ha!ha!
ha!ha!ha!ha!ha!ha!ha!ha!ha!ha!ha!ha!ha!ha!ha!ha!ha!ha!ha!ha!
......
</billion>
```

For an easy to reproduce demonstration, we cut down the Billion Laughs XML in size (to just laugh12) and loaded it with a commonly used Web browser (up to date with all patches) on a fast dual-processor machine with 3GB of memory. Figure 20-2 shows the result—immediately one of the two CPUs was consumed, the system was paging and memory usage quickly spiraled upward. (We killed the process at half a gigabyte so that work on this chapter did not become lost!) To be fair, this scenario crashed every browser we tried, not just the one shown.

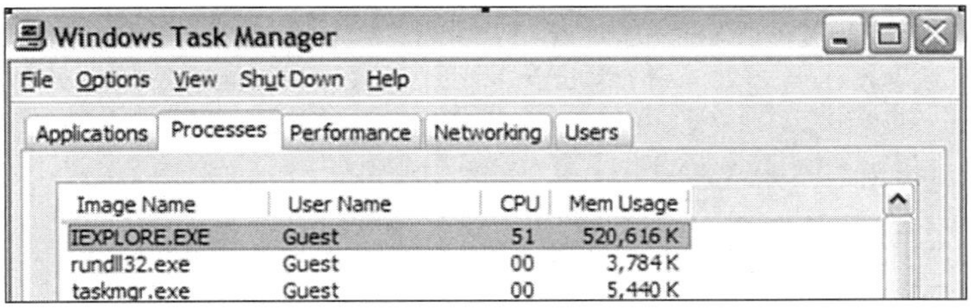

Figure 20-2 A Billion Laughs browser attack.

Mega-* Attacks

The XML specification does not mandate things such as limits on the length of tags (for example element tag names), the number of namespaces in a document, or the maximum number of nested levels in a nodeset. So, we can create well-formed XML documents with mega-tagnames, mega-nesting, mega-namespaces, and so on. These can be used to cause a number of problems. Long element tag names can surprise parsers by exceeding their expectations, causing buffer over-runs in some systems and in others raising system error conditions that may cause processing failures. Extreme levels of nesting can be accomplished by using the recursive techniques we just described. Adding mega-namespaces is trivial, something a person with a rudimentary understanding of XML might understand and attempt (read: young hackers who have had a few intro computer classes). Listing 20-3 shows a SOAP message with 9,999 namespace declarations. (You probably don't need anywhere near that many.)

Listing 20-3 A SOAP Message with Mega-Namespaces

```
<S:Envelope xmlns:S='http://schemas.xmlsoap.org'>
<S:Body xmlns='http://example.com/'>
<X xmlns:X1='http://www.example.com/x1'
   xmlns:X2='http://www.example.com/x2'
   ......
   xmlns:X9998='http://www.example.com/x9998'
   xmlns:X9999='http://www.example.com/x9999'>
</X>
</S:Body>
```

The parser attempts to read and make some sense of these declarations, which causes an extreme amount of overhead. In testing this attack, typically as soon as the input file hits the runtime parser, CPU usage shoots directly to 100 percent utilization and stays there, as shown in Figure 20-3. The system becomes unresponsive to legitimate messages and does not respond to system shutdown commands, leaving the only options as doing a forced power switch shutdown or riding it out. These are not good options—a power off would likely result in a mess of broken transactions to repair, and riding it out means a denial of service to good messages and possibly a full system outage.

Remember, if you have a large cluster of perhaps 20 nodes, an attacker needs only 20 small messages to bring down every server (assuming they are clever enough to send from clients with different IP addresses to avoid stickiness to one particular server). DoS policies set on traditional network equipment would not even blink at 20 messages.

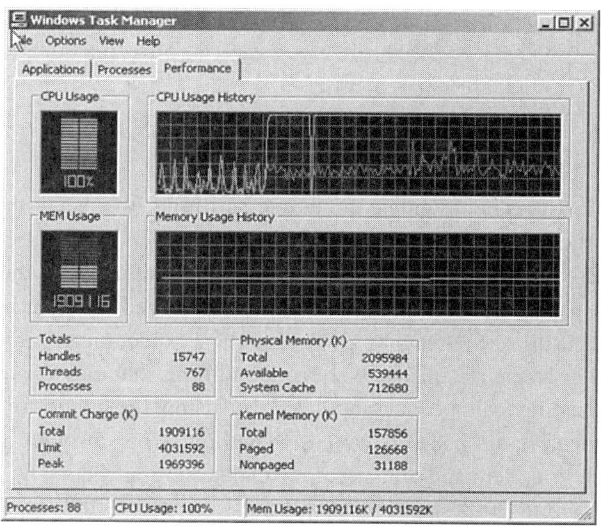

Figure 20-3 CPU consumption during a mega-namespace attack.

Coercive Parsing Attacks

Coercive parsing attacks entail using the sophistication of the XML language to write files that will give the parser fits. Examples might be circular references within or outside of the host document. Legacy systems that implement XML but do not have modern parsers, or have low processing capabilities, are particularly susceptible to these attacks. The Billion Laughs attack could be considered an example of coercive parsing.

Public Key DoS Attacks

In Chapter 18, "DataPower and SSL," and Chapter 19, "Web Services Security," one fundamental point was made clear: Security tasks involving asymmetric keys are expensive computational operations. They consume plenty of resources when working as intended. So what better way to mount an attack than to leverage already powerful and resource-intensive processes like these? Public Key DoS attacks are mounted by sending messages with signatures or encrypted data that use very strong cipher strengths and long key sizes. If certificate chain checking is employed, or if Certificate Revocation Lists (CRLs) are being used, the process can take even longer.

Multiple-Message Denial of Service Attacks

All the attacks in the previous section were contained within a single XML document, and as you have seen, can cause considerable grief for computer systems. Multiple-message attacks are mounted by sending more than a single message to a particular system. Let's look at a few of those.

XML Flood

We've seen the damage a single XML document can cause. Consider the impact if we decide to send a flood of them! That's what the XML Flood attacks are all about. Pick any one of the single-message attacks, or a healthy mix, and set up a script to bombard a system, and you can imagine the result.

Even small, benign messages can be sent in rapid succession by using the type of load-producing tools intended for performance testing to wreak havoc on systems, simply due to the overhead of parsing and error handling, in addition to the other DoS symptoms such as socket/connection saturation.

Resource Hijack

We often think of hackers, or those seeking to compromise our systems, as bad people dressed in dark, shabby clothing and hiding out in remote corners of the world. However, according to studies many attacks originate on the *inside* of corporations, not the outside! Resource hijack attacks involve some knowledge of the applications and their transactional properties.

For example, database deadlock (also known as "deadly embrace") is a problem that has been around for a long time. Despite all the fancy technology out front and in the middle of our topologies, in most cases, it is still ultimately a database that the information is stored in. If someone knows the proper transaction sequence from a client perspective—perhaps a series of Web services calls—to cause resource contention and deadlocks on the backends of our systems, the result can be an outage.

Unauthorized Access Attacks

Unauthorized access attacks are just what they sound like—attempts to gain access to information that one would not normally be permitted to access. There are several known forms of this type of attack, as discussed in the following sections.

Dictionary Attacks

We mentioned earlier in this chapter about our "old friends" coming back to see us, dressed in new clothes and hoping for acceptance this time around. Dictionary attacks have been around for as long as there have been Web login forms. The concept is that people are basically lazy about passwords, because "good" passwords are hard to remember. A great password would be something like '@#GWse5@%&8!_4', but it would be hard to remember, so instead in many cases we might go with the ever so tricky "passw0rd" or the name of our first born child, and then write it on a yellow sticky note and attach that to the underside of our keyboard for layered security.

Attackers know that there are a core set of passwords that many people use. Dictionary attacks are mounted by using an automated script and database of common passwords to "keep on trying" until one password succeeds. In the case of Web login forms, a script would continually enter passwords from the common password database (assuming the userid is known, or else it might be a combination of user ID and password dictionaries) until one works. However, at some point we got smart—and the new "best practice" for login forms became the "three strikes rule"—which means that after three straight bad passwords, you are no longer allowed to log in until calling the help desk (or some 'timeout' period may be enforced).

What about new ways of logging in? User IDs and passwords are found in many different places now—not just login forms. In Chapter 19 we discussed the WS-Security UsernameToken profile, which contains a userid and password. Is anyone enforcing "three strikes" on those? Most likely they are not.

Falsified Message and Replay Attacks

Falsified message and replay attacks depend on intercepting legitimate messages and then altering them. Intercepting messages is also referred to as "man-in-the-middle" and can be thwarted by using the network security techniques we've described throughout this book, such as mutual SSL tunnels and network interface isolation.

An example scenario might be an attack where a SOAP message that updates payroll information is intercepted and studied, and used to submit additional, similar messages later, perhaps modified to provide a "bump" in salary for a particular employee.

The message may have been sent by someone with privileges to make such changes, such as the payroll administrator. But if someone else on the network (perhaps an operator who feels she is not properly compensated) intercepts and modifies that message, it will still be sent with the payroll administrator's identity if that credential is embedded in the message. This highlights the importance of encrypting all network traffic, and setting good timeout values on credentials that are being created for the message payload—they should always have a limited lifetime in order to minimize the time available for such manipulations.

TIP—INTERNAL SSL

Many network topologies show that SSL is used only to protect connections to and from the outside world, and then is not used for internal network connections. This is just the type of configuration that allows man-in-the-middle scenarios. Keep in mind that if a DataPower appliance in the DMZ has an SSL connection to client-facing traffic and a non-SSL connection from the DMZ to the private internal network on the same Ethernet interface, you are still allowing unencrypted sensitive data in the DMZ, which can be sniffed and compromised. This is why using separate interfaces for inbound (client-facing) and backend (to the trusted zone) provides better security through network isolation.

Even for systems completely inside the internal network, without SSL you are opening yourself up to sniffing and information compromise by your employees or contractors, which in some cases may put you at risk of lawsuits or in violation of laws meant to protect others' privacy.

Data Integrity and Confidentiality Attacks

Data integrity and confidentiality attacks can take many forms. They can exploit weaknesses in the access control mechanism that permits the attacker to make unauthorized calls to the Web service to alter or view data on the backend, or by examining all or part of the content of a message to breach the privacy of that message's content. This is called *message snooping*.

Message Snooping Attacks

Snoop attacks can happen to messages being transmitted in the clear or transmitted encrypted but stored in the clear, or by decrypting messages using stolen key or crypto material. This is why we have filled this book with encouragement to use crypto for message integrity and privacy, and above all to protect your private keys!

In Chapter 4, "Advanced DataPower Networking," we covered the basics of the Ethernet protocol, on which almost all networks are based. We discussed how messages bounce around the network until they find their intended target. There are many tools available that are capable of intercepting and displaying messages from the network. These are the type of tools that are employed not only for network troubleshooting, but also sometimes for bad intent. There are many tales of salary information, sensitive email, love letters, embarrassing photographs, and other types of messages being intercepted within a workplace and leading to interoffice mayhem, or worse.

> **TIP—Never Sniff the Network Without Permission!**
>
> Because these network sniffing tools can compromise privacy, their use is a very sensitive issue for corporate IT departments. If you ever feel the need to use one (for legitimate purposes we hope), it is best to ask for permission in writing from the network or IT security team. Network admins and security sentries can actually "sense" when these sniffers are activated over the network. Don't be surprised to get a visit rather quickly at your workstation should you do this—they have ways of tracking you down!

SQL Injection Attacks

SQL injection attacks, of course, attack databases. These are yet another new twist on an old form of attack. In past days, someone figured out that the data that is entered in computer entry forms is, in most cases, inserted directly into a SQL command by the backend application.

For example, if a manager has a form that lets her pull contact information for any of her direct reports, but not others in the company, she would log in and the application might show a form with a drop-down list of only her direct reports from which to choose, based on her login ID. She could choose an employee ID and check off the pieces of info that she wants—address, mobile phone number, and so on. For example, if she selects the ID 'j_smith' from the drop-down and checks off certain fields in the form to get Jerry Smith's business contact info, behind the scenes an application might take what she enters and use it to build a SQL statement with code, such as that shown in Listing 20-4.

Listing 20-4 Typical SQL Statement Built Using Programming Code

```
SQLStmt= "SELECT " + fieldString + " FROM corp_employees WHERE username =
'" + username + "';"
```

Now imagine the effect on that programming code, and the resulting SQL command string, if one were to get access to the data entered in the form and change it before it gets to the backend application. The value 'j_smith' could be substituted with the following malicious values;

- `'*'` would result in all employees' contact info being returned—a breach of privacy because this manager was only allowed to see his own direct reports. "`OR 1=1`" could also be appended to j_smith for the same result.

  `'j_smith');DROP TABLE corp_employeesj--'` uses the semicolon command delimiter to append another command on the end, this one would delete the table!
- `j_smith');INSERT INTO db_admins (user_id, passwd, is_admin) VALUES (badguy01, mypwd, true);--'` would stealthily insert an entry into the database administrator table for the hacker, and from there all bets are off because they have full control of the database.

If the column names to be returned by the SQL query were also changed, for example to compromise the value of fieldsString in Listing 20-4, we could get a lot more information on the employees than just their addresses. For example, if this were changed to "*" then all columns would be returned, possibly exposing salary rates, drivers license numbers, and other sensitive information. Using a value of 1/0 for this field results in a divide by zero, something that is never fun for computer systems to attempt!

Just as we have learned in the past how to protect against attacks like DoS, we have also learned how to protect against these form-based attacks. The solution is to check all field entries on form posts for any suspicious looking strings, such as SQL commands, JavaScript, or system commands. However, in today's world, much of the data heading to backend databases is contained in SOAP messages, and it is unlikely they are being subjected to this type of sanitizing. Not that there is a whole lot funny about cyber attacks, but Figure 20-4 from the wonderful IT comic xkcd (http://www.xkcd.com/) puts SQL injection into a humorous light.

Figure 20-4 A little SQL injection humor.

In fact, there is a documented case of someone using a custom license plate on a vehicle to try to gain revenge against law enforcement using license-plate scanning technology to catch vehicle infractions—the custom license plate reads OR 1=1;-- (see `http://www.areino.com/hackeando/` for more information).

XPath/XQuery Injection

In Chapter 22, "Introduction to DataPower Development," we introduce you to XPath. It is a language for addressing and querying parts of an XML document, as opposed to databases. Similar to SQL, injection attacks can also be applied to XPath statements. With databases, some SQL injection attacks may be denied simply due to the user not having access to the particular columns being requested. Access is often controlled by ACLs on the database itself. However, there is no such method of authorizing for access to specific areas of an XML document with XPath, so it is all the more dangerous.

Follow-on technologies to XPath such as using XQuery with XACML do provide some relief in this area, but again only if these new and somewhat complex tools are implemented in the products you use, understood by your developers, and configured correctly.

WSDL Enumeration

You learned in Chapter 10, "Web Service Proxy," that a WSDL file is a virtual handbook on the details of a Web service application. The available operations are listed, along with the host names, ports, and URIs. This is very convenient for publishing to registries and for building clients, intermediaries, and proxies, such as with DataPower. However, we have talked a great deal in this book about the importance of not exposing "too much" in the way of implementation details so that the information cannot be used to mount an attack. The WSDL in particular poses a problem in this light.

Often, WSDL files are generated blindly from development or directory tools. They will examine a Web services application and spit out everything that is found therein to the resulting WSDL. Consider the normal case, where programmers have not only implemented the services they were tasked with, but along the way built in other services to aid their debugging, or maybe aborted attempts or older versions of the operations that are still laying around in the code. Sometimes programmers will build in their own "back door" services to circumvent things like security for their own testing.

If a WSDL is built with these services exposed, they can be discovered by WSDL enumeration. There are several ways that inquiring minds can get access to the WSDL. If it is published in a public directory, of course the job is easy. Most hackers know that you can simply append ?wsdl to the end of any Web services URL, and as part of the specification, the backend WSDL is returned to the client. Now, wasn't that easy!

The WSDL file should be treated like application code, and as such subject to a thorough review by multiple parties, as part of a stringent process to ensure security. When publishing services to directories, care should be taken to publish only those that are intended to be public.

Schema Substitution

The XML schema definition file is the template that XML input and output files must adhere to. It lays out the acceptable structure of the documents, which elements are required versus optional, and what order things should be in. It is meant to be used to enforce "good" data coming into the system and head off "bad" data at the pass by easily detecting it.

XML files can identify the schema that they should conform to by including a link inside of themselves. Listing 20-5 shows a simple XML document containing a reference to its schema on a remote server, and what that schema file might look like. You can see that the types are tightly defined. Seeing loose definitions such as xs:any for field types should be a red flag, as these will allow any type of content, including perhaps our friend the Billion Laughs!

Listing 20-5 An XML Document with Schema Reference and Its Schema File

```
<product xmlns:xsi="http://www.w3.org/2001/XMLSchema-instance"
xsi:noNamespaceSchemaLocation="http://myserver/schemas/product.xsd">
<prod_id>001234</prod_id>
	<price>42.36</price>
</product>

<xs:schema xmlns:xs="http://www.w3.org/2001/XMLSchema">
	<xs:element name="product" type="product"/>
	<xs:complexType name="product">
		<xs:sequence>
			<xs:element name="prod_id" type="xs:string"/>
			<xs:element name="price" type="xs:decimal"/>
		</xs:sequence>
	</xs:complexType>
</xs:schema>
```

The danger of this approach is in the server hosting that schema possibly becoming compromised, and the schema being replaced with one that allows malicious content. When you are depending on remote servers, you are extending your trust domain, and must do so judiciously, as you are then only as secure as those others servers. Also, in a case where the remote server is down (perhaps due to an attack), you risk being brought down due to the inaccessibility of the files. Remote servers should be highly available and redundant if they are critical.

Routing Detours

Routing detours involve using the SOAP routing header to access internal Web services that perhaps were not meant to be accessed. With technologies such as WS-Addressing, this is even easier if one can get access to and modify or replay the client message. It would then be possible to route messages to an alternate server, perhaps one owned by the hacker. These could even be copies of messages so that it may never become obvious that something bad is happening.

System Compromise Attacks

While some of the previously discussed attacks might be stealthy in nature, there's nothing subtle about this category. The general intention of a system attack is to raise hell in a profound way. Let's look at some examples.

Malicious Include Attacks

Like most programming dialects, XML allows for directives to include other files within a file. So why not take advantage of this by inserting a directive to include a file such as /etc/password? Before you assume the user will not have privileges to access this type of file, keep in mind that many backend server processes that serve up XML responses are running with root privileges.

Memory Space Breach

The memory space breach attack has been around for a long time as well. Like the injection attacks, it relies on inserting some data into an entry form. This time, the goal is to use very large data such that the memory space of the system might be exceeded and the data might "bleed" over into the area of memory that contains processing instructions. And if the data that is being entered contains processing instructions, those instructions might be executed. Memory space breaches are accomplished by causing stack overflows, buffer overruns, and heap errors. While this is more difficult in Java-based systems, it can still be done.

XML Encapsulation

CDATA is an XML construct (short for character data) to include content that is "not XML" in an XML file. Using this tag tells the parser that this is character data, and it should not be parsed. This can be used to include nonlegal characters in XML, including system commands and script. Listing 20-6 shows a CDATA section that you do not want executing on your system!

Listing 20-6 CDATA Being Used for Bad Intent

```
<![CDATA[
badCmd = new ActiveXObject( "WScript.Shell" );
badCmd.Run( "%systemroot%\\SYSTEM32\\CMD.EXE /C DEL C:\\*.*" );
```

XML Viruses

Sound familiar? We've talked a lot about how many of these "XML Threats" are new twists on traditional attacks. Most people who use computers know what viruses are, and how they get them. The common delivery vehicle is through an email attachment. We learned our lesson here as well—these days our email is scanned for any virus-laden attachments at the mail server before it is permitted to be forwarded to the email client inbox on our workstations. The virus scanners are updated frequently (as our desktops are!) with the latest known virus signatures, as new viruses are appearing all the time.

What about SOAP attachments? Is anyone scanning those for viruses? These are even more destructive as they are opened on the server, rather than an email client at a desktop. SOAP attachments are just as capable of carrying viruses as email attachments, yet they are rarely checked.

Threat Protection with DataPower

Now that we've sufficiently scared you from ever using computers again, let's get to the good news. DataPower appliances are an effective way to protect against these types of threats. This is primarily due to the end-to-end XML security focus of the products, as well as having the horsepower to pull off the intense introspection and interrogation of messages for suspicious profiles without a major hit to performance. Let's walk through some of the configurations that can save you.

Characterizing Traffic

Several of the attacks we discussed were based on sending badly formed data. Most traditional DoS attacks send huge quantities of HTTP HEAD requests, which contain no body. One simple first step toward protecting your systems is to characterize the type of messages you are expecting. In Chapter 8, "XML Firewall," we showed the Request Type and Response Type fields. These also appear in the Multi-Protocol Gateway and Web Service Proxy. Figure 20-5 shows these drop-downs and the possible choices.

If your service is intended to receive only SOAP messages, even though the other choices will allow SOAP, by being more specific you are enabling the device to help protect you by telling it to reject anything that is not SOAP (and even badly formed SOAP). Those messages could be malicious. Some might get lazy here and just specify XML, and that will work, as SOAP is an XML vocabulary. But you are then subjecting yourself to any XML-based attacks (such as the Billion Laughs attack) that aren't based on SOAP and would otherwise be rejected.

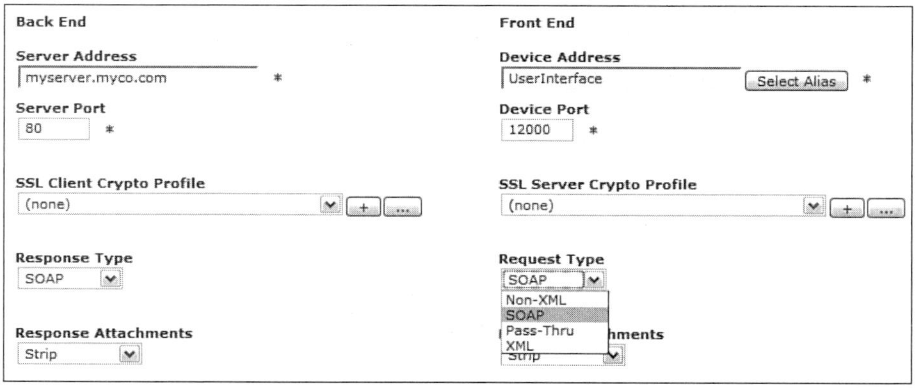

Figure 20-5 Characterizing front and back side traffic.

XML Manager Protections

A deeper level of message characterization can be found in the XML Manager. Figure 20-6 shows the XML Manager XML Parser tab. You should have a good idea of the characteristics for your own request and response documents from your testing procedures. (You do have those, right?) While the defaults here are reasonable, there is no way for the fine engineers at DataPower to know what is "right" for everyone else's applications.

If you know that the maximum nesting depth of your messages is 14 levels, you can tune these settings much more efficiently by lowering the default of 512. This particular setting is useful for preventing recursion attacks that attempt to deeply nest the document.

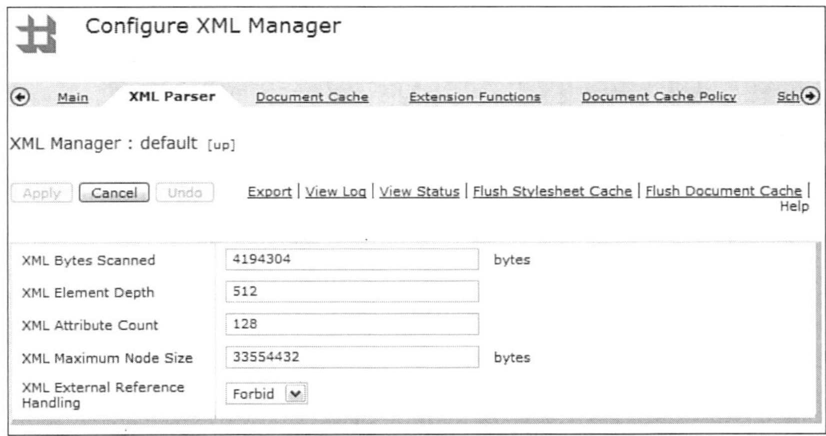

Figure 20-6 XML Manager XML Parser tab for XML characterization.

The other fields shown can (and should) be similarly tuned. The Bytes Scanned, Attribute Count, and Maximum Node Size fields are self-descriptive and can prevent mega and jumbo payload attacks. In particular, the Attribute Count setting would prevent the attack we demonstrated earlier, which depended on a large number of namespace declarations.

One more item of note before we leave this topic, is the XML External Reference Handling field. This can be used to tell DataPower to stop parsing if it encounters an external reference (either to an XSD, entity, or DTD) to ignore these and replace them with empty strings, or to allow them. The most secure setting (Forbid) is the default. This is here specifically to prevent substitution attacks.

Network/Protocol Protection

Figure 20-7 shows the Advanced Networking tab from the XML Firewall (similar options appear on all services or FSHs). We discussed how DoS attacks typically use HTTP HEAD or GET messages as they are lightweight. The Disallow GET (and HEAD) configuration will cause those to be rejected. This is on by default—if your applications use HEAD or GET, turn this off to allow those message types. Disabling GET on the FSH for a Web Service Proxy also prevents the WSDL from being returned to the client with the ?wsdl technique that we discussed in the section on WSDL Enumeration attacks.

The ability to set up ACLs is also seen in Figure 20-7. This allows you to designate only certain other computers that are allowed to connect to your services. While this might not be useful for workstations due to the predominant use of DHCP (although you can specify ranges and netmasks), it can be useful for server-to-server configurations inside the trusted, internal network.

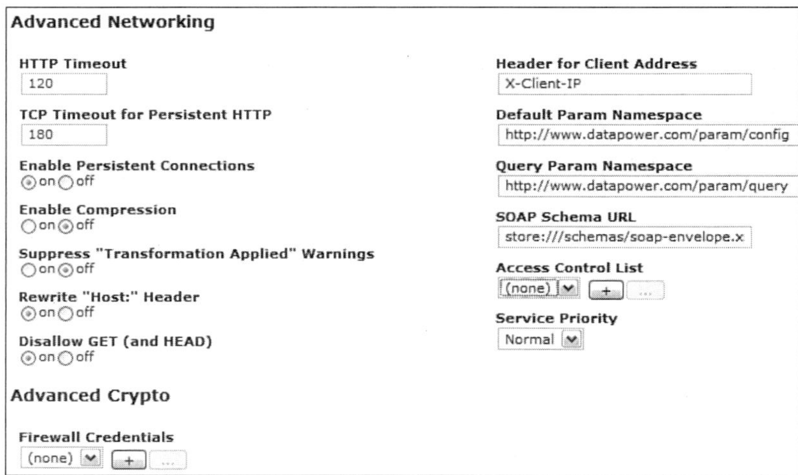

Figure 20-7 The Advanced Networking configuration pane.

> **TIP—DON'T DEPEND ON IP-BASED PROTECTION**
>
> Keep in mind that IP addresses can be spoofed, so any security configuration that depends on them should be used as a front line of defense, with stronger measures backing it up. Security in layers is a good thing!

The XML Threat Protection Tab

The XML Threat Protection tab is the centerpiece for configuring against attacks. It is found on all the primary services, and there are sections within it for many of the major attacks that we have discussed. Let's have a look at those now.

Single-Message DoS Protection

Looking at this section, as shown in Figure 20-8, we can see that it is similar to the XML Manager page shown in Figure 20-6. We see many of the same fields here, and as you can imagine, there would be a conflict if the settings were defined differently in both places. You can use the Override XML Manager parser limits radio button to specify that you want the settings here, on the service, to take precedence over the XML Manager. If you have several services using the same profile settings, it may be more efficient to configure them in an XML Manager and share that between the services. One addition here is the Max. Message Size, which is for the total message size, including headers and other metadata. It defaults to zero, which means no limit is enforced (in lieu of the more specific XML settings in most cases). Another field allows setting limits on the size of any incoming attachments, again to protect against jumbo payload attacks.

Another interesting field in this section is the Recursive Entity Protection, which would protect against recursion attacks. Notice that this field is disabled for changes, meaning it is always on—you don't get a choice for this one!

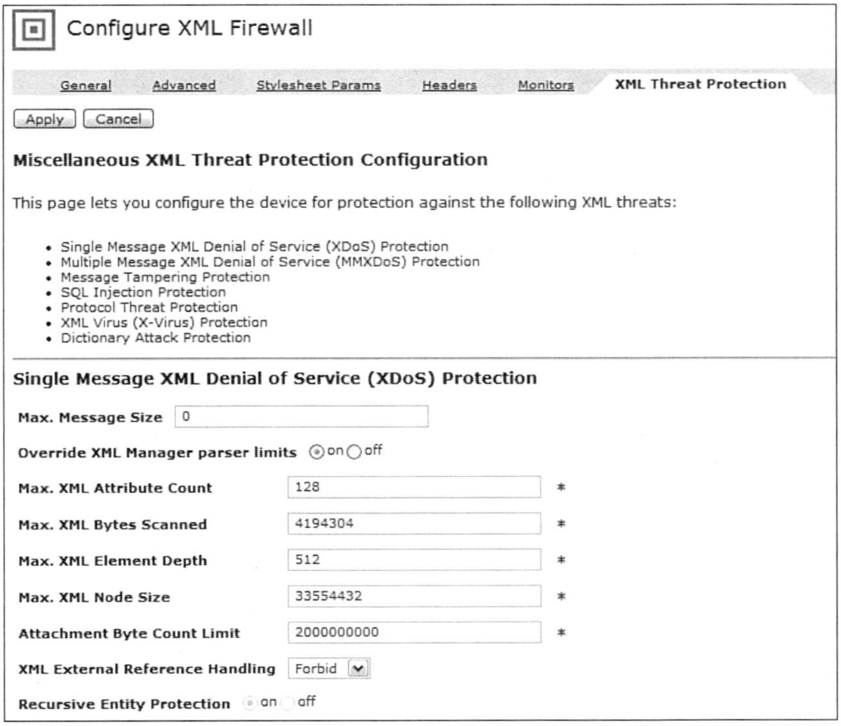

Figure 20-8 XML Threat Protection Tab and Single-Message DoS.

Testing Single-Message DoS on DataPower

Now that we've shown how DataPower can protect against single-message attacks, let's demonstrate what happens when we throw two specific examples we gave earlier at it. For this test, we configured a simple loopback XML Firewall with all defaults. Figure 20-9 shows the result of the Billion Laughs attack. It is apparent here that the single-message default for maximum message size was exceeded and caught this when the input message mushroomed beyond the limit of 4,194,304 bytes.

```
xmlfirewall (SimpleLoopbackFW): No match from processing policy 'SimpleLoopbackFW' for code '0x00030003'
xmlfirewall (SimpleLoopbackFW): XML parser limits exceeded
xmlfirewall (SimpleLoopbackFW): Generated error on URL 'http://192.168.1.130:2048/': <?xml version="1.0" encoding="UTF-8"?>
<env:Envelope
xmlns:env="http://schemas.xmlsoap.org/soap/envelope/"><env:Body><env:Fault><faultcode>env:Client</faultcode><faultstring>Malforme
content (from client)</faultstring></env:Fault></env:Body></env:Envelope>
xmlfirewall (SimpleLoopbackFW): XML parser limits exceeded
xmlfirewall (SimpleLoopbackFW): rule (SimpleLoopbackFW_request): implied action Parse input as XML failed: document size limit of 419430
bytes exceeded, aborting
xmlfirewall (SimpleLoopbackFW): document size limit of 4194304 bytes exceeded, aborting
xmlfirewall (SimpleLoopbackFW): Parsing document 'http://192.168.1.130:2048/'
xmlfirewall (SimpleLoopbackFW): rule (SimpleLoopbackFW_request): selected via match 'SimpleLoopbackFW' from processing policy
'SimpleLoopbackFW'
xmlfirewall (SimpleLoopbackFW): New transaction(conn use=1): POST http://192.168.1.130:2048/ from 192.168.1.107
```

Figure 20-9 Log entries from Billion Laughs message submitted to the device.

Figure 20-10 shows the log entries for a mega-namespace attack. This time, the maximum attribute limit of 128 caught the offending message.

```
xmlfirewall (SimpleLoopbackFW): No match from processing policy 'SimpleLoopbackFW' for code '0x00030003'
xmlfirewall (SimpleLoopbackFW): XML parser limits exceeded
xmlfirewall (SimpleLoopbackFW): Generated error on URL 'http://192.168.1.130:2048/': <?xml version="1.0" encoding="UTF-8"?>
<env:Envelope
xmlns:env="http://schemas.xmlsoap.org/soap/envelope/"><env:Body><env:Fault><faultcode>env:Client</faultcode><faultstring>Malforme
content (from client)</faultstring></env:Fault></env:Body></env:Envelope>
xmlfirewall (SimpleLoopbackFW): XML parser limits exceeded
xmlfirewall (SimpleLoopbackFW): rule (SimpleLoopbackFW_request): implied action Parse input as XML failed: attribute limit of 128 per
element exceeded, aborting at offset 6190 of http://192.168.1.130:2048/
xmlfirewall (SimpleLoopbackFW): attribute limit of 128 per element exceeded, aborting at offset 6190 of http://192.168.1.130:2048/
xmlfirewall (SimpleLoopbackFW): Parsing document 'http://192.168.1.130:2048/'
xmlfirewall (SimpleLoopbackFW): rule (SimpleLoopbackFW_request): selected via match 'SimpleLoopbackFW' from processing policy
'SimpleLoopbackFW'
```

Figure 20-10 Log entries from mega-namespace message submitted to the device.

Multiple-Message DoS Protection

The Multiple-Message DoS Protection, as shown in Figure 20-11, is turned off by default. It is used to set up policies for rates and durations of messages coming into the device.

As the figure demonstrates, we have enabled this and provided some sample values for discussion. Starting from the top, our sample configuration will not allow the maximum duration for any request to exceed 5 seconds.

Next, we are configuring so that more than ten messages per second from any one host (client) will cause an over-threshold condition and subsequent messages within that threshold period (one second) will be denied. Similarly, we are allowing for a maximum of 1,000 messages per second to this service overall (from all clients cumulatively). If either the host or firewall thresholds are exceeded, we have configured a block interval of half-second where no traffic will be permitted. If any of these thresholds are exceeded, a message will be logged at the specified severity.

These settings can be used in conjunction with performance test results from your backend systems to ensure that they are never over-run. For example, if performance testing on your back-end application servers show that the JVM craters when transaction rates hit 1,000 per second, you can set a policy here to ensure that the rate of traffic to that server is never exceeded. However, the SLM policies, where available (WSP and MPGW), are more sophisticated ways to do this, and are also shareable and enforceable between peer devices.

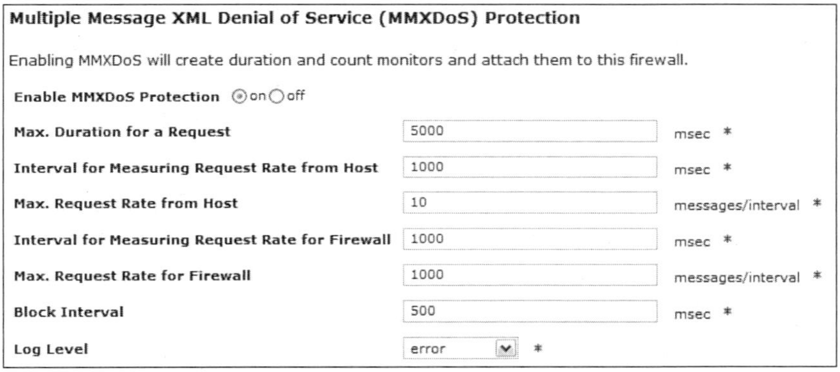

Multiple Message XML Denial of Service (MMXDoS) Protection

Enabling MMXDoS will create duration and count monitors and attach them to this firewall.

Enable MMXDoS Protection	on / off	
Max. Duration for a Request	5000	msec *
Interval for Measuring Request Rate from Host	1000	msec *
Max. Request Rate from Host	10	messages/interval *
Interval for Measuring Request Rate for Firewall	1000	msec *
Max. Request Rate for Firewall	1000	messages/interval *
Block Interval	500	msec *
Log Level	error	*

Figure 20-11 Multiple-Message DoS Protection.

Protocol Threat Protection

Figure 20-12 and Figure 20-13 show the Protocol Threat Protection values for the XML Firewall and Web Service Proxy, respectively. (The MPGW does not have this area in its XML Threat Protection page, but you can specify the HTTP version on any FSH.) The choices for the WSP are the same ones we find for characterizing message types on the other services.

Earlier, we discussed how characterizing the message types could help to filter out some attacks, for example denying straight XML attacks because we have specified to accept only SOAP. These protocol settings are similar—specifying that only HTTP 1.1 connections allowed to the device will filter out any HTTP 1.0 traffic, which may be used on some of the antiquated systems that hackers around the world might target.

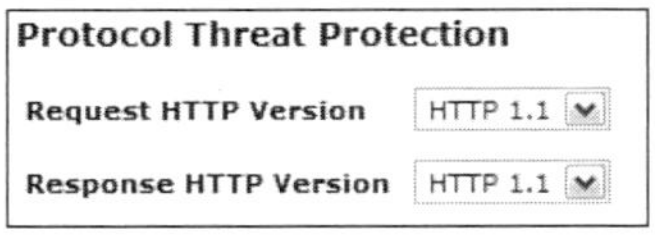

Protocol Threat Protection

Request HTTP Version	HTTP 1.1
Response HTTP Version	HTTP 1.1

Figure 20-12 XML Firewall Protocol Threat Protection.

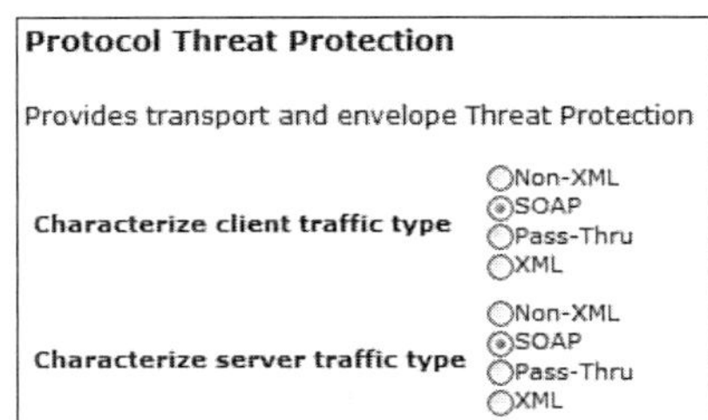

Figure 20-13 Web Service Proxy Protocol Threat Protection.

Message Tampering Protection

This section offers no configuration; it just suggests and acts as a reminder that you add a Validate action to your policies to validate messages against their schema to ensure they have no extra content or other schema violations.

We would like to take this opportunity to reinforce this advice. Schema validation is important, and in too many cases, we see it disabled either due to schema files being out of date or never created, or for fear of performance problems. Of course, schema validation is fundamentally useless unless you have strongly typed and well-defined schemas!

Because you have the massive processing power of DataPower at your disposal, feel free to do all those things you were afraid to do on your software-based systems. This includes schema validation—on both request *and* response messages! Many times when our security hats are on, we are too focused on the front door (incoming traffic), whereas our back door is wide open to attack. Often systems are harmed not by bad guys and gals, but by bad program code by partners and other intermediaries, and yes, sometimes even our own programmers. This is a far more frequent occurrence than being hacked. This is why we should use validation as often as possible. For example, after we transform messages, those transform results should be validated before sending them off to a backend or client that they could potentially crash.

Response validation also makes sure that only the data you want to leave your enterprise does so. Returning too many entries or fields that don't meet the schema could mean an unauthorized access, injection, or other type of data acquisition attack.

> **TIP—VALIDATE EVERYTHING!**
>
> Validate requests, responses, and any time a message is altered on the device. You never know when something might have gone wrong unless you do. Nobody wants to deal with the consequences of "unexpected results." And remember, GIGO (Garbage In, Garbage Out). Unless your schemas are well written and strongly typed, schema validation cannot help!

SQL Injection Protection

Earlier in this chapter, we gave some extensive examples (and a little humor) on SQL injection. Remember, this doesn't necessarily mean that your SOAP messages are passing around SQL statements (although we've seen this in the field). The attack is based on modifying normal input data that is headed to your backend systems, which will in many cases be used to formulate SQL commands. To prevent this, the inputs should be inspected for SQL commands that might have been appended to the input data in an attempt to get them to execute as well.

You can implement protection against this type of attack quite easily in DataPower. In fact, most or all the work is already done for you. Let's walk through an example implementation. To incorporate SQL injection protection, you start by adding a Filter to your Processing Policy and selecting the SQL-Injection-Filter.xsl stylesheet that resides in the device's store: directory, as shown in Figure 20-14.

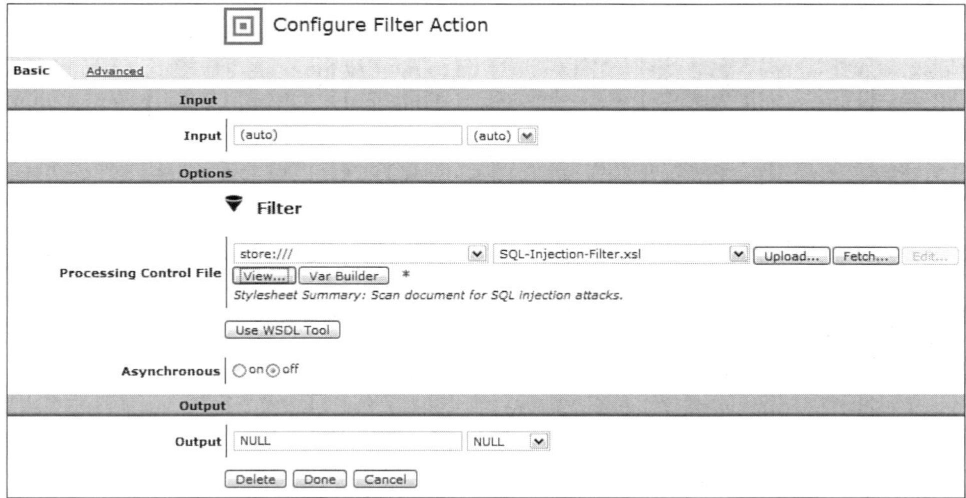

Figure 20-14 Filter action with SQL Injection Filter.

This stylesheet is worth opening and inspecting. There is a lengthy comment prologue that describes how the configuration works, and states a recommended two-step process for preventing SQL injection attacks:

1. Use the SQL injection filter included to capture all common data acquisition and destruction attempts.
2. Schema validate all response data, for example to ensure that if you are only expecting one row of data to return, that multiple rows are not returned. (As you have read, that is a symptom of a SQL injection attack!)

Upon inspection of the stylesheet, you will see that it loads a SQL patterns XML file. This stanza is shown in Listing 20-7.

Listing 20-7 SQL-Injection-Filter.xsl Patterns File Identification

```
    <xsl:param name="dpconfig:SQLPatternFile" select="'store:///SQL-
Injection-Patterns.xml'"/>
    <dp:param name="dpconfig:SQLPatternFile" type="dmFSFile" xmlns="">
        <display>SQL Injection Pattern File</display>
        <location>store:</location>
        <location>local:</location>
        <default>store:///SQL-Injection-Patterns.xml</default>
        <description>The file containing patterns to search for in order to
detect SQL injection attacks.</description>
    </dp:param>
```

Of course, there is always the possibility that some of these patterns could be identical to legitimate SQL that you may be passing in your messages, which would not be good because those valid messages will be rejected! You are free to modify the included XML file and place a modified copy in the local: directory per the instructions in the XSL file. (These are much more detailed than the WebGUI Guide.) If you do this, you must modify the filter parameter SQLPatternFile that is show in Listing 20-7 by setting the parameter in either the firewall or Filter action. (The Add Parameter button appears on the Advanced tab of the Filter action.)

The filter searches through incoming messages and rejects any that match the regular expressions contained within. Let's look at the contents of the included XML file, as shown in Listing 20-8.

Listing 20-8 Top Portion of the SQL-Injection-Patterns.xml File

```
    <pattern>
          <name>SQL LIKE% Match</name>
        <regex>'[\s]*[\%]+</regex>
    </pattern>

    <!-- SQL Escape Sequences -->
      <pattern>
          <name>SQL Escape Sequence</name>

<regex>('[\s]*;|'[\s]*[\)]+|'[\s]*[\+]+|'[\s]*[\*]+|'[\s]*[\=]+)</regex>
      </pattern>

    <!-- SQL keyword injection -->
    <pattern type="element">
        <name>SQL Keyword Injection</name>
        <regex>^(insert|as|select|or|procedure|limit|order
by|asc|desc|delete|update|distinct|having|truncate|replace|handler|like)$</
regex>
    </pattern>
```

```
<! - MS SQL Commands  ->
<pattern>
    <name>MS SQL Commands</name>
    <regex>\b(exec sp|exec xp)\b</regex>
</pattern>
```

The file starts out by looking for and rejecting some typical escape sequences used in SQL, such as the semicolon used to delimit commands or append new commands. Following that, certain keywords are rejected—such as update, delete, and truncate. The last stanza shown in our listing (the file is actually much longer with many additional examples) is one that is specific to Microsoft SQL Server.

You might notice that the pattern with the name SQL Keyword Injection has an attribute named "type" on the pattern element. This tells the stylesheet to search only elements. Correspondingly, if it is not present, or is set to type=global, both elements and attribute values will be scanned for offending values.

To gain a better understanding of how this works at runtime, let's put together an example. We have configured a simple loopback XML Firewall with a Filter action set up as shown in Figure 20-14, using the out-of-the-box SQL Injection stylesheet and XML file. We pass in a file with a SQL command string concatenated to the data, as shown in Listing 20-9.

Listing 20-9 Input File with SQL Injection Attack

```
<?xml version='1.0' ?>
<SOAP-ENV:Envelope
xmlns:SOAP-ENV="http://schemas.xmlsoap.org/soap/envelope/">
  <SOAP-ENV:Body>
    <book>
          <name>Moby Dick';SELECT * FROM BOOK_AUTHORS WHERE AUTHOR_NAME
LIKE '%KEROUAC%</name>
          <author>Herman Melville</author>
    </book>
  </SOAP-ENV:Body>
</SOAP-ENV:Envelope>
```

When the command is submitted, the client sees the rejection message, as shown in Figure 20-15. The resulting message does give evidence as to why the command has failed.

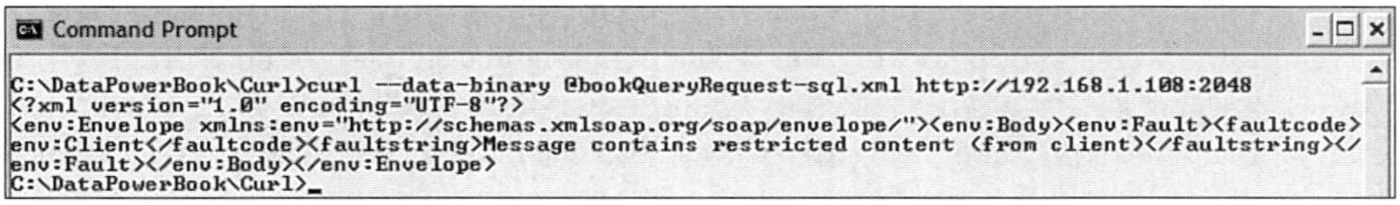

```
Command Prompt
C:\DataPowerBook\Curl>curl --data-binary @bookQueryRequest-sql.xml http://192.168.1.108:2048
<?xml version="1.0" encoding="UTF-8"?>
<env:Envelope xmlns:env="http://schemas.xmlsoap.org/soap/envelope/"><env:Body><env:Fault><faultcode>
env:Client</faultcode><faultstring>Message contains restricted content (from client)</faultstring></
env:Fault></env:Body></env:Envelope>
C:\DataPowerBook\Curl>_
```

Figure 20-15 Client error message indicating restricted content.

For a more detailed analysis, the log messages for the firewall can be viewed. Figure 20-16 shows those log messages, with a detailed explanation of what has transpired and why the transaction was rejected. Notice it tells exactly what pattern has caused the rejection, in this case the one named SQL LIKE% Match, which is the first one shown in Listing 20-8.

```
xmlfirewall (XMLThreatTestFirewall): No match from processing policy 'XMLThreatTestFirewall' for code '0x00d30003'
xmlfirewall (XMLThreatTestFirewall): Rejected by filter; SOAP fault sent
xmlfirewall (XMLThreatTestFirewall): Generated error on URL 'http://192.168.1.108:2048/': <?xml version="1.0" encoding="UTF-8"?>
<env:Envelope
xmlns:env="http://schemas.xmlsoap.org/soap/envelope/"><env:Body><env:Fault><faultcode>env:Client</faultcode><faultstring>Message
contains restricted content (from client)</faultstring></env:Fault></env:Body></env:Envelope>
xmlfirewall (XMLThreatTestFirewall): Rejected by filter; SOAP fault sent
xmlfirewall (XMLThreatTestFirewall): request XMLThreatTestFirewall_request #1 filter: 'INPUT store:///SQL-Injection-Filter.xsl' failed: Message
contains restricted content
xmlfirewall (XMLThreatTestFirewall): Execution of 'store:///SQL-Injection-Filter.xsl' aborted: Message contains restricted content
xmlfirewall (XMLThreatTestFirewall): ***SQL INJECTION FILTER***: Message from 192.168.1.102 contains possible SQL Injection Attack of
type 'SQL LIKE% Match'. Offending content: '%'. Full Message: '&lt;?xml version="1.0" encoding="UTF-8"?> &lt;SOAP-ENV:Envelope
xmlns:SOAP-ENV="http://schemas.xmlsoap.org/soap/envelope/"> &lt;SOAP-ENV:Body> &lt;book> &lt;name>Moby Dick;SELECT * FROM
BOOK_AUTHORS WHERE AUTHOR_NAME LIKE '%KEROUAC%'&lt;/name> &lt;author>Heman Melville&lt;/author> &lt;/book>
&lt;/SOAP-ENV:Body> &lt;/SOAP-ENV:Envelope>'.
xmlfirewall (XMLThreatTestFirewall): Reject set: Message contains restricted content
xmlfirewall (XMLThreatTestFirewall): Finished parsing store:///SQL-Injection-Patterns.xml
xmlfirewall (XMLThreatTestFirewall): Parsing document 'store:///SQL-Injection-Patterns.xml'
xmlfirewall (XMLThreatTestFirewall): Stylesheet URL to compile is 'store:///SQL-Injection-Filter.xsl'
xmlfirewall (XMLThreatTestFirewall): Finished parsing http://192.168.1.108:2048/
xmlfirewall (XMLThreatTestFirewall): Parsing document 'http://192.168.1.108:2048/'
xmlfirewall (XMLThreatTestFirewall): rule (XMLThreatTestFirewall_request): selected via match 'XMLThreatTestFirewall' from processing policy
'XMLThreatTestFirewall'
xmlfirewall (XMLThreatTestFirewall): New transaction(conn use=1): POST http://192.168.1.108:2048/ from 192.168.1.102
```

Figure 20-16 DataPower log showing repulsion of a SQL injection attack.

XML Virus Protection

XML Virus Protection is used for checking messages and attachments for embedded viruses. The types of attacks that can be thwarted by this action are XML Virus Attacks, XML Encapsulation Attacks, Payload Hijack Attacks, and Binary Injection Attacks. Of course, DataPower does not have a built-in virus scanner, or you would have to constantly update it to include new virus signatures, much like you do for your workstation's virus scanner. (You have one of those, right?) The way this works in DataPower is that the device uses the Internet Content Adaptation Protocol (ICAP) to send the content to a virus scanning server, in most all cases the same one that is used to scan your email attachments. You have the option to reject transactions or strip out the attachment and let it proceed, if the virus scanner reports a problem.

In firmware versions prior to 3.6.1, this would be configured similarly to the SQL Injection Protection—by placing a Filter on your policy, assigning a stylesheet store:///Virus-ScanAttachments.xsl, and assigning a value representing the URL of your virus scanning server to the SendTo parameter.

You may still see the instructions to configure virus protection this way on the XML Threat Protection tab, depending on what version of the firmware you are on. However, in 3.6.1 a new Anti-Virus action was introduced to make this process easier.

Figure 20-17 shows the Anti-Virus action configuration, which we arrived at by dragging an Advanced action to our request rule processing line and clicking the Next button.

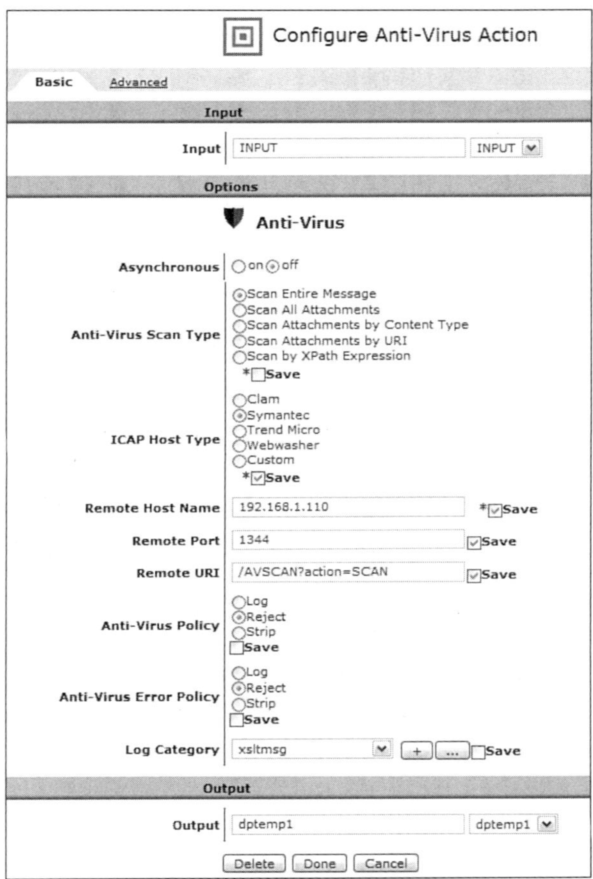

Figure 20-17 Configuration for the Anti-Virus action.

Dictionary Attack Protection

The Dictionary Attack Protection text on the XML Threat Protection pane explains that these are monitored through AAA actions, which makes sense since dictionary attacks are login-based. The policy can be set up to send notification messages to a log target, or put the offending client in "time out" (deny service) for a while. The text goes through some requirements for setting this up, but by far it's easier to just do this from the Post Processing page of the AAA wizard, using the Reject Counter tool, as shown in Figure 20-18. Notice that this field does not have the traditional buttons next to it to add or edit the configuration! We will explain that in a moment.

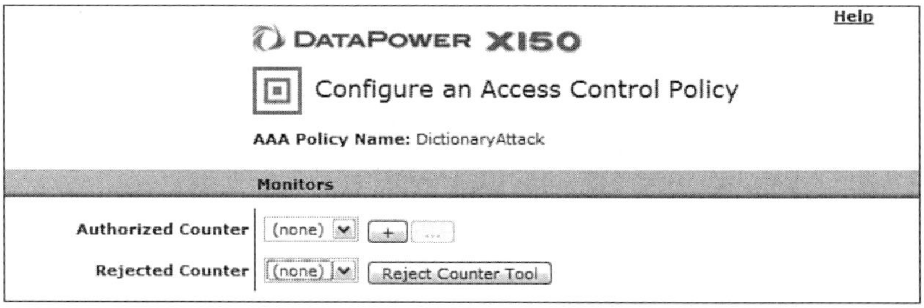

Figure 20-18 The AAA Post Processing Reject Counter tool.

This counter functions regardless of the method chosen for identity extraction and authentication in the earlier pages of the AAA configuration. The configuration is fairly simple as shown in Figure 20-19. We have configured the policy such that if any client gives an invalid authentication more than three times within ten seconds, they may not try again for a minute, and a log message with the severity of warning is issued. Log targets could possibly be set up to send email to an administrative group, or fire an SNMP trap to the datacenter monitoring infrastructure. We covered many options for logging in Chapter 14, "Logging and Monitoring."

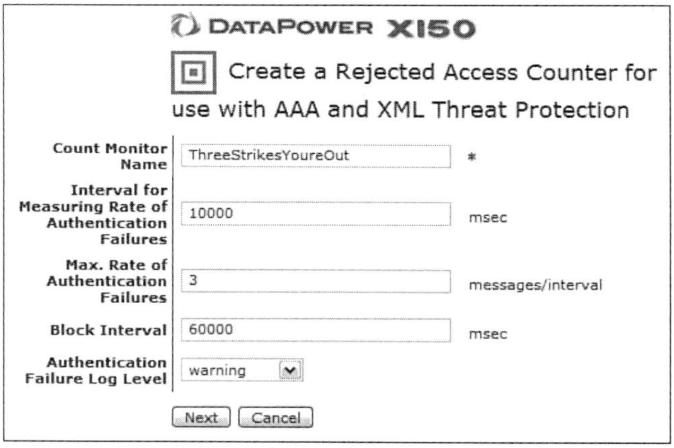

Figure 20-19 A Reject Counter configured for the three strikes rule.

Bear in mind that most dictionary attacks are automated, and the requests will fire in very quickly. Ours was configured somewhat loosely on the time values because we used it from a command shell with a batch file, rather than a sophisticated load generating script or tool. To prevent scripted dictionary attacks, you would set the threshold much lower for the time interval used for detection.

Let's have a look under the covers. What really happened when we built that Reject Counter tool, and why are there no buttons to edit it, in case we made a mistake? What really happens is that DataPower builds a Message Count Monitoring object for you. It uses the data that you have entered from the reject tool and adds defaults for other fields. To view or change this, you would have to go to Objects→Monitoring→Message Count Monitor in the Navigation menu of the WebGUI, and there you will find the object that you named (ThreeStrikesYoureOut in this case). Clicking on it reveals the configuration, as shown in Figure 20-20. Notice here that the X-Client-IP address is being used as a basis for counting—in other words more than three invalid login attempts from the same IP will trigger the time out and log message.

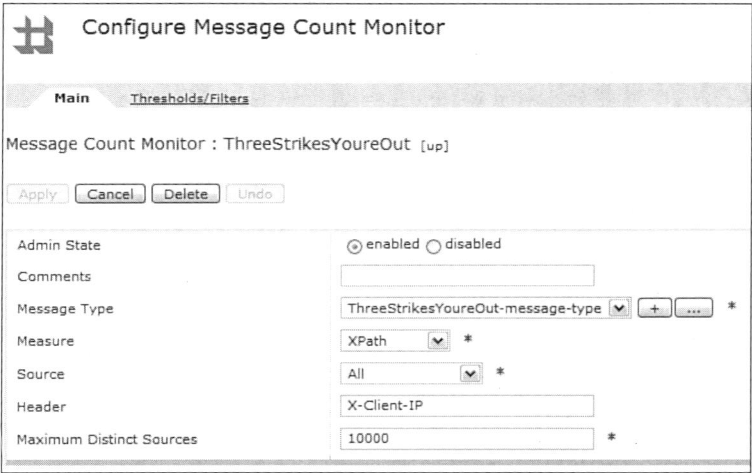

Figure 20-20 The Message Count Monitor object generated by the Reject Counter tool.

Moving over to the Thresholds/Filters tab, the content of which is shown in Figure 20-21, you may notice something suspicious. If you were to test this policy now, by sending four bad logins followed by a good one, the good one would succeed, and the log message and login denial period would not occur. This figure tells us exactly why. The default for the policy allows for "bursts" in the traffic. These might be acceptable in some message counters, but not for the type of Reject Counter on authentications that we are monitoring. You might want to change this default to zero. You should also configure the message count monitor that was created from the AAA policy to be active on your service, for example on the Monitors tab of an XML Firewall or Multi-Protocol Gateway.

Figure 20-21 The Thresholds/Filters settings for the ThreeStrikesYoureOut reject counter.

While we are on this pane, let's have a look at the Message Filter action object that has been built for us. Figure 20-22 shows what we expect—the transaction will be rejected, a log message issued at the level of warning, and a block interval of 60 seconds.

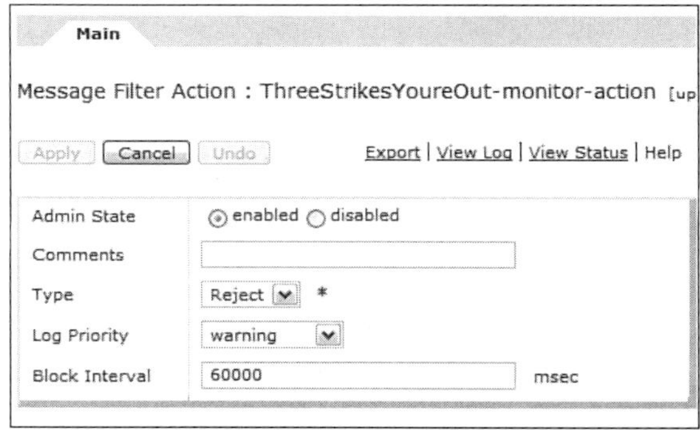

Figure 20-22 The Message Filter action object for the Reject Counter.

Using the Filter Action for Replay Attack Protection

Replay attacks can be prevented by using the Filter action. On the Advanced tab you will find the option to choose a Filter Method of "Replay Filter." This exposes the option to choose a Replay Filter Type, which includes WS-Addressing Message ID, WS-Security Password Digest Nonce, and Custom XPath. This is capability is discussed further in Chapter 19.

SLM Policies

Although service-level management (SLM) is normally thought of in performance, reliability or quality-of-service scenarios, it is also a good way to prevent DoS attacks. By the nature of what SLM does—rate-limiting and shaping traffic—it can be quite useful in thwarting or combating DoS attacks—at least to prevent them from reaching the backend servers. Figure 20-23 shows an SLM policy for a Web Service Proxy that kicks in for one particular backend Web service operation when the traffic reaches 500 transactions per second. This particular policy is set up to use DataPower's unique shaping algorithm, where transactions are queued on the device to introduce slight latencies to smooth out the curve of peak demand. This is covered in Chapter 10.

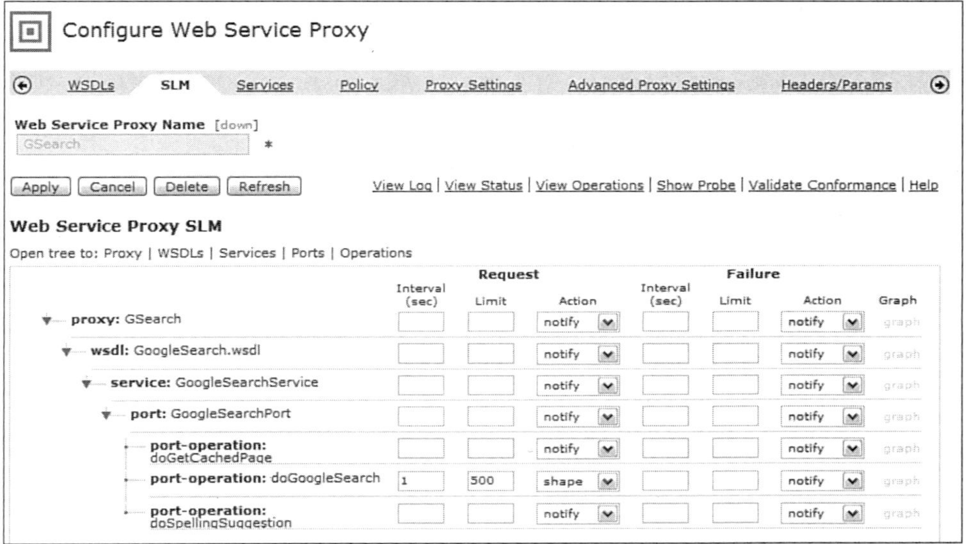

Figure 20-23 The SLM policy for a Web Service Proxy.

Summary

In this chapter, we discussed a wealth of different types of attacks that can be mounted using XML. We built on that to show the many ways that you can protect your systems from those attacks using the features of DataPower SOA appliances. Some of this is incredibly easy (in fact you get a great deal with no additional configuration whatsoever), and some of it takes some investigation into your message metrics, thought, and work on your part. In the end, the results always pay off. The cost of production outages and system compromises is generally staggering.

In conclusion, it's important to note that even though the bad guys are out there, often we simply need to protect ourselves against malformed or rogue messages from our partners, clients, and even our own programmers. Many times the messages that crash our systems are simply a result of bad application code or transforms.

For this reason, we can't stress strongly enough that the advice in this chapter be taken to heart—validate all request and response messages and the results of any transforms or message alterations. Keep the many settings in DataPower that are related to threat protection in mind and make it part of your application acceptance process to review and tune for these, just as you (hopefully) tune your applications and infrastructure for performance.

CHAPTER 21

Security Integration with WebSphere Application Server

This chapter completes Part V, "DataPower Security," and delves into the security integration between DataPower and WebSphere Application Server (WAS) and the related stack products deployed on top of WAS. We offer a brief introduction to these products and discuss the security models that they incorporate. Although this chapter focuses on Web services, we also discuss standard Web applications and security issues in general, all under the chapter context of DataPower-WAS interoperability.

WebSphere Application Server Introduction

IBM WAS has been around quite some time in "IT years," having been born back in 1998 as a fledgling Servlet container, just starting on its growth path into a full-blown Java EE application server. The use of Java and the early design of J2EE and Java EE were in their beginnings back then.

Java EE and the application servers that run it are designed to bring Java runtime environments up to par with corporate IT requirements for things like transaction integrity, maintenance, administration, and high availability. In Java EE, application programs are built into Enterprise Archive (EAR) files, which contain the compiled application code as well as deployment descriptors that tell the Java EE application server containers what requirements the application has (for example, it needs a database). These descriptor entries serve as hints for the admin tools to prompt for connection information for those resources when the application is installed in a particular Java EE application server. For example, when deploying an EAR file that requires a database, the admin tool requires the connection information for the database in the target environment to be specified to satisfy that need. The deployment descriptors also contain security information such as roles and constraints that the application expects the Java EE containers to enforce.

As Java EE and WAS have matured over time, the security model has matured along with it. This is also particularly true in Web services security, which has moved from rough draft status to a standardized and sophisticated framework for providing message integrity and privacy. WAS not only fulfills the requirements of the specification in these areas, but it also extends them to provide its own integration points to customize the security runtime services. We dive into these details shortly.

WAS and Stack Products

Many companies, IBM included, built products on the J2EE and Java EE application server standard. IBM also uses WAS as a platform on which to build and run its other enterprise products. These include WebSphere Portal Server, WebSphere Process Server, WebSphere Enterprise Service Bus, WebSphere Services Registry and Repository (WSRR), and others.

The fact that these products all run on a common base has many advantages. In context with this chapter's subject matter, a big advantage is that they all have a common security model and integration points that are based on standards. Therefore, although this chapter focuses on the core WebSphere Application Server, much of what we say here also applies to integration with these other products, or anything built on WAS for that matter (as long as it is *using* the WAS security infrastructure).

WAS Security Model

There are several aspects of the WAS security model, from the token types supported to specifics related to WS-Security, that are important for the DataPower practitioner to understand. For example, there are some custom integration points similar to the custom AAA techniques shown in Chapter 17, "Advanced AAA." We break all this down for you in this section, so it can be used as context for the rest of our discussion.

Java EE Security

The Java EE security model is declarative in nature, meaning that security constraints for a particular application or its components are "declared" in the deployment descriptors embedded in the EAR file during the application build process. These might specify things such as a Web application requiring basic authentication or a Web service expecting to receive a WS-Security UsernameToken.

The Java EE model uses "lazy authentication," meaning that clients are not challenged until they try to access a particular secured resource. The resources and security policies typically exist on the backend server. For many IT shops, having an unauthenticated, unauthorized request reach the backend—even if the connection is proxied by a secure server—is not acceptable. A current trend is toward perimeter security where all requests are authenticated in the DMZ before they are allowed to proceed to the trusted zone, and the backend Java EE application then uses the credentials verified in a previous step.

Lightweight Third-Party Authentication (LTPA)

LTPA is a security credential format used by WAS and IBM Domino® products. It carries an identity inside a signed, encrypted, limited lifetime binary token. For example, if you were to try to access a WAS application that is designated as protected by security, you would likely be challenged for your identity, and upon providing valid information (userid/password, certificate, or perhaps other means), the WAS security runtime would create an LTPA credential with your identity. It would store the credential in the system cache, and perhaps return a reference to it to your browser (in the form of a session cookie) to be re-sent on subsequent requests as proof of who you are so that you are not troubled to authenticate again.

WAS uses the LTPA credential to provide single sign-on (SSO) within or across groups of application servers called "cells." We mentioned that the LTPA token is encrypted and signed. When the token is created on the application server itself, it is encrypted and signed with the keys in the server's LTPA keystore.

The LTPA token contains little information by default, essentially just the client identity, timestamp, and realm.[1] There is no other information, such as user passwords or group associations about the client. This fact makes LTPA inherently a lossy credential format, meaning that if other information is available about the client at authentication, it is lost due to not being captured in the credential. With the newer LTPA v2 format introduced in WAS 6.0, it is possible to include custom attributes along with the token, but this requires custom programming on the application server side to process and use. We discuss this in more detail shortly.

The normal case is for WAS to do the authentication and create the LTPA token with its own keystore. However, there are two other IBM security products that are capable of creating LTPA credentials: Tivoli Access Manager's (TAM) WebSEAL authentication proxy component and DataPower. When LTPA credentials are created by these intermediaries, WAS will not re-authenticate the user but will need to access the registry to get information needed to create a fully formed Java Subject object. For example, the client's group association and other attributes are necessary to complete the Subject. So as you might guess, it's important in these cases that the authentication proxy and WAS access the same user registry, or registries that contain the same identities. We discuss issues related to choosing this approach later in the chapter.

Trust Association Interceptors/Login Modules

A Trust Association Interceptor (TAI) is an integration point provided by WAS that enables a custom Java module (the TAI) to be written to trust authentications that have been done elsewhere, in place of WAS doing the authentication itself. It is used for Web-based authentication only (which includes Web services). A TAI would normally be called only for requested resources that are configured to require authentication, such as a request for a secured resource that does not carry an LTPA token in its request payload.

[1] A realm name is an abstraction for the user registry used by WAS. For example, if LDAP is used, WAS will generate a realm name that is the LDAP server hostname. This can be changed administratively. Cross-cell single sign-on is facilitated by ensuring that each cell uses the same LTPA keystore and realm name (even if there are different registries used by each cell, as long as they are identical).

When using a TAI, WAS essentially extends its trust domain to include the external authentication mechanism and accept the identity being asserted by it as legitimate. Therefore, this custom code must be written carefully. The critical thing is to ensure there is secure communication between the external authentication mechanism and WAS to prevent a rogue application or hacker from pretending to be the external authentication mechanism.

The TAI is commonly used to facilitate perimeter security using authentication proxies such as DataPower, TAM, Siteminder, and ClearTrust. Some of these products come with a TAI from the vendor to interface with WAS. For others, such as DataPower, a TAI would have to be written. In either case, this code should always be carefully reviewed to ensure that it is truly secure by your *own* standards.

Login modules are similar in nature to TAIs. They are a customized authentication process for Web or Internet Inter-ORB Protocol (IIOP) requests. They are significantly more complicated than TAIs in terms of the configuration and Java code needed.

The benefit that TAIs and login modules have over using an authentication proxy to create the LTPA token is that if there is additional information about the user (such as group associations) available at the time of authentication at the proxy, these can be passed through from the proxy and used to form the Subject on the server. You can also use these to work around the requirement that the authentication proxy and WAS have the same registry. For example, if you were to pass through enough information to create a fully formed Subject, WAS would not attempt to query the registry. If you had DataPower add LTPA attributes to specify additional information about the user and pass that through, you would need to write a TAI or login module to intercept and process that information on WAS.

For an in-depth description of TAIs and login modules in WAS v6, see "Advanced Authentication in WebSphere Application Server" (Keys Botzum, et al) at http://www.ibm.com/developerworks/websphere/techjournal/0508_benantar/0508_benantar.html.

Keys and Certificates in WAS

In WAS version 6.1, self-signed system certificates (such as those used for SSL configurations) are automatically regenerated after 12 months by default. The new certificates are automatically sent to other managed nodes in the WAS infrastructure, but this can cause problems for other infrastructure components (such as Web servers or SOA appliances) that are not WAS-managed nodes and need them. Without the new certificates, SSL connections fail.

For this reason, the general recommendation for WAS installations is to disable automatic certificate generation so that the process can be better managed through other means, such as a well-managed scripted or manual procedure. Of course, proper certificate expiration warnings should be set up on WAS, just as with DataPower. This should be kept in mind for any SSL-based connections to WAS. For example, if action isn't taken before the certificate expires, the WAS certificate that you put in the DataPower SSL client configuration validation credential will no longer be valid, and those connections will fail! We will get into the implications of this for LTPA and DataPower later in the chapter. Because of some WAS critical updates around this particular area of functionality, it is recommended that the WAS install be at least version 6.1.0.11. For any profiles created applying patches at this level, the certs are good for 15 years by default. The automatic replacement of expiring certificates can be changed in the WAS admin console by navigating to SSL certificate and key management→Manage certificate expiration and unchecking the Automatically replace expiring self-signed certificates' checkbox.

WAS uses a different terminology for key/certificate artifacts. For example, the container for signing or trusted certificates is called a trust store, whereas in DataPower it is called a validation credential. Knowing these different terms is important for communicating effectively with the WAS administrator for things such as configuring SSL.

Security Assertion Markup Language (SAML)

DataPower has strong SAML support. For example, if a Web browser made a Representational State Transfer (REST) request through DataPower to WAS, DataPower could consume a SAML token in the payload and generate an LTPA token to change the request into a standard authenticated call to WAS (as we will show shortly).

But if the goal is to use SAML to integrate with WAS for use cases such as identity assertion, the solution would have to include custom code on the WAS side in the form of a login module or TAI to intercept and process the SAML assertion. This may change in the future as SAML support is added to WAS.

WAS Web Services Security Implementation

Support for Web services security has grown quite a bit in recent WAS versions. As shown in Table 21-1, WAS now includes a full complement of WS-* security capabilities (including others not shown here). The middle column in this table represents the enhancements that come with the Web services feature pack for WAS 6.1.

Password digests for UsernameToken profile are not directly supported. Binary Security Token types supported are LTPA, X.509, Kerberos (WSS-Kerberos Token Profile 1.1), and custom.

Table 21-1 Web Services Security Specification Implementations in WAS

	WAS 6.1	WAS 6.1 WSFP	WAS 7
WS-Security	1.0	1.1*	1.1*
UsernameToken Profile	1.0	1.1	1.1
X.509 Token Profile	1.0	1.1	1.1
Kerberos Token Profile			1.1
WS-SecureConversation		1.0	1.3*
WS-Policy			1.5
WS-SecurityPolicy			1.2*
WS-Trust		1.0	1.3*
WSI-Basic Security Profile	1.0	1.0	1.0

* Indicates specifications implemented enough to meet key scenarios.

Key Security Integration Points

Of course, the message privacy and integrity features that we talked about in Chapter 19, "Web Services Security," are included in WS-Security on WAS. WAS can encrypt and sign messages just as DataPower can, as well as process UsernameTokens and everything else encompassed in the specifications shown in Table 21-1.

However, performing these operations on the application server comes at an expensive price. In addition to increasing message/payload sizes, the processing involved in these operations is intensive and, hence, robs processing cycles from business logic. Just as with other expensive operations such as schema validation and transformation, a current trend is to offload these extensive "heavy lifting" security tasks to a fast hardware platform such as DataPower to maximize backend processing power on transactional business logic. And as we said earlier, this allows one to provide for requirements such as perimeter security.

In many cases, the backend runtimes such as application servers or transactional systems do not comply with the latest versions of these specifications. Or several components of a transactional system comply with different versions of the specifications. This encourages the use of DataPower to provide for "spec mediation" between different versions, as well as token mediation due to the numerous token types supported.

In this section we delve into the details of integrating DataPower with WAS to accomplish some of those things.

AAA/LTPA

We've already given extensive coverage of AAA in Chapters 16, "AAA," and 17, but we've intentionally avoided covering the WAS/LTPA particulars—until now. If you recall, LTPA is prominent in the AAA flow. It is listed as a choice on the extract identity, authenticate, and post-processing steps. This is because DataPower can be an LTPA credential consumer or producer. To better understand this, let's walk through a common scenario used in implementing LTPA functionality on DataPower.

DataPower as an LTPA Producer

Our DataPower as an LTPA producer example is a scenario that emulates a simple Web application proxy configuration using an XML firewall. We use the WAS sample application called snoop for our test. Snoop is configured for basic authentication. The concepts shown are just as applicable to proxying Web services with inbound WS-Security UsernameToken headers. We configured our firewall for Web application proxying, as shown in Chapter 11, "Proxying Web Applications with DataPower."

Our next step was to export the LTPA keystore from WAS. This is necessary because DataPower will be creating the credential in place of WAS, and part of that process is encrypting the credential with the keys in the LTPA keystore. Figure 21-1 shows this page in the WAS admin console filled out, including a password that the keystore will be protected with (we have mentioned many times that the private keys within are extremely sensitive data!) and the location and filename for the exported keys. The Export Keys button is used to complete the process.

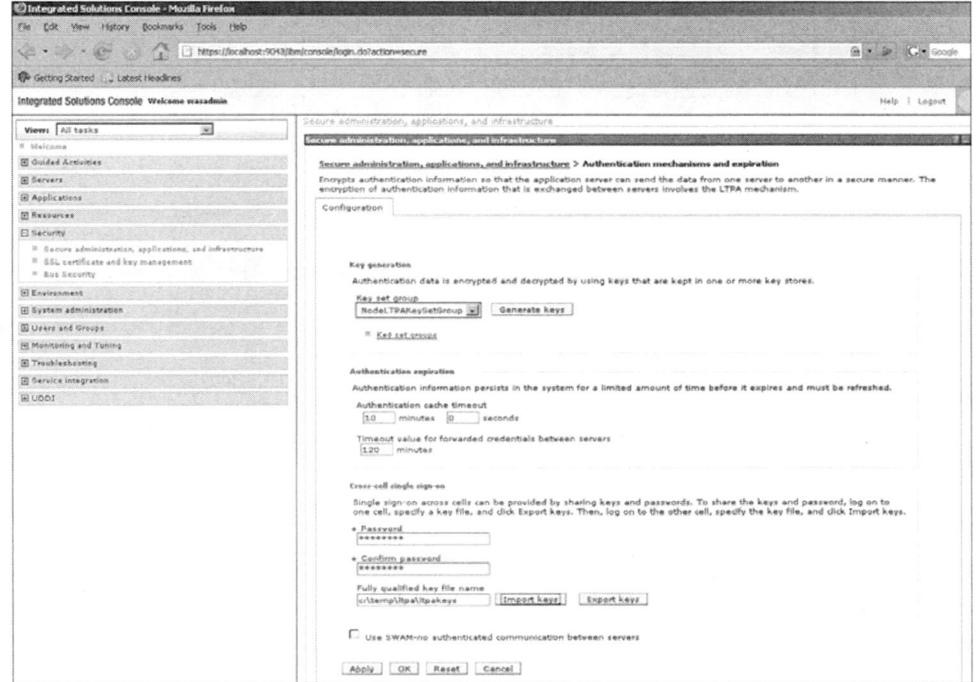

Figure 21-1 Exporting the LTPA keystore from the WAS administrative console.

We then began setting up a AAA Policy for the request. We chose HTTP Basic Authentication Header for our identity extraction method and to authenticate against an LDAP repository for authentication. The LDAP configuration is shown in Figure 21-2.

As mentioned earlier, it is important that this registry used in your AAA Policy be the same one that WAS is configured to use, or else a replica containing the same identities. The reason is that, as mentioned earlier, LTPA contains only the user identity, and when the credential created by DataPower arrives at the application server, the security runtime there will want to form a full Java Subject containing other attributes about the user, such as group memberships. It will read the user repository (LDAP in this case) to obtain the information.

As we discussed earlier, there are ways to prevent WAS from accessing a user repository by putting that information in the LTPA attributes and writing security custom code on the WAS side to process it to create the Subject object, or writing a TAI to receive and process an identity assertion from the AAA Policy rather than generating the LTPA credential on DataPower.

For the AAA Extract Resource and Authorization steps, we selected URL Sent by Client and Allow any Authenticated Client, respectively.

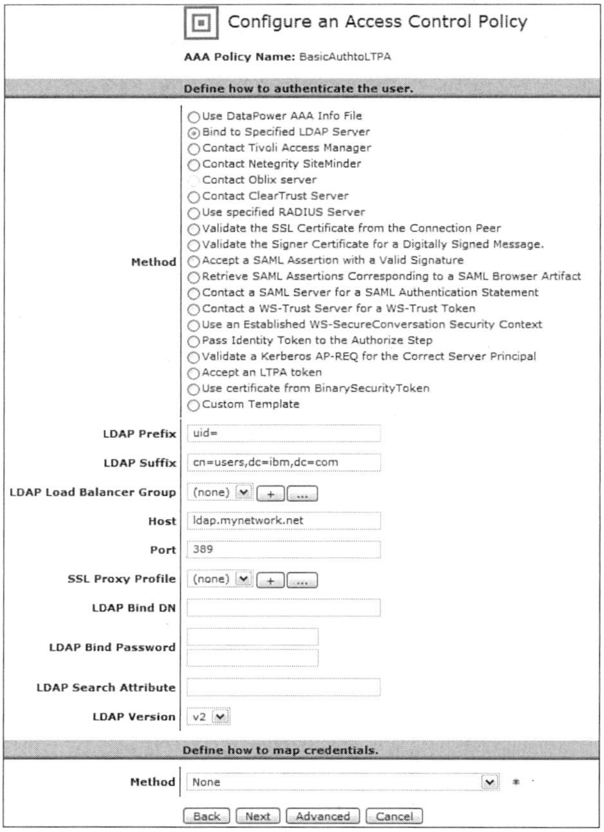

Configure an Access Control Policy

AAA Policy Name: BasicAuthtoLTPA

Define how to authenticate the user.

Method
- Use DataPower AAA Info File
- Bind to Specified LDAP Server
- Contact Tivoli Access Manager
- Contact Netegrity SiteMinder
- Contact Oblix server
- Contact ClearTrust Server
- Use specified RADIUS Server
- Validate the SSL Certificate from the Connection Peer
- Validate the Signer Certificate for a Digitally Signed Message.
- Accept a SAML Assertion with a Valid Signature
- Retrieve SAML Assertions Corresponding to a SAML Browser Artifact
- Contact a SAML Server for a SAML Authentication Statement
- Contact a WS-Trust Server for a WS-Trust Token
- Use an Established WS-SecureConversation Security Context
- Pass Identity Token to the Authorize Step
- Validate a Kerberos AP-REQ for the Correct Server Principal
- Accept an LTPA token
- Use certificate from BinarySecurityToken
- Custom Template

LDAP Prefix: uid=
LDAP Suffix: cn=users,dc=ibm,dc=com
LDAP Load Balancer Group: (none)
Host: ldap.mynetwork.net
Port: 389
SSL Proxy Profile: (none)
LDAP Bind DN:
LDAP Bind Password:
LDAP Search Attribute:
LDAP Version: v2

Define how to map credentials.

Method: None

Back Next Advanced Cancel

Figure 21-2 AAA authentication config for binding against LDAP.

TIP—Security in Layers

For authorization, it is often asked whether application security should be turned off on the backend application server, because we are performing all the usual security steps at the appliance. This is *not* recommended, per the fundamental principal of security in layers. Although some coarse-grained authorization may be done out on the perimeter, there may be additional authorization done on the backend, such as that defined in the Java EE application's deployment descriptors. For example, we may protect a URL or Web service operation at the perimeter, but those requests may trigger Enterprise Java Bean (EJB) calls on the backend, which may also have security constraints in place that need to be met by other (perhaps internal) applications.

In addition, you always want to perform some level of authentication on the perimeter server or device that is asserting the information about the end client to the backend, to prevent man-in-the-middle, end-around, and other types of spoofing attacks. Security must be enabled in order to do this. While network-level configurations add point-to-point trust, this extra user-level authentication is important to be sure that the asserting system is whom it claims to be.

The final post-processing page of the AAA wizard is the interesting part for our example scenario. Our configuration is shown in Figure 21-3. We have turned on the radio button to generate an LTPA token, uploaded the LTPA keystore that we earlier exported from WAS, and supplied the required information such as the keystore password and LTPA timeout value. In keeping with the good practice of ensuring that security credentials have a limited lifetime, we kept the default value of ten minutes. This does not mean that the end user will have to re-authenticate every ten minutes, but that the systems will regenerate the LTPA token, to ensure its integrity.

Also notice that we are using LTPA version 2. This is recommended for all recent versions of WAS, as the encryption and other security are stronger than the older LTPA version 1 format, in addition to the ability to add custom attributes. Of course, this generally depends on what version of WAS you are proxying, but some accept both v1 and v2.

Another setting of interest on the post-processing page is the Wrap Token in a WS-Security Header radio button. When this is off, as is the default setting, the LTPA token is put into the HTTP header, which is standard for Web applications. However, if you are proxying Web services and your backend Web service application on WAS is expecting a WS-Security BinarySecurityToken (BST) containing the LTPA credential, you would set this to On, and DataPower would do all the work to wrap the credential in the WS-Sec SOAP header per the specification. In some cases, even though you use Web services, you might still want to pass the credential in the HTTP header rather than the SOAP header. We show the LTPA BST and touch on this later in the chapter when we discuss Web services security integration in more detail.

One last item you may have noticed in our post-processing configuration is that we are running a custom stylesheet called removeBasicAuthHeader.xsl, shown in Listing 21-1. Although we cover XSLT and programming in the next part of the book, you should still be able to follow this simple logic. Essentially, it removes an HTTP header called Authorization. This is the basic auth header that is inserted by the browser after the user fills out the login screen. It is a good security practice to always remove nonessential security information, such as basic auth headers and WS-Security UsernameTokens. During testing phases, messages should be examined to determine whether they carry any such information. In this case, by the time we get to the post-processing step, we have already extracted the userid and password from the basic auth header and authenticated them against LDAP, so they are no longer needed.

Listing 21-1 Stylesheet to Remove the Basic Authentication Header

```
<?xml version="1.0" encoding="UTF-8"?>
<xsl:stylesheet version="1.0"
      xmlns:dp="http://www.datapower.com/extensions"
      extension-element-prefixes="dp" exclude-result-prefixes="dp"
      xmlns:xsl="http://www.w3.org/1999/XSL/Transform"
      xmlns:tns="http://www.w3.org/1999/xhtml">
<xsl:output method="xml"/>
      <xsl:template match="/">
            <dp:remove-http-request-header name="Authorization"/>
<xsl:copy-of select="."/>
</xsl:template>
</xsl:stylesheet>
```

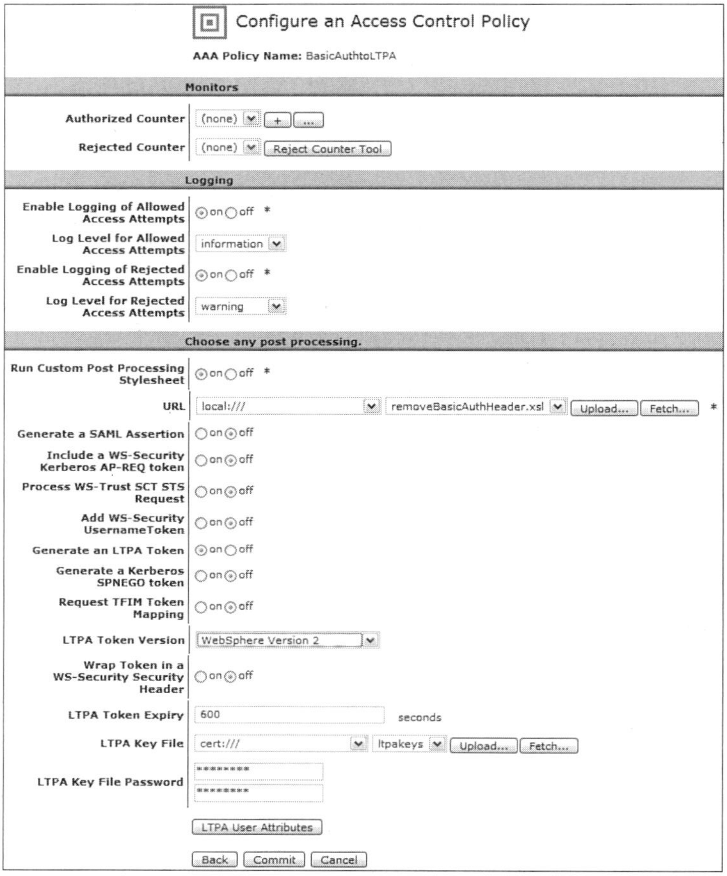

Figure 21-3 AAA Post Processing configuration for generating an LTPA credential.

TIP—Removing Extracted Identities

In addition to being good security practice, removing the extracted identity from the request could also save some troubleshooting headaches.

Consider what would happen if the copy of the LTPA keystore on the appliance were invalid or expired. The credential that is created would be passed to WAS on the backend and then rejected. WAS will then see the basic auth header and repeat the process of authenticating the user against the LDAP server and build the credential all over again!

The worst part is that you may never realize this has happened, as the result is a successful transaction, and the same exact page is returned as if DataPower had done all this, as intended. You would not have gained any of the intended perimeter security or performance benefit of offloading this task to the appliance. Careful inspection of the logs on both sides of the transaction would make it evident that things are not working as desired.

When our example scenario is tested, the user is prompted to enter login information into the basic auth gray form, as shown in Figure 21-4. What occurs here is that DataPower receives the initial request for the URL, realizes that it requires basic authentication per our AAA Policy, notices that there is no basic auth header in the request, and then sends an HTTP 401 to the browser requesting the information. The browser then presents the login dialog to the user, and when the user completes the form, the browser resends the request to DataPower, this time with the basic auth header.

Figure 21-4 User prompted for basic authentication information by DataPower.

When the XML Firewall receives the request containing the basic auth header, it then processes the rest of the AAA steps, such as authenticating the user against the LDAP repository and creating the LTPA credential to send to WAS in the HTTP header. These steps, as well as the HTTP GET sent to WAS and the HTTP 200 OK response code, can be seen in Figure 21-5.

We've shown the successful transaction in the DataPower logs, but what's happening on the WAS side? It's good to have a fundamental understanding of WAS troubleshooting techniques (or know a friendly WAS admin who does) in order to see things more clearly from that side of the transaction. Figure 21-6 shows the details of a WAS security run-time trace using a trace string of com.ibm.wsspi.security.*=all: com.ibm.ws.security.*=all. WAS traces generally output a lot of detail unless they are carefully tuned. In Figure 21-6, we have cut out the less interesting parts in order to focus on the relevant details.

```
xmlfirewall (WASWebAppProxy): Latency: 0 1 1 7 7 1 0 4626 4626 4626 4627 4627 4626 0 0 1 [http://was.mynetwork.net:9080/snoop]
xmlfirewall (WASWebAppProxy): rule (WASWebAppProxy_response): #1 results: 'generated from INPUT' completed ok.
xmlfirewall (WASWebAppProxy): The processing type will pass document through unmodified.
xmlfirewall (WASWebAppProxy): HTTP response code sent to client: 200 OK (url http://was.mynetwork.net:9080/snoop)
xmlfirewall (WASWebAppProxy): rule (WASWebAppProxy_response): selected via match 'WASWebAppProxy' from processing policy
'WASWebAppProxy'
xmlfirewall (WASWebAppProxy): Due to 'non-xml processing' flag, rule 'WASWebAppProxy_response' will be run but content will not be
accessible.
xmlfirewall (WASWebAppProxy): HTTP server side response code: 200 OK (url http://was.mynetwork.net:9080/snoop)
xmlfirewall (WASWebAppProxy): Awaiting response header data
xmlfirewall (WASWebAppProxy): Server side connection made for GET http://was.mynetwork.net:9080/snoop to 192.168.1.143:9080.
Obtaining Response
xmlfirewall (WASWebAppProxy): rule (WASWebAppProxy_request): #2 results: 'generated from PIPE' completed ok.
xmlfirewall (WASWebAppProxy): rule (WASWebAppProxy_request): #1 aaa: 'INPUT BasicAuthtoLTPA stored in PIPE' completed ok.
xmlfirewall (WASWebAppProxy): Policy(BasicAuthtoLTPA): Message allowed
xmlfirewall (WASWebAppProxy): Policy(BasicAuthtoLTPA): Start post processing, local:///removeBasicAuthHeader.xsl
xmlfirewall (WASWebAppProxy): Generated WebSphere v1 FIPS compliant or WebSphere v2 LTPA signature
xmlfirewall (WASWebAppProxy): No special conversion will be done with the credential before calling.
xmlfirewall (WASWebAppProxy): Policy(BasicAuthtoLTPA): anyauthenticated authorization succeeded with credential
'uid=wasadmin,cn=users,dc=ibm,dc=com' for resource '/snoop'
xmlfirewall (WASWebAppProxy): Policy(BasicAuthtoLTPA): Cached Authorize entry
xmlfirewall (WASWebAppProxy): Policy(BasicAuthtoLTPA): Authorizing with "anyauthenticated"
xmlfirewall (WASWebAppProxy): Policy(BasicAuthtoLTPA): Authorize Caching is on: absolute
xmlfirewall (WASWebAppProxy): Policy(BasicAuthtoLTPA): Mapping resources using none
xmlfirewall (WASWebAppProxy): Policy(BasicAuthtoLTPA): Mapping credentials using none
xmlfirewall (WASWebAppProxy): Policy(BasicAuthtoLTPA): ldap authentication succeeded with (http-basic-auth, username='wasadmin'
password='********'configured-realm='login' )
xmlfirewall (WASWebAppProxy): Policy(BasicAuthtoLTPA): Cached Authenticate entry
xmlfirewall (WASWebAppProxy): Policy(BasicAuthtoLTPA): Authenticating with "ldap"
xmlfirewall (WASWebAppProxy): Policy(BasicAuthtoLTPA): Authenticate Caching is on: true
xmlfirewall (WASWebAppProxy): Policy(BasicAuthtoLTPA): Resource "/snoop"
xmlfirewall (WASWebAppProxy): Policy(BasicAuthtoLTPA): Extracting resources using "original-url"
xmlfirewall (WASWebAppProxy): Policy(BasicAuthtoLTPA): Extracting identity using "http-basic-auth"
xmlfirewall (WASWebAppProxy): Stylesheet URL to compile is 'store:///dp/aaapolicy.xsl'
xmlfirewall (WASWebAppProxy): rule (WASWebAppProxy_request): selected via match 'WASWebAppProxy' from processing policy
'WASWebAppProxy'
xmlfirewall (WASWebAppProxy): New transaction(conn use=1): GET http://192.168.1.101:2050/snoop from 192.168.1.114
```

Figure 21-5 DataPower log showing request processing.

In the trace output (which is read top to bottom on WAS), the incoming transaction can be seen. Note the line at the beginning showing the HTTP header names and values—you can see the LTPA credential there. WAS sees, decrypts, and validates (signature verification and timestamp check) the LTPA credential from our AAA Policy and allows the transaction. Because the credential's timestamp is checked, it is obviously important to ensure that the date and time settings on both platforms are in sync; for example, use Network Time Protocol (NTP) on all servers. (They were not exactly in sync for this test, but close enough for success.)

Whew, a lot has happened for our simple Web app request! Figure 21-7 shows the resulting page.

So that's it—we're done, right? Not quite. LTPA is used for single sign-on, as stated earlier. The idea is that after the user authenticates, the credential is held by its client (the browser in this case) and then reused for subsequent requests. This saves the hard work of executing all the AAA steps on every request, such as reading the LDAP server and creating the token over and over again.

```
[8/11/08 16:57:04:156 EDT] 00000023 EJSWebCollabo >  preInvoke Entry
                              com.ibm.ws.webcontainer.srt.SRTServletRequest@17901790
                              com.ibm.ws.webcontainer.srt.SRTServletResponse@cd40cd4
                              /
                              default_host
                              Snoop Servlet
                              true
[8/11/08 16:57:04:156 EDT] 00000023 EJSWebCollabo 3   Http Header names and values:Accept=[image/gif, image/x-xbitmap, image/jpeg, image/pjpeg,
application/vnd.ms-excel, application/vnd.ms-powerpoint, application/msword, application/x-shockwave-flash, */*]Accept-Language=[en-us]User-Agent=
[Mozilla/4.0 (compatible; MSIE 6.0; Windows NT 5.1; SV1; .NET CLR 1.1.4322; .NET CLR 2.0.50727)]Host=[192.168.1.101:2050]Via=[1.1 WASWebAppProxy]
Connection=[Keep-Alive]Cookie=
[LtpaToken2=bTzWYrTMJGdOuNhLOYymp/ocTxcDpEs5ebJ1HGw9DheORlFhjTuxdrWPRf6N5Cb8GwM+zMLDIBPUdoLm7lAlab+8vvGaC9cypm2+ySoUTQn8VJ8ctH/DFqRAjqHwZrqOMTYmoNuLM
vE6/roFaiVX8p/abskLmBpO2kTPbha34bMYpCmLY3xtbd/AFlSPMOxhg4bdM3+JmU16aAC5inzFKXEjvEpJA16Hhr8E16EwrlXHT+6RH6xVuvsfYLzCw9LOnpsar+IeO3Tp2+W8y4PPWQxz9QeVFq
swY5n6nI3FcSh1za+6cZKBWUEPjKJ3pHHNePeWLEoJTfo8EuDSDziwnSx9LCe7yWWBOJ+2ywOKGvM=]Content-Type=[text/xml]X-Client-IP=[192.168.1.114]
[8/11/08 16:57:04:156 EDT] 00000023 EJSWebCollabo 3    Request Context Path=, Servlet Path=/snoop, Path Info=null
[8/11/08 16:57:04:156 EDT] 00000023 webCollaborat 3   Invoked and received Subject are null, setting it anonymous/unauthenticated.
[8/11/08 16:57:04:156 EDT] 00000023 WebAuthentica 3   Attempting primary cookie validation for: LtpaToken2
[8/11/08 16:57:04:156 EDT] 00000023 WebAuthentica >  getCookieValues Entry
                              LtpaToken2
[8/11/08 16:57:04:156 EDT] 00000023 WebAuthentica 3
bTzWYrTMJGdOuNhLOYymp/ocTxcDpEs5ebJ1HGw9DheORlFhjTuxdrWPRf6N5Cb8GwM+zMLDIBPUdoLm7lAlab+8vvGaC9cypm2+ySoUTQn8VJ8ctH/DFqRAjqHwZrqOMTYmoNuLMvE6/roFaiVX8
p/abskLmBpO2kTPbha34bMYpCmLY3xtbd/AFlSPMOxhg4bdM3+JmU16aAC5inzFKXEjvEpJA16Hhr8E16EwrlXHT+6RH6xVuvsfYLzCw9LOnpsar+IeO3Tp2+W8y4PPWQxz9QeVFqswY5n6nI3FcS
h1za+6cZKBWUEPjKJ3pHHNePeWLEoJTfo8EuDSDziwnSx9LCe7yWWBOJ+2ywOKGvM=
[8/11/08 16:57:04:156 EDT] 00000023 LTPAServerObj 3   BEGIN VALIDATING TOKEN: some errors may occur, look for SUCCESS:
[8/11/08 16:57:04:156 EDT] 00000023 LTPAServerObj 3   Calling tokenFactory[1].validateTokenBytes() -> com.ibm.ws.security.ltpa.LTPAToken2Factory
[8/11/08 16:57:04:156 EDT] 00000023 LTPAToken2    >  validate LTPAToken2 from byte[] Entry
[8/11/08 16:57:04:156 EDT] 00000023 LTPAToken2    >  decrypt Entry
[8/11/08 16:57:04:156 EDT] 00000023 LTPACrypto    3   Cipher used to decrypt: AES/CBC/PKCS5Padding
[8/11/08 16:57:04:156 EDT] 00000023 LTPACrypto    3   key size: 24
[8/11/08 16:57:04:156 EDT] 00000023 LTPACrypto    3   The Provider Cipher used to decrypt: IBMJCE version 1.2
[8/11/08 16:57:04:156 EDT] 00000023 LTPACrypto    3   The Algoritm Cipher used to decrypt: AES/CBC/PKCS5Padding
[8/11/08 16:57:04:156 EDT] 00000023 LTPACrypto    3   decrypt() Cipher.doFinal()   tmpMesg: expire:1218488819000
$u:user\:localhost\:389/uid=wasadmin,cn=users,dc=ibm,dc=com%1218488819000%
O82egDGmgIeeNzVoyNbq4+Il5sTeiiUDOi4TCnO1tJaEo2osU78Nxh7hXF6VljD/oW4/CzehTaObpHyAfVnnLLuVhwKik9qqb7CS8dxw+5V53e7VPer7vwM2AbOuZ+7co1fjExCBptb/Kkp8aeW88
gipccNnbVYOQajrQm/ZyTA=
[8/11/08 16:57:04:156 EDT] 00000023 LTPACrypto    3   Total decryption time: 0
[8/11/08 16:57:04:156 EDT] 00000023 LTPAToken2    3   tokenString after decrypt: expire:1218488819000
$u:user\:localhost\:389/uid=wasadmin,cn=users,dc=ibm,dc=com%1218488819000%
O82egDGmgIeeNzVoyNbq4+Il5sTeiiUDOi4TCnO1tJaEo2osU78Nxh7hXF6VljD/oW4/CzehTaObpHyAfVnnLLuVhwKik9qqb7CS8dxw+5V53e7VPer7vwM2AbOuZ+7co1fjExCBptb/Kkp8aeW88
gipccNnbVYOQajrQm/ZyTA=
[8/11/08 16:57:04:156 EDT] 00000023 LTPAToken2    3   Getting expiration from userdata area.
[8/11/08 16:57:04:156 EDT] 00000023 LTPAToken2    3   Expiration returned from expire field in token: Mon Aug 11 17:06:59 EDT 2008
[8/11/08 16:57:04:156 EDT] 00000023 LTPAToken2    3   Expiration set to: Mon Aug 11 17:06:59 EDT 2008
[8/11/08 16:57:04:156 EDT] 00000023 LTPAToken2    3   Expiration returned from expire field in token: Mon Aug 11 17:06:59 EDT 2008
[8/11/08 16:57:04:156 EDT] 00000023 LTPAToken2    3   expire: 1218488819000u: user:localhost:389/uid=wasadmin,cn=users,dc=ibm,dc=comExpiration time:
08.08.11 17:06:59:000 EDT
[8/11/08 16:57:04:156 EDT] 00000023 LTPAToken2    3   verify()   data: expire:1218488819000
$u:user\:localhost\:389/uid=wasadmin,cn=users,dc=ibm,dc=com
[8/11/08 16:57:04:156 EDT] 00000023 LTPAToken2    3   verify()   publicKey: com.ibm.ws.security.ltpa.LTPAPublicKey@755a755a
[8/11/08 16:57:04:171 EDT] 00000023 LTPAToken2    3   verify()   signature:
nullffffffd3ffffffcdffffff9effffff8031ffffffa6ffffff80ffffff87ffffff9e373568ffffffc8ffffffd6ffffffeaffffffe3ffffffe225ffffffe6ffffffc4ffffffdeffffff8
a2503ffffffd22e130a73ffffffb5ffffffb4ffffff96ffffff84ffffffa36a2c53ffffffbf0dffffffc61effffffe15c5effffff95ffffff96377fffffffa16e3f0b37ffffffa14dffff
ffa3ffffff9bffffffa47cffffff807d59ffffffe72cffffffbbffffff95ffffff8702ffffffa2ffffff93ffffffdaffffffaa6ffffffb0ffffff92ffffff1ffffffdc70ffffffbfff
fff9579ffffffddffffffeeffffffd53dffffffeaffffffbfffffbf033601ffffffbd2e67ffffffeeffffffdcffffffa357ffffffe31310ffffff81ffffffa6ffffffd6ffffffff2a4a
7c69ffffffe5ffffffbcffffffff2ffffffa8ffffffa971ffffffc3676effffff60e41ffffffa8ffffffeb426fffffffd9ffffffc930
[8/11/08 16:57:04:171 EDT] 00000023 LTPAServerObj <  validateToken -> SUCCESS: validated using tokenFactoryArray[1]:
com.ibm.ws.security.ltpa.LTPAToken2Factory Exit
[8/11/08 16:57:04:218 EDT] 00000023 WebCollaborat 3   URI - /snoop.GET is protected
[8/11/08 16:57:04:218 EDT] 00000023 WebCollaborat 3   Authorization check for uri: /snoop succeeded.
```

Figure 21-6 WAS trace log output showing transaction details.

If we were to refresh the browser at this point in time, the request would again succeed, and we would see our snoop page results again. However, a close inspection of the logs would reveal that the whole AAA process has repeated—exactly what we wanted to avoid. The reason is that the LTPA credential that WAS returned on the response never made it back to the browser (we will see why when we show the solution to this problem.) So when the page is refreshed, the browser simply replays the basic auth info, which it has held onto. (We only stripped it from our request message, but the browser still has it.) This is used to again read the LDAP registry and create the LTPA credential.

To fix the problem, we need a stylesheet in our *response* rule to look for the credential and set a session (nonpersistent) cookie in the browser so that it is retained and replayed for subsequent requests. Listing 21-2 shows a stylesheet to do this.

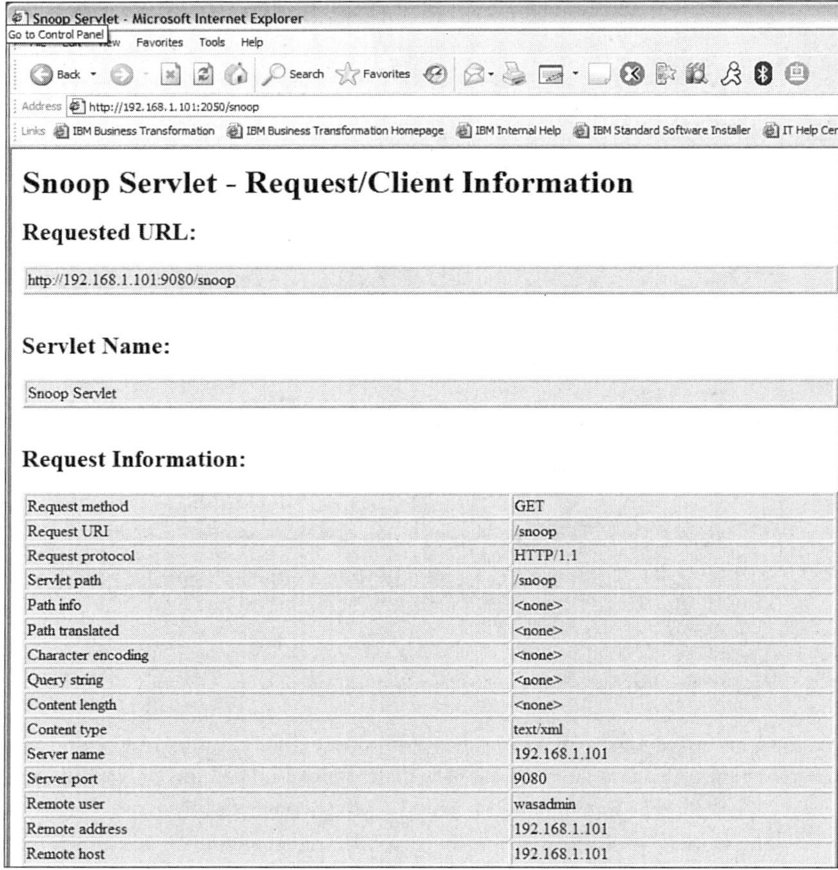

Figure 21-7 Results from the snoop application request.

Listing 21-2 Stylesheet to Set the LTPA Credential as a Browser Cookie

```
<?xml version="1.0" encoding="UTF-8"?>
<xsl:stylesheet xmlns:xsl="http://www.w3.org/1999/XSL/Transform"
version="1.0"
    xmlns:soap="http://schemas.xmlsoap.org/soap/envelope/"
    xmlns:dp="http://www.datapower.com/extensions"
    xmlns:regexp="http://exslt.org/regular-expressions"
    xmlns:dpconfig="http://www.datapower.com/param/config"
    extension-element-prefixes="dp regexp"
    exclude-result-prefixes="dp dpconfig">

    <xsl:template match="/">
      <xsl:message dp:type="aaa" dp:priority="debug">
        LTPA: <xsl:value-of
```

```
select="dp:variable('var://context/AAA/PPLTPA')/LTPAAttribute[./Name=
'LTPAToken']/Value" />
      </xsl:message>
      <! - If LTPA exists, then set it as cookie in the browser -->
      <xsl:if
test="count((dp:variable('var://context/AAA/PPLTPA')/LTPAAttribute[./Name=
'LTPAToken'])) > 0">
          <xsl:variable name="token-value"
select="dp:variable('var://context/AAA/PPLTPA')/LTPAAttribute[./Name=
'LTPAToken']/Value" />
          <dp:append-response-header name="'Set-Cookie'"
value="concat('LtpaToken2=',string($token-value),'; Path=/')" />
      </xsl:if>
      <dp:freeze-headers/>
    </xsl:template>
</xsl:stylesheet>
```

The stylesheet would be configured on our response rule, as shown in Figure 21-8.

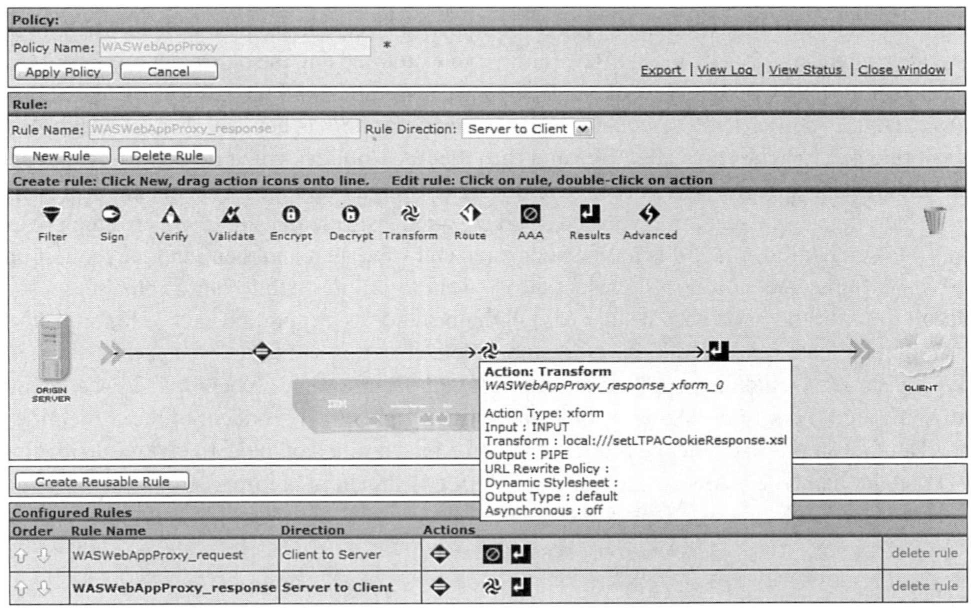

Figure 21-8 A response rule with a stylesheet to set the LTPA credential as a cookie.

With this in place, when the request is fired again, the cookie is set in the browser on the response. Proof of this can be viewed by using a cookie viewing/editing tool, as shown in Figure 21-9. You can also configure your browser options to notify you only when cookies are being set and see the cookie coming through that way. This technique is discussed in Chapter 28, "Problem Determination Using External Tools."

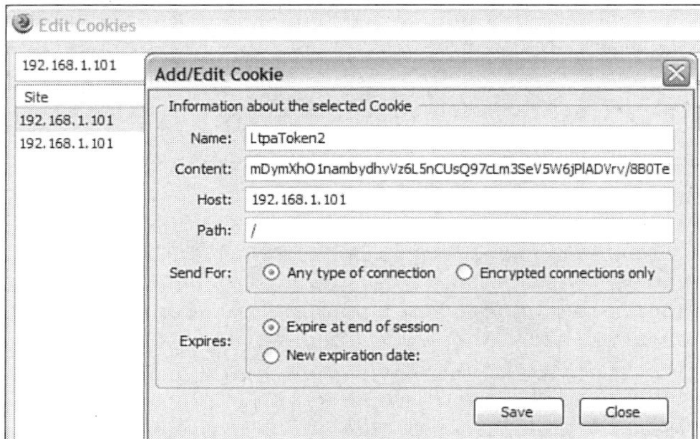

Figure 21-9 Firefox Cookie Editor showing LTPA cookie set in the browser.

DataPower as an LTPA Consumer

So now we are truly done, correct? Again, not so fast! If we were to refresh the browser to send the request again and check the DataPower logs, we would see that the entire AAA policy has *still* been executed. This would include an unnecessary trip to the LDAP repository and all the drudgery of creating another LTPA credential. Think about why this is happening. We have only one request rule that matches on a URL of * and fires the AAA policy, which is still seeing that pesky basic auth header the browser has cached and re-sent, even though the LTPA cookie is present.

To complete our scenario, we need to create a request rule that first looks for the presence of an LTPA credential, and if it is there to consume and validate it and then send the request on its way. Only if this credential is *not* present do we want to fall through to our original request rule that will look for the basic auth header (or tell the browser to prompt the user to log in if it's not there), authenticate, and create the credential. Note that this scenario, with DataPower as an LTPA consumer, would also apply to any cases where DataPower is receiving LTPA credentials from WAS directly, where WAS and not DataPower is the original producer of the credential.

The first step is to create the request rule and a match rule that looks for the credential in the HTTP header named Cookie. An example match rule is shown in Figure 21-10.

Editing Matching Rule property
of **Matching Rule**
Help

Matching Type	HTTP *
HTTP Header Tag	Cookie *
HTTP Value Match	*LtpaToken2* *

Save Cancel

Figure 21-10 Match Rule to look for an LTPA cookie in the request.

The next step is to create a new AAA action and policy on the request rule. LTPA Token is selected for Extract Identity, and Accept an LTPA Token for authentication. Figure 21-11 shows the configuration for validating the LTPA token. Notice that it uses the same LTPA keystore that was imported from WAS and used to create the token in our other AAA policy. We again chose URL Sent by Client for the Extract Resource step and took the defaults on the rest of the AAA wizard pages. There is no need to generate another LTPA credential on the post-processing page, as this one will be passed right along.

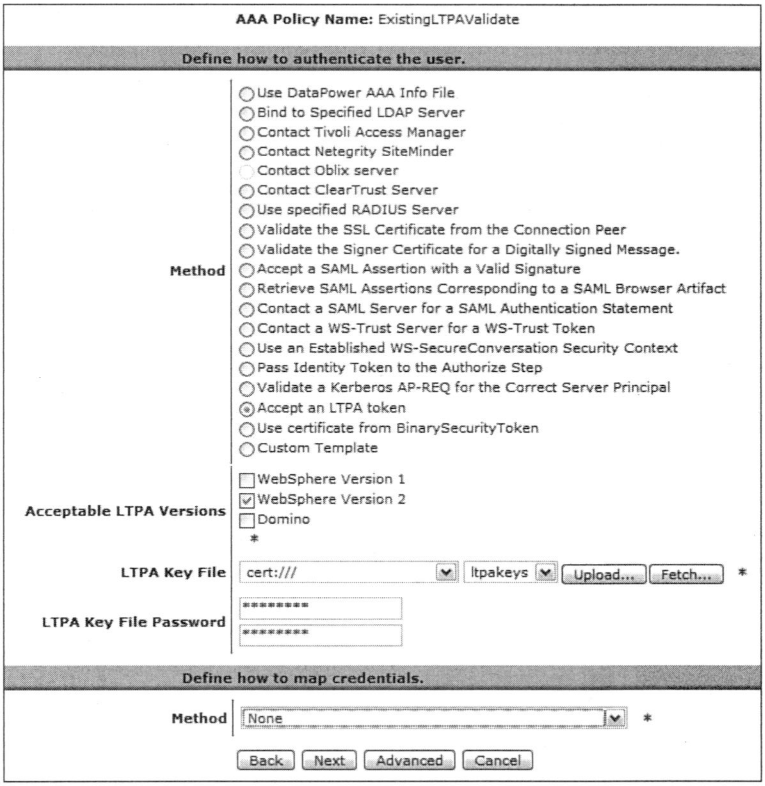

AAA Policy Name: ExistingLTPAValidate

Define how to authenticate the user.

Method

- Use DataPower AAA Info File
- Bind to Specified LDAP Server
- Contact Tivoli Access Manager
- Contact Netegrity SiteMinder
- Contact Oblix server
- Contact ClearTrust Server
- Use specified RADIUS Server
- Validate the SSL Certificate from the Connection Peer
- Validate the Signer Certificate for a Digitally Signed Message.
- Accept a SAML Assertion with a Valid Signature
- Retrieve SAML Assertions Corresponding to a SAML Browser Artifact
- Contact a SAML Server for a SAML Authentication Statement
- Contact a WS-Trust Server for a WS-Trust Token
- Use an Established WS-SecureConversation Security Context
- Pass Identity Token to the Authorize Step
- Validate a Kerberos AP-REQ for the Correct Server Principal
- (selected) Accept an LTPA token
- Use certificate from BinarySecurityToken
- Custom Template

Acceptable LTPA Versions

- [ ] WebSphere Version 1
- [x] WebSphere Version 2
- [ ] Domino

*

LTPA Key File cert:/// ltpakeys Upload... Fetch... *

LTPA Key File Password ******** ********

Define how to map credentials.

Method None *

Back Next Advanced Cancel

Figure 21-11 AAA Authenticate step using LTPA verification.

The final step is to add a Results action and re-order the request rules so that the one that looks for the LTPA credential is first, as shown in Figure 21-12.

Testing our proxy once more by firing the request, logging in, and then refreshing the browser finally gives us the success we desire. Figure 21-13 shows the log for our XML firewall, which indicates that the existing LTPA credential has been found and validated and passed through to WAS for a successful result.

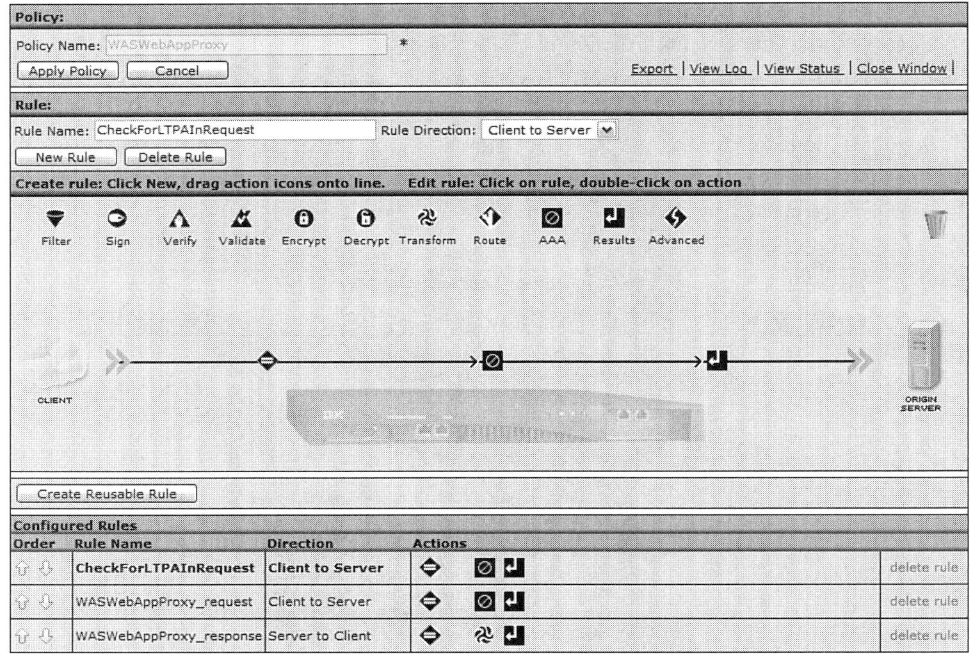

Figure 21-12 Completed Processing Policy for LTPA to WAS.

0x80e0007b	xmlfirewall (WASWebAppProxy): HTTP server side response code: 200 OK (url http://was.mynetwork.net:9080/snoop)
0x80e0014e	xmlfirewall (WASWebAppProxy): Awaiting response header data
0x80e0006f	xmlfirewall (WASWebAppProxy): Server side connection made for GET http://was.mynetwork.net:9080/snoop to 192.168.1.143:9080. Obtaining Response
0x80c00002	xmlfirewall (WASWebAppProxy): rule (CheckForLTPAInRequest): #2 results: 'generated from PIPE' completed ok.
0x80c00002	xmlfirewall (WASWebAppProxy): rule (CheckForLTPAInRequest): #1 aaa: 'INPUT ExistingLTPAValidate stored in PIPE' completed ok.
	xmlfirewall (WASWebAppProxy): Policy(ExistingLTPAValidate): Message allowed
	xmlfirewall (WASWebAppProxy): Policy(ExistingLTPAValidate): anyauthenticated authorization succeeded with credential 'uid=wasadmin,cn=users,dc=ibm,dc=com' for res
	xmlfirewall (WASWebAppProxy): Policy(ExistingLTPAValidate): Cached Authorize entry
	xmlfirewall (WASWebAppProxy): Policy(ExistingLTPAValidate): Authorizing with "anyauthenticated"
	xmlfirewall (WASWebAppProxy): Policy(ExistingLTPAValidate): Authorize Caching is on: absolute
	xmlfirewall (WASWebAppProxy): Policy(ExistingLTPAValidate): Mapping resources using none
	xmlfirewall (WASWebAppProxy): Policy(ExistingLTPAValidate): Mapping credentials using none
	xmlfirewall (WASWebAppProxy): Policy(ExistingLTPAValidate): ltpa authentication succeeded with (LTPA, token=*present*)
	xmlfirewall (WASWebAppProxy): Policy(ExistingLTPAValidate): Cached Authenticate entry
	xmlfirewall (WASWebAppProxy): Policy(ExistingLTPAValidate): Extracted LTPA user: uid=wasadmin,cn=users,dc=ibm,dc=com
0x81600035	xmlfirewall (WASWebAppProxy): WebSphere LTPA v1 FIPS compliant or WebSphere LTPA v2 signature verified
0x8160001e	xmlfirewall (WASWebAppProxy): LTPA attribute name/value decoded from token: u/user:localhost:389/uid=wasadmin,cn=users,dc=ibm,dc=com
0x8160001e	xmlfirewall (WASWebAppProxy): LTPA attribute name/value decoded from token: expire/1218496075000
0x8160000f	xmlfirewall (WASWebAppProxy): Decrypted WebSphere v2 LTPA token: expire:1218496075000$u:user\:localhost\:389/uid=wasadmin,cn=users,dc=ibm,dc=com%121845
0x8160003c	xmlfirewall (WASWebAppProxy): Successfully decrypted LTPA token: expire:1218496075000$u:user\:localhost\:389/uid=wasadmin,cn=users,dc=ibm,dc=com%12184960
0x8160000f	xmlfirewall (WASWebAppProxy): Decrypted WebSphere v2 LTPA token: expire:1218496075000$u:user\:localhost\:389/uid=wasadmin,cn=users,dc=ibm,dc=com%121845
	xmlfirewall (WASWebAppProxy): Policy(ExistingLTPAValidate): Authenticating with "ltpa"
	xmlfirewall (WASWebAppProxy): Policy(ExistingLTPAValidate): Authenticate Caching is on: true
	xmlfirewall (WASWebAppProxy): Policy(ExistingLTPAValidate): Resource "/snoop"
	xmlfirewall (WASWebAppProxy): Policy(ExistingLTPAValidate): Extracting resources using "original-url"
	xmlfirewall (WASWebAppProxy): Policy(ExistingLTPAValidate): Found an LTPA-v2 cookie
	xmlfirewall (WASWebAppProxy): Policy(ExistingLTPAValidate): Extracting identity using "ltpa"
	xmlfirewall (WASWebAppProxy) [XML Firewall Request-Response Type] ore:///dp/aaapolicy.xsl'
0x80e000b4	xmlfirewall (WASWebAppProxy) selected via match 'LTPAMatch' from processing policy 'WASWebAppProxy'
0x80e00077	xmlfirewall (WASWebAppProxy): New transaction(conn use=2): GET http://192.168.1.101:2050/snoop from 192.168.1.114

Figure 21-13 XML firewall logs showing existing LTPA credential being used.

In a real implementation, there would likely be additional steps put in place, such as handling errors caused by an expired LTPA credential on our new rule. (The browser may have been left idle for longer than the LTPA expiration period before sending the next request.) In this case, you would probably want to call the second request rule to generate a new credential. It might be noted that in a real implementation, we would likely not be using basic authentication!

DataPower and WAS Login Forms

We have talked a lot about basic authentication, but another popular form of authentication for WAS-based web applications is the custom HTML login form. Of course, in keeping with the theme of perimeter security for WAS, you might want to intercept the request and produce the login form from the DataPower appliance.

Out of necessity, we cover Web application login forms in Chapter 11. In that chapter, we discussed the requirements for the construction of such forms for POSTing to WAS, assuming that WAS would then do the rest of the security tasks, or perhaps how we might insert DataPower between existing forms to process that same data as a security proxy.

Additional Notes on the LTPA Keystore

Earlier, in our section on keys and certificates, we discussed issues around key and certificate regeneration in WAS v6.1. The LTPA keys are also regenerated by default every 12 weeks (as opposed to the 12 months mentioned earlier for SSL certificates). Now that you've seen how the LTPA keystores are used on intermediaries such as DataPower, you can begin to visualize the problems that could occur should that key regeneration take place.

In fact, two versions of the keys are kept on WAS so that existing LTPA credentials created with the old keys can still be decrypted. So, those keys created on DataPower and destined for WAS will be accepted, but any inbound LTPA credentials to DataPower that were created by WAS using the *new* keys will fail validation. As with the certificate regeneration, the best approach is to turn off the automatic regeneration and script this operation so that the keys are generated and rolled out to the intermediaries at the same time.

The automatic generation of LTPA keystores can be prevented by navigating to SSL certificate and key management→Key set groups→CellLTPAKeySetGroup and unchecking the Automatically Generate Keys checkbox.

Web Services Security

We've spent a lot of time discussing WS-Policy and WS-SecurityPolicy in Chapter 19, and obviously as a Web service-providing platform, most of that applies to WAS. So, we won't repeat the generic topics, but let's focus on a few that are specific to WAS.

LTPA: HTTP Header Versus BST

In the earlier scenario, we showed how DataPower can be used to proxy a WAS Web application by consuming and producing LTPA credentials. In that case, we used the standard HTTP header method to send the token to WAS, which made sense given it was a Web application, but we hinted that the same approach might be viable even for sophisticated technology such as Web services. Why might this be? Many folks assume that given they are doing Web services, the proper approach would be to use a WS-Security Username Token (another form of basic authentication) for claims of identity and Binary Security Token to wrap binary credentials such as X.509 certificates or LTPA credentials. Listing 21-3 shows a SOAP header with the WS-Security header containing the LTPA wrapped in a BST.

Listing 21-3 An LTPA Token Wrapped in a WS-Security Binary Security Token

```
<soapenv:Header>
    <wsse:Security soapenv:mustUnderstand="1"
    xmlns:wsse="http://docs.oasis-open.org/wss/2004/01/oasis-200401-wss-
wssecurity-secext-1.0.xsd">
    <wsse:BinarySecurityToken wsu:Id="SecurityToken-24846c4c-ccd4-4440-
8c4d-8ea41aa02610"       EncodingType="http://docs.oasis-
open.org/wss/2004/01/oasis-200401-wss-soap-message-security-1.0#Base64Binar
y"       ValueType="wsst:LTPA"
    xmlns:wsu="http://docs.oasis-open.org/wss/2004/01/oasis-200401-wss-
wssecurity-utility-1.0.xsd"
xmlns:wsst="http://www.ibm.com/websphere/appserver/tokentype/5.0.2">b7rvnIe
eNPHR8ktaa2mHqFz05//zfQ1AI4In1YPWeJUCFxng4h+rZz9SNLxZVmjVOodVWFz8mr4dgIgRU1
GowLuP1b919dDVeY43wQofG5lxX0B/xX1yNq7M4Lik++TU8ZnyzcrYmPDr2FvFgesB9b7ubFNUA
UyLyRCYBhGcn/MjdPHXr0U43eyjGyLA/h643wz7Y7HBZrExulz6st2yGWTbs2iMwOP8ZCMMJqhx
pCzJilc/0Cs8ypbDvDdth4xNXViBRGMAYzXWcgmIgFQaT/zKPdSCwamFitbNQKyrgnOLNflZKx9
245PvRMbFlyl/ScQHfs454lZ38ogFOaJpU0sX33g2NA+HCHw3Z4OjWYc=</wsse:BinarySecur
ityToken>
</wsse:Security>
</soapenv:Header>
```

Consider your goals carefully. Often the WS-Security approach is viable due to interoperability requirements or mandatory compliance with standards. But if the goal is to simply push the client identity to the backend, there are several advantages to the HTTP header approach over WS-Security:

- **Simplicity**—Placing the credential into the HTTP header could be considered "cleaner" than the resulting storm of XML/SOAP markup that results in placing a binary object into the WS-Security SOAP headers.
- **Security**—Consider that when the identity is placed inside the WS-Security headers, the Web services runtime first parses the message and then passes that identity to the security runtime for validation. So, in essence, you are submitting an unauthenticated message to your parser. (Remember that last chapter on XML threats?) This should scare you, but not so much with DataPower as if this type of thing goes to your WAS backend. When the identity is passed by other means, such as in HTTP headers, the security runtime on WAS is executed first.
- **Functionality**—In the earlier scenario, you saw that when the LTPA credential is passed over HTTP, it is returned to the client for replay. This is not the case when it is

passed in WS-Security headers, as it is assumed that Web services are stateless and there is no vehicle for returning the credential in the spec. The credential is cached on the server side by WAS, however.

- **Performance**—We've already made you aware of the side effects of some of these technologies in terms of message sizes and more complex parsing requirements, which take a toll on performance.
- **Reliability**—Any additional content to the SOAP message must pass schema validation on the backend. If the security headers are unexpected, or if there are mistakes in the XML, this could cause SOAP faults, which means a failed message and the overhead of error handling.

Stripping Out WS-Security Headers

In many cases, the goal is to offload security handling from the backend platform to DataPower. In our earlier scenario, you might remember that we cleaned up the security information by removing the basic authentication header from the message when we were done processing it, before the message passed to the backend.

The same thing should be done in Web services scenarios where you are using the security headers. In fact, DataPower provides a very handy stylesheet in the store directory called strip-security-header.xsl. Just place that into a Transform action before the message is sent (and after the security processing is done), and the WS-Security headers are cleanly removed from the system.

Advanced Web Services Security Integration

There are several predefined policies under store:///policies/templates that are used for integrating DataPower with WAS for Web services security.

wsp-sp-1-1-was-wssecureconversation.xml is a stylesheet used for implementing WS-SecureConversation (WS-SC) between DataPower and WAS. WS-SC is a specification built on WS-Policy and WS-Trust to facilitate secure communication dynamically between Web services, often without the use of common components such as user registries. As you might guess from its conversational nature, it uses symmetric rather than asymmetric crypto operations. It defines mechanisms for creating and sharing security contexts used between endpoints and deriving keys dynamically from those contexts. This is useful for repeated messages between the same parties—to avoid the continual setup and breakdown of crypto artifacts used for traditional security techniques, such as standard WS-Security.

The security context tokens can be created by one of three methods (the third being most common):

- Created by a security token service
- Created by one of the communicating parties and propagated within a message
- Created through dynamic negotiation/exchanges

WS-SC is useful when there are multiple intermediaries who comply with the specification. The session context can be issued by one of the above techniques and used as a temporary ticket between others involved in the message exchange. DataPower and WAS both can interoperate in these exchanges, and this stylesheet would be used as a policy attachment in the Web Service Proxy to facilitate that integration. It identifies the particular requirements on the WAS side for making that integration work. To use it, you would implement this wsp-sp-1-1-was-wssecure-conversation.xml on DataPower and the corresponding built-in policy file on WAS, and then ensure that all key/cert artifacts are in place on both platforms. Two other policy files included under the DataPower store: directory are described in the following:

- **wsp-sp-1-1-was-wssecurity-default.xml**—This stylesheet outlines the basic encryption and signature capabilities required by WAS WS-Security, to either validate and understand messages sent by WAS or to create messages that emulate those sent by WAS. These include an encrypted request message body, a valid signature on the body of the request message, a valid signature on the headers of the request message, and signing/encrypting the body of the response message.
- **wsp-sp-1-1-was-wssecurity-username-default.xml**—This stylesheet is similar to the preceeding policy file, but the policy requires a WS-Security Username Token.

Last Mile Security: Identity Assertion/Propagation from DataPower to Backend Servers

It is common for intermediaries such as DataPower to perform offloaded security tasks, such as client identity authentication for backend servers. But ultimately that identity and message must be passed through or asserted to those backends. This requires the intermediary to send not only the client ID but its own identity as well. Before the client ID and message are accepted by the backend, it must verify that it trusts the sending intermediary, based on a trust relationship. This is true of Web services as well as Web applications. Let's discuss a few approaches for this.

DP-Policy

This is often referred to as "last mile security"; there is a chapter specific to this topic in the WebGUI guide. That chapter shows how to configure last mile security. This involves configuring a Transform action with a stylesheet provided in the store directory. There are two to choose from, depending on whether you are using Public Key Infrastructure (PKI) or Hash Message Authentication Code (HMAC). This Transform inserts a signed DP-Policy block in the SOAP header, which includes a hash of the message body for message integrity.

The backend server would validate the DP-Policy block upon receipt of the message to validate that it is from a trusted intermediary and has not been altered. The WebGUI guide provides sample code to do this verification for Java Web applications (using a Java EE Servlet filter) and Web services (using a JAX RPC handler). Both of these could be used for WAS security integration.

Custom Approaches

The previous approach is a convenient "canned" approach for last mile security. But there are others as well. For example, the client identity can be passed by using an LTPA credential for the client and a WS-Security Username Token (UNT) for DataPower's identity, or vice versa. Virtually any approach could be considered, including custom security credentials similar to LTPA. These solutions should always be audited by security experts and follow the guidelines of being signed, encrypted, and limited in lifetime.

Web Services

WS-Security in WAS supports three trust modes for identity assertion, defined by the idType element in the WS-Security header. The choices are basic authentication, digital signature, or presumed trust. For the first two, the intermediary (DataPower) sends its own credential—usually a UsernameToken or X.509 digital signature. For the third choice, presumed trust is based on something external to WS-Security, such as a mutual SSL tunnel. Of course, the client ID is also sent, usually as a name string, distinguished name, or X.509 certificate. As WAS is a Web services provider, any of these approaches are legitimate.

SAML

Of course, based on its charter, SAML is an excellent fit here. Keep in mind, as we discussed earlier in this chapter, that a TAI or login module may need to be coded with some versions of WAS that do not understand SAML natively.

Summary

In this chapter we took you on a tour of many different options for integrating DataPower appliances with WebSphere Application Server (and stack products) for security. Keep in mind that these techniques are only the basis for ideas to secure your own infrastructure. The correct solution can be determined only after careful discussion and planning by key members of the IT organizations involved. It should be a best fit based on the various products at your disposal, and their compliance with some of the key specifications and standards that we have talked about throughout this book.

Of course we can't recommend strongly enough that integrated security solutions be audited and reviewed by multiple experts in the various areas of security that are touched on—network, Java EE, Web services, key/certificate handling, and others.

This chapter also concludes Part V of our book, which has covered security topics.

PART VI

DataPower Development

CHAPTER 22

Introduction to DataPower Development

As you have now seen, DataPower offers a number of features and functionalities that can be easily implemented in its WebGUI interface.You've seen complex protocol mediation, such as receiving messages over FTP and sending them via WebSphere MQ, done with the creation of a few simple objects and the configuration of a Multi-Protocol Gateway service. You've seen how the Web Service Proxy service can, simply by importing a WSDL, begin protecting the integrity of Web service applications. You have also seen the power of the processing policy and its drag-and-drop editor, including the extensive array of actions such as encryption, digital signature generation, dynamic routing, and more.

DataPower provides these features through a combination of its purpose-built hardware (including cryptographic accelerators and XML processors) and its time-tested and continuously enhanced firmware. In fact, the DataPower appliance is at its core a powerful XML processing machine. It contains an efficient XML parser as well as XSLT compilation, caching, and execution engine.[1]

This chapter teaches you about the inner workings of this architecture and ways in which you can enhance it to meet your fine-grained requirements. It introduces you to the fundamentals, and subsequent chapters will go into more detail with working examples.

Why the Need for DataPower Development?

As practitioners of information technology, you are no doubt aware of the dynamic nature of this industry. Standards are released and extended at a dizzying pace. In addition, as no application exists in a vacuum, integration with other applications often results in having to deal with differing

[1] XSLT, http://www.w3.org/TR/xslt, is the transformation component of XSL, the Extensible Stylesheet Language.

interpretations of specifications. In other instances, integration requires working with applications that have not been written entirely to specification. For example, you could have to change message formats for an individual client that has yet to upgrade to the latest software platforms.

Or in a more practical vein, you may want to simply use the DataPower appliance to perform ad hoc functionality such as message enrichment, cryptographic operations, to transform an incoming message to the schema of another platform, or to generate a customized log of transactions.

DataPower provides all these capabilities and more via the execution of XSLT from within the Transform action of the multistep processing policy. So while many features are available out of the box via the WebGUI interface and the drag-and-drop editor, you may very well find a situation that requires a customized solution, or you may simply want to fully leverage the powerful features we are about to explore.

> **CAUTION**
>
> Be sure that the customized task you are attempting to accomplish is not already available via a WebGUI features. After all, inventing the wheel has already been done.

In this chapter, we present the details of DataPower development, including an introduction to programming with XSLT, XSLT Extension Functions and Elements, XPath,[2] Regular Expressions, DataPower Variables, and the use of EXSLT[3] (a library of extensions to XSLT).

Introduction to XML Technologies

There are many resources dedicated to the understanding of XML and related technologies. The World Wide Web Consortium should be considered the definitive resource for specifications, and its Web site (http://www.w3.org) may be consulted for definitive information. The following sections review some basic XML technologies, such as XPath, XSLT, and XSLT extensions. We assume that you are familiar with basic XML document structure; however if not, please feel free to browse one of the many resources dedicated to its understanding. The XML document in Listing 22-1 is used in the introductions, which follow.

Listing 22-1 Sample XML Document

```
<?xml version="1.0" encoding="UTF-8"?>
<?xml-stylesheet type="text/xsl" href="sayFeeFieFoeFum.xsl"?>
<doc>
     <publication book="Jack and the Beanstalk">Fee</publication>
</doc>
```

[2] XPath is short for XML Path Expressions. Visit http://www.w3.org/TR/xpath for more information.
[3] Visit http://www.exslt.org/ for more information on EXSLT.

Notice that Listing 22-1 contains an XML Document Declaration on the first line that defines information about the version and encoding. The second statement is a processing instruction that defines how the document should be processed, or which XSLT stylesheet should be used to transform it. There are seven types of nodes in an XML document; each type may be uniquely identified and processed:

- Root nodes
- Element nodes
- Text nodes
- Attribute nodes
- Namespace nodes
- Processing instruction nodes
- Comment nodes

So, looking back at our sample XML document in Listing 22-1, we can now see that not only does the document contain the document declaration and processing instruction, but also two elements: doc and publication. It has a root node, which is defined as the parent of the document itself, but it does not actually contain any elements within it. If you look closer at the publication element, you can see that it contains an attribute named book and some text. The text and the attribute are defined as siblings of the publication element—that is, they are independent nodes and not part of the publication node. The book attribute is uniquely addressable, as is the text that it references. The text node contains a text string with the value of Fee, and the book attribute contains a text string of Jack and the Beanstalk. Now that we hopefully have revealed more about XML document structure, let's review some of the techniques used to addresses it. Listing 22-2 shows the XML document with each node labeled.

Listing 22-2 XML Document with Labels

```
<?xml version="1.0" encoding="UTF-8"?>  < - XML Declaration
<?xml-stylesheet type="text/xsl" href="sayFeeFieFoeFum.xsl"?>
                                        < - Processing Instruction
                                        < - Root, (parent of document)
<doc>                                   < - doc node
    <publication                        < - publication node
        book="Jack and the Beanstalk">  < - book attribute
        Fee                             < - Text node
    </publication>                      < - publication node end
</doc>                                  < - doc node end
```

XPath Expressions

XPath was defined as a mechanism to address parts of an XML document. It also provides basic string manipulation, as well as numeric and Boolean operations. It uses a very compact syntax and can quite literally identify any set or a combination of the node types listed previously. In a single word, XPath is cool! However, a word of caution: XPath can be used efficiently and with purpose, or it can be used naively and inefficiently. This is not intended as a complete XPath tutorial—there are Web sites, books, and careers dedicated to that—please refer to those resources if you want.

Let's look at a simple task and see some XPath alternatives. Referring back to our sample XML document in Listing 22-1, what if we wanted to fetch the element named publication that contained an attribute named book with the value Jack and the Beanstalk? The following list shows some examples:

- /doc/publication[@book='Jack and the Beanstalk']
- //publication[@book='Jack and the Beanstalk']
- /doc/child::publication[attribute::book='Jack and the Beanstalk']
- //descendant-or-self::*/publication[attribute::book='Jack and the Beanstalk']

All these expressions return a nodeset containing the element publication that we are interested in. They do so by returning nodes named publication and implementing a filtering construct known as a Predicate Query (the string within brackets, '[]') to examine the book attribute. However, there are some subtle differences in what these statements return and how they go about doing so. The most important differences are in efficiency and the expected results.

Each of these statements begins with a set of XPath Location Expressions that select and return a context node (the current node.) Axes are also used to navigate an XML Document using literal expressions such as child, sibling, and descendant. These operators are evaluated from right to left and may include a rich set of axis and location expressions and their abbreviations, such as those seen in Listing 22-3.

Listing 22-3 Sample Location Paths

```
1) child              - all children of context node
2) descendant         - descendants
3) descendant-or-self - descendants and context node
4) /                  - root node if first, or relative location
5) //                 - descendant-or-self
6) |                  - the union of node-sets, duplicates removed
```

The nasty members of this list of operators in Listing 22-3 are #2, #3, and #5. They use the '//' location path and the descendant-or-self axis. These operations search the entire subtree (beginning with the current context node), looking through all the nodes that follow it. In our simple document, this may be a trivial burden to overcome, but what if the document was a 10MB behemoth and the XPath statement contained not one but many of these XPath operations? Now we are really dealing with inefficiency.

Look out a window and glance at a big tree. When you use the '//' notation, you are telling XPath to search every branch, every twig, and every leaf to satisfy your request, when you could have said, "Go to the first branch, then the third twig, and get the second leaf you find." So, of the four XPath expressions presented, expressions /doc/publication[@book='Jack and the Beanstalk'] and

//publication[@book='Jack and the Beanstalk'] both return the requested node; however, the second searches the entire document and may return additional publication nodes if they are found to contain the aforementioned attribute and value. So while you expected only one, you may get more!

> **CAUTION**
>
> You should never use the descendant-or-self axis or '//' without extreme forethought and caution to avoid excessive and unnecessary document processing.

The XPath expression /doc/publication[@book='Jack and the Beanstalk'] is equivalent to /doc/child::publication[attribute::book='Jack and the Beanstalk'] as is //publication[@book='Jack and the Beanstalk'] to /descendant-or-self::*/publication[attribute::book='Jack and the Beanstalk']. They are just written using axis notation in place of the location abbreviations. You'll find this syntax interchangeable in many XPath statements. If you want to delve deeper into this topic and XPath in general, you are encouraged to seek out one of the many fine resources dedicated to these topics.

XPath also defines a set of core library functions. These are a group of functions that provide the capability to manipulate string, numeric, and Boolean values, and nodesets (parseable lists of XML nodes). You'll find functions to concatenate strings, perform substring parsing, evaluate arithmetic expressions, process arrays, and more.

Namespaces

XML namespaces are used to provide uniqueness to a collection, or vocabulary of XML elements and attributes. When we are dealing with a simple document such as our sample, this is not much of an issue. However, in a real industrial-strength document, you will find elements from multiple sources. You may see WS-Security headers or payroll information from your Human Resources vendor. What if these applications decided to use the same name for an element, and then these elements became comingled? In order to avoid this problem, namespaces were provided to make the various element sources unambiguous. A namespace is simply defined in the XML document, either at the document root or within a particular element. We can add a namespace, mylib, to our sample quite easily. Now the name of the publication element is no longer just publication; its qualified name (QName)[4] is now mylib:publication, as seen Listing 22-4. Although namespace http attributes may appear to reference a well-formed URL, it is important to note that they are, in fact, not used as such. They are simply static strings used to define XML vocabularies, nothing more.

Listing 22-4 Sample XML Document with Namespace

```
<?xml version="1.0" encoding="UTF-8"?>
<?xml-stylesheet type="text/xsl" href="sayFeeFieFoeFum.xsl"?>
<mylib:doc xmlns:mylib="http://Englishfairytales.com">
    <mylib:publication book="Jack and the
Beanstalk">Fee</mylib:publication>
</mylib:doc>
```

[4] The Qualified Name is used for elements and attributes containing both a namespace and node name.

Regular Expressions

We've seen how XPath provides searching and filtering of XML data models. Regular expressions have been used for many years for similar processing of strings. Regular expressions are aptly suited to the searching of character classes, sets of character classes, and patterns such as word boundaries or preceding and following characters, among other string characteristics.

Regular expressions have been implemented on a variety of platforms, and there are differing implementations found. Languages such as Perl[5] have been constructed with regular expression syntax at their foundation. Regular expressions (patterns) in other implementations have strived for compatibility with this functionality via compliance with the Perl Compatible Regular Expression[6] (PCRE) specification. Common browsers such as Microsoft Internet Explorer, Netscape, and Mozilla have created other implementations of the PCRE functionality with their earlier incorporations of JScript and JavaScript. Each currently claims compliance with a standard promoted by ECMA International[7] (an international standards organization) and the ECMAScript[8] specification.

Regular expressions are used within DataPower in many places. As discussed in Chapter 7, "Introduction to Services Configuration," PCREs can be used for the matching of incoming URLs in a Match Rule.

Figure 22-1 shows an example of this use case. Here, a regular expression is created to match URLs that end with .gif or .jpg. Use of patterns on the URL Match Rule implements complex matching rules for the selection of processing policies.

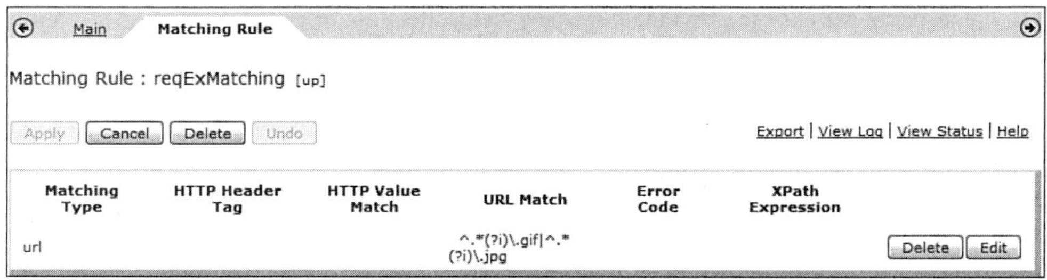

Figure 22-1 Match Rule with regular expression.

[5] For more information on Perl, visit http://www.perl.org/.
[6] For more information on PCRE, visit http://pcre.org/.
[7] For more information on ECMA International, visit http://www.ecma-international.org/.
[8] For more information on ECMAScript, visit http://www.ecma-international.org/publications/files/ECMA-ST/Ecma-262.pdf.

We will shortly see how regular expressions may be used within XSLT, including customized extensions to it such as EXSLT. The EXSLT XSLT function library implements the JavaScript and ECMAScript specifications. Most DataPower functions support PCRE. While they are closely related syntactically, you need to know which version is supported in any given function, and you may need to tweak your patterns to comply with the supported version.

There are many resources available for the study of regular expressions, and it is not our intention to take on that effort here. However, the regular expression in Listing 22-6 is indicative of a typical DataPower use case, the parsing of an incoming URL. It also demonstrates a powerful feature of a PCRE: the ability to capture a back reference, or the contents of grouping parentheses, that is the value of the expression obtained by the portion within the individual parentheses.

Listing 22-6 Typical Regular Expression

```
Incoming URL        http://hostname:port/uri
Pattern             (http://)([^:]*)(:)([0-9]*)(.*)
```

Each of the groupings can be individually identified by the regular expression processor, and are often referenced as $1, $2, and so on. Therefore, in our example, $2 will contain the hostname, $4 the port (assuming it's numeric), and $6 the URI.

XSL Stylesheets

Now that we've completed our basic introduction to XML, XPath, and namespaces, we can use them to construct an XSLT stylesheet. XSLT is used for the transformation of XML documents. The most common case is producing a modified XML document. However, XSLT is not limited to producing XML, and it can be used to produce other data such as Cobol records or comma-delimited text.

It is often useful to think of an XML document as a book, with chapters, pages, verses, letters, figures, and so on. In fact, you may be interested to know that XML is actually an offshoot of SGML[9] defined in 1960s, which was specifically for use with document preparation systems. The process of performing operations for this book involves the selecting of the sections (the sections, chapters, page, paragraph, sentence, word, or the letter perhaps) and the definition of methods to apply to the selected data. In XSLT terminology, a method is known as a template, and we select the data to be processed by applying templates. In both cases, XPath is used to determine the set of nodes to be selected and processed.

Let's look at a simple XSLT stylesheet in Listing 22-7. Now, we get our first look at a stylesheet—it's just XML! It contains a template that matches on the root of the document. Remember from the XPath introduction that '/' represents the document root and establishes the context, or current node for subsequent processing. This template has a single element value-of, which is defined in the XSL namespace. Alternatively, this could be stated as a QName of xsl:value-of.

[9] Standard Generalized Markup Language, http://www.w3.org/MarkUp/SGML/.

This element uses a function named concat, which is defined in the XPath core function library and accepts XPath expressions. It concatenates a string (which may be the result of XPath expressions) and returns a text node. XSLT defines some extensions to the XPath core functions. They can parse an external document, format numbers, and generate meta-data, among other functions. XSLT functions also can return a data model known as a Result Tree Fragment. This is a unique data model that may not be well-formed XML but is treated as a single node. Again, you should consult the XSLT specification for complete information.

Listing 22-7 puts all this together. The mylib namespace has been declared, and the concat function is now referencing the QNames from the sample document:

Listing 22-7 Sample XSLT Containing Function with QName

```
<?xml version="1.0" encoding="UTF-8"?>
<xsl:stylesheet version="1.0"
       xmlns:xsl="http://www.w3.org/1999/XSL/Transform"
       xmlns:mylib="http://Englishfairytales.com">
      <!-- -->
      <xsl:template match="/">
            <xsl:value-of
select="concat(/mylib:doc/mylib:publication/text(), ' Fie Foe Fum, I smell
the blood of an Englishman!')"/>
      </xsl:template>
      <!-- -->
</xsl:stylesheet>
```

Executing this stylesheet against the sample XML document produces the text string in Listing 22-8. It's just a string; XSLT can produce XML or simple unformatted character data.

Listing 22-8 Sample XML Transformed by Sample XSLT

```
Fee Fie Foe Fum, I smell the blood of an Englishman!
```

Introduction to Extension Functions and Elements

To provide for extensions to the XSLT programming model, the specification allows implementers to extend XSLT. There are two types of extensions: Extension Elements, which reside as elements in their own right within the stylesheet, and Extension Functions, which like other functions, are called from within XPath expressions.

There are three types of elements that can be written in an XSLT stylesheet, as presented in Table 22-1.

Table 22-1 XSLT Element Types

Element Type	Description
Result elements	Emitted directly into the result set, defined in any namespace
XSL elements	Defined by their namespace, xmlns:xsl="http://www.w3.org/1999/XSL/Transform, and acted on as instructions
Extension elements	Customized instruction elements

In order to use an extension element, we have to tell the XSLT processor that the namespace associated with it is intended to be used as an extension and not a literal result element. We want to execute the element rather than just write it out to the result set. We do this by the use of the extension-element-prefixes attribute of the xsl:stylesheet element. We can extend our sample stylesheet to prepare for the execution of an extension element defined with the dp prefix by adding extension-element-prefixes="dp" to the stylesheet declaration. The dp prefix is used with DataPower extension functions as we will soon see, and any element that begins with dp: is processed as an extension associated with the http://www.datapower.com/extensions namespace. This definition is seen in Listing 22-9.

Listing 22-9 Sample XSLT with Extension Element Prefix

```
<xsl:stylesheet xmlns:xsl="http://www.w3.org/1999/XSL/Transform"
version="1.0"
xmlns:dp="http://www.datapower.com/extensions"
extension-element-prefixes="dp">
</xsl:stylesheet>
```

We demonstrated the use of the concat XSLT core library function call in our sample XSLT stylesheet, and we can see it again in Listing 22-10.

Listing 22-10 XSLT Function within XPath

```
<xsl:value-of select="concat(/mylib:doc/mylib:publication/text(), ' Fie Foe
Fum, I smell the blood of an Englishman!')"/>
```

If we want to extend the XSLT processor with our own extension function, all that needs to be done is to prefix the function name with a defined namespace. Functions without a namespace prefix, or more specifically without a ':', are known as NCName functions. NCName simply stands for no colon name and when used as a function represents functions within the XSLT core function library. Therefore, any non-NCName function is assumed to be an extension function declared within the associated namespace. If we want to override the implementation of concat, we would use a non-NCName function such as mylib:concat. That is all that has to be done—well, that and implementing the function within the XSLT processor, of course.

Introduction to EXSLT Extension Function and Elements

EXSLT is a widely utilized collection of extensions for XSLT. It is supported by a community of people and organizations who have contributed implementations of functions and features they feel are worthwhile. Its wide distribution means many XSLT processors implement its extensions either by importing packages or rewriting implementations while conforming to its extension signatures.

EXSLT extensions provide quite a few extensions to support dates and times, math, regular expressions, string manipulation, and others. DataPower does not support all EXSLT extensions, but most of the date and time extensions are implemented, as are several of the string and other types. You'll find the supported EXSLT extensions in the DataPower Extension Elements and Functions Catalog documentation available from the DataPower Documentation and Firmware Web site at https://www14.software.ibm.com/iwm/web/swg-datapower/index.shtml.

Introduction to DataPower Extension Functions and Elements

DataPower has defined a large set of extension functions and elements within the implementation of its XSLT 1.0 compliant processor. Each of these is described within the DataPower Extension Elements and Functions Catalog. Earlier we discussed the power of the DataPower WebGUI and the ease with which complex actions such as encryption and decryption could be performed using its powerful tools, such as the drag-and-drop Policy Editor. Now, we can discuss how those actions are really performed. They utilize extension elements and functions that are implemented in DataPower firmware. These extensions leverage the purpose-built hardware, including cryptographic and XML accelerators, to perform these actions. Now you can execute XSLT that also interacts directly with these functions.

While the cryptographic extensions may pique your curiosity with their gee-wiz factor, you'll probably find that you'll use many of the more nuts-and-bolts extensions more often. You'll find extensions to parse and serialize XML, control protocol headers (including accessing, adding, and removing), and to write messages to the log system. You'll also find extensions to provide access to the range of protocols supported by the Multi-Protocol Gateway. If you've read Chapter 9, "Multi-Protocol Gateway," you know that it supports a wide range of protocols, including FTP, NFS, HTTP, HTTPS, WebSphere MQ, and WebSphere JMS. You can use extensions to perform your own protocol level I/O.

We demonstrate several extensions in the following chapters; however, before you start writing your own XSLT, let's take a minute to review what you'll find in the DataPower Extension Elements and Functions Catalog. Each extension is described in the fashion presented in Listing 22-11. This example is for the xset-target extension element, which is used for the setting of backend endpoints in a dynamic routing implementation. Some extensions may be limited to a particular hardware platform, and if so, you will be warned of that. More practical issues, such as the number and type of attributes are defined, as is the return type. You will note that no return type is described for this extension because it is an extension element. Remember that extension elements act as execution instructions; extension functions return data.

Listing 22-11 Sample DataPower Extension Documentation, (abbreviated)

```
xset-target
Specifies a server-side recipient of a client request.

Availability
XA35, XS40, XI50

Namespace Declaration
xmlns:dp="http://www.datapower.com/extensions" extension-element-
prefixes="dp"

Syntax
<dp:xset-target host="hostName" port="portNumber" ssl="true()" | "false()"
sslid="sslProxyProfile"/>

Attributes
host="hostName" (xs:string) Provides the IP address or host name of the
target server.
port="portNumber" (xs:double) Provides the port number of the target
server.

ssl="true()" | "false()" (xs:boolean) Indicates whether the connection to
the target server is secure (SSL-enabled). "true()" Specifies a secure
connection to the target server. "false()" Specifies a nonsecure connection
to the target server.

sslid="sslProxyProfile" (xs:string) Specifies the SSL Proxy Profile to use
to establish the secure connection. This attribute is required when the ssl
attribute is true(); otherwise, it is not used.
```

The actual documentation also contains guidelines for using the element or function and an example. These have been left out of this example for the sake of brevity, and you are again referred to the DataPower Extension Elements and Functions Catalog for complete details.

Putting It All Together

Now that we have presented the necessary technologies, it's time to roll up our sleeves and get to work. There are several integration points in DataPower where you can leverage XSLT and the extensions. You'll find opportunities in the creation of Authentication and Authorization and Auditing (AAA) Policies, for example. But the most likely implementation is in the execution of a Transform or Filter action within a Processing Policy. The Transform action may be used for purposes other than transforming the message, so don't let the name confuse you. It can also be use to set metadata such as protocol headers, write messages to the system log, write to the file system, perform I/O, and more. If you are unfamiliar with the basics of the Processing Policy, you are encouraged to read Chapter 7. Transform actions are executions of XSLT and have many uses. You may need to enrich the incoming message, or you may need to transform the message to a different schema.

We will use as an illustrative example the setting of a dynamic port for backside communication to a service. If you have read the chapters on DataPower service configuration, you will remember that a service may be configured to use a static, hardcoded backend URL. Alternatively, the service may determine the backend at execution time via the execution of the set-route, or its cousin the xset-route extension functions. It is also possible to set the dynamic route via the Route action of a processing policy. We are forsaking that option in this case to demonstrate DataPower extension function capabilities.

First of all, the incoming URL will be fetched from a DataPower service variable. (We will learn much more about these variables in the following chapters.) It will then be interrogated using an EXSLT regular expression extension element to extract the host from the URL. You can see in Figure 22-2 the configuration of our sample XML Firewall; the Firewall Type has been set to Dynamic Backend and a Processing Policy of SetDynamicBackEnd has been defined. The service has been set to accept incoming traffic on port 4002.

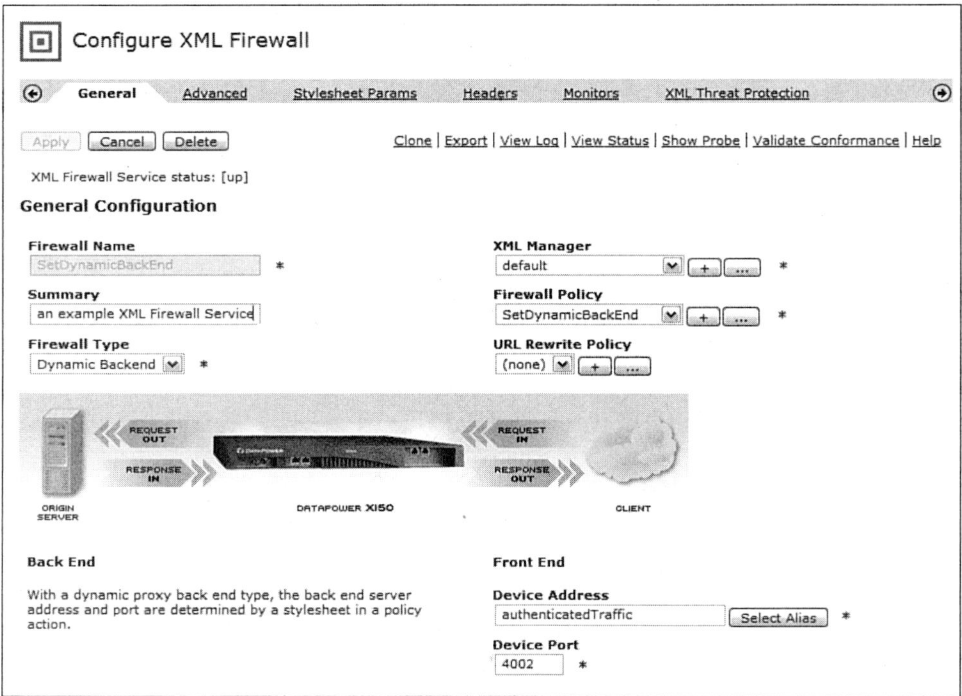

Figure 22-2 XML Firewall with dynamic routing.

The Processing Policy shown in Figure 22-3 consists of three actions. First is the Match Rule, which determines transactions processed by this request side rule. Next is the Transform action, which contains the XSLT as mentioned. Last, a Result action, which sends the incoming message to the dynamically determined backend.

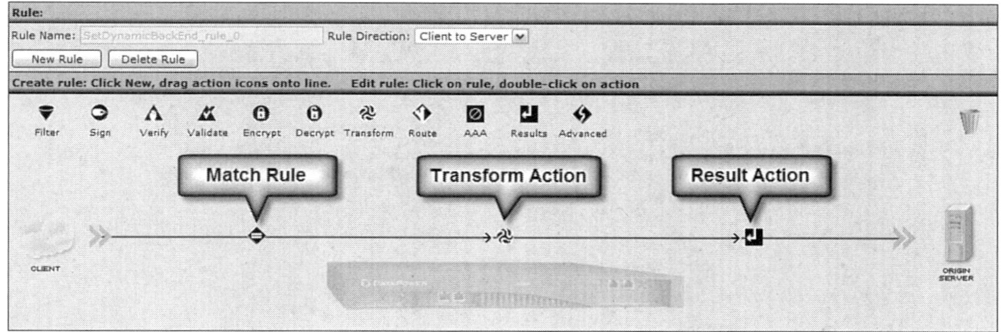

Figure 22-3 Processing Policy with Transformation action.

Figure 22-4 shows the details of the Transform action. It's pretty straightforward—you basically specify the XSLT to process. However, one twist (and again you really need to read the Chapter 7 for this) is the use of the Input and Output contexts. These properties control what the stylesheet will use as its input document, and where the output it produces will be stored. You may not need to access a document as is the case with our example; therefore, we've selected Input and Output contexts of NULL. If we are producing a message to be sent to the backend, modifying the incoming message, transforming the input to another schema, or perhaps adding WS-Security headers, then we must write the modified message to a new context. But if we are only performing functions such as setting the dynamic endpoint, then we do not need to create an Output or read an Input context, and we can set the properties to NULL. This serves a twofold advantage: First, it is more efficient as an input context is not parsed and an additional context is not produced; second, it makes the policy easier to read and comprehend as the intentions of the action are more explicit.

> **TIP—Use NULL as OUTPUT Context when Action Produces No Output**
>
> When not producing an output message (context), use NULL as the Output context to avoid extra processing and to self-document the Transform action functionality.

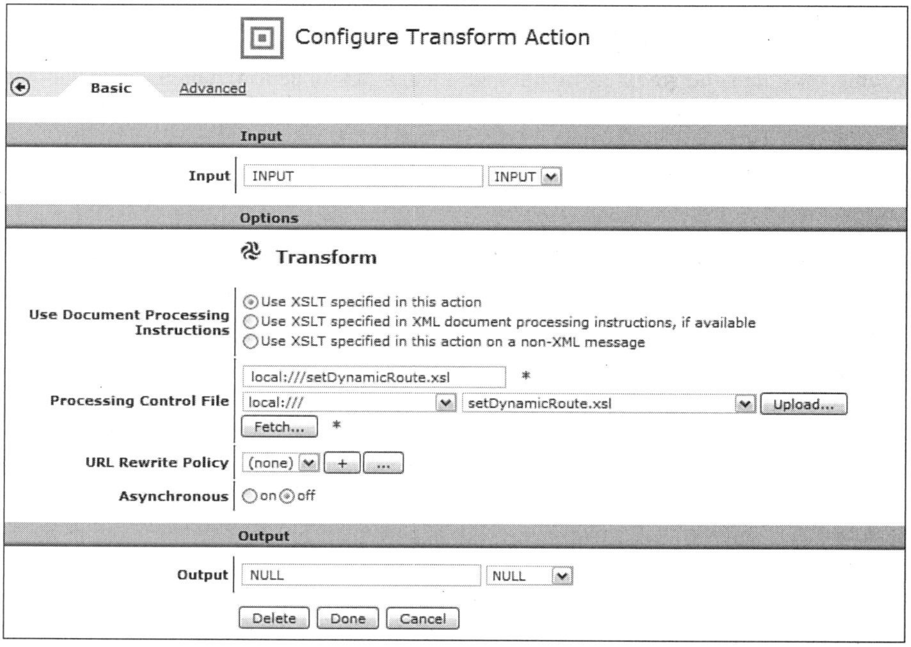

Figure 22-4 Transform action.

Now let's dive into the actual code, where the rubber meets the road (or firmware, more appropriately). Listing 22-12 shows all the XSLT that is required. First the DataPower and EXSLT namespaces are declared. You only need to declare what you are using in the specific stylesheet. Next, the elements that will be presented in these namespaces are declared as extension elements, to differentiate them from the literal result. Finally, to avoid having the XSLT processor writing out our DataPower namespace elements in the result set (output document), we use the exclude-result-prefixes attribute to suppress this.

Getting into the actual XSLT code, the first action performed is to extract the incoming URL by using the DataPower extension function dp:variable. The root template (that template with a '/' match) is always executed even if the input context is NULL. We will take a closer look at this and other elements and functions in the coming chapters, but for now all you need to know is that it gets the incoming URL and stores it in the XSL variable named URL.

Next, an EXSLT extension element, regex:replace, is used to get the hostname from the URL. It takes a PCRE expression and a string as input. Referring back to the introduction of regular expressions, each group (the pattern elements within parentheses) is available in a back reference expression. In this case we are interested in the second group, that section of the URL which falls after the '//' and before a ':'. This pattern would fail if there was no colon (no port), but we are not so much interested in the pattern here as we are in how they are employed.

It's always a good idea to leave a trail of what you are doing, both from a debugging and from an auditing prospective. This is accomplished in this example by using the xsl:message element. This is an element of the XSLT core library, but DataPower has extended it by the implementation of a couple attributes: dp:priority, which specifies the log level for the emitted message, and dp:type, which can be used to specify a log category. You'll find all sorts of information on logging and log targets in Chapter 14, "Logging and Monitoring." But in this example, we've set the log level to info and written a message to the log that is constructed via the XSLT core library concat function. Notice that the XSL variable destinationHost is prefixed with a '$' in the standard XPATH notation.

Finally, we set the dynamic backend via the xset-route extension element. This is not the only way to do this, and again you'll find more examples in the following chapters. But as our intention is to change the port assignment, we do so by using a string literal, and once again referring to the destinationHost that was extracted from the incoming URL. The remainder of the URI is maintained; only the host and port are modified.

Listing 22-12 setDynamicRoute.xsl Stylesheet

```
<! - ->
<xsl:stylesheet xmlns:xsl="http://www.w3.org/1999/XSL/Transform"
version="1.0"
    xmlns:dp="http://www.datapower.com/extensions"
    xmlns:regexp="http://exslt.org/regular-expressions"
    extension-element-prefixes="dp regexp"
    exclude-result-prefixes="dp">
    <! - ->
    <xsl:template match="/">
        <! - ->
        <! - Get the URL ->
        <! - ->
        <xsl:variable name="URL" select="dp:variable('var://service/URL-
in')"/>
        <! - ->
        <! - Get the host ->
        <! - ->
        <xsl:variable name="destinationHost">
            <xsl:value-of
select="regexp:replace($URL,'(http://)([^:]*)(:)([0-9]*)(.*)','','$2')"/>
        </xsl:variable>
        <! - ->
        <! - Tell the log what you are doing ->
        <! - ->
        <xsl:message dp:priority="info">
            <xsl:value-of select="concat('setDynamicRoute.xsl, setting
dynamic route to host(', $destinationHost, ',) hardcoded port 4001')"/>
        </xsl:message>
        <! - ->
        <! - Set the route to port 4001 ->
        <! - ->
        <dp:xset-target host="$destinationHost" port="'4001'"
ssl="false()"/>
        <! - ->
    </xsl:template>
</xsl:stylesheet>
```

In order to exercise our example, we simply send a request to the port exposed by the XML Firewall, port 4002. Listing 22-13 shows this being done (by submitting a document via cURL) and the results displayed.

Listing 22-13 Executing Dynamic Routing Request

```
curl  -data-binary @fee.soap http://192.168.1.35:4002
<?xml version="1.0" encoding="UTF-8"?>
<doc>
 <publication book="Jack and the Beanstalk">Fee</publication>
</doc></soapenv:Envelope>
```

It's always a good idea to check the log to ensure that we've accomplished our goals. And in Figure 22-5, we've done just that. This log display is at the info level to prune out some of the less interesting details that are emitted at the debug level. However, you can see the complete execution of the transaction (it's read from the bottom up), from the initial reception, to the selection of the policy and rule based on the match. Next we see the execution of our stylesheet. Each time a stylesheet is executed, DataPower checks to ensure that the compiled version is up to date with respect to the source code, and if not it will be recompiled. Finally, we see our message and the POST being made to the dynamically chosen backend.

time	category	level	tid	dir	client	msgid	message
09:54:42	latency	info	20929		192.168.1.108	0x80e00073	xmlfirewall (SetDynamicBackEnd): Latency: 0 0 0 1 1 0 0 1 2 2 2 2 2 0 0 0 [http://192.168.1.35:4001/]
09:54:42	xmlfirewall	info	20929	<	192.168.1.108	0x80e000b3	xmlfirewall (SetDynamicBackEnd): No match from processing policy 'SetDynamicBackEnd' - default rule selected.
09:54:42	multistep	info	20929	>	192.168.1.108	0x80c00002	xmlfirewall (SetDynamicBackEnd): rule (SetDynamicBackEnd_rule_0): #2 results: 'generated from INPUT results stored in OUTPUT' completed ok.
09:54:42	multistep	info	20929	>	192.168.1.108	0x80c00002	xmlfirewall (SetDynamicBackEnd): rule (SetDynamicBackEnd_rule_0): #1 xform: 'Transforming INPUT with local:///setDynamicRoute.xsl results stored in NULL' completed ok.
09:54:42	xsltmsg	info	20929	>	192.168.1.108	0x80000001	xmlfirewall (SetDynamicBackEnd): setDynamicRoute.xsl, setting dynamic route to host(192.168.1.35,) hardcoded port 4001
09:54:42	xmlfirewall	info	20929	>	192.168.1.108	0x80e000b4	xmlfirewall (SetDynamicBackEnd): rule (SetDynamicBackEnd_rule_0): selected via match 'matchAll' from processing policy 'SetDynamicBackEnd'
09:54:42	xmlfirewall	info	20929	>	192.168.1.108	0x80e00077	xmlfirewall (SetDynamicBackEnd): New transaction(conn use=1): POST http://192.168.1.35:4002/ from 192.168.1.108

Figure 22-5 Dynamic backend log.

Summary

This chapter brought together the relevant technologies associated with development on the DataPower device. We discussed XML, XPath, Regular Expressions, the concept of DataPower variables, XSLT, and the actual use case of implementing all these in a Transform action.

You now can invoke your own transformations. But you must use this information wisely. As we saw in the XPath discussion, there are ways to optimize processing and ways to write inefficient code. You need to know what you are doing.

As a final thought before you begin your adventure—always consider that the solution you seek may have already been implemented in the DataPower firmware. A time-tested, optimized solution is better than reinventing the wheel; as we said in the introduction, that's already been done.

CHAPTER 23

Programming Within the DataPower Environment

DataPower appliances offer many features through the use of their graphical interfaces and other configuration methodologies. For example, if you have read Chapter 19, "Web Services Security," you have seen the ease in which confidentiality and integrity checking can be performed via the use of the encryption and signature verification actions. If you've read Chapter 22, "Introduction to DataPower Development," you have also seen how DataPower uses its library of extension functions and elements to implement these features.

You may be wondering why it would be necessary to write custom procedures. The reasons are as varied as the environments in which the DataPower devices are deployed. An application may require a customized logging function or you may be required to perform message enrichment (adding or modifying message content) via a programmatic call to an external database.

This chapter provides you with a detailed investigation of the multistep processing policy and its actions. You'll see examples of code to perform fundamental customization processes such as writing messages to the DataPower log and to its file system. You'll see how to manipulate message contents, to parse, serialize, and transform messages in a programmatic fashion. You'll also learn to regulate message flow, accepting and rejecting transactions, and to controlling protocol headers.

You have the background; you now have the tools, let's put them to work!

Variables and Context

DataPower custom programming may be implemented at several integration points within the configuration. For example, you may need to implement a custom Lightweight Directory Access Protocol (LDAP) process as part of the Authentication phase of AAA (Authentication, Authorization, and Auditing). However, the majority of Extensible Stylesheet Language Transformations

(XSLT) programming is invoked via the Transform action of a Processing Policy rule, or the multistep rule as it is also called. Figure 23-1 shows an example of a rule that contains three Transform actions; they are the final three actions. The selected rule, which has been expanded in the display, is a Client to Server (request) rule. A Server to Client (response) rule with a single transformation is also defined and displayed in the Configured Rules table. The following sections introduce the way in which message data and metadata (context) and system, service, and user-defined data (variables) are communicated within the policy.

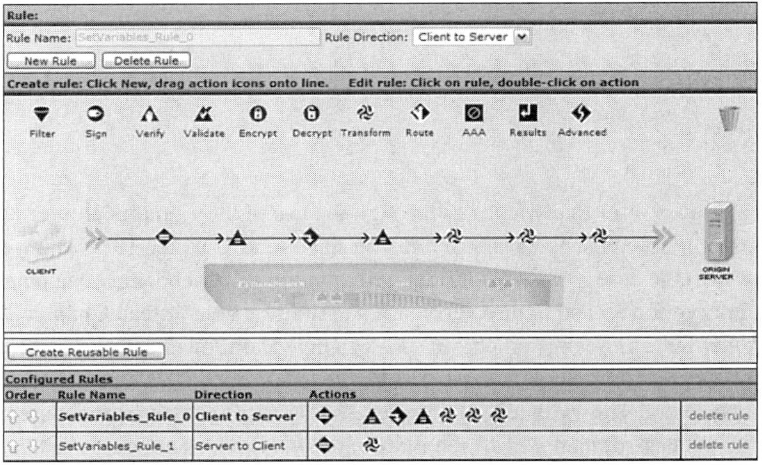

Figure 23-1 Processing Policy rule.

You were introduced to context and document flow in the Chapter 7, " Introduction to Services Configuration." However in order to fully utilize the environment, we need to delve deeper into the way that information flows between the processing policy actions, as this affects what data is available to the XSLT. This is done by passing information within a document structure, known as a context. This contains not only the submitted request message data (if any), but also metadata about the transaction such as content properties, protocol headers, and any attachments that may have been submitted. This data is provided to the actions within the rule, and they, in turn, may create new contexts. This allows for multiple active contexts within a rule. You could have an INPUT context, a signedInput context, and so on. In Figure 23-2, one of the Transform actions from the rule is shown; it uses INPUT as the input context and NULL as the output. (We talk about these contexts later.)

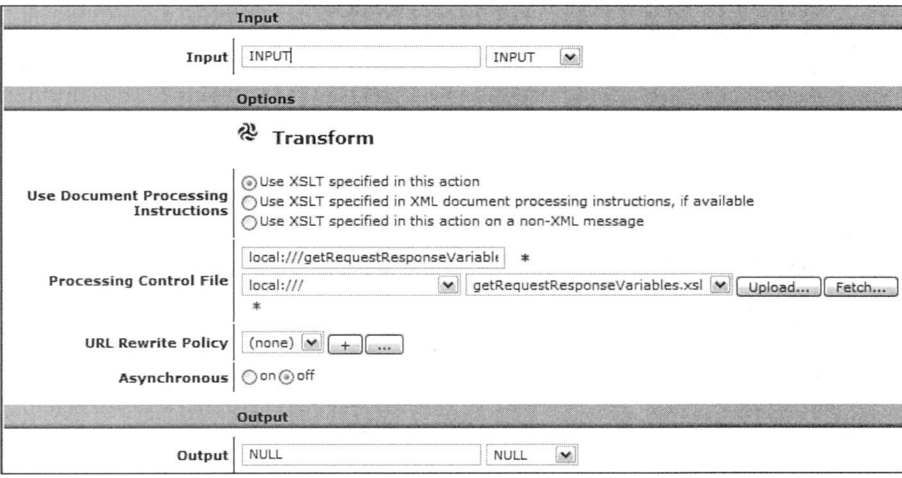

Figure 23-2 Sample input and output context assignments.

The context may be modified within each processing action. Context flow is not necessarily contiguous, and each action may access any of the previously created contexts. Figure 23-3 demonstrates this principle with two transform actions, each accessing the original request context (INPUT) and producing unique contexts (OutPutA and OutPutB) that may be accessed by subsequent actions within the policy rules. This provides the ability to enhance the context (perhaps adding a digital signature) and then the ability to access the modified content (perhaps to write the signed context to a database) after intervening actions have been performed.

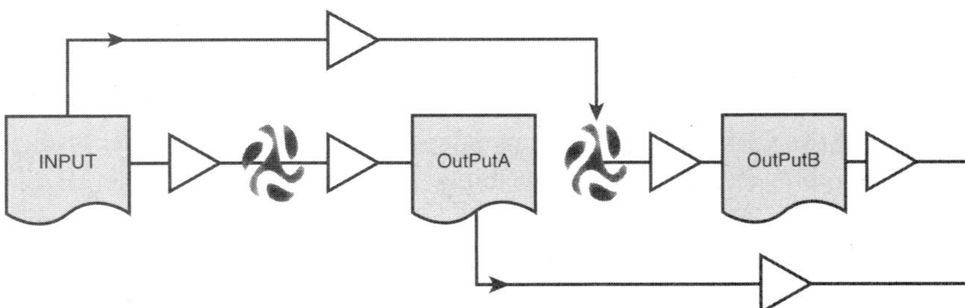

Figure 23-3 Document flow within a rule.

System, Service, and User-Defined Variables

Additionally, important information about the device, the service, and the transaction may be obtained and set via *variables* that are accessible from XSLT. User-defined variables may also be created. Each of these classes of variables is unique in scope (lifespan) and accessibility. Each variable is identified by a naming convention that begins with var:// and may be accessed and set within DataPower extensions. They may also be set graphically via a Set Variable action in a multistep policy.

One class of variables is the Service variables, which define characteristics of the service associated with the current transaction. These variables are available to all actions within the policy to read and some to modify, but new service variables cannot be created. They take the form of var://service/{VariableName}. For example, var://service/multistep/input-context-name is used to access the name of the input context of the current multistep action. While not required, service variables typically are defined in a multi-tiered fashion for organizational purposes as in the previous example.

While service variables allow for the definition and access of service information, system variables provide a similar capability for system-wide metadata. However, while service variables exist only for the duration of the transaction, system variables are long lived. They take the form of var://system/{VariableName}. These variables exist until explicitly assigned a null value, and for that reason must be used with diligence, or else you risk jeopardizing system resources. One powerful characteristic of system variables is that they may be accessed by not just the current service, but by any service on the device, at any time. System variables require a minimum three-tiered URI such as var://system/globalContext/timeOfLastRequest.

A complete list of service and system variables is available in the Extension Functions and Elements Catalog available from the DataPower documentation site.[1] You should definitely become familiar with this resource; it's well-organized and presents valuable information on each variable, including whether the variable is read-only, write-only, or read-write.

User variables (variables that you create) can be created as local to a particular context and accessible only when that context is assigned as the input of a processing action. For example, var://local/LocalVariable defines a variable named LocalVariable. If set, it will be written to the output context specified on the action. This may be the same as the input or it may be a new or existing context. But the point here is the variable LocalVariable can be accessed only when the context it was created in is used as the input context. For example, consider a Transform action that reads the original INPUT context and creates a local variable in a new context named newContext. The local variable created will be accessible only to subsequent actions that define newContext as their input.

Named context variables are created in an independent context, and are accessible from any action within the multistep rule, including across request, response, and error phases. For example, var://context/myContext/ContextVariable, defines a variable named ContextVariable within the myContext context. You can define any number of variables within a context. The context can be newly defined, or one of the contexts previously created within the multistep rule.

While the local and context variable examples used a single level (after var://context/{contextName}) variable name, additional levels can be used. You can use this as a technique for variable organization. For example, var://context/myContext/Routing/CurrentEndPoint and var://context/myContext/Routing/PreviousEndpoint are also acceptable context variable names.

[1] https://www14.software.ibm.com/iwm/web/swg-datapower/index.shtml.

TIP—Use Context Variables for Most Variable Use Cases

Use context variables unless you specifically want a local variable tied directly to a context and accessible only from that context. Context variables are more powerful and less restrictive than local variables.

Variables may be set via XSLT using the DataPower dp:set-variable extension element and read via the dp:variable() extension function. The statements in Listing 23-1 show the assignment of a string to var://local/LocalVariable, and the reading of this variable into an XSL variable. You should note that this does not represent a single XSLT use case; you cannot read a local variable and then fetch it in the same XSLT! Please take care to notice the double quote, single-quote notation in this example. This extension accepts an XPath statement, and using the inner single quote defines this as a string. You can refer to Chapter 22 for more information on XPath.

Listing 23-1 Set-Variable Extension Function

```
<dp:set-variable name="'var://local/LocalVariable'" value="'Local variables
stick with their context!'"/>
...
<xsl:variable name="LocalVariable"
select="dp:variable('var://local/LocalVariable')"/>
```

Variable access is not limited to XSLT, however. The Set Variable action (found within the advanced icon) may be used as well, and Figure 23-4 demonstrates this alternative method. One advantage to this approach is that you do not have to look into XSLT to see what variables are being set. The downside is that you can set only a single variable per Set Variable action.

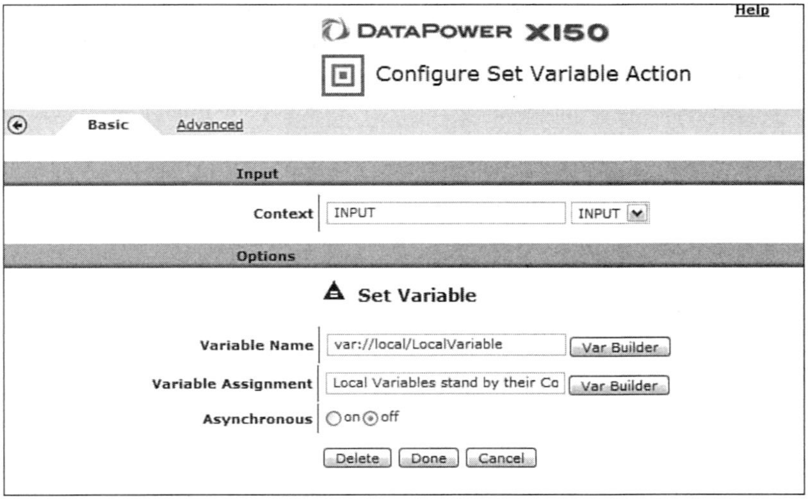

Figure 23-4 Set Variable action.

The Set Variable action also provides a Variable Builder button that takes the guesswork out of variable assignment. It displays all the service, extension, and system variables that may be used as the target or source of set requests (some variables are read-only or write-only as will be noted) and provides input fields for the creation of context variables. Notice that the Var Builder does not provide for a way to create local variables and enforces the preferred context variable. You can see the Var Builder in Figure 23-5.

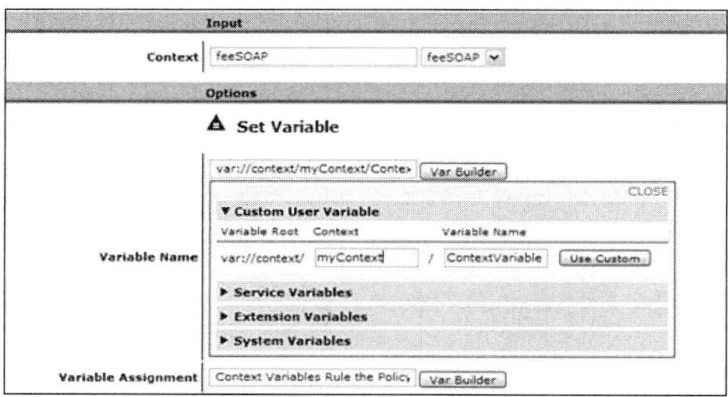

Figure 23-5 Set Variable, Variable Builder.

Variable Usage

Examples of variable usage are as varied as development itself. You can, for example, attach a local variable such as var://local/auditTrack to a context that tracks context modifications. You might use a context variable such as var://context/timeContext/StartTime, which contains the time that a service was invoked. This can be used within any of the multistep actions on either the request or response rule for logging or auditing purposes.

Figure 23-6 demonstrates action context and variable access. The symbol displayed here is for the Transform action. In this case, the action—having been assigned an XSLT stylesheet—is able to read message data, metadata, and local variables from its input context, access and set system, service and context variables, and create an output context that may also include new or previously defined local variables.

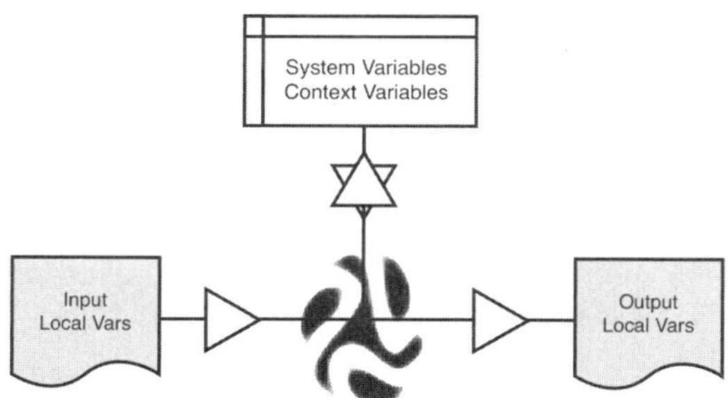

Figure 23-6 Context flow and variable access.

One final note on XSLT utilization of DataPower variables; it may be tempting to use DataPower variables as a convenient enhancement to the immutability attribute of XSL variables. As you may know, XSL variables may not be changed after they are created. Many people struggle with this issue when learning XSLT. However there are metaphors within XSLT such as recursive templates that are well-suited for this problem, and the excessive setting and fetching of DataPower variables may not be the best solution. However it should be noted that DataPower does provide a variant to the set-variable function, set-local-variable that by definition it does not persist the variable beyond the current execution context. It may be considered in those use cases when limited variable mutability is required.

Predefined Contexts

There are a few predefined contexts that you'll need to understand. You are probably already familiar with INPUT. As you've seen previously in this chapter and in Chapter 7, it defines the context of the request. It also defines the input on response rules, which, of course, is not the same as the original input! So a Transform action on a request rule using INPUT sees the client's request. A transformation on the response side sees the server's response.

OUTPUT defines the message sent to the backend server, and every rule that intends to produce a message must write to OUTPUT in some action. OUTPUT on a response rule is the context that is returned to the client.

NULL is a special use case that defines an empty context and can be used when an action does not produce meaningful output, or when it does not read from any previous context. It's an efficiency mechanism as well, as no context processing will be attempted. Even when you use NULL, you'll be able to read system and service variables and execute DataPower extensions.

Finally, PIPE is another special case; it is an efficiency mechanism that describes two contiguous actions that produce and consume a context. The efficiency comes from the second action being prepared to receive its predecessor's output and not going through extra context processing. One side effect of PIPE is that you cannot define local variables within it. So if you plan on this, use another context.

TIP—Use NULL as Output When You Will Not Be Producing an Output Context

Use NULL as output when you will not produce an output context. It's more efficient and self-documents your actions. Use PIPE if two contiguous actions produce and consume a context and no local variables are required.

Writing Messages to the DataPower Log

It is often useful to write messages to the device's log for testing and for auditing purposes. DataPower provides an implementation of the xsl:message element for this purpose. It accepts two attributes defined in the DataPower extensions namespace. The message's log level is assigned via dp:priority, and dp:type is used to assign its log category. You can read more about logging and logging targets in Chapter 14, "Logging and Monitoring." Listing 23-2 demonstrates the writing of a warning message to the default logging target. It uses the xsl:value-of element and concat() XPath function to print out the XSL variables previously established. One interesting XSL attribute of xsl:message (not demonstrated here) is terminate, which, if it is set to yes will cause the current transaction to fail at the end of the current XSLT Transform action. You can use this attribute yourself to force the failure of a transaction, though other techniques such as the use of the Filter action are preferred.

Listing 23-2 XSL Message

```
<xsl:variable name="inputContextName"
select="dp:variable('var://service/multistep/input-context-name')"/>
<xsl:variable name="contextVariable"
select="dp:variable('var://context/myContext/ContextVariable')"/>
<xsl:message dp:priority="'warn'">
      <xsl:value-of select="concat('on Request, Context Name= ',
$inputContextName,
      ', var://context/myContext/ContextVariable= ', $contextVariable)"/>
</xsl:message>
```

Let's put these techniques to use in an example configuration. In this case, Set Variable actions are used to create local and context variables, and a Fetch action obtains a document and places it in a new context. The new variables and context are then accessed by three transform actions that use the same XSLT with differing input contexts to demonstrate variable scope and service variable usage. Figure 23-7 shows the policy. Note that there is both a request and a response rule, and the response also executes the XSLT via a Transform action.

Figure 23-7 Example Style policy.

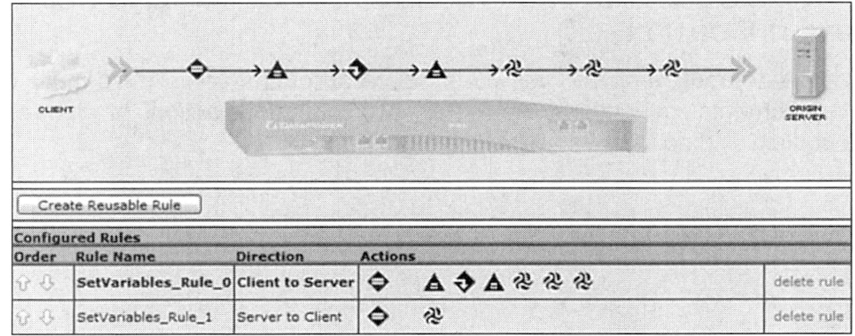

Table 23-1 further describes the actions. Each row in the table represents an action with its input and output context identified. You can match each action in the table to an action in the rules displayed in Figure 23-7. For example, the first action (Set Variable) creates a local variable in the INPUT context. Yes, the output context is named INPUT! Remember, INPUT is just another context name; it is a special one, but it is just a context. The Set Variable action has only an output context. The second action fetches a document from the local directory named fee.soap and places it in a newly created context named feeSoap. The third action is a set variable that assigns a context variable, and it uses NULL as its output. Remember, context variables are independent from any specific named context, so assigning an output context in this case would be unnecessary.

Table 23-1 SetVariables Policy Actions

Action	Input Context	Output Context	Description
Request Actions			
- Set Var		INPUT	var://local/LocalVariable = 'Local Variables stand by their Context!'
- Fetch		feeSoap	Fetches file local:///fee.soap and puts it into new feeSoap context.
- Set Var		NULL	var://context/myContext/ContextVariable = 'Context Variables Rule the Policy!'. NULL is used as output context as this is not a local variable.
- Transform	NULL	NULL	Executes local:///getRequestResponse Variables.xsl against NULL Context, produces no/NULL output.
- Transform	INPUT	NULL	Executes local:///getRequestResponse Variables.xsl against INPUT Context, produces no/NULL output.
- Transform	feeSoap	OUTPUT	Executes local:///getRequestResponse Variables.xsl against feeSoap Context, produces OUTPUT.
Response Actions			
- Transform	INPUT	OUTPUT	Executes local:///getRequestResponse Variables.xsl against INPUT Context of response rule.

So, as the multistep rule is executed and after the variables are defined and the new context is created, the three Transform actions will execute. A single Transform action is also executed in the response rule. The XSLT used in each of the Transform actions, local:///getRequestResponse-Variables.xsl, leverages the DataPower extension functions and elements required to access the local and context variables as we saw in our previous examples.

The point here is to demonstrate the concepts you learned about variable scope and variable access as the XSLT is executed against various contexts. The text of the stylesheet is shown in Listing 23-3. If this is your first look at a complete XSLT on DataPower, hang in there. We know all the techniques it uses! Here are the primary functions of this stylesheet:

- Local and context variables are fetched using dp:variable() and stored in XSL variables.
- The action's input context name is obtained and stored in an XSL variable.
- The dp:responding() extension function is used to determine the rule direction (request or response).
- Messages are printed to the log containing the input context name and the previously fetched variables.
- Finally, the message is written to the currently configured output context via an xsl:copy-of element.

Listing 23-3 XSLT Demonstrating Variable Access

```
<xsl:template match="/">
    <!-- -->
    <!-- get the local and context variables -->
    <!-- -->
    <xsl:variable name="localVariable"
        select="dp:variable('var://local/LocalVariable')"/>
    <xsl:variable name="contextVariable"
select="dp:variable('var://context/myContext/ContextVariable')"/>
    <!-- -->
    <!-- get the Input Context Name -->
    <!-- -->
    <xsl:variable name="inputContextName"
        select="dp:variable('var://service/multistep/input-context-
name')"/>
    <!-- -->
    <xsl:choose>
        <!-- -->
        <!-- Is this a request or response rule? -->
        <!-- -->
        <xsl:when test="dp:responding()=false()">
            <!-- -->
            <!-- It is a request, write a log message with variable
information -->
            <!-- -->
            <xsl:message dp:priority="'warn'">
```

```
                <xsl:value-of select="concat(
                    'on Request, Context Name= ',
                    $inputContextName,
                    ', var://local/LocalVariable= ',
                    $localVariable,
                    ', var://context/myContext/ContextVariable= ',
                    $contextVariable)"/>
            </xsl:message>
            <!-  ->
            <!- If output context is 'OUTPUT', write the message to a
temporary file  ->
            <!-  ->
            <xsl:variable name="outputContextName"
select="dp:variable('var://service/multistep/output-context-name')"/>
            <xsl:if test="$outputContextName='OUTPUT'">
                <dp:dump-nodes file="'temporary:///outputContext.xml'"
nodes="/"/>
            </xsl:if>
        </xsl:when>
        <xsl:otherwise>
            <!-  ->
            <!- It is a response message, write a log message with
variable information  ->
            <!-  ->
            <xsl:message dp:priority="'warn'">
                <xsl:value-of select="concat(
                    'on Request, Context Name= ',
                    $inputContextName,
                    ', var://local/LocalVariable= ',
                    $localVariable,
                    ', var://context/myContext/ContextVariable= ',
                    $contextVariable)"/>
            </xsl:message>
        </xsl:otherwise>
    </xsl:choose>
    <!-  ->
    <!- Now, copy the entire input message to the output stream  ->
    <!-  ->
        <xsl:copy-of select="."/>
    <!-  ->
</xsl:template>
```

Executing a request against the policy (on port 2070), is shown in Listing 23-4. You may have noticed the request document bookQueryRequest.xml; it's the sample BookQueryService request that was presented in the Chapter 8, "XML Firewall." Notice here that what was returned from our SetVariables policy is not the bookQueryRequest, but the fee.soap document that was fetched in our example request rule. It's not the results that we are interested in; this example is about becoming familiar with variables, context, and a few introductory extensions. You may want to refer to Table 23-1 if you want to see that the final request transformation uses the feeSoap context and writes it out to the final OUTPUT context, and the response rule just copies it back to the client.

Listing 23-4 Execution of SetVariables Policy

```
curl  -data-binary @bookQueryRequest.xml http://192.168.1.35:2070
<?xml version="1.0" encoding="UTF-8"?>
<soapenv:Envelope
 xmlns:xsi="http://www.w3.org/2001/XMLSchema-instance"
 xmlns:xsd="http://www.w3.org/2001/XMLSchema"
 xmlns:soapenv="http://schemas.xmlsoap.org/soap/envelope/">

        <soapenv:Header/>
        <soapenv:Body>
                <doc>
                        <fee>enc</fee>
                </doc>
        </soapenv:Body>
</soapenv:Envelope>
```

We have demonstrated the capability to define and access several types of variables. We've put together a fairly complex policy that accesses them, fetches a document, uses an extension function to determine rule direction, references a service variable to get the input context name, and finally uses DataPower's xsl:message implementation to write messages to the log.

Figure 23-8 shows the results of our labor; there are four messages written to the log. A filter of xsltmsg (which shows only the result of xsl:message elements) is used to make the display cleaner. Each message represents an execution of the transformation XLST. There are three on the request rule and one on the response. As expected, the local variable is accessible only in the INPUT context of the request side rule in which it was created, and the context variable is available in all contexts, including NULL, and across rule direction.

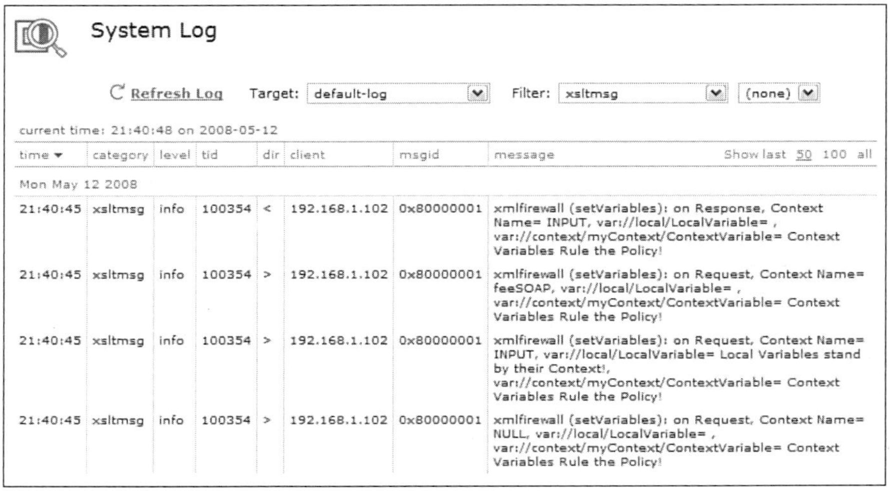

System Log

Refresh Log Target: default-log Filter: xsltmsg (none)

current time: 21:40:48 on 2008-05-12

time	category	level	tid	dir	client	msgid	message (Show last 50 100 all)
Mon May 12 2008							
21:40:45	xsltmsg	info	100354	<	192.168.1.102	0x80000001	xmlfirewall (setVariables): on Response, Context Name= INPUT, var://local/LocalVariable= , var://context/myContext/ContextVariable= Context Variables Rule the Policy!
21:40:45	xsltmsg	info	100354	>	192.168.1.102	0x80000001	xmlfirewall (setVariables): on Request, Context Name= feeSOAP, var://local/LocalVariable= , var://context/myContext/ContextVariable= Context Variables Rule the Policy!
21:40:45	xsltmsg	info	100354	>	192.168.1.102	0x80000001	xmlfirewall (setVariables): on Request, Context Name= INPUT, var://local/LocalVariable= Local Variables stand by their Context!, var://context/myContext/ContextVariable= Context Variables Rule the Policy!
21:40:45	xsltmsg	info	100354	>	192.168.1.102	0x80000001	xmlfirewall (setVariables): on Request, Context Name= NULL, var://local/LocalVariable= , var://context/myContext/ContextVariable= Context Variables Rule the Policy!

Figure 23-8 Execution of SetVariables policy in System Log.

Using the Probe for Variable Display

The Multistep Probe is a valuable tool that provides a graphical display of the contents of contexts within the multistep policy. All of the context details such as message data, metadata, attachments, and system and user variables are available via the device's WebGUI interface. Using this tool gives you valuable information about the characteristics of your policy as each action is performed. You can enable the Probe in several ways. One is to go to the WebGUI Control Panel→Troubleshooting→Debug Probe tab, select the service you are interested in (SetVariables XMLFW in our case), and click the Add Probe button, as shown in Figure 23-9. Now all transactions that traverse this service are captured.

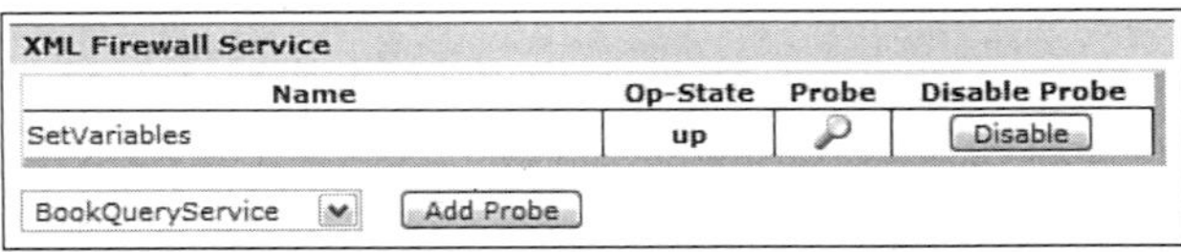

Figure 23-9 Setting Probe from Troubleshooting Panel.

Another method of enabling the Probe is available from the service panel itself. Figure 23-10 shows the Show Probe link, which opens a new window containing the Probe control. Many users find this approach beneficial in that the secondary window created enables you to continue with service configuration.

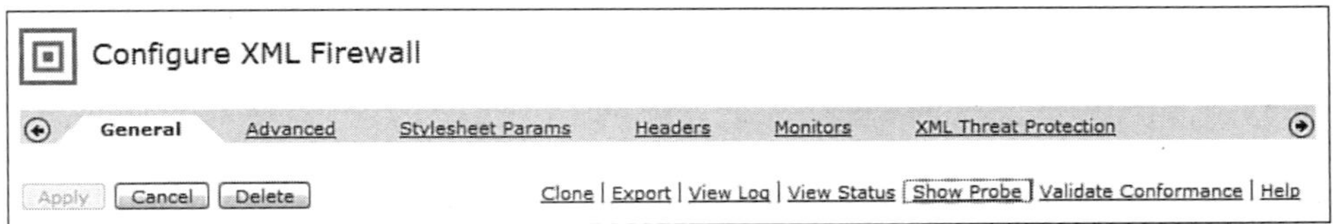

Figure 23-10 Enabling Probe from a service.

An alternative method of setting the Probe is the use of Probe triggers. This is a method that enables the investigation of several pieces of metadata regarding the transaction and automatically turns on the Probe based on this information. For example, if the request comes from a certain IP address or if the request message data contains contents accessible by an XPath statement, the Probe is turned on; otherwise, it is left off. Figure 23-11 shows the Probe trigger screen enabled when the input document contains an element named book; you need to go to the service's object screen (Objects→Services→XML Firewall Service) to set this, and you'll probably need to use this criteria only in selective circumstances. The general methods described via the Debug Probe Tab suffice in most instances.

Figure 23-11 Probe trigger to enable variable Probe control.

Before we go further with the Probe, a couple notes of caution. The Probe is for use only in debugging, and should be turned off during load testing or in a production environment. System performance is degraded with the use of the Probe. Additionally, the Probe creates temporary variables in some instances, such as AAA processing. Make sure you do not rely on these variables in your XSLT. You must test your processing with the Probe off! This ferrets out any such variable dependencies. You can read more about enabling and using the probe in Chapter 27, "Problem Determination Using Built-In Tools." Our discussion here is just to assist you in the DataPower development process.

Executing a transaction against the SetVariables XMLFW and returning to the Probe display provides us with access to captured information. Clicking the magnifying glass (see Figure 23-12) presents the content of the probe capture for the transaction.

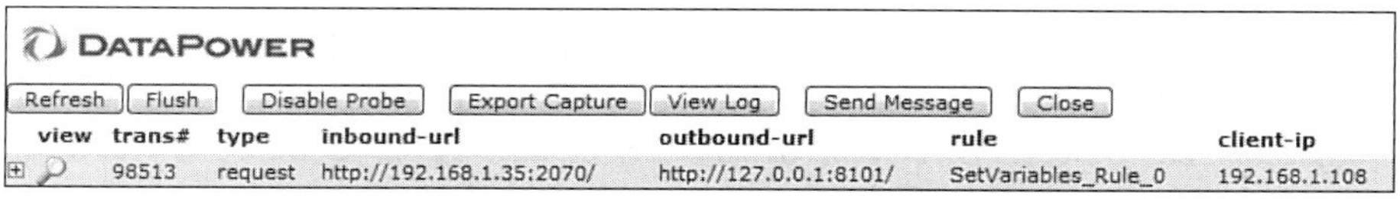

Figure 23-12 Probe list.

Clicking + next to the transaction expands the entry to show both the request and response side of the transaction. If there had been an error that caused an error rule to execute, you'd see that too. You may not see both phases; remember, if the request or response type of the service is set to pass-thru, the policy does not execute and, hence, no Probe is captured. Figure 23-13 displays an example of the request and response rules in our SetVariables service.

DATAPOWER

Refresh | Flush | Disable Probe | Export Capture | View Log | Send Message | Close

view	trans#	type	inbound-url	outbound-url	rule	client-ip
	98513	request	http://192.168.1.35:2070/	http://127.0.0.1:8101/	SetVariables_Rule_0	192.168.1.108
	98513	response	http://192.168.1.35:2070/	http://127.0.0.1:8101/	SetVariables_Rule_1	192.168.1.108

Figure 23-13 Probe request/response.

You can click the magnifying glass next to either entry to begin to display the multistep process. Figure 23-14 shows the initial display of the SetVariables request process. Here, each action is displayed at the top of the panel, and as each action is clicked, or the Next or Previous buttons are clicked, the display presents the context available. In addition to the message itself, you can also view headers, attachments, and local, context, global, and service variables.

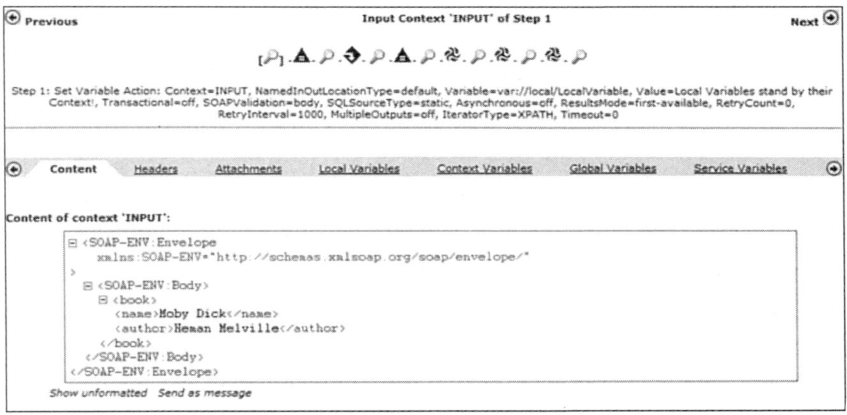

Figure 23-14 Probe INPUT context.

Let's see exactly what is contained in the input context of the fifth step within the rule (the second of our XSLT transforms). In Figure 23-15, the magnifying glass prior to the second transform has been clicked, and the associated context is displayed. In this instance, the Local Variable tab has been selected. Here, you can see the local variable that was set in the first Set Variable action. We can do the same for any of the other actions. You might notice another local variable in the Probe display, var://local/_extension/variables. This is a system-created variable that is a nodeset of local variables that exist in the context. You can use the (show nodeset) button to view it if you like.

The Probe provides a great opportunity to assist in debugging policies and XSLT that is executed within the DataPower system. Using this resource can save you a lot of debugging time and streamline development.

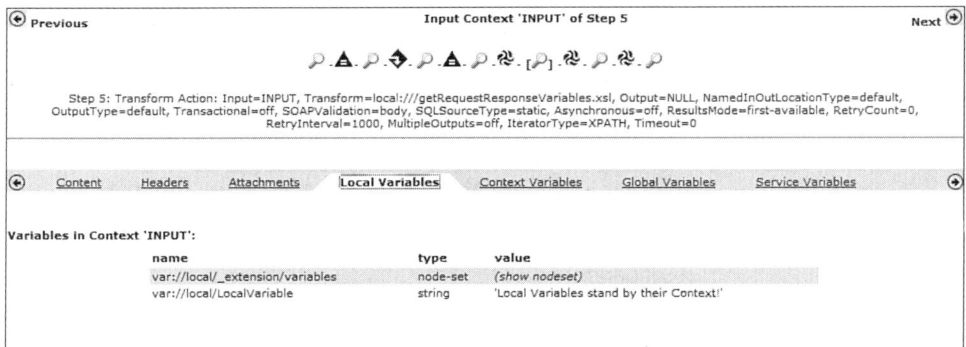

Figure 23-15 Local Variable display of Probe content.

Writing Documents to the File System

It is often convenient to write data to the DataPower file system. This is a great debugging tool, as it allows for the viewing of selective information long after the transaction has ended. However as with every use of the file system, it must be weighed against the size of this finite resource. This problem can be minimized by using the temporary: directory. The temporary: directory is flushed with each reboot of the device, so any unnecessary files or files that you have forgotten about will be removed automatically. You should use temporary: for any such debugging purposes.

> **TIP—USE TEMPORARY: DIRECTORY FOR ANY DEBUGGING PURPOSES**
>
> You should always use temporary: as apposed to local: when doing debugging. It is cleared out on reboot and uses a RAM disk rather than the device's flash memory.

There is a control mechanism that provides some relief from the potential of filling up the temporary file system. These are the Throttle parameters available from Administration→Device→Throttle Settings, as seen in Figure 23-16. Using throttle parameters controls the acceptance of new connections. In the example displayed, if the temporary file system free space is reduced to 20% of capacity (Temp File Space Throttle At), the device will briefly not accept new connections while it pauses (as defined by Timeout) for the file system to be relieved. If the temporary file system free space is reduced to 5% (Temp File Space Terminate At), the device will restart to recapture this file system space.

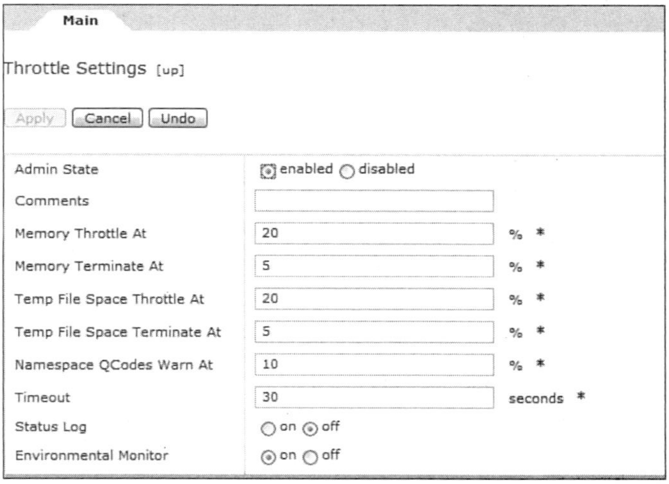

Figure 23-16 Throttle settings for Memory and File Space protection.

Let's go through an example of how to write a document to the file system temporary: directory, and let's make it a little more interesting. This is a good technique for troubleshooting. For example, we can capture the results of the request rule; this is the message data that is written to the OUTPUT context and is written to the backside endpoint of the service. We saw in our previous example that the service variable var://service/multistep/input-context-name can be used to determine the name of the input context for an action. Similarly, var://service/multistep/output-context-name is used to determine the output context, so testing when this is set to OUTPUT provides us with the capability we are interested in.

Let's look at the XSLT that is required. As you can see in Listing 23-5, the xsl:when block that was previously used to determine the direction of the current processing rule is enhanced. First, an xsl:variable is used to extract the output context name from var://service/multistep/output-context-name, then an xsl:if statement is used to test if it is equal to 'OUTPUT'. If this is true, the DataPower extension element dp:dump-nodes is executed placing the contents of the input context (XPath equal to '/') into a file named outputContext.xml in the temporary: directory.

Listing 23-5 XSLT Enhanced to Write File

```
<xsl:when test="dp:responding()=false()">
    <! -  ->
    <! - It is a request, write a log message with variable information  ->
    <! -  ->
    <xsl:message dp:priority="'warn'">
        <xsl:value-of select="concat('on Request, Context Name= ',
$inputContextName,
         ',    var://local/LocalVariable= ', $localVariable,
         ', var://context/myContext/ContextVariable= ',
$contextVariable)"/>
```

```
    </xsl:message>
    <! -  ->
    <! - Is Output Context 'OUTPUT', if so, write the message to a
temporary file  ->
    <! -  ->
    <xsl:variable name="outputContextName"
        select="dp:variable('var://service/multistep/output-context-
name')"/>
    <xsl:if test="$outputContextName='OUTPUT'">
        <dp:dump-nodes file="'temporary:///outputContext.xml'" nodes="/"/>
    </xsl:if>
</xsl:when>
```

Executing the transaction again performs just as expected. The final Transform action, which writes to OUTPUT, has correctly interpreted the system variable and has written the feeSoap message context to the temporary:///outputContext.xml file. Figure 23-17 shows the result of opening this file for edit from the File Management screen.

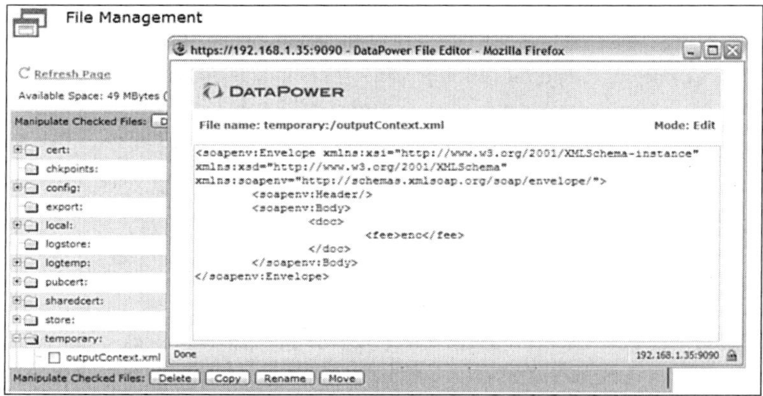

Figure 23-17 File written to file system.

Accessing and Processing Message Context

Our examples so far have dealt primarily with accessing metadata, such as the names of input and output contexts for a given action. There will be many occasions when this information and other metadata information, such as protocol headers, will be all that is needed to implement the functionality desired. However, these examples have not given much attention to the message data itself and have simply used the xsl:copy-of element to blindly copy the input context to the output.

XSLT can do so much more, and there will be occasions when you will want to modify what is found in a request. You may want to change a node's text value, insert additional information (perhaps a username token), or exclude certain nodes from the request. All this is, of course, possible in XSL, and while it is not our intent to provide instruction on XSLT's capabilities (there are so many other resources for that), it will be useful to demonstrate some core principles that will help you in this effort.

Modifying Documents

Let's return to our BookQueryService that was described in the Chapter 8. It receives a request such as the one shown in Listing 23-6.

Listing 23-6 Sample BookQueryService

```
<?xml version="1.0"?>
<SOAP-ENV:Envelope xmlns:SOAP-
ENV="http://schemas.xmlsoap.org/soap/envelope/">
      <SOAP-ENV:Body>
            <book>
                  <name>Moby Dick</name>
                  <author>Herman Melville</author>
            </book>
      </SOAP-ENV:Body>
</SOAP-ENV:Envelope>
```

What if you want to ensure that your friend who is using this service from a known IP address always gets information about your favorite book, such as *IBM WebSphere DataPower SOA Appliance Handbook*, for example. You'll see other examples of accessing message context in Chapter 24, "Real-World Examples of XSLT Programming," but for now this simple example is sufficient to demonstrate some core principles of message manipulation.

First is a simple comment on XSLT programming. This simple technique, if you are not already doing it, will make your XSLT much easier to read and more efficient as well. It relates to the proper construction of templates, match expressions, and patterns. Far too often, for-each loops are used in XSL when a properly formed template would be much more appropriate. This is seen many times, especially when XSLT is constructed as if it were a procedural language rather than the declarative language it is. So, rather than looping though a node, looking for one of interest, it is much more effective to create a pattern that matches the node.

In Listing 23-7, two templates are created to match the name and author; for example, book/name/text() matches the text node of the name node, which is a child of book. Another template is created for the author node. All other elements are styled by the template with a match of '*|@*|text()', which matches all elements, attributes, and text nodes and just copies them.

In this XSL, the client IP is obtained using dp:client-ip-addr() extension function. If it is equal to our address of interest, do the aforementioned modification.

Listing 23-7 XSLT to Change Request

```
<?xml version="1.0" encoding="UTF-8"?>
<xsl:stylesheet version="1.0"
xmlns:xsl="http://www.w3.org/1999/XSL/Transform"
xmlns:fo="http://www.w3.org/1999/XSL/Format"
xmlns:dp="http://www.datapower.com/extensions" extension-element-
prefixes="dp">
    <!-- -->
    <!-- get the client's ip address -->
    <!-- -->
    <xsl:variable name="clientIP">
        <xsl:value-of select="dp:client-ip-addr()"/>
    </xsl:variable>
    <xsl:variable name="friendsIP" select="'192.168.1.108'"/>
    <!-- -->
    <xsl:template match="/">
        <xsl:apply-templates/>
        <!-- -->
    </xsl:template>
    <!-- -->
    <xsl:template match="book/name/text()">
        <xsl:choose>
            <xsl:when test="contains($clientIP, $friendsIP)">
                <xsl:value-of select="'IBM WebSphere DataPower SOA
Appliance Handbook'"/>
            </xsl:when>
            <xsl:otherwise>
                    <xsl:apply-templates select="."/>
            </xsl:otherwise>
        </xsl:choose>
    </xsl:template>
    <!-- -->
    <xsl:template match="book/author/text()">
        <xsl:choose>
            <xsl:when test="contains($clientIP, $friendsIP)">
                <xsl:value-of select="'Bill Hines, John Rasmussen, Jaime
Ryan, Simon Kapadia, Jim Brennan'"/>
            </xsl:when>
            <xsl:otherwise>
                    <xsl:apply-templates select="."/>
            </xsl:otherwise>
        </xsl:choose>
    </xsl:template>
    <!-- -->
    <xsl:template match="*|@*|text()">
        <xsl:copy>
            <xsl:apply-templates select="*|@*|text()"/>
        </xsl:copy>
    </xsl:template>
    <!-- -->
</xsl:stylesheet>
```

Looking in the Probe shows the modified request document. Figure 23-18 shows that the book name and author have been replaced.

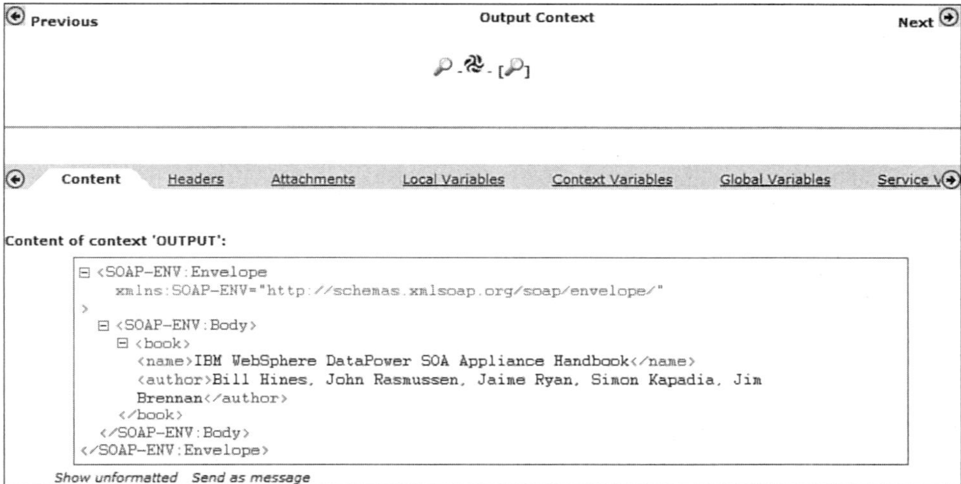

Figure 23-18 Probe display of modified request.

Parsing and Serializing XML

There may be instances when an XML document is received as a text node. For example, it can be contained within the CData section of an XML document, or perhaps as the text of some element. You cannot access the contents of this document using XPath, or any other XML-related methodology because it is just a string. You can, however, parse the string into an actual XML document using the DataPower dp:parse extension element. This extension is used primarily within an xsl:variable element. There is an optional attribute that allows the parsing of a Base64 encoded string as well, and Listing 23-8 demonstrates two examples of its use. Two strings are parsed, one an xml document in string form and one being Base64 encoded. XPath statements are then executed to extract the value of a text nodes contained within.

Listing 23-8 Parse Examples

```
<xsl:template name="parseTest">
    <xsl:variable name="xmlString" select="'&lt;doc>&lt;node>here is the
text!&lt;/node>&lt;/doc>'"/>
    <xsl:variable name="xmlBase64"
select="'PD94bWwgdmVyc2lvbj0iMS4wIj8+PGRvYz48bm9kZT5oZXJlIGlzIHRoZSB0ZXh0IT
wvbm9kZT48L2RvYz4='"/>
    <! -   ->
    <! - Parse the xml string  ->
```

```
    <!- -  ->
    <xsl:variable name="parsedXmlString">
        <dp:parse select="$xmlString"/>
    </xsl:variable>
    <xsl:message>
        <xsl:value-of select="concat('parsedXmlString node text=',
$parsedXmlString/doc/node/text())"/>
    </xsl:message>
    <!- -  ->
    <!- - Parse the base64 encoded xml string  ->
    <!- -  ->
    <xsl:variable name="xmlBase64">
        <dp:parse select="$xmlBase64" encoding="base-64"/>
    </xsl:variable>
    <xsl:message>
        <xsl:value-of select="concat('xmlBase64 node text=',
$xmlBase64/doc/node/text())"/>
    </xsl:message>
</xsl:template>
```

Figure 23-19 shows the results of the parse examples as displayed in the system log. The first message shows the results of using the XPath statement /doc/node/text() on the variable parsedXmlString that contains the parsed version of the variable xmlString. The second log entry (read from bottom up) is the result of converting the base64 encoded string contained in xml-Base64, and again using and /doc/node/text() XPath statement to extract the text node. The results are equivalent as the Base64 encoded string was generated from the text within xmlString.

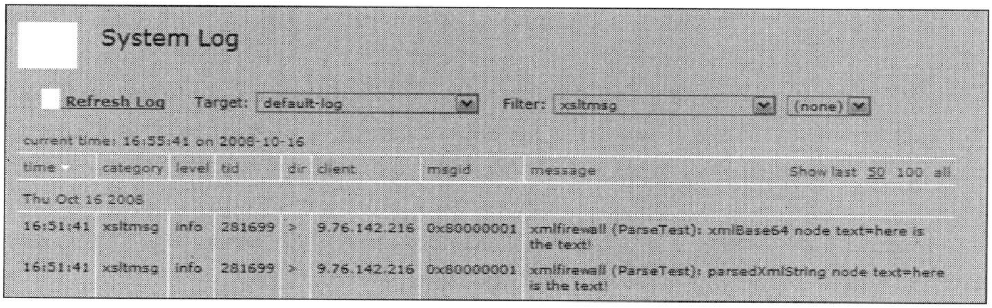

System Log

Refresh Log Target: default-log Filter: xsltmsg (none)

current time: 16:55:41 on 2008-10-16

time	category	level	tid	dir	client	msgid	message
Thu Oct 16 2008							
16:51:41	xsltmsg	info	281699	>	9.76.142.216	0x80000001	xmlfirewall (ParseTest): xmlBase64 node text=here is the text!
16:51:41	xsltmsg	info	281699	>	9.76.142.216	0x80000001	xmlfirewall (ParseTest): parsedXmlString node text=here is the text!

Show last 50 100 all

Figure 23-19 Log display of parse example.

Another example of message manipulation is the serialization of an XML document. In this case, you have a document that you want to convert into a string. An example of this is sending the document context over a protocol such as HTTP, which does not support an XML document model (parsed XML); the document must first be serialized to a string. The DataPower extension element dp:serialize performs this function, and it also can optionally produce or omit the xml declaration normally found as the first line of an XML document. Listing 23-9 displays an example of document serialization. It takes the entire input document using the '/' XPath statement and writes a message to the log with its serialized contents.

Listing 23-9 Serialize Example

```
<xsl:variable name="serializedRequest">
    <dp:serialize select="/" omit-xml-decl="yes"/>
</xsl:variable>
<xsl:message>
    <xsl:value-of select="concat('serializedRequest = ',
$serializedRequest)"/>
</xsl:message>
```

Listing 23-10 shows the results of the dp:serialize element. It has taken a document and converted it into its textual representation. Once again, a document in this context is a parsed representation of an XML string. Serialization is the process of converting it back to a string. You'll notice in the message display that the left brackets, '<', have been converted to character entity format '<'.

Listing 23-10 Sample Serialized Output

```
serializedRequest = &lt;soapenv:Envelope
xmlns:soapenv="http://schemas.xmlsoap.org/soap/envelope/"
xmlns:xsd="http://www.w3.org/2001/XMLSchema"
xmlns:xsi="http://www.w3.org/2001/XMLSchema-instance"> &lt;soapenv:Header/>
&lt;soapenv:Body> &lt;doc> &lt;fee>enc&lt;/fee> &lt;/doc>
&lt;/soapenv:Body> &lt;/soapenv:Envelope>
```

By now, you are familiar with the ability to transform a document via the Transform action of the multistep policy. The DataPower device can also perform transformation in a programmatic fashion within your XSLT. You may, for example, want to look into the contents of an input document to determine a subsequent transformation. The dp:transform extension provides a simple method to perform XSLT-based transformation. The sample in Listing 23-11 shows the XSL necessary; in this case, the $inputNode (a variable containing a parsed XML document) is transformed with a stylesheet contained within the local: directory of the device.

Listing 23-11 Sample dp:transform

```
<xsl:variable name="results">
     <xsl:copy-of select="dp:transform(local:///myXSLT.xsl, $inputNode)"/>
</xsl:variable>
```

Accessing Protocol Headers

There are many occasions when accessing protocol headers is a vital part of transaction processing. Information about the request, such as the user-agent that made the request, can be used to determine the appropriate response format. A browser declares itself using this header, and you can potentially return an HTML document that it can consume. Other HTTP protocol values such as the client IP and content-type are part of the standard manifest of headers that will be received. Other protocols, such as IBM WebSphere MQ (MQ), send headers, such as the Message descriptor (MQMD), that carry not only information about the request type, but details about the queues and queue managers used.

Services allow for header manipulation at configuration time, and we'll see examples of protocol header manipulation in action in the Chapter 24, but for now, let's review the DataPower extension elements and functions available. There are extensions available to get, set, append, and remove protocol headers. There are two basic implementations; the original versions were specific to the HTTP protocol and included the following functions (note response pairs are available for all):

- dp:http-request-header('headerName')—Get a named HTTP header
- dp:remove-http-request-header('headerName')—Remove named headers of all types
- dp:set-http-request-header name="'headerName'" value="'headerValue'"—Set an HTTP header

Newer implementations of these functions were created to remove the HTTP dependency and allow support of the other supported protocols. These include the following request methods (note response pairs are available for all):

- dp:request-header()—Get a named header of all types
- dp:set-request-header()—Set a named header of all types
- dp:append-request-header()—Append a named header of all types

> **TIP—Always Use the Newer Style of Protocol Extensions to Remove Any Protocol Dependencies**
>
> The newer, protocol independent versions of header extension functions work with all supported protocols. The HTTP versions are documented for historical purposes only. You should use the newer version for simplicity.

Listing 23-12 demonstrates an XSL snippet that obtains the value of the Content-Type header. It uses the dp:responding() extension function to determine the phase of the policy, that is, request or response, and issues the appropriate extension function to obtain the header. The returned value is stored in an XSL variable.

Listing 23-12 Header Retrieval

```
<xsl:variable name="contentType">
    <xsl:choose>
        <xsl:when test="dp:responding()">
            <xsl:value-of select="dp:response-header('Content-Type')"/>
        </xsl:when>
        <xsl:otherwise>
            <xsl:value-of select="dp:request-header('Content-Type')"/>
        </xsl:otherwise>
    </xsl:choose>
</xsl:variable>
```

When working with protocol headers, there is an efficiency method that may be employed. When a client is making requests to a server, it cannot write the request stream out until all headers have been written. This delay can be minimized by committing the header stream, which is telling the processor you are finished with header manipulation. This is done by use of the dp:freeze-headers extension element.

The Filter Action

The Filter action is available in all multistep policies. It has a special relationship with two extension elements: dp:accept and dp:reject. These extensions are used to either permit or reject a transaction. The implementation is completely user-defined. In other words, the way that you interpret what is acceptable and what is not is up to you! You can look at protocol headers, message content, metadata, or any combination thereof. You could, in fact, use the dp:accept and dp:reject extensions in a Transform action. However, it is highly preferred to use the Filter action, as this acts as a self-documenting feature of the multistep rule.

You'll see an example of a working Filter policy in Chapter 24, but for now, all that you really need to know is that the Filter action will reject a transaction if the XSLT associated with it emits a DataPower dp:reject element. And while acceptance is not predicated on the dp:accept element, it is a good practice to use one in your stylesheet for auditing purposes. Note that both of these elements can have a body that is written to the log.

Listing 23-13 demonstrates a code snippet that performs the filter function. First the name of the book from the BookQueryRequest is obtained via an XPath statement. Then it is tested to see whether it is equal to 'IBM WebSphere DataPower SOA Appliance Handbook'; if not, the request is rejected! This could, as in all error conditions, cause the execution of an error rule.

Listing 23-13 Sample Filter Execution

```
<xsl:variable name="bookName" select="//*[local-name()='book']/*[local-
name()='name']/text()"/>
<xsl:message>
    <xsl:value-of select="concat('bookName = ', $bookName)"/>
</xsl:message>
<xsl:choose>
    <xsl:when test="$bookName= 'IBM WebSphere DataPower SOA Appliance
Handbook'">
        <dp:accept/>
    </xsl:when>
    <xsl:otherwise>
        <dp:reject>Book != DP Handbook, request rejected!</dp:reject>
    </xsl:otherwise>
</xsl:choose>
```

Routing

Routing is a bread-and-butter operation on the DataPower device, and a widely used procedure. Routing can be performed for a variety of reasons. Perhaps you want to send your high value requests to a set of highly available, redundant, high-performance backend services, and some less critical requests to a less expensive platform. Of course DataPower allows you to do this with the Route action in a multistep policy and in several highly configurable ways. But (maybe you're seeing a pattern here), you can also perform routing directly within XSLT. As we know, the actions within a policy are supported by the extension functions and elements.

Let's look at a couple examples of routing within XSLT. While we are doing so, we will also point out one more layer of detail within the DataPower configuration. We've spoken of extensions and variables, and we've exposed some interesting service variables that allowed us to do things like get the name of contexts, and so on. In many cases the extensions that we use are really methods for the settings of these service variables. The extensions provide a more structured mechanism and remove some of the peculiarities associated with setting the service variables directly. But there may be instances when setting the variables provides a little more flexibility.

Let's see if the examples can make this clear. Our first example in Listing 23-14 shows the use of the dp:xset-target extension element. It enables the setting of host, port, and SSL information. Executing this XSLT changes the backend server address. There is another routing extension, dp:set-target. This is functionally the same as dp:xset-target, but does not enable the use of XPath statements in the attribute assignment, so you will probably just use dp:xset-target in most cases.

Listing 23-14 Sample use of xset-target for Routing

```
<xsl:variable name="ip" select="'10.10.10.15'"/>
<xsl:variable name="port" select="'88'"/>
<xsl:variable name="ssl" select="true()"/>
<xsl:variable name="sslid" select="'someSSLProxyProfile'"/>
<!-- -->
<xsl:template match="/">
    <!-- -->
    <dp:xset-target host="$ip" port="$port" ssl="$ssl" sslid="{$sslid}"/>
    <xsl:message dp:priority="'info'">
        <xsl:value-of select="concat('Setting routing to ', $ip, ':',
$port)"/>
    </xsl:message>
</xsl:template>
```

The next example in Listing 23-15 shows how the same sort of routing can be performed via direct variable setting. In this case, var://service/routing-url is directly modified. This is the core of the routing mechanism and is the variable that the dp:xset-route extension modifies. However, modifying this variable directly allows us to not only change host and port, but also the protocol and Uniform Resource Identifier (URI). You can only change to supported protocols, of course.

Getting back to the ease of use that the extensions provide, an example is a secondary variable associated with routing, var://service/routing-url-sslprofile. This is used to establish the SSL Proxy Profile used for SSL. And it must be set prior to the setting of var://service/routing-url. Using dp:set-route or dp:xset-route does this for you by providing an attribute for the SSL Proxy Profile.

Listing 23-15 Sample Routing-URL Routing

```
<xsl:variable name="newBackSideURL"
select="concat('dpmq://QueueManager/PUT?RequestQueue=', $requestQueue)"/>
<xsl:message dp:priority="'info'">
    <xsl:value-of select="concat('Setting, var://service/routing-url to ',
$newBackSideURL)"/>
</xsl:message>
<! -  ->
<dp:set-variable name="'var://service/routing-url'"
value="$newBackSideURL"/>
```

URL Open

URL Open is an extremely powerful DataPower extension. In fact it rightly deserves the nickname of The Mother of All Extension Functions. If you have read Chapter 9, "Multi-Protocol Gateway," you are aware of all the various protocols supported by the MPGW. Each of these protocols is implemented within the MPGW via Front Side Handlers and Backend URLs. Each of these objects in turn utilizes the URL Open Extension to implement protocol dependant IO. URL Open supports

- FTP/SFTP (File Transfer Protocol)
- HTTP/HTTPS (Hypertext Transfer Protocol)
- ICAP (Internet Content Adaptation Protocol)
- IBM WebSphere MQ (IBM WebSphere Message Queuing)
- NFS (Network File System)
- SMTP (Simple Mail Transfer Protocol)
- SNMP (Simple Network Management Protocol)
- SQL (Structured Query Language)
- TCP (Transmission Control Protocol)
- TIBCO-EMS (TIBCO Enterprise Message Service)
- WAS-JMS (WebSphere Application Server Java Messaging Services)
- IMS (IBM Information Management System)

You can also use the URL Opener within custom XSLT. We will see real-life examples in Chapter 24, but for now let's take a close look at the implementation. Each protocol used with url-open uses a slightly different URL, so you may need to look into the Extension Function Catalog to determine precisely what URL to use. But all protocols share a common format and attributes as shown in Listing 23-16.

Listing 23-16 URL-Open Format

```
<xsl:variable name="response">
    <dp:url-open target="url"
        response="xml | binaryNode | ignore |
            responsecode response code-ignore | savefile"
        resolve-mode="xml | ignore"
        base-uri-node="nodeSet"
        data-type="xml | ignore | filename"
        http-headers="xpathExpression"
        content-type="contentType"
        ssl-proxy="sslProxyName">
    </dp:url-open>
</xsl:variable>
```

The attributes shown in Table 23-2 describe all the potential parameters (attributes), you can use on the url-open element. Most of the parameters are optional; the only required parameter is the target.

Table 23-2 URL-Open Parameters

Parameter	Description
target	Target URL
response	Specifies how to handle response:
	• xml, parse
	• binaryNode, unparsed
	• ignore, discard response
	• responsecode, protocol response is returned with response data
	• responsecode-ignore, only protocol response is returned
resolve-mode	Only used if target is attachment, determines attachment type
base-uri-node	Only if target is relative, used to determine URL
data-type	XML—default
	Base64—input data is Base64
	Filename—local file contains input
http-headers	Optional nodeset of protocol headers
content-type	Optional content-type
ssl-proxy	Optional SSL Proxy Profile to use for SSL

Listing 23-17 shows a simple MQ url-open element. It reads a message from the replyQueue and returns it into the variable "response". The MQ Queue Manager is named QueueManager, and it describes where the actual Queue Manager resides. You can read about Queue Managers in the MPGW chapter if you want. We could have added other parameters to the URL, including timeout values, credential information, and so on. You can read the formal definition of this URL in the Extension Functions Catalog.

Listing 23-17 Sample MQ URL-Open

```
<xsl:variable name="response">
    <dp:url-open target="dpmq://QueueManager/mqGet?ReplyQueue=replyQueue"/>
</xsl:variable>
```

Any data submitted with the request is entered as a child of the url-open element. Listing 23-18 demonstrates the submission of a SOAP request over HTTPS. In this example, the response would be in the $response variable along with the response code due to the use of the response= "responsecode" attribute.

Listing 23-18 Sample HTTPS URL-Open

```
<xsl:variable name="response">
    <dp:url-open target="https://127.0.0.1:5550" response="responsecode">
        <env:Envelope
xmlns:env="http://schemas.xmlsoap.org/soap/envelope/">
            <env:Body>
                <someRequest/>
            </env:Body>
        </env:Envelope>
    </dp:url-open>
</xsl:variable>
```

Summary

This chapter introduced some key methods and DataPower extensions that enable you to perform many different forms of custom transformations in the DataPower environment. We described in detail the manner in which the Processing Policy (multistep policy) passes context and how variables can be accessed and defined. Filtering of transactions, routing of requests, and the ability to create parseable XML from text and Base64-encoded strings have been described, as has the ability to serialize and perform ad-hoc transformation. We have also discussed ways in which to enrich or enhance the message, and to use and manipulate protocol headers.

By now, you have the tools required to handle the corner cases and unique requirements that may be presented to you. Go forth and customize!

CHAPTER 24

Real-World Examples of XSLT Programming

Assuming you have read Chapter 22, "Introduction to DataPower Development," and Chapter 23, "Programming Within the DataPower Environment," you have been introduced to the fundamentals of DataPower development. You have seen the extension functions available to you in the DataPower and EXSLT catalogs, and you are now also familiar with the mechanisms necessary to employ these tools. You also should have a firm understanding of the ways in which document information is traversed and accessed within the multistep policy via its context metaphor.

All you need now is a reason to customize; maybe the examples presented in this chapter will inspire you, but don't customize just for customization's sake! Remember, DataPower has all sorts of capabilities all by itself. Don't reinvent the wheel. But if you need to, you have the tools, you have the power, and you have the technology!

Real-World Examples

This chapter presents examples that explore several aspects of DataPower customization. The following examples are presented:

Example 1: If It's Tuesday, This Must Be Belgium—An example of protocol header inspection and message control

Example 2: Passing Variables to XSLT—An example of passing parameters from the Transform action to XSLT and dynamic XPath execution

Example 3: Error Processing and Control—An example of error capture and processing with protocol response setting and client message creation

Example 4: Dynamic Routing—An example of dynamic routing using a routing XML document and X.509 certificate examination

Example 5: Load Balancer Health Checker—An example of a load balancer group member health check utility based on an Out of Service XML document

Example 1: If It's Tuesday, This Must Be Belgium

We use the title of this 1969 film to demonstrate the ability to control transactions based on the content of protocol headers. In this implementation, the premise is that transactions are allowed to freely execute against a service (we use our BookQueryService) on any day except Tuesday. On Tuesdays, we require that a protocol header named THIS, if found on the request, must contain the value Belgium. If it is not present, the value of Belgium will be used to create the header, which will be passed to the BookQueryService. If the header is present on Tuesday, but has some value other than Belgium, the transaction is rejected.

This fun sample enables us to explore protocol extension elements, DataPower XSLT extensions, EXSLT date extension functions, and some fundamental concepts of transaction analysis and filtering. Figure 24-1 graphically depicts the transaction flow.

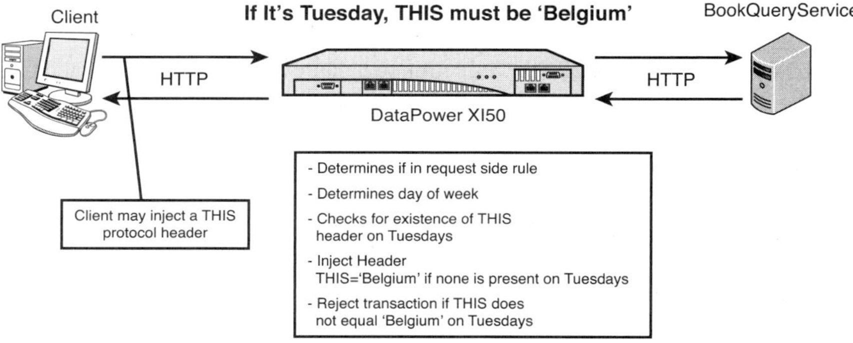

Figure 24-1 If it's Tuesday, this must be Belgium.

Figure 24-2 shows the multistep policy required to implement the example. In this case, there is a single request and response rule. The request rule has a single Filter action that examines the contents. That's where our testing takes place. The Filter action is a transformation (it executes a stylesheet) and has the defined capability to reject or accept incoming requests. As you will see shortly, XSLT is required to implement this.

Figure 24-3 shows the details of the Filter action. As can be seen from the Input context field, the stylesheet will have access to the request message available in the INPUT context, and it will create the final output (that which is written to the backend server) via the OUTPUT context. This will require that our stylesheet copy the input message to the output stream.

Listing 24-1 shows the entire XSLT stylesheet that is executed by the Filter action. Notice the dp and EXSLT date namespace declarations and their entry in the extension-element-prefixes and exclude-result-prefixes attributes of the xsl:stylesheet element. We discussed their definition and requirements in Chapter 22. Please refer to that chapter for a complete description of their utilization.

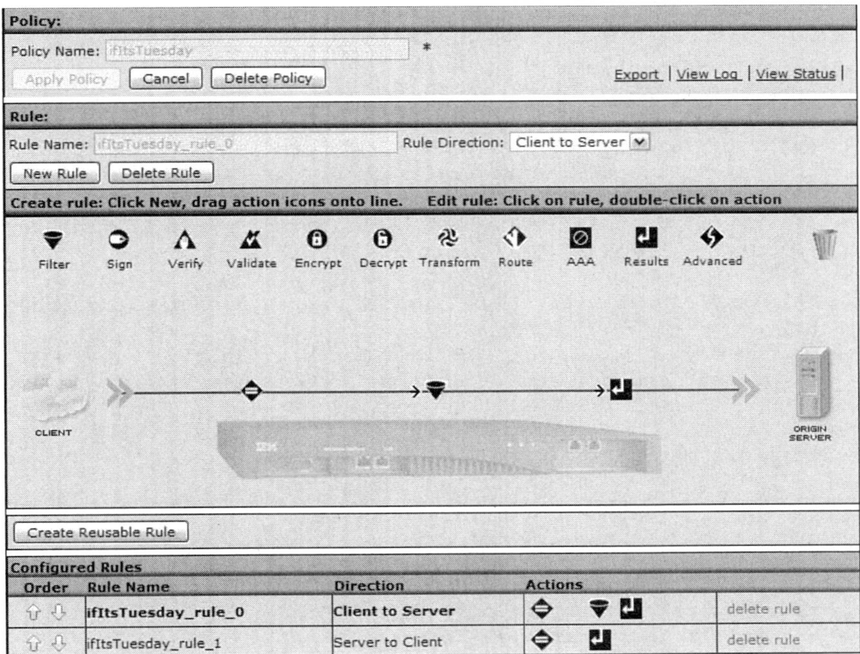

Figure 24-2 IfItsTuesday policy.

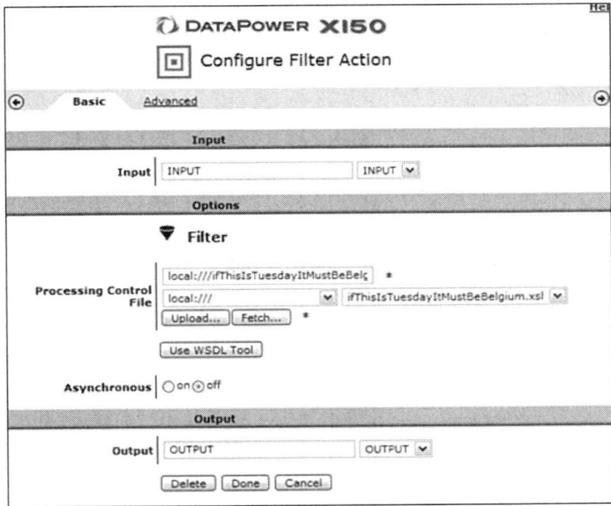

Figure 24-3 Filter action.

Listing 24-1 ifItsTuesdayItMustBeBelgium.xsl

```
<?xml version="1. 0" encoding="UTF-8"?>
<xsl:stylesheet version="1. 0" xmlns:xsl="http://www. w3.
org/1999/XSL/Transform" xmlns:dp="http://www. datapower. com/extensions"
xmlns:date="http://exslt. org/dates-and-times" extension-element-
prefixes="dp date" exclude-result-prefixes="dp date">
    <! -  ->
    <! - IF this is Tuesday, THIS must be Belgium ;-), if Day=Tuesday/3,
Header THIS must = 'Belgium'  ->
    <! -  ->
    <! - This stylesheet will check for the proper use of a protocol header
name 'THIS'  ->
    <! - On Tuesday, if present THIS must contain 'Belgium'  ->
    <! - If present and not equal 'Belgium' the transaction is rejected  ->
    <! - If not present, THIS will be created  ->
    <! -  ->
    <xsl:template match="/">
        <! -  ->
        <! - Make sure this is a request rule, test is made only on
requests  ->
        <! - dp:responding()=false() is true on request rules  ->
        <! -  ->
        <xsl:if test="dp:responding()=false()">
            <xsl:if test="date:day-in-week()=3">
                <xsl:variable name="THIS" select="dp:request-
header('THIS')"/>
                <xsl:choose>
                    <! -  ->
                    <! - There is an THIS Header='Belgium', transaction
accepted  ->
                    <! -  ->
                    <xsl:when test="$THIS='Belgium'">
                        <xsl:message dp:priority="debug">Header THIS =
Belgium</xsl:message>
                    </xsl:when>
                    <! -  ->
                    <! - There is no THIS Header, or THIS is empty  ->
                    <! - Create a THIS Header, set to 'Belgium'  ->
                    <! - Notice the triple quotes!  ->
                    <! -  ->
                    <xsl:when test="$THIS=''">
                        <dp:set-request-header name="'THIS'"
value="'Belgium'"/>
                        <xsl:message dp:priority="debug">Header THIS not
found, set to 'Belgium'</xsl:message>
                    </xsl:when>
                    <! -  ->
                    <! - There is an THIS Header that does not equal
'Belgium', reject transaction  ->
                    <! -  ->
                    <xsl:otherwise>
                        <dp:reject>
```

```
                    <xsl:value-of select="concat(
                    'Transaction ',
                    dp:variable('var://service/transaction-id'),
                    ', Rejected. Header THIS = ',
                    $THIS,
                    '. Must equal Belgium on Tuesdays')"/>
                </dp:reject>
            </xsl:otherwise>
        </xsl:choose>
    </xsl:if>
  </xsl:if>
  <dp:freeze-headers/>
  <xsl:copy-of select="*"/>
 </xsl:template>
</xsl:stylesheet>
```

The first requirement was to ensure that the request transaction complies with the protocol header requirements as described. As this stylesheet could potentially be used in a response side rule, the dp:responding() extension element determines the current direction of the multistep policy. If dp:responding()=false(), we are within a request side policy rule.

Having determined the rule direction, the next requirement is to determine the day of the week. We are concerned only with Tuesdays after all, and there is no reason to perform unnecessary processing if it's another day. The EXSLT extension function date:day-in-week() is used to get the current day of the week. The extension function returns a numeric value with Sunday being 1, Monday 2, and so on. We use Tuesday's value of 3 in this test.

An XSLT variable utilizing the DataPower extension function dp:request-header('THIS') is used to fetch the protocol header. As was discussed in Chapter 22, this is a protocol-independent function that can be used to obtain protocol headers from all the supported protocols such as HTTP, MQ, or JMS, and is preferred over the HTTP protocol specific functions such as dp:http-request-header('THIS'). This header is obtained and is used as the basis of the following xsl:choose statement.

When the header THIS is equal to the string 'Belgium' (It's Tuesday, THIS must be Belgium!) we produce a log message at the debug level and the transaction is on its way. The requirements dictated that this header was not required; only if it is present is its value is tested. If it is not present, a header is created with the required value, a message is written to the log, and all is good.

When the 'THIS' header is found, and if it is Tuesday, and the value is not 'Belgium', the first thing that is done is to reject the transaction by using the dp:reject extension element. As was described in Chapter 22, dp:reject is used to reject incoming requests, and the message created within it (which also contains the transaction id obtained from var://service/transaction-id) is written to the log. Listing 24-2 shows the log message, with the transaction number.

Listing 24-2 If This is Tuesday, Rejection Message

```
xmlfirewall (IfThisIsTuesday): request IfThisIsTuesday_rule_0 #1 filter:
'INPUT local:///ifThisIsTuesdayThisMustBeBelgium.xsl stored in OUTPUT'
failed: Transaction 12433, Rejected.  Header THIS = Amsterdam.  Must equal
Belgium on Tuesdays
```

> **TIP—USE DP:REJECT IN FILTER ACTIONS**
>
> The dp:reject function can, in fact, be used within a Transform action. However, the preference is to use the Filter action to clearly describe the intent of the action and self-document the policy.

The dp:freeze-headers is a simple efficiency statement. A client cannot begin sending its message data until protocol headers have been completely streamed out on the network to the server. The DataPower extension dp:freeze-headers is used here to notify the multistep processor that we have completed header manipulation and that data may be streamed to the intended recipient. This will probably not have a monumental effect on efficiency but is a good practice and acts as a bit of self-documentation in more complex programming.

Copying the request message completes the example. In this statement, xsl:copy-of select="*" is used to copy the entire input message to the output context, which in this action is OUTPUT, or the final message content to the target. Using this statement here (specifically with the assignment to OUTPUT) avoids having to include a Results action within the rule. Some users may prefer to use a Results action, and if you do not specify OUTPUT as the output context for the action, the policy editor will assign one for you. However, using a single Filter, in this case writing to OUTPUT, is the most efficient configuration.

Example Requests

This first example in Listing 24-3 demonstrates a successful execution of a request. It's Tuesday, but because the THIS header was submitted with the correct value (via curl's -H option), the transaction is executed and a response returned from the BookQueryService.

Listing 24-3 Successful If Its Tuesday Request

```
curl  -data-binary @bookQueryRequest. xml http://192.168.1.35:4040 -H
"THIS:Belgium"

<?xml version="1. 0" encoding="UTF-8"?>
<SOAP-ENV:Envelope xmlns:SOAP-
ENV="http://schemas.xmlsoap.org/soap/envelope/">
  <SOAP-ENV:Body>
    <book>
            <name>Moby Dick</name>
            <author>Herman Melville</author>
            <publisher>Longman</publisher>
            <isbn>0321228006</isbn>
            <copyright>2007</copyright>
    </book>
  </SOAP-ENV:Body>
</SOAP-ENV:Envelope>
```

The example in Listing 24-4 demonstrates a failed request. In this case, the THIS header is submitted with the value of Amsterdam, and due to our configuration requirements, the transaction fails. Notice the reject string contained in the SOAP Fault.

Listing 24-4 Unsuccessful If Its Tuesday Request

```
curl  -data-binary @bookQueryRequest. xml http://192.168.1.35:4040 -H
"THIS:Amsterdam"

<?xml version="1. 0" encoding="UTF-8"?>
<env:Envelope xmlns:env="http://schemas.xmlsoap.org/soap/envelope/">
<env:Body><env:Fault><faultcode>env:Client</faultcode>
<faultstring>Transaction 27249, Rejected. Header THIS = Amsterdam. Must
equal Belgium on Tuesdays (from client)</faultstring>
</env:Fault></env:Body></env:Envelope>
```

Example 1 demonstrates some simple concepts in XSLT development with DataPower. We've shown how the direction of a rule can be determined via the dp:responding extension, and we've utilized EXSLT date:day-in-week() functions to determine the day of the week. Finally, we've shown how to reject a transaction and presented some best practices in the use of the dp:reject extension.

Example 2: Passing Variables to XSLT

We've now seen how to write XSLT to enable DataPower to perform transaction validation. However, the values that we tested against in Example 1 were hard-coded, we tested the 'THIS' header for the value of 'Belgium'. Wouldn't it be great if there was a way to modify these static values without having to change the underlying XSLT? Well there is, and this example demonstrates this useful feature of the DataPower multistep policy. We demonstrate the ability to pass variable data to a stylesheet. Constructing the XSLT in this manner provides the device administrator the ability to modify the transformation process without having to change the underlying code. The variable data may be entered via any configuration methodology, and when the WebGUI is used, configurable entry fields can be added to the Transform action's Advanced screen. We show how to create the input fields and how to extract the data from within the XSLT.

In this example, we create a field to enter an XPath expression that will be used to test for the existence of a node within an input request document. We perform this test by the use of an EXSLT extension that dynamically executes the XPath expression, and we report back to the client with the results of the search. Figure 24-4 shows a graphic depiction of this example. The request is sent to a service that invokes the Transform action. The XSLT uses the value entered via the WebGUI to test the input document.

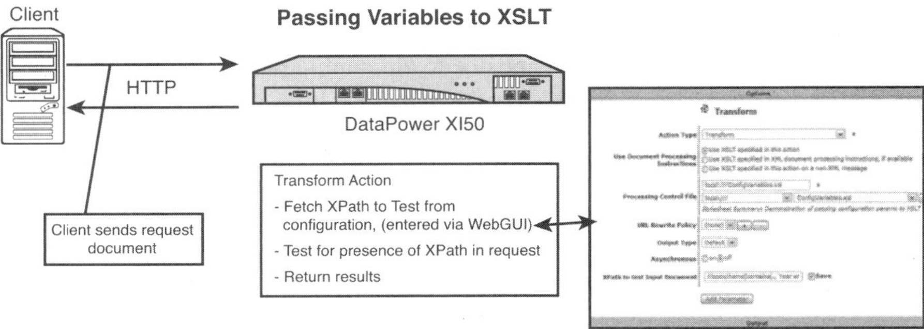

Figure 24-4 Example 2, Passing variables to XSLT.

Figure 24-5 shows the Transform action Advanced tab when the customized XSLT is utilized. Notice the input field "XPath to test Input Document," and the title "Stylesheet Summary: Demonstration of passing configuration params to XSLT" that are displayed. If you were to click the label of the input field, customized help is displayed. These items were dynamically added to the Transform action's Advanced tab based on information in our stylesheet.

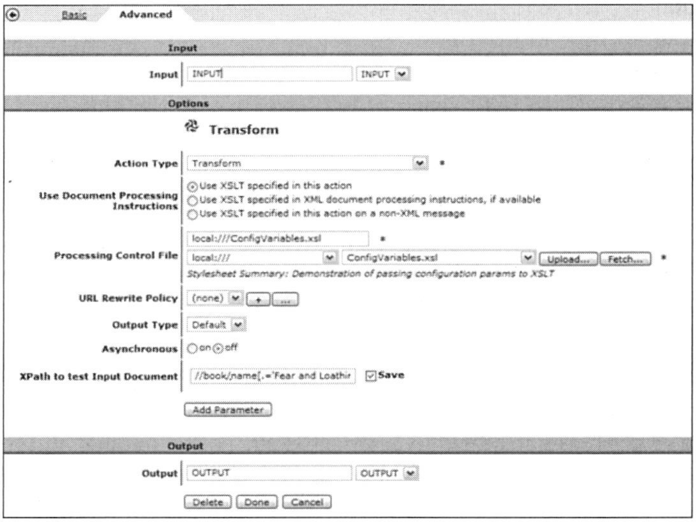

Figure 24-5 Transform action with parameters.

In order to attach custom fields to the Transform action, a few simple commands are required in the XSLT. These statements define the literal values presented on the Advanced screen, such as the summary of the stylesheet, the XSLT field names for each entry field their text label, default values, and online help. The XSLT does not change between the two executions. The configuration variable (config:xpath) utilizes the values entered on the Advanced screen of the Transform action. The action is changed and the policy updated to accept the new book name value.

Listing 24-5 shows the beginning of our stylesheet and the required statements for configuration interaction. The first requirement to note is the namespace list; dpconfig is the special namespace for configuration parameters. You'll notice the standard dp namespace for DataPower extensions, and the dyn for EXSLT dynamic functions (more on this as we discuss the remainder of the code). A summary for the stylesheet, which displays on the WebGUI screens, may be optionally entered as the dp:summary statement demonstrates. Each input field desired requires two statements: an xsl:param to contain the XSLT accessible variable and a dp:param to define the aforementioned label, default value, and online help. If you want additional fields, all that needs to be done is to replicate this statement pair for each new field desired.

Listing 24-5 XSLT Parameter Requirements

```
<?xml version="1.0" encoding="UTF-8"?>
<xsl:stylesheet version="1.0"
xmlns:xsl="http://www.w3.org/1999/XSL/Transform"
xmlns:dpconfig="http://www.datapower.com/param/config"
xmlns:dyn="http://exslt.org/dynamic"
xmlns:dp="http://www.datapower.com/extensions" extension-element-
prefixes="dp" exclude-result-prefixes="dp dpconfig dyn">
    <!-- -->
    <!-- Stylesheet summary for display on Transform action screen in
WebGUI -->
    <!-- -->
    <dp:summary xmlns="">
        <operation>xform</operation>
        <description>Demonstration of passing configuration params to
XSLT</description>
    </dp:summary>
    <!-- -->
    <!-- These fields are extracted from the transform action -->
    <!-- Add an xsl:param and dp:param for each field desired, use dpconfig
namespace -->
    <!-- -->
    <xsl:param name="dpconfig:xpath"/>
    <dp:param name="dpconfig:xpath">
        <display>XPath to test Input Document</display>
        <default>/</default>
        <description>Determine whether document contains XPath
expression</description>
    </dp:param>
```

Now that we have an understanding of the steps required to add our new XPath field, let's look at some demonstrations of its usage and the code necessary to perform the dynamic XPath execution. Listing 24-6 shows two transactions submitted against a service that implements the customized action within its multistep policy. The first is looking for the name of a book that contains the text 'Moby Dick,' and you can see that this string is successfully found in the request document (bookQueryRequest.xml). The second test searches for 'Fear and Loathing in Las Vegas,' which is not found.

Listing 24-6 Examples of XPath Tests Entered from Transform Action Advanced Screen

```
curl  -data-binary @bookQueryRequest. xml http://192.168.1.35:4075
<?xml version="1. 0" encoding="UTF-8"?>
<response><found>//book/name[contains(. , 'Moby Dick')]</found></response>

curl  -data-binary @bookQueryRequest. xml http://192.168.1.35:4075
<?xml version="1. 0" encoding="UTF-8"?>
<response><didNotFind>//book/name[contains(. , 'Fear and Loathing in Las
Vegas')]</didNotFind></response>
```

So let's take a look at the XSLT that is required to obtain this functionality. Listing 24-7 shows the remainder of the stylesheet, the main template that matches against the document root. The dp:serialize statement simply emits a serialized (XML formatted) version of the input message to the log; this could be useful for debugging. The xsl:choose statement is where the results of the XPath evaluation is inspected. The EXSLT function dyn:evaluate() is executed against the input document and returns matching nodes. If the string is found (the count of returned nodes is not equal to zero), the success message is returned and an indication is written to the log. The negative case (the xsl:otherwise statement) again writes a message to the log and returns a not found response.

Listing 24-7 XSLT Utilizing Configuration Variables from Transform Action Advanced Screen

```
<xsl:template match="/">
        <! -  ->
        <! - Put a message to the log showing a serialized display of the
input message  ->
        <! -  ->
        <xsl:message>
            <xsl:value-of select="'Input document'"/>
            <dp:serialize select="/" omit-xml-decl="yes"/>
        </xsl:message>
        <! -  ->
        <! - This choose statement tests the result of dynamically
executing the XPath Statement against the request document  ->
        <! - The count function returns the number of nodes matched by the
XPath, if the count is 0, there is not match  ->
        <! -  ->
        <xsl:choose>
            <! -  ->
            <! - The count is not equal to 0, the node was found, print a
message in the log and return a positive response  ->
            <! -  ->
            <xsl:when test="count(dyn:evaluate($dpconfig:xpath)) != 0">
                <xsl:message>
                    <xsl:value-of select="concat('contains ',
$dpconfig:xpath)"/>
                </xsl:message>
                <response>
                    <found>
```

```
                        <xsl:value-of select="$dpconfig:xpath"/>
                    </found>
                </response>
            </xsl:when>
            <!-- -->
            <!-- The count is 0, the node was not found, print a message in
the log and return a negative response -->
            <!-- -->
            <xsl:otherwise>
                <xsl:message>
                    <xsl:value-of select="concat('does not contain ',
$dpconfig:xpath)"/>
                </xsl:message>
                <response>
                    <didNotFind>
                        <xsl:value-of select="$dpconfig:xpath"/>
                    </didNotFind>
                </response>
            </xsl:otherwise>
        </xsl:choose>
    </xsl:template>
</xsl:stylesheet>
```

This example demonstrates a simple and powerful capability of the DataPower configuration, the ability to pass parameters from the configuration to a stylesheet used within a Transform action. This technique allows change to the XSLT functionality without having to maintain the actual code.

Example 3: Error Processing and Control

DataPower devices are incredibly powerful security tools. And as such, often times they can be restrictive in what they tell violators of configuration policy. Going back again to our BookQueryService, what if our service suddenly starts getting request messages that do not conform to our request schema? Should we tell the client, "Your request did not work because it was in the wrong format?" Should we tell them, "Your request needs to be in this format," and show the required format to them? Maybe this is the right thing to do in this case; after all we are only dealing with books. But what if this was a request to change someone's paycheck? How about if it was a request to schedule the transportation of a certain amount of military hardware? Now telling the requestor what they should do might not be the right thing to do after all. By exposing those implementation details, you may be providing them with information they could use to compromise your system.

So, by its nature, DataPower is restrictive indeed when it comes to telling violators what they have done wrong; in fact, the default action is to simply return a SOAP Fault saying that the transaction failed, nothing more. But now that we have the power of customization in our toolbox, we can enhance this process, we can decide what we want to tell the client, and we can determine how each potential error should be handled.

This next example demonstrates some of the basics of DataPower error processing. We present a unified error mechanism that will leverage a centralized error processor to determine how each potential problem is handled. We also discuss some of the DataPower extensions and variables that play a part in error processing. We show how problems such as schema violations, rejections caused by filters, and backend errors can all be caught and communicated to the client. It's up to you!

As you know, the DataPower device maintains variables that describe details of the system and the current transaction. For example if an error occurs, the error message is maintained in var://service/error-message. However, one of the quirks of error processing is that in some instances the root cause of an error, say schema validation, can be masked by subsequent error generation. For example, the log snippet in Listing 24-8 shows a typical schema validation error. The first message produced shows the actual error; however, the subsequent failure of the multi-step policy generates a Dynamic Execution Error, which, when caught in a traditional error policy, overrides the original schema validation error in var://service/error-message.

Listing 24-8 Schema Validation Log

```
xmlfirewall (ValidatedBookQueryService): No match from processing policy
'ValidatedBookQueryService' for code '0x00230001'

xmlfirewall (ValidatedBookQueryService): Dynamic Execution Error


xmlfirewall (ValidatedBookQueryService): Generated error on URL
'http://192. 168. 1. 35:2115/': <?xml version="1. 0" encoding="UTF-8"?>
<env:Envelope
xmlns:env="http://schemas.xmlsoap.org/soap/envelope/"><env:Body><env:Fault>
<faultcode>env:Client</faultcode><faultstring>Internal Error (from
client)</faultstring></env:Fault></env:Body></env:Envelope>

xmlfirewall (ValidatedBookQueryService): Dynamic Execution Error

xmlfirewall (ValidatedBookQueryService): request
ValidatedBookQueryService_rule_0 #1 validate: 'INPUT schema
local:///bookQueryRequest. xsd' failed: http://192. 168. 1. 35:2115/: cvc-
particle 2. 1: in element book with anonymous type, found <copyright> (in
default namespace), but next item should be author

xmlfirewall (ValidatedBookQueryService): Schema Validation Error

xmlfirewall (ValidatedBookQueryService): Execution of
'local:///bookQueryRequest. xsd' aborted: http://192. 168. 1. 35:2115/:
cvc-particle 2. 1: in element book with anonymous type, found <copyright>
(in default namespace), but next item should be author
```

One solution is to develop a mechanism to catch significant errors via On-Error actions, and to store information about the error in a custom context. This data is then analyzed in a general error processing policy, which produces a meaningful message to the client. If you remember the basics of DataPower service configuration, an On-Error action has the capability to call a rule within another multistep policy. If you're not familiar with On-Error processing, review that mechanism in Chapter 7, "Introduction to Services Configuration."

Figure 24-6 shows the logical flow of this architecture. An On-Error action precedes a Schema Validation action, which, in the event of an error, calls a rule (within another policy) that captures information about the error and establishes a protocol response code to return to the client. This data is stored in context variables, the first via a Set-Variable action (which establishes the protocol response) and the second via a Transform action that gathers several bits of information about the error. The Filter action in this rule forces the execution of an Error rule within the original policy. Its Transform action retrieves the error information from the variables, sets the protocol response code, and formats a message to return to the client. The benefits of this technique are two-fold; first the error data is not overwritten and original messages are captured, and second, a central policy point (the Transform in Error rule), is established to handle all errors.

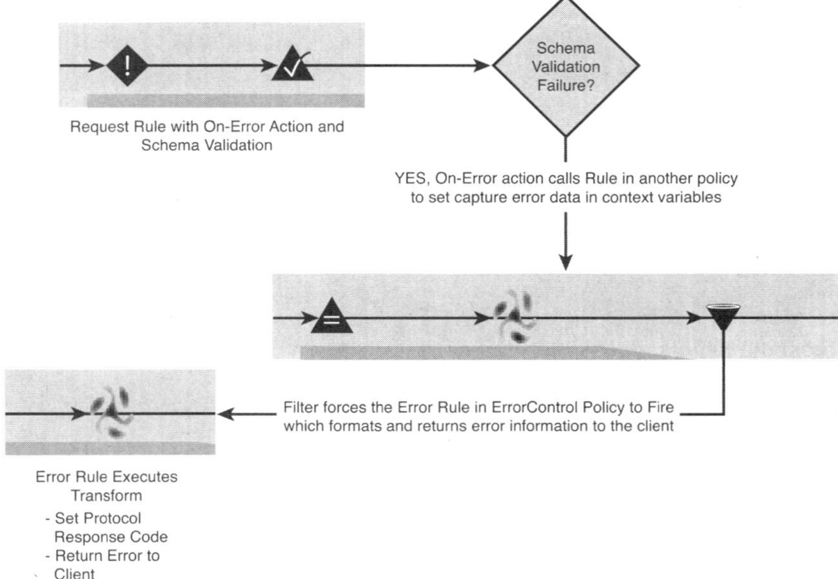

Figure 24-6 Error processing logic.

It's a good practice to create the error capture rules in a separate policy containing all the error rules, and to give the individual rules meaningful names. For example, the error policy in Figure 24-7 shows three request rules named SetErrorVariable_InvalidRequest_440, SetErrorVariable_BadTitle_441, and SetErrorVariable_InvalidResponse_442. These are not error rules, and they do not get fired automatically; they are explicitly called by the On-Error action. They have been given meaningful names so that when they are referred to from an On-Error action, their functionality is apparent. These rules contain two actions that set context variables. The Set-Var uses var://context/errorContext/errorResponse to establish the protocol level error code to send back to the client (for example, 440 in SetErrorVariable_InvalidRequest_440), and the Transform gathers information about the current error message, which is stored in var://context/errorContext/errorInfo. Each rule also contains a Filter action that executes the store:///reject-all.xsl stylesheet. This forces the failure of the transaction and results in an error rule being executed.

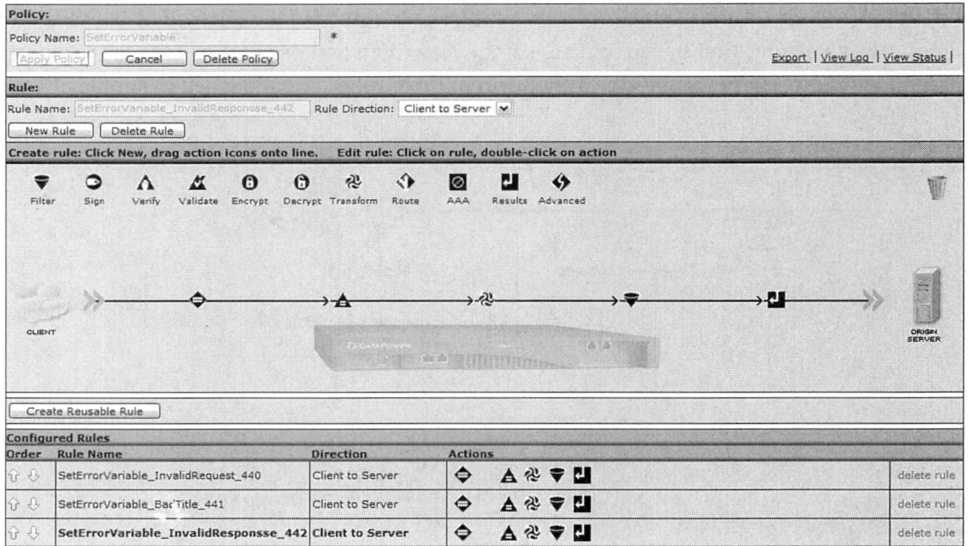

Figure 24-7 SetErrorVariable rule.

The transform action executes a stylesheet, as shown in Listing 24-9. This process gathers up various error data such as the message, codes, headers, reasons, and so on, and stores them in an element named errorInfo, which is then set in var://context/errorContext/errorInfo. This and var://context/errorContext/errorResponse are picked up by the error rule in the original policy. You can see the error data being extracted from the service variables and the errorInfo element being constructed, which is then stored in the context variable var://context/errorContext/errorInfo.

Listing 24-9 XSLT Utilizing Service Variable to Capture Error Data

```
<?xml version="1.0" encoding="UTF-8"?>
<xsl:stylesheet version="1.0"
xmlns:xsl="http://www.w3.org/1999/XSL/Transform"
xmlns:env="http://schemas.xmlsoap.org/soap/envelope/"
xmlns:dp="http://www.datapower.com/extensions" extension-element-
prefixes="dp" xmlns="">
    <!-- -->
    <xsl:template match="/">
        <!-- -->
        <!-- Capture information about the error -->
        <!-- this will be stored in a context variable for   -->
        <!-- later fetching by Error Rule  -->
        <!-- -->
        <xsl:variable name="error-code"
select="dp:variable('var://service/error-code')"/>
        <xsl:variable name="error-headers"
select="dp:variable('var://service/error-headers')"/>
        <xsl:variable name="error-message"
select="dp:variable('var://service/error-message')"/>
        <xsl:variable name="error-protocol-reason-phrase"
select="dp:variable('var://serviceerror-protocol-reason-phrase')"/>
        <xsl:variable name="error-protocol-response"
select="dp:variable('var://service/error-protocol-response')"/>
        <xsl:variable name="error-subcode"
select="dp:variable('var://service/error-subcode')"/>
        <!-- -->
        <!-- Format all the error data -->
        <!-- -->
        <xsl:variable name="errorInfo">
            <errorInfo>
                <error-code>
                    <xsl:value-of select="$error-code"/>
                </error-code>
                <error-headers>
                    <xsl:value-of select="$error-headers"/>
                </error-headers>
                <error-message>
                    <xsl:value-of select="$error-message"/>
                </error-message>
                <error-protocol-reason-phrase>
                    <xsl:value-of select="$error-protocol-reason-phrase"/>
                </error-protocol-reason-phrase>
                <error-protocol-response>
                    <xsl:value-of select="$error-protocol-response"/>
                </error-protocol-response>
                <error-subcode>
                    <xsl:value-of select="$error-subcode"/>
                </error-subcode>
            </errorInfo>
        </xsl:variable>
```

```
        <! -  ->
        <! - Put all the error data in a variable  ->
        <! -  ->
        <xsl:message>
            <xsl:value-of select="concat('errorInfo=', $errorInfo)"/>
        </xsl:message>
        <dp:set-variable name="'var://context/errorContext/errorInfo'"
value="$errorInfo"/>
    </xsl:template>
    <! -  ->
</xsl:stylesheet>
```

Figure 24-8 shows the configuration of the ErrorControl Policy. This policy contains a response, a request, and an error rule. Within the request and response rules, meaningful actions such as the schema validations are prefixed with On-Error actions prepared to call the associated SetErrorVariable rules if something should go wrong. The request rule also contains a Filter action just to spice things up a bit; it tests to ensure that only requests for our DataPower Handbook are made to the BookQueryService. Finally, the policy contains an error rule that executes the centralized error processing stylesheet. We discuss that shortly.

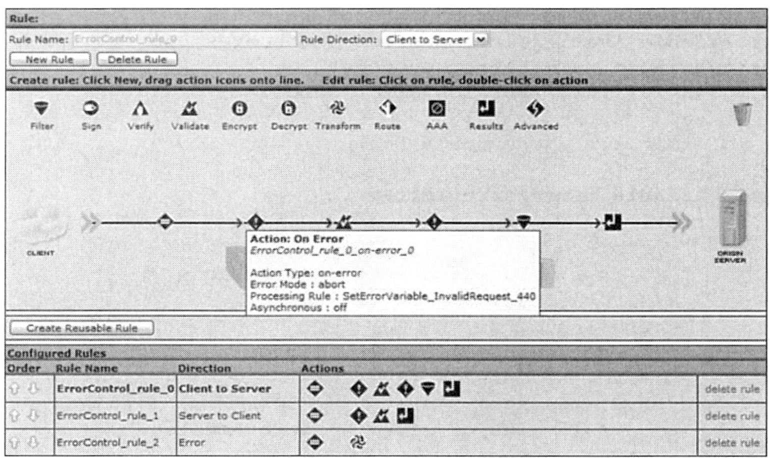

Figure 24-8 ErrorControl Policy with On-Error actions.

Let's review what this configuration does. If, for example, a request is sent to the service that is not valid according to the schema, the On-Error action that prefaces the Schema Validation action will fire. Figure 24-9 shows the On-Error action. It executes the setErrorVariable_InvalidRequest_440 rule, which stores the user defined 440 protocol response and the current system error message in the context variables. The 440 response code is arbitrarily chosen within the 4XX range of HTTP status code. This range defines a client error and 440 is not already assigned. As the On-Error action's error mode property is defined as cancel, the remainder of the actions in the rule are not executed.

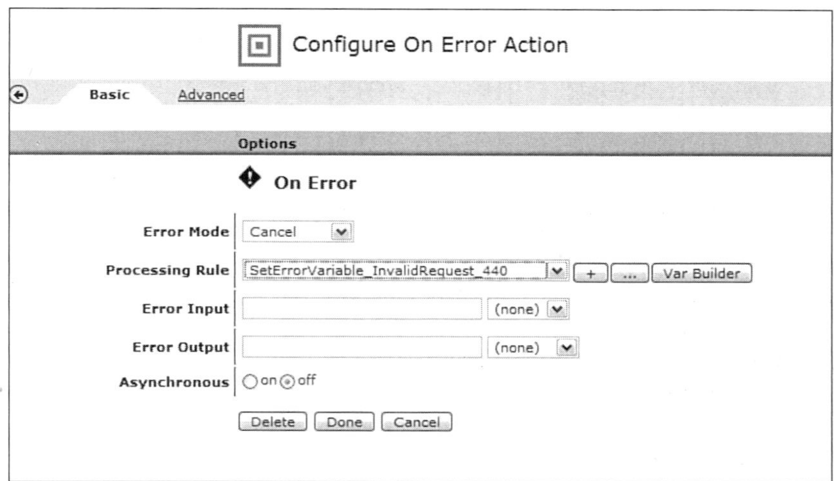

Figure 24-9 Cancel mode On-Error action with execution of Processing Rule.

Listing 24-10 demonstrates a response for the submission of an invalid document to our ErrorControl Service. Some of the details have been eliminated for brevity. Now rather than just returning a generic SOAP Fault with a faultstring of "Internal Error (from client)," the error rule has formatted a SOAP Fault with detailed information about the transaction and the error. The SOAP Fault contains not only information about the schema violation, but also details about the transaction, the client, and the service that was invoked. And in addition, rather than returning a HTTP response code of 500, which would have been the case with the standard SOAP Fault, we have applied control over this, and have returned the 440 that was specified within the error rule.

Listing 24-10 Sample Schema Validation Error

```
<?xml version="1.0" encoding="UTF-8"?>
<env:Fault xmlns:env="http://schemas.xmlsoap.org/soap/envelope/">
    <faultcode>440</faultcode>
    <faultstring/>
    <detail>
        <transactionInfo>
            <transaction-id>161201</transaction-id>
            <transaction-client>192.168.1.100</transaction-client>
            <URL-in>http://192.168.1.35:4010/</URL-in>
            <processor-name>ErrorControl</processor-name>
            <processor-type>XML Firewall</processor-type>
        </transactionInfo>
        <errorInfo>
            <error-code>0x00230001</error-code>
            <error-headers/>
            <error-message>http://127.0.0.1:4000/: cvc-particle 2.1: in
element book with anonymous type, found &lt;copyright> (in default
namespace), but next item should be author</error-message>
```

```
            <error-protocol-reason-phrase/>
            <error-protocol-response>500</error-protocol-response>
            <error-subcode>0x01d30003</error-subcode>
        </errorInfo>
    </detail>
</env:Fault>
```

The XSLT required to return the SOAP Fault and set the protocol response is not so complex. It's been broken down into multiple listings for ease of discussion. Listing 24-11 shows the initial phase of the main template; of course you'll have to declare the dp namespace just like you would with any stylesheet that utilizes DataPower extensions. The first part of the XSLT extracts the context variables that were set by the On-Error rule, and stores the values in XSL variables.

A variable (x-dp-response-code) is used to communicate protocol responses between services. This stylesheet uses this variable to test if a backend service had returned a protocol level error. If so, we'd want to be able to communicate its information to the client. An XSL variable (protocolResponse) is used to determine the response code to send back to the client. If the x-dp-response-code variable has been set (it only would have been if there were a backend failure), it is used; if not, the value set within the On-Error rule is chosen. This is 440 in our schema invalid request document example. The variable protocolResponse is then used to set service/error-protocol-response, which makes the actual response code setting.

Listing 24-11 XSLT Testing and Setting Protocol Response Codes

```
<?xml version="1.0" encoding="UTF-8"?>
<xsl:stylesheet version="1.0"
xmlns:xsl="http://www.w3.org/1999/XSL/Transform"
xmlns:env="http://schemas.xmlsoap.org/soap/envelope/"
xmlns:dp="http://www.datapower.com/extensions" extension-element-
prefixes="dp" xmlns="">
    <! -  ->
    <xsl:template match="/">
        <! -  ->
        <! - Fetch the error information captured by On-Error rule  ->
        <! - Also capture the x-dp-response-code in case this rule  ->
        <! - has been executed by a backend failure  ->
        <! -  ->
        <xsl:variable name="errorResponse"
select="dp:variable('var://context/errorContext/errorResponse')"/>
        <xsl:variable name="errorReason"
select="dp:variable('var://context/errorContext/errorReason')"/>
        <xsl:variable name="x-dp-response-code" select="normalize-
space(dp:response-header('x-dp-response-code'))"/>
        <! -  ->
        <xsl:message>
            <xsl:value-of select="concat('errorResponse=',
$errorResponse)"/>
            <xsl:value-of select="concat(', errorReason=', $errorReason)"/>
            <xsl:value-of select="concat(', x-dp-response-code=', $x-dp-
```

```
response-code)"/>
        </xsl:message>
        <!- -   ->
        <!- - When x-dp-response-code is set, a DP Service on the backend
has failed  ->
        <!- - If so, use its code, else get the code set by the error
rule  ->
        <!- -   ->
        <xsl:variable name="protocolResponse">
            <xsl:choose>
                <xsl:when test="$x-dp-response-code!=''">
                    <xsl:value-of select="substring($x-dp-response-code,
1, 3)"/>
                </xsl:when>
                <xsl:otherwise>
                    <xsl:value-of select="$errorResponse"/>
                </xsl:otherwise>
            </xsl:choose>
        </xsl:variable>
        <!- -   ->
        <!- - Set the services Protocol Reponse  ->
        <!- -   ->
        <dp:set-variable name="'var://service/error-protocol-response'"
value="$protocolResponse"/>
        <xsl:message>
            <xsl:value-of select="concat('var://service/error-protocol-
response set to ', $protocolResponse)"/>
        </xsl:message>
```

Now that the protocol response has been set, the stylesheet begins to construct the response message. Listing 24-12 shows the extraction of various bits of information about the transaction—where the transaction was initiated, the transaction-id, the incoming URL, and which service processed the request.

Listing 24-12 Get Transaction Details

```
<!- -   ->
<!- - Get information about the transaction  ->
<!- -   ->
<xsl:variable name="transaction-client"
     select="dp:variable('var://service/transaction-client')"/>
<xsl:variable name="transaction-id"
     select="dp:variable('var://service/transaction-id')"/>
<xsl:variable name="URL-in"
     select="dp:variable('var://service/URL-in')"/>
<xsl:variable name="processor-name"
     select="dp:variable('var://service/processor-name')"/>
<xsl:variable name="processor-type"
     select="dp:variable('var://service/processor-type')"/>
```

Listing 24-13 constructs the actual SOAP Fault message. You want to ensure that the response is a valid implementation of a SOAP Fault. In this example, the protocol response is returned and the reason information is extracted from the protocolResponse variable. The response string is after the three position number code contained within the protocol response. According to the HTTP specification, the reason phase is not required, and may not be set in all instances. The information about the transaction is retrieved from the variables that were set, and the errorInfo is extracted from the context variable that was stored by the On-Error rule.

Listing 24-13 Complete SOAP Fault

```
<! -  ->
<! - Produce a soap fault with all the acquired information  ->
<! -  ->
<env:Fault>
    <faultcode>
        <xsl:value-of select="$protocolResponse"/>
    </faultcode>
    <faultstring>
        <xsl:value-of select="substring($protocolResponse, 5)"/>
    </faultstring>
    <detail>
        <transactionInfo>
            <transaction-id>
                <xsl:value-of select="$transaction-id"/>
            </transaction-id>
            <transaction-client>
                <xsl:value-of select="$transaction-client"/>
            </transaction-client>
            <URL-in>
                <xsl:value-of select="$URL-in"/>
            </URL-in>
            <processor-name>
                <xsl:value-of select="$processor-name"/>
            </processor-name>
            <processor-type>
                <xsl:value-of select="$processor-type"/>
            </processor-type>
        </transactionInfo>
        <! -  ->
        <! - Get information about the error that was captured in On-Error
rule  ->
        <! -  ->
        <xsl:variable name="errorInfo"
select="dp:variable('var://context/errorContext/errorInfo')"/>
        <xsl:copy-of select="$errorInfo"/>
    </detail>
    </env:Fault>
</xsl:template>
```

This example demonstrates a technique for the management of errors within a policy. A policy was created that contained rules specific to particular errors such as schema violation. These rules defined protocol responses that were returned to the client, and gathered information about the error before any potential overwriting of the information by subsequent multistep policy actions.

Example 4: Dynamic Routing

This next example kicks things up a bit by adding more complexity. This scenario is built around a routing policy. We have sales teams on the East and West coasts who are interested in utilizing our BookQueryService. We would like to route these organizational units to particular BookQueryService implementations. Figure 24-10 shows the network topology. Each team submits their requests over HTTPS, and the SSL certificates will be utilized to determine the requester's identity. BookQueryService-1 and BookQueryService-2 are services running on the DataPower device in this instance. Another implementation might utilize service off the device, perhaps on other DataPower devices.

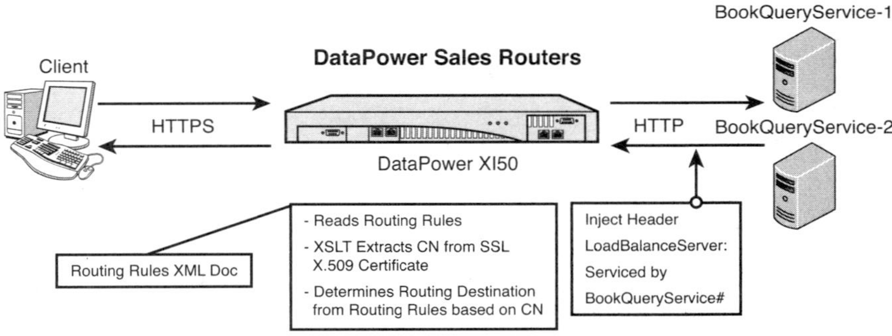

Figure 24-10 DataPower sales team routing.

In addition to determining the destination of the routed request, each client would like to be able to determine which of the load-balanced servers processed the transaction via a custom header. This can easily be done by injecting a protocol header containing a unique string into the response stream, as is referenced in the network topology diagram in Figure 24-10. The actual injection mechanism is accomplished on the service's Header tab and is depicted for BookQueryService-1 in Figure 24-11 with the header named LoadBalanceServer being populated with the string "Serviced by BookQueryService-1." The same process is performed for BookQueryService-2 with a value of "Serviced by BookQueryService-2." Now, each transaction will not only be directed to a particular service, but that service will inject a header (identifying itself) that can be used to track the dynamic routing.

We are going to determine the client's organizational heritage based on the contents of his X.509 SSL certificate. Each sales team has been assigned SSL certificates with distinguishing common name attributes. The east coast team has a common name (CN) of SalesEastCoast; the west coast team uses SalesWestCoast, and we can route the requests based on this.

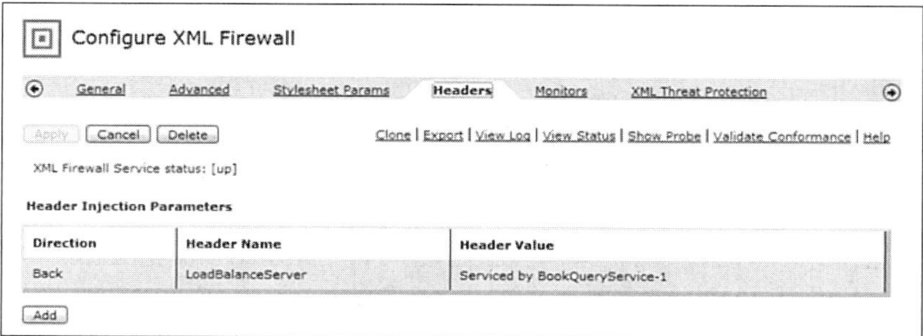

Figure 24-11 BookQueryService-1 Header Injection.

Furthermore, we would like to have a mechanism that enables for future updates to this routing determination that does not require maintaining XSLT code. We want to externalize this decision. This requirement can easily be accomplished by using an XML document to contain the routing data. Listing 24-14 shows a routing table that performs this function. In this implementation, destinations are created with subjectCN attributes containing the client's Common Name, Destination host, port, and an SSL Proxy Profile is potentially matched to the CN.

Listing 24-14 Routing Table

```
<?xml version="1. 0" encoding="UTF-8"?>
<! -    ->
<! - Routing for Sales Teams  ->
<! -    ->
<routingDestinations>
    <destinations subjectCN="CN=SalesEastCoast">
        <host>192.168.1.35</host>
        <port>4051</port>
        <sslid/>
    </destinations>
    <destinations subjectCN="CN=SalesWestCoast">
        <host>192.168.1.35</host>
        <port>4052</port>
        <sslid/>
    </destinations>
</routingDestinations>
```

Figure 24-12 shows the service implementation of the dynamic routing configuration. Make note of the Dynamic Backend selection of the Firewall Type property. We determine the backend URL within the policy. Also notice that an SSL Server Crypto Profile has been defined. This has been configured to require the client to use SSL, and its configuration ensures that the client's certificate is available to the policy by implementing client authentication via the use of an Identification Credential object. You can learn all about SSL configuration in Chapter 18, "DataPower and SSL."

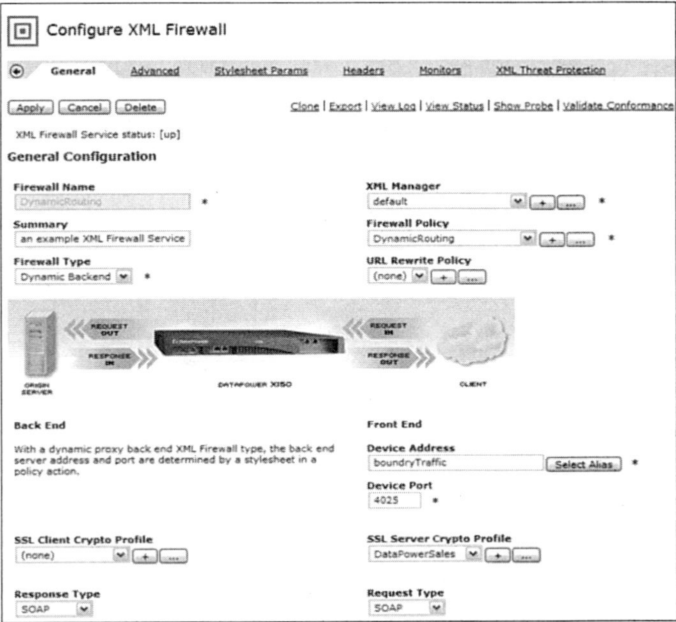

Figure 24-12 Dynamic routing service.

Figure 24-13 shows the multistep policy required to implement our sales routing. The policy consists of a single request and response rule. The request rule contains a Route action (set to use XSLT) from which the routing decision will be made. The Result action simply sends the input message to the intended destination, which was set by the Route action.

Figure 24-14 shows the details of the Route action. The XSLT DynamicSalesRouting.xsl is defined as the processing stylesheet. You may notice that in this action, both the input and output contexts have been defined as NULL. This stylesheet does not look at the contents of the request message or produce any message data. It looks at the client's SSL certificate and makes routing decisions. Neither of these requires message interrogation, and specifying NULL is useful as a self-documenting feature, as well as providing efficiency gained by not having to parse or produce message context.

TIP—Use of NULL in Input and Output Context

Use NULL when you are not consuming or producing message context. It is more efficient and acts as a self-documenting feature of the configuration.

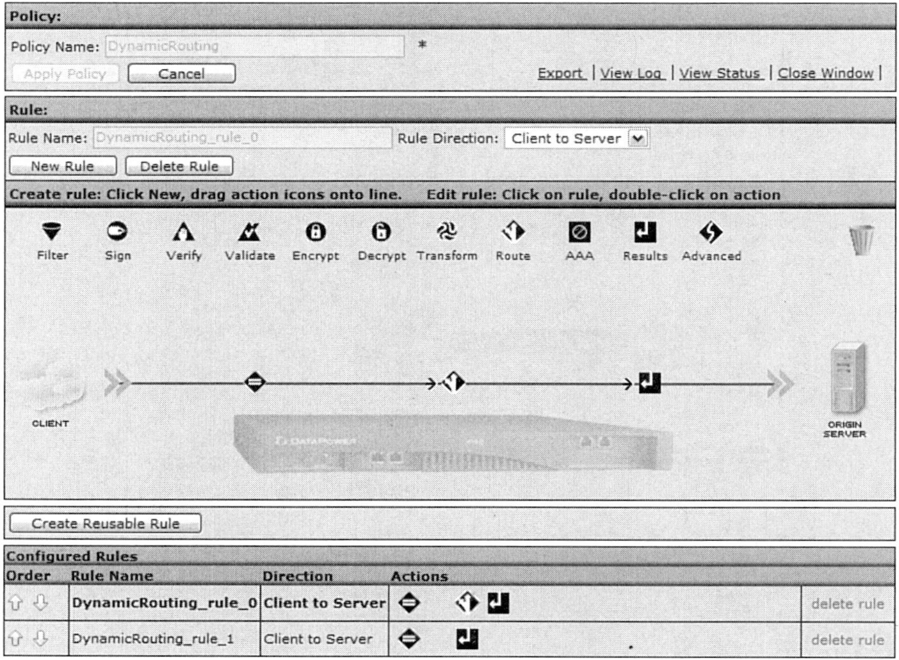

Figure 24-13 Style policy with Route action.

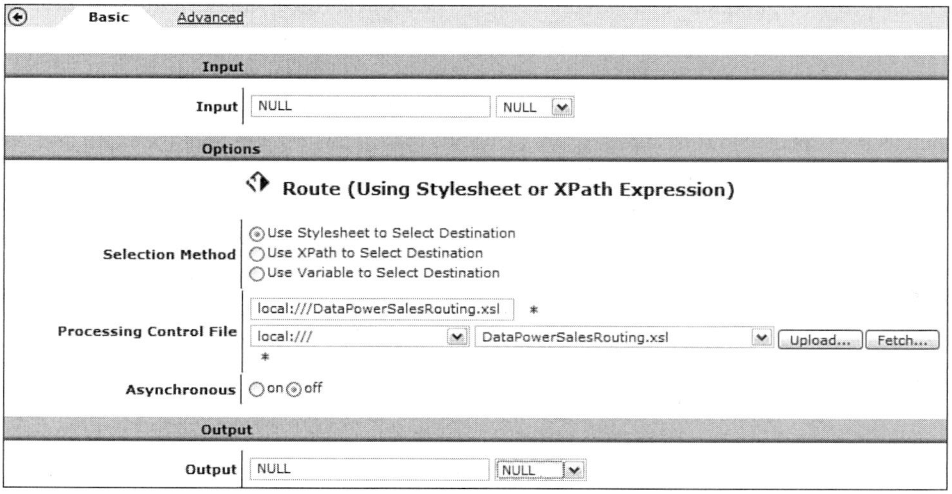

Basic Advanced

Input

Input NULL NULL

Options

Route (Using Stylesheet or XPath Expression)

Selection Method
Use Stylesheet to Select Destination
Use XPath to Select Destination
Use Variable to Select Destination

Processing Control File local:///DataPowerSalesRouting.xsl *
local:/// DataPowerSalesRouting.xsl Upload... Fetch...
*

Asynchronous on off

Output

Output NULL NULL

Figure 24-14 Route action with stylesheet assigned to determine routing determination.

Listing 24-15 shows the completed routing XSLT. The XSLT variable routingDoc is created by parsing the aforementioned routing table XML from within the DataPower file system's local directory. This variable now contains a document that we can access via XPath. It could have also been defined as being on an external server and accessed via HTTP, FTP, or any of the other supported protocols.

Listing 24-15 XSLT Utilizing Routing Document and xset-target for Routing Determination

```
<?xml version="1.0"?>
<! -  ->
<! - Sales Team Routing  ->
<! -  ->
<xsl:stylesheet version="1.0"
xmlns:xsl="http://www.w3.org/1999/XSL/Transform"
xmlns:dp="http://www.datapower.com/extensions"
xmlns:date="http://exslt.org/dates-and-times"
xmlns:str="http://exslt.org/strings" exclude-result-prefixes="dp str"
extension-element-prefixes="dp">
    <! -  ->
    <! - Fetch the DataPower Sales Routing document  ->
    <! -  ->
    <xsl:variable name="routingDoc"
select="document('local:///BookQueryServiceRouting.xml')"/>
    <xsl:template match="/">
        <! -  ->
        <! - Get the clients Distinguished Name from SSL Certificate  ->
        <! - This requires client authentication via Identification
Credentials  ->
        <! - Tokenize it and get the CN  ->
        <! -  ->
        <xsl:variable name="subjectDN" select="dp:client-subject-dn()"/>
        <xsl:variable name="DNTokens"
select="str:tokenize(string($subjectDN), '/')"/>
        <xsl:variable name="CNString"
select="$DNTokens/self::token[substring(text(),1,3)='CN=']/text()"/>
        <! -  ->
        <! - Get the routing information from the routing doc based
on CN  ->
        <! -  ->
        <xsl:variable name="host"
select="$routingDoc/routingDestinations/destinations[@subjectCN=$CNString]/
host/text()"/>
        <xsl:variable name="port"
select="$routingDoc/routingDestinations/destinations[@subjectCN=$CNString]/
port/text()"/>
        <xsl:variable name="sslid"
select="$routingDoc/routingDestinations/destinations[@subjectCN=$CNString]/
sslid/text()"/>
        <! -  ->
        <xsl:choose>
            <! -  ->
```

```
            <! - If the routing requires SSL, use that format of the
dp:xset-target Ext Func  ->
            <! -  ->
            <xsl:when test="$sslid">
                <dp:xset-target host="$host" port="$port" ssl="true()"
sslid="{$sslid}"/>
                <xsl:message>
                    <xsl:value-of select="concat('Routed to ', $host, ':',
$port, 'sslid=', $sslid)"/>
                </xsl:message>
            </xsl:when>
            <! -  ->
            <! - Routing without SSL  ->
            <! -  ->
            <xsl:otherwise>
                <xsl:message>
                    <xsl:value-of select="concat('Routed to ', $host, ':',
$port)"/>
                </xsl:message>
                <dp:xset-target host="$host" port="$port" ssl="false()"/>
            </xsl:otherwise>
        </xsl:choose>
        <! -  ->
    </xsl:template>
</xsl:stylesheet>
```

Having obtained the routing document, the first action in the XSLT is to fetch the client's DN (Distinguished Name) from its SSL public certificate. This is done via the dp:client-subject-dn() extension function. You'll have to use client authentication for this to work or the client will not send its SSL certificate for validation. Having obtained the DN, we need to parse out the CN (Common Name). This is done by utilizing the EXSLT tokenize. It takes the DN string, and by designating the delimiting characters ('/' in this case), produces a nodeset of tokens. So in this example, a DN of C=US/ST=MA/L=Cambridge/O=IBM/OU=DataPower/OU=Sales/CN=SalesEastCoast' will produce a nodeset equal to that shown in Listing 24-16. Take note that this is a nodeset, not an XML Document, as it is missing a root node. This is an important distinction and affects the XPath used to retrieve elements from it.

Listing 24-16 Tokenized DN

```
<token>C=US</token>
<token>ST=MA</token>
<token>L=Cambridge</token>
<token>O=IBM</token>
<token>OU=DataPower</token>
<token>OU=Sales</token>
<token>CN=SalesEastCoast</token>
```

The XPath statement $DNTokens/self::token[substring(text(),1,3)='CN=']/text() is used to extract the CN from the DN. Notice that the Axis 'self' is used; this is required on a nodeset. The CN is then used to XPath into the routing document to obtain the dynamic host, port, and potentially an SSL Profile (though none are used in our examples.)

Finally, the xsl:choose statement is used to determine whether SSL is being used, and then the DataPower dp:xset-target extension element is executed to do the actual routing. There are several methods of routing within XSLT, however dp:xset-target (or its cousin dp:set-target which does not accept XPath in its attributes) is the required routing mechanism in a Route action. You should note in the SSL case, sslid utilizes an attribute value template (an XSLT mechanism) and the variable is required to be wrapped as such within curly brackets. Routing messages are produced and we are done.

Listing 24-17 shows the execution of a sample request using SSL and a public and private key. By using the verbose option of curl (-v), we can see the protocol headers exchanged. As we have requested, the LoadBalanceServer header has been returned with the name of the dynamically selected server that processed the request, BookQueryService-1 in this case. Had BookQueryService-2 serviced the request this header would have represented its injected header containing BookQueryService-2.

Listing 24-17 Sample Dynamic Routing Request

```
curl -k  -data-binary @bookQueryRequest. xml https://192.168.1.35:4025  -
key SalesEastCoast-privkey. pem  -cert SalesEastCoast-sscert. pem  -v

> POST / HTTP/1. 1
> User-Agent: curl/7. 16. 4 (i586-pc-mingw32msvc) libcurl/7. 16. 4
OpenSSL/0. 9. 7e zlib/1. 2. 2
> Host: 192.168.1.35:4025
> Accept: */*
> Content-Length: 246
> Content-Type: application/x-www-form-urlencoded
>
< HTTP/1. 1 200 Good
< User-Agent: curl/7. 16. 4 (i586-pc-mingw32msvc) libcurl/7. 16. 4
OpenSSL/0. 9. 7e zlib/1. 2. 2
< Content-Type: text/xml
< Via: 1. 1 BookQueryService-1,1. 1 DynamicRouting
< X-Client-IP: 192.168.1.35
< Host: 192.168.1.35:4051
< X-Archived-Client-IP: 192. 168. 1. 101
< LoadBalanceServer: Serviced by BookQueryService-1
< Connection: Keep-Alive
< Date: Mon, 09 Jun 2008 13:40:13 GMT
< Transfer-Encoding: chunked
<
<?xml version="1. 0" encoding="UTF-8"?>
<SOAP-ENV:Envelope xmlns:SOAP-
ENV="http://schemas.xmlsoap.org/soap/envelope/">
```

```
  <SOAP-ENV:Body>
    <book>
            <name>Moby Dick</name>
            <author>Herman Melville</author>
            <publisher>Longman</publisher>
            <isbn>0321228006</isbn>
            <copyright>2007</copyright>
    </book>
  </SOAP-ENV:Body>
</SOAP-ENV:Envelope>* Connection #0 to host 192.168.1.35 left intact
* Closing connection #0
```

Example 5: Load Balancer Health Checker

The previous example of dynamic routing demonstrated a simple method of routing traffic to a particular service based on the contents of the client's X.509 SSL certificate. A more likely use case is for traffic to be routed to one of several servers assigned to a pool of potential candidates available to service a request.

If you have read Chapter 7, you are familiar with the Load Balancer object and its implementation on the DataPower device. If you have not read this material, it is highly suggested that you do so, as this example demonstrates how to enable and disable members of a Load Balancer Group based on an Out of Service Schedule. This schedule provides for the ability to define date ranges in which a particular server (member) may be taken out of service (perhaps for scheduled maintenance.) It also provides for a repeating schedule, for example server-1 is taken out of service every Tuesday from 6:00–7:00 PM. There may be multiple occurrences of each type. Server-1 may also be taken out of service on Sundays from 1:00–2:00 AM, for example.

Each Load Balancer object may be configured to utilize a health check routine to ensure the availability of its members, and this example is actually an implementation of a custom health check routine. Figure 24-15 shows the topology of this example; the Out of Service Document is leveraged to manage the availability of the load balancer group members.

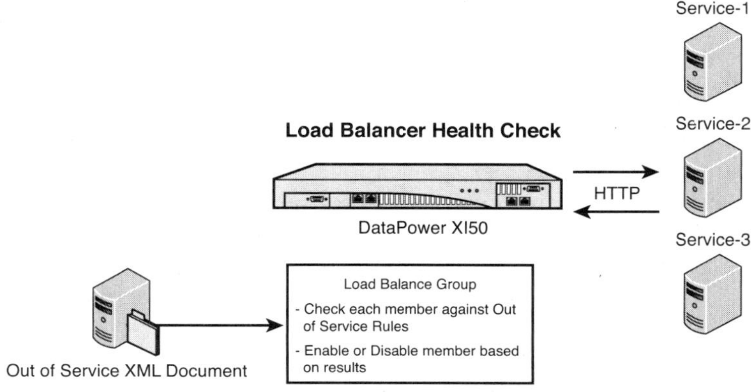

Figure 24-15 Out of Service health check topology.

Figure 24-16 shows the health check screen for the BookServiceLoadBalancerGroup. This Load Balancer acts as an access point for a group of BookQueryService members. You may notice in the XSL Health Check Filter property that the standard HealthCheck.xsl has been replaced with our customized heath check stylesheet bookQueryServiceHealthCheck.xsl . It is, in fact, an extension of the standard health checking stylesheet.

BookQueryService request documents are sent to each member to ensure that it is functioning properly. The location and name of this request document (local:///BookQueryRequest.xml) has been specified in the SOAP Request Document property. To validate the response, we just make sure a book element is found, so the XPath Expression (//*[local-name()='book']) has been set to locate this element.

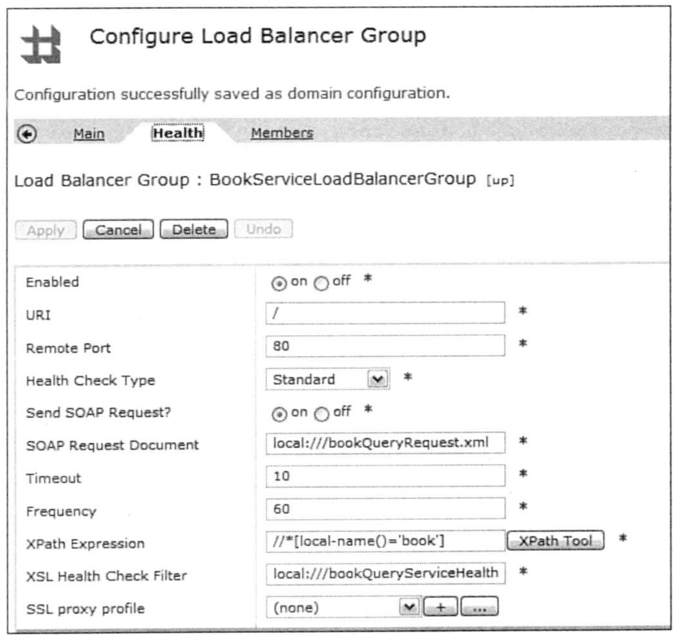

Figure 24-16 Load Balancer Group with customized health checking.

Listing 24-18 demonstrates the Out of Service Schedule XML document. Both ranges and repeating intervals are defined. Dates and times are entered in XML Schema Part 2 Datatypes format ISO 8601 Date format (YYY-MM-DDTHH:MM:SS-TZONE), and multiple entries may be entered for both.

Listing 24-18 Out of Service Schedule

```
<?xml version="1.0" encoding="UTF-8"?>
<! -  ->
<! - Out of Service Schedule for LoadBalancerGroup Members  ->
<! - You can define a range of xs:dateTime values, or a repeating sequence
specifying a day and D/T range  ->
<! - The numbering of days of the week starts at 1 for Sunday, 2 for Monday
and so on up to 7 for Saturday. ->
<! -  ->
<loadBalancerSchedule>
    <outOfService lbGroup="LoadBalancerGroup" lbMember="Service-1">
        <range from="2008-04-30T00:00:01-04:00" to="2008-05-01T00:00:01-
04:00"></range>
        <range from="2008-05-03T00:00:01-04:00" to="2008-05-05T00:00:01-
04:00"></range>
        <range from="2008-05-30T00:00:01-04:00" to="2008-08-30T00:00:01-
04:00"></range>
    </outOfService>
    <outOfService lbGroup="LoadBalancerGroup" lbMember="Service-2">
        <range from="2008-09-30T00:00:01" to="2008-10-30T00:00:01-
04:00"></range>
        <repeating days="6" from="T16:00:01-04:00" to="T18:00:01-04:00"/>
    </outOfService>
    <outOfService lbGroup="LoadBalancerGroup" lbMember="Service-3">
        <range from="2008-05-30T00:00:01-04:00" to="2008-07-30T00:00:01-
04:00"></range>
        <repeating days="1,4" from="T16:00:01-04:00" to="T18:00:01-04:00"/>
    </outOfService>
</loadBalancerSchedule>
```

The configuration of the Load Balancer enables scheduled executions of the health check mechanism. Each member is checked against the assigned health check port. During health check executions, each member is revalidated. So, if a server is brought down, it may well be brought back up if the out of service schedule dictates that. Listing 24-19 shows a log message produced when a Load Balancer member is brought down by our custom health check routine.

Listing 24-19 Out of Service Log Message

```
loadbalancer-group (BookServiceLoadBalancerGroup): LBGroup
(BookServiceLoadBalancerGroup)
LBMemeber (BookQueryService-1) disabled due to Out of Servicerange
from(2008-05-30T00:00:01-04:00),
 to(2008-08-30T00:00:01-04:00)
```

The status of members can also be verified by viewing the load balancer group from the status screens. Simply go to Status→IP Network→Load Balancer Status. You can see from this display that the BookQueryService-1 member has been disabled; its status is down. Figure 24-17 shows the effect of BookQueryService-1 being brought down as the schedule says it should be.

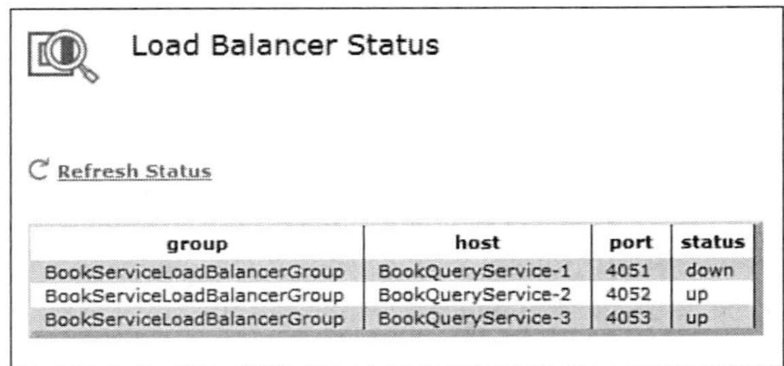

group	host	port	status
BookServiceLoadBalancerGroup	BookQueryService-1	4051	down
BookServiceLoadBalancerGroup	BookQueryService-2	4052	up
BookServiceLoadBalancerGroup	BookQueryService-3	4053	up

Figure 24-17 Load Balancer status.

Before getting into the actual XSLT required, it may be worthwhile to graphically discuss the processing logic. Figure 24-18 is a flowchart of the health check routine, and describes the processing that takes place in the XSLT.

Reading from the top of the chart, the first thing that is done is to fetch the Out of Service Schedule document. Next, the standard health check is validated using the XPath Expression entered on the Load Balancer Health Check screen (//*[local-name()='book']) in our case. If the member does not respond properly, it's declared sick and we're done. If it is active, we begin our custom processing by first checking to see if there are out of service entries for this server. If there are no entries, no further processing is required and we report the server healthy. If there are entries, they are processed and the results will determine if the server is reported as healthy or if it should be taken out of service.

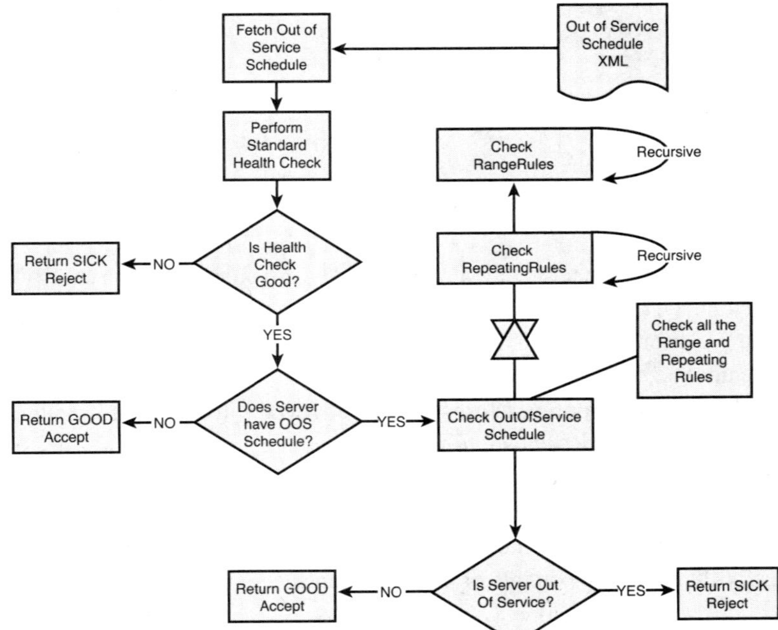

Figure 24-18 Out of service check flowchart.

So, we now have defined the mechanism used to control the members of a Load Balancer Group. Let's take a look at the XSLT required to do so. It's not that complex, and again it's an extension of the DataPower standard healthcheck.xsl stylesheet. We break it down into several listings for ease of discussion.

Listing 24-20 shows the stylesheet declaration. The EXSLT date declarations will be used to process the dates and times in the out of service schedule. The EXSLT dyn namespace is used by the standard health check process to determine the validity of the response from the member service by the execution of the dyn:evaluate element.

The xsl:param elements are standard health check statements. They contain the name of the Load Balancer Group and server being checked and are provided by the main health check processor (the routine that calls our health check routine). The XSL variable type contains the name of a log category we are going to use to send log messages to. You can read about logging targets, custom log categories, and debugging in Chapter 14, "Logging and Monitoring," but as you will see, this makes viewing log messages generated by xsl:message statements in this XSLT easier by allowing filtering to a specific log target.

Listing 24-20 Load Balanced Health Check Preamble

```
<xsl:stylesheet xmlns:xsl=http://www.w3.org/1999/XSL/Transform
version="1.0" xmlns:dp="http://www.datapower.com/extensions"
xmlns:dyn="http://exslt.org/dynamic"
xmlns:dpconfig="http://www.datapower.com/param/config"
xmlns:date="http://exslt.org/dates-and-times" extension-element-
prefixes="dyn dpconfig dp date" exclude-result-prefixes="dyn dpconfig dp
date">
   <! - ->
   <xsl:output method="xml"/>
   <xsl:param name="dpconfig:expression"/>
   <xsl:param name="dpconfig:grp"/>
   <xsl:param name="dpconfig:svr"/>
   <xsl:variable name="type" select="'LoadBalancedBookService'"/>
   <! - ->
```

We will look at the main template of our custom health check function shortly. It may seem a little daunting, maybe more so if you are not familiar with the standard health check routine. So let's go over the basics of what the XSLT is doing, and then address the main statements within it. It's not complicated.

First, the health check routine returns a block of XML with a root of "healthcheckresults" and children of "lbgroup" and "lbhost" to the main health check processor. This structure contains a health child element that indicates the actual results of the check as either "sick," or "good." Invalid checks also invoke the dp:reject function. So the basic premise of our stylesheet is to process the schedule and to return the healthcheckresults block with either a sick or good text string. Listing 24-21 shows an example of this document.

Listing 24-21 Health Check Response

```
<healthcheckresults>
    <lbgroup>loadBalancerGroupName</lbgroup>
    <lbhost>loadBalancerMemberName</lbhost>
    <health>good</health>
</healthcheckresults>
```

Listing 24-22 contains the XSLT main template; let's review what's required. First, we need to fetch and parse the Out of Service Schedule document. The document function does that. Then, as we know the Load Balancer Group and the particular member that is being tested from the parameters passed in, we construct an XPath statement using these variables to see if an out of service schedule exists for it. This is stored in the XSL variable serverSchedule.

Then we begin the process of building the response document. First, we test the standard health check response via the query param $dpconfig:expression. This is the response back from the member just as it would happen in the standard health check stylesheet. After all, if the member is down, there is no point testing it further.

Then, we test the server schedule stored in serverSchedule. If this member has a scheduled rule, we need to test it; if not, we are done. The member is up and we report so. If we are going to test the schedule, a message is written to the log with details about the member. Notice it is written to the custom log category we discussed.

The actual testing of the rules is done in a template named checkOutOfServiceSchedule. This will be presented shortly. For now, all you need to know is that it returns the health element and string that we've just discussed. The call is made to this template, and the results (<health>sick</health>) are potentially stored in an XSL variable named serverScheduleReturn. It gets populated only when the scheduled rules dictate that the member needs to be downed. If that is the case, the <health>sick</health> element is copied to the output stream. If not, then the <health>good</health> element is emitted.

Listing 24-22 Load Balanced Health Check Main Template

```
<xsl:template match="/">
    <! -  ->
    <! - Import the Out of Service Schedule (OOS)  ->
    <! - and get the entries for this LB Group /Server(member) ->
    <! -  ->
    <xsl:variable name="oosSchedule"
select="document('local:///bookQueryServiceOutofServiceSchedule.xml')"/>
    <xsl:variable name="serverSchedule"
select="$oosSchedule/loadBalancerSchedule/outOfService[@lbGroup=$dpconfig:g
rp and @lbMember=$dpconfig:svr]"/>
    <! -  ->
    <! - Standard Health Check entries  ->
    <! - The Main Check processor will looking for these   ->
    <! -  ->
    <healthcheckresults>
```

```
        <lbgroup>
            <xsl:value-of select="$dpconfig:grp"/>
        </lbgroup>
        <lbhost>
            <xsl:value-of select="$dpconfig:svr"/>
        </lbhost>
        <! - ->
        <xsl:choose>
            <! - ->
            <! - The XPath that we are looking for in response is not found ->
            <! - in the response from the server / member ->
            <! - Mark the server sick ->
            <! - ->
            <xsl:when test="count(dyn:evaluate($dpconfig:expression)) = 0">
                <health>sick</health>
                <dp:reject>
                    <xsl:value-of select="concat('Invalid response from ',
$dpconfig:svr, ' in lb-group ', $dpconfig:grp)"/>
                </dp:reject>
            </xsl:when>
            <! - ->
            <! - Are there OOS entries for this server / member? ->
            <! - If so, execute the OOS processing template ->
            <! - ->
            <xsl:when test="$serverSchedule">
                <xsl:message dp:priority="warn" dp:type="{$type}">
                    <xsl:value-of select="concat('dpconfig:grp=',
$dpconfig:grp)"/>
                    <xsl:value-of select="concat(', dpconfig:svr=',
$dpconfig:svr)"/>
                    <xsl:value-of select="concat(', type=', $type)"/>
                    <xsl:value-of select="', SERVER SCHEDULE FOUND'"/>
                </xsl:message>
                <! - ->
                <! - The template checkOutOfServiceSchedule will return the ->
                <! - results of OOS rule testing in $serverScheduleReturn ->
                <! - ->
                <xsl:variable name="serverScheduleReturn">
                    <xsl:call-template name="checkOutOfServiceSchedule">
                        <xsl:with-param name="serverSchedule"
select="$serverSchedule"/>
                    </xsl:call-template>
                </xsl:variable>
                <! - ->
                <! - Test the results of checkOutOfServiceSchedule ->
                <! - If there is anything in it? Only a sick response would be
returned ->
                <! - If nothing is returned the member / server is not OOS ->
                <! - ->
                <xsl:choose>
                    <xsl:when test="string-length($serverScheduleReturn)>1">
                        <xsl:message dp:priority="warn"
```

```
dp:type="{$type}">($serverScheduleReturn)>1</xsl:message>
                        <xsl:copy-of select="$serverScheduleReturn"/>
                    </xsl:when>
                    <! -  ->
                    <! - Otherwise all checked out, its good  ->
                    <! -  ->
                    <xsl:otherwise>
                        <xsl:message dp:priority="warn"
dp:type="{$type}">($serverScheduleReturn) EMPTY </xsl:message>
                        <health>good</health>
                        <dp:accept/>
                    </xsl:otherwise>
                </xsl:choose>
            </xsl:when>
            <! -  ->
            <! - There were no OOS entries found, report healthy  ->
            <! -  ->
            <xsl:otherwise>
                <xsl:message dp:priority="warn" dp:type="{$type}">
                    <xsl:value-of select="concat('dpconfig:grp=',
$dpconfig:grp)"/>
                    <xsl:value-of select="concat(', dpconfig:svr=',
$dpconfig:svr)"/>
                    <xsl:value-of select="', SERVER SCHEDULE NOT FOUND'"/>
                </xsl:message>
                <health>good</health>
                <dp:accept/>
            </xsl:otherwise>
        </xsl:choose>
    </healthcheckresults>
    <! -  ->
</xsl:template>
```

Listing 24-23 shows the checkOutOfServiceSchedule template that was called from Listing 24-22. This is the controlling process for the various rules. Its job is to determine whether there are ranges or repeating rules for this Load Balancer Group member, and to call the appropriate template that does the actual date checking. Then we're done! But this is a robust process here, and it will handle many repeating or range type rules.

The server schedule is extracted from the parameter passed to the template, and stored in the XSL variable serverSchedule. It is then tested to see whether there are range type rules. If so, the date checking template checkRangeRules is called and passed the serverSchedule. Notice that an index (ndx) is also passed so we know which of the potentially multiple rules we are examining. This process is repeated for repeating type rules. Again the date checking template is called, passing the schedule and the index.

The result of the out of service rule checking is then analyzed. First the range rule results are tested; then the repeating rule results are tested. If the range rule has resulted in a health check failure, we emit (xsl:copy-of) the element. The same for the repeating rules. We need only one failure message, hence the choose statement.

Listing 24-23 Template to Test for Existence and Required Processing of Out of Service Schedules

```
<! -  ->
<! - This template processes the OOS Schedule  ->
<! -  ->
<xsl:template name="checkOutOfServiceSchedule">
    <xsl:param name="serverSchedule"/>
    <! -  ->
    <! - First check the range rules starting with the first (ndx=1)  ->
    <! -  ->
    <xsl:variable name="rangeResults">
        <xsl:if test="$serverSchedule/range">
            <xsl:call-template name="checkRangeRules">
                <xsl:with-param name="serverSchedule"
select="$serverSchedule"/>
                <xsl:with-param name="ndx" select="number(1)"/>
            </xsl:call-template>
        </xsl:if>
    </xsl:variable>
    <! -  ->
    <! - Then check the repeating rules starting with the first (ndx=1) ->
    <! -  ->
    <xsl:variable name="repeatingResults">
        <xsl:if test="$serverSchedule/repeating">
            <xsl:call-template name="checkRepeatingRules">
                <xsl:with-param name="serverSchedule"
select="$serverSchedule"/>
                <xsl:with-param name="ndx" select="number(1)"/>
            </xsl:call-template>
        </xsl:if>
    </xsl:variable>
    <! -  ->
    <! - We need to report sick only once, so first check if the repeating
rules reported sick  ->
    <! - If so, copy the <health>sick</health> response  ->
    <! - If not, check the repeating rules  ->
    <! -  ->
    <xsl:choose>
        <xsl:when test="$rangeResults">
            <xsl:copy-of select="$rangeResults"/>
        </xsl:when>
        <xsl:when test="$repeatingResults">
            <xsl:copy-of select="$repeatingResults"/>
        </xsl:when>
    </xsl:choose>
</xsl:template>
```

Listing 24-24 shows the range testing template. It was passed the member's schedule and the index which is initially set to 1 to indicate processing of the first rule found. It determines today's date via the EXSLT date:date-time() function and stores it in the thisDate XSL variable.

We then begin determining whether today's date is within the ranges. That is, is today after the from date-time and before the to date-time? This will be true if the EXSLT date-difference() function returns a negative number for the from date and a positive value for the to date.

If our test is positive (we found an out of service rule), first a variable with some nice debugging information is created, and then written to the log. The health element with "sick" string is produced, and the dp:reject() function is invoked.

We have one final task in this template: what if this rule did not result in an out of service condition but there are more rules? The whole process starts over for the next rule (if there is one.) This is called a recursive template and by incrementing the index, we simply re-run the template using the next rule. The process is repeated until there are no more rules, or we find an out of service condition. Be careful when coding recursive templates, you need to make sure that the processing ends under all possible conditions, or else it just keeps on going!

Listing 24-24 Range Testing Template

```
<!-- -->
<!-- This template processes the OOS Schedule Range rules -->
<!-- The ndx param is used to tell which range rules we are testing -->
<!-- -->
<xsl:template name="checkRangeRules">
    <xsl:param name="serverSchedule"/>
    <xsl:param name="ndx"/>
    <!-- -->
    <!-- Get some date info and calculate -->
    <!-- differences from the from / to dates on rules -->
    <!-- -->
    <xsl:variable name="thisDate" select="date:date-time()"/>
    <xsl:variable name="diffFrom" select="date:difference($thisDate,
$serverSchedule/range[$ndx]/@from)"/>
    <xsl:variable name="diffTo" select="date:difference($thisDate,
$serverSchedule/range[$ndx]/@to)"/>
    <!-- -->
    <!-- If diffFrom is negative and diffTo is positive -->
    <!-- Today's date is in between, i.e. in the range -->
    <!-- Report the server sick (OOS) -->
    <!-- -->
    <xsl:choose>
        <xsl:when test="substring($diffFrom,1,1)='-' and
substring($diffTo,1,1)!='-'">
            <xsl:variable name="rejectString" select="concat(
                    'LBGroup (', $dpconfig:grp,
                    ') LBMemeber (', $dpconfig:svr,
                    ') disabled due to Out of Servicerange',
                    ' from(', $serverSchedule/range[$ndx]/@from,
                    '), to(', $serverSchedule/range[$ndx]/@to, ')')"/>
            <xsl:message dp:priority="warn" dp:type="{$type}">
                <xsl:value-of select="$rejectString"/>
            </xsl:message>
            <health>sick</health>
```

```
            <dp:reject>
                <xsl:value-of select="$rejectString"/>
            </dp:reject>
        </xsl:when>
        <!-- -->
        <!-- Otherwise the server is healthy -->
        <!-- If there are more rules to process, call the template again -->
        <!-- -->
        <xsl:otherwise>
            <xsl:if test="$serverSchedule/range[$ndx+1]">
                <xsl:message dp:priority="warn" dp:type="{$type}">CHECKING
NEXT RANGE</xsl:message>
                <xsl:call-template name="checkRangeRules">
                    <xsl:with-param name="serverSchedule"
select="$serverSchedule"/>
                    <xsl:with-param name="ndx" select="$ndx+1"/>
                </xsl:call-template>
            </xsl:if>
        </xsl:otherwise>
    </xsl:choose>
</xsl:template>
```

The final template for our health check routine processes the repeating rules. It's similar to the previous template that processed the range rules. Listing 24-25 shows the template. Once again, the server's schedule is passed in along with the index. In this case, we need to know not only the date-time but also the day of the week, so the EXSLT date:day-in-week() function is executed. It returns a numeric value starting with 1 for Sunday, and the days for which the rules repeat is extracted from the "days" attribute of the rule.

Again the date:difference() function is executed against the date-time, and the test is performed. In this test, the day is added to the test. You'll notice that the current date is concatenated to the time entered on the rule for the purposes of the test as only time is entered on the rule. As in the range template, a reject string is created if the repeating rule is found to be within the date-time and day of week ranges; if no match is found, the template is recursively called to test additional rules if they are found.

Listing 24-25 Repeating Rule Testing Template

```
<!-- -->
<!-- This template processes the OOS Schedule Repeating rules -->
<!-- This ndx param is used to tell which of repeating rules we are
testing -->
<!-- -->
<xsl:template name="checkRepeatingRules">
    <xsl:param name="serverSchedule"/>
    <xsl:param name="ndx"/>
    <!-- -->
    <!-- Get some date info -->
    <!-- Todays date in prefixed to the time values entered on the rules -->
        <!-- repeating rules do not have a date component -->
```

```
    <! - And calculate differences from the from / to dates on rules  ->
    <! -  ->
    <xsl:variable name="dayOfWeek" select="date:day-in-week()"/>
    <xsl:variable name="days"
select="$serverSchedule/repeating[$ndx]/@days"/>
    <xsl:variable name="thisDate" select="date:date-time()"/>
    <xsl:variable name="from" select="concat(substring-before($thisDate,
'T'), $serverSchedule/repeating[$ndx]/@from)"/>
    <xsl:variable name="to" select="concat(substring-before($thisDate,
'T'),$serverSchedule/repeating[$ndx]/@to)"/>
    <xsl:variable name="diffFrom" select="date:difference($thisDate,
$from)"/>
    <xsl:variable name="diffTo" select="date:difference($thisDate, $to)"/>
    <! -  ->
    <! - If diffFrom is negative and diffTo is positive ->
    <! - Today's date is in between, i.e. in the range  ->
    <! - Report the server sick (OOS)  ->
    <! -  ->
    <xsl:choose>
        <xsl:when test="substring($diffFrom,1,1)='-' and
substring($diffTo,1,1)!='-' and contains($days, $dayOfWeek)">
            <xsl:variable name="rejectString" select="concat(
                    'LBGroup (', $dpconfig:grp,
                    ') LBMemeber (', $dpconfig:svr,
                    ') disabled due to repeating Out of Servicerange,
days(', $days,
                    ') from(', $serverSchedule/repeating[$ndx]/@from,
                    '), to(', $serverSchedule/repeating[$ndx]/@to, ')')"/>
            <xsl:message dp:priority="warn" dp:type="{$type}">
                <xsl:value-of select="$rejectString"/>
            </xsl:message>
            <health>sick</health>
            <dp:reject>
                <xsl:value-of select="$rejectString"/>
            </dp:reject>
        </xsl:when>
        <! -  ->
        <! - Otherwise the server is healthy  ->
        <! - If there are more rules to process, call the template again ->
        <! -  ->
        <xsl:otherwise>
            <xsl:if test="$serverSchedule/repeating[$ndx+1]">
                <xsl:message dp:priority="warn" dp:type="{$type}">CHECKING
NEXT REPEATING</xsl:message>
                <xsl:call-template name="checkRepeatingRules">
                    <xsl:with-param name="serverSchedule"
select="$serverSchedule"/>
                    <xsl:with-param name="ndx" select="$ndx+1"/>
                </xsl:call-template>
            </xsl:if>
        </xsl:otherwise>
    </xsl:choose>
</xsl:template>
```

A look at the custom log target shows the results of the health check. Each member is tested and server-1, having been found to exist in a valid out of service rule, is taken out of service. Figure 24-19 shows the log messages; notice that the target has been selected to exclude all other messages.

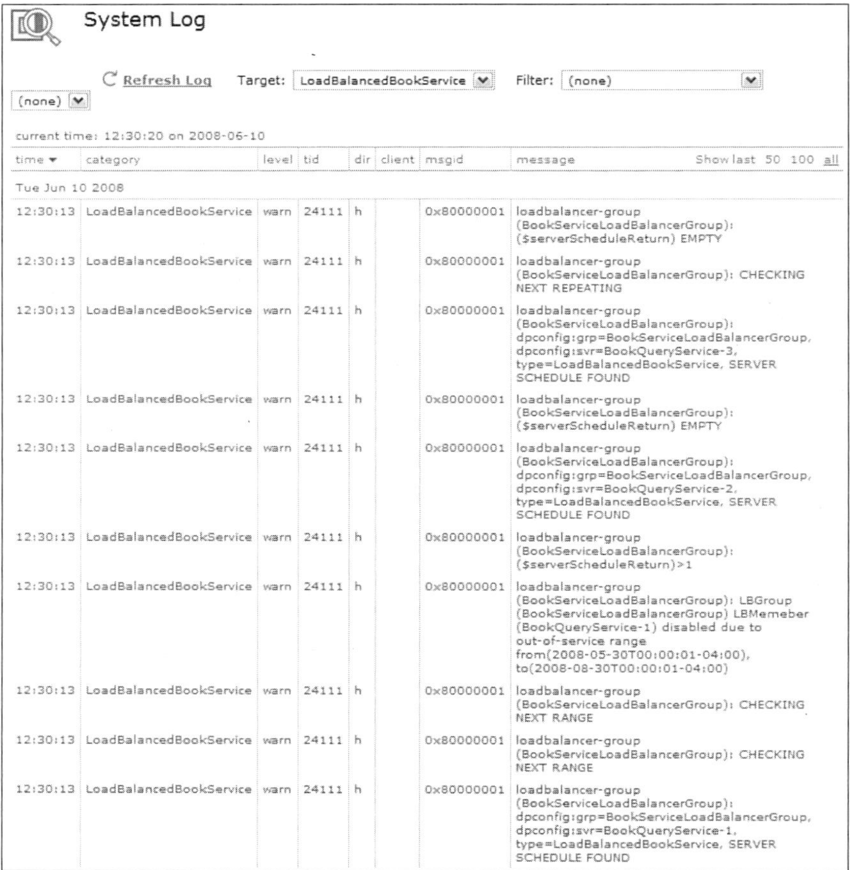

System Log

Refresh Log Target: LoadBalancedBookService Filter: (none) (none)

current time: 12:30:20 on 2008-06-10

time	category	level	tid	dir	client	msgid	message
Tue Jun 10 2008							
12:30:13	LoadBalancedBookService	warn	24111	h		0x80000001	loadbalancer-group (BookServiceLoadBalancerGroup): ($serverScheduleReturn) EMPTY
12:30:13	LoadBalancedBookService	warn	24111	h		0x80000001	loadbalancer-group (BookServiceLoadBalancerGroup): CHECKING NEXT REPEATING
12:30:13	LoadBalancedBookService	warn	24111	h		0x80000001	loadbalancer-group (BookServiceLoadBalancerGroup): dpconfig:grp=BookServiceLoadBalancerGroup, dpconfig:svr=BookQueryService-3, type=LoadBalancedBookService, SERVER SCHEDULE FOUND
12:30:13	LoadBalancedBookService	warn	24111	h		0x80000001	loadbalancer-group (BookServiceLoadBalancerGroup): ($serverScheduleReturn) EMPTY
12:30:13	LoadBalancedBookService	warn	24111	h		0x80000001	loadbalancer-group (BookServiceLoadBalancerGroup): dpconfig:grp=BookServiceLoadBalancerGroup, dpconfig:svr=BookQueryService-2, type=LoadBalancedBookService, SERVER SCHEDULE FOUND
12:30:13	LoadBalancedBookService	warn	24111	h		0x80000001	loadbalancer-group (BookServiceLoadBalancerGroup): ($serverScheduleReturn)>1
12:30:13	LoadBalancedBookService	warn	24111	h		0x80000001	loadbalancer-group (BookServiceLoadBalancerGroup): LBGroup (BookServiceLoadBalancerGroup) LBMemeber (BookQueryService-1) disabled due to out-of-service range from(2008-05-30T00:00:01-04:00), to(2008-08-30T00:00:01-04:00)
12:30:13	LoadBalancedBookService	warn	24111	h		0x80000001	loadbalancer-group (BookServiceLoadBalancerGroup): CHECKING NEXT RANGE
12:30:13	LoadBalancedBookService	warn	24111	h		0x80000001	loadbalancer-group (BookServiceLoadBalancerGroup): CHECKING NEXT RANGE
12:30:13	LoadBalancedBookService	warn	24111	h		0x80000001	loadbalancer-group (BookServiceLoadBalancerGroup): dpconfig:grp=BookServiceLoadBalancerGroup, dpconfig:svr=BookQueryService-1, type=LoadBalancedBookService, SERVER SCHEDULE FOUND

Show last 50 100 all

Figure 24-19 System log showing messages produced by Out of Service health check.

We close our discussion of the load balanced book request by executing a couple of requests against our service. Listing 24-26 shows the requests each being submitted to the dynamic service on port 4020, and each being responded to by a separate service. Extraneous details have been omitted from the listing. We can tell which service executed the request by examining the Load-BalanceServer protocol header. Just as we intended, it is populated by the actual service that satisfied by request, and no request is made against BookQueryService-1, our downed member.

Listing 24-26 Load Balanced Book Requests

```
curl  -data-binary @bookQueryRequest. xml http://192.168.1.35:4020 -v
* About to connect() to 192.168.1.35 port 4020 (#0)
*   Trying 192.168.1.35. . .  connected
* Connected to 192.168.1.35 (192.168.1.35) port 4020 (#0)
> POST / HTTP/1. 1
< HTTP/1. 1 200 Good
< LoadBalanceServer: Serviced by BookQueryService-3
<?xml version="1. 0" encoding="UTF-8"?>
<SOAP-ENV:Envelope xmlns:SOAP-
ENV="http://schemas.xmlsoap.org/soap/envelope/">
  <SOAP-ENV:Body>
    <book>
            <name>Moby Dick</name>
            <author>Herman Melville</author>
            <publisher>Longman</publisher>
            <isbn>0321228006</isbn>
            <copyright>2007</copyright>
    </book>
  </SOAP-ENV:Body>
</SOAP-ENV:Envelope

curl  -data-binary @bookQueryRequest. xml http://192.168.1.35:4020 -v
* About to connect() to 192.168.1.35 port 4020 (#0)
*   Trying 192.168.1.35. . .  connected
* Connected to 192.168.1.35 (192.168.1.35) port 4020 (#0)
> POST / HTTP/1. 1
< HTTP/1. 1 200 Good
< LoadBalanceServer: Serviced by BookQueryService-2
<?xml version="1. 0" encoding="UTF-8"?>
<SOAP-ENV:Envelope xmlns:SOAP-
ENV="http://schemas.xmlsoap.org/soap/envelope/">
  <SOAP-ENV:Body>
    <book>
            <name>Moby Dick</name>
            <author>Herman Melville</author>
            <publisher>Longman</publisher>
            <isbn>0321228006</isbn>
            <copyright>2007</copyright>
    </book>
  </SOAP-ENV:Body>
</ SOAP-ENV:Envelope>
```

Summary

This chapter has demonstrated several examples of DataPower development. We've seen examples of transaction control, SSL certificate interrogation, dynamic routing, custom error processing, and a robust example of load balancer member control. By this time you should have a solid foundation for a wide variety of customization tasks. But again, remember the engineers and architects at DataPower have invested countless man hours to produce an appliance that accomplishes many, many tasks using the power of its configurable services. Look first to these options, and then when you must, open the door to the power within. Have fun!

CHAPTER 25

Development Tools

Now that you have three chapters on development under your belt, you realize that you may have to do some XSLT programming when configuring your services. We have provided you with the basics, some advanced topics, and even some real-world examples. Even after all that, XSLT still might seem a little intimidating. But fear not—help is on the way. As with any other programming language, a developer coding XSLT stylesheets should have a set of tools available for editing, testing, and debugging during the development process. This chapter discusses the tools available for XSLT development, as well as how they can integrate with the DataPower runtime.

Integrated Development Environments

Many "old-school" developers' development environments consist of a basic text editor, and they might claim that's all they need. However, with today's complex programming languages, most realize the benefits of an Integrated Development Environment (IDE). An IDE can be thought of as the developer's tool box. There are many different types available for different programming languages and provided by many different software vendors. Most IDEs provide a robust text editor that offers tools such as code formatting, debugging, and possibly a runtime environment. Because we are programming for the DataPower runtime, we are interested only in XSLT programming and IDEs that support it. Although it is not the intent of this chapter to give you a tutorial on any one product, we will point out the key features of various IDEs that can assist you when coding your XSLT for DataPower services.

Rational Application Developer

The IBM Rational Application Developer (RAD) product is a full-featured IDE that can be used for programming in several different languages. RAD is built on the Eclipse platform with many additional benefits, such as robust testing and debugging tools, code formatting, and much more. It is often used for developing Java EE applications that will be deployed to a WebSphere Application Server (WAS) as it provides many features to aid in the development of Java EE artifacts as well as a built-in WAS test server. RAD also has many built-in features for programming XSLT, such as text formatting, an XSLT runtime engine, and step-by-step debugging. RAD Version 7.0.0 is used for the discussion and examples in this chapter. Some features discussed may not be available in previous versions. Please check your version of RAD for the supported features.

Text Editor

The text editor in RAD is where you create and edit your files. For DataPower development, these are typically XSLT stylesheets and XML files. This is not your typical text editor as it has many built-in features that are available based on the extension of the file you are editing. For example, if you are editing an .xsl file, the editor knows that it is an XSLT stylesheet and enables the built-in features for editing XSLT.

When creating a new file in RAD, you can specify the type of file that you are creating. When you specify that the new file is an XSLT stylesheet, it will create a new XSL file with the mandatory elements and declarations as shown in Listing 25-1.

Listing 25-1 New XSL File Created Within RAD

```
<?xml version="1.0" encoding="UTF-8"?>
<xsl:stylesheet xmlns:xsl="http://www.w3.org/1999/XSL/Transform"
    version="1.0"
    xmlns:xalan="http://xml.apache.org/xslt">
</xsl:stylesheet>
```

After the XSL file is created, the file can be edited in the text editor pane. This is where you see the real power of this IDE. As you first start to code your XSLT, you might notice some pop-ups that display next to the cursor; these contain suggestions for completing the current line of code. For example, when you begin creating your stylesheet, you might start by creating a <xsl:template> element. As you begin to type this code, a pop-up displays with suggestions immediately after typing the '<' in the editor, as shown in Figure 25-1. Any of the elements displayed can be chosen and will be inserted automatically into your code. In this case, you can click the <xsl:template> element. Not only does this save you on some typing, but it is also handy if you don't remember the exact syntax of an element. If you find that this pop-up does not display automatically, you can press CTRL and the spacebar together to activate it.

In addition to this content assist capability, RAD also provides a way of alerting you that there is a syntax error in the code by drawing a red squiggly line underneath the line where the error occurs.

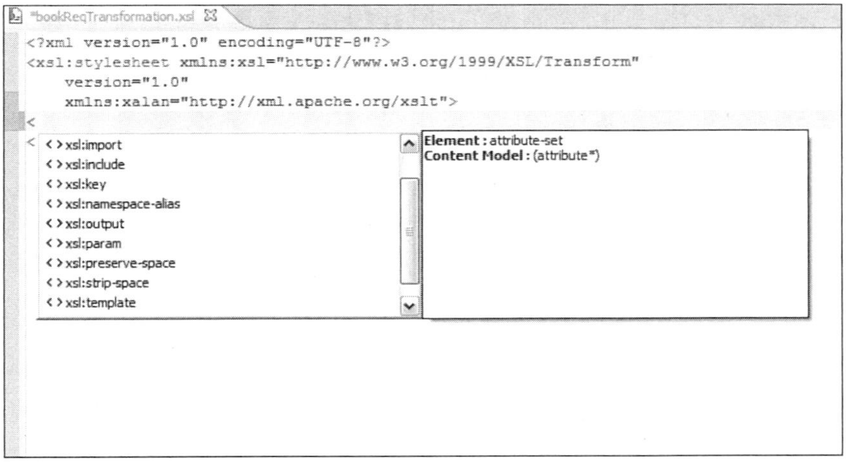

```
*bookReqTransformation.xsl
<?xml version="1.0" encoding="UTF-8"?>
<xsl:stylesheet xmlns:xsl="http://www.w3.org/1999/XSL/Transform"
    version="1.0"
    xmlns:xalan="http://xml.apache.org/xslt">
<
<  <> xsl:import
   <> xsl:include
   <> xsl:key
   <> xsl:namespace-alias
   <> xsl:output
   <> xsl:param
   <> xsl:preserve-space
   <> xsl:strip-space
   <> xsl:template

Element : attribute-set
Content Model : (attribute*)
```

Figure 25-1 Content Assist pop-up.

Figure 25-2 shows an example where the namespace was not added to the ending element for the template. Notice the squiggly line underneath the ending </template> tag. Hovering the cursor over this error provides more details about the error.

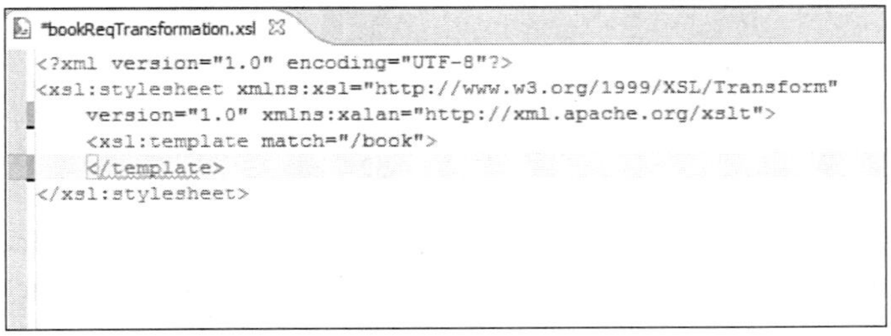

```
*bookReqTransformation.xsl
<?xml version="1.0" encoding="UTF-8"?>
<xsl:stylesheet xmlns:xsl="http://www.w3.org/1999/XSL/Transform"
    version="1.0" xmlns:xalan="http://xml.apache.org/xslt">
    <xsl:template match="/book">
    </template>
</xsl:stylesheet>
```

Figure 25-2 RAD indicating a syntax error.

Many developers do not take the time to write code that is properly formatted, such as indenting between elements and conditional statements. When using RAD, you don't have to worry about this because it provides a feature to format the code for you. You can right-click within your XSL or XML file and select Format→Document, and your document is formatted for you. Figure 25-3 shows a small piece of XSLT within the RAD text editor that has not been properly formatted. After using the Format option, the code is formatted so that all the nested elements are indented, as shown in Figure 25-4.

These formatting parameters are configurable, although the defaults should suffice. Notice how much easier the code is to read after it has been formatted.

*bookReqTransformation.xsl

```
<?xml version="1.0" encoding="UTF-8"?>
<xsl:stylesheet xmlns:xsl="http://www.w3.org/1999/XSL/Transform" version="1.0" xmlns:xalan="http://xml.apache.org/xslt">
<xsl:template match="/book">
<book-request>
<book-name>
<xsl:value-of select="name" />
</book-name>
<book-author>
<xsl:value-of select="author" />
</book-author>
</book-request>
</xsl:template>
</xsl:stylesheet>
```

Figure 25-3 XSL before auto format.

*bookReqTransformation.xsl

```
<?xml version="1.0" encoding="UTF-8"?>
<xsl:stylesheet xmlns:xsl="http://www.w3.org/1999/XSL/Transform"
    version="1.0" xmlns:xalan="http://xml.apache.org/xslt">
    <xsl:template match="/book">
        <book-request>
            <book-name>
                <xsl:value-of select="name" />
            </book-name>
            <book-author>
                <xsl:value-of select="author" />
            </book-author>
        </book-request>
    </xsl:template>
</xsl:stylesheet>
```

Figure 25-4 XSL after auto format.

XPath Expression Builder

When coding XSLT, it is likely that you will be writing many XPath statements to query the XML document being parsed. Many times this will be an easy task that can be accomplished by looking at the XML document itself. There are times however, that even an experienced XSLT developer can use a little help with formulating these XPath expressions for deeply nested, complex XML documents. This is where the XPath expression builder in RAD is invaluable.

As you are coding your XSLT, you will most likely refer back to a sample XML document representing the actual document that will be used as input for the transformation. You will refer to this document for creating XPath expressions that may be used to extract the value of an element or attribute to be used within the transformation. The XPath Expression Builder can be invoked from within the text editor as you are coding at the time where an XPath expression can be used. For example, as you are typing a xsl:value-of element, you can provide the select attribute that would include an XPath expression indicating the data to output. Just after you type the select=" is where you would enter this XPath expression. You can right-click after this parameter and select the XPath Expression option, as shown in Figure 25-5. RAD is smart enough to make this option available only when an XPath expression can be used in the XSLT you are currently typing.

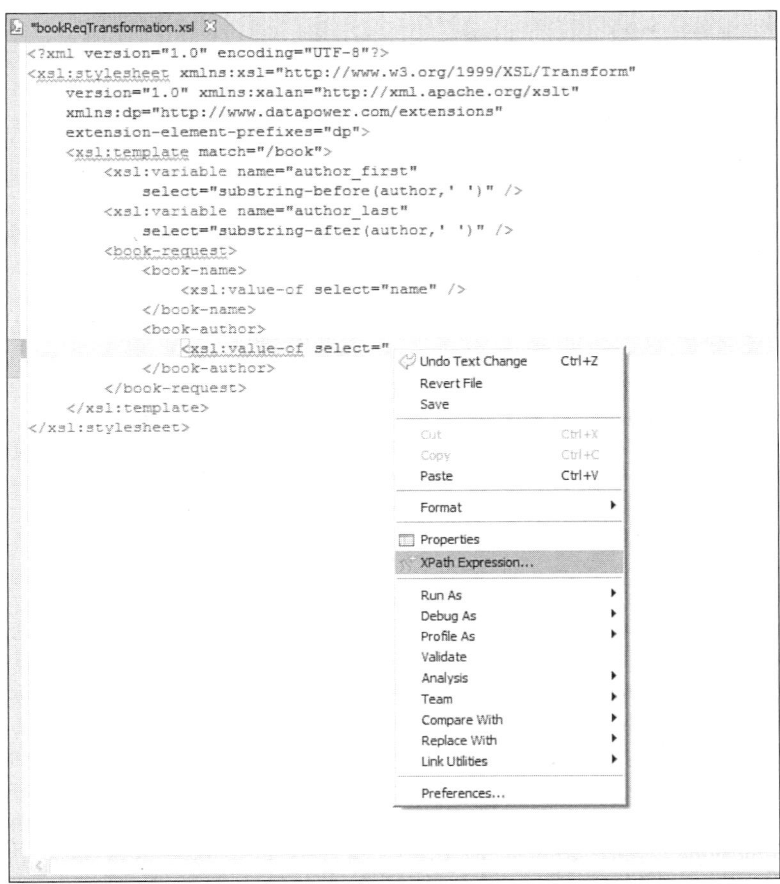

Figure 25-5 Selecting the XPath Expression Builder.

After launching this tool, you need to select an XML document to build the XPath expression from. This is required only the first time that you launch the XPath Expression Builder for a particular XSLT stylesheet. From then on it knows the XML document that you are mapping from. The source XML document is now displayed in the Source Tree window where it can be expanded until you reach the element you are interested in. You can then double-click the element or attribute and the XPath expression is generated for you. Figure 25-6 shows an example of building an XPath expression to extract the name attribute from the element author. For this example, we changed the bookQueryRequest.xml document to contain the author's name in an XML attribute instead of the element itself. After double-clicking this attribute, the XPath expression author/@name is populated in the text box above it. Notice that the tool actually knows the current context within the XSLT being coded. In this example, it knows that the current context is book, so it builds the XPath expression appropriately. You can then highlight the expression that was built for you and click the OK button. The XPath expression is then automatically inserted into the select attribute in your code.

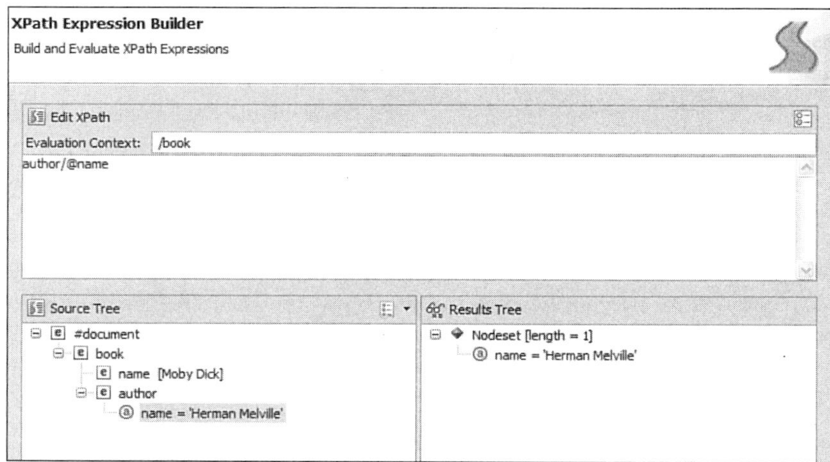

Figure 25-6 XPath Expression Builder.

XSLT Runtime

After you have completed your XSLT development, you might want to test it before deploying it to the DataPower runtime. RAD comes with an XSLT runtime for you to test your code from within the IDE itself. The easiest way to do this is to import the XML that will be used as the input to the transformation into the project. A project is simply a top-level folder containing all the files for the application being developed. When developing stylesheets for DataPower services, you might create a project for each service and store the associated files within it. This keeps your workspace more organized and makes it much easier when it is time to move the code to the DataPower device for a given service. For more information on projects and importing files, please refer to your RAD documentation. After the XML file that will be transformed is in the same project as the XSLT that is being tested, you can highlight the XML and XSL files in the Navigator pane of your RAD environment (hold down Ctrl and click each file), right-click one of them, and select Run As→1 XSL Transformation as shown in Figure 25-7.

After the XSL transformation is complete, the results are written to a new file and shown in the text editor pane. If any errors were encountered during the execution, they will be listed in the console that is typically located just below the text editor. Keep in mind that RAD does not know about any custom functions and elements that your XSLT might be utilizing during a transformation, so using these will cause the transformation to fail. This includes DataPower extension functions and elements and EXSLT functions. After a successful execution, you might notice that the resulting XML file is written out in one single line and may be difficult to read. This is where the Format option comes in handy. As discussed earlier, to format this results document, you right-click in the document and select Format→Document. The results of an XSL transformation after formatting are shown in Figure 25-8.

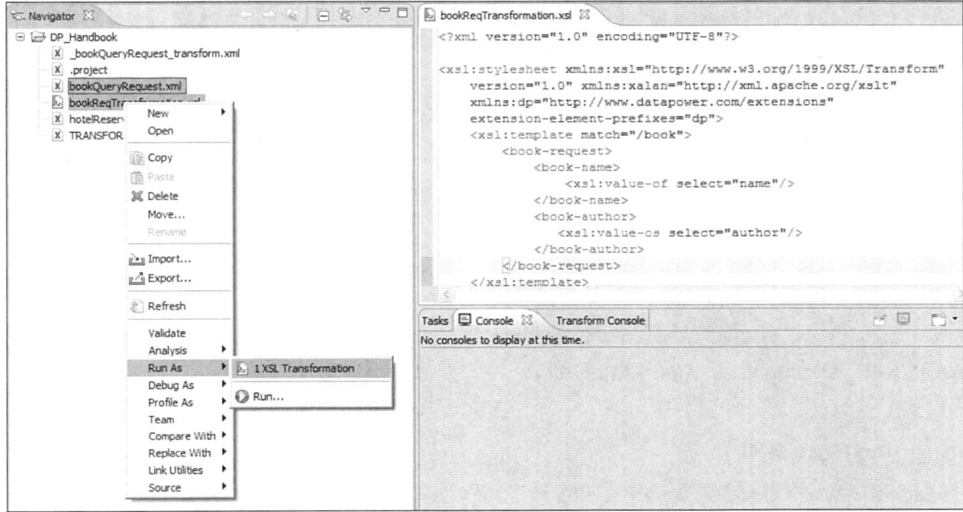

Figure 25-7 Executing XSLT within RAD.

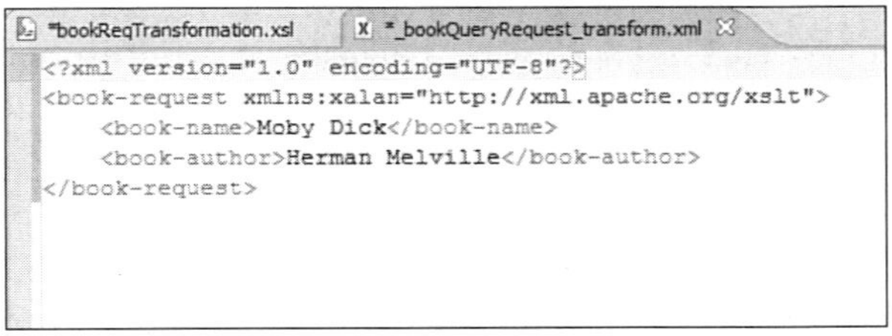

```
*bookReqTransformation.xsl    *_bookQueryRequest_transform.xml
<?xml version="1.0" encoding="UTF-8"?>
<book-request xmlns:xalan="http://xml.apache.org/xslt">
    <book-name>Moby Dick</book-name>
    <book-author>Herman Melville</book-author>
</book-request>
```

Figure 25-8 XSLT execution results.

This example produced a small, simple XML results file that is easy to read. It is likely that your results file will not always be this small. Large XML files, even when formatted, are often difficult to read. Because of this, there is a graphical viewer for your XML files in the text editor. When viewing and editing your XML files, there are two tabs at the bottom of the editor. One is labeled Source and shows you the XML in text format as shown in our examples. The second tab is labeled Design and gives you a graphical representation of the entire XML file, as shown in Figure 25-9. All nested elements can be expanded and collapsed for readability. You can see how this can make reading large XML files much easier.

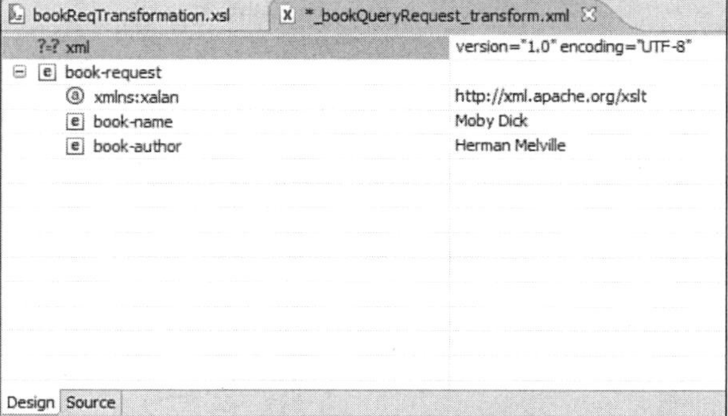

Figure 25-9 Design view of an XML file.

Debugging Your XSLT

Let's face it—when developing any code, it is inevitable that there will be times where errors are thrown or the results produced are not what you expect them to be. Sometimes these will be easy to resolve by reading through the code yourself, and sometimes you just wish you could see what is going on in the code at runtime. This is another area where RAD is extremely powerful; it provides a debugging tool that enables you to step through the code as it executes. You can set breakpoints in your code and view runtime variables and their values at any step during the execution. Figure 25-10 shows this debugging screen as we are stepping through the execution of our XSLT code. Notice the different panes shown in one single view. At the bottom left you can view the code as it executes; the current line of execution is highlighted. In this example, you can see that the current line being executed is the line that outputs the <book-request> element. Next to that in the bottom right, you can view the XML document that is being transformed. The current context is also highlighted as you step through the execution. In this example, we matched on "/book" in our template so the <book> element is the current context as shown. In the upper-right corner, you will notice three tabs. These show breakpoints, current context of the XML document, and the current variables set within the execution. We are showing the Variables tab in Figure 25-10; you can see that there are two variables set. A variable named "author_first" currently has a value of "Herman" and there is a variable named "author_last" with a current value of "Melville." All these screens are updated after each step, providing a snapshot as you step through the execution. This is extremely helpful when debugging those difficult problems. For example, when variables are conditionally set, you can see what condition is true and what the variables are set to during this transformation execution.

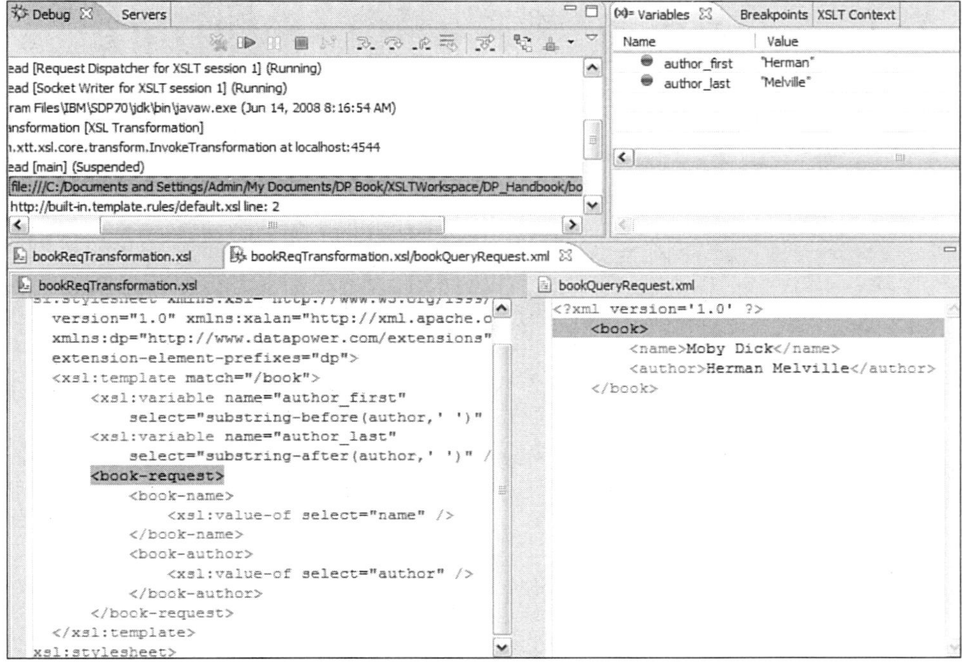

Figure 25-10 Step-by-step debugging.

Building an XML Schema File

Now that your code is developed, tested, and added to your service, you may decide that you would like to validate all incoming requests into the service against the corresponding schema file. You quickly realize that you don't have a schema for the input document that your service is expecting. One thing you do have is the test XML document that you tested your transformations with within RAD. Because you already know that this test file is in the correct format, it would be nice to build a schema right from that. Well, again RAD comes to the rescue.

A convenient feature in RAD is the capability to create a schema from an XML file. By simply right-clicking the XML file in the project and selecting Generate→XML Schema, a new .xsd file is created with the name you provided. This can now be used in your DataPower service to validate all incoming request documents. You should always inspect the resulting schema after it is created because RAD takes a "best guess" at what the schema should be. Although this provides a valid schema for the XML provided, it may not be exactly what you wanted. Figure 25-11 shows the generated XSD file for the bookQueryRequest.xml file.

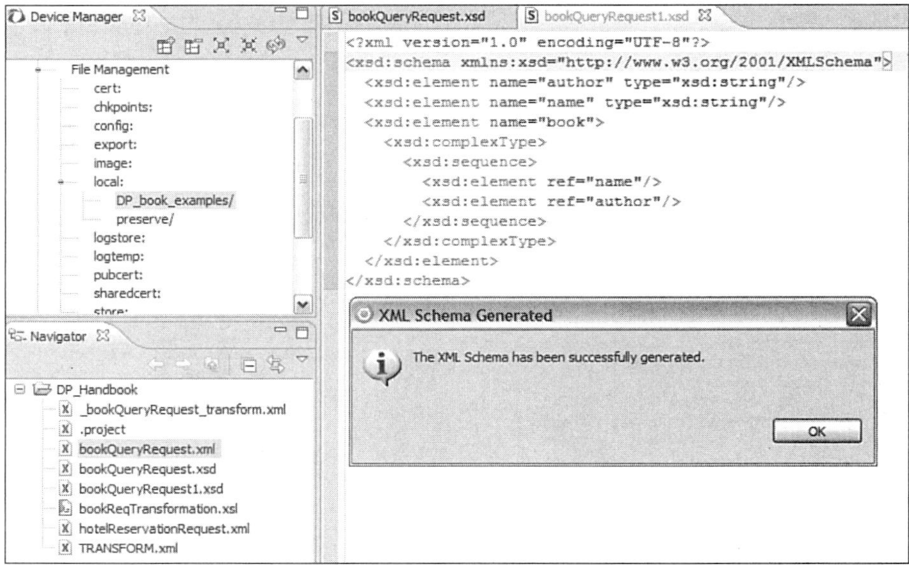

Figure 25-11 Automatically generated schema file for the bookQueryRequest.xml file.

XML Spy

Altova XMLSpy is another popular IDE for working with XML and XSL documents. This IDE is specifically designed to work with XML, XSD, and XSL documents. All the features discussed in this section are demonstrated using the most current version of XMLSpy at the time of this writing and might not be available in all prior versions. Be sure to check the version you are using to see what features are available.

Text Editor

Much like the RAD product, XMLSpy provides a text editor for editing your XML and XSL documents. It provides many similar features as RAD, including auto complete, document formatting, and automatic error identification. Because this product is designed specifically to work with XML documents, it also provides a graphical hierarchical view of the document in the text editor. Each element and its children can be expanded and collapsed within the document. Figure 25-12 shows the text editor displaying an XSL document. Notice how easy it is to identify the start and end of a particular element. It is also convenient to be able to collapse a particular element when you are not working with it.

```
<?xml version="1.0" encoding="UTF-8"?>
<xsl:stylesheet xmlns:xsl="http://www.w3.org/1999/XSL/Transform" version="
1.0" xmlns:xalan="http://xml.apache.org/xslt">
  <xsl:template match="/book">
    <xsl:variable name="author_first" select="substring-before(author,' ')"/>
    <xsl:variable name="author_last" select="substring-after(author,' ')"/>
    <book-request>
      <book-name>
        <xsl:value-of select="name"/>
      </book-name>
      <book-author>
        <author-first><xsl:value-of select="$author_first"/></author-first>
        <author-last><xsl:value-of select="$author_last"/></author-last>
      </book-author>
    </book-request>
  </xsl:template>
</xsl:stylesheet>
```

Text | Grid | Schema/WSDL | Authentic | Browser

Figure 25-12 XMLSpy text editor.

XPath Tool

As mentioned earlier in the chapter, it is likely that you will be coding some XPath expressions in your stylesheets that can sometimes get complex. As with RAD, XMLSpy also comes with a convenient XPath generator tool. By simply referring to the input XML document and the location in the document of interest, this tool can generate the applicable XPath statement. Figure 25-13 shows this feature where the XPath statement is generated for the <author> element, which is a child of the <book> element. Notice the XPath statement "book/author" generated at the bottom of the screen.

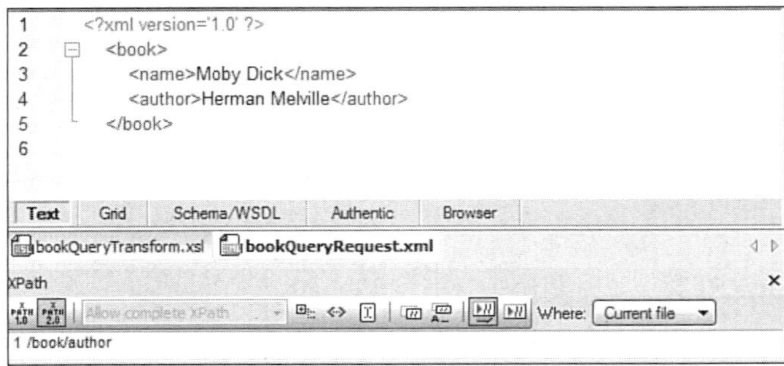

Figure 25-13 XMLSpy XPath feature.

Executing Your XSLT

XMLSpy also includes a built-in XSLT runtime engine, so it is possible to test your XSLT code in this IDE. Just as with RAD, you can specify the input XML document and the XSL file and execute the transformation. The output of the transformation is written to a separate file and displayed. To execute your XSLT in XMLSpy, you first open the XSL file in the text editor. Then from the top menu, select XSL/XQuery→XSL Transformation. You are then asked to select the XML input file, where you can browse to the sample XML to be transformed, as shown in Figure 25-14.

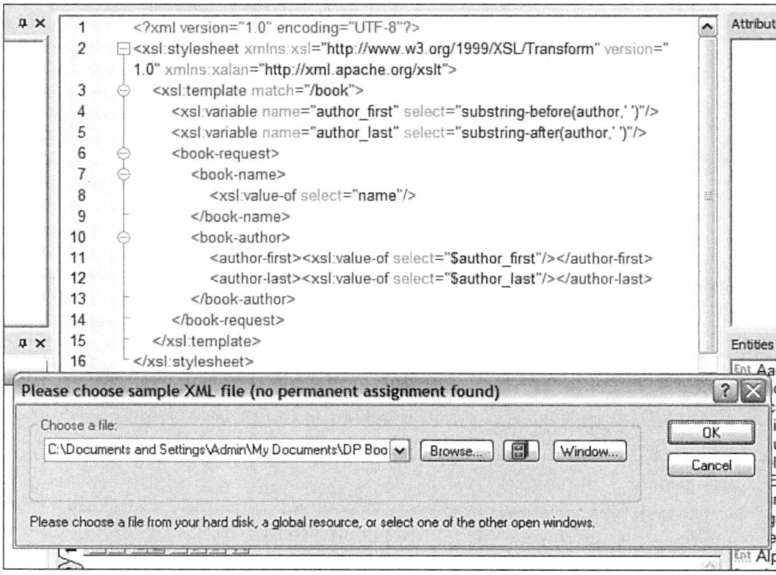

Figure 25-14 Selecting the sample XML input file for transformation.

After selecting the input XML file, the transformation is executed, and the result file is displayed.

Debugging Your XSLT

Just as RAD has a step-by-step debugging tool, so does XMLSpy. It is similar to the RAD debugger in that it provides step-by-step debugging, allowing for breakpoints and displaying the current context, variables, and output document as the XSL executes. To execute the stylesheet in debug mode, you select XSL/XQuery→Start Debugger/Go. You again are asked to select an input XML document. After selecting the input document, you are presented with the debugging screen where you can step through the execution line by line as shown in Figure 25-15.

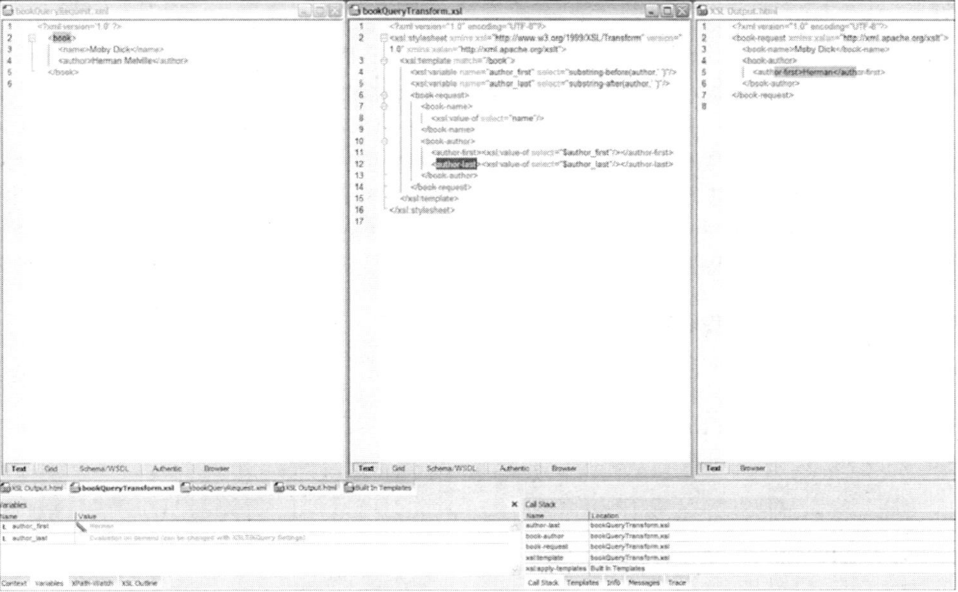

Figure 25-15 XMLSpy debugging.

DataPower Plugins

As you have seen, the two IDEs described previously provide a tremendous amount of value when developing and debugging your XSLT code. The one issue you will find is that they do not know anything about DataPower. That is, they don't know about the DataPower extension functions and elements that can be used in your stylesheets, and are limited to their own runtime environments. This means that if you use any of these custom APIs in your stylesheet and execute them in the IDE's XSLT engine, they will fail. Because using these extension functions within your stylesheets is a common practice, this could become a hindrance. It is for this reason that DataPower provides a plugin for each of these popular IDEs to solve this problem, along with additional functionality.

Eclipse (RAD) XSLT Coproc Plugin

The first plugin that we will discuss is the Eclipse XSLT Coproc Plugin. This plugin can be installed in the Eclipse IDE. It enables you to execute your XSLT code on a DataPower device directly from the IDE itself returning the results back to it. Eclipse is an open source product that can be used for developing different types of applications and code, such as Java and XSLT. RAD is built on Eclipse and adds many robust editing, runtime, and debugging capabilities. It is at its core an Eclipse tool, which is why it can also use this plugin.

As we mentioned before, even with all the capabilities in the RAD product, it is not possible to successfully test your XSL stylesheets if they are using DataPower extension functions. With this plugin installed and configured, you can initiate the execution of your stylesheets in the same tool in which you are editing them. The execution is actually performed on your DataPower device, and the results are returned back to the development environment just as if you executed them locally. Because the stylesheets are executed on the DataPower device, all the extension functions are recognized and executed. Keep in mind that RAD's interactive debugger works only when the transformations are being executed locally, not when they are executed on DataPower.

Installation and Configuration

Preparing your environment for using this plugin is a two-step process. Before you install the plugin within your Eclipse-based tool, you must first configure the DataPower device to listen for requests from the plugin to execute the XSLT that is passed. After this is configured, you can install the plugin.

Setting Up the Coproc Service

You may recall from Chapter 6, "Introduction to DataPower Services," a service type is available on the DataPower device called an XSL Coprocessor service. This service type can be used to offload XSLT processing from applications to the device. This is accomplished by calling the service from a Java application using the JAXP protocol, passing the XSL and the input XML document to be transformed. This service acts as a loopback executing the transformation and returning the results. This is one situation where this service type comes in handy, as the Eclipse Coproc plugin uses it to offload the XSLT execution for you during development and testing. Note that this is for a development environment only and should never be used in a production environment because it listens on a port and attempts to execute any XSLT passed to it without authenticating or authorizing the caller.

The XSL Coprocessor service is one of the simplest services to configure on the device. There is no Processing Policy to configure, so all you need to do is provide a name and a device-listening IP address:port combination and you are finished. To create a new service of this type, it can be accessed via the side navigation menu under Objects→Services→XSL Coprocessor Service. The next screen is the familiar screen that lists all the available services of that type as well as an Add button that you can click to create a new one. Figure 25-16 shows the configuration screen for creating a new service. The three fields that are required are the Name, Local IP Address, and the Port Number. Notice that we still follow the practice of using a host alias even though this service will not be migrated to other environments.

XSL Coprocessor Service : Eclipse_Coproc_plugin_service [up]

Apply | Cancel | Delete | Undo — Export | View Log | View Status

Admin State	enabled / disabled
Local IP Address	PayloadTraffic [Select Alias] *
Comments	
Service Priority	Normal
Port Number	7000 *
XML Manager	default *
URL Rewrite Policy	(none)
Processing Rule	(none)
Connection Timeout	60 seconds
Intermediate Result Timeout	20 seconds
Cache Relative URL	on / off
Use URI Resolver	on / off
Crypto Extensions	on / off
Default parameter namespace	http://www.datapower.com/para
SSL Profile	(none)

Figure 25-16 Coprocessor service configuration screen.

Installing the Plugin

Before installing the Eclipse XSLT Coproc Plugin, it must first be downloaded from the DataPower Appliance Firmware and Documentation Web site at http://www.ibm.com/software/integration/datapower. This is the same Web site from which you download new versions of the DataPower firmware. You will find the plugin listed under the General Firmware, Documentation and Files section of the available downloads. It is also recommended that you download and read the Eclipse Coproc Plugin Instructions that are available in the same section for downloading. The plugin file downloaded will be a .zip file and will have a name such as com.datapower.xml.xslt.coproc.feature_3.6.1.0.bin.dist.zip.

After downloading the .zip file, the plugin can be installed by extracting this file into the appropriate product installation directory. If you are installing it into a base Eclipse product, you must extract this .zip file into the directory that the Eclipse product was installed in. If you are installing it into RAD 7.0, you will extract this file into the SDP70 folder, which can be found in the same folder as your RAD installation. To be sure you are extracting this file to the correct directory, you should see a plugins folder and a features folder in the directory that you are extracting the .zip file into. After extracting this file, you should check to ensure that the DataPower Coproc plugin folder is present in the plugin folder. This folder is named com.datapower.xml.xslt.coproc_x.x.x.x, depending on the version of the plugin that you downloaded. For plugin locations for the version of Eclipse or RAD that you are using, please consult your product documentation.

After the plugin file is extracted to the appropriate directory, you can start the application. If you are just running Eclipse, you can start the application as usual. There is one caveat when starting RAD for the first time after installing the plugin. You must start the application using the –clean option. To do this you need to either create or edit the shortcut to the RAD application. The easiest way is to edit the existing shortcut in your Start→All Programs menu in a Windows environment. You right-click Rational Application Developer and select Properties. You then append –clean to the Target field within the shortcut tab, as shown in Figure 25-17.

Figure 25-17 Rational Application Developer shortcut properties.

After adding this parameter, you can start the application as normal. You do not need to keep this parameter after the initial startup with the plugin installed. This startup parameter forces RAD to clean its cache and refreshes it on startup with the new plugin installed.

After the application has been started, you should see three icons in the top toolbar as shown in Figure 25-18. These are the three buttons that are created by the plugin. This indicates that the plugin has been installed successfully.

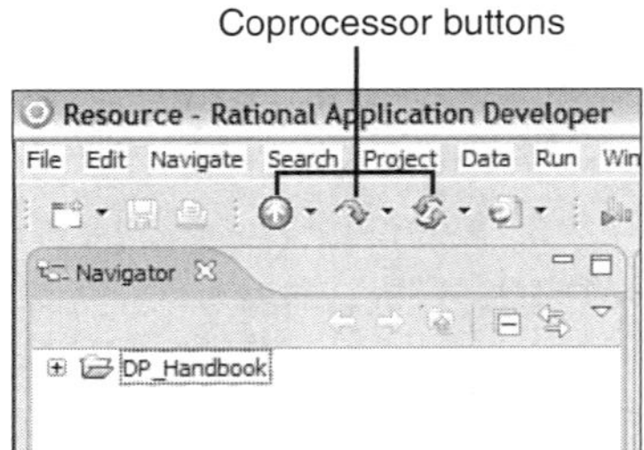

Figure 25-18 DataPower Coproc icons.

After the plugin has been installed, you need to tell it the address and port of the XSL Coprocessor service it will send the transformation requests to. This is the service that you set up in the previous step. To set these configuration parameters in the plugin, navigate to Window→Preferences→DataPower Coprocessor. Here you enter the address and port of the XSL Coprocessor. Figure 25-19 shows the plugin configuration screen referencing the service defined in Figure 25-16. Notice that we also checked the Open Transform Result in editor after transform option. This opens the results from the transformation in the IDE editor after they are sent back from the DataPower service. There is also an Optional Client-ID field for specifying an ID that is sent along with the request to the DataPower service.

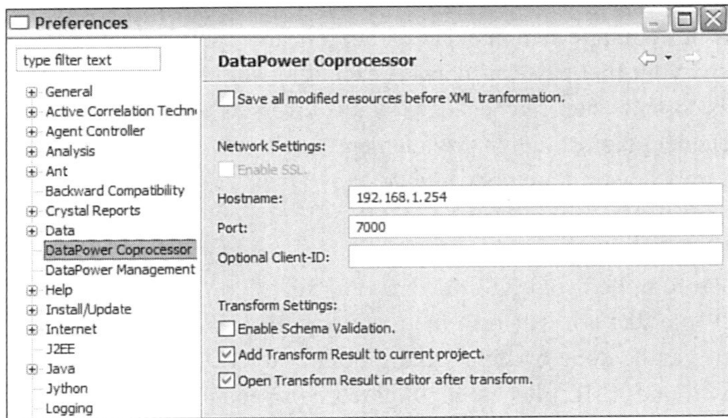

Figure 25-19 Configuring the Eclipse Coproc plugin.

Compiling Your XSLT

The first step in executing an XSLT stylesheet on the DataPower device via the Eclipse Coproc plugin is to compile the XSLT stylesheet. This is accomplished by selecting the XSL file to compile and clicking the middle Coprocessor button on the toolbar. After the compile completes, you get a success message if all went well. Figure 25-20 shows a successful compile of an XSL file named bookReqTransformation.xsl.

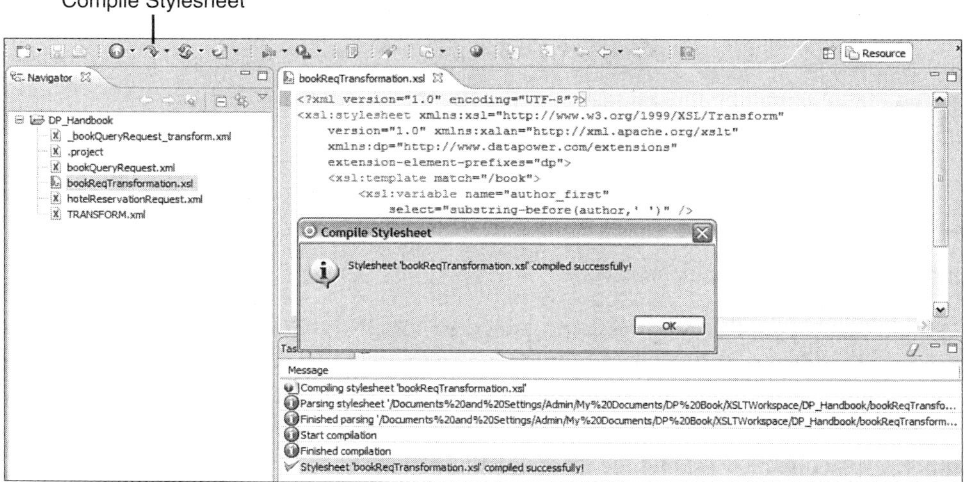

Figure 25-20 Successful compile.

If the compilation was not successful, you receive a pop-up indicating that the transformation has failed. You also see a detailed error message in the Transform Console at the bottom of the screen.

Not only is this compile step mandatory, but it is also useful. If you have coded XSLT, you know that typically your first pass (or more) at executing your stylesheets results in some type of syntax error. This compile step catches these syntax errors as well as any other static errors such as missing end element tags or mandatory elements such as <xsl:stylesheet> before you execute it. Any runtime errors however are not caught.

Executing Your XSLT

Now that you have compiled your XSL file, you can submit it for execution. To do this, you need to select the XSL file that will perform the transformation and the input XML file that will be transformed. This can be done by highlighting both in the IDE (hold down Ctrl and click each file). After the XSL and XML files are highlighted, you then click the plugin's Transform XML Input with XSLT stylesheet button on the toolbar, which is the two green arrows that form a circle. Figure 25-21 shows the initiation of a transformation of the bookQueryRequest.xml file using the bookReqTransformation.xsl stylesheet. This XSL file is also shown in the editor. Notice at the end of the stylesheet that the DataPower extension element set-variable is called. If this were to be executed in the Eclipse/RAD runtime, it would fail.

When the transformation is initiated, a request is sent to the address of the service configured in the plugin. The transformation is then executed via this service, and the results are sent back to the IDE and stored in a file named TRANSFORM.xml, as shown in Figure 25-22.

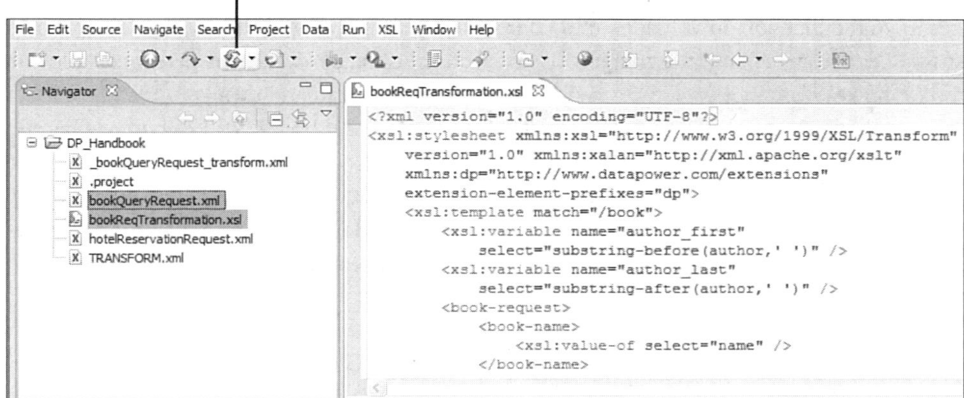

Figure 25-21 Initiating a transformation.

```
bookReqTransformation.xsl    TRANSFORM.xml
<?xml version="1.0" encoding="UTF-8"?>
<book>
        <name>Moby Dick</name>
        <author>Herman Melville</author>
    </book>
```

Figure 25-22 Transformation results.

Eclipse (RAD) Management Plugin

You have now seen how the RAD product with the Coprocessor plugin installed can provide an IDE suitable for developing, compiling, executing, and debugging your XSLT code for DataPower services. There is still one missing piece that would make this IDE a complete "one-stop shopping" tool. That is the ability to copy files to/from the DataPower device to/from the IDE. This is where the Eclipse Management plugin comes in handy. This plugin is intended for managing the DataPower device and lets the developers manage their own domains; it also lets them view the DataPower file system and copy the files to their local Eclipse/RAD project.

Installing the Plugin

As with the coproc plugin, you first need to download the Eclipse Management plugin from the DataPower Appliance Firmware and Documentation site at http://www.ibm.com/software/integration/datapower. This again is a .zip file and is installed into your Eclipse/RAD product in the same manner that the Coproc plugin was installed. In addition to the plugin, you must also download the Eclipse Management Plugin Certificate: root-ca-cert.pem.

After the plugin .zip file is extracted into the appropriate directory, you must import the root-ca-cert.pem file that you downloaded into your Java keystore. This tells the Eclipse environment to trust this certificate when making the SSL connection to DataPower. This certificate file can be added to the keystore in a Windows environment using the command shown in Listing 25-2. This command should be executed at a command prompt within the Java-Dir/lib/security where Java-Dir is the location of the JRE that is being used by RAD. Also notice that this command points to the certificate file in the \tmp directory. This assumes that the root-ca-cert.pem file was copied here. This can be changed to the directory that you have saved this certificate file to. This process is documented in the Eclipse Management Plugin instructions that can also be downloaded.

Listing 25-2 Adding a certificate to the Java Keystore.

```
..\..\bin\keytool.exe -import -alias dproot -file \tmp\root-ca-cert.pem
-keystore cacerts
```

After the plugin is installed and the certificate is added to the keystore, you can launch the Eclipse/RAD application. Remember that if you are using RAD, you must first start the application using the –clean option as discussed in the coproc plugin section.

After the application starts, you can open the DataPower Management perspective that enables you to work with your DataPower devices. To do this, navigate to Window→Open Perspective→Other… and select DataPower Management from the list. If you do not see this perspective in the list, you can select the Show All box at the bottom of the list. An icon for switching to this perspective is also added to the left side of the toolbar next to the Coproc plugin icons. It is the icon showing the DataPower logo.

Adding a DataPower Device

Now that you have installed the plugin and have the DataPower management perspective open, you can add your DataPower device. When in the DataPower Management perspective, you will see a window in the upper-left of the screen named Device Manager. This is where we can add a device by clicking the Add Device or Device Group button. This button is the left-most button at the top of the Device Manager window. Next, you enter the information for the new DataPower device to be added as shown in Figure 25-23. Notice that the XML Management port is required. This is because the XML Management Interface is used to communicate with the device from the plugin. A username and password are also required for communicating with the device. This is a DataPower username that must have the appropriate permissions to access the device via the XML Management Interface. This user ID should also have full privileges to the Default domain, such as the sysadmin group.

Because the XML Management Interface is used for communicating with DataPower, you must ensure that this interface is enabled on the device you are adding, along with the SOAP Configuration Management service within it. This can be enabled and viewed within the DataPower WebGUI by navigating in the default domain to Network→XML Management Interface. Here you can also see the Local IP Address, port, and URI that are required in the device profile shown in Figure 25-23. For more information on the XML Management Interface please refer to Chapter 13, "Alternate Management Interfaces."

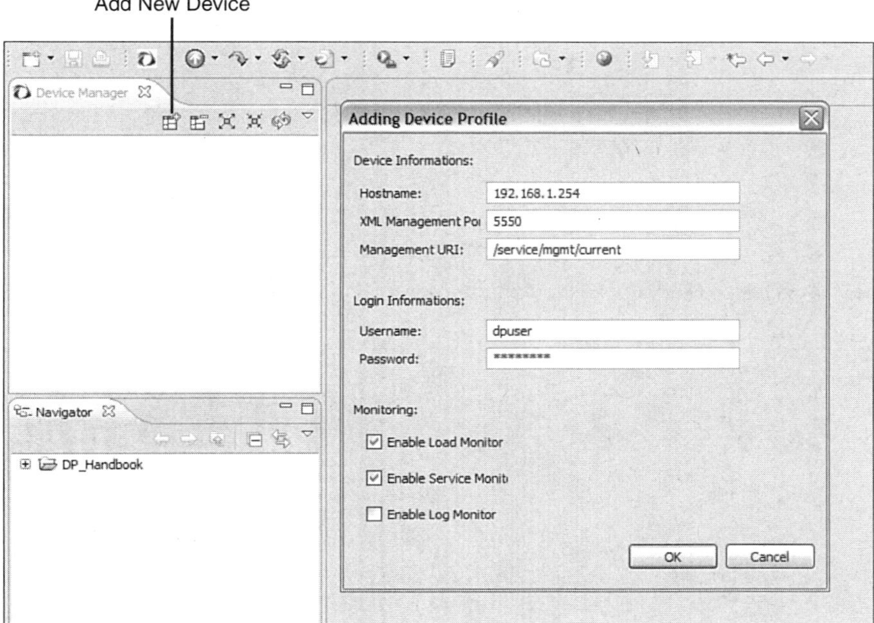

Figure 25-23 Adding a new device.

After adding and applying the device information, you will know that the connection to the device was successful if the device address is listed in the Device Manager with a blue dot before it. If the device address is in a red font, there is an issue with connecting to the device.

If the plugin is not able to communicate with the DataPower device added, the best place to start your investigation is in the system logs within DataPower. This might tell you if there was a connection attempted and why it failed. This could be a permissions error or possibly that the XML Management Interface is not enabled. If there is no sign of communication from the plugin within the system logs, the next step would be to make sure that you can ping the device from your local workstation. You might also ensure that the port that the plugin is attempting to send requests to is not being blocked by a network firewall.

Working with the DataPower File System Within Eclipse/RAD

As mentioned earlier, the Device Management plugin is intended to be used for managing the entire device; however, for our discussion on development tools, we only introduce the file management capabilities. To work with the device file system, expand the tree under the device in the Device Manager window down to File Management→Local. You can then select the domain for the file system that you want to work with, as shown in Figure 25-24.

After you select the domain name for the file system that you want to see, the contents of that file system appear in the main window. From here you can drag files from this window to your local project, as shown in Figure 25-25.

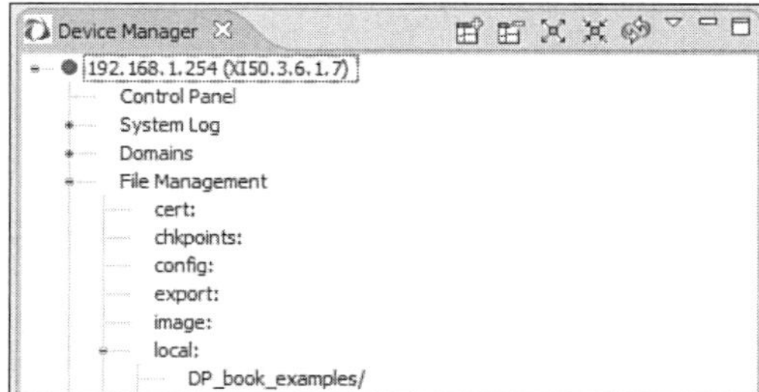

Figure 25-24 Device Manager - File Management.

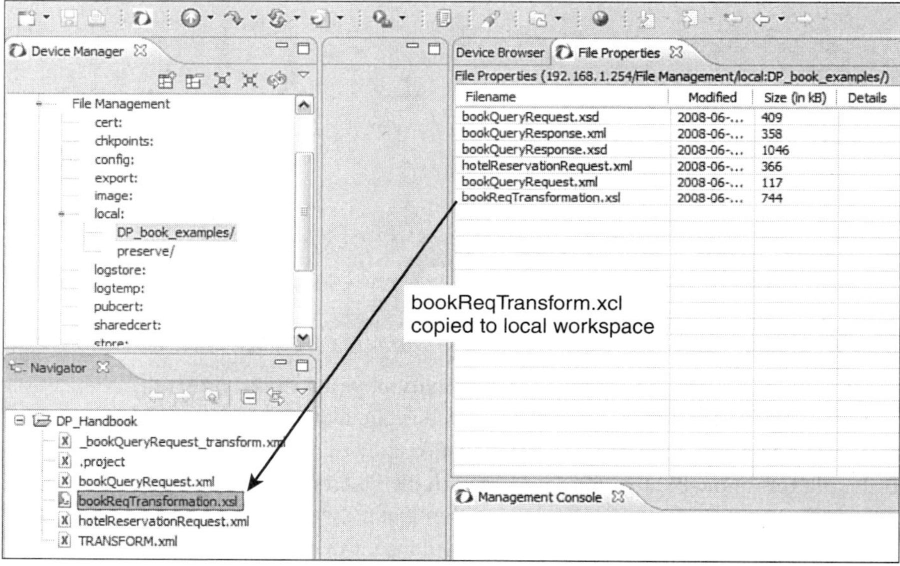

Figure 25-25 Dragging a file from the device to a project.

After you have dragged a file from the DataPower device to your project, you can double-click it within the project to edit it in the text editor as shown in Figure 25-26. Notice that the file system remains to the right of the editor. This is very convenient because after you make your changes to the file, you can drag it back onto the device file system. Note that dragging the file back to the device file system does not cause the device cache to be refreshed with this new version. Further steps must be taken to refresh the cache with this new file, such as manually refreshing the stylesheet cache in the XML manager, creating a URL Refresh Policy, or not caching them at all while developing. Remember, this should only be done in the development environment for the sake of convenience and efficiency. Stylesheets should be cached in all other environments to increase performance. For more information on stylesheet and document caching within DataPower, please refer to Chapter 7, "Introduction to Services Configuration."

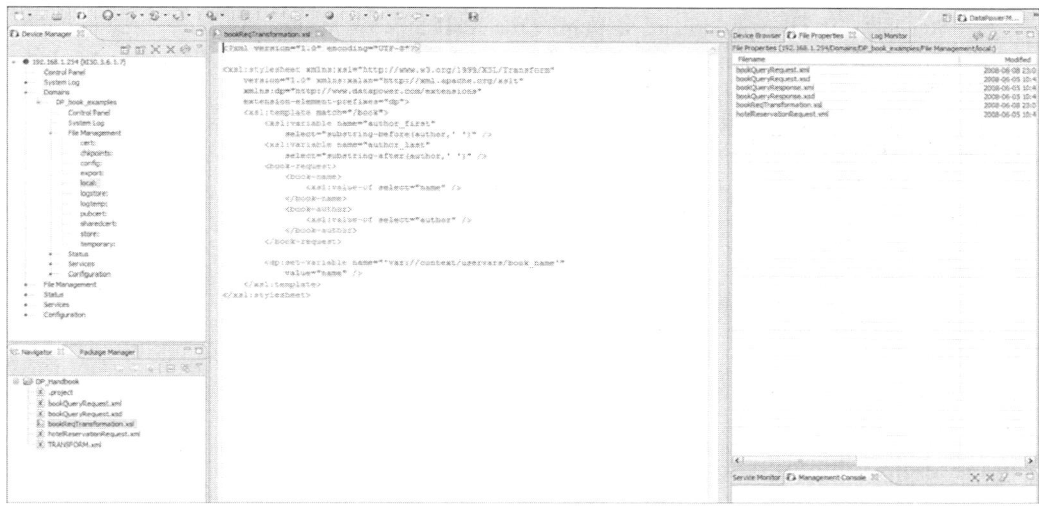

Figure 25-26 Editing the file.

Now that you have seen the RAD IDE capabilities as well as the additional benefits provided by the DataPower plugins, you can see how using the product features in conjunction with both Eclipse plugins can provide a complete development environment for working with XSLT stylesheets to be executed within a DataPower service. In one single screen, you can code, compile, test, debug, and deploy your XSLT. If your source code repository is supported within RAD/Eclipse, you can even integrate it into this complete solution to include checking in and out files.

XMLSpy Plugin

We discussed earlier in the chapter that the Altova XMLSpy product is also a popular and useful XML and XSLT IDE, providing XSLT editing, executing, and debugging features. As with the RAD/Eclipse product, you cannot execute a stylesheet within XMLSpy that contains DataPower extension functions and elements. Because of this, DataPower also offers a plugin for this product that makes it possible to execute your XSLT on a DataPower device from the IDE.

Installing the Plugin

As with the other plugins, the XMLSpy plugin must be downloaded from the DataPower Appliance Firmware and Documentation site at http://www.ibm.com/software/integration/datapower. The file that is downloaded is an executable file named setup.exe. Installation of this plugin is done by simply executing this executable file. After the executable completes, the installation is done.

The XMLSpy plugin also requires an XSL Coprocessor service to be set up on the DataPower device that performs the execution of the transformations. Once this service is configured, you can configure your plugin to point to it.

After installing the plugin and launching the XMLSpy application, you are presented with a pop-up to configure the plugin. You need to edit these fields by selecting Change and adding the device address and port that the XSL Coprocessor service is listening on. You also are required to add a DataPower user ID and password. This configuration screen is shown in Figure 25-27.

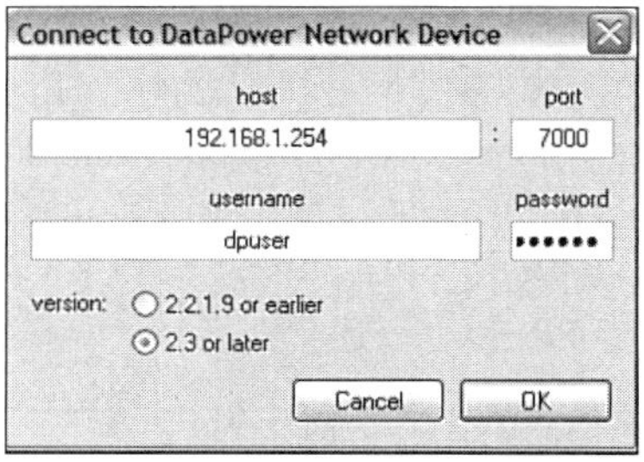

Figure 25-27 XMLSpy plugin configuration.

After you have configured the DataPower device setting, you need to configure XMLSpy to execute all XSLT transformations using the plugin to submit the request to DataPower. This can be set by navigating to Tools→Options from the XMLSpy toolbar. You then select the XSL tab where you select the DataPower XA35 option as shown in Figure 25-28. Even though the name of this plugin references the XA35 device, it is supported on all other DataPower devices.

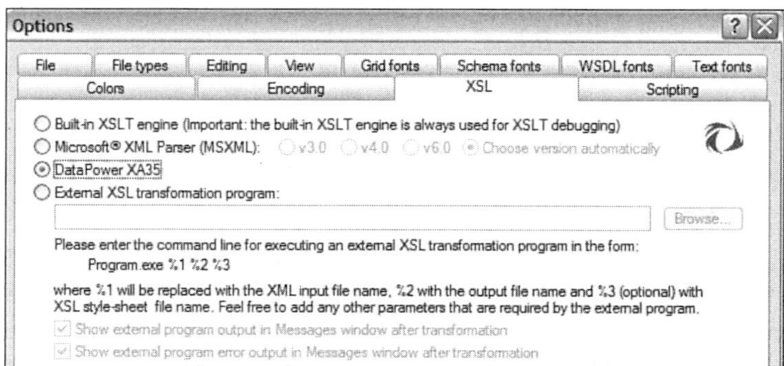

Figure 25-28 Setting the XSL options.

Executing Your XSLT

After the plugin has been installed and configured to point to the DataPower XSL Coprocessor service, you can begin to send XSL transformation requests from XMLSpy. This is done the same way you would execute a transformation within XMLSpy without the plugin. Because you configured the IDE to send all transformation requests to the DataPower device, it is automatically sent and the results are displayed as if the transformation was performed locally.

Summary

As with any programming language, coding XSLT for your DataPower service can be a tedious task, especially in the more complex scenarios. Having an IDE that will provide tools for coding, formatting, executing, and debugging is almost mandatory for any developer. We have discussed the major products that offer this capability for XSLT development as well as the DataPower plug-ins that can help when using DataPower specific extension functions and elements. You have seen how you can have a complete "one-stop shopping" development environment for developing, debugging, and deploying your XSLT code to a DataPower device. Some of these products are customizable so that you can set up your development environment to your liking. Using the tips provided in this chapter and your own personal preferences, you can create your own ideal environment for developing XSLT for DataPower.

CHAPTER 26

Transforming Non-XML Data

This chapter wraps up Part VI on DataPower development. We cover the topic of processing non-XML data and show that while there are some capabilities for hand-coding in XSLT, developers generally utilize specialized tooling due to the complexity of the transforms. We cover both programmatic and nonprogrammatic aspects of transforming non-XML data, and the use of common tools for doing so.

While DataPower is an XML-centric product, it can also apply its processing power to non-XML transformations, which can be more intensive than XML transforms. In fact, the DataPower XI50 has a specialized, optimized runtime engine called DataGlue just for processing non-XML data.

Common Non-XML Data Formats and Scenarios

Often, you will hear non-XML data referred to as binary data. We prefer to say "non-XML" because a typical representation is a text-based format such as comma-separated value (CSV), EDI, or COBOL Copybook.

Two of the tools that we discuss in this chapter use an XML schema to describe the non-XML data. There is currently no widely adopted standard for this,[1] so you will see that each tool uses its own proprietary schema. What they all have in common is that they describe the field layouts, positioning, and other constraints and metadata such as whether each field is numeric, string, date/time, and so on.

[1] There is an emerging standard for describing binary and textual files using XML called Data Format Definition Language (DFDL or "daffodil"). It is currently in draft status from the Open Grid Forum (http://forge.gridforum.org/sf/projects/dfdl-wg).

Although sales presentations, conferences, and trade publications may lead one to believe that modern systems have all fully embraced SOA and are all XML-based, this is often not the case. Most businesses find themselves with only one foot in the door, and they have to leverage multiple data formats—perhaps a more modern Java EE or Web services front-end passing data to a legacy environment consisting of mainframes and messaging systems such as WebSphere MQ. Often, these robust backend platforms remain in place because they are reliable and work well!

Or a business may find itself in a situation where it simply doesn't have the budget or time necessary to upgrade its legacy infrastructure. To better understand, let's explore a few of those scenarios.

Legacy Backend/Pseudo Web Service Frontend

Consider a hypothetical company that has been doing business the same way for many years—it accepts and processes data from its customers (in this case, other businesses) using the EDI message format and protocol backed by mainframe platforms and messaging systems. Although the EDI message format is certainly still viable, and many of the older protocols used for transmission have been replaced by Internet protocols, their partners have stated that they will no longer support EDI at all. The partners have moved on to XML-based message formats and more modern delivery mechanisms, such as SOAP-based Web services.

The first approach our company might take is to rewrite its backend applications and replace its infrastructure in order to "get with the times" and not lose the business from partners and clients. This would likely be quite an expensive and lengthy process; programmers need to be retrained, and there needs to be extensive testing and an elaborate changeover process.

A much better alternative is to use DataPower as a Web services provider to present a modern face to the outside world, and then accept the messages sent in by clients and transform them to the legacy formats and send over the existing protocols to the backend—which in most cases would not need to change at all!

To accomplish this, a WSDL file should be created to represent the agreed-upon service, port, binding, and operation details. There are many tools (for example, Rational Application Developer and Apache Axis JAVA2WSDL) that can be used to create a WSDL from various artifacts such as JavaBeans, "plain old Java objects," and sample XML messages. This resulting WSDL can be used to create a Web Service Proxy, which we cover in Chapter 10, "Web Service Proxy."

As part of the processing policy, a Transform Binary (xformbin) action will be necessary to do the data conversion (XML to EDI in this case). We get into the methods of creating these types of transforms and using the xformbin action later in the chapter.

And lastly, a protocol handler is configured to pass the message to the backend. Typically for Web services, this would be HTTP(s); however, in these situations it's not uncommon to see protocols such as MQ, FTP, IMS, or NFS. The capability to do this accentuates the flexibility of DataPower's protocol mediation features.

Multiple Non-XML Data Formats

Some organizations, by their nature, must process several different types of information in various formats and from various sources. Examples are news, intelligence, and law enforcement agencies. Data can arrive via fax, email, over phone conversation transcripts, teletype terminals, or by other means, and preferably is distilled to a common format (for example an XML "golden schema"), processed, and saved to a backend persistent store such as a database. One of the major use cases for the non-XML processing power of these appliances is to reduce the amount of business application code on the backend—from having to handle and transform many different formats to dealing only with this one "golden" format. As we all know, each line of application code is expensive to maintain, not to mention the huge gain in performance by doing this on a dedicated hardware platform.

For example, a law enforcement agency typically receives daily information from weather services on impending severe weather conditions, from transportation agencies on major accidents, from environmental protection agencies on hazardous chemical spills, and from the general public on just about any "emergency," such as lost pets. The fact that these data streams may be over multiple protocols lends nicely to the use cases for the Multi-Protocol Gateway, as described in Chapter 9, "Multi-Protocol Gateway."

Tooling for Transforming Non-XML Data

There are several options for working with non-XML data. These range from simple (hand-coding in XSLT) to powerful workstation development tools. In this section we familiarize you with a few of these options.

Good Old XSLT

Those familiar with Extensible Stylesheet Language (XSL) already know there are options available for processing non-XML data. XSL is the parent of XSL Transformations (XSLT) and its sibling XSL-Formatting Objects (XSL-FO). XSL-FO is used to generate human-readable documents such as PDF, PostScript, Rich Text Format (RTF), and even GUI components. However, XSL-FO is not a good fit for the type of machine-to-machine translations that are the bailiwick of DataPower. XSLT is a good fit, of course, and there we also find a solution—you can declare <xsl:output method="text"> at the top of your stylesheet to indicate that the output of this transform will be text, rather than the more common XML or HTML. When using this option, a full XML result tree is formed internally, but then the string value is emitted as output. Let's review a simple example. Listing 26-1 shows an example stylesheet to operate on the XML input file shown in Listing 26-2. Note the xsl:output declaration in the stylesheet.

Listing 26-1 XSLT to Create Comma-Separated Text Output from XML Input

```
<?xml version="1.0" encoding="UTF-8"?>
<xsl:stylesheet xmlns:xsl="http://www.w3.org/1999/XSL/Transform"
version="1.0">
    <xsl:output method="text"/>
    <xsl:template match="Customer">
        <xsl:value-of select="firstName"/>,<xsl:value-of
select="lastName"/>,<xsl:value-of select="street"/>,<xsl:value-of
select="city"/>,<xsl:value-of select="state"/>
    </xsl:template>
</xsl:stylesheet>
```

Listing 26-2 Sample XML Input File for XML to Text

```
<?xml version="1.0" encoding="UTF-8" ?>
<Customer>
    <firstName>Dean</firstName>
    <lastName>Moriarity</lastName>
    <street>42 Bleeker St</street>
    <city>Denver</city>
    <state>CO</state>
</Customer>
```

We configured this stylesheet on an XML Firewall with a normal Transform action. We did not modify any values other than to change the Request Type from the default of SOAP to XML. The results are shown in Figure 26-1: text CSV output from an XSLT stylesheet. The first drawback of this approach is that the conversion can only be done "one way" from XML to text. The second drawback is that it would be rather tedious and cumbersome to apply this to many of the "real world" scenarios involving complex data types and large files, such as COBOL Copybooks and EDI documents. It also doesn't support other encoding types.

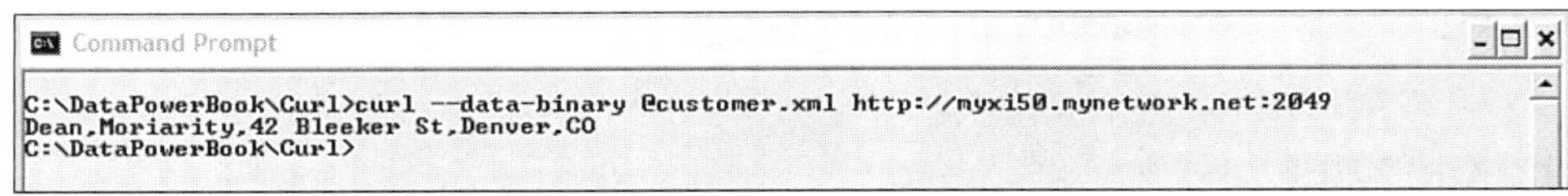

Figure 26-1 Output of XML to text example.

Third-Party Development Tools for Non-XML Transform Development

We have discussed how simple XML-to-text scenarios can be done with XSLT code. However, as we stated earlier, most scenarios involve large amounts of complex data. To develop these types of transformations, some type of external tooling is necessary. There are two options that are used for DataPower: Liaison Contivo Analyst and IBM WebSphere Transformation Extender (WTX).

Both products are similar in nature—they provide graphical integrated development environments (IDE) that enable various inputs and outputs to be described (such as the field delimiters and types) and to lay out the mapping from one datatype to another.

For example, one might import a schema definition file to the tooling to describe the input, and a COBOL Copybook definition to describe what the output should look like. From there, a graphical mapping component is used to drag and drop fields from the XML input card to the COBOL field definition. It can really be this simple in many cases!

Another component of these tools is the testing engine. Both products are used for transformation development outside of DataPower and contain runtime engines that can be added to an application server and other environments for this purpose. For example, the WTX runtime can be purchased as an add-on for IBM WebSphere Message Broker. These runtime environments are included for testing purposes with the development tools from both products we are discussing. Both tools can test the transforms that are being developed against the local runtime as well as directly on a DataPower device. It would be most beneficial to test against the DataPower runtime to ensure that the transforms will work in that environment. For both products, there is not 100 percent compatibility between their native runtimes and the DataGlue implementation on DataPower.

The products require a zip file (available on the DataPower product Web site or the Resource CD) that is imported to the DataPower device to create a special application domain and XML Firewalls. The test tooling uses those firewalls to send the artifacts to real time, to execute and test the maps that are being developed against the appliance runtime. This provides for iterative development/testing and gives immediate feedback to the developer.

When the testing cycle is complete, the artifacts are exported from the tooling and imported to the DataPower device as part of a Processing Policy using the Transform Binary (xformbin) action that we will discuss shortly.

Now that we've talked about what these two products have in common, let's discuss each in more detail.

Liaison Contivo Analyst

The Flat File Descriptor (FFD) is an XML schema developed by DataPower and Contivo to describe non-XML data files. Listing 26-3 shows a sample FFD file to describe a simple comma-separated value text file that can contain from zero to unlimited records.

Listing 26-3 Sample FFD File for Comma-Separated Values

```
<File name="CSVFILE">
      <Group name="CSVLine" minOccurs="0" maxOccurs="unbounded" delim="\n">
            <Field name="id" delim=","/>
            <Field name="fname" delim=","/>
            <Field name="lname" delim=","/>
            <Field name="title" delim=","/>
            <Field name="dept" delim=","/>
            <Field name="org"/>
      </Group>
</File>
```

When you are describing data using Analyst from your workstation, the FFD files are generated for you by the tool and used in conjunction with annotated XSLT, which is also generated. The FFD files describe the data and the XSLT acts as the programmatic code to do the mapping at runtime. For testing, an XML Firewall called contivo_policy, which is included with Analyst, must be imported. This firewall is contained in the domain export contivo-analyst-policy.zip and listens on port 2321 by default. Figure 26-2 shows the Analyst configuration page for setting up DataPower as the runtime test platform.

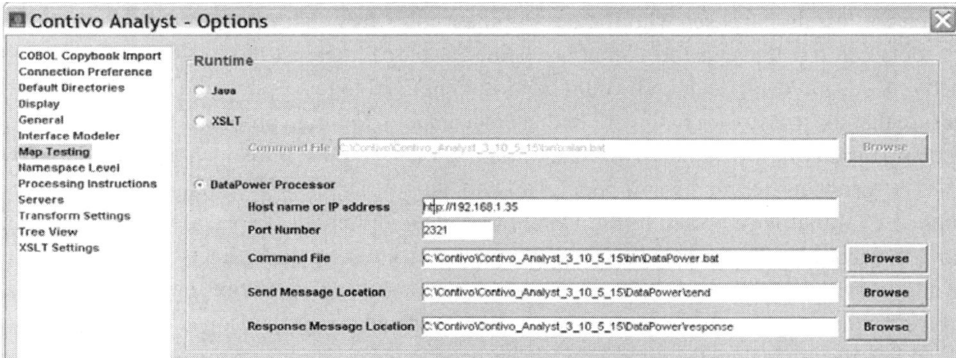

Figure 26-2 Contivo Analyst configuration for DataPower testing.

The Analyst component for describing data layouts is called the Interface Modeler. Figure 26-3 shows a COBOL Copybook description using that tool. Note the use of the OCCURS DEPENDING ON clause for repeating groups. The Layout tab is shown in this figure, but the Basic tab can be used to describe the minimum and maximum occurrences of each field individually, and the Advanced tab can be used to describe the data type of each field (integer, decimal, date/time, and so on).

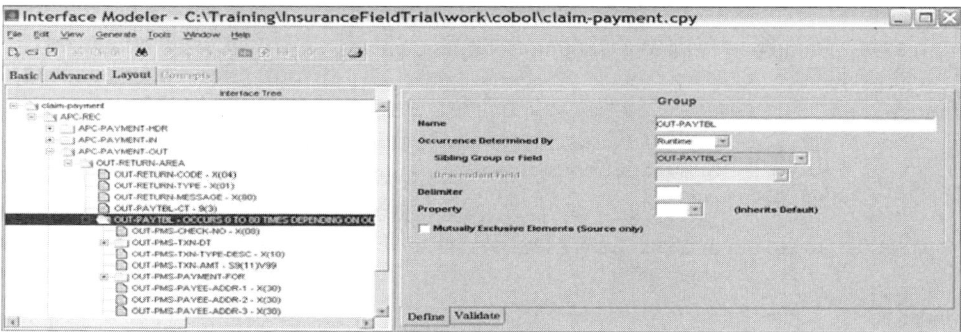

Figure 26-3 Analyst Interface Modeler describing COBOL data.

After the data types have been described, the Analyst Mapping Studio is used to define the relationships between the input and output data by dragging the fields. Figure 26-4 shows a SOAP to COBOL Copybook example using the Map tab.

When the mapping is complete, the next step is to test. Figure 26-5 shows the result of the test for the scenario we have been describing. You can witness how the values have correctly been transferred from the input SOAP message to the output COBOL Copybook, indicating a successful test.

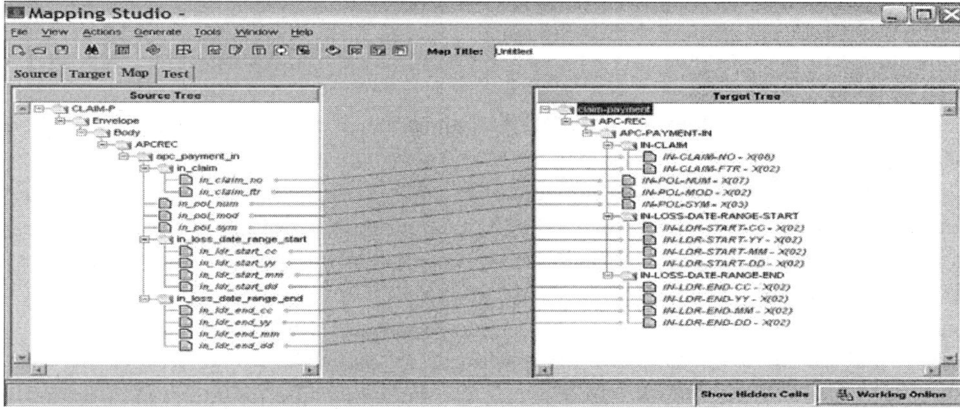

Figure 26-4 Analyst Mapping Studio drag-and-drop paradigm.

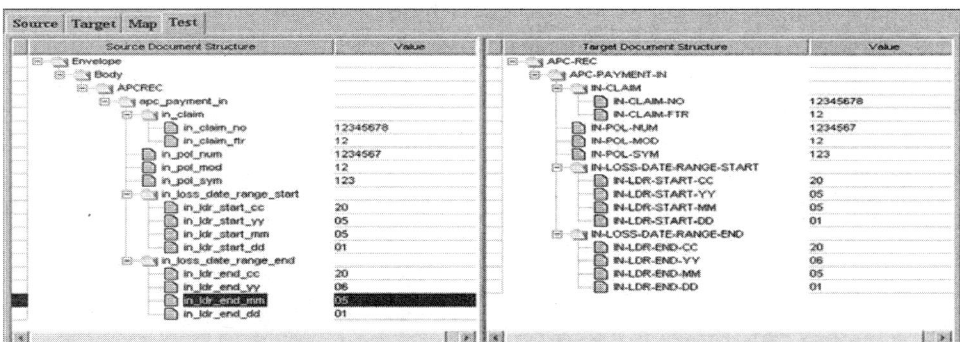

Figure 26-5 Analyst test results.

When testing is done through Analyst to the DataPower platform, a MIME package containing the FFD and XSLT files as well as the test data is sent to the contivo_policy firewall mentioned earlier. The results are processed and sent back for analysis within the Analyst development environment. There are tools for troubleshooting within Analyst, and debugging can also be done on the DataPower side, using the logs, probes, and other troubleshooting techniques described throughout this book.

WebSphere Transformation Extender Design Studio

The second product we will discuss is the IBM WebSphere Transformation Extender (WTX) Design Studio. WTX has several advantages: It is inexpensive, runs in the open and extensible Eclipse platform, and has multiple available runtimes (making it a strategic product for shops with many different environments). This is actually a family of products, including runtime transformation engines for different platforms, a software development kit, an IDE called Design Studio, resource adapters for databases and other platforms, an Integration Flow Designer, and a

Business-to-Business Manager. There are enterprise and industry "packs" available for things like the Health Insurance Portability and Accountability Act (HIPAA), EDI, and Financial Information Exchange (FIX).

Some of these pieces are part of the WTX runtime, which is used for much broader purposes than the "mission" of the DataPower appliances, and hence are not available for running transformations on the DataPower DataGlue engine. For example, DataPower has its own database interface code and does not need to include the WTX runtime for that. DataPower has its own process editor—the Processing Policy. See the WTX documentation for specifics on what features are available when building transformations targeted for DataPower. We will focus on the WTX Design Studio, which is the integrated development environment for describing data and designing maps, and the only part of the WTX suite relevant to DataPower. *To be clear: If you are purchasing WTX solely to use with DataPower, you only need the Design Studio—you do not need any of the other runtime products.*

This chapter is based on version 8.2 of the product, which is a major re-architecture from previous versions that brings the tooling under the Eclipse platform. Prior to this version, the major pieces of the product were separate. These major pieces are the Type Tree Designer, which is used for describing data, and the Map Designer, which is used to build maps to do the actual transforms by operating on those type trees as input and output cards.

The features and usage of Design Studio are similar to that of Contivo Analyst. Maps can be designed and debugged against the local WTX runtime engine, or they can be sent to a DataPower appliance (again a special XML Firewall in a domain that you would import) for development testing of map execution. There are graphical tools for importing XML schema and COBOL Copybook definitions, as well as other data types.

Because many non-XML scenarios involve interaction with legacy backends, a useful feature for WTX is the seamless conversion between various codepages, such as ASCII to EBCDIC, when transforming data.

An old expression states that "talk is cheap," so let's actually look at how to design non-XML transformations for DataPower using WTX Design Studio. Our next section does precisely that!

Creating Non-XML Transformations with WebSphere TX Design Studio

Let's go back to our example scenario where a company has a backend legacy environment that processes COBOL Copybook files with employee records that are sent to them via a legacy transport or protocol. Its business partners have grown tired of the expense of supporting this platform and are insisting on a more modern infrastructure, and are threatening to discontinue doing business with the company if it does not provide an XML-based interface. This presents a big problem for the company. The expense and time involved in retraining programmers, rewriting and testing applications, and converting infrastructure are daunting. However, someone has heard about these "magical appliances" that can act as proxies and that have amazing message transformation and mediation capabilities. DataPower to the rescue!

To solve this problem, we can insert an XI50 between the business partner and that backend. We can then create a WSDL file to use as the basis for a partner-facing Web service and publish that interface to the business partner, who could then send SOAP messages over HTTP. (To focus on the WTX capabilities and keep to a reasonable length, we use a simple XML file and firewall for our example.) When these messages arrive at the appliance, as part of the Processing Policy, we transform them to COBOL Copybook format and transport them to the backend via any supported protocol such as MQ, TIBCO, or FTP. Of course, all other Processing Policy actions are available for things such as crypto, dynamic routing, AAA, logging, auditing, and so on.

Listing 26-4 shows the example XML input file we are using for this scenario. Of course, there is an accompanying schema that describes this document and can be used for validation purposes.

Listing 26-4 Sample XML Employees Input Data

```
<?xml version="1.0" encoding="UTF-8"?>
<NewEmployees>
      <Employee>
            <EmployeeNumber>12345</EmployeeNumber>
            <FirstName>Joe</FirstName>
            <LastName>Smith</LastName>
            <MiddleInitial>L</MiddleInitial>
            <HireDate>20080701</HireDate>
            <StartingSalary>24000</StartingSalary>
      </Employee>
      <Employee>
            <EmployeeNumber>67890</EmployeeNumber>
            <FirstName>Mary</FirstName>
            <LastName>Thomas</LastName>
            <MiddleInitial>R</MiddleInitial>
            <HireDate>20080628</HireDate>
            <StartingSalary>32500</StartingSalary>
      </Employee>
      <Employee>
            <EmployeeNumber>23897</EmployeeNumber>
            <FirstName>Laurie</FirstName>
            <LastName>Jones</LastName>
            <MiddleInitial>T</MiddleInitial>
            <HireDate>20080629</HireDate>
            <StartingSalary>22000</StartingSalary>
      </Employee>
</NewEmployees>
```

The COBOL Copybook for our output data is shown in Listing 26-5. Note that this contains a rather tricky construct for repeating data—the OCCURS DEPENDING ON clause. The file should begin with a record count and then be followed by some number of employee records.

Listing 26-5 COBOL Copybook Definition for the Employee Output Data

```
01 EMPLOYEE-RECS.
   02 EMPLOYEE-COUNT PIC 9(2) COMP.
   02 EMPLOYEE-RECORD OCCURS 0 TO 99 DEPENDING ON EMPLOYEE-COUNT.
      03 EMPLOYEENUMBER PIC 9(5).
      03 FIRSTNAME       PIC A(20).
      03 MIDDLEINITIAL   PIC A(1).
      03 LASTNAME        PIC A(20).
      03 HIREDATE        PIC 9(8).
      03 STARTSALARY     PIC 9(7).
```

Now that we know what we're dealing with, the remainder of this chapter walks you through some of the major steps in creating such a solution. This being a DataPower book, our intention is not to train the reader on WTX Design Studio. The following scenario shows the major points of configuration through an intermediate example. There are many additional powerful features that can be leveraged by the combined strength of DataPower and WTX, so additional reading is recommended!

Configuring DataPower for WTX

We mentioned earlier that the Design Studio enables iterative testing and development against the DataPower runtime. After the Design Studio software is installed on your workstation, the next step is to configure the DataPower appliance with the export-wtx-dev.zip file, which contains the WTX domain. This is on the DataPower Resource CD and can also be obtained from the DataPower support Web site.

There is nothing different about importing this domain than any other, so we do not show the details here. After the import, switching to the newly created WTX domain and clicking on the XML Firewalls icon in the Control Panel reveals a view as shown in Figure 26-6.

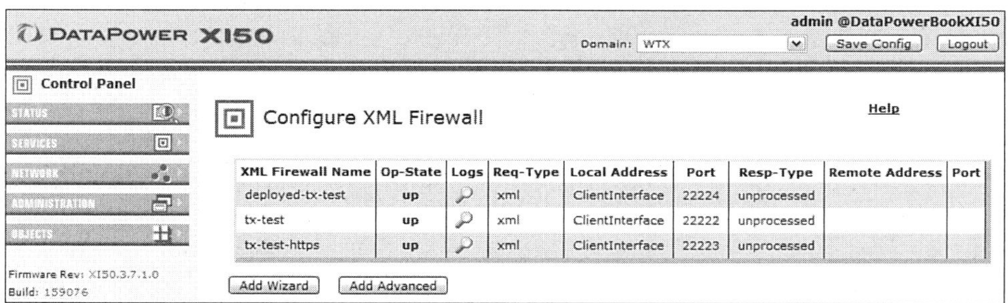

Figure 26-6 XML Firewalls in the imported WTX domain.

As you can see, three firewalls have been created; tx-test and tx-test-https are used by Design Studio to send test cases to the device for iterative testing. As you might guess from the firewall names, one is configured for HTTP and the other for HTTPS. The third firewall, deployed-tx-test, contains a number of example transformations in its processing policy, including some with multiple input and output cards.

Per our recommended practice, we have modified the default listening addresses from 0.0.0.0 to use our client-facing host alias. The default ports can also be changed. There are certificates included with the domain import zip that can be used to configure the SSL firewall, or you can create your own from inside of WTX and then import to DataPower.

Another file that is included with the WTX artifacts on the Resource CD is a test file (wtx.swa) that can be sent to the firewall to test the configuration after the import. You might notice by the extension that this is a SOAP with Attachments file—this is the format that Design Studio uses to package the artifacts and test data, sending them to the firewall when the developer is testing a map. This is also an indication that this information can be specified dynamically at runtime, a powerful capability for dynamic, content-based transforms that we discuss later in the chapter.

Building the Scenario Transformation

At a high level, the scenario consists of a few steps:

1. Create Type Trees to describe the input and output data format. Type Trees are hierarchical objects used by WTX for this purpose. They contain a definition for each distinct field found in the dataset and all attributes about that field, such as its type (numeric, date/time, and so on), its length, what delimiter indicates the end of the field, whether it should be padded, and so forth. Type Trees also contain group objects that can hold those fields in a defined relationship and order, such as how they might appear in an EDI file or Copybook. Type Trees can be created manually or they can be created by importing files such as XML schema definitions, Copybooks, or text/binary example files.
2. Use the Map Designer to describe how the data should be transformed from the input type tree(s) to the output type tree(s). Maps in WTX are held in a container called a Map Source. Each map has some number of input and output cards. These cards represent the datasets used for the transforms. In most cases, you will use Type Trees created earlier for these cards, although there are exceptions—for example, rather than create a Type Tree from an XSD file, you can skip that step and identify the XSD file directly on an input or output card when designing a map. When the input and output cards are defined, they can then be used to lay out the transform by dragging fields from one card to the other, or by using functions from the WTX library or creating your own.
3. Test the transformation first on the WTX runtime and then on DataPower.
4. Deploy the artifacts to a DataPower domain and Processing Policy.

In our following scenario, WTX Design Studio has been installed, and the mundane steps of creating a workspace and project have been completed. We have created a project with the name XMLToCOBOL.

Creating Type Trees

To build our example scenario, first we imported the file for the Copybook that was shown in Listing 26-5. Figure 26-7 shows the numerous choices for data type imports. If the data type is not a known format—for example, custom text or binary files—the type tree can be built manually by describing the field delimiters and types. Importing is much easier!

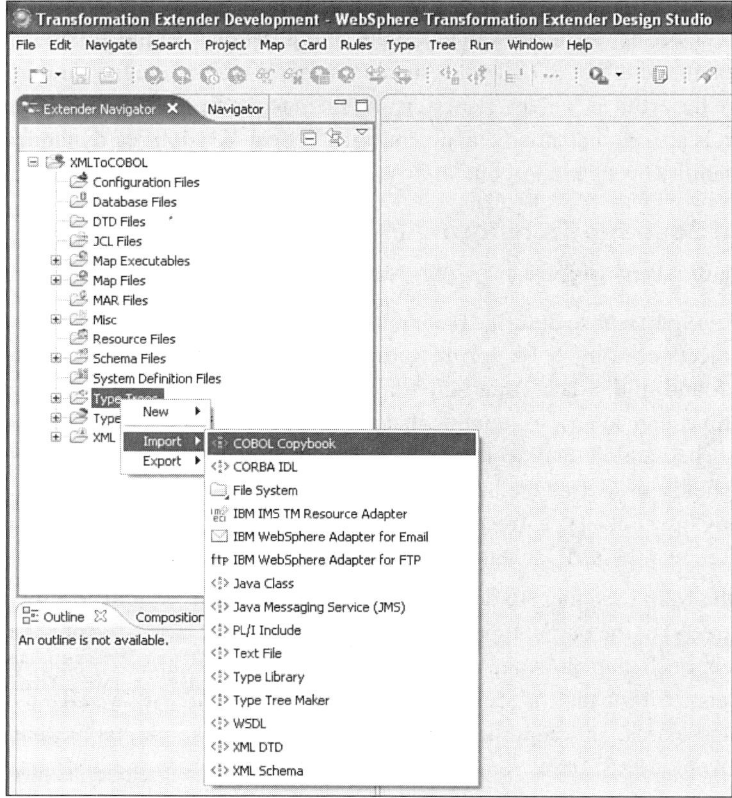

Figure 26-7 Type Tree import selections.

During the import process, we named the new type tree EmployeesCPY, which results in a generated file of the same name with an .mtt extension. The results are shown in Figure 26-8. Notice that the fields are not in the same order they are listed in the Copybook. This is because at this point they are simple, unrelated field definitions.

Clicking on each field results in a properties pane that shows the specifics, such as the field's data type and padding information. Figure 26-9 shows the properties of the STARTSALARY field. Notice that it is numeric (integer), a max length of 7, and will be padded right-justified with leading zeros. Other capabilities shown are the ability to specify the national language (Western, Italian, German, and so forth) and data language (such as Native, ASCII, EBCDIC).

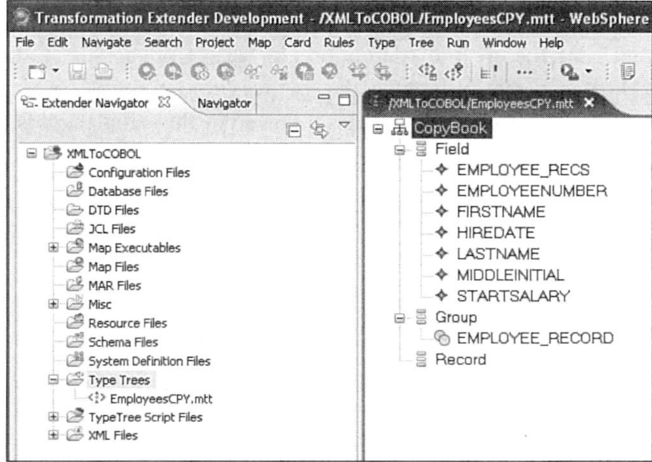

Figure 26-8 Import of COBOL Copybook to type tree.

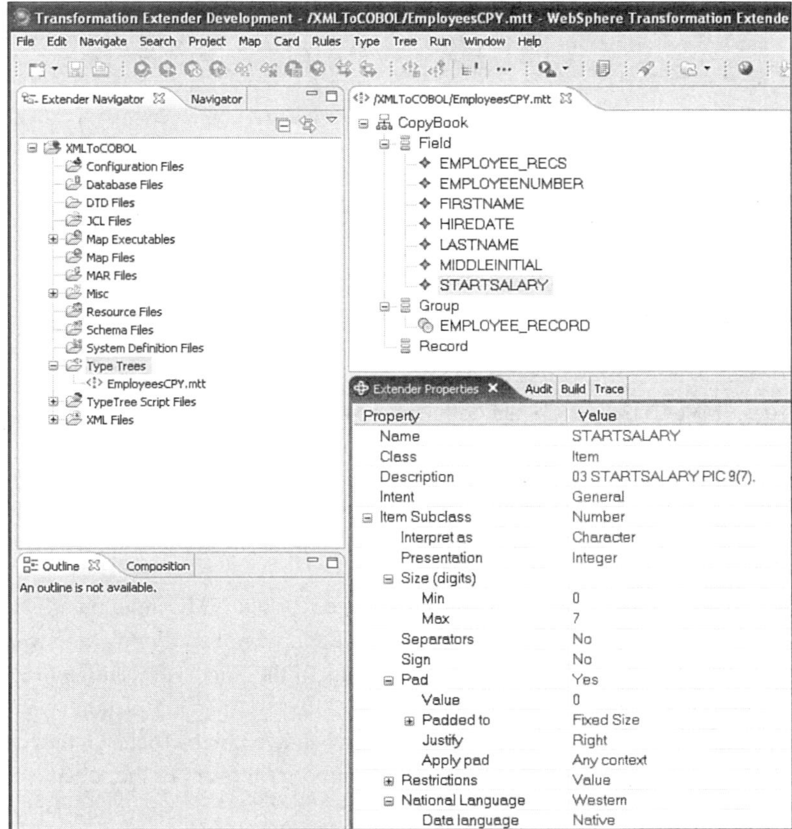

Figure 26-9 Property pane for the STARTSALARY field.

You may have noticed in Figure 26-8 that the importer created an EMPLOYEE_RECORD group object based on the record definition in the Copybook. It also generated an EMPLOYEE_RECS object that is really the entire file definition, which starts with the EMPLOYEE_COUNT record counter field and is followed by the actual records, as shown in Figure 26-10. It is also evident in this figure that the fields are now in their proper order in the record object.

Figure 26-10 EMPLOYEE_RECS file definition object created.

At this point we have completed our definition of the type tree for the COBOL output file. The final step of this process is typically to analyze the logic and structure of the type tree to see if it is formatted properly. Figure 26-11 shows the menu choices used and the analysis results; in this case there are no errors or warnings.

Next we imported the XSD file to build a type tree for our XML input data. The process for this is the same one we used for importing the COBOL Copybook, only this time we chose XML Schema from the list shown in Figure 26-7. The results of the import are shown in Figure 26-12. Noticeable in Figure 26-12 are elements of the XML file, such as the prolog (where the XML version, encoding, and other attributes can be found). We have put the focus on the StartingSalary field to display its attributes, which you can see are numeric/integer per the schema definition for this field.

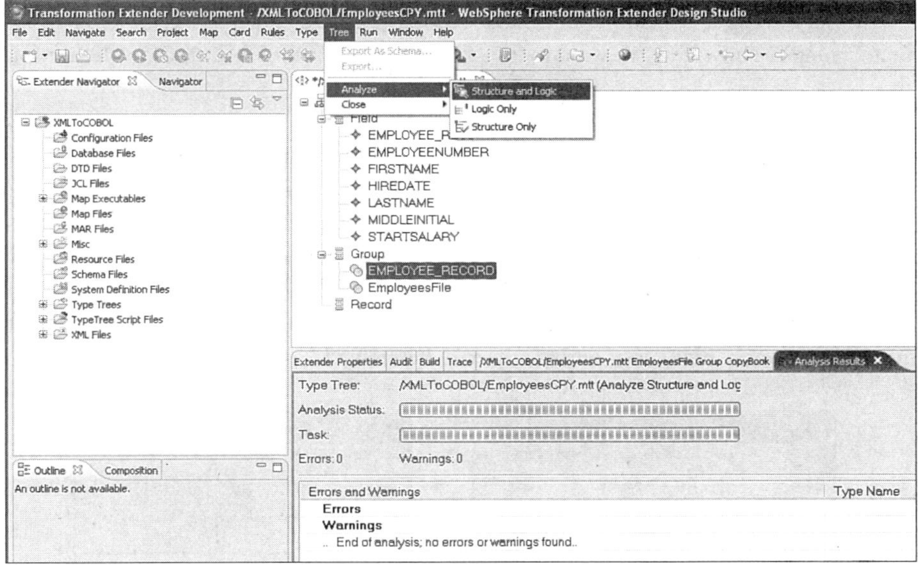

Figure 26-11 Analysis of the COBOL Type Tree with no errors.

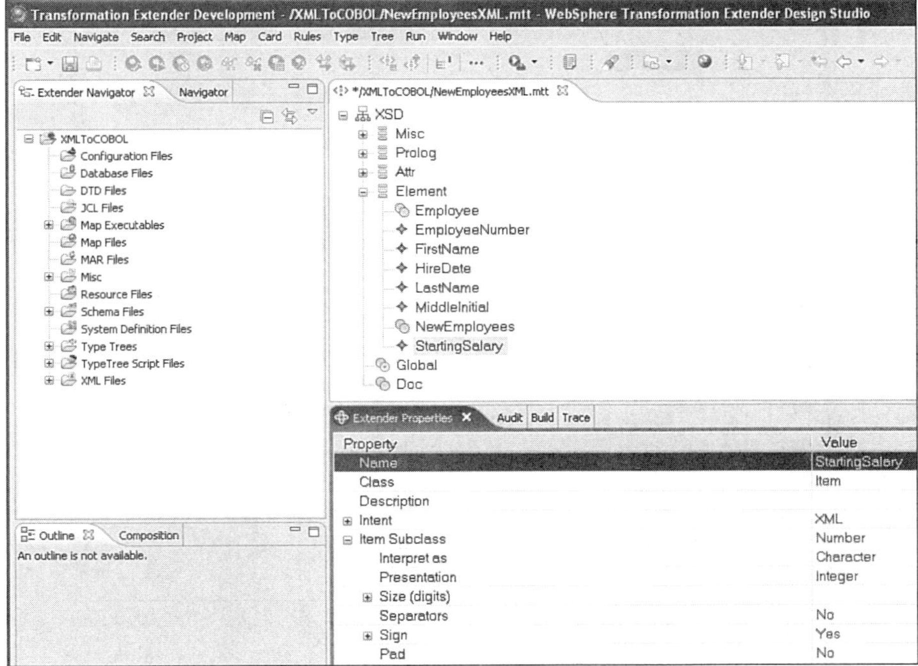

Figure 26-12 Type tree import of the XML schema definition.

Now that our input and output data have been described by the type trees we have built, we can create a map to show how we want to transform the data from XML to COBOL at runtime.

Using the Map Designer

The Map Designer is where the actual logic for the transform is described. In WTX, maps are held in containers called Map Source Files, so one of those must be created prior to any maps. Figure 26-13 shows that we have created a map source called EmployeeMaps by right-clicking on the Map Files folder in the Extender Navigator, and we subsequently created a new map under that called EmployeesXMLtoCPY in the Outline pane just below. Take note of the structure under the map file. There is a section for declaring the inputs and outputs for the map, and then an Organizer area where various logs and results can be viewed.

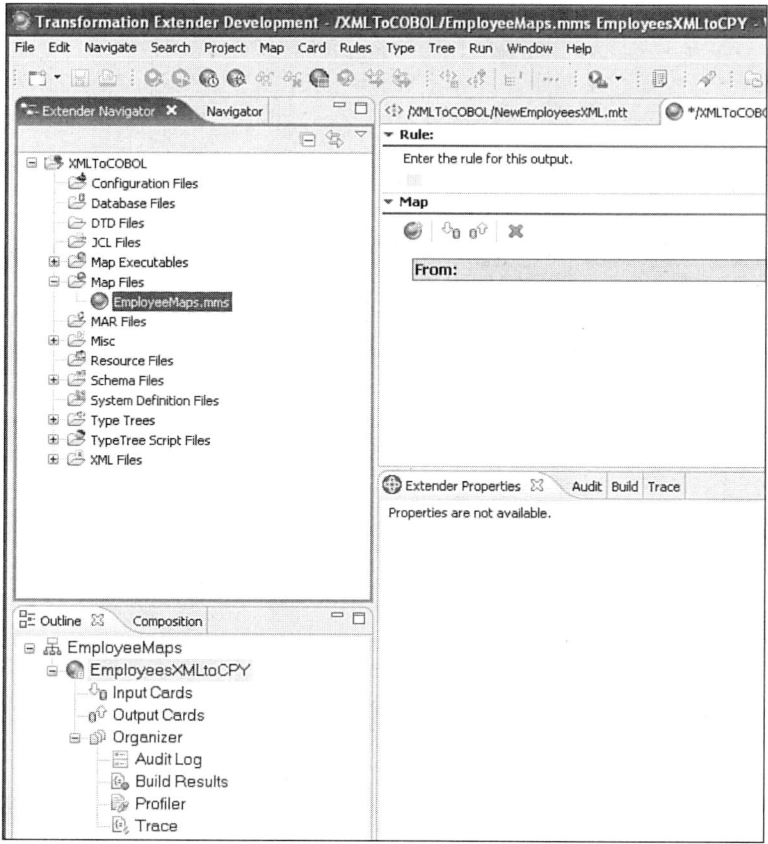

Figure 26-13 Creating a map source and map file.

> **TIP—CREATING NEW MAPS**
>
> After right-clicking on the Map Files folder in the Extender Navigator and selecting New to create a new map source, it may seem intuitive to right-click on the map source name and expect to create a map under that map source. In fact, you must do this in the Outline pane below—right-clicking on the map source there will yield the New→Map selection.

The next step is to define the input and output cards. Figure 26-14 shows the card we created by right-clicking on the Input Cards folder and selecting New. We have given this card a name of EmployeesXMLInput and selected our previously built type tree. When you have identified the type tree, you must populate the Type field to tell the map where in that type tree you want to operate. Remember that the type tree is hierarchical in nature. We have selected the Doc level element, which represents the structured data in the XML file (as can be seen in Figure 26-12). We have also selected a previously created sample input file NewEmployees.xml in the FilePath field, which will be used as input when we tell Design Studio to do a transform to test our map. The file contains the data shown in Listing 26-4.

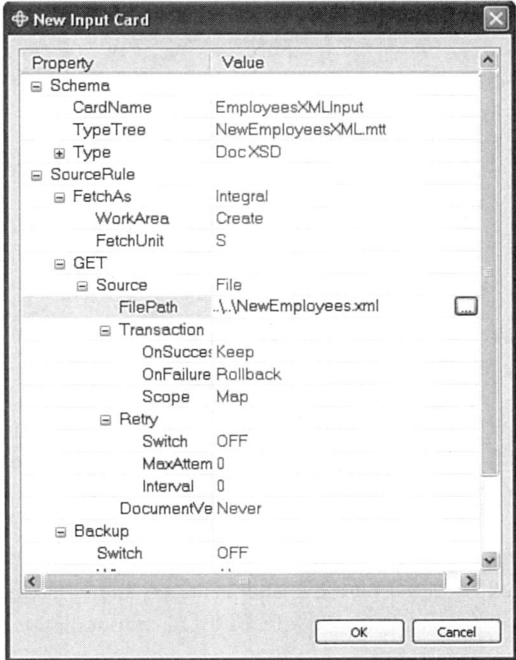

Figure 26-14 Input card for the Employee XML data.

> **TIP—NATIVE SCHEMA SUPPORT**
>
> Note that with version 8.2 and up of WTX Design Studio, the XML schema can be specified directly on the input card in the TypeTree field, rather than the .mtt file that was created by importing the schema. This enables you to avoid the step of importing the schema and creating a type tree.

Next, the output card is defined, using the same process. Figure 26-15 shows the card name, the previously created COBOL type tree, and the type and name of the output file that we would like created when we do our testing. We have chosen the file object created earlier as the type for the transform.

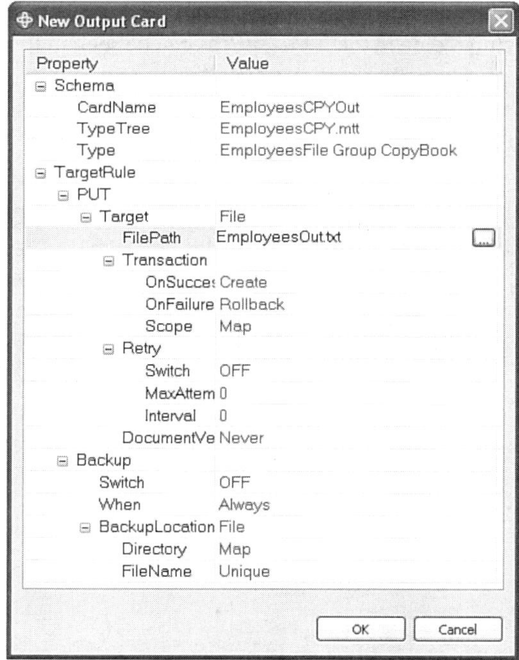

Figure 26-15 Output card defined for Employee COBOL Copybook data.

Now that the cards are defined, the actual transform logic can be described. We have double-clicked on the input and output cards and arranged them side by side to facilitate this, as shown in Figure 26-16—XML input on the left, COBOL output on the right.

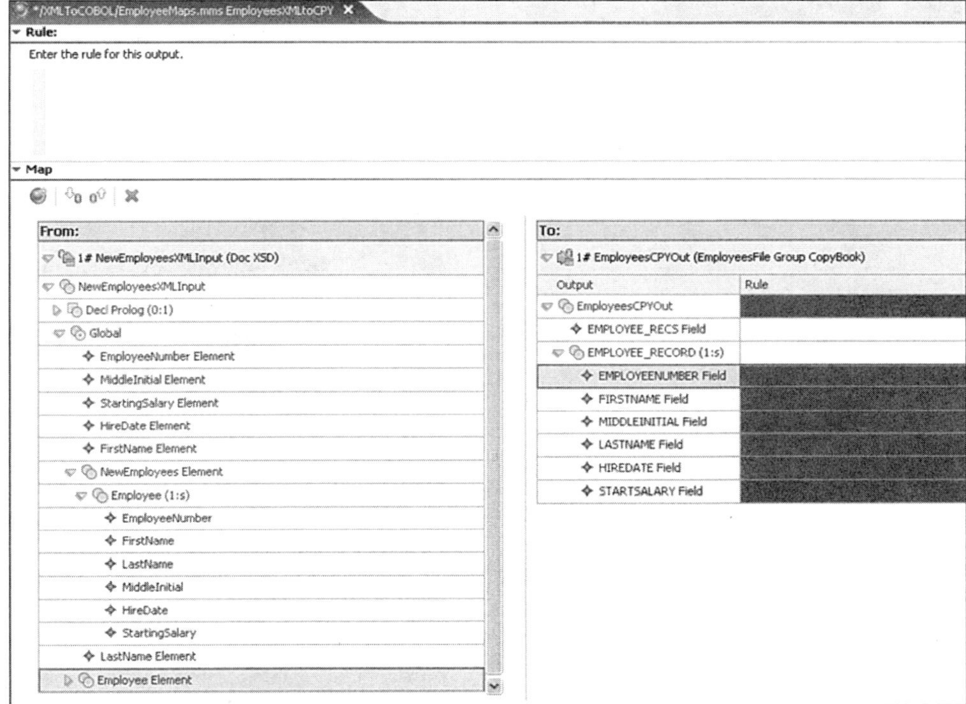

Figure 26-16 Input and output card layouts prior to designing transform logic.

This is the point at which the true power of WTX can be appreciated. What would normally be complex coding can be achieved by simply dragging and dropping. For example, we can simply drag fields such as FirstName from the input card to the corresponding output card rather than having to program those conversions.

However, this example was intentionally created to be nontrivial, containing some of the challenges you might expect in the real world. For example, it is apparent that there is no corresponding XML input field to populate the EMPLOYEE_REC record counter field in the output. This problem can be solved by using one of the WTX built-in programming functions, "COUNT." Figure 26-17 shows this function in place for that field. To create it, we placed our cursor in the Rule column next to that field in the To: card, and then typed "COUNT(" in the Rule pane above that, as seen in the figure. It takes the Employee (1:s) nodeset (which can be dragged directly up rather than typing it) from the input XML document as its input parameter, so the total count of those nodesets found in the XML will be used for the value in the output record.

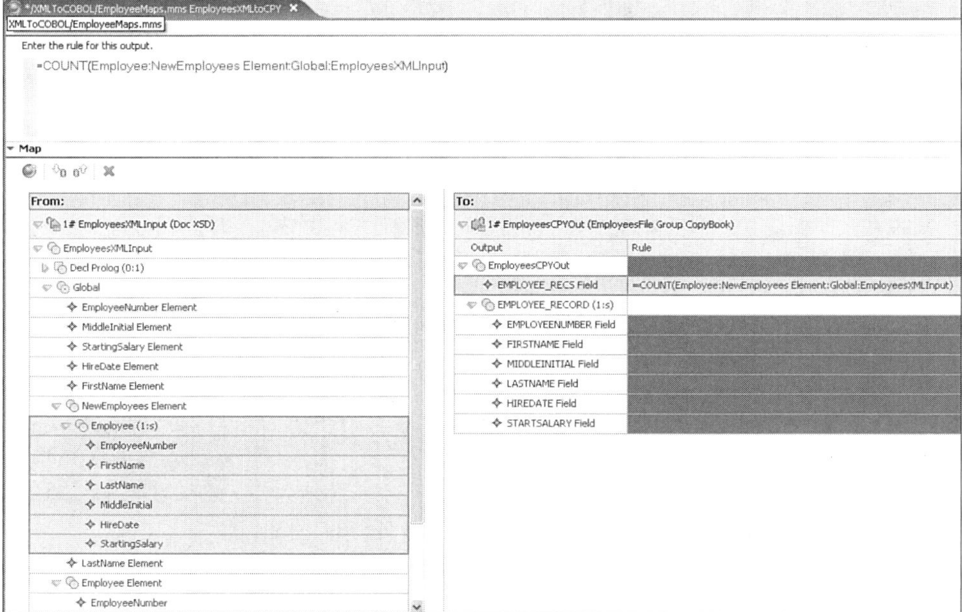

Figure 26-17 COUNT function used to generate the EMPLOYEE_RECS field.

The second challenge presented by our example scenario is that of the repeating records in the output datasets. We need some way to loop through the employee nodesets in the input document and create output COBOL records. To do this in WTX, you use something called a functional map. The standard convention is to begin any new functional map name with "F_" to indicate that this is a functional map rather than a built-in function.

Figure 26-18 shows the functional map call in place, created the same way that the COUNT function was created. However, this is just a call; the function itself has not as yet been created. This would be the next logical step.

For those with a programmatic mindset, it might seem daunting to have to create code to do this looping. You might be saying "Ah hah! Here is where we're going to be forced to write some code...." But this is not the case. By right-clicking on the call that we just created in the Rule cell of the To: card, and selecting Functional Map Wizard from the context menu, we get a dialog like the one shown in Figure 26-19; the wizard selects the proper levels of the hierarchy from both input and output cards for us. Note that this is simply a "very good guess" from the tool and should always be checked for accuracy.

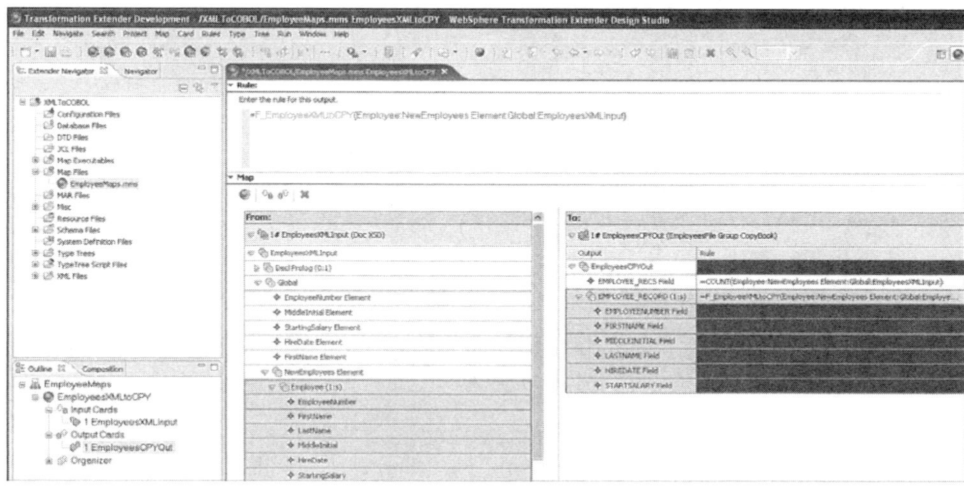

Figure 26-18 Functional Map Call for employee records.

Figure 26-19 Functional Map Wizard for the employee records loop.

All we need to do at this point is click the Create button, and the functional map definition is created for us. Figure 26-20 shows the results. The functional map is shown listed under the Map Executables folder in the Extender Navigator pane, and the Outline pane now contains this new map along with the associated input and output cards, which were also generated for us. These cards are displayed in panes side by side, so that all we need to do now is drag the fields from the input card to the output card to finish defining the transform logic. This has already been done in the figure.

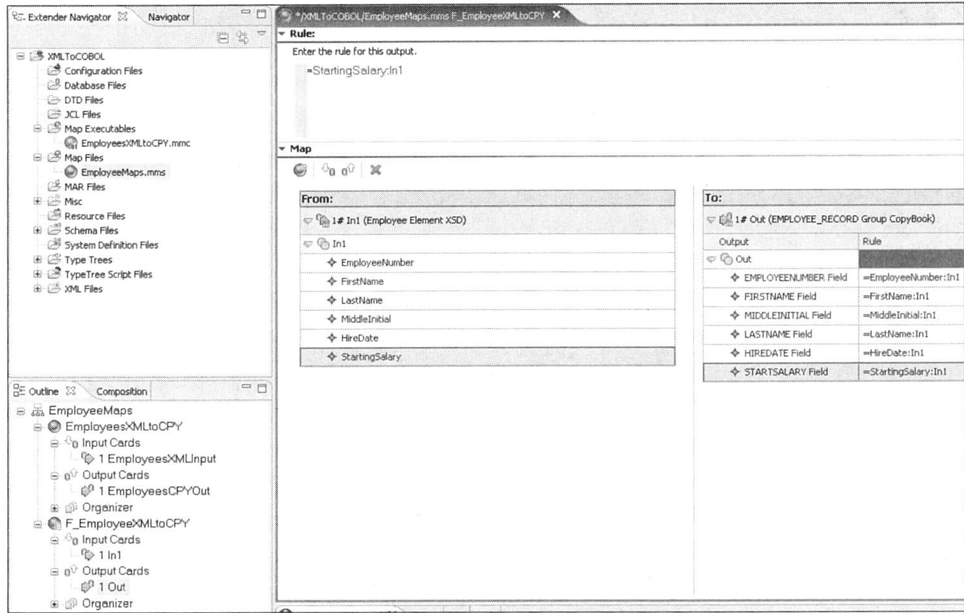

Figure 26-20 Functional map with transform design complete.

Our map is complete at this point, so now on to testing! In Figure 26-20, you might have noticed that the icon next to our map is the purple ball, which represents WTX. This means that WTX is the current runtime designated for this map. We can build the map (in essence, this is a compile step) by right-clicking on the map name in the Outline pane and choosing Build. If there are no errors, the build dialog will flash momentarily and then disappear. We can then run the map by again going to the context menu and choosing Run.

The result at this point is an error that says "One or more inputs was invalid." Something is wrong. What a great time to investigate some of the troubleshooting tools! By right-clicking on the map name in the Outline pane and choosing Map Settings, you can access the map trace settings. Figure 26-21 shows how we have enabled the trace with all settings On.

After the map is rebuilt and rerun, the tools under the Organizer folder can be leveraged. Double-clicking on the Trace folder will load the trace into a new pane for inspection, as shown in Figure 26-22. Reading this, it becomes evident that the runtime is trying to read the schema file, which has not been imported into the project. When we built the type tree based on this schema earlier, it did not get imported automatically as a result.

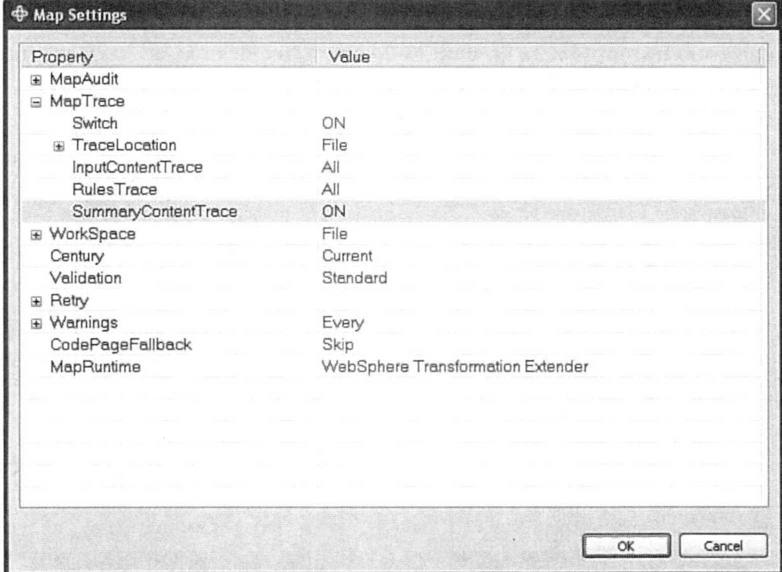

Figure 26-21 Map trace set on for our employee Map transformation.

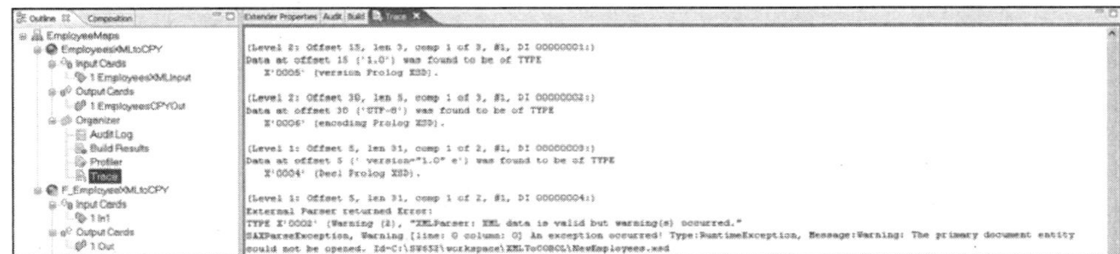

Figure 26-22 Trace output for debugging WTX transform problems.

If we go to the Extender Navigator and right-click on the Schema Files directory, import the schema, and then build and run the map once more, we get a much better result, as seen in Figure 26-23.

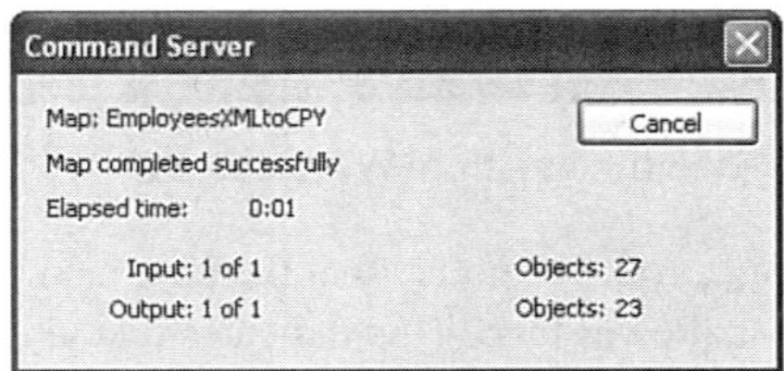

Figure 26-23 A successful map execution for the employee transformation.

Seeing is believing, as they say. To look at the actual results of this run, right-click the map name again and choose Run Results. Figure 26-24 shows the desired results: the binary two-byte field for our record counter followed by several employee records. The output COBOL data matches what our XML input data had.

Figure 26-24 Run results for the employee XML to COBOL transformation.

Keep in mind what we said earlier that not all WTX runtime functions are supported on DataPower. So testing against WTX as a first step is fine, particularly since you can take advantage of the debugging and profiling tools in that mode. But keep in mind that the maps may work there, but not against DataPower. For this reason, you may want to specify DataPower as the runtime engine as a default and leave it that way.

To change the runtime for a map, you must right-click the map and go to the map settings, as shown in Figure 26-25.

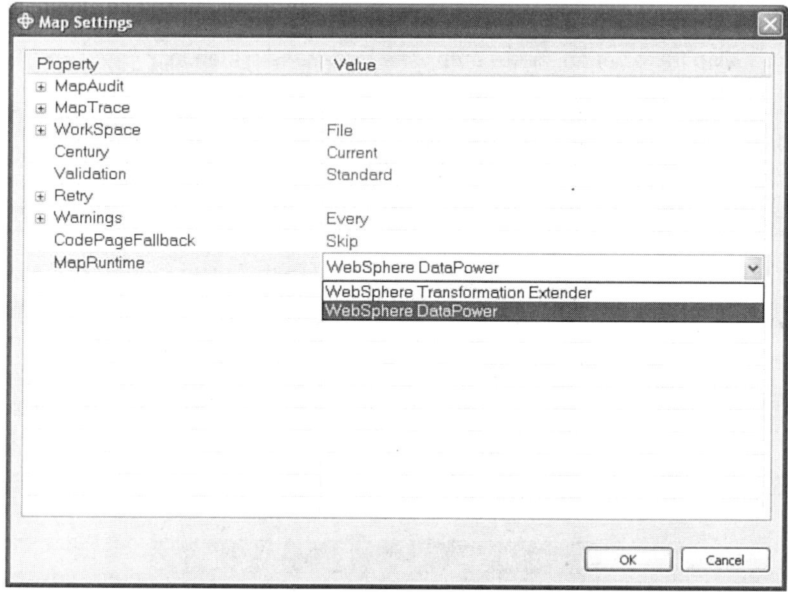

Figure 26-25 Changing the map runtime from WTX to DataPower.

After making this change, you will notice that the icon next to the map has changed from the WTX purple ball to the DataPower logo. This indicates that when the map is run, it will execute against the DataPower runtime. Obviously, we must tell the Design Studio where our device is located. This can be accomplished by going to the Window→Preferences menu and navigating to the DataPower settings, as shown in Figure 26-26. You can see in this figure where the 22222 port from the HTTP XML Firewall in the WTX domain (way back in Figure 26-6) is used, where you can configure the SSL settings should you choose to use that, and that DataPower should be the default runtime. You would generally "set and forget" these after installing Design Studio.

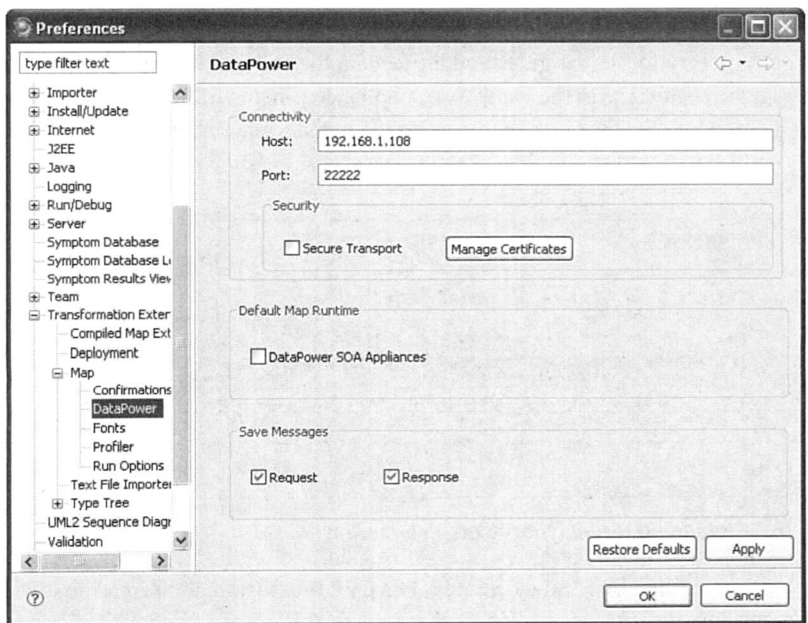

Figure 26-26 Configuring WTX Design Studio for DataPower runtime.

Rebuilding and running the map now (assuming the DataPower device is up and running, with the WTX domain installed) results in a successful run. There is indication on the results dialog that the test was run against the appliance, as shown by the IP address and port in Figure 26-27. The results can be inspected again and are the same. The DataPower logs in the WTX domain can also be viewed for additional confirmation or debugging.

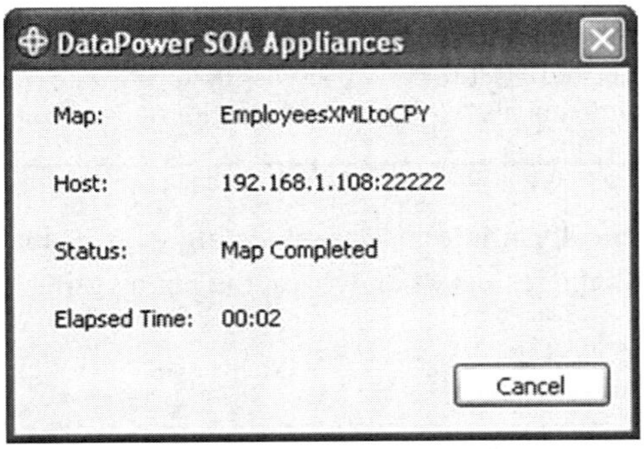

DataPower SOA Appliances

Map: EmployeesXMLtoCPY

Host: 192.168.1.108:22222

Status: Map Completed

Elapsed Time: 00:02

Cancel

Figure 26-27 Successful map execution on DataPower.

Deploying to DataPower

As we've seen, changing, testing, and debugging to fine-tune the maps can be done very easily in an iterative fashion, with very little effort by the developer. But at some point, the developer will be satisfied with the changes and will want to move the transform to a real DataPower service running in some domain.

The first step is to locate the generated artifacts in the Design Studio workspace directory for your project, and upload those to the DataPower appliance. There will be an XML file, which is the metadata to be used by the DataGlue engine to do the transformation, and two .mts files, which are the descriptions of the data, the type trees. The upload process is shown in Figure 26-28.

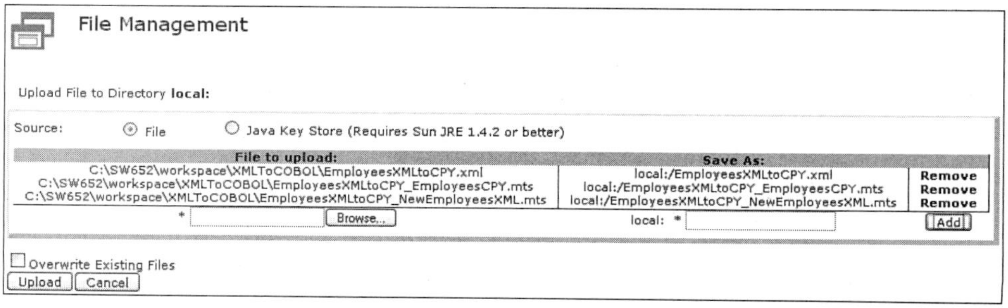

File Management

Upload File to Directory **local:**

Source: ⦿ File ○ Java Key Store (Requires Sun JRE 1.4.2 or better)

File to upload:	Save As:	
C:\SW652\workspace\XMLToCOBOL\EmployeesXMLtoCPY.xml	local:/EmployeesXMLtoCPY.xml	Remove
C:\SW652\workspace\XMLToCOBOL\EmployeesXMLtoCPY_EmployeesCPY.mts	local:/EmployeesXMLtoCPY_EmployeesCPY.mts	Remove
C:\SW652\workspace\XMLToCOBOL\EmployeesXMLtoCPY_NewEmployeesXML.mts	local:/EmployeesXMLtoCPY_NewEmployeesXML.mts	Remove
* Browse...	local: *	Add

☐ Overwrite Existing Files

Upload Cancel

Figure 26-28 Uploading the WTX artifacts to DataPower.

These files can then be used to create a Binary Transform action in a request or response rule in a Processing Policy. Figure 26-29 shows how this is accomplished. First a Transform action is dragged onto the rule and configured. The "Use XSLT specified in this action on a non-XML message" option is chosen, which you may notice changes the action title and icon from Transform to Transform Binary. Next, the XML file that was just uploaded must be specified in the WTX Map file field. There is no need to specify the MTS files anywhere—they are referenced inside the XML file.

TIP—Be Careful Where You Type!

It is a common mistake to type the path to the XML file in the Processing Control File field just above, rather than in the WTX Map file field, or to look for it in the drop-down list, which only contains .xsl files and not .xml files in the local directory.

After placing this transform into a service, testing can be done using any of the normal means. Figure 26-30 shows the results when we test the policy using curl.

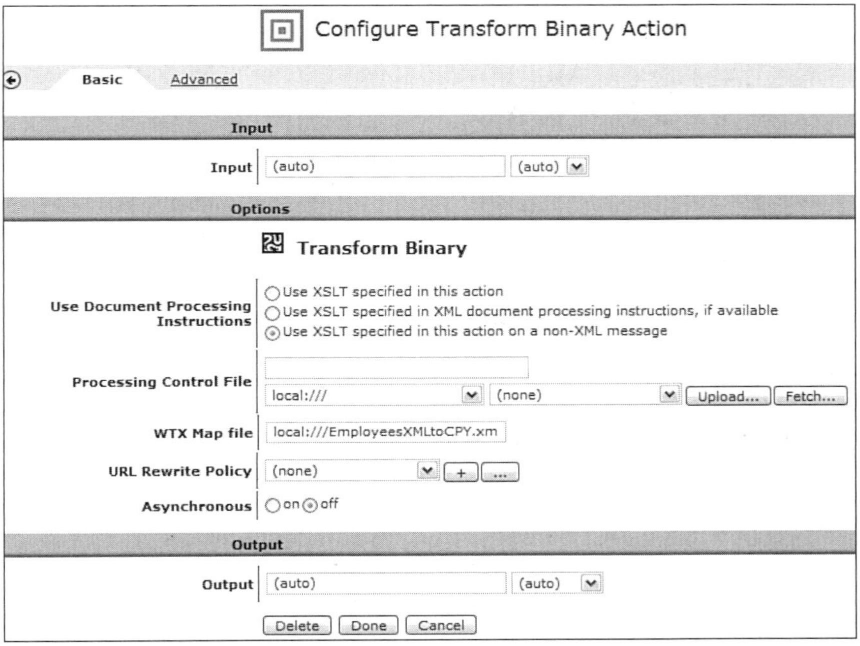

Figure 26-29 Configuring a Transform Binary action in the Processing Policy.

Figure 26-30 Run results for sample non-XML transforming firewall.

Advanced Transform Binary Features

There are often complex requirements for non-XML transformations, like any other business scenario. Let's explore some of the more advanced techniques in this area.

Multiple Input and Output Cards

The scenario we showed you was simple: one input and one output dataset. In the real world, one scenario might be to have multiple input or output datasets. As you know by now, the advanced features for any DataPower object can be found in the WebGUI only by accessing it through the Navigation menu. Figure 26-31 shows our example Transform Binary action (accessed from Objects→XML Processing→Processing Action), and it is obvious how much more there is in the way of configuration than what we saw earlier when opening this through the policy editor. In this figure, the Locate Named Inputs and Outputs drop-down has been exposed to show the choices—default, dynamic, and explicit.

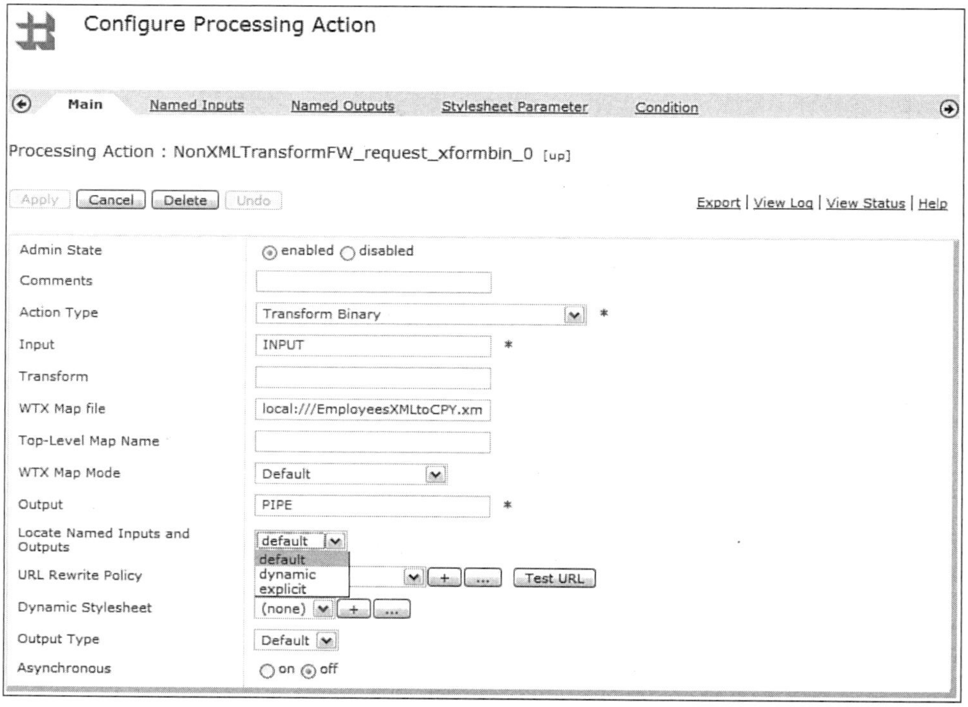

Configure Processing Action

Main | Named Inputs | Named Outputs | Stylesheet Parameter | Condition

Processing Action : NonXMLTransformFW_request_xformbin_0 [up]

Apply | Cancel | Delete | Undo

Export | View Log | View Status | Help

Admin State	enabled disabled
Comments	
Action Type	Transform Binary *
Input	INPUT *
Transform	
WTX Map file	local:///EmployeesXMLtoCPY.xm
Top-Level Map Name	
WTX Map Mode	Default
Output	PIPE *
Locate Named Inputs and Outputs	default (default / dynamic / explicit)
URL Rewrite Policy	+ ... Test URL
Dynamic Stylesheet	(none) + ...
Output Type	Default
Asynchronous	on off

Figure 26-31 Transform Binary action accessed through the Navigation menu.

The default choice enables one input and one output context, as used in our example scenario.

The explicit choice requires you to name the inputs and outputs directly. This can be done by using the Named Inputs and Named Outputs tabs shown in the figure. As an example, if you had a transform that requires input from an EDI file and an MQ message, your configuration might appear as shown in Figure 26-32. This would require you to have cards named EDIFile-Card and MQMessageCard in the map you built in WTX, and to have contexts named EDIFile-Context and MQMessageContext with the appropriate data available to the action and visible at runtime when the policy executes. Multiple outputs would be configured similarly.

To use the dynamic option, you must at runtime populate one or more DataPower variables in the form var://local/named-input/map-input-name, where map-input-name corresponds to a named card in the WTX map (such as the EDIFileCard we used in the last explicit example). You can have one or more of these variables. The value of this variable should be the name of the context that will hold the data at runtime (for example, EDIFileContext as shown previously). There is a corresponding named-output variable for the outputs. This dynamic content could come from message attachments, external sources, content enrichment techniques such as data fetched with the dp:url-open() extension function, using the Fetch action, or any number of ways, making this quite powerful.

Figure 26-32 Multiple named inputs for a Transform Binary action.

Precompiling Maps for DataPower

WTX Design Studio comes with a number of useful tools, one of which is a command-shell utility for precompiling maps. This has a parameter to compile maps for DataPower, which might be useful in batch deployment scenarios. The result of this is the same XML and MTS files that are generated when you choose the Build command from the Design Studio context menu for the map. An example is shown in Figure 26-33.

```
C:\WINDOWS\system32\cmd.exe

C:\IBM\WebSphere Transformation Extender 8.2>mcompile \sw652\workspace\XMLToCOBO
L\EmployeeMaps.mms -DP
================================================================================
===
IBM Utility :    mcompile (Map compile utility)
Version :               8.2.0.2(52)
Map Source File :       C:\sw652\workspace\XMLToCOBOL\EmployeeMaps.mms

Executable Map :        EmployeesXMLtoCPY

Map compiled successfully.

================================================================================
===

C:\IBM\WebSphere Transformation Extender 8.2>_
```

Figure 26-33 Batch compilation of DataPower maps with mcompile.

Detecting Non-XML Files

In some situations, the message content may need to be analyzed dynamically at runtime to determine whether it is XML or non-XML, or perhaps if non-XML to look for certain values inside the file to determine which transform should be used.

One way to determine whether the file is XML is to set up a Binary Transform action to look for the XML declaration within an incoming message, and then use a callable rule to fire the appropriate processing rule for XML or non-XML data.

Another approach would be to use the dp:parse() extension function to attempt to parse the data, and check for a failure (indicating that this is non-XML). To use this technique, you need to use a binary transform to turn the input into base64 encoded data, and then dp:parse the Base64-encoded node.

Summary

This chapter has taken you deep into the world of non-XML transformations on the DataPower appliances. We have discussed some of the tools and techniques that are involved. When the transforms are built, they can be used with any service, commonly the Multi-Protocol Gateway due to its many supported protocols, and the Web Service Proxy as in some of the scenarios we've discussed.

This is a topic that can be quite complex, and perhaps even merit a book of its own! We recommend exploring the example files in the sample XML Firewall in the WTX domain. There is an additional DataPower sample under the install directory for Design Studio that has a scenario for converting a comma-separated text contact information file to mailing labels.

Many shops have data specialists that focus on the taxonomy of the data structures used by their applications. This is further evidence that working with DataPower often requires cooperation among the many factions that comprise an enterprise IT shop!

PART VII

Problem Determination and Tools

CHAPTER 27

Problem Determination Using Built-In Tools

Troubleshooting of applications running through a DataPower appliance, and of the appliance itself, can take place at two different stages in an application's lifecycle. During service development, unit testing, load testing, and quality assurance, the main concern is creating a service, getting it running, and making sure that processing is taking place as desired. In a production setting, much of the troubleshooting will be related to hardware or networking issues, as well as making sure any runtime application errors are received by the appropriate party. DataPower provides built-in tools for tracking down any issues during development, testing, and production. This chapter details common issues and the on-board tools available for debugging and resolving them.

We discuss the creation of new services and some of the challenges that can arise during development. We demonstrate how to drill down into a nonfunctioning service and verify that all dependent objects are working as desired. We also show how to read the logs to gather more information and how to debug initial connectivity issues. For troubleshooting a service that is up and running, we discuss how to avoid some common mistakes and how to track them down when they arise. From an operational perspective, we will also discuss troubleshooting in a production environment. We cover critical events that may occur on the hardware, logging and monitoring of those events, and possible remediation steps.

Configuration Troubleshooting

We have discussed the development of various types of DataPower services throughout this book, and we have mostly focused on the right way to do things. What happens when things are done the wrong way? Generally, these problems present themselves in two different fashions. It's possible that an object created by you (or created automatically by DataPower during the development process) has a down status; a down object can prevent a service from functioning. If you get past that point, it's possible to have a working service that generates unexpected behavior or causes an error at runtime. For now we'll focus on the development portion, and then examine unexpected behavior later in the chapter.

Object Status

Every DataPower service consists of many objects. A Multi-Protocol Gateway (MPGW) is essentially an object that references a Processing Policy, a Front Side Handler, an XML manager, and many other subordinate objects. Each of those objects, in turn, can depend on others; a Processing Policy contains rules, which contain actions, which may rely on a file or additional configuration objects. Each object must be active and working as intended in order for the service to work as a whole. This might sound a bit scary, but we've seen how easy it is to configure these services, and each object is arranged in a logical hierarchy that makes it simple to debug. We've seen the hierarchy in previous chapters, so now we'll focus on making sure each layer is working properly.

Most problems are noticed when a service becomes inoperable. Each service type has a list of configured services that contains basic metadata and is accessible from the Control Panel or the Services section of the left-side menu. An XML Firewall (XMLFW) list is shown in Figure 27-1. There is a bright red status indicator under the Op-State column that suggests the service's operational state is currently down.

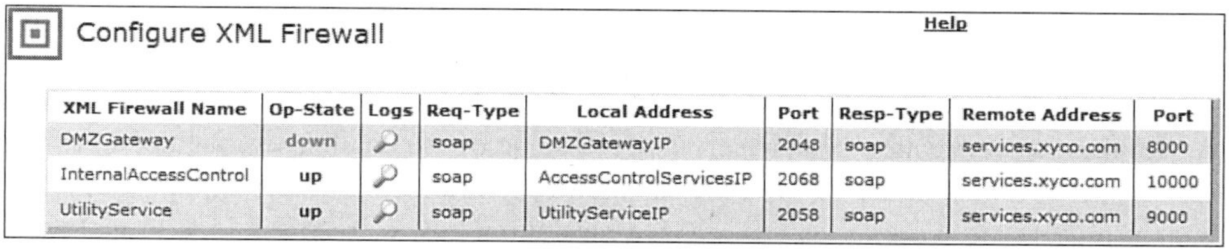

Configure XML Firewall

Help

XML Firewall Name	Op-State	Logs	Req-Type	Local Address	Port	Resp-Type	Remote Address	Port
DMZGateway	down		soap	DMZGatewayIP	2048	soap	services.xyco.com	8000
InternalAccessControl	up		soap	AccessControlServicesIP	2068	soap	services.xyco.com	10000
UtilityService	up		soap	UtilityServiceIP	2058	soap	services.xyco.com	9000

Figure 27-1 Viewing a down service in the service list.

This can also be seen at the top of the service configuration page itself, next to the status: indicator as shown in Figure 27-2. In this second case, the root cause of the problem is somewhat apparent, as the SSL Server Crypto Profile field also has a down indicator. However, the problem isn't always this obvious, and the root cause may be deeper than the SSL Profile itself.

In order to gather more information about an object that is down, click on the View Status link that is at the top of every object configuration screen. This opens a new window with status information about that object and every object on which it depends. Each of the items has three status fields and a detail field, as shown in Figure 27-3.

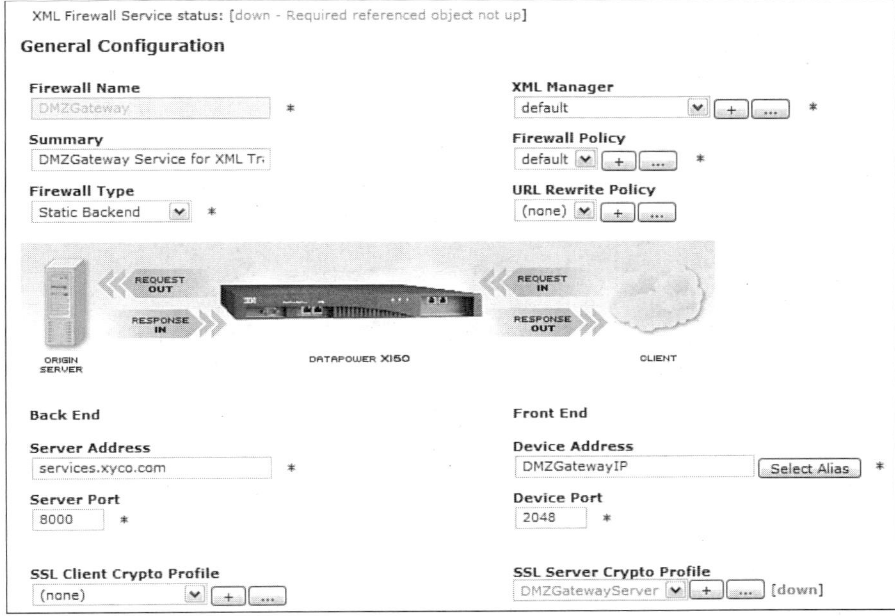

Figure 27-2 Viewing a down service from within the configuration page.

name	config-state	op-state	admin-state	detail	logs
XML Firewall Service					
⊟ DMZGateway [XML Firewall Service]	new	down	enabled	Required referenced object not up	
⊟ default [XML Manager]	saved	up	enabled		
default [User Agent]	saved	up	enabled		
⊟ DMZGateway [SSL Proxy Profile]	new	down	enabled	Required referenced object not up	
⊟ DMZGatewayServer [Crypto Profile]	new	down	enabled	Required referenced object not up	
⊟ DMZGateway [Crypto Identification Credentials]	new	down	enabled	Required referenced object not up	
DMZGateway [Crypto Key]	new	up	enabled		
DMZGateway [Crypto Certificate]	new	down	enabled	File is expired	
default [Processing Policy]	saved	up	enabled		

Figure 27-3 Viewing the status page for an XML Firewall Service.

Configuration State

An object's configuration state describes its creation/modification status, and is designated by the config-state field. There are a few options for this field's value:

- **New**—The object has just been created and has not been saved to the device's persisted configuration.
- **Modified**—The object exists in the persisted configuration but has been modified since it was last saved.
- **Saved**—The object has been saved to the persisted configuration and has not been modified.

Operational State

An object's operational state reflects whether the object is currently functional and is defined in the op-state field. There are only two options for this field:

- **Up**—The object is active and operational.
- **Down**—The object is inactive due to a misconfiguration, a dependent object that is also down, or an administrative choice to disable that object.

Administrative State

An object's administrative state is defined by the user and is represented by the admin-state field. This state is modified from the object's configuration screen and has two possible values:

- **Enabled**—The object should be active (if configured properly).
- **Disabled**—The object has been selectively removed from service by the user. A disabled object may affect any objects that depend on it, as its operational state will be down.

For some objects such as services, the admin state can only be modified from the Objects menu. That is, to disable an XML Firewall Service using its admin state, you must navigate to Objects→Services→XML Firewall Service in the left-side menu, click the appropriate firewall, select the disabled radio button, and then click Apply. You do not see the admin state field when editing the service from the Control Panel as it is intended to provide a simpler, more streamlined view.

Detail Field

The object status screen's detail column provides any additional information that is applicable to each object's current status. If the object is down, the detail will be a message that suggests a reason for that status; in Figure 27-3, most of the down objects suggest that the problem is due to a required referenced object not being up. The crypto certificate object called DMZGateway indicates that its certificate file is expired, and this is the root cause of the problem we have been discussing.

Object Branches

The status page is hierarchical so that referenced objects are listed below the referencing object, and are indented to suggest a parent-child relationship. In the example in Figure 27-3, the branch that is causing the problem contains (from highest-level to lowest-level object) the following: XML Firewall→SSL Proxy Profile→SSL Crypto Profile→Identification Credentials→Crypto Certificate. Notice that the XML Manager and the Processing Policy are unaffected by the down crypto certificate, as they are not dependent on any of the objects in this branch.

Domain-Level Service Status

Though every object has its own status page that references only that object and any referenced objects, there is also a global status page that references every object within a domain. Navigate to Status→Main→Object Status in the left-side menu to see the status of every service defined in this domain, as shown in Figure 27-4.

name	config-state	op-state	admin-state	detail	logs
⊟ HTTP Service					
⊟ WebSphere MQ Gateway					
⊟ WebSphere MQ Host					
⊟ WebSphere MQ Proxy					
⊟ Multi-Protocol Gateway					
⊞ DMZGateway [Multi-Protocol Gateway]	saved	up	enabled		
⊟ SSL Proxy Service					
⊟ TCP Proxy Service					
⊟ UDDI Subscription					
⊟ Web Application Firewall					
⊟ Web Service Proxy					
⊞ HRServices [Web Service Proxy]	saved	up	enabled		
⊟ WSRR Subscription					
⊟ XML Firewall Service					
⊞ DMZGateway [XML Firewall Service]	modified	down	enabled	Required referenced object not up	
⊟ XSL Coprocessor Service					
⊟ XSL Proxy Service					

Figure 27-4 Viewing the domain-level object status page.

By default, this page is indexed only by services, and all referenced objects are collapsed under the services that reference them. You might want to drill into a particular service, such as one with an operational state marked as down. You can click the plus sign (+) next to any service to expand by one level. At each level, there should be at least one object that is also down, until you reach the object that is causing the problem. In Figure 27-5, we have expanded the same firewall object that we reviewed earlier.

⊟ XML Firewall Service					
⊟ DMZGateway [XML Firewall Service]	modified	down	enabled	Required referenced object not up	
⊞ default [XML Manager]	saved	up	enabled		
⊟ DMZGateway [SSL Proxy Profile]	saved	down	enabled	Required referenced object not up	
⊟ DMZGatewayServer [Crypto Profile]	saved	down	enabled	Required referenced object not up	
⊟ DMZGateway [Crypto Identification Credentials]	saved	down	enabled	Required referenced object not up	
DMZGateway [Crypto Key]	saved	up	enabled		
DMZGateway [Crypto Certificate]	saved	down	enabled	File is expired	
default [Processing Policy]	saved	up	enabled		

Figure 27-5 Viewing a service status from the Object Status page.

Clicking the Open All button at the top of the page expands all referenced objects. This is a useful way to determine whether any object is down in any service, but it can quickly grow to a long list in domains with many services. You can filter the list to only up or down services by selecting the desired state from the Show only op-state: drop-down at the top of the page. Clicking the magnifying glass next to any of the object entries shows any recent log messages for these objects; clicking it for the DMZGateway Crypto Certificate object displays the logs shown in Figure 27-6.

02:13:21	mgmt	error	HRServices	495			0x00f30008	certificate (DMZGateway): File is expired
02:13:21	crypto	error	HRServices	495			0x8060008b	certificate (DMZGateway): certificate 'cert:///DMZGateway-sscert.pem' is expired

Figure 27-6 Viewing the logs for a down certificate object.

Domain-Level Object Status

In some cases, low-level objects not tied directly to a service may be down without that status being reflected in a higher-level object; the Object Status page can show these as well. For a different perspective on all objects in a domain, rather than just those referenced by services, select types (instead of services) from the View by: drop-down at the top of the page. This displays all objects, sorted alphabetically by object name, and their current operational states. Figure 27-7 shows some of this display; we've also chosen to filter by only down objects. This is a great method for getting an overview of the current health of all objects in a particular domain. It is especially useful after importing configurations into a different device/domain than the one on which they were developed.

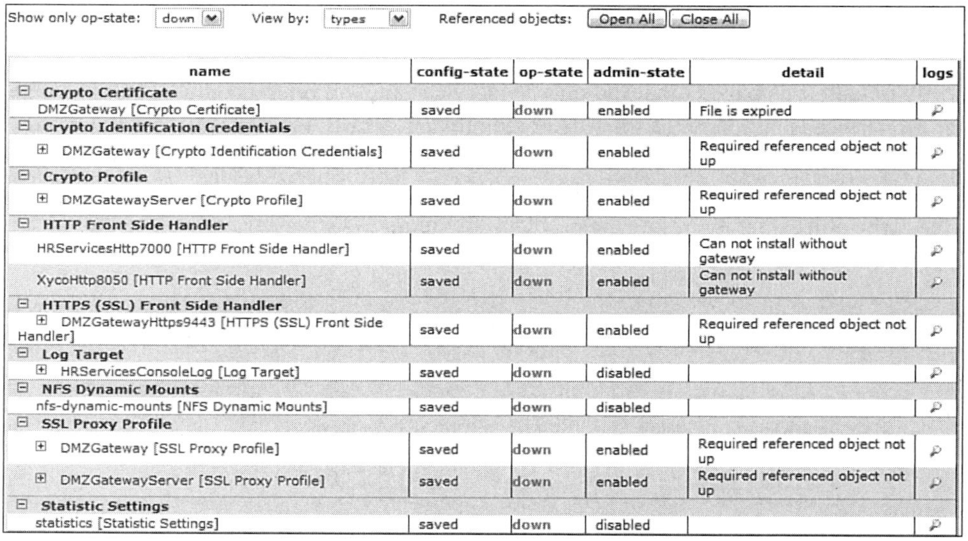

Show only op-state: down View by: types Referenced objects: Open All Close All

name	config-state	op-state	admin-state	detail	logs
⊟ **Crypto Certificate**					
DMZGateway [Crypto Certificate]	saved	down	enabled	File is expired	
⊟ **Crypto Identification Credentials**					
⊞ DMZGateway [Crypto Identification Credentials]	saved	down	enabled	Required referenced object not up	
⊟ **Crypto Profile**					
⊞ DMZGatewayServer [Crypto Profile]	saved	down	enabled	Required referenced object not up	
⊟ **HTTP Front Side Handler**					
HRServicesHttp7000 [HTTP Front Side Handler]	saved	down	enabled	Can not install without gateway	
XycoHttp8050 [HTTP Front Side Handler]	saved	down	enabled	Can not install without gateway	
⊟ **HTTPS (SSL) Front Side Handler**					
⊞ DMZGatewayHttps9443 [HTTPS (SSL) Front Side Handler]	saved	down	enabled	Required referenced object not up	
⊟ **Log Target**					
⊞ HRServicesConsoleLog [Log Target]	saved	down	disabled		
⊟ **NFS Dynamic Mounts**					
nfs-dynamic-mounts [NFS Dynamic Mounts]	saved	down	disabled		
⊟ **SSL Proxy Profile**					
⊞ DMZGateway [SSL Proxy Profile]	saved	down	enabled	Required referenced object not up	
⊞ DMZGatewayServer [SSL Proxy Profile]	saved	down	enabled	Required referenced object not up	
⊟ **Statistic Settings**					
statistics [Statistic Settings]	saved	down	disabled		

Figure 27-7 Viewing object status indexed by object name.

Reasons for Down Handlers

There are a myriad of reasons an object might be down, and they are too numerous to list in this setting. However, each of these reasons is generally evident from the detail field on the object status page. By following a branch of down objects, the lowest-level object can be fixed; each object name is clickable and will open that object's configuration page. When the object has been modified and the changes have been applied, click Refresh on the object status page to see whether the problem has been solved. If so, the entire branch of objects should revert to an up operational state. Let's walk through some common examples, including expired certificates, missing key files, down messaging server objects, improperly configured protocol handlers, and network-level conflicts.

Expired Certificates

Services that require SSL communication or that contain actions relying on cryptographic material are subject to a couple of common issues. First, certificates can expire. It is important that certificates on the device are monitored for expiration, as you have seen in our previous examples; one expired certificate can bring down an entire service. Fortunately, this problem can be avoided before it ever arises, using a special object on the appliance. The Crypto Certificate Monitor was discussed in Chapter 14, "Logging and Monitoring." This object monitors certificates for upcoming expiration, and begins sending warnings to the log at a user-configurable interval. By default, the warnings begin 30 days before expiration and are sent once per day. A sample log message delivered by the certificate monitor is shown in Figure 27-8.

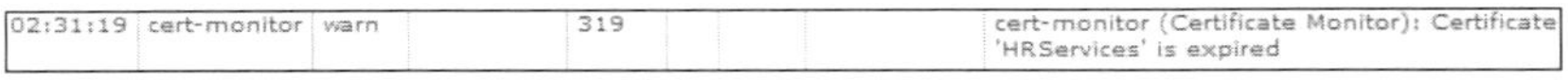

02:31:19 cert-monitor warn 319 cert-monitor (Certificate Monitor): Certificate 'HRServices' is expired

Figure 27-8 Viewing logs generated by the certificate monitor.

A log target can also be created to email an appropriate administrator when this event occurs. Enforcing a proactive certificate management policy prevents potential problems that could bring down your services.

Missing Cryptographic Files

Another common issue with services relying on keys and certificates arises during configuration export and import. None of the items in the cert: and sharedcert: directories, including keys and certificates, can be exported or removed from a device in any way. When a service is exported that relies on these files, keys and certificates must be backed up (during their creation) and moved manually. If you forget this step, you'll see some of the same behavior as in previous examples. In the case of a certificate used for SSL in an XML Firewall, the entire service will be brought down, as it depends entirely on the single frontend or backend interface that uses the expired certificate. However, MPGW and Web Service Proxy (WSP) objects separate the network interfaces from the service implementation using Front Side Handlers (FSH). In these services, an FSH can be down due to a missing key/certificate file, but the service itself will be up. You'll notice in the front side settings that a particular FSH is down, as shown in Figure 27-9.

Front side settings

Front Side Protocol

Type	Name	Op-State	
HTTPS (SSL) Front Side Handler	DMZGatewayHttps9443	[down - Required referenced object not up]	Remove

HRServicesHttp7000

Add Create new...

Figure 27-9 Examining a down FSH.

Whether or not the service itself is down, you can still click the View Status link at the top of the service configuration page. This shows all the underlying objects for easy debugging. If a key or certificate is missing, the object detail will mention that the File is unreadable, as shown in Figure 27-10; this is exactly what will be seen if you import a service or domain and forget to bring in the keys and certificates separately. This error is also true for existing files that are in a format that can't be read, so check for both cases when receiving this detail message.

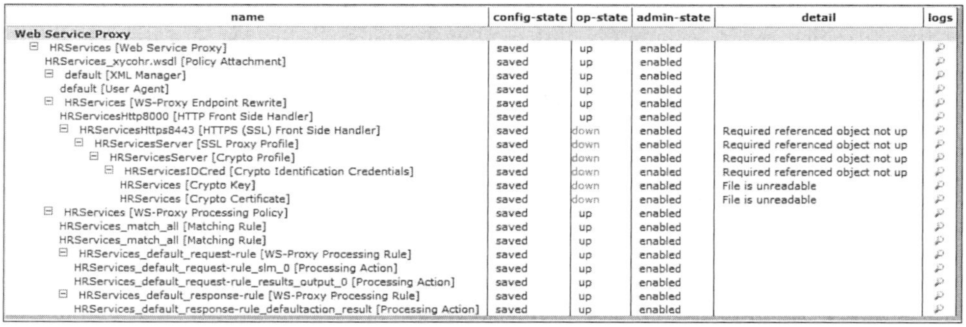

name	config-state	op-state	admin-state	detail	logs
Web Service Proxy					
⊟ HRServices [Web Service Proxy]	saved	up	enabled		
HRServices_xycohr.wsdl [Policy Attachment]	saved	up	enabled		
⊟ default [XML Manager]	saved	up	enabled		
default [User Agent]	saved	up	enabled		
⊟ HRServices [WS-Proxy Endpoint Rewrite]	saved	up	enabled		
HRServicesHttp8000 [HTTP Front Side Handler]	saved	up	enabled		
⊟ HRServicesHttps8443 [HTTPS (SSL) Front Side Handler]	saved	down	enabled	Required referenced object not up	
⊟ HRServicesServer [SSL Proxy Profile]	saved	down	enabled	Required referenced object not up	
⊟ HRServicesServer [Crypto Profile]	saved	down	enabled	Required referenced object not up	
⊟ HRServicesIDCred [Crypto Identification Credentials]	saved	down	enabled	Required referenced object not up	
HRServices [Crypto Key]	saved	down	enabled	File is unreadable	
HRServices [Crypto Certificate]	saved	down	enabled	File is unreadable	
⊟ HRServices [WS-Proxy Processing Policy]	saved	up	enabled		
HRServices_match_all [Matching Rule]	saved	up	enabled		
HRServices_match_all [Matching Rule]	saved	up	enabled		
⊟ HRServices_default_request-rule [WS-Proxy Processing Rule]	saved	up	enabled		
HRServices_default_request-rule_slm_0 [Processing Action]	saved	up	enabled		
HRServices_default_request-rule_results_output_0 [Processing Action]	saved	up	enabled		
⊟ HRServices_default_response-rule [WS-Proxy Processing Rule]	saved	up	enabled		
HRServices_default_response-rule_defaultaction_result [Processing Action]	saved	up	enabled		

Figure 27-10 Viewing the object status for a service with missing crypto files.

Sometimes the cryptographic files are intended to be different between various environments, as the SSL hostnames and encryption keys should change between preproduction and production. If you have the new files available to you, the fix is simple. Just click the key name in the Object Status screen to open the key configuration page. Select the file (if it is on the device but misnamed), or upload a new file using the Upload button. In Figure 27-11, we've selected the appropriate key file from the drop-down. Click Apply to save your changes and close the window; you'll be taken back to the Object Status screen.

Crypto Key : HRServices [down - File is unreadable]

Apply | Cancel | Undo

Admin State	(•) enabled ( ) disabled
File Name	cert:/// ▾ HRServices-privkey.pem ▾

Figure 27-11 Selecting a new key file for a private key object.

You'll have to perform the same steps for the certificate object; click the name, select/upload the right file, and click Apply. Please note that if the files were uploaded separately (perhaps from the File Management page), the key and certificate objects will not retry a previously unreadable file. To force the new files to be recognized, open the objects (you can click on their names from Object Status), modify something to enable the Apply button, and then click it. This can be as simple as typing and then deleting a space in the comment field, or clicking the radio buttons for disable and then enable; applying these "changes" causes the object to reread the file. When done, click Refresh on the object status page to verify that the problem has been solved. Chapter 15, "Build and Deploy Techniques," contains more information about possible migration strategies.

Down Messaging Server Objects

To this point, we've only discussed problems with crypto objects, which are often used in HTTP and HTTPS FSHs. Other FSH objects can also run into issues during initial configuration; just as HTTP problems often arise from a missing or expired referenced object, the other protocols also use lower-level objects. For example, MQ FSHs require an MQ Queue Manager object to be defined; if there is a problem with this definition (or the queue manager itself), the object will be down. Even if there isn't a problem, there is occasionally an initial delay while the device communicates with the queue manager. In this case, the object will be marked as Down—Pending as shown in Figure 27-12, which means down until the connection is made. The object status page shows an operational state of Down, with a detail of Pending.

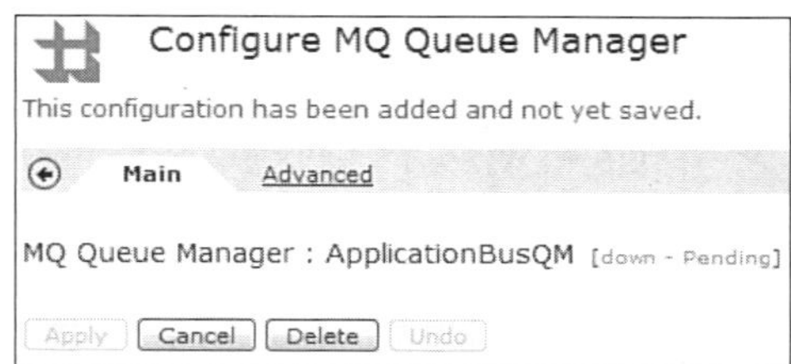

Figure 27-12 Configuring a queue manager.

Refreshing the object status page gets the latest information; after the initial connection is complete, the object is marked as Up if successful, or Down if unsuccessful. If it is still down, the detail field will provide more information. In Figure 27-13, the DataPower queue manager object is down because the remote queue manager itself is down.

name	config-state	op-state	admin-state	detail	logs
MQ Queue Manager					
⊟ ApplicationBusQM [MQ Queue Manager]	new	down	enabled	QM down	
⊟ default [XML Manager]	saved	up	enabled		
default [User Agent]	saved	up	enabled		

Figure 27-13 Viewing a down queue manager.

These protocol-specific connection sequences often have more information about the specific error that occurred. To see the logs relating to the queue manager object, click the magnifying glass in the logs column. Error messages could include references to an invalid user, a bad channel name, or simple connectivity issues. In Figure 27-14, the log mentions that DataPower failed to connect to the queue manager, and provides an MQ error message (2059) that suggests the queue manager is down.

05:52:49	mq	error	74738			0x80e00107	mq-qm (ApplicationBusQM): Queue Manager Error: '192.168.1.201' 'DPMQ'. Reason code - 2009
05:52:49	mq	error	74738			0x80e0015f	mq-qm (ApplicationBusQM): test connection failed (2059)
05:52:45	mgmt	error	495			0x00330019	mq-qm (ApplicationBusQM): Operation state transition to up failed

Figure 27-14 Viewing the logs for a failed queue manager connection.

Other common MQ-related issues often arise when using nonstandard configurations on the WebSphere MQ side. Listeners not defined on the default port (1414), configured user accounts without appropriate access rights, and disabling of the default channel names could all lead to a mismatch between DataPower and MQ settings. Check the logs and double-check the WebSphere MQ deployment.

Misconfigured Handlers

These same suggestions apply to all the messaging protocols, including WebSphere MQ, Tibco EMS, and WebSphere JMS. Each requires an object for managing connections to the server, and each must be configured correctly to avoid FSH object errors. For nonmessaging protocols such as FTP and Raw XML, there is no underlying object, but proper configuration is still just as important. If the handler is configured incorrectly, it will appear as Down in the object status page, and a combination of the detail field and the object logs should be used to fix the error.

These simple mistakes can happen on HTTP handlers as well, as shown in Figure 27-15. In this case, there was a simple typographical error when defining the host alias used for the local IP. After clicking Apply, the handler remains down, and the status shows an invalid local address; the same error would occur if an invalid IP was defined manually. This demonstrates the importance of using Host Aliases and the Select Alias helper, as you won't have to type anything by hand and open yourself to the possibility of errors.

Figure 27-15 Causing a down handler with a typographical error.

Network Conflicts

We've talked about the power of application domains, and how services and other objects created in one domain are logically partitioned from those in other domains, thus reducing potential conflicts and duplication. The exception to this concept exists at a network level, as any given device can have only a single listener on an IP:port combination. Port conflicts generally result in a down handler, with priority going to the first one enabled. Any subsequent listener that is installed on the same port fails. The first indicator of a problem depends on the service type; an XMLFW will be entirely down, an MPGW will have a single down handler, and a WSP will display a statistic about down endpoints in the WSDL tab, as shown in Figure 27-16.

Web Service Proxy WSDLs

- (•) Edit WSDL/Subscription
- ( ) Add WSDL
- ( ) Add UDDI Subscription
- ( ) Add WSRR Subscription

WSDL Source Location	Endpoint Handler Summary	WSDL Status	WS-I BP Status	Action
⊞ http://server1:5005/xycohr.wsdl	0 up / 1 configured	Okay	Okay	Remove

Figure 27-16 Down handlers in a Web Service Proxy.

We have seen that there are multiple reasons why a configured FSH might be down, so the simple fact that zero of one configured handlers are up does not provide all the necessary information for determining the source of the problem. Again, we turn to the object status by clicking View Status at the top of the WSP configuration page. In this case, we see a new error message in the detail column, Failed to install on port, as shown in Figure 27-17.

Unused properties: Show Hide

name	config-state	op-state	admin-state	detail	logs
Web Service Proxy					
⊟ HRServices [Web Service Proxy]	modified	up	enabled		
HRServices_xycohr.wsdl [Policy Attachment]	new	up	enabled		
⊟ default [XML Manager]	saved	up	enabled		
default [User Agent]	saved	up	enabled		
⊟ HRServices [WS-Proxy Endpoint Rewrite]	modified	up	enabled		
HRServicesHttp7000 [HTTP Front Side Handler]	new	down	enabled	Failed to install on port	
⊟ HRServices [WS-Proxy Processing Policy]	saved	up	enabled		
HRServices_match_all [Matching Rule]	saved	up	enabled		
HRServices_match_all [Matching Rule]	saved	up	enabled		
⊟ HRServices_default_request-rule [WS-Proxy Processing Rule]	saved	up	enabled		
HRServices_default_request-rule_defaultaction_slm [Processing Action]	saved	up	enabled		
HRServices_default_request-rule_defaultaction_result [Processing Action]	saved	up	enabled		
⊟ HRServices_default_response-rule [WS-Proxy Processing Rule]	saved	up	enabled		
HRServices_default_response-rule_defaultaction_result [Processing Action]	saved	up	enabled		

Figure 27-17 Failing to configure a listener on a specified port.

Although this error message almost always suggests a port conflict, we can get even more information by clicking the log magnifying glass next to the HTTP FSH. This gives us the full set of error messages that were generated during creation of the listener, as shown in Figure 27-18. First, reading from the bottom up, we receive an error message that the handler cannot install without a gateway. This suggests that the handler was created before the initial service definition was completed; until the service is up and running, the listener has nothing to listen for. This is not a problem as long as you finish the service configuration and click Apply. As we can see in the log, the service was completed 15 seconds later and the handler tried to come up again; this time, the port conflict prevented it from becoming active.

To solve this issue, simply change the port number for the HTTP handler to an unused port. To determine which ports are already in use and which are not, you can navigate to Status→IP-Network→TCP Port Status. The domain, service type, and object name for each listener will be displayed. Notice that these are sorted first by interface, and then by port; even if you don't see a particular port being used on one interface, make sure it's also not used with the 0.0.0.0 designation for all interfaces.

System Log for HTTP Front Side Handler "HRServicesHttp7000"

Refresh Log Target: default-log Filter: (none) (none)

current time: 01:38:52 on 2008-06-08

time	category	level	tid	dir	client	msgid	message
Sun Jun 08 2008							
01:37:23	mgmt	error	495			0x00330019	source-http (HRServicesHttp7000): Operation state transition to up failed
01:37:23	mgmt	error	495			0x00b30002	source-http (HRServicesHttp7000): Failed to install on port
01:37:23	mpgw	error	495			0x80e00135	source-http (HRServicesHttp7000): Protocol Handler failed to go active
01:37:08	mgmt	error	495			0x00330019	source-http (HRServicesHttp7000): Operation state transition to up failed
01:37:08	mgmt	error	495			0x00b3000a	source-http (HRServicesHttp7000): Can not install without gateway

Show last 50 100 all

Figure 27-18 Viewing the logs for a newly created HTTP handler.

Other Down Helper Objects

As we've seen in various examples, nonoperational objects are commonly caused by connectivity issues when talking to messaging servers or trying to install a listener on a port. We've also seen them caused by typographical errors or other mistaken configuration parameters. Because FSH objects often require both detailed connection information and reliable network connectivity, they tend to see the most development-time errors. However, other configuration objects that rely on these same needs, connectivity and configuration, can also cause problems when defining a service. Two examples are the SQL Data Source object and the Tivoli Access Manager object.

SQL Data Source Object

A SQL data source object, which is used within a SQL action in a Processing Policy, needs to be able to both connect to the database server and to begin making connections to the database instance itself. Configuration parameters are important, just as they would be if you were defining a database connection string during application development. If there are network connectivity issues, the object will be marked as down—Pending—and it will continue to retry until it achieves a connection to the database. The log messages for the object appear similar to those shown in Figure 27-19.

16:53:21	sql	error	2916			0x81800038	sql-source (OracleApplicationDB): Attempt to start SQL endpoint failed; will continue to attempt to establish the connection
16:53:21	sql	error	2916			0x8180001b	sql-source (OracleApplicationDB): Message from SQL endpoint: Connection refused. Verify Host Name and Port Number.
16:53:21	sql	error	2916			0x8180001d	sql-source (OracleApplicationDB): Error creating SQL endpoint
16:52:50	mgmt	info	2916			0x00360001	sql-source (OracleApplicationDB): Pending
16:52:50	sql	notice	2916			0x8180001e	sql-source (OracleApplicationDB): Signaled SQL endpoint startup

Figure 27-19 Debugging a SQL data source connectivity error.

Always check the log in these circumstances, as various network issues can distinguish themselves: DNS resolution errors, hostname errors, and invalid port errors. If the error is due to a bad configuration rather than a connectivity issue, then the object status will reflect that as shown in Figure 27-20. An invalid DB configuration template refers to a known problem with a specific field, possibly a typographical error or other simple issue. Check the error logs for more specific information.

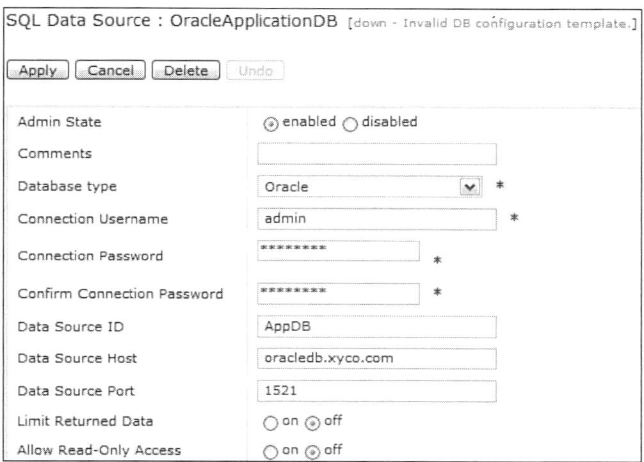

Figure 27-20 Defining an invalid SQL data source configuration.

Tivoli Access Manager Object

Definition of a Tivoli Access Manager (TAM) object is really a two-part process. First, you must generate the key, stash, and configuration files necessary to make the connection, and then you must define the object and reference those files. Alternatively, you can manually define the configuration file and import the key and stash files from your TAM server. Either way, you must be careful with the initial configuration parameters, as any mistake can cause a failure during file generation. To generate the files from the device, navigate to Administration→Miscellaneous→IBM TAM Tools in the left-side menu. Enter the configuration parameters for the instance of the Tivoli Access Manager that you want to connect to, and then click the button to create the files. DataPower will actually connect to the TAM server, create a new user (for performing authorization requests), and generate a key and stash file to be used for communication with the server. If you check the system logs after an attempt, you can see any errors that occurred during file generation, as shown in Figure 27-21.

In this case, the host information could not be resolved from the hostname. Other possibilities for connectivity errors are incorrect ports or inability to connect to a host. Notice that because DataPower failed to connect, it also failed to generate the necessary configuration files. If successful, this process should generate three files named according to the Output Configuration File Name field; the three files are a configuration file in the local: directory and a key and stash pair in the cert: directory.

18:02:33	tam	error				0x81a0004d	Failed to copy newly-created key files to temporary:
18:02:33	tam	error				0x81a00040	Failed to generate Tivoli Access Manager client files
18:02:33	tam	error				0x81a0001e	Failed to create Tivoli Access Manager host runtime configuration file
18:02:33	tam	error				0x81a00027	Getting Tivoli Access Manager CA cert failed: 2008-06-08-18:02:37.289-04:00I----- 0x106520DE bassslcfg FATAL bas mts mtsclient.cpp 1817 0xb7599ab0 HPDBA0222E The TCP/IP host information could not be determined from the server hostname. Ensure that the server hostname is correct.
18:02:32	tam	debug				0x81a00026	Starting Tivoli Access Manager file creation process
18:02:32	tam	info	7139			0x81a0000d	Signaling Tivoli Access Manager client file creation
18:02:32	tam	info	7139			0x81a0000d	Signaling Tivoli Access Manager client file creation
18:02:32	cli	debug	7139				(admin:web-gui:192.168.1.101): create-tam-files create-copy "on" file "InternalTAMDomain" admin "sec_master" password "password" tam-domain "Default" application "TAMDomain20080922" host "tamserver.xyco.com" port "7135" ssl-key-expiry "183" ssl-timeout "30" ldap-host "tamserver.xyco.com" ldap-port "389" ldap-password "password" ldap-auth-timeout "30" ldap-search-timeout "30" use-ldap-cache "off" ldap-user-cache-size "256" ldap-policy-cache-size "20"

Figure 27-21 Viewing errors during TAM configuration file generation.

TAM Application IDs

One of the fields necessary during TAM configuration file generation is the Application ID. This ID needs to be a unique value for each creation of these files; it is combined with the DataPower hostname/IP and used as the TAM user during authentication and authorization operations. If you generate a second set of TAM config files for the same instance, use a different application ID or the process will fail. This also applies in cases where the initial configuration works, but file generation fails; when retrying, use a new application ID or it will fail due to a duplicate ID.

Connectivity Issues

Many of the problems we have discussed in this chapter have revolved around connectivity issues. Failing to connect to a SQL data source or a messaging server can have serious consequences, as no objects that depend on these connections will function as intended. To get past this hurdle, there are several connection tests that can be performed from any of the appliance's interfaces. From the Web interface, these tools are located in the Troubleshooting page, which is accessible from the Control Panel. The Networking section contains the Ping and TCP Connection tools. For additional network troubleshooting using the Command Line Interface (CLI) and XML Management Interface, including the traceroute command discussed shortly, see Chapter 13, "Alternate Management Interfaces."

Ping

A ping test is probably the most common networking troubleshooting test in the IT industry. It's available on almost all platforms and operating systems, and can test whether a particular host or IP is accessible via the network. Ping sends ICMP echo request packets to a target server and waits for the corresponding response packets. This ability is hampered when the target server has its ICMP interfaces disabled; therefore, a failed ping should not be a definitive indicator of a bad connection. To perform this test, simply enter a remote hostname or IP and click Ping Remote.

TCP Connection Test

A TCP connection test is a much better indicator of server connectivity, as it is specifically targeted to a port on the remote host. The test can then be tailored to the interface that is potentially unreachable. Enter a host and port and click the TCP connection test to verify connectivity. This often helps to track down remote servers that are using nonstandard ports; for example, if you're connecting to an LDAP server that doesn't respond on port 389, you might need to contact an administrator. Though most databases and TAM have default ports, many administrators change these ports during installation; the TCP connection test helps clarify these problems. Firewall issues are also commonly found using this test, as particular ports can be blocked by firewalls between enterprise domains. If ping works and the TCP connection doesn't, it's likely a firewall blocking the port or a backend process not running.

Traceroute

The traceroute command is executed from the CLI and determines the route between the DataPower device and any given IP address. If a route does not exist, this suggests that the server is on a network that is not accessible to the device. This can happen when attempting to bridge two internal domains and is sometimes seen when moving a configuration from an appliance in one environment to one in another environment. Server references often need to be modified between development and preproduction environments, and we recommend the use of host aliases and static routes to make this process as easy as possible. See Chapter 3, "DataPower as a Network Device" and Chapter 4, "Advanced DataPower Networking" for more details on appropriate network configurations and analyzing routing tables.

Application Troubleshooting

We've covered the service development process in detail, from service types to processing rules to actions, as well as all the standard objects that go along with services. We've also covered specific use cases around security, protocol mediation, and message transformation; we've even discussed custom development techniques using stylesheets and extension functions. If some portion of that development resulted in a nonfunctional service, the first portion of this chapter discussed using the object status page, object logs, and networking tools to get the service up and running.

Now you have a full configuration built for an application round-trip, including the client, proxy (DataPower), and backend application logic. However, what happens if you start testing your service and the output isn't what you expected? Even worse, what happens if everything works and then suddenly it doesn't, or if it works for you but not for someone else? Let's talk about troubleshooting tools provided on the appliance for runtime debugging.

System Logs

The system logs are really the go-to source for information about what's occurring on the appliance. We've mentioned them before in other chapters, and even earlier in this chapter, as the first place to look for a detailed explanation of device behavior. In Chapter 14 we took an exhaustive look at each of the log fields and how to interpret its contents. We also demonstrated the creation of various log targets that subscribe to particular events and deliver those events to remote log servers, SNMP monitoring tools, and even the command line console. That chapter has most of the details and options, so we'll take this opportunity to delve deeper into the on-board log files.

Let's say you've just created a Web Service Proxy that performs various security and transformation tasks before and after connecting to a backend service. You send your first test message, expecting a Web service response, but all you get back is a SOAP fault with a painfully vague fault string: Internal Error (from client). This message is vague for a reason—you never want to provide a potentially malicious user with enough information to circumvent your security. Your legitimate partners and internal users should have the WSDL and other service information, and should know how to make a successful invocation. However, DataPower provides details about the fault in the error log so that you can work with those legitimate users to debug any unforeseen complications.

To get to the on-device logs, you have several options. You can simply click View Logs from the Control Panel to get the default log for the entire domain. To focus on a specific service, you can open that service configuration page and click View Log at the top of the screen; this filters the log for this service and its related objects. For maximum flexibility, you can go to Control Panel→Troubleshooting and click View System Logs in the Logging section; this opens the domain's logs in a new window so that you can continue development and maintain an open view of the logs. Whichever method you prefer, open the logs to get more information about the error you've received. A sample log is shown in Figure 27-22.

System Log

Refresh Log Target: default-log Filter: (none) (none)

current time: 01:54:19 on 2008-06-09

time	category	level	tid	dir	client	msgid	message Show last 50 100 all
Sun Jun 08 2008							
22:39:19	ws-proxy	info	44865	e	192.168.1.101	0x80e000b6	wsgw (HRServices): No match from processing policy 'HRServices' for code '0x00230001'
22:39:19	ws-proxy	debug	44865		192.168.1.101	0x81000089	wsgw (HRServices): WSDL component type 'all' matches .
22:39:19	ws-proxy	debug	44865		192.168.1.101	0x81000089	wsgw (HRServices): WSDL component type 'all' matches .
22:39:19	ws-proxy	error	44865	e	192.168.1.101	0x00230001	wsgw (HRServices): Dynamic Execution Error
22:39:19	multistep	error	44865	>	192.168.1.101	0x80c00008	wsgw (HRServices): rule (HRServices_default_request-rule): Pipeline beginning at implied action Parse input as SOAP, attempt pipeline failed: http://192.168.1.199:8000/HRService:15: cvc-particle 2.1: in element {http://xycohr.com/hrservices}request of type {http://xycohr.com/hrservices}hrrequest, found <EmployeeID> (in default namespace), but next item should be Employee_ID
22:39:19	xmlparse	error	44865	>	192.168.1.101		wsgw (HRServices): http://192.168.1.199:8000/HRService:15: cvc-particle 2.1: in element {http://xycohr.com/hrservices}request of type {http://xycohr.com/hrservices}hrrequest, found <EmployeeID> (in default namespace), but next item should be Employee_ID
22:39:19	xmlparse	debug	44865	>	192.168.1.101		wsgw (HRServices): Parsing document 'http://192.168.1.199:8000/HRService'
22:39:19	ws-proxy	debug	44865		192.168.1.101		xmlmgr (default): wsdl Compilation Request: Found in cache (http://server1:5005/xycohr.wsdl)
22:39:19	ws-proxy	debug	44865		192.168.1.101		xmlmgr (default): wsdl Compilation Request: Checking cache for URL http://server1:5005/xycohr.wsdl

Figure 27-22 Reviewing logs generated by a failed request.

The most recent event is always listed at the top of the logs, so you would read from the bottom up if you desired a chronological order. You can see that the log includes events at all priorities, including debug, which means that the default system log has been set to a debug level. Setting this value determines which events are gathered by the log; because the filtering is done at event creation, there is no way to "get back" an event recorded at a level that was not being monitored. During development, you can set the log to a debug level and then filter as desired.

The log displays the last 50 items by default; click 100 or all in the top right to show more events. In Figure 27-22, we show only the last nine entries from the transaction, as all of the previous events completed as intended. The goal is to determine what caused the error, which you can pick out in red text when looking at your log. In this case, the problem was a schema validation error—the incoming request had an EmployeeID field, but the schemas defined in the WSDL specified the name as Employee_ID. This should certainly be enough to fix the input messages being sent by your client, or to tell your business partner what the problem with their request was. The log will almost always provide additional information about the processing of each step and the errors encountered during the transaction.

You've modified your request message and fixed your first error using the logs for guidance. You send the message again, and get back another fault: Rejected by policy (from client). Again, after working with the appliance for a while, you might realize this means an authentication or authorization error in a AAA policy. Going back to the logs, you could filter by AAA events by selecting that category from the Filter drop-down at the top of the screen. If you only wanted to see problems, you could also filter by priority, as shown in Figure 27-23. If you're new to the appliance and its purposely obtuse error messages, you can just filter by priority and look at the recent errors. You can also click on a transaction ID to get only those messages related to a particular transaction.

System Log

Refresh Log Target: default-log Filter: aaa warn

current time: 02:36:54 on 2008-06-09

time	category	level	tid	dir	client	msgid	message Show last 50 100 all
Mon Jun 09 2008							
02:30:27	aaa	warn	63649	>	192.168.1.101		wsgw (HRServices): Policy(UsernameTokenToLDAP): Message rejected
02:30:27	aaa	warn	63649	>	192.168.1.101		wsgw (HRServices): Policy(UsernameTokenToLDAP): anyauthenticated authorization failed with credential 'SPECIAL-FORMAT-NOT-PRINTED' for resource '/HRService'
02:30:27	aaa	warn	63649	>	192.168.1.101		wsgw (HRServices): Policy(UsernameTokenToLDAP): ldap authentication failed with (wssec-username, username='wilma' password='********')

Figure 27-23 Filtering on AAA events at a warning level.

You can see that authentication of the credentials provided with the incoming request failed when checked against LDAP. Check the credentials being provided, and check your LDAP server to make sure the user has a valid entry. Hopefully this solves the problem; if not, you might be interested to see exactly what is being sent to the LDAP server. For more insight into the payload and processing at each step, you can use the transaction probe.

Transaction Probe

The transaction probe is definitely close behind the system logs in terms of usefulness during the application debugging process. Where the log focuses on specific events (file reads, cache hits/misses, transformations, schema validations, and so on), the transaction probe is focused on the message flowing through the device, the processing rule being executed, and the metadata surrounding each transaction. Similar to debug-level logging, the probe is a development-only tool that will assist in debugging but should not be used in production for performance reasons. To enable the probe for a specific service, click on Show Probe at the top of the service configuration page. An empty transaction list pops up; click Enable Probe to turn on the probe and subsequent requests will be gathered for review. Send your test message again and refresh the transaction list; you will see the new transaction appear as shown in Figure 27-24.

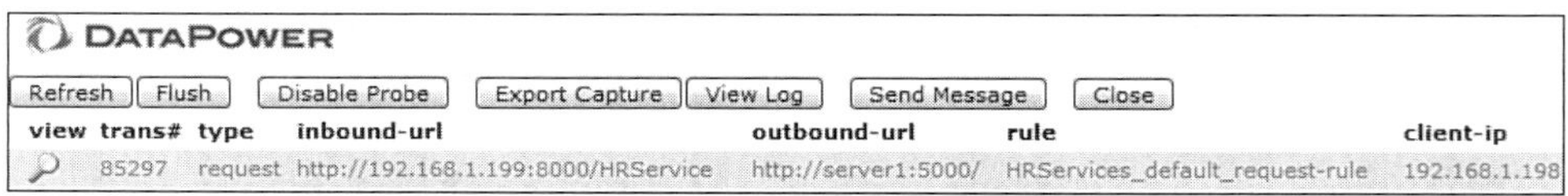

Figure 27-24 Inspecting transactions using the probe.

The probe shows quite a bit of information in the transaction list, even before drilling into a particular transaction. The transaction ID, inbound URL (provided by the client), outbound URL (sent to the backend service), processing rule, and client IP all distinguish one service execution from another. Find the transaction you'd like to review (use the system log for correlating the transaction ID if necessary) and click the magnifying glass in the View column. A new window for the transaction opens as shown in Figure 27-25.

The transaction view is divided into sections. The upper portion shows the processing rule currently being examined; there are brackets around the context or action that is selected. The tabs across the middle determine what will be shown in the bottom window. In our example, we are viewing the content of the message before it reaches the SLM processing step in the rule. If we clicked on the headers tab, we would see the HTTP headers at this point in the execution. Each tab contains metadata or content relating to this transaction, including device variables. These tabs are particularly useful when using extension functions to extend some functionality in the appliance, or when using Set Variable or Extract actions to set variable values.

At the moment, we're interested in the LDAP interaction, so we can click on the icon for the AAA action. For actions, the available tabs are a bit different, and focus on parameters provided to the action and execution of the underlying stylesheets; the Extension Trace tab shows any extension functions used during execution. In our example, we are interested in the LDAP request, which appears as an ldap-authen execution as shown in Figure 27-26.

Figure 27-25 Examining a specific transaction input using the probe.

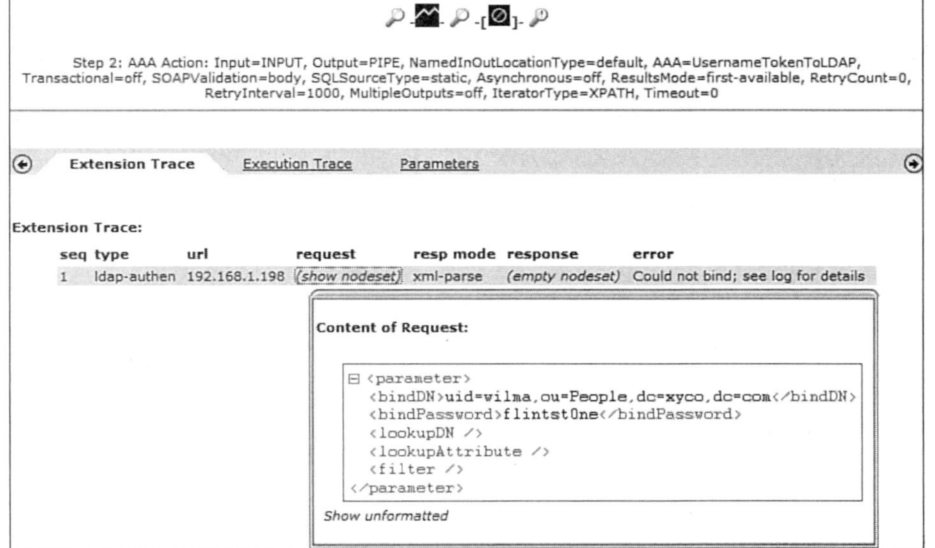

Figure 27-26 Viewing an LDAP authentication call in the probe.

We can see the call to LDAP and we know that it couldn't bind, resulting in an unsuccessful authentication. To see the distinguished name (DN) with which the device attempted to bind, click show nodeset on the extension's request field. This opens a new window with the parameters of our authentication call, so you can verify the appropriate DN and password. Note that passwords will be in the clear—another reason not to use the probe in a production environment. Seeing the DN should give even more information with which to verify your LDAP server configuration and check for existence of the user. On a subsequent successful request, the ldap-authen call would have a response nodeset containing the entry returned by the server.

Common Configuration Mistakes

Now that you've made sure your DataPower AAA configuration matches your LDAP configuration with some help from the transaction probe, you send a new test message with a valid username. This time you get a response, but it's not what you expected. Perhaps you were expecting an encrypted response, or a digital signature, or even an entirely transformed message payload. What happened?

Context Mismatches

One common configuration error, especially when dealing with several named contexts in a processing rule, is the creation of a context mismatch. That is, the input context to an action is not the input you desired—this can result in the wrong context being processed by an action, or even in the wrong context being returned as output. Open your Processing Policy and check the input and output context for each action. This can be done without opening the actions themselves; just hover over each one for a moment. An example of this is shown in Figure 27-27.

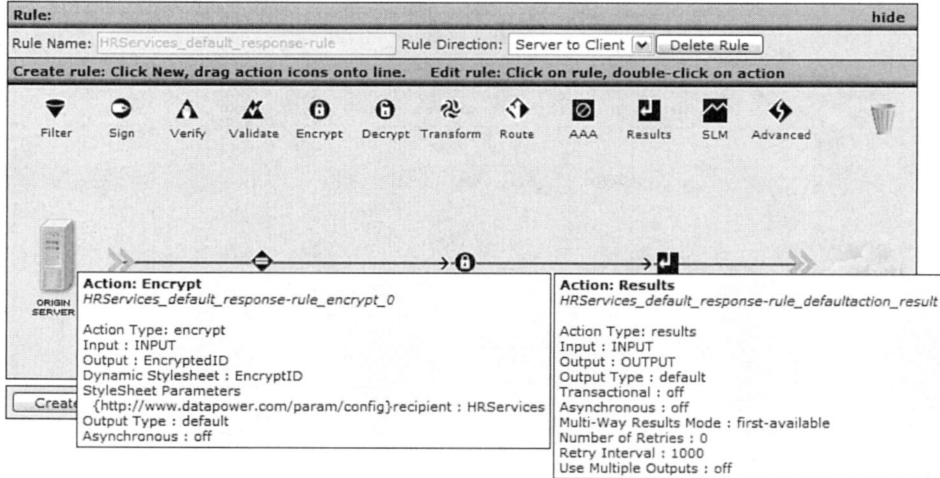

Figure 27-27 Diagnosing a context mismatch.

In this case, the Encrypt action is processing the INPUT context and generating a new EncryptedID context. Instead of responding to the client with this new context, the Results action is sending out the INPUT context, which represents the original response from the backend server. To fix this problem, you would change the input context of the Results action to be EncryptedID. By default, DataPower chains together contexts in a generic pipeline, expecting that each action that produces an output will have that output context consumed by the following action. In fact, the preceding example would have been configured correctly by DataPower's policy editor. However, when moving back and forth between named contexts in a more complex, nonstandard pipeline, you may accidentally match an input to an inappropriate output; keep an eye out for this behavior.

> **TIP—NAME YOUR CONTEXTS**
>
> When dealing with multiple contexts in a scenario that doesn't call for PIPE contexts between actions, it's best to name all your output contexts, and specifically use those named contexts as your input contexts. This provides a method for documentation of processing logic, and it reduces context mismatch errors.

Unordered Match Rules

This has been discussed in prior chapters, but it bears repeating in a debugging chapter such as this: When defining multiple rules in a Processing Policy, each rule is evaluated individually, starting at the top and moving down. The Match action will be checked; if there is a match, then that rule (and only that rule) will be executed. This makes the order important, as some rules might never be executed if the rules are sorted incorrectly. In the example in Figure 27-28, the processing behavior and subsequent output depends entirely on which rule is matched; however, there is a MatchAll rule at the top of the list. If this indeed matches all incoming messages, then the other three rules will never be executed, no matter what the input.

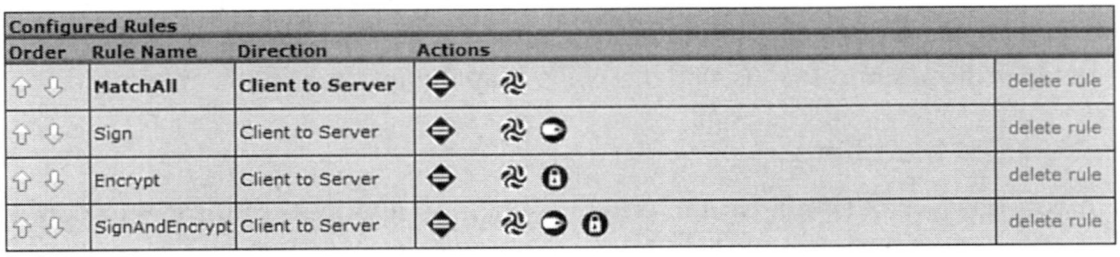

Configured Rules				
Order	Rule Name	Direction	Actions	
	MatchAll	**Client to Server**		delete rule
	Sign	Client to Server		delete rule
	Encrypt	Client to Server		delete rule
	SignAndEncrypt	Client to Server		delete rule

Figure 27-28 Diagnosing a context mismatch.

The most generic rules should always be placed at the bottom of the list, with more specific rules above. In general, try to avoid any order which would eliminate one rule from ever being executed.

Overlooked Parameters

Some objects have parameters that are not required by the GUI but will cause unexpected behavior if not present. These are often overlooked when on background tabs in the configuration page, such as in the Match action and Log Targets. A Match action requires at least one matching rule to function, but the Matching Rule tab can easily be overlooked; the Main tab contains only the name field and parameters to modify the matching behavior. An object without a matching rule will eventually be marked as Down as shown in Figure 27-29, but this may not be noticed during configuration.

Figure 27-29 Viewing a match rule without any rules defined.

The log target object is defined similarly. The Main tab contains configuration data about the target location, but no events will be sent to that target unless at least one Event Subscription is defined; we'll discuss how to debug this later in this chapter.

In general, be aware of which fields are necessary for any given configuration. Enter a value for each required field, and then consider the object you are defining and whether it will need any additional parameter values. For example, the Crypto Key object does not require a Password value, as not all key files are password protected. However, if you have uploaded a key file protected by a password, make sure to also provide the password. Some other example fields that act the same way are the Document Crypto Map in a field-level Encrypt/Sign action, the certificate and key fields in those same actions, and the WTX Map file in a non-XML transformation.

Overlooked List Members

This common mistake is similar to the previous one, but applies specifically to configuration parameters that allow lists of multiple options. This includes certificate objects in a validation credential, permission profiles on a custom user group, and FSHs on a MPGW or WSP. It is easy to define a new item (a FSH, for example) and then forget to add it to the list of listeners for your service. The noticeable behavior will, of course, depend upon the type of object. A missing FSH might not be noticed until you try to send a message to the service and fail to connect. It may be up and listening on other interfaces, but until that particular handler is added to the list, it will not apply to the service. If a certificate is left out of a validation credential, it's possible that all but one of your customers will be able to invoke a service using SSL with mutual authentication. If a permission profile is forgotten in a user group object, a whole category of users may not have access to the appropriate objects in the administration consoles. Keep these possibilities in mind whenever configuring list-based parameters—don't forget one!

Web Services Errors

Web services are an integral part of many enterprise IT infrastructures because they represent a standards-based method for defining machine-readable request and response structures. However, interoperability can sometimes be an issue due to evolving standards and toolkits. Here are a few configuration issues that are specific to Web services:

- A SOAPAction header is often required by backend services. Make sure this header is either passed by the client or added by DataPower using header injection techniques.
- There is no universally accepted method for describing endpoints using non-HTTP protocols in WSDLs. In addition, some toolkits support nonstandard bindings. These WSDL files might need to be edited before being uploaded to the DataPower appliance.
- When using a Web Service Proxy, policies defined at an operation or service level supersede those defined at the (default) proxy level. If some default actions need to be executed on *every* request, create a callable rule to share this functionality.
- Many Web services backends require that requests are tagged with an HTTP Content-Type of text/xml. Additionally, some require an explicit character set (usually UTF-8). Together, this would require a header of Content-Type: text/xml; charset=utf-8.

Send a Test Message

We've just discussed some of the challenges of interacting with Web service providers. These configurations can certainly be tested and debugged using external tools; in fact, that will be covered in Chapter 28, "Problem Determination Using External Tools." However, sometimes it is useful to isolate DataPower and its backends from an external client. DataPower provides an onboard client for this purpose. Navigate to Administration→Debug→Send a Test Message. In the new window, define the endpoint URL, any necessary headers, and the sample message that will be sent. An example is shown in Figure 27-30.

Click Make Call to submit the request and receive a response. If necessary, depending on any errors returned from the server, you can add additional headers or modify the payload and then resubmit the request. A successful response is shown in Figure 27-31. The HTTP response code and response headers are provided as well, to assist in debugging.

Figure 27-30 Sending a test message using the on-device client.

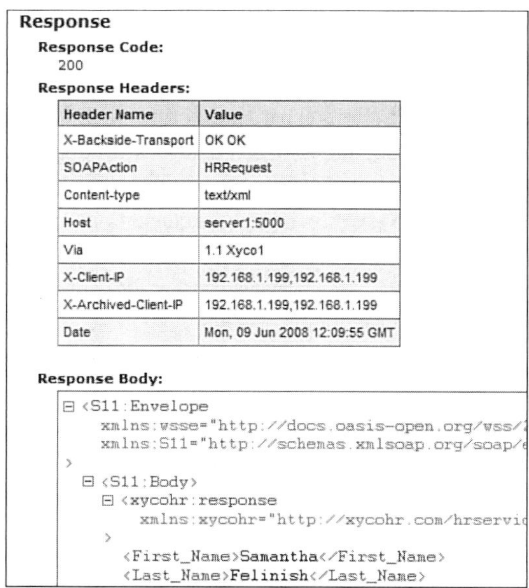

Figure 27-31 Receiving a response from a submitted test message.

XML File Capture

We've already discussed using the transaction probe for targeted inspection of certain service transactions on the appliance. Occasionally, you might need to collect a broader array of inputs and outputs for analysis. The appliance provides an XML file capture utility for recording all inputs and outputs to all services. If the service contains a transformation, the captured files also contain metadata about the stylesheet executions. Due to the verbose nature of this broad capture technique, consider carefully before enabling it, and don't use it in a production environment unless absolutely necessary. It is only available from the default domain, and applies to the entire device. To enable XML file capture, navigate to Administration→Debug→XML File Capture (in the default domain) and switch the admin state to enabled, as shown in Figure 27-32.

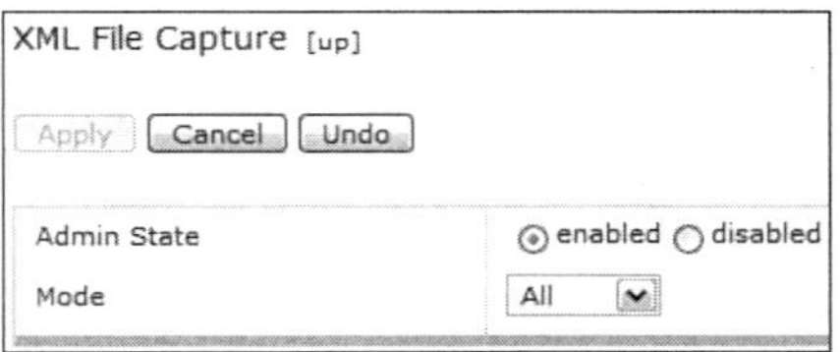

Figure 27-32 Enabling XML file capture on an appliance.

Modify the mode to choose whether to capture all messages or only error messages. Input, output, and metadata for every request/error will be captured and saved to a temporary portion of the filesystem. If this saved data needs to be cleared due to low memory, captures will be removed in the order that they were created. To browse the files that have been captured, navigate to Administration→Debug→Browse Captured Files. A new window opens with transactions, grouped by service hostname, then by service URI, and then by transaction. In the example in Figure 27-33, you can see transactions from two different services. Clicking on a service narrows the transactions by URI.

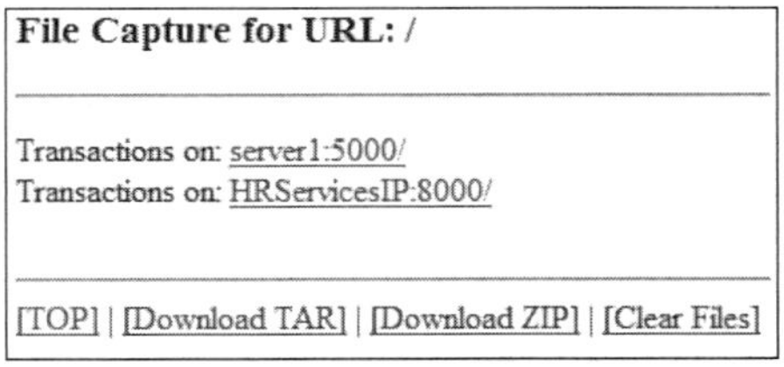

File Capture for URL: /

Transactions on: server1:5000/
Transactions on: HRServicesIP:8000/

[TOP] | [Download TAR] | [Download ZIP] | [Clear Files]

Figure 27-33 Browsing captured files.

At any point in the captured hierarchy, you can choose to download a compressed copy of that portion of the directory. You can also remove all saved files by clicking on Clear Files. When you have explored the directory structure all the way to the individual transactions, you have the option to view or download the input and output files, as shown in Figure 27-34.

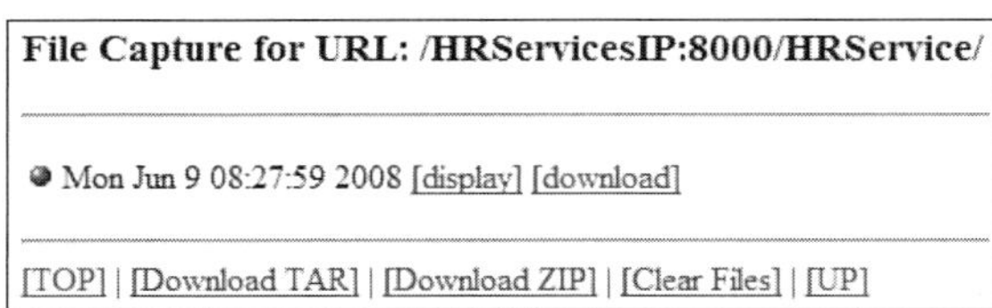

Figure 27-34 Browsing a single captured transaction.

Clicking display loads the file in a browser window, while clicking download provides a text file (filecap.txt) containing the XML content. Download or view the important files and then disable the file capture mechanism when finished.

Operations Troubleshooting

After an appliance is live in production and being monitored by operations, much of the monitoring process will be exactly the same as your current processes for other hardware devices such as load balancers and IP firewalls. Chapter 12, "Device Administration" and Chapter 14 walk through the steps necessary to set up an appliance for inclusion into your monitoring operations. Log targets should be delivering event messages to your logging servers; SNMP monitoring tools should be polling the device for health metrics and receiving traps in case of critical hardware events. When set up correctly, this should all work without additional development; however, you might want to debug whether event messages are being delivered accurately.

Log Target Troubleshooting

If you suspect that log messages are not being communicated appropriately to their designated log targets, there are a few places to verify this behavior. For general target information, navigate to Status→Main→Logging Targets to view the current status of all targets defined within the current domain. The display shows the name, current status, and any error information, as shown in Figure 27-35.

Logging Targets

Refresh Status

name	status	processed	dropped	pending	error info
default-log	active	1693	0	0	none
HRServicesCacheLog	active	500	186	1000	none
HRServicesConsoleLog	suspended	0	0	0	Operational state is down

Figure 27-35 Checking the status of configured log targets.

The status page also shows the number of messages processed, dropped, and pending for each target. The number of messages dropped depends on the target type and the maximum event rate defined. In this example, the cache target is capped at 1000 events, which are held in memory until viewed in the logs. They are viewed in 500 event increments, and any messages over the maximum 1000 are dropped. The HRServicesConsoleLog has been disabled, so it is not currently gathering any events.

If there are no dropped messages for a particular target, all messages sent over the TCP protocol should have reached their destination as intended. If a particular event message was expected but never received by the target, double-check the log target settings. As discussed earlier in this chapter, it is easy to configure the Main tab of the Log Target object, but to forget to add message types and priorities on the Event Subscriptions tab. Without any subscriptions, the target will never receive any messages; verify that all of the intended subscriptions are in place. Also verify that the event is not being filtered by either an Object Filter or an Event Filter. If the event does not meet the filter criteria, or is being excluded with an Event Suppression Filter, it will never reach its intended destination.

After you have your log targets defined as desired, you can make one last check for connectivity and message delivery. Navigate to Control Panel→Troubleshooting and go to the Logging section. The Generate Log Event tool creates an event on the appliance; this event will be treated like any other, in that it will be gathered by any log targets subscribed to the event's category and priority. In the example in Figure 27-36, a cert-monitor message will be sent at a warning level, and targets designated for these messages should receive the text as written.

Figure 27-36 Generating a sample log event from the Troubleshooting page.

These tests should be performed on any newly installed and configured device before going to production, as they verify both connectivity and functional log targets. These targets are the lifeline between the appliance and your monitoring and logging infrastructure, and it is important that they function as intended to notify you of any critical event.

Critical Events

There are some events which will likely always require some sort of attention, either from the hardware, networking, or application personnel. These include a device throttling due to high memory usage, notification of an unexpected device restart, and hardware events such as power supply or fan failures. Your operational policies should determine the appropriate audience for each of these events, and action should be taken when the event occurs. Ideally, this notification should take place automatically—for example, an SNMP trap marked as critical can be parsed and forwarded by most SNMP tools via email. Error remediation depends on the environment, the current device status, and the error itself.

Last Resorts

Okay, so you've tested and debugged your services and something still isn't working as intended. Or you just got an email that Power Supply #2 has failed. Or you need some more information about a particular use case. What resources are available beyond this book in general and this chapter specifically? Let's discuss the procedures for contacting support and obtaining more information online.

Hardware Failures

If a portion of the appliance hardware fails, including a power supply, a NIC, or an entire device, you need to contact IBM Customer Support for a replacement. The best location for up-to-date contact information is from the DataPower support site located at http://www.ibm.com/software/integration/datapower/support/.

Telephone numbers are listed by geography and provide a direct link to a DataPower support engineer that can initiate the replacement process; the turnaround time for a new device will be dependent upon your level of support.

With more recent hardware models, some items (including batteries, power supplies, and fans) are user-replaceable. Contact customer support for verification of a failed part and to order a replacement.

Suspected Product Defects

If you suspect that a feature on the device is not working as intended, or not working at all, you can contact customer support through one of the phone numbers on the support site, or you can email the support organization at csupport@us.ibm.com. The Web site describes the information that will be necessary to provide for support entitlement, including the device serial number and firmware version, your IBM customer number and contact information, and an issue severity. It also defines the steps needed to gather additional data.

The support engineer that takes your case will likely ask for this additional information regarding the error or unexpected behavior that you are encountering. A description of the problem, an export of the related configuration, and a list of steps to repeat the problem will be very useful to DataPower support and will help drive a speedy resolution. An error report can be generated by the device, and will include log information that might be of some help. To generate an error report, navigate to Control Panel→Troubleshooting and click the Generate Error Report button under the Reporting section. Turn on the Include Internal State parameter to include additional potentially useful information.

If you are not running the latest version of the appliance firmware, you should also probably check the release notes from the most recent version. These notes are available from the support site as well, along with all current firmware and documentation downloads. Make sure the issue you are seeing is not described in the current documentation, or fixed as reported by the release notes. If so, we would suggest an upgrade to the most recent firmware version.

Additional Information

Sometimes there's nothing really *wrong*, but you need some additional help with device configuration, architecting a use case, or understanding the full capabilities of the appliance. For formal assistance, IBM offers both education services through WebSphere Education and consulting services through IBM Software Services for WebSphere. These are paid engagements; contact your IBM Sales representative for pricing and scheduling. For less formal assistance, there is a DataPower SOA Appliance forum on the IBM developerWorks Web site. A community of users is available to ask and answer questions about common DataPower development tasks.

Summary

We have demonstrated that there are a number of on-board tools that can be used for debugging DataPower applications throughout the entire development lifecycle. We've shown how to obtain more information about down objects during configuration, how to follow the execution of services during runtime, and how to troubleshoot operations issues once an appliance is in production. When combined with Chapter 28, you should have a complete picture of application troubleshooting on DataPower SOA Appliances.

CHAPTER 28

Problem Determination Using External Tools

In Chapter 27, "Problem Determination Using Built-In Tools," we discussed some of the out-of-the-box options for troubleshooting and debugging application messages flowing through a DataPower SOA Appliance. While these tools provide significant insight into the messages received and processed by the appliance, a true production application likely involves many other systems. Clients will execute the service and must make sure they are sending the appropriate message; on DataPower's backend, it must connect to an appropriate service endpoint and receive a response message. Side calls might be made to supplementary servers for user authentication, event logging, and other external tasks. Additionally, some portions of the processing policy (especially XSLT stylesheets and XML configuration files) may have been created in peripheral tools and might need to be modified or updated during troubleshooting.

This chapter explores a number of external tools that may help during the development and debugging process. We explore tools for application testing, for SOAP, XML, and browser-based requests, and we discuss methods for testing additional protocols for delivering request messages without using HTTP. We also take a look at a broad spectrum of toolkits: authentication server browsers, XSLT development environments, log servers, and SNMP toolkits.

Specifically relating to connectivity, we suggest various methods of debugging failed connections from both a network level and an application level. If your request message is being rejected for an unknown reason and you want to simplify your environment, we'll show you how to strip down a request to its barest elements, eliminating potential sources of errors until the problem is solved.

We take a look at a number of applications that have made our lives easier and can assist you in a successful deployment of an architecture including DataPower appliances. Our set of tools has been formed over years of experience with DataPower implementations, but there may be many others that work equally as well. Your organization might already use similar tools; in the end, only you can choose the tools that will best suit your needs.

Application Testing

After a message reaches a DataPower appliance, there is full visibility into the payload and accompanying headers that are received; they are available using the event log, through the troubleshooting probe, and various XSLT debugging methodologies. However, many production Web service clients abstract away the actual message payload using a complicated API, custom code, and built-in "optimizations" such as automated header construction or sample data insertion. When something goes wrong, it's often helpful to get back to the basics and use simple tools to deliver a known message. This allows more control over the incoming request and can assist in debugging. In the end, the goal is message visibility, so here are some tools that provide that insight.

cURL

One of the most powerful clients you can use is also one of the simplest. Curl (actually cURL—we altered the capitalization for readability) is a command line application used for sending requests using HTTP, HTTPS, and several other protocols. It is freely available at http://curl.haxx.se for multiple platforms. Its power lies in its transparency. Curl sends exactly what you tell it to, and not much else. This enables you to control the payload, headers, and other protocol options without seeing unexpected behavior caused by overly ambitious clients. Curl comes with an extensive man page and command-line syntax suggestions (curl --help); let's talk about some common usages in a DataPower environment.

Basic Usage

Though curl can be used for testing Web applications and DataPower Web Application Firewalls, we focus on curl for Web service scenarios. Although useful for document submission, curl will not actually generate a Web service request from a WSDL; thus, the first step to using curl for Web service requests is to assemble a payload document. Many tools create an example message from a schema, but they will fill in dummy data—it's up to you to generate a realistic message, with data that will produce a successful response. You can capture this data from an existing request using the Troubleshooting Probe or XML File Capture mechanisms, both discussed in Chapter 27. Save this data in a file so that it can be edited separately. Then, POSTing your message to a DataPower service is as simple as the following command:

```
curl --data-binary @input.xml http://services.xyco.com/bookQuery
```

Though there are flags for posting ASCII data (--data-ascii or -d) and URL-encoded data (--data-urlencode), these could potentially modify the data or URL before sending. Using --data-binary will send the payload with no extra processing, ensuring a clean POST; you should use this even when sending plain text. The @ sign preceding the filename tells curl to read the payload from the file rather than from the command line.

There are two things to watch out for:

- If you forget the @ sign, curl will attempt to send the filename as your input; this will obviously fail
- If you mistype the filename, curl will send an empty POST and you'll get this message: "Warning: Couldn't read data from file "inpyt.xml", this makes an empty POST."

For more information about exactly what is traveling over the wire, you can add a -v flag to make the interaction verbose. This shows you the basic connection information (including the SSL handshake), the headers and request message that are being sent to the destination (prefixed with a >), and the headers and response message sent back by the server (prefixed with a <). For GET requests, simply leave out the data flag and the filename, and the page residing at the given URL will be retrieved.

Some versions of curl have slightly different flag styles for verbose output and filename selection; double-check the appropriate style for your version with the curl --help command.

To save any response document (also useful for debugging), you can redirect the output from the command line (where you can see it scroll by) to a file. Simply add a redirect statement ("> output.xml" or "-o output.xml") to the end of the command. The following command retrieves Google's front page and saves it to a local file:

```
curl http://www.google.com/ > GoogleFrontPage.html
```

Adding Headers

The basic curl commands result in the payload being sent to the defined URL with only some simple headers, most of which are required by the HTTP specification. Fortunately, these can be overridden if necessary using the -H flag. Some application servers (and DataPower's XSL Proxy service) will complain if the content type and character set are not defined appropriately in the HTTP headers; this command adds the most commonly anticipated content type for a Web service message:

```
curl  -data-binary @input.xml -H "Content-type: text/xml;charset=UTF-8"
http://services.xyco.com/bookQuery
```

To add a SOAPAction header to a Web service request, the command is similar:

```
curl  -data-binary @input.xml -H "SOAPAction: requestHoliday" ...
```

If multiple headers are required on a single request, several -H parameters can be added to the command, or multiple headers can be included in a single double-quoted -H parameter. This building-block style of sending requests can help you determine exactly what is required by the backend, and what is extraneous. Start with the payload and add the minimal amount of additional headers until you receive a successful response.

Adding Credentials

If you have implemented access control in your DataPower service, your client will need to provide user credentials with the request. For a Web service request using a WS-Security UsernameToken, this task is as simple as adding the appropriate header to the payload document. Because the credentials travel in the message itself, rather than the protocol headers, nothing needs to be changed in the curl command.

If the service requires protocol-based credentials (although we do not recommend this as a credential delivery method), adding them is as simple as adding a new flag. To add a basic-authentication header, use the -u flag:

```
curl  -data-binary @input.xml -u username:password
http://services.xyco.com/bookQuery
```

This creates an Authorization header containing the word Basic and the Base-64 encoded version of the username and password, according to the HTTP basic authentication header specification. For instance, providing -u username:password produces the following header:

```
Authorization: Basic dXNlcm5hbWU6cGFzc3dvcmQ=
```

Keep in mind that sending a basic-authentication header is only as secure as the protocol over which it is sent. Unless there is some form of protocol-level encryption, the client's username and password can be intercepted and easily unencoded. More robust forms of credential delivery are recommended in most cases, such as using HTTP over SSL.

Cleaning Up Output

The response from a command-line application like curl is often unformatted and difficult to read; its output is often one long line of XML. To make sense of the document, it is helpful to clean it up—there are various tools for this purpose. As mentioned earlier, output can be saved to a file, enabling you to use a syntax-highlighting editor for viewing purposes. To output a clean, indented response in real time, you can use a command line tool like xmllint or xmltidy. These are freely available online for various platforms from multiple sources. The output of curl can then be piped to one of these applications, as shown in Listing 28-1.

Listing 28-1 Cleaning Up Output Using XML Tidy

```
> curl  -data-binary @input.xml http://services.xyco.com/bookQuery | java -
jar xmltidy.jar

<?xml version="1.0" encoding="UTF-8"?>
<SOAP-ENV:Envelope
          xmlns:SOAP-ENV="http://schemas.xmlsoap.org/soap/envelope/">
   <SOAP-ENV:Body>
      <book>
         <name>Moby Dick</name>
         <author>Herman Melville</author>
```

```
        <publisher>Longman</publisher>
        <isbn>0321228006</isbn>
        <copyright>2007</copyright>
    </book>
  </SOAP-ENV:Body>
</SOAP-ENV:Envelope>
```

Overriding Default Behavior

Curl can make service requests over HTTP or HTTPS (as well as other protocols). When making SSL requests, the handshake between the client and the server (or DataPower) uses server certificates to validate the server identity. Curl uses its built-in certificate bundle to attempt validation—if the certificate is not present, the connection will fail with an error. To turn off validation of the certificate during testing or for self-signed certificates that will be validated by "real" clients, add a -k flag to the request. See the curl documentation for instructions on adding certificates to the bundle for true verification; inclusion of client-side certificates for mutual authentication is discussed later in this chapter.

Curl is perhaps the most flexible client for DataPower testing, as it can support both POST and GET methods, does not require any application-specific files (WSDL or XSD), and can emulate output from Web service clients, browsers, and various other toolkits. With hundreds of additional features described in the documentation, there are few requests that cannot be generated with this powerful tool.

SoapUI

SoapUI provides an easy and effective way to create and send Web service requests using a WSDL for service configuration. It is available from http://www.soapui.org/ in both free and commercial flavors, and has a graphical interface used to set up projects for multiple service invocations. In addition, it can set up mock service backends, modify protocol and message headers, and build automated, multistep test cases. There is significant online documentation that will take you through the advanced features, but let's discuss some of the basic usages.

Basic Usage

All testing using SoapUI is done from a workspace containing projects—one project for each service that is being tested. New workspaces can be created using File→New Workspace. Right-click on the workspace icon that appears and select New WSDL Project to begin the project definition process. You can give the project a name and upload a WSDL file for introspection. The Create Requests check box automatically generates a sample input message for each Web service operation, producing a service hierarchy similar to that shown in Figure 28-1.

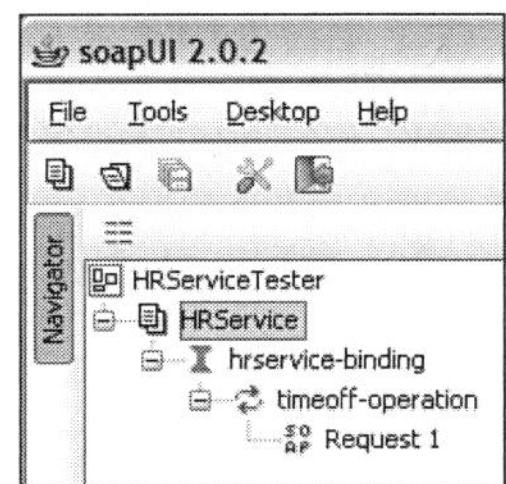

Figure 28-1 Creating a new service hierarchy in SoapUI.

Double-clicking the Request 1 request node in the example opens a window for the request and response messages. Each field that requires input data is filled in with a question mark; replace these with known good data for the service invocation. For a simple execution of the service using the default endpoint and standard HTTP headers, simply clicking the button with a green Play arrow submits the request and fills in the response side of the window.

To change the endpoint for the request, you can use the URL drop-down at the top of the window. You can add multiple backends with the Add New Endpoint selection, or use Edit Current to modify the selected endpoint. This enables you to switch back and forth between implementations on two different servers (or DataPower devices).

Adding Headers

Adding headers is a simple matter of extending the Headers section at the bottom of the input window. Click on the Headers (0) tab to open it, and then click the plus sign (+) to create a new header, as shown in Figure 28-2.

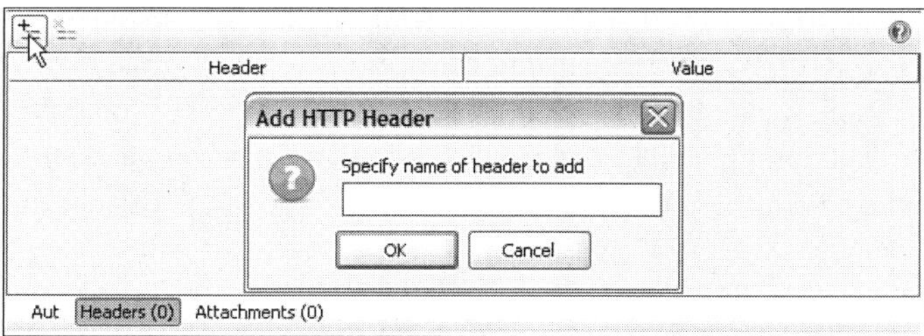

Figure 28-2 Adding an arbitrary header to a SoapUI request.

Specify the name of the header and it is added to the list; then type a value. The header count is increased appropriately. Select a header and click the X to remove it from the list.

Adding Credentials

Various types of credentials can be added to a SoapUI request. Use the Request Properties section shown in Figure 28-3 to modify various request parameters, including credential values such as username and password.

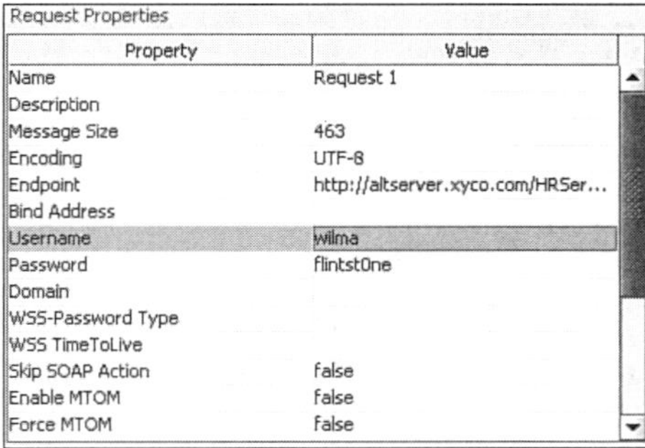
Request Properties

Property	Value
Name	Request 1
Description	
Message Size	463
Encoding	UTF-8
Endpoint	http://altserver.xyco.com/HRSer...
Bind Address	
Username	wilma
Password	flintst0ne
Domain	
WSS-Password Type	
WSS TimeToLive	
Skip SOAP Action	false
Enable MTOM	false
Force MTOM	false

Figure 28-3 Adding a username and password to a SoapUI request.

Simply typing a username and password generates an HTTP Basic Authentication header, which contains the defined values. If either the WSS-Password Type or WSS TimeToLive fields—which control the password encoding and header timestamp—are defined, a WS-Security UsernameToken is added to the SOAP Header node in the request message. This happens automatically and is reflected in the logs (and in the raw request). For instance, selecting a password type of PasswordText produces a plaintext password in a UsernameToken, whereas PasswordDigest computes a hashed version of the password. As an alternative, you can simply type (or paste) a UsernameToken into the request message by hand.

SoapUI can also be used to simulate a Web services server, and this functionality is covered in more detail, along with more examples, later in this chapter.

Browser Tools

SoapUI and curl are useful for sending SOAP requests, but what happens if you're testing a Web application? Simple interactions can be executed with curl, but the most useful tools are those that provide some insight into the message (and headers) that flow between your browser and the DataPower appliance. In fact, one of the best tools is the browser itself—Mozilla Firefox allows add-ons that dramatically increase the functionality of the browser, and can greatly add to a developer's toolkit. There are plugins available for Microsoft Internet Explorer (IE) as well, but these are not as strongly supported by the open source community. This section discusses some plugins that you might find useful.

Header Manipulation

There are header plugins available for both Firefox and IE. One of the most popular is Live HTTP Headers, which adds several menu items to Firefox. First, it adds a Headers tab to the Page Info screen for each site visited. This tab displays request and response headers for the current page, as shown in Figure 28-4.

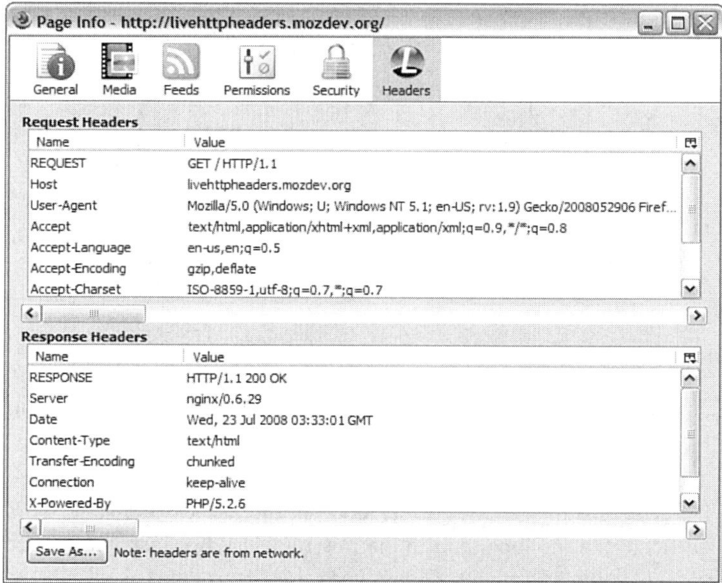

Figure 28-4 Viewing headers using a Firefox add-on.

Although it may be helpful to view the headers for the current page, it's often more useful to see a full stream of all the headers as they flow to and from the browser. This shows all HTTP requests from the browser for accessory files (images, JavaScript, stylesheets, and so on). You can view this stream by selecting Tools→Live HTTP Headers from the Firefox menu. The view is initially empty, as you must have the window open while making the request in order for the headers to be captured.

If you determine from the captured headers that something is being sent incorrectly or if you want to mimic a header that might be sent from a different browser or client, you can replay a request and modify the headers before they are sent. Selecting a request and clicking the Replay button displays the request in a new window, as shown in Figure 28-5.

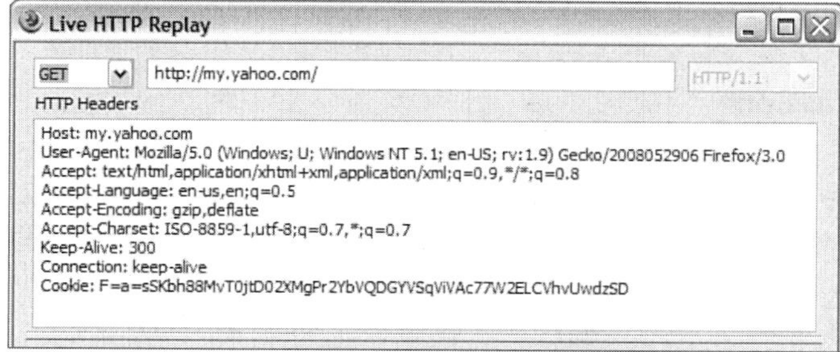

Figure 28-5 Replaying an HTTP request with modified headers.

You can change any of the headers and resubmit the request by clicking Replay. If the request is a POST, you can also change the payload that is sent. This is a valuable tool for testing online forms being POSTed to DataPower and for unit testing applications that respond differently to various user agents. The Live HTTP Headers extension is available from the built-in Add-ons page in Firefox (Tools→Add-ons). Search there to get the latest Mozilla-approved version.

On the Internet Explorer side of things, the ieHTTPHeaders plugin enables you to perform some of the same tasks. For any request, you can see the request and response headers. You can also filter those headers by Content-type or HTTP status code; selecting a content type can narrow down the requests to certain file types (only image requests, for example), while choosing a status code can help pick out requests with errors or redirects. This capability is especially useful when debugging a Web application being proxied by DataPower. The ieHTTPHeaders plugin is free for personal use but licensed for professional use.

Cookie Manipulation

Cookies, though technically just part of another HTTP header, are somewhat of a special case, as they contain additional data and are tailored to the site being visited. There are several Firefox extensions that can view and manipulate plaintext cookies; search the Firefox Add-ons page for the latest and most popular. A good cookie editor is able to view all cookies sent to a site, modify the content of each cookie individually, and manipulate the expiration dates contained therein. In a DataPower environment, cookies are generally used by Web applications to provide credentials for access control, to correlate the browser session with the backend session, to maintain user state, or to pass user information to the backend application server. Using cookie manipulation extensions allows you to test access control policy enforcement, impersonate various users for the backend, and verify appropriate behavior upon cookie expiration.

Non-HTTP Protocol Tools

To this point, we have discussed HTTP-based clients. However, it is just as important to gain visibility into messages arriving using other protocols. Testing headers, payloads, and connection issues for protocols such as WebSphere MQ, WebSphere JMS, and Tibco EMS requires tools geared toward those proprietary formats.

MQ Tools

There are useful tools that come with WebSphere MQ for both administration of queues and reading and writing of messages to and from those queues. IBM WebSphere MQ Explorer enables you to create and manage the MQ objects necessary for connection to DataPower appliances. The various objects that can be managed are seen in Figure 28-6.

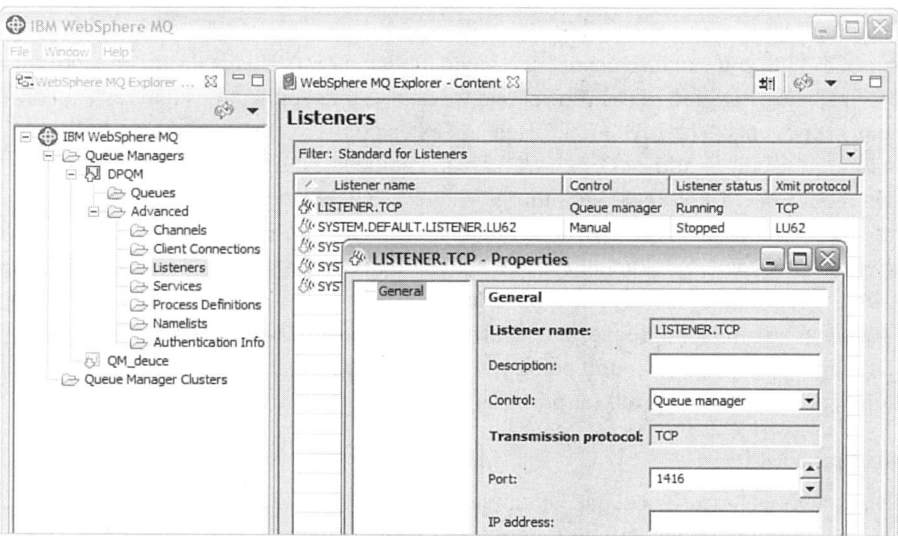

Figure 28-6 Browsing WebSphere MQ objects.

Beginning with the queue managers defined in this instance of WebSphere MQ, you can browse the hierarchy of lower-level objects. Selecting an object type will display a list in the right-side window. Double-clicking a particular object opens the Properties page for modification. Make any necessary changes and then click Apply. The objects needed for connection to DataPower are as follows—though these were covered in Chapter 9, "Multi-Protocol Gateway," it is useful to view them in the context of an MQ Explorer to verify successful connection parameters. They are

- **Queue Manager (QM)**—A QM is the root service responsible for handling messages and transferring those messages to other queue managers via message channels. A DataPower Queue Manager object requires the QM name.
- **Channel**—A channel defines communication between local and remote queue managers. A channel name is required by DataPower QM objects and defaults to SYSTEM.DEF.SVRCONN, which is defined by default in new WebSphere MQ installations.
- **Listener**—A listener defines the local IP address and port on which the queue manager listens. DataPower requires these values in the Host Name field in the QM object. MQ listener ports are usually expressed in parentheses and default to 1414; a valid entry can be something like mqserver1.xyco.com(1414).
- **Queues**—A queue is a storage location for an incoming or outgoing message. Queues can be browsed for messages, and then those messages can be PUT to or GET from the queue, which will be discussed shortly. For DataPower configuration, you need the names of an input queue and an output queue.

After the queue-related objects have been configured using MQ Explorer, you can use a tool called rfhutil to deliver and manipulate messages on the queues. This tool is included in the WebSphere MQ Support Pack, and provides many useful features.

The first step for using rfhutil is to define the queue manager and queue name that you want to interact with. When submitting a message that is picked up by an MQ Front Side Handler (FSH) on DataPower, you connect to the same queue manager that has been configured on the appliance. Type the name of the queue being used as DataPower's request queue. Now you have several options, as shown in Figure 28-7.

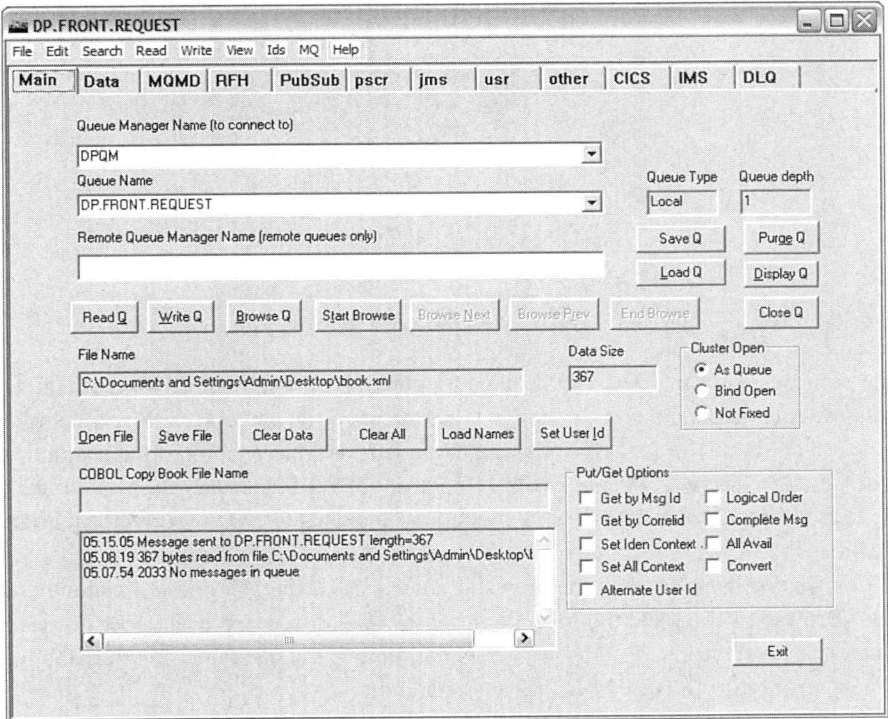

Figure 28-7 Using rfhutil to browse and manipulate messages on a queue.

The log area at the bottom of the window shows the results of commands that have been applied; the entries are read from the bottom up, as they are in reverse chronological order. You can see the first entry in the example said that there were no messages in the queue—this is generated when you try to Read Q when the queue is empty. The next entry says that bytes were read from a file—to read an input file into the tool, select Open File and then browse to a local request message. This process places the message in memory, waiting to be PUT to the queue. You can select Write Q to send the message to the queue. The message is picked up by DataPower's MQ FSH and processed by a processing policy. The service response is then delivered to the response queue.

To retrieve a response message from another queue, it's a simple modification of the queue name to the appropriate response queue. You can read the first message and remove it from the queue by selecting Read Q; if you'd like to view the messages without removing them, you can use the Browse Q (one message) or Start Browse (multiple messages, one at a time) buttons. Starting the browse process will read the first message into memory—you can inspect the message that has been retrieved by switching to the Data tab, as shown in Figure 28-8.

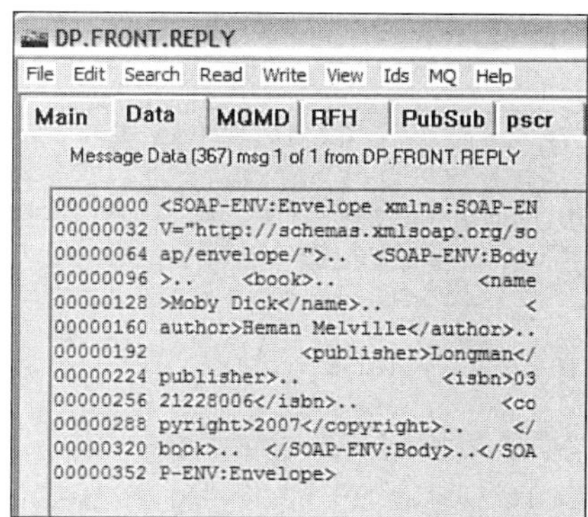

Figure 28-8 Viewing data contained within a browsed message using rfhutil.

In addition, you can view MQ headers by clicking on the other tabs across the top. The MQMD header contains fields for message type, message ID, and correlation ID, among many others. These fields can be set before writing to a queue as well, enabling total customization of the input message. These tabs represent the equivalent of HTTP headers for MQ—there may be specific uses for modifying the fields they contain. See Chapter 9 for more on MQMD header modification.

Click Browse Next to continue browsing messages (if there are more than one), and then click End Browse to complete the browsing process. The queue depth (number of messages in the queue) remains constant, as a browse does not remove the messages. To clear the messages from the queue, perform a Read Q or Purge Q operation.

JMS/EMS Tools

For a more generic tool that supports Tibco EMS, WebSphere JMS, and WebSphere MQ (among others), HermesJMS is a cross-protocol tool for browsing and modifying messages on various queues. Hermes is free software and is available from http://www.hermesjms.com/ for download. Though the interaction with queues is different, all the same connection parameters and PUT and GET commands are still applicable. For full documentation, see the Hermes Web site.

Authentication and Authorization Server Tools

If a DataPower appliance is used for access control, it is likely that there will be some interaction between the device and an external server for authentication, authorization, or both. Many of the supported servers are proprietary and have their own consoles or command-line applications for configuration and testing. However, even those proprietary tools are often built on an LDAP registry (such as SiteMinder), or expose an LDAP interface (such as Active Directory). This makes the need for an LDAP browser common. When your AAA policy isn't working as expected, these LDAP tools can often determine the root cause.

LDAP Admin

LDAP Admin is a free, simple, lightweight tool for browsing and searching an LDAP repository. It is located at http://ldapadmin.sourceforge.net/ and is available in both single-file executable and full-source formats. To begin using LDAP Admin, click Connect and define a new connection to an LDAP server. Enter the server information as shown in Figure 28-9.

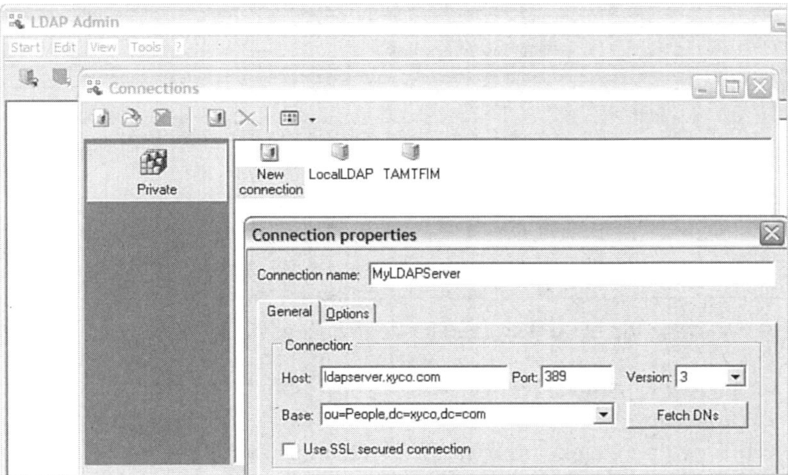

Figure 28-9 Creating a new connection in LDAP Admin.

If your LDAP server supports version 3, you can define the host and port and then click Fetch DNs to retrieve a list of possible hierarchies to use as a base. If your repository uses SSL for secure connections, click the appropriate check box. Enter your authentication information if you want to connect as an administrator or a specific user; otherwise you may be able to create an Anonymous Connection for simple browsing purposes.

After the connection is made, you can browse your identity repository and view the users and groups to which you have access. Permissions are granted based upon the authentication information provided during connection configuration. Click on a user or group to retrieve more information about that entity. You can right-click to perform various operations on the user, or to begin a search query from a given hierarchical location.

The out-of-the-box LDAP authentication step in a DataPower AAA policy requires you to define a prefix and suffix for mapping an incoming credential to an LDAP distinguished name (DN).

The DN that is created and used for binding can be displayed in the troubleshooting probe as shown in Figure 28-10. See Chapter 27 for more details on how to initiate the probe and discover this data.

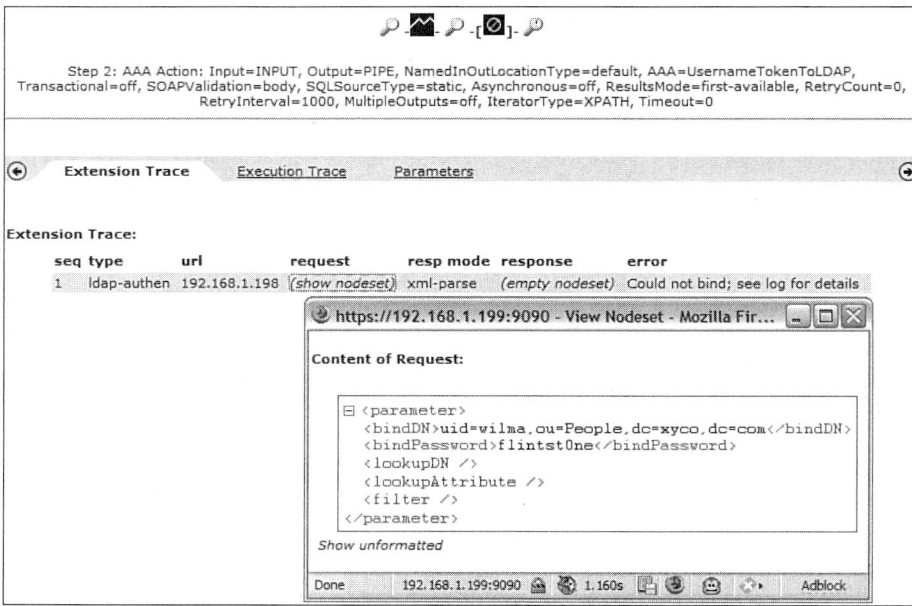

Figure 28-10 Viewing the LDAP DN used for an unsuccessful bind.

How do we know that the DN that we're trying to bind with is actually in our repository? LDAP Admin can retrieve the actual DN of an existing user by right-clicking on the user's entry. You can select Copy dn to clipboard from the menu, as shown in Figure 28-11, or click Ctrl+N while the user is selected; this places the full DN in your clipboard. It can then be pasted into the DataPower AAA policy wizard—the first portion (before the user ID) is the prefix and the last portion (after the user ID and trailing comma) is the suffix. The user ID itself should be removed from the DN, as it is filled in at runtime. See Chapter 16, "AAA," for more configuration details.

While LDAP Admin supports moving and copying trees in the repository, it is not meant to be used as a full management tool. Other tools are available when your needs are more sophisticated.

Softerra LDAP Administrator

The Softerra LDAP Administrator provides many of the same browsing capabilities as LDAP Admin, but also contains significant administrative functionality. The full, professional (commercial) version includes wizards for such tasks as attribute creation, profile creation, and entry creation using either a schema or a template. Customizable dialogs and interfaces, sophisticated filter and DN editors, and drag-and-drop capabilities make this product quite robust. Softerra also offers a free LDAP Browser that provides limited functionality related to basic browsing and takes advantage of the same helpful interface.

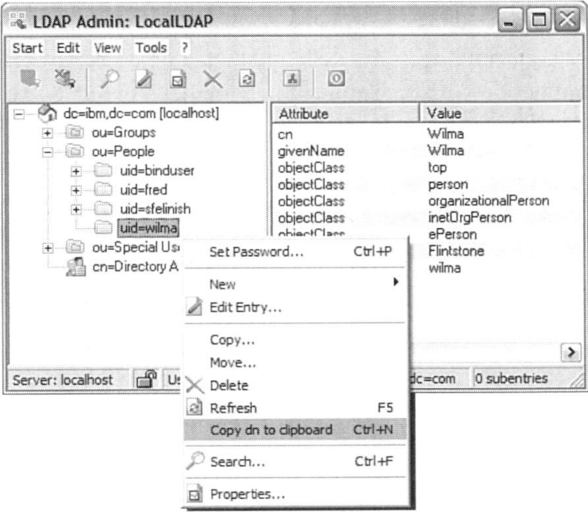

Figure 28-11 Retrieving the LDAP Distinguished Name for an existing user.

XSLT Debugging

In Chapter 25, "Development Tools," we took a close look at two Integrated Development Environments (IDE) for which there is a DataPower plugin for stylesheet development: IBM's Rational Application Developer and Altova's XMLSpy. These tools integrate with the appliance for real-time execution of stylesheets during development, and represent powerful solutions for DataPower custom programming. They can also serve as XSLT debuggers, used when a transformation does not produce the expected output.

When writing a stylesheet for basic transformation purposes, similar to those that would be executed by a software application, you can simply use the integrated debuggers provided by the products. However, creating stylesheets that use DataPower extension functions requires some additional effort for debugging, as the integrated debuggers cannot be used when being executed on a device through the plugin. We have discussed the xsl:message element several times; in Chapter 23, "Programming Within the DataPower Environment," we showed you how to use these message elements to write events to the log. A combination of an IDE for development, DataPower for remote execution, and custom log messages for insight into stylesheet behavior provide the best opportunity for XSLT debugging.

However, some users are more comfortable with a simpler approach—a basic text editor with or without syntax highlighting. Fans of emacs and vi will find built-in features, external plugins, and custom macro development as powerful as even the friendliest IDE.

Backend Spoofing

The tools that we have discussed to this point have dealt almost entirely with the frontend execution of services deployed on a DataPower device, and with debugging the processing that happens during execution. However, it is just as important to make sure that the backend server being accessed by a service is connected appropriately and behaving correctly. Often, DataPower development happens in conjunction with backend application development—so what do you do when you need to test a service that isn't deployed or functional? You fake it!

SoapUI Mock Service

There are several ways to create a simulated backend service, including using one of the tools we have already discussed. SoapUI can create a mock service to serve as the backend for an existing project. Simply right-click on the service name and select New MockService, as shown in Figure 28-12. Provide a name for the new faux backend.

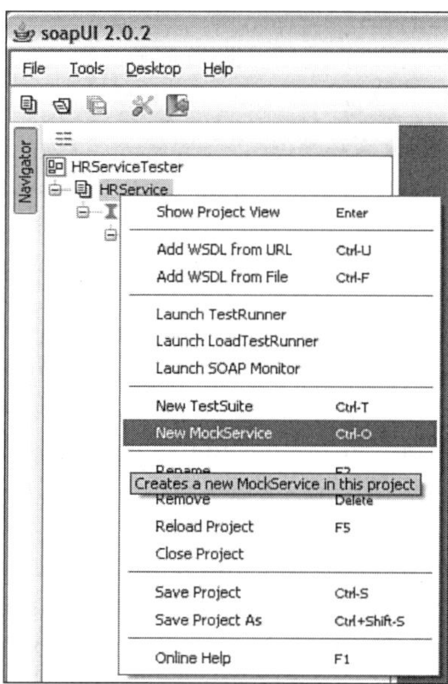

Figure 28-12 Creating a mock backend for a service in SoapUI.

The backend is created with default parameters that can be seen in the MockService Properties window; the port and path (URI) parameters define where the service listens on the local machine. Right-click on the mock service and select New MockOperation; select the operation you'd like to simulate from the drop-down list. This generates an operation and a sample response window. SoapUI provides a sample message that is created from the operation's response schema, as defined in the service's WSDL. An example is shown in Figure 28-13.

As you can see, field values are initially left as question marks that can be modified to add real-life data. It goes without saying that the service response document should be as realistic as possible, so that the full service (including processing of the response in DataPower) can mimic actual behavior.

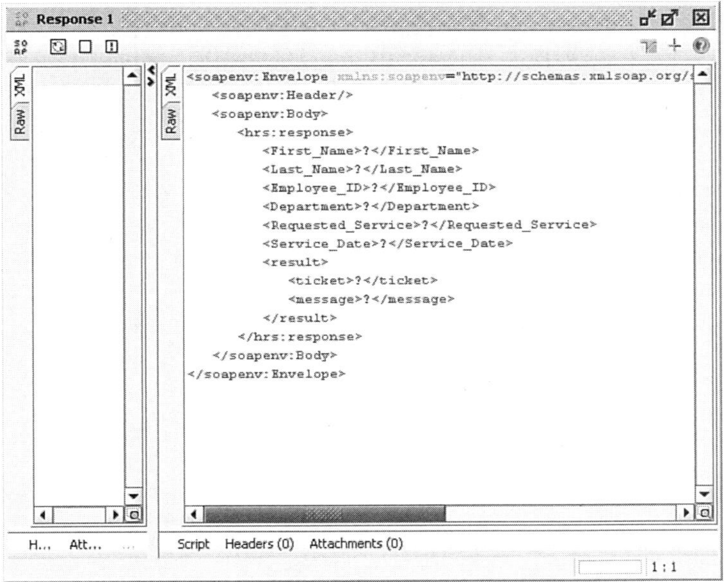

Figure 28-13 Defining a sample response document for a mock service.

To prepare the mock service to handle requests, double-click the service name to open the listener window, as shown in Figure 28-14. If you want to change the default port and URI, you can do so by clicking the options button on the toolbar. Click the green Start this MockService button to put the service into listening mode. Now any requests sent to the appropriate URL are processed by the mock service, and the sample message is sent back to the client.

Figure 28-14 Starting a mock service listener.

To test the mock service from SoapUI itself, without going through DataPower, simply edit your request endpoint as discussed earlier in this chapter. The default URL (from the local machine) would be http://127.0.0.1:8080/. Any requests made will result in a notification in the message log, along with a response time; any errors will also be displayed there.

This is useful for a simple response that doesn't change from request to request and doesn't require any specific input from the client; SoapUI also enables you to create multiple canned responses that can be staged and selected dynamically or randomly. Double-click on an operation in your MockService to view the available responses for that operation, as shown in Figure 28-15.

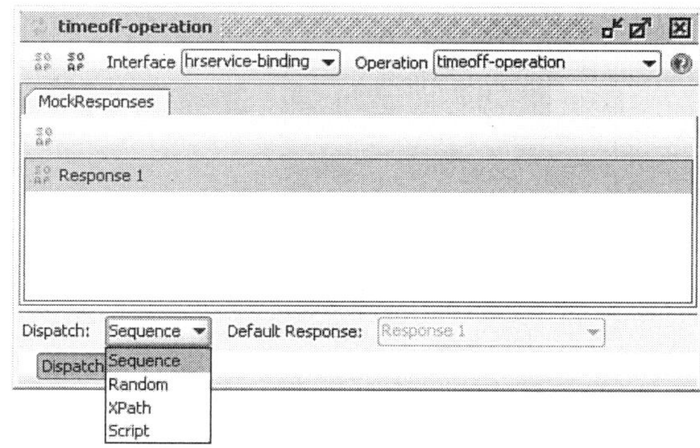

Figure 28-15 Adding additional responses to a MockService.

Right-click in the MockResponses section and select New MockResponse to open a new MockResponse window. Fill in the appropriate values for your second response. You can determine which response message is served on a given request using the Dispatch drop-down. The options are as follows:

- Sequence simply cycles through each response in a round-robin pattern.
- Random selects a random response to return.
- XPath enables you to use a node in the incoming message to determine which response is used.
- Script enables you to write a script (in the Java-like programming language Groovy) to determine which response is returned.

Of particular usefulness is the XPath option, which enables you to dynamically determine which response is sent using a field in the incoming message. For example, you can look at an incoming WS-Security UsernameToken and send back a message that was appropriate to a particular user. Which response is chosen is tied to the name of the response message; that is, the XPath statement executes and returns a value—SoapUI then selects the response with a name equal to that value. Define a Default Response for any messages that can't determine an appropriate response. In the example shown in Figure 28-16, usernames of fred or wilma generate the responses meant for those users; any message without a WS-Security username, or containing a username other than those values, will receive the AuthenticationError response.

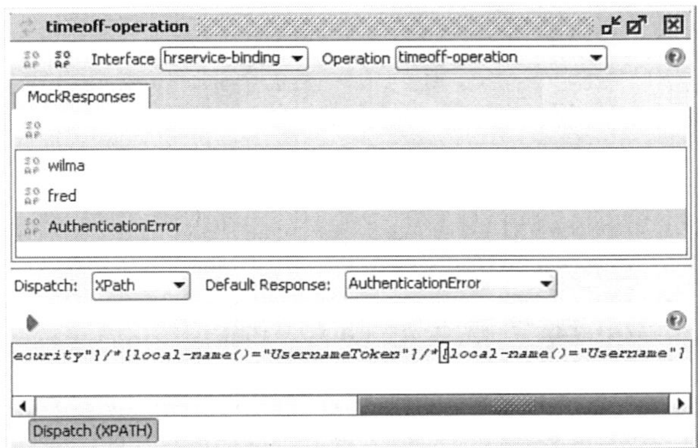

Figure 28-16 Selecting an appropriate response using an XPath statement.

This AuthenticationError is one of a number of errors that might be useful for testing purposes. In these cases, you can open the response message and click the exclamation point on the toolbar—this generates a SOAP Fault response, which you can then customize to return potential errors. This allows you to verify that DataPower is processing each error (and each successful response) appropriately.

Loopback XML Firewall

Though this chapter relates to external tools, you can create these mock backends using DataPower as well. In Chapter 8, "XML Firewall," we discussed the loopback firewall, a service that accepts a request, performs some processing, and returns a response without ever connecting to a backend server. Using this functionality as a service backend enables you to take advantage of the appliance's full capabilities in creating a mock response. If you are using the device to send an encrypted message to a partner, but the partner's service isn't ready, then simulate it with an XML firewall that performs the decryption and processes it as your partner would.

HTTP Service

Some DataPower services simply retrieve a file from a backend Web server; this could be used for a portal or content-rendering application, in which an XML file is transformed by the appliance into a useful format for the client. If the backend Web server isn't available yet, DataPower can simulate that as well. Navigate to Services→Other Services→HTTP Service and click Add to create a new Web server. Define an IP and port on which to listen, and then choose a base directory from which to serve files; you may want to create a subdirectory within the local: directory, as shown in Figure 28-17.

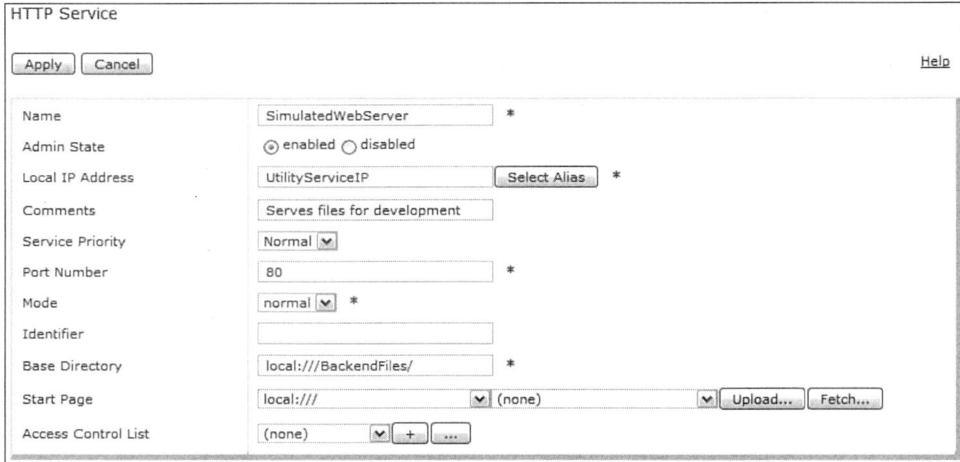

Figure 28-17 Creating an HTTP service to use as a file server for testing.

If you define a start page, it is served for requests without a URI; if undefined, a directory listing is returned. If you would prefer the server to simply return an exact copy of the GET or POST request, change the Mode to echo.

Remote Data Collection

Many of the off-device tools helpful in the debugging process will be data collection systems such as log servers and SNMP monitoring tools. In Chapter 14, "Logging and Monitoring," we discussed the various options for log targets, including syslog, SMTP, and file upload. With the appropriate event subscriptions, any interested groups should already be receiving the messages that may be useful to them for troubleshooting. Similarly, tools using SNMP-based polling to monitor the health of the device should be configured to alert the proper personnel when the values for certain parameters exceed a defined threshold.

The exact methodologies required to configure proprietary monitoring and logging toolkits or generate reports and alerts are beyond the scope of this book, but definitely an important part of the troubleshooting process. See Chapter 14 to make sure that you are taking full advantage of this integration with your existing infrastructure.

Connection and Networking Issues

We have discussed message visibility and manipulation at three important points: the client, the processing policy, and the backend. However, visibility into the wire-level data being transmitted between DataPower and other machines is just as important. Sometimes the only way to truly debug a connection issue is to see exactly what is happening at the transport and network layers. Through a combination of on-board and external tools, we have access to this level of detail as well.

Packet Captures

Perhaps the most revealing method for debugging a transport-layer issue is through the use of packet captures. Though these could technically be captured at any point in the network, it is often difficult to achieve on a backend server or remote client system. DataPower provides access to packet captures on each interface of the device, so that the exact incoming and outgoing communication can be analyzed.

Generating a Packet Capture

To create a packet capture, first navigate to Control Panel→Troubleshooting→Packet Capture. This task can only be performed in the default domain, as network-level access is denied to application domains. There are two possible modes for packet captures: timed and continuous. A timed capture saves everything (up to a user-defined limit) that goes in and out of the interface for a set period of time. A continuous capture continues until it is manually turned off (up to that same user-defined limit). When unexpected behavior is reproducible, it is often more helpful to perform a continuous packet capture, as you can turn it on, send a request, and then turn it off without gathering too much extraneous data.

Configuration of a continuous packet capture is shown in Figure 28-18. Clicking Start Packet Capture opens a confirmation window, and the capture begins as soon as you click Confirm. Stopping the capture also requires a confirmation, at which point the capture terminates. When performing a timed capture, there is no need to manually stop the process; it ends when the maximum duration has been reached.

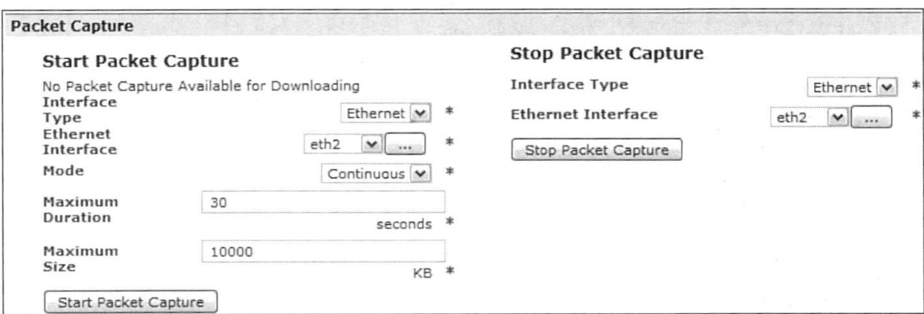

Figure 28-18 Initiating a continuous packet capture on the eth2 interface.

After a packet capture has been started, a new icon displays in this area, as shown in Figure 28-19. Clicking Download Packet Capture will prompt you to save a file; the default filename is simply pcap, but you should rename it to something useful that represents the transaction being tested (BackendConnectionError.pcap). Using a .pcap filename extension ensures that packet capture browsers are able to read the file.

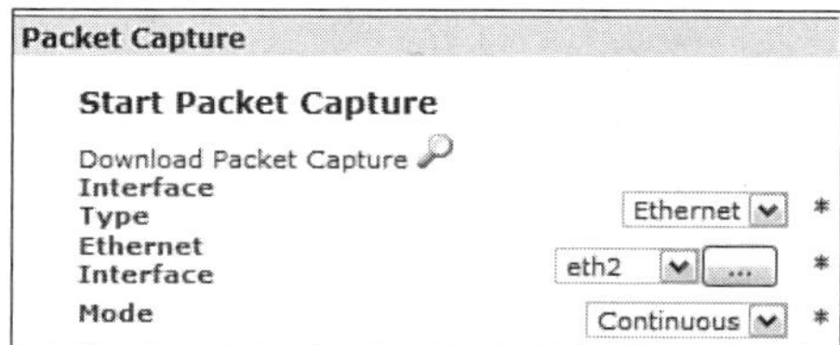

Figure 28-19 Downloading a packet capture file.

Analyzing a Packet Capture

Wireshark is a free packet capture analysis tool available from http://www.wireshark.org/. During the installation process, you can decide whether to install a local network sniffer as well, to monitor interfaces on the local PC; this is not required to analyze captures exported from the appliance. If you chose to associate .pcap files with Wireshark, simply double-click on the downloaded file; otherwise, open Wireshark, click File→Open, and select the packet capture file.

Basic data about each packet is separated into columns in the upper section of the screen, as shown in Figure 28-20. The columns are sortable and searchable, which is helpful when there are thousands of packets captured in just a few seconds. You can define search filters to apply to the list in order to narrow it down to a manageable number. To understand what to filter on, you must first understand what each field means.

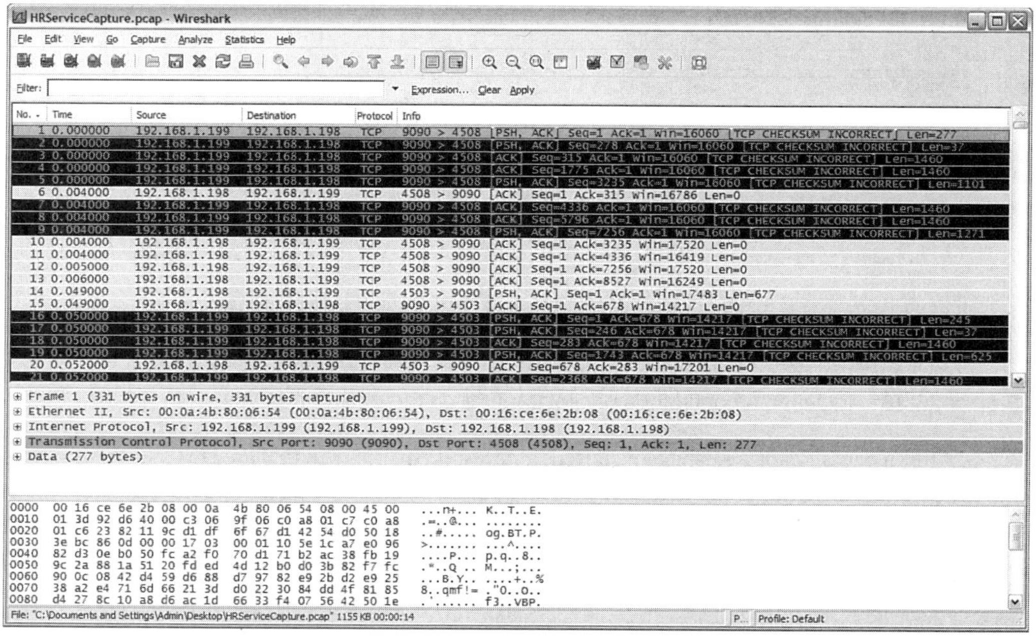

Figure 28-20 Browsing captured packets.

Each field represents a different bit of information about the packet. The columns are as follows:

- **Number**—Packets are numbered in chronological order, starting with number one.
- **Time**—Associated timestamps start at zero and count up in milliseconds from the capture initiation.
- **Source**—The IP of the source machine; there is an option during file load so that you can resolve MAC or network addresses to provide name-based records.
- **Destination**—The IP (or name) of the destination machine.
- **Protocol**—The protocol used by the packet being transmitted; though most will be TCP, other valid protocols include UDP, ARP, LDAP, MQ, and so on.
- **Info**—Additional information regarding the packet; this field begins with the request and response ports, type of command, sequence number, acknowledgment number, and length.

Clicking on a specific packet displays additional information in the two lower sections. The middle contains supplementary timing information, network details, MAC addresses, checksums, network flags, and so on. The bottom section contains a decoded version of all those details, in both hexadecimal and ASCII. As you click on a field in the middle section, the decoded portion is highlighted in the lower area, as shown in Figure 28-21. For more information about what each section means, see Chapter 4, "Advanced DataPower Networking."

```
    [Next sequence number: 1295    (relative sequence number)]
    Acknowledgement number: 1    (relative ack number)
    Header length: 20 bytes
  ⊟ Flags: 0x18 (PSH, ACK)
      0... .... = Congestion Window Reduced (CWR): Not set
      .0.. .... = ECN-Echo: Not set

0020  01 c7 11 a8 1b 58 5f 1d  03 fe d4 91 21 b9 50 18   .....X_. ....!.P.
0030  44 70 83 37 00 00 50 4f  53 54 20 2f 48 52 53 65   Dp.7..PO ST /HRSe
0040  72 76 69 63 65 20 48 54  54 50 2f 31 2e 31 0d 0a   rvice HT TP/1.1..
0050  43 6f 6e 74 65 6e 74 2d  54 79 70 65 3a 20 74 65   Content- Type: te
0060  78 74 2f 78 6d 6c 3b 63  68 61 72 73 65 74 3d 55   xt/xml;c harset=U
0070  54 46 2d 38 0d 0a 53 4f  41 50 41 63 74 69 6f 6e   TF-8..SO APAction
0080  3a 20 22 22 0d 0a 55 73  65 72 2d 41 67 65 6e 74   : ""..Us er-Agent
0090  3a 20 4a 61 6b 61 72 74  61 20 43 6f 6d 6d 6f 6e   : Jakart a Common
00a0  73 2d 48 74 74 70 43 6c  69 65 6e 74 2f 33 2e 30   s-HttpCl ient/3.0
00b0  2e 31 0d 0a 48 6f 73 74  3a 20 31 39 32 2e 31 36   .1..Host : 192.16
00c0  38 2e 31 2e 31 39 39 3a  37 30 30 30 0d 0a 43 6f   8.1.199: 7000..Co
00d0  6e 74 65 6e 74 2d 4c 65  6e 67 74 68 3a 20 31 31   ntent-Le ngth: 11
00e0  31 38 0d 0a 0d 0a 3c 73  6f 61 70 65 6e 76 3a 45   18....<s oapenv:E
00f0  6e 76 65 6c 6f 70 65 20  78 6d 6c 6e 73 3a 68 72   nvelope  xmlns:hr

Acknowledgement number (tcp.ack), 4 bytes
```

Figure 28-21 Viewing data within a packet.

To debug a particular transaction, it might help to significantly filter the packets involved. Use the filter field at the top to narrow them down. The online documentation has the full set of possible field names, but here are a few that are particularly useful:

- **ip.addr eq 192.168.1.199**—This displays only packets that are coming from or going to a particular address; to require that the IP is either the source or the destination, you can use ip.src or ip.dst.

- **tcp.port eq 7000**—This displays only packets directed to (or coming from) a particular port.
- **ldap**—Many protocols have their own search filters; as an example, this will retrieve only LDAP requests, and can be made more specific with ldap.bindRequest.
- **ip.src eq 192.168.1.199 and tcp.port eq 389**—Filters can be combined to create more advanced lookups.

After you've narrowed it down a bit, perhaps to all communications between one client and the DataPower appliance, you can select one particular transaction. Choose a packet that you know is in the transaction (either request or response). Right-click the packet and choose Follow TCP Stream. A new window opens with the full request-response content, including headers and payloads, as shown in Figure 28-22. The request and response are color-coded so they are easier to distinguish from one another.

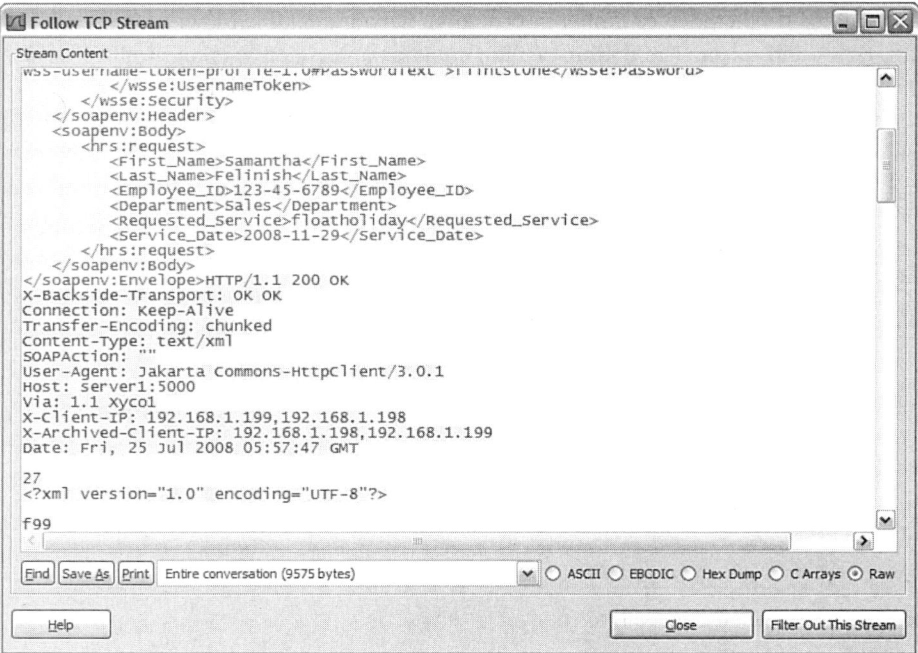

Figure 28-22 Following a TCP stream.

The options at the bottom of the window enable text conversion, saving, printing, and additional filtering of the stream. You can use Find to search for text within the transaction; if you select Filter Out This Stream, the entire transaction is removed from the original packet capture.

When you exit this window, the capture will display only the packets that were involved in your selected stream. The filter that has been auto-generated may give you interesting ideas about how to manipulate your capture.

SSL Packet Captures

In the previous example, it was easy to debug the content of the message because it was all visible in plain text. However, this will not be the case when a connection is using transport-level encryption such as SSL. There are two solutions to this problem. The first possible solution is to import the private key being used for SSL connectivity and let Wireshark decode the messages. The second solution is to modify the ciphers being used in the SSL connection so that the content appears in plain text. In Chapter 18, "DataPower and SSL," we described the configuration of SSL-related crypto objects. In the Crypto Profile being used for the connection, change the Ciphers to NULL as shown in Figure 28-23.

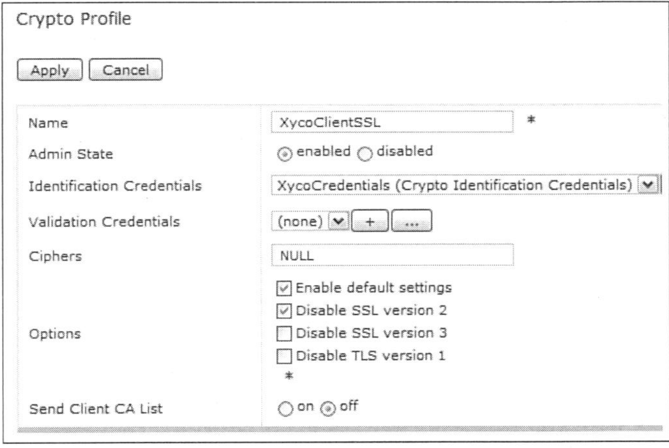

Figure 28-23 Setting SSL ciphers to NULL for plaintext connections.

Setting the ciphers to NULL does not prevent an SSL connection from being created. Instead, the handshake is performed and the connection is created, but the data is not encrypted in transit. In this case, the client must also allow for null ciphers. However, keep in mind that this is a serious security vulnerability in a production system; use this only for internal debugging during development, and make sure to switch the ciphers back to their appropriate value (the default is DEFAULT) when the problem has been resolved.

Simple Network Capture

Full packet captures and analysis using Wireshark provide the best visibility into transport-level errors; sometimes they provide *too* much information. For a simpler method of insight into these transactions at a transport level, TCPMon is a useful alternative. TCPMon is a free download available from http://tcpmon.dev.java.net/. It can also be run directly from the Web site using Java Web Start.

The interface for TCPMon is extremely simple (see Figure 28-24). Define a local listener port for requests, and then select a host and port to forward those requests to. Click Add Monitor to create the listener and display messages as they are sent through the tool. This provides much of the basic capture functionality inherent in Wireshark, but uses a much cleaner GUI—in cases where you just need to view the header and message over the wire, this may be a simpler solution.

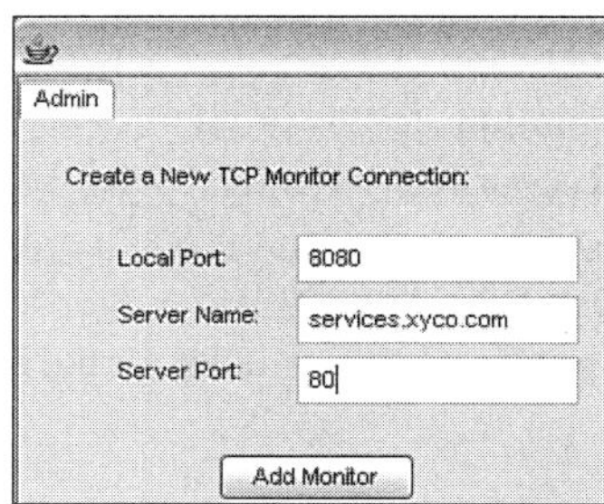

Figure 28-24 Creating a TCPMon listener for message sniffing.

Testing Connections

Our focus to this point has been at both a high level, for message creation and manipulation, and at a low level, for packet-level transport issues. Now let's focus on basic connectivity—how do we make sure we can create successful connections between a client and a DataPower service? Because DataPower is often deployed in topologies using multiple networks, routers, and firewalls, debugging connectivity issues is often required.

Connectivity Tools

For testing basic connectivity, many of the external tools are the same as those provided by the DataPower appliance. In Chapter 13, "Alternate Management Interfaces," we discussed the command-line applications ping and traceroute. Most operating systems have exact duplicates of these two commands. Ping can verify a simple connection to a remote service—just type ping services.xyco.com from a command line within Windows, Linux, and so on. Assuming that DNS resolution is working correctly (and ping responses have not been disabled), ping will look up the IP and start sending packets to the server in question. Traceroute is similar, but it determines the full route from the local machine to a remote host, reporting each network hop in between. On Windows environments, the exact command name is tracert; it remains traceroute on most other operating systems. Note that ping and traceroute test basic machine-to-machine connectivity, but do not test the actual ports being used by the various servers in your topology.

SSL Connection Issues

Before you ever get to a packet-level issue with SSL, you have to be able to make the initial connection and encryption handshake. Depending upon the parameters defined on DataPower, this might be one-way SSL, where the client needs to validate only the server's credentials (or ignore them). If defined as two-way SSL (mutual authentication), then the client also needs to send its own certificate, which will be validated by DataPower and used in the handshake. If you are attempting a connection to an HTTPS URL but are receiving an error message, this could be the problem. In curl, this issue reveals itself with the following error message:

```
curl: (35) error:14094410:SSL routines:SSL3_READ_BYTES:sslv3 alert
handshake failure
```

If you had a key and certificate in the right format, you could send them with your curl request. For this and other related issues, you might need to convert from one crypto format to another. Fortunately, there are tools to assist with this process.

OpenSSL

Let's say you want to generate a key/certificate pair on the device, but your client doesn't support the .pem files DataPower produces. OpenSSL is a free software product that can perform key conversions (among many other features). It is included in many Linux distributions, and the source can be downloaded from http://www.openssl.org/. This site also contains links to partner sites that provide a self-executing installer.

Once OpenSSL is installed, much of its work must be done from the command line. If you have generated .pem files on a DataPower appliance, you can convert them to DER-formatted files with the following commands. First, the private key needs to be converted from PEM to DER format, and is output as a .key file:

```
openssl rsa -in XycoClient-privkey.pem -inform PEM -outform DER -out
XycoClient-privkey.key
```

Next, the certificate needs to be converted into a plain X509 cert with a .crt extension, also in a DER format:

```
openssl x509 -in XycoClient-sscert.pem -inform PEM -outform DER -out
XycoClient-sscert.crt
```

See the OpenSSL documentation for the full range of formats and options that are supported. In this case, a PEM file is simply a Base64 encoded version of a DER file, with descriptive headers added. Once the key and certificate are in the desired format, you can import them into your service client. In curl, there's no need to actually perform an import—they can be referenced directly from the command line. Here is the appropriate command:

```
curl -data-binary @input.xml https://services.xyco.com:7443/HRService -
key XycoClient-privkey.key -key-type DER -cert XycoClient-sscert.crt -
cert-type DER -k
```

For clients that can also perform WS-Security encryption and digital signatures, these new crypto files can be used for the same purpose. Just convert the files to the desired format and then import them into the client. In this same manner, OpenSSL can also convert files to base64 and back using the openssl enc command; see the documentation for usage details.

Summary

Yes, this is a DataPower book, but even DataPower can't do everything. We have demonstrated some of the most useful external tools for generating meaningful requests, manipulating those requests, adding headers, creating a network connection over various protocols, delivering the message, preparing an on-device transformation for that message, generating a backend server response, and sending that response all the way back to the client. Along with the internal tools discussed in Chapter 27, you should now have a good base for troubleshooting any applications flowing through the DataPower appliance. Have fun!

CHAPTER 29

Multiple Device Management Tools

Despite robust construction and a very low mean-time-between-failures rate, a single DataPower device is just that—a single point of failure in the eyes of high-availability specialists. For that reason, it is common to employ multiple devices in production and preproduction environments. Whether they are deployed as active-active or active-standby, the essential requirement is that the application domains on the devices be duplicates of each other. This begs the question, "How do we keep these devices in sync?" In this chapter, we show a few approaches.

Scripted Approaches

In Chapter 15, "Build and Deploy Techniques," we showed how to script the build and deployment of DataPower configurations using a few different approaches. These could be expanded to script the deployment of configurations to multiple devices.

When using this approach, it is common to do so by removing one device or domain at a time from the active configuration so that the updates can be applied without affecting traffic. Care must be taken to quiesce (or drain) current transactions without allowing new ones, and then check to ensure there are no incomplete transactions on the target before making the changes. These types of rolling updates are usually done by having the network team manage the traffic from device to device. As load balancers are often employed to front groups of devices, this can be done by using features of the load-balancing products.

For example, in an environment with three devices, the steps at a high level might be as follows:

1. Use the load balancer configuration to quiesce traffic away from device one.
2. When device one has drained, apply changes, bring it back online, and allow new transactions.

3. Use the load balancer configuration to quiesce traffic away from device two.
4. When device two has drained (for example, all existing requests for this device have completed and device one is now back online and receiving requests), apply changes, bring it back online, and allow new transactions.
5. Use the load balancer configuration to quiesce traffic away from device three.
6. When device three has drained, apply changes, bring it back online, and allow new transactions.

You should ensure that the new configuration works properly on the first two devices before updating device three. If there is a problem, you can always stay at the old configuration by just using device three until the problem is resolved.

Of course, when using approaches like this, it is imperative that the smaller set of online appliances be able to handle any expected (or unexpected) traffic. You may also want to take additional steps, such as doing regression testing on each device before it is added back into the available pool, or sending priming commands to prime caches. We are assuming a highly available configuration as well, where there cannot be downtime for maintenance. If your service-level agreements (SLA) provide for a maintenance window where the devices can be brought down periodically, maintenance is much less complicated.

Load Balancers or VRRP?

The question about how to make multiple devices highly available is often asked. While there are built-in capabilities on the appliances based on Virtual Router Redundancy Protocol (VRRP), these are typically for active/standby configurations, which are not as widely used as active-active. You can create a pseudo active-active config by using it across two sets of interfaces, but more often, load balancers are used for their more flexible and rich feature sets.

Operating system shell scripts by themselves, or in conjunction with more powerful and common scripting environments such as Ant, Perl, and Python, are all reasonable choices for these types of operations. The scripts should be used to deploy the configuration for preproduction environments as well so that the benefit of having the scripts tested is achieved.

ITCAM SE for DataPower

IBM Tivoli Composite Application Manager System Edition for DataPower (ITCAMSEDP) is a utility that runs on a version of Tivoli's Enterprise Portal (TEP) software, on supported Windows and Linux operating systems. It is on the Resource CD that comes with the appliances and can also be downloaded from the DataPower firmware and documentation Web site.

This powerful software runs on WebSphere Application Server (WAS) and stores its data in database tables. It installs those components on its own, but if they are already available in your environment, you can configure ITCAMSEDP to use the existing installed versions, as long as they meet the prerequisites.

All prerequisites should be checked carefully before installing, as with any enterprise software package. The install and user guide should be reviewed to familiarize yourself with the install process and options. This utility is normally installed on a server, where it can continuously monitor the appliances it is configured for.

The features of this tool enable it to be used to keep a centralized list of all addressable devices, back up their configurations and domains, and act as a repository for various versions of firmware. When the devices are identified, they can be organized into "managed sets." For example, you may have one managed set represent production devices and another for preproduction test environment devices. One device in each managed set is indicated as the master for that set, and from there the selected device's configuration settings can be shared across the set (for example SNMP or Network Time Protocol properties). Also, application domains can be clustered together so that when a change is made to the master device, it is propagated to the other devices in the managed set. These changes are made intelligently so that existing transactions are not disrupted. Firmware updates (or rollbacks) can be automatically distributed in order to keep the appliances in the managed set in sync.

As this utility runs on TEP, there are some SNMP capabilities as well, but they are not discussed in this chapter. See the ITCAMSEDP User Guide for that information.

Let's walk through a sample scenario in order to understand better how this works. Figure 29-1 shows a device being added to ITCAMSEDP. This is done by right-clicking on the Devices label in the middle pane and choosing Add from the context menu. The device is assigned a name, and the IP address (or hostname), XML Management port, admin ID, and password are supplied. The XML Management settings for the device must have the AMP Endpoint box selected, as this is the message format used for communication between ITCAMSEDP and the devices it manages.

When the OK button is clicked, ITCAMSEDP interrogates the device over the network and presents the list of application domains found and other device properties, as shown in Figure 29-2.

A second device is added in the same fashion, as shown in Figure 29-3. Notice that while this device has some similarly named application domains on it, they are completely separate at this point from the domains in the first device.

Now that two devices are known to ITCAMSEDP, a managed set can be created. Similar to adding a device, this is done by right-clicking the Managed Sets label and choosing Add. Figure 29-4 shows a managed set called ProductionDataPowerAppliances being created.

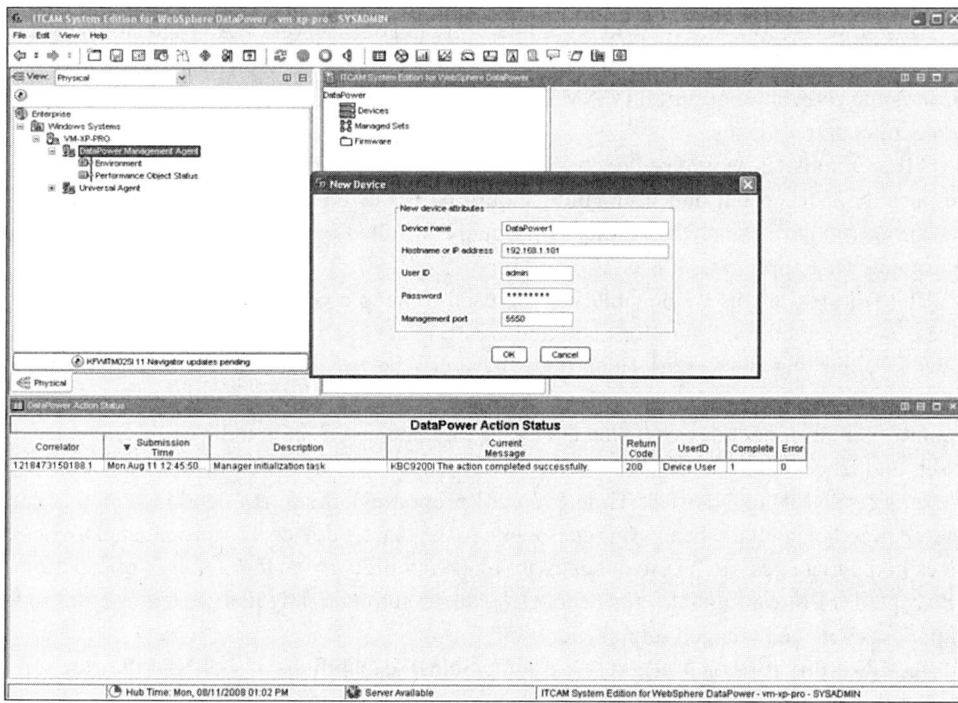

Figure 29-1 Adding devices to an ITCAMSEDP install.

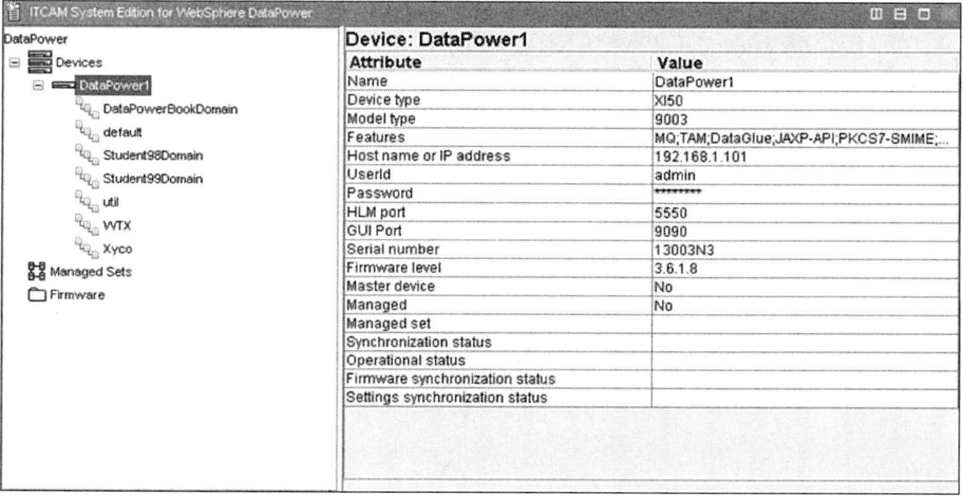

Figure 29-2 Newly added device properties and domains.

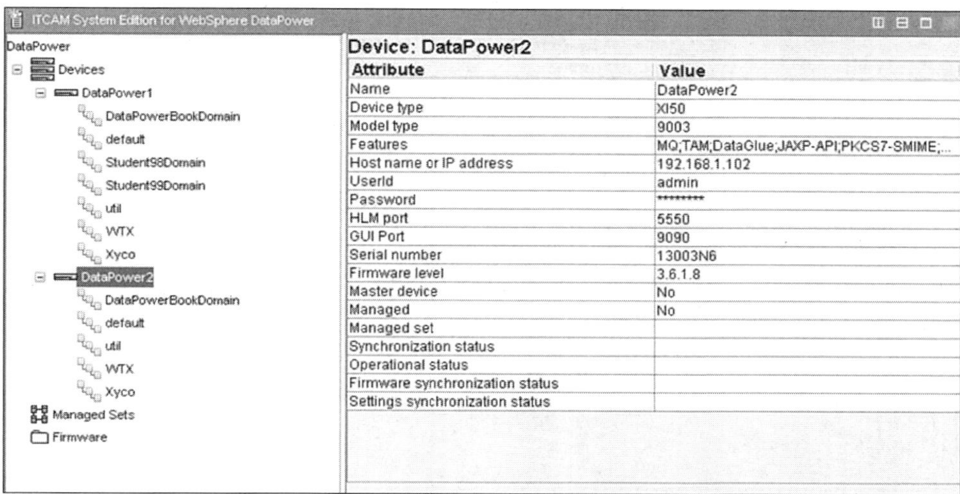

Figure 29-3 A second device is identified.

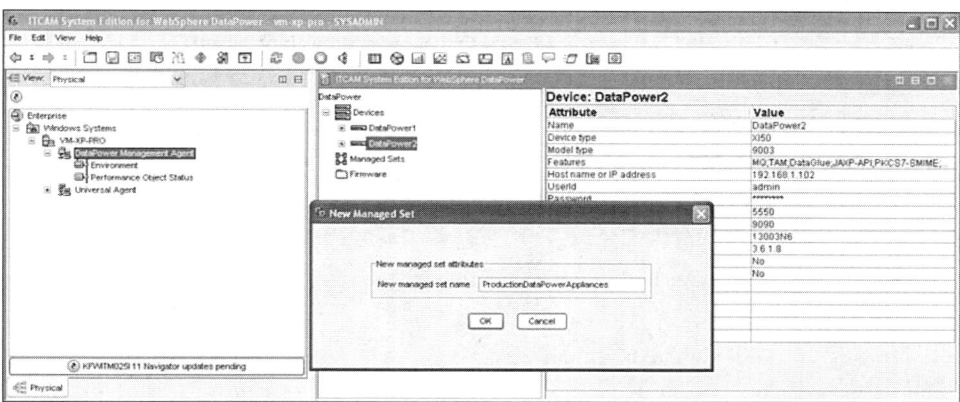

Figure 29-4 A managed set is created.

Nothing special happens at this point. Now that the managed set exists, we can load devices into it by dragging the device on top of the managed set name. When this is done, the system prompts to ask whether this device should be the master, as shown in Figure 29-5. We chose to make this one the master.

Now that there is a device in the managed set, indicated as master, the system backs up the device settings, as shown in Figure 29-6. This can be used to later replicate the settings across the other devices that might be in the managed set, and also to roll forward or backward to different versions of the settings that have been captured by the tool. Each time the system detects a change, it automatically creates a new version of the settings.

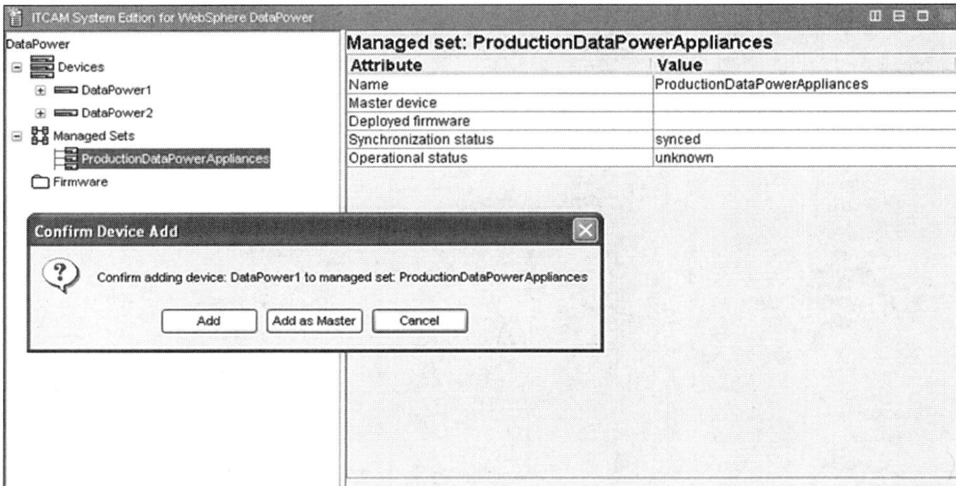

Figure 29-5 Device DataPower1 is being added to the managed set as master.

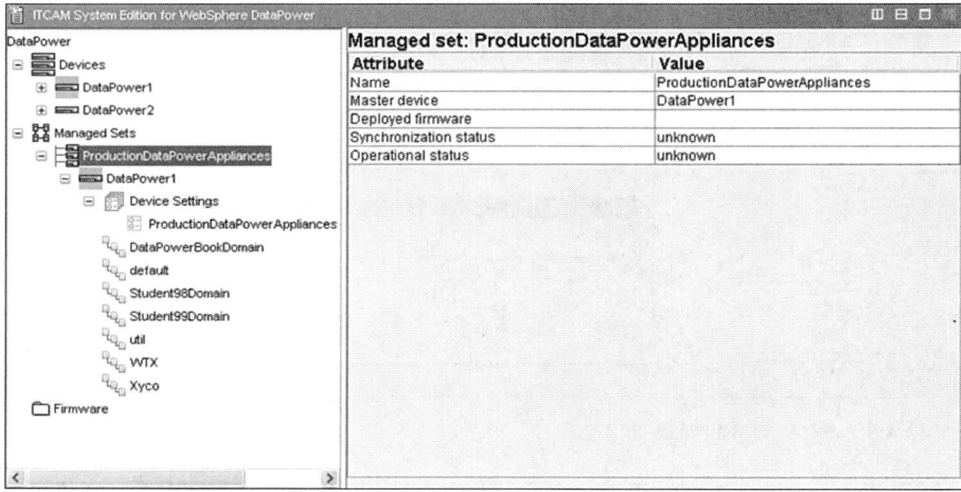

Figure 29-6 DataPower1 in the managed set with a device settings backup.

A firmware image is added next, before bringing the second device into the managed set. It is a requirement, so normally a version that is equivalent to the version currently running on the first device is uploaded. This is done by right-clicking the Firmware label and choosing Add Firmware Image from the context menu. Figure 29-7 shows this simple operation. Of course, you want to choose only firmware images that have features licensed for your devices!

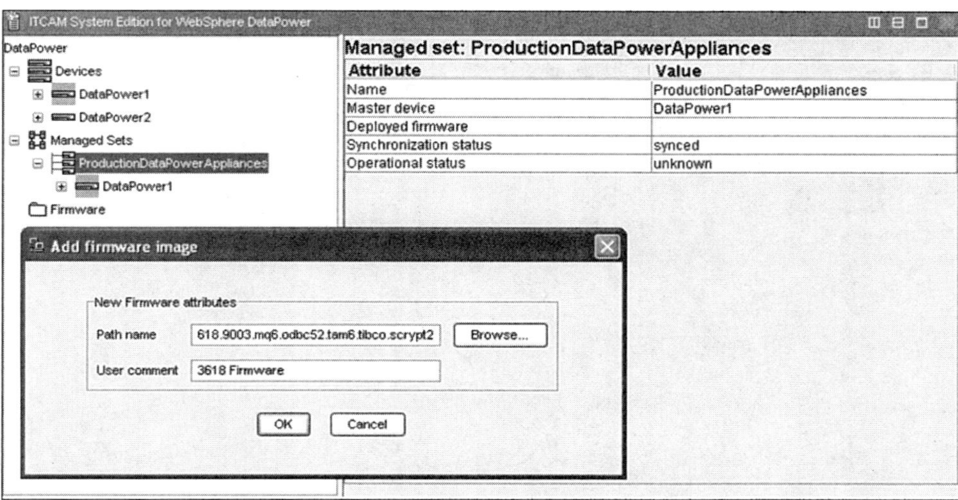

Figure 29-7 Loading a firmware image to ITCAMSEDP.

After the firmware is loaded into the tool (this may take a few moments depending on the size), it is displayed along with the features that are determined by ITCAMSEDP interrogating the binary file. This is shown in Figure 29-8. Note that the tool has determined that our master device already has this version installed and is indicating a status of "synced."

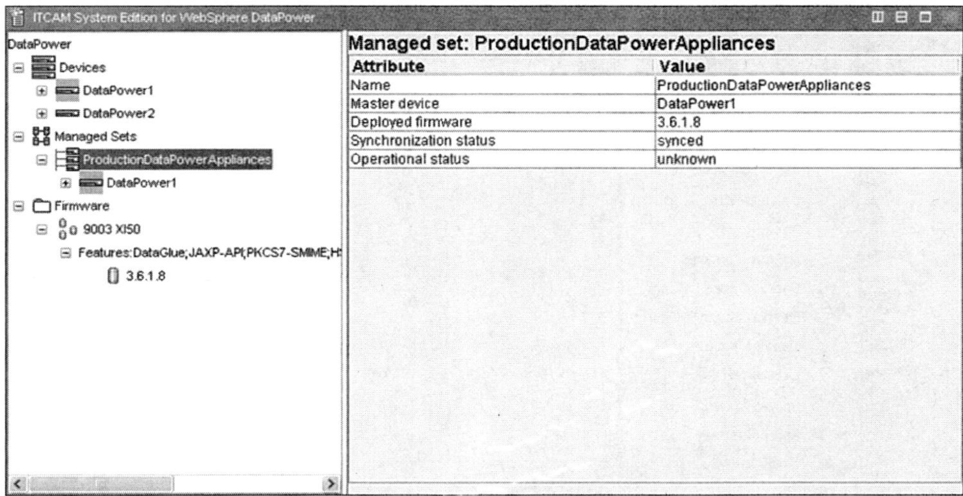

Figure 29-8 Firmware image added to ITCAMSEDP.

Now the second device can be added to the managed set. This is done just as the first one was added, with the key difference being that we click the Add button rather than Add as Master. Figure 29-9 shows both devices in the managed set. ITCAMSEDP color codes these to tell the master apart from the other members of the managed set.

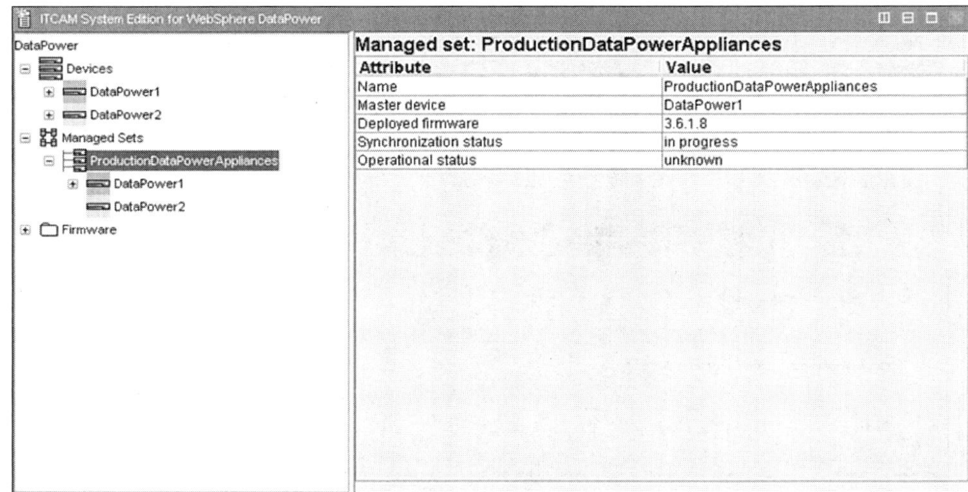

Figure 29-9 Two devices in a managed set.

A number of options appear on the context menu for the devices after they are added to the managed set. Figure 29-10 shows some of these, such as the ability to manually synchronize, launch the WebGUI for a particular device, and manually back up and restore settings.

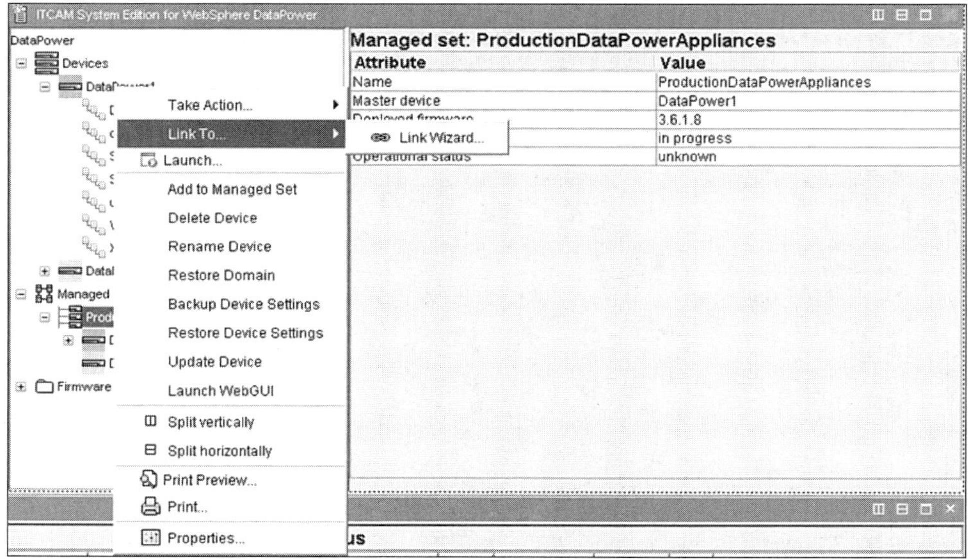

Figure 29-10 Device capabilities through ITCAMSEDP.

After the managed set is created, we are free to flag individual domains within the master device as managed domains. This means that the domain is replicated from the master device across the other devices in the managed set. As soon as the synchronization is completed, the domain should appear on all devices and the services in the domain should be available for use, unless there are problems. Figure 29-11 shows the context menu choice to indicate that a domain should be managed. This essentially gives you a clustered, redundant group of the managed domains, similar to a cluster of application server JVMs on WAS.

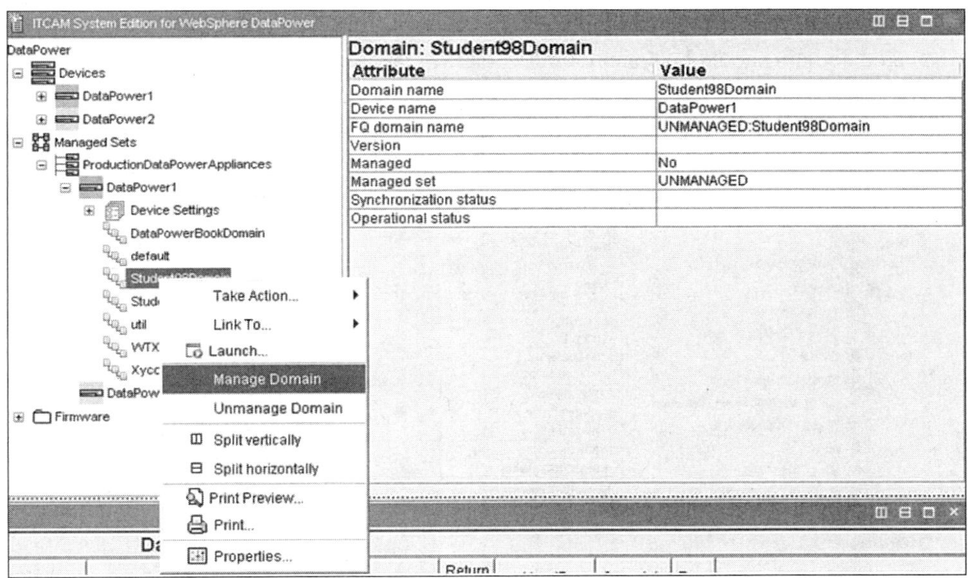

Figure 29-11 Managing a domain in a managed set.

There are certain caveats to managing a domain. The first goes back to a concept that we have stressed throughout this book: When keys and certificates are placed in the appliance's cert: directory, they cannot be copied from there. The impact for managed domains in ITCAMSEDP is that any configurations which depend on certs or keys from that directory will not work unless they are placed in advance. For this reason, a separate (perhaps scripted) process to distribute these crypto artifacts should be put in place as part of the process of configuring each device. This is not as big a problem as it might sound—these typically change once per year and remain fairly static. Most changes in a domain are configuration changes to the services running within it, or new versions of those services, which will be replicated to the managed set.

The second caveat revolves around the issues related to the IP addresses and ports used by the services. We have discussed techniques for keeping your configurations environment-agnostic and device-independent at length in Chapter 15, and those can be used successfully here as well. For example, it would be a problem if you ignored our advice and assigned specific hard-coded IP addresses in the listening front-side handlers for your services, and then those services were replicated throughout the managed set. The services would fail on startup when deployed to these other appliances, as the IP addresses would likely either be invalid for that subnet or seen as duplicates on the network should the source devices be addressable. However, if you used the Host Alias technique, all would be fine! The other solution would be to use 0.0.0.0 for all listening addresses, which we do not recommend. The listening ports used, of course, would have to be the same on all devices.

When the domain is flagged as managed, ITCAMSEDP backs up the domain configuration much like it did for the device settings when the device was added as master to the managed set. This is shown in Figure 29-12. At this point in the process, the synchronization is completed and the managed domain should be up and running on the DataPower2 device.

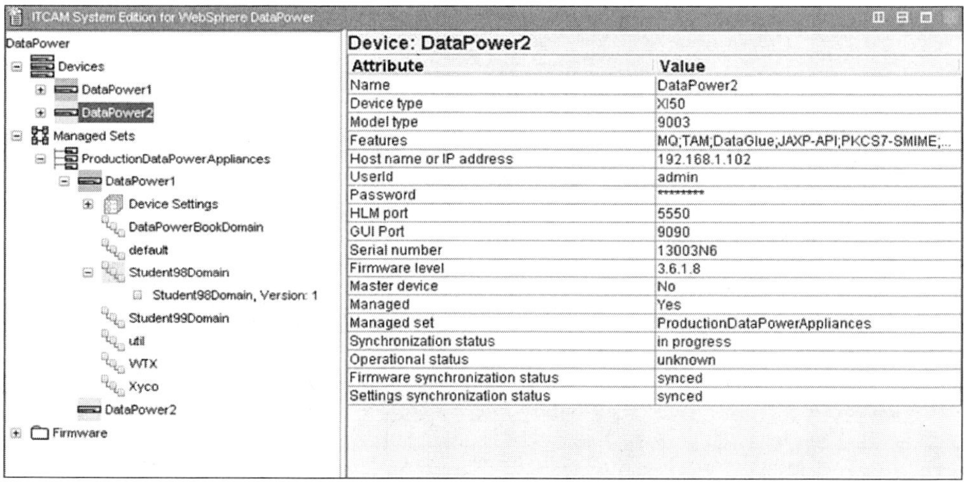

Figure 29-12 Backup completed for the new managed domain.

You may be wondering what "behind the scenes" mechanisms actually keep the devices in sync via the ITCAMSEDP utility. The utility actually configures a log target called DeMI on the master device. The log target notifies ITCAMSEDP when any significant events occur. This log target is shown in Figure 29-13. Notice that it sends the events to the server running ITCAMSEDP, which is listening on port 5555. The log format is Common Base Event (CBE), a standardized SOAP schema for logging events. Keep in mind that this port must be open on your firewalls for these messages to flow between DataPower and the utility.

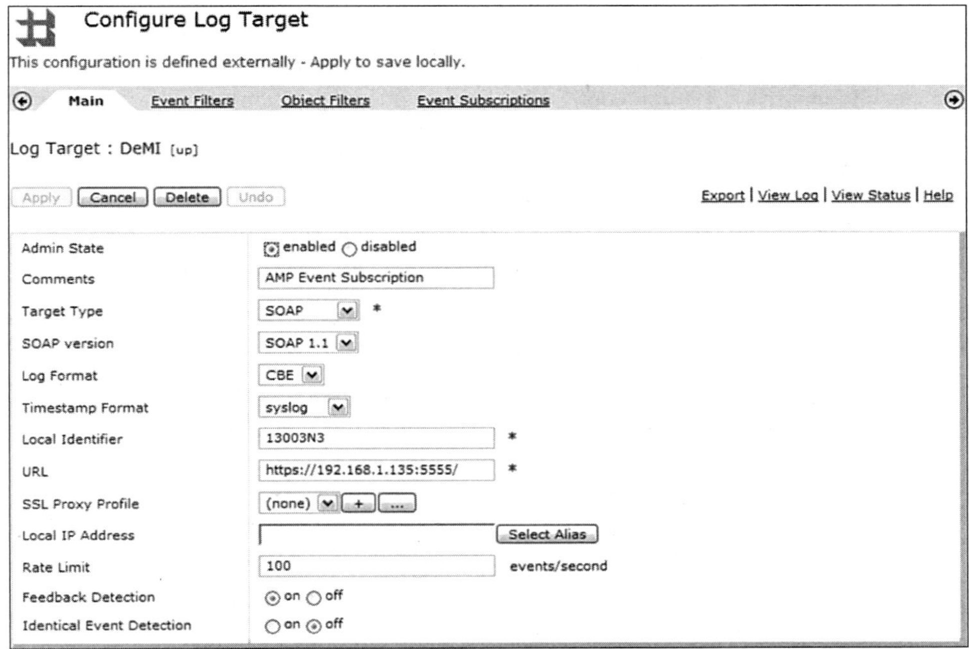

Figure 29-13 Log target for significant events to ITCAMSEDP.

The specific events that this log target is configured to listen for on the Event Filters tab as shown in Listing 29-1.

Listing 29-1 Event Filters Configured for the DeMI Log Target

```
Event Code 0x080400003 - The system will be shutdown.
Event Code 0x08100006a - The domain has been disabled.
Event Code 0x08100006b - The domain has been enabled.
Event Code 0x08100006c - The device firmware has been updated
Event Code 0x08100006e - The startup config for the device is executed.
Event Code 0x8100003b - The domain has been configured successfully.
Event Code 0x8100003e - Unpersisted configuration changes have been
reverted.
Event Code 0x8100003f - The domain configuration contains unpersisted
changes.
Event Code 0x81000040 - The domain configuration has been saved.
Event Code 0x81000041 - Domain restart has been initiated.
```

The most common sequence of events is that some administrative change is made to the master device, and when the configuration is saved (via the Save Config link in the WebGUI, write mem CLI command, or save-config XML Management operation), a notification is sent to ITCAMSEDP, which then calculates the changes and pushes them to the other devices in the managed set. This is the same sequence for both device settings and the managed domains. As you can imagine, it would be a better approach to batch up the changes by scripting your administration and then commit them in one shot, rather than use the WebGUI and take the chance that someone will click the Save Config link when changes are only partially in place.

TIP—CHANGE ONLY THE MASTER DEVICE!

It is important to realize that changing the non-master members of the managed sets in the area of shared device settings or any managed domains will result in those changes being overwritten at the next synchronization!

In summary, you can now see how using a disciplined, scripted approach to doing build and deploys of the configurations to each environment, as shown in Chapter 15, would need to update the master device only in each lifecycle area, and ITCAMSEDP would take care of the rest.

WebSphere Application Server v7 Administration Console

WebSphere Application Server (WAS) is IBM's flagship Java Platform, Enterprise Edition (Java EE) application server and Web services provider platform. WAS is used as the foundation run-time for many other IBM software products, and as such there is a unified administrative interface for these products, used with Web browsers, which is referred to as the Integrated Solutions Console (ISC).

Version 7 of WAS introduced some powerful new management capabilities for DataPower so that users of both WAS and DataPower could have a "one-stop shopping" solution for this type of administration. Essentially, these are the same features (minus SNMP) that the ITCAMSEDP utility provides, as discussed in the previous section. In fact, both tools act as a user interface shell over the same runtime code.

Out of necessity, there is some WAS-specific jargon used in this section. For those unfamiliar with some of these terms, see Chapter 21, "Security Integration with WebSphere Application Server."

To compare and contrast the two utilities, we will use the same scenario as discussed previously, but this time, we use the WAS ISC. This should all look familiar if you read the previous section.

Figure 29-14 shows a new device being added to the configuration, as was the first step in our prior scenario. The same bits of information are required as when adding the device in ITCAMSEDP.

After the device is added, it is interrogated by the ISC for its configuration. Figure 29-15 shows the result of this operation.

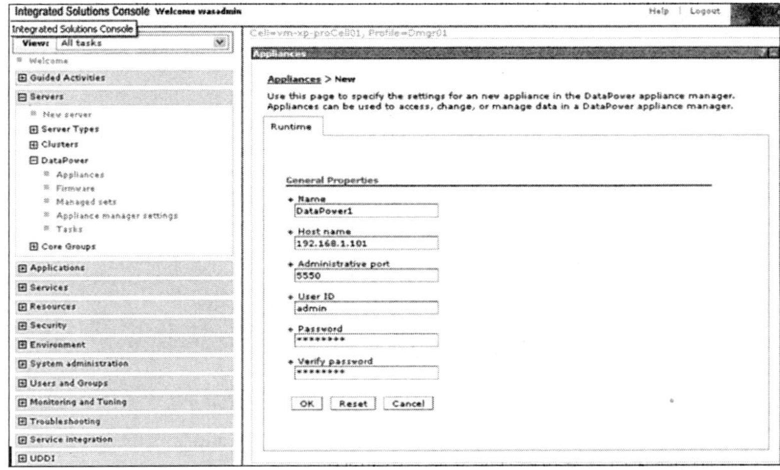

Figure 29-14 WAS ISC page for adding a new DataPower device.

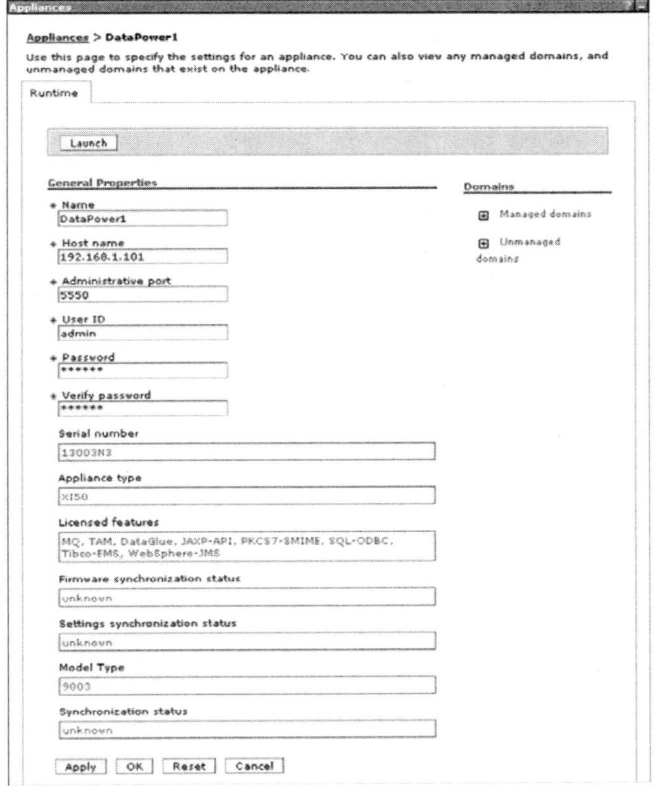

Figure 29-15 Device configuration as interrogated by the WAS ISC.

As with ITCAMSEDP, the ISC can act as a firmware repository to distribute firmware to the members of a managed set. Figure 29-16 shows a firmware version that has been loaded into the console.

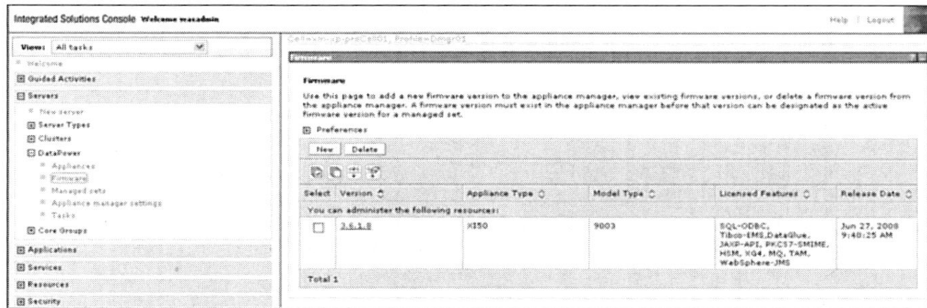

Figure 29-16 A firmware image added to the ISC.

With a device and firmware configured, a managed set can now be added. Figure 29-17 shows the name and device provided to the ISC.

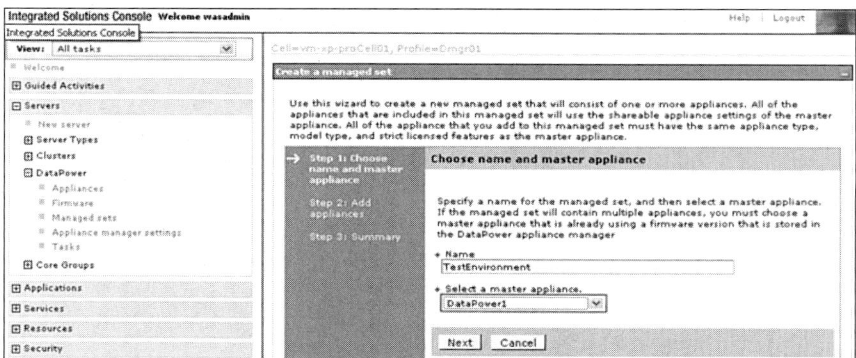

Figure 29-17 A managed set being created.

In Figure 29-18, a second device named DataPower2 is identified to the ISC to be included in the managed set. Notice in this figure how DataPower1 is indicated as the master appliance.

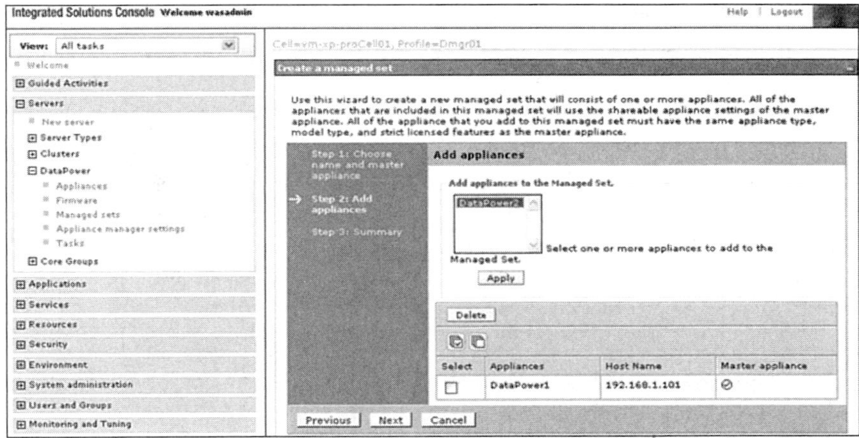

Figure 29-18 Adding DataPower2 to the managed set.

In Figure 29-19, a managed set with two appliances is now configured.

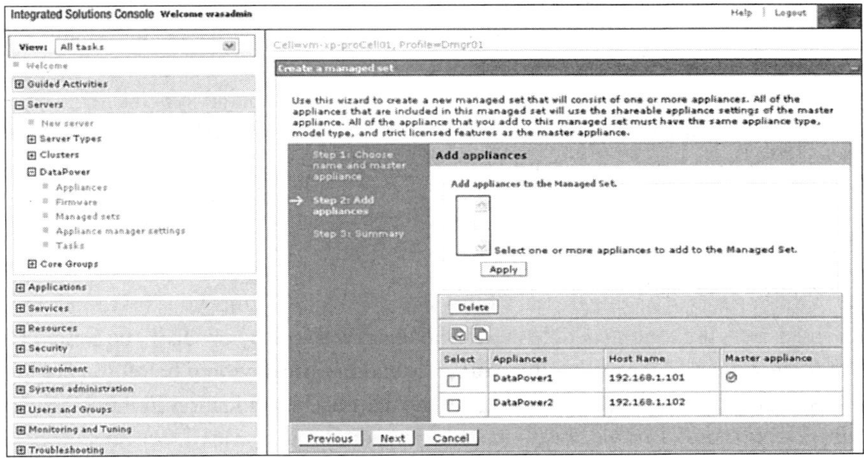

Figure 29-19 A managed set consisting of two devices.

While these administrative changes are being made, the ISC logs events to its own console. These can be viewed from the left-side Servers→DataPower→Tasks menu, as shown in Figure 29-20.

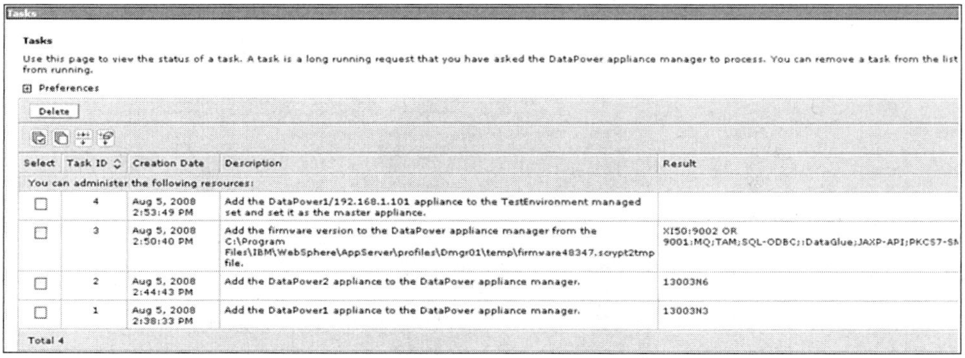

Tasks

Tasks

Use this page to view the status of a task. A task is a long running request that you have asked the DataPower appliance manager to process. You can remove a task from the list from running.

Preferences

Delete

Select	Task ID	Creation Date	Description	Result
You can administer the following resources:				
☐	4	Aug 5, 2008 2:53:49 PM	Add the DataPower1/192.168.1.101 appliance to the TestEnvironment managed set and set it as the master appliance.	
☐	3	Aug 5, 2008 2:50:40 PM	Add the firmware version to the DataPower appliance manager from the C:\Program Files\IBM\WebSphere\AppServer\profiles\Dmgr01\temp\firmware48347.scrypt2tmp file.	XI50:9002 OR 9001:MQ;TAM;SQL-ODBC;:DataGlue;JAXP-API;PKCS7-SM
☐	2	Aug 5, 2008 2:44:43 PM	Add the DataPower2 appliance to the DataPower appliance manager.	13003N6
☐	1	Aug 5, 2008 2:38:33 PM	Add the DataPower1 appliance to the DataPower appliance manager.	13003N3

Total 4

Figure 29-20 Log messages showing administrative activity.

Most of the work for administering the managed sets of devices can be done from the Servers→DataPower→Managed sets menu choice. In Figure 29-21, we have selected our managed set, and you can see that there are many options on this one page. The firmware level for the managed set can be changed, version history can be perused, the WebGUI can be launched (a nice feature here is that you are automatically logged in), and devices and managed domains can be added or removed.

Figure 29-21 also shows that we have expanded the list of unmanaged domains on the master appliance, right-clicked the DataPowerBookDomain domain, and selected to manage it. It then appears in the Managed domains list, and the same set of backup and synchronization operations occur as discussed when we did this in the ITCAMSEDP tool. The figure shows that both devices in the managed set have been successfully synchronized.

As with ITCAMSEDP, a log target named DeMI is created on the master appliance. This log target reports significant events to the WAS ISC. The set of event filters that is configured is the same as those used by ITCAMSEDP.

One of the benefits of having this capability in the WAS ISC is that you have access to the wealth of logging and debugging tools available there. Major errors should show up in the SystemOut.log file in the WAS Deployment Manager log directory. If you don't see anything helpful in the log, you can turn on WAS tracing by using com.ibm.datapower.*=all trace specification in the WAS Deployment Manager trace. By default, that will result in a file named trace.log (with a lot of detail) being created in the Deployment Manager log directory. Of course, you can also view the log target on the DataPower appliances to look for problems.

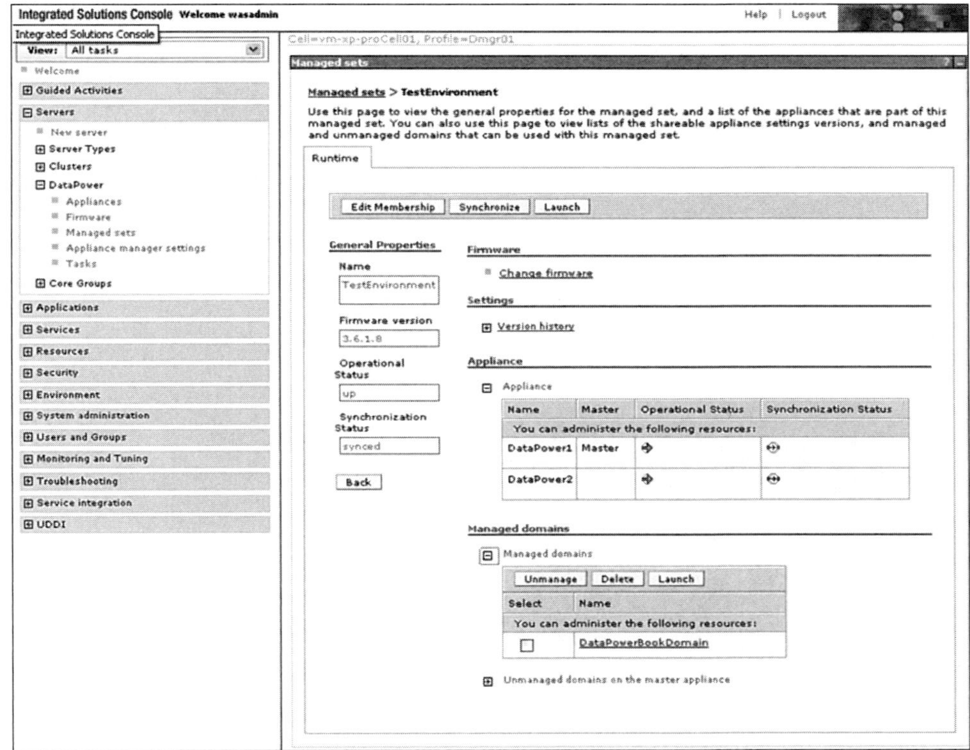

Figure 29-21 The ISC page for administering the managed set.

Summary

In this chapter, we introduced you to one custom technique and two "productized" techniques for managing multiple DataPower appliances in an environment. These techniques enable you to keep device configurations in sync, to cluster specific application domains, and replicate firmware versions across groups of devices called managed sets. Used in conjunction with the deployment approaches discussed in Chapter 15, these combine for powerful administrative processes when used properly. As you can tell, we heavily favor scripted approaches to deployment for a well-tested, reproducible systematic process rather than relying on humans using the WebGUI.

Part VIII

Appendixes

APPENDIX A

DataPower Naming Conventions

This appendix is designed to give some insight into the process of naming DataPower configuration objects, as well as providing some example names that follow the guidelines. Though every enterprise will have its own internal naming conventions that must be taken into account during a DataPower implementation, it is almost guaranteed that those conventions will not extend to the specificity needed by the multitude of internal DataPower objects.

Developers and administrators also have their own preferences for case, concatenation, and abbreviation. Feel free to impose those preferences on these guidelines. This text uses CamelCase[1]; however, hyphenated (-) names, underscored (_) names, and ALL_CAPS names are also acceptable (syntactically) as DataPower object names. Use your favorite. Even if you don't agree with these conventions, it's important to follow standard naming rules in your DataPower configurations for reusability and for collaboration.

Note that the examples in this book are just that, examples. As such, they do not always follow these naming guidelines; they are designed more for demonstration purposes than for true configuration creation.

General Guidelines

These guidelines are designed for maximum reusability, from both configuration management and environment promotion perspectives. Though ideal conditions may dictate that each logical environment (development, testing, preproduction, and production) have its own DataPower device, this is sometimes not the case in real-world situations. Usually, there is a load-balanced group of

[1] CamelCase is the practice of concatenating capitalized words without spaces to allow for syntax requirements that disallow whitespace. This document specifically uses UpperCamelCase, in which the first letter is also capitalized.

two or more devices in production, hopefully with an exact replica in pre-production and/or disaster recovery. Occasionally, all other environments are shared on a single device. This setup is definitely *not* recommended and introduces additional complexity for environment promotion.

Although this is essentially a configuration management issue, it has an effect on naming conventions as well. Objects should be able to be moved from domain to domain (and device to device) with minimal manual modifications, as described in Chapter 15, "Build and Deploy Techniques." Ideally, this will be a completely automated process, and the more changes that have to be made (to an XML config file, CLI script, or XML Management request), the more complicated and error-prone the process becomes. So, when in doubt, design for clarity and reusability.

The other important principle to keep in mind is functional explanation. In a clear but concise manner, an object's name should represent the functional logic of the configuration held within. It should be instantly recognizable by both you and any of your colleagues, and when seen in context with its object type, it should represent the task it performs.

> **Name Changes**
>
> After an object has been created with a given name, that name cannot be easily modified. As such, make sure you get the name right the first time and verify that your name will represent the object in every environment to which it can potentially be deployed.

Names

The suggested naming conventions are grouped by object or object category. Each contains the naming scheme, at least one example, and some explicative reasoning for why the naming choice has been made.

Device

There are few places where devices actually require names (other than their several TCP/IP hostnames for connectivity). They usually require a name when used as an identifier to external servers, such as syslog daemons, or as a notice on the login page. The audience for these names will sometimes be different than the DataPower development audience and, thus, may be designated by personnel in other departments (typically, networking or security). These names must differentiate between multiple devices in a given environment, sometimes even between this and other nonappliance servers and routers, and may need to contain hints about physical location. As such, this is one of the least standardized names. We strongly suggest you name all of your devices by navigating to Administration→Device→System Settings in the left-side menu and choosing a System Identifier; here are a few examples:

- XmlGwDMZ01
- XS40Dev03
- DPProd17
- XI50TucsonStaging02

Application Domain

The name of an application domain depends quite a bit on your designated architecture, from device management, project management, and environment promotion perspectives. Domains can be created for a development team, a project team, or even for a single user (in a development setting). Single user and other sandbox domain names are less important than those that might travel between appliances, but their names should still be descriptive. For those that will be promoted between environments, the name should contain the development group or project name. If DataPower appliances are deployed in multiple corporate security zones, each with its own version of a domain, then the name should also reflect its eventual destination, even if all development is done on a single internal device. Here are a few options:

- HRServices
- AccountServicesDMZ
- AccountServicesInternal
- NextGenInfrastructure
- JoeSmith
- MainframeServices

Service

A service name should give some indication of what is represented by the configuration. In a Web Service Proxy (WSP), this generally means the service it protects; however, WSPs can also contain multiple WSDLs, each referencing a related service with unique features. In these cases, the name should be more generic, representing the full cluster of categorized services. In these cases, when built upon one or more Web services, the name will often be followed by "Service" or "Services." For services without an existing Web service name, you should consider the full path of a message that might be flowing through this service: it will enter the device in a particular format on a given protocol, be processed in some fashion, and be delivered to a backend server in (perhaps) another format or protocol. Your name should reflect the full progression, especially if there will be a format, protocol, or message transformation involved. Here are some examples:

- ImagingService/ImagingServices
- MapHTTPToMQ
- ConvertEDIToXML
- BillingServices
- BridgeMQToEMS

What these names should *not* do is contain the name of the environment in which the service resides. Even if this is a development environment, naming your Web Service Proxy ImagingServiceDev will only cause problems when you go to promote this environment to QA. You should always look for this balance between generality and descriptiveness; keep it general enough to move between domains and environments, while still providing clues to the processing contained therein. Services are also always grouped by type when displayed by the administrative tools, so there's no need to distinguish between ImagingServiceMPGW, ImagingServiceXMLFW, and ImagingServiceWSP—just call it ImagingService.

> **Service Types**
>
> These service naming criteria apply to all major service types, including XML Firewall, Multiprotocol Gateway, Web Service Proxy, Web Application Firewall, XSL Proxy, and the lesser-known services available from the left-side menus.

Processing Policy

A processing policy is tied closely to the service in which it resides, as each service can contain only one policy. As such, a processing policy usually has the same name as its service, minus any reference to the protocols being invoked. A policy can be used by multiple services, perhaps of different types with different protocols; this name should focus entirely on the processing taking place within and ignore the type of service or the protocols for frontend and backend connections. ConvertEDIToXML is still a valid name because it focuses on the message format rather than the protocol; MapHTTPToMQ would be significantly less useful. In these cases, focus on the actions within: AddMQHeaders or RouteToMQBackend would be more appropriate. Note that policies within a Web Service Proxy are not named by the user and are not reusable in other services.

Processing Rule

A processing rule name should be much more specific than a processing policy, as a policy can contain multiple rules that perform different tasks. These objects are named automatically according to the processing policy if a name is not manually defined, but this simply appends a number to the policy name, such as PolicyName_rule_0. For more specificity and potential reuse, a rule should be named according to its processing logic. More importantly, the name should distinguish between different rules within the same policy; you should be able to determine their functional differences without inspecting the actions contained therein. A rule named StripAttachments is completely distinguishable from another named VirusCheckAttachments. If the rule performs more than one major function, feel free to concatenate the important ones. Focusing on the main purpose of a processing rule will result in names such as the following:

- ProcessAttachments
- StripAttachments
- SignEncrypt
- TransformSignEncrypt

If you are not interested in taking advantage of the reusability of these rules, and they will appear only in the processing policy in which they've been defined, you may want to include the processing policy name as a prefix. In this case, AttachmentServiceProcessAttachments and AttachmentServiceStripAttachments could be separate rules in the AttachmentService processing policy.

Match Rule

Each processing rule begins with a match action that defines which incoming messages will be executed by that rule. Match rules are reusable, so they should be named according to their matching criteria so that they may be used appropriately and easily. These criteria can vary widely because matching can take place on headers, URLs, error codes, and even message content. The following could all be useful matching rule names:

- MatchAll
- SAMLAssertion
- BackendConnectionError
- BinarySecurityToken

Front Side Handlers

Each MPGW or WSP service can have multiple Front Side Handlers, listening for requests on various protocols. These should be named according to the service to which they are attached and should include the protocol. For Web Service Proxies, this may reference a group of services. In addition, HTTP and HTTPS listeners can include a port, but *only* if this port will not be modified between environments. The port addition is especially useful when looking at a list of services or at a list of FSH within a service—the port is not shown unless you open the FSH object itself, so including the number (in an accurate and consistent manner) can save a step. Examples are as follows:

- ImagingServiceMQ
- HRServicesHttps443
- CreditServiceFTP

Keep in mind that these names can't be easily changed. If the HRServicesHttps443 Front Side Handler might be copied to another domain and modified to listen on 8443, then *don't* include the port number in the name!

XML Manager

Although many services can use the default XML Manager, simple changes often need to be made, such as the addition of a Load Balancer Group, modification of parser behavior, or definition of a caching policy. In these cases, you should always create a new XML Manager (don't modify the default one!) and name it after the modifications. This would result in names similar to the following:

- ParseRestrictions
- CacheDocuments
- BackendLoadBalancer

If you simply modify the default XML Manager, there is the potential to unwittingly impose those modifications on a new service that you (or someone else in the same domain) create in the future. That object is also less likely to be noticed and successfully imported when moving objects between domains or devices.

User Agent

In the same fashion that an XML Manager controls parsing and caching behavior for the incoming message, a user agent controls connection behavior between DataPower and any backend servers. Any user agent requirements should be created in a new object (don't modify the default one!) and should be named after the modifications contained therein. This results in names similar to the following:

- InjectSOAPActions
- FTPCredentials
- ProxyServerConfig
- HTTP10Policy

AAA Policy

Within a processing rule, a AAA policy can provide access control for inbound messages. These are highly reusable, as the accepted input credentials, authentication/authorization methodologies, and backend token formats are likely to be similar for various services. If the policy is being used for token exchange, its name should reflect the input and output token formats. BasicAuthToSAML and UsernameTokenToLTPA would be useful in this case. If the policy is simply authenticating and authorizing without producing a backend token, then you should name the policy based on the servers being used for each. LDAPAuth and TAMAuAz are both distinctive and descriptive.

Certificate

Certificate objects on the DataPower appliance encapsulate certificate files for abstraction purposes. This allows the actual file to have a name descriptive of the environment for which it is used, while keeping the object name generic enough to be promoted to a new environment without a need for modification. The object name should describe its place in the logical architecture rather than referencing a specific hostname. A certificate imported from an LDAP server for LDAPS interaction should be called LDAPServer, rather than DevLDAP. WASBackend could be another internal server, while InternalHRClient could represent a certificate used for mutual authentication to an internal HR application. XYCorpServices could represent the server certificate delivered by services.xyco.com; it is nonrepresentative of an application environment, but still self-explanatory.

Key

Key objects are generally paired to certificate objects that will be used on the device for encryption by a partner, SSL server identification, or digital signature creation. As such, the names of objects referencing key files should be tied very closely to the names of the objects referencing the certificate files with which they are paired. Because keys can be tied to multiple certificates, the common name included in a particular certificate should be excluded from the key name; aside from that, they should be exactly the same.

Identification Credential

An Identification Credential represents the pairing of a key object to a certificate object. They are then used for SSL server identification and other document encryption and decryption tasks. ID credentials should be named the same as the certificate they contain so that it is obvious which key pair they are referencing.

Validation Credential

A validation credential is used for verifying incoming certificates used for SSL mutual authentication and other cryptographic tasks. Because this object can contain multiple certificates, it is often impossible to reference them all in the object name. Focus on the group of certificate owners that need to be validated or the type of certificates expected. Sample names can be similar to the following:

- PublicCerts
- InternalCARoot
- DotNetWAS
- ApprovedExternalClients

Crypto Profile

A crypto profile provides a method for combining cryptographic objects for use in an SSL connection. The included objects depend on whether the appliance is acting as a server (backend) or a client (frontend) and whether Mutual Authentication is necessary. These two criteria, as well as an indication of the service itself, should be included in the crypto profile name. Use the service name, followed by the type of SSL (client or server) then followed by an optional MA for mutual authentication. This results in sample names such as the following:

- InternalServicesServer
- BackendServicesClient
- HRServicesServerMA

SSL Proxy Profile

A SSL proxy profile consists of either one or two Crypto Profile objects, tying those objects to a particular service as either a reverse (server) SSL connection, a forward (client) SSL connection, or a two-way (both server and client) connection. For forward or reverse, the object should have the exact same name as the crypto profiles they reference. For two-way SSL, remove the reference to Client or Server and replace it with the phrase TwoWay. This results in a name such as HRServicesTwoWayMA.

Queuing Technologies

The general category of queuing technologies encompasses several different DataPower objects. The same naming guidelines apply to each, as they all require an initial configuration of the connection to the management server—that object is then referenced in the actual connection URL or Front Side Handler. These objects include the MQ Queue Manager, Tibco EMS server, and WebSphereJMS; nonmessaging server interface objects such as IMS Connect and SQL Data Source would have similar naming conventions. Names for these objects should reference the logical architecture rather than their physical location or application environment. Avoid hostnames, references to development, QA, production, and datacenter names. If the queuing server will act as a bridge between two architectural zones, reference them both. There is no need to reference the protocol itself, as these objects are each in their own lists, categorized by object. Examples are as follows:

- DMZInternet
- DMZIntranet
- InternalWASCluster
- HRMainframeApp

Log Target

Log targets represent a subscription to a set of log events that will be designated to be sent to a specific target over any one of a number of protocols. A log target name should represent the type and priority of the events to which it is subscribed, as well as the target of those events. If there are filters on the events, the object or event being filtered should be included as well. Examples can include

- EmergencyToSNMP
- AlertToSMTP
- CertMonitorToAppSyslog
- AAAToSecuritySyslog
- HRServicesProxyErrorToFTP

Transforms (XSLT)

There are many cases in which files need to be uploaded to the device (or referenced from a remote location). There may be existing corporate naming conventions for files containing code; these conventions are available otherwise. For XSLT stylesheet files that will be used in Transform actions, names should represent the logic inherent within. Here are some examples:

- CheckAttachment.xsl
- StripWSSecurity.xsl
- AuthorizeLDAPGroups.xsl

Filters (XSLT)

Filter files are also XSLT transformations and should also be named by logic. However, because these will be used in a Filter action, that should be appended to the end of the filename. An example of a filter that checks for negative inputs would be SQLInjectionFilter.xsl, while one that checks for valid inputs would be ValidFormContentsFilter.xsl.

Configuration Files (XML)

Additional XML files used for configurations, user data, and other on-board uses should be named for the data contained within. Example names could be UserRegistry.xml, RoutingTable.xml, or AAAForHR.xml.

Summary

There are many objects that can be configured on the DataPower appliance, including some that are not explicitly referenced in this chapter. As long as you keep in mind the two guiding principles for name creation—descriptiveness and reusability/portability—you should be able to extend the concepts laid out here to fit any other object on the device. The names will then become common sense, and you can create objects named HRServicesDevelopers (for a User-Group), PerMappedCredential (for a SLM Credential Class), and EncryptSocSecNbr (for a Document Crypto Map). Following these guidelines will assist with collaboration, reuse, and easy documentation among development groups. Use them to finalize your own naming conventions that will be used and enforced in your environment.

APPENDIX B

Deployment Checklist

DataPower is well known for its ease of configuration. Those quick configuration exercises are great for demos and quick one-off tests, but when it comes to rolling out anything into production, great care must be taken. Often, the best-laid deployment plans go awry due to haste, lack of planning, or miscommunication. It takes only one missed step during deployment to thwart the careful planning and hard work of entire teams of architects, developers, and testers. Backing out a botched deploy isn't pleasant. The deployment process is something that is best done quickly and efficiently, particularly because, in some cases, systems are down or applications are unavailable during deployment. This appendix provides a checklist of things to think about before the actual process starts. This can (and should) be augmented with many of the other environment-specific tips and techniques found in the text of this book.

Testing

T1. Have unit, integrated, performance, functional, and acceptance testing been completed satisfactorily? Just because DataPower is an appliance does not mean that testing should not be done. Testing against this platform using the same tools and methodologies you test your transactional backend systems with is important. What are the detailed, reproducible, and carefully reviewed results of these tests? (Yes, those things are all important.)

T2. Can all Service Level Agreements (SLA), such as response time under a peak-simulated load, be met, including the overhead of authentication/authorization if they are required? Is this also the case when failover occurs during reasonable failure scenarios? If DataPower is configured for high availability and some of the dependent components (such as LDAP directories) are not, then you do not have high availability. The system has a single point of failure (SPOF) and can be brought down by the failure of a single component.

T3. Has failover been verified by "disconnecting" components to simulate runtime failures? Do any single points of failure exist and has the "Rule of Threes" (if it takes two of something to handle peak load, then you need three in case one fails) been taken into account? Has failover testing been done while load testing is under way to test the behavior under duress? Remember, high availability is a systemwide thing, and should also be tested (no matter how painful it is to pull that plug).

T4. Were the final pre-production or staging tests done in an environment identical to production? (Or if not, are the deltas and associated risks well documented?)

T5. Have members of other infrastructure areas (network, database, and operating system) been involved in testing and have they made tuning changes to accommodate the new deployment?

T6. Have all functional and nonfunctional requirements been signed off?

T7. Have the users been prepared and trained? Will they have the opportunity to use the prior version for some period of time?

Security

S1. Have security requirements been carefully defined and the system implementation evaluated against those requirements? Has a security expert reviewed the system design and implementation? Have all system components outside of DataPower been hardened? Has the network topology been reviewed for possible sensitive traffic "in the clear"?

S2. Has the DataPower system certificate been replaced with a self-signed certificate or certificate from a legitimate Certificate Authority? Instructions for doing this are in the WebGUI Guide.

S3. Has any form of ethical hacking been done, at a minimum turning some of the more "creative" employees loose on the system as a challenge?

S4. Have expiration dates been checked and documented on all certificates and passwords? Is there a clear plan for updating these when needed? Is monitoring in place to alert administrators when they near expiration? (Don't depend on someone checking the logs on a regular basis!)

S5. Has it been verified that all identities used for connecting to backend resources, such as databases, are valid for the new environment being deployed to and have the correct privileges assigned to them?

S6. Have access violations been captured in a Log Target and rolled off the device to a persistent location? Tracking these may help to identify attempts to compromise the system.

S7. Has administrative access to the device been limited to a well-defined group of users connecting on a management network? Make sure everyone isn't sharing a single admin account, particularly not the "admin" userid.

S8. Have password policies been established to ensure they meet internal security policies and are changed periodically?

Environment

E1. Will all necessary userids/passwords for DataPower and other components be available for the deployment? It is a common theme to get to the deployment date and not have correct privileges to deploy some component into the target environment—for example, not having the admin

password for a firewall to allow traffic to pass from DataPower to the backend over the configured port(s).
E2. Has it been verified that all infrastructure components are fully operational, with no errors occurring in the logs? As part of "sanity checking," all logs should be checked for DataPower and other system components to ensure there are no early warning signs of production failure when the go switch is flipped.
E3. Is all necessary information (for example, server names and port numbers) available for resources such as databases or legacy systems? Has connectivity to these resources from the target environment been verified?
E4. Have all network traffic routes through firewalls, switches, and routers been verified? Are documents showing the topology, firewall rules, and so on up to date and available for troubleshooting?
E5. Are Log Targets being used to capture critical log events and are they being moved off the device to persistent locations?
E6. Is there plenty of space on persistent volumes used for logging? Has capacity planning been done for all system components?
E7. Has configuration data for both pre-deploy and post-deploy been checked into change management?
E8. Has it been verified that there is appropriate monitoring and that alerts go to the appropriate places?
E9. Are all commercial software infrastructure components at the appropriate version/fixpack levels? Are all vendor prerequisites in place?
E10. Have all "test harnesses" or test-only configurations and stubs been removed?
E11. Have configurations for logging been turned down to production levels? You don't want to go live with logging set at the debug level!
E12. Have all probes been disabled in all domains in all devices? Having these enabled can impact performance as well as the security of sensitive production data.

Deployment Process

D1. Have all team member responsibilities and their status for the deployment date been verified?
D2. Is there a well-defined reproducible deployment process? There should be a clear document describing the process. Is the deployment process automated? If not, see Chapter 15, "Build and Deploy Techniques."
D3. Have deployment scripts (where used) been verified prior to deployment in production-like environments? It is important to test and exercise these scripts as part of moving the configuration through the various stages of testing—unit, integration, performance, QA, failover, system, preproduction—to ensure that the deployment scripts themselves work and will not fail at the critical hour. Deployment should be a fast and boring job!
D4. Has the build been verified to include all components at the correct version level if you are building your domains in a granular fashion (for example, creating a new domain and importing services or below in the object hierarchy from version control)?

D5. Have all team members reviewed the rollout plan (downtime, rolling servers, and so on)?

D6. Have arrangements been made to have representatives of various infrastructure areas such as network, operating system, legacy system, and database admins available in case there are problems? Have those persons been briefed on how the new DataPower applications interact with their areas, so they can anticipate problems or react more quickly should they occur?

D7. Will the DataPower application architect and key developers be available for troubleshooting in case there are problems?

D8. Are initialization scripts—such as those to "prime" the application's listeners and caches after it has been deployed, or precompile stylesheets, or test for successful response codes from applications—in place and tested?

D9. Is there a test for success for the production deployment and a backout plan in case of problems? Has the backup plan been tested? This is a critical step that is often forgotten due to teams focusing on the "happy path."

D10. Are all team members in agreement that the deployment should proceed? Ask one more time to "speak now or forever hold your peace."

D11. Have separate provisions been made to deploy artifacts that are not exported by DataPower (and related tools such as ITCAM SE for DataPower), such as keys and certificates and user account passwords?

Administration

A1. Are all DataPower administrative IDs/roles in place on the device or for RBM?

A2. Is there a process for log file review and archival?

A3. Have all operational procedures (such as backup, disaster recovery) been tested?

A4. Are all product licenses and support agreements up to date for the intended environment?

A5. Has the help desk received proper training and documentation on the new deployment? Is there a well-defined process for fixing production problems? This includes well-defined phone numbers, pager access numbers, call lists, and escalation procedures.

A6. Have the IBM Customer Account information and contact procedures been supplied to the help desk should they need to contact IBM DataPower Support?

A7. Is a system monitoring process in place? How will the system be monitored to ensure that it is running? How will its logs and errors be monitored to capture potential problems before they become serious?

A8. Does the monitoring process include monitoring load and other resource usage? Is that information being used to predict future load and system needs? Have you taken into account load spikes that might be based on calendar events or perhaps special marketing events?

We've tried to pick out the "usual suspects" in terms of things to look out for as deployment to production nears. We're sure there are others that have occurred to you as you read this. This list should be customized for your own environment and requirements. It's meant to be just a start, but hopefully a good one!

APPENDIX C

DataPower Evolution

Just like any hardware or software product, DataPower has evolved over time and will continue to advance to meet the changing needs of its customers and the evolving IT industry. This appendix takes a brief look at the past, present, and future of DataPower and its product line. We discuss its history (both corporate and technical) to demonstrate how the DataPower product line has grown with the market for such devices. We discuss specific updates in both hardware and firmware, and the progression of the appliance model as applied to industry verticals.

DataPower History

DataPower was originally formed by a group of MIT alumni with an interest in using hardware appliances to solve problems that were traditionally approached with a focus on software solutions. In the process, they created a new market for network devices geared toward service-oriented architectures. IBM acquired DataPower in October 2005; it now exists as the SOA Appliance division within IBM's WebSphere brand. Through it all, DataPower's technical solutions have continued to evolve with the changing of the IT landscape.

Performance

DataPower appeared in 1999 as a response to the advent and increasing popularity of XML as a message format. Though much more human-readable and self-descriptive than previously defined formats such as EDI, CSV, and Cobol Copybooks, XML is also verbose, resulting in a large memory and CPU footprint when parsed or transformed. Existing software parsers based solely on Document Object Model (DOM) or Simple API for XML (SAX) methodologies were slow and had significant drawbacks; transformation and schema validation engines were even less efficient. DataPower overcame these performance implications using a new, patented parser technology to create a secure, efficient platform for XML processing and transformation. When combined with specialized hardware for execution of these expensive operations, the eventual result of these efforts was the DataPower XA35 XML Acceleration appliance.

Security

XML parsing performance improvements made DataPower appliances an invaluable addition to many IT architectures requiring accelerated rendering of XML content as HTML, WML (Wireless Markup Language), and other browser-based formats. As XML usage matured, however, it began to be used for more than just content storage; communication of XML formatted messages to business partners allowed for easy data exchange. Message structures could be defined using standard specifications (XML Schema), and data arrived in a self-descriptive format that required less in the way of tight coupling between applications and software platforms. The ability to share data, even at high speeds, came with a price; DataPower recognized that the security of this data (privacy, integrity, and access control) was paramount to the success of this new paradigm. As the initial specifications around Web services arose (SOAP and WSDL, especially), the need for related security standards became obvious. The WS-Security specifications fit the bill but were complex and difficult to implement. The DataPower XS40 Security Appliance addresses this challenge, enforcing security policies and implementing complex encryption and digital signature specifications at wire speed through a user-friendly click-to-configure GUI. With a sophisticated interface and full support for many industry-standard security protocols, the XS40 shortened time-to-market and increased confidence in application security.

Integration

Often, industry trends come full circle. Though the popularity of XML is in part a response to the complex, machine-readable data formats of yesteryear, those old formats (and the applications that rely on them) will not soon fade away. Instead, the challenge is to re-use those existing applications and make them available as services, while at the same time incorporating advanced security and performance characteristics. The DataPower XI50 Integration Appliance addresses this need through support for many protocols, including messaging technologies (WebSphere MQ, WebSphere JMS, and Tibco EMS), common mainframe interfaces such as IMS, and database and file interfaces (SQL, FTP, and NFS). In addition, the XI50 can perform any-to-any message format transformation, allowing access to applications written in COBOL and other legacy languages.

DataPower Hardware

Though DataPower hardware has had several revisions in the many years since the company's founding, the truly important evolution has been in the area of firmware. The firmware contains the patented technologies used for message processing; the SSL and cryptographic hardware accelerators don't need to be updated to add additional features. In fact, many devices from the original hardware generation (known as the 9001 generation) are still in production with customers today, though IBM support for this hardware was withdrawn effective December 31, 2008.

Subsequent hardware generations (9002 and 9003) were very similar to the 9001, with minor updates in certain components. Both have four Ethernet interfaces and use flash memory as an on-device store; the 9003 hardware also has dual power supplies.

The hardware model known as the 9004 generation (or machine type 9235) adds additional on-board storage, with a choice between a RAID-mirrored pair of hard drives and a user-replaceable Compact Flash drive. It also contains iSCSI support for connections to Storage Area Networks (SAN). These additions allow for significant local logging if desired; the Compact Flash support continues to provide an alternative option with no spinning media. Prior to the 9004 hardware, any hardware issues were subject to the replacement of the entire device. The 9004 model introduced user-swappable power supplies, hard drives, fans, and battery.

DataPower Firmware

As mentioned earlier, the true power of DataPower functionality lies within the device's firmware. This user-upgradeable firmware image contains all the features and specification support used by the device and is constantly evolving with changing IT and Web services standards.

DataPower maintains a firmware release schedule dedicated to providing maximum customer value with a manageable volume of new releases. Releases come approximately four times per year, with two major and two minor revisions. In addition, point releases are made available for bug fixes and other minor modifications. Each image is accompanied by release notes describing any behavior changes, documentation updates, and known issues.

Though this book is focused on recent firmware releases and includes discussion of new and evolving features, previous firmware revisions may not contain some of the functionality we have discussed. The release notes and user documentation for your firmware image should be used as the final authority on what features are available.

Similarly, DataPower is constantly adding new features, some of which may not be described within this book. As the specifications surrounding Web services evolve, so too does the DataPower firmware. As an example, some past additions have involved support for nonstandard (Microsoft and BEA) WS-Policy implementations, enhancements to the existing Tibco EMS support, and even additional protocol support in the form of SFTP Server functionality on a Front Side Handler. Check the release notes for all the latest changes.

As Web services standards rapidly change to meet a fluid marketplace, DataPower shields applications from needing to update their programming. DataPower is dedicated to keeping up with these evolving standards, and firmware releases are frequent enough to support new standard levels as they become accepted within the industry.

Additional Appliances

The value of using a network device to commoditize complex processes with simple configurations has been well demonstrated by IBM's success with the DataPower product line. However, broad concepts such as security and integration are not the only arenas that can benefit from this technology. Companies in some industries can also gain a competitive edge using the appliance model for more specific challenges.

B2B Appliance

The DataPower XB60 B2B Appliance provides a high throughput secure entry point at the edge for routing data into the enterprise. Specifically geared toward protocols such as AS2 and AS3, this device leverages DataPower's core performance, security, and integration features to provide value in a B2B environment.

Core capabilities of the XB60, which is purple in color, include trading partner profile management, a B2B transaction viewer, and end-to-end document correlation. This device provides a hardened infrastructure for protocol and message level security in DMZ deployments and a full-featured user interface for simplified B2B configuration, management, and deployment.

Low Latency Messaging Appliance

The DataPower XM70 Low Latency Messaging (LLM) Appliance provides a simplified, configuration-driven approach to low-latency publish-subscribe messaging and content-based routing. It combines the power of a drop-in network solution with powerful LLM technologies to achieve enhanced quality of service and performance. In financial, government, and energy markets, this appliance can act as a highly available messaging backbone for data feeds and other high-volume transactions.

Principal features of the XM70, which is silver in color, include highly scalable unicast and multicast messaging with minimal latency, native XML and FIX parsers for routing based on destination, property, or message content, and optimized bridging to standard messaging protocols such as MQ, Tibco, WebSphere JMS, and HTTP(S). Simplified interfaces for configuration and management of messaging destinations and routing provide quicker time to value than non-appliance solutions.

Other Appliances?

Though the precise nature of any future appliances is confidential, consider some of the potential realms in which a high-performance, easily configurable appliance form factor could assist in your IT architecture. Add to that IBM's existing investments in identity management, data storage, messaging, and mainframe form factors, and you may be able to guess at some possible additions to the product line. The IT industry is also filled with verticals requiring their own protocols and data formats—appliances could assist in these realms as well. In the end, the IBM WebSphere DataPower Appliance division has an incredibly broad potential—our success is limited only by our imagination.

Summary

This appendix and this book focuses on various aspects of the DataPower SOA Appliances, from hardware to firmware to features. You've learned how these devices are purpose-built to solve IT problems and how you can configure them to perform valuable, reusable tasks in a variety of different use cases. We hope you have gained enough insight to use these appliances, introduce them into your architectures, and love them as much as we do. Good luck!

APPENDIX D

Acronyms Glossary

Acronym	Meaning
AAA	Authentication, Authorization, Auditing
ACL	Access Control List
AJAX	Asynchronous JavaScript and XML
ARP	Address Resolution Protocol
BST	Binary Security Token
CA	Certificate Authority
CIDR	Classless Inter-Domain Routing
CLI	Command Line Interface
CSV	Comma Separated Values
DHCP	Dynamic Host Configuration Protocol
DIME	Direct Internet Message Encapsulation
DMZ	Demilitarized Zone
DN	Distinguished Name
DNS	Domain Name System
DOM	Document Object Model
DSIG	Digital Signature
DTD	Data Type Definition

Acronym	Meaning
EDI	Electronic Data Interchange
EMS	Enhanced Messaging Service or Enterprise Messaging Service
ESB	Enterprise Service Bus
FFD	Flat File Descriptor
FTP	File Transfer Protocol
FTPS	File Transfer Protocol over Secure Socket Layer
HMAC	Hash Message Authentication Code
HSM	Hardware Storage Module
HTTP	Hypertext Transfer Protocol
HTTPS	Hypertext Transfer Protocol over Secure Socket Layer
ICAP	Internet Content Adaptation Protocol
ICMP	Internet Control Message Protocol
IDE	Integrated Development Environment
IDS	Intrusion Detection System
IMS	Information Management System
IP	Internet Protocol
iSCSI	Internet Small Computer System Interface
Java EE	Java Enterprise Edition
JDBC	Java Database Connectivity
JMS	Java Message Service
JVM	Java Virtual Machine
KDC	Key Distribution Center
LDAP	Lightweight Directory Access Protocol
LTPA	Lightweight Third-Party Authentication
MAC	Media Access Control
MD5	Message Digest Algorithm Number 5
MIB	Management Information Base
MIME	Multipurpose Internet Mail Extensions
MQ	IBM WebSphere MQ

Acronym	Meaning
MQMD	MQ Message Descriptor
MTOM	Message Transmission Optimization Mechanism
NFS	Network File System
NTP	Network Time Protocol
ODBC	Open Database Connectivity
OID	Object Identifier
PDP	Policy Decision Point
PEP	Policy Enforcement Point
PKI	Public Key Infrastructure
PCRE	Perl Compatible Regular Expression
QA	Quality Assurance
QM	Queue Manager
RAID	Redundant Array of Independent Disks
REST	Representational State Transfer
RFC	Request For Comments
RFH	MQ Rules and Formatting Header
RFH2	MQ Rules and Formatting Header 2
SAML	Security Assertion Markup Language
SAN	Storage Area Network
SAX	Simple API for XML
SCM	Source Configuration Management
SCP	Secure Copy Protocol
SFTP	Secure File Transfer Protocol
SHA-1	Secure Hash Algorithm number 1
SLA	Service Level Agreement
SLM	Service Level Monitoring or Service Level Management
SMTP	Simple Mail Transfer Protocol
SNMP	Simple Network Management Protocol
SOA	Service Oriented Architecture

Acronym	Meaning
SOAP	Once known as Simple Object Access Protocol, though no longer an acronym
SPNEGO	Simple and Protected GSS API Negotiation Mechanism
SQL	Structured Query Language
SSH	Secure Shell
SSL	Secure Sockets Layer
TAM	Tivoli Access Manager
TCP	Transmission Control Protocol
TFIM	Tivoli Federated Identity Manager
TLS	Transport Layer Security
UDDI	Universal Description Discovery and Integration
UDP	User Datagram Protocol
UNT	Username Token
URI	Uniform Resource Identifier
URL	Uniform Resource Locator
WSDL	Web Services Description Language
WSRR	IBM WebSphere Service Registry and Repository
WAS	IBM WebSphere Application Server
WML	Wireless Markup Language
WTX	IBM WebSphere Transformation Extender
XACML	XML Access Control Markup Language
XML	Extensible Markup Language
XMLDSIG	XML Digital Signature
XMLENC	XML Encryption
XPath	XML Path Language
XSD	XML Schema Definition
XSL	Extensible Stylesheet Language
XSLT	Extensible Stylesheet Language for Transformations

Index

B

D

E

F

G

H

J–K

L

O

Q

R

S

W

X–Z